Child Welfare Law and Practice

Representing Children,
Parents, and State Agencies in
Abuse, Neglect, and Dependency Cases

2nd Edition

Donald N. Duquette & Ann M. Haralambie
General Editors

BRADFORD PUBLISHING COMPANY
Denver, Colorado

DISCLAIMER

This book is intended to provide general information with regard to the subject matter covered. It is not meant to provide legal opinions or to offer advice, nor to serve as a substitute for advice by licensed, legal or other professionals. This book is sold with the understanding that Bradford Publishing Company and the author(s), by virtue of its publication, are not engaged in rendering legal or other professional services to the reader.

Bradford Publishing Company and the author(s) do not warrant that the information contained in this book is complete or accurate, and do not assume and hereby disclaim any liability to any person for any loss or damage caused by errors, inaccuracies or omissions, or usage of this book.

Laws, and interpretations of those laws, change frequently, and the subject matter of this book can have important legal consequences that may vary from one individual to the next. It is therefore the responsibility of the reader to know whether, and to what extent, this information is applicable to his or her situation, and if necessary, to consult legal, tax, or other counsel.

Library of Congress Cataloging-in-Publication Data

Child welfare law and practice : representing children, parents, and state agencies in abuse, neglect, and dependency cases / [editors] Donald N. Duquette and Ann M. Haralambie. -- 2nd ed.
   p. cm.
 Includes index.
 ISBN 978-1-932779-96-7
 1. Children--Legal status, laws, etc.--United States. I. Duquette, Donald N. II. Haralambie, Ann M.
 KF3735.Z9C47 2010
 344.7303'27--dc22

               2010036887

Published 2010 by Bradford Publishing Company
1743 Wazee Street, Denver, Colorado 80202
www.bradfordpublishing.com

ABOUT THE EDITORS

Ann M. Haralambie, J.D., is a Certified Family Law Specialist, Arizona Board of Legal Specialization and a Martindale-Hubbell AV® Preeminent™ rated attorney in private practice in Tucson, Arizona since 1977. Her practice is restricted to family and child welfare cases, with an emphasis on custody and child abuse. She is the author of numerous articles, book chapters, and books, including the three volume treatise, *Handling Child Custody, Abuse and Adoption Cases, 3d* (Thomson West), *Child Sexual Abuse in Civil Cases: A Guide to Custody and Tort Actions* (American Bar Association), and *The Child's Attorney: A Guide to Representing Children in Custody, Adoption, and Protection Cases* (American Bar Association). Ms. Haralambie was on the drafting committees for the American Bar Association's *Standards of Practice for Lawyers Who Represent Children in Child Abuse and Neglect Cases*, the *Standards of Practice for Lawyers Who Represent Children in Custody Cases*, and the *Standards of Practice for Lawyers Who Represent Parents in Child Abuse and Neglect Cases*. She was the ABA Advisor to the National Conference of Commissioners on Uniform State Laws, Drafting Committee on Uniform Representation of Children in Abuse and Neglect and Custody Proceedings Act and the ABA Family Law Section Advisor to the NCCUSL Drafting Committee on the Uniform Taking Testimony from Children Act. She is an active national and international speaker on legal topics dealing with custody and child welfare law. Ms. Haralambie is the recipient of several awards, including the Arizona Council of Attorneys for Children Child Advocacy Award, ABA YLD Child Advocacy National Certificate of Recognition, and the ALI-ABA Harrison Tweed Special Merit Award. She is a past president and former board member of the NACC and currently serves as the trainer for the NACC's Child Welfare Law Specialist certification program.

Donald N. Duquette, J.D., Clinical Professor of Law, is the founder (in 1976) and director of the Child Advocacy Law Clinic at the University of Michigan Law School, the oldest clinical law program in the country specializing in child abuse and neglect and foster care cases. Don has developed one of the most respected and influential child advocacy law programs in the country. His research and teaching interests focus on interdisciplinary approaches to child welfare law and policy. He manages the Law School's Bergstrom Child Welfare Law Summer Fellowship Program and in winter 2004 started the Law School's first mediation clinic. Since October 2009 Don has been Director of the National Quality Improvement Center on the Representation of Children in the Child Welfare System, a five-year, $5 million project focusing on improving justice for children in the child welfare system through empirical studies and knowledge development and dissemination. A graduate of Michigan State University, he was a social worker specializing in child protection and foster care before earning his J.D. at Michigan Law School. He then served as an assistant professor of pediatrics and human development at Michigan State University's medical school from 1975 to 1976. His 1990 book, *Advocating for the Child in*

Protection Proceedings, formed the conceptual framework for the first national evaluation of child representation as mandated by the U.S. Congress. During a leave from the Law School, he managed an expert work group for the U.S. Children's Bureau and drafted *Permanency for Children: Guidelines for Public Policy and State Legislation* as part of President Clinton's Adoption 2002 Initiative. Don was co-director of the National Association of Counsel for Children's national project to certify lawyers as specialists in child welfare law. The NACC child welfare specialty gained American Bar Association accreditation in February 2004.

CONTRIBUTING AUTHORS

Lauren Girard Adams, J.D., is co-chair of the Children's Rights Litigation Committee of the American Bar Association Section of Litigation. She specializes in juvenile law and currently resides in Norwich, Vermont.

Susan Badeau is currently the Director of the Cross Systems Integration team within the Knowledge Management department of Casey Family Programs. She has been a child welfare professional for thirty years and was a Public Policy Fellow in the U.S. Senate in 1999.

Terri James Banks, M.S.W., L.C.S.W., is Director of the Under Sixes Program, and Therapist for the Perinatal Mental Health Programs for the Kempe National Center for the Prevention and Treatment of Child Abuse and Neglect.

Katherine Brady, J.D., a senior staff attorney at the Immigration Legal Resource Center in San Francisco, California, is the author of several manuals and articles about immigration law.

Donald C. Bross, J.D., Ph.D., is Professor of Pediatrics (Family Law), University of Colorado School of Medicine, and Director of Education and Legal Counsel for the Kempe National Center for the Prevention and Treatment of Child Abuse and Neglect, (bross.donald@tchden.org).

Howard Davidson, J.D., is Director of the ABA Center on Children and the Law, a program of the American Bar Association based in Washington, DC.

Melanie Delgado, J.D., is an attorney at the Children's Advocacy Institute (CAI) and director of CAI's Foster Youth Transition Project.

Donald N. Duquette, J.D., is Clinical Professor of Law and Director of the Child Advocacy Law Clinic of the University of Michigan Law School.

Robert Fellmeth, J.D., is the Price Professor of Public Interest Law, University of San Diego School of Law and Director of the Children's Advocacy Institute.

Donna Furth, J.D., practices law in San Francisco. She has authored the chapters on appeals and writs in several books.

Ann M. Haralambie, J.D., is a certified family law specialist practicing in Tucson, Arizona. She is also an author and speaker in the fields of family and children's law.

...ren Aileen Howze, J.D., is a Magistrate Judge, Superior Court of the District of Columbia. She is the author of *Making Differences Work: Cultural Context in Abuse and Neglect Cases* (American Bar Association 1996), which established the framework which is discussed in Chapter 8 for examining culture in abuse and neglect practice.

Anne Kellogg, J.D., is a Staff Attorney and the Resources Director at the National Association of Counsel for Children.

Kristin Kelly, J.D., is a staff attorney with the American Bar Association Center on Children and the Law and works on the Legal Center for Foster Care and Education.

Mimi Laver, J.D., is the Director of Legal Education at the ABA Center on Children and the Law, Washington, D.C. She previously was a Deputy City Solicitor representing the Department of Human Services and the Department of Health in Philadelphia, Pennsylvania.

Steven Lubet, J.D., is Williams Memorial Professor of Law and Director of the Bartlit Center for Trial Strategy at Northwestern University School of Law in Chicago, Illinois.

Therese Roe Lund, M.S.W., is Director of Staff Development for ACTION for Child Protection and Associate Director of the National Resource Center for Child Protective Services.

Thomas D. Lyon, J.D., Ph.D., is the Judge Edward J. and Ruey L. Guirado Chair in Law and Psychology at the USC Gould School of Law.

Kathleen McNaught, J.D., is an assistant director at the American Bar Association Center on Children and the Law and directs the Legal Center for Foster Care and Education, a national technical assistance resource and information clearinghouse on legal and policy matters affecting the education of children and youth in foster care.

John E. B. Myers, J.D., is Professor of Law at University of the Pacific, McGeorge School of Law.

Bernard P. Perlmutter, J.D., is Director and Associate Clinical Professor at the Children & Youth Law Clinic, University of Miami School of Law.

Jennifer Renne, J.D., is Director of the National Resource Center on Legal and Judicial Issues with the American Bar Association.

Colene Flynn Robinson, J.D., is an Associate Clinical Professor at the University of Colorado Law School and the director of the Juvenile Law Clinic. From 2001 to 2004 she was Senior Staff Attorney at the National Association of Counsel for Children.

Vivek S. Sankaran, J.D., CWLS, is a clinical assistant professor of law in the Child Advocacy Law Clinic and Director of the Detroit Center for Family Advocacy. Professor Sankaran's research and policy interests center on improving outcomes for children in child abuse and neglect cases by empowering parents and strengthening due process protections in the child welfare system. Professor Sankaran sits on the Steering Committee of the ABA National Project to Improve Representation for Parents Involved in the Child Welfare System and chairs the Michigan Court Improvement Project subcommittee on parent representation.

Janet Stotland, J.D., is the co-director of the Education Law Center (PA).

David B. Thronson, J.D., Professor of Law, Michigan State University College of Law, researches and writes about the intersection of immigration and family law.

Frank E. Vandervort, J.D., is Clinical Assistant Professor of Law at the University of Michigan Law School where he teaches in the Child Advocacy Law Clinic and the Juvenile Justice Clinic, teaches Juvenile Justice, and consults with the School of Social Work on child maltreatment issues. He is co-author of the recently released book: K. Staller, K. C. Faller, F. Vandervort, W. C. Birdsall & J. Henry, *Seeking Justice in Child Sexual Abuse: Shifting Burdens & Sharing Responsibilities* (Columbia University Press 2010).

Marvin Ventrell, J.D., is the Executive Director of the Juvenile Law Society (JLS) in Denver, CO, www.juvenilelawsociety.org. He was the CEO of the NACC from 1994 to 2009.

TABLE OF CONTENTS

I. THE CONTEXT OF CHILD WELFARE LAW

II. LEGAL FRAMEWORK

III. THE CHILD WELFARE LEGAL PROCESS

Chapter 13: The Practice of Child Welfare Casework: A Primer for Lawyers

IV. THE ROLE AND DUTIES OF LEGAL COUNSEL

V. COURTROOM ADVOCACY

FOREWORD

The setting for this book is the child welfare court, often referred to as the dependency court. Approximately 800,000 children in the United States are subject to its jurisdiction. For many of these children, state courts, in essence, become their legal parents until adoptions or guardianships are arranged and for many until they age into adulthood. As such, child welfare courts make significant, often life-altering decisions for these children, decisions that have long-lasting impacts.

Courts often determine the critical details of living for these children, exceeded in intrusion and detailed supervision only by those caught up in the criminal justice system. Courts often decide where and with whom the child lives. Many of these children also have direct or indirect court direction as to who they see, the schools they attend, and whether they are given help with disabilities, special education, and other services and supports they may need.

This legal setting of intervention and reliance properly commends attorneys to competently and effectively represent all three parties before the court—children, parents, and social service agencies. The National Association of Counsel for Children (NACC) has long believed that the best results for children and their families come from full and professional representation of all these parties.

As we know, courts fundamentally make decisions based on what is brought before them. To that end, the attorneys so functioning *must* be competent in applicable law and practice. They must combine typical litigation acumen with uncommon expertise—knowledge about child development, knowledge about the signs of abuse, and the ability to communicate with and understand youth. They must also have enough knowledge and information about the ancillary help that might be needed, such as special education plans, mental health treatment, higher education opportunities, and transitional supports for youth aging out of foster care.

Since its inception, the NACC has strived to promote the best possible legal representation of children, families, and agencies involved in juvenile law cases, especially child welfare cases.

To that end the NACC has provided training and technical assistance to attorneys and other multi-disciplinary professionals in the field. The NACC has also worked diligently to establish the practice of child welfare law as a distinct legal specialty that promotes the highest quality legal representation to our nation's most vulnerable children and families. This is accomplished through the Child Welfare Law Certification Program launched by the NACC in 2000. Attorneys are certified as child welfare law specialists and hold themselves out as such under the Standards set by the NACC and the American Bar Association. CWLS status is now a recognized specialty in 14 states and the District of Columbia and is expected to expand to all jurisdictions that permit specialization.

The second edition of this book provides detailed and in-depth analysis and instruction on the multitude of issues involved in child welfare law practice. Its overall purpose is to serve as a major resource for ensuring that attorneys have the knowledge needed to engage in high quality legal representation in this area of practice. While this book is more than a primer and less than a comprehensive treatise, it tries to cover enough areas in adequate depth for the lawyer to develop a specialist's competence.

The NACC also encourages you to review and use, as appropriate, the additional resources referred to throughout the text.

It is our hope that the second edition of *Child Welfare Law and Practice* will better inform and guide advocates in this most important and complex area of practice that impacts the lives of vulnerable children and families.

Robert C. Fellmeth, Chairman, Board of Directors
On Behalf of the Board and Staff,
National Association of Counsel for Children

INTRODUCTION TO THE SECOND EDITION

Child Welfare Law and Practice: Purpose and Use of this Publication

Child welfare law has become an increasingly complex area of practice that requires lawyers to not only understand complex federal and state law and procedure, but also detailed institutional information regarding child welfare funding streams, treatment and placement options, medicine, mental health, and child development. All of this takes place in a context of heart-wrenching abuse, neglect, and poverty and a complex and under-resourced bureaucracy which both under-responds and over-responds to presenting problems. What was once a cause has become a profession for highly trained and skilled attorneys. Child welfare law has arrived as a distinct legal specialty, as evidenced by the extensive body of state and federal law and procedure, law school curriculum, scholarship, continuing legal education, and national and state standards of practice for attorneys.

Yet the profession is still young and has not yet fully matured. Children are not simply small adults, and our assumptions and rules of lawyering are not automatically transferable to the child welfare law context. The role and duties of the child's attorney are still developing. Likewise, the nuances of representing parents and state agencies present special challenges for the child welfare attorney. The result is that, while the practice of child welfare law has arrived as a professional legal specialty, there is much work to be done to create a high-functioning child welfare system throughout the country. A critical piece in that process is a comprehensive understanding of the competencies of child welfare. This book is intended to facilitate that understanding.

This book and national certification standards would not have been possible, even a few years ago. Historically, child welfare law and practice have varied significantly from state to state. Recently, however, a national model of child welfare law with applicability to every state has emerged through a culmination of federal law and policy and through widely accepted national standards of lawyer practice. From the Child Abuse Prevention and Treatment Act, the Adoption and Safe Families Act, the Fostering Connections Act, and other federal laws, there is now considerable federal statutory direction with which states must comply to secure significant amounts of federal funding for child protection and child welfare services. Additionally, the NACC and ABA have adopted national standards of practice for representing children, and the ABA has adopted national standards for agency and parent attorneys. State Program Improvement Plans resulting from the Child and Family Service Review (CFSR) process further define performance standards for attorneys and call for training and education consistent with the emerging national model. While child welfare law technically remains the province of state law, it is heavily influenced by federal policy. What was once a local practice, varying considerably from state to state, has increasingly become a national model of practice. The benefit of these developments is an increasing uniformity of the legal representation of children, parents, and state agencies. Now it is possible to produce a meaningful national practice book and to award specialty certification based on a mastery of the knowledge and skills presented here.

This book is intended to serve as a resource for agency, parent, and children's attorneys preparing for the NACC child welfare law certification exam. But the NACC "Red Book" has become more than an exam study guide for it represents the body of knowledge that defines child welfare law as a specialized field of legal practice. The first edition also became widely used as a basis for attorney training, a guide and reference for judges and lawyers representing all parties, and a teaching tool in law school substantive and clinical courses. We are very pleased about the widespread and strong acceptance of "Red Book I." Now, having the benefit of five years of experience with the book, we tried to consolidate some chapters and keep them concise and informative. This second edition includes ten new chapters and contributions from the leading authorities in the country. In most cases this book discusses what the law is and can reasonably be interpreted to mean rather than advocating for policy changes we would like to see accomplished. The field of child welfare law continues to develop rapidly, and we have endeavored to provide Web site addresses to assist the reader in keeping abreast of changes.

We are struck by the different tone we can adopt now in this Introduction. Five years ago the Introduction seemed to press hard for recognition of child welfare law as a real and legitimate specialty. Now there is no need to do that. The legitimacy and importance of our specialty is well established. Improved training and greater professionalization of child welfare lawyers is happening in nearly all states. NACC specialty certification is recognized in 14 states and the District of Columbia with more on the way. The federal government has just created a National Quality Improvement Center on Child Representation in the Child Welfare System, at the University of Michigan Law School which is to develop and disseminate empirical knowledge on child representation. Child Welfare law attorneys are increasingly recognized for the serious work we do. Our hope is that this book can continue to support the maturing of the field.

Donald N. Duquette, Editor
Director Child Advocacy Law Clinic, University of Michigan Law School
Director, National Quality Improvement Center on Child Representation in the Child Welfare System

Ann M. Haralambie, Editor
Attorney at Law, Certified Family Law Specialist, Arizona Board of Legal Specialization

I. THE CONTEXT OF CHILD WELFARE LAW

Chapter 1: America's Children

by Anne Kellogg[1]

§ 1.1 The Well-Being of America's Children

The United States is considered the wealthiest nation in the world based on gross domestic product.[2] Yet, when it comes to child maltreatment, the U.S. is failing, according to the *Innocenti Report Card 7*, a publication produced by The United Nation Children's Fund. Out of the 21 developed nations profiled in the Report Card, the U.S. ranked 20th based on overall child well-being.[3] Similarly, the U.S. ranked 25 out of 27 for the rate of child deaths resulting from abuse and neglect.[4]

Although America and its children have made noteworthy progress, America is still failing its children. Children make up a significant proportion of the U.S. population. The total U.S. population in 2009 was over 307 million people.[5] Of those 307 million, 73,942,000 were children.[6] Still, the nation with the highest GDP is failing 24% of its citizenry, a group that can easily be categorized as the most vulnerable and helpless group in America.

Child maltreatment is a serious public health problem with extensive short- and long-term health consequences.[7] The small numbers of child maltreatment cases heard

---

[1] Anne Kellogg, J.D., is a Staff Attorney and the Resources Director at the National Association of Counsel for Children.

[2] World Bank, *World Development Indicators Database (Gross Domestic Product 2008)*, p. 1 (Apr. 19, 2010), *available at* http://siteresources.worldbank.org/DATASTATISTICS/Resources/GDP.pdf.

[3] Innocenti Research Centre, UNICEF, *Report Card 7, Child Poverty in Perspective: An Overview of Child Well-Being in Rich Countries*, p. 2 (2007) (provides a comprehensive assessment of the lives and well-being of children and young people in 21 nations of the industrialized world, using six categories of child well-being: material well-being, health and safety, educational well-being, family and peer relationships, behaviors and risks, subjective well-being).

[4] *Id.* at 4.

[5] U.S. Census Bureau, Annual Estimates of the Resident Population for the United States, Regions, States, and Puerto Rico: April 1, 2000 to July 1, 2009 (NST-EST2009-01), *available at* http://www.census.gov/popest/states/tables/NST-EST2009-01.xls.

[6] U.S. Census Bureau, Annual Estimates of the Resident Population by Sex and Age for States and for Puerto Rico: April 1, 2000 to July 1, 2008 (May 14, 2009), available at http://www.census.gov/popest/states/asrh/SC-EST2008-02.html.

[7] Centers for Disease Control and Prevention, *Understanding Child Maltreatment: Fact Sheet 2010*, *available at* http://www.cdc.gov/violenceprevention/pdf/CM-FactSheet-a.pdf.

in the news are only a fraction of the reality that is child maltreatment. Many cases of abuse and neglect go unnoticed and/or unreported to police or social services. However, the statistics speak for themselves with regard to its prevalence: 1,760 children died in the U.S. in 2007 from abuse and neglect and 794,000 children were found to be victims of maltreatment.[8] Based on a study using self- and parent reports, about 8,755,000 children were victims of child maltreatment during a one-year period.[9] This means that more than 1 out of 7 children between the ages of 2 and 17 experienced some form of maltreatment.

§ 1.1.1 Indicators of Well-Being

When evaluating the well-being of America's children, there are many factors to consider. The 20th annual *Kids Count Data Book*, produced by the Annie E. Casey Foundation, is intended to illuminate the status of America's children and to assess trends in their well-being. The book profiles the well-being of America's children on a state-by-state basis and ranks states on 10 key measures of child well-being.[10] Although the 10 key measures cannot capture the full range of conditions shaping children's lives, research shows that the key indicators capture most of the yearly variation in child well-being reflected in other indices that use a much larger number of indicators.[11]

In 2009, Kids Count used the following 10 measures to rank the well-being of America's children: Percent of low birth weight babies; infant mortality rate; child death rate; teen death rate; teen birth rate; percent of teens who are high school dropouts; percent of teens not attending school and not working; percent of children living in families where no parent has full-time, year-round employment; percent of children in poverty; percent of children in single-parent families.

§ 1.1.2 National Trends in Child Well-Being

According to the Kids Count data, there has been very little change in child well-being since 2000. At the national level, 6 of the 10 indicators of child well-being showed that conditions improved since 2000, while child well-being worsened on 4 indicators.

The lack of change in child well-being since 2000 stands in stark contrast to the pre-2000 data. Between 1996 and 2000, 8 of the 10 key indicators improved, and

---

[8] U.S. Department of Health & Human Services, Administration on Children, Youth and Families, *Child Maltreatment 2007* (U.S. Government Printing Office 2009), *available at* http://www.acf.hhs.gov/programs/cb/pubs/cm07/.

[9] David Finkelhor, Richard K. Ormrod, Heather Turner & Sherry L. Hamby, *The Victimization of Children and Youth: A Comprehensive National Survey*, 10/1 CHILD MALTREAT. 5 (2005).

[10] Annie E. Casey Foundation, *2009 Kids Count Data Book* (July 28, 2009), *available at* www.aecf.org/kidscount.

[11] *Id.*

several improved dramatically. The improvement was experienced by every racial group and in almost every state.

The contrast in trends pre- and post-2000 mirror the changes in the child poverty rate since the mid-1990s. Between 1994 and 2000, the child poverty rate fell by 30%—the largest decrease since the 1960s. In contrast, since 2000, such improvements in child poverty have stalled. Sadly, the child poverty rate has increased by 6%, which translates to nearly 900,000 more children living in poverty in 2007 than in 2000.[12]

§ 1.1.3 Kids Count Indicator Summaries

The 2009 Kids Count Indicator Briefs[13] provide the following summaries of data concerning recent trends in the 10 indicators of child well-being.

Low Birth Weight

Low birth weight (less than 2,500 grams, or 5 pounds, 8 ounces) remains a major public health concern. Preterm birth (birth prior to 37 weeks of gestation) is the most common cause of low birth weight. Since 1990, the U.S. low birth weight rate has increased by 19%, and the preterm birth rate has increased by 21%. There are persistent disparities for different racial and ethnic groups.

Infant Mortality

Between 1960 and 2000 the United State's infant mortality rate (the death rate for infants during the first year of life) decreased steadily. This decline can be attributed to advancement in addressing congenital malformation (a physical defect present at birth, irrespective of whether the defect is caused by a genetic factor or by prenatal events that are not genetic[14]) and sudden infant death syndrome. Progress stalled from 2000 to 2006 as low birth weight and preterm birth have been difficult to overcome.

The Child Death Rate

From 2000 to 2006, the mortality rate for children ages 1 to 14 years fell by 14%, dropping from 22 to 19 deaths per 100,000 children. Despite this progress, the child death rate in the United States remains higher than in many other wealthy nations. Many of these deaths are preventable. Injury continues to be the chief cause of death for the nation's children and youth. Moreover, despite decades of progress, geographic, racial, and ethnic disparities in the child mortality rate persist.

---

[12] This Kids Count *Data Book* does not reflect the current period of economic recession at the national level. The economic indicators included in the *Data Book* come from the 2007 American Community Survey, which reflects information for the 12 months prior to the survey date. The effects of the economic downturn were not felt by most U.S. families until well into 2008 and 2009.

[13] 2009 Kids Count Indicator Briefs, *available at* http://datacenter.kidscount.org/databook/2009/IndicatorBriefs.aspx.

[14] MedicineNet.com, *Definition of Congenital Malformation, available at* http://www.medterms.com/script/main/art.asp?articlekey=2820.

The Teen Death Rate

Life continues to hold considerable risk for adolescents in the United States. In 2006, the teen death rate stood at 64 deaths per 100,000 teens (13,739 teens). Although it has declined by 4% since 2000, the rate of teen death in our country remains substantially higher than in many peer nations, based largely on higher rates for the three most prevalent causes of death among adolescents and young adults: motor vehicle accidents, homicide, and suicide.

The Teen Birth Rate

In 2006, the teen birth rate for 15- to 19-year-olds increased for the first time in 14 years, reaching 24 per 1,000 teens. There is no single explanation for this increase. Researchers point to a trend toward earlier puberty (and early sexual activity) for girls; an overall rise in teen sexual activity; a decline in contraception use by teens; a lessening of the stigma associated with teen birth; and diminished educational and career opportunities stemming from changing economic conditions. Some observers cite a redirection of public attention and resources to other issues, following years of downtrend in the teen pregnancy rate.

The High School Dropout Rate

Researchers use many different methods to calculate the high school dropout rate, and depending on the approach, the numbers can look very different. Using data from the U.S. Census Bureau, the Kids Count Data Center reports the number and percentage of youth ages 16 to 19 who are not enrolled in high school and are not high school graduates in a given year. Using this yardstick, in 2007, there were 1.2 million dropouts in the United States, and the nation's dropout rate was 7%. Five states and 11 urban school districts have dropout rates that were 10% or higher.

The Number of Disconnected Youth

As they move toward adulthood, most young Americans are either in school, in the workforce, or in the military. But far too many are disconnected from the roles and relationships that set young people on pathways toward productive adult lives. In 2007, 8% of youth 16 to19 were disconnected by virtue of being out of school and not working. American Indian (15%), African American (13%) and Hispanic (12%) youth were more likely to be disconnected than their White and Asian counterparts.

The Number of Children Whose Parents Have Stable Employment

When parents have secure employment and earn enough to meet their families' basic needs, children benefit in many ways. Today, many children grow up without these advantages. In 2007, more than 24 million children (33%) lived in households in which no parent had full-time and year-round employment. The economic recession that began in late 2007 has placed more children at risk.

The Child Poverty Rate

In 2007, nearly one in five or 18% of U.S. children lived in poverty. African American (35%), American Indian (33%) and Hispanic (27%) children are more likely to live in poverty than White (11%) and Asian (12%) children. Although many children live in poverty, many more lack a decent standard of living as their families hover near the poverty line or move in and out of official poverty from year to year. The trend is worsening. Between 2000 and 2007, the number of children living in poverty increased by 14.7%, from 12.2 million to 13.1 million.

The Percentage of Children Living in Two-Parent Families

Parents raising children together tend to have more money, more flexibility and more time to supervise their children, offer emotional support, take an active part in their education, and arrange other activities for them. Today, many children go without these benefits. In 2007, 32% of children in the United States were living with one parent. The percentage has nearly tripled since 1970. This trend disproportionately affects disadvantaged children and children of color.

§ 1.2 Child Maltreatment

Child maltreatment includes all types of abuse and neglect that occur among children under the age of 18. Child maltreatment includes any act or series of acts of commission or omission by a parent or other caregiver that results in harm, potential for harm, or threat of harm to a child. There are four common types of abuse:

(1) Physical abuse – occurs when a child's body is injured as a result of hitting, kicking, shaking, burning, or other show of force.

(2) Sexual abuse – involves engaging a child in sexual acts (i.e., fondling, rape, and exposing a child to other sexual activities).

(3) Emotional abuse – refers to behaviors that harm a child's self-worth or emotional well-being. Examples include name calling, shaming, rejection, withholding love, and threatening.

(4) Neglect – the failure to meet a child's basic needs. These needs include housing, food, clothing, education, and access to medical care.

In 2007, U.S. state and local child protective services (CPS) investigated 3.2 million reports of children being abused or neglected.[15] CPS classified 794,000 (10.6 per 1,000) of these children as victims. Approximately three quarters of them had no history of prior victimization. Of these children, 59% were classified as victims of

---

[15] U.S. Department of Health & Human Services, Administration on Children, Youth and Families, *Child Maltreatment 2007* (U.S. Government Printing Office 2009), *available at* http://www.acf.hhs.gov/programs/cb/pubs/cm07/. Note: *A child is counted each time she or he is a subject of a report, which means a child may be counted more than once as a victim of child maltreatment.*

child neglect; 4% as victims of emotional abuse; 8% as victims of sexual abuse; and 11% as victims of physical abuse.[16] A non-CPS study reported that 14% of U.S. children experienced some form of child maltreatment: 8% were victims of sexual abuse; 22% were victims of child neglect; 48% were victims of physical abuse; and 75% were victims of emotional abuse.[17]

In 2007, CPS reported the approximate rates of child maltreatment based on reports of suspected child abuse and neglect:[18]

> 21.9 per 1,000 for 0 to 1 year-olds
> 13.0 per 1,000 for 1 year-olds
> 12.6 per 1,000 for 2 year-olds
> 11.9 per 1,000 for 3 year-olds
> 11.5 per 1,000 for 4 to 7 year-olds
> 9.4 per 1,000 for 8 to 11 year-olds
> 8.7 per 1,000 for 12 to 15 year-olds
> 5.4 per 1,000 for 16 to 17 year-olds

Non-CPS studies have reported higher rates of nonfatal child maltreatment cases, ranging from 43 to 49 per 1,000 children.[19]

In 2007, 1,760 children died from abuse or neglect—a rate of 2.35 per 100,000 children.[20] Over 75% of the deaths occurred among children younger than age 4; 13% among 4- to 7-year-olds; 5% among 8- to 11-year-olds; 5% among 12- to 15-year-olds; and 2% among 16- to 17-year-olds. Over 40% of deaths were non-Hispanic White children, 26% were African American children, and 17% were Hispanic children.

The characteristics of perpetrators are as follows: Female perpetrators, mostly mothers, are typically younger than male perpetrators, who are mostly fathers; more women (56%) than men (42%) are perpetrators of all forms of child maltreatment;[21] the racial distribution of perpetrators was similar to the race of their victims—in 2007, nearly one-half (48.5%) of perpetrators were White and one-fifth (19.0%) were

---

[16] *Id.*

[17] David Finkelhor, Richard K. Ormrod, Heather Turner & Sherry L. Hamby, *The Victimization of Children and Youth: A Comprehensive National Survey*, 10/1 CHILD MALTREAT. 5 (2005).

[18] U.S. Department of Health & Human Services, Administration on Children, Youth and Families, *Child Maltreatment 2007* (U.S. Government Printing Office 2009), *available at* http://www.acf.hhs.gov/programs/cb/pubs/cm07/.

[19] David Finkelhor, Richard K. Ormrod, Heather Turner & Sherry L. Hamby, *The Victimization of Children and Youth: A Comprehensive National Survey*, 10/1 CHILD MALTREAT. 5 (2005); Adrea D. Theodore, Jen Jen Chang, Desmond K. Runyan, Wanda M. Hunter, Shrikant I. Bangdewala & Robert Agans, *Epidemiologic Features of the Physical and Sexual Maltreatment of Children in the Carolinas*, 115/3 PEDIATRICS e331 (2005).

[20] U.S. Department of Health & Human Services, Administration on Children, Youth and Families, *Child Maltreatment 2007* (U.S. Government Printing Office 2009), *available at* http://www.acf.hhs.gov/programs/cb/pubs/cm07/.

[21] *Id.*

African American; approximately 20% (19.8%) of perpetrators were Hispanic. These proportions also have remained consistent for the past few years.[22]

§ 1.2.1 Poverty, Race, and Child Maltreatment

It is undeniable that racial disparities exist among children involved in the child welfare system. In 2007, some children had higher rates of victimization: African American children, American Indian or Alaska Native children, and children of multiple races had the highest rates of victimization at 16.7, 14.2, and 14.0 per 1,000 children of the same race or ethnicity, respectively. Hispanic children and White children had rates of 10.3 and 9.1 per 1,000 children of the same race or ethnicity, respectively. Asian children had the lowest rate of 2.4 per 1,000 children of the same race or ethnicity. Nearly one-half of all victims were White (46.1%), one-fifth (21.7%) were African American, and one-fifth (20.8%) were Hispanic.[23]

When looking at the maltreatment types by race, some disproportionality issues become apparent. "Disproportionality" refers to the extent to which children are over- or underrepresented in the child welfare system relative to their proportions in the census population. Of the victims of all maltreatments, 45.4% were White, but only 36.4% of medical neglect victims were White. African Americans comprised 21.4% of all victims, but 35.3% of medical neglect victims. Of the sexual abuse victims, more than one-half (51.5%) were White, compared with 45.4% of all victims who were White.[24]

On September 30, 2008, there were 463,000 children in foster care. The chart below contains a breakdown of their race/ethnicity:[25]

Alaska Native/American Indian	2%	8,802
Asian	1%	2,631
African American	31%	142,502
Hawaiian/Other Pacific Islander	0%	877
Hispanic (of any race)	20%	92,464
White	40%	183,149
Unknown/Unable to Determine	2%	10,753
Two or more races	5%	21,822

Racial disproportionality in the child welfare system has been a major concern for decades. Although minority children comprise about 40% of all children in the nation,

---

[22] *Id.* at Ch. 5.

[23] *Id.* at Ch. 3.

[24] *Id.* at Ch. 3.

[25] U.S. Department of Health & Human Services, Administration on Children, Youth and Families, The AFCARS Report: *Preliminary FY 2008 Estimates as of October 2009, available at* http://www.acf.hhs.gov/programs/cb/stats_research/afcars/tar/report16.htm.

they account for 50% of the more than 500,000 children in foster care.[26] However, three phases of the National Incidence Studies (1980, 1986, and 1993) found that children of color are not abused at higher rates than White children.[27] Further, children of color, while under state-mandated care, suffer far worse outcomes—in terms of physical and mental health, educational performance, and access to basic services and resources—despite evidence that parents of color are no more likely than White parents to abuse or neglect their children.[28]

Overrepresentation of minority children in the child welfare system has not always existed. In the 19th century, orphanages were established. However, minority children were entirely excluded, and this exclusion continued through the first half of the 20th century.[29] African American children had limited access to segregated orphanages. In the 1950s and 1960s, the number of African American children in White child welfare institutions began to steadily grow. According to Robert Hill, this increase was a direct result of (1) the surge in African American migrants from rural areas to cities, (2) the civil rights anti-segregation movements, and (3) the mass departure of Whites from cities to suburbs.[30]

Theories about causation of minority disproportionality have classified three types of factors: (1) parent and family risk factors; (2) community risk factors; and (3) organizational and systemic factors.[31] According to theories about parent and family risk factors, minorities are overrepresented in the child welfare system because they have disproportionate needs. These children come from families that are more likely to have risk factors such as unemployment, teen parenthood, poverty, substance abuse, incarceration, domestic violence, and mental illness, factors that result in high levels of child maltreatment.[32] Proponents of community risk factors assert that overrepresentation has less to do with race or class and more to do with residing in neighborhoods and communities that have many risk factors, such as high levels of poverty, welfare assistance, unemployment, homelessness, single-parent families, and crime and street violence, factors that make residents more visible to surveillance from public authorities.[33] But theories about organizational and systemic factors contend that minority overrepresentation results from the decision-making processes

---

[26] Robert B. Hill, *Synthesis of Research on Disproportionality in Child Welfare: An Update*, p. 7 (Casey-CSSP Alliance for Racial Equity in the Child Welfare System, Oct. 2006), *available at* http://www.racemattersconsortium.org/docs/BobHillPaper_FINAL.pdf.

[27] *Id.*

[28] *Id.*

[29] *Id.*

[30] *Id.*

[31] *Id.* at 8.

[32] *Id.*

[33] *Id.*

of CPS agencies, the cultural insensitivity and biases of workers, governmental policies, and institutional or structural racism.[34]

It is undeniable that minority children experience disparate outcomes. For a more detailed analysis of disparity, see Chapters 8 and 16.

§ 1.2.2 Risk Factors for Child Maltreatment

Some factors can increase the risk for abuse or neglect. A combination of individual, relational, community, and societal factors contribute to the risk of child maltreatment. Although children are never to blame for the harm inflicted upon them, certain characteristics have been found to increase their risk of being maltreated. Risk factors are those characteristics associated with child maltreatment- they may or may not be direct causes.

Individual risk factors for victimization relate to age and special needs. Children younger than four years of age are at greatest risk for severe injury and death from abuse. Children with special needs that may increase caregiver burden (e.g., disabilities, mental retardation, mental health issues, and chronic physical illnesses) are also at a greater risk of harm.

Risk factors for perpetration are classified into three categories: (1) individual risk factors; (2) family risk factors, and (3) community risk factors.

Individual risk factors include:

- Parents' lack of understanding of children's needs and child development and parenting skills
- Parents' history of child abuse in family of origin
- Substance abuse and/or mental health issues, including depression, in the family
- Parental characteristics such as young age, low education, single parenthood
- Large number of dependent children
- Low income
- Nonbiological, transient caregivers in the home (e.g., mother's male partner)
- Parental thoughts and emotions that tend to support or justify maltreatment behaviors

Family risk factors include:

- Social isolation (family lacks nearby friends, relatives, and other social support)

---

[34] *Id.*

- Family disorganization, dissolution, and violence, including intimate partner violence
- Family stress (which can result from a family history of violence, drug or alcohol abuse, poverty, and chronic health problems)
- Parenting stress
- Poor parent-child relationships
- Negative interactions

Community risk factors include:

- Community violence (ongoing violence in the community may create an environment where child abuse is accepted)
- Concentrated neighborhood disadvantage (e.g., high poverty and residential instability, high unemployment rates, and high density of alcohol outlets)
- Poor social connections

§ 1.2.3 Consequences of Child Maltreatment

Most of the studies examining the consequences of child maltreatment have used a retrospective approach. This requires conducting studies to determine if any association exists between a history of childhood abuse and/or neglect and current health conditions in adults. Fewer studies have been conducted using a longitudinal research strategy, which identifies maltreated children and/or at-risk children and follows them for a long period of time, sometimes decades, to see what conditions develop. Regardless of the approach, it is undeniable that child maltreatment negatively impacts the physical, psychological, and behavioral health of maltreated children.

Abused children often suffer physical injuries including cuts, bruises, burns, and broken bones. A child may suffer severe or fatal head trauma. Where the head trauma is severe but not fatal, the child may result in varying degrees of visual impairment (i.e., blindness), motor impairment (i.e., cerebral palsy), and/or cognitive impairments.[35]

In addition, child maltreatment that causes excessive stress can disrupt early brain development.[36] Extreme stress can also harm the development of the nervous and immune systems.[37] The stress resulting from chronic abuse may cause a "hyperarousal" response in certain areas of the brain, which may result in hyperactivity, sleep disturbances, and anxiety. Chronic abuse may also make victims

---

[35] National Center on Shaken Baby Syndrome, *All About SBS/AHT*, *available at* http://www.dontshake.org/sbs.php?topNavID=3&subNavID=317.

[36] National Scientific Council on the Developing Child, *Excessive Stress Disrupts the Architecture of the Developing Brain, Working Paper No. 3* [online], 2005, *available at* www.developingchild.net.

[37] *Id.*

more vulnerable to problems such as post-traumatic stress disorder, conduct disorder, and learning, attention, and memory difficulties.[38]

Maltreatment that occurs during infancy or early childhood can cause important regions of the brain to form and function improperly, with long-term consequences on cognitive, language, and socioemotional development.[39]

In addition to the physical health consequences, some maltreated children experience psychological health problems. In one long-term study, 80% of young adults who had been abused met the diagnostic criteria for at least one psychiatric disorder by age 21. These young adults exhibited many problems, including depression, anxiety, eating disorders, and suicide attempts.[40]

Further, maltreated children often experience behavioral health problems. Maltreated children are 25% more likely to experience problems such as delinquency, teen pregnancy, low academic achievement, drug use, and mental health problems.[41] A longitudinal study conducted by the National Institute of Justice study found that childhood abuse or neglect increased the likelihood of arrest as a juvenile by 59%.[42] This same study also found that abused youth were less likely to have graduated from high school and more likely to have been a teen parent.[43]

Not only do maltreated children experience behavioral health problems in their minority, but these children also are at an increased risk for behavioral and mental health problems as adults, including smoking, alcoholism, depression, drug abuse, eating disorders, obesity, suicide, sexual promiscuity, and certain chronic diseases.[44]

---

[38] S. J. Dallam, *The Long-Term Medical Consequences of Childhood Maltreatment, in* THE COST OF CHILD MALTREATMENT: WHO PAYS? WE ALL DO (K. Franey, R. Geffner & R. Falconer eds., Family Violence & Sexual Assault Institute 2001); Bruce D. Perry, *The Neurodevelopmental Impact of Violence in Childhood, in* TEXTBOOK OF CHILD AND ADOLESCENT FORENSIC PSYCHIATRY 221–38 (D. Schetky & E. Benedek eds., American Psychiatric Press 2001).

[39] U.S. Department of Health & Human Services, Administration on Children, Youth, and Families, *Understanding the Effects of Maltreatment on Early Brain Development* (2001), *available at* http://dcfs.co.la.ca.us/katieA/docs/Maltreatmnet%20on%20Early%20Brain%20Development.pdf.

[40] Amy B. Silverman, Helen Z. Reinherz & Rose M. Giaconia, *The Long-Term Sequelae of Child and Adolescent Abuse: A Longitudinal Community Study*, 20/8 CHILD ABUSE & NEGLECT 709 (1996).

[41] BARBARA T. KELLEY, TERENCE P. THORNBERRY & CAROLYN A. SMITH, IN THE WAKE OF CHILDHOOD MALTREATMENT (National Institute of Justice 1997).

[42] Jennifer E. Langsford, Shari Miller-Johnson, Lisa J. Berlin, Kenneth A. Dodge, John E. Bates & Gregory S. Pettit, *Early Physical Abuse and Later Violent Delinquency: A Prospective Longitudinal Study*, 12/3 CHILD MALTREAT. 233 (2007).

[43] *Id.*

[44] V. J. Felitti, R. F. Anda, D. Nordenberg, D. F. Williamson, A. M. Spitz, V. Edwards, M. P. Koss & J. S. Marks, *Relationship of Childhood Abuse and Household Dysfunction to Many of the Leading Causes of Death in Adults: The Adverse Childhood Experiences (ACE) Study*, 14/4 AM. J. PREV. MED. 245 (1998); D. Runyan, C. Wattam, R. Ikeda, F. Hassan & L. Ramiro, *Child Abuse and Neglect by Parents and Other Caregivers, in* WORLD REPORT ON VIOLENCE AND HEALTH 59–86 (E. Krug et al. eds., World Health Organization 2002), *available at* http://www.who.int/violence_injury_prevention/violence/global_campaign/en/chap3.pdf.

Individuals who were maltreated as children are 1.5 times more likely to use illicit drugs—marijuana in particular—in middle adulthood.[45] Abuse and neglect also increase the likelihood of adult criminal behavior by 28% and perpetration of violent crime by 30%.[46] Early child maltreatment can have a negative effect on the ability of both men and women to establish and maintain healthy intimate relationships in adulthood.[47]

In sum, children who are abused or neglected are at higher risk for physical, psychological, and behavioral health problems as juveniles, and those risks continue through adulthood.

§ 1.2.4 Child Maltreatment and the American Economy

The costs associated with the short-term and long-term care of victims significantly impacts the U.S. economy. These expenditures include direct costs associated with treatment of victims (i.e., doctor and hospital visits) as well as indirect costs related to lost productivity, disability, decreased quality of life, and premature death.

Child maltreatment also has an economic impact on the American legal system, state child welfare agencies, and other institutions.

Child poverty itself is a terrific drag on the American economy. In January 2007, poverty experts testified before Congress that children who grow up poor cost the economy $500 billion a year because they are less productive, earn less money, commit more crimes, and have more health-related expenses.[48] "The high cost of childhood poverty to the United States suggests that investing significant resources in poverty reduction might be more cost effective over time than we previously thought."[49]

Children in the child welfare system are nearly always from poor families. This is not to say that poor people are necessarily poorer parents, but rather that they are under greater scrutiny than others in our society and that they often lack the basic tools and resources to allow them to succeed as parents. The *Third National Incidence Study of Child Abuse and Neglect* found that 47% of children with demonstrable harm from abuse or neglect and 95.5% of endangered children came from families whose

---

[45] Cathy Spatz Widom, Naomi R. Marmorstein & Helene Raskin White, *Childhood Victimization and Illicit Drug Use in Middle Adulthood*, 20/4 PSYCHOL. ADDICT. BEHAV. 394 (2006).

[46] Cathy Spatz Widom & Michael G. Maxfield, *An Update on the "Cycle of Violence"* (National Institute of Justice Feb. 2001), *available at* http://www.ncjrs.gov/pdffiles1/nij/184894.pdf.

[47] Rebecca A. Colman & Cathy Spatz Widom, *Childhood Abuse and Neglect and Adult Intimate Relationships: A Prospective Study*, 28/11 CHILD ABUSE & NEGLECT 1133 (2004).

[48] The Economic Costs of Child Poverty: Testimony Before the U.S. House Committee on Ways & Means, 110th Cong. (2007) (statement of Harry J. Holzer, professor and visiting fellow at the Urban Institute, Georgetown University Public Policy Institute), *available at* http://www.urban.org/publications/901032.html.

[49] *Id.*

income was less than $15,000 per year.[50] A poor child is 22 to 27 times more likely to be identified as harmed by abuse or neglect.[51]

Poverty is inexorably linked to child maltreatment. Impoverished communities lack the capacity to assist children. "High poverty rates indicate what may be insurmountable problems for the child welfare system. . . . The child welfare system, in isolation, is unlikely to be able to demonstrate a positive impact in the well-being of the majority of children in its care."[52]

In a recent study by UNICEF, America's child poverty rate was dead last among 24 developed counties.[53] According to the U.S. Census Bureau, America's child poverty rate remains just below 18%.[54]

§ 1.3 The Lawyer Role

Child maltreatment is a serious public health problem. But it also affects fundamental issues of personal liberty and social justice. Recognition and awareness of child maltreatment, although essential for successful prevention, are only a start to the solution. Prevention efforts and policies must directly address children, caregivers, and communities in order to prevent child abuse from occurring and to appropriately respond to abuse that has already occurred. But even though the ultimate goal is to stop child maltreatment before it starts, maltreatment in its various forms does and will occur. It is critical that state child protection systems respond to reports of abuse, investigate allegations properly, and intervene appropriately in family relationships when necessary. When intervention in the family does occur, well-trained and committed child welfare lawyers are necessary to ensure that the rights and interests of children, parents, and the society at large are fully protected.

§ 1.4 Additional Resources

- To report abuse or get help, contact the National Child Abuse Hotline at 1-800-4-A-CHILD (1-800-422-4453).

- Centers for Disease Control and Prevention: www.cdc.gov/injury

- Children's Bureau, Administration for Children and Families: www.acf.hhs.gov/programs/cb

---

[50] Andrea J. Sedlack & Diane D. Broadhurst, U.S. Department of Health & Human Services, *Third National Incidence Study of Child Abuse and Neglect: Final Report*, 5–3 tbl.5–1, 5–11 tbl.5–2 (1996).

[51] *Id.*

[52] Sarah H. Ramsey, *Child Well-Being: A Beneficial Advocacy Framework for Improving the Child Welfare System?*, 41 U. MICH. J.L. REFORM 9 (2007).

[53] Innocenti Research Centre, UNICEF, *Report Card 7, Child Poverty in Perspective: An Overview of Child Well-Being in Rich Countries*, p. 6, fig. 1.1 (2007).

[54] U.S. Census Bureau, Current Population Reports Series, *Income, Poverty, and Health Insurance Coverage in the United States: 2006*, Report P60-233, 15 tbl.4 (Aug. 2007), *available at* http://www.census.gov/prod/2007pubs/p60-233.pdf.

- Child Welfare Information Gateway: www.childwelfare.gov
- FRIENDS National Resource Center: www.friendsnrc.org
- National Scientific Council on the Developing Child: www.developingchild.net

Chapter 2: Physical, Sexual, and Emotional Child Abuse and Neglect[*]

by Ann M. Haralambie[1]

§ 2.1 Physical Abuse

Physical abuse is a serious problem in the United States. According to the National Child Abuse and Neglect Data System (NCANDS),[2] in 2007 there were 3.2 million referrals to child welfare agencies throughout the country, resulting in an initial assessment of 5.8 million children. Of these referrals, 25% were substantiated. As a result, it was identified that in 2007, 794,000 children were found to be victims of maltreatment (10.6 per 1,000 children in the United States), and 24% of these children were placed in foster care. There were 1,760 deaths attributed to abuse and neglect with a death rate of 2.35 deaths per 100,000 children. The NCANDS data identified the following categories: neglect, 59%; physical abuse, 10.8%; sexual abuse, 7.6%; psychological maltreatment, 4.2%; multiple maltreatments, 13.1%; and other 4.2%; and medical neglect, 0.9%.[3]

The actual number of children physically abused is probably much higher because the abuse is both undetected and under-reported. The American Academy of Pediatrics' Committee on Child Abuse and Neglect has written that the "detection and diagnosis of child physical abuse depends on the clinician's ability to recognize suspicious injuries, conduct a careful and complete physical examination with judicious use of auxiliary tests, and consider whether the caregivers' explanation is supported by the characteristics of the injury or injuries and the child's developmental capabilities."[4]

The modern child welfare system was largely a response to the concerns of pediatricians such as C. Henry Kempe and his colleagues, who coined the term

---

[*] Reprinted from *Handling Child Custody, Abuse and Adoption Cases, Third Edition*, with permission of Thomson Reuters. For more information about this publication, please visit www.west.thomson.com. *Author's Note*: This chapter is based in part on chapters 16, 17, and 18 of ANN M. HARALAMBIE, HANDLING CHILD CUSTODY, ABUSE AND ADOPTION CASES 3D (Thomson West 2009).

[1] Ann M. Haralambie, J.D., is a certified family law specialist practicing in Tucson, Arizona. She is also an author and speaker in the fields of family and children's law. The NACC is grateful to John H. Stuemky, M.D. Section Chief, Pediatric Emergency Medicine Children's Hospital at Oklahoma University Medical Center, for his services editing this chapter.

[2] National Child Abuse and Neglect Data System (NCANDS) Combined Aggregate File, FFY-2007.

[3] For information on NCANDS and the National Data Archive on Child Abuse and Neglect, see http://www.ndacan.cornell.edu/index.html.

[4] Nancy D. Kellogg & Committee on Child Abuse and Neglect, *Evaluation of Suspected Child Physical Abuse*, 119/6 PEDIATRICS 1232 (2007).

"battered child syndrome" to describe, in part, the existence of multiple fractures in different stages of healing.[5] Physicians now have more than half a century of study and training in forensic pediatrics to assist in diagnosing physical child abuse, and what began as a response to physical abuse has now come to also incorporate a legal response to sexual and emotional abuse as well as physical, medical, and educational neglect.[6] However, not all physicians are well-versed in this information, and child welfare attorneys must ensure that the experts they use are well-trained and that their knowledge is up-to-date. For example, a family doctor may not be alert for signs of abuse and may accept a superficially plausible explanation from the parents.

One of the most common ways of diagnosing any non-accidental injury is recognizing a discrepancy between the physical findings and the parent's explanation of how the injury occurred. The Committee on Child Abuse and Neglect wrote:

> Explanations that are concerning for intentional trauma include:
>
> 1. no explanation or vague explanation for a significant injury;
>
> 2. an important detail of the explanation changes dramatically;
>
> 3. an explanation that is inconsistent with the pattern, age, or severity of the injury or injuries;
>
> 4. an explanation that is inconsistent with the child's physical and/or developmental capabilities; and
>
> 5. different witnesses provide markedly different explanations for the injury or injuries.[7]

Parents who are abusive may not report information about the abuse in a manner that is totally consistent with the physical findings. Some parents change their versions of what occurred when questioned more than once or when questioned separately. It is important to identify any inconsistencies in their responses because such inconsistencies demonstrate that the information reported does not reflect reality and contradicts the physical findings.

Parents of young children and infants may explain that the child received the injury by doing something the child was developmentally incapable of doing. For example, parents of babies who cannot crawl or even creep may say that the baby fell after being left in the middle of a bed. The parents may say that the child injured himself or herself deliberately, but children rarely deliberately injure themselves. Other children are often accused of dropping, pushing, or hitting a younger sibling

---

[5] *See, e.g.,* C. Henry Kempe, Frederic N. Silverman, Brandt F. Steele, William Droegemueller & Henry K. Silver, *The Battered-Child Syndrome,* 181/1 JAMA 17 (1962).

[6] For a full description of the condition of children in America and the incidence of child maltreatment, see Chapter 1, America's Children.

[7] *See* Nancy D. Kellogg & Committee on Child Abuse and Neglect, *Evaluation of Suspected Child Physical Abuse,* 119/6 PEDIATRICS 1232 (2007).

when the older child lacks the physical strength or agility to do so or to strike a blow with enough force to cause the injury sustained.

Generally parents of children with accidental injuries seek medical help immediately. However, parents who have inflicted the injuries on the child may fear detection of the abuse and, therefore, delay in seeking help. Any delay and the explanations offered for the delay are important parts of the medical history. The attorney attempting to prove physical abuse should obtain all chart notes and personal notes reflecting the history given, especially the parent's first explanation. Often, the parents' behavior, such as absence of stress and flat affect, might be noted by the emergency room doctor or intake social worker, and would be incongruent with what one might expect from a concerned parent. In addition, the attorney should direct discovery to the parent, whether through interrogatories, depositions, or requests for admissions, seeking the parent's detailed explanation of how the injury occurred and a recitation of every explanation the parent has given, including the timeline reported by the parents and who the parents say first "discovered" the child's condition. The physician to be used as an expert witness at trial should be provided with detailed information about each explanation, because he or she must be able to express an opinion as to whether that explanation is consistent with the findings.

§ 2.1.1 Fractures

What is relevant in proving abuse is not that the child has suffered a fracture, but that the fracture was received nonaccidentally. Certain types of fractures are caused by different mechanisms. The biomechanics of the type of force used to result in a particular type of fracture can be explained, and the forces necessary to result in the fracture can be calculated,[8] although the amount of force varies depending on the age and skeletal development of the child. The most important factor to consider is whether or not the explanation given for the injury is consistent with the type of force required to cause the injury. The types of biomechanical forces involved in abusive fractures have been summarized as including:

- Transverse/greenstick fractures (bending or direct impact from a hand or other blunt object)
- Spiral/oblique fractures and periosteal striping with subperiosteal hemorrhage (twisting or torsion of the limb)
- Metaphyseal as well as epiphyseal complex fractures (shaking or pulling on the end of a limb)[9]

---

[8]   *See, e.g.,* Betty Spivak, *Biomechanics of Nonaccidental Trauma, in* CHILD ABUSE: A MEDICAL REFERENCE 61–78 (Stephen Ludwig & Allan Kornberg eds., 1992).

[9]   *See* D. Merten et al., *Skeletal Manifestations of Child Abuse, in* CHILD ABUSE: MEDICAL DIAGNOSIS AND MANAGEMENT 26 (Robert M. Reece ed.,1994).

The expert who testifies at trial should be prepared to explain the mechanism of the fracture. Although the expert may not be able to calculate the actual amount of force needed to cause the injury, he or she should be able to testify that:

- The degree of force necessary to produce such a fracture would exceed that of normal child care

- The force is great enough that any reasonable person would recognize that it would hurt a child

- Given the child's response, it did hurt the child

Skeletal models or diagrams may be helpful in demonstrating how the fracture was inflicted. Some medical conditions and diseases may produce findings similar to those of abusive fractures and should be considered and ruled out by the medical expert. These include osteogenesis imperfecta, osteomyelitis, congenital syphilis, rickets, scurvy, leukemia, and Menkes' syndrome.[10]

The age of the fracture or fractures may be important to a determination of who had access to the child when the injury was inflicted and whether multiple fractures occurred on different occasions.[11] Very recent fractures may be accompanied by swelling or bruising, although there is frequently no external indication of fractures in abused children. Very recent fractures, particularly those in a very young infant, may be difficult to detect on initial radiographic evaluation and may be first identified at the time of a repeat x-ray taken at a two- or three-week follow-up. As fractures heal, they calcify, leaving a radiological record called a callous. New bone formation does not show up on x-rays initially, but in 5 to 14 days a thin layer of new bone is formed.[12] The younger the child, the more quickly healing will occur.[13] Additionally, a fracture may completely resolve in six months, so the absence of a fracture at the time of presentation does not absolutely exclude previous injury that has completely healed. It may be useful to consider the assistance of a pediatric radiologist to testify about the timing of a fracture.

§ 2.1.2 Bruises

Some of the most obvious physical injuries abused children display are bruises. Medical records may use several terms to describe a bruise. The terms used most often are:

---

[10] *See, e.g.*, Carole Jenny, for the Committee on Child Abuse and Neglect, *Evaluating Infants and Young Children With Multiple Fractures*, 118/3 PEDIATRICS 1299 (2006); Paul W. Brill & Patricia Winchester, *Differential Diagnosis of Child Abuse, in* DIAGNOSTIC IMAGING OF CHILD ABUSE 221 (Paul Kleinman ed., 1987).

[11] *See generally* John F. O'Connor & Jonathan Cohen, *Dating Fractures, in* DIAGNOSTIC IMAGING OF CHILD ABUSE 103–13 (Paul Kleinman ed., 1987).

[12] *See* Sandy C. Marks, *The Structural and Developmental Context of Skeletal Injury, in* DIAGNOSTIC IMAGING OF CHILD ABUSE 67 (Paul Kleinman ed., 1987).

[13] *See* John F. O'Connor & Jonathan Cohen, *Dating Fractures, in* DIAGNOSTIC IMAGING OF CHILD ABUSE 107 (P. Kleinman ed., 1987).

- "Contusion" (any injury, usually caused by a blow, in which the skin is not broken)
- "Ecchymosis" (a purplish patch on the skin caused by an extravasation of blood into the surrounding tissue)
- "Petechiae" (tiny red or purple spots caused by an effusion of blood from ruptured capillaries)

A violent blow to the skin may cause petechiae when the blood is forced "out of the capillaries under the area of contact into the surrounding unsupported vessels which rupture under the strain."[14] Strangulation injuries may produce something called Tardieu's ecchymoses, Tardieu's petechiae, or Tardieu's spots. The attorney may also see the word "purpura" in medical charts to describe a hemorrhage into the skin, which may be caused by disease, allergies, or fever rather than abuse. Redness of the skin produced by inflammation may be called "erythema."

As with other signs of physical abuse, the significant issue is not that the child has one or more bruises, but whether the bruises were received accidentally or not. Most children who play actively have bruises on their bodies most of the time. They may not be able to remember how they received them. Typical accidental bruises occur on the skin overlying the bony prominences, such as elbows, knees, shins, chin, cheek bone, and forehead. Children who are not yet pulling to stand and walk along furniture, called cruising, should not have bruises, and the presence of bruises in these children should raise the suspicion of non-accidental trauma. Conversely, toddlers who are just learning to walk are particularly prone to falling and bumping into things. But bruises received from such falls and bumps are typically circular with irregular borders. Generally bruises received in a fall are on one plane of the body, unless it was a tumbling fall. In contrast, abusive bruises may be seen on unlikely parts of the body, such as the backs of the knees, genitals, lateral thighs, buttocks, back, fleshy part of the arm, neck, soft tissues of the cheek, or earlobes. Such bruises may result from blows to the child's body, or the child being grabbed, pinched, or squeezed. Two black eyes are almost always indicative of physical abuse[15] unless the child has a large bump on the forehead, in which case the blood can track down into the more dependant areas, such the area below the eyes. Bruises on the back, buttocks, and lateral thighs are generally the result of excessive discipline.[16]

Many times the implement that inflicted the injury leaves its outline in the bruise. Pinch mark bruises are round or oval bruises the size of fingertips. A larger thumb print bruise may be the appropriate distance away. Grab marks generally have the thumb bruise on one side of the limb and the fingertip bruises on the other side. Handprints may leave the outline of the hand, even including the spaces between the

---

[14] *See* C. Cooper, *Child Abuse and Neglect: Medical Aspects, in* THE MALTREATMENT OF CHILDREN 9, 21 (Selwyn M. Smith ed., 1978).

[15] *Id.* at 22.

[16] *See, e.g.*, Baron D. Schmitt, *The Child with Nonaccidental Trauma, in* THE BATTERED CHILD 178, 180 (Ray Helfer & Ruth Kempe eds., 4th ed. 1987).

fingers and the lines of the finger joints. The shape of part of the implement may be quite visible in the bruise. For example, the loops of an electrical cord may be seen. Similarly, the width of a belt, sometimes even showing the holes, may be seen. The tapered end of a belt might leave a triangular bruise at the end of the linear bruise. This underscores the importance of the investigator's effort to obtain potential weapons from the scene, which the medical expert can correlate with the injury. Sometimes there are ligature marks when the child has been bound or strangled. Ligature marks are typically seen as circumferential wounds around the extremities, particularly the wrists and ankles, or in the case of an attempted strangulation, around the neck. There may be abrasions and bruises around the ligature mark or grab marks elsewhere where the child was restrained while being bound. Bite marks also leave crescent-shaped linear bruises, often paired with individual tooth marks that are visible. A physician or dentist can measure the distances seen in the bruise and match them with the size of the abuser's bite. Parents often blame bite marks on other children; however, there is a significant variation between the size of a child's bite and that of an adult.

There are some medical conditions that cause bruise-like markings, such as leukemia and idiopathic thrombocytopenic purpura. In addition, some kinds of birth marks, such as Mongolian spots, nevi, or hemangiomas, may look like bruises but are not. Some disorders, such as hemophilia and Von Willebrand's disease, result in bruising with very little force. Bleeding disorder screens provide laboratory evidence concerning whether a bruise could have been spontaneous or the result of minor injury because of a coagulation disorder. Some cultures have medical practices, such as coining, which produce abrasions or bruises, and when accompanied by hot oil, may include some burning. Other potential causes of bruising should always be ruled out by a physician.

§ 2.1.3 Lacerations

Lacerations are cuts on the skin. Sometimes the pattern of the lacerations indicates abuse. If the child is hit with a switch, for example, there may be a number of parallel linear lacerations on the child's back or the back of the child's legs. The child may receive a torn frenulum of the upper lip or tongue from having a bottle forcibly shoved into his or her mouth. Such injuries are often seen in child abuse cases. Older children may tear the frenulum accidentally in a fall, but there is a history to fit the injury as these injuries typically bleed considerably. Lacerations in the mouth heal very quickly, and even within a few days there may be no evidence of the laceration. The impact of a fist, boot, or an object may leave a laceration as well as a bruise. Sometimes lacerations are intentionally inflicted by a knife or razor.

§ 2.1.4 Burns

Because children's skin is thinner than adults' skin, contact with a hot object for the same amount of time will leave a more severe burn on the child than on the adult.

The burn pattern may well contain clues suggesting the agent, mode, direction, and time of injury. Dry burns often show the imprint of what caused them. Irons, electric range coils, hot plates, curling irons, radiator grates, fireplace pokers, branding irons, cigarettes, and cigars all may leave burns clearly indicative of what was used to burn the child. Inflicted burns tend to have sharp, clear borders from direct and sustained contact with the hot object. Accidental burns tend to be glancing burns, as the child pulls back from the accidental contact. Because the skin is in contact with the hot object for a shorter time, the resulting burns tend to be less severe than inflicted burns. The margins of the burn may be more diffuse and the depth of the burn both shallower and less symmetrical. For example, a child who accidentally walks into a lighted cigarette may have an oval or oblong burn deeper on one end than the other. In contrast, an inflicted cigarette burn may be perfectly round and deep. Especially in hot climates, accidental burns may result from contact with metal objects heated by the sun. For example, a seat belt buckle may leave a burn with distinct borders showing the shape of the buckle. Car seats may also burn the child. Sometimes children are "branded" with heated metal objects such as knife blades, fireplace pokers, and the metal tops of cigarette lighters. Cigarette lighters may also be used to inflict burns by holding a part of the child's body, often the palm, over the open flame.

Immersion burns leave imprints of the water level, with or without splash marks, which can allow a physician to recreate the child's exact posture when he or she was burned. "Stocking" and "glove" burns result from a child's foot or hand, respectively, being dunked in scalding water, leaving a burn pattern where the water touched the child. Frequently there is an absence of splash marks in these burns. A "doughnut" scalding burn occurs when a child is held down in a bathtub of scalding water. The pressure of the child's skin that is touching the relatively cool bottom of the tub is not burned, while the surrounding areas are burned from the scalding water. If the child was standing in the tub, the soles of the feet might not be burned for the same reason. Some children are held under running scalding water, causing particularly deep burns, because the water coming from the spigot is uniformly hot, with no time to cool down. Children who are still in diapers or who are being toilet trained are at particular risk of dunking burns. The parent may be frustrated at having to clean the child or may be angry that the child was not able to wait to use the toilet. The child is immersed in hot water either to clean the child's genital area or to punish the child for the lapse in toilet training.

Accidental scalds may be caused by a child tipping a pot or cup of boiling liquid. The hot liquid generally flows off the child and cools relatively quickly in the air, causing a less severe burn. The hot pot or tea kettle may also fall on the child, leaving a non-scald burn. If the child accidentally pulled the container of hot liquid onto himself or herself, the child will be burned mostly on the face, arms, and upper trunk, often including the underside of the chin and armpit on injured side, with the most severe burn at the point of initial impact and less severely burned areas flowing down from that area of burn. If those areas are not burned, it suggests that the hot liquid was actually thrown at or poured on the child. Correlation with history given is always critical.

Splash marks are often seen with scald burns, and their location indicates the direction from which the water or other hot liquid came. If the liquid was pulled down from above the child, the splash marks will be seen below the primary burn. If the liquid was thrown at the child, the splash marks may be at the same height, but beyond the primary burn, or may even be above the primary burn. If the child is restrained while being immersed in scalding water, there will be relatively few splash marks. There may be some from the water from the spigot splashing back when it hits the rest of the water in the tub. If the child is able to flail about, there may be many splash marks.

Scald burns around the mouth may result from hot liquid or a corrosive agent being forced into the child's mouth. Corrosive burns around and in the mouth and throat may also be caused accidentally if the child ingests corrosive agents found around the house. Poison control centers routinely deal with such mishaps. It is important to identify the corrosive agent causing the burn and to determine whether the child would have had access to it.

In all burns, scene investigations are extremely important to assist in the reconstruction of the circumstances around the injury. Additionally, as with all injuries, the element of delay in seeking medical treatment may help to differentiate between inflicted and accidental burns.

There are some things that produce injuries that look like inflicted burns but are not. For example, impetigo, a contagious infection, may look similar to an inflicted cigarette burn. Moxibustion is the burning of herbal agents on the skin as a counter-irritant in the treatment of disease in traditional Chinese and Japanese medicine. It is important to be sure that the physician who testifies has considered and ruled out any such alternative explanation. The physician should also be asked to rule out conditions that may mimic burns, such as cutaneous infections, hypersensitivity reactions, and allergic reactions.

§ 2.1.5 Internal (Abdominal and Thoracic) Injuries

Serious internal injuries may occur as a result of abuse, frequently without any evidence of outward signs, such as bruises or lacerations. Such injuries may be the result of being punched, kicked, or thrown. Abdominal blows and severe crushing or squeezing of the trunk may cause internal injuries without leaving any bruises or other marks on the skin. When the child's abdominal wall is relaxed at the time of the blow, the internal organs absorb most of the energy from the blow, so there may be no abdominal bruising.[17] The most likely internal injuries will be to the abdominal organs, such as the liver, spleen, pancreas, gastrointestinal tract, or bladder, because the thoracic organs are protected by the rib cage.

---

[17] *Id.* at 190.

Abusive abdominal and thoracic (chest) injuries have a poorer prognosis than those that occur as a result of an accidental cause. This is largely as a result of a delay in seeking care as well as poor or no history for the injury, making diagnosis and treatment difficult. Children who have sustained these injuries typically exhibit signs of the injury initially, but this may be followed by a period when the child seems to get better. This period ends when the child's injury progresses as a result of infection or other complications. Therefore, establishing the timing of the injury is challenging and dependant on careful history from the caregivers.

§ 2.1.6 Abusive Head Trauma

Head injury is a common presentation for child abuse and is the most common cause of death in fatal child abuse cases. The American Academy of Pediatrics has issued a policy statement strongly advocating that the diagnosis of "abusive head trauma," and not "shaken baby syndrome," be used because this term more accurately describes the events that have occurred to the child.[18] The statement explains the need for changed terminology as follows: "Although shaking an infant has the potential to cause neurologic injury, blunt impact or a combination of shaking and blunt impact cause injury as well. Spinal cord injury and secondary hypoxicischemic injury can contribute to poor outcomes of victims. The use of broad medical terminology that is inclusive of all mechanisms of injury, including shaking, is required."[19] Children may sustain a head injury in an accidental manner, but there are certain features that are suggestive of and, in some cases, diagnostic of non-accidental injury. As with all child abuse, it is important to correlate the injury that the child sustains with the explanation given for that injury.

Very serious injuries or even death may result from shaking a child, especially an infant. Because infants have relatively large heads compared to their body size, and because they have relatively weak neck muscles, shaking an infant may cause serious injury or death. This injury may or may not be followed by rapid deceleration of the head against an object, constituting an impact that further increases the severity of the injury. The constellation of injuries commonly seen with shaking include intracranial head injuries, eye injuries, and skeletal injuries.

When a child is shaken, the rapid acceleration and deceleration of the child's head tears the cerebral veins, causing bleeding between the arachnoid and the dura mater (fibrous tissue layers that surround the brain), resulting in a subdural hematoma.[20] Subarachnoid hematomas may also occur when blood accumulates in subarachnoid space. Additionally, damage to the brain parenchyma (brain tissue) may occur as a result of the shaking itself as the axons (main nerve fibers that carry impulses) are

---

[18] *See* Cindy W. Christian, Robert Block & the Committee on Child Abuse and Neglect, *Abusive Head Trauma in Infants and Children*, 123/5 PEDIATRICS 1409 (2009).

[19] *Id.*

[20] Baron D. Schmitt, *The Child With Nonaccidental Trauma*, *in* THE BATTERED CHILD 188 (Ray Helfer & Ruth Kempe eds., 4th ed. 1987).

injured. This may cause brain edema (swelling), which can be further exacerbated by apnea (intermittent cessation of breathing causing lack of oxygen to the tissues) and, frequently, delay in seeking medical care.

Eye injuries are frequently seen in children injured by a shaking mechanism. Retinal hemorrhages are the most common eye injury seen, but there may also be bleeding in the area behind the eye or around the optic nerve (seen only at autopsy). Retinal hemorrhages are described by their type, extent, and location. Severe retinal hemorrhaging may result in folding of the retina (called retinoschesis) or a detached retina.

Several skeletal injuries may also be seen in a child injured by shaking with or without impact. A skull fracture confirms some element of impact. Rib fractures may also be sustained when the perpetrator grabs the child around the chest during the shaking episode. Lateral rib fractures arise from anterior to posterior squeezing of the ribs, and posterior rib fractures are the result of the back of the rib bending against the spine, which acts as a fulcrum for the rib. These injuries are quite specific for a squeezing mechanism. As mentioned earlier, there may also be fractures to the end of the long bones called metaphyseal fractures. In addition to the acceleration and deceleration involved in shaking, shaking may involve sudden extension and flexion, which may result in spinal fractures or other neck injury.

Epidural hematomas occur when blood accumulates between the dura mater and the skull where arteries traverse. These injuries are the result of blunt force trauma to the head and are more commonly the result of an accidental injury. Subgaleal hematomas may form under the scalp from blunt trauma or as the result of a child's hair being pulled forcefully. Because subgaleal hematomas are between the scull and the scalp, they do not present the serious danger that subdural, subarachnoidal, and epidural hematomas do.

Other potential causes for the above injuries need to be ruled out, including accidental injury, infection, and metabolic illness. Serious head injury or death very rarely result from short falls or falls down stairs, although this is a common explanation given for these injuries, and when they do, the injury is either an epidural bleed or, rarely, a space-occupying subdural hematoma.

§ 2.1.7 Munchausen Syndrome by Proxy[21]

Munchausen syndrome by proxy involves fabricating, simulating, or inducing symptoms in a child or tampering with laboratory samples or monitors, which in turn, results in unnecessary medical procedures being performed on the child for diagnosis or treatment.[22] It is also known as "Pediatric Condition Falsification" (PCF) from the

---

[21] For further discussion of Munchausen by proxy syndrome, see § 31.3.3, Munchausen Syndrome by Proxy.

[22] *See generally* HERBERT A. SCHREIER & JUDITH A. LIBOW, HURTING FOR LOVE: MUNCHAUSEN BY PROXY SYNDROME (1993); Roy Meadow, *What Is and What Is Not Munchausen Syndrome by Proxy?*, 72/6 ARCH. DIS. CHILD. 534 (1995); Donna Andrea Rosenberg, *Munchausen Syndrome by Proxy, in*

child's perspective and as "Factitious Disorder by Proxy" (FDP) (300.19) from the perpetrator's perspective.[23] Parents with Munchausen syndrome by proxy often have some medical knowledge; therefore, they may be quite clever in the fabrications. The parents, almost always mothers, are generally quite concerned and cooperative with the medical personnel, who become a team of medical detectives to explain and treat the child's problem. In retrospect, the mothers can be described as being overly involved and constantly with the child. The father is typically absent or very uninvolved. Preverbal children are the most likely victims of this type of maltreatment because they are not only under their parent's control, but they are also unable to give their own history to the medical personnel. The child's physicians may begin to suspect Munchausen syndrome by proxy only long after repeated testing fails to uncover the etiology of the child's problems. While occasionally the parent's action is captured on videotape (such as covert video surveillance in a hospital room recording a parent suffocating a child or contaminating an intravenous line), the diagnosis of Munchausen syndrome by proxy is most often made only after careful and exhaustive medical detective work.

Munchausen syndrome by proxy is a controversial diagnosis,[24] which is part of the reason why the term "Pediatric Condition Falsification" (PCF) is now used to describe a medical diagnosis in the child.[25]

§ 2.1.8 Medical Ramifications

In addition to diagnosing the child maltreatment, the medical expert should explain the ramifications of the maltreatment, both short-term and long-term. If the child will need special care, then the parent's ability and willingness to provide that care must be determined. The attorneys for the agency and child, in particular, will need to address any ancillary services the child will require, including follow-up medical care. The parent's attorney will need to determine whether specialized services are available to assist the parent in learning how to care for the child.

CHILD ABUSE: MEDICAL DIAGNOSIS & MANAGEMENT 513–63 (Robert M. Reece & Cindy W. Christian eds., 3d ed. 2009); Donna A. Rosenberg, *Munchausen Syndrome by Proxy: Medical Diagnostic Criteria*, 27/4 CHILD ABUSE & NEGLECT 421 (2003).

[23] AMERICAN PSYCHIATRIC ASSOCIATION, DIAGNOSTIC AND STATISTICAL MANUAL OF MENTAL DISORDERS, TEXT REVISION 517 (4th ed. 2000).

[24] *See, e.g.*, ERIC G. MART, MUNCHAUSEN'S SYNDROME BY PROXY RECONSIDERED (2002); DAVID B. ALLISON & MARK S. ROBERTS, DISORDERED MOTHER OR DISORDERED DIAGNOSIS? MUNCHAUSEN BY PROXY SYNDROME (1998).

[25] *See, e.g.*, Loren Pankratz, *Persistent Problems With the Munchausen Syndrome by Proxy Label*, 34/1 J. AM. ACAD. PSYCHIATRY LAW 90 (2006); Herbert Schreier, *Munchausen by Proxy Defined*, 110/5 PEDIATRICS 985 (2002). *See generally* CAROLE JENNY, CHILD ABUSE AND NEGLECT: DIAGNOSIS, TREATMENT AND EVIDENCE (2010).

§ 2.2 Sexual Abuse

The Child Abuse Prevention and Treatment and Adoption Reform Act[26] defines sexual abuse for the purposes of that Act as including:

> (A) the employment, use, persuasion, inducement, enticement, or coercion of any child to engage in, or assist any other person to engage in, any sexually explicit conduct or simulation of such conduct for the purpose of producing a visual depiction of such conduct; or

> (B) the rape, and in cases of caretaker or inter-familial relationships, statutory rape, molestation, prostitution, or other form of sexual exploitation of children, or incest with children.

A more conceptual definition was provided by Drs. Ruth and C. Henry Kempe, who saw sexual abuse as "the involvement of dependent, developmentally immature children and adolescents in sexual activities that they do not fully comprehend, to which they are unable to give informed consent, or that violate the social taboos of family roles."[27]

It is important to understand that children who have not been sexually abused exhibit a broad range of sexual behaviors. Therefore, attorneys, experts, and courts should be aware of empirical research concerning normative sexual behavior among children.[28]

§ 2.2.1 Intrafamilial Child Sexual Abuse

Intrafamilial child sexual abuse involves sexual contact or activity with a member of one's family or household, including sexual activity with one's natural or adopted children, stepchildren, or children of one's "significant other." It is often referred to as incest. Such sexual abuse does not require that there be intercourse, or even that there be actual contact. Having a child watch one masturbate or taking pornographic pictures of a child constitutes sexual abuse even when the adult never touches the

---

[26] 42 U.S.C. § 5106g(4).

[27] *See* RUTH S. KEMPE & C. HENRY KEMPE, CHILD ABUSE 43 (1978).

[28] *See, e.g.*, William N. Friedrich, Jennifer Fisher, Daniel Broughton, Margaret Houston & Constance R. Shafran, *Normative Sexual Behavior in Children: A Contemporary Sample*, 101/4 PEDIATRICS e9 (1998), *available at* http://pediatrics.aappublications.org/cgi/reprint/101/4/e9; S. Lamb & M. Coakley, *"Normal" Childhood Sexual Play in Games: Differentiating Play from Abuse*, 17/4 CHILD ABUSE & NEGLECT 515 (1993); THOMAS M. ACHENBACH, MANUAL FOR THE CHILD BEHAVIOR CHECKLIST 2–3, 1992 PROFILE (1992); W. N. Friedrich, P. Grambsch & L. Damon et al., *Child Sexual Behavior Inventory: Normative and Clinical Comparisons*, 4/3 PSYCHOL. ASSESS. 303 (1992); THOMAS M. ACHENBACH, MANUAL FOR THE CHILD BEHAVIOR CHECKLIST 4–18, 1991 PROFILE (1991); William N. Friedrich, Patricia Grambsch, Daniel Broughton, James Kuiper & Robert L. Bielke, *Normative Sexual Behavior in Children*, 88/3 PEDIATRICS 456 (1991); B. N. Gordon, C. S. Schroeder & J. M. Abrams, *Age Differences in Children's Knowledge of Sexuality*, 19 J. CLIN. CHILD PSYCHOL. 33 (1991).

child. Similarly, having children engage in sexual contact with one another while the adult watches constitutes sexual abuse. Fondling over clothing can also be sexual abuse. Fondling, oral-genital contact, romantic kissing, inserting objects in a child's vagina or anus, digital penetration, and penile penetration are other forms of sexual abuse.[29] In some cases, both parents or parent-figures are actively engaged in molesting the child. More frequently, however, only one parent or parental figure molests the child. The other—whether out of ignorance, impotence, complicity, or denial—simply fails to protect the child from the abuse.

§ 2.2.2 Pedophilia

The *Diagnostic and Statistical Manual of Mental Disorders (DSM-IV-TR)*,[30] referring specifically to the disorder of pedophilia (302.2) states that:

> Some individuals with Pedophilia are sexually attracted only to children (Exclusive Type), whereas others are sometimes attracted to adults (Nonexclusive Type).
>
> Individuals with Pedophilia who act on their urges with children may limit their activity to undressing the child and looking, exposing themselves, masturbating in the presence of the child, or gentle touching and fondling of the child.
>
> Others, however, perform fellatio or cunnilingus on the child or penetrate the child's vagina, mouth, or anus with their fingers, foreign objects, or penis and use varying degrees of force to do so.
>
> These activities are commonly explained with excuses or rationalizations that they have "educational value" for the child, that the child derives "sexual pleasure" from them, or that the child was "sexually provocative" – themes that are also common in pedophilic pornography.[31]

In addition to the actual abuse, a person who molests a child may bribe or threaten the child to secure his or her acquiescence. This "complicity" by the child in the act of

---

[29] Psychiatrist David Jones divides "child sexual abuse" into direct sexual acts (contacting child's genital or anal area; anal, vaginal or oral penetration; and "other acts in which the child is the object of the adult's gratification," such as bondage, frotteurism, ejaculation onto the child, and fondling of a postpubertal child's breasts) and indirect sexual acts (genital exposure, production of pornographic material, encouraging children to have sex together, and exposing children to pornographic material). He defines "child sexual abuse" as "the actual or likely occurrence of a sexual act (or acts) perpetrated on a child by another person." *See* David P. H. Jones, *Assessment of Suspected Child Sexual Abuse, in* THE BATTERED CHILD 296, 296–97 & nn.1–2 (Mary Edna Helfer et al. eds., 5th ed. 1997).

[30] AMERICAN PSYCHIATRIC ASSOCIATION, DIAGNOSTIC AND STATISTICAL MANUAL OF MENTAL DISORDERS, TEXT REVISION (4th ed. 2000).

[31] AMERICAN PSYCHIATRIC ASSOCIATION, DIAGNOSTIC AND STATISTICAL MANUAL OF MENTAL DISORDERS, TEXT REVISION 571 (4th ed. 2000).

abuse may make the child feel responsible or guilty, especially if the child derived some pleasure from the molestation. This may contribute to the child's reluctance or unwillingness to disclose the abuse. The child may also be directly threatened not to disclose.

Prentky, Knight, and Lee report that while the DSM-IV diagnostic criteria "may succeed in isolating the 'pedophilic' child molester, it fails to capture those incest and extrafamilial offenders without known 6-month histories of sexualized interest in children . . . . [which will] inevitably screen out a large number of child molesters."[32] Therefore, Prentky believes that the DSM-IV will fail to provide adequate coverage in classifying most child molesters.[33]

The stereotypical picture of a child molester is the "dirty old man" in a trench coat hanging around playgrounds and elementary school fences. Such a person is typically a predatory pedophile, whose primary or only sexual attraction is to children. Most pedophiles do not fit this stereotype. Some people are sexually attracted to children in general and may seek out opportunities to be with children, often in socially accepted positions such as scout leader, coach, or Sunday school teacher. The DSM-IV-TR points out that except where pedophilia is associated with sexual sadism, "the person may be attentive to the child's needs in order to gain the child's affection, interest, and loyalty and to prevent the child from reporting the sexual activity."[34] Other persons do not have primary sexual attraction to children but end up molesting children in their own household out of their improper responses to various stressful situations.[35] The DSM-IV-TR classifies pedophilia, 302.2, as either Exclusive Type, where the sexual attraction is only towards children, or Nonexclusive Type, where the sexual attraction may also be to adults.[36]

The DSM-IV states that some pedophiles, particularly those who frequently victimize children, "develop complicated techniques for obtaining access to children" that can include winning the trust of the child's mother, marrying a woman who has an attractive child, trading children with other pedophiles, or "in rare instances, taking in foster children from nonindustrialized countries or abducting children from strangers."[37]

---

[32] *See* ROBERT A. PRENTKY ET AL., U.S. DEPARTMENT OF JUSTICE, CHILD SEXUAL MOLESTATION: RESEARCH ISSUES 4 (NIJ Research Report NCJ 163390, 1997).

[33] *See* Robert A. Prentky, *Child Sexual Molestation, in* HANDBOOK OF PSYCHOLOGICAL APPROACHES WITH VIOLENT OFFENDERS: CONTEMPORARY STRATEGIES AND ISSUES (Michel Hersen & Vincent B. Van Hasselt eds., 1999).

[34] AMERICAN PSYCHIATRIC ASSOCIATION, DIAGNOSTIC AND STATISTICAL MANUAL OF MENTAL DISORDERS, TEXT REVISION 571 (4th ed. 2000).

[35] The DSM-IV states that "[i]ndividuals may limit their activities to their own children, stepchildren, or relatives or may victimize children outside their families." *Id.*

[36] *Id.*

[37] *Id.*

Further, the person may be attracted just to males, just to females, or to both.[38] While the disorder generally begins in adolescence, some pedophiles report "that they did not become aroused by children until middle age."[39] The frequency of the sexual activity "often fluctuates with psychosocial stress."[40] Marital discord, divorce, moving out of the family home, and the tension that often accompanies visitation and other communications during domestic relations litigation certainly constitute psychosocial stress, which may exacerbate the inappropriate sexual behavior.

§ 2.2.3 Diagnosing Sexual Abuse

The social sciences have developed some practice standards for the assessment of child sexual abuse in response to the McMartin Preschool case and others, in which legal and mental health professionals made some significant mistakes.[41] Because the alleged victim and the alleged perpetrator are most often the only two sources of information about the sexual abuse event or history (absent any medical evidence), use of an assessment model that considers multiple hypotheses has become a gold standard in the specialized field of child sexual abuse assessment. As psychologist Kathryn Kuehnle has stated, "child sexual abuse is an event or a series of events, not a psychiatric disorder. The view of sexual abuse as a trigger that sets off an internal process in the child that surfaces as predictable behavioral and emotional symptoms does not have an empirically based foundation."[42] Kuehnle recommends the scientist-practitioner model for child sexual abuse evaluations.[43] It is important for evaluators to use alternative hypotheses in assessing allegations.[44]

The alleged perpetrator does not have to be an adult for the activity to constitute child sexual abuse. Any time there is a great disparity in power and authority, such as between a teenage child and a young sibling or step-sibling, sexual contact takes on

---

[38] *Id.*

[39] *Id.*

[40] *Id.*

[41] *See* John E. B. Myers, *Introduction: Improved Forensic Interviewing: The Legacy of the McMartin Preschool Case, in* THE EVALUATION OF CHILD SEXUAL ABUSE ALLEGATIONS: A COMPREHENSIVE GUIDE TO ASSESSMENT AND TESTIMONY (Kathryn Kuehnle & Mary Connell eds., 2009). *See also* KATHLEEN COULBOURN FALLER, INTERVIEWING CHILDREN ABOUT SEXUAL ABUSE: CONTROVERSIES AND BEST PRACTICE (2007).

[42] Kathryn Kuehnle, *Child Sexual Abuse Evaluations, in* COMPREHENSIVE HANDBOOK OF PSYCHOLOGY: VOLUME 11, FORENSIC PSYCHOLOGY 437–60 (Alan M. Goldstein & Irving B. Weiner eds., 2002).

[43] See Kathryn Kuehnle, *Child Sexual Abuse Evaluations: The Scientist-Practitioner Model*, 16/1 BEHAV. SCI. LAW 5 (1998).

[44] *See, e.g.,* CHILD CUSTODY LITIGATION: ALLEGATIONS OF CHILD SEXUAL ABUSE (Kathryn Kuehnle & Leslie Drozd eds., 2005), published simultaneously as 2/3 J. CHILD CUSTODY (2005); KATHLEEN COULBORN FALLER, UNDERSTANDING AND ASSESSING CHILD SEXUAL MALTREATMENT (2003); SANDRA K. HEWITT, ASSESSING ALLEGATIONS OF SEXUAL ABUSE IN PRESCHOOL CHILDREN: UNDERSTANDING SMALL VOICES (1999).

the characterization of abuse.[45] Children under the age of 13 perform 13% to 18% of all childhood sexual abuse.[46] There are data to indicate that the social and legal view adopted by the United States on youth sexual offending has moved away from rehabilitation and toward punishment. It is important for the child advocate to consider the continuum of children's sexual behavior that runs from normative to psychopathological.[47]

It is important to understand that while the presence of physical (medical) evidence is probative of sexual abuse, negative findings *are not* probative. History is probably the most important criterion in diagnosing child sexual abuse.[48] It is not uncommon for sexually abused children to have normal physical examinations, including normal genital examinations.[49] Most acts of child molestation would not be expected to leave evidence: fondling, oral-genital contact, digital penetration, exhibitionism, and nude photography. Many children are not injured in any way during the molestation. Young children might not have any sense that the contact is "wrong," and would not be expected, therefore, to exhibit signs of psychological trauma from the abuse. The attorney must keep in mind the entire context of the molestation and make sure that expert testimony is presented that will focus the judge on what is really relevant information.

There is sometimes medical evidence of vaginal or anal penetration in a child. Very recent traumatic penetration may be revealed by lacerations or bruising. Because the hymen is an elastic tissue, it is possible for there to have been penetration without tearing the hymen or leaving an enlarged opening.[50] Even pregnant adolescents, who have had intercourse, may have normal genital findings.[51] Sometimes medical findings have causes other than abuse.[52] For example, children may sustain straddle

---

[45] For example, the DSM-IV-TR diagnostic criteria for pedophilia require for that particular diagnosis that the perpetrator be at least 16 years old and at least 5 years older than the victim. AMERICAN PSYCHIATRIC ASSOCIATION, DIAGNOSTIC AND STATISTICAL MANUAL OF MENTAL DISORDERS, TEXT REVISION 572 (4th ed. 2000).

[46] Alison Stickrod Gray & William D. Pithers, *Relapse Prevention with Sexually Aggressive Adolescents and Children: Expanding Treatment and Supervision, in* THE JUVENILE SEX OFFENDER 289–319 (Howard E. Barbaree, William L. Marshall & Stephen M. Hudson eds., 1993).

[47] Jessica Gurley, Kathryn Kuehnle & H. D. Kirkpatrick, *The Continuum of Children's Sexual Behavior: Discriminative Categories and the Need for Public Policy Change, in* THE EVALUATION OF CHILD SEXUAL ABUSE: A COMPREHENSIVE GUIDE TO ASSESSMENT AND TESTIMONY 129–50 (Kathryn Kuehnle & Mary Connell eds., 2009).

[48] *See, e.g.*, Carolyn J. Levitt, *The Medical Examination in Child Sexual Abuse: A Balance Between History and Exam*, 1/4 J. CHILD SEXUAL ABUSE 113 (1992).

[49] *Id.* at 114.

[50] *Id.* at 116.

[51] *See, e.g.*, Nancy D. Kellogg, Shirley W. Menard & Annette Santos, *Genital Anatomy in Pregnant Adolescents: "Normal" Does Not Mean "Nothing Happened,"* 113/1 PEDIATRICS e67 (2004) (noting vaginal penetration generally does not result in observable evidence of healed injury to perihymenal tissues; only 2 of the 36 subjects had definitive findings of penetration).

[52] *See generally* Joyce Adams, *Significance of Medical Findings in Suspected Sexual Abuse: Moving Towards Consensus*, 1/3 J. CHILD SEXUAL ABUSE 91, 93 (1992) (listing the following findings as non-

injuries from falling on playground equipment or bicycle bars. The abrasions and bruises resulting from such accidental injuries, however, tend to appear on the more exposed, superficial parts of the body, with areas such as the hymen and vagina not receiving the blunt trauma.[53] Accidental penetrating injuries are much rarer.[54]

Infections may also create genital inflammations, rashes, and even bleeding.[55] Foreign objects in the vagina, such as pieces of toilet paper or feces, may cause vaginal discharge, which may be blood-tinged. Passage of large, hard stools may result in fairly superficial, straight, and narrow anal fissures.[56] However, if the fissures are deep, irregular, extending beyond the rugal folds, or are accompanied by swelling, bleeding, or hematomas, there is some suspicion of an abusive etiology.[57]

Medical findings that are suggestive of sexual abuse include abrasions, lacerations, swelling, bruising (only if the abuse was very recent), scarring or tearing of the hymen, absent or narrow hymenal tissue, scars, the presence of semen or sperm, bite marks, and the presence of sexually transmitted diseases.[58] A child who has been forcibly sexually abused may have grab mark bruises on the thighs. Because the vagina is very vascular, injuries heal quickly, often without leaving behind any medical evidence, even under magnification.[59] Therefore, negative medical findings may not be inconsistent with a history of trauma that is not very recent.

§ 2.3 Emotional Abuse

Emotional abuse is difficult to define, but it can damage a child in more far-reaching and pervasive ways than the more obvious physical abuse.[60] While emotional abuse may accompany physical or sexual abuse, it may also exist in the absence of other forms of maltreatment. The DSM-IV-TR does not include a diagnosis for emotional abuse. The American Academy of Pediatrics Committee on Child Abuse and Neglect defines "psychological maltreatment"[61] as "a repeated pattern of

---

specific: irregular vascularity, erythema of the vestibule, labial adhesions, urethral dilatation with labial traction, friability of the posterior fourchette, hymenal septa, transverse measurements of the hymenal orifice over 5 mm, using labial separation (supine), and vaginal discharge).

[53] *See, e.g.,* DAVID L. CHADWICK ET AL., COLOR ATLAS OF CHILD SEXUAL ABUSE 57 (1989).

[54] *Id.*

[55] *Id.* at 58–59 (1989) (listing vulvovaginitis, streptococcal perianal disease, diaper dermatitis, lichen sclerosis et atrophicus, and postinflammatory labial adhesions).

[56] *Id.* at 60.

[57] *Id.*

[58] *See, e.g.,* American Academy of Pediatrics, Committee on Child Abuse and Neglect, *Guidelines for the Evaluation of Sexual Abuse of Children,* 87/2 PEDIATRICS 254 (1991).

[59] *See, e.g.,* Joyce Adams, *Significance of Medical Findings in Suspected Sexual Abuse: Moving Towards Consensus,* 1/3 J. CHILD SEXUAL ABUSE 91, 97 (1992).

[60] *See, e.g.,* JAMES GARBARINO ET AL., THE PSYCHOLOGICALLY BATTERED CHILD (Jossey-Bass, 1st ed. 1986).

[61] Although emotional and psychological abuse are used synonymously here, they may be distinguishable for professional diagnostic purposes.

damaging interactions between parent(s) and child that becomes typical of the relationship" and "occurs when a person conveys to a child that he or she is worthless, flawed, unloved, unwanted, endangered, or only of value in meeting another's needs. The perpetrator may spurn, terrorize, isolate, or ignore or impair the child's socialization."[62] The committee stated that:

> If severe and/or repetitious, the following behaviors may constitute psychological maltreatment:
>
> 1. Spurning (belittling, degrading, shaming, or ridiculing a child; singling out a child to criticize or punish; and humiliating a child in public).
>
> 2. Terrorizing (committing life-threatening acts; making a child feel unsafe; setting unrealistic expectations with threat of loss, harm, or danger if they are not met; and threatening or perpetrating violence against a child or child's loved ones or objects).
>
> 3. Exploiting or corrupting that encourages a child to develop inappropriate behaviors (modeling, permitting, or encouraging antisocial or developmentally inappropriate behavior; encouraging or coercing abandonment of developmentally appropriate autonomy; restricting or interfering with cognitive development).
>
> 4. Denying emotional responsiveness (ignoring a child or failing to express affection, caring, and love for a child).
>
> 5. Rejecting (avoiding or pushing away).
>
> 6. Isolating (confining, placing unreasonable limitations on freedom of movement or social interactions).
>
> 7. Unreliable or inconsistent parenting (contradictory and ambivalent demands).
>
> 8. Neglecting mental health, medical, and educational needs (ignoring, preventing, or failing to provide treatments or services for emotional, behavioral, physical, or educational needs or problems).
>
> 9. Witnessing intimate partner violence (domestic violence).[63]

Some state statutes tie the definition of emotional abuse to a psychological or psychiatric diagnosis in the child and a causal connection between the disorder and

---

[62] *See* Steven W. Kairys, Charles F. Johnson & Committee on Child Abuse and Neglect, *The Psychological Maltreatment of Children—Technical Report*, 109/4 PEDIATRICS e68 (2002).

[63] *Id.*; *see also* Stephanie Hamarman & William Bernet, *Evaluating and Reporting Emotional Abuse in Children: Parent-Based, Action-Based Focus Aids in Clinical Decision-Making*, 39/7 J. AM. ACAD. CHILD ADOLESC. PSYCHIATRY 928 (2000).

improper conduct by the parent.[64] The statutes may require that emotional abuse be proven based on the testimony of a licensed physician or psychologist.[65]

§ 2.4 Neglect

In this section, the following types of neglect are discussed: emotional neglect, physical neglect, medical neglect, failure to thrive, and educational neglect.

§ 2.4.1 Emotional Neglect

Even if the parent provides for the child's physical needs, the child's emotional needs may be neglected. Children who experience chronic emotional neglect may grow up without the ability to form emotional bonds, resulting in antisocial behavior and crime. It is difficult to define what constitutes psychological or emotional neglect. Garbarino, Guttmann, and Seeley identify five forms of "psychically destructive behavior": rejecting, isolating, terrorizing, ignoring, and corrupting.[66] It might be said that the rejecting, isolating, and ignoring forms constitute emotional neglect, while the terrorizing and corrupting forms constitute emotional abuse. Emotional or psychological neglect may also arise from the emotional unavailability of the parent to the child. The DSM-IV-TR describes the psychiatric diagnosis of Reactive Attachment Disorder of Infancy or Early Childhood (313.89) as involving "pathogenic care," evidenced by at least one of the following:

(1) persistent disregard of the child's basic emotional needs for comfort, stimulation, and affection

(2) persistent disregard of the child's basic physical needs

(3) repeated changes of primary caregiver that prevent formation of stable attachments (e.g., frequent changes in foster care).[67]

Despite the adverse consequences to the emotionally neglected child, courts are not as likely to sustain an adjudication based on emotional or psychological neglect as for physical or medical neglect.

---

[64] *See, e.g.*, COLO. REV. STAT. § 19-1-103(1)(a)(IV), which defines emotional abuse as "an identifiable and substantial impairment of the child's intellectual or psychological functioning or development or a substantial risk of impairment of the child's intellectual or psychological functioning or development."

[65] For a useful set of guidelines on evaluating emotional abuse, see AMERICAN PROFESSIONAL SOCIETY ON THE ABUSE OF CHILDREN, GUIDELINES FOR PSYCHOSOCIAL EVALUATION OF SUSPECTED PSYCHOLOGICAL MALTREATMENT IN CHILDREN AND ADOLESCENTS.

[66] JAMES GARBARINO ET AL., THE PSYCHOLOGICALLY BATTERED CHILD (Jossey-Bass, 1st ed. 1986).

[67] AMERICAN PSYCHIATRIC ASSOCIATION, DIAGNOSTIC AND STATISTICAL MANUAL OF MENTAL DISORDERS, TEXT REVISION (4th ed. 2000).

§ 2.4.2 Physical Neglect

There are a number of types of neglect, including physical neglect, medical neglect, failure to thrive, educational neglect, and emotional neglect. Neglect can be based on the parent's own actions or inactions or by the parent's failure to protect the child from abuse or neglect by others. Neglect does not require a finding of parental fault, only the inability or unwillingness to provide proper care for the child. The failure to perform an affirmative parental duty constitutes neglect. Neglect can encompass neglect of physical needs (such as food, shelter, and clothing), medical needs (either regular care or a special medical procedure), supervision, or emotional needs (such as attention, affection, and intellectual stimulation). In its most extreme form, neglect may result in abandonment, the *de facto* forfeiture of parental care for a child. While society often views neglect as being more benign than abuse, research has shown that neglect, particularly emotional neglect, can leave far deeper and more debilitating scars in a child.

It is important to distinguish neglect from poverty. There are often various programs available to assist parents who find it difficult to meet their children's needs because of their poverty. A parent who is unable to provide personally for the child's physical needs, but who leaves the child in a good environment that does provide for those needs, has not neglected the child. However, the fact that a parent is poor is not a defense to the failure to meet the child's basic needs. In proving neglect, it is important to address the role that poverty plays in the failure to provide what the child needs, with particular emphasis placed on the parent's refusal or misuse of available services and assistance.

It is also important for the attorney to be aware of the broad range of cultural standards sometimes labeled as neglect. By keeping in mind the need to *prove* some actual detriment or unacceptable risk of harm to the child, the attorney should be able to differentiate between neglect warranting court intervention and simply different, but acceptable, cultural norms.

§ 2.4.3 Medical Neglect

In *Parham v J.R.*, the United States Supreme Court stated that parents have "a 'high duty' to recognize symptoms of illness and to seek and follow medical advice."[68] Failure to obtain appropriate medical care for a child may constitute medical neglect. If the parent never takes the child for medical care, and the child's health is adversely affected because of that failure, the court may find medical neglect. The important issue of proof is the adverse affect of the failure on the child's medical (or psychiatric) health. Most medical neglect cases come to the attention of the court when a child has a particular medical crisis or condition and the parent refuses to follow a physician's advice concerning treatment. Where the parent acts

---

[68] 442 U.S. 584, 602 (1979) (ruling on requirements for parents voluntarily admitting their minor children to mental health institutions).

contrary to medical advice without competent medical advice supporting the parent's decision, the court may find medical neglect. However, where there is considerable risk in the proposed procedure or the parents are acting on medical advice, courts have accorded great deference to the parents' judgment in choosing medical treatment. Where the medical condition is life-threatening, and the risks of withholding the proposed treatment are much greater than the risks associated with the treatment, courts are more likely to find medical neglect and order the recommended treatment.

Medical neglect cases often involve religious issues, and a number of states have specific statutory provisions providing some special protections in such circumstances. However, in *Prince v. Massachusetts* the U.S. Supreme Court stated that the "right to practice religion freely does not include liberty to expose the community or the child to communicable disease or the latter to ill health or death."[69] The Supreme Court has held that the constitution does not forbid a finding of medical neglect when the parent's religiously motivated failure to provide medical care seriously endangers the child.[70]

§ 2.4.4 Failure to Thrive

Babies who are denied attention and affection may suffer from nonorganic failure to thrive syndrome (FTT).[71] These babies are born with a normal weight but do not gain weight and develop normally. Their failure to grow as expected is not because of a physical problem. Sometimes the baby does not gain weight normally at home because the family is too poor to obtain proper food or formula or because the inexperienced parents do not know how or how often to feed the child. This possible cause for the baby's condition is usually determined by an initial interview by a doctor, nurse, or social worker. Such a cause is not FTT, but may constitute neglect by virtue of the failure to provide adequate nutrition. Sometimes the child has an organic defect or disease that prevents proper absorption of nutrients. Sometimes the child is genetically small for gestational age (SGA), just as some adults are short. The parents are not to blame for these conditions, and no neglect is involved, except to the extent that the parents of a child with an organic problem did not seek proper medical attention or follow through with the medical advice prescribed. Such children are not FTT babies. The final diagnosis of FTT is often made by placing the baby in a

---

[69] 321 U.S. 158, 166–67 (1944) (ruling on whether a parent may be convicted for providing children with religious literature to sell on the street in violation of child labor laws).

[70] *See* Jehovah's Witnesses in State of Washington v. King County Hosp. Unit No. 1, 390 U.S. 598 (1968) (per curiam), *aff'g* 278 F. Supp. 488 (W.D. Wash. 1967) (upholding a state statute authorizing dependency when parents refuse to allow their children to have blood transfusions).

[71] *See generally* Robert W. Block, Nancy F. Krebs & Committee on Child Abuse and Neglect and the Committee on Nutrition, *Failure to Thrive as a Manifestation of Child Neglect*, 116/5 PEDIATRICS 1234 (2005); Deborah A. Frank, *Failure to Thrive, in* DEVELOPMENTAL AND BEHAVIORAL PEDIATRICS: A HANDBOOK FOR PRIMARY CARE 183 (Steven Parker, Barry S. Zuckerman & Marilyn Augustyn eds., 2d ed. 2004); American Academy of Pediatrics, *Failure To Thrive (Pediatric Undernutrition), in* PEDIATRIC NUTRITION HANDBOOK 443 (Ronald E. Kleinman ed., 5th ed. 2003).

controlled environment, sometimes a foster home, but more typically a hospital, where the baby gains weight rapidly.

§ 2.4.5 Educational Neglect

States generally require children to attend school through a certain grade or until a certain age. The parent is not required to send the child to public school,[72] although the child must be given an adequate education in the private school. If the parent does not send the child to school or is unable to enforce school attendance, the parent may be said to have educationally neglected the child.

States that permit home-schooling generally have some prerequisites or require certain performance on standardized tests. Where there are specific statutory requirements, the first place to begin an analysis of the case is to determine whether those statutory requirements have been met. Where home schooling is inadequate, the child may found to be neglected. Where the state requires certain qualifications of the home teacher, proof that the parent lacks the minimum qualifications may be sufficient to show educational neglect.

---

[72] *See, e.g.*, Pierce v. Society of Sisters, 268 U.S. 510, 45 S.Ct. 571 (1925).

Chapter 3: Mental Health and Related Professional Evaluations in Child Welfare Proceedings[*]

by Ann M. Haralambie[1]

§ 3.1 Introduction

Mental health and related professional evaluations of child and adult parties involved in child welfare proceedings are essential in terms of clinical and forensic assessment and case disposition. The relationships between parents and children and among family systems are always an important part of child welfare cases. Parents involved in child welfare proceedings often have diagnosed or diagnosable mental health or substance abuse conditions and require proper identification and treatment.[2] Children also often have developmental, medical, or mental health conditions that can challenge parenting and require specialized services.[3]

Many states' laws provide that the mental illness of a parent may constitute grounds for dependency or termination of parental rights. The mere fact of a diagnosis, however, is only the beginning of the inquiry. The crucial determination is the effect of the mental illness on the parent's ability to care for the child. If the parent neglects or abuses the child or places the child in physical or emotional jeopardy, then the mental illness is relevant. A parent's mental illness may also impair his or her ability to benefit from services, or it may impact which types of services are effective. On the

---

[*] Reprinted from *Handling Child Custody, Abuse and Adoption Cases, Third Edition*, with permission of Thomson Reuters. For more information about this publication, please visit www.west.thomson.com. *Author's Note:* Portions of this chapter were adapted from ANN M. HARALAMBIE, 3 HANDLING CHILD CUSTODY, ABUSE, AND ADOPTION CASES 3D, Ch. 22 (Thomson West 2009). Additionally, portions were adapted with permission from other works by Ann Haralambie. The excerpts were previously published in THE CHILD'S ATTORNEY: A GUIDE TO REPRESENTING CHILDREN IN CUSTODY, ADOPTION, AND PROTECTION CASES AND CHILD SEXUAL ABUSE IN CIVIL CASES: A GUIDE TO CUSTODY AND TORT ACTIONS, published by the American Bar Association, copyright 1993 and 1999, respectively. All rights reserved. Reprinted by Permission. *This information or any portion thereof may not be copied or disseminated in any form or by any means or downloaded or stored in an electronic database or retrieval system without the express written consent of the American Bar Association.*

[1] Ann M. Haralambie, J.D., is a certified family law specialist practicing in Tucson, Arizona. She is also an author and speaker in the fields of family and children's law. The NACC is grateful to Christina Little, Ph.D., a clinical psychologist and Senior Instructor of Pediatrics, University of Colorado School of Medicine, for her contribution to the original version of this chapter.

[2] U.S. DEP'T OF HEALTH AND HUMAN SERVS., BLENDING PERSPECTIVES AND BUILDING COMMON GROUND: A REPORT TO CONGRESS ON SUBSTANCE ABUSE AND CHILD PROTECTION (1999).

[3] Robert B. Clyman, Brenda Jones Harden & Christina Little, *Assessment, Intervention, and Research with Infants in Out-of-Home Placement*, 23/5 INFANT MENT. HEALTH J. 435 (2002).

other hand, if the mental illness manifests itself as nothing more serious than eccentricity or problems similar to those of parents who are not labeled mentally ill, or if the mental illness is being controlled by medication or other therapy and the parent is treatment adherent, then it is not relevant.

If the state removes a child from a parent's custody, the state is obligated under the Adoption and Safe Families Act (ASFA)[4] to provide rehabilitative services to reunify the family if possible. Before a parent's rights may be terminated, however, courts generally require a finding that the parent is unfit and unlikely to become fit within a reasonable period of time. Mere progress by a parent, however, will not be sufficient if the child is still at risk. Under ASFA, the relevant time periods have been shortened. Therefore, the parent's attorney should move quickly to get the parent involved in effective treatment.

§ 3.2 Mental Health Professionals

While different types of mental health professionals may be involved in the child welfare case, the following professionals have the general capacity to evaluate and treat mental illness and should be certified or licensed by a governing body.[5] The disciplines of psychiatry, psychology, and social work each have diverse aspects of training and, by nature of the discipline, these professionals often possess specialized expertise in one or more areas. Further specialization is possible within each discipline. Infants and toddlers are a critical population within the child welfare system that often benefits from specialized expertise in evaluation and treatment. Children three years and under were the largest single group of victims, and were more likely than older children to re-experience maltreatment within six months of the first substantial report.[6] The large majority of children entering foster care is under three years old, and infants and toddlers tend to remain in foster care longer than older children.[7] While resources may be scarce in many communities, there are mental health professionals who sub-specialize in the field of infant mental health.[8]

Some other people holding themselves out as mental health practitioners may or may not be licensed or certified. There are many degrees and acronyms behind

---

[4] Pub. L. No. 105-89, 111 Stat. 2115 (codified as amended in scattered sections of 42 U.S.C.).

[5] For further information on using experts and treatises, see ANN M. HARALAMBIE, 3 HANDLING CHILD CUSTODY, ABUSE, AND ADOPTION CASES 3D, Ch. 22 (West 2009).

[6] ADMIN. FOR CHILDREN & FAMILIES, U.S. DEP'T OF HEALTH AND HUMAN SERVS., CHILD MALTREATMENT 2002: REPORTS FROM THE STATES TO THE NATIONAL CHILD ABUSE AND NEGLECT DATA SYSTEMS – NATIONAL STATISTICS ON CHILD ABUSE AND NEGLECT (2004).

[7] R. M. Goerge & F. Wulczyn, *Placement Experiences of the Youngest Foster Care Population: Findings from the Multistate Foster Care Data Archive*, 19/3 ZERO TO THREE 8 (1998).

[8] The Zero to Three organization published a diagnostic manual specific to the birth to three population. *See* Zero to Three: National Center for Infants, Toddlers, and Families, *Diagnostic Classification of Mental Health and Developmental Disorders of Infancy and Early Childhood* (1994) (DC: 0-3). For information and resources on infant mental health resources, see the Zero to Three Web site at http://zerotothree.org/.

people's names which purport to identify the holders as "mental health professionals." Further, there are various "diplomas" or other credentials that can be purchased over the Internet or through the mail which can create the illusion that the person possesses specialized training. Licensure or certification allows the lawyer and the court to have an "objective evaluation" of a professional's *entry-level* competence for practice.[9] For all professionals, the theoretical underpinnings of various types of training may be quite different.

Further, even well-educated and experienced mental health professionals may have *clinical* training and experience but lack *forensic* training and experience. Both the purposes and some of the methods of clinical evaluation and forensic evaluations differ, and these differences are important.[10] Forensic evaluations are specifically tailored to answer legal questions. Forensic experts are trained to maintain a healthy skepticism about what they hear from parties and to seek corroboration and multiple sources of information. Several professional organizations have adopted guidelines for forensic evaluations. For example, Division 41 of the American Psychological Association and the American Psychology-Law Society have jointly adopted guidelines applicable to all forensic psychology situations.[11] A number of organizations now have developed professional guidelines for forensic evaluations in child custody and child sexual abuse cases.[12]

---

[9] Celia B. Fisher, *American Psychological Association's (1992) Ethics and the Validation of Sexual Abuse in Day-Care Settings*, 1/2 PSYCHOL. PUB. POL'Y & L. 4 (1995).

[10] *See, e.g.,* Alicia Pellegrin, *Daubert and Forensic Psychological Evaluations, in* STANDING AT THE FOREFRONT: EFFECTIVE ADVOCACY IN TODAY'S WORLD 271, 275 (Anne Kellogg ed., NACC Children's Law Manual Series, 2009 Edition) ("the fact that tests may be appropriate and useful in a clinical situation, yet not be admissible in a court, is a significant example of the difference between clinical and forensic psychology"). *See generally* THE SCIENTIFIC BASIS OF CHILD CUSTODY DECISIONS (Robert M. Galatzer-Levy, Louis Kraus & Jeanne Galatzer-Levy eds., 2d ed. 2009); GARY B. MELTON, JOHN PETRILA, NORMAN G. POYTHRESS & CHRISTOPHER SLOBOGIN, PSYCHOLOGICAL EVALUATIONS FOR THE COURTS: A HANDBOOK FOR MENTAL HEALTH PROFESSIONALS AND LAWYERS (3d ed. 2007); JONATHAN W. GOULD & DAVID A. MARTINDALE, THE ART AND SCIENCE OF CHILD CUSTODY EVALUATIONS (2007); FORENSIC MENTAL HEALTH ASSESSMENT OF CHILDREN AND ADOLESCENTS (Steven N. Sparta & Gerald P. Koocher eds., 2006); KIRK S. HEILBRUN, PRINCIPLES OF FORENSIC MENTAL HEALTH ASSESSMENT (2001); Jonathan W. Gould, H. D. Kirkpatrick, William G. Austin & David A. Martindale, *Critiquing a Colleague's Forensic Advisory Report: A Suggested Protocol for Application to Child Custody Evaluations*, 1/3 J. CHILD CUSTODY 37 (2004).

[11] *See, e.g.,* Committee on Ethical Guidelines for Forensic Psychologists, *Specialty Guidelines for Forensic Psychologists*, 15/6 LAW & HUM. BEHAV. 655 (1991).

[12] American Academy of Child and Adolescent Psychiatry, *Practice Parameters for the Forensic Evaluation of Children and Adolescents Who May Have Been Physically or Sexually Abused*, 36/3 J. AM. ACAD. CHILD ADOLESC. PSYCHIATRY 423 (1997); American Professional Society on the Abuse of Children, *APSAC Guidelines for Practice: Psychosocial Evaluation of Suspected Sexual Abuse in Children* (2d ed. 1997); American Professional Society on the Abuse of Children, *APSAC Guidelines for Practice: Psychosocial Evaluation of Suspected Psychological Maltreatment in Children and Adolescents* (1995); American Medical Association *Diagnostic and Treatment Guidelines on Child Sexual Abuse* (American Medical Association 1992); American Academy of Pediatrics, Committee on Child Abuse and Neglect, *Guidelines for the Evaluation of Sexual Abuse of Children*, 87/2 PEDIATRICS 254 (1991).

§ 3.2.1 Psychiatrists

A psychiatrist is a licensed medical doctor who chooses to practice in the mental health area. Psychiatrists diagnose and treat mental illness. It is not necessary that the doctor have had any more training in psychiatry than other doctors, but the majority of psychiatrists have had an internship and residency in psychiatry following graduation from medical school. Psychiatrists are generally not trained in the administration or interpretation of psychological testing. If a psychiatrist is "board certified" it usually means that he or she has met national criteria and passed a rigorous examination in the field by the American Board of Psychiatry and Neurology, which certifies physicians in psychiatry, child psychiatry, and neurology, or the American Board of Forensic Psychiatry, which certifies physicians in forensic psychiatry, also based on an examination. There are also a number of professional organizations that do not certify members. These organizations include the American Academy of Psychiatry and Law and the American Academy of Adolescent and Child Psychiatry.

Psychiatrists follow the code of ethics of the American Psychiatric Association. Psychiatrists may be the experts of choice where a party has complex psychiatric diagnoses or is on psychotropic medication. Many psychiatrists pursue training and board certification in subspecialty areas with relevance to child welfare proceedings, including: child and adolescent psychiatry and substance abuse. In cases where children need to be evaluated and possibly treated with medication, it is important for a psychiatrist specifically trained in child and adolescent psychiatry to be involved.

§ 3.2.2 Psychologists[13]

A psychologist is a licensed or certified mental health professional who has a doctorate in a field of psychology. Psychologists deal with their patients' experiences, thoughts, and emotions, and evaluate and treat healthy as well as mentally ill patients. There are many types of psychologists, such as clinical psychologists, rehabilitation psychologists, research psychologists, industrial psychologists, and occupational psychologists. It is important to understand what degree and type of training the psychologist has. For example, Psy.D (doctor of psychology) psychologists receive less training in research than do Ph.D. (doctor of philosophy) psychologists, even though both have doctoral level degrees.[14] Psychologists in each field are trained differently and approach problems differently. One type of psychologist may be well trained to do therapy, while another type has had no clinical experience whatsoever. Forensic psychologists have specialized training in doing forensic assessments, which address the specific legal issues at hand. They are less likely than clinical

---

[13] *See* AMERICAN PSYCHOLOGICAL ASSOCIATION COMMITTEE ON PROFESSIONAL PRACTICE AND STANDARDS, GUIDELINES FOR PSYCHOLOGICAL EVALUATIONS IN CHILD PROTECTION MATTERS (American Psychological Association 1998), *available at* http://www.apa.org/practice/guidelines/child-protection.pdf.

[14] *See* Richard A. Crain, *Choosing the Best Custody Expert Witness*, 30 FAM. ADVOC. 12, 13 (2008).

psychologists without forensic training to accept at face value the reports of the client and to seek collateral sources of information and corroboration.

In some states, professionals with a Master's degree in Clinical Psychology can also practice as psychologists. In order to be licensed as a psychologist, supervised pre- and post-doctoral mental health internships must be completed and a state licensing examination must be passed. Each state has its own certification or licensing requirements. In addition to the diagnosis and treatment of mental illness and other psychosocial problems, psychologists are extensively trained in psychometric testing and research methodology. Clinical psychologists generally have more extensive training and skill in all types of psychometric testing than do other types of psychologists.

Psychologists follow the code of ethics of the American Psychological Association (APA). A psychologist may be called a "Fellow" of the APA for making "unusual and outstanding contributions in the field of psychology." The requirements to become a Fellow are more rigorous than they used to be, so it is important to know when a psychologist became a Fellow. Two Boards confer *diplomate* status on psychologists based on examinations: the American Board of Professional Psychology and the American Board of Forensic Psychology. Certification by those boards is not as frequent among psychologists as board certification is for psychiatrists. There is an annual national register of psychologists that lists all psychologists who are certified as health service providers, showing particular qualifications to provide treatment.[15]

§ 3.2.3 Social Workers

Social workers are concerned with how a person or family functions, with reference to external influences as well as individual capabilities and mental and emotional status. For example, social workers assess the pressures and supports of the parties' finances, employment, and extended family. Social workers are virtually always primary witnesses in dependency, termination of parental rights, and adoption cases. They are particularly useful in cases of child abuse and neglect and family dysfunction. More frequently than most other professionals, social workers make home visits and coordinate referrals to various other professionals and agencies. Social workers are also qualified to do counseling. Some attorneys and judges seriously underestimate the knowledge, training, and experience of good social workers. Although they may informally be referred to as "social workers," many "caseworkers" are not, in fact, trained social workers.

Social workers who practice mental health evaluation and treatment are specifically titled "Clinical Social Workers." They must complete a Master's Degree in Social Work and are trained in the diagnosis and treatment of mental illness. As part of this degree, they complete extensive internships in clinical settings. Licensing

---

[15] COUNCIL FOR THE NAT'L REGISTER OF HEALTH SERV. PROVIDERS IN PSYCHOLOGY, NATIONAL REGISTER OF HEALTH SERVICE PROVIDERS IN PSYCHOLOGY, http://www.nationalregister.com.

is certified by each state and licenses are not necessarily transferable across states. To become a licensed clinical social worker, L.C.S.W., the social worker must pass an examination and meet other state requirements. Social workers follow a code of ethics adopted by the National Association of Social Workers (NASW). A social worker with A.C.S.W. after his or her name has been certified by the Academy of Certified Social Workers, part of the NASW, after taking a national examination and providing evidence of superior skill. The National Organization of Forensic Social Work certifies social workers based on training, experience, and examination. Diplomates must have at least a Masters of Social Work Degree and three years of experience following their masters degree. Social workers may also pursue doctoral degrees in social work.

§ 3.2.4 Evidentiary Privilege and Confidentiality

In general, patients have an evidentiary privilege protecting their communications with mental health professionals. The privilege is based on state law. States frequently provide such a privilege for psychiatrists, physicians, and psychologists. Some states also extend the privilege to other certified mental health professionals, such as social workers, marriage counselors, and rape crisis counselors. However, the privilege does not arise for communications made during a court-ordered evaluation.[16]

An attorney may use a mental health professional as a consultant or advisor, and that professional may even evaluate the client. An expert serving in this capacity is part of the attorney's "team," whose file and recommendations come within the attorney's work-product privilege so long as the expert will not be used as a witness.

§ 3.3 Evaluations

Child welfare attorneys and evaluation professionals should be mutually clear on the purpose of an evaluation and how it is to be subsequently used. In any written evaluation report, the evaluator should describe the methods used and the reasoning for conclusions and recommendations. The specific reason for an evaluation referral should dictate what type of assessment methods are used and, at times, by what type of professional. A mental health, psychiatric, or psychological evaluation addresses an individual's mental and emotional status, provides diagnostic information, and offers recommendations if appropriate. However, the comprehensive child welfare evaluation should include more than merely a psychiatric or psychological evaluation of each party. In terms of treatment planning for the family and information regarding case disposition, evaluations geared specifically to parenting competencies and the quality of the parent-child relationship are often the most useful for child welfare proceedings.

---

[16] For a discussion of confidentiality in reporting and investigating child maltreatment, see Chapter 18, Confidentiality.

Three United States Supreme Court cases have changed the foundational requirements for expert testimony: *Daubert v. Merrell Dow Pharmaceuticals, Inc.,*[17] *G.E. Co. v. Joiner,*[18] and *Kumho Tire Co. v. Carmichael.*[19] Taken together, these cases place great responsibility on the trial court as gatekeepers for determining the reliability of expert testimony and the methods by which the experts arrived at their opinions and conclusions. Therefore, it is important for attorneys to understand the different types of psychological testing and other methods used in an evaluation.

§ 3.3.1 Evaluating the Evaluation

The first thing the attorney needs to do is to evaluate the evaluation on several levels. In child welfare evaluations, the mental health professional should adhere to the same ethical and practice principles that would be used in any other type of evaluation specific to his or her field. Evaluation methods that are culturally insensitive or inappropriately used or interpreted, overstating the reliability or validity of instruments, and otherwise inadequate evaluations can result in unwise decisions by the court in the child welfare proceeding. The credibility and persuasiveness of the report can never exceed those of the expert who made the evaluation. Therefore, the attorney must review the qualifications of the evaluator. The attorney should determine what type of expert conducted the evaluation and how much expertise he or she has in the particular areas involved in the case. For example, if psychometric tests are administered or interpreted as part of the evaluation, the expert should have training in psychometric testing. In child evaluations, the expert must have specialized training in child development and assessment.

It is also essential for the evaluator to consider the emotional status of the persons being evaluated. Involvement in child welfare proceedings occur in the context of stress and possible crisis for the family, and the timing of any evaluation in the course of the proceedings should be kept in mind. Examples may include whether or not a traumatizing physical or psychological event has just occurred or the presence of possible separation effects on both parents and children if the child has been removed from the home. Behavior and performance in evaluations may change over time. For example, performance may change in response to intervention, or for children, placement changes. It is recommended that all types of evaluations be based on multiple methods, multiple sources, and multiple sessions.[20] It is important to know exactly how much time the evaluator spent with the persons being evaluated and how that time was used. For example, the attorney should know who participated in the evaluation (some of the parties, all of the parties, friends and relatives, teachers,

---

[17] 509 U.S. 579 (1993).

[18] 522 U.S. 136 (1997).

[19] 526 U.S. 137 (1999).

[20] Karen S. Budd, Erika D. Felix, LaShaunda M. Poindexter, Anjali T. Naik-Polan & Christine F. Sloss, *Clinical Assessment of Children in Child Protection Cases: An Empirical Analysis*, 33/1 Prof. Psychol. Res. Pract. 3 (2002).

physicians, and other professionals involved with the child or parents), the length of the evaluation, and the procedures used. Further, the attorney should ascertain whether various people were seen individually or together. An evaluation made over a period of time is more likely to be reliable than one made after a one-time visit; however, most agency evaluations of parents or children are made after only one visit. Therefore, there may be a question about whether the findings, particularly those based on one method or source of information, can be generalized. The mental health professional should address the limitations of the evaluation and the generalizability of the findings in the report.

The conclusions reached should be based on articulatable grounds and should be supported by clear reasoning. Often experts who are basing their recommendations on purely subjective factors will write reports that are so vague or full of imprecise jargon that they would not be acceptable by the standards of their profession. The attorney and his or her own expert should understand the report and the evaluator's reasoning. Claims to a scientific basis for the recommendation should be well supported by use of scientific methodology and empirical evidence. Clinical judgment should be labeled as such.

§ 3.3.2 Mental Health Evaluations and Diagnoses

Psychological and psychiatric evaluations are performed for many different reasons, and they address problems and competencies that may or may not be relevant to the legal and social issues presented by child welfare proceedings. Therefore, child welfare attorneys need to understand the context and purpose of any procedures and records that are being used. From a mental health professional's standpoint, evaluations can be thought of as forensic or clinical. Forensic evaluations are intended to address a legal issue or question, while clinical assessments are most relevant for treatment needs and planning.[21] Mental health professionals must be cautious not to engage in "multiple relationships," which generally contraindicates the same professional acting as both an evaluator and mental health treatment provider.[22] To understand the treatment needs of a parent or child, a mental health evaluation could focus on one or more different domains, including but not limited to the need for services targeted toward a specific diagnosis of mental illness, substance abuse treatment, or the potential need for psychiatric medication. Specific referral questions regarding a child

---

[21] American Academy of Child and Adolescent Psychiatry, *Practice Parameters for the Forensic Evaluation of Children and Adolescents Who May Have Been Physically or Sexually Abused*, 36/10 J. AM. ACAD. CHILD ADOLESC. PSYCHIATRY 37S (1997).

[22] American Psychological Association, *Ethical Principles of Psychologists and Code of Conduct*, 57/12 AM. PSYCHOL. 1060 (2002); Karen S. Budd, Erika D. Felix, LaShaunda M. Poindexter, Anjali T. Naik-Polan & Christine F. Sloss, *Clinical Assessment of Children in Child Protection Cases: An Empirical Analysis*, 33/1 PROF. PSYCHOL. RES. PRACT. 3 (2002); David E. Arredondo & Hon. Leonard P. Edwards, *Attachment, Bonding, and Reciprocal Connectedness: Limitations of Attachment Theory in the Juvenile and Family Court*, 2 J. CENTER FOR FAMILIES, CHILDREN & COURTS 109 (2000), *available at* http://www.courtinfo.ca.gov/programs/cfcc/pdffiles/109arredando.pdf.

could also address the psychological and developmental impacts of maltreatment or separation from family, types of services needed in multiple domains, or the impact of visitation or reunification with the birth family.

The attorney should be familiar with the current edition of the American Psychiatric Association's DIAGNOSTIC AND STATISTICAL MANUAL OF MENTAL DISORDERS (DSM),[23] which represents the most recent classification of mental disorders for both adults and children. Disorders are arranged by categories, and within the categories, more specific disorders are described and assigned a diagnostic number. Each category is explained in general terms, and each specific disorder is described according to essential features, associated features, predisposing factors, and other parameters. Some disorders are further broken down into subtypes, and differential diagnoses for those are listed. The most useful features for attorneys are the diagnostic criteria and differential diagnosis sections. Psychiatric and psychological evaluations frequently contain the DSM diagnosis number. The DSM sets forth five axes on which the individual is to be evaluated. They are:

- Clinical syndromes (Axis I)
- Personality disorders and specific developmental disorders (Axis II)
- Physical disorders and conditions (Axis III)
- Severity of psycho-social stressors (Axis IV)
- Highest level of functioning past year (Axis V)

The Axis I clinical syndromes include disorders such as those involving depression, anxiety (including Post-Traumatic Stress Disorder), psychosis, and substance abuse. Axis I clinical syndromes may be acute or chronic. Axis II disorders, such as Borderline Personality Disorder, tend to be fairly persistent parts of the person's make-up, but currently there are treatment strategies targeted toward some personality disorders.[24] Both Axis I and Axis II conditions require treatment by mental health professionals with expertise in that specific disorder.

§ 3.3.3 Parent-Child Relationship Evaluations

Evaluations of the parent-child relationship are complex and require a great deal of specialized expertise. Evaluations should incorporate multiple methods of gaining information including direct observation of parent and child interactions, preferably in multiple sessions and in natural surroundings, and a consideration of strengths as well as problems. Although there are some general professional guidelines for parent-child

---

[23] AMERICAN PSYCHIATRIC ASSOCIATION, DIAGNOSTIC AND STATISTICAL MANUAL FOR MENTAL DISORDERS, TEXT REVISION (DSM–IV–TR) (4th ed. 2000) is the current edition.

[24] Marsha M. Linehan, Bryan N. Cochran & Constance A. Kehrer, *Dialectical Behavior Therapy for Borderline Personality Disorder, in* CLINICAL HANDBOOK OF PSYCHOLOGICAL DISORDERS: A STEP-BY-STEP TREATMENT MANUAL 470–522 (David H. Barlow ed., 3d ed. 2001).

evaluations,[25] there are currently no standardized protocols that are widely used. However, promising measures include clinical adaptations of the Crowell Assessment[26] and the Emotional Availability Scales.[27] Relationship evaluations may be useful in many aspects of a child welfare case, such as providing specific parent and child mental health treatment recommendations, and providing information for making placement and visitation decisions and case dispositions. In very general terms, this type of evaluation should assess the relationships among the relevant adult parties and the child, the needs of the child, and the abilities of the parents or other caregivers to meet those needs.[28]

Specific referrals for evaluation regarding parental capacities, parent-child treatment planning, and case disposition are often variably termed "parent-child interactionals," "attachment studies/evaluations," or "bonding studies/evaluations." There are important distinctions between the meaning of the terms "attachment" and "bonding" from a theoretical child development perspective, and there has been some criticism that the terms are used with a lack of precision in forensic/clinical practice.[29] The concepts of secure and insecure attachment derived from theory and research[30] can be useful in describing child behavior with the caregiver. But from a research perspective, attachment is one aspect of the caregiver-child relationship, and it refers specifically to behavior exhibited by the child in the context of separations and reunions. Empirical research has shown that the majority of maltreated children exhibit disorganized attachment patterns;[31] therefore, observing the specific behaviors of each adult and child with one another is crucial. In making treatment or dispositional recommendations, it is not sufficient to rely solely on broadly termed

---

[25] AMERICAN PSYCHOLOGICAL ASSOCIATION COMMITTEE ON PROFESSIONAL PRACTICE AND STANDARDS, GUIDELINES FOR PSYCHOLOGICAL EVALUATIONS IN CHILD PROTECTION MATTERS (American Psychological Association 1998), *available at* http://www.apa.org/practice/guidelines/child-protection.pdf.

[26] Cindy S. Lederman & Joy D. Osofsky, *Infant Mental Health Interventions in Juvenile Court: Ameliorating the Effects of Maltreatment and Deprivation,* 10/1 PSYCH. PUB. POL'Y & L. 162 (2004); Judith A. Crowell & Melissa A. Fleischmann, *Use of Structured Research Procedures in Clinical Assessments of Infants,* in HANDBOOK OF INFANT MENTAL HEALTH 210–21 (Charles H. Zeanah, Jr. ed., The Guilford Press 2000).

[27] Z. Biringen, J. L. Robinson & R. N. Emde, *The Emotional Availability Scales,* Unpublished Manuscript, University of Colorado, Health Science Center, Denver (1998, 1993).

[28] AMERICAN PSYCHOLOGICAL ASSOCIATION COMMITTEE ON PROFESSIONAL PRACTICE AND STANDARDS, GUIDELINES FOR PSYCHOLOGICAL EVALUATIONS IN CHILD PROTECTION MATTERS (American Psychological Association 1998), *available at* http://www.apa.org/practice/guidelines/child-protection.pdf .

[29] David E. Arredondo & Hon. Leonard P. Edwards, *Attachment, Bonding, and Reciprocal Connectedness: Limitations of Attachment Theory in the Juvenile and Family Court,* 2 J. CENTER FOR FAMILIES, CHILDREN & COURTS 109 (2000), *available at* http://www.courtinfo.ca.gov/programs/cfcc/pdffiles/109arredando.pdf.

[30] *See* Chapter 4, Child Development and the Impact of Maltreatment.

[31] *See* Dante Cicchetti & Sheree L. Toth, *A Developmental Psychopathology Perspective on Child Abuse and Neglect,* 34/5 J. AM. ACAD. CHILD ADOLESC. PSYCHIATRY 541 (1995).

attachment behavior in a forensic or clinical evaluation. The evaluation should focus on *reciprocal* relationship behaviors between adult and child on a number of dimensions (e.g., parental warmth and control, the ability to read child cues appropriately, and child responsivity to the parent). Additionally, an evaluation of parenting capacity should consider the ability to provide adequately for a child's basic needs and safety.

It is possible that the particular needs (i.e., developmental, medical, or mental health) of a specific child may exceed the ability of a specific parent to address them.[32] Prior experience with problematic caregiving can promote child behaviors that, while adaptive in the previous context with an abusive or neglectful parent,[33] can challenge even a typically sensitive caregiver. The child's developmental stage should also be considered in conjunction with specific parenting capacities. If the evaluation identifies parenting deficiencies, the evaluation should include: (1) a description of the specific nature of the deficiencies; (2) a prognosis and recommendations for what would be needed to remediate the problems; and (3) a reasonable estimate of the time the remediation might take. A time estimate is important to assist the parties and the court to determine whether the remediation is likely to occur within the state- and federally-mandated time frames. Subsequent treatment that targets parenting problems should be provided by a mental health professional experienced in parent-child therapy. For infants and toddlers, treatment needs to take place jointly with the primary caregivers and the child. If the child is in non-parental care and reunification is indicated, treatment should occur with the parent and child, for example through therapeutic visitation.[34]

§ 3.4 Psychological Tests

For both adults and children, referral for testing by a psychologist can target functioning in different domains of cognition or other development, provide further information regarding emotional issues, and provide further recommendations for treatment. Child welfare attorneys should be familiar with the most commonly used

---

[32] AMERICAN PSYCHOLOGICAL ASSOCIATION COMMITTEE ON PROFESSIONAL PRACTICE AND STANDARDS, GUIDELINES FOR PSYCHOLOGICAL EVALUATIONS IN CHILD PROTECTION MATTERS (American Psychological Association 1998), *available at* http://www.apa.org/practice/guidelines/child-protection.pdf; Corina Benjet, Sandra T. Azar & Regina Kuersten-Hogan, *Evaluating the Parental Fitness of Psychiatrically Diagnosed Individuals: Advocating a Functional-Contextual Analysis of Parenting*, 17/2 J. FAM. PSYCHOL. 238 (2003).

[33] P. M. Crittenden, *Attachment and Risk for Psychopathology: The Early Years*, 16/3 J. DEV. BEHAV. PEDIATR. S12 (1995).

[34] A. F. Lieberman, R. Silverman & J. Pawl, *Infant-Parent Psychotherapy: Core Concepts and Current Approaches*, *in* HANDBOOK OF INFANT MENTAL HEALTH 472–84 (Charles H. Zeanah, Jr. ed., The Guilford Press 2000); Mary Dozier, Elizabeth Higley, Kathleen E. Albus & Anna Nutter, *Intervening with Foster Infants' Caregivers: Targeting Three Critical Needs*, 23/5 INFANT MENT. HEALTH J. 541 (2002); C. H. Zeanah, J. A. Larrieu, S. S. Heller, J. Valliere, S. Hinshaw-Fuselier, Y. Aoki & M. Drilling, *Evaluation of a Preventive Intervention for Maltreated Infants and Toddlers in Foster Care*, 40/2 J. AM. ACAD. CHILD ADOLESC. PSYCHIATRY 214 (2001).

psychological tests. Consultation with a qualified psychologist can be very useful in helping to understand the tests used in an evaluation, the appropriateness of using the tests, and how they were used and interpreted. There are hundreds of psychological (psychometric) tests. Some are widely used, and others are not. Some have a solid empirical basis, and others do not. Methods of finding information on test characteristics, test usage, and tester qualifications can be accessed through the American Psychological Association.[35]

If the evaluator used psychological tests, the attorney should know what the tests were, whether they were used properly, and whether the evaluator personally administered the tests and interpreted the results. Tests used as the basis for expert testimony should be used widely in the profession, the norms should be standardized for the population to whom they are being applied, and the tests should be validated for the purposes for which they are used.[36] "Reliability" in a psychological instrument refers to a test being administered and interpreted in the same way by different clinicians. "Validity" refers to whether the instrument really measures what it claims to measure. Attorneys should find out whether the psychological tests used have been established as both reliable and valid. The education, reading ability, and language fluency of the test-taker all affect whether the person being evaluated understands the task he or she is being asked to complete. A perfectly acceptable test can be useless if the test-taker is not able to understand and comply with the requirements of the test. In many evaluation contexts, test takers can be prone to give socially desirable answers and have varying motivation to fully participate. In child welfare proceedings, these issues can be heightened and many factors may influence the willingness of the test taker's compliance, honesty, and willingness to be complete in giving answers. The evaluator should explicitly take the assessment context and the test taker's behavior into consideration when interpreting the results and offering recommendations.

§ 3.4.1 Psychometric Tests

Psychometric tests sample certain information, and the interpretation generalizes from the responses, making assumptions and predictions about a person based on that sampling in comparison to the scores obtained by other people. Psychometric tests are either objective or projective. Objective tests involve standardized administration, scoring, and interpretation that does not require clinical judgment, although clinical judgment should be used to interpret test results for the particular person and context. Projective tests generally examine how a person responds to ambiguous stimuli and rely on clinical interpretation to score as well as to interpret the results. They permit great flexibility in how the person tested responds to the stimulus given. Some tests are based

---

[35] *See* http://www.apa.org.

[36] A test can be valid and reliable for some uses but not for others. For example, the MMPI (discussed in the section below in *Personality Tests*), is useful for many purposes, but it cannot diagnose someone as a pedophile. Therefore, it is important to know whether there is empirical support for using the test to answer the specific questions being addressed.

on self-reports, others involve completion of checklists by lay persons such as parents, foster parents and teachers, and still others rely on direct measurement of performance.

There are thousands of psychometric tests. Some are widely used, and others are not. Most are not designed for use in forensic settings. Where psychologists are involved in child welfare cases, psychometric tests are likely to be part of the evaluation process. It is important for attorneys to have at least a general knowledge of the tests used in evaluations, and if particular tests are used in an evaluation, the attorney should look specifically at those tests.[37] There are some valid and reliable pure forensic instruments, some which are forensically relevant, and others which are designed for use in clinical settings but from which clinicians who testify sometimes extrapolate inappropriately.[38] The attorney should review books that discuss various psychological tests to become familiar with the background, purposes, and use of any tests that have been administered to the parties,[39] and should also review books on forensic evaluations.[40]

---

[37] For critical reviews of commercially available, English-language instruments, the attorney should look at the Buros Institute's Mental Measurements Yearbook series. The most current version is THE EIGHTEENTH MENTAL MEASUREMENTS YEARBOOK (Robert A. Spies, Janet F. Carlson & Kurt F. Geisinger eds., 2010). For $15 per test, one can download reviews for over 2,500 tests that include specifics on test purpose, population, publication date, administration time, and descriptive test evaluations. *See* the Web site of the Buros Institute of Mental Measurements, http://buros.unl.edu/buros/jsp/search.jsp.

[38] The Association of Family and Conciliation Courts, Model Standards of Practice for Child Custody Evaluation, Standard 6.4 (2006), specifically provides that "[e]valuators shall not use instruments for purposes other than those for which they have been previously validated."

[39] *See, e.g.*, JAMES N. BUTCHER, JOHN R. GRAHAM, CAROLYN L. WILLIAMS & YOSSEF S. BEN-PORATH, DEVELOPMENT AND USE OF THE MMPI-2 CONTENT SCALES (MMPI-2 MONOGRAPH SERIES) (2007); KENNETH S. POPE, JAMES N. BUTCHER & JOYCE SEELEN, THE MMPI, MMPI-2 & MMPI-A IN COURT: A PRACTICAL GUIDE FOR EXPERT WITNESSES AND ATTORNEYS (2006); JOHN E. EXNER, THE RORSCHACH: BASIC FOUNDATIONS AND PRINCIPLES OF INTERPRETATION (Vol. 1) (2002); DONALD P. OGDON, PSYCHODIAGNOSTICS AND PERSONALITY ASSESSMENT: A HANDBOOK (2d ed. 1998); ALAN F. FRIEDMAN, RICHARD LEWAK, DAVID S. NICHOLS & JAMES. T. WEBB, PSYCHOLOGICAL ASSESSMENT WITH THE MMPI-2 (Lawrence Erlbaum 2001); THEODORE MILLON, THE MILLON CLINICAL MULTIAXIAL INVENTORY-III MANUAL (Pearson NCS, Inc. 4th ed. 2009); A. T. BECK, R. A. STEER & G. K. BROWN, BECK DEPRESSION INVENTORY MANUAL, SECOND EDITION (The Psychological Corporation 1996); LARRY H. BROWN & MICHAEL A. UNGER, SENTENCE COMPLETION SERIES: PROFESSIONAL USER'S GUIDE (Psychological Assessment Resources 1992); J. N. BUTCHER, J. R. GRAHAM, Y. S. BEN-PORATH, A. TELLEGEN, W. G. DAHLSTROM & B. KAEMMER, THE MINNESOTA MULTIPHASIC PERSONALITY INVENTORY-2 (MMPI-2): MANUAL FOR ADMINISTRATION, SCORING, AND INTERPRETATION (Rev. ed. 2001); MEASURING MENTAL ILLNESS: PSYCHOMETRIC ASSESSMENT FOR CLINICIANS (Scott Wetzler ed., 1989); HANDBOOK OF CLINICAL ASSESSMENT OF CHILDREN AND ADOLESCENTS (Clarice Kestenbaum & Daniel Williams eds., 1988); THE ASSESSMENT OF CHILD AND ADOLESCENT PERSONALITY (Howard M. Knoff ed., 1986); THOMAS GRISSO, EVALUATING COMPETENCIES: FORENSIC ASSESSMENTS AND INSTRUMENTS (2d ed. 2003).

[40] *See, e.g.*, GARY B. MELTON, JOHN PETRILA, NORMAN G. POYTHRESS & CHRISTOPHER SLOBOGIN, PSYCHOLOGICAL EVALUATIONS FOR THE COURTS: A HANDBOOK FOR MENTAL HEALTH PROFESSIONALS AND LAWYERS (3d ed. 2007); JOANNA BUNKER ROHRBAUGH, A COMPREHENSIVE GUIDE TO CHILD CUSTODY EVALUATIONS: MENTAL HEALTH AND LEGAL PERSPECTIVES (2007); FORENSIC MENTAL HEALTH ASSESSMENT OF CHILDREN AND ADOLESCENTS (Steven N. Sparta & Gerald P. Koocher eds., 2006); MARK J. ACKERMAN & ANDREW W. KANE, PSYCHOLOGICAL EXPERTS IN DIVORCE ACTIONS (4th

§ 3.4.2 Personality Tests

Personality tests are used in most evaluations in child welfare cases. They measure personality traits, temperament, psychological functioning, and adjustment. They can be either objective or projective tests. The best known objective personality test is the Minnesota Multiphasic Personality Inventory (MMPI), now in a revised edition (MMPI-2),[41] for adults and the MMPI-Adolescent Version (MMPI-A)[42] for adolescents. The test publisher, the University of Minnesota, does not continue to sell the original MMPI, supporting only the MMPI-2. The MMPI-2 is a 567-item true/false test that the test-taker answers by filling in a scoring sheet. Interpretation includes validity scales, clinical scales, and a number of supplemental scales. Because the validity and clinical scales are based only on the first 370 items, it is acceptable for a clinician to administer only those first 370 items, rather than including all 567 items, which are necessary for using the content subscales. In 2008 a restructured form of the MMPI, called the MMPI-2-RF, was published as a more psychometrically up-to-date version of the instrument.[43] It has been pared down to 338 items and uses 50 scales, many of which are new. It eliminated all of the older MMPI-2 clinical scales in favor of using the MMPI-2 Restructured Content (RC) scales, which were developed in 2003 using more rigorous empirical methods and study,[44] and the Fake Bad Scale (FBS), which was added to the MMPI-2 in 2007. In the MMPI-2-RF, no item is repeated in more than one of the RC scales, which reduces the correlations among the scales . The MMPI-2-RF also added a new validity scale, an over reporting scale of somatic symptoms scale (Fs). The use of the RC scales has created some controversy within the mental health professions.[45] Not all psychologists are using the newest

---

ed. 2005); KIRK S. HEILBRUN, PRINCIPLES OF FORENSIC MENTAL HEALTH ASSESSMENT (2001); THOMAS GRISSO, EVALUATING COMPETENCIES: FORENSIC ASSESSMENTS AND INSTRUMENTS (2d ed. 2003).

[41] STARKE R. HATHAWAY & J. CHARLNEY MCKINLEY, MINNESOTA MULTIPHASIC PERSONALITY INVENTORY-2 (1989).

[42] JAMES N. BUTCHER ET AL., MMPI-A: MINNESOTA MULTIPHASIC PERSONALITY INVENTORY-ADOLESCENT: MANUAL FOR ADMINISTRATION, SCORING, AND INTERPRETATION (The University of Minnesota Press MMPI Adolescent Project Committee 1992).

[43] YOSSEF S. BEN-PORATH & AUKE TELLEGEN, MINNESOTA MULTIPHASIC PERSONALITY INVENTORY-2-RESTRUCTURED FORM (2008).

[44] *See, e.g.*, A. TELLEGEN, Y. S. BEN-PORATH, J. L. MCNULTY, P. A. ARBISI, J. R. GRAHAM & B. KAEMMER, B., THE MMPI-2 RESTRUCTURED CLINICAL SCALES: DEVELOPMENT, VALIDATION, AND INTERPRETATION (2003).

[45] *See, e.g.*, James N. Butcher & Carolyn L. Williams, *Personality Assessment with the MMPI-2: Historical Roots, International Adaptations, and Current Challenges*, 1/1 APPLIED PSYCHOL. HEALTH & WELL-BEING 105 (2009); R. Rogers, K. W. Sewell, K. S. Harrison & M. J. Jordan, *The MMPI-2 Restructured Clinical Scales: A Paradigmatic Shift in Scale Development*, 87/2 J. PERSONALITY ASSESS. 139 (2006); A. Tellegen, Y. S. Ben-Porath, M. Sellbom, P. A. Arbisi, J. L. McNulty & J. R. Graham, *Further Validity of the MMPI-2 Restructured Clinical (RC) Scales: Addressing Questions Raised by Rogers et al. and Nichols*, 87/2 J. PERSONALITY ASSESS. 148 (2006); R. P. Archer, *A Perspective on the Restructured Clinical (RC) Scale Project*, 87/2 J. PERSONALITY ASSESS. 179 (2006); James N. Butcher, Cassia K. Hamilton, Steven V. Rouse & Edward J. Cumella, *The Deconstruction of the Hy Scale of MMPI-2: Failure of RC3 in Measuring Somatic Symptom Expression*, 87/2 J. PERSONALITY ASSESS. 186 (2006); A. B. Caldwell, *Maximal Measurement or*

form of the instrument, so it is important to know exactly which MMPI was administered and how it was scored and interpreted. If the MMPI-2-RF was used in an evaluation, it is critical to refer to an authoritative book on the subject[46] and experts who are familiar with this new instrument.

Another personality test is the Millon Clinical Multiaxial Inventory, now in a revised edition (MCMI-III)[47] and Millon Adolescent Clinical Inventory (MACI).[48] The MCMI-III is a 175-item true/false test that the test-taker answers by filling in a scoring sheet. Interpretation includes validity and clinical scales. The MACI is a similar, 160-item true/false test administered to adolescents between 13 and 19 years of age.

§ 3.4.3 Projective Tests

Projective tests, such as the Rorschach Ink Blot Technique,[49] are very subjectively interpreted. In a projective test, the test taker explains what various ambiguous pictures or situations look like or mean to him or her. The theory behind projective testing is that people will project their personality, experiences, and thought structure into their stories, explanations, or drawings. While the explanations may suggest certain personality characteristics or psychological traits or dynamics, they are not conclusive. There may or may not be well accepted methods for interpreting the results of particular projective tests. For example, the Rorschach may be interpreted based on the Comprehensive System.[50] In the Rorschach, the test-taker observes ten abstract inkblot cards and describes what he or she sees. Responses on the Rorschach or other projective tests, such as the various Draw-a-Person Tests (DAP),[51] and

---

Meaningful Measurement: The Interpretive Challenges of the MMPI-2 Restructured Clinical (RC) Scales, 87/2 J. PERSONALITY ASSESS. 193 (2006); M. Sellbom, Y. S. Ben-Porath, J. R. Graham, P. A. Arbisi & R. M. Bagby, *Susceptibility of the MMPI-2 Clinical, Restructured Clinical (RC), and Content Scales to Overreporting and Underreporting*, 12/1 ASSESSMENT 79 (2005); M. Sellbom & Y. S. Ben-Porath, *Mapping the MMPI-2 Restructured Clinical (RC) Scales onto Normal Personality Traits: Evidence of Construct Validity*, 85/2 J. PERSONALITY ASSESS. 179 (2005); Yossef S. Ben-Porath, *Introducing the MMPI-2 Restructured Clinical (RC) Scales* (workshop presented for the Society for Personality Assessment, San Francisco , CA, March 2003).

[46] *See, e.g.*, YOSSEF S. BEN-PORATH, INTERPRETING THE MMPI-2-RF (in press); Y. S. BEN-PORATH & A. TELLEGEN, MMPI-2-RF (MINNESOTA MULTIPHASIC PERSONALITY INVENTORY-2): MANUAL FOR ADMINISTRATION, SCORING, AND INTERPRETATION (2008); Y. S. BEN-PORATH & A. TELLEGEN, MMPI-2-RF (MINNESOTA MULTIPHASIC PERSONALITY INVENTORY-2): TECHNICAL MANUAL (2008); Y. S. BEN-PORATH & A. TELLEGEN, MMPI-2-RF (MINNESOTA MULTIPHASIC PERSONALITY INVENTORY-2): USER'S GUIDE FOR REPORTS (2008).

[47] THEODORE MILLON, THE MILLON CLINICAL MULTIAXIAL INVENTORY-III MANUAL (Pearson NCS, Inc., 4th ed. 2009).

[48] THEODORE MILLON ET AL., MANUAL: THE MILLON ADOLESCENT CLINICAL INVENTORY (1994).

[49] HERMANN RORSCHACH, PSYCHODIAGNOSTIK (1932).

[50] JOHN E. EXNER, 1 THE RORSCHACH: A COMPREHENSIVE SYSTEM: BASIC FOUNDATIONS (Wiley 1993).

[51] *See* EDWARD STEINBERG, CLINICAL JUDGMENT AND THE VALIDATION OF THE DAP (University Microfilms 1973).

Sentence Completion Tests,[52] Thematic Apperception Test (TAT)[53] and Children's Apperception Test (CAT),[54] may be less reliable when administered to highly creative people, whose unusual responses may be a function of their creativity rather than personality traits or emotional disturbances. With the TAT and CAT, the test-taker is shown a number of cards depicting an ambiguous activity and asked to tell a story about what is depicted.

If interpretation of a child's drawings or paintings is part of the evaluation, the attorney should become familiar with the methodology used in interpreting artwork. The attorney should also determine whether the artwork was created as part of a therapeutic exercise or done outside of the direct evaluative process. If the art was produced outside of the evaluation, it is important to know the circumstances of the creation. For example, the interpretation of a drawing made during free play may differ from that of a drawing responsive to a particular school assignment. While projective tests are often used in clinical practice, because of lack of validity and reliability, they are less useful in a forensic child welfare evaluation.

§ 3.4.4 Developmental and Intelligence Tests

Because children involved with the child welfare system often show developmental delays and because developmental levels are relevant to child welfare proceedings, tests are often given to locate the child's progress and functioning relative to other children of the same age. Even very young babies can be evaluated in terms of their achievement of developmental milestones as well as the quality of their developmental progress (e.g., motor movement quality). Specialized training in infant assessment is necessary for identifying problems and competencies in this age group. Common developmental tests for infants and toddlers are the Denver Development Screening Test[55] and the Bayley Scales of Infant Development-II.[56] Developmental evaluations for all children should take into account the child's prenatal experience (e.g., exposure to alcohol and illegal substances), risk factors at birth (e.g., low birth weight, prematurity), and other pediatric issues. It is important for the attorney to facilitate the evaluator's ability to review this collateral information because it can be very difficult to obtain for children involved in the child welfare system.

There are several intelligence tests, the most widely used being the various Wechsler Intelligence Scales. The current version for adults, the Wechsler Adult

---

[52] *See generally* JAMES QUINTER HOLSOPPLE & FLORENCE R. MIALE, SENTENCE COMPLETION: A PROJECTIVE METHOD FOR THE STUDY OF PERSONALITY (Charles C. Thomas 1954).

[53] HENRY MURRAY AND LEOPOLD BELLAK, THEMATIC APPERCEPTION TEST (1973); *see also* LEOPOLD BELLAK, THEMATIC APPERCEPTION TEST, THE CHILDREN'S APPERCEPTION TEST, AND THE SENIOR APPERCEPTION TECHNIQUE IN CLINICAL USE (Allyn and Bacon 1997).

[54] HENRY MURRAY AND LEOPOLD BELLAK, CHILDREN'S APPERCEPTION TEST (1974).

[55] WILLIAM FRANKENBURG, DENVER DEVELOPMENTAL SCREENING TEST (Ladoca Project & Publishing Foundation 1970).

[56] N. BAYLEY, MANUAL FOR THE BAYLEY SCALES OF INFANT DEVELOPMENT (The Psychological Corporation, 2d ed. 1993).

Intelligence Scale (WAIS-IV) was published in 2008 in recognition of emerging demographic and clinical trends.[57] It is intended for use with adults ages 16 to 90 and measures cognitive ability using 10 core subtests that focus on four specific domains of intelligence yielding: verbal comprehension index (VCI), perceptual reasoning index (PRI), working memory index (WMI), and processing speed index (PRI).[58] These index scores replaced the previous Verbal IQ and Performance IQ scores. The combined performance on all four index scores yields the Full Scale IQ score (FSIQ). The combined performance on just the VCI and PRI scores yields the General Ability Index (GAI). The Full Scale IQ scores on the Wechsler scales are labeled as follows:

Extremely Low	below 69
Borderline	70-79
Low Average	80-89
Average	90-109
High Average	110-119
Superior	120-129
Very Superior	130 and above

The current version of the Wechsler Intelligence Scale for Children is the WISC-IV, published in 2003.[59] It eliminated some of the subtests of the WISC-III and added other new subtests, reflecting advances in understanding neurological components of cognitive functioning. It uses 10 core subtests and 5 supplemental subtests and focuses on the same four domains as the WAIS-IV. It is intended for use with children between 6 years and 16 years 11 months. The full scale IQ score ranges from 40 to 160, and the full scale score on the WISC-IV may show a 5 point drop from the full scale IQ score of the same person taking the WISC-III based on "new aspects of the test, and the novelty of some of the new items and subtests."[60]

Children from 2 years, 6 months to 7 years, 3 months may be tested with the Wechsler Preschool and Primary Scale of Intelligence (WPPSI). The current version is the WPPSI-III,[61] published in 2002. The WPPSI-III uses 14 subtests. There is less

---

[57] DAVID WECHSLER, WECHSLER ADULT INTELLIGENCE SCALE – FOURTH EDITION (2008). The current Spanish language version, standardized in Puerto Rico, is DAVID WECHSLER, ESCALA DE INTELIGENCIA DE WECHSLER PARA ADULTOS—TERCERA EDICION (EIWA-III), used for persons age 16 through 64 years, 11 months.

[58] *See generally* ELIZABETH O. LICHTENBERGER & ALAN S. KAUFMAN, ESSENTIALS OF WAIS-IV ASSESSMENT (2009); WAIS-IV TECHNICAL AND INTERPRETIVE MANUAL (2008).

[59] DAVID WECHSLER, WECHSLER INTELLIGENCE SCALE FOR CHILDREN – FOURTH EDITION (2003). There is also a Spanish version of the WISC-IV, DAVID WECHSLER, WISC-IV SPANISH (2004).

[60] See Inderbir Kaur Sandhu, *The Wechsler Intelligence Scale for Children – Fourth Edition (WISC–IV)*, *available at* http://www.brainy-child.com/expert/WISC_IV.shtml.

[61] DAVID WECHSLER, WECHSLER PRESCHOOL AND PRIMARY SCALE OF INTELLIGENCE –THIRD EDITION (2002). *See generally* ELIZABETH O. LICHTENBERGER & ALAN S. KAUFMAN, ESSENTIALS OF WPPSI-III ASSESSMENT (2003); DAVID WECHSLER, WPPSI-III–TECHNICAL AND INTERPRETIVE MANUAL (2002).

support for the reliable use of intelligence tests with preschoolers than with older children.

§ 3.4.5 Neuropsychological Tests

Neuropsychological testing can help to identify behavioral indicators of organic brain disorders and provide more specific information about cognitive functioning and thought processes. Neuropsychological testing can illuminate possible connections between brain functioning and specific types of problematic behaviors and help to differentiate them from more psychologically-based disorders. A common test used to measure vulnerabilities in brain functioning is the Bender Visual-Motor Gestalt Test. (Bender-Gestalt II).[62] It measures psychomotor development, orientation, memory, calculation, learning, knowledge, and judgment abilities and changes. A leading group of neuropsychological tests is the Halstead-Reitan Neuropsychological Battery.[63] The battery evaluates a number of neurological functions to determine brain damage. The attorney should make sure that any expert who testifies concerning organicity is properly qualified and has administered the appropriate tests.[64]

§ 3.4.6 Achievement Tests

Achievement tests measure mastery over specific fields of information. Schools are required to administer some achievement tests to their students. Commonly used achievement tests are the Stanford Achievement Test, 10th edition (SAT-10),[65] the Peabody Individual Achievement Test (PIAT-R/NU),[66] Wide Range Achievement Test-4 (WRAT-4),[67] and the Woodcock-Johnson III Complete Battery.[68] The use of achievement tests in conjunction with intelligence tests and other cognitive tests can provide information regarding psycho-social or other issues that may interfere with school or vocational achievement. For example, a pattern of average or high cognitive

---

[62] LAURETTA BENDER & THE AMERICAN. ORTHOPSYCHIATRIC ASSOCIATION, INC., BENDER VISUAL-MOTOR GESTALT TEST (Bender-Gestalt II).

[63] WARD HALSTEAD & RALPH REITAN, HALSTEAD-REITAN NEUROLOGICAL BATTERY (1959, 1979).

[64] *See generally* Donna K. Broshek & Jeffrey T. Barth, *The Halstead-Reitan Neuropsychological Test Battery*, in NEUROPSYCHOLOGICAL ASSESSMENT IN CLINICAL PRACTICE: A GUIDE TO TEST INTERPRETATION AND INTEGRATION (Gary Groth-Marnat ed., 2000); Jovier D Evans, Walden S. Miller, Desiree A. Byrd & Robert K. Heaton, *Cross-cultural Applications of the Halstead-Reitan Batteries*, in HANDBOOK OF CROSS-CULTURAL NEUROPSYCHOLOGY: CRITICAL ISSUES IN NEUROPSYCHOLOGY (Elaine Fletcher-Janzen, Tony L. Stickland, & Cecil R. Reynolds eds., 2000).

[65] HARCOURT ASSESSMENT, STANFORD ACHIEVEMENT TEST (Harcourt Assessment, Gallaudet Research Institute, 10th ed. 2003).

[66] FREDERICK C. MARKWARDT, JR., PEABODY INDIVIDUAL ACHIEVEMENT TEST-REVISED-NORMATIVE UPDATE (1998).

[67] GARY S. WILKINSON & GARY J. ROBERTSON, WIDE RANGE ACHIEVEMENT TEST 4 (2006).

[68] RICHARD W. WOODCOCK ET AL., WOODCOCK-JOHNSON III COMPLETE BATTERY (The Riverside Publishing Company 2001).

abilities in combination with low achievement suggests that further assessment is warranted.

§ 3.4.7 Checklists and Inventories

There are also a variety of checklists and inventories for use with children and adults, such as the Achenbach Child Behavior Checklist,[69] Beck Depression Inventory (2nd edition),[70] Parenting Stress Index (3rd edition),[71] Parent-Child Relationship Inventory,[72] the Child Abuse Potential Inventory,[73] and the Child Sexual Behavior Inventory.[74] The information provided in these checklists and inventories varies in usefulness based on who is filling out the form.

§ 3.4.8 Scoring and Interpreting Tests Results

Some experts have the tests interpreted by a computer program or another person. For example, the MMPI-2 and the MCMI-III are often scored by computer. A computer report, in addition to listing the various scores, may also contain text interpretations. However, these interpretations do not take into account various relevant clinical factors and case-specific facts that are important to understanding the family functioning and creating a usable case plan. For many tests, clinical interpretation, based on the evaluator's knowledge of the client, is essential in interpreting the test results. In addition, some test results are affected by race, sex, socioeconomic group, or education. Standardized tests compare the test-taker's answers with those of other persons. Therefore, it is important that the standard group be fairly representative. Some tests have never been standardized. Some tests are standardized to a very small or a racially skewed sample. Some tests are standardized on a clinical or incarcerated population, which may, therefore, suggest a higher level of pathology.

Computer scoring can be extremely helpful to reduce scoring errors and to compile various subsets of information, such as scoring the supplemental scales in the MMPI-2. Computer-generated interpretations of tests, particularly personality tests raise difficult problems because they are based on assumptions that may not apply to

---

[69] THOMAS M. ACHENBACH, CHILD BEHAVIOR CHECKLIST (University of Vermont Psychiatry Department 1991).

[70] AARON BECK, ROBERT A. STEER & GREGORY K. BROWN, BECK DEPRESSION INVENTORY MANUAL (Psychological Corporation, 2d ed. 1996).

[71] RICHARD ABIDIN, PARENTING STRESS INDEX (PSYCHOLOGICAL ASSESSMENT RESOURCES, 3d ed. 1995).

[72] ANTHONY B. GERARD, PARENT-CHILD RELATIONSHIP INVENTORY (Western Psychological Services 1994).

[73] JOEL S. MILNER, CHILD ABUSE POTENTIAL INVENTORY MANUAL (Psychological Assessment Resources, 2d ed. 1986).

[74] *See* William N. Friedrich, Patricia Grambsch, Linda Damon, Sandra K. Hewitt, Catherine Koverola, Reuben A. Lang, Vicki Wolfe & Daniel Broughton, *Child Sexual Behavior Inventory: Normative and Clinical Comparisons*, 4/3 PSYCHOL. ASSESS. 303 (1992); William N. Friedrich, Jennifer L. Fisher & Carrie Anne Dittner et al., *Child Sexual Behavior Inventory: Normative, Psychiatric, and Sexual Abuse Comparisons*, 6/1 CHILD MALTREAT. 37 (2001).

the person being tested and can be oversimplified. It is important for clinical information to be included in any interpretation of results. For example, the test taker's education, socioeconomic background, occupation, and context of taking the test must be taken into consideration. Results for people in a forensic setting may need to be interpreted differently than for people in a clinic or research setting.

Assuming that the tests used are accepted, standardized, and validated, the attorney should ascertain whether they were administered according to the instructions provided with the tests. Standardized tests are always accompanied by detailed instructions on how the test should be administered and scoring manuals on how the results should be tabulated and interpreted. More often than one might expect, the tests are not administered or interpreted according to the instructions. Many clinicians develop their own procedures for administering and interpreting psychometric tests. Even if the test has been validated for the purpose for which it is being used, the validation rests on proper administration and scoring. Conclusions based on an improperly used test are not entitled to the same weight as those based on a properly used test and should not survive a *Daubert* test. The credibility of an expert who has not properly administered or interpreted a test is also diminished.

§ 3.5 Child Sexual Abuse Evaluations

Most child sexual abuse cases do not have any positive medical findings,[75] making the mental health evaluation particularly important. However, evaluations in the area of child sexual abuse raise many issues, and the empirical data continues to be compiled concerning best practices.[76] Several professional organizations have provided practice guidelines regarding the evaluation of child sexual abuse.[77] In addition, structured interview protocols have also been developed, but they are not widely used in clinical practice.[78] Child welfare attorneys should keep up-to-date with the professional literature to assist them in critically reviewing evaluations of alleged victims and alleged perpetrators, and evaluating "risk assessments," which attempt to address whether a person is likely to have molested a child or whether someone who has molested a child is likely to re-molest.

---

[75] For further discussion of sexual abuse, see § 2.2, Sexual Abuse.

[76] *See generally* ANN M. HARALAMBIE, CHILD SEXUAL ABUSE IN CIVIL CASES: A GUIDE TO CUSTODY AND TORT ACTIONS, Ch. 6 (American Bar Association 1999); ANN M. HARALAMBIE, 3 HANDLING CHILD CUSTODY, ABUSE, AND ADOPTION CASES 3D Ch. 16 (West 2009).

[77] W. Bernet, *Practice Parameters for the Forensic Evaluation of Children and Adolescents Who May Have Been Physically or Sexually Abused*, 36/10 J. AM. ACAD. CHILD ADOLESC. PSYCHIATRY 37S (1997).

[78] Yael Orbach, Irit Hershkowitz, Michael E. Lamb, Kathleen J. Sternberg, Phillip W. Esplin & Dvora Horowitz, *Assessing the Value of Structured Protocols for Forensic Interviews of Alleged Child Abuse Victims*, 24/6 CHILD ABUSE & NEGLECT 733 (2000); Web site for the National Institute of Child Health and Human Development (NICHD) at http://www.nichd.nih.gov; Web site for the National Institutes of Health at http://www.nih.gov.

While practice guidelines vary, there are some general consistencies regarding interviewing children in sexual abuse evaluations largely due to continuing research in child development and related fields. For example, most guidelines recommend the reliance on free-recall prompts (i.e., invitations to report remembered information without input from the interviewer)[79] at least as an initial strategy when interviewing children because this method provides greater accuracy.[80] The diagnostic use of anatomically detailed dolls is specifically disapproved by all of the protocols and guidelines that mention the issue. There is no MMPI scale or profile that can identify an incestuous offender or a molested child. Similarly, there is no item or cluster of items on the Child Sexual Behavior Inventory (CSBI) that can determine whether a child has or has not been sexually abused. The Multiphasic Sex Inventory II[81] (MSI II), which is sometimes used as a part of an evaluation of offenders, is not able to tell whether a person *who does not admit* to the abuse has molested the child.[82] A National Institute of Justice Research Report says:

> The sexual abusers of children are highly dissimilar in terms of personal characteristics, life experiences, and criminal histories. No single "molester profile" exists. Child molesters arrive at deviancy via multiple pathways and engage in many different sexual and nonsexual "acting out" behaviors.[83]

While there may not be a profile or syndrome that is diagnostic of child sexual abuse, experts may testify that various behaviors, symptoms, and disorders are consistent with sexual abuse. Testimony about any such patterns or profiles, however, must be based on the foundational showing of reliability and acceptance in the field of the pattern or profile. Explicit sexualized play in the absence of a history explaining the child's knowledge (such as exposure to watching people engaged in sexual activity or exposure to sexually explicit pornographic material) is a frequently discussed behavior that may be indicative of sexual abuse.[84] However, not all

---

[79] Jan Aldridge, Michael E. Lamb, Kathleen J. Sternberg, Yael Orbach, Phillip W. Esplin & Lynn Bowler, *Using a Human Figure Drawing to Elicit Information from Alleged Victims of Child Sexual Abuse*, 72/2 J. CONSULT. CLIN. PSYCHOL. 304 (2004).

[80] AMERICAN PROFESSIONAL SOCIETY ON THE ABUSE OF CHILDREN, GUIDELINES FOR PSYCHOSOCIAL EVALUATION OF SUSPECTED SEXUAL ABUSE IN YOUNG CHILDREN (APSAC, rev. ed. 2002).

[81] H. NICHOLS & I. MOLINDER, MULTIPHASIC SEX INVENTORY II (1990).

[82] *See* H. NICHOLS & I. MOLINDER, MULTIPHASIC SEX INVENTORY MANUAL 39 (1984): "Finally, it is important to remember that the MSI is not appropriate for use in the legal pursuit of guilt or innocence. The alledged [sic] offender must acknowledge culpability in order for the inventory to be used."

[82] ROBERT A. PRENTKY ET AL., U.S. DEPARTMENT OF JUSTICE, CHILD SEXUAL MOLESTATION: RESEARCH ISSUES 2 (NIJ Research Report NCJ 163390, 1997).

[83] ROBERT A. PRENTKY ET AL., U.S. DEPARTMENT OF JUSTICE, CHILD SEXUAL MOLESTATION: RESEARCH ISSUES 2 (NIJ Research Report NCJ 163390, 1997).

[84] *See generally* William N. Friedrich, *Sexual Victimization and Sexual Behavior in Children: A Review of Recent Literature*, 17/1 CHILD ABUSE & NEGLECT 59 (1993).

molested children engage in sexualized play, and not all children who engage in sexualized play have been molested.

The term "syndrome" has been used very loosely, with a great deal of confusion in the legal arena. The syndromes used in sexual abuse cases are generally not really syndromes in the diagnostic sense. The most prominent syndrome that had been used to understand children's behavior is the Child Sexual Abuse Accommodation Syndrome (CSAAS),[85] which suggested that many children share a pattern of response to sexual abuse that includes feelings and behaviors of secrecy, helplessness, entrapment and accommodation, and delayed, conflicted, and unconvincing disclosures and retraction. While sexually abused children may individually experience these feelings and show these behaviors, the validity of the CSAAS is not widely accepted,[86] and there has been little empirical evidence supporting this theory. One exception is that research has consistently indicated that the majority of children who have been sexually abused do considerably delay disclosure of the abuse.[87]

Not every physician or mental health professional is an expert in intrafamilial child sexual abuse, which is an extremely specialized field. Especially where the sexual abuse allegations arise where there is also family law litigation, a circumstance that often raises a high level of skepticism, it is essential that a properly qualified expert evaluate the allegations. As with other areas of forensic evaluation, sexual abuse evaluators must keep current with the latest research on relevant scientific topics, such as children's memory and response to interviewing techniques, in addition to professional practice guidelines.

§ 3.6 Conclusion

Several types of evaluations performed by mental health professionals can be helpful in appropriate treatment planning and to assist the court in case disposition at all stages. As child welfare cases overwhelmingly involve families with multiple problems and service needs, evaluations tapping into different domains of functioning will likely be required to identify the individual needs of parents and children, as well as the quality and treatment of the parent-child relationship itself. When involved in making referrals it is important for the child welfare lawyer to communicate to the evaluator what specific information is necessary for the case and how the evaluation results and recommendations are intended to be utilized. Familiarity with the

---

[85] *See, e.g.*, Roland Summit, *The Child Sexual Abuse Accommodation Syndrome*, 7/2 CHILD ABUSE & NEGLECT 177 (1983).

[86] Kamala London, Maggie Bruck, Stephen J. Ceci & Daniel W. Shuman, *Disclosure of Child Sexual Abuse: What Does the Research Tell Us About the Ways that Children Tell?*, 11/1 PSYCHOL. PUB. POL'Y & L. 194 (2005); Celia B. Fisher, American Psychological Association's (1992); *Ethics and the Validation of Sexual Abuse in Day-Care Settings*, 1/2 PSYCHOL. PUB. POL'Y & L. 461 (1995).

[87] Kamala London, Maggie Bruck, Stephen J. Ceci & Daniel W. Shuman, *Disclosure of Child Sexual Abuse: What Does the Research Tell Us About the Ways that Children Tell?*, 11/1 PSYCHOL. PUB. POL'Y & L. 194 (2005).

professional codes of ethics and most recent practice guidelines for varied mental health professionals will assist the child welfare attorney in ensuring that evaluations provided on the behalf of parent and child clients will be of high quality and useful in directing treatment planning and case disposition.

Chapter 4: Child Development and the Impact of Maltreatment[*]

by Ann M. Haralambie[1]

§ 4.1 Child Development

Child welfare attorneys need to have a general understanding of child development and a realization that children's needs will vary significantly, depending on the age and developmental stage of the child. All attorneys in the case need to review the child's statements and behaviors in light of the individual child's developmental level. Additionally, as the ABA and NACC/ABA Standards[2] provide, the child's attorney should always consider the child's developmental level—both when communicating with the child and when making legal decisions for the child. This should include an assessment of the child's "emerging behavioral repertoire, cognitive and language functions, social and emotional processes, and changes occurring in anatomical structures and physiological process of the brain."[3]

From birth through adolescence, the needs of children are ever changing. Development involves progressive changes throughout the life span, with changes being more rapid and definitive in the early years than in later years. "Developmental psychopathologists perceive development as consisting of a number of important age and stage-appropriate tasks which, upon emergence, remain critical to the child's continual adaptation, although decreasing in salience relative to newly emerging

---

[*] Reprinted from *Handling Child Custody, Abuse and Adoption Cases, Third Edition*, with permission of Thomson Reuters. For more information about this publication, please visit www.west.thomson.com. *Author's Note*: Portions of this chapter were adapted from ANN M. HARALAMBIE, 3 HANDLING CHILD CUSTODY, ABUSE, AND ADOPTION CASES 3D, Ch. 24 (Thomson West 2009). The relevant portions of chapter 24 were co-authored by Ann Haralambie and psychologists Jean M. Baker, Ph.D. and Rachel B. Burkholder, Ph.D. Additionally, portions of this chapter were adapted from Jean M. Baker & Rachel B. Burkholder, *Child Development and Child Custody*, previously published in The Child's Attorney: A Guide to Representing Children in Custody, Adoption, and Protection Cases, published by the American Bar Association, copyright 1993. All rights reserved. Reprinted by Permission. *This information or any portion thereof may not be copied or disseminated in any form or by any means or downloaded or stored in an electronic database or retrieval system without the express written consent of the American Bar Association.*

[1] Ann M. Haralambie, J.D., is a certified family law specialist practicing in Tucson, Arizona. She is also an author and speaker in the fields of family and children's law. The NACC is grateful to Stacy A. Klapper, Psy.D in clinical psychology, for her contribution to the original version of this chapter.

[2] *See* American Bar Association Standards of Practice for Lawyers Who Represent Children in Abuse and Neglect Cases.

[3] Dante Cicchetti & Sheree L. Toth, *A Developmental Psychopathology Perspective on Child Abuse and Neglect*, 34/5 J. AM. ACAD. CHILD ADOLESC. PSYCHIATRY 541 (1995).

tasks."[4] Chronological age provides only an estimate of a child's developmental level, as typical development often follows an uneven course.[5] For example, a child may be verbally precocious, but lack age-appropriate competency in peer skills or emotional regulation. Developmental competencies in many areas, such as emotional regulation and attachment, continue to unfold across the lifespan, with new experiences shaping new opportunities for growth.[6] "As such, individuals will experience the same events differently depending on their level of functioning across all domains of psychological and biological development."[7] This has important implications for understanding the developmental consequences resulting from childhood maltreatment.

The experience of being maltreated will have different meaning for individual children according to their level of functioning at the time of the maltreatment.[8] For example, a child with well-developed language skills will have a different skill set for understanding and containing the maltreatment experience than a pre-verbal child.[9] While not all children who have been maltreated will display symptoms at the time of court involvement, there is clear evidence that abuse and neglect impact interconnected areas of development across the lifespan.[10] Therefore, even the asymptomatic child warrants assessment following the experience of maltreatment, and children who have completed a successful course of treatment may experience a resurgence of symptomatology as new developmental challenges emerge.

Although there is no one unified approach, child development is historically described as an unvarying series of stages, each one being qualitatively distinct from the preceding one, and being reflected by dramatic changes in physical, cognitive, language, and social/emotional characteristics. There are numerous theories of child development, each of which traces the child's growth through a number of distinct stages. Each of these theories describes the particular activities or behaviors that are

---

[4] John W. Pearce & Terry D. Pezzot-Pearce, *Attachment Theory and its Implications for Psychotherapy with Maltreated Children,* 18/5 CHILD ABUSE & NEGLECT 425 (1994).

[5] T. B. BRAZELTON, TOUCHPOINTS: YOUR CHILD'S EMOTIONAL AND BEHAVIORAL DEVELOPMENT (Perseus Books 1992).

[6] Dante Cicchetti & Sheree L. Toth, *A Developmental Psychopathology Perspective on Child Abuse and Neglect,* 34/5 J. AM. ACAD. CHILD ADOLESC. PSYCHIATRY 541 (1995).

[7] *Id.*

[8] *Id.*

[9] Theodore J. Gaensbauer, *Trauma in the Preverbal Period: Symptoms, Memories, and Developmental Impact,* 50 PSYCHOANAL. STUDY CHILD 122 (1995); Max Sugar, *Toddlers' Traumatic Memories,* 13/3 INFANT MENT. HEALTH J. 245 (1992); Ross A. Thompson & Jennifer M. Wyatt, *Current Research on Child Maltreatment: Implications for Educators,* 11/3 EDUC. PSYCHOL. REV. 173 (1999).

[10] D. J. Kolko, *Child Physical Abuse, in* THE APSAC HANDBOOK ON CHILD MALTREATMENT 21–50 (John Briere & Lucy Berliner eds., Sage Publications 1996); Robin Malinosky-Rummell & David J. Hansen, *Long-term Consequences of Child Physical Abuse,* 114/1 PSYCHOLOGICAL BULLETIN 68 (1993); R. C. Pianta, B. Egeland & M. F. Erickson, *The Antecedents of Maltreatment: Results of the Mother-Child Interaction Research Project, in* CHILD MALTREATMENT: THEORY AND RESEARCH ON THE CAUSES AND CONSEQUENCES OF CHILD ABUSE AND NEGLECT 203–53 (D. Cicchetti & V. Carlson eds., Cambridge University Press 1989); Ross A. Thompson & Jennifer M. Wyatt, *Current Research on Child Maltreatment: Implications for Educators,* 11/3 EDUC. PSYCHOL. REV. 173 (1999).

most significant for the child at the given stages of development. Certain developmental theorists have focused on specific aspects of development. For example, Piaget[11] focused on cognitive development, and Erik Erikson[12] focused on psychosocial development. Others have taken a more comprehensive approach and have written detailed descriptions of children's overall growth and development at various ages.[13]

While stage models of development provide a framework for placing skills and abilities within a predictable context, it is important to remember that the range of normal behavior is vast and varied. Brazelton notes that, "no developmental line in a child proceeds in a continuous upward course."[14] Typically developing children display widely divergent behaviors, and tasks of infancy have implications across the lifespan.[15] With maturation, a child will re-work earlier developmental stages, consolidating skills and acquiring more sophisticated understanding and solutions to problems. In this way, developmental tasks of childhood remain salient throughout the lifespan, as greater maturational strength is applied to previously acquired competencies. Similarly, stressors such as losses, illness, moves, and changes in caregiving relationships can impact developmental functioning, such that children appear to lose competencies for a time. For example, a child who has successfully completed toilet training may lose this skill under stress. In addition, as new developmental challenges emerge, such as the onset of walking, children may experience a brief regression in skills in other areas, such as verbal communication.[16]

> We have at all times to think in terms of the interactions and transactions that are constantly occurring between an ever-developing personality and the environment, especially the people in it. This means that it is necessary to think of each personality as moving through life along some developmental pathway, with the particular pathway followed always being determined by the interaction of the personality as it has so far developed and the environment in which it then finds itself.[17]

---

[11] *See, e.g.*, JEAN PIAGET, THE LANGUAGE AND THOUGHT OF THE CHILD (1955).

[12] *See, e.g.*, ERIC ERICKSON, CHILDHOOD AND SOCIETY (1950).

[13] *See, e.g.*, ARNOLD GESELL & FRANCES L. ILG, THE CHILD FROM FIVE TO TEN (1946); BURTON WHITE, THE FIRST THREE YEARS OF LIFE (2d ed. 1985).

[14] T. B. BRAZELTON, TOUCHPOINTS: YOUR CHILD'S EMOTIONAL AND BEHAVIORAL DEVELOPMENT (Perseus Books 1992).

[15] JOHN BOWLBY, 1 ATTACHMENT AND LOSS: ATTACHMENT (1969); DANIEL STERN, THE INTERPERSONAL WORLD OF THE INFANT: A VIEW FROM PSYCHOANALYSIS AND DEVELOPMENTAL PSYCHOLOGY (Basic Books 1985).

[16] T. B. BRAZELTON, TOUCHPOINTS: YOUR CHILD'S EMOTIONAL AND BEHAVIORAL DEVELOPMENT (Perseus Books 1992).

[17] John Bowlby, *Developmental Psychiatry Comes of Age*, 145 AM. J. PSYCHIATRY 1 (1988).

Most importantly, successful development depends on the health of the relationship between the child and the caregiving environment. The child and the caregiver bring particular strengths and challenges to the relationship, and the "goodness of fit" between what the child needs and what the parent has to offer sets the stage for developmental risk or healthy outcomes. "Virtually all contemporary researchers agree that the development of children is a highly complex process that is influenced by the interplay of nature and nurture . . . In simple terms, children affect their environments at the same time that their environments are affecting them."[18]

§ 4.1.1 Physical Development

Children require a caregiving environment that supports their physical growth. "Despite a tendency to see infants as objects existing in a material world where their talents unfold in some maturational sequence, the reality is that, from conception, the infant is embedded in relationships with others who provide the nutrition for both physical and psychological growth."[19] Studies of children who have experienced severe environmental deprivation reveal that when a child lacks appropriate environmental stimulation and support for exploration, the child's physical development, in addition to his or her cognitive and social-emotional development, may move off track.[20] The physical development of children follows a sequential course that is quite consistent in all normal children who are raised without any extreme environmental deprivations. A child's muscle control will develop without any attempt on the parent's part to teach the child, however parents can optimize their child's motor development by providing opportunities for supervised play and exploration, encouraging the child to use his or her body to actively learn about the child's surroundings.[21] The elemental human desire to explore one's environment and gain mastery through experience drives much of early motor development.[22] The age range during which the various motor skills typically emerge is relatively narrow. Here are some of the physical milestones of young children:

---

[18] National Research Council, Institute of Medicine, Committee on Integrating the Science of Early Childhood Development & Board on Children, Youth, and Families, FROM NEURONS TO NEIGHBORHOODS: THE SCIENCE OF EARLY CHILDHOOD DEVELOPMENT (Jack P. Shonkoff & Deborah A. Phillips eds., 2000), *available at* http://books.nap.edu/catalog/9824.html?onpi_newsdoc100300.

[19] A. J. Sameroff & B. H. Fiese, *Models of Development and Developmental Risk, in* C. H. Zeanah, Jr. (Ed). HANDBOOK OF INFANT MENTAL HEALTH (The Guilford Press, 2d ed. 2000).

[20] National Research Council, Institute of Medicine, Committee on Integrating the Science of Early Childhood Development & Board on Children, Youth, and Families, FROM NEURONS TO NEIGHBORHOODS: THE SCIENCE OF EARLY CHILDHOOD DEVELOPMENT 24 (Jack P. Shonkoff & Deborah A. Phillips eds., 2000), *available at* http://books.nap.edu/catalog/9824.html?onpi_news doc100300.

[21] T. B. BRAZELTON, TOUCHPOINTS: YOUR CHILD'S EMOTIONAL AND BEHAVIORAL DEVELOPMENT (Perseus Books 1992).

[22] MASTERY MOTIVATION: ORIGINS, CONCEPTUALIZATIONS, AND APPLICATIONS: ADVANCES IN APPLIED DEVELOPMENTAL PSYCHOLOGY, Vol. 12 (Robert MacTurk & George Morgan eds., Ablex Publishing Corp. 1995).

turning	4-6 months
reaching for objects	4-6 months
unaided sitting	5-8 months
crawling, scooting	6-12 months
climbing (up to 6 inches)	8-10 months
walking while holding onto support	9-15 months
climbing (up to 12 inches)	11-12 months
unaided walking	9-15 months
unaided stair climbing	25-30 months
ability to turn door knob	25-30 months
ability to remove jar lids	25-30 months
anal sphincter muscles in control	31-36 months

Between the ages of three to six, children's gross and fine motor skills expand significantly. Their movements smooth out and become more automatic. Their sense of balance improves, and the ability to draw, copy, cut, and pick up tiny objects becomes increasingly proficient. By age six many children can ride a small bicycle and will attempt to accomplish many physical feats that involve increasingly refined coordination and skill. Physical growth for the school-aged child tends to slow down. Body proportions become more similar to those of adults. Both gross and fine motor skills improve until they gradually almost resemble those of adults.

§ 4.1.2 Cognitive Development

Cognitive development refers to the process of intellectual growth. "Abundant evidence indicates that brain development begins well before birth, extends into the adult years, and is specifically designed to recruit and incorporate experience into its emerging architecture and functioning."[23] The process of cognitive development enables a human being to progress from the initial state of infancy to a well-organized, well-ordered understanding of the world typical of the average adult. For this to occur, all children must pass through certain developmental sequences in each important area of intellectual understanding. This means that a child must have reached a given stage of maturation and experience before certain concepts can be taught or understood. The exact age at which individual children will reach given

---

[23] National Research Council, Institute of Medicine, Committee on Integrating the Science of Early Childhood Development & Board on Children, Youth, and Families, FROM NEURONS TO NEIGHBORHOODS: THE SCIENCE OF EARLY CHILDHOOD DEVELOPMENT 216 (Jack P. Shonkoff & Deborah A. Phillips eds., 2000), *available at* http://books.nap.edu/catalog/9824.html?onpi_news doc100300.

stages of cognitive development can vary considerably, and children's capacities to make sense of the world is embedded in relational, familial, and cultural contexts.[24]

Overall, cognitive development seems to be robust in young children. "Both language development and the emergence of early learning capabilities appear to be relatively resilient processes. This means that they are relatively protected from adverse circumstances, that it may take more to undermine these processes than is the case for other aspects of development, and that they can show surprising recovery if children exhibiting delays are placed in more advantageous environments."[25] Fortunately, even children who have experienced extreme cognitive deprivation and trauma show a remarkable capacity for learning and growth once provided with a reparative circumstance.[26] Nonetheless, deficits in attention, emotional regulation, and behavioral control often remain.[27] "The neuroscientific research on early brain development says that the young children warranting the greatest concern are those growing up in environments, starting before birth, that fail to provide them with adequate nutrition and other growth-fostering inputs, expose them to biological insults, and subject them to abusive and neglectful care."[28]

In typically developing children, the progression of cognitive development in early years has been described by Piaget as following a fairly predictable course, with the evolution of competencies being acquired in a universal manner. "Children from birth to age five engage in making sense of the world on many levels: language, human interactions, counting and quantification, spatial reasoning, physical causality, problem solving, categorization. Indeed, even pre-verbal infants show surprisingly sophisticated understandings in each of these areas."[29] Piaget organized his theory of cognitive development into four stages. The first stage is called the sensorimotor period and lasts from birth to around eighteen months or two years. The sensorimotor stage describes the development of object permanence and causality. "A baby's expectations for certain kinds of reactions from important individuals around the baby are signs of learning about predictability. As early as one month, a baby will have different expectations for a father and a mother,"[30] demonstrating a capacity for

---

[24] *Id.*

[25] *Id.* at 125.

[26] E. W. Ames, *The Development of Romanian Orphanage Children Adopted to Canada: Final Report to the National Welfare Grants Program: Human Resources Development Canada* (Burnaby, British Columbia: Simon Fraser University 1997); M. Rutter & the English and Romanian Adoptees (ERA) Study Team, *Developmental Catch-up, and Deficit, Following Adoption After Severe Global Early Privation*, 39/4 J. CHILD PSYCHOL. PSYCHIATRY 465 (1998).

[27] National Research Council, Institute of Medicine, Committee on Integrating the Science of Early Childhood Development & Board on Children, Youth, and Families, FROM NEURONS TO NEIGHBORHOODS: THE SCIENCE OF EARLY CHILDHOOD DEVELOPMENT (Jack P. Shonkoff & Deborah A. Phillips eds., 2000), *available at* http://books.nap.edu/catalog/9824.html?onpi_newsdoc100300.

[28] *Id.* at 271.

[29] *Id.* at 147.

[30] T. B. BRAZELTON, TOUCHPOINTS: YOUR CHILD'S EMOTIONAL AND BEHAVIORAL DEVELOPMENT (Perseus Books 1992).

memory based on patterns of interaction over time. In the first two years of life, babies "prefer consequences that they control directly over those that are uncontrollable. Infants 12 and 18 months old respond more positively to strangers who act in predictable ways that allow them more control to strangers who are less predictable."[31] During this period, the child's thinking is displayed in concrete actions rather than language. The child is focused on building motor and sensory skills, on his body movements, and on manipulation of concrete objects.

The next broad phase of cognitive development is called preoperational, during which language begins to govern the child's mental life. The emergence of language marks the development of a symbolic function, allowing play to serve an important role in communicating thoughts and feelings. The first part of this stage, which lasts roughly from two to four years, is called preconceptual. During this time thought is extremely egocentric and still quite concrete. Children's reasoning at this stage is often distorted because they are able to focus on only one salient aspect of a situation at a time. The second half of the preoperational stage lasts from age four to about age seven and is referred to as the intuitive phase. The child during this period is gradually becoming able to construct more complex thoughts and images. "By age five [the ability to take on another's perspective] has developed into a full-blown theory of mind, in which children can predict others' intentions, deceive others successfully, and recognize that beliefs don't always correspond to reality."[32]

Piaget's third broad stage is called concrete-operational and lasts from about age seven to approximately age eleven. Caplan and Caplan describe this stage as follows: "During this time the child develops the ability to do in his head what he previously would have had to do through physical action. He can make estimates and is able to understand the concepts of relative length, amount, etc. His ways of thinking are becoming increasingly like those of an adult."[33]

Piaget's fourth stage is called the stage of formal operations. It begins at about age twelve. The child is now able to think abstractly and use abstract rules and is also capable of considering a number of different hypothetical possibilities in a given situation or in solving a given problem.

Research on early learning and brain development reveals that infants come into the world "wired to learn" with "inborn motivation to develop competencies."[34] "The

---

[31] National Research Council, Institute of Medicine, Committee on Integrating the Science of Early Childhood Development & Board on Children, Youth, and Families, FROM NEURONS TO NEIGHBORHOODS: THE SCIENCE OF EARLY CHILDHOOD DEVELOPMENT 147 (Jack P. Shonkoff & Deborah A. Phillips eds., 2000), *available at* http://books.nap.edu/catalog/9824.html?onpi_news doc100300.

[32] *Id.* at 148.

[33] *See* TERESA CAPLAN & FRANK CAPLAN, THE EARLY CHILDHOOD YEARS: THE 2 TO 6 YEAR OLD 1 (1983).

[34] National Research Council, Institute of Medicine, Committee on Integrating the Science of Early Childhood Development & Board on Children, Youth, and Families, FROM NEURONS TO NEIGHBORHOODS: THE SCIENCE OF EARLY CHILDHOOD DEVELOPMENT 148 (Jack P. Shonkoff &

exciting discoveries that have characterized research on cognitive development have led some to argue that young minds—so active and capable—require special, heightened cognitive stimulation. Certainly, as more is learned about the remarkable capabilities of young children and their eagerness to learn, one naturally wants to provide them with environments that will support them in their task of becoming the most competent children, and ultimately adults, that they can be."[35] However, research has not shown that special toys or exposure to certain music, such as Mozart, optimizes cognitive growth. Instead, "as with every other task of early development . . . this literature emphasizes parents' interactions with their young children, their beliefs about learning and their children's capabilities, the home learning environment, and family organization."[36]

§ 4.1.3 Language Development

Language development, like other aspects of development, follows a regular sequential course in all children who are not physically, mentally, or emotionally impaired. However, there is a great deal of variation in the ages at which language acquisition and usage takes place. Also, language development is highly influenced by the environment, particularly by the amount of language stimulation provided by the parents or other adults. "Language learning turns out to be remarkably similar across cultures. Children exposed to markedly different languages follow similar developmental trajectories as they learn their native language."[37] At all given stages of language acquisition, the child usually comprehends approximately twice as many words as he or she is able to speak.

The period from age two to age five is the most notable in terms of the acquisition and mastery of language. However, the precursors of language are evident almost from birth. For example, during the second and third month, infants usually begin to make non-crying, squalling, gurgling sounds called cooing. By the end of the fourth or fifth month the infant has started to babble, i.e., make sounds that resemble one syllable utterances such as ma, mu, da, etc. Babbling becomes more frequent with identifiable, single words emerging around the end of the first year. Signs of understanding some words and commands is also evident at this time. Children usually start to combine words into simple two word sentences at 18 to 24 months. By 36 months the child's utterances consist of at least two words, and the child may even use three to five word sentences. By the age of four language is usually well established, and the child is starting to master the complex rules of grammar. By this age the average number of words in the child's spoken vocabulary is about 1,500.

Deborah A. Phillips eds., 2000), *available at* http://books.nap.edu/catalog/9824.html?onpi_newsdoc 100300.

[35] *Id.* at 155.

[36] *Id.* at 156–58.

[37] *Id.* at 127.

By the age of five, speech is becoming more fluent and grammatically correct. The child can usually give his or her name, age, and address. The number of words of the vocabulary of the average five-year-old is approximately 2,200.[38] Even though five- and six-year-old children are becoming more and more competent in language skills, there are limits to what children under seven can convey with words alone. The adult needs to observe the child's nonverbal behavior in order to fully comprehend the meaning of the child's language. The young child's language is closely tied to action and is embedded in the ongoing situation. The child of this age is very easy to misunderstand, and it is not until about the age of six, at the earliest, that the child can pay attention to language per se without external support, actions, or physical cues.

After age six or seven, the child's expressive language gradually becomes more and more adult-like, and communication with others is significantly easier to understand. Written language expands, and as children move into elementary school age, they can express much more clearly their ideas and intentions. The language and communication skills of adolescents differ little from those of adults.

§ 4.1.4 Social and Emotional Child Development

The child's experiences with adult caretakers during the first few years of life lay the foundation for his or her social, emotional functioning throughout life. Thus, rejection, neglect, and abuse during childhood may result in serious interference with the child's social and emotional development. Erik Erikson has described a series of psychosocial stages that children move through as they mature.[39] During each of the stages there is a major task for the individual to accomplish if development is to proceed normally and positively. These stages will be described in some detail because Erikson's theories are highly applicable to child welfare cases. An understanding of these stages and the tasks associated with each will help the attorney to understand children's social and emotional growth at different times of their lives, and thus, what children may need in terms of parenting at each of these developmental stages.

Stage 1 – Basic Trust vs. Mistrust

This stage lasts from birth until approximately 18 months of age. The major developmental task to be accomplished by the developing infant is to establish "basic trust." This sense of trust is established during the first year or so of life. "By the end of the first year of life, infants are acutely sensitive to the emotional cues of other people, especially in uncertain or potentially threatening circumstances. In a process researchers call social referencing, infants take their cues from the reassuring or anxious expression of a caregiver, which, in turn, can affect whether they continue to

---

[38] *See, e.g.,* FRANK CAPLAN, THE PARENTING ADVISOR 301 (1978).

[39] *See* ERIC ERICKSON, CHILDHOOD AND SOCIETY (1950).

play comfortably or freeze in their tracks."[40] Infants require consistent, responsive interactions to develop a secure belief that their needs will be met. The child's ability to love other people and to relate positively to others is also best established during this very important period of development.

The infant learns to trust by having his or her physical and emotional needs met by a nurturing, responsive, non-abusive caretaker. If these needs are not met during the first year or so of life, the child's capacity to relate to and trust other people is likely to be permanently impaired. "The findings on the prevalence and stability of insecure and atypical attachments in maltreated children point to the extreme risks these children face in achieving adaptive outcomes in other domains of interpersonal relationships."[41] It is during this stage that the child is, thus, particularly vulnerable to physical or emotional neglect. Neglect at this stage includes not meeting the child's needs for food, comfort, soothing, physical contact, and appropriate stimulation. The promptness with which the child's needs are met is especially important at this stage. The young infant does not have the capacity to wait for long periods of time while the parent takes care of other things.

Infants are at much greater risk of physical abuse and neglect than older children due to their physical fragility and extreme helplessness. Also, the consequences of certain types of physical maltreatment (e.g., shaking, tossing in the air, jerking an arm or leg, hitting, or spanking) can be extremely damaging to the young child and can result in serious physical injury, neurological damage, and even death. The same acts perpetrated upon an older child might result in only minor injury. Therefore, physical abuse of the child at this particular development level must be considered a much more serious event than at older age levels.

Even though children at this very early developmental stage are more at risk of abuse or neglect, they are also more at risk of being emotionally damaged by being removed from a parent to whom they are attached even though that parent may be abusive or neglectful. It is generally accepted among health professionals and child development specialists that it can be extremely damaging to separate a young child from a primary caretaker. Bowlby, among others, has expressed the opinion that states of anxiety, depression, and other forms of adult pathology may have their origins in earlier experiences of separation and loss.[42]

Despite the risks associated with removal, however, there are certain types of abuse, particularly at this early stage of development, where the risk of severe injury or death is so great that nothing but removal should be considered. A parent who is

---

[40] National Research Council, Institute of Medicine, Committee on Integrating the Science of Early Childhood Development & Board on Children, Youth, and Families, FROM NEURONS TO NEIGHBORHOODS: THE SCIENCE OF EARLY CHILDHOOD DEVELOPMENT 107 (Jack P. Shonkoff & Deborah A. Phillips eds., 2000), *available at* http://books.nap.edu/catalog/9824.html?onpi_news doc100300.

[41] Dante Cicchetti & Sheree L. Toth, *A Developmental Psychopathology Perspective on Child Abuse and Neglect*, 34/5 J. AM. ACAD. CHILD ADOLESC. PSYCHIATRY 541 (1995).

[42] *See, e.g.*, JOHN BOWLBY, 2 ATTACHMENT AND LOSS: SEPARATION, ANXIETY, AND ANGER (1973).

capable of intentionally and severely abusing a tiny infant is not likely to be rehabilitated, and termination of parental rights should be considered. There are also parents who, even though they may not severely abuse their child, are so inadequate and so unable to recognize the helplessness of a baby that their ability to provide protection must be questioned. Bolton,[43] in his discussion of parents who are unable to form attachments, warns that a failure to view the infant's helplessness realistically suggests that such a parent, because of his or her own selfishness and inability to care for a helpless infant, may never be able to adequately fulfill a parental role, nor is such a parent likely to benefit from treatment or education. In these instances, it is necessary to consider the termination of parental rights as early as possible.

Stage 2 – Autonomy vs. Shame and Guilt

Sometime beginning in the second year of life and extending until around the age of three years, the child goes through the second stage of development. Erikson has called this the stage of autonomy. He describes the child's primary developmental task during this period as that of developing a sense of independence and self-control. The child's striving for independence during this stage repeatedly brings the child into conflict with what society and parents expect. The child begins to encounter the word "no" and to resist the prohibitions that accompany this word. The child at this stage needs opportunities to assert his or her will to some extent, to make choices, and to feel he or she is having an impact on the world in which the child lives. At the same time, the child needs to learn that there are limits and some external controls over his or her behavior. The capacity for later self-control may be very much related to the opportunity to practice making mistakes and experiencing natural consequences. As the child gets closer to the age of two, the child often becomes more and more negative and rebellious. This negativism is actually a positive sign of good emotional adjustment. The child is learning to assert himself or herself and to develop confidence in his or her own abilities. Failure to receive proper support and guidance during this period of life may result in deep-seated feelings of shame and guilt.

The risk for physical abuse at this stage often revolves around the child's struggle for independence and need to explore. At this stage of development, the child requires a parent who can allow the child to make choices and decisions while not becoming punitive or overly invasive in an attempt to control the child's behavior. The parent of a child at this stage needs to be patient and not overly rigid. The capacity for later self-control requires that the child be allowed some freedom at this stage and not be shamed for making mistakes. Because language and cognitive development are still limited, children at this stage often do not comprehend verbal instructions, and may require reminders of what is expected. When the parents do not understand these limitations and they lack understanding of positive ways to manage the child's

---

[43] *See, e.g.*, FRANK BOLTON, WHEN BONDING FAILS: CLINICAL ASSESSMENT OF HIGH RISK FAMILIES 184 (1983).

negativistic and rebellious behavior, they may falsely assign malevolent intentions to their child's attempts at autonomous exploration.

Simple punishments such as light spanking may escalate to increasingly punitive and abusive treatment of the child. Again, parents often have unrealistic expectations of children's capabilities. When the child does not obey verbal instructions or is uncooperative with toilet training or does not pick up the toys, the parent may interpret the child's behavior as disrespectful or disobedient rather than as a function of his or her developmental level. This may lead to excessive punishment and abuse. Children at this age are physically fragile and unable to defend themselves. Therefore, although they are not quite as vulnerable as during the first year or so of life, children in this stage are still at high risk for very serious physical abuse.

It is also at this stage that emotional abuse and emotional neglect may become more evident. Although emotional abuse is a complex phenomenon and there are no clear-cut guidelines as to when it exists, it is important to realize that emotional abuse may be as damaging—or even more damaging—than physical abuse. Diagnosis of emotional abuse usually requires an evaluation by a child psychologist or child psychiatrist who can differentiate between emotional abuse and psychiatric disturbance arising from other causes. For example, Attention Deficit Disorder with or without Hyperactivity, Pervasive Developmental Disorders, and organic problems may need to be ruled out. Emotional abuse and neglect are often manifested at this stage by a lack of parental responsiveness to the child's normal needs for attention, approval, and affection. At this stage, the child is also particularly vulnerable to being shamed or belittled, especially around the issues of toilet training and obedience. During toilet training, a parent who is critical and negative can seriously damage the child's sense of autonomy and self respect.

Children in this age range are also extremely vulnerable to physical neglect as they are still dependent upon an adult to provide a safe and healthy environment. Lack of supervision is often a serious neglect issue because the child cannot provide for his or her own physical needs, does not have a cognitive understanding of danger, and requires protection in almost all settings.

Separation of children from their parents is still extremely traumatic at this age, and alternatives to removal should be considered, except in very high risk situations. If a child of this age has been removed from parental custody because of abuse or neglect, a careful assessment should be made by a qualified professional in creating a visitation plan.

Stage 3 – Initiative vs. Self-Doubt

The third stage is the stage of initiative. It develops during the third year and lasts up until around six years. The child's growth in physical coordination, in language, and in imagination is most important in terms of development. These developmental skills enable the child to accomplish the main developmental task of this period, which is to find out what kind of person he or she is going to be. The child's great store of energy and growing skills allow the child to plan and carry out many new activities. A child at this stage may be more aware of sexual impulses. One of the problems at this stage may be that of excessive feelings of guilt.

Excessive guilt can result in an overly strict conscience. The child does need to learn to experience some guilt about his or her inappropriate behavior because this is the stage when the conscience (feelings of right and wrong) is being established. However, it is also possible for the child to feel very little remorse about destructive or negative behaviors and thus fail to develop appropriate feelings about right and wrong.

At this stage, the child is particularly interested in the activities of adults and may imitate and identify with the parents even more than he or she did at younger ages. Because of the increase in imaginative powers and the desire to imitate adults, the child engages in a great deal of fantasy and playing out the roles of adults. A child who successfully negotiates this phase of development will establish a sense of playfulness and creativity.

At this stage the child is more active and physically coordinated and also can move about much more freely. Children at this stage are at a high risk of neglect, especially lack of appropriate parental supervision and exposure to household and neighborhood dangers. Unrealistic expectations for the child may lead the parent to believe the child is capable of avoiding these dangers and may also lead the parent to treat the child as older than he or she is developmentally. For example, parents may leave three- to six-year-olds alone in the house or may even leave them alone to supervise younger children. Parents may also expect children at this age to be able to assume household responsibilities that they are not capable of—such as cleaning the house, keeping their rooms picked up and neat, and preparing their own meals—all without adult supervision. When the child does not perform these tasks or performs them poorly, the parent may believe that the child is being deliberately disobedient and, thus, deserving of punishment that can be excessive, physical, and even abusive.

At this stage, the risk from physical abuse is still quite high, but the likelihood of serious physical injury is not quite as great as at earlier ages because the child is less fragile physically and more mobile (e.g., the child can run away from a momentarily angry parent). Also, because children at this age have significantly better language and cognitive skills, they can understand simple verbal instructions and explanations, making it somewhat easier to discipline them without resorting to physical punishment.

Children at the stage of initiative need opportunities to plan and initiate their own activities and develop competencies and confidence. They need help in language development and encouragement in pre-school and school attendance and activities. Rewarding a child's accomplishments and achievements with attention and praise helps the child to experience success and not develop feelings of hopelessness and failure. Encouraging a child to establish good relationships with peers and providing opportunities for this to occur are important goals at this stage. The parent must have the willingness and the time to carry out these many parenting responsibilities. If parents berate or make fun of their children or prevent them from participating in activities and experiences in which they can achieve mastery and competence, children begin to doubt themselves and suffer impairment of self-esteem. Such treatment can reach the level of emotional abuse, wherein the child may feel totally rejected or terrorized by the parent's threats or by their extremely harsh punishments.

Sexual abuse in the family is an increasing danger at this age, even more so when the adult male in the home is not biologically related to the child.[44] It is also possible that a child may have repeatedly observed adult intercourse in the home or may have viewed explicit sexual activities on cable or satellite television channels or on video or DVD movies. These kinds of experiences, by prematurely exposing a child to sexual stimuli, can lead to early sexualization of the child. Thus, some children who are observed to behave in very sexualized ways and are thought to have been sexually molested, may have, instead, witnessed adult sexual activity. Some authorities consider such experiences to be a form of sexual abuse. Elevated sexual behavior, particularly certain types of sexual behavior, has been found to occur more frequently in sexually abused children.[45]

Although temporary separation from a primary parenting figure can be better tolerated than at younger ages, regular contact with the parents is still very important and should be maintained except in extreme situations.

Stage 4 – Industry vs. Inferiority

Stage 4 begins at about the time the child enters elementary school and lasts until puberty begins. This stage is sometimes referred to as the latency period, during which a child earns recognition from others by learning to apply himself or herself to skills and tasks that go beyond play and pleasure. The child's major task is to develop a sense of industry, both at home and at school, learning the basic skills of survival and thereby avoiding feelings of inferiority and inadequacy. This is also a very decisive stage socially because it involves doing things cooperatively with others, resulting in a sense of self-worth.

Of prime importance during this stage of development is the parents' support of and interaction with their child's educational program and activities. This is also the time in a child's life when the development of social skills and strong peer relationships become highly significant. The child needs to have numerous successes to avoid a sense of inferiority. Providing consistent and fair rules and guidelines during these developmental years helps the child to learn to live within societal limits and develop a sense of right and wrong. The child's participation in school and social activities is very important and should not be disrupted if possible. Peers are also extremely important at this stage of development, and disruption of peer relationships can be damaging to the child's social and emotional development.

---

[44] *See, e.g.,* DIANA RUSSELL, THE SEXUAL TRAUMA: INCEST IN THE LIVES OF GIRLS AND WOMEN (1986).

[45] *See, e.g.,* WILLIAM N. FRIEDRICH, PSYCHOTHERAPY OF SEXUALLY ABUSED CHILDREN AND THEIR FAMILIES (1990). Friedrich has published a CHILD SEXUAL BEHAVIOR INVENTORY FOR CHILDREN, AGES 2 TO 12 (1990), which has been helpful in distinguishing those specific sexual behaviors which are more diagnostic of sexual abuse from those which are exhibited generally in non-abused children.

The child at this developmental stage is gradually becoming more and more independent and is not so helpless or physically fragile. He or she is less vulnerable to serious injury from abuse and less in danger from neglect or lack of supervision. Because the child is cognitively and linguistically more advanced, he or she is able to listen to reasoning and to respond to verbal discipline. However, because children at this stage can reason, they may talk back to parents when the parents are illogical or ill informed. This talking back is often perceived as a lack of respect and may lead to abuse.

The child's emotional and social needs during this stage include the establishment and maintenance of peer relationships. Achieving some independence from parental figures is another important need, particularly toward the end of this age period. The parent who is unable to recognize the child's emotional and social needs is likely to become involved in conflict with the child. School is particularly important during this stage of development, and success in school helps the child to avoid feelings of inferiority. However, if the child is not doing well in school and the parental expectations are for school success, serious conflict may occur in the parent-child relationship. Slow-learning children or children with unidentified learning disabilities are especially vulnerable to parental abuse when they bring home poor grades. Punishment related to poor grades is common and often so severe that it can be considered abusive.

Children who have attention deficit or hyperactivity disorders are particularly susceptible to abuse because they are so impulsive and do not learn as readily from consequences as do other children. Children who are suspected of being hyperactive are usually not identified as hyperactive until they enter school. These children, whether in abuse/neglect cases or divorce cases, need thorough evaluations by a child psychiatrist and a child psychologist because they may need medical management and other forms of psychological treatment.

Another significant issue at this developmental stage is sexual abuse. Research studies have found that children are most vulnerable to sexual abuse between the ages of eight to twelve years old.[46] In addition, there are risks of inappropriate exposure to adult sexuality through observation of adults in the home or from watching overtly sexual videotapes or movies in the home.

At this developmental stage, separation from abusive parents through removal from parental custody does not usually result in the severe trauma that separation at younger ages does. Separation may be dangerous to the child's mental health, however, due to disruption of schooling and peer relationships, particularly if the child is moved to a different neighborhood because of being placed in foster care or with relatives. Also, children at this age may be extremely resistant to removal from their home, despite the abuse. The child's own desires are particularly important to the child's attorney, even when the child's desires may not represent what the attorney

---

[46] *See, e.g.*, David Finkelhor & Larry Baron, *High-Risk Children, in* A SOURCEBOOK ON CHILD SEXUAL ABUSE 60 (David Finkelhor ed., 1986).

considers to be the child's best interest. All of these issues must be taken into consideration by the child's attorney in making legal recommendations.

If it is necessary to remove the child from the home, an attempt should be made to locate an appropriate placement for the child that will be in or close to the child's own neighborhood and in the same school district. The child may be able to suggest relatives or friends who may be willing to take the child in or even to become specially licensed foster parents for the child. If not, placement should be sought in a foster home as close as possible to the child's parents' home, with the child to be transported to the same school and, if at all possible, be allowed to continue established activities and maintain contact with his or her family.

Stage 5 – Identity vs. Role Confusion

This final developmental stage before reaching adulthood is one of rapid physical growth and evolving sexual maturity. Each youth is now faced with the formidable task of integrating his or her physiological upheaval with his or her natural aptitudes, acquired skills, and newly developing social roles into a sense of personal identity. The danger at this stage is one of "role confusion" sexually, vocationally, and socially, which may result in a tendency to over identify with accessible heroes who are revered by those in his or her age group. In particular, the young individual is eager to be affirmed by his or her peers while grappling with the morality he or she learned as a child and the ethics to be developed for the adult years ahead.

When children enter the changing turbulent years of adolescence, the role of the parent also changes. As the young person attempts to clarify and solidify his or her identity, parents often become the foil against whom the child tries out new and sometimes controversial ideas. Walking the fine line between maintaining necessary and consistent boundaries and rules, while allowing the child to gradually become more self-sufficient and independent is a parental requirement at this stage. As a result of the drastic changes involved in the rapid physical growth and maturation, adolescents generally experience a great deal of emotional turmoil. A child who has previously been compliant and easy to get along with may suddenly become rebellious and demanding. This places pressure on parents, who may have gotten along relatively well with the child so long as the child was following family rules and adhering to family values. As the child's cognitive and language abilities mature and he or she is trying to establish a healthy sense of his or her own identity, the parents may become increasingly frustrated in their attempts to control the child. Conflict can erupt, leading to escalation of discipline on the part of the parents, which in turn may result in actual physical or emotional abuse.

Although the risk of serious harm or injury is much less at this age than when the child was younger, there still may be some situations in which the child is so at risk that removal from parental custody may need to be considered. However, the attorney should recognize that alternative placements in state custody are quite limited for adolescents and that few foster homes are equipped to deal with a rebellious adolescent. In addition, many adolescents, despite their conflict with their parents and even abuse by one or both parents, may still not wish to be removed from their present home or placed in foster care. Also, because adolescents are able to reason and think abstractly, much like an adult, they are able to consider various alternatives to their family situations and the consequences of these alternatives. Therefore, the adolescent's choice must be respected, unless remaining in parental custody would involve extreme risk. Attorneys should be reluctant to recommend asking the state to take custody of adolescent clients. An alternative may be to consider placing the adolescent in a temporary shelter facility to reduce immediate stress, to allow mediation between parent and child, and to locate therapy services that might resolve the family conflicts.

Emotional abuse may be more likely to occur with adolescents than physical abuse. However, again, attempting to define and prove emotional abuse is a very difficult task, and the diagnosis usually requires the services of a psychiatrist or psychologist who can differentiate between emotional symptoms that are caused by emotional abuse and those where the cause lies elsewhere. The most serious neglect, as well as abuse, may arise in situations where parents are severe alcoholics or drug abusers. Such situations present very complex legal decisions, requiring a delicate balance between risk of leaving the adolescent in such a family situation versus the risk of removing the child and all the attendant problems that go along with that removal, such as: changing schools, separation from friends, and the difficulties of adjusting to foster families.

Another area of family conflict that often emerges during adolescence is related to the adolescent's interest and involvement in sexual experimentation. This is likely to create significant anxiety on the part of the parents, often leading to attempts to control the child's sexual activity and consequently to situations that may become abusive. Another significant issue that may first emerge at this developmental level is that of a child's emerging homosexual orientation. Gay and lesbian youth are more likely to be abused and rejected by their families than are heterosexual youth, and research indicates that many run away from home, attempt suicide, and abuse substances.[47] The unusually high rate of suicide among gay adolescents has been repeatedly demonstrated, and is a phenomenon with which child welfare attorneys should be familiar.

§ 4.1.5 Attachment, Separation, and Loss

The concepts of attachment, separation, and loss are significant in understanding children's social and emotional needs at different developmental stages. John Bowlby[48] and Mary Ainsworth[49] were among the earliest professionals to describe the

---

[47] *See, e.g.,* Gary Remafedi, *Adolescent Homosexuality: Medical and Psychological Implications*, 79/3 PEDIATRICS 331 (1987); Gary Remafedi, *Homosexual Youth: A Challenge to Contemporary Society*, 258/2 JAMA 222 (1987).

[48] *See, e.g.,* JOHN BOWLBY, 1 ATTACHMENT AND LOSS: ATTACHMENT (1969); JOHN BOWLBY, 2 ATTACHMENT AND LOSS: SEPARATION, ANXIETY AND ANGER (1973).

importance of a child's attachment to his or her primary caretaker as well as the child's reactions to separation from that caretaker. It is extremely important for a child's attorney to be knowledgeable about these issues because of their significance at different stages of a child's development. For example, in Bowlby's description of attachment, he states that most infants have begun to respond differently to the mother (or other primary caretaker) as compared to other people in the infant's life.[50] It is now commonly believed that the attachment process continues to develop over the course of the first year of life and beyond. If the child's basic physical needs and the needs for comfort, touch, nurturing, and stimulation have been met, the child will develop an increasing attachment to the caretaker who meets these needs most consistently.

Ainsworth described three patterns of attachment: secure, anxious/avoidant, and anxious/resistant. These types of attachment are observed in the "Strange Situation," in which a child between one and two years old is separated from and reunited with a parent or primary caretaker, and the evaluator observes the child's reactions.[51] The securely attached child protests the separation and is happy and easy to console upon reunification. Securely attached children have a secure base from which to explore their environment. They are expected to show separation anxiety and to be more easily consoled by their parents than by other adults. The insecurely attached, anxious/avoidant child is not distressed during separation and avoids the parent at the time of reunification. Children with anxious/avoidant attachment are presumed to have had experiences where their emotional arousal was not reestablished by the parent or where they were overly aroused through intrusive parenting; so they over-regulate their affect and avoid situations that are likely to be distressing. The insecurely attached, anxious/resistant child is clingy from the beginning, anxious during separation, and angry upon reunification. Children with anxious/resistant attachment under-regulate their affect, heightening their expression of distress and becoming preoccupied with having contact with the parent, but becoming frustrated even when the parent is available.

Main and Solomon have identified a fourth pattern of attachment, with the child demonstrating seemingly undirected behavior, freezing, hand clapping, head banging, and the wish to escape the situation even in the presence of the parent. They call this pattern of attachment "disorganized/disoriented."[52] Children with disorganized/disoriented attachment are presumed to have had experiences where the parent was a source of both fear and reassurance, so arousal of the attachment behavioral system

---

[49] *See, e.g.,* Mary D. Salter Ainsworth, *Infant-Mother Attachment,* 34/10 AM. PSYCHOL. 932 (1979); Mary D. Salter Ainsworth, *Attachments Beyond Infancy,* 44/4 AM. PSYCHOL. 709 (1989).

[50] *See* JOHN BOWLBY, 1 ATTACHMENT AND LOSS: ATTACHMENT (1969).

[51] *See, e.g.,* M. D. S. AINSWORTH ET AL., PATTERNS OF ATTACHMENT: A PSYCHOLOGICAL STUDY OF THE STRANGE SITUATION (1978).

[52] *See, e.g.,* Mary Main & Judith Solomon, *Procedures for Identifying Infants as Disorganized/Disoriented during the Ainsworth Strange Situation, in* ATTACHMENT DURING THE PRESCHOOL YEARS: THEORY, RESEARCH AND INTERVENTION 121–60 (Mark T. Greenberg et al. eds., 1990).

produces strong conflicting motivations. A history of serious neglect or physical or sexual abuse is often associated with this pattern.[53]

Attachment patterns in infancy affect a child's ability to form future attachments, including attachments to subsequent caretakers. Children whose attachments are repeatedly broken—by being placed in multiple placements, for example—may have difficulty forming secure attachments anywhere. Children with insecure attachments from their homes of origin or multiple out-of-home placements need stability and specialized therapy to increase the likelihood of their being able to form secure attachments, even in their subsequent adult relationships.

A great deal has been written about children's reactions to separation from their primary caretakers.[54] It is generally accepted among mental health professionals and child development specialists that it can be extremely damaging to separate a child from a primary caretaker. Among the first writers to point out the extremity of children's reactions to such separations were Dorothy Burlingham and Anna Freud.[55] They describe their experiences with young children who were separated from their parents in England during World War II to protect them from bombing raids. Concerning children who they observed in the Hampstead Nursery where they were cared for during this separation, Burlingham and Freud commented that the child who was between the ages of one and three was particularly affected. "Reactions to parting at this time of life are particularly violent. . . . This new ability to love finds itself deprived of the accustomed objects (parents) and his greed for affection remains unsatisfied. His longing for his mother becomes intolerable and throws him into states of despair."[56] Bowlby, among others, has referred to these findings and expressed the opinion that states of anxiety, depression, and other forms of adult pathology may have their origins in earlier experiences of separation and loss.[57]

Because the attachment process is important to the child's sense of security and trust, it is necessary to carefully consider the child's possible reactions to separation from, or loss of, his or her primary attachment figures, whether these result from parental divorce or from involvement by the child welfare system. The risks

---

[53] *See, e.g.*, Dante Cicchetti & Marjorie Beeghly, *Symbolic Development in Maltreated Youngsters: An Organizational Perspective, in* ATYPICAL SYMBOLIC DEVELOPMENT: NEW DIRECTIONS FOR CHILD DEVELOPMENT 5–29 (Dante Cicchetti & Marjorie Beeghly eds., 1987); Mary Main & Erik Hesse, *Parents' Unresolved Traumatic Experiences Are Related to Infant Disorganized Attachment Status: Is Frightened and/or Frightening Parental Behavior the Linking Mechanism?, in* ATTACHMENT IN THE PRESCHOOL YEARS: THEORY, RESEARCH AND INTERVENTION 161–82 (Mark T. Greenberg et al. eds., 1990).

[54] *See, e.g.*, Mary D. Salter Ainsworth & M. Boston, *Psychodiagnostic Assessments of a Child After Prolonged Separation in Early Childhood*, 25/4 BR. J. MED. PSYCHOL. 169 (1952); JOHN BOWLBY, 1 ATTACHMENT AND LOSS: ATTACHMENT (1969); JOHN BOWLBY, 2 ATTACHMENT AND LOSS: SEPARATION, ANXIETY AND ANGER (1973).

[55] *See, e.g.*, DOROTHY BURLINGHAM & ANNA FREUD, INFANTS WITHOUT FAMILIES (1944); DOROTHY BURLINGHAM & ANNA FREUD, YOUNG CHILDREN IN WAR-TIME (1942).

[56] *See* DOROTHY BURLINGHAM & ANNA FREUD, YOUNG CHILDREN IN WAR-TIME 388 (1942).

[57] *See, e.g.*, JOHN BOWLBY, 2 ATTACHMENT AND LOSS: SEPARATION, ANXIETY AND ANGER (1973).

associated with separation vary at different stages of the child's development and with the length of the separation. In general, the younger the child, the more difficult a separation will be. After the age of three, some children can tolerate temporary separation from parent figures more readily than at earlier ages. Because of their increased language and cognitive abilities, the parent's absence can be explained to the older child, and the child has the ability to understand that the absence will be temporary.

It is extremely important for the child's attorney to recognize the risks of separation and to realize that even in cases of abuse and neglect, it is necessary to weigh the risks of removal of the child from the home just as carefully as the risks of leaving the child in the home with an abusive or neglecting parent. In abuse or neglect situations, one possible solution may be for the attorney to recommend that the state take legal custody but leave the child in the physical custody of the parent. Danger can be minimized by asking the court to order monitoring and intensive services to be provided to the family in the home in order to ensure that the child's developmental needs are being met and that the child is not in danger of serious abuse or neglect.

§ 4.2 Long-Term Effects of Maltreatment

§ 4.2.1 Generally

Abuse and neglect may have long-term physical consequences. Children of alcoholic and substance-abusing mothers may be born with physical limitations. For example, children whose mothers consume alcohol during their pregnancy may be born with fetal alcohol syndrome, which can include physical, behavioral, and learning disabilities that may persist into adulthood. Infants and toddlers who are violently shaken may suffer from shaken baby syndrome, which can cause death, paralysis, blindness, brain damage, learning disabilities, and mental retardation. Being exposed to a violent or chaotic home in the earliest years of life can change the way neurons form in the brain, affecting the child cognitively, emotionally, and behaviorally. Inadequate nutrition in infancy and early childhood can alter all types of physical development, including development of the brain. Serious physical injuries can result in life-long disabilities and deficits. Beyond these direct, physical consequences, maltreatment can change who the child is: how the child views himself or herself, the child's worth, and the child's ability to relate to his or her world and the people in it.[58] Maltreated children may suffer from post-traumatic stress disorder, depression, anxiety disorders, dissociative disorders, eating disorders, and attachment disorders as a result of their maltreatment. These disorders may affect the child for his or her lifetime.

Children who are abused and neglected may be more likely to have various social problems, including substance abuse, school disciplinary problems, and delinquency.

---

[58] *See generally* YOUNG CHILDREN AND TRAUMA (Joy D. Ofofsky ed., 2004).

These problems may persist into adulthood, particularly when children age out of the child welfare system with multiple foster care and group home placements. These children are at a greater risk of experiencing homelessness and incarceration as young adults. Adults who have juvenile histories of poor academic performance, behavioral problems, substance abuse, and delinquency are less likely to be welcomed into good schools or to be offered good jobs.

Responses to child abuse and neglect are very individual. Some resilient children are able to overcome even serious abuse and flourish, while other children are seriously impaired in their life-long ability to function as adults. A number of factors have been identified that affect outcomes, including:

- The child's age and stage of development when the abuse occurred
- The severity, frequency, duration, and type of the abuse
- The relationship between the child and the abuser
- The child's temperament
- The child's physical and emotional health
- The degree of family or community support systems
- The presence of a healthy, nurturing relationship between the child and an adult, who need not be a relative

§ 4.2.2 The ACE Study

The Centers for Disease Control and Prevention and Kaiser Permanente's Health Appraisal Clinic in San Diego, California, is running "one of the largest investigations ever conducted on the links between childhood maltreatment and later-life health and well-being,"[59] known as the Adverse Childhood Experiences (ACE) Study. This study, which is still ongoing, has included over 17,000 members of Kaiser Permanente's HMO "undergoing a comprehensive physical examination provided detailed information about their childhood experience of abuse, neglect, and family dysfunction."[60]

The ACE Study findings "suggest that these experiences are major risk factors for the leading causes of illness and death as well as poor quality of life in the United States."[61] These include:

---

[59] *See* Department of Health and Human Services, Centers for Disease Control and Prevention, Web page titled "Adverse Childhood Experiences Study" at http://www.cdc.gov/nccdphp/ACE/.

[60] *Id.*

[61] *Id. See generally* Vincent Felitti & Robert Anda et al., *Relationship of Childhood Abuse and Household Dysfunction to Many of the Leading Causes of Death in Adults: The Adverse Childhood Experiences (ACE) Study,* 14/4 AM. J. PREV. MED. 245 (1998) ("Persons who had experienced four or more categories of childhood exposure, compared to those who had experienced none, had 4- to 12-fold increased health risks for alcoholism, drug abuse, depression, and suicide attempt; a 2- to 4-fold increase in smoking, poor self-rated health, ≥50 sexual intercourse partners, and sexually transmitted disease; and a 1.4- to 1.6-fold increase in physical inactivity and severe obesity. The number of

- Alcoholism and alcohol abuse
- Chronic obstructive pulmonary disease (COPD)
- Depression
- Fetal death
- Health-related quality of life
- Illicit drug use
- Ischemic heart disease (IHD)
- Liver diseases
- Risk for intimate partner violence
- Multiple sexual partners
- Sexually transmitted diseases (STDs)
- Smoking
- Suicide attempts
- Unintended pregnancies

The ACE Score is calculated by identifying the following adverse childhood experiences:

- Abuse
  - Emotional Abuse: Often or very often a parent or other adult in the household swore at you, insulted you, or put you down and/or sometimes, often or very often acted in a way that made you think that you might be physically hurt.
  - Physical Abuse: Sometimes, often, or very often pushed, grabbed, slapped, or had something thrown at you and/or ever hit so hard that you had marks or were injured.
  - Sexual Abuse: An adult or someone at least five years older ever touched or fondled you in a sexual way, and/or had you touch their body in a sexual way, and/or attempted oral, anal, or vaginal intercourse with you and/or actually had oral, anal, or vaginal intercourse with you.
- Neglect
  - Emotional Neglect: Respondents were asked whether their family made them feel special, loved, and if their family was a source of strength, support, and protection. Emotional neglect was defined

---

categories of adverse childhood exposures showed a graded relationship to the presence of adult diseases including ischemic heart disease, cancer, chronic lung disease, skeletal fractures, and liver disease. The seven categories of adverse childhood categories of childhood exposure were likely to have multiple health risk factors later in life.")

using scale scores that represent moderate to extreme exposure on the Emotional Neglect subscale of the Childhood Trauma Questionnaire (CTQ) short form.

- o Physical Neglect: Respondents were asked whether there was enough to eat, if their parents drinking interfered with their care, if they ever wore dirty clothes, and if there was someone to take them to the doctor. Physical neglect was defined using scale scores that represent moderate to extreme exposure on the Physical Neglect subscale of the Childhood Trauma Questionnaire (CTQ) short form constituted physical neglect.

- Household Dysfunction
  - o Mother Treated Violently: Your mother or stepmother was sometimes, often, or very often pushed, grabbed, slapped, or had something thrown at her and/or sometimes often, or very often kicked, bitten, hit with a fist, or hit with something hard, and/or ever repeatedly hit over at least a few minutes and/or ever threatened or hurt by a knife or gun.
  - o Household Substance Abuse: Lived with anyone who was a problem drinker or alcoholic and/or lived with anyone who used street drugs.
  - o Household Mental Illness: A household member was depressed or mentally ill and/or a household member attempted suicide.
  - o Parental Separation or Divorce: Parents were ever separated or divorced.
  - o Incarcerated Household Member: A household member went to prison.

§ 4.3 Importance of Developmental Level for Child Abuse/Neglect Issues

Many researchers and child abuse specialists have observed that the likelihood of being abused is greatest for children who are from three months to three years of age. Possible reasons for this phenomenon are that the younger children tend to place much higher emotional and physical demands on their parents. Also, they are more disruptive to the parents' activities than are older children. Thus, it should be recognized that the period of greatest risk for children coincides with the period of greatest vulnerability, helplessness, and need. Certain children are even more at risk during this age period, such as children who have any type of physical or developmental handicap, children who are born prematurely, children with difficult temperaments who may cry excessively, or children who, for any reason, require more than the usual amount of attention and care giving. These children tend to remain at high risk of abuse throughout their childhood.

Since children have differing cognitive, physical, emotional, and language capabilities at different stages of their development, the parents need to take these capabilities into account when forming expectations for their children. Abusive parents have often been found to have unrealistic expectations for their children, based on their lack of understanding of the child's developmental needs. When the child does not respond according to the parents' expectations, this may lead to anger in the parents, and abuse may occur.

It is important to understand that abuse and maltreatment exist on a continuum of severity. Bolton describes that "the maltreating family may be drawn from a wide distribution of social/emotional/parenting pathology. These families range from those who repeatedly inflict grievous injury on their children and seem impervious to treatment to those who make minor child care errors out of ignorance."[62] Depending on the nature and severity of abuse and the parent's potential for benefiting from treatment, intervention approaches other than removing a child from an abusive home should be considered. Since separation from a primary caretaker is known to be extremely damaging, particularly to very young children, other alternatives should usually be considered. The following are among the possible alternative interventions:

- Parent education
- Parent counseling
- Supervision and close monitoring by Child Protective Services
- In-home family therapy
- Parent aides in the home

Use of multidisciplinary teams can be extremely valuable in long term planning for difficult cases.

It is important to recognize that children who have been victims of abuse and/or neglect often need mental health treatment themselves. For example, if the child appears to be displaying signs of anxiety, depression, aggression, or extreme noncompliance, evaluation and treatment by a mental health professional may be necessary. Abused children who need treatment and do not receive it at the appropriate time may experience life-long adjustment and emotional problems.

§ 4.4 Conclusion

While not every child who experiences abuse or neglect will develop a diagnosable disorder, many children do display symptoms that warrant treatment. Children who experience abuse and neglect are at risk for developing complex, interconnected developmental problems. In order to better meet the needs of maltreated children, we must understand the developmental challenges occurring at

---

[62] *See, e.g.*, FRANK BOLTON, WHEN BONDING FAILS: CLINICAL ASSESSMENT OF HIGH RISK FAMILIES 184 (1983).

the time of the trauma. Because there exists a variety of responses to maltreatment, careful assessment and diagnosis by a qualified professional is imperative.

Diagnosing problems in young children is difficult for many reasons. Adults often assume that problems of childhood will work themselves out over time—that children go through stages and that problems don't require intervention. Adults worry about labeling young children and fear that labels will become self-fulfilling prophecies. Recognizing problems in children forces adults to examine painful feelings of guilt and inadequacy, especially when the child is experiencing problems as a result of adult behavior. These difficulties are particularly present in cases of child maltreatment.

Children look different from adults in terms of their physical, social, cognitive, emotional, neurological, and developmental capacities. Despite the difficulty of recognizing problems, young children continue to experience symptoms that benefit from intervention. Children who have experienced maltreatment should receive a thorough professional evaluation. Even subtle delays in motor planning, speech-language, and social-emotional arenas can negatively impact a child's functioning and interfere with effective learning. While typically developing children can focus on gaining new skills and taking good advantage of a stimulating environment, children who suffer from abuse and neglect are often more focused on basic survival. Their systems are revved up and they are exquisitely aware of events in their environment. This hypervigilance served a protective function at one point for the child who needed to be aware of his or her surroundings in order to find protection from a perpetrator of abuse. Unfortunately, children often hang onto old patterns of behavior long beyond their usefulness has been served. Children must feel safe and secure in order to begin to let go of protective defenses. This is particularly relevant in terms of children's relational functioning. The experience of being abused or neglected at the hands of adults who are supposed to love and protect their children has repercussions across the lifespan. Maltreated children are faced with the challenge of re-working maladaptive relationship patterns—a task requiring new, reparative models of interaction and a safe environment that promotes growth and healing.

Chapter 5: Investigative Interviewing of the Child

by Thomas D. Lyon[1]

§ 5.1 Introduction

The research on children's abilities as witnesses has made great progress over the past few decades. In the 1980s a series of high-profile allegations of ritualistic abuse in day care centers uncovered highly coercive questioning methods. Researchers were inspired to mimic the methods in the laboratory, and a number of studies provided dramatic demonstrations the suggestibility of children, particularly preschool children.[2] The message was largely negative, telling interviewers what to avoid, without producing alternative interviewing approaches. Fortunately, subsequent research suggested that most forensic interviews are not as coercive as the infamous cases, but nevertheless concluded that most interviewers are unnecessarily direct in their questioning, and that they do little to encourage children to provide a complete narrative of their abusive experiences.[3]

More recently, researchers have turned their attention to finding means of questioning children that maximize productivity while avoiding suggestiveness.[4] These researchers have demonstrated that children, if questioned in a supportive manner, are capable of providing enormous amounts of productive information in response to open-ended questions. The irony is that many direct and suggestive methods once thought necessary to overcome abused children's reluctance to disclose abuse have been found counterproductive in two ways: they minimize the number of details in true allegations at the same time that they increase the risk of false allegations. If children are questioned suboptimally, it is more difficult to distinguish true reports from false ones.

---

[1] Thomas D. Lyon, J.D., Ph.D., is the Judge Edward J. and Ruey L. Guirado Chair in Law and Psychology at the USC Gould School of Law.

[2] Stephen J. Ceci & Maggie Bruck, *Children's Suggestibility: Characteristics and Mechanisms*, 34 ADV. CHILD DEV. BEH. 247 (2006).

[3] Nadja Schreiber, Lisa D. Bellah, Yolanda Martinez, Kristin A. McLaurin, Renata Strok, Sena Garve & James M. Wood, *Suggestive Interviewing in the McMartin Preschool and Kelly Michaels Daycare Abuse Cases: A Case Study*, 1/1 SOCIAL INFLUENCE 16 (2006).

[4] *See, e.g.*, MICHAEL E. LAMB, IRIT HERSHKOWITZ, YAEL ORBACH & PHILLIP W. ESPLIN, TELL ME WHAT HAPPENED: STRUCTURED INVESTIGATIVE INTERVIEWS OF CHILD VICTIMS AND WITNESSES (2008); Karen J. Saywitz, Thomas D. Lyon & Gail S. Goodman, *Interviewing Children, in* THE APSAC HANDBOOK ON CHILD MALTREATMENT (John E. B. Myers ed., 3d ed. 2010).

Research on child witnesses is useful to attorneys who work with children in several ways. First, it enables attorneys to evaluate the quality of interviews conducted with children to determine whether the reports are likely accurate. Second, it provides clear guidance for how attorneys can best interview children. Third, it suggests how attorneys can better elicit testimony from children testifying in court.

This chapter will emphasize how the research on child interviewing can help attorneys better question children.[5] A great deal has been written about investigative interviewing, largely because of efforts to improve the quality of interviewing conducted by social workers, police, and therapists. The fact that the newer interviewing techniques can be used by attorneys, and even implemented in court, has largely been overlooked.

§ 5.2 Ask Open-Ended Questions

If you could only change one thing about the kind of questioning you use with children, you should ask more open-ended questions and fewer closed-ended questions. Closed-ended questions include yes–no questions, forced-choice questions, and questions that can be answered with a single word.

§ 5.2.1 Question Types: Closed-Ended vs. Open-Ended

The first step toward avoiding closed-ended questions is to become more aware of question types, so that one can closely monitor one's questions (and the questions of others). Yes–no questions are, of course, questions that can be answered yes or no. If the questions start with "Did" or "Was," or if the child is nodding or shaking his or her head in response, the questions are yes–no. Forced-choice questions are questions that ask the child to choose among options, and they always include the word "or." For example, one might ask, "Was it inside or outside?"

Some questions are unintentionally yes–no. For example, if one asks a child, "Do you remember when it was?" one is implicitly asking "When was it?" but literally one is asking a yes–no question. The same is true of questions that start with "can you tell me." As we'll see, "tell me . . ." can be a very productive question, but by adding "can you," the interviewer makes it easy for the child to simply say "no." Interviewers often ask questions intended to clarify or elicit further information that are phrased as yes–no questions. For example, interviewers will paraphrase the child's words ("You said he hurt you?") or follow-up a denial with an "are you sure?"

Analyses of child interviews (and work we have done with court transcripts) reveals that most questions are closed-ended, and yes–no questions predominate. Other examples of closed-ended questions are more difficult to spot because they require consideration of the specificity of the information requested. Wh– questions

---

[5] Because this chapter designed to introduce attorneys to the area, I only selectively cite research. However, readers should be aware that the approach is research-based, and those interested in accessing the original sources should consult the sources cited in the previous footnote.

are questions that begin with who, what, where, when, why, and how. Wh– questions move along a spectrum from open-ended to closed-ended as the information requested becomes more explicit. "What happened" is open-ended but "what color was his hat" is closed-ended.

§ 5.2.2 Why Minimize Closed-Ended Questions

Children tend to respond to closed-ended questions with no more information than the answer requires. As a result, they will provide very little information on their own, and the interviewer will do most of the talking. The more the interviewer talks, the more the interview is about the interviewers' suppositions rather than the child's memory. If the words are almost all the interviewers' the likelihood the child will be confused by the wording or structure of the questions increases. Finally, closed-ended questions increase the likelihood that the questions will be suggestive and that the answers will reflect response biases or guessing rather than the truth.

(1) Children often answer closed-ended questions with a single word, rather than elaborate with their own words and their own memories.

The basic difficulty in asking children closed-ended questions is that *if the question can be answered with one word, it almost always will be.* This is particularly true of young children, but it is also true with older children questioned in an intimidating environment, such as a courtroom. Children's tendency to answer closed-ended questions with a single word is perhaps the most striking difference between conversations with children and with adults. When we speak with other adults, we often ask yes–no questions, but adults will elaborate rather than simply answer "yes" or "no." For example, if at the end of the day one asks one's spouse "did you have a good day today?" one would be quite surprised, and perhaps have reason to worry, if the response was a one-word "yes" or "no." A single word response would be viewed as uncooperative because although the question is literally a yes–no question, the questioner is implicitly asking "tell me about your day." Children, however, without any apparent intention to be uncooperative, will frequently answer such questions with a curt response.

Single word responses have a number of obvious disadvantages. If the question is general (such as "did you have a good day?") then a simple "yes" or "no" is relatively uninformative. If the question is specific (such as "did you play on the swings today?"), then a "yes" or "no" is informative, but provides no details beyond those contained in the question. In either case, the questioner is forced to ask a further question. Moreover, as we discuss below, the other problems with specific closed-ended questions (suggestibility, incomprehension, and response biases) come into play.

If the interviewer is asking a series of closed-ended questions, and the child is providing limited responses, then the interviewer is doing all the talking, and anyone observing the interview (including the interviewer) is unable to obtain a sense of the child's capacities or attitudes or personality.

A number of studies have demonstrated that open-ended questions reliably elicit more details from children questioned about abuse than closed-ended questions. For example, Michael Lamb and his colleagues conducted interviews with children who were disclosing sexual abuse.[6] The authors found that a particular type of open-ended question, invitations, elicited several times as many details per question as closed-ended questions. Invitations are among the most open-ended of questions because they consist of requests for the child to "tell me more about" details that the child has produced. Even young children were more productive when asked invitations than closed-ended questions. This was somewhat surprising because laboratory research had suggested that young children are deficient in recall memory, in which they must generate the to-be-remembered information, as compared to recognition memory, which is tapped through yes–no questions. Another important finding that was that when asked closed-ended questions, older children were about as unproductive as younger children. In other words, if one asked an older child a series of yes–no questions, that child would appear about as reticent as a younger child—probably not a good thing for courts and others asked to evaluate the child's credibility.

(2) Closed-ended questions state what the interviewer thinks rather than what the child knows.

Most of the information in a closed-ended question is contained in the question. That is why it is possible to answer such a question with a single word. The disadvantage of this fact should be obvious: the information the interviewer can obtain is limited to the facts that the interviewer brings to the interview. If the interviewer is basing questions on information already obtained, then the likelihood that the child will provide any new information is minimal. If the interviewer is speculating, then the kinds of information that can be obtained is limited by the interviewer's imagination. Moreover, many of the interviewer's speculations are likely to be incorrect, in which case the questions will be unproductive at best.

For example, imagine you are trying to find out about a child's day at school. If you ask a series of yes–no questions (e.g., "did you play soccer") or forced-choice questions ("did you go outside or stay inside at recess"), then you will learn about activities that you are already aware of. If something exceptional happened (e.g., a clown visited the child's school), you are unlikely to find out.

Before we address the next problem with closed-ended questions, it is important to stop and recognize that the problems thus far occur regardless of accuracy. That is, even if closed-ended questions elicit *accurate* responses from children, they are less likely than open-ended questions to elicit *complete* responses from children. Some

---

[6] *See* Michael E. Lamb, Kathleen J. Sternberg & Phillip W. Esplin, *Effects of Age and Delay on the Amount of Information Provided by Alleged Sex Abuse Victims in Investigative Interviews*, 71/6 CHILD DEV. 1586 (2000).

interviewers have argued that closed-ended questions are necessary to overcome children's reluctance to disclose abuse. The problem with this argument is that reliance on closed-ended questions may actually *facilitate* reluctance. The fact that closed-ended questions may be answered with a single word means that a child who does not wish to provide details may more easily avoid doing so. And, as we shall see when we discuss accuracy problems, if the question is a yes–no question, then the reluctant child can simply answer "no."

(3) Closed-ended questions rely on the interviewer's words, and those words may be difficult or ambiguous.

If the interviewer asks a series of closed-ended questions and receives a series of single word answers, then the interviewer is doing almost all the talking. It follows that most of the words used are also the interviewer's. In any interview, it is a problem if the interviewee does not understand words that the interviewer uses.

This problem is magnified for children in three ways. First, children's vocabularies tend to be smaller than adults'. It is particularly hard for attorneys to speak to children because attorneys have internalized a substantial amount of legal jargon that is second nature to them but alien to most children. Moreover, even if one simplifies one's word use, children can be hamstrung by difficult syntax (sentence structure) and a lack of understanding of pragmatics (the implicit messages in language). Second, a child is less likely than an adult to inform you when he or she does not understand the words in a question. The child is particularly likely to fail to report incomprehension when the question is closed-ended because one can easily provide answers to closed-ended questions (particularly yes–no and forced-choice questions) without fully understanding the question (e.g., one can simply answer "yes" or "no" and appear to be following the questioning). Third, very young children are not even aware of their own incomprehension. The ability to reflect on what one understands and does not understand is called comprehension monitoring, and developmental psychologists have shown that comprehension monitoring substantially develops during the preschool years.

One might object that open-ended questions may also contain words that children do not understand. However, simply by virtue of the fact that open-ended questions increase the proportion of words provided by the child, the dangers of incomprehension are reduced. (The child is less likely to say things the interviewer does not understand than vice versa). Furthermore, the best open-ended questions are questions like "tell me everything that happened" or "what happened next," which do not introduce potentially difficult vocabulary. Also productive are "tell me more" questions, in which the interviewer repeats an aspect of the child's report and asks the child to "tell me more" (e.g., "you said he touched you. Tell me more about the touching"). Finally, because open-ended questions lead to multi-word answers, the interviewer is more likely able to detect incomprehension in the child.

Some interviewers are aware of children's limitations but adopt ineffective means of attempting to avoid the problem of difficult language. First, interviewers may watch for incomprehension in the child's expressions, and change their language if they spot signs of confusion. The problem is that children often fail to exhibit incomprehension, particularly if they misinterpret the interviewers' language rather than lack any understanding of the question's meaning. In other words, a child who mistakenly thinks he or she understands the question will not exhibit any signs of incomprehension.

Second, interviewers might test for comprehension, by pausing and asking the child if the child understands potentially difficult words. Because tests for comprehension are typically yes–no questions (e.g., "do you understand?" "do you know what a trial is?"), all of the problems with closed-ended questions arise. The child may answer "yes" without truly understanding. If the child answers "no," the interviewer often feels compelled to provide an on-the-spot lesson, which risks being long-winded and digresses from the purpose of the interview, which is to elicit information from the child. Alternatively, if the interviewer avoids the yes–no question and asks the child to define the term, then the child is put in the difficult position of providing definitions, but children are likely to understand words that they cannot define. Hence, the interviewer will underestimate the child's understanding.

Third, interviewers may try to learn guidelines describing the words that children understand or do not understand at various ages. For example, some interview guides suggest the ages at which children understand various prepositions (e.g., in, on, or under) or various concepts (such as words about time). This is a very difficult task, and is often of limited utility. First, children vary enormously in their understanding of concepts, so that age guides are only very rough guides to what any individual child will understand. Second, guides are likely to exaggerate children's understanding. When researchers in developmental psychology test children's comprehension, they work hard to make the tasks as sensitive to understanding as possible, and they often report ages at which some children exhibit understanding (rather than the age at which one can feel confident that most children, of whatever aptitude, will perform well). Finally, avoiding difficult words only scratches the surface of linguistic difficulties; as noted above, questions can be complicated because of their structure and their implications, not just because of their words.

The simplest means of avoiding difficult language is to ask questions in which the *child* does the talking, not the interviewer, and in which the follow-up questions rely as much as possible on information (and language) that the child has used. This can be accomplished through an emphasis on open-ended questions.

(4) Closed-ended questions tend to be more suggestive and more prone to response biases than open-ended questions.

We have just discussed one way in which closed-ended questions can increase error: if the child misunderstands the words used by the interviewer, then the child may be answering a different question than the interviewer intended. The interviewer will come away with a false perception of the experiences the child described.

Closed-ended questions also lead to other types of errors. From the interviewer's perspective, closed-ended questions are more likely than open-ended questions to communicate biases or suggestions. From the child's perspective, closed ended questions are more likely to lead to response biases, which reflect habits of responding to certain types of questions in certain ways, regardless of the accuracy of the response. Unfortunately, children are more suggestible to interviewer biases and more subject to response biases.

Yes–no questions are not necessarily leading, but they often are. Interviewers tend to ask questions that they expect to be answered in the affirmative. If the questions are highly specific, they become more objectionable (compare "did you see the defendant do something" with "did you see the defendant murder the victim") Yes–no questions can be made clearly leading by changing their structure. One can add a "tag" and turn "did he hurt you" into "he hurt you, didn't he?" Alternatively, one can place the tag at the beginning of the question: "didn't he hurt you?" (technically, this is a "negative term" question). Attorneys understand these distinctions; they will not object to all yes–no questions, but they will certainly recognize tag questions and negative term questions as leading.

Forced-choice questions are leading to the extent that they assume that one of the options provided is correct. Interviewers often overlook the possibility that there is a third option. For example, interviewers often ask children disclosing sexual abuse whether their clothes (or the perpetrator's clothes) were "on or off." The problem is that abuse often occurs with the clothes disheveled but not removed.

Wh– questions (who, what, where, when, why, and how) are generally considered less leading than yes–no questions (compare "what color was his hat" with "was his hat red?"). But wh– questions can be highly leading in a subtle way. They may be suppositional, in that they presuppose information that the child has not provided. "What color was his hat" would be very leading if the child had not mentioned that the person wore a hat!

There are several kinds of response biases often found in children. Forced-choice questions sometimes elicit a last response bias, in which the child chooses the last choice offered. This reflects the fact that whatever is mentioned last is easiest to recall. Some researchers have found that children exhibit a "yes" bias to yes–no questions, although the results are inconsistent. It seems fair to conclude that the risks of yes-bias increase among younger children and children who are cognitively less mature. The inconsistencies may be due to the fact that younger children initially use "yes" and "no" to reflect their desires rather than their beliefs. Hence, there is some evidence that young children will exhibit a "no" bias if asked about unpleasant topics.

If a young child responds to yes–no questions in line with his or her desires rather than reality, this wreaks havoc for the interviewer who relies on yes–no questions. If the questions are obviously unpleasant (e.g., if they involve physical abuse, or sexual touching that the child recognizes as inappropriate), then such a child would simply deny abuse. If the questions are about apparently innocuous events (e.g., if they are about sexual touching under the guise of play) or ambiguous, then the child might appear to acknowledge abuse. In either case the truth is unclear.

If one restricts one's questions to open-ended questions, one both minimizes suggestiveness and reduces the likelihood that a child's response bias will lead one astray.

(5) Closed-ended questions encourage guessing and are less likely to be answered with "I don't know."

For a number of reasons children may be disinclined to tell you when they don't know the answer to a question. One reason is that they regard an interviewer's questions as analogous to questions they receive from other adults, such as parents and teachers, which are often less requests for information that the child is privy to and more tests of the child's knowledge. If one is taking a test, a reasonable strategy is to hazard a guess rather than leave the answer blank. This is a disastrous strategy if others are relying on one's answers as a key to the truth. Another reason is that younger children are less aware of what they know and do not know; in other words, they are less cognizant of the differences between knowing and guessing. This limitation is similar to children's problems with comprehension monitoring mentioned above; just as very young children have limited awareness of whether they understand, they have limited understanding of when they are knowledgeable.

If a child does not know the answer but does not want to appear ignorant, he or she must hazard a guess. Guesses are much easier when one is asked closed-ended questions because one only has to produce a single word (or concept) in response. Yes–no and forced-choice questions are particularly subject to guessing because it is so easy to simply choose "yes" or "no" or one of the choices offered by the forced-choice. Some types of closed-ended wh– questions are also quite susceptible to guessing because children may answer with respect to their expectations or their general knowledge of the world. For example, in one classic study of children's suggestibility, children were asked "What color was the man's beard?" Despite the fact that the man did not wear a beard, most children responded "black," something obviously borrowed from their knowledge of beards in general.

§ 5.3 Begin the Interview with Interview Instructions

In only two minutes, it is possible to provide children a bit of instruction on how investigative interviews work. Instructions are helpful because interviews are unlike other kinds of adult-child interactions. Children are accustomed to interactions with adults in which the adult knows the answer and the child is either being taught the answer, or should have learned the answer and is now being tested. If the adult knows the answer, and the child is expected to know the answer, then the child will be inclined to accept the adults' suggestions and to guess at answers rather than acknowledge incomprehension or ignorance. These are obviously dangerous inclinations in an investigative interview in which the interviewer is sincerely interested in only what the child knows and remembers.

There are a few general rules for instructions. Instructions should be worded as simply and as succinctly as possible. They should be provided one at a time. They should be given with feedback, to ensure that the child understands the instruction and so that the child recognizes that the interviewer truly wants the child to follow the instruction. These general rules lead to the recommendation that interviewers follow a carefully scripted list of instructions that they become accustomed to giving in every interview. It is dangerous for an interviewer to think "I'm good with kids, and so I can wing this." When interviewers ad lib, they tend to leave out instructions, or combine them, or use unnecessarily complicated words, or forget to provide feedback.

The Ten Step Investigative Interview, modeled after the NICHD structured interview, includes four instructions and elicitation of a promise to tell the truth.[7] After a brief self-introduction (e.g., "My name is Tom and I talk to kids about things that have happened to them"), the interviewer then directly moves to the first instruction.

§ 5.3.1 Give the "I Don't Know" Instruction

The interviewer tells the child "If I ask you a question and you don't know the answer, then just say 'I don't know.'" The interviewer then provides an example, "So if I ask you, 'what is my dog's name?' what do you say?" When the child answers "I don't know," the interviewer responds, "O.K.! Because you don't know." The interviewer then provides a counter-example. "But what if I ask you, 'Do you have a dog?'" After the child answers, the interviewer concludes, "O.K.! Because you do know."

As discussed above in § 5.2.2, children are often reluctant to answer "I don't know," particularly when asked closed-ended questions. Asking as many open-ended questions as possible is clearly the best strategy to avoid this problem, but the "I don't know" instruction is also valuable. A number of studies have found that instructing children that "I don't know" answers are acceptable reduces children's suggestibility to misleading questions.[8]

It is important to emphasize that this instruction is different than simply telling the child that it is o.k. to indicate when they don't know the answer. A simple "tell me when you don't know" is likely to be ineffective because the example ("what is my

---

[7] *See* Thomas D. Lyon, *Ten Step Investigative Interview* (2005), *available at* http://works.bepress.com/thomaslyon/5/. For the NICHD protocol, *see* MICHAEL E. LAMB, IRIT HERSHKOWITZ, YAEL ORBACH & PHILLIP W. ESPLIN, TELL ME WHAT HAPPENED: STRUCTURED INVESTIGATIVE INTERVIEWS OF CHILD VICTIMS AND WITNESSES (2008).

[8] *See, e.g.,* Susan Gee, Marian Gregory & Margaret Ellen Pipe, *"What Colour is Your Pet Dinosaur?": The Impact of Pre-interview Training and Question Type on Children's Answers*, 4/1 LEGAL & CRIM. PSYCHOL. 111 (1999); Karen Saywitz & Susan Moan-Hardie, *Reducing the Potential for Distortion of Childhood Memories*, 3 CONSCIOUSNESS & COGNITION 408 (1994).

dog's name") both tests the child's comprehension of the instruction and enables the interviewer to reinforce the don't know response. In cases in which the child guesses the name of the interviewer's dog, the interviewer can respond, "No, you don't know my dog's name. Remember that if you don't know you can tell me. Let's try another, 'what is my sister's name?'" Moreover, it is important to provide a counterexample— to reinforce giving an answer when the child does know. Researchers have found that children reinforced only for don't know responses overuse the don't know response; in other words, they respond "I don't know" even when they do know.

The instruction is also different than waiting for the child to spontaneously respond "I don't know" during the course of the interview and providing reinforcement at that point. Some children will never spontaneously indicate ignorance, and they will obviously fail to benefit from an instruction. Worse, children will provide don't knows in cases in which the interviewer has no idea whether the child does or does not really know. Children's don't knows during the interview may evince reluctance rather than ignorance. Reinforcing the child for reluctant-based don't knows may reinforce evasive responding.

§ 5.3.2 Give the "I Don't Understand" Instruction

The interviewer tells the child, "If I ask you a question and you don't know what I mean or what I am saying, you can say 'I don't know what you mean.' I will ask it in a different way." The interviewer provides an example, "So if I ask you, 'what is your gender?' what do you say?" When the child answers "I don't know" or something like "what's gender?" the interviewer responds, "Good, because 'gender' is a big word. So then I would ask, "are you a boy or a girl?"

As discussed above in § 5.2.2, children often fail to indicate when they do not understand questions, particularly when they are asked closed-ended questions. The wording of the question is designed to avoid the word "understand," because of the ironic fact that young children may not know what it means. As with the don't know instruction, this instruction is more effective if provided with feedback, and it is important to reword the question so that the child understands that the purpose of their response is for the question to be rephrased (rather than avoided). In case the child knows the word "gender," the interviewer should have in mind a different example; one possibility is to ask the child "what is my orientation," and when they express incomprehension, follow-up with "Am I standing up or sitting down?"

§ 5.3.3 Give the "You're Wrong" Instruction

The interviewer tells the child, "Sometimes I make mistakes or say the wrong thing. When I do, you can tell me that I am wrong." The interviewer provides an example, "So if I say, 'you are thirty years old,' what do you say?" When the child answers "you're wrong" or something like "I'm not thirty years old" the interviewer responds "Okay. So how old are you?"

This instruction has some value in encouraging the child to resist suggestions from the interviewer. An example is particularly important to convince the child that it is indeed appropriate to contradict an authoritative adult.

§ 5.3.4 Give the Ignorant Interviewer Instruction

The interviewer tells the child, "I don't know what's happened to you. I won't be able to tell you the answers to my questions." This simple instruction has been found to reduce children's suggestibility. One of the reasons children are suggestible is that they assume adults are knowledgeable. Children may make this assumption for several reasons. First, as noted above § 5.2.2, children are accustomed to interactions where adults ask questions as a means of testing children, and already know the answers to their questions. Second, children involved in legal disputes may naturally assume that the questioner has spoken to the others and is aware of any prior statements that the child has made.

§ 5.3.5 Elicit a Promise to Tell the Truth

The interviewer tells the child, "It's really important that you tell me the truth," and then asks "Do you promise that you will tell me the truth?" After the child responds, the interviewer asks, "Are you going to tell me any lies?" Research with children, including children who have been maltreated, has demonstrated that a promise to tell the truth increases children's honesty, even if they have been coached to cover up a transgression or to make a false report.[9]

The wording of the promise is important. Young children are likely to know the meaning of the word "will" even if they do not know the meaning of the word "promise"; hence, asking the child "do you promise that you will" should have some meaning for even quite young children. Asking for both a "yes" response (to "do you promise") and a "no" response ("are you going to tell me any lies") reduces the likelihood that a child mindlessly replies "yes" to the questions. Furthermore, asking "do you promise that you won't tell any lies" is not recommended; many children will respond "no," probably intending to assert that "no, I won't tell any lies."

§ 5.3.6 Limitations of Instructions

Interview instructions improve interviews, but they do not solve all problems, and their effect can easily be overridden by a suggestive interview. Because some of the instructions require the child to monitor his or her mental state (e.g., knowledge, understanding), they are likely less effective with younger children. When interview instructions are ad-libbed, they are often confusing and likely to be forgotten by the child.

---

[9] *See, e.g.*, Thomas D. Lyon, Lindsay C. Malloy, Jodi A. Quas & Victoria Talwar, *Coaching, Truth Induction, and Young Maltreated Children's False Allegations and False Denials*, 79/4 CHILD DEV. 914 (2008).

Consider the following instruction, which was given by a judge to a 10-year-old witness in a child sexual abuse criminal trial:

> THE COURT: If you don't know the answer to a question, I don't want you to guess. I just want you to tell us if you don't understand, or if you don't know the answer. Okay?
>
> THE WITNESS: Okay.[10]

Although the judge is well-meaning, the instruction is very likely to be ineffective. The judge combines the don't know and don't understand instructions and provides no examples or feedback to the child. With a little patience and a willingness to "follow the script," questioners can increase the likelihood that their interview instructions will make a difference.

§ 5.4 Use Open-Ended Rapport Building, Including Narrative Practice, Before Moving to the Interview Topic

Interview instructions allow the interviewer to begin building rapport with the child, but the interviewer does almost all the talking. To increase the child's comfort level and to encourage the child to speak, it is helpful to discuss innocuous events in the child's life before introducing the topic of interest. It is during this phase of the interview that the interviewer begins to use open-ended questions, and in particular "tell me more" and "what happened next" questions.

The interviewer starts by asking the child, "tell me about things you like to do." At this point the interviewer should take care to give the child time to respond, and should restrain any impulse to step in and provide assistance should the child falter. For example, if the child falls silent, and the interviewer then suggests "do you like school?" the child is likely to simply respond "yes," and the interviewer has gotten off on the wrong foot. If the interviewer is patient, the child is quite likely to provide something, even if only a word or phrase. With just a few words (e.g., "I like soccer,"), the interviewer has an opening, and can follow-up with "you like soccer! Tell me about playing soccer." If the child provides a list, the interviewer can ask for a little elaboration of each item of the list in turn. The purpose is to communicate to the child that in this interview, the more the child says (and the less the interviewer talks) the better. In the Ten Step interview,[11] the interviewer also asks "tell me about things you don't like to do," and follows up in the same manner.

---

[10] People v. Hilaire, YA035220 (Los Angeles County Superior Court, 1998).

[11] *See* Thomas D. Lyon, Lindsay C. Malloy, Jodi A. Quas & Victoria Talwar, *Coaching, Truth Induction, and Young Maltreated Children's False Allegations and False Denials*, 79/4 CHILD DEV. 914 (2008).

The interviewer then asks the child to provide a narrative of a recent event, an approach called narrative practice. For example, the interviewer asks the child, "Tell me everything that happened on your last birthday," following up with "tell me more" questions ("You said you hit a piñata. Tell me more about hitting the piñata") and "what happened next" questions ("You said you ate cake. What happened next?"). It is not essential that narrative practice ask about the child's last birthday, although we have found that this is routinely quite productive. The interviewer could ask about other recent events, even what the child had done on the day of the interview ("Tell me everything that you did from when you woke up until when you came here").

Research has demonstrated that when children questioned about sexual abuse were asked open-ended narrative practice questions during the rapport-building phase (in contrast to closed-ended questions), they provided longer and more detailed responses to the first question about abuse.[12] Laboratory research has shown that the additional information is not less likely to be accurate. The narrative practice need not take long; five minutes appears to be optimal (and 15 minutes may be too long because of fatigue).

§ 5.5 Introduce the Interview Topic with Open-Ended Questions

To transition into the interview topic, the interviewer says to the child, "Now that I know you better, I want to talk about why you came to see me today. Tell me why you came to see me." Remarkably, children disclosing sexual abuse (and questioned with open-ended rapport building and narrative practice) are likely to initiate their report of abuse at this point about half the time. If a child does mention the interview topic, the interviewer's first follow-up is as general as possible. For example, if the child says something like "my uncle touched me," the interviewer follows up with as open-ended a question as possible, such as "Your uncle touched you. Tell me everything that happened, from the beginning to the end."

Interviewers have to be very careful at this point not to step in with closed-ended questions designed to disambiguate the child's initial statement. For example, one might worry about which uncle, or whether the touching was truly inappropriate. Many interviewers would ask "where did he touch you" and, anticipating embarrassment, produce a drawing and ask the child to point. Some interviewers would ask for the uncle's name, and ask where the uncle lived, before attempting to elicit any details. The problem with these strategies is that they entail asking closed-ended questions, and will undermine the purpose of the rapport building and the narrative practice, which is to enable (and encourage) children to provide a narrative of their experience. Moreover, closed-ended clarification questions at this point are

---

[12] *See* Kathleen Sternberg, Michael E. Lamb, Irit Hershkowitz, Liora Yudilevitch &Yael Orbach, *Effects of Introductory Style on Children's Abilities to Describe Experiences of Sexual Abuse*, 21/11 Child Abuse & Neglect 1133 (1997).

unnecessary because the child's narrative will often provide the necessary details and because clarification questions can always be asked, if necessary, after the narrative report.

It is also important to give the child plenty of time to respond to one's questions, particularly at the beginning of the interview. Teachers are taught to use "wait-time," in which they allow children plenty of time to think about a question before they assume the child does not know the answer. Wait-time is also effective in enabling children to build up the courage to discuss unpleasant subjects.

Although the "tell me why" question is effective for about half of children who do disclose, it is necessary to ask further questions to elicit disclosures from the other half. Furthermore, it is important to acknowledge that the research proving the efficacy of the "tell me why" question in interviews with abused children assumes that children know why they are being interviewed, which in turn depends on the child having discussed abuse at some prior time. In sexual abuse cases, this is not a problematic assumption because abuse tends to be suspected and substantiated on the basis of a disclosure by the child.

Indeed, other interview topic questions, which are asked only if the "tell me why" question is unproductive, take advantage of any prior disclosures by the child. The interviewer refers to a person to whom the child disclosed (preferably an impartial recipient, if there was one): "I heard you talked to a police lady. Tell me what you talked about." This question can be used with multiple recipients; the point is to cue the child to the topic without overtly suggesting that something untoward occurred. The interviewer only gradually moves toward more direct suggestions; for example, in sexual abuse interviews, the interviewer may ask if adults are "worried about" the child and if "somebody did something that was wrong." These questions are necessarily less desirable; they are not only more direct, but by being yes–no, they are less productive (they risk a curt "yes" and a recanting "no").

An obvious problem is that an interviewer cannot rely on a child's prior words if the child has never disclosed any information. It is extremely common, however, for children to have said *something* about the allegation in question. In sexual abuse, for example, abuse is most often discovered because the child makes some sort of disclosure. A good investigative interviewer will find out as much as possible about the child's prior statements. Those statements can be referred to obliquely in the allegation phase of the interview, if necessary to cue the child to what the interview is about, and at the end of the child's initial narrative, the interview can also refer to details to probe for additional details and to assess possible inconsistencies.

§ 5.6 Use Optimal Interviewing Strategies in Court

Although interviewing protocols were largely designed for investigative interviewing, there is no reason why attorneys could not use the protocols to elicit testimony from children in court. Research has documented what experienced attorneys already know: children are less productive when questioned in a courtroom than in a less formal setting. Testifying in an open courtroom, particularly in criminal cases in which the witness faces the jury and the accused, is extremely stressful, even for adult witnesses.

Indeed, attorneys frequently attempt to build rapport with child witnesses before introducing the topic of their testimony. Although the opponent might argue that such questions are irrelevant, these questions can be justified in several ways. First, the court has a responsibility to ensure that witnesses are not unduly intimidated by questioning. Under Federal Rule of Evidence 611(a), a version of which has been adopted by most of the states, the court is required to control the mode of questioning so as to "protect witnesses from harassment or undue embarrassment." The propriety of preliminary questioning with child witnesses alleging abuse seems self-evident, making it difficult to find opinions even addressing the practice. In the single case I have been able to locate, the appellate court approved a "series of questions concerning whether [child witness] had pets, what kind of dog she had, what she liked to do in her spare time, who she played softball for, what kind of music she liked, what kind of subjects she liked in school, and what kind of food she preferred" that "were asked to help [the child] feel comfortable on the stand, before delving into the sexual conduct at issue in the case."[13] Second, preliminary questions about a child witness' background are relevant in that they help the fact-finder assess the credibility of the witness.[14] Third, in states that require a preliminary finding of testimonial competency (not to be confused with oath-taking competency, which entails understanding of truth and lies), questions about recent events in the child's life are relevant in determining whether the child can answer questions and relate past experiences.

The problem with attorney-conducted rapport building is that attorneys tend to ask a series of closed-ended factual questions (such as "how old are you," "what school to you go to," "what is your teacher's name") that are demonstrably poor in increasing children's subsequent productivity. Indeed, the reader may have noticed that the questions asked in the appellate case approving introductory questions, although about the child's likes, were quite specific and likely to have been asked as yes–no ("do you have pets?") or closed-ended wh– questions ("what is your pet's name"). Hence the challenge is not to obtain the right to ask rapport-building questions, but to ask the questions in the right way.

Attorneys can also elicit children's substantive testimony through open-ended questions. One often hears the objection, "calls for a narrative," but there is nothing inherently objectionable about narrative questions.[15] Indeed, legal commentators have recognized the virtues of narrative testimony: "Truth can be promoted because a

---

[13] State v. Hanna, 2003 WL 22843592, at 2 (Ohio App. 5 Dist. Nov. 25, 2003).

[14] *See* State v. Brewer, 26 Ariz. App. 408, 549 P.2d 188, 195 (1976) ("It is commonly accepted that a person may be examined about his background, occupation and the like for the purpose of aiding the jury to evaluate his testimony and credibility").

[15] State v. Abril, 76 P.3d 644, 648 n. 1 (N.M. Ct. App. 2003) ("There is no per se rule against narrative testimony").

witness who testifies in the form of a narrative has not been prompted by specific questions suggesting which facts are important. Time can be saved since the cumbersome back and forth of numerous questions and answers is economically replaced with a single question and answer."[16] The potential disadvantages of the narrative question are that the witness may make statements that are irrelevant or prejudicial.[17] However, these risks are slight in a proceeding in which a child is questioned about abuse. Virtually everything the child reports will be admissible because the child's responses will enable the court to assess the child's competence and credibility. The child's reports of the perpetrator's statements will generally be admissible as party admissions or as non-hearsay statements that explain the child's actions. Second, any statements that are irrelevant can be struck. In bench trials (which of course are most common in child welfare cases) one worries little about prejudice because the court knows what is inadmissible.

§ 5.7 Case Studies

§ 5.7.1 Narrative Practice and Young Children's Responses to Open-Ended Questions: The Case of Four-Year-Old J.

Interviewers who have extensive experience with children, particularly child abuse victims, are often extremely skeptical when advised to move away from closed-ended questions. They are likely to have had experience with children who refused to talk, or appeared incapable of responding to questions, particularly when the children were very young and the allegations extremely serious.

Consider four-year-old J., who was a potential eyewitness in a double homicide case. The victims were J.'s great grandmother (J. knew her as "Gramma Great") and the grandmother's caretaker. Gramma Great and her caretaker were found stabbed to death in Gramma Great's one-bedroom apartment. Gramma Great's body was found next to an exercise bike in the living room, and the caretaker's body was found in the bathtub. The chief suspect was K., J.'s mother, who had been staying with Gramma Great, but who had moved out of the apartment at about the time the murder occurred. If questioned, K. was likely to acknowledge that she had an argument with Gramma Great, which led her to leave with J. (and her other children, a 6-year-old, P., and a two-year-old, A.), but that the murders occurred after K. had left. She might have pinned the blame on her mother, Gramma Great's daughter, who also stayed in the apartment. Hence, J.s' testimony might prove crucial. J. was questioned by two homicide detectives the day after the bodies were discovered.

> Q: Let me ask you something J., you're a very smart girl and because the
> other police officers were telling me you're very smart, we wanted to

---

[16] Wright & Gold, 28 FED. PRAC. & PROC. EVID. § 6164 (1997).

[17] *Id.*

know what happened yesterday at the house, at the apartment on C. avenue there. Can you tell me in your own words what happened yesterday?

A: Hm?

Q: Can you tell me what happened?

A: [Nods]

Q: What happened?

A: Hm?

Q: What happened yesterday? At the apartment. Did somebody get hurt?

A: Hm?

Q: Did somebody get hurt yesterday?

A: [Nods]

Q: Who got hurt? Who got hurt?

A: K. [J.'s mother].

Q: K. got hurt. How did she get hurt?

A: 'Cause she was fight Gramma Great.

Q: She got in a fight with Gramma Great?

A: [Nods]

Q: What happened?

A: Hm?

Q: What happened?

A: Hm?

Q: What did you see?

A: K.

Q: What did, what, what happened though? What happened between K. and [trails off] How did she get hurt? [3 second pause] Do you remember how she got hurt?

A: [Nods]

Q: Can you tell me?

A: Hm?

Q: Could, could, can you tell me what happened?

A: Yes.

Q: Okay, what happened? [child fiddles with ring in her hand] Can I see that for a sec? [detective takes object from the child] Okay, I'll give you that in just a second. Wondering what happened?

A: Hm?

Q: What happened yesterday?

A: Huh?

Q: [Second detective] Can you, can you show us what happened?

A: Hm?

Q: Well, did you hear what happened?

A: [Nods]

Q: What did you hear?

A: Hm?

Q: Did you hear some noises?

A: [Nods]

Q: Oh, what kind of noises?

One might conclude that J. was obviously traumatized from witnessing the stabbing death of her great grandmother and another adult. She appeared stymied by the general nature of the questions; perhaps "what happened" was too open-ended for a child who is extremely young, frightened, and inarticulate. Many interviewers would conclude that direct (and perhaps some leading) questions are required. However, J. responded to the yes–no questions with nods or non-committal "hm"s. The "hm" is particularly worrisome because J. may have been using the "hm" to reflect acknowledgement, but she may also have been expressing incomprehension. A series of yes–no questions outlining the detectives' theory of the case would be very hazardous.

The reader should also take note that open-ended questions phrased as yes–no questions also elicit a single word response: for example J. responded "yes" to "can you tell me what happened." Finally, the reader should consider how many of the detectives' words may have been incomprehensible to a young four-year-old child. Is it likely that J. understood that she was staying in an "apartment" and that it was on "C. avenue"?

The interview continued for several minutes in the same vein. The detectives were quite conscientious in avoiding any overtly leading questions (e.g., they never asked "did you see K. kill Gramma Great?"), but had little success in eliciting details using open-ended questions (such as "what happened"). Many interviews would not have been so patient.

The reader should notice that the detectives did little to build rapport with J. or to get J. talking before moving to the interview topic. How would J. have responded to open-ended questions after rapport building and narrative practice? Less than a week later, I questioned J. using the Ten Step interview (which, as noted above, is a modification of the NICHD structured interview protocol). After interview instructions, I asked J. about her last birthday as part of narrative practice:

Q: Tell me everything that happened on your last birthday.

A: You remember I had ice cream and chocolate and cake.

Q. You had what?

A: Ice cream and chocolate and cake.

Q: Oh. Ice cream and chocolate and cake. Tell me more about. . .

A: K. made it for me.

Q: K. made it for you.

A: Yes. K. put chocolate on the cake, 'cause it wasn't sweet when it was no chocolate on it.

Q: Oh, it wasn't sweet when there was no chocolate on it. Tell me what you did before—

A: A.'s two now!

Q: What?

A: A.'s two now.

Q: A.'s two now, Oh who's A.?

A: He's two.

Q: Um hmm. But who is he?

A: He's just A.

Q: Oh he's just A. But you were telling me about your birthday. Tell me what you did before you ate the ice cream. What'd you do before the ice cream?

A: First I just mixed it up and ate it.

Q: First you just mixed it up and ate it.

A: Yes.

Q: Oh okay. Now what else did you do for your birthday?

A: I just. . .I just shared A. and P. some.

Q: You shared?

A: Yes, they had their own bowls, and. . .

Q: They had their own bowls and you. . .Now what did you do after you had ice cream and cake? What'd you do after for your birthday?

A: I did turn into. . .[holds up four fingers].

Q: Oh you turned into four, okay. Okay, alright. Did you get anything for your birthday?

A: I just got cake from the store.

Q: I see. Okay, okay.

After narrative practice was complete, I introduced the interview topic:

Q: Now that I know you a little better, J., tell me why you came to talk to me. Tell me why you came to talk to me.

A: Hm?

Q: Tell me why you came to talk to me.

[9 second pause]

Q: Tell me why.

[6 second pause]

Q: Well, I heard, I heard something about, I heard something about K. Tell me what happened.

A: Hm?

Q: Tell me what happened.

A: I heard K. fighting Gramma Great.

Q: Oh.

A: Yes. K. was killing her. By the bike, Yes. My grandmother's bike. That's what K. was doing.

Q: Ok. So you said you heard K. was killing her? Tell me everything you heard.

A: K. was killing her by Gramma Great's bike. . .

Q: Mmkay, So you said you heard K. killing her. What was she doing? What was K. doing?

> A: She was killing her by the bike.

> Q: I see. And how did she kill her?

> A: With a sharp knife.

During narrative practice, J. clearly showed that she could comprehend the questions and that she was capable of providing multi-word responses (sometimes even in response to yes–no questions). She was also obviously engaged, and she spontaneously mentioned both her brothers (A. and P.), which facilitated asking about their whereabouts during the murders later in the interview. Knowing that she was comprehending my questions and capable of providing a great deal of information made it easier for me to provide some wait-time at the beginning of the interview topic.

I can be criticized for first mentioning K. because K. was a suspect. A better question might be "I heard something about Gramma Great." Indeed, it is simple to construct topic questions for homicide interviews because merely mentioning the victim is frequently sufficient to elicit a report. On the other hand, I mentioned K. without suggesting that K. had done something wrong. Indeed, J. had told the detectives that it was K. who had been hurt (which probably reflected the cuts on K.'s hands that K. received from the murder weapon).

J. remained difficult to interview, providing relatively cursory responses. She was, after all, a 4-year-old child. However, she was clearly responsive to open-ended questioning. Once the child disclosed the murder, it was no longer necessary to introduce outside information. The key was to build the child's own words into the follow-up questions, which were open-ended, preferably "tell me more" questions and open-ended wh– questions (such as "how did she kill her?").

§ 5.7.2 Older Children's Narratives: The Case of Eleven-Year-Old A.

Whereas younger children are often somewhat reticent even under the best of conditions, older children are impressively productive in response to open-ended questions. Consider 11-year-old A., who watched her father kill her mother while her mother was in the driver's seat and A. was in the passenger seat of their car. I interviewed A. because the D.A. was concerned that A. was too traumatized and would not be able to testify at the father's murder trial. She was also concerned that the father might claim self-defense, claiming that he thought the mother was reaching for a gun in the car when he shot her. She was specifically interested in proving that the mother was in fact reaching for a cell phone and attempting to dial 911.

After interview instructions and rapport building (during which A. described a recent basketball game in which she played), I moved to the interview topic.

> Q: Now that I know you a little bit better, I wanna talk to you about why you came to talk to me today. Tell me why you came to talk to me today.

A: 'Cause my dad shot my mom.

Q: Uh-huh. Okay, now I need you to tell me everything that happened, from the beginning to the end.

[16 second pause]

A: Do I have to?

Q: It's really important that we know everything that happened. Okay? So I need you to tell me everything that happened.

[10 second pause]

A: I was coming back from my Uncle Sammy's, 'cause I went to spend the night over there. And then I went with my mom, and when I came back, my mom was there with my brother, and my brother was sick. And then we went to the store to go buy him Gatorade. And then we seen my mom's car up the hill where my dad go'ed. And my mom went to the corner, she stopped, she went around the block, stopped at the corner, and got the license plate number, 'cause the police officer said to get it. And when she got the police officer, she called my grandma and told her. And then we went to the store to go buy Gatorade, and then when we parked, we were gonna get out the car, but then we seen him, and he blocked us in, and we couldn't get out. And then he comed and shouted to my mom to get out the car, get out the car. And he told me to get out the car, and I said, "No." And then after, he got a little rock, he threw it at the window and cracked the window. He got the bottom part in the front and hit it. He hit the window and then broke the window. And my mom got out of the car. When she was getting out of the car [trails off] When, no, when. When after he broke the window, he went to the car, to his car to go get bullets for the gun, 'cause it didn't have any. And then, he came back, and my mom was getting out of the car, and he started shooting my mom, and that's when I got out of the car and went into the store and told them to call the police. And then after, I came back outside and started screaming at him, and he told me to shut up and get in the car. And then after, I told him, "Why did you do it?" And he said 'cause my mom was a whore and a slut. And then he took me to my grandma's house. And he told my grandma that he had shot my mom. And then my grandma said, "You freakin' liar, you freakin' son of a [trails off] bitch." And then [trails off] And then he shot her, and my grandma was holding my baby cousin, and then after, he shot her two times, I got out the car, and I hid behind my mom's van. And then after, my grandpa was coming outside with my uncles, and he was shouting at my grandpa, and he hit the door, and it skinned him in the arm, and then that's when he left and I ran up the stairs, and everybody went to go see what happened.

Wait-time appeared effective for A. She seemed to gather her courage during this time. When she asked, "do I have to?" I refrained from a long-winded explanation (for obvious reasons, it was inadvisable to say something like "you can help us keep your dad in jail"), but simply emphasized the importance of knowing everything.

Although I did not ask any questions during A's narrative, I was not silent. In addition to taking careful notes, after every sentence or so I would let her know that I was listening by uttering an "uh-huh" or an "o.k." These utterances are called facilitators, and they are known to increase children's productivity.

The reader may have noticed that A. did not mention her mother's cell phone or a 911 call. I recall being tempted to interject this question during A.'s initial narrative, knowing this was a detail the D.A. was particularly interested in, but I refrained from doing so as not to interrupt the narrative. Significantly, A. then provided an unexpected detail that would rebut any self-defense claim; her father's own explanation for the shooting. With respect to the cell phone, it was easy to come back to this point in the follow-up questions, when I asked "I heard something about a phone. Tell me about that," and A. confirmed the fact that her mother was attempting to make a call when the defendant shot her. This detail was also easy to corroborate because the police found the cell phone in the car, and 911 was the last number dialed.

Chapter 6: Interviewing and Counseling Legal Clients Who Are Children[*]

by Ann M. Haralambie[1] and Lauren Adams[2]

§ 6.1 Introduction

To effectively represent a child, it is important to understand the child's developmental stage and competencies, as discussed in Chapter 4, Child Development and the Impact of Maltreatment. That understanding comes not only from reading records and consulting relevant parties and experts in the case, but also through spending time with the child. It is difficult to represent a child, either as a client-directed attorney, a best interests attorney, or a guardian ad litem, without developing a relationship with the child. It is only through talking and visiting with a child over a period of time that the child's special needs and interests may begin to emerge. Often this requires meeting with the child client under a variety of circumstances, both inside and outside of the child's home environment. Older children may be able to articulate their own needs quite accurately. Younger children may demonstrate their needs more through their behavior or emotions. Therapists and teachers are particularly helpful resources in assisting the attorney in interpreting the child's behaviors and statements.

§ 6.2 Building Trust and Establishing Rapport

Building a relationship and communicating effectively with a child client gives the child a voice in the proceedings and enables the attorney to get the information required to represent the child effectively. To this end, a critical component of any attorney-client relationship is trust, especially when the client is a child. The child client may be exposed to myriad state actors and court officials during the course of the case, many before the child meets his or her lawyer. In addition, the child client may have had prior involvement with the courts or administrative bodies (e.g.,

---

[*] Portions of this chapter are based on and adapted from a previous work by Ann M. Haralambie. The excerpts were previously published in THE CHILD'S ATTORNEY: A GUIDE TO REPRESENTING CHILDREN IN CUSTODY, ADOPTION, AND PROTECTION CASES (American Bar Association 1993), used with permission. *This information or any portion thereof may not be copied or disseminated in any form or by any means or downloaded or stored in an electronic database or retrieval system without the express written consent of the American Bar Association.*

[1] Ann M. Haralambie, J.D., is a certified family law specialist practicing in Tucson, Arizona. She is also an author and speaker in the fields of family and children's law.

[2] Lauren Girard Adams. J.D., is co-chair of the Children's Rights Litigation Committee of the American Bar Association Section of Litigation. She specializes in juvenile law and currently resides in Norwich, Vermont.

juvenile delinquency or immigration). These prior encounters may have been unpleasant or even traumatic for the child, leaving the child with a distrust of adults in the system. Knowing this, and approaching the representation of a child client with consideration of his or her past and/or concurrent involvement in other matters, will help the attorney establish the trust necessary for a positive attorney-client relationship.

§ 6.2.1 Explaining the Role of the Attorney

The role of an attorney for a child will differ depending on the jurisdiction and/or the role the judge has asked the attorney to fill in a particular case. In all cases, before beginning to gather information from a child client, the attorney must explain who he or she is, including the attorney's specific role in the case. The attorney should regularly remind her child client of her role. Young children in particular are not likely to remember what the attorney's role is and may have been told erroneous information about the attorney's role by other people. Thus, it is imperative that the attorney take the time at the outset to differentiate himself or herself from other adults in the system, and to make sure that the child understands how the child's attorney's role differs from that of the judge, caseworkers, state's attorney, or other official.

One of the most important concepts for an attorney to explain is the attorney-client privilege (where applicable) and the role that confidentiality plays in the particular case.[3] To develop trust, the child client must understand whether, and to what extent, the information he or she tells the attorney will remain confidential. The child needs to know whether his or her statements to the attorney can or will be repeated to the child's parents, the judge, the social worker, the therapist, or anybody else. The attorney should explain this to the child in developmentally appropriate language, keeping in mind that children who are abused may be threatened with dire consequences if they reveal family secrets. Therefore, confidentiality should be explained in a way that the child understands, and in a way that distinguishes it from the kind of "secret" cover-up of abuse that the parent or other family member has required. In some jurisdictions, the attorney may be able to use information gathered from the child (i.e., take action based on the information) without revealing that the child was the original source of the information. In such cases, the attorney should explain that the information will be used, but that he or she will not tell anyone that the information came from the child.

Finally, the attorney should confirm that the child understands the attorney's role, the attorney-client privilege, and the role of confidentiality. To that end, the attorney should have the child explain, in the child's own words, what these concepts mean to the child. Engaging the child client in this way lets the child know that the attorney values what the child thinks, which will be invaluable in building trust and establishing rapport.

---

[3] For more information on confidentiality, see Chapter 18.

§ 6.2.2 Planning for the Initial Client Contact

Preparation is the key to success. The attorney should obtain as much background information as possible prior to speaking with a child client for the first time. Sources of background information include caseworkers, social workers, teachers, coaches, family members, and friends. In addition, professionals already involved in the case may be able to provide the attorney with copies of some school records, case reports, medical records, police reports, and other historical documents that provide additional background information.[4] By gathering background information from other sources first, the attorney will be in a better position to evaluate what the child is saying to the lawyer or showing through behavior. Because young children have short attention spans, they are generally not good sources for a detailed history. Gathering information in advance of the initial meeting will allow the attorney more time to focus on building trust and establishing rapport during the initial interview, as well as getting the child's unique perspective on the case.

Another way to start establishing trust early and to facilitate a more productive initial interview is a brief pre-interview phone call. This gives the child client an opportunity to learn the attorney's name, hear the attorney's voice, get used to the idea of meeting with an attorney in person, and to begin to understand that the attorney is the child's advocate and is someone the child can trust.

During this brief pre-interview phone conversation, the attorney should give the child client a chance to ask questions. The attorney also should explain that the child will have additional opportunities to ask questions both in person as well as over the phone. At this point, the attorney should find out what means of communication works best for the child. If the child is not available to speak by phone, the attorney could send a short introductory note instead. Either way, the time the attorney spends gathering information and reaching out to a child in advance of the initial meeting will go a long way toward establishing a trusting a productive attorney-client relationship.

§ 6.3 Meeting with a Child Client

Meeting with a child client on a regular basis is essential to building a relationship, and may tell the attorney a great deal about the child and his or her environment and relationships with siblings, friends, and caretakers. It is important to strike a balance between having a safe, familiar adult nearby for the child's security and having the interview stifled by the presence of one of the parties or another person with a stake in the outcome. Children, unlike adults, are not used to talking to people they do not know well. The attorney must establish at least some level of relationship with the child before the child is likely to say anything at all that will be useful. Major

---

[4]   Unless your jurisdiction provides legal authority for the child's attorney to gain any and all information regarding the child, you may need a court order or a release to obtain certain records. The release may require the signature of the child and/or the parent. In such a case, think carefully about when and where to introduce the release.

adjustments are necessary in one's usual interviewing techniques when children are involved. A good start is to begin thinking about "listening to," rather than "interviewing," the child.

§ 6.3.1 Choosing a Location

In many cases, having the child come to the office, sit in a big chair across from a big desk, and discuss the case will not be productive. The child may feel ill at ease or intimidated. It is usually easier to build rapport with children on their own turf: at their house, in the school playground, or at the local ice cream or hamburger shop. Meeting with a child client in his or her environment and getting to know the child client's community also provides the attorney with information that is essential to the representation. For example, what are the child client's living arrangements? Where are siblings and other important family members? How close is the child to school and after-school activities? What resources are available to the child and the child's family in the community? Knowing this information will enable the attorney to advocate more successfully for the client.

A playroom with child-sized furniture and toys is another good location for interviewing children. Some attorneys get down on the floor to talk to the child. It is important that the attorney be comfortable; if sitting on the floor is awkward, it will only appear condescending and phony to the child. Even without a playroom, the very young child should be allowed some play at the beginning of the meeting.

A teenager may enjoy meeting the attorney in the office and may be able to speak openly there. During the pre-interview phone call, the attorney should consider asking the teenage client if he or she prefers to meet in the office or elsewhere. Teenagers may be insulted if they are treated as anything other than adults. It is important, therefore, to get a sense of how the child client feels before making assumptions about how and where to meet.

Finally, in determining where to meet a child client, consider the logistical challenges the child may face. For example, the child may be totally dependent on family to get to the meeting. The child also may have limited access to a phone, which would make it difficult for the child to inform his or her attorney to ask to reschedule a meeting at the last minute. All of these considerations are also relevant to choosing a location for the interview.

Getting to know a child client in his or her community and meeting with the child in a safe and accessible location will help the attorney develop the rapport and trust necessary for a positive and successful attorney-client relationship.

§ 6.3.2 Helping the Child Feel Comfortable

Many times children will speak about difficult topics more easily if they can hold on to a stuffed animal or doll or play with a toy while they talk. For many children, it is very uncomfortable to make eye contact while discussing very personal or painful things. It is easier for them to talk if they have the option of playing with a distracting toy. Sometimes the location itself can be the distraction: walking through the zoo or duck pond, playing at a park or playground, or visiting an amusement park. Some snack or juice should be available for the child to increase the child's comfort level during the interview, especially if it is conducted at the attorney's office. Children who are hungry or thirsty or have to go to the bathroom will have even less concentration than normal.

Another major factor to consider is whether to include the parents or other legal guardian or siblings, and if so, for how much of any particular client meeting. Especially at the beginning of the attorney- client relationship, it may put the child at ease to have a familiar and trusted adult or sibling present. The trusted person can facilitate a "relationship transfer" in that the words and mere presence of the trusted person tells the child that the attorney too is a person they can trust. However, the attorney must be mindful of ethical obligations with respect to confidentiality and the attorney-client privilege. Moreover, as the attorney and child build trust and establish rapport, the child may become more willing to share sensitive information with the attorney if no family member, caseworker, foster parent, or legal guardian is present.

§ 6.3.3 Keeping Promises

Keeping promises is one of the most effective measures an attorney can take to quickly and effectively build trust and establish rapport with a young client. Even small steps can lead to huge strides in the relationship. Breaking promises, on the other hand, will impair communication and hinder the attorney-client relationship.

First, an attorney should promise only what they attorney is certain he or she can deliver. One way to do this is for the attorney to tell the child client that he or she will call the child at a specific time on a specific day and then follow through. This type of communication, if done on a consistent basis, will signal to the client that the attorney is trustworthy.

Second, honesty is key. At all times, the attorney should be honest with the client. While it may be difficult to deliver unpleasant news to a child, for example telling a child that he or she cannot have a sibling visit this week, it is critical to the success of the representation that the attorney is up front and honest with the client. Honesty builds credibility and will help solidify a client's trust in the attorney.

Third, it is the attorney's responsibility to manage a young client's expectations. A client may seek his or her attorney's assistance on a number of collateral issues. The attorney must make clear to the child what is within the attorney's control versus what decisions will be made by other people, such as the judge, school official, caseworker, or family member.

Building trust and establishing rapport with a child client are crucial to a successful attorney-client relationship. The attorney should consider these elements at the beginning of the case, as well as throughout the representation. In so doing, the attorney maximizes the ability to gather information and represent the child client.

§ 6.3.4 Informing the Client About the Case

The child's attorney is responsible for keeping the child informed about what is going on in the child's case, and the child's attorney must be available to explain the process to the child. It is extremely important that the child does not feel a sense of responsibility for the judge's decision. The child needs to understand that the judge, not the child, makes the final decision. The attorney should explain what will happen at different stages and that it may take "a long time" for a final decision to be made. If the attorney knows when the trial is set and how long the judge takes to render a decision, a time frame the child can relate to may be used, such as "after Christmas," "not until you're in second grade," or "before summer." Often the child does not need to know about the intricacies of the litigation, but a general idea of what will happen will ease the child's mind.

It is a mistake to think that a child will spontaneously ask questions that may be very pressing to the child. Some children will ask, but many will not. It is helpful to ask the child periodically whether he or she has any questions about why the attorney is there or about what is going on in court. Keep in mind that children have a strong desire to please authority figures. Thus, a child may indicate that he or she understands what is going on, when in fact he or she does not. The onus is on the attorney to ensure the child's understanding. One way to do so is for the attorney to ask the child to explain what is happening in the child's own words.

The child also should be given the opportunity to ask any final questions and should be encouraged to contact the attorney if any other questions arise. The child should be told how to get in touch with his or her attorney.

§ 6.4 Child-Centered Interviewing

The trust and rapport an attorney develops with a child client are invaluable as the attorney begins to gather the information that is critical to the child's representation. This section discusses some techniques that will help attorneys gather accurate information while protecting and further building their relationships with their child clients.[5]

§ 6.4.1 Communicating at the Child's Level

Many adults find it difficult to understand what attorneys are talking about. For children, the communication barriers can be immense. Children do not usually volunteer that they do not understand something, and they often give an answer regardless of whether they actually know what they were asked. It is important, therefore, for the attorney to understand how to talk to children at their own level. One excellent resource is Ann Graffam Walker's book, *Handbook on Questioning Children: A*

---

[5] For a discussion of investigative child interviewing, see Chapter 5.

Linguistic Perspective,[6] which is brief enough to review before an attorney speaks to a child client. The book gives specific, practical guidance for every age group. Dr. Walker's general advice is:

- DO use simple, common, everyday English words and phrases. "Attorney," "Court," "deny," "subsequent," "take the witness stand," "at that point in time," and the like do not fall into that category.

- DO put names and places back in where pronouns once lived. Ask, "What did Albert say?" instead of "What did *he* say?" Ask, "Were there a lot of people in the kitchen?" instead of "Were there a lot of people there?"

- DO stay away from negatives. Phrase your questions positively, whenever possible.

- DO use questions and comments that keep the number of ideas to a minimum. The younger the child, the smaller the number. One main idea is good.

- DO start your questions and comments off with the main idea. "Did the bell ring when you were eating?" instead of, "When you were eating, did the bell ring?"

- DO remember: this is a child. Children are not short adults. Try to listen to the proceedings with a child's ears. You might be surprised at what you hear.[7]

Dr. Walker provides 18 principles for communicating with children, including the following:

- Language is shaped by experience.
- Language is not an all-or-nothing affair.
- Inconsistency in children's statements is normal.
- Children are very literal in their approach to language.
- Adult-like use of language does not necessarily reflect adult-like linguistic or cognitive capabilities.
- Young children in particular have difficulty attending to more than one or two things at once (including multi-part, multi-idea questions).
- Pausing is productive.
- Children will not necessarily tell you that they do not understand you.
- Framing is good (letting them know what the subject is and why you are asking the question).

---

[6] ANN GRAFFAM WALKER, HANDBOOK ON QUESTIONING CHILDREN: A LINGUISTIC PERSPECTIVE (American Bar Association, 2d. ed. 1999).

[7] *Id.* at 5–6.

- Children's responses to your questions are not necessarily answers to your questions.

- The ability to recite a list is not the same as the ability to understand its contents.

- Children are not born with the ability to give adult-like accounts of their personal experiences.

- Not all families talk to each other.

- Familiarity and culture matter.[8]

It behooves the attorney to prepare carefully in advance of talking to children when the purpose of the discussion is to obtain information from the child.[9]

§ 6.4.2 Strengthening Rapport

One way to continue to strengthen the rapport an attorney has developed with a child client is to begin each meeting discussing subjects that are comfortable and familiar to the child, such as friends or activities. Attorneys can talk to the child about things in their own life, where they went on vacation, something their children or grandchildren used to do at the client's age, or activities they participate in—whatever might draw them into the child's sphere of experience. Anything that can build a bridge between the attorney and child, any common ground, can help build the relationship.

Children cannot be rushed. They are very inefficient interviewees. They quickly tire from answering a string of questions. They tend to ramble and jump from topic to topic as one comment reminds them of something else. They do not like to be brought back "on track" constantly, just when their answers are getting into interesting, if legally irrelevant, ground. It is all too easy for attorneys with rushed schedules to forget that children shut down under time constraints. Even if the attorney has made a list of questions to be asked, it is important not to be tied to the list. If the child's discussion goes in another direction, the attorney should follow the child's lead. One can always cover an important topic later, even if it is not in the order most helpful for note-taking.

§ 6.4.3 Being Aware of Your Own Responses

It is preferable to allow children to say what they think is important in their own words, using questions only when necessary. The attorney should be aware of his or her own verbal and nonverbal responses. Nods, facial expressions, and filler comments such as "really?" and "wow!" may be interpreted as carrying a value judgment or other substantive reaction to the content of what the child has said. Surprise or an

---

[8] *Id.* at 9–24.

[9] For a more complete discussion of talking to children in order to obtain information, see Chapter 5, Investigative Interviewing of the Child.

intended expression of sympathy, especially where a child has been abused or molested, may be interpreted as disgust or disapproval. Some animation and expression of interest is important for the development of a relationship, but the attorney should be very careful about what is being conveyed.

§ 6.4.4 Active Listening

Active listening is an invaluable tool in the representation of child clients. Children can be particularly sensitive not only to an adult's words, but also to the adult's body language and tone of voice. Thus, a child's attorney must be aware of his or her tone, facial expressions, and body language, and the messages that these cues may send to the child client. During each conversation, the attorney also should take time to observe the client, including the client's body language.

Specific active listening techniques that an attorney can use to improve information gathering include:

- *Be aware.* An attorney should be sensitive to what the child client may have been through before the meeting. For example, a meeting that takes place soon after a crisis should be short and simple. A child in crisis is less able to participate in a meaningful discussion.

- *Repeat key phrases.* Repetition signals to a child client that the attorney is listening, that the attorney values what the client is saying, and that the attorney understands. This in turn encourages the child client to continue the dialogue.

- *Use probing phrases.* Short phrases, such as "tell me more," encourage the child client to provide more detail on a particular subject.

- *Use conventional building blocks.* Having prepared in advance, the attorney will come to an interview with an idea of what information needs to be gathered. Rather than sticking firm to a pre-set list of questions, the attorney should base each question on the child client's previous answer. For example, an attorney asks her client about school. The child answers, "I don't like school, I like video games." An active listener might respond, "Tell me what you like about playing video games."

- *Show empathy.* When a child opens up about a difficult situation, an active listener could respond, "How did that make you feel?" or "That must be hard." The attorney should provide a comfortable space for the child to show emotions and then acknowledge those emotions. The attorney, however, should not show emotion, but rather remain professional.

- *Stay positive.* Questions should be framed in a positive light and avoid value judgments. For example, instead of asking "Why didn't anyone stay with you in the house?", a more positive way to elicit information on the same subject would be "Were you alone in the house? Where was everyone else?"

- *Avoid "why" questions*. For many children, asking "why" may seem accusatory.

- *Avoid assumptions*. The attorney and child client may come from very different backgrounds. The attorney should avoid assumptions about the client's neighborhood, background, family, friends, and school. An attorney who approaches the facts from a neutral position will better understand the facts from the client's perspective, which will enable the attorney to more effectively advocate on the client's behalf.

- *Encourage questions*. An attorney can empower the child client by welcoming questions and encouraging active participation and ownership in the case. To that end, the attorney should make sure that the client has his or her contact information and feels comfortable calling.

- *Do not be patronizing*. Sometimes interviewers using "active listening" techniques can become patronizing, rephrasing every statement that the child is making: "so what you're saying is . . ." or "what I'm hearing is . . ." While such comments can be helpful in ensuring that the attorney in fact understands what the child has said, continually making such statements can be very patronizing and offensive, especially to older children who may feel that they are clear and articulate on their own.

§ 6.4.5 Using the Funnel Technique

The funnel technique is a powerful tool a child's attorney can use in conjunction with active listening to gather information about the child client and his or her case. There are three stages to the funnel technique.

Stage 1. The attorney should first ask the child client to tell his or her story from start to finish, with no interruptions. Children have a natural inclination to please authority figures, so letting them tell their story without any interruption or outside input is invaluable. The first time the child client tells the story, it may not make sense, or there may be significant gaps in the story line. Nonetheless, it is crucial that the attorney refrain from interrupting. Rather, the role of the attorney during this initial stage is to encourage the client to speak. To that end, the attorney can ask questions such as "tell me more" and "what happened next," which will encourage the child.

By giving the child the opportunity to tell his or her story from start to finish, the attorney learns more than just the facts. The attorney also learns which parts of the story are most important to the child. The facts emphasized by the child might not be crucial to a case theory, but knowing this information will provide invaluable insight and help the attorney build trust and establish rapport. It also demonstrates to the child that the attorney respects the child and what he or she is saying, thus encouraging continued communication.

Stage 2. The attorney should then use open-ended questions to clarify and fill in missing information. In addition to wanting to please authority, children also are quite suggestible. If the attorney focuses on a particular set of facts too soon, the child may believe that those are the only facts that matter and stop offering other facts. To avoid losing valuable information, the attorney should keep the questioning open at this point and maximize the child's control of how the information is disseminated. Pointed questions such as who, where, and when are effective in getting more detailed information without altering the child's story or willingness to offer new facts.

In addition to asking who, where, and when questions, another way for an attorney to clarify the facts through open-ended questioning is by repeating a word or phrase that the child used, giving the child an opportunity to elaborate and/or clarify. For example, a child might say, "He poked me." The attorney could say, "poked," giving the child an opportunity either to confirm or to describe further what the child meant by the word "poked." Attorneys should avoid negative clarifications, such as, "Did you really mean to say 'poked'?", which signals to the child that he or she used the wrong word in the first place.

Demonstration is another important tool the attorney can use to clarify facts during Stage 2. The attorney can ask the child to role-play, or act out, the facts that he or she described during Stage 1. Children tend to describe time and space differently than do adults. Thus, giving them an opportunity to demonstrate these facts, rather than describe them with words, may provide clarity to an otherwise confusing story.

Stages 1 and 2 involve open-ended questions designed to allow the child to tell his or her story fully, through the child's lens, without interruption or significant input from the attorney. It may take several sessions to get through both stages. At the end of stage 2, the attorney should have a clear picture of what happened, but may still need to solidify some key facts.

Stage 3. Lastly, stage 3 is when the attorney can direct the child's attention to specific facts for further clarification. In this final stage, the attorney also should make sure the child understands certain legal terms so that the child can answer specific questions about the case if he or she testifies at a hearing or at trial. Attorneys should be careful to prepare, but not unduly influence, the child client. The attorney should be confident of the answers to questions that the child may be asked at trial, while ensuring that the answers are in the child's words.

§ 6.5 Counseling the Child Client

Representing children involves more than investigation and advocacy. Some of the criticism of the client-directed model of child representation is based on the concern that client-directed attorneys will merely act as mouth pieces for what immature and emotionally vulnerable children say they want. However, all attorneys have an obligation to counsel their clients. This duty is not diminished for children's attorneys. Indeed, attorneys for children have a heightened duty to ensure that their clients understand the relevant issues involved in the case, the actual alternatives available, and the pros and cons of each decision for which the client's input is sought.

If the attorney has developed a good rapport with the child and has taken the time to understand the child's perspective and what is important to the child, the decision-making process will usually lead to a position that the attorney can support. Children rarely appreciate the long-term consequences of decisions they make, but the attorney can help to explain these to the child. At the same time, the attorney must understand the child's perspective. The child's life is richly textured far beyond the immediate legal issues before the court. It is easy to lose sight of the entire context of the child's world in trying to address the immediate concern.

Counseling the child client starts with really listening to the child and understanding the short-term and long-term consequences of any positions taken on the entire fabric of the child's life. The attorney should keep this in mind when explaining options to the child. The attorney's counseling function can be very empowering for a child, who can feel that his or her voice is being heard and feelings are considered. The best representation of children involves a decision-making partnership, which requires sensitive legal counseling.

See Chapter 29, Representing Children and Youth, for full discussion of the law governing the child's lawyer, including guidance on determining the child's capacity to direct counsel, the place of child's stated wishes in determining the goals of the case, and representation of a client with diminished capacity.

Chapter 7: Family Dynamics and Treatment of Child Abuse and Neglect

by Donald C. Bross[1] and Terri James-Banks[2]

> "Every happy family is the same, but every unhappy family is different."
>
> —The opening lines of <u>Anna Karenina</u> by Leo Tolstoy

§ 7.1 Introduction

Clinical observations, rather than controlled research, form the primary basis for current beliefs and understanding about family dynamics in child abuse. No single explanation for child maltreatment has been established, but there are many risk factors and indicators of the psychological, social-psychological and situational, contextual or ecological realities most likely to be present when children are abused. Thus, even though each specific situation of child maltreatment is unique, such factors as how parents were cared for in their own childhood, the existence of one or more types of "crisis" in the home, some feature or behavior of the child that "triggers" parental anger or falls short of parental expectations, isolation from needed support or intervention from other adults, are present singly or in combination in almost every confirmed child abuse or neglect case.

Adequate legal representation requires the child's lawyer to know enough about contemporary views of child abuse dynamics to ask informed questions before hearings, of witnesses at trial, and of treatment plans that purport to address the question of whether a given parent can safely and at least minimally adequately respond to the needs of the child client. Addressed below are various behavioral theories of child maltreatment, important features of children's development that challenge parents, the limited research on treatment interventions, and assessment of treatment progress, treatment failure and cases in which treatment is most unlikely to be successful.

---

[1] Donald C. Bross, J.D., Ph.D., is Professor of Pediatrics (Family Law), University of Colorado School of Medicine, and Director of Education and Legal Counsel for the Kempe National Center for the Prevention and Treatment of Child Abuse and Neglect, (bross.donald@tchden.org).

[2] Terri James Banks, M.S.W., L.C.S.W., is Director of the Under Sixes Program, and Therapist for the Perinatal Mental Health Programs for the Kempe National Center for the Prevention and Treatment of Child Abuse and Neglect.

§ 7.2 Circumstances Under Which Child Maltreatment Occurs

"The term child maltreatment covers a large, complex group of human behaviors characterized by traumatic interactions between parents or other caretakers and the infants and children of all ages under their care."[3] There are many differences in how parents view children, and how parents were themselves cared for in their own childhood. The inherent vulnerability of infants and toddlers makes manifest that children need parents. On the other hand, to what extent does a parent "need" the child? Normal child development requires parents who can meet the needs of their child, subordinating the parents' own needs, such as emotional reassurance that they are not inadequate, emotional closeness, or love. Maltreatment can occur whenever a parent's needs overwhelm his or her ability to give a dependent child what the child must have to be safe and develop normally.

Knowledge about children's changing needs as each develops over time is essential for every adequate caregiver. How does someone learn to be a parent? Books can help, but clinical observation suggests that much of what parents carry with them into the parenting role is the experience of being cared for by others. Just as we best learn dancing by the act of having someone dance with us, we best learn caregiving by being cared for. Parents who did not receive adequate care themselves as children must acquire not only cognitive but also social and emotional facility if they are to provide adequate care. The difficulty in understanding the challenge can be illustrated by the difference between the words empathy and sympathy. If one is sympathetic, it is because one is similar to another person or has similar experiences on which to draw. If one is empathic, it is because one can, to some degree, accurately assess how the other person might be feeling without necessarily being like the other person. With empathy, the differences between the two persons do not block meaningful and appropriate interaction. Developmentally, children are always different from their adult caregivers. Parents who expect developmentally unrealistic ideas, attitudes, or behaviors from their children, such as, for example, about crying or toilet training, are not demonstrating empathy. Instead, the parent's behavior might be based entirely on the parent's needs or the parent's acting as if that the child must think or understand in the same way the parent does.

When parents themselves have not been empathically cared for, they can be less resilient and less prepared to deal with the many types of "crisis" that can occur in a home. Crises can include substance abuse, marital discord, domestic violence, job loss and job demands, mental illness, mental retardation, or physical illness. While the parent might contribute to these problems, parents cannot control all aspects of their lives and it is a mistake to assume that "fault" is at the core of resolving these crises even though improved self-efficacy is usually part of treatable situations. Few would

---

[3] Brandt F. Steele, *Psychodynamics and Biological Factors in Child Maltreatment, in* THE BATTERED CHILD 73 (Mary Edna Helfer et al. eds., 5th ed. 1997).

consider mental illness or mental retardation as the "fault" of the parent. Many would, however, think that parents can control how they respond to each of these problems. From the perspective of child protection, the essential question is not whether a parent is at "fault" but whether the parent has the "competency" to provide minimally adequate (or preferably reasonably adequate) care for a given child.

While parents vary greatly in their ability to adapt to the needs of different types of children, everyone would have difficulty caring for some children. Even for children fairly easy to care for, there might be some feature or behavior of a child that can "trigger" an angry or non-empathic response to the child's behavior. For example, when a child falls short of parental expectations, even expectations that can be unrealistic such as an infant not crying, this small bit of "misbehavior" might be intolerable. The parent's competency to care must be measured in terms of the child's needs, and the standard is higher for the children for whom it is much more demanding to provide care. In addition to crying, other "triggers" identified in child abuse fatalities are feeding difficulties and toilet training accidents. Again, in each of these areas the child's behavior can be completely understood, tolerated, and responded to empathically by experienced caregivers, but is often seen as a personal affront, deliberate disobedience, or intolerable to the abusive individual.

Many maltreating parents are isolated from supportive family and friends, and thus lack a "life line" that could change the parental and family dynamic. If parents have extended family who reinforce parental abuse or neglect, they are still "isolated" from healthy support systems. If nothing else, once a child is abused or neglected, appropriate intervention decreases the damaging isolation of families in which maltreatment is occurring.

§ 7.3 Perspectives for Understanding Abusive or Neglectful Parenting

Following identification of the battered child syndrome in 1962[4], psychodynamic theory and practice provided an early foundation for understanding maltreating families. From the beginning, early life experience was identified as an important feature of why some parents abused their children and others did not. Attachment and bonding research extended this approach to a detailed examination of early mother-child interaction patterns, including a range of secure to insecure attachments between mothers and infants. Almost from the beginning of modern attention to child maltreatment, it has been understood that some children are resilient, do not seem as devastated by their abuse as one might expect, but rather survive the harm done to them extremely well despite their mistreatment. It has also repeatedly been noted that many children who were abused will not later abuse their own children. As also noted below, however, some maltreated children do very poorly.

---

[4]   C. H. Kempe, F. N. Silverman, B. F. Steele, W. Droegemueller & H. K. Silver, *The Battered Child Syndrome*, 18/1 JAMA 17 (1962).

Social and economic ecology, including different cultural traditions and degrees of economic poverty, have also been shown to create risk for abuse and neglect. While no culture has been shown to be immune to child abuse, some seem to experience less abuse and others more.[5] Poverty in the U.S. is associated with physical abuse and neglect more strongly than with sexual abuse, which is more likely to be reported from all of the socio-economic classes.[6] To address all of the possible factors in child maltreatment, "Brofenbrenner's 1979 ecological model often has been used to integrate research on multiple risks for family violence at four levels of analysis: (a) individual characteristics, (b) the immediate social context, (c) the broader ecological context, and (d) the societal and cultural context."[7]

More recently, developing knowledge of human biology has been evaluated for the possible influences of intrinsic biological differences in parents and children on the risk for child abuse and risk from the consequences of child maltreatment. Genetics, which might underpin some of the risk for post-natal depression, and in one prospective study has been shown to create higher odds for physically abused males to exhibit negative behavioral effects from abuse than females, is currently a major focus of research. Other factors with genetic underpinnings, such as substance abuse especially and mental illness to a lesser extent, are known to be significant co-factors in many maltreating families, and different studies are being undertaken to develop tailored approaches when these factors are present.

Developmental psychopathology is a newly evolving approach that combines many different disciplines and theories to understand individual pathology as it relates to a multitude of risk factors and developmental pathways.

> Theorists and researchers in the field of developmental psycho-pathology seek to unify, within a life-span framework, the many contributions to the study of individuals at high risk for developing mental disorders and those who have already manifested such disorders. Developmental psychopathologists strive to engage in a comprehensive evaluation of biological, psychological, social and cultural processes and to ascertain how these multiple levels of analysis may influence individual differences, the continuity of discontinuity of adaptive or maladaptive behavioral patterns, and the pathways by which the same developmental outcomes may be achieved. In a discussion of the importance of basic and applied research, and of a multidomain and interdisciplinary perspective for the field of neuroscience Miller (1995) enunciated the view that all of

---

[5]   *See, e.g.,* Jill E. Korbin, *Culture and Child Maltreatment, in* THE BATTERED CHILD 29 (Mary Edna Helfer et al. eds., 5th ed. 1997).

[6]   *See* DAVID FINKELHOR, A SOURCEBOOK OF CHILD SEXUAL ABUSE (1986).

[7]   *See* Robert E. Emery & Lisa Laumann-Billings, *An Overview of the Nature, Causes, and Consequences of Abusive Family Relationships: Toward Differentiating Maltreatment and Violence,* 53/2 AM. PSYCHOL. 121, 135 (1998).

the different specialties—ranging from the basic to the applied and from the biological to the social and cultural—are needed to advance our common goal of better understanding human behavior.[8]

The literature shows that both trauma and resilience interplay in complex ways that are only barely appreciated. Yet early intervention is relevant to all theoretical frameworks, given studies that suggest that reduction of maltreatment can yield both short-term and long-term beneficial effects.[9] Anyone hoping to represent a maltreated child well must continue learning about the developments that are leading to the most appropriate, effective interventions.

§ 7.4 Consequences of Maltreatment

The consequences of child abuse and neglect have been better documented during the last 40 years.[10] The consequences vary depending on many factors, such as the gender of the victim, with males more likely to "externalize" the effects of maltreatment and females more likely to "internalize" various forms of maltreatment. Cathy Spaatz Widom followed more than 1,000 young males from a midwestern American state, some of whom had official records of having been abused or neglected and others without such a record, but from the same neighborhood. Widom found that a history of physical abuse or neglect increased the odds of arrest as a minor or as an adult by 60%.[11] Dorothy Otnow Lewis[12] and her colleague Jonathan Pincus, a neurologist, have interviewed hundreds of violent offenders in the U.S. over a period of more than two decades, and found that a combination of severe child maltreatment and organic brain injury, from accident or abuse, is associated with the most violent offenders, including serial killers. More recent research is broadening and deepening our understanding of childhood trauma. For example, Martin Teicher and colleagues at Harvard have used functional magnetic resonance imaging (fMRI), in combination with questionnaires with purposeful groups and other methods to

---

[8] Dante Cicchetti & L. Alan Sroufe, *Editorial: The Past as Prologue to the Future: The Times, They Have Been A-Changing*, 12/3 Dev. Psychopathol. 264 (2000).

[9] *See, e.g.*, David L. Olds, John Eckenrode & Charles R. Henderson et al., *Long-term Effects of Home Visitation on Maternal Life Course and Child Abuse and Neglect*, 278/8 JAMA 637 (1997). Note that this article won the 1997 NIHCM Foundation Health Care Research Award.

[10] For an excellent and detailed list of references on developmental consequences of child abuse and treatment of child abuse and neglect, see Child Welfare Information Gateway, *Long-Term Consequences of Child Abuse and Neglect* (2008), *available at* http://www.childwelfare.gov/pubs/factsheets/long_term_consequences.cfm.

[11] *See* Cathy S. Widom & Michael G. Maxfield, *A Prospective Examination of Risk for Violence among Abused and Neglected Children*, 794/1 Ann. N. Y. Acad. Sci. 224 (1996). *See also* Cathy S. Widom & Michael G. Maxfield, *An Update on the "Cycle of Violence"* (National Institute of Justice Research in Brief, Feb. 2001), available at http://www.ncjrs.gov/txtfiles1/nij/184894.txt.

[12] Dorothy Otnow Lewis, Guilty by Reason of Insanity: A Psychiatrist Explores the Minds of Killers (1998). This book is written for a general audience but summarizes results published in peer-reviewed journals and will make readers familiar with an entire line of research.

demonstrate the association between persistent limbic irritability in the brains of individuals who have suffered verbal abuse, witnessed domestic violence, been victimized by sexual abuse, or a combination of one or more of these experiences.[13]

Moeller, Bachmann, and Moeller reported on the results of interviews with 668 middle-class women, 47% of who reported experiencing one or more forms of child maltreatment.[14] The physical and psychological health problems reported by the women were significantly different for the two groups. For example, none of the non-abused group reported being alcoholic or experiencing a drug overdose, but 2.5% of the abused group were alcoholic and 1.4% had experienced a drug overdose, and 5.4% reported excessive drug use (as compared to 0.3% of the non-abused group). For the abused group, being a victim of a crime was 6 times more likely (6.2% vs. 1%), suicide attempts were 6 times more likely (4.5% vs. 0.7%), and thoughts of hurting oneself were 9 times more likely (9.6% vs. 1.0%). Other areas in which the maltreated group experienced more problems were with physical health, missing work due to illness, depressed feelings, frequent emotional outbursts, frequent conflicts, and problems in many other areas. The authors provided data indicating that physical abuse, neglect, or sexual abuse, alone or in combination, can each increase the risk of many different problems for adults who were maltreated as children.

Working with a small but scientifically defined population, researchers in Minnesota reported statistically significant differences between a group of children under age five with a history of abuse or neglect and a control group of children with no such history. Maltreated children in general were more negative, non-affectionate, and avoidant of their mothers, and they lacked enthusiasm and persistence in age appropriate tasks. They were more likely to be angry, showed a lack of self-control, and were judged to be avoidant and low in self-esteem. At age 54 months through kindergarten, physically abused children were identified by teachers as "extremely inattentive, unpopular, aggressive, and overactive. They were more likely than children in the control group to engage in self-destructive and obsessive-compulsive behavior."[15]

With time, there has been increasingly careful documentation of the short- and long-term harms to children who are abused and neglected. The resiliency and specific vulnerabilities of each child, for example a child with disabilities,[16] are known to be part of the picture of both who is targeted and how experiencing trauma

---

[13] *See* Martin H. Teicher, Jacqueline A. Samson, Ann Polcari & Cynthia E. McGreenery, *Sticks, Stones, and Hurtful Words: Relative Effects of Various Forms of Childhood Maltreatment*, 163/6 AM. J. PSYCHIATRY 993 (2006).

[14] *See* T. P. Moeller, G. A. Bachmann & J. R. Moeller, *The Combined Effects of Physical, Sexual, and Emotional Abuse During Childhood: Long-term Health Consequences for Women*, 17/5 CHILD ABUSE & NEGLECT 623 (1993).

[15] *See* M. F. Erickson, B. Egeland & R. Planta, *The Effects of Maltreatment on the Development of Young Children, in* CHILD MALTREATMENT: THEORY AND RESEARCH ON THE CAUSES AND CONSEQUENCES OF CHILD ABUSE AND NEGLECT 647 (Dante Cicchetti & Vicki Carlson eds., 1989).

[16] *See* DICK SOBSEY, VIOLENCE AND ABUSE IN THE LIVES OF PEOPLE WITH DISABILITIES: THE END OF SILENT ACCEPTANCE? (1994).

plays out for individuals. The impact of traumatic events on infants, toddlers, and preschoolers is well documented yet has failed to engage sufficient clinical and legal attention. There continues to be a misconception among some that young children are immune to trauma because they are too cognitively immature to understand, remember, or be badly harmed. However, research on trauma in the first five years of life consistently reveals a high risk of negative biological, emotional, social, and cognitive consequences. In particular, the immediate postpartum period is a particularly vulnerable time: one third of maltreated infants younger than one year of age are injured in the first week of life.[17] Contextual violence is also prevalent in young children's environments. Children younger than five are disproportionately represented in homes with domestic violence, and exposure to domestic violence in the first six months of life is a significant predictor of child abuse through five years of age.[18] This information clearly indicates a need for mental health professionals trained in infant and early childhood mental health and family systems theory utilizing treatment interventions that have been demonstrated to be effective with this population. These facts speak to the essential role of the nonverbal child's legal representative, who must in turn challenge any failure to respect and address the needs of these children.

§ 7.5 Treatment

Family dynamics depend not only on the nature of individual parents but also on the nature of individual children. Some children are much more difficult to parent than others. Children who have been maltreated can need care and treatment that is well above average in quality for the child to recover and develop normally. Thus treatment is needed for abused and neglected children, their parents, and the child and parents together.

Over the past 20 years, more practices informed by research have developed. Sometimes referred to as EBP, "evidence-based practice" typically will have "well-developed treatment manuals, establishing training protocols for clinicians, and ongoing assessment of clinical fidelity to the treatment model. EBP is unique from more traditional practices given that treatment effectiveness is demonstrated incrementally through well-designed, randomized clinical trails using outcomes that are tied to specific treatment goals."[19]

---

[17] *See* Centers for Disease Control and Prevention, *Nonfatal Maltreatment of Infants—United States, October 2005–September 2006*, 57 MORB. MORTAL. WKLY. REP. 336 (2008).

[18] *See, e.g.*, John W. Fantuzzo & Rachel A. Fusco, *Children's Direct Exposure to Types of Domestic Violence Crime: A Population-based Investigation*, 22/7 J. FAM. VIOL. 543 (2007); William M. McGuigan & Clara C. Pratt, *The Predictive Impact of Domestic Violence on Three Types of Child Maltreatment*, 25/7 CHILD ABUSE & NEGLECT 869 (2001).

[19] Kimberly Shipman & Heather Taussig, *Mental Health Treatment of Child Abuse and Neglect: The Promise of Evidence-Based Practice*, 56/2 PEDIATR. CLIN. NORTH AM. 417 (2009).

§ 7.5.1 Treatment for Abused and Neglected Children

Trauma-focused cognitive behavioral therapy is a model now used to treat children who have suffered multiple types of trauma.[20] Improvements in the areas of post-traumatic symptoms such as anxiety, depression, externalizing behaviors, sexualized behaviors and shame have been documented, with gains maintained at one- and two-year follow ups, and with application in diverse populations including African American and Latino populations.[21] Child psychotherapy for children ages birth to six years can demonstrate parent-child relationship improvements and improvements in children's behaviors such as decreased anger, avoidance, resistance, and increased partnership with the mother.[22]

While studies of treatment for parents who abuse or neglect children and studies of the effects of therapy for maltreated children[23] are still too few in number and quality, new studies continue to be reported.[24] Notwithstanding limits on available research, it appears that children who actually receive competent psychotherapy appear to do better than children who receive no competent therapy; yet children do not receive treatment to the extent needed. In the United States, approximately 20% of all children have a diagnosable emotional or behavioral disorder.[25] As discussed previously, maltreated children are at a greatly increased risk of experiencing a wide variety of emotional and behavioral disorders. Unfortunately, this fact generally has not led to specific treatment for abused children other than any benefit that might accrue from being in foster care, being engaged in the child welfare system, and any improvements that might or might not occur indirectly in the children's lives through treatment of the parents.

Placing a label of "Evidence-Based Practice" (EBT) on an intervention or therapy does not imply that it is a panacea for the complex problems confronted by children and parents in child welfare systems. The absence of the label EBT, does not mean automatically that an intervention is without merit.[26] Other treatment modalities,

---

[20] *Id.*

[21] *Id.* at 421.

[22] *Id.* at 421–22.

[23] *See, e.g.,* R. Kim Oates & Donald C. Bross, *What Have We Learned About Treating Child Physical Abuse? A Literature Review of the Last Decade,* 19/4 CHILD ABUSE & NEGLECT 463 (1995); David Finkelhor &Lucy Berliner, *Research on the Treatment of Sexually Abused Children: A Review and Recommendations,* 34/11 J. AM. ACAD. CHILD ADOLESC. PSYCHIATRY 1408 (1995).

[24] For a good, quick source of information on the treatment of abused and neglected children, see the list of manuals provided on the Child Welfare Information Gateway's page titled "Child Abuse and Neglect User Manual Series 1990s" at http://www.childwelfare.gov/pubs/umnineties.cfm; *see especially* U.S. Department of Health & Human Services, A. J. Urquiza & C. Winn, *Treatment for Abused and Neglected Children: Infancy to Age 18* (1994), *available at* http://www.childwelfare.gov/pubs/usermanuals/treatmen/index.cfm.

[25] *See, e.g.,* A. Angold & E. J. Costello, *Assessment to Intervention, in* ASSESSMENT AND TREATMENT OF CHILDHOOD PROBLEMS (Carolyn S. Schroeder & Betty N. Gordon eds., 1995).

[26] *See, e.g.,* Arthur C. Bohart, *Evidence-based Psychotherapy Means Evidence-informed, Not Evidence-driven,* 35/1 J. CONTEMP. PSYCHOTHER. 39 (2005).

including therapeutic preschools, individual therapy, group therapy, home-based services with a multi-systemic approach, treatment that helps foster parents address children's needs, and case work, have promising indicators of success. "Evidence-based," psychotropic medications can be helpful, but they often cannot alone address the needs of maltreated children.[27] Only rarely do maltreated children receive direct benefits from any of these therapies. This represents one of the major challenges to the child's attorney or guardian ad litem, i.e., to assure that abused and neglected children have a "right to treatment" that is enforced. When asking questions and challenging treatment professionals to address the treatment needs of abused and neglected children, the attorney or guardian ad litem should avoid any formulaic approach to the client's needs and be the best possible "consumer" on behalf of the child to increase the chances of an appropriate, scientifically-based where possible, and individually tailored plan.

In many respects, foster care has become the default mental health intervention in the lives of maltreated children. Children can do both worse and better in foster care. To the extent that they do much better in foster care, it is a diagnostic indication that their previous home environment was sorely lacking in the physical, emotional, and psychological support needed. Gradually, a picture is being established of improvements in the life prospects for many children who, for good and sufficient reasons, must be placed in foster care, notwithstanding losses in relationships with families of origin.[28]

§ 7.5.2 Treatment for Parents

The goals of treatment for parents include: topping abuse or reversing neglect; ensuring adequate caregiving; improving the parental competency for positive interpersonal relationship with any child in the family who has been the subject of maltreatment and other family members; addressing any symptoms of psychological disorder; and managing any sexually aggressive, violent, or exploitative behavior that is directed toward the child. The phases of treatment include acknowledgment of abuse and its effects and the development of increased parental competence and sensitivity to the child. Resolution is the beginning of more adaptive family functioning so far as the child is concerned.[29]

A number of evidence-based practices (EBP) for parents are receiving additional empirical support. Parent-Child Interaction Therapy (PCIT) and Abuse-Focused Cognitive Behavioral therapy (AF-CBT) result in reducing child behavior problems,

---

[27] *See, e.g.,* D. C. Bross, B. Stafford & T. James-Banks, *Uses and Misuses of Psychiatric Knowledge for Advocacy for Children, in* THE SPECIALIZED PRACTICE OF JUVENILE AND FAMILY LAW 171–92 (Anne Kellogg ed., 2008).

[28] *See, e.g.,* Kimberly Shipman & Heather Taussig, *Mental Health Treatment of Child Abuse and Neglect: The Promise of Evidence-based Practice,* 56/2 PEDIATR. CLIN. NORTH AM. 417, 422–24 (2009).

[29] *See, e.g.,* David P. H. Jones, *Treatment of the Child and Family, in* THE BATTERED CHILD 521, 524–25 (Mary Edna Helfer et al. eds., 5th ed. 1997).

better child-parent relationships, and many improvements in psychological and social functioning.[30]

One of the important assumptions of the American child protection system and of court involvement in the lives of maltreating families is that mandatory, rather than voluntary, intervention can be protective of children and help parents more than it will harm them. The earliest attempt to determine if court-ordered intervention might have a positive effect was published in 1980.[31] With 71 physically abusing parents referred for treatment, 46 of whom voluntarily agreed to treatment, and 25 of whom were court-ordered to treatment, the court-ordered families were found to have been five times more likely to have completed treatment. The percentage of court-ordered families viewed as "successful" from treatment (17 of 25 or 68%) was also much higher than the percentage of voluntary families who were successfully treated (6 of 46 or 13%). A later study also concluded that families in both voluntary and involuntary treatment significantly increased their use of praise in interaction with their children and drastically reduced their use of criticism.[32] A five-year follow up study of 53 infants born positive for substance abuse exposure, all of whose mothers were court-ordered into treatment, found that 66% of the infants were reunited with at least one parent and that only one child (whose mother did not attend therapy or comply with toxicology screening) was subsequently abused.[33] A study published in 1990 asked parents whether their families were either better off or worse off after involuntary reports and services.[34] Of the 176 parents responding, 20% of the parents did not answer the question, 20% said their families were "worse off," and 60% of the parents responding said their families were "better off." All of the studies cited are limited by relatively small numbers of subjects and a lack of randomized control groups, or even matched individuals, for comparison purposes. The results are enough to suggest, however, that the effects of legally mandated intervention are not necessarily bad and indeed seem to be beneficial beyond mere protection, when warranted by underlying documented abuse or neglect.

Nothing in the EBP interventions described here appear to have occurred with an entirely voluntary population, unless giving a parent an option of going to court or going into therapy is considered to be voluntary therapy. Given that many of the practices outlined here are not available in every community or jurisdiction, an

---

[30] *See, e.g.*, Kimberly Shipman & Heather Taussig, *Mental Health Treatment of Child Abuse and Neglect: The Promise of Evidence-based Practice*, 56/2 PEDIATR. CLIN. NORTH AM. 417, 420–21 (2009).

[31] *See* David A. Wolfe, John Aragona, Keith Kaufman & Jack Sandler, *The Importance of Adjudication in the Treatment of Child Abusers: Some Preliminary Findings*, 4/2 CHILD ABUSE & NEGLECT 127 (1980).

[32] *See* Ana Maria Irueste-Montes & Francisco Montes, *Court-ordered vs. Voluntary Treatment of Abusive and Neglectful Parents*, 12/1 CHILD ABUSE & NEGLECT 33 (1988).

[33] *See* James R. MacMahon, *Perinatal Substance Abuse: The Impact of Reporting Infants to Child Protective Services*, 100/5 PEDIATRICS e1 (1997).

[34] George E. Fryer, Jr., Donald C. Bross, Richard D. Krugman, David Denson & Diane Baird, *Good News for CPS Workers: An Iowa Survey Shows Parents Value Services*, 48/1 PUBLIC WELFARE 38 (1990).

attorney working in this field can learn by keeping up with research and innovative practice what is possible and then advocate for the best empirically-based treatment for both children and parents.

§ 7.5.3 Parents Who Are the Most Difficult to Treat

David P. H. Jones, a child psychiatrist in Oxford, England, published a typology of "treatability" or "untreatability" in the mid-1980s that has not been replaced by any better approach:[35]

- There are some families who simply will not change. They do not want or intend to change.
- Some parents persistently deny abusive behavior in the face of clear evidence to the contrary.
- Some families cannot change in spite of a will to do so. There may be a subgroup of families who are willing to change but resources to help them are not available.
- Some parents can change, but not "in time" for their child's developmental needs. For example, abusive parents of a six-month-old baby become less impulsive and dangerous after two years, but in the meantime their baby has developed a strong attachment to a surrogate parent.
- Similarly, other parents may change in time for their next child but not for the index one.
- Finally, there is the category of untreatable parents who fail to respond to one treatment approach but who may be amenable to another agency or approach.

There are many additional characteristics of parents making them less amenable to treatment, while it must also be noted that a single indicator is not necessarily a determining factor. These factors include: parental history of severe childhood abuse, persistent denial of abusive behavior, severe personality disorder (sociopathy, grossly inadequate personality), mental handicap associated with personality disorder, psychotic parents with delusions involving their own children, a schizoid personality with respect to pervasive detachment, antisocial personality with respect to total disregard for others, criminally insane, persistently addicted to drugs or alcohol, persistent violent sexual fantasies. In sexual abuse cases the following factors are considered as signs of poor prognosis for treatment of the parent: pedophilia, lack of empathic feeling for the child, failure to see the child's need as separate from own, child is seen as having sexual needs/desires identical to parent's needs/desires, previous violent acts (increasing in number), degree of sadism or sexual deviancy, drug or substance abuse at the time of the event—continuing if the individual in

---

[35] *See* David P. H. Jones, *The Untreatable Family*, 11/3 CHILD ABUSE & NEGLECT 409 (1987).

question is dependent on drugs or other substances. Other problems that have been associated with treatment difficulty are severe failure to thrive, fabrication of pediatric illness, vaginal or anal intercourse, and sadism.

Parents with personality disorders (i.e., those who have a disorder on Axis II in DSM-IV-TR) are an example of a persons who can be particularly difficult to treat, and who present a type of problem not uncommon to abusive situations. Included within this general diagnostic category are narcissistic, borderline, obsessive-compulsive, and antisocial personalities. With these diagnoses it is common for the parent to lack the ability to recognize and respond to the needs of anyone except themselves. In treatment, they often are unable to see any problem with their behavior, tending to define the problem in terms of the failures of others. The same features that make addressing the needs of children difficult for a parent with a personality disorder tend to make treatment of the same individual both intensive and long-term.

As another example of treatment difficulty, persons with multiple problems, such as dual diagnoses of mental illness and substance abuse, require carefully tailored and often prolonged courses of treatment. It is not always possible for parents confronting a more difficult course of treatment to improve sufficiently in time to meet the minimal needs of developing children, who cannot wait for adequate care.

§ 7.6 Measuring Change in Parenting Competency and Motivation

In 1993 the National Research Council published a review of available research on the etiology of child maltreatment.[36] They identified more than 55 variables that had been associated with occurrence of child maltreatment, and 12 of the variables specifically related to aspects of the interaction between child and caregiver. Among the reported findings regarding a caregiver's relationship with the child were:

1. Unrealistic expectations of the child
2. Views child's behavior as extremely stressful
3. Negative attitudes about the child's behavior
4. Perceives the child as more aggressive, intentionally disobedient, annoying and less intelligent
5. Abusive mothers are more likely to perceive their child's negative behavior as the result of stable internal factors such as a personality trait, but her behaviors as a result of unstable external factors
6. Low involvement, nurturance, control, and monitoring
7. Authoritarian, involving punitiveness, coercion, restrictiveness, and low warmth and respect

---

[36] NATIONAL RESEARCH COUNCIL, UNDERSTANDING CHILD ABUSE AND NEGLECT (1993).

8. Less supportive, affectionate, playful and are less responsive with their children

9. With infants, abusing parents are more controlling, interfering, and covertly if not overtly hostile

10. Neglectful parents tend to be unresponsive to infants and children

11. Neglectful parents do not initiate interaction with their children and do not respond to initiations by their children

12. Abusive parents are more likely to use punishment, threats, coercion, and power, and they are less likely to use reasoning and affection in controlling their children

In considering the development of case or treatment plans, this information suggests that evaluators responsible for determining whether change has occurred in important problems of caregiving that might have lead the case to court should be able to understand and measure parental attitudes and behaviors in the areas noted by the National Science Foundation and in similar areas of interaction and caregiving. While psychological testing might be sensitive enough to measure change in some situations, the ability to interview and observe parents and children will almost always form the basis for the most compelling insights. Sometimes observation of parent-child interactions, if not too distressing to the child, is essential for clarity.

Sometimes the individual behaviors of either parent or child in isolation from each other can be so dramatic that the information is compelling. Thus a child's significant improvement in foster care can provide evidence that whatever the nature of some of the parent's interactions with the child, there are also prevailing parental acts or omissions that are destructive of the child's chances for reasonable development. It is important to attend to the more subtle and unique aspects of caregiver and child interactions, rather than to rely solely on identifying issues such as substance abuse, mental health issues, or domestic violence as the primary guide for intervention strategies. A major challenge for the child's advocate is to become a "good consumer" of evaluation and therapeutic providers to determine if they are able to perform reliably and validly at the level of understanding and insight required.

Maltreatment may be exacerbated or caused by conditions such as substance abuse, mental illness, and domestic violence, but clinical experience and reports suggest that harm to children also separately derives from certain aspects of the interactions of caretaker and child. A fundamental need in assessing prognosis for change is to conduct a family assessment and/or an evaluation of interactions between parent and child with the purpose of identifying the relative strengths and deficits in the caregiver-child relationship.

Concomitantly, adjunctive psychological evaluations of the caregivers can also provide additional insight into the personality structure of the individuals, which can be incorporated into treatment planning and evaluation of treatment progress. Evaluations conducted at the onset of a child protective case can provide a "base line" for ongoing evaluation of the prognosis for change rather than waiting for evaluation after efforts at reunification have failed. When such evaluations are conducted with knowledge of attachment theory, psychodynamic theory, social learning theory, child development, family systems theory, and including the bio-ecological model, the evaluation can inform individualized treatment plans and clarify criteria for evaluating whether change is occurring that reduces the potential for recidivism of abuse and neglectful behavior. Individual assessments are useful and sometimes essential in child protection. However, the core challenge for child protection is to understand how the caretaker's own dynamics are leading to abusive and neglectful behavior in the context of the specific parent-child relationships.

§ 7.7 Decisions Regarding Placement, Reunification, and Termination

Thanks to the work of Goldstein, Freud and Solnit[37] in their seminal series on the "best interests of children," any attorney who has represented infants and very young children especially is aware that time can be of the essence in the secure attachment of children. In other words, it is not good for children to be moved from one caregiver, parent, or foster parent to another for more than a very limited time, generally measured in hours for infants and days for toddlers, without very important reasons of safety or, in some situations, a clear diagnostic purpose. Every move must have an impact on the child, and unless carefully considered, may cause the child to experience a sense of loss and even depression. Thoughtful and planned changes with transition objects, preparation, and support for the child and caregivers throughout the process are essential to the child's well-being. Applying attachment or bonding criteria is not the only technique or consideration in evaluating child and parent relationships, of course, and the meaning of the terms and the proper application of the concepts is only part of the reciprocal connectedness that courts must consider when making decisions about child placements.[38]

Safety is always the first consideration in decisions for reunification. If issues of safety have been addressed, then reunification must encompass the needs of the child and caregivers for continued support because reunification also means a different set of hourly and daily interactions between child and parent and every other person in the environment of each. This means lots of work and stress for the child and the parent, as understanding and reciprocity are renegotiated.

Termination may be the only option for not only the child but the parent needing to transcend significant parental limitations. Necessary criteria for termination include: court-adjudicated abuse or neglect, a court-approved treatment plan that has

---

[37] *See, e.g.,* JOSEPH GOLDSTEIN, ANNA FREUD & ALBERT J. SOLNIT, BEYOND THE BEST INTERESTS OF THE CHILD (1985).

[38] *See, e.g.,* David E. Arredondo & Leonard P. Edwards, *Attachment, Bonding, and Reciprocal Connectedness: Limitations of Attachment Theory in the Juvenile and Family Court,* 2 J. CENTER FOR FAMILIES, CHILDREN & COURTS 109 (2000).

been refused or failed, continued parental incapacity that relates directly to meeting the child's minimally adequate needs, and if and when involuntary dissolution of the child-parent legal relationship is otherwise in the child's best interests. However, a child who is much older or appears very difficult to adopt might not benefit from termination.

§ 7.8 Summary

An understanding of the family dynamics that create risk and precede child abuse, child sexual abuse, and various forms of neglect is important for adequate evaluation of the existence of maltreatment, is essential for crafting interventions to address the child's and family's problems of abuse and neglect, and is the foundation for determining where children can be placed appropriately at any stage of child protection proceedings. Intrinsic biological factors of the parent and child, risk factors from the parent's childhood, and the nature of relationships that have developed between the child, parent, and significant others in the child's life are all informed by experience and research on family dynamics in child abuse and neglect settings. Each child's attorney has the responsibility to address both the importance of general factors of maltreatment and resiliency and the uniqueness of each child's situation.

Chapter 8: Cultural Context in Abuse and Neglect Practice: Tips for Attorneys

by Karen Aileen Howze[1]

§ 8.1 Introduction

The men and women who serve as attorneys, judges, and social workers in abuse and neglect cases bring their total life experiences—and the assumptions that those experiences create—to each case. It is a lofty goal to expect that attorneys, judges, and social workers can set aside assumptions that are based on our perceptions of race, ethnic background, religion, poverty, substance abuse, literacy, language differences, gender, age, and sexual orientation.

Yet, central to the role of attorneys for children, parents, and child welfare agencies is the examination of the specific needs of each family and each child so that permanency can be achieved in a timely manner. To determine the specific needs of the family and child and to choose appropriate services that will promote permanency, it is crucial to explore the cultural and subcultural context within which each child, parent, and substitute caretaker lives.

§ 8.2 The Rule of Law: Safety, Well-Being, and Permanency

The effective application of and compliance with federal, state, and tribal law has an impact on the length of time children remain under court supervision. The Adoption and Safe Families Act (ASFA) requires that, to achieve permanency, the focus *must* be on the specific needs of each child and parent or custodian.[2] ASFA—with its tight timeframes for achieving permanency and its focus on the well-being and safety of children under court supervision—requires that attorneys understand and employ different approaches to management of their cases, regardless of whether they represent parents, children, or agencies.

Attention to the cultural context of a child is also within the mandates and limits of the Multi-Ethnic Placement Act (MEPA).[3] MEPA prohibits denying any person the

---

[1] Karen Aileen Howze, J.D., is a Magistrate Judge, Superior Court of the District of Columbia. She is the author of MAKING DIFFERENCES WORK: CULTURAL CONTEXT IN ABUSE AND NEGLECT CASES (American Bar Association 1996), which established the framework on which this chapter is based for examining culture in abuse and neglect practice.

[2] 42 U.S.C. §§ 671–679(b). For a more detailed discussion of establishing permanency, see Chapter 25, Establishing Legal Permanence for the Child.

[3] 42 U.S.C. § 1996b; 42 U.S.C. § 671(a)(18); 42 U.S.C. § 674(d)(2).

opportunity to become an adoptive or foster parent on the basis of race, color, or national origin. The Act also requires diligent recruitment of potential adoptive and foster parents that reflect the ethnic and racial diversity of children in the state for whom foster and adoptive homes are needed.[4]

In addition, the Indian Child Welfare Act (ICWA)[5] provides a framework for the states to ensure tribal sovereignty in the determinations of placement of Native American children who are in need of protection, out-of-home care, or adoption. MEPA carves out an exception for considerations mandated by ICWA.

Finally, the Chafee Foster Care Independence Act[6] requires that services for adolescents in care meet the specific needs of each young person to ensure successful transition from foster care to emancipation. In short, determining the specific needs of each child and each family turns on an examination of the cultural and subcultural context of each child and each family.

Indeed, compliance with the law in abuse and neglect cases mandates an examination and responsiveness to the specific needs of each child and each family. Case planning is more likely to meet the unique needs of each child and family if the cultural and subcultural context of the parties is considered from the initial hearing through case resolution. Considering the context increases the likelihood that the services provided to resolve these cases will help to ameliorate the conditions that affect the child's safety and well-being and ensure compliance with the timeframes for case resolution.

§ 8.3 Defining Cultural and Subcultural Context

As attorneys, judges, and social workers work to rebuild families in abuse and neglect cases, the reality is clear: The law is color blind. The law is blind to economic differences. The law balances the interests of the parties based solely on the facts presented. These are the cornerstones of the culture of American jurisprudence.

At the same time, our society is filled with differences that affect a person's interpretation of the facts that are central to the application of the rule of law. In no other area of law are the differences more pronounced and more likely to affect the outcome of a case than in the area of child abuse and neglect, as the research regarding disproportionality confirms.

The facts:

- The majority of child welfare cases across the United States involve people who live at or below the poverty line.[7]

---

[4] For a full discussion of MEPA, see § 10.4, Multiethnic Placement Act and the Interethnic Adoption Provisions.

[5] 25 U.S.C. §§ 1901–1963.

[6] 42 U.S.C. §§ 677 *et seq.*

[7] *See* DOROTHY E. ROBERTS, POVERTY, RACE, AND NEW DIRECTIONS IN CHILD WELFARE POLICY 69 (1999).

- Frequently, mothers in abuse and neglect cases are single and rearing more than one child.[8]

- Drug addiction, mental illness, developmental issues, and cognitive issues create permanent disabilities that impact services and planning for permanency.[9]

- The number of African-American and Hispanic children in foster care is disproportionate to their representation in the general population across the United States.[10]

- Youth in foster care have a greater incidence of emotional, behavioral, and developmental problems than other adolescents.[11]

"Cultural and subcultural context" is the intersection of culture and subculture with the application of the law. It is the application of culture (race, ethnicity, and religion) and subculture (poverty, language, mental and physical disability, literacy, gender, sexual identity, age, religion, or faith) to improve the decision-making and quality of the services that are designed to meet the needs of children and families as they move toward a permanent resolution of conditions that necessitated court intervention. The context provides a framework for judges, attorneys and social workers to effectively address the safety and well-being of children under court supervision, as well as the timely achievement of permanency.

§ 8.4 Race, Ethnicity, and Child Protection

Children of all races are equally likely to suffer from abuse and neglect, according to the U.S. Department of Health and Human Services' periodic *National Incidence Study of Child Abuse and Neglect*, which is mandated by Congress.[12] Yet, the over-representation of children of color in the child welfare and juvenile justice systems

---

[8] U.S. Department of Health & Human Services, Administration on Children, Youth and Families, *Child Maltreatment 2007* (U.S. Government Printing Office 2009), p. 27, *available at* http://www.acf.hhs.gov/programs/cb/pubs/cm07/.

[9] Child Welfare Information Gateway, *Parental Substance Use and the Child Welfare System: Service Delivery Issues* (2009), *available at* http://www.childwelfare.gov/pubs/factsheets/parentalsubabuse.cfm#6; National Mental Health Information Center, *Critical Issues for Parents with Mental Illness and their Families: Chapter V*, *available at* http://mentalhealth.samhsa.gov/publications/allpubs/KEN-01-0109/ch5.asp.

[10] For an excellent discussion of the history of data collection regarding overrepresentation in the juvenile justice system and the child welfare system, along with a discussion of the meaning of overrepresentation, underrepresentation, disproportionality, and disparity, see Center for Juvenile Justice Reform & Chapin Hall, *Racial and Ethnic Disparity and Disproportionality in Child Welfare and Juvenile Justice: A Compendium* (Jan. 2009), *available at* http://cjjr.georgetown.edu/pdfs/cjjr_ch_final.pdf.

[11] American Academy of Pediatrics: Committee on Early Childhood, Adoption and Dependent Care, *Developmental Issues for Young Children in Foster Care*, 106/5 PEDIATRICS 1145 (2000).

[12] *See* National Incidence Study of Child Abuse and Neglect (NIS-4) (2004–2009), *available at* www.childwelfare.gov/systemwide/statistics/nis.cfm.

has been documented and persisted since 1972.[13] The following information provides an overview of some of the studies that address disproportionality—the over-representation of children of color in child welfare when compared to their numbers in the general child population.[14]

In 2004, the Center for the Study of Social Policy found that states vary considerably in the degree of overrepresentation of African American children in the child welfare system compared to White children. The Center reported the following findings based on 2000 Census and Child Welfare (AFCARS) data:[15]

- African American children accounted for 37% of the total number of children placed in foster care in 2000, and approximately 46% were accounted for by non-Hispanic White children, even though African American children comprised only 15% of the total U.S. child population under 18 (U.S. Census).

- Forty-six states have disproportionate representations of African American children in their child welfare systems, which means that in these states the proportion of African American children in foster care is more than two times the proportion of African American children in the state's total child population 18 years and younger.

- In seven states, the proportion of Black children in foster care is four times what you would expect based on their occurrence in the general child population of those states. The states with the highest African American disproportionality ratios based on 2000 AFCARS and Census data are: California, Oregon, Wyoming, Minnesota, Idaho, New Hampshire, and Wisconsin.

- *In every state*, the occurrence of White children in the child welfare system is *at least* proportional to their occurrence in the states' total child population under 18. In all but four states, the proportion of White children in the foster care population is less than what would be expected given the proportion of all children under 18.

- The states were divided into three categories that define the level of disproportionality by dividing the proportion of African American (or non-Hispanic White) children in foster care by the proportion of African

---

[13] *See* Center for Juvenile Justice Reform & Chapin Hall, *Racial and Ethnic Disparity and Disproportionality in Child Welfare and Juvenile Justice: A Compendium* (Jan. 2009), *available at* http://cjjr.georgetown.edu/pdfs/cjjr_ch_final.pdf.

[14] Although most data available reports on disproportionality and the disparity in treatment and services between African American and White children, recent data, gleaned from reports required of state systems by the U.S. Department of Health and Human Services, provide data for Hispanic, Asian/Pacific Islander, and Native American children and families.

[15] Center for the Study of Social Policy, *The Race & Child Welfare Project: Fact Sheet 1 – Basic Facts on Disproportionate Representation of African Americans in the Foster Care System, available at* http://www.cssp.org/uploadFiles/factSheet1.pdf.

American (or non-Hispanic White) children under the age of 18 in the state population.

- o *Moderate Disproportion (15 states)*: Louisiana, South Carolina, Alabama, Georgia, Arkansas, Tennessee, North Carolina, Washington, Florida, Virginia, Maine, New York, Oklahoma, Maryland and Alaska.

- o *High Disproportion (15 states)*: Kentucky, Texas, Delaware, Nevada, Missouri, Utah, Vermont, Nebraska, West Virginia, Kansas, Colorado, North Dakota, South Dakota, Ohio and Connecticut.

- o *Extreme Disproportion (16 states)*: Rhode Island, New Jersey, New Mexico, Iowa, Indiana, Pennsylvania, Arizona, Montana, Illinois, California, Oregon, Wyoming, Minnesota, Idaho, New Hampshire and Wisconsin.

§ 8.4.1 Disproportionality Facts

The investigation and substantiation of child abuse and neglect is clearly the purview of state and county agencies charged with child and community safety. However, attorneys who represent children, parents, and caretakers—along with judges who are responsible for monitoring the safety, well-being, and permanency of each child—play a pivotal role in addressing disproportionality and the unequal treatment of children in care after the child and the family are under court supervision.

The following are of particular concern:

- • The length of time children of color remain in foster care, whether the case goal is reunification, guardianship, or adoption

- • The quality of the preparation and services provided to those children who will, by plan, emancipate at the age of majority

Finally, the research clearly supports the conclusion that the overrepresentation of children of color in foster care leads to and is indicative of unequal treatment (disparity of treatment). The Annie E. Casey Foundation and the U.S. Department of Health and Human Services reported that most Black children requiring intervention are placed in foster care, while most White children receive in-home services.[16] The first reports on length of time to reunification by race and ethnicity gleaned from the Child and Family Services Reviews shows that White children achieve permanency outcomes at a higher rate than children of color.[17] Recent research shows that

---

[16] Robert B. Hill, *Synthesis of Research on Disproportionality in Child Welfare: An Update* (Oct. 2006), pp.22–23, *available at* http://www.racemattersconsortium.org/docs/BobHillPaper_FINAL.pdf.

[17] CRS Report for Congress, *Child Welfare: State Performance on Child and Family Services Reviews* (June 2005), pp. CRS-60, CRS-61, *available at* http://www.policyarchive.org/handle/10207/bitstreams/2481.pdf.

disproportionality and the resultant unequal treatment has not changed since the 1990s. Robert Hill, PhD, of Westat, reviewed current and historical data, including data gleaned from the Department of Health and Human Services child and family services reviews. The report reveals:[18]

- White and Asian/Pacific Islanders are less likely to be investigated and substantiated for abuse and neglect, and these children are less likely to be placed in foster care after abuse or neglect is substantiated.

- Nationally, Black and Native American parents and caretakers are twice as likely as White parents and caretakers to be investigated and substantiated for abuse and neglect, but their children are three or four times more likely than White children to be placed in foster care.

- Hispanics across the nation are less likely than Whites to be investigated or substantiated, but Hispanic children are somewhat more likely than White children to be placed in foster care.

- Even when risk factors such as poverty, substance abuse, parental employment readiness, and the availability of services needed to support the family are taken into consideration, race remains a strong predictor of reunification. In 2005, White children were about four times more likely to be reunified with their families than Black children.

- Race is not as great a predictor for Black and White children exiting the system through adoption; however, adoptions took longer to finalize for Black children than for White children.

Finally, in 2007, the U.S. Government Accountability Office reported the findings of a survey of 21 state agencies in which social workers and administrators reported the following as strong contributors to disproportionality and disparities in treatment, services, and outcomes for children of color in the child welfare system:[19]

- Poverty, which increases the contacts of children and families with social and other government agencies

- Challenges to accessing services in impoverished communities including housing, mental health services, and substance abuse treatment

- Racial bias or cultural misunderstanding among decision-makers including social workers, attorneys, and judges

---

[18] Robert B. Hill, *Synthesis of Research on Disproportionality in Child Welfare: An Update* (Oct. 2006), pp. 22–23, *available at* http://www.racemattersconsortium.org/docs/BobHillPaper_FINAL.pdf.

[19] U.S. Government Accountability Office, Report to the Chairman, Committee on Ways and Means, House of Representatives, GAO-07-816, *African American Children in Foster Care, Additional HHS Assistance Needed to Help States Reduce the Proportion in Care*, p. 1, (2007), *available at* http://www.gao.gov/new.items/d07816.pdf.

§ 8.5 The Players

The greatest challenge facing attorneys is the development of a professional framework rooted in law to recognize when the attorney's individual perceptions and assumptions of cultural and subcultural context are getting in the way of effective advocacy and decision-making. In most areas of the law, the assumptions and perceptions of attorneys and judges are of little if any consequence because resolution of the issues before the court depends on the application of the law to the facts of the case.

In abuse and neglect cases, the law also rules, but the facts are always colored by cultural and subcultural context. Once the law is applied, case resolution depends on the appropriate application of the cultural and subcultural context that is wrapped around each child, each parent, and each permanent placement family. Although an adversarial stance is required at various stages in child abuse and neglect proceedings, attorneys who are successful are also able to create a cooperative, problem-solving atmosphere while keeping in mind the context of the children and their families.

§ 8.5.1 Parents' Attorney

Parents' attorneys serve as advocates and counselors. As advocate, the attorney guides the parent in making choices early in the case in the hopes that those choices will facilitate rebuilding family and the return of the child to the home. As counselor, the attorney encourages parents to put aside their reactions and feelings that "they took my child" so the rebuilding process can begin immediately.

§ 8.5.2 Child's Attorney/Guardian Ad Litem

Assisting the court as representative of the child is a powerful position with an awesome responsibility. If that representative does not understand how to evaluate and use cultural and subcultural context in performing these responsibilities, the child is disserved. Consider this: How can the attorney purport to speak for the child when the attorney does not understand who the child is? If the attorney is to advocate for the best interests of the child, under whose norms or standards will "best interests" be defined?

There are no clear-cut answers to these questions. Good practice requires that each attorney acting as a child's representative understand who the child is and what the child's context is. In short, the child's attorney has a special duty that requires constant self-awareness and the ability to set aside one's background and discern what is important to a child who may not be able to define what is important for himself or herself.

The exploration of cultural and subcultural context is not as complex as it may seem. The information that follows is designed to help attorneys develop a framework for understanding cultural context in abuse and neglect cases.

§ 8.6 Eliminating Assumptions and Perceptions

The critical issue for attorneys—whether they represent the agency, children, or adults—is understanding their own cultural and subcultural assumptions and perceptions. Once there is an awareness of one's perceptions and assumptions about race, religion, poverty, substance abuse, mental illness, and other cultural and subcultural markers, attorneys must let those assumptions and perceptions give way to a methodical approach to questioning the reality of the lives of the children, parents, and caretakers that the attorneys serve.

§ 8.6.1 Beginning the Process

Creating a balance between cultural context and compliance with the law at every stage of abuse and neglect proceedings is a challenge. The populations that are frequently before the court in these matters are overwhelmingly poor. They have less education. They are often mentally ill or developmentally delayed. Many cannot read or write. Many do not speak English. Many are immigrants. Yet each has a unique family system and structure that may not mirror the personal histories of the lawyers who represent them. The following principles apply to all:

- Each family is unique.
- Each family is different in key aspects of each family member's life.
- The solutions needed to repair the family or to successfully move toward adoption, guardianship or an alternate plan must be based on a clear and careful examination of family differences and family uniqueness.
- To accomplish permanency for children, attorneys must develop a disciplined method of questioning the facts in each case to determine what role culture plays throughout each phase of the abuse and neglect proceedings.

The first step in the examination process requires that the scope of relevant facts be expanded to include the total life experiences of adults and children before the court.

The principles guiding the examination are:

- *Culture does not shape the law within the abuse and neglect framework.* Rather, cultural and subcultural context provide a backdrop upon which judges, attorneys, and social service agencies can determine the levels of service, the types of services, and the anticipated impact of those services on the outcome of each case.

- *Cultural context encompasses more than race and ethnicity.* Other areas that must be explored in each case are: economic status, literacy, language, immigration status, mental and physical disabilities, education, gender, age, and sexual orientation.

- *Learning a few generalizations about the characteristics of African-Americans, Hispanics, Asians, Native Americans, or the poor does not meet the requirements for working within cultural context.* Rather, learning to question why parents or children respond the way they do will lead to an effective use of cultural and subcultural context.

- *Cultural and subcultural context must be explored through methodical questioning.* The facts of abuse and neglect must be balanced against the law with a constant eye on the impact of culture and subculture in shaping the permanency outcome.

- *Cultural and subcultural context requires an understanding of when and how cultural factors affect the way families function.* Examine each family with the assumption that each is a unique entity working within its own environment, which is affected by race, economics, language, disabilities, and more.

§ 8.6.2 Begin at the Commencement of the Case

Attorneys are in a unique position to lead the assessment of the cultural and subcultural context as each case moves from petition through permanency. Attorneys cannot assume that cultural and subcultural context is the purview of the social workers just because they are specially trained in working with people. Attorneys must look at cultural and subcultural context as a critical element in their management of each case. Whether advocating for the child or representing the parent, the context of the client must be in the forefront to determine whether reunification is in the best interest of the child or whether adoption, guardianship or an alternate plan are appropriate. It is through the examination of cultural and subcultural context that attorneys, judges and social workers can evaluate the individual service needs of each family member and determine whether the services will be effective based on the individual needs of each family member.

Central to the ability of attorneys to address the issues raised through the examination of cultural and subcultural context is the need to look beyond what we know through our personal life experiences. Attorneys must develop a method of interacting, assessing, and communicating with children and families through a methodical questioning process that assumes there is validity in examining the total family environment in each case to determine how we can assist families toward permanency without negating their histories. Judges, commissioners, and referees must ask the questions that may not be asked by the attorneys, social workers, or other professionals so that cultural and subcultural context is applied appropriately during all phases of each case.

§ 8.7 The Questioning Process

Applying cultural context to child abuse and neglect cases is a complex process. It requires:

- Knowledge of the overall community and the resources available to children and families in their communities of origin

- Understanding of the meaning of community diversity and what community diversity means to those children and families

- Understanding how culture and subculture affect the ability of children and families to participate in the rehabilitation process and achieve permanency while ensuring the well-being and safety of each child

§ 8.7.1 At the Initial Hearing

From the instant a case is petitioned, the court's goal must be to remove the child from neglectful or abusive relationships without removing the cultural context that may be at the heart of the child's sense of self. At the initial hearing, decisions are made regarding where the child should be placed. The court enters orders to initiate services for the family and the child. Often these processes occur with little chance for a full investigation of the social and emotional status of the parents and the children. The quality of the questioning by the court, attorneys for the parties, and social workers between the initial hearing and disposition often have a greater impact on case resolution than at any other time in the proceedings.

CASE SCENARIO:

James is one of three children. He is five years old and has lived in his inner-city neighborhood his entire life. His mother allegedly beat him with a belt; marks were left on his back and legs. At the initial hearing, the mother is present. It is alleged that she beat her 5-year-old son, James, with a belt. Her attorney talks with her about the case and the case is called. The child is removed and placed in the home of an unrelated foster parent in a rural community about 50 miles from home. The guardian ad litem has not met with the child; however, the maternal grandmother tells her that the 5-year-old has physical and emotional issues. The grandmother is unable to care for the child. The plan: Once the mother is drug free, the child will be allowed to return home. The mother also must secure her GED.

The case plan does not explore or address the cultural and subcultural context of James' life. What information is missing that could be gleaned before, during and after the hearing to develop a sense of the cultural and subcultural context of the mother and child, and thus shape the case plan?

CULTURAL CONTEXT: There are no apparent issues of race, ethnicity, or religion.

SUBCULTURAL CONTEXT: Consider possible mental illness, emotional and developmental issues for parent and child, religion/faith community, and neighborhood.

Why is information regarding cultural and subcultural context needed at the initial hearing? The mother may be mentally ill or cognitively impaired, requiring more specialized treatment than is provided in a standard drug treatment program. If the mother begins and fails in an inappropriate program, the clock continues to tick, and reunification may become less and less likely as the mother moves from program to program or gives up because the services provided did not meet her specific needs. Without at least an inquiry about the child's functioning, the child may be placed inappropriately based on his functioning and also based on the impact of moving the child a distance from whatever level of security the child may have had in his home environment.

Examine the questions that should be asked to provide context.

THE QUESTIONS:

- *The child*: What is the child's relationship with the maternal grandmother and, though she cannot care for him, does she wish to be involved in his life? How? Does the child participate in a church? Do the foster parents participate in church? How important is church participation to the respondent? To his family? Can the family participate in ensuring that his connections to his church are maintained? Are the religious affiliations of the foster parent compatible with the church affiliation that the child is accustomed to? What issues should be addressed to ensure that the respondent, a city kid, is comfortable and feels safe in a rural environment 50 miles from home?

- *The mother*: Though drug addiction is not a subcultural context, other issues related to mental health and cognitive functioning are. Is the birth mother diagnosed with a mental illness? Is she literate? Is English her primary language? If she is not literate or is developmentally disabled, is the plan to secure a GED realistic in the context of her life and the timelines required under ASFA?

Even though the answers to these questions may not be available at the initial hearing, the mere questioning begins to shape services and case planning at the earliest possible point in the case. The goal in the questioning process is to address issues that may affect the well-being of the child when in foster care, and ensure that a realistic plan is developed to move toward return home because the birth mother is able to comply with the orders entered as early as the initial hearing.

§ 8.7.2 Between Disposition and the Permanency Hearing

Disposition—and the reviews that follow—is one of the most critical stages in abuse and neglect cases. The timelines for reunification are short; termination of parental rights may loom on the horizon; the child experiences many changes, including the loss of a parent figure in many cases and adjustment to new ways of living when the child is placed in a non-relative foster placement. Between removal and disposition, some children change placements multiple times. Each move affects the child in unique ways, and each move affects the ability of the attorneys, social workers, and judges to assure timely permanency as required by law. On the other hand, once disposition occurs, the court will regularly examine progress made by the parents to achieve the dispositional goal. Without an early examination of the cultural and subcultural context of the child's life and the parent's life, achieving permanency will become an elusive and somewhat painful process for all.

DISPOSITION CASE SCENARIO #1:

Joseph is a 15-year-old Vietnamese youth who resided with his mother, father and two siblings (ages 5 and 9) in a community that is primarily African American. Joseph called the authorities to ask that he and his siblings be removed. He says he cannot live with his dumb parents any longer. Joseph says his parents use drugs and, because of that, the family is facing eviction. He and his younger siblings were placed in a foster home in a predominantly White community in a different city than his home of origin. The goal at disposition is reunification for all three children. The birth mother speaks some English. The birth father does not speak English. The children speak both English and Vietnamese. The birth parents have substance abuse issues. For reunification to occur, the birth mother must secure housing, undergo drug treatment, and participate in individual and family therapy to address the domestic violence between the parents. The disposition hearing sets a six-month deadline for reunification. The birth mother says she will kick her drug habit on her own. The birth father claims he does not have a drug habit.

CULTURAL CONTEXT: Ethnicity and race (Vietnamese family).

SUBCULTURAL CONTEXT: Language barriers (internal and external to the family), possible mental health issues, literacy issues.

THE QUESTIONS:

- How do we determine whether traditional cultural practices should be a factor in the services that are provided to the family? Are there differences in the level of receptiveness to those services by the parents and each child?

- How do we determine what is an appropriate placement for an adolescent (family foster placement vs. group home setting) who is slowly losing the connection between the family's culture of origin and the adolescent's acculturation into American culture? Does the ethnic or racial composition of the foster home matter if a family setting is appropriate?

- How do we communicate with an adolescent when English is not the first language and nuances of communication are lost because of the lack of proficiency in English?

- What are Joseph's views of his culture of origin? Can his positive views be used to help him understand that he may be able to function in the world of his family's culture and in his new American world? How do we address the apparent lack of interest and disrespect that Joseph exhibits toward his culture of origin in a manner that will make it easier for him to "live in two worlds?"

- Can we identify service providers to assist in developing the service plan, explore the issues presented by Joseph and his family, and possibly provide direct services to this family beginning soon after the removal?

- Does the reunification plan include helping the birth parents understand and cope with Joseph's Americanized behaviors?

- What services will be needed to ensure a successful reunification for Joseph? Does the language spoken by the service provider matter? Who will provide the services, and will they be able to work effectively with Joseph and other family members?

- What will the parents need to help them understand the cultural and subcultural context of their son's life to ensure the success of the reunification effort?

- Are service providers who are experienced in working with these cultural issues available to work with the family consistently until permanency is resolved?

Clearly, there are no pat answers or cookie-cutter solutions to this scenario or those that follow. However, by simply raising the questions that arise from the facts of the case, the attorney will provide invaluable assistance to the court in setting realistic timeframes for reunification and defining the quality and type of service needed by the birth family. Raising the questions may assist in predicting issues that the children may face as the reunification effort progresses, and raising the questions early in the case reduces the likelihood that the issues will divert attention from rebuilding the family of origin on stronger footing to achieve the permanency goal. By raising the questions, the attorney has a basis to question whether the disposition plan should be the same for all three children or whether the time frame for reunification may differ based on the needs of each child.

Frequently, the failure to identify cultural and subcultural context derails or delays the achievement of permanency. Ultimately, the judicial officers who are responsible for the lives of the children and families must hold the child's attorney, the social worker, counsel for the birth parents where appropriate, agency counsel, and service providers accountable for ensuring that the questioning process is in full force at the disposition hearing—and at all subsequent permanency hearings.

THE GUIDELINES:

- Recognize that the cultural framework of each family of origin and each member of the family remains with each child no matter how long the youth is in foster care.

- While the child is in care, the cultural framework must continue to be nurtured or the child will lose an important part of who that child is, which will affect dispositional planning, permanency planning, and the child's well-being as the case moves forward.

- Question the cultural and subcultural context as early in the case as possible. Failing to address context at each stage may create safety issues for the respondent and missteps that will ultimately delay case resolution.

§ 8.7.3 Permanency Hearing Through Case Resolution

No matter how long a child has been away from his or her birth family, the reintegration into the family after foster care is often fraught with cultural and subcultural issues that were not explored while the family received reunification services. Joseph's case provides an example of the need to address cultural and subcultural issues immediately upon removal or state intervention. Take a look at Joseph's situation as permanency planning proceeds:

DISPOSITION CASE SCENARIO #1 (CONT.):

Joseph decides that he does not wish to return home even though his sister and brother will be going home in a few months. Joseph says he no longer considers himself Vietnamese. He is American. He also does not want to live in a White community because he is more comfortable around African Americans. A permanency plan must be developed for Joseph. The case has been open for 16 months.

Joseph's circumstances present a clear picture of the impact that failing to explore cultural and subcultural context can have on the resolution of the case.

THE QUESTIONS:

- The primary question: Is adoption an option for Joseph? Is there anyone who is a possible adoptive resource for him?

- What impact does Joseph's rejection of his culture of origin have on his continued relationship with his siblings? His parents?

- What is the view of adoption in the Vietnamese community?

- Would the change in the goal and identification of an appropriate pre-adoptive family have been easier if Joseph's familiarity and comfort with one culture (African Americans) had been taken into account at his—and his siblings'—placement in shelter care?

Questions like these are central to the effective exploration and preparation of children for any permanency plan. Failing to ask cultural and subcultural context questions can and does result in frustration during permanency planning, and it may mean the difference between successful resolution and continued foster care for some children.[20]

If reunification cannot be achieved and Joseph is to find permanency, attention must be focused on the best solution. It is never too late to begin the questioning process.

PERMANENCY PLANNING SCENARIO #1:

Mary is 16 years old. She was reared by her maternal grandmother who is a devoted member of a Christian church that requires strict adherence to the church leaders' interpretation of the Bible. The church also condones and encourages corporal punishment as a means of ensuring that children comply with the word of God and obey their caretakers. Mary, whose family is originally from the Dominican Republic, was removed from her grand-mother's care after her uncle beat her repeatedly, causing physical injury. Between the removal hearing and disposition, Mary told her social worker that she is in love with a girl in her class and has been attending a church that is open to gays and lesbians. Mary did not share this information with anyone else, and her guardian ad litem has recommended that Mary begin transitioning back home to her grandmother rather than remaining in a

---

[20] Forty-seven states, the District of Columbia, American Somoa, Guam, and the Northern Mariana Islands, Puerto Rico, and the Virgin Islands require that adolescents consent to their adoption. Twenty-three states and the Virgin Islands require 14-year-olds to consent; eighteen states, American Somoa, and Guam require consent from 12-year-olds; and seven states, the Northern Mariana Islands, and Puerto Rico require the consent of youth age 10 and above. Similar laws apply in custody and guardianship proceedings. For Native American children, when ICWA applies and the tribal court holds jurisdiction, the issue of whether an adolescent must consent to adoption, guardianship, or custody is based on the tribe's laws. In cases where the state has guardianship or custody of the adolescent, state consent laws apply.

group home placement. The social worker did not share the information regarding Mary's sexual orientation with the court, the GAL, the agency attorney, or the grandmother's attorney. The social worker believes Mary is going through a phase of sexual exploration that is not related to her family circumstances.

CULTURAL CONTEXT: Race and ethnicity (Hispanic/Dominican Republic); religious beliefs

SUBCULTURAL CONTEXT: Sexual identity; religious beliefs and practices.

THE QUESTIONS:

- What cultural and subcultural issues are paramount in planning for Mary's placement? Race and ethnicity? Religious beliefs and practices of Mary's family of origin? Mary's sexual identity? Mary's religious beliefs and practices? Is the context different for each member of this family?

- Does Mary wish to return home to her grandmother's care? What does she say she needs to make her feel safe if she returns home?

- How do we determine whether the family's strict adherence to their religious beliefs and practices may have contributed to Mary not being safe within her family of origin? Is the primary issue her sexual identity? Are they separate issues or inextricably linked?

- How can the issue of Mary's sexual identity be addressed with family members within either the racial/ethnic framework or the context of their religious beliefs?

- What role does the uncle played in the rearing of Mary? What role will he play if she is returned to her grandmother's care?

- What services are needed to prepare Mary for discussions with her grandmother and her uncle about her life choices, including her religious choices and her sexual identity?

- Can we identify service providers to help develop the service plan, explore the issues presented by Mary and her family, and possibly provide direct services to this family beginning soon after disposition?

- Does the reunification plan include helping Mary's family—including any extended family—understand her sexual identity as well as her choice of a house of worship? What services will the grandmother and uncle need to help them understand the cultural and subcultural context of Mary's life to ensure the success of a reunification effort if and when Mary agrees to return home to the family? What will the family need to help them build a new relationship with Mary if she chooses not to return home?

- What services will be needed to ensure a successful reunification for Mary? Does it matter which language the service provider speaks? Does it matter whether the service provider is Christian? Does it matter whether the service provider is Hispanic? Does it matter what the service provider, if Hispanic, is from the Dominican Republic, Puerto Rico, Cuba, El Salvador, etc.?

The complexities of cultural and subcultural context are evident in Mary's case. In fact, depending on who the analysis focuses on, the issues of gender, sexual identity, faith and race or ethnicity may rise to the level of cultural rather than subcultural context. For Mary, as an adolescent, the convergence of race and ethnicity, sexual identity, and religious beliefs may require a concerted effort to address these issues fully as Mary's cultural context. While the race and ethnicity and the mandates of the family's religious beliefs may be cultural for the grandmother and uncle, Mary's sexual identity may be subcultural in the context of the caretakers.[21]

PERMANENCY PLANNING SCENARIO #2:

Jeremiah is a 12-year-old African American who visits with his birth family occasionally. Substance abuse was the primary issue that led to the finding of neglect in his case. For two years, his goal has been adoption. He has been placed with one foster family since his removal. The foster parents are African American and they are Muslim. Jeremiah grew up participating in services with his grandmother, who is a Jehovah's Witness. The foster family has written a letter informing the agency that they intend to adopt Jeremiah even though he has stated he is not willing to explore adoption by the foster parents. In addition, he is not enthusiastic about meeting other prospective adoptive parents. The social worker recommends that Jeremiah's goal be changed to an Alternate Planned Permanent Living Arrangement so that he can remain with the current foster parents until he is emancipated.

CULTURAL CONTEXT: Religion (Muslim faith of the foster parents).

SUBCULTURAL CONTEXT: Religion (faith community of the family of origin).

THE QUESTIONS:

- Did anyone involved in the case know that Jeremiah was a Jehovah's Witness?

---

[21] *See* MIMI LAVER & ANDREA KHOURY, OPENING DOORS FOR LGBTQ YOUTH IN FOSTER CARE: A GUIDE FOR LAWYERS AND JUDGES (American Bar Association 2008).

- Was the Agency aware of the foster family's practices and beliefs before the placement?

- Were the foster parents provided with guidance regarding how to introduce their religious and cultural practices to Jeremiah before his placement? Has there been any discussion regarding his feelings about abandoning the religious experiences he had with his grandmother prior to his placement in foster care?

- Was there an opportunity for Jeremiah to learn about their practices and beliefs before he was placed in the home?

- Once he was in the family home did anyone discuss how Jeremiah felt about the Muslim faith? After he was placed in foster care, was he given an opportunity to participate in services and activities through his grandmother's church?

- Is Jeremiah's reluctance to be adopted by the foster parents based on their beliefs, practices, and traditions, or is it based on his conflicts regarding his birth family?

- Has anyone discussed the conflicts facing Jeremiah with his birth parents?

Because these cultural and subcultural context questions were not explored at the time of placement, the opportunity has more than likely been lost for this foster home to serve as the permanent placement should an Alternate Planned Permanent Living Arrangement be set as Jeremiah's permanency plan. Again, there are no pat answers or cookie-cutter solutions, and it is never too late to begin the questioning process.

PERMANENCY PLANNING SCENARIO:

Maria is a 10-year-old who was born in Mexico. She and her five siblings have been placed in a foster home where no one speaks Spanish. English is the second language for the children. They visit their birth mother weekly and attempt to keep up their native language skills during those visits. The adoption goal was set six months ago during the first permanency hearing and within weeks of their placement in the current foster home. The foster family has indicated an interest in adopting the children, but Maria is not interested. Recently, Maria informed the court that she does not want to remain in the home because the family does not allow the children to speak Spanish. Her siblings are three and four years old, and Maria does not want to leave her siblings.

CULTURAL CONTEXT: Ethnicity and race.

SUBCULTURAL CONTEXT: Language.

THE QUESTIONS:

- What can be done to resolve the issues presented for Maria and her siblings? Should there be a search for a placement that will respect the language and culture of all three children?

- What should be done to determine whether the pre-adoptive family has the capacity to view the children's culture and language with respect and allow them to continue to participate actively in that culture? Who will assess their capacity?

- Even with appropriate assessment and intervention, is it too late to rectify the situation for Maria? What will become the best permanency option for Maria and her siblings, and what interventions will be necessary to ensure that they can remain together and have a permanent home?

- Has the situation with the current foster parents affected Maria's interest in pursuing adoption as a goal, or is her refusal to participate in the adoption process based on her relationship with her birth mother?

- What harm will be caused to Maria if she is placed elsewhere and the younger children remain in the current foster home? What harm will be caused to the younger children if they remain in a home that does not value their heritage? What impact will this dynamic have on their overall development? What impact will the lack of respect for culture have on their relationships with each other and with Maria if she begins to resist remaining in the home as adoption plans progress?

- What is the family of origin's cultural view of adoption? Termination of Parental Rights?

Consider the following permanency scenarios:

- How do the cultural norms of the 7-year-old Native-American boy affect his ability to integrate into a new family structure and a new community that is primarily White and in a new state? What supports will be required if he is placed in a Caucasian family for adoption?[22]

---

[22] The Indian Child Welfare Act (ICWA), 25 U.S.C. §§ 1901–1963, governs jurisdiction for certain Native American children. ICWA is based on the recognition that child welfare officials and workers do not share the same values as Indian families and authorities. The Act requires the involvement of the tribe in decisions related to children and families and promotes the placement of Native American children with Native families. Two excellent resources for permanency planning for this population are NATIONAL COUNCIL OF JUVENILE AND FAMILY COURT JUDGES, INDIAN CHILD WELFARE ACT CHECKLIST, PERMANENCY PLANNING FOR CHILDREN DEPARTMENT (2003), and PERMANENCY PLANNING FOR CHILDREN DEPARTMENT, NATIONAL COUNCIL OF JUVENILE AND FAMILY COURT JUDGES, THE NATIVE AMERICAN RESOURCE DIRECTORY FOR JUVENILE AND FAMILY COURT JUDGES (2003). For a comprehensive discussion of ICWA, see B. J. JONES, KELLY GAINES-STONER & MARK TILDEN, THE INDIAN CHILD WELFARE ACT HANDBOOK: A LEGAL GUIDE TO THE CUSTODY AND ADOPTION OF NATIVE

- A 16-year-old girl from a farming community in the South is placed with a family in a metropolitan area in New York State. What assistance will this adolescent need to help her become acclimated to her new environment? What assistance will she and her new family need to help her adjustment in the home, at school, and in the community?

If attention is not paid to the cultural and subcultural context, opportunities are missed to ensure appropriate placement to meet the contextual needs of each child. Each of the reunification and adoption scenarios presented above rest on the edge of an alternate planned permanent living arrangement because cultural and subcultural context were not addressed early in the permanency planning process. What will be the goal for Maria, Jeremiah, and Joseph if the questions are not explored and issues resolved with an eye to cultural and subcultural context?

§ 8.7.4 APPLA is the Final Option

APPLA SCENARIO:

Catherine is 15 years old. She has been in foster care since she was 10. She has been involved in two failed attempts to reunify with her birth mother and has decided she does not wish to live with her mother. Catherine's family— maternal and paternal—are very religious. Over the past 18 months, she was placed successively with her maternal grandmother and a paternal aunt. Each relative asked for her removal because of the friends she associates with and her mode of dress. She says she is a lesbian, though she states she has never had a relationship with anyone. She is seriously depressed and has tested as mildly mentally retarded. The Agency has identified a foster home, but Catherine is not interested in placement in a family setting.

CULTURAL CONTEXT: Religion.

SUBCULTURAL CONTEXT: Sexual identity, mental health issues, emotional/ developmental issues, and faith/religion.

THE QUESTIONS:

- Can the social worker and the court ensure that Catherine is placed in a safe environment where she is able to grow into herself without feeling she is not a healthy person? If safety cannot be certain in a group setting, what discussions will the worker have with Catherine to determine whether she will agree to a foster home placement and under what circumstances?

AMERICAN CHILDREN (American Bar Association, 2d ed. 2008). The Indian Child Welfare Act is discussed in this book in Chapter 12.

- What role does faith play in Catherine's life? Is there a faith organization that will be accepting of Catherine where she can continue to maintain a faith connection despite her past rejection?

- Has anyone explored identifying a specialized placement for Catherine with a foster parent who has been trained in working with adolescents who have sexual identity issues?

- Has anyone explored whether a safe group setting can be identified that does not leave Catherine vulnerable to attack because of her dress, her friends and associates, and her intellectual functioning?

- What impact does Catherine's diagnosis as mildly mentally retarded have on her ability to process and advocate for herself regarding her sexual identity issues?

- Has Catherine been referred to community-based organizations that assist youth who are questioning their sexual identity? Has anyone helped Catherine identify a professional who can assist her in resolving the rejection that she has experienced from her family members because of her dress and her friends?

APPLA CASE SCENARIO:

Michael is a 17-year-old Native American who is under state court jurisdiction. The tribal court agreed to state jurisdiction because services were available through the state that would not have been available through the tribe. Michael was discharged from residential treatment six months ago. He has done well in his placement and in the community, and he is excelling in school. Michael, whose parents are deceased, remains connected to the tribe. The social worker who was assigned to the case two months ago reports to the court that she is frustrated because Michael seems to not be fully invested in his emancipation planning. He arrives late for critical meetings and can never look her in the eye. That behavior, she says, makes her believe she cannot trust him or the information he provides to her about his compliance with his Independence Transition Plan. She recommends that the court end supervision because Michael is not participating in the process and says that he has members of his tribe who will provide support for him once court supervision ends. The social worker has not met with any of Michael's support network from the tribe.

CULTURAL CONTEXT: Ethnicity and race.

SUBCULTURAL CONTEXT: Age and neighborhood.

THE QUESTIONS:

- Are the conclusions of the social worker based in reality or are they perceptions of Michael's presentation that do not reflect his involvement in his emancipation planning? Is there any relevance in knowing what specific tribe Michael is a member of and whether some of the social worker's complaints about him, such as eye contact and punctuality, are based on norms within his specific tribe?

- What can the court do to bring together Michael's supportive adults from the tribe to participate in the last year of planning for Michael and place his response in the process in the proper perspective so that Michael can be successful?

- How can Michael be encouraged to involve the tribe in the planning process? Who can help him in this process? Can the judge contact the tribal court to discuss Michael's situation and forge a partnership with the tribe, regardless of who has jurisdiction?

§ 8.8 Context and Reasonable Efforts

The examination of cultural and subcultural context helps judges determine whether reasonable efforts have been made to prevent removal, to reunify the family, or to achieve permanency in each case as required under the Adoption and Safe Families Act. If the services proposed at each stage of the case do not address the individual needs of the child and the family, it is questionable that the proffer that reasonable efforts have been made can support a finding of reasonable efforts under ASFA.

The answers to the questions posed in each scenario presented in this chapter may lead counsel for parents or children to conclude that the individual services needed to ensure the timely resolution of each case have not been provided and, therefore, that reasonable efforts have not been made.

In preparing for an examination of reasonable efforts in each case, most of the scenarios in this chapter provide issues that may allow attorneys to more effectively participate in shaping the court's response to the adequacy of services provided to children, parents, and caretakers while promoting safety and well-being for each child under court supervision. Reexamine each scenario and see whether the answers can lead to the framing of either a proffer of reasonable efforts or a proffer that reasonable efforts have not been made, and ponder whether there are any issues that should be addressed to inform the court's reasonable efforts findings and the orders to bring the case into compliance. A few points to ponder:

- What will happen if Mary is returned home to her grandmother because the social worker does not delve into her needs and the functioning of the family but rather concludes that Mary is just a rebellious teen who is exploring her sexuality?

- What will happen if Jeremiah and the pre-adoptive family are not provided interventions to address the issues of faith as an impediment to adoption early in the case?

- What will happen if Joseph's parents are not provided treatment for mental health issues and substance abuse by service providers who speak their language?

§ 8.9 Conclusion

The methodical questioning process presented here is designed to help attorneys ensure that the cultural and subcultural context of each child and each family is carefully considered at all stages of abuse and neglect proceedings. The methodical questioning approach provides an opportunity to explore the individual needs of children and parents if the time under court supervision is to result in the rehabilitation and restoration of family life or alternative placements when return home is not in a child's best interest.

Indeed, the exploration of cultural and subcultural context is a process that may also help shorten the time that youth remain in foster care, shorten the time that it takes to identify and complete adoptive placements or kinship placements, increase and encourage the involvement of birth fathers and their kin, and promote the successful emancipation of youth who will remain in foster care until they reach the age of majority. In some cases, the examination of cultural and subcultural context can mean the difference between a permanent home through reunification, adoption, or guardianship versus an Another Planned Permanent Living Arrangement.

The questions in each scenario clearly exhibit that by asking questions, attorneys, judges, and social workers begin to peel the onion to reach the core issues that may ensure that each child in foster care reaches permanency in a timely and appropriate manner.

Meanwhile, the answers that are developed through this methodical approach provide the fodder for uncovering the true mosaic of each child and each family so that the life-altering decisions that are made in abuse and neglect cases can begin to reflect the specific and unique needs and realities of each child and family.

These are the critical factors that ring true in all cases:

- There are numerous cultural and subcultural issues involved in each case. No one can decide which issue is paramount.

- The family defines which issues are paramount—even if the professionals believe the priorities set by the family do not comport with the professional's view of what will be required to achieve permanency. Attorneys, social workers, and judges will not be able to craft a plan that

will be successful without the understanding of the cultural and
subcultural context of the family and each member involved in the case.

In the end, by working with the cultural context of each child and adult in abuse and neglect cases, we will make the differences within our communities work to maximize the potential of each child and adult to rebuild their families or successfully move children to new families with their cultural and subcultural context in tact if reunification is not possible.

II. LEGAL FRAMEWORK

Chapter 9: The History of Child Welfare Law[*]

by Marvin Ventrell[1]

§ 9.1 Why History? Author's Note

History provides context and guidance for current decision-making. As practitioners and policy-makers, we make judgments each day for our court system and its litigants. These judgments can be informed by a sound working knowledge of past experience or they can be uninformed by neglect of history.

The lessons of history are the lessons of what has succeeded and what has failed. Our juvenile court history is replete with both. As professionals in the field, we should avoid the mistakes of the past. Above all, we should do no harm[2] to children and families, and our experience can help ensure that we do not. We now know that well-intentioned zeal to protect children can create a population without permanent homes, and our removal and reunification decisions are guided by this experience.

History also helps us create solutions. Experiential data informs good decision-making. Some "new ideas" may have succeeded before. Safe, anonymous infant abandonment locations such as fire stations, introduced in the 1990s, for example, were first used successfully in Sixth Century France where convents had receptacles for the safe abandonment of infants, and with maternal anonymity.

---

[*] This chapter, as modified, first appeared as a journal article commemorating the 100th anniversary of the Juvenile Court in, Marvin Ventrell, *Evolution of the Dependency Component of the Juvenile Court*, 49/4 Juv. & Fam. Ct. J. 17 (Fall 1998). It was reprinted in the first edition of this text. It has been revised by and is printed here with the permission of Marvin Ventrell.

[1] Marvin Ventrell, J.D., is the Executive Director of the Juvenile Law Society (JLS) in Denver, CO, www.juvenilelawsociety.org. He was the CEO of the NACC from 1994 to 2009.

[2] Ann Haralambie makes the apt analogy of this medical axiom to the practice of child welfare law in her book, THE CHILD'S ATTORNEY (American Bar Association 1993).

History can provide inspiration. It can be difficult to advocate for an unpopular or still developing remedy. Such was likely the case for attorney Amelia Dietrich Lewis who represented Gerry Gault in the mid 1960s. Ms. Lewis was on new legal ground when she demanded that her minor client be given a due process hearing before detention. It took Ms. Lewis's courage to give us the *Gault*[3] decision and its mandate of due process and the right to counsel for juveniles.

This chapter attempts to describe some history of the American Juvenile Court within the context of two competing ideological forces: outcome motivated problem solving and due process based advocacy. Attorneys representing children in delinquency and dependency actions in the pre-*Gault* era and the 1960s recall the practice of sitting down with the judge, unencumbered by bureaucratic process, and working out a resolution for a child. It is an attractive proposition. But these attorneys also report the unintended and sometimes harmful consequences of these "comfortable resolutions" and the difficulty of pursuing a remedy that was not amenable to consensus. These pre-*Gault* era court conventions, as contrasted with post-*Gault* era more formalized procedures, illustrate a fundamental context of the history of the juvenile court and beg the question: Do we serve children, families, and society through a legalized process that ensures rights but can restrict outcomes, or should we de-legalize procedures and focus on outcomes which seem best? History should provide some guidance.

§ 9.2 The Historical Context of Child Welfare Law: From Child Saving to Empowerment, from Cause to Profession[4]

"Child saving" is a term used to describe the work of late nineteenth-century social reformers who sought to "save" neglected, abandoned, and abused children from the effects of poverty largely brought on by the industrialization and urbanization of America.[5] The "saving" typically took the form of removal of poor children from their families and placement in reformatories where, through an inculcation of White, Protestant, middle class values, children, the child savers believed, could become proper citizens. Some of these children avoided lives of destitution because of the child savers, but there is also evidence that many children grew up without family in harsh environments that provided little respect for the individual or opportunity for quality of life.

The child savers' paternalistic and authoritarian methods do not necessarily withstand the scrutiny of modern progressive thought. While well intentioned, the

---

[3]   *In re* Gault, 387 U.S. 1 (1967).

[4]   This work has been adapted from its original form as published in *The Colorado Lawyer* at: Vol 32, No. 1 (Jan. 2003). *See* Marvin Ventrell, *From Cause to Profession: The Development of Children's Law and Practice*, 32/1 COLO. LAW. 65 (2003).

[5]   ANTHONY M. PLATT, THE CHILD SAVERS: THE INVENTION OF DELINQUENCY (1969, 1977).

child savers often exercised unbridled discretion over the lives of children and families. Due process of law was ignored and seen as an impediment to producing good outcomes. The child savers believed they knew what was best for children and had the right to implement it.

Given the benefit of historical hindsight, it is easy to criticize the child savers as self-important and misguided. Yet their sympathy for the plight of children was real and formed the basis for the child advocacy movement of the twentieth century. They were the early child advocates from which current child welfare practice has grown. They identified a cause that has now become a profession.

As we work to improve the practice of child welfare law in the twenty-first century, we should be both students and critics of the child savers. We are moved to action by the same sympathy for the plight of children in need of care, yet the experience of over a century has taught us that children deserve more than sympathy. Children also deserve fair processes that respect their autonomy and dignity as individuals, family members, and rights-based American citizens. The lesson of *In re Gault*[6] in the development of juvenile delinquency law is that due process, more than benevolent intentions, produces fair outcomes. The *Gault* decision exposed the myth of child saving and the inherent abuses of a system without due process, which ignores the rights of the individual for the proclaimed "good of the individual."

The development of the practice of law for children is very much about the development of children from a sympathetic underclass worthy of welfare to a rights-based citizenry, capable of demanding justice through due process.[7] Children at the opening of the twenty-first century certainly do not, and most would agree should not, hold all of the rights of adults. But children have become something they were not in the nineteenth and much of the twentieth centuries—persons under the law who may demand certain things, including due process of law. This is important because the development of these rights gives rise to a legal profession to protect those rights. The historical development of children's rights teaches us a great deal about the relationship between our view of children and the quantity and quality of services we provide. Children's status can be viewed as a movement from children as property, to children as welfare recipients, to children as rights-based citizens. The degree of legal services available to children corresponds to these stages. Children viewed as property receive no legal services because property holders may do essentially as they wish with their property. Children as a welfare class will receive the services that the state chooses to grant. These services promote the state's interest or, at best, what the state views as the child's interest. But children as rights-based citizens are situated to receive the full benefit of independent legal counsel as they demand the enforcement of their rights.[8]

---

[6] 387 U.S. 1 (1967).

[7] Marvin Ventrell, *Preface, in* ROBERT C. FELLMETH, CHILD RIGHTS & REMEDIES: HOW THE US LEGAL SYSTEM AFFECTS CHILDREN (2002).

[8] *See* Marvin Ventrell, *The Practice of Law for Children*, 66 MONT. L. REV. 1 (2005).

Although children occasionally have been represented by legal counsel throughout American history, it was not until the 1960s and 1970s that we began to see a practice of law for children. A legal specialty requires a body of law at its base, and until society and the law began to view children as having protectable legal interests, there was not much for lawyers to do.

But as this body of law developed, a corresponding practice of law developed around it. The early child representatives were the lay advocates of the child saving movement. They were passionate advocates driven by a single-minded vision of what was best for children. They functioned without legal process or professional standards. While they undoubtedly helped many children, their service was limited. That changed with the development of proceedings based on due process and on federal and state child protection law. While it is true that there has been no *Gault* decision in the federal dependency context giving children a constitutional right to legal counsel,[9] the dependency system has become a process-based system that creates important work for the lawyers representing children, parents, and state agencies.

Child protection cases are now handled in a rights-based legal process where unrepresented parties do not fare well. Ours is a system premised on the notion that competing independent advocacy produces just results. Courts' decisions are only as good as the information on which they are based. Information comes to the court through the presentation of evidence by trained legal advocates. Litigants are not qualified to "speak for themselves" in this complex arena. Children in particular are unable to speak for themselves in court. They require legal counsel, particularly when one considers that the outcomes of these proceedings involve basic human needs, family relationships, and safety decisions that can be a matter of life and death.

The challenge to provide quality legal representation for children, parents, and agencies is enormous. Recent federal statistics show 3.2 million reports of child maltreatment involving 5.8 million children in 2007.[10] Approximately 794,000 of these cases were substantiated after investigation.[11] CAPTA mandates a representative for these children,[12] and many state laws require the child's representative to be an attorney.[13]

At the same time, child welfare law has become an increasingly complex area of practice that requires lawyers to not only understand complex federal and state law

---

[9] But see *Kenny A. ex rel. Winn v. Perdue*, 218 F.R.D. 277 (N.D. Ga. 2003), a class action suit brought by foster children in DeKalb and Fulton Counties in Georgia for the counties' failure to provide adequate and effective legal representation to children in their care. The federal district court of Georgia issued an order denying the defendants' motions for summary judgment on the grounds that dependent children in Georgia have both a statutory and constitutional right to counsel.

[10] U.S. Department of Health and Human Services, Administration on Children, Youth and Families, *Child Maltreatment 2007* (2009), p.5, *available at* http://www.acf.hhs.gov/programs/cb/pubs/cm07/cm07.pdf.

[11] *Id.*

[12] 42 U.S.C. § 5106a(b)(2)(A)(xiii).

[13] *See, e.g.*, COLO. REV. STAT. §§ 19-1-111, 19-1-103(59).

and procedure, but also detailed institutional information regarding child welfare funding streams, treatment and placement options, medicine, mental health, and child development. And all of this takes place in a context of devastating abuse, neglect, and poverty, which makes the work emotionally taxing.

What was once a cause has become a profession for highly trained and skilled attorneys. Child welfare law has arrived as a distinct legal specialty, as evidenced by the extensive body of state and federal law and procedure, law school curriculum, scholarship, continuing legal education, and national and state standards of practice for attorneys.

Yet the profession is still young and underdeveloped. Children are not simply small adults, and our assumptions and rules of lawyering are not automatically transferable to the child law context. The role and duties of the child's attorney are still developing. Likewise, the nuances of representing parents and state agencies present special challenges for the child welfare attorney.

§ 9.3 Juvenile Law

Juvenile law and the juvenile court are comprised of two distinct but historically related components: delinquency (juvenile justice) and dependency (child welfare).[14] Much has been written about the history of delinquency but very little about dependency. The history of child welfare law and the dependency side of the juvenile court are commonly seen as beginning with the anomaly of the child abuse case of "Little Mary Ellen" toward the end of the nineteenth century, followed many years later by society's recognition of child maltreatment in the 1960s, culminating in the federal Child Abuse Prevention and Treatment Act in 1974. Although these are significant events leading to the current child welfare system, they do not explain the whole story. The early juvenile court actually had a dependency component that evolved into the modern dependency system. That dependency component, like its delinquency counterpart, has a lengthy and important history. To more fully understand current child welfare law and policy and to inform system improvement, it is useful to know something about its development. What follows is primarily an attempt to summarize and give context to existing research[15] on the development of child welfare law and the dependency court.

---

[14] *See* Leonard P. Edwards, *The Juvenile Court and the Role of the Juvenile Court Judge*, 43/2 Juv. & Fam. Ct. J. 5 (1992).

[15] This analysis draws heavily on the scholarship of Sanford J. Fox (former Professor of Law, Boston College School of Law), Jean Koh Peters (Clinical Professor of Law, Yale University School of Law), John C. Watkins, Jr. (University of Alabama), Mason P. Thomas, Jr. (Professor of Public Law and Government, Institute of Government, University of North Carolina), and Douglas R. Rendleman (Professor of Law, University of Alabama School of Law).

§ 9.4 Dependency Court Jurisdiction

The dependency court is that part of the juvenile court that handles child maltreatment cases. A child who has been adjudicated maltreated or is under state custody is often referred to as a dependent child.[16] Child maltreatment is the general term used to describe all forms of child abuse and neglect that give rise to dependency court jurisdiction.[17] There is no one commonly accepted definition of child abuse and neglect. The federal government defines child abuse and neglect in the Child Abuse Prevention and Treatment Act (CAPTA) as "at a minimum, any recent act or failure to act on the part of a parent or caretaker, which results in death, serious physical or emotional harm, sexual abuse or exploitation, or an act or failure to act which presents an imminent risk of serious harm"[18] Each state provides its own definition of child abuse and neglect.[19] Child maltreatment encompasses physical abuse, sexual abuse, neglect, and emotional abuse, which can be defined as follows:

- *Physical Abuse*: Nonaccidental physical injury as a result of caretaker acts. Physical abuse frequently includes shaking, slapping, punching, beating, kicking, biting, and burning.[20]

- *Sexual Abuse*: Involvement of dependent, developmentally immature children and adolescents in sexual activities that they do not fully comprehend and to which they are unable to give informed consent. Sexual abuse includes touching, fondling, and penetration.[21]

- *Neglect*: Failure of caretakers to provide for a child's fundamental needs. Although neglect can include children's necessary emotional needs, neglect typically concerns adequate food, housing, clothing, medical care, and education.[22]

- *Emotional or Psychological Abuse*: The habitual verbal harassment of a child by disparagement, criticism, threat, and ridicule. Emotional or psychological abuse includes behavior that threatens or intimidates a child. It includes threats, name calling, belittling, and shaming.[23]

These categories make up the jurisdiction of the modern juvenile dependency court. The first juvenile court was founded in Chicago in 1899, and the dependency

---

[16] *See* INGER SAGATUN & LEONARD EDWARDS, CHILD ABUSE AND THE LEGAL SYSTEM 17 (1995).

[17] *Id.*

[18] 42 U.S.C. § 5106(g)(2) (2004).

[19] *See*, 1 NAT'L CENTER ON CHILD ABUSE AND NEGLECT, CHILD ABUSE AND NEGLECT STATE STATUTES SERIES (1997), for a compilation of state maltreatment statutes.

[20] KIM OATES, THE SPECTRUM OF CHILD ABUSE (1996); *see also* INGER SAGATUN & LEONARD EDWARDS, CHILD ABUSE AND THE LEGAL SYSTEM 17 (1995).

[21] KIM OATES, THE SPECTRUM OF CHILD ABUSE (1996).

[22] *Id.*

[23] *Id.*

categories then were quite different.[24] The word "abuse" does not appear in the act, although parental neglect and cruelty are mentioned. While with a little ingenuity, modern categories of child abuse and neglect can be made to fit the 1899 categories, the jurisdictional dependency language of the early court suggests a different emphasis. Tracking the evolution of current dependency court jurisdiction begins with a review of the historical treatment of children.

§ 9.5 Origins of Child Maltreatment and Protection

§ 9.5.1 Maltreatment

In 2007, there were an estimated 3.2 million referrals involving the alleged maltreatment of approximately 5.8 million children.[25] Approximately 62% of these referrals were investigated, and 794,000 children were confirmed victims of child maltreatment.[26] As a result of child welfare system action, approximately 500,000 children live in foster care.[27] Nearly half of these children are in non-relative foster care.[28] Forty percent of foster children are between the ages of 13 and 21, and each year over 20,000 young adults age out of the foster care system.[29] The average time spent in foster care is significant and varies by state.[30] More than 20% of children in care move at least three times and there are many instances of children moving seven or more times.[31] In 2001, approximately 65,000 children experienced termination of parental rights.[32]

The foregoing snapshot of America's maltreated children reveals the critical need for improved child advocacy. For those children receiving foster care services in 2007, best estimates are that court action, requiring the appointment of a CAPTA

---

[24] *See* § 9.5.6 for a detailed discussion of the dependency categories of the 1899 court.

[25] U.S. Department of Health and Human Services, Administration on Children, Youth and Families. *Child Maltreatment 2007* (2009), p.xii, *available at* http://www.acf.hhs.gov/programs/cb/pubs/cm07/cm07.pdf.

[26] *Id.* at p.5.

[27] Child Welfare Information Gateway, *Foster Care Statistics* (2009) , *available at* http://www.childwelfare.gov/pubs/factsheets/foster.cfm#child.

[28] *Id.*

[29] The PEW Charitable Trusts, *Time for Reform: Preventing Youth from Aging Out on Their Own* (Sept. 2008), *available at* http://kidsarewaiting.org/tools/reports/files/Aging-Out-2008AL.pdf, (citing M. B. Kushel, I. H. Yen, L. Gee & M. E. Courtney, *Homelessness and Health Care Access After Emancipation: Results From the Midwest Evaluation of Adult Functioning of Former Foster Youth*, 161/10 ARCH. PEDIATR. ADOLESC. MED. 986 (2007).

[30] See the "Foster Care Fact Sheets" prepared by the National Resource Center for Permanency and Family Connections, detailing foster care statistics for each state and the District of Columbia, *available at* http://www.hunter.cuny.edu/socwork/nrcfcpp/info_services/fact-sheets.html.

[31] Kathy Barbell & Madelyn Freundlich, *Foster Care Today*, p. 3–4 (Casey Family Programs 2001). These figures were based on 1994 data from the U.S. House of Representatives, 2000.

[32] U.S. Department of Health and Human Services, Children's Bureau, *The AFCARS Report #8* (March 2003), *available at* www.acf.dhhs.gov/programs/cb/publications/afcars/report8.htm

compliant attorney, CASA, or GAL (attorney or lay) occurs in approximately 43% of cases affecting more than 53,000 children.[33]

Child maltreatment was appropriately described by the U.S. Advisory Board on Child Abuse and Neglect as a national emergency to which inadequate attention and resources are paid.[34] Child maltreatment is not a recent phenomenon, nor is it unique to certain nations and cultures.[35] It appears children have always been abused and neglected.[36] A number of essays on child maltreatment have included the familiar quote by Lloyd deMause:

> The history of childhood is a nightmare from which we have only recently begun to awaken. The further back in history one goes, the lower the level of child care, and the more likely children are to be killed, abandoned, beaten, terrorized, and sexually abused.[37]

One the one hand, history seems to bear out deMause. History is replete with incidents of infanticide, sexual abuse, beatings, and inadequate responses to these tragedies.[38] At the same time, it is a mistake to assume that the history of childhood has been a nightmare for most children or that significant efforts have not been made to protect children. To the contrary, one can make the case, as does John E.B. Myers, that history shows continual humanitarian progress to value and protect children. Professor Myers begins his recent book on the history of child protection as follows:

> Throughout history, parents adored their children. Something deep within us created a bond between parent and child; a bond that is without parallel in human experience. Because of this bond, and for other reasons as well, the vast majority of parents do not abuse or neglect their children. Competent parenting is the rule, abuse and

---

[33] See the "Foster Care Fact Sheets" prepared by the National Resource Center for Permanency and Family Connections, detailing foster care statistics for each state and the District of Columbia, *available at* http://www.hunter.cuny.edu/socwork/nrcfcpp/info_services/fact-sheets.html.

[34] U. S. Advisory Board on Child Abuse and Neglect, *Child Abuse and Neglect: Critical First Steps in Response to a National Emergency* (National Clearinghouse on Child Abuse and Neglect Information, Aug. 1990).

[35] Robert W. ten Bensel et al., *Children in a World of Violence: The Roots of Child Maltreatment, in* THE BATTERED CHILD 3, 3–5 (Mary Edna Helfer et al. eds., 5th ed. 1997).

[36] *Id.*

[37] Lloyd deMause, *The Evolution of Childhood, in* THE HISTORY OF CHILDHOOD 1 (Lloyd deMause ed., 1995).

[38] Lloyd deMause, *The Evolution of Childhood, in* THE HISTORY OF CHILDHOOD 1 (Lloyd deMause ed., 1995); William L. Langer, *Foreword, in* THE HISTORY OF CHILDHOOD i, i–ii (Lloyd deMause ed., 1974); Robert W. ten Bensel et al., *Children in a World of Violence: The Roots of Child Maltreatment, in* THE BATTERED CHILD 3, 4–5 (Mary Edna Helfer et al. eds., 5th ed. 1997).

neglect the exception. . . . Efforts to protect children from abuse and neglect are as old as maltreatment itself.[39]

These two views are entirely reconcilable. From the perspective of education and awareness, it is necessary to point out the horrors of child maltreatment and society's inadequate response. At the same time, we should be mindful that most children are not abused or neglected and that while we are not there yet, great strides have been made in child protection.

§ 9.5.2 Child Protection

Before the sixteenth-century legal and humanitarian efforts to protect maltreated children were minimal. To the extent that services or prohibitions against maltreatment were afforded to children, the work was private or church driven. A review of some historic pro-child developments does reveal a gradual increase in child protection and children's rights. Robert W. ten Bensel[40] reports that esteem for the child slowly began to appear in the following historic events:

- The Bible commands, "Do not sin against the child" (Gen. 42:22).
- The laws of Solon, in 600 B.C., required the commander of an army to protect and raise, at government expense, children of citizens killed in battle.
- Athens and Rome had orphan homes.
- The Christian church fathers in the fourth century, in line with the Judaic injunction "Thou shalt not kill," equated infanticide with murder. A succession of imperial edicts after that guaranteed a child's right to life.
- Orphanages were mentioned in 529 in the laws of Justinian.
- By the sixth century, the "orphanage" at Trier included a marble receptacle in which a child could be safely deposited.
- The first foundling hospital was established in Milan in 787.
- Pope Innocent III started the Hospital of the Holy Spirit in 1066.
- A foundling hospital was established in Florence in 1444, and was known as the Hospital of the Innocents.
- Vincent de Paul established a foundling hospital in Paris in 1650 when he became concerned about the children abandoned on the steps of Notre Dame.

While these events may in some way represent the origins of modern child protection, it is difficult to argue that children's status, even as late as the sixteenth

---

[39] John E. B. Myers, A History of Child Protection in America 17 (2004).

[40] Robert W. ten Bensel et al., *Children in a World of Violence: The Roots of Child Maltreatment, in* The Battered Child 3, 16–21 (Mary Edna Helfer et al. eds., 5th ed. 1997).

and seventeenth centuries, was such that children were meaningfully protected from maltreatment. The family's autonomy to do essentially as it saw fit with its children was untouched. The first direct link with juvenile dependency court protections appears in sixteenth-century England.

§ 9.5.3 Sixteenth- and Seventeenth-Century England: Creation of a System of Family Law

The development of American family law most likely has its origins in the sixteenth and seventeenth centuries, when society moved from communal living arrangements to family groups.[41] From there, it is argued that the relationship of those family groups to the church and state, and the institutions that resulted from them, form the basis of the law that led to the creation of the juvenile court.[42] This period is characterized by nonintervention into the family except to the extent a driving social policy warranting intervention arose.[43] The two driving policies that justified intervention were the regulation of poverty and the regulation of wealth.

Jacobus tenBroek describes the family law of sixteenth- and seventeenth-century England as a "dual system."[44] More recently, Jean Koh Peters has supplemented this analysis by reviewing the theory of the dual system of family law in the context of the development of child protection law.[45] The theory of the dual system of family law is that, to the extent that families of sixteenth- and seventeenth-century England experienced legal intervention, they experienced one of two distinct types of intervention according to their social class. On one side of the spectrum was a legal system designed to ensure the orderly passage of property of the rich. On the other side of the spectrum was a legal system of intervention designed to control the family relationships of the poor. In the middle were the majority of people who experienced no legal intervention into the accepted patriarchal system.[46]

Family Law for the Wealthy

The wealthy experienced no family intervention except to the extent that it was necessary to insure the passage of wealth. The state had an interest in taxing the transfer of property from one generation to the next. Under primogeniture, court or crown involvement was generally unnecessary. However, where a patriarch died prior to his heir's majority, or where there was a dispute as to the identity of the heir or the

---

[41] *See* Douglas R. Rendleman, *Parens Patriae: From Chancery to the Juvenile Court,* 23 S.C. L. REV. 205 (1971) (tracing the evolution of the juvenile court system from feudal England to modern times).

[42] *See, e.g., id.*

[43] JEAN KOH PETERS, REPRESENTING CHILDREN IN CHILD PROTECTIVE PROCEEDINGS: ETHICAL AND PRACTICAL DIMENSIONS app. (2d ed. 2001).

[44] Jacobus tenBroek, *California's Dual System of Family Law: Its Origin, Development and Present Status* (pt. 1), 16 STAN. L. REV. 257, 257–58 (1964).

[45] JEAN KOH PETERS, REPRESENTING CHILDREN IN CHILD PROTECTIVE PROCEEDINGS: ETHICAL AND PRACTICAL DIMENSIONS app. (2d ed. 2001).

[46] *Id.*

character of land tenure, the crown became interested in the child to ensure proper passage of wealth and to collect tax on the property. It is in these proceedings that we first see the appointment of a representative for the child in the form of the guardian ad litem.[47]

Family Law for the Poor

As the chancery court was deciding the property and custody issues of the aristocracy, a statutory scheme dealing with the custody of poor children was developing.[48] Two concepts began to emerge in sixteenth-century England out of what became the Elizabethan Poor Laws, which serve to connect this period in history to the juvenile court. The first is the government's assumption of the authority and obligation to care for poor children as a kind of ultimate parent. The second is the mechanism of apprenticeships as a means of that parentage.

At the decline of the feudal age, motivated by the emergence of an underclass of poor children, and the vagrancy and crime attributed to the poor, combined with the post reformation decline of the church as an instrument of social welfare, Parliament passed the Statute of Artificers[49] in 1562 and later the Poor Law Act of 1601.[50] The Statute of Artificers provided that poor children could be involuntarily taken from their parents and apprenticed. The Poor Laws were a series of statutes authorizing the removal of poor children from their parents at the discretion of overseer officials and the "bounding out" of children to a local resident as an apprentice until the age of majority.[51] In addition to this forced labor, the Poor Laws also provided for cash for those unable to work.[52] These laws resulted in considerable family intervention and are seen as the beginning of "state-run welfare."[53]

The Elizabethan state-run welfare program was cleverly structured without state funding. The law provided that each community, through its parish, would administer the law by providing relief, removing children, apprenticing children, and using punishment.[54] Peters points out that the Poor Laws effected the poor in three basic ways:[55]

---

[47] *Id.*

[48] *See, e.g.,* Douglas R. Rendleman, *Parens Patriae: From Chancery to the Juvenile Court,* 23 S.C. L. Rev. 205, 210 (1971).

[49] 5 Eliz. c. 4 (1562).

[50] 43 Eliz. c. 2 (1601).

[51] Jacobus tenBroek, *California's Dual System of Family Law: Its Origin, Development and Present Status* (pt. 1), 16 Stan. L. Rev. 257, 279–82 (1964).

[52] Douglas R. Rendleman, *Parens Patriae: From Chancery to the Juvenile Court,* 23 S.C. L. Rev. 205, 211 (1971).

[53] Jean Koh Peters, Representing Children in Child Protective Proceedings: Ethical and Practical Dimensions 238 (2d ed. 2001).

[54] 43 Eliz. c. 2 s.1. (1601).

[55] Jean Koh Peters, Representing Children in Child Protective Proceedings: Ethical and Practical Dimensions 239–40 (2d ed. 2001).

1. *Labor.* The Poor Laws controlled labor of the poor in the following ways:

   - By mandating that an unmarried laborer could not refuse work in his apprenticed trade.
   - Laborers' wages were capped.
   - Women who labored had to be over 12, under 40, and unmarried.
   - There were to be restrictions on both apprenticeship and laboring.
   - Rules were to be adopted regarding the dismissal of an apprentice.
   - The apprenticing of nonpoor children was to be regulated by provided rules.

2. *Travel.* Poor persons' travel and residency were restricted in these ways:

   - Poor persons were often restricted from moving to healthier economies.
   - The parish had the authority to remove the poor.
   - Regulations determined who were local and foreign and not the responsibility of the parish.

3. *Family Support.* The Poor Laws shaped family life for poor persons by:

   - The doctrine of intra-familial support that demanded three generations of ascending and descending support, mandating parental support of children.
   - Restricting the freedom of the poor to marry through tactics to prevent the poor from marrying and producing children.
   - Restricting a poor woman's right to bear children through bastardy laws that could result in punishments for mothers of illegitimate children of up to one year labor in a house of corrections.[56]

It is generally accepted that the Poor Laws authorized significant intervention into the lives of the poor in exchange for poverty relief. In truth, the Poor Laws served less as a system of welfare and more as a mechanism of social control of the poor.[57]

In a frequently used quote, William Blackstone summarized the dual system of family law and the rise of the state as the ultimate parent:

> Our laws, though their defects in this particular cannot be denied, have in one instance made a wise provision for breeding up the rising generation; since the poor and laborious part of the community, when past the age of nurture, are taken out of the hands of their parents, by the statutes for apprenticing poor children; and are placed out by the

---

[56] Mothers could also be forced to pay relief to the state for having an illegitimate child and then receive no state assistance with which to feed the child. This practice led to an increase in infanticide, which was itself punished. *Id.* at 249 n.76 (quoting PETER C. HOFFER & N. E. HULL, MURDERING MOTHERS: INFANTICIDE IN ENGLAND AND NEW ENGLAND, 1558–1803 (1981)).

[57] *Id.* at 241.

public in such manner, as may render their abilities . . . of the greatest advantage to the commonwealth. The rich indeed are left at their own option, whether they will breed up their children to be ornaments or disgraces to their family.[58]

§ 9.5.4 Colonial America: Transplanting and Developing the English System

The English dual system of family law was transplanted with the colonists into seventeenth- and eighteenth-century America[59] and then modified in a number of ways.[60] For the majority of colonists, there continued to be little or no intervention into patriarchal, autonomous family life. Only the rich and poor were affected, and the rich only minimally. In fact, it is argued that the system for the rich in colonial America is characterized by even less intervention than occurred in England. Peters argues that the American colonists actually expanded the autonomous, nuclear patriarchal family for the nonpoor through two major changes:

1. *Abolition of Feudal Land Tenures*. The most significant example of this was the creation of private bequeathal such that property passed not by primogeniture, but by the choice of the testator. In this way, the transfer of property bypassed any feudal structure that ensured payment of taxes to the government.

2. *Private Property Matters in Secular Chancery Courts*. Correspondingly, private property matters were taken away from church or crown control and placed in local secular chancery courts.

These actions seem consistent with the view that colonists settled America in rejection of excessive governmental and religious intervention into their lives.[61]

The English Poor Law, however, was transplanted firmly into the colonies and even enhanced. Mobility restrictions were transplanted as part of the colonial poor laws. The New Plymouth code required settlements to take responsibility for their poor and restrict settlement; the Massachusetts Bay code prohibited new settlers coming in without town council approval; Connecticut codes required proof of

---

[58] *Id.* at 235 (quoting WILLIAM BLACKSTONE, COMMENTARIES ON THE LAWS OF ENGLAND 452 (1826)); *see also* Douglas R. Rendleman, *Parens Patriae: From Chancery to the Juvenile Court,* 23 S.C. L. REV. 205, 211 (1971).

[59] Stefan A. Riesenfeld, *The Formative Era of American Public Assistance Law,* 43 CAL. L. REV. 175, 177–78 (1955).

[60] Douglas R. Rendleman, *Parens Patriae: From Chancery to the Juvenile Court,* 23 S.C. L. REV. 205, 211 (1971); JEAN KOH PETERS, REPRESENTING CHILDREN IN CHILD PROTECTIVE PROCEEDINGS: ETHICAL AND PRACTICAL DIMENSIONS 242 (2d ed. 2001).

[61] JEAN KOH PETERS, REPRESENTING CHILDREN IN CHILD PROTECTIVE PROCEEDINGS: ETHICAL AND PRACTICAL DIMENSIONS 242 (2001); *see* John Seymour, *Parens Patriae and Wardship Powers: Their Nature and Origins,* 14 OXFORD J. LEGAL STUD. 159, 164–65 (1994); HASSELTINE BYRD TAYLOR, LAW OF GUARDIAN AND WARD 23–24 (1935).

property ownership for settlement; and New York provided relief to poor nonresidents only if they brought proof that their community had no funds to support them.[62]

Involuntary apprenticeship of poor children became an integral part of colonial North American Poor Law.[63] Such apprenticeships were frequently used throughout the colonies.[64] Douglas Rendleman makes the case that it is at this point we see an enhancement of English Poor Law into a "poor plus" system.[65] In eighteenth-century Virginia for example, children could be removed and apprenticed not only because of their poverty but because their parents were not providing "good breeding, neglecting their formal education, not teaching a trade, or were idle, dissolute, unchristian or uncapable."[66] Rendleman suggests this is an example of the state's belief that poor children needed to be protected, not just from poverty, but from certain environmental influences commonly associated with the poor.[67] Apprenticeships were in many ways the ideal anchor in the poor law system because the child paid his or her own way, the child was trained in skilled labor, relief costs were kept down, and society experienced reduced idleness and unemployment.[68] As a reflection of the state in the role of beneficent ultimate parent, however, the system left much to be desired, since the quality of the child's care was suspect and the child operated frequently as nothing more than a slave subject to a business proposition.[69]

In addition to Rendleman's "poor plus" modification of the dual system of family law, Peters has suggested that an additional condition unique to the colonies created a third system of family law for the black slave family.[70] Prior to the civil war, there was no legal recognition of the black slave family. Legally, blacks were not persons, but were instead property of their masters, and secondarily subject to all White people.[71] Black men and woman living in a long-term committed relationship were not

---

[62] JEAN KOH PETERS, REPRESENTING CHILDREN IN CHILD PROTECTIVE PROCEEDINGS: ETHICAL AND PRACTICAL DIMENSIONS 243 (2d ed. 2001). For an examination of poor law statutes in the American colonies, see Judith Areen, *Intervention Between Parent and Child: A Reprisal of the State's Role in Child Neglect and Abuse Cases,* 63 GEO. L.J. 887, 899–900 (1975); Gerald L. Neuman, *The Lost Century of American Immigration Law 1776–1875,* 93 COLUM. L. REV. 1833, 1846 (1993); Stefan A. Riesenfeld, *The Formative Era of American Public Assistance Law,* 43 CAL. L. REV. 175, 206 & n.179, 212, 219 (1955).

[63] Stefan A. Riesenfeld, *The Formative Era of American Public Assistance Law,* 43 CAL. L. REV. 175, 214 (1955).

[64] MARCUS WILSON JERNEGAN, THE LABORING AND DEPENDENT CLASSES IN COLONIAL AMERICA, 1607–1783, at 157 (1960).

[65] Douglas R. Rendleman, *Parens Patriae: From Chancery to the Juvenile Court,* 23 S.C. L. REV. 205, 212 (1971).

[66] *Id.* at 212 (citing MARCUS WILSON JERNEGAN, THE LABORING AND DEPENDENT CLASSES IN COLONIAL AMERICA, 1607–1783, at 104, 151, 149, 161 (1960)).

[67] *Id.*

[68] *Id.*

[69] *Id.*

[70] JEAN KOH PETERS, REPRESENTING CHILDREN IN CHILD PROTECTIVE PROCEEDINGS: ETHICAL AND PRACTICAL DIMENSIONS 243 (2d ed. 2001).

[71] *Id.; see also* GEORGE M. STROUD, A SKETCH OF THE LAWS RELATING TO SLAVERY 154 (2d ed. 1856).

recognized as lawfully married, and therefore their children were considered illegitimate.[72]

Peters points out that it was even difficult for blacks to maintain a *de facto* family life because the White master exercised total control over the slave's education, labor, diet, living arrangements, mates, and children. The result was the creation of a unique "family relationship" in which slave families lived apart and children were regularly sold away from their biological parents. A third system of family law clearly did exist in the colonies as to black slave families, a system that prohibited traditional family relationships for an entire segment of society.[73]

While governmental intervention due to child abuse per se was exceptionally rare in colonial America, Robert Bremner has recorded three seventeenth-century American cases. The 1655 Massachusetts case of twelve-year-old apprentice John Walker who was killed by his master may be the first recorded American case of child abuse. John was brutally beaten and neglected until his death. His master was convicted of manslaughter. In addition, in Massachusetts, Samuel Morison in 1675 and Robert Styles in 1678 had their children removed by the court for failure to provide suitable homes.[74]

In summary, the developing American system of intervention into the life of the child was characterized by the absence of intervention except on very rare occasions or where the very poor were concerned. Family autonomy for the self-sufficient was paramount. The majority of children in Colonial America received no protection from abuse and neglect. The Massachusetts Stubborn Child Law of 1646, for example, even allowed parents to classify their child as stubborn and seek state punishment, including capital punishment.[75] In the case of the poor, the state felt authorized to remove poor children and apprentice them for the common good. It was in no way, however, a system designed to protect maltreated children, and little welfare was actually provided to children and their families in exchange for lost autonomy. This doctrine remained intact and was emulated in the states and territories of the west through the eighteenth century.[76]

---

[72] JEAN KOH PETERS, REPRESENTING CHILDREN IN CHILD PROTECTIVE PROCEEDINGS: ETHICAL AND PRACTICAL DIMENSIONS 243 (2d ed. 2001); *see also* HERBERT G. GUTMAN, THE BLACK FAMILY IN SLAVERY AND FREEDOM 1750–1925, 9 (1976).

[73] JEAN KOH PETERS, REPRESENTING CHILDREN IN CHILD PROTECTIVE PROCEEDINGS: ETHICAL AND PRACTICAL DIMENSIONS 245 (2d ed. 2001). Peters also points out the importance of studying this neglected area of the development of child intervention law as black families struggle for normalcy and develop family models following the civil war.

[74] 1 CHILDREN AND YOUTH IN AMERICA 41–42,123–24 (Robert H. Bremner ed., 1970).

[75] NATHANIAL B. SHURTLEFF, RECORDS OF THE GOVERNOR AND COMPANY OF THE MASSACHUSETTS BAY IN NEW ENGLAND 1628–1686, at 101 (1854).

[76] Douglas R. Rendleman, *Parens Patriae: From Chancery to the Juvenile Court,* 23 S.C. L. REV. 205, 212 (1971). For a discussion of specific jurisdictions, see, e.g., JOHN LEWIS GILLIN, HISTORY OF POOR RELIEF LEGISLATION IN IOWA (1914); ROBERT W. KELSO, HISTORY OF PUBLIC POOR RELIEF IN MASSACHUSETTS 1620–1920 (1922); ISABEL BRUCE & EDITH EICKHOFF, THE MICHIGAN POOR LAW (1936); Jacobus tenBroek, *California's Dual System of Family Law: Its Origin, Development and*

§ 9.5.5 Nineteenth-Century America: The Rise of the *Parens Patriae* System

Although children in the twentieth century existed as a recognized social class,[77] children first developed class identification in the nineteenth century. The child's identity as it developed was as both a resource and a danger to society.[78]

Major social change is a theme of the nineteenth century. Early nineteenth-century America was dominated by the "rural-communitarian-protestant triad."[79] That triad began to come apart in the nineteenth century with the industrialization and urbanization of America. Additionally, the industrialized urban areas became populated with European and Asian immigrants. An 1824 report concluded, for example, that there were approximately 9,000 children under age 14 living in poverty in New York State, and that three-fourths of the children receiving public relief were immigrant children.[80] The response to this condition gives rise to a special system for treatment of children.

The House of Refuge Movement

In response to the creation of the underclass of urban poor children, the House of Refuge Movement, a movement that has been called the first great event in child welfare, was launched.[81] The movement began with the Society for Prevention of Pauperism, which believed that poverty was a cause, if not the primary cause, of crime committed by children. The Society issued a report in 1819 raising concern for the number of children confined with adults in Bellevue Prison, and in 1823 the Society issued a now famous statement describing the streets as overrun with pauper children in need of saving. On January 1, 1825, New York City opened the first "House of Refuge."[82]

The New York House of Refuge was authorized by New York Law[83] that provided a charter to the Society for the Reformation of Juvenile Delinquents, the

---

Present Status (pt. 2), 16 STAN. L. REV. 900, 965 (1964). *See also generally* Stefan A. Riesenfeld, *Lawmaking and Legislation Precedent in American Legal History,* 33 MINN. L. REV. 103 (1949).

[77] Whether we treat the class of children empathically, or merely as a "reflection of adult concerns and agendas" is debatable, but children are seen in the twentieth century as an identifiable interest group. *See* JEAN KOH PETERS, REPRESENTING CHILDREN IN CHILD PROTECTIVE PROCEEDINGS: ETHICAL AND PRACTICAL DIMENSIONS 249 (2d ed. 2001).

[78] JOHN C. WATKINS, JR., THE JUVENILE JUSTICE CENTURY 3 (1998).

[79] *Id.* at 4.

[80] Sanford J. Fox, *Juvenile Justice Reform: An Historical Perspective*, 22 Stan. L. Rev. 1187, 1200 & n.72 (1970) (citing J. YATES, REPORT OF THE SECRETARY OF STATE IN 1824 ON THE RELIEF AND SETTLEMENT OF THE POOR, *reprinted in* I NEW YORK STATE BOARD OF CHARITIES, ANNUAL REPORT NO. 34, at 937, 942).

[81] *Id.* at 1187; *see also* DAVID M. SCHNEIDER, THE HISTORY OF PUBLIC WELFARE IN NEW YORK STATE 1609–1866, AT 317 (1938).

[82] JOHN C. WATKINS, JR., THE JUVENILE JUSTICE CENTURY 4 (1998).

[83] *See* Sanford J. Fox, *Juvenile Justice Reform: An Historical Perspective,* 22 STAN. L. REV. 1187, 1190 & n.20 (1970) (referring to Laws of New York, 47th Session, Ch. CXXVI at 110 (1824)).

successor to the Society for Prevention of Pauperism.[84] The authorizing legislation allowed managers of the Society to take into the house children committed as vagrants or convicted of crimes by authorities. Criminal conviction was not a condition to incarceration in the House of Refuge. Children could even be committed by administrative order or application of their parents.[85] Neither was there any right to indictment or jury trial,[86] as summary conviction of disorderly persons had previously been upheld in New York in the case *In re Goodhue*.[87]

It is a mistake to assume that the House of Refuge served as a haven for youth otherwise guilty of serious crime. Those youth were still maintained in the adult system. In the first two years of operation of the New York House of Refuge, approximately 90% of the children were housed as a result of vagrancy or minor offenses.[88] Since such minor offenses tended to go unpunished by the law, it is unlikely that these children would have fallen under the authority of the state without a House of Refuge.[89]

Neither, however, was the Refuge movement one to protect abused children from their caretaker's authority. There is no evidence that children were placed as a result of caretaker cruelty. To the contrary, severe corporal punishment was clearly part of the House of Refuge system. In fact, conditions in many Houses were quite abusive by modern standards, including solitary confinement and beatings.[90]

Poor "vagrant" children were the focus of the Refuge movement. In short, seriously criminal children tended to remain in the adult system, the majority of children in families saw no intervention, and children who might today be considered status offender cases, were rounded up off the streets. The Refuge movement was a pre-delinquency movement, which focused on saving "salvageable," probably neglected, poor children. In that sense, as Sanford Fox has pointed out, the Refuge movement was, although motivated in part by humanitarianism, very much a "retrenchment in correctional practices" and "a regression in poor-law policy."[91] The movement also involved a coercive religious intolerance, as all children were required to adopt the Protestant teachings of their reformers.[92] When viewed in the context of

---

[84] *Id.*

[85] THOMAS J. BERNARD, THE CYCLE OF JUVENILE JUSTICE (1992).

[86] Sanford J. Fox, *Juvenile Justice Reform: An Historical Perspective*, 22 STAN. L. REV. 1187, 1191 (1970).

[87] *Id.* at n.28 (citing *In re* Goodhue, 1 N.Y. City Hall Recorder 153 (1816)).

[88] *Id.* at 1192.

[89] *Id.* at 1194.

[90] *Id.* at 1195 (citing SOCIETY FOR THE REFORMATION OF JUVENILE DELINQUENTS, ANNUAL REPORT NO. 3 (1828), *reprinted in* SOCIETY FOR THE REFORMATION OF JUVENILE DELINQUENTS, DOCUMENTS RELATIVE TO THE HOUSE OF REFUGE 138 (N. Hart ed. 1832) and R. PICKETT, HOUSE OF REFUGE 24 (1969)).

[91] Sanford J. Fox, *Juvenile Justice Reform: An Historical Perspective*, 22 STAN. L. REV. 1187, 1195 (1970).

[92] *Id.*

protection for abused and neglected children, it did not represent progress. It did represent continued intervention, but little welfare, for neglected poor children.

The Refuge movement spread from New York to Boston (1826) to Philadelphia (1828) to New Orleans (1847) to Baltimore (1849) to Cincinnati (1850) to Pittsburgh and St. Louis (1854). By 1860, 16 Houses of Refuge were opened in the United States.[93] Legislation authorizing the intervention and placement of delinquent and dependent children similarly spread throughout the jurisdictions.[94]

In addition to Houses of Refuge, Reformatories, which were entirely state-financed, began to emerge toward the middle of the century. John Watkins points out that the reformatory movement was initiated by a number of influential individuals who believed the House of Refuge system had not slowed the rate of delinquency.[95] Reformatories were to be progressive institutions where, through civic and moral training, the youth would be reformed by his or her surrogate parent. In reality, Reformatories tended to be coercive, labor-intensive incarceration.[96]

Houses of Refuge dominated the first half, and Reformatories the last half of the century. They were characterized by an ultimate parent philosophy toward the poor, which ties the movement to the poor laws. Another link to the past was the use of apprenticeship in the Refuge movement. As Houses of Refuge became overcrowded, many children were "placed out" by being transported to rural areas of the state or placed on trains headed to the developing west where they were apprenticed until they reached age 21. It was thought, or at least stated, that rural agrarian lifestyle would reform children from the effects of urban poverty.[97]

Ex parte Crouse *and* Parens Patriae

The House of Refuge movement may not have had significant impact on the ultimate development of the juvenile court if the judicial system had not validated it. In a number of cases during this period, courts affirmed and authorized the practice of intervention into the lives of children through the English doctrine of *parens patriae,* which means ultimate parent or parent of the country. The courts accepted the Reformers' logic that they were entitled to take custody of a child, regardless of the child's status as victim or offender, without due process of law, because of the state's authority and obligation to save children from becoming criminal.

The 1839 Pennsylvania decision of *Ex parte Crouse*[98] is thought to be the first case upholding the Refuge System. The child, Mary Ann Crouse, was committed to the Philadelphia House of Refuge by a Justice of the Peace Warrant. The warrant,

---

[93] JOHN C. WATKINS, JR., THE JUVENILE JUSTICE CENTURY: A SOCIOLEGAL COMMENTARY ON AMERICAN JUVENILE COURTS 5 (1998).

[94] *Id.* at 7.

[95] *Id.* at 8.

[96] *Id.* at 9.

[97] *Id.* at 7.

[98] 4 Whart. 9 (Pa. 1839).

executed by Mary Ann's mother, essentially provided that it would be in Mary Ann's interests to be incarcerated in the House because she was "beyond her parent's control." The reported case is an appeal from a denial of the father's subsequent *habeas corpus* petition for his daughter's return. The father argued that the law allowing commitment of children without a trial was unconstitutional. The court summarily rejected the father's argument on the basis that the House was not a prison (even though Mary Ann was not free to leave), and the child was there for her own reformation, not punishment (even though Mary Ann was probably treated very harshly, a fact the court did not review). The court essentially accepted the rhetoric of the representatives of the House of Refuge. In doing so, the court acknowledged and sanctioned the state's authority to intervene into the family as ultimate parent via the doctrine of *parens patriae*. The case and the doctrine became the cornerstones of juvenile proceedings throughout the century and through the pre-*Gault* years of the juvenile court. The case was generally relied on to support "the right of the state to make coercive predictions about deviant children."[99] Although the distinction may have been irrelevant at the time, the case involved a dependent—not delinquent—child, and in dicta, as Rendleman points out, the court argued that the state has authority to intervene into the parent-child relationship for the good of the child:

> To this end may not the natural parents, when unequal to the task of education, or unworthy of it, be superseded by the parens patriae, or common guardian of the community? . . . . That parents are ordinarily intrusted with it is because it can seldom be put into better hands; but where they are incompetent or corrupt, what is there to prevent the public from withdrawing their faculties, held, as they obviously are, at its sufferance? The right of parental control is a natural, but not an unalienable one.[100]

The *Crouse* court was making the case for state intervention into the family where the parents fail, in the state's view, to perform adequately, and the state is needed to care for the child. The reality that the state was probably caring for the child very poorly does not diminish the precedent for intervention in dependency cases.

The lead of the *Crouse* court was followed in a series of cases involving delinquent and dependent children. In Maryland, *Roth v. House of Refuge*,[101] in Ohio, *Prescott v. State*,[102] in Wisconsin, *Milwaukee Indus. School v. Supervisors of Milwaukee County*,[103] and in Illinois, *In re Ferrier*,[104] courts adopted the *Crouse*

---

[99] Sanford J. Fox, *Juvenile Justice Reform: An Historical Perspective*, 22 STAN. L. REV. 1187, 1207 (1970).

[100] *Ex parte Crouse*, 4 Whart. 9, 11 (Pa. 1839).

[101] 31 Md. 329 (1869).

[102] 19 Ohio St. 184 (1869).

[103] 40 Wis. 328 (1876).

[104] 103 Ill. 367 (1882).

policy that the state's *parens patriae* duty and authority permitted seemingly unlimited intervention into family autonomy, including the child's deprivation of liberty.

The 1882 Illinois *Ferrier* case is particularly illustrative of the development of child protection law for two reasons. First, it involved a very young dependent, rather than delinquent, child. Nine-year-old Winifred Bean came to the court's attention, in significant part because her parents were viewed as incompetent to provide necessary parental care. Testimony was even taken that the parents were neglectful. Winifred was adjudicated dependent by a jury and committed to an industrial school for girls. In language typical of *Crouse* and its progeny, the court approved of both the state's authority to interrupt the rights of parents and children to the parent-child legal relationship, as well as the right to deprive the child of a degree of personal liberty through a state placement. While acknowledging that the Refuge movement did not distinguish between dependent and delinquent children (as the focus was delinquency prevention, not humanitarian protection), *Ferrier* was not just another case of picking up a vagrant child. It was a case of forced removal due to parental neglect.

Second, *Ferrier* repudiated a serious effort to create precedent limiting the state's *parens patriae* authority. Twelve years earlier, in *People ex rel. O'Connell v. Turner,*[105] the Illinois court had issued a decision that, if followed, would have repudiated the *parens patriae* Refuge system. The Illinois court released Daniel O'Connell from the custody of the Chicago Reform School because his confinement as a dependent child was unconstitutional. The court wrote: "in our solicitude to form youth for the duties of civil life, we should not forget the rights which inhere both in parents and children. The principle of the absorption of the child in, and its complete subjection to the despotism of, the State, is wholly inadmissible in the modern civilized world."[106] The case was not followed, however, and was then overruled by *Ferrier*. "The decision was ultimately looked upon as an aberrant pronouncement that could not and would not stand in the way of Progressive social engineering."[107]

As the final third of the nineteenth century approached, state legislatures had created, and the courts had approved, a system of family law and intervention that focused on "saving" children of the expanding poor urban population by removal and placement. In doing so, authorization was given to disrupt the parent-child legal relationship and infringe on children's liberty solely because the child was not, in the state's view, cared for properly. The focus of the intervention was status-offending poor street children, with an occasional neglect scenario and, although an occasional reference to parental cruelty was made, little if any intervention for the abused child.

---

[105] 55 Ill. 280 (1870).

[106] *Id.* at 284.

[107] JOHN C. WATKINS, JR., THE JUVENILE JUSTICE CENTURY 25 (1998).

Special Cases of Child Abuse

Absent from many histories of the dependency court, but present in histories of child abuse and neglect, are the several documented nineteenth-century cases of legal intervention on behalf of children who were physically abused by their caretakers. Clearly, these are not the types of cases the Reformers of the nineteenth century envisioned as part of the movement to save children. Society did not view even severe corporal punishment or discipline as beyond the autonomy of the family, except in particularly heinous cases. In addition, even in such cases, criminal punishment of the parent, rather than removal and care of the child, was the focus.[108] Mason Thomas points out that the lack of civil cases can be explained in part by the then existing common law doctrine that a minor could not sue his parents in tort. The view that, at best, a child may get protection by way of criminal prosecution of parents was stated in the 1891 Mississippi case, *Hewellette v. George*,[109] where the court wrote: "The state, through its criminal laws, will give the minor child protection from parental violence and wrongdoing, and this is all the child can be heard to demand."[110]

Why these cases did not come to the developing *parens patriae* court's attention is not entirely clear, but the explanation is probably basic—those officials in charge of executing the Reformers' child-saving plans did not include caretaker-abused children within their net, and society did not view even brutal treatment of children by their nonpoor caretakers as outside the bounds of family autonomy. Such an illustration is found in the 1840 Tennessee case, *Johnson v. State*,[111] where the court reversed the parents' criminal conviction for the brutal treatment of their daughter. The court's analysis of whether the parents' exceeded their authority to control and discipline included the following language:

> The right of parents to chastise their refractory and disobedient children is so necessary to the government of families, to the good order of society, that no moralist or lawgiver has ever thought of interfering with its existence, or of calling upon them to account for the manner of its exercise, upon light or frivolous pretenses. But, at the same time that the law has created and preserved this right, in its regard for the safety of the child it has prescribed bounds beyond which it shall not be carried.[112]

---

[108] 2 CHILDREN AND YOUTH IN AMERICA 119–24 (Robert H. Bremner ed., 1971).

[109] 68 Miss. 703 (1891).

[110] Mason P. Thomas, Jr., *Child Abuse and Neglect*, 50 N.C. L. REV. 293, 304 & n.43 (1972) (quoting Hewellette v. George, 68 Miss. 703, 711 (1891)).

[111] 21 Tenn. (2 Hum.) 282 (1840).

[112] Mason P. Thomas, Jr., *Child Abuse and Neglect*, 50 N.C. L. REV. 293, 305 (1972) (citing Johnson v. State, 21 Tenn. (2 Hum.) 282, 283 (1840)).

Nonetheless, some jurisdictions specifically mentioned cruelty as a justification for removal in their reform laws, and those that did not could have accommodated abused children in their dependency statutory scheme, but they did not.

This brings us to the myth that the Mary Ellen case is the first documented child abuse case. That is not accurate for the reasons just discussed. Additionally, it now appears there was a similar case, also involving Henry Bergh (who intervened for Mary Ellen), before Mary Ellen. Steven Lazoritz and Eric Shelman published an article entitled *Before Mary Ellen*[113] that, based on the unpublished notes of the biographer of Henry Bergh, recounts the story of the intervention to protect the child Emily Thompson several years before the case of Mary Ellen. As the biographer's notes state, according to Lazoritz and Shelman, in June of 1871, a woman approached Henry Bergh, founder of the Society for Prevention of Cruelty to Animals, and sought his assistance to save 8-year-old Emily Thompson, who she said she frequently observed from her window being brutally beaten and whipped for up to an hour at a time. Bergh sent investigators who found the child to be battered. Additional neighbors came forward to confirm the almost daily beatings. Bergh acquired a writ— probably the same writ later used in Mary Ellen's case—and the child was removed. Emily was presented to New York Court of Special Sessions where Judge Barnard took jurisdiction, apparently as a criminal matter. Although the child was visibly battered, Mary Ann Larkin, who was Emily's nonbiological caretaker, denied the abuse, as did Emily. The judge found Ms. Larkin "guilty," suspended her sentence, and returned the child to her care. Later, however, Emily's grandmother, who thought the child dead, read a newspaper account of the matter and contacted Bergh. Bergh brought Emily again to Judge Bernard on a writ. Judge Bernard then removed Emily from Ms. Larkin and placed her with her grandmother. It is not indicated whether the court viewed the removal and placement as a continuation of the criminal action against the caretaker or under some theory of protection jurisdiction. The trial-level action was apparently never reviewed.

As for Mary Ellen, the case has traditionally been used to support the proposition that at the time of the case, society had no child protection law, and after the case, due to the clever use of an animal rights theory and sympathy created by the case, child abuse protection began. As we have seen, that proposition is not supported by fact. New York, Mary Ellen's residence, as we have seen, had a massive child welfare scheme, albeit not focused on removing middle class children, but prevalent enough to have had a hand in placing the child in the abusive setting in the first place. Using Bremner's documentary history, Thomas sorted out the facts as follows:

> The case arose in 1874, when Mary Ellen probably was ten years old. Laws to protect children (criminal laws forbidding assault and statutes dealing with the neglect of children) were not lacking but were not enforced systematically. The case was not brought into court

---

[113] Stephen Lazoritz & Eric A. Shelman, *Before Mary Ellen*, 20/3 CHILD ABUSE & NEGLECT 235, 235–37 (1996).

by the Society for the Prevention of Cruelty to Animals on the theory that this child was entitled to the legal protection afforded animals; rather, it was initiated by the founder of this society acting as an individual, using the Society's attorney, by a petition for a writ *de homine replegiando*, on the basis of which the court issued a special warrant to bring the child before the court. Mary Ellen was not placed with the church worker but instead was placed temporarily (exactly where is unknown) for seven months pending efforts to locate relatives; when none could be found, she was committed to the "Sheltering Arms," an orphan asylum.

Various issues of the *New York Times* during April 1874 summarize the evidence presented in the several court hearings that involved this case: Mary Ellen Wilson, an infant girl whose birth date apparently was unknown, was left at the office of the Superintendent of Outdoor Poor, Department of Charities, New York City, on May 21, 1864, by a woman who had cared for the child while she received eight dollars per month for her support. When the support stopped, she turned the child over to the Department. When Mary Ellen was eighteen months old, she was apprenticed to Mary and Thomas McCormack under an indenture that required the foster parents to teach her that there was a God, and what it meant to lie, and to instruct her "in the art and mystery of housekeeping." The indenture also required the foster parents to report to the Department annually on the child's condition. The placement was made on January 2, 1866, and the indenture was signed on February 15. When the placement was made, the Department checked with one reference – Mrs. McCormack's physician. Unbeknown to the Department of Public Charities, Mary Ellen Wilson was actually the illegitimate child of Thomas McCormack by a "good-for-nothing" woman whose name was unknown.

The case arose in 1874, when Mary Ellen was about ten years old. By that time, Thomas McCormack had died and Mary McCormack had married Francis Connolly. Mary Ellen could not remember having lived with anyone other than the Connollys. She believed that her parents were dead; she did not know her exact age; and she called Mrs. Connolly "Mamma." She could not recall ever having been kissed by anyone.

The Superintendent of Outdoor Poor, who had made the placement, testified that he could remember nothing about the case except what was contained in his written record, since he had placed five hundred children through his department during 1874. Clearly, the Department of Charities had lost contact with Mary Ellen and the

Connollys, as only two of the required annual reports on the child's condition had been made between 1866 and 1874.

The evidence indicated both abuse and neglect: Mrs. Connolly had whipped Mary Ellen almost every day with a cane and a twisted whip – a rawhide that left black and blue marks – and had struck her with a pair of scissors (which were produced in court) that had cut her on the forehead; the child was locked in the bedroom whenever "Mama" left home; she was not allowed to leave the room where the Connollys were; she was not allowed to play outside or with other children; and she was inadequately clothed and slept on a piece of rug on the floor.

Mrs. Connolly was prosecuted under indictments for felonious assault with a pair of scissors on April 7, 1874, and for a series of assaults during 1873 and 1874. The jury found her guilty of assault and battery and sentenced her to one year in the penitentiary at hard labor.[114]

The Mary Ellen case, together with the founding of the New York Society for Prevention of Cruelty to Children (NYSPCC), did have significant impact on child welfare. Its founder, Elbridge Gerry, recognized the void in the Refuge system for abused and neglected children outside the pre-delinquency net. He also recognized that law enforcement did not typically become involved in "family matters." Eventually, the NYSPCC acquired police power and controlled the welfare of many of New York's abused and neglected children. By 1900, 161 similar "cruelty" societies existed in the United States.

By the end of the nineteenth century, there was a developing *parens patriae* jurisprudence that enabled saving children from the effects of poverty and a related movement began to concern itself with child abuse and neglect within the family.

A Scientific Development

An important scientific development in the recognition of child abuse and neglect occurred in France in 1860. A French physician, Ambrose Tardieu, conducted a study of 32 children whom he believed died of child abuse. Tardieu's findings describe medical, psychiatric, social, and demographic features of the condition of child abuse as a syndrome.[115] This groundbreaking work went largely unrecognized until the mid-twentieth century.

---

[114] Mason P. Thomas, Jr., *Child Abuse and Neglect*, 50 N. C. L. REV. 293, 308–10 (1972) (citations omitted); for a description of events in Mary Ellen's later life, see Stephen Lazoritz, *Whatever Happened to Mary Ellen?*, 14/2 CHILD ABUSE & NEGLECT 143 (1990).

[115] SELWYN M. SMITH, TARDIEU, ETUDE MEDICO-LEGALE SUR LES SERVICES ET MAUVAIS TRAITEMENTS EXERCES SUR DES ENFANTS (1860), THE BATTERED CHILD SYNDROME (1975).

§ 9.5.6 The Juvenile Court: Institutionalizing and Developing the *Parens Patriae* System

Founding and Dependency Philosophy

The events of the last decades of the nineteenth century that lead to the founding of the first juvenile court were very much an extension of the nineteenth-century refuge/reform movement, which in turn were an outgrowth of poor law policy. While the founding of the court has traditionally been treated as a revolutionary humanitarian advancement for children, more recent scholarship has shown the inaccuracy of that belief.[116] This is not to say the founding of the court was not an historic event; it was just not a revolutionary one. It was a culmination of, not a departure from, nineteenth-century reform.

The legislation that led to the creation of a special tribunal, which came to be called the juvenile court, was "An Act to Regulate the Treatment and Control of Dependent, Neglected and Delinquent Children."[117] The Juvenile Court of Cook County, Illinois opened on July 1, 1899.[118] Although it is accurate that the Cook County Court was the first fully formalized tribunal of its kind, Massachusetts (in 1874) and New York (in 1892) had actually passed laws separating minors' trials from adults. While it is a mistake to assume all subsequent juvenile courts simply copied the Illinois legislation, it did serve as a model, and in less than 20 years similar legislation had been passed in all but three states.[119]

The Illinois legislation was largely the product of a Progressive Era movement called Child Saving. The Child Savers were individuals who viewed their cause of saving "those less fortunately placed in the social order"[120] as a matter of morality. The Child Savers were dominated by bourgeois women, although many were considered liberals. The movement, which was supported by the propertied and powerful, "tried to do for the criminal justice system what industrialists and corporate leaders were trying to do for the economy—that is, achieve order, stability, and control, while preserving the existing class system and distribution of wealth."[121] The Child Savers' rhetoric envisioned a juvenile court that would serve children and society by removing children from the criminal law process and placing them in special programs.[122] The movement in Chicago was supported by the Illinois Conference of Charities, The Chicago Bar Association, and the Chicago Woman's Club.

---

[116] Sanford J. Fox, *Juvenile Justice Reform: An Historical Perspective*, 22 STAN. L. REV. 1187 (1970).

[117] Act of Apr. 21, 1899, [1899] Ill. Laws 131.

[118] J. WATKINS, JR., THE JUVENILE JUSTICE CENTURY: A SOCIOLEGAL COMMENTARY ON AMERICAN JUVENILE COURTS 43 (1998).

[119] ANTHONY M. PLATT, THE CHILD SAVERS 10 (2D ED. 1977).

[120] *Id.* at 3.

[121] *Id.* at xxii.

[122] *Id.* at 10.

The Illinois act provided for jurisdiction in a special court for delinquent and dependent and neglected children. A delinquent child was any child under age 16 who violated a law or ordinance, except capital offenses.[123] Dependency and neglect was defined as follows:

1. Any child who for any reason is destitute or homeless or abandoned;

2. Has not proper parental care or guardianship;

3. Who habitually begs or receives alms;

4. Who is found living in any house of ill fame or with any vicious or disreputable person;

5. Whose home, by reason of neglect, cruelty, or depravity on the part of its parents, guardian or other person in whose care it may be, is an unfit place for such a child;

6. Any child under the age of 8 years who is found peddling or selling any article or singing or playing any musical instrument upon the street or giving any public entertainment.[124]

The categories are remarkably familiar to the Refuge movement conditions of eliminating vagrancy through confinement. As Fox has noted, the juvenile court was very much a continuation of a system of coercive predictions begun at the beginning of the century.[125]

There also appears to be little, if any, support for the proposition that the juvenile court began a system of benevolent caretaking of youth by substituting a kind of therapeutic jurisprudence for harsher and limited criminal procedure. First, older serious offenders stayed in the adult criminal system. Second, the nineteenth-century case law reveals that juveniles brought to court under delinquency and dependency concepts received no due process. *Ex parte Crouse*[126] served to inform us they were entitled to none.

This is not to suggest that the juvenile court was a step backward. It was progress in the form of codification and institutionalization of the nineteenth-century *parens patriae* system. As an institution, the juvenile court stressed centrality for dependent children. Rather than being subject to random placements without follow up, it was believed that a court could function as a centralized agency responsible for all such children from start to finish. The new court implemented the concept of probation, and the founders made minimal progress toward improving placement conditions for children. Dependent children could be placed with an agency or put on probation. To

---

[123] Act of Apr. 21, 1899, [1899] Ill. Laws 131.

[124] Act of Apr. 21, 1899, [1899] Ill. Laws 131.

[125] Sanford J. Fox, *Juvenile Justice Reform: An Historical Perspective*, 22 STAN. L. REV. 1187 (1970).

[126] 4 Whart. 9 (Pa. 1839). *See* § 9.5.5, Nineteenth-Century America: The Rise of the *Parens Patriae* System.

at least some extent, the Child Savers' mission of creating a juvenile "statutory, non-criminal, stigma-neutral, treatment-oriented" system was achieved.[127]

As for abused and neglected children, although cruelty societies helped, state intervention under the juvenile court acts was modest. The condition of poverty, which brought children into the Refuge system, continued as a *de facto* prerequisite for juvenile court intervention. Saving nonpoor abused and neglected children from their lawful caretakers was not a goal of the Child Savers either. Nonetheless, the *parens patriae* authority to do so became the central component of the juvenile court.

The early years of the court were characterized by continued commingling of dependency and delinquency under the courts' *parens patriae* authority. Minimal numbers of appeals validated that authority. Families remained autonomous.

The delinquency and dependency components of the juvenile court, historically connected by a "child saving" philosophy, began to separate into distinct functions in the 1960s. Driven by judicial process in delinquency, and social progress in dependency, both components were transformed.

Gault *and the Transformation of Delinquency out from* Parens Patriae

The delinquency component of juvenile court was transformed in the late 1960s by two U. S. Supreme Court cases. In 1966, in *Kent v. United Sates*, the court set the stage for dismantling the *parens patriae* authority of the juvenile delinquency court by holding that the action of transferring a juvenile to criminal court required procedural due process.[128] Then, in 1967, the Court struck down the *parens patriae* authority of the juvenile court in the context of delinquency adjudication in *In re Gault*.[129] The Court declared that "neither the Fourteenth Amendment nor the Bill of Rights is for adults alone."[130] In his famous opinion, Justice Fortas reviewed the shortcomings of the juvenile process, which had been in operation since the founding of the court. Justice Fortas stated that the belief that the juvenile court could best care for children without the distractions of due process was a myth, and that due process, not benevolent intentions, produced justice. Among the rights *Gault* created for juveniles were notice of charges, confrontation and cross-examination, prohibition against self-incrimination, and the right to counsel. The decision continues to be hailed by some as a great advancement in children's rights and by others as the criminalization of the juvenile court and the beginning of the end of the court's authority to treat children like children rather than adults. The difference of opinion goes to the heart of the debate over the purpose and future of the delinquency court.

---

[127] John C. Watkins, Jr., The Juvenile Justice Century: A Sociolegal Commentary on American Juvenile Courts 50 (1998).

[128] 383 U.S. 541 (1966).

[129] 387 U.S. 1 (1967).

[130] *Id.* at 13.

While *Gault* did not instruct juvenile courts across the country to wholly substitute adult criminal procedure for juvenile practice, that is very much what happened. The delinquency court separated from the dependency court, and the traditional commingling of all children in a predelinquency/criminal prevention program began to come to an end.

For the future of dependency proceedings it is critical to focus on what *Gault* did *not* do: *Gault* did not dismantle, or even limit, the *parens patriae* authority of the dependency court. The *Gault* Court focused on juvenile misconduct, as opposed to victimization, and stated, "[w]e do not in this opinion consider the impact of these constitutional provisions upon the totality of the relationship of the juvenile and the state."[131] The state, therefore, was free to continue separately "saving" dependent children, whoever they may be, under the *parens patriae* duty and authority of the state.

The Battered Child, *CAPTA, and the Evolution of Dependency within* Parens Patriae

The dependency court underwent a transformation in the last half of the twentieth century, not away from, but within the state's *parens patriae* authority. Grounded in a new public awareness of the need to protect children from maltreatment, the dependency court moved from a system of coercive predictions for poor dependent children to a system of intervention into the family to protect abused and neglected children. This "evolution" can be seen in the following events:[132]

- In 1912, as a result of President Roosevelt's 1909 White House Conference on Children, Congress created the United States Children's Bureau.

- In 1921, Congress passed the Shappard-Towner Act, which established Children's Bureaus at the state level and promoted maternal-infant health.

- In 1944, the Supreme Court of the United States confirmed the state's authority to intervene in family relationships to protect children in *Prince v. Massachusetts*.[133]

- In 1946, Aid to Dependent Children was added to the Social Security Act.

- In 1946, Dr. Caffey, a pediatric radiologist in Pittsburgh, published the results of his research showing that subdural hematomas and fractures of the long bones in infants were inconsistent with accidental trauma.[134]

---

[131] *Id.*

[132] *See generally* INGER SAGATUN & LEONARD EDWARDS, CHILD ABUSE AND THE LEGAL SYSTEM (1995) (describing and identifying many of these events).

[133] 321 U.S. 158 (1944).

[134] John Caffey, *Multiple Fractures in the Long Bones of Infants Suffering from Chronic Subdural Hematoma*, 56 AM. J. ROENTGENOLOGY 163 (1946).

- In 1962, following a medical symposium the previous year, several physicians headed by Denver physician C. Henry Kempe, published the landmark article *The Battered Child Syndrome* in the Journal of the American Medical Association. Through the article, Kempe and his colleagues exposed the reality that significant numbers of parents and caretakers batter their children, even to death. The Battered Child Syndrome describes a pattern of child abuse resulting in certain clinical conditions and establishes a medical and psychiatric model of the cause of child abuse. The article marked the development of child abuse as a distinct academic subject. The work is generally regarded as one of the most significant events leading to professional and public awareness of the existence and magnitude of child abuse and neglect in the United States and throughout the world.[135]

- In 1962, in response to *The Battered Child*, the Children's Bureau held a symposium on child abuse, which produced a recommendation for a model child abuse reporting law.

- By 1967, 44 states had adopted mandatory reporting laws. The remaining six states adopted voluntary reporting laws. All states now have mandatory reporting laws. Generally, the laws require physicians to report reasonable suspicion of child abuse. Reporting laws, now expanded to include other professionals and voluntary reporting by the public, together with immunity for good faith reporting, are recognized as one of the most significant measures ever taken to protect abused and neglected children. Reporting is recognized as the primary reason for the dramatic increases in cases of child abuse and neglect.

- In 1971, the California Court of Appeals recognized the Battered Child Syndrome as a medical diagnosis and a legal syndrome in *People v. Jackson*.[136]

- In 1974, Congress passed landmark legislation in the federal Child Abuse Prevention and Treatment Act (CAPTA).[137] The Act provides states with funding for the investigation and prevention of child maltreatment, conditioned on states' adoption of mandatory reporting law. The Act also conditions funding on reporter immunity, confidentiality, and appointment of guardians ad litem for children. The Act also created the National Center on Child Abuse and Neglect (NCCAN) to serve as an

---

[135] C. Henry Kempe, Frederic N. Silverman, Brandt F. Steele, William Droegemueller & Henry K. Silver, *The Battered Child Syndrome,* 181/1 JAMA 17 (1962).

[136] 18 Cal. App. 3d 504, 506–08 (1971); *see also* Estelle v. McGuire, 502 U.S. 62 (1991) *and* State v. Henson, 33 N.Y.2d 63 (1973) (describing Battered Child Syndrome).

[137] Pub. L. No. 93-273, 88 Stat. 93; 42 U.S.C. §§ 5101–5119 (1996) (current version amended and reenacted through the Keeping Children and Families Safe Act of 2003, Pub. L. No. 108-36, 117 Stat. 800).

information clearinghouse. In 1978, The Adoption Reform Act was added to CAPTA. In 1984, CAPTA was amended to include medically disabled infants, the reporting of medical neglect and maltreatment in out-of-home care, and the expansion of sexual abuse to include sexual exploitation.

- In 1980, Congress passed the Adoption Assistance and Child Welfare Act,[138] designed to remedy problems in the foster care system. The Act made federal funding for foster care dependent on certain reforms. In 1983 the Act was amended to include "reasonable efforts." The reasonable efforts amendment provided for special procedures before removing a child and reunification strategies after removal. Important provisions for case review were also included. The Act and its amendment essentially provided fiscal incentives to encourage states to prevent unnecessary foster care placements and to provide permanent homes for children in placement as quickly as possible. The law also gave courts a new oversight role.

- In 1981, Title XX of the Social Security Act was amended to include the Social Services Block Grant to provide child protective services funding to states. This became the major source of state social service funding.

- In 1986, Congress passed the Child Abuse Victims' Rights Act, which gave a civil damage claim to child victims of violations of federal sexual exploitation law.

- In 1991, Congress passed the Victims of Child Abuse Act of 1990, aimed at improving the investigation and prosecution of child abuse cases.

- In 1993, as part of the Omnibus Budget and Reconciliation Act, Congress provided funding for state courts to assess the impact of Public Law 96-272 (the Adoption Assistance and Child Welfare Act) on foster care proceedings, to study the handling of child protection cases, and to develop a plan for improvement. Funds were made available to states through a grant program called the State Court Improvement Program. The program was the impetus behind a nationwide movement to improve court practice in dependency cases.

- In 1997, Congress passed the Adoption and Safe Families Act of 1997 (ASFA).[139] ASFA represents the most significant change in federal child welfare law since the Adoption Assistance and Child Welfare Act of 1980. ASFA includes provisions for legal representation, state funding of child welfare and adoption, and state performance requirements. In general, ASFA is intended to promote primacy of child safety and timely decisions while clarifying "reasonable efforts" and continuing family

---

[138] Pub. L. No. 96-272, 94 Stat. 500 (codified as amended in 42 U.S.C. §§ 670–676 (2004)).

[139] Pub. L. No. 105-89, 111 Stat. 215 (codified as amended in scattered sections of 42 U.S.C.).

preservation. ASFA also includes continuation funding for court improvement.[140]

These events, particularly recognition of the "battered child," mandatory reporting and the passage of CAPTA, exemplified a new recognition of both the presence of child maltreatment and the need to protect its victims. As a result, the dependency court, once reserved primarily for pre-delinquent vagrant children of the poor, was transformed into an active tribunal to determine whether a child is abused and neglected, and if so, what disposition is appropriate. Criminal prosecutions of adults for child maltreatment were no longer viewed as the child's exclusive "remedy."

As juvenile court legislation was transformed in the delinquency context to provide procedures to satisfy the *Gault* requirements, the dependency court was left to continue its *parens patriae* jurisdiction over children and families. Within that context, states' dependency codes were modified to provide special processes for the intake, adjudication, and disposition of the newly recognized class of maltreated children. The result is child protection codes that contain language describing child abuse and neglect, rather than the early dependency language that described social conditions warranting intervention. Although vestiges of the commingling of delinquency and dependency can still be seen in some juvenile codes, the combination of the *Gault* influence on delinquency and the recognition of child maltreatment on dependency cause a clear separation of the two components of the juvenile court.[141]

The Dependency Court in the Twenty-First Century

The early twenty-first-century dependency court is very different from the "vagrancy" dependency court that began the twentieth century. Child abuse and neglect cases, once unrecognized, dominate the court calendar.

INCIDENCE OF MALTREATMENT

Although it is difficult to accumulate precise statistics for child maltreatment nationally, methodology has been developed for accumulating the incidence of child maltreatment from the states.[142] Once thought to be a problem involving only a few thousand children a year, child maltreatment has since been identified as nothing less than a national emergency.[143].

---

[140] Rollin, *Legislative Update*, 16/11 CHILD LAW PRAC. 166 (1998).

[141] It is even uncommon for attorneys representing children to "cross over" from one forum to the other. Katner, *Addressing the "Unmet Need" for Counsel to Handle Delinquency As Well As Dependency Cases*, 20 GUARDIAN 2, 3 (1998).

[142] ANDREA J. SEDLAK & DIANE D. BROADHURST, U.S. DEPARTMENT OF HEALTH & HUMAN SERVICES, THE THIRD NATIONAL INCIDENCE STUDY OF CHILD ABUSE AND NEGLECT (1996); *see also* CHILDREN'S BUREAU, U.S. DEPARTMENT OF HEALTH AND HUMAN SERVICES, CHILD MALTREATMENT 2002.

[143] U.S. Advisory Committee on Child Abuse and Neglect, *Child Abuse and Neglect: Critical First Steps in Response to a National Emergency* (National Clearinghouse on Child Abuse and Neglect Information, Aug. 1990). For a full description of the condition of children in America and the incidence of child maltreatment, see Chapter1, America's Children.

In response to growing evidence of child maltreatment, state legislatures enacted child protection legal procedures within their juvenile dependency codes. The juvenile dependency court became the primary forum for the oversight and the resolution of these child maltreatment and foster care cases. Where once child maltreatment cases occupied little, if any, of the juvenile court's time, they have recently become the central business of the dependency court.

Today's abused children were simply not part of the early dependency court. Likewise, the current dependency system reaches far beyond the neglected "pauper" children before the emergence of the juvenile court and during the early juvenile court. A significant number of abused and neglected children come to the system from the middle class.[144] These statistics reflect a legal and social willingness to intervene in the family and protect children. The dependency court can no longer be classified as a system of coercive predictions for pre-delinquent children. The poor law philosophy, which clearly found its way into the early court, no longer dominates the dependency court. There is considerable evidence of continuing class bias in the contemporary dependency court, however. The Third National Incidence Study of Child Abuse and Neglect (NIS-3) reports the highest correlation of family income to maltreatment exists in families with an annual income of $15,000 or less, and the lowest correlation in families with annual income of $30,000 or more.[145] This and the disproportionate representation of minority children in dependency cases should be taken seriously, particularly in light of the medical view that child abuse knows no class or race boundaries.[146] Whether reporting accurately captures maltreatment in higher income households, and whether intervention is racially and culturally competent, are critical matters.[147]

TOWARD BALANCE: BEST INTERESTS AND FAMILY PRESERVATION

While *parens patriae* continues as the underlying theory for intervention, the modern dependency court is not without legal process. The process is intended, within limitations protecting parental autonomy, to serve "the best interests of the child." The best interests standard is the governing principle of the modern dependency court. "Best interests" represents advancement in child protection compared with the early court, which tended to view child welfare through society's eyes. "Best interests" is a child-centered principle that represents real progress in the dependency system.

"Best interests" is not, however, an entirely objective standard, and as we are quick to congratulate the current court for the principle, we must recognize that the

---

[144] ANDREA J. SEDLAK & DIANE D. BROADHURST, U.S. DEPARTMENT OF HEALTH & HUMAN SERVICES, THE THIRD NATIONAL INCIDENCE STUDY OF CHILD ABUSE AND NEGLECT 5–3 (1996).

[145] *Id.*; *see also* MICHAEL R. PETIT & PATRICK A. CURTIS, CHILD ABUSE AND NEGLECT: A LOOK AT THE STATES (Child Welfare League of America 1997).

[146] Jill E. Korbin, *Culture and Child Maltreatment, in* THE BATTERED CHILD 29, 29–48 (Mary Edna Helfer et al. eds., 5th ed. 1997).

[147] Apart from *parens patriae* jurisdiction, this may be the thread that ties the late twentieth century dependency court to its poor laws heritage.

litigants' perspectives influence the position taken on the child's interests. The caretakers' interest in parental rights and the state's fiscal concerns may prohibit empathic consideration from the child's perspective. One of the most significant innovations of the modern juvenile court is the use of a representative for the child whose function is to view the best interests standard through the eyes of the child. CAPTA requires the appointment of a guardian ad litem, a vestige of the dual system of English family law, to protect the child's interest.[148] While attorney representatives for children were absent from the early court, there is now a consensus among dependency court professionals that quality legal representation for children is necessary to a high functioning court process.[149]

Coexisting with the "best interests" is the dependency court policy of "family preservation and reunification." Begun as an amendment to the federal Adoption Assistance and Child Welfare Act, the policy continues, as modified, in the federal Adoption and Safe Families Act (ASFA). While keeping child safety paramount, the policy calls for recognition that families should be kept together. While more and different types of families experience intervention in the modern dependency court, the intervention occurs within the context of a policy of family integrity. Today's courts operate with "best interests of the child" and "family preservation" as the guideposts, using the three-tiered federal directive of child safety, permanence, and well-being.[150]

§ 9.6 Evolving Dependency Philosophy and Operation

Evaluation and criticism produce improvement. Criticism of the current juvenile dependency court philosophy tends to take several forms.

§ 9.6.1 Parental Rights

A "parental rights" criticism suggests that families should be allowed, without governmental interference, to raise, educate, and discipline their children as they see fit. This view requires one to accept either that children are not, in reality, seriously maltreated by their caretakers, or that society should allow vast numbers of children to be maltreated by their caretakers as a price of parental autonomy. In reality, child

---

[148] 42 U.S.C. § 5106(a) (1988).

[149] MARK HARDIN ET AL., A.B.A. CENTER ON CHILDREN AND THE LAW, COURT IMPROVEMENT PROGRESS REPORT, 1998 (1998). Additionally, the representation of children in the dependency court has also evolved from the 1970s paternal model to the current tendency toward an independent child's attorney. *See, e.g.,* Brian G. Fraser, *Independent Representation for the Abused and Neglected Child: The Guardian Ad Litem,* 13 CAL. W. L. REV. 16 (1976); Ann M. Haralambie, *Current Trends in Children's Legal Representation,* 2/3 CHILD MALTREAT. 193 (1997); Marvin R. Ventrell, *Rights and Duties: An Overview of the Attorney-Child Client Relationship,* 26 LOY. U. CHI. L. J. 259 (1995).

[150] *See* DONALD N. DUQUETTE & MARK HARDIN, GUIDELINES FOR PUBLIC POLICY AND STATE LEGISLATION GOVERNING PERMANENCE FOR CHILDREN (Children's Bureau 1999).

maltreatment data, if flawed, is probably understated.[151] Further, an argument that societal tolerance of large-scale child maltreatment is the legitimate price of parental autonomy violates core principles of social justice.

Another component of the "parental rights" criticism is that the child protective system generally overreaches unnecessarily into the autonomy of the family. There is however, an absence of data showing overreaching. While system accountability and awareness of abuse of authority must be part of the process, there is a lack of evidence that the child protective system unfairly intrudes into the American family. The vast majority of families will simply never experience any form of intervention from the state. It is a myth that the state possesses unfettered authority to substitute its parenting judgment for that of parents. States may not substitute judgment of a child's interests except in rare circumstances. The "best interests of the child" standard is invoked only where a threshold finding of abuse or neglect is supported through a judicial determination after a hearing in which parental fitness is presumed. Further, even where dependency adjudications are made, many children are never, even temporarily, removed from the home. The state's authority to terminate the parent-child legal relationship is even further restricted. Family preservation remains the underlying policy of the juvenile court under federal law.[152] Additionally, parents have a constitutionally protected right to raise their biological children, and the minimum burden of proof required to terminate parental rights is clear and convincing evidence. Under the due process clause of the Fourteenth Amendment, "the fundamental liberty interest of natural parents . . . does not evaporate simply because they have not been model parents or have lost temporary custody of their child to the State."[153]

§ 9.6.2 Cultural Context

Good policy notwithstanding, the facts do not lie. Race and poverty play significant roles in the entry, treatment, and exit of children and families in our child welfare system. Poverty was the condition for entry into the first child welfare system in Elizabethan England, it was the condition for entry into the Refuge and Reform Systems of 19th Century America, and it remains, coupled with race, an undeniable factor in the current system. The majority of child welfare cases are brought on grounds of neglect. The majority of child welfare cases involve families living at or below the poverty level. African American and Hispanic children are disproportionately represented in the system. Cultural competence provisions of federal law including ASFA and MEPA begin to address these issues. We have reached some

---

[151] CHILDREN'S BUREAU, U.S. DEPARTMENT OF HEALTH AND HUMAN SERVICES, CHILD MALTREATMENT 2002.

[152] DONALD N. DUQUETTE & MARK HARDIN, GUIDELINES FOR PUBLIC POLICY AND STATE LEGISLATION GOVERNING PERMANENCE FOR CHILDREN (Children's Bureau 1999).

[153] Santosky v. Kramer, 455 U.S. 745, 753 (1982).

level of awareness. [154] We know that child maltreatment is not confined to one or several racial, religious, or economic groups. We also know that poverty impacts maltreatment in terms of its incidence and our interpretation thereof.

§ 9.6.3 System Operation

Criticism of the dependency court process includes the view that the system does not produce adequate outcomes for adequate numbers of children. While many children are well served by the system, the criticism is valid. Problems including failure to remove children in danger, inappropriate removal, inadequate services to children at home and in placement, lack of high quality social work, untimeliness of proceedings, inadequate legal representation, and failures to develop permanent solutions exist and must be acknowledged and corrected.

The huge increase in maltreatment cases and removals of the 1970s and 1980s produced a population of 500,000 children living and frequently drifting in foster care, without permanent plans. Our zeal to protect children, to be "child savers" once again, and perhaps our failure to value "adequate parenting" over removal, taught us one of our biggest lessons. Our efforts can and sometimes do harm children. Efforts such as the federal Child and Family Service Reviews and the corresponding Program Improvement Plans, together with the Court Improvement Program, address many of these issues.

§ 9.7 The Child Welfare Law Attorney

This chapter appears in a book about proficient legal representation of children, parents, and state agencies. It is only recently widely accepted that just judicial outcomes are dependent on proficient legal representation of all parties: agencies, parents, and children. This can be seen as the outgrowth of the recognition of children as rights-based citizens rather than objects of our welfare or sympathy. As our view of children and the law of children and families has developed, so has the procedure for applying the law. A system that adjudicates the rights of litigants requires legal counsel to advocate for those rights. This is the current state of the evolution of juvenile law from a welfare system to a rights-based system, and from child advocacy as a cause to a legal specialty within the legal profession.

---

[154] For a discussion of cultural context in child welfare cases, see Chapter 8.

Chapter 10: Federal Child Welfare Legislation[*]

by Frank E. Vandervort[1]

§ 10.1 Introduction

This chapter provides a brief overview of federal statutes that impact the practice of child welfare law. Since the enactment of the Child Abuse Prevention and Treatment Act in 1974 (CAPTA), the federal government has played an ever increasing role in handling child maltreatment cases.

In the early history of America, the welfare of children who were abused, neglected, or abandoned was addressed only by local authorities. Later, individual states developed responses to cases of child maltreatment.[2] Over the past four decades the federal government has played an ever increasing role in child welfare. With few exceptions, federal child welfare legislation is not substantive.[3] That is, the federal government cannot tell any state how it must handle individual cases of child maltreatment. Rather, most federal legislation establishes funding schemes by which an individual state may avail itself of federal funds if it complies with various requirements established by the federal government. While a state may decline to take the federal dollars offered through the various programs, and thereby release itself from any duty to comply with the federal requirements, as a practical matter the funding provided by the federal government is essential to states' efforts to deliver

---

[*] Portions of this chapter are adapted from the earlier version, Miriam Rollin, Frank Vandervort & Ann Haralambie, *Federal Child Welfare and Policy: Understanding the Federal Law and Funding Process*, in CHILD WELFARE LAW AND PRACTICE: REPRESENTING CHILDREN, PARENTS, AND STATE AGENCIES IN ABUSE, NEGLECT, AND DEPENDENCY CASES (Marvin Ventrell & Donald N. Duquette eds., 2005). I wish to thank Jonathan Fazzola for his helpful research assistance in preparing this chapter.

[1] Frank E. Vandervort, J.D., is Clinical Assistant Professor of Law at the University of Michigan Law School where he teaches in the Child Advocacy Law Clinic and the Juvenile Justice Clinic, teaches Juvenile Justice, and consults with the School of Social Work on child maltreatment issues. He is co-author of the recently released book: K. STALLER, K. C. FALLER, F. VANDERVORT, W. C. BIRDSALL & J. HENRY, SEEKING JUSTICE IN CHILD SEXUAL ABUSE: SHIFTING BURDENS & SHARING RESPONSIBILITIES (Columbia University Press 2010).

[2] *See* Chapter 9, The History of Child Welfare Law.

[3] A notable exception is the Indian Child Welfare Act (ICWA), 25 U.S.C. §§ 1901 *et seq*. For a discussion of the ICWA, see Chapter 12.

child welfare services. Today every state accepts federal funding; they are at pains to comply with the requirements of the various federal statutes.

§ 10.2 The Early Years

Since the earliest days after European contact with America, the law has provided for the protection of children from maltreatment by their parents or legal custodians.[4] During the pre-Civil War period, the protection of children was primarily the responsibility of local authorities, who were assisted by various private organizations.[5] In the 1860s, state governments began playing a role in child protection by providing funding assistance to local communities and oversight regarding the use of those monies.[6]

The federal government's role in child welfare began with the 1909 White House Conference on the Care of Dependent Children.[7] Among the recommendations that emerged from this meeting of the national child welfare leadership was the creation of an office within the federal government to address the needs of abused, neglected, and dependent children.[8] In April of 1912 the Children's Bureau was established and charged with the duty to "'Investigate and report . . . upon all matters pertaining to the welfare of children. . . .'"[9]

The role of the federal government in child well-being began with the passage of the Social Security Act of 1935 (SSA). Among other efforts on behalf of children and families, the SSA provided for the Children's Bureau to work with state authorities to improve the provision of child welfare services to abused and neglected children.[10] For four decades following the enactment of the SSA, the federal government's role in child welfare was modest, limited to the provision of AFDC benefits for eligible children placed in the foster care system. But in the 1970s the federal government, acting pursuant to the spending clause of the United States Constitution,[11] dramatically increased its role in all phases of preventing and responding to child maltreatment. Since then, the federal role in the child welfare system has steadily increased to the point that today it plays a dominant role.[12]

---

[4] JOHN E. B. MYERS, CHILD PROTECTION IN AMERICA: PAST, PRESENT, AND FUTURE 11–13 (2006). *See also* Chapter 9, The History of Child Welfare Law.

[5] *Id.* at 11, 58.

[6] *Id.* at 58.

[7] *Id.* at 58–59.

[8] *Id.* at 59, 61.

[9] *Id.* at 61 (citation omitted).

[10] *Id.* at 63.

[11] U.S. CONST. art. I, § 8, cl. 1.

[12] JOHN E. B. MYERS, CHILD PROTECTION IN AMERICA: PAST, PRESENT, AND FUTURE 64 (2006).

§ 10.3 Current Federal Law

Current federal law provides a detailed scheme for funding all areas of child welfare practice. Although federal law provides funding for all phases along the child welfare continuum—from primary prevention through early intervention to termination of parental rights and adoption—it still provides inadequate amounts of money to deal with the problem of child maltreatment comprehensively.

§ 10.3.1 Child Abuse Prevention and Treatment Act

Congress expanded its involvement in child welfare in 1974 with the enactment of the Child Abuse Prevention and Treatment Act (CAPTA).[13] CAPTA must be periodically reauthorized. Broadly speaking, CAPTA accomplishes two goals. First, it establishes federal programs for research on the causes of child abuse and neglect and for implementation of programs of best practice in the states. CAPTA permits the Secretary of the Department of Health and Human Services (DHHS) to appoint an advisory board on child abuse and neglect for the purpose of making recommendations to the Secretary and to congressional committees "concerning specific issues relating to child abuse and neglect."[14] Additionally, the statute requires that the DHHS establish a Clearinghouse for child welfare information.[15] The purpose of the Clearinghouse is to "maintain, coordinate and disseminate information" regarding programs aimed at the "prevention, assessment, identification, and treatment of child abuse and neglect and hold the potential for broad scale implementation and replication."[16] The Secretary of DHHS is also charged with "carry[ing] out a continuing interdisciplinary program of research . . . that is designed to provide information needed to better protect children from abuse or neglect and to improve the well-being of abused or neglected children."[17] Additionally, the DHHS must conduct research regarding the national incidence of child abuse and neglect.[18]

Secondly, the statute provides states with a mechanism for accessing federal dollars to support their efforts to prevent and respond to cases of child maltreatment, including but not limited to neglect, physical abuse, and sexual abuse. The Secretary of DHHS must make grants to states "based on the population of children under the age of 18 in each state that applies for a grant."[19] If a state wishes to draw down the

---

[13] 42 U.S.C. §§ 5101 *et seq.* For a comprehensive treatment of the most recent version of CAPTA, see U.S. Department of Health & Human Services et al., *Child Abuse Prevention and Treatment Act: Including Adoption Opportunities and the Abandoned Infants Assistance Act, as Amended by the Keeping Children and Families Safe Act of 2003* (June 25, 2003), *available at* www.acf.hhs.gov/programs/cb/laws_policies/cblaws/capta03/capta_manual.pdf.

[14] 42 U.S.C. § 5102(a).

[15] 42 U.S.C. § 5104.

[16] 42 U.S.C. § 5104(b).

[17] 42 U.S.C. § 5105(a)(1).

[18] 42 U.S.C. § 5105(a)(2).

[19] 42 U.S.C. § 5106a(a).

financial support provided by CAPTA, it must present to the DHHS for approval a state plan that complies with the commands of the statute.[20] The application must address each of the areas of concern established in the statute. Basically, the state's application must establish a comprehensive program for: (1) mandated reporting of suspected child abuse or neglect; (2) responding to those reports with assessment methods that will distinguish valid from invalid reports; and (3) taking action that is appropriate to the level of risk of harm to the child involved.[21]

Among CAPTA's numerous provisions are several that may be of particular interest to child welfare lawyers. First, the statute provides that if judicial proceedings are necessary to protect a child, a guardian ad litem (GAL) must be appointed to represent the child's interests. That GAL "may be an attorney."[22] The state must ensure that GALs appointed to represent children in child protective proceedings have received "training appropriate to the role."[23] A GAL appointed to represent a child in a protective proceeding is to "obtain first-hand, a clear understanding of the situation and the needs of the child" as well as "make recommendations to the court concerning the best interests of the child."[24]

A portion of the federal dollars provided to the states through CAPTA may be used to train professionals, including GALs, regarding the prevention of and response to child maltreatment.[25] If implemented, these training programs may include information regarding the legal rights of children and families.[26]

Additionally, CAPTA provides federal funding for states to improve their child protection systems, by "improving legal preparation and representation" relating to "(i) procedures for appealing and responding to appeals of substantiated reports of abuse and neglect; and (ii) provisions for the appointment of an individual . . . to represent a child in judicial proceedings."[27] That is, a state may use a portion of its federal CAPTA dollars to ensure there is a process in place for a parent to appeal a CPS finding that he or she maltreated his or her child and for the appointment of a representative for the child when a child protection action is filed with the court. Finally, when CAPTA was reauthorized and amended in 2003 as part of the Keeping Children and Families Safe Act, among the additions to the statute was one that permits each state to decide whether court proceedings regarding child abuse and neglect will be open to the public.[28]

---

[20] The commands of state plans are comprehensive and detailed. Space limitations do not permit a truly detailed discussion of the requirements of a state plan. *See* 42 U.S.C. § 5106a(b) (detailing the requirements of a state plan).

[21] 42 U.S.C. § 5106a.

[22] 42 U.S.C. 5106a(b)(2)(A)(xiii).

[23] 42 U.S.C. 5106a(b)(2)(A)(xiii).

[24] 42 U.S.C. § 5106a(b)(2)(A)(xiii).

[25] 42 U.S.C. 5106(a)(1).

[26] 42 U.S.C. § 5106(a)(1)(F).

[27] 42 U.S.C. § 5106a(a)(2)(B).

[28] 42 U.S.C. § 5106a(b)(2)(D).

CAPTA mandates that a state plan submitted pursuant to its requirements be coordinated with the state's plan submitted under Title IV-B of the Social Security Act, which seeks to preserve families in which child abuse or neglect have been found to exist and to prevent children from entering the foster care system.[29] Thus, when taken together with Titles IV-B and IV-E, CAPTA attempts to provide a comprehensive funding scheme to respond to reports of child maltreatment.

§ 10.3.2 Titles IV-B and IV-E

By the late 1970s, in part as a result of heightened awareness of child maltreatment and mandated reporting, the number of children in the foster care system nationally had grown to more than a quarter of a million. Throughout the decade of the 1970s child advocates grew increasingly concerned about the number of children in foster care and the length of time those children spent in the foster care system. At that time, children who entered foster care often spent years in the legal "limbo" of the system, which was intended to provide temporary care for the children, not returning to their parents yet never being freed for adoption. The facts in two United States Supreme Court cases from that era provide vivid and typical examples of this problem. In *Smith v. Organization of Foster Families for Equity and Reform (OFFER)*[30] foster parents brought suit alleging that their constitutional rights were violated when state child welfare workers moved foster children who had been in their care for extended periods of time, sometimes for years, without adequate due process. In its opinion, the Court noted that, on average, children in New York's foster care system stayed in temporary foster care for more than four years, with some children having lived with their foster parents for 10 years.[31] Similarly, the oft cited *Santosky v Kramer*,[32] in which the court established the constitutionally mandated standard for termination of parental rights as clear and convincing, involved three children. One child entered foster care in November 1973, the other two in September 1974. In September 1976, the state sought to terminate parental rights. The court, however, denied the state's request. The children remained in foster care until October 1978 before the state again sought to free the children for adoption.[33]

In addition to the problem of foster care "limbo," there was concern about "foster care drift," the phenomenon of children being moved from one placement to another, often repeatedly. For instance, in *Smith v OFFER*[34] the court pointed out that in 1973-

---

[29] *See* 42 U.S.C. §§ 621 *et seq.*

[30] 431 U.S. 816 (1977).

[31] *Id.* at 836.

[32] 455 U.S. 745 (1982).

[33] Of course, the Supreme Court did not issue its opinion in the case until March 1982, so the final resolution of the children's legal status took more than eight-and-one-half years.

[34] 431 U.S. 816 (1977).

1974 approximately 80% of child who were removed after spending at least one year in a foster home were removed to be placed in another foster home.[35]

The Adoption Assistance and Child Welfare Act of 1980

Concern about the numbers of children entering the foster care system, as well as the length of time they remained subject to placement instability, led Congress to pass and President Jimmy Carter to sign into law the Adoption Assistance and Child Welfare Act of 1980 (AACWA), which established Titles IV-B and IV-E of the Social Security Act.[36] The act's overarching goal was to reduce the number of children entering foster care and to reduce the length of time they remained in the system after they entered. Broadly speaking, the legislation addressed the problem in three ways. First, it sought to reduce the number of children entering foster care by requiring that "reasonable efforts" be made to keep children in their families. Next, the statute attempted to reduce children's lengths of stay by mandating that "reasonable efforts" be made to reunify children with their parents.[37] The statute also introduced for the first time the idea of permanency planning. Specifically, the law mandated that either the state child welfare agency or the court hold periodic reviews of cases to monitor progress (at least every six months) and that a permanency planning hearing be held after the child was in out-of-home care for 18 months. Finally, the legislation provided, for the first time, federally funded adoption subsidies in an effort to move special needs children—older children and those with emotional or behavioral problems—from the temporary status of foster care into permanent homes.

Like CAPTA, the legislation sought to accomplish its goals by establishing a program of contingent funding for the states. If states developed child welfare and foster care programming consistent with the federal government's requirements, the state would be eligible to receive federal funding to support those efforts. Typically, the funds provided by the federal government require a state match, which varies from 25% to 80% depending on the nature of the expenditure.[38]

---

[35] *Id.* at 829, n. 23. While there has been some improvement in placement instability, it remains a substantial problem. For instance, a 2004 study conducted by the Children and Family Research Center at the University of Illinois Urbana-Champaign found that 40% of Illinois' foster children experience placement instability, which was defined as having at least four placements while in foster care. *See* Children and Family Research Center, *Multiple Placements in Foster Care: Literature Review of Correlates and Predictors* (2004), *available at* www.cfrc.illinois.edu/LRpdfs/Placement Stability.LR.pdf.

[36] 42 U.S.C. §§ 621 *et seq.*; 42 U.S.C. §§ 670 *et seq.*

[37] The AACWA did not define "reasonable efforts," nor have subsequent amendments to the statute. For helpful guidance in understanding the reasonable efforts concept and its application in practice, see ABA CENTER ON CHILDREN AND THE LAW, MAKING SENSE OF THE ASFA REGULATIONS: A ROADMAP FOR EFFECTIVE IMPLEMENTATION (2001); CECILIA FIERMONTE & JENNIFER RENNE, ABA CENTER ON CHILDREN AND THE LAW, MAKING IT PERMANENT: REASONABLE EFFORTS TO FINALIZE PERMANENCY PLANS FOR FOSTER CHILDREN (2002).

[38] 42 U.S.C. § 674 (detailing percentages of reimbursements on expenditures).

Federal funds available pursuant to Title IV-B are intended for use in preventing and responding to cases of child maltreatment. Its purposes are broadly outlined in the statute:

> The purpose of [Title IV-B] is to promote State flexibility in the development and expansion of a coordinated child and family services program that utilizes community-based agencies and ensures all children are raised in safe, loving families, by—
>
> (1) protecting and promoting the welfare of all children;
>
> (2) preventing the neglect, abuse, or exploitation of children;
>
> (3) supporting at-risk families through services which allow children, where appropriate, to remain safely with their families or return to their families in a timely manner;
>
> (4) promoting the safety, permanence, and well-being of children in foster care and adoptive families; and
>
> (5) providing training, professional development and support to ensure a well-qualified child welfare workforce.[39]

In order to be eligible to draw down the federal money, the state, together with the Secretary of DHHS, must develop a state plan for the provision of child welfare services that meets certain federal requirements.[40] The statute requires that the state's Title IV-B plan be coordinated with the state's other child welfare plans pursuant to various other federal child welfare legislation.[41] The state's child welfare agency must also "demonstrate substantial, ongoing, and meaningful collaboration with state courts" in implementing their plans.[42]

Title IV-E funds provide federal assistance to states to help offset the costs of placing abused and neglected children into the foster care system when they cannot be safely maintained in their homes. It has long required states to develop a plan for the delivery of child welfare services, which must be approved by the federal government. Among its many requirements are that each child that enters foster care must have a plan that articulates the permanency goal for the child, establishes a schedule of services that the parents and child are to receive to facilitate reunification or, if reunification is not the permanency goal, a plan for achieving the identified permanent goal.

The AACWA began to have its intended impact. By 1982 the number of children in foster care began to decline.[43] But two phenomena converged shortly thereafter to

---

[39] 42 U.S.C. § 621.

[40] 42 U.S.C. § 622.

[41] 42 U.S.C. § 622(b)(2).

[42] 42 U.S.C. § 622(b)(13).

[43] RICHARD GELLES, THE BOOK OF DAVID: HOW PRESERVING FAMILIES CAN COST CHILDREN THEIR LIVES 130–31 (1996).

dramatically increase the number of children entering the nation's foster care system. First, in response to the election of Ronald Reagan as President, a more conservative government began to cut economic benefits to poor and working families. Between 1982 and 1984 nearly a half million families were removed from public assistance and another half million lost their Social Security disability payments.[44] Secondly, new social forces emerged—crack cocaine and HIV/AIDS—that dramatically increased the demand for child welfare services, and professionals began to see more families with multiple problems.[45] Whereas in 1982 there were about a quarter of a million children in the nation's foster care system, by 1993 that number had grown to 464,000.[46]

One response to the increased demand for child welfare services through the decade of the 1980s that was consistent with the federal mandate of the AACWA to preserve families was the increased use of family preservation programs. In hindsight, these politically popular programs may have been utilized beyond what the evidence of their efficacy would support.[47] As Professor Elizabeth Bartholet has observed, advocates for these programs often measured their success by whether they maintained children in their homes rather than whether children were safe and well cared for.[48] In a number of high profile cases, children were seriously injured or killed by parents in families in which child protective services had been involved.[49] This led policy makers to act once again.

Adoption and Safe Families Act

Concerned that its intent with regard to the handling of child welfare cases—and especially that its intentions regarding the application of the "reasonable efforts" and family preservation provisions of the AACWA—had been misunderstood and misapplied,[50] Congress, in 1997, passed the Adoption and Safe Families Act (ASFA), which became law in November of that year.[51] ASFA amended Titles IV-B and IV-E to clarify the intent of Congress with regard to the provision of child welfare services.

ASFA maintained the basic formula established in the AACWA. First, it reaffirmed the federal government's commitment to family preservation as a means of reducing the number of children removed from their homes and placed into the foster care system. It maintained the requirement that in most cases state child welfare

---

[44]   *Id.*

[45]   *Id.* at 131–32.

[46]   *Id.* at 131.

[47]   *Id.* at 132–33; *see also* ELIZABETH BARTHOLET, NOBODY'S CHILDREN: ABUSE, NEGLECT, FOSTER DRIFT, AND THE ADOPTION ALTERNATIVE (1999).

[48]   *Id.* at 113–121.

[49]   *See, e.g.*, RICHARD GELLES, THE BOOK OF DAVID: HOW PRESERVING FAMILIES CAN COST CHILDREN THEIR LIVES (1996).

[50]   *Id.* (arguing that family preservation had become the "central mission" of the child welfare system and that it placed children at unacceptable risk of harm).

[51]   Pub. L. No. 105-89, 111 Stat. 2115 (as codified in scattered sections of 42 U.S.C.).

agencies should make "reasonable efforts" to maintain familial integrity, and it substantially increased the funding available to states for family preservation services. In doing so, however, the Congress specifically sought to make clear that "in determining reasonable efforts to be made with respect to a child . . . the child's health and safety shall be the paramount concern."[52]

Next, when a child's safety in the familial home cannot be guaranteed, ASFA provides for a differential response depending on the nature of the harm done to the child. In cases of serious abuse in which the child or a sibling of the child has suffered grave harm, that has resulted in a criminal conviction of the parent for killing or inflicting serious harm on a child or where a parent has experienced previous involuntary termination of parental rights, ASFA eliminates the reasonable efforts requirement altogether and requires that the state child welfare agency immediately initiate or join an effort to terminate the parent's rights or otherwise place the child permanently.[53] Thus, for the first time, the federal law demanded that states seek immediate termination of parental rights or that another alternative permanent plan be sought in order to protect the child from abuse, neglect, or abandonment.

ASFA also invited, but did not require, each state to establish for itself a set of "aggravated circumstances" cases, which the state determines by either statute or policy will render a parent ineligible for either family preservation or family reunification services.[54] That is, ASFA permitted each state to define for itself a category of cases in which it will immediately seek to terminate the parents' rights or implement an alternative permanency plan. While the federal legislation allows each state to determine the specific types of cases that will fall within the "aggravated circumstances" designation, it suggests that appropriate cases may include situations where the parent has subjected the child to "abandonment, torture, chronic abuse, and sexual abuse."[55] Finally, ASFA permits the state child welfare agency to seek,[56] and the court to grant,[57] a request for immediate or early termination of parental rights in any case

---

[52] 42 U.S.C. § 671(a)(15).

[53] *See* 42 U.S.C. § 671(a)(15)(D)(ii). *See also* 45 C.F.R. § 1356.21(b)(3) (requiring that the parent be convicted of the relevant crime before ASFA's mandatory termination requirement is triggered).

[54] 42 U.S.C. § 671(a)(15)(D)(i).

[55] *Id.* Note, again, that this list is merely suggestive and that each state is free to determine for itself whether or not to include these or other types of cases in its definition of "aggravated circumstances" cases. For example, Michigan has adopted a definition of "aggravated circumstances" cases that includes child sexual abuse involving penetration or an attempt to penetrate, but has excluded those sexual abuse cases which involve only fondling. *See* MICH. COMP. LAWS ANN. § 722.638 (requiring state child protection agency to petition the court and seek termination of parental rights at the initial dispositional hearing); MICH. COMP. LAWS ANN. § 712A.19b(3)(k) (establishing aggravated circumstances as a basis for termination of parental rights). For more information regarding the bases for involuntary termination of parental rights, including information as to how individual states have defined "aggravated circumstances," see the following page on the Children's Bureau's Child Welfare Information Gateway: http://www.childwelfare.gov/systemwide/laws_policies/statutes/reunify.cfm#4.

[56] *See* Rule of Construction following 42 U.S.C. § 675 (Pub. L. No. 105-89, § 103(d)); *see generally* U.S. v Weldon, 377 U.S. 95, n. 4 (1964).

[57] 42 U.S.C. § 678.

where the facts and circumstances of that particular child's situation warrant such action. Illinois has, for instance, adopted a statute that codifies this authority. Its law permits an appropriate party to seek termination of parental rights "in those extreme cases in which the parent's incapacity to care for the child, combined with an extremely poor prognosis for treatment or rehabilitation, justifies expedited termination of parental rights."[58] Statutes such as this may place an additional burden on the child's attorney. For instance, some states allow the child's advocate to petition the court to terminate parental rights or to otherwise move to permanency at any time after the case is filed. In a state that permits such action, it is a good practice for the child's advocate to consider at each stage of every case whether the facts merit an effort to pursue early permanency or whether continued efforts to reunify the family will best serve the child.

Unless the court has determined that no "reasonable efforts" are required and permits a party to immediately implement an alternative permanent plan, the state must make "reasonable efforts" to reunify the child with his or her parent. While the federal law requires "reasonable efforts" be made in most cases, it does not define what constitutes "reasonable efforts." Defining "reasonable efforts" in a way that is truly helpful and provides practitioners with guidance has proven elusive. Missouri, for example, uses this definition:

> "Reasonable efforts" means the exercise of reasonable diligence and care . . . to utilize all available services related to meeting the needs of the juvenile and the family. In determining reasonable efforts to be made and in making such reasonable efforts, the child's present and ongoing health and safety shall be the paramount consideration.[59]

In order to operationalize the definition, some states have combined a definition of "reasonable efforts" with criteria to help courts determine whether the state agency has undertaken the necessary steps to comply with the requirement. The Iowa statute provides an example of this approach:

> "reasonable efforts" means the efforts made to preserve and unify a family prior to the out-of-home placement of a child in foster care or to eliminate the need for removal of the child or make it possible for the child to safely return to the family's home. Reasonable efforts shall include but are not limited to giving consideration, if appropriate, to interstate placement of a child in the permanency planning decisions involving the child and giving consideration to in-state and out-of-state placement options at a permanency hearing and when using concurrent planning. If returning the child to the family's home is not appropriate or not possible, reasonable efforts shall

---

[58] *See, e.g.,* 705 ILL. COMP. STAT. ANN. § 405/1-2(1)(c).

[59] MO. ANN. REV. STAT. § 211.183(2).

include the efforts made in a timely manner to finalize a permanency plan for the child. A child's health and safety shall be the paramount concern in making reasonable efforts. Reasonable efforts may include but are not limited to family-centered services, if the child's safety in the home can be maintained during the time the services are provided. In determining whether reasonable efforts have been made, the court shall consider both of the following:

(1)   The type, duration, and intensity of services or support offered or provided to the child and the child's family. If family-centered services were not provided, the court record shall enumerate the reasons the services were not provided, including but not limited to whether the services were not available, not accepted by the child's family, judged to be unable to protect the child and the child's family during the time the services would have been provided, judged to be unlikely to be successful in resolving the problems which would lead to removal of the child, or other services were found to be more appropriate.

(2)   The relative risk to the child of remaining in the child's home versus removal of the child.[60]

Despite the definitional difficulties, when "reasonable efforts" must be made the state's child welfare agency must establish a written case plan. That plan must include a description of the child's placement and a schedule of services to be provided to the child, the child's parents, and the foster parents to facilitate reunification.[61] Additionally, the plan must contain information about the child's health care, schooling, and related information.[62] If the child is 16 years of age or older, the case plan typically must contain a schedule of services aimed at helping the youth develop independence.[63] If the permanency planning goal is adoption or some other alternative (e.g., permanent guardianship), then the case plan must include a description of the "reasonable efforts" made to achieve the identified goal.[64]

In addition to the provisions that more clearly define the need to make "reasonable efforts," ASFA made numerous procedural changes aimed at expediting children's moves through the foster care system.[65] The state's plan for providing

---

[60]   Iowa Code § 232.102(10)(a).

[61]   42 U.S.C. § 675(1) (defining "case plan" and detailing the contents of that plan).

[62]   42 U.S.C. § 675(1).

[63]   *See* § 10.5, The Foster Care Independence Act (Chaffee Act). It should be noted that some states have made these independent living skills programs and services available to youth younger than 16. You should consult your state laws and policy to determine your state's approach to this question.

[64]   42 U.S.C. § 675(1)(E).

[65]   42 U.S.C. § 675(5).

foster care services must include a "case review system" that provides for periodic review of the case by a court or an administrative agency at least every six months, as well as a permanency planning hearing to be held at least once every 12 months for as long as the child remains in foster care.[66] Subject to several specific exceptions, when a child has been in foster care for 15 of the most recent 22 months, ASFA requires that the state child welfare agency pursue termination of parental rights.[67] At least one state's supreme court has held, however, that more than the mere passage of time is necessary when considering termination based on the child's being in foster care for a defined period of time.[68]

Several other provisions of ASFA focused on expediting children's moves through foster care. ASFA continued AACWA's effort to move children out of the foster care system and into permanent placement by permitting the use of concurrent planning.[69] Concurrent planning allows the state to simultaneously pursue efforts aimed at reunification as well as efforts to place the child in an alternative permanent setting if family reunification cannot be achieved. Such a concurrent approach, as opposed to the seriatim approach often used by child welfare agencies, may shorten substantially the child's stay in temporary foster care.

Next, in addition to continuing the subsidies available to individual families to assist with expenses associated with adoption, ASFA provided each state a financial incentive to focus on efforts to move children who could not be returned to their family of origin into adoptive homes. It did so by establishing a baseline number of adoptions and then paying the state a bonus for each adoption from foster care finalized in excess of that baseline.[70]

Finally, the ASFA expanded the permanency options available for resolving cases.[71] For instance, permanent guardianship was specifically recognized as a form of permanency.[72] As a last resort for those children who could not be returned to their family of origin but for whom more complete legal permanency could not be achieved, ASFA permitted the state to use "another planned permanent living arrangement" (APPLA).[73] APPLA "is a case plan designation for children in out-of-home care for

---

[66] 42 U.S.C. § 675(5).

[67] 42 U.S.C. § 675(5)(E).

[68] *In re* H.G., 757 N.E.2d 864 (Ill. 2001) (termination based merely on child's placement in foster care for 15 of 22 months violated parent's substantive due process right to custody of the child).

[69] 42 U.S.C. § 671(a)(15)(F).

[70] 42 U.S.C. § 673b.

[71] *See generally* DONALD N. DUQUETTE & MARK HARDIN, GUIDELINES FOR PUBLIC POLICY AND STATE LEGISLATION GOVERNING PERMANENCE FOR CHILDREN (Children's Bureau 1999).

[72] 42 U.S.C. § 675(7) (defining "legal guardianship" as a judicially created relationship that is intended to be permanent). It should be noted here that additional amendments to Title IV-E enacted as part of the Fostering Connections Act have further ensconced legal guardianship as a permanency plan and provides federal funding to assist in the establishment of permanent, subsidized legal guardianships. These changes are discussed in more detail later in this chapter.

[73] *See* 42 U.S.C. § 675(5)(C).

whom there is no goal for placement with a legal, permanent family."[74] Before using an APPLA, the caseworker must document and present to the court compelling reasons why a more appropriate, legally permanent placement option (e.g., return home, adoption, permanent placement with a willing relative) is not available for the child or youth.[75] APPLA may include independent living for an older foster youth who does not wish to be adopted, long-term foster care placement for a youth who has a strong bond with his or her natural parent but whose parent is unable to care for the youth or, in the case of an Indian child, a situation where the child's tribe has established a different plan for the child's permanent placement.[76]

§ 10.4 Multiethnic Placement Act and the Interethnic Adoption Provisions

§ 10.4.1 History

Through much of American history, minority children—and particularly African American children—were excluded from receiving publicly funded child welfare services or received fewer services in less family-like settings than Caucasian children.[77] Some non-governmental child welfare programs provided services to children without regard to race, yet the needs of children of color often went unmet or were improperly addressed.[78] In the early decades of the twentieth century, African American women began establishing privately funded programs to provide services for Black children in need of such services.[79] Over time, these organizations contracted with public authorities to provide services to children of color. Today it would be illegal to deny a child services to a child or family based on race.

In recent years, the concern of child welfare professionals has not been the lack of services to children of color,[80] but rather the overrepresentation of minority children,

---

[74] Child Welfare Information Gateway, *APPLA and LTFC, available at* www.childwelfare.gov/out of home/types/appla_ltfc.cfm.

[75] 42 U.S.C. § 675(5).

[76] *See* Jennifer Renne & Gerald P. Mallon, *Facilitating Permanency for Youth: The Overuse of Long-Term Foster Care and the Appropriate Use of Another Planned Permanent Living Arrangement as Options for Youth in Foster Care, in* CHILD WELFARE FOR THE 21ST CENTURY: A HANDBOOK OF PRACTICES, POLICIES, AND PROGRAMS (Gerald P. Mallon & Peg McCartt Hess eds., 2005).

[77] Wilma Peebles-Wilkins, *Janie Porter Barrett and the Virginia Industrial School for Colored Girls: Community Response to the Needs of African American Children,* 74/1 CHILD WELFARE 143 (1995); JOHN E. B. MYERS, CHILD PROTECTION IN AMERICA: PAST, PRESENT, AND FUTURE 184–85 (2006). *See generally* RANDALL KENNEDY, INTERRACIAL INTIMACIES: SEX, MARRIAGE, IDENTITY, AND ADOPTION (2003).

[78] *Id.*

[79] Wilma Peebles-Wilkins, *Janie Porter Barrett and the Virginia Industrial School for Colored Girls: Community Response to the Needs of African American Children,* 74/1 CHILD WELFARE 143, 145–46 (1995).

[80] A number of commentators have argued, of course, that children and families of color are provided the wrong or inadequate services. *See* JOHN E. B. MYERS, CHILD PROTECTION IN AMERICA: PAST,

and particularly African American children, in the nation's public child welfare system.[81] As African American children began to be served by the public system, a number of controversies emerged. Among these, few have been more contentious than the placement of children across racial lines, principally, although not exclusively, the placement of African American children with Caucasian families.[82] On the one hand, the failure to place children across racial lines means that there is a smaller foster family pool to draw from, and this may deprive children of a family and condemn them to shuffle from temporary foster home to temporary foster home or institutional care.[83] On the other hand, there is concern that placing children across racial lines may dislocate children from their racial and ethnic identity and will not adequately prepare minority children for dealing with a racist society.[84]

Placement of children across racial lines for foster care and adoption has had a contentious history in this country.[85] This may in part stem from a long-standing misperception that African Americans families were unwilling to adopt.[86] But it also has its roots in the historical failure of public authorities to license African American homes to provide foster care to children, sometimes because of overt racism and sometimes because of the application of race neutral licensing criteria, which historically have had a disproportionate negative impact on African Americans. In 1972, the National Association of Black Social Workers adopted a policy position opposing the adoption of African-American children by non-African-American parents.[87] While over the years the organization's position has developed nuance, it continues to oppose the trans-racial adoption of African-American children in most circumstances.[88] For decades, child welfare agencies maintained race matching

---

PRESENT, AND FUTURE 185 (2006) (citing DOROTHY ROBERTS, SHATTERED BONDS: THE COLOR OF CHILD WELFARE (2002)).

[81] JOHN E. B. MYERS, CHILD PROTECTION IN AMERICA: PAST, PRESENT, AND FUTURE 198 (2006).

[82] The removal Indian children from their families and placement with White families for adoption was a major impetus for the enactment of the Indian Child Welfare Act, 25 U.S.C. §§ 1901 *et seq.* For a full discussion of the reasons for the enactment of the Indian Child Welfare Act, see § 12.2, History.

[83] *See generally* RANDALL KENNEDY, INTERRACIAL INTIMACIES: SEX, MARRIAGE, IDENTITY, AND ADOPTION 402–79 (2003).

[84] *Id.* at 395–96.

[85] *See generally Id.* (discussing the conflict surrounding interracial adoption); ELIZABETH BARTHOLET, NOBODY'S CHILDREN: ABUSE, NEGLECT, FOSTER DRIFT, AND THE ADOPTION ALTERNATIVE 123–40 (1999) (discussing the history of the controversy surrounding race matching in adoption).

[86] ANDREW BILLINGSLEY, CLIMBING JACOB'S LADDER: THE ENDURING LEGACY OF AFRICAN-AMERICAN FAMILIES 29 (1992).

[87] *See* National Association of Black Social Workers, *Preserving Families of African Ancestry* (adopted by the NABSW National Steering Committee, Jan. 10, 1993), *available at* www.nabsw.org/mserver/ PreservingFamilies.aspx (describing the organization's position on adoption and preservation of African-American Families).

[88] *Id.*

policies for foster children and those in need of adoption services.[89] During that time, placement of a child across racial lines was permitted only as a last resort.[90] Too frequently, however, children were removed from stable trans-racial foster home placements only to prevent the possibility of a trans-racial adoption.[91] Those polices often resulted in minority children remaining in temporary foster care for unnecessarily long periods of time.[92]

In an effort to address these issues, Congress passed the Multi-Ethnic Placement Act (MEPA) in 1994, which amended portions of Title IV-B and IV-E of the Social Security Act.[93] The Act sought to eliminate—or at least dramatically reduce—race, color, and national origin as considerations in making foster care and adoptive placement decisions. The original statute, however, contained language that was easily interpreted to permit just what it intended to prohibit—the consideration of race, color, or national origin of the child or the parent when making foster care or adoptive placement decisions.[94] For example, the statute prohibited the "routine" consideration of race, color, or national when making placement decisions, which implied that these factors were legitimate considerations rather than wholly prohibited.

Two years after the enactment of MEPA, Congress enacted the Interethnic Adoption Provisions of the Small Business Job Protection Act (IEP). These amendments sought to clarify Congress's intent that, consistent with other civil rights legislation, considerations of race, color, or national origin were not to be permitted when making placement decisions in the public child welfare system.[95] The IEP also engrafted significant financial penalties in the form of loss of Title IV-E funding onto the law for violation of its terms.[96] Moreover, the amendments explicitly provided a right to sue to any child or adult aggrieved by its violation.[97]

Broadly speaking, the MEPA-IEP seeks to achieve three goals. First, it seeks to eliminate the consideration of a person's race, color, or national origin with regard to licensing foster parents. The current law provides that:

---

[89] JOAN HEIFETZ HOLLNGER & THE ABA CENTER ON CHILDREN AND THE LAW, A GUIDE TO THE MULTIETHNIC PLACEMENT ACT OF 1994 AS AMENDED BY THE INTERETHNIC ADOPTION PROVISIONS OF 1996 at 4–6 (American Bar Association 1998).

[90] *Id.* at 4.

[91] *Id.*

[92] *Id.* at 5.

[93] *See* 42 U.S.C. § 622(b)(7); 42 U.S.C. § 671(a)(18); 42 U.S.C. § 674(d)(2).

[94] ELIZABETH BARTHOLET, NOBODY'S CHILDREN: ABUSE, NEGLECT, FOSTER DRIFT, AND THE ADOPTION ALTERNATIVE 130–31 (1999).

[95] *Id.* at 131.

[96] 42 U.S.C. § 674(d)(1).

[97] *See* 42 U.S.C. § 674(d)(3).

... neither the State nor any other entity in the State that receives funds from the Federal Government and is involved in adoption or foster care placements may—

(A) deny to any person the opportunity to become an adoptive or a foster parent, on the basis of race, color, or national origin of the person, or of the child, involved.[98]

Next, it prohibits state child welfare agencies, their workers or agents, and the courts from considering the race, color, or national origin of either a child or a parent when making decisions regarding foster care or adoptive placement of a child. The law provides that state agencies or their agents shall not "delay or deny the placement of a child for adoption or into foster care, on the basis of the race, color, or national origin of the adoptive or foster parent, or the child, involved."[99]

Finally, it requires state child welfare authorities to make diligent efforts to recruit foster and adoptive parents "that reflect the ethnic and racial diversity of children in the State for whom foster and adoptive homes are needed."[100] Specifically, the law, as interpreted by the Department of Health and Human Services, mandates that, among other things, state authorities do all of the following:

- Develop recruitment plans that reach all parts of the community
- Use diverse methods and avenues for disseminating information about fostering and adopting
- Ensure all prospective foster or adoptive parents have timely access to the home study process
- Train workers to work with diverse cultures
- Develop methods to overcome language barriers[101]

§ 10.4.2 Delay

Any delay in placement based on race, color, or national origin is prohibited by the statute. Thus, for instance, using "holding periods" for the purpose of placing a child in racially congruent foster or adoptive home would violate the law.

---

[98] 42 U.S.C. § 671(a)(18)(A).

[99] 42 U.S.C. § 671(a)(18)(B).

[100] 42 U.S.C. § 622(b)(7); *see also* JOAN HEIFETZ HOLLNGER & THE ABA CENTER ON CHILDREN AND THE LAW, A GUIDE TO THE MULTIETHNIC PLACEMENT ACT OF 1994 AS AMENDED BY THE INTERETHNIC ADOPTION PROVISIONS OF 1996 at 2 (American Bar Association 1998).

[101] JOAN HEIFETZ HOLLNGER & THE ABA CENTER ON CHILDREN AND THE LAW, A GUIDE TO THE MULTIETHNIC PLACEMENT ACT OF 1994 AS AMENDED BY THE INTERETHNIC ADOPTION PROVISIONS OF 1996 at 13 (American Bar Association 1998).

§ 10.4.3 Denial

Under MEPA-IEP, race, color, or national origin cannot be used to render a child ineligible for foster care or adoption or to deny a person the opportunity to become a foster parent. Additionally, the agency must not take race, color, or national origin into consideration when making decisions regarding efforts aimed at reunification, concurrent planning, or the termination of parental rights.

Although race, color, and national origin may not be considerations used to deny foster care or adoptive placement, MEPA-IEP does not prohibit all consideration of these factors when assessing the needs of a particular child in an individual case.[102] Guidance published by the DHHS in 1997 and 1998 provides that in certain, narrowly tailored situations, the best interests of a particular child may support some consideration of race, color, or national origin in placement decision-making.[103] To be legitimate, however, consideration of these factors must grow out of the unique needs of a particular child. The 1997 policy guidance provides insight into the types of consideration which may be permissible:

> [I]t is conceivable that an older child or adolescent might express an unwillingness to be placed with a family of a particular race. In some states older children and adolescents must consent to their adoption by a particular family. In such an individual situation, an agency is not required to dismiss the child's express unwillingness to consent in evaluating placements.[104]

In very carefully circumscribed instances such as these, consideration of race, color, or national origin may be appropriate under the law. Even in situations such as these, however, the caseworker should not blindly defer to the young person. Rather, this should be seen as a situation in which the child may need counseling. Agencies' actions in such cases will be carefully scrutinized to ensure that there are not more narrowly tailored responses available to meet the child's expressed reluctance.

When a child has a specific need relating to race, color, or national origin, that need as well as less impactful methods of addressing the child's need should be carefully documented in the child's case file. Doing so will help prevent the routine consideration of race, color, or national origin that the law so clearly prohibits. Race, color, or national origin, then, should only rarely be taken into consideration when making placement decisions.

Two important issues must be accounted for when race, color, or national origin influence a placement decision. First, race, color, or national origin cannot be considered for certain categories of children. For instance, infants are presumed to have

---

[102] *See* U.S. Department of Health & Human Services, Administration for Children and Families, *Guidance for Federal Legislation—The Small Business and Job Protection Act of 1996* (IM-97-04) (June 5, 1997).

[103] *Id.*

[104] *Id.* at 4.

no special needs concerning race, color, or national origin. As such, consideration of race, color, or national origin during placement decision-making for an infant cannot grow out of the unique needs of the individual child, and any consideration of them when making decisions regarding infants is prohibited. Secondly, any consideration of race, color, or national origin will be subjected to strict scrutiny and must be narrowly tailored to meet a compelling governmental interest. Thus, even in a situation where race, color, or national origin may be properly considered, the agency's response must not be overly broad and the agency must seek out the least restrictive means of addressing the individualized needs of the specific child. Responses to a child's individualized needs regarding race, color, or national origin must be narrowly tailored to meet that specifically articulated need.

§ 10.4.4 MEPA-IEP and the Indian Child Welfare Act

MEPA-IEP specifically provides that its provisions do not apply to any child who qualifies as an "Indian child" under the ICWA.[105] Because ICWA applies only to children who are members of or eligible for membership in a federally recognized Indian tribe (i.e., one who meets the definition of "Indian child"), MEPA-IEP's provisions would apply to those children who are of Native American heritage but who are not member of or eligible for membership in a tribe.

§ 10.4.5 Enforcement

MEPA-IEP contains strict enforcement mechanisms. First, violations of the MEPA-IEP's requirements may constitute a violation of Title VI of the Civil Rights Act of 1964.[106] Next, failure to comply with the statute's mandates may result in substantial financial penalties for the state in the form of lost Title IV-B funding.[107] Similarly, a state may lose Title IV-E funds if it violates the statute.[108] Specifically, the statute provides for a penalty of a 2-percent reduction in the state's Title IV-E funds for the fiscal year for a first violation, a 3-percent reduction for a second violation, and a 5-percent reduction for the third violation. These penalties could easily run into the tens of millions of dollars. Finally, the statute explicitly provides an individual cause of action for any individual child or prospective foster or adoptive parent who has been aggrieved as a result of a violation of the statute.[109] MEPA-IEP provides a two-year statute of limitations for bringing an action.[110]

---

[105] 42 U.S.C. § 674(d)(4); 42 U.S.C. § 1996b(3).

[106] 42 U.S.C. § 1996b(2); *see also* JOAN HEIFETZ HOLLNGER & THE ABA CENTER ON CHILDREN AND THE LAW, A GUIDE TO THE MULTIETHNIC PLACEMENT ACT OF 1994 AS AMENDED BY THE INTERETHNIC ADOPTION PROVISIONS OF 1996 at 16 (American Bar Association 1998).

[107] 42 U.S.C. § 623(a); 45 C.F.R. § 201.6(a).

[108] 42 U.S.C. § 674(d).

[109] 42 U.S.C. § 674(d)(3).

[110] 42 U.S.C. § 674(d)(3).

§ 10.5 The Foster Care Independence Act (Chaffee Act)

Although discussed in more detail in Chapter 23, the Foster Care Independence Act (commonly referred to as the Chaffee Act) merits a brief mention here. For some time it has been clear that youth who age out of the foster care system without having found a stable family face major obstacles in their transition to young adulthood.[111] Among the challenges these young people face are lack of adequate education, lack of marketable job skills, homelessness, poverty, teen pregnancy, and involvement in the juvenile and criminal justice systems. To address these problems, in 1986 Congress amended Title IV-E to establish the Independent Living Program. The Program aims to provide services to older foster youth to prepare them for adulthood. In 1999 Congress expanded the services available to these youth by amending various provisions of Title IV-E. Basically, the Chaffee Act established the Chaffee Foster Care Independence Program, which allowed states to provide Medicaid coverage to youth 18 to 21 years of age who are in foster care on their 18th birthday, permitted foster care youth to have assets valued at up to $10,000 and remain eligible for Title IV-E funding (up from only $1000), required state child welfare authorities to ensure that foster parents are prepared initially and on an ongoing basis to care for the youth placed in their homes, and authorized increased adoption incentive payments to states to aide in establishing permanent homes for these youth.

§ 10.6 Fostering Connections to Success and Increasing Adoptions Act

The Fostering Connections to Success and Increasing Adoptions Act (Fostering Connections Act),[112] which amends numerous provisions of Titles IV-B and IV-E, became law on October 7, 2008. In broad terms, these amendments seek to maintain a child's ties with family, expedite children's passage through the foster care system, provide prompt permanency, and achieve better outcomes for youth once they leave the foster care system. More specifically, the Fostering Connections Act: (1) expands permanency options for foster children and youth; (2) requires increased efforts of state child welfare authorities to locate members of a child's kinship network where that child is in or at risk of entering the child welfare system; (3) requires state child welfare authorities to undertake more aggressive efforts to notify a child's adult relatives that the child has entered the foster care system; (4) permits waiver of certain foster home licensing rules in order to place a child with relatives; (5) permits states to maintain youth in foster care until age 21 under certain circumstances; (6) requires that the agency work with youth close to aging out of foster care to develop a plan for

---

[111] Martha Shirk & Gary Strangler, On Their Own: What Happens to Kids When They Age Out of the Foster Care System? (Westview Press 2004).

[112] 42 U.S.C. §§ 621 *et seq.*; 42 U.S.C. §§ 670 *et seq.*

transitioning to independence; (7) encourages educational stability by requiring state child welfare authorities to coordinate with educational providers; (8) ensures children in foster care have access to health care; (9) ensures that when possible siblings are placed together; (10) permits Indian tribes to directly access Title IV-E funds rather than having to work through states to receive these funds; (11) provides incentives for adoption of children from the foster care system. Each of these goals will be discussed briefly.

§ 10.6.1 Expanded Permanency Options

The Fostering Connections Act permits each state to establish a subsidized kinship guardianship program. Under such a program "grandparents and other relatives" who have cared for a child in the role of foster parents and who are willing to make a permanent commitment to raising the child may become legal guardians of the child. This program would work much the same way as the adoption assistance program. The adult relative would be given guardianship over the foster child that is intended to be permanent. The relative-guardian would receive financial assistance to provide care for that child. Among other requirements, to be eligible for a subsidized guardianship, the relative must have cared for the child as a foster care provider for six consecutive months. Additionally, the state can be reimbursed by the federal government for up to $2000 per child for nonrecurring expenses related to getting the guardianship put in place (e.g., filing fees). Before a relative-guardian may receive kinship guardianship assistance payments, the agency must conduct a criminal background check using national crime information data bases of the guardian and any other adult living in the home. Moreover, before placing a child in a kinship guardianship, the case worker must document the steps that were taken to determine that returning the child to the parent is not an appropriate permanency plan, why placement with a relative in a permanent guardianship will serve the child's best interests, that adoption by the relative has been discussed and why adoption is not being pursued, and what efforts were made to discuss the matter with the child's parents.

§ 10.6.2 Locating Adult Relatives

The amendments permit the DHHS to make a limited number of matching grants to the individual states, local, tribal, or private agencies to help children who are in or are at risk of entering the foster care system to reconnect with adult relatives. Among the services that may be made available through these grants are kinship navigator programs, which assist adult caregivers in locating services that will assist them in providing for the needs of a child who is placed with them. Included in the bundle of services that should be made available through the kinship navigator program is assistance in locating and obtaining legal counsel.

These grants may also be used to implement "intensive family-finding efforts" to locate members of the child's extended family, to work toward reestablishment of relationships with these newly located relatives, and to find permanent family placements for children.

Family connection grants may also be used to fund "residential family treatment" programs that would "enable parents and their children to live in a safe environment for a period of not less than 6 months" and which would provide various services to the child and the parent, either in that program or by way of referral to another program.[113]

§ 10.6.3 Providing Notice to Relatives

The Fostering Connections Act amends Title IV-E to require that each state's plan provide that within 30 days of the child's removal from the parental home state authorities will "exercise due diligence to identify and provide notice to all adult grandparents and other adult relatives of the child" unless there has been family or domestic violence involving that adult.[114] The statute contains a number of requirements for the information that must be provided in such a notification.

§ 10.6.4 Waiving Licensing Rules

The statute clarifies that non-safety related licensing rules may be waived to facilitate placement of children into relative foster homes.[115] However, such waivers must be made on a case-by-case basis and may not be made as a matter of policy. Each state may define for itself what constitutes a "non-safety" licensing rule.

§ 10.6.5 Extending Age of Foster Care Placement

While it is the federal government's general policy to move children out of the foster care system and into permanent placements as soon as possible, for older youth, remaining in the foster care system longer may actually enhance the young person's chances of a successful transition into adulthood.[116] For instance, in a study comparing the outcomes of youth who were released from the foster care system at 18 and those who were maintained in the system until age 21, researchers at Chapin Hall found evidence that youth maintained in the system until age 21 had improved outcomes in terms of education, earnings from employment, and delayed teen pregnancy.[117] In part as a result of this research, effective October 1, 2010, the Act

---

[113] 42 U.S.C. § 627(a)(4).

[114] 42 U.S.C. § 671(a)(29).

[115] 42 U.S.C. § 671(a)(10).

[116] For a summary of this research, see Mark E. Courtney, Amy Dworsky & Harold Pollack, *Issue Brief: When Should the State Cease Parenting? Evidence from the Midwest Study* (Chapin Hall Center for Children, Dec. 2007). For a more detailed discussion of this research, see Mark E. Courtney, A. Dworsky, G. R. Cusick, J. Havlicek, A. Perez & T. Keller, *Midwest Evaluation of Adult Functioning of Former Foster Youth: Outcomes at Age 21* (Chapin Hall Center for Children 2007).

[117] Mark E. Courtney, Amy Dworsky & Harold Pollack, *Issue Brief: When Should the State Cease Parenting? Evidence from the Midwest Study* (Chapin Hall Center for Children, Dec. 2007).

permits the federal government to provide funding to support youth if a state elects to extend their stays in the foster care system to the age of 21. To be eligible for Title IV-E funding between the ages of 18 and 21, the youth must be completing high school or an equivalent program, be enrolled in college or a program of vocational education, be engaged in a program to obtain employment, be employed for at least 80 hours per month, or be unable to be involved in one of these programs because of a medical condition.[118]

§ 10.6.6 Transition Plan

The Fostering Connections amendments require that during the 90 days immediately preceding a youth's emancipation from foster care, whether at age 18 or older if the state chooses, agency caseworkers must meet with the youth and others who are supportive of the youth for the purpose of developing a transition plan for exiting the foster care system.[119] The plan must be "personalized at the direction of the child" and must specifically address the youth's housing, health insurance, education, available mentors, continuing support services that are available to the youth, work force supports, and employment services. The plan must be as detailed as the youth chooses.

§ 10.6.7 Educational Stability

Children entering the foster care system have often been required to move to a new school system. These moves have inevitably resulted in foster children losing momentum in their educational progress. The Fostering Connections Act seeks to address this problem by requiring that State child welfare authorities work with relevant educational authorities to ensure that children who are removed from the homes of their biological parents can remain in their elementary or secondary school after the move.[120] Thus, each state's plan for foster care must contain assurances that: (1) the appropriateness of the child's educational placement is taken into consideration when making decisions about moving the child, and (2) foster placements, whenever possible, are coordinated to ensure the child can remain in his or her school if doing so is in the best interests of the child. Where remaining in the school in which the child was enrolled at the time of placement is not in the child's best interests, then the state plan must provide for the immediate placement of the child is an appropriate school setting. The federal government will also reimburse states for travel expenses associated with maintaining a child in his or her pre-placement school.

---

[118] 42 U.S.C. § 675(8).

[119] 42 U.S.C. § 675(5)(H).

[120] 42 U.S.C. § 675(1)(G).

§ 10.6.8 Health Care

Children entering the foster care system have numerous health care needs, sometimes due to naturally occurring maladies or due to the neglect and abuse they have experienced before entering the system.[121] There has been long-standing concern about the promptness, continuity, and quality of health care foster children receive while in care. Fostering Connections requires that states' plans for delivery of services to children in foster care include a strategy to ensure that children are provided appropriate health care,[122] including for mental and dental health. In addition to initial and periodic physical exams, the state may develop a plan for ensuring that the child's medical records are created and stored electronically and are accessible as health care providers may change. The state must also include in its plan for delivery of foster care services a plan to ensure continuity of medical care and the agency may establish a medical home for the child.

§ 10.6.9 Keeping Siblings Together

Fostering Connections establishes a preference that when removed from the home of their parents, siblings will be placed together.[123] Thus, it amends Title IV-E to require each state's plan for providing foster care services must include a commitment that the state will make "reasonable efforts" to place siblings together—whether in the home of a relative, foster home with an unrelated person, or for adoption—unless placing the children in the same home would not protect the safety and well-being of one or more of the children. When siblings cannot be placed in the same home, the agency must provide for "frequent visitation or other ongoing interaction between the siblings" unless such frequent contact would not serve the child's interests.[124]

§ 10.6.10 Tribal Access to Title IV-E Funds

Historically Indian tribes have not had direct access to Title IV-E funds. To gain access to this money, tribes have been required to develop agreements with state child welfare authorities to draw down their share of these federal dollars. Only about half the federally recognized tribes have such an agreement in place.[125] The Fostering Connections Act attempts to change this by establishing a system that permits tribes or tribal consortiums to develop their own plans for providing child welfare services, thereby gaining direct access to federal financial assistance.[126]

---

[121] *See* Jan McCarthy & Maria Woolverton, *Healthcare Needs of Children and Youth in Foster Care, in* CHILD WELFARE FOR THE 21ST CENTURY: A HANDBOOK OF PRACTICES, POLICIES, AND PROGRAMS 129–47 (Gerald P. Mallon & Peg McCartt Hess eds., 2005).

[122] 42 U.S.C. § 622(b)(15).

[123] 42.U.S.C. § 671(a).

[124] 42 U.S.C. § 671(a)(31)(B).

[125] Visit the Fostering Connections Resource Center at www.fosteringconnections.org.

[126] 42 U.S.C. § 679c.

To avail itself of this direct federal funding, the tribe or tribal consortium must develop a plan for delivery of child welfare services similar to the plans states have been required to have in place. Each such plan must ensure that it has the capacity to provide for adequate fiscal management of federal programs and must describe the service areas and the populations that will benefit from the tribe's child welfare services program. The law requires that the Secretary of DHHS provide technical assistance to tribes to assist them in developing a Title IV-E plan for the delivery of child welfare services. Additionally, tribes are eligible for a one time grant of up to $300,000 to offset the costs of developing and submitting the plan.[127]

§ 10.6.11 Adoption Incentives

To encourage states to press for the adoption of foster children who are in need of adoption services, the Fostering Connections Act increases adoption incentive payments to states. Since the enactment of ASFA, states have been able to receive incentive payments for each adoption of an older child or a child with special needs above the state's base number of adoptions. The way this works is that the state has a base number of adoptions completed as of a certain date. For each adoption of an older child or a child with special needs beyond this base number, the state will be eligible to receive an incentive payment from the federal government.

Fostering Connections enhances these payments in several ways. First, it increases adoption incentive payment to the state for each child adopted beyond the base number from $2000 to $4000. If the adopted child is a special needs child, the state will receive an additional $4000. Finally, when the adoption involves an older child the state will be eligible for the $4000 incentive payment plus an additional $8000 payment (note that this payment is only available for each adoption exceeding the state's base number of adoptions of older children). The intent of these incentives is to motivate the states to focus on the adoption of special needs and older children from the foster care system.

§ 10.7 Child Well-Being Statutes

Numerous federal statutes unrelated to preventing and responding to child maltreatment play a crucial role in supporting families and promoting child well-being. Some of these establish federal programs to assist particular children or families (e.g., Temporary Assistance to Needy Families (TANF), Medicaid, and the food stamps program), while others provide block grants to the states to provide particular services (e.g., Social Services Block Grants (SSBG) and Maternal and Child Health Block grants). For this latter type of program, the state must establish the program, then individuals apply to the state to gain the benefit of the program. Some of these programs include at least some amount of direct funding for child welfare

---

[127] 42 U.S.C. § 676(c).

purposes (e.g., Temporary Assistance to Needy Families, Social Services Block Grants); others are supports generally available to assist categories of children and families, with some children and families who are involved in the child welfare system included in those categories (e.g., Child Care, Title I Education for the Disadvantaged). Some are open-ended entitlements, meaning that federal funding automatically expands or contracts annually to provide a defined benefit for all eligible persons (e.g., foster care, adoption assistances). Most programs are funded at specific levels rather than being limited only by the level of need (e.g., TANF and SSBG).

The following are the significant programs that provide assistance to qualifying individuals and include substantial child welfare services funding.

§ 10.7.1 Temporary Assistance to Needy Families

TANF is a block grant program created in 1996 to replace Aid to Families with Dependent Children (AFDC), which was an open-ended entitlement.[128] TANF funds time-limited cash assistance to low income families with children. Receipt of TANF funds is contingent on meeting work-hour requirements. The program provides some work supports for participants (e.g., training, child care, transportation). Most TANF beneficiaries are children living with their parents, but a substantial percentage are children residing with relatives, some of whom are placed with that relative as a result of a child welfare proceeding. Indeed, TANF is a significant source of funding for child welfare services including support for children in relative placements as just mentioned, adoption, and related services. Additionally, individual states may choose to transfer a portion of their TANF funds to the SSBG program under Title XX, which funds may be used to provide child welfare services.

§ 10.7.2 Medicaid

Medicaid is an entitlement program that provides health care benefits to low income persons.[129] Eligibility requirements, the specific services covered, and the level of reimbursement for medical services provided vary from state to state.

Eligibility

States are required to cover pregnant women and children under 6 years of age with a family income below 133% of the federally established poverty rate, and children between 5 and 19 years of age whose family income is below the poverty line. Individual states may choose to also cover pregnant women and children whose family income is between 133% and 185% of the federally established poverty line. States must also provide Medicaid benefits to recipients of Title IV-E foster care and adoption assistance to age 18. Individual states may choose, under the Chaffee Act, to

---

[128] Pub. L. No. 104-193, 110 Stat. 2105 (codified as amended at 42 U.S.C. §§ 601–619).

[129] 42 U.S.C. §§ 1396–1396v.

provide Medicaid benefits to young people who are or were in foster care to age 21. States may also choose to cover some children and youth who do not fall within these categories of recipients, and some states elect to provide services to foster children. States are prohibited from imposing cost sharing on services provided to children under age 18 or for services related to pregnancy.

Benefits

Medicaid includes both mandatory services (e.g., hospitalization, lab and x-ray fees, family planning and pregnancy-related services) and optional services (e.g., eyeglasses, prescription drugs, dental care, and case management). Those under age 21 are entitled to receive preventative care through "Early and Periodic Screening, Diagnosis and Treatment," including comprehensive physical exams, immunizations, lead screening, vision and dental services, and other healthcare services necessary to address medical need identified through the exams. Children receiving Medicaid services may receive those services through managed care organizations.

§ 10.7.3 State Children's Health Insurance Program

In 1997 Congress enacted the State Children's Health Insurance Program (SCHIP).[130] The program was reauthorized and expanded to cover more children in 2009. The SCHIP program establishes a defined federal financial commitment to provide medical care to children who are ineligible for Medicaid because their family income is too high yet who lack health insurance. Often these children hail from working poor families. Currently, the program covers children and youth under age 19 whose families earn less that approximately $36,200 per years (for a family of four).[131] States may implement their SCHIP programs by expanding their Medicaid program, by establishing an entirely separate program, or by combining the two programs.

§ 10.7.4 Supplemental Security Income

The Supplemental Security Income (SSI) program is a means tested program, administered by the federal government, which was established in 1972.[132] To receive benefits under this program, the individual must meet income eligibility requirements and have a qualifying disability (e.g., physical handicap, mental illness, etc.). SSI is fully federally funded and individual states do not have to match the federal funds.

---

[130] Pub. L. No. 105-33, 111 Stat. 251 (codified as amended at 42 U.S.C. §§ 1397aa–1397f).

[131] Robert Longley, *Health Insurance for Uninsured Children: About the SCHIP Program, available at* http://usgovinfo.about.com/od/medicarehealthinsurance/a/schip.htm.

[132] Pub. L. No. 92-603; 42 U.S.C. §§ 1381–1383(d).

§ 10.7.5 Other Federal Programs

In addition to the programs already discussed, there are numerous other programs that may provide aide to children and families involved in child welfare proceedings. These include:

- Food Stamps – a means tested entitlement program.[133]

- The Special Supplemental Nutrition Program for Women, Infants, and Children (WIC) – a non-entitlement program that provides nutritional support to low income pregnant women and their children to age 5.[134]

- Child Nutrition Program – funds, among other things, school breakfast and lunch programs.[135]

- Section 8 housing – not an entitlement program, but it provides rental assistance to low income persons.[136]

- The Child Care and Development Block Grant – provides child care assistance to low-income working parents.[137]

- Head Start – a non-entitlement program aimed at providing quality early childhood education and comprehensive services to low-income, pre-school aged children.[138]

§ 10.8 Miscellaneous Federal Statutes

In addition to the child welfare and child well-being legislation discussed above, child welfare lawyers should be aware that other federal statutes may impact your handling of child welfare cases. In this portion of this chapter, we will discuss two statutes of this sort.

§ 10.8.1 Americans with Disabilities Act

The Americans with Disabilities Act (ADA)[139] was enacted to address the long-standing and pervasive discrimination against persons with physical and mental disabilities.[140] The statute intends to guarantee that persons with disabilities have the same access to services, programs, and activities as persons without disabilities. Thus,

---

[133] Pub. L. No. 88-525; 7 U.S.C. §§ 2011–2036.

[134] 42 U.S.C. § 1786.

[135] 42 U.S.C. §§ 1751–1790.

[136] 42 U.S.C. §§ 1437–13664.

[137] 42 U.S.C. § 9858.

[138] 42 U.S.C. §§ 9831–9843a.

[139] 42 U.S.C. §§ 12101 *et seq.*

[140] 42 U.S.C. § 12101(a)(1).

the ADA requires that in certain circumstances public bodies make reasonable accommodations for persons with qualifying disabilities.[141]

There are three general areas of concern regarding the application of the ADA to child welfare cases. First, the ADA guarantees that all litigants have reasonable access to legal proceedings.[142] The states must make reasonable accommodations for parents and children with disabilities to ensure that they may participate in the proceedings. This would include such things as physical access to the courthouse and assistive listening devices or sign language interpreters for the deaf.

The second area of concern relates to the substantive application of the ADA to efforts by state child welfare agencies to preserve and reunify families in which child maltreatment has occurred. It appears that the ADA does not directly apply to child welfare cases.[143] To the extent that the ADA applies in the child welfare context, most courts have held that proceedings involving the termination of parental rights do not constitute "services, programs and activities" within the meaning of the ADA, so the ADA does not act to bar proceedings to terminate parental rights.[144] Some courts have held that the ADA applies to a limited extent to child welfare proceedings.[145] These courts have generally held that if the state has met the "reasonable efforts" requirement it has also met the ADA's "reasonable accommodation" requirement.[146] Although the ADA may apply to the agency's efforts to reunify and the types of services offered, it does not provide a defense to a termination of parental rights action.[147]

Finally, the ADA applies to children who are the subject of child protective proceedings to protect them from discrimination based on a disability. For instance, a child care center must make an individualized determination as to whether a particular child's disability should be accommodated by the program.[148]

---

[141] *See* 42 U.S.C. §§ 12131 *et seq.*

[142] *See* Tennessee v. Lane, 541 U.S. 509 (2004) (upholding against Eleventh Amendment immunity attack Title II of ADA requiring that disabled persons have access to courthouses and that their disabilities be accommodated so that they may participate in legal proceedings); *see generally* Peter Blanck, Ann Wilichowski & James Schmeling, *Disability Civil Rights Law and Policy: Accessible Courtroom Technology*, 12 WM. & MARY BILL OF RTS. J. 825 (2004).

[143] *In re* B.S., 166 Vt. 345, 693 A.2d 716, 720 (1997); State v Raymond C. *(In re* Torrance P.), 187 Wis. 2d 10, 522 N.W.2d 243 (1994).

[144] *Id.; see also* Adoption of Gregory, 434 Mass. 117, 747 N.E.2d 120 (2001); *In re* Anthony P., 84 Cal. App. 4th 1112, 101 Cal. Rptr. 2d 423 (2000); Stone v. Daviess County Div. Child. & Fam. Servs., 656 N.E.2d 824 (Ind. App. 1995).

[145] *See, e.g., In re* Terry, 240 Mich. App. 14, 610 N.W.2d 563 (2000).

[146] *See, e.g.,* J.T. v. Arkansas Dep't of Human Servs., 329 Ark. 243, 947 S.W.2d 761 (1997); *In re* Welfare of A.J.R., 78 Wash. App. 222, 896 P.2d 1302 (1995); *In re* Angel B., 659 A.2d 277 (Me. 1995); In Interest of C.M., 526 N.W.2d 562 (Iowa App. 1994).

[147] *See, e.g.,* People v. T.B., 12 P.3d 1221 (Colo. App. 2000); *In re* Terry, 240 Mich. App. 14, 610 N.W.2d 563 (2000).

[148] *See* U.S. Department of Justice, Civil Rights Division, *Commonly Asked Questions About Child Care Centers and the Americans with Disabilities Act* (Oct. 1997), *available at* www.usdoj.gov/crt/ada/childq&a.htm.

§ 10.8.2 Children's Health Act of 2000

The Children's Health Act of 2000 includes provisions regarding the rights of children who are placed in a "non-medical, community-based facility for children" such as group homes or residential treatment facilities.[149] The Act protects children placed in such facilities from physical or mental abuse, corporal punishment, and restraints or involuntary seclusion imposed for the purpose of discipline or for convenience. The statute strictly limits the use of restraints and seclusion to those members of the staff of such programs certified by the state and trained in taking such action.[150]

§ 10.9 Case Example: Applying Selected Federal Funding Streams and Statutory Requirements

To understand how the various federal statutes interact, it may be instructive to consider them in the context of a specific child welfare case:

Laura is a 22-year-old single young woman who is pregnant with her first child and is staying in the home of friends. Laura had an unfortunate childhood. Her mother is a long-standing polysubstance abuser whose drugs of choice are marijuana, cocaine, and alcohol, although she has sometimes used other substances. To support her drug habit, Laura's mother sometimes resorted to prostitution. During her childhood, Laura was sexually abused by several of her mother's male partners. Laura was removed from her mother's care at the age of 11 and placed into the foster care system. By the time she aged out of foster care at 18, Laura had lived in nine foster homes, a residential treatment facility, and a group home. Laura did not finish high school and has struggled with homelessness and poverty since her emancipation. Although Laura has no contact with her baby's father at this time, he is a 38-year-old man she met in her neighborhood.

Because she is living in poverty, Laura receives public assistance under the TANF program and receives monthly food stamps, as well. Also, because of her pregnancy, she is eligible to receive supplemental nutritional services through the WIC program. In addition to these more general services, because there is an elevated risk of child abuse or neglect, Laura is eligible to receive nurse home-visitor services paid for by Title IV-B's Promoting Safe and Stable Families program as well as early intervention services provided through CAPTA. The nurse home-visitor provides educational support to Laura about her pregnancy, provides developmental information about the baby Laura will soon have, and acts as a conduit to other services. For instance, the nurse referred Laura to the local housing office for Section 8 housing. Unfortunately, there are no current housing units available, and the wait list is long.

---

[149] 42 U.S.C. § 290jj.

[150] 42 U.S.C. § 290jj.

Despite these efforts, at the time Laura gave birth to her son, Michael, he was born with both THC and cocaine metabolites in his system. When interviewed by a hospital social worker, Laura admitted that she smoked marijuana off and on throughout her pregnancy—most recently three days before her delivery—and used cocaine only the day before giving birth to Michael. Michael was born two weeks prematurely, although he is 5 pounds and 13 ounces. While in the hospital, he experienced some mild tremors and rigidity, which the doctors ascribe to his prenatal exposure to illicit drugs. Because of Michael's condition, CAPTA's mandatory reporting law, which has been integrated into the state's child protection law, the doctor who attended his birth files the necessary report with children's protective services. A caseworker is assigned to investigate the report—which is financially supported, in part, by CAPTA.

The worker interviews Laura and observes Michael. During the interview, Laura explains that her drug use is the result of the stress of her pregnancy and her poverty. She has no place to go because her friends have informed her that she cannot return to live with them. She says that she very much wants help for her drug usage and that she desperately wants to raise Michael and does not want him placed into foster care. At the conclusion of the worker's investigation, he substantiates that Michael is a neglected child. He files a petition with the local family court and, accessing funds provided through Title IV-E by the Fostering Connections Act, and after an assessment of her needs, he places Laura into a residential drug treatment program where Michael will join her when he is ready for release from the hospital in a few days.

Because a court petition was filed, the court, consistent with the requisite provisions of CAPTA, appoints an attorney to represent Michael's interests as his guardian ad litem. At the initial hearing, held within 48 hours of the filing of the petition, the court finds that there is sufficient evidence of neglect to permit the case to proceed, that reasonable efforts were made or were unnecessary to preserve the family, and that placement with Laura without court intervention would be contrary to Michael's welfare, meeting the requirements of Title IV-E. Under state law, Michael "entered" foster care on the day the court authorized the case to proceed, so the state must conduct a permanency planning hearing in 12 months unless the case is resolved earlier.

Michael is released from the hospital and is placed with Laura in the drug treatment program. Laura is very happy that she is able to see her son daily and to parent him, although she quickly learns that it will be difficult to care for him while working to overcome her addiction. Her daily therapy sessions are very difficult as she begins to deal with the underlying traumas that have led her to use drugs. Laura's substance abuse related treatment is paid for, in part, by the state's substance abuse block grant while other portions of her treatment are covered under the state's Title XX Social Services Block Grant, and Michael's well baby visits are paid for by Medicaid. She continues to receive WIC, which pays for Michael's formula.

The residential program is designed to last 90 days to six months depending on the severity of the parent's substance abuse. For the first couple of weeks, Laura does well. But as her treatment proceeds, she finds it harder to confront her past and to work through the trauma she has experienced. The stress is enormous and she sometimes lacks the energy to care for Michael. When a staff member of the program raises this issue with her, she has an angry outburst and leaves the program, leaving Michael behind. The program immediately contacts the CPS worker. The worker is unaware of any relative who could care for Michael, so he is placed into a foster home on an emergency basis while the worker seeks out possible relatives with which to place Michael. When Laura returns to the program three days later, she is informed that she has been expelled and Michael placed in foster care. She meets with her worker and identifies several members of her extended family who may be able to provide for Michael. Consistent with federal law as adopted by the state, Michael is shortly thereafter placed in the home of Laura's aunt who will pursue foster care licensing, a placement which is supported, in part, by Title IV-E funds.

By this time, the workers, using the federally funded parent locator system, have contacted Michael's father, William. Paternity is established but William indicates that he is in no position to care for his son. He relates an extensive history of drug usage, a long criminal record including two convictions for domestic violence, and a general unwillingness to parent the baby.

The court case proceeds. Michael is adjudicated a neglected child after Laura and William each admit various allegations in the agency's petition. Michael's placement continues to be funding through Title IV-E. Also consistent with the Fostering Connections Act, the agency makes a concerted effort to identify other relatives on both sides of Michael's family, and several other potential relative caregivers are identified. These relatives are provided notice of the proceeding.

At the dispositional hearing, the agency recommends, and the court adopts, a permanency goal of reunification with Laura. By this time, she has reentered drug treatment, albeit in an intensive outpatient program. She is ordered to continue and complete the substance abuse treatment program, undergo psychological and psychiatric assessments, and to follow any recommendations regarding medication and mental health treatment, to complete parenting classes and, to visit Michael at least two times per week under the supervision of her aunt. Her substance abuse treatment is paid for from Title XX and from state funds received through the federal Substance Abuse and Mental Health Services Administration, and the other services are paid for by IV-E funds as matched with state money.

After a couple of months in treatment, Laura again drops out. She continues to visit Michael; however, her aunt reports that she is belligerent and has come to some of the visits appearing to be intoxicated. The aunt reports that at the last visit Laura showed up with a man who scared the aunt and who, like Laura, was obviously high. The aunt is fed up and is no longer willing to care for Michael because of Laura's behavior. The aunt says she believes a different permanent plan needs to be made for Michael.

The agency convenes a case meeting with the relevant parties to consider options. At the meeting are the workers, Michael's guardian ad litem, Laura, and several relatives. There is a consensus that Laura has not made adequate progress. It is decided that the time has come, consistent with the ASFA, to institute a concurrent plan for Michael. He needs to be placed in a placement that will commit to providing for him permanently in the event that Laura or William cannot regain custody. Laura says she has heard on the street that William is back in prison on a parole violation. Unfortunately, for one reason or another, none of the relatives is willing to commit to caring for Michael permanently. No other relatives can be identified, so Michael is placed with foster parents who are interested in adopting a child. Laura again insists that she wants to get clean and care for Michael, so she re-enters drug treatment.

Within a few weeks, however, Laura again drops out of treatment, and her whereabouts are unknown. Meanwhile, Michael has begun to show signs of developmental delay, which medical professionals attributed at least in part to prenatal exposure to illicit drugs. Another case conference is held. Michael's lawyer explains that she recently attended some training funded by Title IV-E in which early termination of parental rights was one of the issues discussed. She believes the permanency goal should change to termination of parental rights and adoption. The workers were resistant. Even if Laura could get clean, the lawyer argued, she would not be able to meet Michael's special needs.

In the end, the worker agrees, and a termination petition was filed. At the pretrial hearing on the petition, the judge referred the matter to the county's new child protection mediation program. Laura had resurfaced and agreed to appear at the mediation. After carefully listening to the workers and Michael's lawyer, Laura agreed that it was not fair to Michael to have to wait longer for her to be in a position to care for him. After consulting with her attorney, she decided to release her parental rights.

A hearing was scheduled at which Laura released her parental rights. William's rights were involuntarily terminated. Michael is adopted by his foster parents. Because of his special needs, the foster parents will be eligible for a Title IV-E funded adoption subsidy, which will provide both a cash subsidy and Medicaid to help provide for his needs throughout his childhood.

§ 10.10 Conclusion

Since the federal government entered the child protection and foster care arena in the 1960s, its role and influence has steadily expanded. As the case of Laura and Michael demonstrates, today virtually no aspect of a child welfare case is free of the impact of federal law, either directly or indirectly. Thus, it is incumbent upon child welfare law practitioners, whether representing the child, the parents, or the agency, to be intimately familiar with the workings of the various federal statutes in the field.

Chapter 11: U.S. Supreme Court Cases Regarding Child Welfare

by Ann M. Haralambie[1]

§ 11.1 Introduction

The following U.S. Supreme Court cases form the constitutional parameters for the relationship between the state, parents, and children. Many do not deal directly with child welfare, but they are used to define the constitutional boundaries that apply in child welfare cases. They provide that parental rights are fundamental and entitled to great deference. However, they are not absolute. Children have their own liberty interests worthy of constitutional protection. The state has the right to act to protect children, but cannot always be held responsible for its failure to protect those not directly in its custody. Even when the state is motivated by a desire to protect children, it is limited in the circumstances and means it can use to undertake that protection.

§ 11.2 Constitutional Rights of Parents

§ 11.2.1 *Meyer v. Nebraska*

The Supreme Court, in *Meyer v. Nebraska*,[2] addressed a parent's right to control the education of his or her child. A parochial school teacher was criminally charged and convicted for teaching German to a ten-year-old child in violation of a statute prohibiting teaching in a language other than English or teaching a foreign language to children who had not completed the eighth grade. The Supreme Court held that the concept of liberty, as protected by the Fourteenth Amendment, denotes "not merely freedom from bodily restraint but also the right of the individual to contract, to engage in any of the common occupations of life, to acquire useful knowledge, to marry, establish a home and bring up children, to worship God according to the dictates of his own conscience, and generally to enjoy those privileges long recognized at common law as essential to the orderly pursuit of happiness by free men."[3]

The Court concluded that the statute was unconstitutional. It held that the teacher had a constitutionally protected liberty interest in teaching. Furthermore, the parents

---

[1] Ann M. Haralambie, J.D., is a certified family law specialist practicing in Tucson, Arizona. She is also an author and speaker in the fields of family and children's law.

[2] 262 U.S. 390 (1923).

[3] *Id.* at 399.

had a constitutionally protected liberty interest in educating their children as they saw fit. The Court noted that "[m]ere knowledge of the German language cannot reasonably be regarded as harmful. Heretofore it has been commonly looked upon as helpful and desirable. Plaintiff in error taught this language in school as part of his occupation. His right thus to teach and the right of parents to engage him so to instruct their children, we think, are within the liberty of the Amendment. . . . Latin, Greek, Hebrew are not proscribed; but German, French, Spanish, Italian, and every other alien speech are within the ban. Evidently the Legislature has attempted materially to interfere with the calling of modern language teachers, with the opportunities of pupils to acquire knowledge, and with the power of parents to control the education of their own."[4] This case is often cited in appellate child welfare cases as a foundational case recognizing that parents' family rights are a fundamental liberty interest and entitled to constitutional protection.

§ 11.2.2 *Pierce v. Society of Sisters*

In *Pierce v. Society of Sisters*,[5] the Supreme Court addressed a parent's right to decide the school his or her child attends. The constitutionality of a compulsory education law that required that children be educated in public schools was at issue. The Oregon Compulsory Education Act required every child between the ages of 8 and 16 years to attend public schools. Oregon argued that the state had the authority to require children to attend schools, and that compulsory public school attendance did not deprive parents of their rights. A parochial school and a private military school sought to enjoin the law, which prevented parents from sending children to their schools. The Supreme Court held that the statute was unconstitutional. The Court upheld an injunction issued against enforcement of the law as an arbitrary, unreasonable, and unlawful interference with the school's patronage, destroying their business and property. The Court held that the Act unreasonably interfered with the liberty of parents and guardians to direct the upbringing and education of children under their control. Although the state had the power to require children to attend school, it could not dictate which school a child attends. The Court stated: "The child is not the mere creature of the state; those who nurture him and direct his destiny have the right, coupled with the high duty, to recognize and prepare him for additional obligations."[6] This case is also frequently cited in child welfare cases to establish the right of parents to raise their children without undo government interference.

---

[4] *Id.* at 400–01.

[5] 268 U.S. 510 (1925).

[6] *Id.* at 535.

§ 11.2.3 *Prince v. Massachusetts*

In *Prince v. Massachusetts*,[7] a woman who was the guardian of her niece was criminally convicted for violating child labor laws, which prohibited boys under 12 and girls under 18 from selling newspapers, magazines, or other merchandise on any street or public place. She furnished her niece with Jehovah's Witness magazines, which the child then sold in the street. The aunt claimed her right to permit the actions by her niece both as a First Amendment matter of freedom of religion and as a Fourteenth Amendment due process parental right. The Supreme Court explained that state law restricting child labor did not impermissibly violate the parent's or guardian's First Amendment right to religious freedom.

The Court stated:

> The parent's conflict with the state over control of the child and his training is serious enough when only secular matters are concerned. It becomes the more so when an element of religious conviction enters. Against these sacred private interests, basic in a democracy, stand the interests of society to protect the welfare of children, and the state's assertion of authority to that end, made here in a manner conceded valid if only secular things were involved. The last is no mere corporate concern of official authority. It is the interest of youth itself, and of the whole community, that children be both safeguarded from abuses and given opportunities for growth into free and independent well-developed men and citizens.[8]

The Court recognized the "rights of children to exercise their religion, and of parents to give them religious training and to encourage them in the practice of religious belief, as against preponderant sentiment and assertion of state power voicing it . . . ."[9]

However, the Court also noted that

> the family itself is not beyond regulation in the public interest, as against a claim of religious liberty. And neither rights of religion nor rights of parenthood are beyond limitation. Acting to guard the general interest in youth's well being, the state as parens patriae may restrict the parent's control by requiring school attendance, regulating or prohibiting the child's labor, and in many other ways. Its authority is not nullified merely because the parent grounds his claim to control the child's course of conduct on religion or conscience. Thus, he cannot claim freedom from compulsory vaccination for the child more than for himself on religious grounds. The right to practice religion freely does not include liberty to expose the community or

---

[7] 321 U.S. 158 (1944).

[8] *Id.* at 165.

[9] *Id.*

the child to communicable disease or the latter to ill health or death. The catalogue need not be lengthened. It is sufficient to show . . . that the state has a wide range of power for limiting parental freedom and authority in things affecting the child's welfare; and that this includes, to some extent, matters of conscience and religious conviction.[10]

The court also noted that the state has broader power to regulate the conduct of children than its power to regulate adult behavior. The legislative intent behind the child labor law was to prevent the negative effects of child employment and the possible harms inherent in street activities. Although the child's aunt accompanied her during the sales, the court concluded that this activity nonetheless violated the state law. Many subsequent cases quote the Court's statement that "[p]arents may be free to become martyrs themselves. But it does not follow they are free, in identical circumstances, to make martyrs of their children before they have reached the age of full and legal discretion when they can make that choice for themselves."[11]

§ 11.2.4 *Wisconsin v. Yoder*

Wisconsin v. Yoder[12] involved a Wisconsin law that required children to attend school until age 16. Amish and Mennonite families in Wisconsin objected to the law because the period from the end of eighth grade to their adult baptism was very important for indoctrination into the Amish faith. The parents contended that if their children went to public high school the opportunity for religious education would be lost. The Court found for the Amish and Mennonite parents stating that the children continued to receive education at home and that the state's interest in using education to produce productive members of society was met by the vocational schooling the youth received from their parents. Therefore, the Court held that the Amish parents had the protection of the religious clause and their right to freedom of religion dominated the state's interests.

The Court conceded that "activities of individuals, even when religiously based, are often subject to regulation by the States in the exercise of their undoubted power to promote the health, safety, and general welfare, or the Federal Government in the exercise of its delegated powers."[13] However, the Court pointed out that the issue raised in this case "is not one in which any harm to the physical or mental health of the child or to the public safety, peace, order, or welfare has been demonstrated or may be properly inferred."[14]

Justice Burger, writing for the Supreme Court, concluded that "the record in this case abundantly supports the claim that the traditional way of life of the Amish is not

---

[10] *Id.* at 166–76 (citations and footnotes omitted).

[11] *Id.* at 170.

[12] 406 U.S. 205 (1972).

[13] *Id.* at 220.

[14] *Id.* at 230 (footnote omitted).

merely a matter of personal preference, but one of deep religious conviction, shared by an organized group, and intimately related to daily living."[15] The Court detailed how the compulsory education law interfered with the Amish and Mennonite parents' right to free exercise of religion for their families and children and concluded that the compulsory education law violated their First Amendment rights.

In a famous dissent, Justice William O. Douglas noted that the wishes of the people most directly affected—two of the teenage students involved, Vernon Yutzy and Barbara Miller—were not considered. The students were not parties, nor were they consulted. Justice Douglas stated in part, "The Court's analysis assumes that the only interests at stake in the case are those of the Amish parents on the one hand, and those of the State on the other. The difficulty with this approach is that, despite the Court's claim, the parents are seeking to vindicate not only their own free exercise claims, but also those of their high-school-age children."[16]

§ 11.2.5 *Troxel v. Granville*

Troxel v. Granville[17] involved the constitutionality of Washington's third-party visitation statute. The statute provided that any person could petition the court for visitation rights at any time and that the court could grant visitation rights whenever visitation may serve the best interest of the child. The grandparents of children born out of wedlock petitioned a Washington court for the right to visit their grand-daughters. The children's mother agreed to grandparent visitation but wanted the visits to be limited to one day each month. The court granted the grandparent's request for more visitation over the objections of the children's mother. The children's mother appealed the visitation order. The court of appeals reversed the lower court's order. The grandparent's appealed, and the Washington Supreme Court affirmed the appellate court's decision. The U.S. Supreme Court granted certiorari to consider the constitutionality of the Washington statute.

In a plurality opinion, the U.S. Supreme Court found that the statute violated the mother's due process liberty interest in the care, custody, and control of her children. The Court pointed out that the statute did not provide any deference to the parent's wishes and left the question of what was in the children's best interest solely to the judge. The Court reaffirmed the presumption that fit parents can make decisions that are in the best interests of their children and affirmed the Washington Supreme Court's order. The Court stated that "if a fit parent's decision of the kind at issue here becomes subject to judicial review, the court must accord at least some special weight to the parent's own determination."[18] The Court noted that it was not holding that all

---

[15] *Id.* at 216.

[16] *Id.* at 241 (Douglas, J., dissenting).

[17] 530 U.S. 57 (2000).

[18] *Id.* at 70.

nonparental visitation statutes violated the due process clause per se. The decision in this case was based on the breadth of the Washington statute.

NOTE: Parameters of Parents' Rights. Taken together, these early cases, *Meyer*, *Pierce*, and *Prince*, set the basic parameters of the relationship between parent and state. They establish the principle that parents have a fundamental liberty interest in directing the upbringing of their children, which is protected by the Due Process Clause of the Fourteenth Amendment on which the state may infringe only for compelling reason and only insofar as that infringement is necessary to protect the state's interest. This basic framework has guided the courts' analysis of issues involving family life in a variety of circumstances, including matters pertaining to child welfare law.[19]

§ 11.3 Constitutional Rights of Children and Youth

§ 11.3.1 *In re Gault*

In this landmark case, *In re Gault*,[20] the Supreme Court declared that neither the Fourteenth Amendment nor the Bill of Rights is exclusively for adults. The Arizona juvenile court committed Gerald Gault, a 15-year-old delinquent, to the state industrial school until his 21st birthday. The court administered a typically informal proceeding. The proceeding took place in chambers where the judge questioned the juvenile. The alleged victim was not present, no witnesses were sworn, and no transcript was made of the proceeding. Gault was given no notice of charges, no counsel, no protection from self-incrimination, and no opportunity to confront and cross-examine his accuser. The juvenile court reasoned that because children had no right to liberty they could be denied due process. Furthermore, the juvenile court argued that the lack of procedural protection did not violate any rights because a child had none.

The Supreme Court held that the due process clause of the Fourteenth Amendment applied to delinquency adjudicatory proceedings. Specifically, the Court included the right to notice of charges, the right to confrontation, the right to cross-examination, the prohibition against self-incrimination, and the right to counsel. Under *Gault*, youth accused of violating the law have essentially the same rights as adults and they are recognized as independent persons, not merely property of their parents.

---

[19] *See generally* Wisconsin v. Yoder, 406 U.S. 205 (1972) (right of Amish parents to direct educational aspects of their children's upbringing pursuant to their religious convictions); Moore v. East Cleveland, 431 U.S. 494 (1977) (invalidating housing ordinance making it illegal for a grandchild to live in grandparent's home); Troxel v. Granville, 530 U.S. 57 (2000) (right of fit parent to determine grandparent visitation).

[20] 387 U.S. 1 (1967).

NOTE: It is important to recognize that *Gault* did not address the representation of children in abuse, neglect, and dependency proceedings. As of 2010, there does not exist a federal requirement for legal representation of children involved in dependency proceedings. Child Abuse Prevention and Treatment Act Programs (CAPTA)[21] requires that a "representative" be appointed to children involved in dependency proceedings. The CAPTA requirement, however, may be fulfilled by but does not mandate an attorney representative. Therefore, many children are appointed lay representatives who can be court-appointed special advocates, lay guardians ad litem, or other volunteers. Advocates have argued for the establishment of *Gault*-like requirements for dependency proceedings, including a right to client-directed counsel.[22] One argument in support of a child's entitlement to legal counsel in dependency cases is premised on the *Mathews v. Eldridge*[23] due process test, described below,[24] as a basis.

In *Mathews v. Eldridge*,[25] the U.S. Supreme Court applied a three-part test to determine whether a state action deprived a citizen of his due process rights. While this case does not deal with children's law, it is important because it outlined the factors the court must look at in determining whether due process rights have been violated. The Court, citing *Morrissey v. Brewer*, 408 U.S. 471, 481 (1972), stated that "[D]ue process is flexible and calls for such procedural protections as the particular situation demands."[26] To determine what the "situation demands," courts must weigh three factors: (1) "The private interest that will be affected;" (2) "The risk of an erroneous deprivation" of the private individual's interest "through the procedures used" and the probable benefits of additional procedural requirements; and (3) the Government's interest, including "fiscal and administrative burdens" that might result from additional procedural requirements.[27]

Recently, applying the three-part *Matthews* test to the question of whether a child has a due process right to legal counsel in neglect proceedings, the United States District Court for the Northern District of Georgia held that the Due Process Clause of the Georgia state constitution requires the appointment of legal counsel for a child when the state seeks to remove the child from parental custody.[28]

---

[21] 42 U.S.C. §§ 5101–5107.

[22] *See* LaShanda Taylor, *A Lawyer for Every Child: Client-Directed Representation in Dependency Cases*, 47/4 FAM. CT. REV. 605 (2009).

[23] 424 U.S. 319 (1976).

[24] Jacob E. Smiles, *A Child's Due Process Right to Legal Counsel in Abuse and Neglect Dependency Proceedings*, 37 FAM. L. Q. 485 (2003).

[25] *Id.*

[26] *Id.* at 334.

[27] *Id.* at 335.

[28] *See* Kenny A. *ex rel.* Winn v. Perdue, 356 F. Supp. 2d 1353 (N.D. Ga. 2005).

§ 11.3.2 *Tinker v. Des Moines Independent Community School District*

In *Tinker v. Des Moines Independent Community School District*,[29] the Supreme Court held that students had a First Amendment right to wear arm bands in school to protest the Vietnam War. Justice Fortas, writing for the Court, wrote: "It can hardly be argued that either students or teachers shed their constitutional rights to freedom of speech or expression at the schoolhouse gate."[30] This case is most frequently cited for the proposition that a student's constitutional right to freedom of speech is of utmost importance and warrants protection.

The Court noted that "[s]chool officials do not possess absolute authority over their students. Students in school as well as out of school are 'persons' under our Constitution. They are possessed of fundamental rights which the State must respect . . . ."[31] The Court stated that "[i]n order for the State . . . to justify prohibition of a particular expression of opinion, it must be able to show that its action was caused by something more than a mere desire to avoid the discomfort and unpleasantness that always accompany an unpopular viewpoint. Certainly where there is no finding and no showing that engaging in the forbidden conduct would 'materially and substantially interfere with the requirements of appropriate discipline in the operation of the school,' the prohibition cannot be sustained."[32]

§ 11.3.3 *Bellotti v. Baird*

In *Bellotti v. Baird*,[33] the Supreme Court held that pregnant girls cannot be required to obtain parental consent for an abortion without providing them a hearing as to their maturity to make the decision without anyone else's consent. The Massachusetts statute required that a minor received consent from both of her parents before she could have an abortion. If her parents refused to consent, she could obtain consent from a judicial order for good cause based on the judge's decision that an abortion was in her best interest. The Court concluded that the statute placed an undue burden on a minor's right to access abortion. It stated that every pregnant minor must be able to go directly to a court and request judicial consent for an abortion without being required to first consult her parents.

The Court stated that a "child, merely on account of his minority, is not beyond the protection of the Constitution."[34] The Court went on to describe three reasons for treating a child's constitutional rights differently than those of adults: "the peculiar vulnerability of children; their inability to make critical decisions in an informed,

---

[29] 393 U.S. 503 (1969).

[30] *Id.* at 506.

[31] *Id.* at 511.

[32] *Id.* at 509 (citation omitted).

[33] 443 U.S. 622 (1979).

[34] *Id.* at 633.

mature manner; and the importance of the parental role in child rearing."[35] With respect to the first reason, the Court noted that its concern "is demonstrated in its decisions dealing with minors' claims to constitutional protection against deprivations of liberty or property interests by the State. With respect to many of these claims, we have concluded that the child's right is virtually coextensive with that of an adult."[36] Further, "[v]iewed together, our cases show that although children generally are protected by the same constitutional guarantees against governmental deprivations as are adults, the State is entitled to adjust its legal system to account for children's vulnerability and their needs for 'concern, . . . sympathy, and . . . paternal attention.'"[37] With respect to the second reason, the Court stated that "States validly may limit the freedom of children to choose for themselves in the making of important, affirmative choices with potentially serious consequences. These rulings have been grounded in the recognition that, during the formative years of childhood and adolescence, minors often lack the experience, perspective, and judgment to recognize and avoid choices that could be detrimental to them."[38] With respect to the third reason, the Court explained:

> [T]he guiding role of parents in the upbringing of their children justifies limitations on the freedoms of minors. The State commonly protects its youth from adverse governmental action and from their own immaturity by requiring parental consent to or involvement in important decisions by minors. But an additional and more important justification for state deference to parental control over children is that . . . [the] affirmative process of teaching, guiding, and inspiring by precept and example is essential to the growth of young people into mature, socially responsible citizens.
>
> We have believed in this country that this process, in large part, is beyond the competence of impersonal political institutions. Indeed, affirmative sponsorship of particular ethical, religious, or political beliefs is something we expect the State *not* to attempt in a society constitutionally committed to the ideal of individual liberty and freedom of choice.[39]

The Court emphasized the special character of decisions regarding abortion, because that decision had been given the status of a constitutional right.[40] The Court

---

[35] *Id.* at 634.

[36] *Id.*

[37] *Id.* at 635 (citation omitted).

[38] *Id.* (footnote omitted).

[39] *Id.* at 637–38 (citations and footnote omitted).

[40] *Id.* at 641 ("But we are concerned here with a constitutional right to seek an abortion. The abortion decision differs in important ways from other decisions that may be made during minority. The need to preserve the constitutional right and the unique nature of the abortion decision, especially when

also noted the exigency of the abortion decision, which unlike a decision such as whether to marry, may not be delayed without being be made "by default with far-reaching consequences."[41]

The Court held that the statute was unconstitutional and that to be constitutional, a statute must provide that:

> every minor must have the opportunity—if she so desires—to go directly to a court without first consulting or notifying her parents. If she satisfies the court that she is mature and well enough informed to make intelligently the abortion decision on her own, the court must authorize her to act without parental consultation or consent. If she fails to satisfy the court that she is competent to make this decision independently, she must be permitted to show that an abortion nevertheless would be in her best interests. If the court is persuaded that it is, the court must authorize the abortion. If, however, the court is not persuaded by the minor that she is mature or that the abortion would be in her best interests, it may decline to sanction the operation.[42]

The Court did say that "the court may deny the abortion request of an immature minor in the absence of parental consultation if it concludes that her best interests would be served thereby, or the court may in such a case defer decision until there is parental consultation in which the court may participate. But this is the full extent to which parental involvement may be required."[43]

§ 11.3.4 *Parham v. J.R.*

Parham v. J.R.[44] was a class action brought by Georgia children who had been voluntarily committed to state mental health institutions by their parents or guardians. The Georgia District Court ruled in favor of the children finding that the state statutory scheme was unconstitutional because in did not protect the children's due process rights. The court held that minors who are going to be voluntarily committed are entitled to an adversary-type hearing before an impartial tribunal. The State appealed the decision to the U.S. Supreme Court. The Court concluded that the medical fact-finding process was consistent with due process guarantees.

The Court considered whether Georgia's procedures for voluntarily commitment of minors to state mental hospitals violated the children's Fourteenth Amendment due process rights. The state statute provided that for the voluntary commitment of a child

---

made by a minor, require a State to act with particular sensitivity when it legislates to foster parental involvement in this matter.").

[41] *Id.* at 643.

[42] *Id.* at 647–48.

[43] *Id.* at 648.

[44] 442 U.S. 584 (1979).

there must be an application from the child's parent or guardian. The statute permitted any child who had been voluntarily committed for more than five days to be discharged at the request of his or her guardian. Additionally, it required the hospital superintendent to re-evaluate patients who were voluntarily committed and release them if they no longer need to be hospitalized.

The Court concluded that Georgia's practice did satisfy due process requirements. It noted that children have a liberty interest in not being unnecessarily confined and an interest in not being erroneously labeled mentally ill. The Court, however, found that the law sufficiently protected the children's interests. Parents did not have absolute discretion to have their child committed. Furthermore, the medical fact-finders who admitted children had the authority to refuse to admit any patients, and they periodically reviewed continued commitment. The Court held that Georgia's statutory and administrative procedure for the voluntary commitment of children was not unconstitutional.

§ 11.4 Constitutional Rights of Putative Fathers of Children Born Out of Wedlock

§ 11.4.1 *Stanley v. Illinois*

Stanley v. Illinois[45] established rights for fathers whose children were born out of wedlock. The Illinois statute provided that children of unmarried fathers, upon the death of the mother, were declared dependents without any hearing on parental fitness and without proof of neglect, even though a hearing on parental fitness and proof of neglect were required before the state assumed custody of children of married or divorced parents and unmarried mothers. With respect to fathers of children born out of wedlock, there was an irrebuttable presumption of unfitness. The facts of this case are particularly compelling because the father and mother had lived together intermittently over 18 years, during which time their three children were born. Upon the mother's death, the state filed a dependency action, and the children were placed with court-appointed guardians. Nothing in the record indicated that the father was unfit or neglectful of his children in any way.

The state argued that most fathers of children born out of wedlock are unfit and that the statutory scheme appropriately served the needs of most children. The Supreme Court rejected this argument and found that parental unfitness must be established on the basis of individualized proof. The Court stated that "the interest of a parent in the companionship, care, custody, and management of his or her children 'come(s) to this Court with a momentum for respect lacking when appeal is made to liberties which derive merely from shifting economic arrangements.'"[46] The Court found it irrelevant that the father could have applied for adoption or for custody and

---

[45]   405 U.S. 645 (1972).

[46]   *Id.* at 651 (citation omitted).

control of his children, especially in light of the fact that he would not be afforded any priority and would bear the burden of proof that he should be permitted to serve as the children's guardian or adoptive parent. The Court concluded that the state's practice violated the Equal Protection Clause because parents are entitled to a hearing on their fitness before their children are removed. The Court noted that "[p]rocedure by presumption is always cheaper and easier than individualized determination. But when, as here, the procedure forecloses the determinative issues of competence and care, when it explicitly disdains present realities in deference to past formalities, it needlessly risks running roughshod over the important interests of both parent and child. It therefore cannot stand."[47] The Supreme Court held that under the Due Process Clause of the Fourteenth Amendment, all parents, including fathers of children born out of wedlock, are constitutionally entitled to a hearing on fitness before their children are removed from their custody in dependency proceedings.

§ 11.4.2 *Quilloin v. Walcott*

In *Quilloin v. Walcott,*[48] the U.S. Supreme Court considered whether the state of Georgia could constitutionally deny an unwed father the authority to object to the adoption of his child. The case involved a stepparent adoption of a child born out of wedlock, over the objection of the birth father. The child had lived with his mother since birth, and had never lived with his biological father. When the child was approximately 3 years old, his mother married another man. When the child was 11 years old, his mother consented to the child's adoption by her husband, and he filed an adoption petition. The Georgia statute provided that only the mother's consent was required for the adoption of a child born out of wedlock. The biological father, however, could acquire veto authority over the adoption if he had legitimated the child. A child born in wedlock could not be adopted without the consent of each living parent who had not voluntarily surrendered rights of the child or been adjudicated unfit. The father in this case had not legitimated the child prior to the filing of the adoption petition. Using the "best interests of the child" standard, the trial court granted the stepparent adoption over the father's objection and denied the biological father's petition for legitimization, in which he sought visitation rights but not custody. The trial court did not find the father to be an unfit parent. The court did find that, although the child had never been abandoned or deprived, the father had provided support only on an irregular basis.

The Supreme Court limited the constitutional rights of fathers of children born out of wedlock to those who had evidenced a substantial interest in their children's welfare. The Court held that under the circumstances of the case, the father's substantive rights were not violated by application of a "best interests of the child"

---

[47] *Id.* at 656–57 (footnote omitted).

[48] 434 U.S. 246 (1978).

standard.[49] The biological father had never sought custody. For equal protection purposes, the Court found that the rights of a father who was never married to the mother are distinguishable from those of a separated or divorced father. The state, therefore, could permissibly give such a father less veto authority than it provides to a married father.

§ 11.4.3 *Caban v. Mohammed*

In *Caban v. Mohammed,*[50] the Supreme Court struck down as violative of equal protection a statute requiring the mother's consent, but not the father's consent, to adoption of the a child born out of wedlock. This case involved children born out of wedlock whose mother subsequently married and had the stepfather adopt the children over the birth father's objection. The biological father in this case was more involved in the children's lives than the father in *Quilloin*. The children's biological father was married to someone else, but he lived with their mother and held himself out as married to her for several years. During that time two children were born. He was named on the birth certificates and contributed to the children's support. After the parents separated, the mother took the children and married another man. During the next two years the father maintained contact with the children. When the children were four and six years old, their mother and her husband filed for a stepparent adoption. The birth father cross-petitioned for adoption. The surrogate court granted the stepparent adoption over the father's objection. The New York statutory and case law required the mother's consent for the adoption of children born out of wedlock but did not require the father's consent, even when his parental relationship was substantial. The father did have a right to notice and the opportunity to be heard, but he could prevent the termination of his parental rights only by showing that adoption was not in the best interests of the child.

The Supreme Court noted that this case demonstrated that an unwed father may have a relationship with his children fully comparable to that of the mother. The Court addressed the issue it had reserved in *Quilloin* and held that the New York statute unconstitutionally distinguished unwed parents according to their gender. The Court also found that the distinction did not bear a substantial relation to the state's interest in providing adoptive homes for illegitimate children. Therefore, the statute was unconstitutional under the Equal Protection Clause of the Fourteenth Amendment.

§ 11.4.4 *Lehr v. Robertson*

Lehr v. Robertson[51] involved a statutory scheme that allowed fathers of children born out of wedlock to acquire legal rights to object to adoption comparable to those of mothers by signing up on a putative father's registry. The father had lived with the

---

[49] *Id.* at 254.

[50] 441 U.S. 380 (1979).

[51] 463 U.S. 248 (1983).

mother prior to the child's birth and visited her in the hospital when the baby was born. His name, however, did not appear on the birth certificate. He did not live with the mother or child after the child's birth, never provided them with any financial support, never offered to marry the mother, and never registered on the state's putative father registry. The mother married another man eight months after the child's birth, and he filed a stepparent adoption petition when the child was two years old. The father was not given or entitled to notice of the adoption because he had not registered on the putative father's registry. The father learned of the adoption proceeding when he filed a paternity action and sought visitation. The Court noted that equal protection did not prevent a state from according parents separate legal rights when one parent had a continuous relationship with the child and the other parent had never established a relationship with the child.

The Supreme Court held that the New York statute did not violate the father's Fourteenth Amendment due process or equal protection rights by granting an adoption without notice to or consent by him. The statutory scheme provided him ample opportunity to put himself in a position of being entitled to receive notice, which he did not use. Justice Stevens summarized the varying constitutional protections given to fathers of various degrees of involvement with their children born out of wedlock:

> The difference between the developed parent-child relationship that was implicated in Stanley and Caban, and the potential relationship involved in Quilloin and this case, is both clear and significant. When an unwed father demonstrates a full commitment to the responsibilities of parenthood by "[coming] forward to participate in the rearing of his child," Caban, 441 U.S., at 392, his interest in personal contact with his child acquires substantial protection under the Due Process Clause. At that point it may be said that he "[acts] as a father toward his children." Id., at 389, n. 7. But the mere existence of a biological link does not merit equivalent constitutional protection. . . .

> The significance of the biological connection is that it offers the natural father an opportunity that no other male possesses to develop a relationship with his offspring. If he grasps that opportunity and accepts some measure of responsibility for the child's future, he may enjoy the blessings of the parent-child relationship and make uniquely valuable contributions to the child's development. If he fails to do so, the Federal Constitution will not automatically compel a state to listen to his opinion of where the child's best interests lie. . . .

> In this case, we are not assessing the constitutional adequacy of New York's procedures for terminating a developed relationship. Appellant has never had any significant custodial, personal, or financial relationship with Jessica, and he did not seek to establish a legal tie until after she was two years old. We are concerned only

with whether New York has adequately protected his opportunity to form such a relationship.[52]

§ 11.4.5 *Michael H. v. Gerald D.*

Michael H. v. *Gerald D.*[53] addressed the constitutionality of Section 621 of the California Evidence Code, which provided that "the issue of a wife cohabitating with her husband, who is not impotent or sterile, is conclusively presumed to be a child of the marriage."[54] Paternity tests established that Michael H. was the biological father of Victoria D. Victoria's mother had lived with Michael H. in an on-again, off-again manner and asserted that he was the child's father. At the time of Victoria's birth, she was married to Gerald D., who was named as Victoria's father on her birth certificate. Eventually, Victoria and her mother went to live with Gerald D., and Michael H. filed an action to establish his paternity and visitation rights. The California courts denied his request, finding that Section 621 of the California Evidence Code prevented a putative father from establishing paternity and California law denied visitation requests by a putative father against the wishes of the mother. Michael H. asserted on appeal to the U.S. Supreme Court that Section 621 violated his substantive and procedural due process rights.

Michael H. first contended that procedural due process prevented the state from terminating his relationship with his child without permitting him an opportunity to prove his paternity in an evidentiary hearing. The Supreme Court rejected this argument. It found that the California legislature devised the statute to prohibit paternity inquiries when a child was born to a married couple to protect family privacy and integrity. Next, Michael H. argued that because he had established a relationship with Victoria, as a matter of substantive due process the state's interest in protecting marriage was insufficient to terminate his relationship with his daughter. The Court also rejected this argument, and concluded that in the history of the United States the relationship between a putative father and his child has never been constitutionally protected. Finally, the Court considered whether Victoria had a liberty interest in maintaining a relationship with Michael H. and Gerald D. The Court rejected this claim and concluded that there is no historical support to recognize multiple fathers.

---

[52] *Id.* at 261–63 (citations omitted).

[53] 491 U.S. 110 (1989).

[54] *Id.* at 117.

§ 11.5 Termination of Parental Rights

§ 11.5.1 *Lassiter v. Department of Social Services*

In *Lassiter v. Department of Social Services* [55] the Supreme Court held 5-4 that states are not constitutionally required to provide appointed counsel for indigent parents in all termination of parental rights cases. In the present case, the child was removed from the mother's custody as an infant based on her failure to provide proper medical care. The mother was subsequently convicted of second degree murder and sentenced to 25 to 40 years incarceration. Three years after the child's initial removal, the county department of social services filed a petition to terminate the mother's parental rights. The petition was based on her lack of contact with the child, and the fact that she left the child in foster care without showing substantial progress, a positive response to the agency's efforts, or constructive planning for the child's future. The mother had retained counsel in order to seek invalidation of the criminal conviction, but she had failed to mention the termination proceeding to him. The agency arranged to have the mother transported to the termination hearing. The trial court found that the mother's failure to have counsel was without just cause. Further, she did not allege that she was indigent. After the trial court held that she was not entitled to court appointed counsel, Ms. Lassiter represented herself at the hearing.

In this case, the Court emphasized, there were no allegations of abuse or neglect that might result in criminal prosecution, no expert witnesses were called, nor were there any substantively or procedurally difficult points of law. Additionally, the mother had previously failed to attend a custody hearing, she hadn't bothered to mention the case to her criminal attorney, and she had not evidenced much interest in the child after his removal. It did not appear that the presence of counsel would have made a determinative difference. While the Court held that the mother in this case was not constitutionally entitled to appointed counsel under the circumstances, it noted that there may be termination of parental rights cases in which the nature of the allegations and the evidence to be presented give rise to a due process right to the appointment of counsel. The Court noted that "33 States and the District of Columbia provide statutorily for the appointment of counsel in termination cases. The Court's opinion today in no way implies that the standards increasingly urged by informed public opinion and now widely followed by the States are other than enlightened and wise."[56] Moreover, the Court encouraged state courts to appoint counsel in termination cases, stating that a "wise public policy . . . may require that higher standards be adopted than those minimally tolerable under the Constitution. Informed opinion has clearly come to hold that an indigent parent is entitled to the assistance of appointed counsel not only in parental termination proceedings, but in dependency and neglect proceedings as well."[57]

---

[55] 452 U.S. 18 (1981).

[56] *Id.* at 34.

[57] *Id.* at 33–34.

Despite the Court's holding in *Lassiter*, a number of state appellate courts have held that their state constitution demands that a parent alleged to be abusive or neglectful has the right to the appointment of counsel.[58]

§ 11.5.2 *Santosky v. Kramer*

A 5–4 majority of the Supreme Court held in *Santosky v. Kramer*[59] that under the due process clause of the Fourteenth Amendment, in state-initiated termination of parental rights cases, the state must prove its case by at least clear and convincing evidence. The Court ruled, therefore, that New York's statutory scheme, which required only proof by a preponderance of the evidence, was unconstitutional.

The Court discussed a parent's fundamental liberty interest in the care, custody, and management of his or her children. It noted that even those who have lost custody of their children or who are not model parents still retain an interest in maintaining their parental rights. The Court concluded that the state must provide parents with fundamentally fair procedures. The Court found that in termination of parental rights proceedings, "the private interest affected is commanding; the risk of error from using a preponderance standard is substantial; and the countervailing governmental interest favoring that standard is comparatively slight. Evaluation of the three *Eldridge* factors compels the conclusion that use of a 'fair preponderance of the evidence' standard in such proceedings is inconsistent with due process."[60] The Court found that a clear and convincing standard was necessary to protect a parent's due process rights.

§ 11.5.3 *M.L.B. v. S.L.J.*

In *M.L.B. v. S.L.J.*,[61] the Supreme Court held that when an indigent parent appeals the termination of his or her parental rights, the Fourteenth Amendment's Due Process Clause requires that he or she be provided "a record of sufficient completeness to permit proper appellate consideration of her claims" at public expense.[62] M.L.B. was the mother of two children, a boy and a girl. M.L.B.'s ex-husband, S.L.J., and his new wife sought to terminate M.L.B.'s parental rights so that S.L.J.'s new wife could adopt the children. The trial court found that "there had been a 'substantial erosion of the relationship between the natural mother, [M.L.B.], and the minor

---

[58] *See, e.g.*, In the Interest of D.B. and D.S., 385 So. 2d 83 (Fla. 1980); Reist v. Bay County Circuit Judge, 396 Mich. 326, 241 N.W.2d 55 (Mich. 1976); Danforth v. State Dep't of Health & Welfare, 303 A.2d 794 (1973). Some states also require appointment of counsel for parents by statute. *See, e.g.*, ARIZ. REV. STAT. ANN. § 8-2215(B); 705 ILL. COMP. STAT. ANN. §405/1-5(1) (2009); CAL. WELF. & INST. CODE § 317 (mandatory if child is in out-of-home placement or agency is requesting out-of-home placement); VA. CODE §16.1-266(DC) (mandatory where parent or guardian could be subjected to the loss of residual parental rights and responsibilities); WIS. STAT. ANN. § 48.23(2).

[59] 455 U.S. 745 (1982).

[60] *Id.* at 758.

[61] 519 U.S. 102 (1996).

[62] *Id.* at 106 (internal quotation marks omitted).

children' which has been caused 'at least in part by [M.L.B.'s] serious neglect, abuse, prolonged and unreasonable absence or unreasonable failure to visit or communicate with her minor children.'"[63] M.L.B. sought to appeal and paid a $100 filing fee. M.L.B. was unable to pay the additional $3253.36 fee for the production of the record necessary to prosecute the appeal. After examining a number of precedents in both the criminal and civil spheres regarding the appointment of counsel or the provision of transcripts at public expense and relating to the termination of parental rights, the court framed the precise question to be answered: "Does the Fourteenth Amendment require Mississippi to accord M.L.B. access to an appeal—available but for her inability to advance required costs—before she is forever branded unfit for affiliation with her children?"[64]

The majority observed that "termination decrees 'work a unique kind of deprivation.'. . . In contrast to matters modifiable at the parties' will or based on changed circumstances, termination adjudications involve the awesome authority of the State 'to destroy permanently all legal recognition of the parental relationship.'. . . Our *Lassiter* and *Santosky* decisions, recognizing that parental termination decrees are among the most severe forms of state action . . . have not served as precedent in other areas. . . . We are therefore satisfied that the label 'civil' should not entice us to leave undisturbed the Mississippi courts' disposition of this case."[65] Because of the importance of the rights at stake for the parent, and the relatively minimal financial burden placed on the state if it is compelled to provide a court record at public expense, the court held that the State is required to provide an indigent parent enough of the record to permit appellate consideration of his or her case.

§ 11.6 Foster Parent Relationships

§ 11.6.1 *Smith v. Organization of Foster Families for Equality & Reform*

Smith v. Organization of Foster Families for Equality & Reform[66] was brought by foster parents and a foster parents' organization seeking declaratory and injunctive relief challenging procedures for removal of foster children from their foster homes. The applicable New York statutes and New York City regulations provided for notice and an opportunity to be heard before a foster child could be removed except in an emergency. The foster parents had the right to be advised of the reasons for the removal, to appear with counsel, and to submit reasons why the child should not be removed. If the child was being transferred to another foster home, but not if the child was being returned to his parents, the foster parents could also request a full trial-type

---

[63] *Id.* at 108 (citations omitted).

[64] *Id.* at 119.

[65] *Id.* at 127.

[66] 431 U.S. 816 (1977).

hearing before the child's removal. Finally, if the child had been in foster care longer than 18 months, the foster parents were made parties to the proceeding and could request review of the child's status by the family court, which could result in a court order that the agency leave the child with the foster parents.

The foster parents contended that when a child has lived in a foster home for a year or more, the foster family becomes the true "psychological family" of the child, and the foster family acquires a Fourteenth Amendment liberty interest in maintaining that family unit, which requires a higher level of due process before a foster child is removed.[67] The trial court did not recognize such a right, and instead granted relief based on an independent right of the foster child to be heard before being "condemned to suffer grievous loss," namely, disruption of a stable foster placement.[68] On appeal, the state alleged that the trial court's analysis was not constitutionally sound.

The Supreme Court pointed out a significant constitutional difference between foster family relationships and natural family relationships, even when the child has been with the foster family for a long time: "[U]nlike the earlier cases recognizing a right to family privacy, the State here seeks to interfere, not with a relationship having its origins entirely apart from the power of the State, but rather with a foster family which has its source in state law and contractual arrangements.... In this case, the limited recognition accorded to the foster family by the New York statutes and the contracts executed by the foster parents argue against any but the most limited constitutional "liberty" in the foster family."[69] The Court also pointed out that while "ordinarily procedural protection may be afforded to a liberty interest of one person without derogating from the substantive liberty of another," in this case, the foster parents' interest is in derogation of the interests of "the natural parent of a foster child in voluntary placement [who] has an absolute right to the return of his child in the absence of a court order obtainable only upon compliance with rigorous substantive and procedural standards, which reflect the constitutional protection accorded the natural family."[70] Therefore, the Court concluded that "[w]hatever liberty interest might otherwise exist in the foster family as an institution, that interest must be substantially attenuated where the proposed removal from the foster family is to return the child to his natural parents."[71]

The Court did not need to decide the constitutional limits of the foster parents' interest, however, because it found that the procedures offered by New York were not constitutionally defective.[72]

The Supreme Court rejected the argument that the foster child's interest was impaired by the lack of a right to request a hearing, stating, "if [the foster parents] do

---

[67] *Id.* at 839.

[68] *Id.* at 840.

[69] *Id.* at 845.

[70] *Id.* at 846.

[71] *Id.* at 846–47.

[72] *Id.* at 847.

not request a hearing, it is difficult to see what right or interest of the foster child is protected by holding a hearing to determine whether removal would unduly impair his emotional attachments to a foster parent who does not care enough about the child to contest the removal."[73] The Court then considered the private interests of the foster families, the risk of erroneous deprivation of that interest, and the state's interest. The Court reversed the lower court's decision. It concluded that foster parents' rights were sufficiently protected by the procedure provided, noting that the case concerned "issues of unusual delicacy, in an area where professional judgments regarding desirable procedures are constantly and rapidly changing. In such a context, restraint is appropriate on the part of courts called upon to adjudicate whether a particular procedural scheme is adequate under the Constitution."[74]

§ 11.7 State Agency Duties

§ 11.7.1 *DeShaney v. Winnebago County Department of Social Services*

In *DeShaney v. Winnebago County Department of Social Services*,[75] the Court concluded that the state did not have a duty to act to protect a child that was not in the state's custody. This case involved a civil rights action under 42 U.S.C. §1983, filed on behalf of a severely abused child against social workers and local officials who had received complaints that he was being abused by his father and had reason to believe that he was abused. They initially removed the child for three days to evaluate him in a hospital, but he was returned to his father's care. The department provided voluntary services. The juvenile court dismissed the child protection case and returned the child to the custody of his father. The caseworker did not take action after a report from an emergency room physician, but made monthly visits to the child's home. During this time, she observed a number of suspicious injuries on the child's head and noticed that the father had not followed through with some of his voluntary agreements. She noted in the record these problems and her suspicion that the child was being abused but took no action to protect the child. The caseworker responded to the home two additional times following another report from the emergency room and was told that the child was too ill to see her. She took no further action. Finally, the child was beaten so severely that he suffered brain damage so severe that he is expected to spend the rest of his life confined to an institution for the profoundly retarded.

The Supreme Court considered whether the child's due process rights were violated by Child Protective Services when they failed to protect him from the abuse. The Court concluded that nothing in the language of the due process clause required the state to protect citizens from private actors. The Court stated that there is no

---

[73] *Id.* at 850 (footnote omitted).

[74] *Id.* at 855–56.

[75] 489 U.S. 189 (1989).

"affirmative right to governmental aid, even where such aid may be necessary to secure life, liberty, or property interests of which the government itself may not deprive the individual."[76] The Court additionally concluded that if "the Due Process Clause does not require the State to provide its citizens with particular protective services, it follows that the State cannot be held liable under the Clause for injuries that could have been averted had it chosen to provide them."[77]

The Supreme Court rejected the argument that a "special relationship" existed between the agency and the child in this case.[78] The petitioner's argued the relationship existed because the State knew that the child faced a special danger of abuse at his father's hands, and specifically proclaimed, by word and by deed, its intention to protect him against that danger, thereby creating a duty to act reasonably. The Court found that such a duty would arise only where "the State by the affirmative exercise of its power so restrains an individual's liberty that it renders him unable to care for himself, and at the same time fails to provide for his basic human needs . . . . The affirmative duty to protect arises not from the State's knowledge of the individual's predicament or from its expressions of intent to help him, but from the limitation which it has imposed on his freedom to act on his own behalf."[79] The Court reasoned that the Fourteenth Amendment does not require a state agency to protect citizens from private conduct that is not attributable to the agency's employees. It concluded that because the child was not in the state's custody, there was no duty to act.

§ 11.7.2 *Youngberg v. Romeo*

The Court held, in *Youngberg v. Romeo*,[80] that a mentally retarded man who was involuntarily confined in a state institution had constitutionally protected liberty interests under the due process clause of the Fourteenth Amendment to reasonably safe conditions of confinement, freedom from unreasonable bodily restraints, and such minimally adequate training as reasonably might be required by these interests. This case involved a 33-year-old man who had the mental capacity of an 18-month-old child. He was involuntarily committed to a state institution. Shortly after his commitment, he sustained a number of injuries. His mother filed suit on behalf of him against the institution officials under 42 U.S.C. § 1983. She alleged that his rights under the Eighth and Fourteenth Amendments were violated.

The Court concluded that when a person is institutionalized and dependent on the state, the state has a duty to provide certain services and care. The Court expanded the State's responsibilities to include: (1) providing patients with safe conditions; (2) freedom from restraint; and (3) adequately trained employees. The Court stated that

---

[76] *Id.* at 196.

[77] *Id.* at 196–97.

[78] *Id.* at 197.

[79] *Id.* at 200.

[80] 457 U.S. 307 (1982).

the proper test to determine whether the State violated a patient's rights is to consider whether the State adequately protected those rights and whether the State exercised professional judgment.

NOTE: Taken together, *DeShaney* and *Youngberg* suggest a rule that while the State has no duty to intervene to protect a child from parental maltreatment, when the State does intervene and removes a child from his or her home, the federal civil rights statutes require that the child not be placed in a home that the state actors know or suspect may be abusive.[81]

§ 11.7.3 *Suter v. Artist M.*

Suter v. Artist M.[82] involved an action for injunctive and declaratory relief filed on behalf of children adjudicated dependent. They sought to enforce the state agency's duty under the Adoption Assistance and Child Welfare Act (Act) and the state plan adopted pursuant to the Act to provide reasonable efforts to maintain an abused or neglected child in his home or return the child to his home from foster care. The Act provided the federal government with the authority to reduce or eliminate payments to a State on finding that the state's plan did not comply with the Act's requirements. The Court held that the Act did not create enforceable rights for dependent children.

The Court determined that although the Act placed requirements on the States, the only requirement was that the States have a plan approved by the Secretary of Health and Human Services and that the plan called for reasonable efforts. The Court held that there was no private cause of action created under the Act. The Court concluded that "the 'reasonable efforts' language does not unambiguously confer an enforceable right upon the Act's beneficiaries. The term 'reasonable efforts' in this context is at least as plausibly read to impose only a rather generalized duty on the State, to be enforced not by private individuals, but by the Secretary in the manner previously discussed."[83]

NOTE: Following *Suter v. Artist M*, the Second Circuit Court of Appeals allowed certification of a class action lawsuit on behalf of children in New York City's child welfare system.[84] The D.C. Circuit Court of Appeals also permitted a class action lawsuit on behalf of foster children in the District of Columbia.[85] The Supreme Court's decision in *Suter v. Artist M.* was limited by statute in 1994 when Congress amended the Social Security Act.[86] The amendments did not, however, alter the

---

[81] *See, e.g.*, K.H. *ex rel.* Murphy v. Morgan, 914 F.2d 846 (7th Cir. 1990); Lewis v. Anderson, 308 F.3d 768 (7th Cir. 2002), *cert. denied sub nom.* Lewis v. Stolle, 538 U.S. 908, 123 S.Ct. 1500 (2003).

[82] 503 U.S. 347 (1992).

[83] Suter v. Artist M., 503 U.S. 345, 363 (1992).

[84] *See* Marisol A. v. Giuliani, 126 F.3d 372 (2d Cir. 1997).

[85] *See* LaShawn A. by Moore v. Kelly, 990 F.2d 1319 (D.C. Cir. 1993).

[86] 42 U.S.C. §§ 1320a-2, 1320a-10.

the state had concerns about the child's well-being. The court noted that the foregoing circumstances lessened the parent's right to invoke the Fifth Amendment privilege.

§ 11.11 Prenatal Drug Testing; Criminal vs. Civil Child Protection Investigations

§ 11.11.1 *Ferguson v. City of Charleston*

Ferguson v. City of Charleston[92] involved a city's response to the perceived problem of pregnant women receiving prenatal care who were using cocaine, causing their babies to be born with cocaine in their systems. The local public hospital agreed to cooperate with the City of Charleston and law enforcement by performing urinalysis testing on pregnant women suspected of drug use, the results of which would be used as evidence against the women. The policy required: (1) that a chain of custody be followed when obtaining and testing patients' urine samples; (2) educated hospital personnel in police procedures; and (3) criteria for arresting women who tested positive for drugs. A group of mothers sued to overturn the policy, arguing that the warrantless and nonconsensual drug tests conducted for criminal investigatory purposes were unconstitutional searches. The Supreme Court agreed and held that the state hospital's performance of a diagnostic test to obtain evidence of a patient's criminal conduct for law enforcement purposes is an unreasonable search if the patient has not consented to the procedure and, therefore, it violated the Fourth Amendment. The Court noted that "[w]hile the ultimate goal of the program may well have been to get the women in question into substance abuse treatment and off of drugs, the immediate objective of the searches was to generate evidence *for law enforcement purposes* in order to reach that goal."[93] The primary purpose of the policy was to use the threat of arrest and prosecution to force women into treatment. The Court stated that "[w]hile state hospital employees, like other citizens, may have a duty to provide the police with evidence of criminal conduct that they inadvertently acquire in the course of routine treatment, when they undertake to obtain such evidence from their patients *for the specific purpose of incriminating those patients,* they have a special obligation to make sure that the patients are fully informed about their constitutional rights, as standards of knowing waiver require."[94]

---

[92] 532 U.S. 82 (2001).

[93] *Id.* at 82–83 (footnote omitted; emphasis in the original).

[94] *Id.* at 84–85 (footnote omitted; emphasis in the original).

Chapter 12: The Indian Child Welfare Act

by Frank E. Vandervort[1]

§ 12.1 Introduction

Few child welfare lawyers routinely confront the application of the Indian Child Welfare Act (ICWA or "the Act"). When the statute applies, however, it is crucial that its provisions be strictly followed. There are at least three reasons why counsel should attempt to ensure that ICWA's provisions are carefully applied. First, ICWA's provisions are jurisdictional. Failure to abide by its requirements invalidates the proceeding from its inception. Indeed, any party or the court may invoke ICWA at any time in the proceeding, including for the first time on appeal.[2] Second, unlike most federal child welfare legislation which provides funding streams to states and therefore may not be enforceable in trial level proceedings, ICWA is substantive law that provides minimum federal standards for addressing any case involving a child who qualifies as an "Indian child."[3] Finally, the failure to adhere to the law's requirements can be disruptive for children, harmful to families, and undermining to tribal authority; it is also burdensome for courts and child welfare agencies.[4] For instance, where the Act's provisions were not properly followed, the United States Supreme Court invalidated an adoption some three years after the completion of the proceedings in the trial court and remanded the case for further proceedings.[5] In addition to the statute itself, counsel should carefully consider the application of the Bureau of Indian Affairs, *Guidelines for State Courts; Indian Child Custody Proceedings* (BIA Guidelines),[6] which, while they do not have binding effect, are entitled to great weight

---

[1] Frank E. Vandervort, J.D., is Clinical Assistant Professor of Law at the University of Michigan Law School where he teaches in the Child Advocacy Law Clinic and the Juvenile Justice Clinic, teaches Juvenile Justice, and consults with the School of Social Work on child maltreatment issues. He is co-author of the recently released book: K. STALLER, K. C. FALLER, F. VANDERVORT, W. C. BIRDSALL & J. HENRY, SEEKING JUSTICE IN CHILD SEXUAL ABUSE: SHIFTING BURDENS & SHARING RESPONSIBILITIES (Columbia University Press 2010).

[2] *See In re* S.R.M., 153 P.3d 438 (Colo. App. 2006); *In re* S.M.H., 33 Kan. App. 2d 424, 103 P.3d 976 (2005); *In re* J.T., 166 Vt. 173, 693 A.2d 283, 287–88 (1997).

[3] *See* 25 U.S.C. § 1902. It should be noted that there are many children who are Native American but who would not qualify as an "Indian child" within the meaning of the statute. *See* § 12.3, The Indian Child Welfare Act.

[4] *See, e.g.*, Mississippi Band of Choctaw Indians v. Holyfield, 490 U.S. 30 (1989).

[5] *Id.*

[6] *See* Bureau of Indian Affairs, *Guidelines for State Courts; Indian Child Custody Proceedings*, 44 Fed. Reg. 67584 (Nov. 26, 1979), *available at* www.nicwa.org/policy/regulations/icwa/ICWA_guidelines.pdf.

represent the construction of the statute by the administrative agency
_ _ ..... implementing the Act's provisions.[7]

Courts in a number of jurisdictions have affirmed ICWA's constitutionality in the
face of equal protection challenges.[8] These courts have reasoned in part that the
treatment of Indian people is unique not because they belong to a discrete racial group
but because they are members of a quasi-sovereign tribe.[9]

§ 12.2 History[10]

For many decades the policy of the United States government was to assimilate
Native American people into White European-based culture.[11] Among the methods
used to accomplish this assimilation were large scale removals of Native children from
their families by child welfare authorities.[12] Studies conducted by the Association on
American Indian Affairs in 1968 and 1974 found that 25% to 35% of all Indian
children were removed from their families for placement in foster homes or institutions
or for adoption.[13] Most of these children were adopted into Caucasian families or
placed in federally funded Indian Boarding Schools.[14] Conditions in the boarding
schools were often brutal, and many children suffered physical and sexual abuse.[15]

---

[7] *See* In the Matter of E.S., 92 Wash. App. 762, 964 P.2d 404, 409 (1998) (citing *In re* Junious M., 144
Cal. App. 3d 786, 793 n.7 (1983)).

[8] *See, e.g., In re* Angus, 655 P.2d 208 (Or. App. 1982); Matter of Appeal in Pima County Juvenile
Action No. S-903, 130 Ariz. 202, 635 P.2d 187 (1981); Matter of Guardianship of D. L. L., 291
N.W.2d 278 (S.D. 1980).

[9] *See generally* Fisher v. District Court, 424 U.S. 382, 390–91 (1976) (stating that exclusive
jurisdiction of the tribal court does not derive from the plaintiff's race but rather from the tribe's
quasi-sovereign status under federal law and that, "even if a jurisdictional holding occasionally results
in denying an Indian plaintiff a forum to which a non-Indian has access, such disparate treatment of
the Indian is justified because it is intended to benefit the class of which he is a member by furthering
the congressional policy of Indian self-government").

[10] For more detailed discussions of the historical rationales for the statute's enactment, see Marc Mannes,
Factors and Events Leading to the Passage of the Indian Child Welfare Act, 74 CHILD WELFARE 264
(1995). This chapter will address only Subchapter I of the statute and will do so in a limited fashion.
For more detailed discussions of the statute and its application, see B. J. JONES, KELLY GAINES-
STONER & MARK TILDEN, THE INDIAN CHILD WELFARE ACT HANDBOOK: A LEGAL GUIDE TO THE
CUSTODY AND ADOPTION OF NATIVE AMERICAN CHILDREN (2d ed. 2008); THE NATIVE AMERICAN
RIGHTS FUND, A PRACTICAL GUIDE TO THE INDIAN CHILD WELFARE ACT (2007), *available at*
www.narf.org/icwa.

[11] *See, e.g.,* Carol A. Hand, *An Ojibwe Perspective on the Welfare of Children: Lessons of the Past and
Visions for the Future*, 28/1 CHILD. YOUTH SERV. REV. 20, 27 (2006).

[12] *See, e.g.,* H.R. Rep. No. 95-1386, at 9 (1978).

[13] *Id.*

[14] *See* Carol A. Hand, *An Ojibwe Perspective on the Welfare of Children: Lessons of the Past and
Visions for the Future*, 28/1 CHILD. YOUTH SERV. REV. 20, n. 3 (2006).

[15] *Id.* at n. 3 (noting that children placed in boarding schools "were subjected to military discipline,
malnutrition, hard manual labor, and religious and political indoctrination. Harsh physical punishment
and abuse, as well as sexual abuse, were not uncommon. Contagious diseases spread easily in these
unhealthy conditions leading to many deaths.").

Moreover, the separation from family and culture left many Native American children, now adults, with psychological scars that persist even today.[16]

Congress has unique authority to regulate the relationship between Indian tribes and the federal government.[17] In 1832 the Supreme Court reaffirmed this authority in *Worcester v. Georgia*.[18] The special relationship between the United States government and Indian tribes and their members provides Congress plenary power over Indian affairs.[19] Thus it was that in the late 1960s American Indian advocacy groups began to press Congress to redress long-standing grievances regarding unnecessary removals.[20]

In 1978, after a decade of advocacy and numerous efforts by federal agencies to provide appropriate child welfare services to Indian children and families, Congress enacted the Indian Child Welfare Act.[21] In doing so, Congress made a number of findings based on studies of the number of children removed from their families as well as emotional antidotal reports of removals of Indian children and the impact such removals had on families, children, and tribes.[22] Congress found.

- "that there is no resource that is more vital to the continued existence and integrity of Indian tribes than their children"

- "that an alarmingly high percentage of Indian families are broken up by the removal, often unwarranted, of their children from them by nontribal public and private agencies and that an alarmingly high percentage of children are placed in non-Indian foster and adoptive homes and institutions"

- "that the States . . . have often failed to recognize the essential tribal relations of Indian people and the cultural and social standards prevailing in Indian communities and families"[23]

With this backdrop, Congress enacted ICWA in an attempt to remedy the unwarranted removals of Indian children from their families and tribal communities.

---

[16] *Id.* at 26.

[17] *See* U.S. CONST. art. I, § 8, cl. 3; 25 U.S.C. § 1901.

[18] 31 U.S. 515 (1832) (overruled on other grounds). *See also* Mescalero Apache Tribe v. Jones, 411 U.S. 145, 148 (1973) (noting that the Supreme Court has repeatedly stated that state laws cannot be applied on Indian reservations if the laws would impair a right guaranteed or reserved by federal law).

[19] Morton v. Mancari, 417 U.S. 535, 551–52 (1974).

[20] *See* Marc Mannes, *Factors and Events Leading to the Passage of the Indian Child Welfare Act*, 74 CHILD WELFARE 264 (1995).

[21] 25 U.S.C. §§ 1901 *et seq.*; *see* Marc Mannes, *Factors and Events Leading to the Passage of the Indian Child Welfare Act*, 74 CHILD WELFARE 264 (1995).

[22] *See* H.R. Rep. No. 95-1386 (1978); Marc Mannes, *Factors and Events Leading to the Passage of the Indian Child Welfare Act*, 74 CHILD WELFARE 264, 274–78 (1995). *But see* RANDALL KENNEDY, INTERRACIAL INTIMACIES: SEX, MARRIAGE, IDENTITY, AND ADOPTION 489–99 (2003) (questioning the soundness of the evidence on which Congress based the ICWA).

[23] 25 U.S.C. § 1901.

Following the lead of the federal government, at least two states have enacted their own versions of ICWA.[24]

§ 12.3 The Indian Child Welfare Act

§ 12.3.1 Overview

Because of the history of unnecessary and precipitous removals, in enacting ICWA Congress put in place procedural protections to make it more difficult to remove an Indian child from home than is typically the case with non-Indian children. As is explained in the BIA Guidelines, "[p]roceedings in state courts involving the custody of Indian children shall follow strict procedures and meet stringent require-ments."[25] It is clear that the intent of the Act is to preserve Indian families by making it difficult to remove an Indian child from the home. It begins this effort by defining several important terms.[26] For our purposes, it will suffice to begin with the three essential terms that define the cases to which the Act applies.

First, the statute defines a "child custody proceeding" as any action involving the placement of a child into foster care, into a pre-adoptive home, for adoption, or a proceeding to terminate parental rights.[27] By its terms, ICWA does not apply to child custody disputes between parents.[28]

Next, ICWA defines an "Indian child" as "any unmarried person who is under age eighteen and is either (a) a member of an Indian tribe or (b) is eligible for membership in an Indian tribe and is the biological child of a member of an Indian tribe."[29]

Third, an "Indian tribe" refers to any organization of Native Americans or Alaska Native village that is formally recognized by the Secretary of the Interior.[30] Accordingly, ICWA's mandate does not apply to tribes or bands that are not so recognized.[31] Each tribe is the sole arbiter of its membership.[32] Tribes may have different methods of keeping track of their membership because ICWA imposes no

---

[24] *See, e.g.*, Iowa Indian Child Welfare Act, Iowa Code §§ 232B.1 *et seq.*; Minnesota Indian Family Preservation Act, Minn. Stat. §§ 260.751 *et seq.*

[25] 44 Fed. Reg. 67586 (Nov. 26, 1979).

[26] 25 U.S.C. § 1903.

[27] 25 U.S.C. § 1903(1).

[28] 25 U.S.C. § 1903(1). *See also* Comanche Indian Tribe v. Hovis, 53 F.3d 298 (10th Cir. 1995), *cert. denied*, 516 U.S. 916 (1995).

[29] 25 U.S.C. § 1903(4).

[30] 25 U.S.C. § 1903(8). For a list of federally recognized tribes, see 53 Fed. Reg. 52829 (Dec. 29, 1988).

[31] *In re* Fried, 266 Mich. App. 535, 702 N.W.2d 192 (2005); *In re* A.D.L., 169 N.C. App. 701, 612 S.E.2d 639 (2005).

[32] *See, e.g.*, 44 Fed. Reg. 67584 (Nov. 26, 1979) (determination by the tribe that a child is or is not eligible for membership is conclusive); *see also* People *ex rel.* J.A.S., 160 P.3d 257 (Colo. App. 2007); *In re* Welfare of S.N.R., 617 N.W.2d 77 (Minn. App. 2000); Matter of Adoption of Riffle, 277 Mont. 388, 922 P.2d 510 (1996); In the Matter of Phillip A.C., 149 P.3d 51 (Nev. 2006); *In re* Dependency of T.L.G., 126 Wash. App. 181, 108 P.3d 156 (2005).

standardized method of doing so.[33] Consequently, the method of proving membership will vary from tribe to tribe.[34]

The statute applies where there is a child custody dispute involving an "Indian child." Several courts have held that the statute applies only if the child or the family has sufficient ties to the tribe or Indian culture so as to constitute an "existing Indian family."[35] Most state courts that have considered the question of the so-called existing Indian family exception, however, have rejected it,[36] and ICWA itself contains no requirement that the child have particular ties to the tribe beyond what the statute sets forth. In fact, in some jurisdictions where appellate courts have held the existing Indian family exception to apply, the state legislature has rejected it by statute. For instance, in both California and Oklahoma the legislatures overrode the courts' adoption of the exception by enacting statutes that explicitly invalidate this exception.[37] If ICWA applies to the child and the proceeding, its provisions and protections pertain to both Native and non-Native parents and family members.

§ 12.3.2 Exclusive Tribal Jurisdiction

ICWA seeks to protect not only the interests of individual children and their parents but also the interests of the child's tribe.[38] Accordingly, the statute provides that tribes have exclusive jurisdiction over an Indian child who "resides or is domiciled within the reservation" or "is a ward of the tribal court."[39] A state court's authority to enter orders relating to an Indian child who is the ward of a tribal court or domiciled on a reservation but who is temporarily located off the reservation is sharply circumscribed. In such a situation, the court may order the child removed from a parent or Indian custodian only "to prevent imminent physical damage or harm to the child" and such an emergency order placing the child must terminate immediately when "no longer necessary to prevent imminent physical damage or harm to the child."[40] Where a state court has issued emergency orders regarding an Indian child who is domiciled on a reservation but temporarily off the reservation, it must transfer the case to tribal

---

[33] *In re* Angus, 655 P.2d 208, 212 (Or. App. 1982).

[34] *Id.*

[35] *See, e.g., In re* Santos Y., 92 Cal. App. 4th 1274, 112 Cal. Rptr. 2d 692 (2001); *In re* J.J.G., 32 Kan. App. 2d 448, 83 P.3d 1264 (2004); Rye v. Weasel, 934 S.W.2d 257 (Ky. 1996); Hampton v. J.A.L., 658 So. 2d 331 (La. App. 2d Cir. 1995), *writ denied*, 662 So. 2d 478 (La. 1995).

[36] *See, e.g.,* Matter of Adoption of Riffle, 277 Mont. 388, 922 P.2d 510 (1996); Michael J., Jr. v. Michael J., Sr., 198 Ariz. 154, 7 P.3d 960 (Ct. App. 2000); *In re* Vincent M., 150 Cal. App. 4th 1247, 59 Cal. Rptr. 3d 321 (2007), *rev. denied* (2007); *In re* Welfare of S.N.R., 617 N.W.2d 77 (Minn. App. 2000); *In re* Baby Boy C., 27 A.D.3d 34, 805 N.Y.S.2d 313 (2005); *In re* A.B., 663 N.W.2d 625 (N.D. 2003); *In re* Matter of Baby Boy L., 103 P.3d 1099 (Okla. 2004).

[37] *See* Cal. Welf. & Inst. Code § 224(a)(1) (2006); Okla. Stat. § 10-40.1 (1994).

[38] *See* Mississippi Band of Choctaw Indians v. Holyfield, 490 U.S. 30 (1989).

[39] 25 U.S.C. § 1911(a).

[40] 25 U.S.C. § 1922.

jurisdiction, begin proceedings in the state court which are subject to the ICWA, or release the child to the parent or Indian custodian.[41]

Because exclusive tribal court jurisdiction is determined by the child's domicile and residence, rather than mere presence in a particular place, it is crucial that an investigation regarding the child's domicile be undertaken. For an adult, domicile is determined by physical presence in a given place coupled with intent to remain in that place.[42] The Supreme Court has observed that a child obtains a "domicile of origin" at birth which remains the child's domicile until he or she establishes a "domicile of choice" later in life (which may, of course, be different than the "domicile of origin").[43] A child is unable to form the mental intent to stay in a particular place, and therefore the child's domicile is the domicile of his or her parents (or in the case of a child born to a single mother, that of the mother).[44] Thus, it is possible for a child to be domiciled in a place where she has never in fact been.[45] Such was the case in *Mississippi Band of Choctaw Indians v Holyfield*,[46] in which a mother traveled some 200 miles from her reservation to give birth to twins whom she wished to place directly for adoption without involving her tribe. The tribe, after learning of the adoption, brought an action arguing that its right to notice of the adoption proceedings under the ICWA had been violated. The Mississippi Supreme Court ruled that the babies were never domiciled on the reservation and upheld the adoptions. The United State Supreme Court reversed, applying a federal definition of domicile and holding that although the children had been born off and had never been physically present on the reservation, they were domiciled on the reservation because that was their parents' domicile.[47]

§ 12.3.3 Concurrent Jurisdiction

In cases in which the child is an "Indian child" but resides off reservation, the state and tribal courts have concurrent jurisdiction.[48] However, ICWA provides that the state court, "in the absence of good cause to the contrary, shall transfer such proceeding to the jurisdiction of the tribe, absent objection by either parent, upon the petition of either parent or the Indian custodian or the Indian child's tribe: *Provided*, That such transfer shall be subject to declination by the tribal court of such tribe."[49] When a parent objects to transfer, the state trial court is prohibited from transferring

---

[41] 25 U.S.C. § 1922.

[42] *See* Mississippi Band of Choctaw Indians v. Holyfield, 490 U.S. 30, 48 (1989).

[43] *Id.*

[44] *Id.*

[45] *Id.* at 49–50.

[46] *Id.*

[47] *Id.* at 48–49.

[48] 25 U.S.C § 1911(b).

[49] 25 U.S.C. § 1911(b) (emphasis in original).

the case to a tribal court.[50] That is, while any party may object to a request to transfer the case, if a parent does so, that parent's objection acts as a veto prohibiting the transfer.

Alternatively, the child's parent, Indian custodian, or tribe may seek transfer of the case from the state to the tribal court.[51] Conspicuously absent from the list of parties that may seek transfer is the child himself or herself. Absent objection by either parent or a "good cause" showing not to transfer the case, the state court must transfer jurisdiction to the tribal court. The BIA Guidelines provide that a request to transfer may be made orally or in writing.[52] The purpose for permitting oral requests is to expedite the procedure.[53]

ICWA does not define what constitutes "good cause" for declining transfer of the case to tribal court. However, the BIA Guidelines suggest that a state trial court could find "good cause" to decline to transfer a case if: (1) the tribe does not have a tribal court; (2) the proceeding is at an "advanced stage" when transfer is sought and the petitioner for transfer did not make the request promptly after receiving notice of the proceeding; (3) the Indian child is over 12 years of age and objects to the transfer of the case; (4) the presentation of evidence to the tribal court would present an undue hardship to the parties or the witnesses; or (5) the child is over 5 years of age, the parents "are not available," and the child has had little or no contact with the tribe.[54] The BIA Guidelines make clear that the perceived inadequacy of a tribal court or tribal social services programs does not constitute good cause and cannot provide a state trial court with a rationale for denying transfer.[55] The burden of establishing good cause to deny transfer is on the person opposing transfer.[56] Even though the state court may be willing to grant a transfer request, the tribal court may decline.[57]

If the state court retains jurisdiction, the child's "Indian custodian"[58] or tribe may move to intervene in the state court proceeding.[59] Both the statute and case law make clear that the child's tribe may intervene in state court proceedings at any point in those proceedings.[60] If the tribe intervenes in the state court proceedings, it becomes a

---

[50]   *In re* Maricopa County Juvenile Action No. JD-6982, 922 P2d. 319 (Ariz. App. 1996).

[51]   25 U.S.C. § 1911(b).

[52]   44 Fed. Reg. 67590 at C.1.

[53]   *See* Commentary to Guideline C.1. *Id.*

[54]   44 Fed. Reg. 67591 at C3.

[55]   44 Fed. Reg. 67591 at C.3.(c).

[56]   44 Fed. Reg. 67591 at C.3.(d).

[57]   25 U.S.C. § 1911(b). Note that the tribe's exercise of its right to decline transfer does not obviate the need for the state court to apply the ICWA in an appropriate case.

[58]   The ICWA defines "Indian custodian" as "any Indian person who has legal custody of an Indian child under tribal law or custom or under State law or to whom temporary physical care, custody, and control has been transferred by the parent of such child." 42 U.S.C. § 1903(6).

[59]   25 U.S.C. § 1911(c).

[60]   25 U.S.C. § 1911(c). *See, e.g.*, In the Matter of Phillip A.C., 149 P.3d 51 (Nev. 2006); *In re* J.J., 454 N.W.2d 317, 331 (S.D. 1990).

party to the case with the rights and responsibilities of any party, including the right to access all documents regarding the case.[61]

§ 12.3.4 Notice

ICWA's notice provisions[62] are arguably its most important. In addition to mandating that states notify the parent or Indian custodian, the Act also requires that the child's tribe be notified. If the child's tribal affiliation is uncertain because he or she may belong to more than one tribe, then notification must be provided to "any tribe that may be the Indian child's tribe."[63] In cases in which tribal affiliation is unknown, then notice must be sent to the Secretary of the Interior.[64] Some courts have broadly construed the tribal notice requirement so that if there is any hint of possible Native American heritage the state court must provide notice pursuant to the statute.[65] Therefore, in practice, whenever tribal affiliation is at all unclear, notice should be sent to the Secretary of the Interior.

There are sometimes disagreements as to which entity—the petitioning child protection agency or the court—has the duty to provide notice. The statute provides that "the party seeking the foster care placement of, or termination of parental rights to, an Indian child shall notify" the relevant parties.[66] This provision of the law clearly suggests that the individual or agency petitioning the court to take protective action regarding the child is responsible for fulfilling the notice requirement, and a number of courts have so held.[67] Other courts, however, have made clear that the duty to provide proper notification must be borne by the court as well.[68]

§ 12.3.5 Appointment of Counsel

The United States Supreme Court has held that a parent has only a limited right to appointment of counsel at public expense in a child welfare proceeding.[69] ICWA,

---

[61] 25 U.S.C. § 1912(c). *See* In the Matter of Baby Girl Doe, 262 Mont. 380, 865 P.2d 1090 (1993) (noting that the right to intervene means the right to meaningful intervention).

[62] 25 U.S.C. § 1912(a).

[63] 44 Fed. Reg. 67588 at B.5(b).

[64] 25 U.S.C. § 1912(a). The best practice when tribal affiliation is uncertain is to send notice to any potential tribe and to notify the Secretary of the Interior. The Secretary may be noticed by sending the appropriate paperwork to the regional office of the BIA.

[65] *See, e.g., In re* Desiree F., 83 Cal. App. 4th 460, 99 Cal. Rptr. 2d 688, 696 (2000) ("The Indian status of the child need not be certain to invoke the notice requirement."); *In re* I.E.M., 233 Mich. App. 438, 592 N.W.2d 751 (1999) (notice required where "at least suggests" that child's mother and child "potentially qualify as tribal members").

[66] 25 U.S.C. § 1912(a).

[67] *See, e.g., In re* Desiree F., 83 Cal. App. 4th 460, 99 Cal. Rptr. 2d 688, 695 (2000); *In re* I.E.M., 233 Mich. App. 438, 592 N.W.2d 751 (1999).

[68] *In re* J.T., 166 Vt. 173, 693 A.2d 283 (1997); *In re* H.A.M., 25 Kan. App. 2d 289, 961 P.2d 716 (1998).

[69] Lassiter v. Dep't of Soc. Servs. of Durham County, N.C., 452 U.S. 18 (1981).

however, greatly expands the right to appointment of counsel for a parent or Indian custodian who is responding to a child protection action.[70] Under the Act, whenever a state trial court determines that a parent is indigent, it must appoint counsel for any "removal, placement, or termination proceeding."[71] Moreover, if the court believes that appointing counsel for the child would serve the child's best interests, the court may appoint counsel to represent the child.[72] The Child Abuse Prevention and Treatment Act requires, as a contingency to receiving federal funding, that states provide a guardian ad litem to represent a child.[73] ICWA requires the appointment of "counsel" if the court chooses to appoint a representative for the child. To ensure compliance with both CAPTA and ICWA, courts should appoint an attorney to represent the child in every child protective proceeding to which ICWA applies. In those states that do not routinely provide counsel to indigent parents or children in child protection proceedings, the court may seek reimbursement from the Secretary of the Interior for "reasonable fees and expenses" related to the appointment of counsel.[74]

§ 12.3.6 Removal

The law seeks to preserve Indian families by requiring a higher standard of evidence to support the removal of an Indian child from home. Before a state court removes an Indian child from his or her parent the court must make a finding based on clear and convincing evidence "that the continued custody of the child by the parent or Indian custodian is likely to result in serious emotional or physical damage to the child."[75] To address the historical imposition of middle class, White values onto Native American families, Congress mandated that the court must have "qualified expert witness" testimony on this point.[76] The statute does not define "qualified expert witness." Again, the BIA Guidelines provide helpful embellishment of the statutory provision. First, to be qualified, an expert should be able "to speak specifically to the issue of whether continued custody by the parents or Indian custodian is likely to result in serious physical or emotional damage to the child."[77] Persons who may fulfill this requirement include: (1) a member of the child's tribe who has expertise in the family organization and childrearing practices of the tribe; (2) a non-Indian expert who has "substantial experience" in providing family services to Indians and "extensive knowledge of prevailing social and cultural standards and childrearing practices" within that child's particular tribe; or (3) a "professional person having substantial education

---

[70] 25 U.S.C. § 1912(b).

[71] 25 U.S.C. § 1912(b).

[72] 25 U.S.C. § 1912(b).

[73] 42 U.S.C. § 5106a(b)(2)(A)(xiii).

[74] 25 U.S.C. § 1912(b).

[75] 25 U.S.C. § 1912(e).

[76] 25 U.S.C. § 1912(e).

[77] 44 Fed. Reg. 67593 at D.4.

and experience in the area of his or her specialty."[78] The expert witness requirement is a direct effort on Congress's part to counteract the imposition of cultural bias by state officials. Thus, as the Oklahoma Supreme Court has noted, ICWA's expert witness requirement is intended "to provide the Court with knowledge of the social and cultural aspects of Indian life to diminish the risk of any cultural bias."[79]

Some states have refined these definitions in their state ICWAs, and some of these refinements have led to more exacting standards than the federal law demands. For instance, Iowa's statutory law provides that a "'qualified expert witness' may include, but is not limited to, a social worker, sociologist, physician, psychologist, traditional tribal therapist and healer, spiritual leader, historian, or elder."[80] It also contains stricter definitions of "qualified expert witness" and makes clear that a professional person who is not recognized by the child's tribe and who lacks extensive knowledge of and experience with the child's particular tribe may only be used after the petitioner has satisfied the court a more appropriate "qualified expert witness" is not available.[81] On the other hand, some state appellate courts have held that so long as the expert is otherwise qualified, he or she is not required to have more specific expertise in Indian culture or Indian families.[82]

§ 12.3.7 Active Efforts

Before a state court may order a child removed from his or her home for placement in foster care, the petitioner must "satisfy the court that active efforts have been made to provide remedial services and rehabilitative programs designed to prevent the breakup of the Indian family."[83] A similar showing must be made when the petitioner is seeking termination of parental rights.[84] ICWA does not define "active efforts." The BIA Guidelines provide that when determining whether active efforts have been made, courts should consider the "prevailing social and cultural and way of life of the Indian child's tribe."[85] The Act's "active efforts" requirement is generally thought to demand more of the petitioning state authorities than the "reasonable efforts" requirement of other federal laws. As the Court of Civil Appeals

---

[78] 44 Fed. Reg. 67593 at D.4.

[79] *In re* N.L., 754 P.2d 863, 867 (Okla. 1988) (citing State *ex rel.* Juvenile Dep't v. Tucker, 76 Or. App. 673, 710 P.2d 793, 799 (1985)).

[80] Iowa Code § 232B.10.

[81] Iowa Code § 232B.10.

[82] *See, e.g.,* Rachelle S. v. Arizona Dep't of Econ. Sec., 191 Ariz. 518, 958 P.2d 459 (1998); People In Interest of R.L., 961 P.2d 606 (Colo. App. 1998); State *ex rel.* Juvenile Dep't v. Tucker, 76 Or. App. 673, 710 P.2d 793, 799 (1985); *In re* Mahaney, 146 Wash. 2d 878, 51 P.3d 776 (2002).

[83] 25 U.S.C. § 1912(d).

[84] 25 U.S.C. § 1912(d).

[85] 44 Fed. Reg. 67592 (Nov. 26, 1979).

of Oklahoma observed, "the 'active efforts' standard requires more effort than the 'reasonable effort' standard in non-ICWA cases."[86]

While this more demanding standard is generally required, several state appellate courts have held that "active efforts" are not required if making such efforts would be futile.[87] Other courts have rejected this futility test.[88]

§ 12.3.8 Placement Preferences

When an Indian child is removed from the parental home and placed, the statute imposes the general rule applicable to all children that placement be in the least restrictive, most family-like setting that will meet the child's needs and that that placement be reasonably proximate to the child's home.[89] Further, ICWA imposes, in the absence of a determination to the contrary by the child's individual tribe, a descending order of placement preferences when a child is removed from the parent or Indian custodian.[90] First, the statute requires that an Indian child be placed in the home of a member of the extended family.[91] If no family member is able to provide for the child, then the statute permits placement in a foster home that has been licensed or otherwise approved by the child's tribe.[92] Only if one of these preferred placements is not available may the child be placed in an Indian foster home licensed by a "non-Indian licensing authority."[93] ICWA does not explicitly provide for placement with a non-Indian foster home licensed by a non-Indian licensing authority. When institutional care is needed, the statute limits that care to an institution that is either approved by a tribe or operated by an "Indian organization."[94]

A state court may deviate from these placement preferences only when the child's tribe has established a different order of placement priorities[95] or for good cause.[96]

---

[86] *See In re* J.S., 177 P.3d 590, 593–94 (Okla. Civ. App. 2008). *See also In re* A.N., 325 Mont. 329, 106 P.3d 556 (2005); A.M. v. State, 945 P.2d 296 (Alas. 1997).

[87] *See, e.g.*, Wilson W. v. State, 185 P.3d 94 (Alas. 2008); *In re* K.D., 155 P.3d 634 (Colo. App. 2007); Letitia v. Superior Court, 81 Cal. App. 4th 1009, 97 Cal. Rptr. 2d 303 (2000).

[88] *See, e.g.*, *In re* J.L., 483 Mich. 300, 770 N.W.2d 853, 867 (2009).

[89] 42 U.S.C. § 1915(b).

[90] 25 U.S.C. §§ 1915(b).

[91] 25 U.S.C. § 1915(b)(i). ICWA does not distinguish between Native and non-Native family members in the placement priorities.

[92] 25 U.S.C. § 1915(b)(ii).

[93] 25 U.S.C. § 1915(b)(iii).

[94] 25 U.S.C. § 1915(b)(iv). Note that "Indian organization" as used in the statute is a term of art. See 25 U.S.C. § 1903(7).

[95] 25 U.S.C. § 1915(c).

[96] 25 U.S.C. § 1915(b).

The BIA Guidelines provide direction regarding what constitutes good cause for deviating from the statutory placement preferences.[97]

§ 12.3.9 Termination of Parental Rights

Just as ICWA demands a higher standard of proof of harm before removing an Indian child from his or her home, it requires a state court to find beyond a reasonable doubt that "the continued custody of the child by the parent or Indian custodian is likely to result in serious emotional or physical damage to the child" before the court may terminate the parental rights of an Indian child's parents.[98] Note that this compares to the clear and convincing standard of evidence that the Supreme Court has held is mandated in non-Indian cases.[99] As is the case with removal, a proceeding for termination of parental rights must include testimony of at least one "qualified expert witness,"[100] and the court must find that "active efforts" have been made to preserve or return the child to his or her family before entering an order terminating the parents' rights.[101]

§ 12.3.10 Adoption Placement Preferences

When a state court terminates the parental rights of an Indian child's parents and the goal for the case changes to adoption, the Act again delineates a set of placement preferences.[102] These are, in descending order of preference, placement with: (1) a member of the extended family; (2) another member of the child's tribe; or (3) another Indian family. Note that the first preference, that the child be placed with extended family, does not require that that the child be placed with a Native American person or that the child be placed with the nearest blood relative.[103]

---

[97] *See* 44 Fed. Reg. 67594 at F.3 (one of the following may constitute good cause to alter the placement preference: (1) the parent or child request a different placement; (2) extraordinary physical or emotional needs of the child; (3) no family meeting the preference is available after a diligent search).

[98] 25 U.S.C. § 1912(f).

[99] *See* Santosky v. Kramer, 455 U.S. 745 (1982).

[100] 25 U.S.C. § 1912(f); see the discussion of "qualified expert witness" in § 12.3.6, Removal.

[101] 25 U.S.C. § 1912(d) ("Any party seeking to effect a foster care placement of, or termination of parental rights to, an Indian child under State law shall satisfy the court that active efforts have been made to provide remedial services and rehabilitative programs designed to prevent the breakup of the Indian family and that these efforts have proved unsuccessful.").

[102] 25 U.S.C. § 1915(a).

[103] For instance, in *In re Adoption of Bernard A.*, 77 P.3d 4 (Alas. 2003), the Supreme Court of Alaska held that the trial court did not commit error by placing the child for adoption with a second cousin once removed rather than with the maternal grandparents. The grandparents argued that they were the closer blood relatives and should have received placement under the ICWA's adoption placement preferences. The court rejected this argument, and deferred to the tribe's determination that the cousin was part of the child's extended family. *Id.* at 9–10 (citing C.L. & C.L. v. P.C.S., 17 P.3d 769 (Alas. 2001)).

§ 12.3.11 Miscellaneous Provisions

The statute contains several additional provisions of which counsel should be aware.[104] First, because ICWA's provisions are jurisdictional, it appears that any party can bring a petition to invalidate state court action undertaken in violation of the Act at any time.[105] Certainly, the statute contains no time limit by which an action to invalidate must be filed. Thus, even if the court applies the state's statute of limitations, as some courts have done, such an action may delay permanency for the child and could have a disruptive effect on the stability of the child's situation. Counsel can largely avoid such problems by taking steps to ensure that ICWA's provisions are strictly adhered to.

Next, state courts and child welfare agencies must give full faith and credit to the "public acts, records, and judicial proceedings of any Indian tribe . . . to the same extent that such entities give full faith and credit to the public acts, records, and judicial proceedings of any other entity."[106] States, however, are not required to provide more full faith and credit to the orders of tribal courts than they do other entities.[107]

Finally, ICWA makes clear that where state and federal laws are inconsistent, state courts must apply the law that provides "a higher standard of protection to the rights of the parent or Indian custodian of an Indian child."[108] For instance, where state law provides a higher notice standard than ICWA, the higher state standard must be applied.[109] It appears that the higher standard rule contained in ICWA applies not just to individual litigants, but also to Indian tribes.[110]

§ 12.4 Conclusion

Although the Indian Child Welfare Act was enacted more than 30 years ago, significant problems with the statute's implementation remain.[111] One major problem, which is indicative of other implementation challenges, is the overrepresentation of

---

[104] Space limitations do not permit a more detailed discussion of these provisions; however, this is not to suggest that these portions of the statute are of less importance.

[105] 25 U.S.C. § 1914. *See generally* Mississippi Band of Choctaw Indians v. Holyfield, 490 U.S. 30 (1989) (petition brought by tribe after state adoption proceedings were complete in the trial court; adoption ultimately set aside three years after adoption complete).

[106] 25 U.S.C. § 1911(d). *See also* Native Village of Stevens v. Smith, 770 F.2d 1486 (9th Cir. 1985), *cert. denied,* 475 U.S. 1121 (1986).

[107] Navajo Nation v. Dist. Court for Utah County, 624 F. Supp. 130 (D. Utah 1985), *aff'd,* 831 F.2d 928 (10th Cir. 1987).

[108] 25 U.S.C. § 1921.

[109] *See In re* Elliott, 218 Mich. App. 196, 554 N.W.2d 32 (1996).

[110] *See, e.g.,* Cherokee Nation v. Nomura, 160 P.3d 967 (Okla. 2007).

[111] *See* U.S. General Accounting Office, *Indian Child Welfare Act, Existing Information on Implementation Issues Could be Used to Target Guidance and Assistance to States* (2005).

Indian children placed in out of home care.[112] In 2005, the General Accounting Office found that nationally American Indian children comprised 3% of the foster care population in fiscal year 2003 while they make up only approximately 1.8% of the country's population of children under age eighteen.[113] To better serve Indian children and their parents, it is important that counsel become familiar with the detailed provisions of ICWA and that counsel take every reasonable step to ensure that its provisions are carefully and faithfully applied.

---

[112] *Id.* at 11. *See also* Carol A. Hand, *An Ojibwe Perspective on the Welfare of Children: Lessons of the Past and Visions for the Future*, 28/1 CHILD. YOUTH SERV. REV. 20, 27 (2006).

[113] U.S. General Accounting Office, *Indian Child Welfare Act, Existing Information on Implementation Issues Could be Used to Target Guidance and Assistance to States*, p. 1 (2005).

III. THE CHILD WELFARE LEGAL PROCESS

Chapter 13: The Practice of Child Welfare Casework: A Primer for Lawyers

by Therese Roe Lund[1]

§ 13.1 Introduction

A popular cartoon depicts a child lawyer cross-examining Santa Claus to learn the precise methods used to determine whether his client was bad or good.[2] Beyond the cartoon's witty absurdity, the hapless look of the witness is reminiscent of how difficult it can be for child welfare social workers to describe their casework practice. The listener must sift through acronyms and jargon. One hears about bureaucratic forms and processes that seem to have undergone an anthropomorphosis to the degree that the agency's *forms* are "deciding" issues of critical importance rather than the social workers and supervisors themselves. It is not unusual to hear child welfare staff explain a decision by placing responsibility on their agency's form's acronym (e.g., "FORMAP"). For example, "The FORMAP says the child must be placed out of the home."

Who are these staff struggling to describe their work? There are an estimated 870,000 child welfare workers, and the vast majority female. Depending on whether they work in the public sector or for a subcontracted private nonprofit agency, they earn on average between $27,000 and $33,000 a year.[3] While there is some variation, many child welfare agencies experience considerable staff turnover (20% to 40% a year), causing the average tenure of child welfare staff to be two years, and the tenure of the supervisors charged with casework oversight, three years.[4]

Job titles for these staff differ across agencies: Child Protective Services (CPS) social workers, caseworkers, child welfare workers, investigators, child and family

---

[1] Therese Roe Lund, M.S.W., is Director of Staff Development for ACTION for Child Protection and Associate Director of the National Resource Center for Child Protective Services.

[2] Newsbreak, "We Don't Want To Hear About It Department," *The New Yorker* (December 28, 1998), p. 57.

[3] Annie E. Casey Foundation, The Unsolved Challenge of System Reform: The Condition of the Frontline Human Services Workforce (2003).

[4] U.S. General Accounting Office, Report to Congressional Requesters, GAO-03-357, Child Welfare: HHS Could Play a Greater Role in Helping Child Welfare Agencies Recruit and Retain Staff (Mar. 2003).

workers, case managers, permanency workers, reunification and/or family preservation workers, and other titles are used depending on the agency's classification system. In some agencies, one social worker carries out the bulk of the tasks and responsibilities for a child welfare case. In others, particularly in larger agencies, job titles might differ because job functions are specialized. One worker may only conduct child protection investigations. After an investigation is complete, another worker may work only with intact families, while other staff focus on working with families whose children are in placement.

There is significant diversity among agencies' minimum requirements for a job in child welfare.[5] While some agencies have many staff who have a master's degree in Social Work (MSW), many other agencies have staff with only a bachelor's degree in Social Work. Not all child welfare workers are trained social workers. Many agencies only require a bachelor's degree, with wide latitude as to the major field of study.[6]

With such a salary, questionable rigor of education requirements, and fairly inexperienced staff, it might be reasonable to assume that the job responsibilities of child welfare staff are correspondingly streamlined, with little autonomy allowed regarding critical decision-making. In truth, child welfare workers handle several dozen cases concurrently, carry out complex tasks, and follow myriad policies, regulations, and laws. They work with involuntary clients who have serious and multiple needs. The work is difficult and taxing and demands a breadth of knowledge and depth of understanding of dynamics of child maltreatment. While few child welfare workers might feel autonomous working in a bureaucracy, the level and quality of supervision provided can be insufficient. More significant is the fact that the bulk of the work of interacting with children, parents, and other family members occurs when the child welfare worker is out alone in the field—deciding what to do, what t say, what to pay close attention to, and what to ignore.

The vast majority of families seen by child welfare staff are never involved with the court or any of the legal community. While the need for placement is what often creates the request for court intervention, only about 21% of identified child victims are placed in foster care.[7] Most reports of alleged maltreatment received by CPS are assessed/investigated and either closed for further services or served voluntarily (i.e., without court involvement) by the agency or the community. When child welfare workers determine intrusive actions are needed, judges and attorneys must be able to ascertain what methods were used to make those determinations. This goes beyond

---

[5] Joan Zlotnik, Diane DePanfilis, Clara Daining & Melissa McDermott Lane, Factors Influencing the Retention of Child Welfare Staff: A Systematic Review of Research – A Report from the Institute for the Advancement of Social Work Research (2005).

[6] U.S. General Accounting Office, Report to Congressional Requesters, GAO-03-357, Child Welfare: HHS Could Play a Greater Role in Helping Child Welfare Agencies Recruit and Retain Staff (Mar. 2003).

[7] U.S. Department of Health & Human Services, Administration on Children, *Youth and Families, Child Maltreatment* 2007 (U.S. Government Printing Office 2009), *available at* http://www.acf.hhs.gov/programs/cb/pubs/cm07/.

examining the form used by the agency for decision-making. Every agency's form and every model of practice is built on an assumption that a worker will meet families, learn about them, and understand their strengths and their needs.

This chapter provides a roadmap of what attorneys can reasonably expect from the child welfare staff who make decisions about the families for whom the attorney advocates. Every child welfare agency has a similar case process or chronology, even if the terminology is different and/or there is variation in how many different workers (with different titles) might be involved.

This chapter does not describe an ideal best practice model of child welfare casework practice. Rather, based on current law and professional standards of practice, it offers a description of the activity that any agency staff should be carrying out to arrive at specific conclusions, recommendations, and strategies. While fidelity to the implementation of casework practice greatly varies across child welfare agencies, the steps and behaviors described in this chapter are generally acknowledged as the state of the art.[8] Steps presented are consistent with the principles of critical thinking, fairness regarding level of intrusion, helpfulness, and with the outcomes of safety, permanency, and well-being.

§ 13.2 Stages of the Child Welfare Case Process

Figure 1 shows the fundamental stages families go through when involved with child welfare/child protection agencies. This graphic does not represent who within the agency carries out these functions, nor is it a "decision-tree" to depict various alternative pathways. The stages are consistent whether the agency is rural or urban, public or subcontracted. Some agencies use additional methods to help carry out each stage, such as family group conferences or mediation services. Still, the fundamental stages remain the same.

---

[8]   OFFICE ON CHILD ABUSE AND NEGLECT (DHHS), DIANE DEPANFILIS & MARSHA K. SALUS, CHILD PROTECTIVE SERVICES: A GUIDE FOR CASEWORKERS (2003); U.S. Department of Health & Human Services, *Rethinking Child Welfare Practice under the Adoption and Safe Families Act of 1997: A Resource Guide* (2000); Child Welfare League of America, *CWLA Standards of Excellence for Services for Abused or Neglected Children and Their Families* (1999).

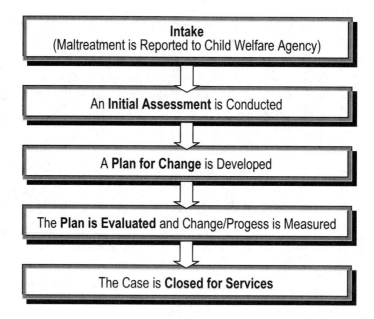

Figure 1

This chapter will not address reporting suspected child maltreatment and agency intake procedures. It will discuss each stage of the process beyond intake: initial assessment, developing a plan for change, evaluating progress, and closing the case. To promote confidence that the decisions or recommendations made by the child welfare agency are justified, attorneys advocating for the agency, children, or parents should know what must be decided and accomplished by the conclusion of each of these stages and what sufficient casework practice looks like.

§ 13.3 The Initial Assessment

While the term "investigation" is still used, many agencies call this step the "initial assessment." Commonly this stage is just beginning when the court becomes involved. The allowed time period for the initial assessment, as set by law or agency policy, is usually between 30 to 60 days. By the end of this stage the assigned worker must conclude:

- Did the alleged maltreatment happen, and if so, who is the maltreater?
- Has other maltreatment happened, to whom, and by whom?
- Is the family in crisis, and/or are there immediate needs to be addressed?
- Are all the children in the home safe?
  - If not safe, what actions are needed to make them safe?
  - Is court action necessary to authorize the needed actions?
- Without some type of help, will things get worse?

- Should the agency remain involved with the family beyond this assessment/investigation stage?

- Does the family need any referrals to community resources?

- Are there other ways the worker can help the family?

- If court action was not initiated earlier in this step, does information by the end of the initial assessment/investigation suggest that court action is necessary to protect the child?

To justify these conclusions, the worker's case practice should include:

✓ A review of relevant background information regarding the family: CPS history, criminal background, and other available records to understand how long problems have been occurring, what has worked before, and what might explain the current context.

✓ A protocol that assures that information is not compromised: The worker should observe and talk with family members privately, with short time gaps between interviews, and should collect collateral information (e.g., medical, school, relatives).

✓ Information collection that is comprehensive enough to understand the family and the functioning of the individuals in the family, rather than simply the alleged incident of maltreatment

✓ An analysis of the meaning of the collected information in consideration of the agency's standardized criteria for risk, safety assessment, and management and substantiation decisions.

✓ An approach to the work that demonstrates respect, seeks genuine involvement of the family in the provision of a plan to control for safety, and provides explanation of decisions and future steps.

✓ Agency supervision throughout this stage to help direct the worker and assure quality of decision-making.

Evaluating the Sufficiency of Casework Practice at Initial Assessment

Because child welfare and other professionals often treat the initial assessment stage as a legalistic investigation rather than a social work assessment having significant impact on a family, the attorney should consider:

- The focus of the worker during this step: Was it only about the alleged child victim or all of the children? Were all adults in the household met and interviewed? Did information gathering focus only on the alleged incident of maltreatment?

- What was the level of effort? How much time was spent collecting information and talking with family members? Did the worker try to reconcile inconsistencies in information? Is there adequate attention to detail?

- Are the actions taken by the worker to control for safety (i.e., the safety plan) logical? Are they too intrusive, suggesting that not all information beyond the maltreatment incident was gathered or considered? Common thinking errors made by workers regarding safety decision-making to watch for:

  - Thinking a child is unsafe because there has been maltreatment

  - Thinking a child needs placement because the child is unsafe

- How does the worker talk about the family? Are there indications that the approach is one of "processing a case" versus helping people? The approach to casework influences the quality and quantity of information learned, and therefore has a direct effect on the accuracy of decisions.

Not all families continue working with the child welfare agency after the conclusion of the initial assessment. The attorney representing the agency, child, or parents may find that the family has had previous involvement with the child welfare agency, but not past the initial assessment or investigation stage. Some child welfare agencies' policies are silent about who they serve (i.e., which families remain involved with the agency post-investigation), but many agencies have begun identifying a *practice model* and the families for whom services will be provided. These policy decisions about whom to serve are often based on a combination of philosophy, community standards, statutory criteria, and available resources. Categories of families served may be: families whose children have been assessed as unsafe, families with children assessed as at risk, families whose incidents of maltreatment that have been substantiated, or other categories.

§ 13.4 The Plan for Change

The stage of developing the *plan for change* has myriad names across child welfare agencies. This may be called the case plan, treatment plan, service plan, dispositional plan, permanency plan, or another term. Some agencies have adopted a practice of simply submitting a court report with recommendations for what the family must do, and the court's order is, in effect, the plan for change. Regardless of terminology, this plan is about identifying strategies for *change*; this plan operates *concurrently* with a plan for *control*, i.e., the safety plan.

The time frame for the conclusion of this stage is determined by law or agency policy, and is often 30 to 60 days. In some communities this stage has been tied to the court time frames. For example, if the dispositional hearing is scheduled within 10 days of the jurisdictional hearing, the court may expect this stage to be completed in time for the hearing. Child welfare agencies have most often acquiesced to these kinds of court policies. As a result, the case practice that is outlined below may very well be short-changed to meet the court's time frame.

By the conclusion of developing the plan for change, the worker must address these questions:

- Have the criteria for why the case remains open post-investigation been met? For example, are safety threats present?

- Is the current plan to control for child safety sufficient? Is it working?

- What is the perspective of the parents/caregivers related to the issues that cause the case to remain open?

- What protective capacities exist that could be enhanced?

- What protective capacities are missing that would be needed for the parents to protect the children on their own?

- What are the realities: the caregiver's readiness and willingness to change, the expectations of the court, and what is not negotiable (e.g., safety of the children)?

- What strategies for making some changes on the part of the parents will target the top priorities? Which will have a "ripple effect" on other issues needing change? What are the issues parents are most ready to focus on?

- Are there services that could help with these strategies and when are they available?

- What will be the benchmarks for progress that will help the parents and worker know the strategies are having the desired effect?

- What will be the worker's role in helping the family, and how often will the worker have contact?

- How will the worker coordinate, manage, and oversee the case plan and all the service providers? (This includes assuring the children remain safe, whether they live at home or are in placement.)

- How and when will this plan be communicated to the court and parties?

§ 13.5 When Children Are Placed: Additional Conclusions Regarding the Plan for Change

Beyond the above conclusions, when one or more of the children are in placement, the worker has additional responsibilities, which include addressing:

- What is the plan for contact between the child and parents? Between the child and siblings?

- What are the circumstances that must be present before the child can return home with an in-home safety plan (i.e., the conditions for return)?

- What is the prognosis or the likelihood for change?
    - Based on the likelihood, what is the permanency goal (e.g., reunification), and what is the concurrent plan for an alternate form of permanency should the goal fail?

- Who are family members who might be resources for an alternate plan for permanency if change is not likely?

- What realities and consequences must be discussed, such as time limits for change and concurrent planning actions that will be taken?

- What do the substitute caregivers need to be able to provide sufficient and safe care to the child, and how will these needs be addressed?

- What are the medical, mental health, and educational needs of the child, and how will they be addressed?

To justify all of these conclusions, the worker's case practice should include:

- ✓ A review of the case record, including the current initial assessment/investigation, for accuracy, logical conclusions, and sufficiency of the safety plan.

- ✓ A plan to reconcile any gaps in information.

- ✓ Contact with all parties involved in the safety plan to assure it is operating effectively. Action is taken, if necessary, to secure child safety.

- ✓ Contact with the children to assess needs, using collateral consultations as needed as well as information from the parents and substitute caregivers.

- ✓ Contact with parents/caregivers, separately and together, including conversations about what has happened thus far. Parental input and perspectives are actively sought.

✓ Exploration with the parents, through conversations and observation, of how safety threats or other problems or risk issues play out in the family. Consideration is given to duration, frequency, and effects of these issues.

✓ An understanding of the parents' awareness, agreement with these issues, and what they have done to try to control these issues themselves. This helps identify protective capacities.

✓ Listening to what parents say has prevented them from sufficiently and consistently controlling for child safety. Sharing observations of other issues that might stand in the way and seek parents' reactions.

✓ Seeking areas of agreement on what things parents would like to change and how they could behave differently if they were to be solely in charge of protecting their children.

✓ Clearly identifying the consequences if things do not change (e.g., an alternate permanent plan if the children are in placement, court-ordered services for some issues regardless of agreement, etc.).

✓ Seeking information from the parents and other relatives about who might be a permanent caregiver for the children if change does not occur and reunification is not possible.

✓ Enlisting parents' help in developing incremental goals that they seem ready to take on and will have an effect on some of the other problem areas.

✓ Discussions with parents (and children if appropriate) and collaterals such as relatives and caregivers about how everyone will know that behavior, emotions, patterns, etc. are beginning to change (i.e., what will be measured?).

✓ Discussing what type of help the parents might want or be willing to try in order to achieve the goals (i.e., types of services, formal or informal).

✓ Discussing with substitute caregivers their needs in caring for the children.

✓ Identifying the role the worker will play in arranging and coordinating the plan.

✓ Identifying the responsibilities the caregivers will have. Clarifying the methods and frequency of contact between the caregivers and the worker, the caregivers and the children (if in placement), the worker and the children, the worker and any service providers, and (if applicable) the children's substitute caregiver.

✓ Formalizing the plan with a date for evaluating progress (no longer than 90 days).

✓ Supervision by the agency throughout this process to direct the worker and assure quality of the process and decision-making.

Evaluating the Sufficiency of Casework Practice at Case Planning

The common error to watch for regarding the plan for change is whether the plan's strategies involve a rudimentary, simplistic "identified problem matched with a service" approach (e.g., physically abusing your child means you need to attend parenting classes). The consequence of this error is that only compliance (usually meaning attending something) can be measured rather than actual change in behavior. Another common error is that specific conditions for return are not identified so the plan is to reunify the child when the parent completes all the services. As a result, children are reunified later than necessary, instead of when an in-home safety plan could sufficiently control for any threats.

Regarding the practice and process that led to the development of the case plan, consider:

- How much time was spent talking with the parents, and what was the focus of the conversations?

- What is the level of involvement, awareness, and readiness to change on the part of the parents? What level of effort did the worker make to understand and listen to them? Put reservations aside regarding "second-guessing" social work and consider the implications of a worker who does not genuinely involve parents in the strategies for change. Review the research that demonstrates that involuntary clients are more likely to be invested in the plan when they have been a part of creating it.[9]

- How much time did the court process allow for this stage? Was the amount of time reasonable for what must be accomplished during this stage or should the court extend its time frame for the next hearing?

- If the children are in placement, are there conditions for return that are not the same as the parents resolving all the issues? How does the worker describe the difference between what must happen to bring the children home (with an in-home safety plan) and what must happen to close the case?

- Can the parents describe their understanding of what may happen if changes are not made (i.e., is there concurrent planning activity that has genuinely included the parents)?

---

[9] Ken Barter, *Building Relationships With Involuntary Clients in Child Protection: Lessons From Successful Practice, in* THE CARROT OR THE STICK?: TOWARDS EFFECTIVE PRACTICE WITH INVOLUNTARY CLIENTS IN SAFEGUARDING CHILDREN WORK (Martin C. Calder ed., 2008); Kari Dawson & Marianne Berry, *Evidence-Based Best Practices in the Engagement of Families* (report for Kansas Department of Social and Rehabilitation Services, 2001), *available at* http://vafamilyconnections.com/documents/Evidenced%20Based%20Best%20Practices%20in%20the%20Engagement%20of%20Families.pdf.

- While this stage must result in a product (i.e., a logical, feasible plan for change), place equal if not greater weight on examining the process that led to the plan's creation.

§ 13.6 Evaluating the Plan's Effectiveness and Measuring Change/Progress

Intervention by the child welfare agency and the court is intrusive, and a regular evaluation of its merits is critical. When children are placed outside of their home, the law establishes time limits regarding how long children should wait in care before an alternate plan for permanency is justified.[10] Working with involuntary family members who often have multiple and complex problems creates a perfect storm for mistakes to be made when creating the plan for change: wrong issues are prioritized, service providers are not suitable to the task, and changes have occurred in the family that impinge on progress.

These issues compel a frequent examination of how effective the case plan is by measuring the reduction of behaviors and other conditions that influence risk and safety and the increase in behaviors and other conditions that are associated with protective capacities. This stage is sometimes called case evaluation, case review, administrative review, or permanency review. As with other stages described in this chapter, *methods* used to carry out this stage may include family team meetings, going to court, or consulting with professionals.

The time frame for an evaluation of the plan should be in agency policy and/or in state law. When children are in placement, the law provides time frames for review. Usually these policy and legal time frames provide for a review or evaluation no more frequently than every six months. With a plan that establishes incremental behavioral goals and with so much at stake, a 90-day time frame for measuring progress is imperative.

Regardless of the name, methods used, or frequency, by the end of this evaluation stage the worker must conclude:

- To what degree are the safety threats (or problems that were the basis for the agency's and/or court's involvement) eliminated or reduced?

- To what degree are the protective capacities that were absent or diminished now present and/or strengthened?

- What are the observable behaviors that suggest progress or the lack of it?

- What are the parental perceptions of any changes taking place: growing awareness, indications of strength needed to make further changes, and increasing motivation to keep working?

---

[10] *See* Chapters 16 and 25.

- What are the perceptions of service providers and other involved parties regarding progress, the children's needs, and the overall effectiveness of the plan?

- What changes should be made to the plan?

- What must be communicated to the court and parties and when?

§ 13.7 When Children Are Placed—Additional Conclusions Regarding the Evaluation of the Plan for Change

§ 13.7.1 Evaluation Process if Children Are in Placement

When one or more of the children are in placement, the worker has additional responsibilities, which include addressing this question: Are the conditions for return established at the time of placement now met, allowing an in-home safety plan to be implemented while the case plan continues? In other words, can reunification occur through the use of an in-home safety plan?

To arrive at conclusions regarding the progress of the case plan, the worker's case practice should include:

- ✓ A review of contact notes, observations made, progress summaries, and any evaluations completed (e.g., psychological evaluation or children's school records) to identify trends in progress.

- ✓ Conversations with the parents regarding their perceptions of how things are changing (with a focus on specific behaviors connected to safety threats or protective capacities).

- ✓ Discussion with parents as to their general understanding of the issues that caused agency/court involvement. With parents, share and contrast how perceptions of the worker and the parents are the same or different.

- ✓ Conversations with the children regarding their perceptions and observing their needs.

- ✓ Collateral contacts with: service providers, school, health care providers (if relevant), substitute care providers, relatives, and others regarding their perceptions of the plan and its progress.

- ✓ If the children have been placed to keep them safe, regardless of treatment progress (i.e., actual change or even compliance), discuss with all parties whether the conditions for return have been met.

§ 13.7.2 If the Conditions for Return Are Met

Different issues must be addressed by the worker depending on the conclusion drawn regarding the conditions for return. If conditions for return are met, the worker must address the following questions:

- What will the process and preparation for reunification involve?
- Exactly what will the in-home safety plan include, and when can it be put into operation?

The case practice to justify these conclusions should include:

✓ Development of a reunification plan involving the parents, substitute caregivers, appropriate relatives, professionals, and others who may be part of the plan.

✓ Ensuring that a specific, detailed in-home safety plan is ready to be in place from the first day of reunification.

✓ Active preparation for reunification, including all of the following:

- Increasing visits between children and parents
- Preparing the substitute caregiver to support reunification
- Ensuring that all parties (school, health care providers, etc) are aware of the plan
- Involving extended family, as appropriate
- Preparing parents and solving practical issues (e.g., school transportation, clothing needs, daycare, etc.)
- Identifying the level of involvement between the worker and the family during the initial months after reunification
- Specifying the date for reunification
- Planning for continued involvement of the substitute care providers, if possible

§ 13.7.3 If the Conditions for Return Are Not Met

If the conditions for return are not yet met, the worker must address the following:

- What is the plan for contact between the child and the parents? Between the child and siblings? What changes in the plan for contact should be made?
- What is the prognosis or the likelihood for change (usually regarding parental behaviors, emotions, other conditions)?
  - Based on this likelihood, are changes to the permanency goal needed?
  - Is the concurrent planning activity sufficient in case an alternate plan for permanency must be realized? What activity must be carried out

to prepare the child, family, and substitute caregivers for an alternate permanent plan (e.g., adoption, transfer of legal guardianship)?

- o Are legal and other consultations necessary for permanency goal changes?

- Are the child's medical, mental health, and educational needs being met?
- Are the needs of the substitute caregivers being met so they can continue to provide safe and sufficient care to the child?
- Is the child still safe in the placement?

To justify and explain the conclusions drawn, case practice should include discussions with the parents and the service providers regarding the reasons for the lack of progress on the case plan goals and/or the conditions for return. The following issues should be discussed:

- Are the goals feasible and do the goals target the correct issues?
- Are the service providers sufficiently capable of helping the parents?
- If the plan does not need adjustment, what is the prognosis for change?
- If the children are in placement, what are the ramifications of the lack of change for their right to permanency?
- What are the realities and natural consequences for the lack of change, and what updates to concurrent planning activity are needed?
- What are the parents' perceptions regarding an alternate plan for permanency, such as voluntary termination of parental rights, guardianship with kin, etc.?
- When and how will the court and parties be informed of the results of the case plan evaluation?
- If progress is not occurring and appears unlikely, an alternate permanent plan must be ready and preparations made with the agency attorney and guardian ad litem to ensure the casework and information fully justify this recommendation.
- Provision of supervision by the agency throughout this stage for any direct intervention tasks, to help direct the worker and assure quality of decision-making.

Evaluating the Sufficiency of Casework Practice at Case Plan Evaluation

This stage of the case process should result in decisions of utmost importance, namely, the direction of intervention. The range of options to decide at this juncture include: (1) correcting the plan to ensure time is not wasted on a flawed strategy; (2) reunification of the children and family; (3) changing the permanency goal if progress is not made and increasing court and casework activity to ensure an alternate plan for permanence (e.g., adoption, transfer of guardianship) is secured; and (4) closing the case for services. Consider:

- How frequently is the plan evaluated?

- Is the worker focusing on behavioral change or merely on compliance?

- Are the methods for gathering information and measuring progress including the appropriate parties? (i.e., parents, substitute caregivers, children, service providers, etc.)

- If there are differences of opinion regarding progress, does the worker attempt to reconcile those differences?

- Is the worker open to considering any lack of progress as connected to: (1) a lack of parental involvement in the plan's creation, (2) a poorly conceived strategy, or (3) service providers who are not suited for the tasks?

- Is there a genuine concurrent plan that has been actively pursued in the event that change is not likely to occur in a timely way?

- Are the behaviors and conditions that are measured related to the central issues: the safety threats and gaps in protective capacities?

- Is there a thoughtful distinction made between all the central problems being resolved and enough of a change that an in-home safety plan can be implemented (and sustained while further change occurs)?

- Is this step carried out as a deliberate *process* or does it have characteristics of collecting reports and filling out required forms?

- If reunification (with an in-home safety plan) is considered feasible, is there a corresponding "uptick" of casework activity to thoroughly plan for this? Is the level of frequency the worker (and others) will have contact with the family post-reunification sufficient to assure safety and prevent a return to foster care?

If the case plan is targeting the correct issues and casework practice meets the above expectations, there should be abundant information supporting conclusions reached at the progress evaluation stage. The process should be sufficient to demonstrate that reunification is warranted, or it should be sufficient to demonstrate that reasonable efforts have been made to reunify but an alternate plan for permanency is required.

§ 13.8 Closing the Case for Services

The stage of evaluating the case plan is logically the time when a decision is reached about the readiness to close a case. To close the case for court and agency involvement, the worker must reach the following conclusions:

- The original reason for involvement no longer exists (i.e., if the child had originally been unsafe, the child is now safe; if risk of maltreatment was the original basis for involvement, risk is now eliminated or sufficiently reduced).

- The results of case plan evaluations over the past months demonstrate that a *safe home* now exists, meaning:
  - Threats to child safety are absent
  - Protective capacities are present
  - A sense of refuge exists in the family by all family members
  - Family members feel safe and secure
  - There is confidence that these characteristics will exist consistently

- Alternatively, the worker could conclude that case plan evaluations continue to demonstrate that the family cannot become sufficiently functional to protect the children and the parents are unwilling or unable to use community resources to augment their efforts to be protective. An alternate permanent placement of the child has been secured, such as transfer of legal guardianship or adoption. (The decision to pursue the implementation of the alternate plan for permanency occurs at case plan evaluation. Casework and legal activity at that time endeavor to ensure the alternate plan can be carried out. Once permanency is secured, the case can be closed for services.)

To justify all of these conclusions, the worker's case practice should include:

- ✓ Reviewing with the family and service providers the progress that has been made as demonstrated through past case plan evaluations.

- ✓ Assuring that an in-home safety plan is no longer needed: the family has demonstrated and can talk about what they now do differently to protect the children and keep them safe.

- ✓ Observing and, as appropriate, discussing with the children how they are feeling and what home life is now like to assess their functioning for indications or characteristics consistent with children who live in safe environments.

- ✓ Observing and discussing with parents (and seeking observations of others) to assess parental functioning for indications or characteristics consistent with a family who live in a safe environment.

✓ Discussing with parents and children, as appropriate, their plans to ensure that their progress is sustained, considering connections to the community and the level of familial and other support.

✓ Deciding how and when the court and parties will be involved in this decision.

✓ Provision of supervision by the agency throughout this stage to help direct the worker and assure quality of decision-making.

Evaluating the Sufficiency of Casework Practice at Case Closure

The most common errors made at this stage are on opposite ends of the continuum: the case is closed too quickly after reunification (or if no placement had occurred, too quickly after superficial or marginal progress), or the case continues to remain open with the agency (if not the court) "just to be sure," when the intrusion is no longer justified. Consider:

- Is the worker confusing compliance with services with actual behavioral change?

- Are there differences of opinion among involved parties (including the parents) about readiness for closure? How are differences reconciled?

- Is closure really about diminished threats and enhanced protective capacities (i.e., safety) or is it simply corresponding with a scheduled court date for a review?

- How long has the family been reunified? Has there been sufficient time to assure that the family has adjusted to this change and that an in-home safety plan is no longer necessary?

- Is the plan for supporting the family sufficient?

---

§ 13.9 Conclusion

The procedures relied on and the pace kept by the children's court system can sometimes serve to obfuscate the practice issues and thinking errors surrounding the child welfare agency's conclusions and recommendations. Diligent legal representation should include understanding what casework practice entails for accurate decision-making at each stage of the case process. This lends greater confidence that intervention is justified, fair, likely to be helpful, and will produce outcomes of safety, permanency, and well-being.

Editor's Note: A caseworker must have a variety of information from other professions and agencies to perform his or her task. What are the skills needed to work well with mental health, physicians, substance abuse providers, police officers, teachers, and developmental disabilities specialists? The lawyer might need to have this information directly because a typical caseworker should not be expected to completely understand these areas of knowledge in sufficient detail to provide certain facts or opinions necessary to make decisions in the case. By making "modern" caseworkers more and more "managers of cases" instead of "clinicians," some of the clinical skill and insight available in some CPS agencies cannot uniformly be expected of the caseworker. This is a very real detriment to the attorney and the attorney has to be prepared to look elsewhere, e.g., by going directly to the contracted or outside service providers to ensure that such knowledge is brought to bear in understanding the case and then transmitted to the court. In locations where multidisciplinary teams are legally required, this problem is sometimes abated, but such teams are not a panacea. Members of the CPT are often not providers, although they can help remind all involved of the necessity of finding out what is needed from non-CPS agency professionals.

§ 13.10 Resources for Further Information

Web Sites

Children's Bureau, Administration for Children, Youth and Families, Department of Health and Human Services
http://www.acf.hhs.gov/programs/cb/

National Resource Center for Child Protective Services
http://www.nrccps.org

National Resource Center for Permanency and Family Connections
http://www.hunter.cuny.edu/socwork/nrcfcpp/

National Resource Center for Youth Development
http://www.nrcys.ou.edu/yd/

National Resource Center for Adoption
http://www.nrcadoption.org/

National Child Welfare Resource Center on Legal and Judicial Issues
http://www.abanet.org/child/rclji

Child Welfare Information Gateway
http://www.childwelfare.gov/

The State of the Art of Child Welfare Practice

AMERICAN HUMANE ASSOCIATION, HELPING IN CHILD PROTECTIVE SERVICES: A COMPETENCY-BASED CASEWORK HANDBOOK (Charmaine Brittain & Deborah Hunt eds., 2d ed. 2004)

CHILD WELFARE FOR THE TWENTY-FIRST CENTURY: A HANDBOOK OF PRACTICES, POLICIES, AND PROGRAMS (Gerald P. Mallon & Peg McCartt Hess eds., 2005)

HANDBOOK FOR CHILD PROTECTION PRACTICE (Howard Dubowitz & Diane DePanfilis eds., 2000)

OFFICE ON CHILD ABUSE AND NEGLECT (DHHS), DIANE DEPANFILIS, & MARSHA K. SALUS, CHILD PROTECTIVE SERVICES: A GUIDE FOR CASEWORKERS (2003)

Child Welfare Reforms and Initiatives

U.S. Department of Health and Human Services, *Recent Trends in Local Child Protective Services Practices* (July 2, 2009), *available at* http://aspe.hhs.gov/hsp/09/TrendsinCPS/index.shtml

U.S. Department of Health and Human Services & Office of the Assistant Secretary for Planning and Evaluation, *National Study of Child Protective Services Systems and Reform Efforts: Findings on Local CPS Practices* (May 2003), *available at* http://aspe.hhs.gov/hsp/cps-status03/cps-practices03/index.htm

Chapter 14: Child Safety:
What Judges and Lawyers Need to Know[*]

by Therese Roe Lund[1] and Jennifer Renne[2]

§ 14.1 Introduction

How do you know whether a child's severe injury represents a pattern of dangerous conditions or is a one-time incident? What criteria do you use to determine whether a child is safe? How do you determine whether you can make the child safe without removal? (Can you remove the danger and not the child?) How do you decide whether to return a child home?

The purpose of this chapter is to provide judges and attorneys with a practical summary about key aspects regarding child safety by presenting tools to logically and methodically assess the threat of danger facing a child, the child's vulnerability, and the protective capacities of the parent(s). This chapter will also distinguish between safety plans and case plans and explore whether it is possible to *remove the danger*

---

[1] Therese Roe Lund, M.S.W., is Director of Staff Development for ACTION for Child Protection and Associate Director of the National Resource Center for Child Protective Services.

[2] Jennifer Renne, J.D., is Director of the National Resource Center on Legal and Judicial Issues with the American Bar Association.

and not the child. For children who are placed out of home, this chapter provides guidance on how to determine when it is safe to return a child by looking beyond mere compliance with a case plan, and linking conditions for return to the elimination or amelioration of threats of danger. It references and connects the analysis to current federal law governing foster care placement and reasonable efforts.

Safety planning in the child welfare system is a shared responsibility, but ultimately the court must make critical safety decisions such as whether to remove a child and when to return a child home. Judges often lack a decision-making structure when making these decisions, which can lead to following agency recommendations without a thorough inquiry. This lack of structure can lead to an over-removal problem, i.e., rubber-stamping agency recommendations without knowing what is driving the safety decision, or an under-removal problem, i.e., leaving children in unsafe conditions or returning them home prematurely. This chapter offers the basic outline of an approach to child safety decision-making, including safety assessments and safety planning.

Safety decisions must be made throughout the life of the case. Often after the initial removal, attorneys, caseworkers, and judges lose sight of original safety concerns. Parents, children, and even judges and attorneys are often unclear as to what needs to be accomplished for the child to be returned. The lack of clear standards leads to frustration for families and their attorneys and causes children to linger in foster care. Children are kept in out of home placements inappropriately for reasons that would not have justified removal in the first place. This chapter lays out clear standards, or "conditions for return," that must be met before a child can be returned and refers the reader to checklists to help courts make reunification decisions. Finally, this chapter provides assistance to judges on what to consider before closing the case.

§ 14.2 Understanding the Terms

State statutes use different terms to describe safe and unsafe children. Many statutes use language such as "imminent risk," "risk of harm," "immediate physical danger," or "threat of imminent harm." Regardless of the terms in the statute, the critical question is whether or not the child is safe. Whether or not a child is safe depends on a *threat of danger*, the child's *vulnerability*, and a family's *protective capacity*. Each term is described in this chapter, and is part of the following definitions of the safe and unsafe child.

Safe child:

Vulnerable children are safe when:

- there are no threats of danger within the family or
- the parents possess sufficient protective capacity to manage any threats.

Unsafe **child:**

Children are unsafe when:

- threats of danger exist within the family and
- children are vulnerable to such threats and
- parents have insufficient protective capacities to manage or control threats.

Child Protective Services (CPS) or child welfare agency staff frequently confuse the concepts of *risk* and *safety*, and use the words interchangeably. For a child to be unsafe, the consequences must be severe and imminent.

A conclusion about *safety* means considering:

- how s*oon* something may occur
- how *severe* the consequences will be to a child
- how *out-of-control* conditions are

A conclusion about *risk* assesses the *likelihood* of maltreatment and has:

- an *open-ended* time frame
- *consequences* that may be *mild or serious*

This distinction is important so the judge stays focused on the critical question: *Is this child safe?*

§ 14.3 Information Drives Decisions About Safety: Six Crucial Questions

Concluding whether a child is safe is based on information observed or gathered from credible sources. The following are six background questions that should guide safety in each case. The answers will help the court assess threats of danger, child vulnerability, and protective capacities. The information will also help judges decide what to do about an unsafe child.

Six Questions to Guide Safety Decisions

1 – What is the nature and extent of the maltreatment?

2 – What circumstances accompany the maltreatment?

3 – How does the child function day-to-day?

4 – How does the parent discipline the child?

5 – What are the overall parenting practices?

6 – How does the parent manage his or her own life?

Without this information, courts can have little confidence in their decisions about safety.

Judges, attorneys, and caseworkers tend to focus on the maltreatment and exclude gathering and considering more information. Although circumstances may initially seem threatening to the child, continuing to gather information helps confirm if patterns and threats actually exist. More information also helps one to determine if the family can manage safety without court intervention or with court intervention but without removal and placement.

Below is a detailed explanation of the six broad questions the court needs CPS workers and other parties to answer. *The answers provide the minimum information a judge needs to make safety decisions.*

§ 14.3.1 What Is the Nature and Extent of the Maltreatment?

In answering this question, the CPS worker should be able to describe the maltreating behavior (i.e., what is happening) and the immediate physical effects on a child (i.e., the child's injuries). Answering this question also results in a maltreatment finding. This question is typically the focus of most investigations. When explaining the nature and extent of the maltreatment, the CPS worker should include:

- Type of maltreatment
- Severity of the maltreatment and the injuries
- Maltreatment history, including similar incidents
- Description of the events, including what happened, such as hitting or pushing
- Description of the emotional and physical symptoms
- Identification of the child and the maltreating parent

However, relying only on the immediate behavior and its effects is inadequate for deciding whether a child is unsafe or what to do about it if the child is unsafe.

§ 14.3.2 What Circumstances Accompany the Maltreatment?

The worker should be able to describe what is going on when the maltreatment occurs. This description helps the court understand contributing factors. Answering this question includes considering:

- How long the maltreatment has been occurring
- Parental intent concerning the maltreatment
- Whether the parent was impaired by substance use or was otherwise out-of-control when maltreatment occurred
- How the parent explains maltreatment and family conditions

- Whether the parent acknowledges maltreatment, and what is the parent's attitude
- Other problems connected with the maltreatment, such as mental health problems

§ 14.3.3 How Does the Child Function Day-to-Day?

The worker should know the following about *all* children in the home: general behavior, emotions, temperament, and physical capacity. Information should address how a child functions generally rather than at points in time, such as the time of CPS contact or maltreatment. The worker should answer this question and include the following information about the child compared to other children of the child's age:

- Capacity for attachment (close emotional relationships with parents and siblings)
- General mood and temperament
- Intellectual functioning
- Communication and social skills
- Expressions of emotions/feelings
- Behavior
- Peer relations
- School performance
- Independence
- Motor skills
- Physical and mental health

§ 14.3.4 How Does the Parent Discipline the Child?

The worker should learn how the parents approach discipline and child guidance. Discipline is considered in the context of socialization, teaching, and guiding the child. The worker should find out about:

- Disciplinary methods
- Concept and purpose of discipline
- Context in which discipline occurs, e.g., is the parent impaired by drugs or alcohol when administering discipline?
- Cultural practices

§ 14.3.5 What Are the Overall Parenting Practices?

Beyond discipline, the worker should learn more about the parent's general nature, the parent's approach to parenting, and the parent-child interaction by finding out each parent's:

- Reasons for being a parent
- Satisfaction in being a parent
- Knowledge and skill in parenting and child development
- Parental expectations and empathy for the child
- Decision-making in parenting practices
- Parenting style
- History of parenting behavior
- Protectiveness
- Cultural context for the parenting approach[3]

§ 14.3.6 How Does the Parent Manage His or Her Own life?

The worker should learn how the parents feel, think, and act daily, not limited to times and circumstances surrounding the maltreatment. The worker should focus on the adults, separate from their parenting role or interaction with CPS, and should provide information about each parent's:

- Communication and social skills
- Coping and stress management
- Self control
- Problem-solving
- Judgment and decision-making
- Independence
- Home and financial management
- Employment
- Community involvement
- Rationality
- Self-care and self-preservation
- Substance use, abuse, or addiction
- Mental health
- Physical health and capacity
- Functioning within cultural norms

Conclusions must be supported by sufficient information. This information supports the court's conclusions about threats, protective capacities, and methods to keep the child safe.

---

[3] For a discussion of understanding cultural context, see Chapter 8.

§ 14.4 Collecting Information: Availability During the Court Process

A court's safety decisions can be thorough only if the agency has had time to assemble comprehensive information. Depending on the court proceeding, the worker may not have sufficient information to provide a full picture. For example, at an emergency removal hearing, the worker may know information only about an incident that happened the previous night. The worker needs to collect more information so the agency can argue for an emergency removal decision. The judge needs to hear, at a minimum, information about the extent of this maltreatment and the surrounding circumstances.

After that initial hearing, however, the CPS worker should gather and assess comprehensive information. By the adjudicatory hearing, judges and attorneys can expect CPS staff to provide complete information.

The agency's safety decision-making process is not always consistent with court time frames, so the court may need to hold additional hearings after information has been gathered and the assessment is complete. This practice may differ from traditional court practice, where decisions are made with limited information and a belief that "this is just the way it must be" to expedite the case.

The Adoption and Safe Families Act[4] (ASFA) requires the court to make the initial reasonable efforts determination (reasonable efforts to prevent removal) within 60 days of removal, or to make a finding that an emergency at the time of removal made services to prevent removal impractical. The majority of states, whether by statute or practice, make this finding much earlier than 60 days, usually within a few days of filing the petition. Similarly, the "contrary to the welfare" finding must be made even earlier in the case, as part of the first court order authorizing removal. The timing of these findings means the court often has insufficient information at early stages to make a well-informed decision.

Regardless of when original reasonable efforts and "contrary to the welfare" findings are made, the court must revisit the issue of the child's safety after the court has complete information. While an emergency may have existed at removal, the child may be safe at home later with an in-home safety plan.

While federal law does not require a subsequent reasonable efforts finding to finalize the permanency plan until 12 months after the child enters foster care, the court can rule on reasonable efforts to reunify earlier than that. Once the agency has gathered sufficient information on the above six safety-related questions, the court should reconsider whether the child can be safely returned home. Indeed, the court may reconsider whether a safety plan can be put in place to return the child *at any point in the case.* If the agency fails to provide this safety-related information, *the court may find the agency failed to make reasonable efforts to finalize the reunification plan under ASFA.* The attorney should ask the court to direct the agency

---

4   Pub. L. No. 105-89, 111 Stat. 2115 (codified at 42 U.S.C. §§ 621 *et seq.* and 42 U.S. C. §§ 670 *et seq.*).

to collect and provide additional information to allow the court to make an informed decision concerning the child's safety. A hearing should be scheduled to allow the court to make a follow-up decision based on full information.

§ 14.5 Key Elements for Safety Decision-Making: Standardizing Criteria for Threats, Vulnerability, and Protective Capacity

§ 14.5.1 The First Element: Threats of Danger

A *threat of danger* is a specific family situation or behavior, emotion, motive, perception, or capacity of a family member that meets each of the following criteria: (1) it is specific and can be observed or described; (2) it is out of control; (3) it is immediate or liable to happen soon; and (4) it has severe consequences. Understanding what is happening in a family depends on how volatile and transparent the threats of danger are.

Threats of danger observed by the CPS worker demonstrate the need for protection and urgent response. These threats are the basis for emergency removal decisions. Because little is known, often the only protective action the agency can make is removing the child. Typically, at the emergency removal hearing little information has been gathered besides information about the maltreatment. However, information collection must continue. *The protective action, removal, is temporary until a more complete picture can be offered to the court about ensuring the child's safety.*

By collecting answers to the six safety questions discussed in Section 14.3, the worker and the court should learn which, if any, of the 15 threats of danger listed below are present. At each review hearing, the judge should ask if, and to what degree, threats still exist. Often at review hearings, the parties and the court forget the original safety concerns surrounding the removal.

Factors to Consider When Assessing Threats

Evaluate the child's safety in his or her own home. The threats appeared in the original home, so don't be distracted if the child is temporarily placed. Would these threats exist if the child were now home with his or her parents?

Who are the parents, and who is the family? Consider who interacts or responds with the child as a parent, e.g., the biological parents, the boyfriend who sleeps over, and the live-in grandmother.

Would these threats exist if the temporarily absent abuser returns home?

You may need to consider more than one household if the child spends time in the home of both parents.

---

15 Threats of Danger Defined

The following list identifies 15 threats of danger, with definitions and examples. The threats of danger may be present in parental behavior, emotion, attitude, perception, or general situations.

1. No adult in the home is routinely performing basic and essential parenting duties and responsibilities.

2. The family lacks sufficient resources, such as food and shelter, to meet the child's needs.

3. One or both parents lack the parenting knowledge, skills, and motivation necessary to assure a child's basic needs are met.

4. One or both parents' behavior is violent and/or they are behaving dangerously.

5. One or both parents' behavior is dangerously impulsive or they will not or cannot control their behavior.

6. Parents' perceptions of a child are extremely negative.

7. One or both parents are threatening to severely harm a child, are fearful they will maltreat the child, and/or request placement.

8. One or both parents intend(ed) to seriously hurt the child.

9. The parents largely reject CPS intervention, refuse access to a child, and/or the parents may flee.

10. Parent refuses and/or fails to meet the child's exceptional needs that do/can result in severe consequences to the child.

11. The child's living arrangements seriously endanger the child's physical health.

12. A child has serious physical injuries or serious physical symptoms from maltreatment, and the parents are unwilling or unable to arrange or provide care.

13. A child shows serious emotional symptoms requiring immediate help and/or lacks behavioral control or exhibits self-destructive behavior and the parents are unwilling or unable to arrange or provide care.

14. A child is profoundly fearful of the home situation or people within the home.

15. The parents cannot, will not, or do not explain a child's injuries or threatening family conditions.

§ 14.5.2 The Second Element: Child Vulnerability

For a child to be unsafe, there must be a threat of danger, *and* the child must be vulnerable to the threat. Children are vulnerable because they depend on others for protection and care. Considering vulnerability involves knowing about the child's ability to protect himself or herself from threats and how the child is able to care for himself or herself. The information from the six safety questions provided by CPS helps the judge decide about the child's vulnerability. Criteria to consider include age, physical ability, cognitive ability, developmental status, emotional security, and family loyalty.

CPS must provide sufficient information to the court regarding the family conditions that shape the child's vulnerability. While the vulnerability of some children (e.g., an infant) is obvious, determining the vulnerability of many children depends on the worker or other parties having a good understanding of the child and family.

Vulnerability must be judged against threats occurring in a family. Vulnerability is not judged in degree; children are either vulnerable to threats or they are not.

If a threat of danger is present, presume the child is vulnerable and, therefore, unsafe. If, however, the child possesses certain strengths, then the child may not be vulnerable to that particular threat. *Vulnerability is presented as a key element of safety assessment because workers, attorneys, and judges often skip or oversimplify whether a child is vulnerable to a threat of danger.* For example, a judge may assume the child is not vulnerable because of the child's age. However, an older child may be unable or unwilling to protect himself or herself due to fear, family loyalty, or not comprehending the seriousness of the threats.

Assessing child vulnerability is more complex than merely assessing the age or intelligence of the child. The analysis should focus more on ways that safety threats manifest in the family and the child's qualities that may or may not make the child vulnerable to those threats. The following child characteristics contribute to a child's vulnerability:

- Inability to self-protect
- Susceptibility to harm based on the child's size, mobility, or social/emotional state
- Young in age (generally 0-6 years of age)
- Physical or mental developmental disabilities
- Isolation from the community
- Inability to anticipate and judge the presence of danger
- Consciously or unknowingly provokes or stimulates threats and reactions
- Poor physical health and/or limited physical capacity
- Physical frailty and potential physical harm from future maltreatment
- Emotional vulnerability
- Impact of prior maltreatment
- Feelings toward the parent – attachment, fear, insecurity, or security
- Ability to attach and vulnerability to future separations
- Ability to articulate problems and danger

§ 14.5.3 The Third Element: Protective Capacities

Remember, a child is safe when threats of danger are absent, the child is not vulnerable to the threat that may exist, *or* sufficient protective capacity exists to manage threats. This section will discuss "protective capacity." It will also detail how the judge can decide the child is safe even though threats exist.

Protective capacity is the ability to be protective towards one's young. Protective capacities are cognitive, behavioral, and emotional qualities supporting vigilant protectiveness of children. Protective capacities are fundamental strengths preparing and empowering the person to protect.

Judges should weigh parents' protective capacities against existing threat(s) of danger. Do some protective capacities exist? Are they sufficient to control and manage the threats? When threats of danger exist, lack of sufficient protective capacity can mean that the court orders CPS to do what the parent cannot. The child may or may not require placement. What substitutes for a parent's insufficient protective capacity and keeps the child safe will be discussed later.

Information detailing what protective capacities exist should be included in answers to the six safety questions discussed in Section 14.3. CPS workers should inform the court about the parent's observable qualities, behaviors, and actions that make the parent protective.

All adults living in the home should be assessed for protective capacities, including those who do not maltreat and are not sources of any threats of danger. The CPS worker should determine each adult's contribution to the family unit and whether their capacities are strong enough to control or manage the specific threats of danger.

The following subsections contain descriptions of cognitive, behavioral, and emotional protective capacities and examples of how a parent might demonstrate these strengths.

Cognitive Protective Capacities

Cognitive protective capacity refers to knowledge, understanding, and perceptions contributing to protective vigilance. Although this aspect of protective capacity has some relationship to intellectual or cognitive functioning, parents with low intellectual functioning can still protect their children. Cognitive protective capacity has to do with the parent recognizing that he or she is responsible for the child and recognizing clues or alerts that danger is pending.

Cognitive protective capacities can be demonstrated when the parent:

- Articulates a plan to protect the child
- Is aligned with the child
- Has adequate knowledge to fulfill care-giving responsibilities and tasks
- Is reality oriented and perceives reality accurately
- Has accurate perceptions of the child
- Understands his or her protective role

- Is self-aware as a parent

Behavioral Protective Capacities

Behavioral protective capacity refers to actions, activities, and performance that result in protective vigilance. Behavioral aspects show that the parent not only knows what must be done or recognizes what might be dangerous to a child, but that the parent will *act*.

Behavioral protective capacities can be demonstrated when the parent:

- Is physically able
- Has a history of protecting others
- Acts to correct problems or challenges
- Demonstrates impulse control
- Demonstrates adequate skill to fulfill care-giving responsibilities
- Possesses adequate energy
- Sets aside his or her needs in favor of a child
- Is adaptive and assertive
- Uses resources necessary to meet the child's basic needs

Emotional Protective Capacities

Emotional protective capacity refers to feelings, attitudes, and identification with the child and motivation resulting in protective vigilance. Two issues influence the strength of emotional protective capacity: the attachment between parent and child and the parent's own emotional strength.

Emotional protective capacities can be demonstrated when the parent:

- Is able to meet his or her own emotional needs
- Is emotionally able to intervene to protect the child
- Realizes that the child cannot produce gratification and self-esteem for the parent
- Is tolerant as a parent
- Displays concern for the child and the child's experience and is intent on emotionally protecting the child
- Has a strong bond with the child, knowing that a parent's first priority is the well-being of the child
- Expresses love, empathy, and sensitivity toward the child; experiences specific empathy with the child's perspective and feelings

How to Determine if Sufficient Protective Capacity Exists

There is no formula for determining if sufficient protective capacities exist. Rather, if the court finds that these capacities exist, the court must remember that: (1)

it has concluded that there are active threats of danger; and (2) it now concludes that no further judicial action is necessary to assure safety because the parent can do it without judicial oversight. Sufficient information must justify this recommendation. It is not a matter of a well-intentioned parent wanting or promising to do the right thing. The court must have confidence that credible information supports its conclusion.

§ 14.6 Using the Information to Make a Safety Decision

Determining whether the child is safe means considering three elements: threats of danger, the child's vulnerability, and protective capacities. This decision is distinct from other pending issues. This specific decision demands a logical, sequential process built on credible information supplied to the judge. Carefully analyzing and applying the three safety decision elements helps avoid confused thinking and respects the rights of the child and family.

Here is an overview of the decision process:

1. The court is given sufficient information about the family based on the six safety questions.

2. The court weighs the information against criteria for threat of danger (15 threats) and determines if one or more threats exist.

3. The court is given sufficient information to understand whether the children are vulnerable, analyzes the information, and then determines whether the children are vulnerable.

4. The court considers the criteria for protective capacities, then determines whether protective capacities exist and whether they are sufficient to manage specific threats.

5. If no threats are present, the child is safe.

6. If threats are present, but the child is not vulnerable, the child is safe.

7. If threats are present with a vulnerable child, but sufficient protective capacities exist, the child is safe.

8. If threats are present, the child is vulnerable, and protective capacities are insufficient, the child is unsafe.

An illustration of this process follows:

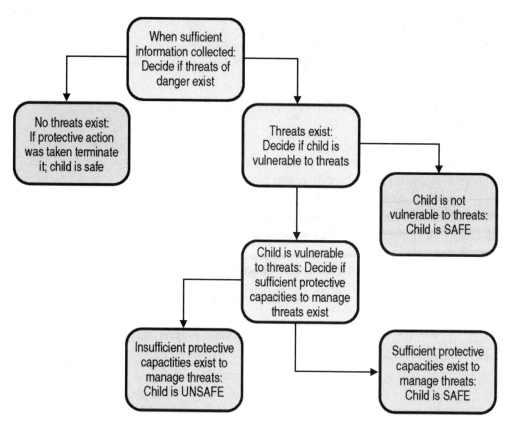

§ 14.7 Safety Plans

§ 14.7.1 When a Safety Plan Is Necessary

A safety plan is necessary when the child is unsafe. When threats of danger are present with a vulnerable child and the parents do not have sufficient protective capacities, the court decides what will temporarily substitute for the parents' inability to control the threats on their own. These substitute actions, tasks, services, and people focus on controlling threats of danger and create the components of the *safety plan*. A safety plan ensures the child's safety while working with the family. It is different from a case plan or treatment plan.

Nothing in the safety plan identifies how the parent must change. The case plan or treatment plan, which will be discussed later, identifies changes the parent must make to protect and assure the child's safety.

§ 14.7.2 Criteria the Safety Plan Must Meet

- The safety plan only controls or manages threats of danger. There must be a direct and logical connection between plan tasks and the way threats operate in the family.

- The safety plan must have an immediate effect in controlling threats. Strategies designed for long-term change, i.e., counseling or anger management classes, may be appropriate for the case plan or treatment plan but will not have an immediate effect and do not belong in a safety plan.

- People and services identified in the safety plan must be accessible and available when threats are present.

- Safety plans will have more concrete, action-oriented activities and tasks than case plans. For example, a safety plan might require providing day care or supervising/monitoring the home while a case plan might require the parent to attend therapy or parenting classes.

- Safety plans never rely on parental promises to stop the threatening behavior, e.g., "I will stop drinking" or "I will always supervise the child." Since a criterion for a threat of danger is out-of-control behavior, it is useless to rely on an out-of-control parent to be in control.

§ 14.7.3 The Range of Safety Plans

An unsafe child does not automatically require placement outside the home. Safety plans range from entirely in-home to exclusively out-of-home care. A safety plan's objective is to control threats in the least intrusive manner. Using respite care or short-term foster care to separate children from threats can be combined with time at home. When recommending an out-of-home safety plan, the parties must inform the court why an in-home safety plan cannot work as part of demonstrating reasonable efforts.

§ 14.7.4 Safety Plan Actions and Services that Help Control Threats

Devising a safety plan that is not full-time out-of-home placement requires knowing about other actions or methods that might immediately control threats of danger. The following are actions and strategies that can help substitute for a parent's lack of protective capacities. Most actions do not have to be carried out by a professional or a paid service provider. For example, child care can be provided by a daycare facility or a church volunteer. A grandmother, mentor, family preservation worker, or CPS worker can monitor whether and how parents are providing children with meals. The court should consider including these actions and strategies in the court order.

Actions and Services to Control or Manage Threatening Behavior

This type of service in a safety plan is concerned with aggressive behavior, passive behavior, and the absence of behavior—any of which threatens a child's safety. Activities and services that are consistent with this action can include, for example:

- In-home health care
- Supervision and monitoring
- Stress reduction
- Outpatient or inpatient medical treatment
- Substance abuse intervention, detoxification
- Emergency medical care
- Emergency mental health care

Actions and Services that Will Manage Crises

Crisis management aims to halt a crisis, return a family to a state of calm, and solve problems that fuel threats of danger. Appropriate crisis management handles precipitating events or sudden conditions that immobilize parents' capacity to protect and care for children. Examples include:

- Crisis intervention
- Counseling
- Resource acquisition, such as obtaining financial assistance or help with basic parenting tasks

Actions and Services Providing Social Support

These services may be useful with young, inexperienced parents failing to meet basic protective responsibilities, anxious or emotionally immobilized parents, parents needing encouragement and support, parents overwhelmed with parenting responsibilities, and developmentally disabled parents. Examples include:

- Friendly visitor
- Basic parenting assistance and teaching
- Homemaker services
- Home management
- Supervision and monitoring
- Social support
- In-home babysitting

Actions and Services that Can Briefly Separate Parent and Child

Separation is a temporary action that can last from one hour to a weekend to several days. It may involve hourly babysitting, temporary out-of-home placement, or both. Besides ensuring safety, separation may provide: (1) respite for parents and children; (2) alternatives to family routine, scheduling, and daily pressures; and (3) supervisory or oversight functions. Examples include:

- Planned parental absence from home
- Respite care
- Day care
- After school care
- Planned activities for the children
- Short term out-of-home placement of child for weekends, several days, or several weeks
- Extended foster care

Actions and Services to Provide Resources

These actions and services provide the family with practical benefits that they otherwise might not be able to afford and without which the child's safety is threatened.

- Resource acquisition, such as obtaining financial assistance or help with basic parenting tasks
- Transportation services
- Employment assistance
- Housing assistance

§ 14.7.5 When an In-Home Safety Plan Is Sufficient, Feasible, and Sustainable: Reasonable Efforts to Prevent Placement

This section describes how judges decide if the agency made reasonable efforts to prevent removal as required by ASFA regulations.[5] To make this determination, the judge must first decide on a safety plan that is sufficient, feasible, and sustainable.

Deciding about reasonable efforts goes beyond the identifying information previously discussed to determine if the child is safe. The real question is whether an in- or out-of-home safety plan, or some combination, is the least intrusive approach to keep the child safe and still be sufficient. *If an in-home safety plan would be sufficient, and the agency fails to consider or implement one, then the agency has failed to provide reasonable efforts to prevent removal.*

---

[5] *See* 45 C.F.R. § 1356.21(b)(1).

The court moves from analyzing whether the family can manage safety on their own (least intrusive state intervention) to whether an in-home safety plan involving others will work (more intrusive intervention). If the analysis reveals that no practical in-home safety plan is sufficient, feasible, or sustainable, the court must order an *out-of-home safety plan* (most intrusive intervention).

A Note About Reasonable Efforts Findings

Often, in lieu of a finding that the agency made reasonable efforts to prevent removal, courts find that an emergency existed at the time of removal. The agency is required to provide reasonable efforts to reunify immediately. The next required reasonable efforts finding is whether the agency made reasonable efforts to finalize the permanency goal.[6] This finding must be made within 12 months of foster care entry, but can be made earlier.[7]

This reasonable efforts finding may be more meaningful if the court considers whether the agency explored, developed, and implemented a sufficient safety plan. At any point in the case, the court can order the agency to accomplish these objectives. Failing to follow the court's order or to develop a sufficient safety plan can be the court's basis for finding the agency failed to finalize a permanency plan of reunification. The threat of such a finding may serve as added incentive for the agency to implement the safety plan because the agency will not receive Title IV-E funding unless and until a positive finding is made.

---

[6] 45 C.F.R. § 1356.21(b)(2).

[7] 45 C.F.R. § 1356.21(b)(2)(ii).

Safety Decision-Making: Developing the Safety Plan through Terminating Court Jurisdiction

After the court orders the safety plan, review hearings continue to address safety and other issues. Steps to resolve safety issues are depicted in the following chart:

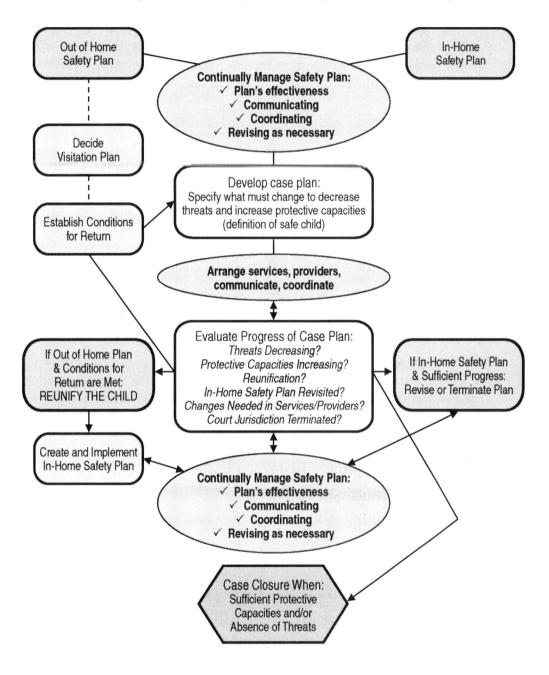

§ 14.8 The Out-of-Home Safety Plan

An out-of-home safety plan becomes necessary whenever an in-home safety plan is not sufficient, feasible, or sustainable. The out-of-home safety plan involves placement with a relative, foster home, or other court-ordered placement. An out-of-home safety plan poses two issues for the court to decide:

    (1)   What kind and amount of contact (i.e., visitation) will there be between the children and parents?

    (2)   What are the minimum expectations or conditions for the child to return home?

This section will help judges consider *visitation* and the *conditions for return home* within the framework of safety decision-making.

§ 14.8.1 Visitation: Contact Between Children and Family

Immediate and frequent contact between the child and parent(s) helps maintain the child's identity and reduces trauma. It also influences future safety decision-making. Visitation is less helpful to future safety decisions when it is identical in every case, such as:

- Supervised regardless of need for, or level of, supervision
- Carried out at the same location: the CPS agency
- Has the same frequency

Cookie-cutter visitation plans often place needless restrictions on parent-child contact and miss opportunities to achieve safety expediently. CPS, the parties, and the judge should use visits to assess and develop parental protective capacities that could make the child safe at home without state intervention. When ordering visitation, judges should consider why the child was removed.

§ 14.8.2 Components of Visitation Plans

At a minimum, visitation plans should include:

- Face-to-face contact between child and parent (unless shown why not) no more than five days after placement. Contact should occur weekly and, in many cases, more frequently.
- Face-to-face contact between siblings at least once per month
- Other contacts including phone calls, letters, email, text messaging, and attending church, school, and other appointments together
- A court order or visitation document, provided to everyone involved in visitation, specifying the times, duration, location, and conditions of supervision

- An assurance that the frequency or length of visits will not be used as punishment or reward but is a right of all family members unless child's safety is jeopardized

- A statement that CPS will oversee visitation, including logistics, and will ensure the child's safety

- Steps to maintain parent-child attachment and help parents practice or learn greater protective capacity

- Dates when visitation terms will be routinely reviewed

- Ideally, a statement that visits will take place in the foster home, providing a more natural setting and letting the foster parent model parenting techniques

§ 14.8.3 Conditions for Return: Establishing Clear Objectives

Conditions for return are what must happen for the child to return home. Conditions should be detailed in a court order and include the circumstances that must exist in the home before that child can return. Circumstances should include the parents' behaviors, skills, understandings, emotions, and attitudes, as well as other conditions that must be met.

The judge and CPS must be clear about what the conditions mean and provide that information to the parents. This expectation is consistent with federal law requiring the court to hold annual permanency hearings (administrative reviews every six months) and determine all of the following:

- Safety of the child

- Continuing necessity for and appropriateness of the placement

- Extent of compliance with the case plan

- Extent of the progress that has been made toward alleviating or mitigating the causes necessitating placement in foster care

- A likely date by which the child may be returned to and safely maintained in the home or placed for adoption or legal guardianship[8]

Having unclear, imprecise, or vague conditions for the child's return produces bad outcomes and frustration for parents and children. The parents' confusion about what they must accomplish creates barriers to the child's safe and timely return. Failing to identify and explain conditions for return leads to lower rates of reunification.

The judge can use the safety decision-making process as the logical foundation for identifying conditions for return. Conditions for return are the benchmarks for reunification. These benchmarks guide services, provide clarity for parents, and help parties focus on whether *safety can be achieved in the home*, not whether treatment programs were completed or treatment goals accomplished. Some courts and agencies

---

[8]   42 U.S.C. § 675(5)(B).

decide to reunify based entirely on parents following case plan requirements, such as attending service classes or appointments. More important is whether parents' participation in services changes the skills, behavior, attitudes, and conditions that brought the family to court. Perfect attendance may do nothing to make the home safe. Conversely, a parent may not attend services and yet still satisfy conditions for return.

§ 14.8.4 Using Safety-Related Information and Logical Decision-Making When Establishing Conditions for Return

Conditions for return are based on what the child needs to be safe, with a sufficient, feasible, and sustainable in-home safety plan. What happens when threats of danger and gaps in protective capacities have been identified and an in-home safety plan is insufficient? Knowing why an in-home safety plan cannot work suggests what circumstances or conditions must change for the child to return. What must change to be safe *now* becomes the conditions for return.

Can Return Be Made Safe?

Conditions for return should not be confused with long-term service needs or what must change over time. *It is not necessary to wait until the family is able to protect the child before returning the child home.* Threats of danger need to be controlled, not eradicated, before children can be reunified with families. Likewise, parents do not have to change before children can be reunified. When deciding to return a child, the court should focus on whether *return can be made safe,* not on parents complying, completing or even improving with treatment.

Conditions for return should specify the people, behaviors, and circumstances (including alternatives and options) that, if in place and active, would resolve why an in-home safety plan was insufficient. One example:

One or both parents lack parenting knowledge, skills, and motivation necessary to assure a child's basic needs are met.	Bryan and Sheila are the 19-year-old parents of a newborn, Heather. Both adults are intellectually limited and socially immature. They lack fundamental knowledge and skills needed to provide basic care to the infant (i.e., food, clothing, protection). In addition to the basic care problems, they mishandle the child and behave toward her as if she were a doll.
	Conditions for Return:
	• A person with suitable knowledge and skill to meet the basic care needs of Heather is present in the home every day to help care for her.
	• Bryan and Sheila agree to accept help in learning how to care for and physically handle the child.

> - Bryan and Sheila demonstrate the ability to handle Heather gently and carefully and understand the importance of doing so.

§ 14.9 The Court-Ordered Case Plan

The *case plan* is different from the safety plan in two respects:

1. **It details what must change to be "successful,"** e.g., terminating court jurisdiction, versus a safety plan detailing what must be controlled for the child to be placed at home.

2. **Its effect can be achieved over time,** versus a safety plan that controls threats of danger immediately and on a day-by-day basis.

Federal and state laws and policies specify requirements for case plans, including requirements about the child and foster parents, and these are discussed below.

This section shows judges and advocates how to determine whether a case plan recommended by the parties: (a) is consistent with federal safety requirements; (b) is consistent with a logical process for safety decision-making; and (c) has a high likelihood of achieving "success."

§ 14.9.1 Federal Foster Care Requirements

The federal law governing foster care can be found in Titles IV-B and IV-E of the Social Security Act, as Amended by the Adoption and Safe Families Act (ASFA).

When children are deemed unsafe and are placed out-of-home to assure safety, ASFA requires a case plan. The case plan sets forth the services for the child, parents, and foster parents "to improve the conditions in the parents' home [and] facilitate return of the child to his own safe home . . . ."[9] ASFA also requires that case plan progress be reviewed at least every six months.[10]

Federal law also establishes time limits for children in an out-of-home placement. These time limits make it essential that the case plan: (1) sets forth an effective and expedient strategy to prepare parents to ensure children's safety; and (2) evaluates progress frequently and is revised when needed.

The case plan should contain a logical strategy for addressing the reasons the court became involved: threats of danger to the child and the parents' insufficient protective capacity.

The case plan outcome should be a home environment with no threats of danger or, at least, a home where one or both parents have sufficient protective capacities to manage such threats. The case plan should include goals, tasks, and timetables for services facilitating changes. Again, keep in mind that while the case plan should

---

[9] 42 U.S.C. § 675(1)(B).

[10] 42 U.S.C. § 675(5)(B).

reduce threats of danger over time, the safety plan ensures the child's safety now. While the case plan and safety plan may be included in the same document, their purposes are distinct.

Note that a case plan covers more than safety outcomes; it also outlines how to meet the children's needs. This chapter addresses only the safety aspects of case plans.

§ 14.9.2 Increasing the Case Plan's Likelihood for Success

The judge should consider:

☐ **Does the case plan include goals or tasks addressing changes** in behaviors, commitments, and attitudes related to safety? Listing required services and directing parents to "follow all treatment recommendations" does not allow the court to measure progress, only attendance or participation. A more specific example: "Alan will demonstrate an ability and willingness to delay his own needs to provide food, supervision, and attention for his daughter Kayla."

☐ **Does the case plan follow logically from the threats** and gaps in protective capacities in the home? Be precise when detailing a case plan's strategy, and specify what must change.

☐ **Does the case plan duplicate the safety plan**? If yes, one plan (or both) is not fulfilling its purpose. These plans work concurrently. The case plan addresses changes so the parents, in time, can keep their child safe without court intervention; the safety plan addresses how the child stays safe from threats.

☐ **Does the case plan target issues that influence threats of danger** and conditions interfering with parent protective capacity? Some parents must deal with their own victimizing experiences and/or mental health issues before they can develop protective capacities. A case plan calling for a parent to "learn about child development" will fail if it does not address these crucial problems.

☐ **How do parents react to the case plan?** An experienced judge knows how to gauge a parent's hope, fear, or remorse.

☐ **Does the case plan focus on reducing threats without also increasing protective capacities?** The family has the best chance for success if they reduce threats *and* increase protective capacity. For example, compare the benefits of (a) having a single mother end her live-in relationship with her boyfriend who physically abused her and her child with (b) helping that mother develop her alertness to danger and willingness to put her child first. If the first succeeds, one threat is eliminated. If the second succeeds, the mother manages future threats. Both strategies can be in the case plan. While focusing solely on reducing threats is more obvious, lack of this dual strategy will likely limit long-term success.

§ 14.9.3 Evaluating Progress Using Safety Criteria

Progress towards achieving case plan goals will be measured in behavioral, emotional, and mental health changes. Simply measuring attendance or participation in services is insufficient. The judge can order a more frequent evaluation of progress, i.e., more often than twice per year.

The judge must evaluate safety plan progress during the review hearing no matter what other issues need to be resolved. The judge evaluates progress to determine whether:

- The safety plan and case plan are appropriate
- Services, actions, tasks, and responsibilities are being carried out according to plan
- Parents and others are participating according to commitments made in both plans
- Progress is occurring
- Conditions for return have been met
- The safety plan or case plan must be modified or revised

If the judge raises these issues in every hearing, it can influence how diligently the parties meet their case plan responsibilities. *The judge's influence is often critical to achieving a safe home for the child and completing a successful plan.*

Judges and attorneys should focus on critical safety issues. This focus can help deter parties from overemphasizing attending services and can avoid confusing *child well-being*, such as appropriateness of the child's education while in care, with *child safety.*

Safety-Related Questions for the Judge to Consider

☐ **What do the parties know about child safety issues, including progress under the case plan?** Are the six safety questions about the family being answered today with current information? Can they be answered with credible information free from bias?

☐ **What is the status of the threats of danger and what, if any, additional threats of danger have emerged?** Does information suggest threats are diminishing or emerging differently? Ask for information about each original threat. What, if any, information has come forth concerning new threats of danger?

☐ **What is the status of the parents' protective capacities?** Have the parents demonstrated enhanced capacity? Will the parents protect the child without intervention? Has there been any change in their willingness, awareness, and ability to protect the child from threats of danger? Judges should get information about each protective capacity identified in the case plan.

☐ **Are there differences of opinion among the parties?** Learn why differences are present. Resist listening to one opinion or relying on the most credentialed "expert." Challenge the parties to reconcile differences of opinion and consider their rationales.

☐ **Have conditions for return been met?** This question must be asked, regardless of how well treatment is or is not progressing. Resist "raising the bar" by having higher standards for returning the child than for removing the child. Is an in-home safety plan now sufficient, feasible, and sustainable until the parent is able to protect the child without help?

☐ **Can the in-home safety plan be revised to be less intrusive?** The answer to this question depends on how threats are emerging, any changes in parent awareness, and parents acknowledging that a safety plan is important and necessary.

☐ **If there has been little progress, consider:**
  • Does the case plan contain the right strategies?
  • Are the services and/or the providers appropriate for the task?
  • Does the parent want the same changes as the other parties?
  • Does the lack of progress affect permanency issues if an out-of-home safety plan is in effect? There is a solid link between safety outcomes and permanency, with one influencing the other. Consider how long it will take for the conditions for return to be met, and how long it is reasonable to continue working on the reunification goal without ongoing parental supervision.

§ 14.10 Reunification: A Safety Decision

Deciding when a child can be reunified and stay home safely is one decision that troubles most judges. This section reinforces the idea that the reunification decision has the same threshold as the out-of-home safety plan decision. In other words, the standard for return home is often higher than the standard for the initial removal and children are often left in out-of-home care despite the lack of threats to safety. Practical help will be offered on identifying essential information and how to weigh its significance.

The formal case plan evaluation informs the reunification decision. Tracking progress should be continual, occurring at and between court review hearings.

§ 14.10.1 Issues Central to the Reunification Decision

  • Parents do not have to complete treatment nor do all safety threats need to disappear before reunification can occur.

  • The conditions for return are reunification benchmarks, not case plan goals.

- The fundamental issues are:
  - o Has there been enough change in threats, in protective capacities, and in *circumstances*, so that the earlier reason an in-home safety plan was insufficient is no longer accurate?
  - o Does an analysis using the same criteria that required an out-of-home safety plan, now find that an in-home safety plan is sufficient to control the threats, is feasible, and can be sustained? At least until the parent can protect without help?
- Deciding to reunify the child and family is the same as determining an in-home safety plan can replace an out-of-home safety plan.

§ 14.10.2 Determining Whether to Reunify

While deciding whether to reunify, the judge requires the following information:

☐ The status of the original threats of danger and any newly emerged threats.

☐ The nature, quality, and length of visits between child and parent. (By the time reunification is considered, visits should have been frequent, consistent, and unsupervised).

☐ Specific information about changes in parent behavior, attitudes, motivation, and interactions.

☐ Parental willingness and capacity to support reunification and an in-home safety plan. (Gaining parental promises to control situations determined out-of-control is irrelevant).

☐ Information and observations from the out-of-home care provider. What are patterns of child or parent behavior before, during, and after visits? Will changes in the child since placement influence successful reunification?

☐ The preparation given by the out-of home care provider to support reunification. The natural loss experienced by the providers if reunification occurs does not nullify the value of their information; consider how their support or lack of it will influence reunification.

☐ Progress noted by providers, opinions of providers regarding reunification, and recommendations from providers about what is needed for the in-home safety plan to be sufficient. Scrutinize differences of opinion and resist relying on one party or the person with the most credentials.

☐ An independent recommendation and its justification from the CPS worker. The worker should not rely solely on another professional recommendation, but should make and defend an independent recommendation.

☐ The specifics of a reunification plan. Having a reunification plan means that when the court orders reunification, it happens with preparation, not at 6:00 pm tonight.

Neither should it wait until the end of the school semester or another lengthy time frame. Plan specifics should include:

- o Changes to the visitation schedule, i.e., how will visits increase and still be used to keep measuring and building confidence in the reunification decision?

- o Involvement of the extended family, as appropriate.

- o Involvement of the out-of-home care provider, foster parent.

- o Specific time frames.

- o The plan to prepare the child. Who will discuss it with the child? What will the child miss in the placement home? What other issues are important to the child?

- o The plan to prepare the family and the home for child's return. Parents may have unspoken issues they feel guilty about raising, or they may fear that they will be considered unready if they do raise those issues. There also must be a plan for solving practical issues (e.g., school) and emotional issues (e.g., anxiety). Do not assume that the therapist will handle these issues; get specifics on resolution of these issues.

- o Specific details of the in-home safety plan, e.g., actions, frequency, providers, and roles.

- o The CPS worker's role and responsibility for actively managing the safety plan. Reunification is the most dangerous time for the child. The court should be alert because agency and service providers may reduce contact with the family. The court should order specifics for aggressive supervision of the safety plan.

§ 14.10.3 Safety Criteria Help Determine When to Terminate Court Jurisdiction

Case plan evaluation informs the reunification decision and provides the basis for terminating court jurisdiction. Using criteria for what makes a child safe helps avoid premature dismissal at reunification. If the court dismisses the case when a child returns home, either that dismissal is too early or the child was returned home too late.

Another common error is arbitrarily using the calendar for ending court supervision, e.g., at six months after reunification. Deciding to dismiss the case should be based on analyzing safety, i.e., showing that threats of danger no longer exist or sufficient protective capacities are present.

Only consider terminating court jurisdiction if the child is safe. Safety is achieved by eliminating threats of danger, reducing the vulnerability of the child, improving the parents' protective capacities to control threats, or a combination of these.

§ 14.11 Summary

Decisions about child safety must be methodical, logical, and thorough, following a careful sequence of critical thinking. Good decisions about safety require extensive information about the family. The judge should know the extent of maltreatment; circumstances contributing to the maltreatment; the child's vulnerabilities and strengths; the attitudes, behavior, and condition of the parents; and how the parents care for and discipline the child.

This information guides the judge in determining whether there is a sufficient "threat of danger" to justify court intervention and what out-of-control circumstances will result in immediate and severe harm to a vulnerable child. The child is unsafe if threats of danger exist, the child is vulnerable, and parents have insufficient protective capacities to control the danger.

If the child is unsafe, a safety plan must then temporarily compensate for the parents' inability to control the threats of danger. Safety plans may be 100% in-home plans, 100% out-of-home plans, or some combination of both. The safety plan employed in a specific case should be the least intrusive needed to ensure the child's safety. Regardless of the plan, CPS must manage it to ensure it is working and to determine if it needs revision.

If an out-of-home safety plan is required, it must provide details about the child's contacts with parents and siblings, and should specify conditions for the child's return home. These conditions should be based on the exact threats of danger and the reasons why an in-home safety plan was not sufficient, feasible, and sustainable.

The case plan (as opposed to the safety plan) identifies what must change for the child to be fully safe so the court can ultimately dismiss the case. The case plan identifies long-term goals and services that reduce specific threats of danger and increase parents' protective capacities. Case plan progress should be evaluated frequently, i.e., a minimum of every 90 days.

Family reunification should occur when an in-home safety plan is now sufficient, feasible, and sustainable. The child is safely returned home, while the parties work to end court intervention. The court should dismiss the case when sufficient information supports the judgment that threats of danger are now absent, parents have sufficient protective capacities, or both.

Chapter 15: Due Process of Law and Child Protection

by Howard Davidson[1]

§ 15.1 Introduction to Federal Due Process Issues in CPS Activities

This chapter provides an overview of constitutional due process of law issues that relate to the operation of child protective services (CPS) agencies. As a result of a June 2003 reauthorization of the federal Child Abuse Prevention and Treatment Act[2] (CAPTA), all states receiving federal funding under that Act are required to promptly notify every individual who is the subject of a child abuse and neglect investigation of the allegations against him or her. This must be done in such a way as to protect each person's individual rights. CAPTA also now requires that child protective services agency (CPS) workers be trained in how to conduct abuse/neglect investigations in a way that protects the legal rights of the children and their family. This means, among other things, that CPS workers must comply with Fourth Amendment requirements against unreasonable warrantless entries (or entries not authorized by a prior valid court order) and searches of parents' homes, and against unlawful seizures of minor children during their investigations. Such prior court orders (or warrants), when required, must issue from a judge (or other designated judicial hearing officer) and be initially based on a reasonable suspicion or probable cause that child abuse/neglect has occurred.

There are a number of important principles and cases that child welfare attorneys should be aware of related to the rights of parents and children in connection with CPS agency operations, particularly in regard to investigations, confidentiality of records, and emergency removal of children. Some of those principles are elaborated upon in state statutes that constrain certain agency practices. These statutes often specify the parameters of the lawful authority of police officers or CPS caseworkers when investigating child abuse/neglect reports. This can include provisions on entering homes, interviewing children without prior parental notification or consent, or conducting other investigatory actions. In some states, there are explicit requirements for obtaining judicial orders, including on an *ex parte* emergency basis, to permit home entries where parents have refused them, or other judicial authorization for completion of a child protection investigation when impediments arise.

---

[1] Howard Davidson, J.D., is Director of the ABA Center on Children and the Law, a program of the American Bar Association based in Washington, DC.

[2] Pub. L. No. 108-36, 117 Stat. 800.

In addition to these Fourth Amendment issues related to the investigation of reported child maltreatment cases, this chapter will also summarize litigation that has challenged the preservation and use of information about parents and children in CPS central registries. These are data preservation systems, not necessarily titled "central registries," where information on children alleged to have been abused or neglected, and their alleged parent perpetrators, are maintained. Some states preserve such data even if cases are "unsubstantiated" or disproven after an investigation is completed. Others keep this data only upon "substantiation" of allegations by CPS or if there is a judicial finding that the abuse/neglect occurred. Litigation has arisen over the use of central registry information in employment and licensing decisions where an adult is listed in the registry as a perpetrator of abuse or neglect.

§ 15.2 Exceptions to the Requirement of a Court Order or Warrant Before Certain CPS Actions

The general rule is that with three exceptions discussed below, CPS workers and the police or others assisting them must have a warrant or court order to enter a home, conduct searches, or remove a child into placement. The three very important exceptions to the prior court order or warrant requirement are consent, exigent circumstances (emergencies), and special needs. In each area, a summary of relevant court decisions applying these principles is included below.

§ 15.2.1 Need for Consent to Enter a Child's Home

The most common exception to the Fourth Amendment warrant requirement occurs when the CPS worker obtains consent of one or both parents to enter and inspect the premises and the child.

Case Law

- In *Coleman v. New Jersey Division of Youth and Family Services*,[3] plaintiffs contended that, during the investigation of the mother, caseworkers made improper allegations concerning a prior incident of sexual abuse of one of the children and made improper reference to the mother's infidelity and her husband's resulting suicide. Plaintiffs also asserted that the caseworkers' conduct was motivated by racial bias and that the caseworkers searched plaintiffs' house and interviewed the children without consent. The court found the CPS workers did not violate the mother's Fourth Amendment rights because she had consented to entry into the home and voluntarily escorted caseworkers through the house, and the caseworkers ceased interviewing the children when the mother revoked her consent to the interviews.

---

[3] 246 F. Supp. 2d 384 (N.J. 2003).

- In *Walsh v. Erie County Department of Job and Family Services,*[4] caseworkers searched the parents' home during an investigation into an anonymous tip that their children were living in unsafe conditions. The court found that the defendants failed to obtain consent to enter the home where they used force and threats of arrest and/or removal of the children if the parents failed to allow CPS workers to enter and search the home. The court held that consent requires the absence of any overt act or threat of force against parents and the absence of any promise to the parents or any indication of more subtle forms of coercion that may flaw their judgment. Valid consent also requires the absence of any indication that parents are newcomers to the law, mentally deficient, or unable in the face of custodial arrest to exercise a free choice.

- In *Calabretta v. Floyd,*[5] a CPS worker and police officer entered the parents' house without a search warrant to investigate an anonymous tip of child abuse. While in the house, the CPS worker required the mother to remove a child's clothes to check for bruises. The court held that the consent of the parent to enter the home was not obtained when the CPS worker used a police officer to intimidate the mother into opening the door and allow their entry. The court also held that the CPS worker and police officer were not entitled to qualified immunity where the court found that a reasonable officer would have known that warrantless entry was illegal and no exigent circumstance existed.

- In *Wildauer v. Frederick County,*[6] a county attorney, social worker, and county sheriffs went to the foster mother's home to obtain release of four children in her care and recover them. The social worker brought nurses to the foster mother's home to examine the other nine children. CPS determined that all the children had been neglected and sought custody. The court held that the CPS workers were entitled to qualified immunity because the foster mother granted consent to enter the home and conduct a search and exam the children. The court also found that the foster mother did not have a constitutionally protectable interest because she did not have legal custody of the other children.

Implications for CPS Practice

In general, the above cases conclude that any consent given by a parent to enter their home or examine their child's body must be given freely, without intimidation, threat of arrest, or threats of removal of the child from the home. Such consent can be explicitly stated or implied by the parent's actions (i.e., setting an appointment for a home visit, escorting the CPS worker into the home). However, a parent also has the

---

[4]   240 F. Supp. 2d 731 (N.D. Ohio 2003).

[5]   189 F.3d 808 (9th Cir. 1999).

[6]   993 F.2d 369 (4th Cir. 1993).

right to revoke the freely given consent at any point during the investigation, meaning that the CPS workers must stop their investigation, search, or interview and obtain a warrant or court order before proceeding further (unless one of the exceptions described below applies).

§ 15.2.2 Need for Consent to a Physical Examination of a Child by a Caseworker

Case Law

- In *Greene v. Camreta*,[7] the children's mother brought a 42 U.S.C. § 1983 action against a CPS caseworker and deputy sheriff, alleging violations of Fourth and Fourteenth Amendment rights under the Due Process Clause. The Ninth Circuit Court of Appeals held that the decision to seize and interrogate child at school, in the absence of a warrant, court order, exigent circumstances, or parental consent, violated the Fourth Amendment, stating that the "special needs" exception was not applicable in child abuse investigations, and holding that a caseworker might still be liable for removing a child from her mother's custody and for excluding the mother from being present at a medical center while her children underwent physical examinations.

- In *Roe v. Texas Department of Protective and Regulatory Services*,[8] upon receiving a report of alleged sexual abuse, a CPS worker made an unannounced home visit after unsuccessfully trying to reach the mother by phone and left her card requesting that the mother get in touch with her to discuss the allegations of abuse. The mother called the CPS worker and set up an appointment for the next day. The mother allowed the CPS worker into the home to interview her child. The CPS worker also conducted a physical examination and took pictures of child over the mother's protests. The court found that the CPS worker did not violate the mother's Fourth Amendment right against unreasonable search because the mother gave her consent when she set up an appointment over the phone for the worker to make a home visit. However, with respect to the body cavity search of the child, the court found that the CPS worker did violate the child's right to bodily integrity and privacy. The court also found a question of fact as to whether one of the parents had consented to the search, given that the CPS worker ignored the parent's protests over the necessity of such an invasive search.

- In *Darryl H. v. Coler*,[9] the plaintiffs' children were required to disrobe and allow a CPS worker to examine their bodies for signs of abuse and neglect. The plaintiffs challenged the constitutionality of the CPS policy that allowed caseworkers to conduct physical examinations of children's bodies when

---

[7]   588 F.3d 1011 (9th Cir. 2009).

[8]   299 F.3d 395 (5th Cir. 2002).

[9]   801 F.2d 893 (7th Cir, 1986).

investigating allegations of abuse or neglect, arguing that it violates fundamental Fourth and Fourteenth Amendment rights to privacy and protection from unreasonable searches and seizures. Affirming the district court's ruling, the Seventh Circuit Court of Appeals found that a caseworker could conduct a physical examination of a child without probable cause or a warrant when investigating alleged abuse that met the criteria of the abuse hotline, without violating the Fourth Amendment. The court reasoned that what was to be considered a reasonable search depended on the circumstances under which the search occurred, and that if an allegation of abuse met the hotline criteria, then it would be reasonable for the caseworker to conduct a physical examination of the alleged victim of abuse. The court did, however, express reservations that the state's hotline criteria, as they were then written, would serve to make all physical examinations reasonable as a matter of law and not in violation of the Fourth Amendment.

Implications for CPS Practice

The issue of parental consent to a child's physical examination by a caseworker invokes greater concern over violation of Fourth Amendment rights than other areas, and CPS workers should tread very carefully in this area. Courts are more likely to apply tougher standards when addressing this topic and require a CPS worker to show probable cause as to why a physical examination had to occur at *that point* in the investigation, rather than obtaining a warrant or (a more common route) having the child examined by a medical professional. Because physical exams are by their nature very intrusive and violations of bodily integrity, CPS workers need to be very clear as to whether they have obtained parental consent, and stop examinations at the first sign of protest from a parent. If the parent is not home, workers would be advised to wait until they meet with the parent and seek their consent, unless they consider examining the child *at that moment* to be a necessity based on an immediate need to take appropriate protective action for that child to protect that child from serious harm.

§ 15.2.3 Need for Consent to Enter a Child's School to Interview/Examine a Child

Case Law

- In *Doe v. Heck*,[10] several weeks after learning that private school administrators used corporal punishment as a form of discipline, caseworkers initiated an investigation for child abuse. Over the objection of a school's principal, and without a warrant or parental notification or consent, caseworkers removed an 11-year-old student from his classroom and interviewed him about corporal punishment that he and other students may have received,

---

[10] 327 F.3d 492 (7th Cir. 2003). *See also* Michael C. v. Gresbach, 526 F.3d 1008 (7th Cir. 2008) (worker could be liable for under-the-clothes examination of child at *private* school while investigating abuse report).

as well as about certain family matters. Thereafter, they unsuccessfully attempted to interview other family members, and caseworkers threatened to remove the children from their parents' custody. They were unsuccessful at an attempt to interview other students at the school. The court held that although the CPS workers were entitled to qualified immunity, they had violated the Fourth Amendment rights of the school and student when they interviewed the child on school premises with the aid of a police officer and without the school's or parents' consent.

Implications for CPS Practice

Just as parents have the right to privacy and freedom from intrusion into their homes, at least one federal court has held that schools have this same right, since parents have sent their children there with the expectation that the children will be afforded relative privacy and be free from state intrusion. However, if a school administrator gives consent to enter, then a CPS worker may enter the school. Some state laws specifically require public schools to cooperate with CPS investigations.

§ 15.2.4 The Exception of Exigent Circumstances/Emergencies

The second exception to the warrant requirement of the Fourth Amendment, and the one most commonly used, involves the "emergency doctrine" where a child is considered to be in imminent danger of physical harm and a CPS worker reasonably believes he or she must act immediately to prevent that harm. Every state allows a child to be removed from the home without a court order in certain situations of abuse or neglect in which it would be impossible to obtain a court order without placing that child at further risk of harm. Many states, however, allow for children to be removed from home in emergency situations only by *law enforcement officials.*

Some state laws specifically mention police officers as being authorized to remove children, while others also allow probation officers or authorized officers of the court to remove them. Some states allow both law enforcement officials and CPS caseworkers to remove children. Others only specifically allow for emergency removal by CPS and make no specific mention of law enforcement.

State statutes vary in the language used to describe situations or circumstances in which a child may be taken into protective custody without a court order, although most are similar. Some require that the child be in "imminent" or "immediate" danger, or that there exists an "imminent harm" or "immediate threat" to the child's life, safety, or health. Other statutes require the child to be "seriously endangered" in his or her surroundings, and other statutes require the child to be "endangered" in his or her surroundings or unable to be cared for without endangering the child's health or safety. A few states are far more restrictive, authorizing removal when necessary only to protect a child's life, while some are broader, such as authorizing removal to protect a child from injury. Surprisingly, in light of the federal "reasonable efforts" requirement in effect since 1980, only a few states' statutes specifically require a determination that there is no less drastic alternative available before making a removal.

Case Law

- In *Gates v. Texas Department of Protective and Regulatory Services*,[11] the court held that caseworkers cannot seize children from home without a court order, parental consent, or exigent circumstances (defined as "reasonable cause" to believe that the child is in imminent danger of physical or sexual abuse if remaining in the home). The agency, after this court decision, issued a follow-up memo to the effect that caseworkers should get consent or a court order unless a child's "life or limb is in immediate jeopardy or sexual abuse is about to occur" and that they should weigh each child's case separately.

- In *In re Texas Department of Family and Protective Services*,[12] removals of 468 children during a CPS investigation of the Yearning for Zion Ranch led to dependency proceedings. The Texas Supreme Court affirmed that the removals were not legally warranted, that the agency failed to carry its statutory burden of proof *to maintain custody* of children (and there was no evidence each child was in immediate or urgent danger to physical health or safety, and that there was no evidence that "reasonable efforts" were made to eliminate or prevent a need for removal).

- In *Wallis v. Spencer*,[13] two children had been seized from home on the basis of a nonexistent court order, placed in a county-run institution, and subjected to intrusive anal and vaginal physical examinations. These exams were conducted without court authorization or notifying the parents that such exams would occur. The court held that the heinousness of a suspected crime did not constitute an emergency sufficient to allow ignoring the substantive and procedural guarantees of the Constitution.

- In *Roska v. Sneddon*,[14] a school had reported possible medical neglect of child. After getting legal advice from an assistant attorney general, the agency caseworker had a child removed from home based on suspicions of

---

[11] 537 F.3d 404 (5th Cir. 2008). *See also* Smith v. Texas Dep't of Family & Protective Servs., 2009 WL 2998202 (W.D. Tex. 2009) (court dismissed case, finding that defendant was entitled to qualified immunity for interview of allegedly abused child at school, for seizure of the child (based on ruling in the *Gates* case), for claims of deprivation of the right to family integrity, and for placement with the mother who was in a shelter at the time); Burke v. County of Alameda, 586 F.3d 725 (9th Cir. 2009) (police officer who removed child from parents' custody reasonably relied on child's statements in finding she was in imminent danger of abuse).

[12] 255 S.W.3d 613 (Tex. 2008).

[13] 202 F.3d 1126 (9th Cir. 2000).

[14] 437 F.3d 964 (10th Cir. 2006) [*see also* 437 F.3d 964 (10th Cir. 2003) and 304 F.3d 982 (10th Cir. 2002)]. See also *Gomes v. Wood*, 451 F.3d 1122 (10th Cir. 2006), another case involving a CPS caseworker's removal of a child from home, in which the court affirmed that defendants had qualified immunity.

Munchausen Syndrome by Proxy. After two hearings, the child was returned to the parents, and the child and family then sued under Section 1983 of the federal Civil Rights Act, claiming violations of their Fourth and Fourteenth Amendment rights. The federal district court first granted summary judgment in favor of the defendants based on qualified immunity principles, then after remand from the initial appeal, the defendants were found *not to be entitled* to qualified immunity. After a second appeal, the Court of Appeals held that the plaintiffs had proved that their child's removal without a warrant or hearing deprived them of their constitutional right to maintain a family relationship. The lower court had found that the defendants failed to comply with a state law requiring provision of services to prevent the need for removal, especially in light of information from the child's physician that removal might harm him.

- In *Roska v. Peterson*,[15] based on reports of suspected abuse from school officials, CPS workers entered the plaintiff's home without knocking and without a warrant to gain custody of a child. The CPS workers claimed that, based on reports from school officials and descriptions of the child's medical history, exigent circumstances existed that justified entering the home without knocking and without a warrant. They also based their actions on consultation with an assistant attorney general who told them they had probable cause to remove the child from home.

The court held that in order for CPS to use exigent circumstances as a defense they must show that they have *reasonable* grounds that there is:

    (1) an immediate need to protect their lives or others or their property or that of others;

    (2) the search is not motivated by an intent to arrest and seize evidence; and

    (3) there is some reasonable basis, *approaching probable cause*, to associate an emergency with the area or place to be searched. What is considered reasonable depends on the context in which the search takes place.

In this case, the court found there were not reasonable grounds for the CPS workers to believe that exigent circumstances existed to permit their entry into the home and removal of the child.

---

[15] 328 F.3d 1230 (10th Cir. 2003). *See also* Arredondo v. Locklear, 462 F.3d 1292 (10th Cir. 2006) (emergency removal, due to reasonable suspicion of imminent risk of harm, did not violate parents' due process rights); Rogers v. County of San Joaquin, 487 F.3d 1288 (9th Cir. 2007) (exigent circumstances for removal and imminent risk of serious bodily harm did not exist; worker who had time to get warrant before removal was not entitled to qualified immunity); Kovacic v. Cuyahoga County Dep't of Children & Fam. Servs., 2007 WL 2027326 (not reported, N.D. OH 2007) (warrantless entry was not supported by exigent circumstances of imminent risk of harm).

The court also held that Fourth Amendment warrant requirements do apply to CPS workers in the performance of their duties because the state's interest in protecting children from harm does not outweigh a parent's interest in maintaining family integrity.

This case contrasts directly with *Franz v. Lytle*,[16] where the same court made a distinction between a police officer and a social worker. The court in that case denied qualified immunity to a police officer who made a warrantless entry into a home to investigate a report of abuse, but stated that a CPS worker would have received qualified immunity under the same circumstances.

- In *Doe v. Kearney*,[17] a suit was brought against a CPS caseworker after she removed three children from their parents' care without a warrant, under what they asserted were non-emergency circumstances. The court reasoned that state law allows CPS workers to make an emergency removal without a court order where they have probable cause to believe a child has been abused or is at imminent risk of harm. The court found that the caseworker was entitled to qualified immunity because her actions were based on the evidence before her and found that she did have probable cause to believe the children were at imminent risk of harm.

- In *Walsh v. Erie County Department of Job and Family Services*,[18] caseworkers had searched the parents' home during an investigation into an anonymous tip that their children were living in unsafe conditions. The court held that the defendants failed to show a risk of imminent or likely harm sufficient to justify warrantless entry under the exigent circumstances requirement. The exigent circumstances doctrine requires a showing that prompt action is needed and that delay to secure a warrant would be unacceptable or place someone at risk of harm, under the factual circumstances of the case.

- In *Moodian v. County of Alameda Social Services Agency*,[19] without first obtaining a warrant, a social worker removed the mother's children from home based on the social worker's concern that the children were in imminent danger of emotional harm. A second social worker investigated the allegations of abuse and eventually filed a dependency petition against the mother. Months later, the children were returned to the mother. The court found that the CPS worker was liable for violating the mother's and children's Fourth Amendment rights when she removed the children. The court ruled that the emergency or exigent circumstance exception for removing children without a warrant is limited to imminent risk of physical, not emotional, harm.

---

[16] 997 F.2d 784 (10th Cir. 1993).

[17] 329 F.3d 1286 (11th Cir. 2003).

[18] 240 F. Supp. 2d 731 (N.D. Ohio 2003).

[19] 206 F. Supp. 2d 1030 (N.D. Cal. 2002).

- In *Hatch v. Department for Children, Youth and Their Families (State of Rhode Island)*,[20] Richard Hatch sued the state child welfare agency, claiming constitutional violations, after his adopted son was removed without a warrant. The removal was based on allegations that the child was abused. Finding that the welfare of the child was the paramount consideration when investigating abuse, the court found the CPS worker had acted properly when he removed the boy without first securing a warrant. The court reasoned that based on the evidence available to the CPS worker at the time, and because the child's doctor had placed him under a 72-hour medical hold, the CPS worker had the basis for a reasonable suspicion that the child had been abused and was in danger of imminent abuse.

- In *Brokaw v. Mercer County*,[21] when a child was six years old, he and his three-year-old sister were forcibly removed from their home. After he turned 18, he filed suit against his grandfather and aunt, whom he contended conspired with his uncle, a deputy sheriff, to violate his constitutional rights. He also sued the social worker and other officers involved in removing him from home, along with the state judge who presided over various hearings. The court found that the sheriff's officers and the CPS caseworkers were not justified in removing these children without a warrant because their removal was based on fabricated and vague allegations of neglect by other family members and that there was not probable cause to believe that the children were at imminent risk of harm.

- In *Tenenbaum v. Williams*,[22] a caseworker removed a developmentally delayed five-year-old from kindergarten under an emergency protection law but without a court order or notification and took her to an emergency room, where she was examined by two doctors for signs of sexual abuse. When no signs were found, she was returned to her parents, and the case was closed as "unfounded." The court found that the CPS worker was not entitled to qualified immunity when investigating allegations of sexual abuse under the emergency doctrine because although she had probable cause to believe the allegations were true, she also had time to obtain a court order because her purpose was not to remove the child from harm but to investigate the allegation of abuse.

Implications for CPS Practice

While an emergency does not have to constitute a life or death situation, a CPS caseworker must have reasonable cause to believe that if she or he does not act, a child will be put in, or remain at, imminent risk of physical harm. Emotional harm or neglect may not be sufficient to meet the requirements of the emergency doctrine,

---

[20] 274 F.3d 12 (1st Cir. 2001).

[21] 235 F.3d 1000 (7th Cir. 2000).

[22] 193 F.3d 581 (2nd Cir. 1999).

unless these parental actions or omissions rise to the level of placing the child at imminent risk of physical harm. What is to be considered imminent will depend on the circumstances of each case, as well as the statutory or regulatory guidelines that define the criteria for emergency removal of the child in a particular state. In such cases, it is better for CPS caseworkers to err on the side of caution and obtain a warrant or court order if the situation reasonably allows them to do so. The safest route is as follows: If there is time to get court approval without endangering the child, caseworkers should do that.

§ 15.2.5 Exception of Special Needs

The final exception to the warrant or court order requirement involves cases that fall beyond the normal needs of law enforcement and make the warrant and probable cause requirements impracticable. Such "special needs" cases *are rare* and require a showing of why the circumstances were such that obtaining a warrant was impracticable, if the case was not an emergency. Examples of where the "special needs" doctrine has been applied include enforcement of school discipline,[23] allowing administrative searches of the business premises of closely regulated industries,[24] and taking inventory of seized items for "caretaking" purposes.[25]

Case Law

- In *Roska v. Peterson,*[26] the court held that in cases asserting the "*special needs doctrine*" exception to warrant or consent requirements, the nature of the need addressed must make particularized suspicion impossible or otherwise render the warrant requirement impractical. If a "special need" renders the warrant requirement impracticable, then the court will balance the nature of the privacy interest upon which the search intrudes and the degree of intrusion occasioned by the search against the nature and immediacy of the governmental concern at issue and the efficacy of the means for meeting it. In this case, the court found that CPS caseworkers could not avail themselves of a "special needs" exception.

- In *Walsh v. Erie County Department of Job and Family Services,*[27] the court rejected the defendant's argument that the state had a special need to verify the report of abuse that overrode the plaintiff's right to be secure from warrantless searches and seizures. The defendant contended that the state's statutory framework for learning about and investigating allegations of child abuse and neglect superseded their obligations under the Fourth Amendment. The court noted that while the state does have an interest in protecting the

---

[23] New Jersey v. T.L.O., 469 U.S. 325 (1985).

[24] New York v. Burger, 482 U.S. 691 (1987).

[25] Cady v. Dombrowski, 413 U.S. 433 (1973).

[26] 328 F.3d 1230 (10th Cir. 2003).

[27] 240 F. Supp. 2d 731 (N.D. Ohio 2003).

safety and welfare of children from abuse, they must exercise that interest within constitutional boundaries.

- In *J.B. v. Washington County*,[28] CPS workers seized a child under an *ex parte* order for approximately 18 hours to interview the child outside of the presence of her parents, for the purposes of investigating a report of sexual abuse. The court found the CPS workers and police did not violate the parents' constitutional rights when they removed the child from the home. The court found that there was probable cause to believe the child had been abused and the officers acted in such a way as to balance their need to interview the child without undue influence from the parents with the family's rights under the Fourth Amendment.

Implications for CPS Practice

The cases that have been examined suggest that the *special needs exception* to the warrant requirement probably will not be applied to CPS cases. Without exigent or emergency circumstances, there are very few reasons a CPS worker would not be able to procure a warrant before entering the child's home. Also, the test applied by courts to determine whether the special needs exception has been met is stricter than that for the consent or emergency exception to the warrant requirement. Generally, verifying that abuse occurred will not be sufficient to meet the special needs requirement, even where the CPS worker is mandated to protect the interests of the child.

§ 15.3 Understanding the Concept of Qualified Immunity for CPS Workers

It has been noted that "Government officials receive qualified immunity so that they will be protected from 'undue interference with their duties and from potentially disabling threats of liability.'"[29] CPS workers are entitled to use qualified or absolute immunity as a defense in civil law suits when they were performing the *discretionary functions* of their job, if their conduct does not violate clearly established statutory or constitutional rights of which a reasonable person would or should have known.[30] A clearly established constitutional right was defined by the Supreme Court in *Anderson v. Creighton*,[31] as follows:

> The contours of the right must be sufficiently clear that a reasonable official would understand that what he is doing violates that right. This is not to say that an official action is protected against qualified immunity unless the very action in question has previously been held

---

[28] 127 F.3d 919 (10th Cir. 1997).

[29] Patrick E. O'Neill, Note: *Time for Direction: The Need for a Clear, Uniform Rule Regarding Searches During Child Abuse Investigations*, 83 KY. L.J. 529 (1994-1995).

[30] Chavez v. Bd. of County Comm'rs of Curry County, 130 N.M. 753, 31 P.3d 1027 (2001).

[31] 483 U.S. 635, 640 (1987).

unlawful, but it is to say that in light of pre-existing law the unlawfulness must be apparent.

The determination whether a constitutional right has been violated is determined by a judge as a matter of law and is done by performing the following two-part test:

(1) First, the courts ask whether, taken in the light most favorable to the party asserting the injury, the facts alleged show the official conduct violated a constitutional right. If no constitutional right would have been violated were the allegations established, there is no necessity for further inquiry;

(2) If on the other hand, a violation could be made out on a favorable view of the parties' submissions, the next sequential step for the court is to ask whether the right violated was clearly established.[32]

Case Law

- In *Defore v. Premore*,[33] a runaway girl alleged sexual abuse by her father. Her mother signed a voluntary placement agreement, which the father refused to sign. The girl was placed in foster care but later hospitalized after she had made several suicide attempts. The parents brought a civil rights suit against CPS agency personnel, alleging a violation of the constitutional right of parental control, since medical treatment was provided to the girl that they did not consent to. The allegations of abuse later were unfounded. The court nonetheless found that defendant's actions in arranging the girl's hospitalization were reasonable, thus a finding of qualified immunity was affirmed.

- In *Dornheim v. Sholes*,[34] a Section 1983 action was brought against agency social workers, the child's court-appointed guardian ad litem, and others based on mandated evaluations and therapy following allegations of child abuse allegedly tied to a custody dispute between the plaintiff mother and her ex-husband. The child had never been removed from the mother's home. The Court of Appeals affirmed the lower court's judgment dismissing the lawsuit based on qualified immunity.

---

[32] Doe v. Heck, 327 F.3d 492 (7th Cir. 2003).

[33] 86 F.3d 48 (2nd Cir. 2006). *See also* Carter v. Lindgren, 502 F.3d 26 (1st Cir. 2007) (imminent serious risk of neglect— mother's attempted suicide—qualified immunity for worker who removed child); Beltran v. Santa Clara County, 491 F.3d 1097 (9th Cir. 2007) (absolute worker immunity in temporary removal and placement attempts and preparing and filing dependency and custody petitions); Hopkins v. Rhode Island, 491 F. Supp. 2d 266 (D.R.I. 2007) (qualified immunity for worker who investigated and petitioned against foster parent for alleged child sexual abuse); Beltran v. Santa Clara County, 514 F.3d 906 (9th Cir. 2008) (worker who made alleged fabricated statements in both dependency and custody petitions leading to removal was not entitled to absolute immunity); Southerland v. City of New York, 521 F. Supp. 2d 218 (E.D.N.Y. 2007) (no "removal" liability could be based on inadequate CPS training or alleged racial motivation in implementing an alleged "when in doubt, yank them out" policy).

[34] 430 F.3d 919 (8th Cir. 2005).

- In *Kauch v. Department for Children, Youth and Their Families*,[35] the plaintiff brought suit against a CPS worker and the agency because the worker investigating allegations of abuse against his son took into consideration a 1994 allegation of sexual abuse against his daughter. He objected to the worker's use of that information because it had been ordered expunged from the Department's records. The court found that the worker was entitled to a qualified immunity defense. While it was not proper for the CPS worker to consider an expunged record in her investigation, she did not violate a constitutionally protected right.

- In *Roska v. Peterson*,[36] applying the two-part test outlined above, the court found that there was enough ambiguity in the law, as it stood at the time CPS workers removed the child from the home, to hold that CPS did not violate a clearly established constitutional right under the Fourth Amendment, and they were therefore entitled to a qualified immunity defense. With respect to the violation of the child's constitutional rights when they removed him from the home without a hearing and notice, the Court of Appeals remanded the case to the lower court for further review.

In their argument for dismissal of this part of the case on qualified immunity grounds, the CPS workers claimed to have relied on several state statutes as the basis for authorizing their conduct. The court ruled, however, that "the appropriate inquiry is not whether a reasonable state officer could have concluded that the statute authorized the unconstitutional conduct in question. Rather, a court must consider whether reliance on the statute rendered the officer's conduct 'objectively reasonable,' considering such factors as:

(1) the degree of specificity with which the statute authorized the conduct in question;

(2) whether the officer in fact complied with the statute;

(3) whether the statute had fallen in desuetude; and

(4) whether the officer could have reasonably concluded that the statute was constitutional."

On this basis, the court remanded the case to the lower court for determination of whether the CPS workers' reliance on the two state statutes in question was reasonable enough for them to assert a qualified immunity defense.

- In *Tower v. Leslie-Brown*,[37] plaintiffs sued the State Police and Department of Human Services after their five children were removed from their care. They alleged that the state trooper and CPS caseworker violated their constitutional

---

[35] 321 F.3d 1 (1st Cir. 2003).

[36] 328 F.3d 1230 (10th Cir. 2003).

[37] 326 F.3d 290 (1st Cir. 2003).

rights when the father was arrested in his home for abuse of three older children and the two younger children were removed without a warrant. The court found that both the state trooper and the CPS caseworker were entitled to qualified immunity because the trooper was operating under the assumption that a valid warrant had been issued, even though he did not have it in hand, and the CPS worker was entitled to remove the children without a warrant if there were emergency or exigent circumstances that warranted such action.

- In *Mabe v. San Bernardino County Department of Public Social Services*,[38] a CPS caseworker removed without a court order a 14-year-old child from her home one month after receiving an initial report of alleged sexual abuse and four days after her initial home visit with the family. In ruling that the CPS worker was not entitled to a qualified immunity defense, the court found that the parents' right to the care and custody of their child was clearly established and that there was a material question of fact as to whether it was reasonable for the CPS worker to believe her conduct was lawful, under the circumstances of the case, given that it was unclear that the child was in imminent danger of harm.

- In *Kiser v. Garrett*,[39] a child was removed from home during an investigation of child abuse after severely fracturing his arm. The family sued the CPS worker and Texas Department of Human Services, claiming constitutional violations. Applying the first part of the two-part test to determine if a CPS worker is entitled to qualified immunity, the court found that because, at the time the child was removed from the home, the constitutional violations complained of were not "clearly established," the CPS worker and Department of Human Services were entitled to qualified immunity.

- In *Millspaugh v. County Department of Public Welfare of Wabash County*,[40] two mothers brought suit against CPS when their children were removed from their care. The removal was based on allegations that the mothers were unable to provide for their children because they had no furnishings or provisions in the home, for religious reasons, and they had withdrawn the children from school. The court found that the CPS worker was entitled to qualified immunity from liability, even if she did have other motives in removing the children (preventing the mothers from practicing their religion and turning the children away from the religion), because the objective facts of the case were such as to justify the worker's actions in removing the children.

---

[38] 237 F.3d 1101 (9th Cir. 2001).

[39] 67 F.3d 1166 (5th Cir. 1995).

[40] 937 F.2d 1172 (7th Cir. 1991).

- In *Good v. Dauphin County Social Services for Children and Youth*,[41] a mother brought suit against a CPS caseworker, police officer, and a CPS supervisor alleging violation of her constitutional rights when the mother allowed the worker into her home, believing she was compelled to do so, after the police officer told her that they did not need a warrant to enter her home for purposes of a child abuse investigation. The mother also continued to protest verbally throughout the search of her home and child. The court held that the CPS worker and police officer were not entitled to qualified immunity because it was *not reasonable* for either the caseworker or police officer to believe, *in light of decided case law*, that their conduct was lawful or that their conduct followed established constitutional principles.

- In *Hodorowski v. Ray*,[42] CPS caseworkers, investigating allegations of child abuse, removed two children from home without a court order after finding them home alone and one child with visible bruising on the exposed parts of her body, even though neither child was in need of emergency medical attention. The court held that while the CPS workers were not entitled to absolute immunity, they were entitled to qualified immunity. Finding that family integrity was a nebulous right and that the CPS workers' actions were objectively reasonable when they removed the children, the court found that the workers had violated no clearly established constitutional right.

- In *Darryl H. v. Coler*,[43] the plaintiffs' children were required to disrobe and allow a CPS caseworker to examine their bodies for signs of abuse and neglect. The plaintiffs challenged the constitutionality of the CPS policy that allowed caseworkers to conduct physical examinations of children's bodies when investigating allegations of abuse or neglect, arguing that it violated fundamental Fourth and Fourteenth Amendment rights to privacy and protection from unreasonable searches and seizures. The court found that because, at the time of the alleged violation, the constitutional right for children to be free from unreasonable searches was not "clearly established," the CPS workers who conducted the physical examinations of the children were entitled to qualified immunity.

Implications for CPS Practice

As the above cases illustrate, a CPS worker will be protected from liability so long as he or she is acting within his or her official capacity and is performing a discretionary function of his or her job that does not violate some clearly defined constitutional right of the child or family. As more such cases go to trial, however, the constitutional rights of the child and family are becoming more clearly defined. CPS workers and agency attorneys need to remain abreast of these changes in the

---

[41] 891 F.2d 1087 (3rd Cir. 1989).

[42] 844 F.2d 1210 (5th Cir. 1988).

[43] 801 F.2d 893 (7th Cir. 1986).

interpretation of the law through continuing education classes and seminars because it will change how they proceed with their abuse investigations. To be safe, CPS should seek court orders, when possible without endangering children: (1) before removing a child; (2) before entering the home without consent; or (3) before disrobing a child for a physical examination without parental consent.

§ 15.4 Due Process Rights Regarding Child Abuse/ Neglect Central Registries

Every state has procedures for maintaining records of child abuse and neglect. Most states maintain, through a statutory requirement, what they call a *central registry*, which is a centralized database of child abuse and neglect investigation records or summaries. In other states, records on reports of abuse/neglect and their investigative outcomes are maintained as a matter of administrative or agency policy rather than statutory mandate. Central registries, and the systematic record keeping of child abuse/neglect information, were intended to assist in the identification and protection of abused and neglected children. Information in registries is typically used to aid CPS in investigation, treatment, and prevention of child maltreatment, and to maintain statistical information for staffing and funding purposes.

In many states, central registry records are used to screen persons who will be entrusted with the care of children, especially for persons applying to be child or youth care providers. Such information can be made available to employers in the child care, school, or other child-related fields. States are required to check criminal records of prospective foster and adoptive parents, and in many states there is also a check of central registry records as part of the background check.

Information contained in central registries and related databases varies, but it usually includes the child's name and address, the name of the mother, father, or guardian, the names of any siblings, the nature of the reported maltreatment, the name of the alleged perpetrator(s), and the findings of investigations into the reported abuse or neglect. Some states maintain information on all investigated reports of abuse and neglect in their central registries, while others maintain only substantiated reports. Access to information maintained in registries and CPS records also varies, as does the length of time information is held and the conditions for expunging the information.

§ 15.4.1 Due Process Violations Alleged in Central Registry Entries, Use, and Maintenance

Because many States use central registry records for background checks for persons seeking employment or volunteer positions to work with children and for prospective foster and adoptive parents, several due process issues arise when a state maintains information that identifies individuals accused of and found by CPS to have committed child abuse or neglect. Persons listed as alleged or "substantiated" perpetrators in a central registry have claimed that their listing in the registry deprives them of a constitutionally protected interest without due process of law.

Most states provide written notice to adults that they have been listed on the registry, and they have the right to request an administrative review or hearing to contest CPS findings of an investigation and the right to have an inaccurate report expunged or corrected. In some states, an aggrieved person can directly petition the court to have his or her name removed from a registry.

Under the federal Child Abuse Prevention and Treatment Act (CAPTA), in order to receive a federal grant, states must submit plans that include provisions and procedures for the prompt expunction of records of unsubstantiated or false cases if the records are accessible to the general public or are used for purposes of employment or other background checks. However, this law does allow CPS agencies to retain information on unsubstantiated reports in their casework files to assist in future risk and safety assessment. There is also a requirement that individuals who disagree with an official finding of abuse or neglect be provided with a process through which they can appeal a CPS substantiation finding.[44]

The federal Adam Walsh Child Protection and Safety Act of 2006 contained a provision mandating certain CPS central registry checks in prospective foster and adoptive parent screening. The registries of all states where an applicant indicates they have lived in the past five years must be checked to see if the applicant is listed by CPS as a perpetrator of abuse or neglect.[45]

§ 15.4.2 When Central Registry Listings Violate Fundamental Liberty or Property Interests

In determining whether an adult has a fundamental liberty interest *to protect his or her reputation*, courts apply the "stigma plus" test. Proof of stigma, the first prong, requires proof that inclusion on a registry will damage one's reputation. Inclusion on a child abuse registry labels an individual as a child abuser, which courts have held is very damaging to reputation, especially if employed in a child-related position. Plaintiffs must also show that, as a result of being placed on a registry, a right or status previously recognized by state law was distinctly altered or ended. Individuals have a liberty interest in pursuing a job, and even if a person does not lose a job as a result of a central registry listing stigma, that person still may meet this criterion if the label in essence prevents him or her from pursuing a career. This prong of the test is most often met when people who work with children are unable to maintain or obtain employment because state law *requires* a registry check before hiring.

- In *Finch v. N.Y. State Office of Children and Family Services*,[46] the plaintiffs alleged that inordinate delays in scheduling administrative hearings to challenge their listing in the central registry violated their due process rights and that those delays unconstitutionally infringed upon their protected liberty

---

[44] 42 U.S.C. § 5106a(b)(2).

[45] Pub. L. No. 109-248, 120 Stat. 587, § 152 (2006).

[46] U.S. District Court, Southern District of N.Y, Docket No. 04 Civ. 1668, Memorandum Opinion and Order, 2008 WL 5330616 (S.D.N.Y. 2008).

interests to pursue employment of their choice. On February 19, 2010, the federal district court approved a settlement under which New York agreed to notify about 25,000 people on the registry whose hearing requests were terminated between 2003 and 2007. The notice will inform them they may have a right to request a new hearing. Those who so request will have their records reviewed by the state, which must produce documentation of a hearing decision. If the State is unable to produce that decision, a new hearing will be scheduled. At some later point in this litigation, it is expected that the judge will determine the maximum time allowed for scheduling hearings to challenge registry entities (now estimated to take 8-10 months before a decision is reached).

- In *Humphries v. County of Los Angeles*,[47] the plaintiffs successfully argued that a fundamental liberty interest was violated under the "stigma plus test." The court found that being labeled a child abuser through placement on the state registry was "unquestionably stigmatizing." The court held that the plaintiffs satisfied the "plus" prong because state law requires agencies to check the registry before granting certain licenses and benefits, preventing one plaintiff from renewing teaching credentials. The court also stated that the "plus" prong is satisfied when the law "creates a framework under which agencies reflexively check the stigmatizing listing—whether by internal regulation or custom—prior to conferring a legal right or benefit." The court concluded that the state offers no mechanism for people to get off the registry, even if they were placed there in error, and that this database is accessible to a wide array of state and private entities. The court ruled that the state violates the Fourteenth Amendment's Due Process Clause because people like the plaintiffs are not given a fair opportunity to challenge their placement on that database.[48]

- In *Dupuy v. Samuels*,[49] the court found that having one's name on a registry was stigmatizing. It also found that the "plus" prong was met by current and potential child care workers who challenged their registry placement, reasoning that because state law requires registry background checks of all current and future child care workers, being listed on the registry bars the plaintiffs from work in their chosen profession. The court refused to extend

---

[47] 554 F.3d 1170 (9th Cir. 2009).

[48] On February 22, 2010, the U.S. Supreme Court agreed to hear an appeal of this decision. Certiorari granted in part, Los Angeles County, Cal. v. Humphries, 130 S. Ct. 1501 (2010). The issue the Court agreed to decide was whether plaintiffs must demonstrate that a constitutional violation was the result of a policy, custom, or practice attributable to a local public entity, since there is a split of opinion on this among the federal circuit courts of appeal.

[49] 397 F.3d 493 (7th Cir. 2005). *See also* Behrens v. Regier, 422 F.3d 1255 (11th Cir. 2005) (where plaintiff, who had adopted one child, argued that his name on the registry prevented him from adopting again, the court rejected the argument that his substantive right to familial relations was violated, since the court found that individuals do not have a fundamental right to adopt).

the analysis to foster parents, however, holding that foster parenting is not a "career" but rather a contractual agreement with the state to assist victims of abuse/neglect. It also held that foster parents did not have a property interest in foster parenting, because typical foster care contracts grant broad discretionary authority to remove a child from foster parents, and thus there is no legal entitlement to providing foster care.

- In *Valmonte v. Bane*,[50] the plaintiff successfully argued that her fundamental liberty interest was violated by a state registry process. Applying the stigma-plus test, the court found that even though the plaintiff had not actually been deprived of employment in the child care field, the law's requirement that current or future employers review the registry, and file an exception if they chose to hire someone on the registry, places a tangible obstacle to employment prospects.

- In *Hodge v. Jones*,[51] the parents' names were left on a state registry after investigations were classified as "unsubstantiated." The court found that the parents' national security clearances for their jobs, which could have been affected by registry placement, did not constitute a property entitlement under the due process clause. The court also rejected a liberty interest argument relating to familial privacy, noting that having their names on the registry did not impact their family's functioning. The court also rejected a reputational harm argument because it found that the plaintiffs were not stigmatized by the registry entries, which were only accessible to agency representatives.

§ 15.5 Conclusion

As this chapter suggests, more constitutional scrutiny is being given to child welfare agency actions that affect the rights of parents. The courts are likely to continue to refine how to balance the protective and safety rights of children, the privacy and autonomy rights of parents, and the *parens patriae* duty of the state. As such, this is an area of law that will continue to be the subject of litigation and appellate court attention. Lawyers who practice in the child welfare arena should understand that due process of law violations might be raised within the context of government involvement in the lives of families. This chapter has provided a basic overview of two principal areas where federal due process rights may be asserted: actions taken within the CPS investigative process and in CPS "central registry" recordkeeping and sharing.

---

[50] 18 F.3d 992 (2d Cir. 1994).
[51] 31 F.3d 157 (4th Cir. 1994).

Chapter 16: A Child's Journey Through the Child Welfare System*

by Susan Badeau, Ann M. Haralambie, and Donald N. Duquette[1]

§ 16.1 Introduction

While 463,000 children were in foster care on September 30, 2008,[2] *nearly 750,000 spent some time in care over the course of that year.*[3]

Children in care in 2008 had been in foster care for an average of 27.2 months. More than 12% (53,763) of the children had been in care for five or more years.[4]

Once a child is known to the government child welfare agency, the child and his or her family become subject to a series of decisions made by judges, caseworkers, legal representatives, and others—all of whom have an important role to play. A child may encounter dozens of other new adults, including foster parents, counselors, and doctors.

Most children enter foster care when removed from their homes by a child protective agency because of abuse or neglect, or both. Others enter care because of the absence of their parents, resulting from illness, death, disability, or other problems. Some children enter care because of delinquent behavior or because they have committed a juvenile status offense, such as running away or truancy. A small

---

* The authors thank Sarah Gesiriech for her contribution to this chapter which is based on the original work *A Child's Journey through the Child Welfare System*, Copyright 2003 by The Pew Commission on Children in Foster Care by Sue Badeau and Sarah Gesiriech.

[1] Susan Badeau is currently the Director of the Cross Systems Integration team within the Knowledge Management department of Casey Family Programs. She has been a child welfare professional for thirty years and was a Public Policy Fellow in the U.S. Senate in 1999.

Ann M. Haralambie, J.D., is a certified family law specialist practicing in Tucson, Arizona. She is also an author and speaker in the fields of family and children's law.

Donald N. Duquette, J.D., is Clinical Professor of Law and Director of the Child Advocacy Law Clinic of the University of Michigan Law School.

[2] U.S. Department of Health and Human Services, Administration for Children & Families, Children's Bureau, *The AFCARS Report Preliminary FY 2008 Estimates as of October 2009*, *available at* http://www.acf.hhs.gov/programs/cb/stats_research/afcars/tar/report16.htm.

[3] *Id.*

[4] *Id.*

percentage of children enter care because of a disability.[5] For many, foster care represents their only access to disability services, such as mental health care for a child with severe emotional disturbance. In these rare instances, in states that allow such placements, a child is placed in foster care voluntarily at the request of the child's parents.

Foster care is intended to provide a safe temporary home to a child until the child can be safely provided with a permanent family in which to grow up, through reunification, legal guardianship (often with a relative), or adoption. However, being removed from home and placed in foster care is traumatic for a child, and the period of time a child may spend in foster care can be filled with uncertainty and change.

A child in foster care is affected by a myriad of decisions established by federal and state laws designed to help the child. At each decision point, action or inaction can profoundly influence the child's current circumstances and future prospects. The discussion that follows highlights typical decision points on a child's journey through foster care. Although the format is based on federal and typical state law and practice, it is only a model. Laws vary across states, as do the capacity and practices of child welfare agencies and courts to manage their caseloads. While some of these variations are intended to expedite the child's journey, often these factors create delays that complicate a child's journey through the child welfare system and often extend the child's time there.

---

[5]   U.S. Government Accountability Office, Report to the Chairman, Committee on Ways and Means, House of Representatives, GAO-07-816, *African American Children in Foster Care, Additional HHS Assistance Needed to Help States Reduce the Proportion in Care*, p. 1, (2007), *available at* http://www.gao.gov/new.items/d07816.pdf.

A Child's Journey through the Child Welfare System

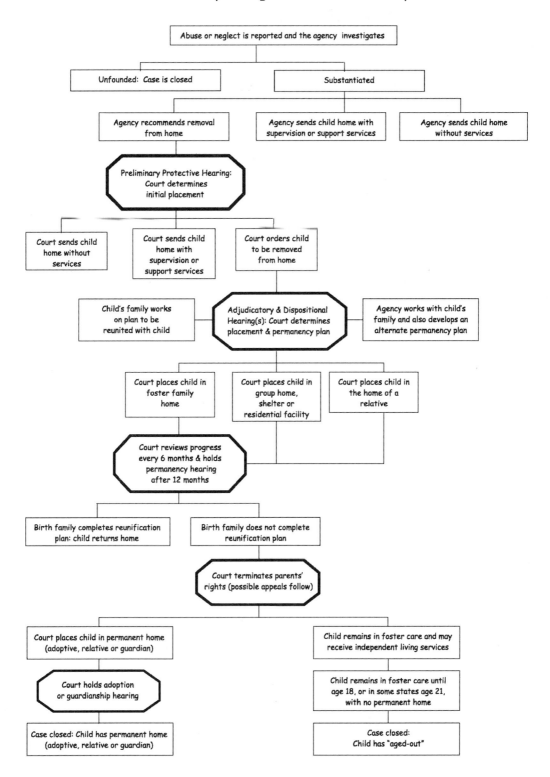

§ 16.2 Reporting Child Maltreatment

The child's journey through foster care usually begins when a mandated reporter[6] or concerned citizen makes a report of abuse or neglect to a state agency. For example, a doctor delivers a baby who has drugs in his or her system; a neighbor notices bruises on a child; a toddler is found abandoned in a public place; or a teacher notices a student who is unclean, unfed, or severely ill.

In 1974, Congress passed landmark legislation in the federal Child Abuse Prevention and Treatment Act (CAPTA).[7] The Act provided states with funding for the investigation and prevention of child maltreatment, conditioned on states adopting mandatory reporting laws. The Act also conditioned funding on reporter immunity, confidentiality, and the appointment of guardians ad litem for children. Although there is no one commonly accepted definition of "child abuse and neglect," the federal government defines child abuse and neglect in CAPTA as, at minimum, "any recent act or failure to act on the part of a parent or caretaker which results in death, serious physical or emotional harm, sexual abuse or exploitation; or an act or failure to act which presents an imminent risk of serious harm." Based on the minimum standards set by federal law, each state provides its own definition of child maltreatment.[8] Abuse is often defined by states as "harm or threatened harm" or "serious threat or serious harm" to a child. All states have mandatory reporting statutes, but there are some differences among the various states concerning who must report and the circumstances under which reports must be made.

The U.S. Department of Health and Human Services (HHS) estimates that in 2007 (the last year for which data is available), CPS agencies received 3.2 million referrals of maltreatment involving 5.8 million children. Approximately 794,000 of these cases were substantiated after investigation.[9]

The following types of abuse and neglect occurred (some in combination with others):

Type of Abuse	Percentage
Neglect	59%
Multiple Maltreatments	13.1%
Physical Abuse	16.8%

---

[6] State laws identify certain professionals who are mandated to report suspected abuse. They generally include medical professionals, teachers, coaches, child care workers, photo lab developers, and law enforcement.

[7] Pub. L. No. 93-247, 88 Stat. 4 (codified as amended at 42 U.S.C. §§ 5101 *et seq.*).

[8] Child Welfare Information Gateway, *What is Child Abuse and Neglect?*, p. 1 (2008), *available at* http://www.childwelfare.gov/pubs/factsheets/whatiscan.pdf.

[9] U.S. Department of Health and Human Services, Administration on Children, Youth and Families, *Child Maltreatment 2007* (U.S. Government Printing Office 2009), p. 5, *available at* http://www.acf.hhs.gov/programs/cb/pubs/cm07/cm07.pdf.

Sexual Abuse	77.6%
Psychological maltreatment	44.2%
Medical Neglect	.9%
Other (abandonment, congenital drug addiction)	44.3%[10]

The ages of the victims ranged as follows:

Age	Percentage
Birth to 3 years	31.9%
4-7	23.8%
8-11	19%
12-15	18.5%
16-17 or unknown	6.9%[11]

More than half (57.7%) of substantiated reports were made by professionals, including teachers, law enforcement officers, lawyers, social services staff, and physicians. The remaining 42.3% were made by family members, friends, neighbors, and other members of the community.[12] The majority (80.1%) of the victims were maltreated by a parent, including stepparent. The breakdown is as follows:

Relationship to the Child	Percentage
Mothers (acting alone or with a non-parent)	44.4%
Fathers (acting alone or with a non-parent)	18.8%
Mother and Father	16.8%
Non-parent	10%
Unknown	9.8%[13]

In 2007, an estimated 1,760 children died from abuse or neglect. Three-quarters (75.7%) of child fatality victims were younger than four years.[14]

§ 16.2.1 Reporting by Professionals

Typically, professionals who deal with children are required to report suspicion of abuse. If they fail to do so, they may suffer criminal or civil penalties. Under some statutes, professionals are required to report suspicion of abuse if the suspicion originates from the professional's observation or examination of the child (as opposed

---

[10] *Id.* at 26.

[11] *Id.* at 25.

[12] *Id.* at 66.

[13] *Id.* at 52.

[14] *Id.* at 55.

to merely hearing about the abuse from a person other than the child). Doctors, nurses, teachers, psychologists, and daycare workers who have a reasonable *suspicion* of abuse generally must make a report, even if they would not be in a position to testify that they held a professional opinion that abuse had occurred. In other words, it is the duty of child protective services or law enforcement to investigate suspected abuse. It is not the reporter's obligation to conduct an investigation. Tort liability may lie against a mandated reporter who delays making a report because he or she has not determined whether, in fact, the child's injuries were caused by abuse. Similarly, the obligation to report is personal to the mandated reporter and may not be discharged by reporting to an administrative supervisor who decides not to report.

Professional privileges for confidential communications are generally abrogated by the mandatory reporting laws. However, in some states a few privileges remain and excuse an otherwise mandated reporter from making a report if the source of the suspicion is a privileged communications.

§ 16.2.2 Reporting by Nonprofessionals

Any person *may* report cases of suspected child abuse or neglect. But in some states family members or neighbors *must* report suspicions of child maltreatment. Approximately eighteen states and Puerto Rico require all citizens, regardless of their profession, to report suspected child maltreatment and neglect.[15] Additionally, some states require any individual who has contact with children to report suspected child abuse or neglect. For example, Arizona requires all parents and anyone responsible for the treatment or care of a child to report suspected child abuse or neglect.[16]

§ 16.2.3 Good Faith: Immunity from Civil Liability

Even if a person is not mandated to make a report, discretionary reports may be made, even anonymously. In most cases, the reporter is entitled to immunity from civil suit by the parents based on the report, so long as the report was made in good faith.

§ 16.2.4 Liability for Making False or Malicious Report

Many states now provide specifically for tort liability against people making malicious reports. The California penal code addresses liability for persons making false reports; the statute provides in part:

> No mandated reporter shall be civilly or criminally liable for any report required or authorized by this article . . . Any other person reporting a known or suspected instance of child abuse or neglect

---

[15] Child Welfare Information Gateway, *Mandatory Reporters of Child Abuse and Neglect* (2008), *available at* www.childwelfare.gov/systemwide/laws_policies/statutes/manda.cfm.

[16] ARIZ. REV. STAT. ANN. § 13-3620 (2009).

shall not incur civil or criminal liability as a result of any report authorized by this article unless it can be proven that a false report was made and the person knew that the report was false or was made with reckless disregard of the truth or falsity of the report, and any person who makes a report of child abuse or neglect known to be false or with reckless disregard of the truth or falsity of the report is liable for any damages caused . . .[17]

Similarly, the Idaho Code states that any person who reports suspected child abuse or neglect in bad faith or with malice is not provided immunity for reporting.[18]

§ 16.3 Investigating Child Maltreatment

Once a report of maltreatment has been made, the CPS agency investigates whether abuse or neglect has occurred and assesses the risks to the child. According to the National Child Abuse and Neglect Data System, a total of 3.2 million referrals to child protective services, involving 5.8 million children, were made in federal fiscal year 2007.[19] More than one-third (38.3%) of reports made to child protective services were "screened out" and not investigated.[20] The remainder of the referrals were either investigated by CPS to determine if a child was maltreated or assessed for risk of maltreatment. Of the reports that were investigated, 25.2% resulted in a substantiated report of child maltreatment.[21]

§ 16.3.1 Time Frame

Once a report is made, child protective services or law enforcement must investigate within a specific period of time unless the facts alleged would not constitute abuse or neglect under the requisite state statutes. Most states designate reports as higher or lower priority and respond accordingly.[22] Higher-priority reports of child maltreatment are generally investigated within 1 to 24 hours of the report; child protective services agencies respond to lower-priority reports of abuse between 24 hours and 14 days of the report.[23] An example of a lower-priority case could be when there are no specific allegations of abuse or neglect or where the child is over a certain age, whereas reports about children under the age of three are nearly always

---

[17] Cal. Penal Code § 11172(a) (2004).

[18] Idaho Code Ann. § 16-1606 (2009).

[19] U.S. Department of Health & Human Services, Administration on Children, Youth and Families, *Child Maltreatment 2007* (Washington, DC: U.S. Government Printing Office 2009), p. xii, *available at* http://www.acf.hhs.gov/programs/cb/pubs/cm07/cm07.pdf.

[20] *Id.* at 6.

[21] *Id.* at 5.

[22] *Id.* at 9, 16.

[23] *Id.* at 9, 16.

considered "higher-priority" cases. Given limited funding for child protective services, there is always some degree of triage involved. Sometimes all required investigations are not performed in a timely manner or at all. Other cases are investigated in only a cursory manner.

§ 16.3.2 Risk Assessment

For ongoing safety assessment beyond the stage of the initial child protection intervention, see Chapter 14, Child Safety: What Judges and Lawyers Need to Know.

Initially, child protective services must assess the situation to determine if the child has been maltreated or if the child is at a substantial risk of maltreatment.[24] Most states use risk assessment models designed to structure decision-making, predict future harm, aid in resource management by identifying service needs for children and families, and facilitate communication between the agency and community.[25] The assessment may include a visit to the family home and interviews with the family and persons outside the family. The family may help identify services that may be needed to better care for their child, such as parenting skills training or addiction services. The majority of children entered foster care because of neglect, often the result of a parent's failure to provide necessary physical (food and shelter), medical, educational, or emotional care,[26] which are conditions that may often be ameliorated by community-based interventions, thus avoiding placing the child in out-of-home care. These approaches are called "alternative" or "differential" responses.[27]

Agencies analyze the risk assessment information and evaluate the situation of the child and family, their strengths and resources, and community services. Child protective services then determines whether there is sufficient and believable information to confirm maltreatment and assigns significance to the risks and family strengths. Additional risk assessment criteria are considered in cases involving substance abusing families, families where partner abuse is an issue, and families with unique cultural backgrounds. Child protective services then evaluates the child's safety.

§ 16.3.3 Safety Assessment

The Adoption and Safe Families Act of 1997 (ASFA) requires states to provide safe environments for children in birth families, out-of-home care, and adoptive homes.[28] The risk of child maltreatment and the safety of a child are two separate

---

[24] DIANE DEPANFILIS & MARSHA K. SALUS, U.S. DEPARTMENT OF HEALTH AND HUMAN SERVICES, CHILD PROTECTIVE SERVICES: A GUIDE FOR CASEWORKERS (2003), *available at* http://www.childwelfare.gov/pubs/usermanuals/cps/cps.pdf.

[25] *Id.* at 43–45 (internal citations omitted).

[26] Child Welfare Information Gateway, *What is Child Abuse and Neglect?*, p. 2–3 (2008), *available at* http://www.childwelfare.gov/pubs/factsheets/whatiscan.pdf.

[27] *Id.*

[28] Pub. L. No. 105-89, 111 Stat. 2115 (codified as amended in 42 U.S.C. §§ 670–676 (2004)).

inquiries. Safety assessment requires the caseworker to make two determinations. First, when the caseworker initially meets with the family, he or she must determine if the child is currently in danger. Second, at the end of the initial assessment, the caseworker must consider the following factors:

- Whether the child will be safe in the home without further involvement by child protective services.

- Under what circumstances the case could be moved to community partners.

- Whether home-based services are necessary to protect the child.

- Ultimately, whether the child needs to be placed in out-of-home care.

Child protective services use the findings of the risk assessment to determine the child's safety at the conclusion of the initial assessment.[29]

§ 16.3.4 Investigating Evidence of Child Maltreatment

Child protective services also considers whether the harm to the child constitutes child maltreatment and whether there is sufficient evidence to support a case of child maltreatment. For example, a thorough investigation of a report involving physical abuse includes collecting information about the injury and photographing the child as soon as possible.[30] Additionally the investigator should interview the child and possible witnesses, including siblings, neighbors, teachers, caregivers, and medical personnel. It is crucial that the investigation is conducted using trauma-informed practices and is well documented; legally it is very important to be able to trace what exactly was asked during interviews.[31] The child's medical records, school or daycare records, and family history should also be reviewed.[32]

If the investigation reveals problems that do not pose an immediate danger to the child, and if the family will cooperate with services, the agency might refer the family to voluntary services without filing a court action. The family might agree to an informal period of out-of-home placement of the child with a relative, friend, or foster home. The agency might require the parents to file a written contract covering this arrangement. If the parent does not cooperate with the voluntary services or does not remedy the problem, the agency might choose to pursue court action.

---

[29] For a discussion of assessing the child's safety, see Chapter 14, Child Safety: What Judges and Lawyers Need to Know.

[30] Some state statutes explicitly permit photographing children as part of an investigation into child maltreatment. *See* FLA. STAT. § 39.301(19) (2003); ARIZ. REV. STAT. § 13-3620 (I) (2004).

[31] JOHN E. B. MYERS, LEGAL ISSUES IN CHILD ABUSE AND NEGLECT PRACTICE 166 (2d ed. 1998).

[32] *Id.* at 58; *see generally* OFFICE OF JUVENILE JUSTICE AND DELINQUENCY PREVENTION, U.S. DEPARTMENT OF JUSTICE, PORTABLE GUIDES TO INVESTIGATING CHILD ABUSE (1996–1998).

§ 16.3.5 Interpreting Labels of "Founded" or "Unfounded" on Agency Reports

Attorneys involved in child welfare cases must understand the limitations of investigations in some circumstances and not assume that reports labeled "unfounded," "unsubstantiated," or otherwise closed without a finding of abuse or neglect mean that there was an affirmative determination that abuse or neglect did or did not occur. Many child protective services agencies are limited to two choices (such as "founded" and "unfounded") and are not permitted to indicate varying degrees of suspicion. In some agencies, reports are designated "unfounded" if the family cannot be located. Sometimes, even with a good investigation, a report may be labeled "unfounded" because there is simply insufficient evidence to prove what the investigator feels was real abuse. Sometimes a series of "unfounded" reports reflects a malicious or hypervigilant reporter. Often it reflects limitations of proof, limitations of time or experience of the investigator, or children and families unwilling to speak honestly. Attorneys need to look carefully at the facts of each case without making assumptions based on the labels assigned to reports.

§ 16.3.6 Emergency Protective Custody

Some states provide that child protective services or law enforcement may take a child into emergency protective custody for an investigative period without the parent's consent or a court order. When a child is taken into emergency protective custody, there must be a judicial review of the state's action within a specified amount of time, generally between 48 and 96 hours. For example, in Florida, a law enforcement officer or a social worker may take a child into custody without a court order if he or she has probable cause to believe the child has been abused or is in imminent danger of injury.[33] The child's parents must be notified immediately and there must be a shelter hearing within 24 hours of removal.[34] State legislatures are challenged with striking a balance between providing law enforcement and child protective services with the authority to protect children, on the one hand, and safeguarding the rights of parents and the integrity of families, on the other.[35] In addition, every effort must be made to minimize the infliction of additional trauma on the child caused by removal from parents or caregivers.

In most states, child protective services or law enforcement may enter a home without a search warrant if they believe a child is in imminent danger. Additionally, many states provide statutory authority for social services, law enforcement, or school

---

[33] FLA. STAT. § 39.401 (2003).

[34] FLA. STAT. § 39.402 (2003).

[35] For a discussion of the constitutional issues relevant to removal of children from their parent's custody, see Chapter 15, Due Process of Law and Child Protection.

personnel to conduct an initial interview with a child at school without giving the child's parents prior notice.[36]

§ 16.4 Initiating Court Action

Every child welfare court case begins with either the filing of a petition or an emergency removal. The case then proceeds to a detention hearing to determine whether the child should be removed from his or her home or returned if he or she was previously removed. The case then proceeds through several procedural stages:

- The temporary custody or emergency hearing
- The adjudicatory (fact-finding) hearing
- The disposition hearing
- A series of periodic review hearings
- The permanency planning hearings
- A termination of parental rights hearing or other final orders
- Further review hearings
- An adoption or guardianship hearing if that is the final plan

A child welfare case can be dismissed at any time during the case process, and appeals or writs can be taken at different stages throughout the life of the case.[37]

If the investigator determines that court action is necessary, the agency will file a petition. Many states restrict the ability to file dependency petitions to the state or county agency. Sometimes a private child welfare agency is given standing to file. In some states, designated private individuals may file. In a few states, any person having a legitimate interest in the child may file a petition; in those states, even if the agency's investigation is closed without the filing of a petition, a concerned adult may nevertheless seek court intervention. Local law determines whether such actions are filed in juvenile court, family court, probate court, or other courts. For purposes of this chapter, we will refer to the relevant court generically as "juvenile court."

§ 16.5 Emergency Removal/Detention

In most cases, the temporary custody order is obtained *ex parte*. Usually, all that is required is a *prima facie* showing that the child is likely to be in danger of imminent harm. In some jurisdictions, the *prima facie* showing may be established by hearsay, written declarations, or other procedures short of a full evidentiary hearing. If a child is placed in temporary custody, the parents and, arguably, the child are entitled to an expedited hearing to review custody. This may be called an "emergency

---

[36] ME. REV. STAT. ANN. tit. 22, § 4021(3) (2003).

[37] For a discussion of appellate practice, see Chapter 26, Child Welfare Appellate Law and Practice.

hearing," "shelter care hearing," or "preliminary hearing" and is typically held 24 to 72 hours after an emergency removal of the child. Some courts use mediation, family group conferencing, family group decision-making, or other procedures to attempt to work out temporary orders involving placement, access, and pretrial services to address the family's problems and secure safe, stable permanence for the child at the earliest possible stage.[38] The temporary custody hearing may also address other temporary orders, such as establishing initial services to be provided to the parents and children, visitation if the child is not returned to the parent, diligent search for and notification of fathers and kin/relatives, and the designation of financial responsibility for the child.[39]

The court may provide third parties, such as relatives, limited party status. For example, the court may permit a relative who desires to be a placement for the child to appear at the temporary custody hearing and to participate on the issue of placement. Full intervening party status might be granted under certain circumstances.

The Fostering Connections to Success and Increasing Adoptions Act of 2008 requires a notice of placement to relatives "within 30 days after the removal of a child from the custody of the parent" and requires the state to "exercise due diligence to identify and provide notice to all adult grandparents and other adult relatives of the child."[40] Moreover, the state must inform relatives of their options "to participate in the care and placement of the child" including the requirements "to become a foster family home and the additional services and supports that are available for children placed in such a home."[41]

If the child is placed in a shelter, the state's statute may require interim review hearings of temporary custody until the child is placed in a foster home or other more long-term placement. In such cases, the agency is required to make reasonable efforts to find a more appropriate placement for the child.[42]

The agency has a duty to make reasonable efforts to prevent or eliminate the need for removal of the child from the home, as long as the child's health and safety is assured. Reasonable efforts are not required under certain circumstances.[43] The agency must be prepared to explain to the court what efforts it has made, why the child must be removed, or why reasonable efforts were not required under the statutory criteria.[44] The agency must develop a case plan for the child within 60 days

---

[38] For a further discussion of alternative dispute resolution, *see* Chapter 24, Non-Adversarial Case Resolution.

[39] For a fuller discussion of the legal requirement to identify extended family, including a discussion of The Fostering Connections to Success and Increasing Adoptions Act, see §10.6, Fostering Connections to Success and Increasing Adoptions Act.

[40] Pub. L. No. 110-351, § 103 (codified at 42 U.S.C. § 671(a)(29)).

[41] *Id. See also* the Fostering Connections Resource Center, *Kinship/Guardianship: Relevant Sections of P.L. 110-351* at http://www.fosteringconnections.org/resources/sections?id=0004.

[42] 45 C.F.R. § 1356.21(b).

[43] 45 C.F.R. § 1356.21(b)(3).

[44] 45 C.F.R. § 1356.21(b)(3).

of the child's removal from home.[45] The parents or guardians have a right to be involved in developing the case plan.[46] Once a child is removed, the agency has a duty to make reasonable efforts to maintain the family unit and make it possible for the child to return home safely as long as the child's health and safety is assured.[47] Reasonable efforts are not required under certain circumstances.[48]

The court's determination at a temporary custody hearing is non-appealable, but it may be reviewed by filing for an extraordinary writ. Child placement decisions are time-sensitive for children, and extraordinary writs are an appropriate means for reviewing a temporary custody order or order denying temporary custody.[49]

§ 16.6 Pretrial Discovery and Motion Practice

Child welfare law includes trial practice, and child welfare law specialists should be capable trial lawyers. Because many courts schedule only short hearings in child welfare cases, it is particularly important to be well prepared, well organized, efficient, and compelling in presenting evidence and cross-examining witnesses.

In most states, the state rules of civil procedure apply to child welfare cases. In some states, there are additional juvenile court rules or local rules. In states that follow the Federal Rules of Civil Procedure, parties to child welfare cases may have an affirmative duty to provide disclosure.[50] In addition, discovery should be available, at least with respect to the adjudicatory dependency or termination hearings. Children's attorneys, as well as agency attorneys and parent's attorneys, should avail themselves of discovery techniques when appropriate. Appointed counsel may or may not be given funds with which to conduct discovery. In such cases, while it may not be possible to take depositions, the attorney can still use less costly methods of discovery, such as requests for admission, requests for production of documents, and interrogatories. Requests for admission are particularly helpful in narrowing the contested trial issues. Where discovery is permitted after adjudication, interrogatories can be used to clarify expectations and to monitor the compliance and progress of all parties with rehabilitative services.

Attorneys for each of the parties should develop a trial strategy, plan and prepare witnesses and exhibits, and present a cogent, efficient case.[51]

---

[45] 45 C.F.R. § 1356.21(g)(2).

[46] 45 C.F.R. § 1356.21(g)(1).

[47] 45 C.F.R. § 1356.21(b).

[48] 45 C.F.R. § 1356.21(b)(3).

[49] For a discussion of writs, see Chapter 26, Child Welfare Appellate Law and Practice.

[50] FED. R. CIV. P. 26.

[51] For in-depth treatment of trial practice issues, see Chapter 32, Trial Advocacy.

§ 16.7 Adjudication

The court at the dependency trial determines whether or not the facts alleged have been proven true by a preponderance of the evidence[52] and whether the case meets the statutory requirements for a dependency adjudication under state law. Under the federal Child Abuse Prevention and Treatment Act (CAPTA), the court must provide representation for the child by an attorney, guardian ad litem, or court appointed special advocate who has received training appropriate to the role.[53] Various states have different requirements for who provides such representation and the role of that person. Although not required as a matter of federal constitutional law,[54] most states appoint attorneys for indigent parents.

State law determines how quickly the adjudicatory hearing must be held. If the child is placed out-of-home, the hearing may be accelerated. The hearing may have to be completed in as little as 60 days from the date of filing the petition.[55]

The petitioner has the burden of proving the abuse or neglect by a preponderance of the evidence, except in ICWA cases. A heightened standard of proof is not required because dependency cases balance the interests of the child as well as those of the parents and the state or county. While a parent's criminal conviction for abuse or neglect involving the same facts may establish the grounds for dependency, acquittal on the criminal charges is not relevant because of the heightened criminal standard of proof and the different statutory requirements for the juvenile court proceeding.

§ 16.8 Disposition

If the child is adjudicated dependent, the court may enter dispositional orders at the same time as the adjudication, or it may set a separate dispositional hearing. The child may be adjudicated dependent but permitted to remain in the home, under the supervision of the agency and court. The dispositional hearing will determine: (1) the child's custodial placement; (2) terms of contact between child and parent if the child is not placed in the home; and (3) services to be provided to both the parent and child. ICWA contains special requirements if the child is an "Indian child."[56]

---

[52] Except that the standard for at least some findings is clear and convincing evidence in cases falling under the Indian Child Welfare Act (ICWA). 25 U.S.C. § 1912(f). For further discussion of ICWA, see Chapter 12, The Indian Child Welfare Act.

[53] 42 U.S.C. § 5106a(b)(2)(A)(xiii). For a more detailed discussion of CAPTA, see Chapter 10, Federal Child Welfare Legislation.

[54] *See* Lassiter v. Dep't of Soc. Servs., 452 U.S. 18, 30 (1981).

[55] For a discussion of adjudication times, see NATIONAL COUNCIL OF JUVENILE AND FAMILY COURT JUDGES, RESOURCE GUIDELINES: IMPROVING COURT PRACTICE IN CHILD ABUSE & NEGLECT CASES (1995).

[56] *See* Chapter 12, The Indian Child Welfare Act.

The permanency plan for the family should be specified. In 2008, the case goals of 463,000 children in state custody were:

Case Goal	Percentage	(number)
Reunify with Parent(s) or Principal Caretaker(s)	49%	(226,867)
Adoption	24%	(111,225)
Case Plan Goal Not Yet Established	5%	(22,642)
Long Term Foster Care	8%	(37,522)
Emancipation	6%	(29,556)
Live with Other Relative(s)	4%	(16,922)
Guardianship	4%	(18,266)[57]

In 2008, the placement settings for children in state custody were:

Placement Setting	Percentage	(number)
Foster Family Home (Non-relative)	47%	(217,243)
Foster Family Home (Relative)	24%	(112,643)
Institution	10%	(47,165)
Group Home	6%	(29,122)
Pre-Adoptive Home	4%	(17,485)
Trial Home Visit	5%	(24,358)
Runaway	2%	(9,766)
Supervised Independent Living	1%	(5,217)[58]

Placement of the child is reevaluated at disposition and remains an essential and ongoing concern of the case. Placement at home may be risky for a child, but out-of-home placement can carry its own hazards. Children may have multiple change of placement. Children move for many reasons, including attrition and lack of training or support for foster families, lack of resources to address a child's special needs, or because the child's behavior may be difficult for some foster parents to manage. Lawyers for all the parties are well advised to see placement "through the eyes of the child." If the child is removed from his or her home, the child is separated from his or her parents and may be separated from siblings, as well. The child will meet new temporary "parents" and adjust to their lifestyle and house rules. Foster parents may have their own children or other foster children in their homes. The child may have to

---

[57] U.S. Department of Health and Human Services, Administration for Children & Families, Children's Bureau, *The AFCARS Report Preliminary FY 2008 Estimates as of October 2009, available at* http://www.acf.hhs.gov/programs/cb/stats_research/afcars/tar/report16.htm; U.S. Department of Health and Human Services, Children's Bureau, *The AFCARS Report #8* (March 2003), *available at* http://www.acf.dhhs.gov/programs/cb/publications/afcars/report8.htm.

[58] *Id.*

attend a new school, leaving old friends behind and adjusting to a new teacher, new classmates, and new rules. The emotional adjustments may differ for children placed with relatives or placed in their own neighborhood. The child will have to make these adjustments each time he or she is moved. All of these moves and adjustments can create or exacerbate a child's experience of trauma. Attorneys involved in child welfare cases should become familiar with the impact of trauma on children and work to ensure that trauma is reduced or mitigated whenever possible.[59]

Federal law recognizes a preference for placement with relatives.[60] However, the regulations clarify that health and safety are the paramount considerations when any placement decision is made regarding a child in foster care, including care with a relative.[61] Generally, relatives do not receive foster care payments unless they are licensed foster care providers.

In some jurisdictions, mediation, family group conferencing, or family group decision-making are available to assist the parties in reaching a dispositional agreement. The best dispositional orders are clear and specific in outlining the terms of placement, and in setting forth the specific expectations of all the parties.

§ 16.9 Case Plans

At any time the child is removed from the parent's home, federal law requires that the agency develop a case plan within a reasonable time, not to exceed 60 days.[62] Parents, guardians, and youth are entitled to participate in developing the case plan.[63] The case plan should outline the responsibilities of each party, including what services the agency will provide and what is expected of the parents and child. Any party may suggest alternate services, different visitation, participation of the child in ongoing activities, or different time lines.[64] The goals and objectives of the case plan and the services provided should always be permanency-oriented, and reflect the court's findings and the statutory bases for the dependency adjudication. The services should be designed to remedy or address the problems identified and should include realistic time lines by which each party is expected to be responsible for meeting the goals and objectives. The case plan should build on the strengths and resources of the parents, child, and family. The case plan should address both the reasonable needs of the child and the deficits of the parents.[65] The case plan should also address ICWA

---

[59] See the National Child Traumatic Stress Network, www.nctsn.org.

[60] 42 U.S.C. § 671(a)(19).

[61] Title IV-E Foster Care Eligibility Reviews and Child and Family Services State Plan Reviews, 65 FED. REG. 4020-01 (January 25, 2000), pp. 4032–33.

[62] 45 C.F.R. § 1356.21(g)(2).

[63] 45 C.F.R. § 1356.21(g)(1).

[64] 45 C.F.R. § 1356.21(g)(3).

[65] 45 C.F.R. § 1356.21(g)(3). *See also* Adoption and Safe Families Act of 1997, Pub. L. No. 105-89, 11 Stat. 2115.

compliance and/or issues related to any child's connection to his or her cultural, racial, ethnic and religious heritage. The child's needs are broader than those merely designed to return the child home or find an alternative permanency plan—addressing the child's needs could also include responding to the child's educational, medical, mental health, sibling connections, extracurricular, and associational needs. The more specific and objectively measurable the case plan is, the easier it will be for the parties to determine when and whether each party is in compliance. Such specificity also assists the court in determining whether the agency has made reasonable efforts toward achieving the case plan, and whether the parents have made reasonable efforts at compliance.

Concurrent planning is explicitly permitted.[66] Therefore, even if the permanency plan is return to the child to his or her parent, the agency may also prepare for a different plan in the event that the reunification does not occur. For example, if it appears that the agency must provide reasonable efforts to reunify the family, but reunification seems unlikely, the agency might choose to place the child in a foster-adoptive home so that if the plan changes to termination of parental rights, the child's foster parents could adopt the child. Such concurrent planning shortens the time to permanency and increases the likelihood that the child will not have to move if the plan changes.[67]

§ 16.10 Review Hearings

Federal law requires review hearings must be held at least every twelve months from the previous hearing until the child is reunified, adopted, or until an alternate permanent plan has been effectuated.[68] Some states hold review hearings quarterly or even more frequently. Federal law permits review hearings to be conducted by the court or an administrative body (including a citizen review panel). But state law may specify that review hearings must be heard by the court. Notice of the review hearings must be provided not only to the parties, but also to foster parents, foster-adopt parents, and relative caregivers who are entitled to be heard at review hearings even though they are not parties.[69] In some states, review hearings may include hearsay reports, so long as the caseworker providing the report is available for cross-examination. One particular type of review hearing, the permanency planning hearing, is discussed separately below.

In a review hearing, the court needs to be able to determine from the evidence whether the child is safe, whether additional or different steps must be made to ensure

---

[66] 45 C.F.R. § 1356.21(b)(4).

[67] *See* Child Welfare Information Gateway, *Concurrent Planning for Permanency for Children: Summary of State Laws, available at* www.childwelfare.gov/systemwide/laws_policies/statutes/concurrent.cfm.

[68] 45 C.F.R. § 1356.21(b)(2)(1).

[69] 45 C.F.R. § 1356.21(o).

the child's safety, or whether the child may now be safely returned to the parent.[70] The court needs to be able to determine whether the parent has achieved the case plan objectives, and if so, whether there should be changes to the child's placement or visitation, or whether there need to be changes in the services offered. If the parent has not yet achieved any of the case plan objectives, the court needs to be able to determine whether there should be changes in the objectives, changes in the services, or changes in the case plan or whether the parent should be given more time to achieve the objectives. The case review must also set a target date for the child's return home, adoption, or other permanent placement. This thorough review must be conducted for each child within a sibling group while also addressing the collective needs of the sibling group as a whole. Efforts to place siblings together and maintain their connections should be given priority consideration.

As well as reviewing the parent's progress, the court will review whether the agency has provided timely and appropriate services. Unless the case circumstances fall within an exception, the agency has a continuing duty to make reasonable efforts to prevent the need for removal of the child from the home or to reunify the child with the family if the child has been removed.[71] At each review hearing, the court must make specific findings concerning whether the child continues to be dependent and whether the agency is making reasonable efforts to reunify the family or pursue another approved permanency plan. The court will review the appropriateness of the current case plan and order appropriate changes or additions to the case plan.

§ 16.11 Permanency Hearings

The Adoption and Safe Families Act (ASFA)[72] requires that the court must hold a permanency planning hearing within 12 months from the time the child enters foster care.[73] If the court determines that the agency is not required to make any or further reasonable efforts at reunification, the permanency hearing must be held within 30 days of that determination.[74]

There are a variety of permanency plans other than simply the choice between return to parent and termination of parental rights followed by adoption.[75] For example, in some cases an appropriate plan could be permanent guardianship or a relative placement. While independent living is a legally acceptable permanency plan, it is recognized that this does not give the same lifelong stability, security, or rights to a young person that are conferred by other family-based permanency options.

---

[70] For a more detailed discussion, see Chapter 14, Child Safety: What Judges and Lawyers Need to Know.

[71] 42 U.S.C. § 671(a)(15)(B), (C).

[72] The Adoption and Safe Families Act of 1997 (ASFA), Pub. L. No. 105-89, 111 Stat. 2115.

[73] 42 U.S.C. § 675(5)(C).

[74] 42 U.S.C. § 671(a)(15)(E)(i).

[75] See Chapter 25, Establishing Legal Permanence for the Child.

Therefore, the use of independent living as a permanency plan should be rare. All youth, however, can benefit from and are entitled to skill-building services that will help prepare them for a successful transition to adulthood. Such services can include independent living skills, post-secondary education, employment, and other supports. These services can occur concurrently with permanency planning and should not replace efforts to seek a family-based permanent connection for each youth.[76] It is important that permanency plans be made thoughtfully, based on an individualized assessment of the particular child's needs and family circumstances, rather than on generalized philosophical positions. The agency must propose a permanency plan and engage the parents and youth in the development of the plan.

Under special circumstances, the courts are allowed to extend foster care for an additional period to continue reunification efforts. This is particularly likely when there have been defects in the services offered by the agency. For example, the agency may not have been diligent in obtaining appropriate services, or long waiting lists may have precluded a parent from participating in a service identified in the case plan, despite the parent's best efforts. If the parent has been diligent in participating in the case plan and is making good progress but is not yet ready to assume custody of the child, and if reunification is in the child's best interests, the court may continue the child in foster care.

A court may choose from among several permanency options for the child. In 2008 285,000 children exited foster care in the following ways:

Outcomes for Children Exiting Foster Care	Percentage	(number)
Reunification with Parent/Primary Caretaker	52%	(148,340)
Living with Other Relative(s)	8%	(23,944)
Adoption	19%	(54,284)
Guardianship	7%	(19,941)
Emancipation	10%	(29,516)
Transfer to Another Agency	2%	(5,195)
Runaway	1%	(3,324)
Death of Child[77]	less than 1%	(456)[78]

If the parents are successful with the court-ordered treatment plan, the child is reunited with his or her parents, and the case is closed. Many states are beginning to offer post-reunification services to support the success and stability of the reunified family, and attorneys for children should advocate for such services when available.

---

[76] See Chapter 23, Foster Youth: Transitioning from Foster Care into Self-Sufficient Adulthood.

[77] These deaths resulted from all causes, including accidental and natural. Only 18 deaths resulted from abuse.

[78] U.S. Department of Health and Human Services, Administration for Children & Families, Children's Bureau, *The AFCARS Report Preliminary FY 2008 Estimates as of October 2009, available at* http://www.acf.hhs.gov/programs/cb/stats_research/afcars/tar/report16.htm.

In 2007, more than 52% (148,340) of children in out-of-home care were reunited with their families.[79]

However, other studies have noted that approximately 33% of children who are reunified with their families re-entered foster care within three years.[80] And, approximately 17% of children who entered foster care had been in foster care before.[81]

§ 16.12 Termination of Parental Rights

If a parent fails to comply with the reunification plan, the child welfare agency will petition the court to terminate the parent's rights to the child. At any point during the court process, a parent may seek to voluntarily relinquish his or her parental rights. When the parent's rights are terminated, a permanent plan for the child will be created.

Federal law requires states to initiate Termination of Parental Rights (TPR) proceedings for: (1) children who have been in foster care for 15 of the most recent 22 months; (2) infants determined to be abandoned; (3) cases in which a parent has killed another of his/her children; or (4) certain other egregious situations. States may opt not to initiate TPR if: (1) at the option of the State, the child is in a relative's care; (2) the child welfare agency has documented a compelling reason that TPR would not be in the child's best interest; or (3) the state has not provided necessary services to the family.[82]

In FY 2008, the living parents of more than 75,000 children had their parental rights terminated.[83]

As a matter of federal constitutional law, the petition must prove the grounds for termination by clear and convincing evidence.[84] Typically, the petitioner must also prove by a preponderance of the evidence that termination is in the best interests of the child. Even if the parent's actions or inactions constitute statutory grounds for termination, the child's circumstances may be such that maintaining the legal parent-

---

[79] *Id.*

[80] *Id.*

[81] U.S. Department of Health and Human Services, Administration for Children & Families, National Clearinghouse on Child Abuse and Neglect Information, *Foster Care National Statistics* (April 2001), (2000b).

[82] 42 U.S.C. § 675(1)(5)(E). In the case of an abandoned child, regulations require States to initiate TPR within 60 days of a court determination of abandonment and in the case of a child whose parent has been convicted of a felony specified in the law 60 days of a court determination that reasonable efforts to reunite are not required.

[83] U.S. Department of Health and Human Services, Administration for Children & Families, Children's Bureau, *The AFCARS Report Preliminary FY 2008 Estimates as of October 2009, available at* http://www.acf.hhs.gov/programs/cb/stats_research/afcars/tar/report16.htm.

[84] *See* Santosky v. Kramer, 455 U.S. 745, 747–49 (1982).

child relationship promotes the child's best interests. With the accelerated time lines provided by ASFA, agencies are moving more quickly to termination. For some children, however, termination does not result in the child having a permanent home. Some children will reach 18 and leave foster care without being reunited with their families, adopted, or placed in another permanent home. In these cases, the child welfare agency may provide basic living skills training, housing assistance, and educational and employment opportunities through federally funded independent living programs or extension of foster care to the age of 21 for the purpose of providing continuing services and continued efforts to achieve permanence.[85]

> *In FY2008, approximately 29,516 youth left foster care when they reached the age of 18 (or 21, in some cases).*[86]

If the case falls within the federal Indian Child Welfare Act (ICWA),[87] then notice must also be provided to the child's Indian tribe or Native Alaskan Village.[88] The tribe or village may have the right to have the case transferred to tribal court.[89] If the case proceeds in state court, the tribe or village has the right to participate in the state proceeding.[90] The standard of proof, at least for the required ICWA findings, is proof beyond a reasonable doubt; this is true even when applied to the non-Indian parent of an Indian child.[91] ICWA also requires that certain findings be supported by expert testimony.[92]

§ 16.13 Post-Termination Review Hearings

When a child is not immediately adopted, so long as the court maintains jurisdiction over the child, review hearings will continue, even after termination of parental rights. Post-termination reviews are like regular review hearings, with some additional features. Family reunification is no longer a goal, but the court must still ensure that adequate services are provided to the child and that a realistic placement plan is aggressively pursued.[93] Continuation of sibling and other familial relationships may also be an appropriate part of the case plan. The Fostering Connections to

---

[85] For further discussion see Chapter 23, Foster Youth: Transitioning from Foster Care into Self-Sufficient Adulthood.

[86] U.S. Department of Health and Human Services, Administration for Children & Families, Children's Bureau, *The AFCARS Report Preliminary FY 2008 Estimates as of October 2009*, *available at* http://www.acf.hhs.gov/programs/cb/stats_research/afcars/tar/report16.htm.

[87] 25 U.S.C. §§ 1901–1963. For a more detailed discussion of ICWA, see Chapter 12.

[88] 25 U.S.C. § 1912(a) (2004).

[89] 25 U.S.C. § 1911(b) (2004).

[90] 25 U.S.C. § 1911(c) (2004).

[91] 25 U.S.C. § 1912(f) (2004).

[92] 25 U.S.C. § 1912(f) (2004).

[93] National Council of Juvenile and Family Court Judges, Resource Guidelines: Improving Court Practice in Child Abuse & Neglect Cases 94 (1995).

Success and Increasing Adoptions Act of 2008 (Pub. L. No. 110-351) added a new requirement that case plans also ensure the educational stability of the child.[94] Because the child is a "legal orphan," having no legal parent, the court and agency or other legal guardian have a particularly important role to play in the child's life, especially in preparing the child for transition to adulthood.

§ 16.14 Achieving Permanence for the Child

Achieving safe, legal permanence for every child is a primary responsibility of the State, and the child's journey is not complete until he or she as a safe, stable, loving, permanent family. Options for legal permanence for the child are discussed in Chapter 25, Establishing Legal Permanence for the Child.

---

[94] 42 U.S.C. § 675(1)(G) (2008).

Chapter 17: Interstate and International Issues[*]

by Ann M. Haralambie[1]

§ 17.1 Introduction

Historically, courts had subject matter jurisdiction to deal with the child welfare concerns of any child found within the state. However, now state and federal statutes, interstate compacts, and international treaties govern where such cases may be heard and how courts and agencies must deal with interstate and international cases.

§ 17.2 Uniform Child Custody Jurisdiction and Enforcement Act

The Uniform Child Custody and Jurisdiction and Enforcement Act (UCCJEA)[2] is an updated version of the Uniform Child Custody Jurisdiction Act (UCCJA). It resolved the ambiguities in the UCCJA and made explicit the requirements of the federal Parental Kidnapping Prevention Act (PKPA).[3] While not a federal law, the UCCJEA has been enacted in 48 states and the District of Columbia, with the Act pending in the Massachusetts and Vermont legislatures as of the summer of 2010. Personal jurisdiction is neither necessary nor sufficient for UCCJEA subject matter jurisdiction. The UCCJEA provides for jurisdiction for a state when: (1) the state is a home state; (2) the state has significant connections; (3) other states with higher priority have declined jurisdiction in favor of the state; or (4) there is no state that fulfills the other jurisdictional requirements. The home state is the state in which a child lived with a parent or a person acting as a parent for at least six consecutive months immediately before the commencement of a child custody proceeding. The UCCJEA prioritizes home state above the other jurisdictional bases, in conformity to the Parental Kidnapping Prevention Act.[4] If there is a home state, in the absence of the

---

[*] Reprinted from *Handling Child Custody, Abuse and Adoption Cases, Third Edition*, with permission of Thomson Reuters. For more information about this publication, please visit www.west.thomson.com. *Author's Note:* Portions of this chapter were adapted from ANN M. HARALAMBIE, 1 HANDLING CHILD CUSTODY, ABUSE, AND ADOPTION CASES 3D, CH 2 (Thomson West 2009).

[1] Ann M. Haralambie, J.D., is a certified family law specialist practicing in Tucson, Arizona. She is also an author and speaker in the fields of family and children's law.

[2] For a detailed discussion of the UCCJEA, see ANN M. HARALAMBIE, 1 HANDLING CHILD CUSTODY, ABUSE, AND ADOPTION CASES 3D §§ 2:2–2:16 (West 2009).

[3] 28 U.S.C. § 1738A.

[4] 28 U.S.C. § 1738A.

home state's declination of jurisdiction, another state may not assume jurisdiction, even based on the child's best interests, although under certain circumstances another state may assume temporary "emergency" jurisdiction to enter orders that are necessary to protect and provide for the child. If there is no home state, or if the home state has declined to exercise jurisdiction in favor of another court because it is a more appropriate forum, that state may exercise significant connections jurisdiction if: (1) both the child and at least one parent, or person acting as a parent, have a significant connection with the state other than mere physical presence; and (2) substantial evidence is available in the state concerning the child's care, protection, training, and personal relationships.

A court that has exercised jurisdiction consistent with the UCCJEA retains exclusive, continuing jurisdiction over the determination until that court determines that either: (1) neither the child, parents, nor person acting as a parent have a significant connection with the state and that substantial evidence is no longer available in the state concerning the child's care, protection, training, and personal relationships; or (2) the child, parents, or person acting as a parent do not presently reside in the state. Alternatively, a court with continuing jurisdiction may decline to exercise its jurisdiction in favor of another court that it finds to be more appropriate. Except for temporary orders made in an emergency, a court may not exercise modification jurisdiction so long as another state has exclusive continuing jurisdiction and has not declined to exercise its superior jurisdiction.

The UCCJEA provides for inter-court communication and specifies more clearly than the UCCJA how such communications should be handled. The court may permit the parties to participate in those communications, but if they do not participate, they must be given the opportunity to present facts and legal arguments prior to a decision being made on jurisdiction. A record must be made of substantive communications.

The UCCJEA also provides for taking the testimony of witnesses, including parties and the child, by deposition or otherwise in another state, or in a manner that the court prescribes. Out-of-state testimony may also be offered by telephone, audiovisual means, or other electronic means before a designated court or at another location in that state. A court may request the court of another state to do any of the following:

- Hold an evidentiary hearing
- Produce or give evidence pursuant to the procedures of that state
- Order a custody evaluation
- Have a person appear with or without the child
- Transmit a certified copy of the transcript or evaluation

Orders that comply with the UCCJEA are entitled to full faith and credit in other states and must be enforced. UCCJEA enforcement actions are expedited procedures. Generally, a hearing must be held on the next judicial day after service of an order directing the respondent to appear (with or without the child), unless that date is impossible, in which case the hearing must be held on the first judicial day possible.

These statutes become important when a parent with custody of a child takes the child from one state to another and becomes involved with the child protection system in the subsequent state. For example, imagine a case in which Mr. and Mrs. Smith are married in California. Mrs. Smith gives birth to Sally. When Sally is five years old, Mr. and Mrs. Smith divorce in California. Mrs. Smith, who is awarded primary custody of Sally, is allowed to move with Sally to New York. In New York, when Sally is seven years old, Mrs. Smith becomes involved with an abusive boyfriend, drugs, and the excessive use of alcohol, which causes her to leave Sally alone for days at a time. When Sally tells a school teacher what is happening at her home, the school authorities report their concern to child protection authorities.

In general, the UCCJA and the UCCJEA establish a child's "home state" as the jurisdiction with authority to make determinations regarding custody of a child. In our case example, California was Sally's "home state" at the time of the original custody determination (in the divorce). California had jurisdiction and properly resolved the custody dispute between Sally's parents. Under the UCCJEA, California retains jurisdiction to make custody determinations regarding Sally because her father continues to reside there. New York, however, has "emergency" jurisdiction over Sally because her health and safety are impaired by her mother's inability to provide a fit home environment for Sally. Under the UCCJEA, New York has "emergency" jurisdiction to enter orders that are necessary to protect and provide for Sally. However, these orders may only be temporary, and unless California declines to exercise its jurisdiction, the child welfare case must be brought in California and dismissed in New York.

§ 17.3 Parental Kidnapping Prevention Act

Despite the efforts of the uniform state law—then just the UCCJA—to resolve jurisdictional disputes, there continued to be struggles regarding which of two states' courts had jurisdiction over child custody actions. In 1980 Congress responded to these concerns by enacting the Parental Kidnapping Prevention Act (PKPA),[5] which is intended to "specify which types of custody decrees must be afforded full faith and credit, as well as the circumstances that would allow states to modify an outstanding custody decree of another state."[6] The PKPA establishes a federal standard for giving effect to child custody orders.[7] If a child custody order has been issued by a court with proper jurisdiction under state law, the PKPA ensures that that order will be entitled

---

[5] 28 U.S.C. § 1738A.

[6] JOHN DEWITT GREGORY, PETER N. SWISHER & SHERYL L. WOLF, UNDERSTANDING FAMILY LAW 435 n. 109 (2001).

[7] For a detailed discussion of the PKPA, see ANN M. HARALAMBIE, 1 HANDLING CHILD CUSTODY, ABUSE, AND ADOPTION CASES 3D §§ 2:17–2:21 (West 2009).

to full faith and credit in another state. The UCCJEA incorporated the requirements of the PKPA into the updated uniform act in order to resolve any ambiguities found in the UCCJA.

Regarding child maltreatment, the PKPA provides that a state court has jurisdiction if state law grants that court jurisdiction over child maltreatment cases and "the child is physically present in such State and (i) the child has been abandoned, or (ii) it is necessary in an emergency to protect the child because the child, a sibling, or parent of the child has been subjected to or threatened with mistreatment or abuse."[8]

Returning briefly to our example involving Sally and her parents, while the California court's order would generally be entitled to full faith and credit under PKPA, the PKPA would permit the New York court to take steps to protect Sally from parental maltreatment. The California court, however, retains jurisdiction to modify its original custody order.[9] This is true even though the divorce decree was not being directly modified, because the effect of the child welfare action would be to modify the custody determination contained in the divorce decree.

The PKPA contains no requirement that the New York court notify either Sally's father or the California court of its protective actions regarding Sally. The UCCJEA, however, contains mechanisms for the New York court to notify the father in California and for the New York court to communicate with the California court.[10]

When child welfare proceedings trigger concerns regarding these uniform jurisdictional acts or the PKPA, these issues must be carefully analyzed and the requirements of the relevant statutes adhered to.

§ 17.4 Interstate Compacts

Interstate compacts are reciprocal, contractual agreements between and among states. As treaties work among countries, and unlike federal laws, interstate compacts apply only between states that have enacted them. The National Center for Interstate Compacts has explained that:

> an interstate compact differs from a uniform state law in several ways, most notably that a uniform law does not depend on contractual obligations and a state can therefore change any portion of the law, thus losing any degree of uniformity initially intended. Second, courts of different states may interpret the provisions of a uniform state law differently and since the highest court in a state is the final arbiter on legal issues within that state, there is no satisfactory way to achieve a reconciliation of divergent interpretations.

---

[8]   28 U.S.C. § 1738A(c)(2)(C).

[9]   *See* 28 U.S.C. § 1738A(f).

[10] *See, e.g.*, Section 108 of the UCCJEA (notice to party outside of the state); Section 110 of the UCCJEA (communicate with court with prior jurisdiction).

> Compacts are created when an offer is made by one state, usually by statute that adopts the terms of a compact requiring approval by one or more other states to become effective. Other states accept the offer by adopting identical compact language. Once the required number of states has adopted the pact, the "contract" among them is valid and becomes effective as provided.[11]

There are several Interstate Compacts now in effect that impact child welfare cases. This section will briefly describe three of them.

§ 17.4.1 Interstate Compact on the Placement of Children (ICPC)

The Interstate Compact on the Placement of Children (ICPC)[12] has been adopted by all 50 states, the District of Columbia, and the U.S. Virgin Islands.[13] The intention of the Compact is to establish uniform legal and administrative procedures governing the interstate placement of foster children. Before sending a child to a foster home, child care institution,[14] or pre-adoptive placement, the ICPC requires that the sending state must notify the receiving state and receive back from that state notice that the proposed placement does not appear to be contrary to the interests of the child.[15] The purpose of the notice requirement is to permit the receiving state to investigate the proposed placement and to inform the sending state of the results of the investigation. The requirements of the Compact apply to placements arranged by courts, agencies, and by private persons[16] other than parents, stepparents, grandparents, adult siblings,

---

[11] *See* Council of State Governments—National Center for Interstate Compacts, *Understanding Interstate Compacts, available at* http://www.cglg.org/projects/water/CompactEducation/Understanding_Interstate_Compacts--CSGNCIC.pdf.

[12] The Interstate Compact on the Placement of Children is available at http://www.aphsa.org/Home/Doc/Interstate-Compact-for-the-Placement-of-Children.pdf.

[13] A revised ICPC has been drafted, but it will not come into force until 35 states have adopted it. As of December 2009, only Alaska, Delaware, Florida, Indiana, Maine, Minnesota, Missouri, Nebraska, and Ohio had adopted the new version. For an up-to-date chart on state enactments, see http://www.aphsa.org/Policy/icpc2006rewrite.htm. For a side-by-side comparison of the two versions, see *Side by Side Comparison of the New ICPC and the Current ICPC, available at* http://www.aphsa.org/Policy/ICPC-REWRITE/NewICPCSidebySide.pdf. The revised ICPC has proven to be controversial. *See, e.g.,* Robert G. Spector & Cara N. Rodriguez, *Jurisdiction Over Children in Interstate Placement: The UCCJEA, Not the ICPC, Is the Answer,* 41 FAM. L.Q. 145 (2007); John C. Lore III, *Protecting Abused, Neglected, and Abandoned Children: A Proposal for Provisional Out-of-State Kinship Placements Pursuant to the Interstate Compact on the Placement of Children,* 40 U. MICH. J. L. REFORM 57 (2006); Vivek Sankaran, *Perpetuating the Impermanence of Foster Children: A Critical Analysis of Efforts to Reform the Interstate Compact on the Placement of Children,* 40 FAM. L.Q. 435 (2006).

[14] Except for institutions caring for the mentally ill, mentally defective, or epileptic, or institutions that are primarily educational or medical facilities. *See* ICPC, art II(d).

[15] ICPC, art III.

[16] ICPC, art II(b), (c).

aunts, uncles, and guardians for the purpose of placing the child with any such relative or nonagency guardian in the receiving state.[17]

Each state has a designated compact administrator who helps to administer the Compact and works with other compact administrators to promulgate model rules and regulations with respect to the compact.[18] Notice of a proposed placement is initiated by filing a specific form with the Compact Administrators of both states. Prior to the child being placed in the other jurisdiction, the Compact Administrators in both jurisdictions must approve the interstate placements of children covered by the ICPC. Delays in obtaining the approval of both Compact Administrators has been one problem with the implementation of ICPC placements. However, failure to comply with the compact and its regulations may render the placement illegal.[19]

The sending state retains jurisdiction after the child's interstate placement, and it also retains legal and financial responsibility for the child in the other state. The receiving state conducts a pre-placement home study to determine the appropriateness of the proposed placement and provides post-placement supervision, including making reports to the sending state. The receiving state may also coordinate post-placement services at the expense of the sending state.

The Compact covers placement only and does not deprive the sending state of continuing jurisdiction over the placement. Similarly, it does not relieve the sending agency of financial responsibility with respect to the child.[20] However, the agency may contract with persons or agencies in the receiving state to provide services to the child or family.[21]

The Association of Administrators of the Compact, which is comprised of Compact Administrators from various states, has drafted model regulations governing the implementation of the Compact. Model Regulation III states that the ICPC applies to the interstate placement of an adjudicated dependent child with his or her parent except in limited situations involving non-custodial parents. Despite this model regulation, there is a split in the case law concerning whether the Compact applies to placements with a parent in another state.[22] Some courts have held that the model

---

[17] ICPC, art VIII(a).

[18] ICPC, art VII.

[19] ICPC, art IV.

[20] ICPC, art I.

[21] ICPC, art V(b).

[22] For cases holding that the Compact does apply, see, e.g., Green v. Div. of Family Servs., 864 A.2d 921 (Del. Supr., 2004); *In re* T.N.H., 70 S.W.3d 2 (Mo. Ct. App. E.D. 2002); Arizona Dep't of Economic Sec. v. Leonardo, 200 Ariz. 74, 22 P.3d 513 (Ct. App. Div. 2 2001); Dep't of Children & Families v. Benway, 745 So. 2d 437 (Fla. Dist. Ct. App. 5th Dist. 1999); Adoption of Warren, 44 Mass. App. Ct. 620, 623, 693 N.E.2d 1021, 1024 (1998). For cases holding that the Compact does not apply, see, e.g., *In re* Alexis O., 157 N.H. 781, 959 A.2d 176 (2008); Arkansas Dep't of Human Servs. v. Huff, 347 Ark. 553, 65 S.W.3d 880 (2002); *In re* Johnny S., 40 Cal. App. 4th 969, 47 Cal. Rptr. 2d 94 (1995); Nance v. Arkansas Dep't of Human Servs., 316 Ark. 43, 870 S.W.2d 721 (1994); McComb v. Wambaugh, 934 F.2d 474 (3rd Cir. 1991).

regulations are not binding and cannot expand the scope of the statute.[23] Scholars and commentators have also challenged the application of the ICPC to out-of-state parents as inconsistent with the underlying statutory authority and as a deprivation of constitutional due process.[24] Similarly, some courts have held that the Compact also does not apply to placements of foster children with their relatives.[25]

An attorney representing a party in which the ICPC is implicated must carefully assess whether the provisions of the Compact are applicable and, if so, how to expedite such placements.[26]

§ 17.4.2 Interstate Compact on Adoption and Medical Assistance (ICAMA)

The Interstate Compact on Adoption and Medical Assistance (ICAMA)[27] addresses the need for assistance with special needs adoptions. At least 48 states and the District of Columbia have adopted the ICAMA. The ICAMA provides for the "establishment and maintenance of suitable substantive guarantees and workable procedures for interstate cooperation and payments to assist with the necessary costs of child maintenance, the procurement of services, and the provision of medical assistance."[28] ICAMA requires the use of specific forms and administrative procedures, which facilitates and coordinates subsidies, services, and medical benefits, including Medicaid, Title IV-E and Title XX payments, and state subsidies, across state lines.

§ 17.4.3 Interstate Compact on Mental Health (ICMH)

The Interstate Compact on Mental Health (ICMH) applies to coordinate appropriate treatment for patients with mental illness or mental disability, including

---

[23] *See* McComb v. Wambaugh, 934 F.2d 474 (3d Cir. 1991). Courts are split on the applicability of ICPC regulations to courts and its compliance with constitutional due process. For a compilation of ICPC cases and other resources for the child welfare attorney, see *ICPC Resources, available at* http://www.law.umich.edu/centersandprograms/ccl/specialprojects/Documents/ICPCCaselist.pdf.

[24] *See, e.g.*, Vivek Sankaran, *Out of State and Out of Luck: The Treatment of Non-Custodial Parents Under the Interstate Compact on the Placement of Children*, 25 YALE L. & POL'Y REV. 63 (2006). For a compilation of case law and resources compiled by Professor Sankaran, see the University of Michigan Law School Web page titled "ICPC Advocacy" at http://www.law.umich.edu/CENTERS ANDPROGRAMS/CCL/SPECIALPROJECTS/Pages/ICPCAdvocacy.aspx.

[25] *See, e.g.*, Arkansas Dep't of Health & Human Servs. v. Jones, 97 Ark. App. 267, 248 S.W.3d 507 (2007);Cabinet for Health & Family Servs., Commonwealth of Kentucky v. G.C., 2009 Ky. App. Unpub. LEXIS 27 (Ct. App. Ky. May 1, 2009); *In re* J.E., 182 N.C. App. 612, 643 S.E.2d 70 (2007); N.J. Div. of Youth & Family Servs. v. K.F., 353 N.J. Super. 623, 803 A.2d 721 (App. Div. 2002); *In re* Crystal A., 818 N.Y.S.2d 443, 13 Misc.3d 235 (2006).

[26] *See* Vivek S. Sankaran, *Navigating the Interstate Compact on the Placement of Children: Advocacy Tips for Child Welfare Attorneys*, 27 ABA CHILD L. PRAC. 33 (2008).

[27] Interstate Compact on Adoption and Medical Assistance, *available at* http://aaicama.org/cms/icama-aaicama-docs/Articles_of_ICAMA.pdf.

[28] *Id.* at § 1(d).

children and youth, by providing a procedure for transferring patients between states to allow for inpatient or aftercare treatment and for returning civilly committed patients who absconded from state treatment facilities. The ICMH also provides that patients in need of treatment should receive treatment where the person is present, without regard to residency. Member states are also permitted by the Compact to enter into supplemental agreements with one another to provide services or facilities. At least 45 states and the District of Columbia have adopted the ICMH.

§ 17.5 International Treaties and Enabling Laws

§ 17.5.1 Hague Convention on the Civil Aspects of International Child Abduction (Hague Abduction Convention) and ICARA

The Hague Convention on Child Abduction and its implementing legislation, the International Child Abduction Remedies Act (ICARA),[29] came into force in the United States in April 1988. The Convention provides civil procedures and remedies for obtaining the return of a child who has been wrongfully removed from, or retained in a country other than, the "state of habitual residence." The Convention addresses only *which* country has the right to make orders regarding custody and does not address the substantive custody issues. The U.S. State Department is the designated "Central Authority" for the United States, and the Bureau of Consular Affairs, Office of Children's Issues, has primary responsibility for implementing the Convention. The State Department formerly contracted with the National Center for Missing and Exploited Children (NCMEC) to provide services but since 2009 now provides those services directly. The Convention applies between the United States and original participating countries and countries who subsequently acceded to the Convention and whose accessions have been accepted by the United States. A list of participating countries may be found on the Web site of the U.S. Department of State.[30] The wrongful removal or retention must have occurred after the effective date.

In general, the Convention requires that a child under the age of 16 who was habitually resident in one country, but who was wrongfully removed to or retained in another country while the non-abducting parent was exercising custodial rights, must be returned to the country of habitual residence. The Convention can also be used to help parents exercise their access rights in another country. Most countries (but not the United States) provide legal counsel for aggrieved parents. However, the State department maintains a referral panel, which includes the availability of some pro

---

[29] Pub. L. No. 100-300, 102 Stat.437 (codified as amended at 42 U.S.C. §§ 11601–11610 (1988)).

[30] *See* http://www.adoption.state.gov/hague/overview/countries.html. For a list of countries and the dates on which the Convention became effective, see the Web site of the Hague Permanent Bureau at http://www.hcch.net/index_en.php?act=conventions.status&cid=69.

bono counsel. In the United States, applications under the Convention may be filed in state or federal court, or both.

The remedy of automatic return may be lost if the aggrieved custodian does not file an application under the Convention within one year. There are also limited defenses to return even when an application has been timely filed. A court may deny return of a child to the habitual residence if the person, institution, or other body having the care of the person of the child was not actually exercising the custody rights at the time of removal or retention, or had consented to or subsequently acquiesced in the removal or retention. Most courts have held that the exercise of access rights only is not sufficient to constitute the exercise of custody rights. Access rights are also protected by the Convention, but to a lesser extent that does not involve return of the child to the country of habitual residence. There is a "maturity" exception to return, but the Convention does not give any guidance with respect to how old a child must be before his or her wishes are considered as a part of the exception.

A defense to return that may arise in a child welfare context is the Article 13(b) exception for "grave risk" of physical or psychological harm to the child or of placing the child in an intolerable situation. This defense requires more than showing that the child has been abused in the country of habitual residence. Most courts construe the exception very narrowly and require a showing that the courts in the country of habitual residence are unable or unwilling to provide proper protection for the child pending the substantive hearing.

A free Internet research tool is the International Child Abduction Database (INCADAT), which contains leading international case law under the Convention.[31] The State Department also provides a free, downloadable handbook on handling Hague Abduction Convention cases.[32]

§ 17.5.2 Hague Convention on Protection of Children and Co-operation in Respect of Intercountry Adoption (Hague Adoption Convention) and IAA

The Hague Convention on Intercountry Adoption and its implementing legislation, the Intercountry Adoption Act of 2000 (IAA),[33] came into force in the United States in October 2000. Federal regulations will be promulgated to further govern adoptions under the Convention and the IAA. The U.S. State Department is the designated "Central Authority" for the United States, and the Bureau of Consular Affairs, Office

---

[31] *See* http://www.incadat.com. The search form in English can be accessed at http://www.incadat.com/index.cfm?act=search.detailed&sl=2&lng=1.

[32] Kilpatrick Stockton, *Litigating International Child Abduction Cases Under the Hague Convention* (National Center for Missing and Exploited Children, 2007), *available at* http://www.missingkids.com/missingkids/servlet/ResourceServlet?LanguageCountry=en_US&PageId =3411.

[33] Pub. L. No. 106-279, 114 Stat. 825.

of Children's Issues, has primary responsibility. The Convention applies to the adoption of children between the United States and the other signatory countries. The Convention provides that adoptions must take place in the best interests of the child and prevents the abduction, sale, or traffic in children. Participating countries must regulate agencies and individuals who are involved in intercountry adoptions between the participating countries. Only competent bodies may be accredited. Authorities in the country of origin must verify that the child has been legally made free for adoption and that all necessary consents have been freely given in writing and have not been withdrawn. The Convention provides that:

- Consents to adoption may not be induced by payment or compensation in kind.

- Mothers may not consent until after the child is born.

- Children are to be counseled concerning the effects of adoption (having regard to the child's age and maturity).

- Consideration must be given to the child's wishes and opinions.

- No one shall derive improper financial or other gain from an activity related to an intercountry adoption.

- Only costs and expenses, including reasonable professional fees of persons involved in the adoption, may be charged or paid.

- Directors, administrators, and employees of bodies involved in an adoption shall not receive remuneration that is unreasonably high in relation to services rendered.

- The authorities in the receiving country must ensure that the adoptive parents are qualified to adopt the child and have been counseled as necessary.

- The Central Authorities of both countries must take all necessary steps to secure permission for the child to leave the country of origin and to enter and permanently reside in the receiving country.

The Convention prohibits contact between prospective adoptive parents and birth parents or other caretakers until certain prerequisites have been met, unless it is a relative adoption or the contact complies with conditions established by the competent authority in the country of origin. The Central Authority of the country of origin must provide the receiving country with a report including information about the child's identity, adoptability, background, social environment, family history, medical history, and any special needs of the child and must give due consideration to the child's upbringing, ethnic, religious, and cultural background. If there is a probationary period, the Central Authorities of both countries are required to keep each other informed about the progress of the adoption. If the adoptive placement disrupts or is no longer in the child's best interests after the child is in the receiving country, the Central Authority of the receiving country is required to take steps to protect the child, including removing the child from the prospective adoptive parents and arranging alternate adoptive or foster care in consultation with the Central Authority of the country of origin. The Central Authority of the country of origin must be informed in advance of any adoption by another family. As a last resort, the child may need to be returned to the country of origin.

The Immigration and Nationality Act was amended to provide that children may be qualified to receive immigrant visas either because of their Convention adoption abroad or their placement abroad with U.S. prospective adoptive parents for Convention adoption in the United States.[34]

§ 17.6 United Nations Conventions and Protocols

The United Nations has sponsored a number of protocols and conventions that countries may ratify. Two are of particular relevance to the child welfare field. One has been ratified by the United States, and Congress has enacted implementing legislation. The other has not been ratified by Congress, and therefore, does not have the force of law in the United States. It is included in this book because of its wide acceptance elsewhere and the importance of the rights it expresses for children.

§ 17.6.1 UN Protocol to Prevent, Suppress and Punish Trafficking in Persons, Especially Women and Children, supplementing the United Nations Convention against Transnational Organized Crime

The United Nations Protocol to Prevent, Suppress and Punish Trafficking in Persons, Especially Women and Children, supplementing the United Nations Convention against Transnational Organized Crime,[35] and its implementing legislation, the Trafficking Victims Protection Act of 2000 (TVPA),[36] came into force in the United States in October 2000.

The Protocol defines "trafficking in persons" as "the recruitment, transportation, transfer, harbouring or receipt of persons, by means of the threat or use of force or other forms of coercion, of abduction, of fraud, of deception, of the abuse of power or of a position of vulnerability or of the giving or receiving of payments or benefits to achieve the consent of a person having control over another person, for the purpose of exploitation. Exploitation shall include, at a minimum, the exploitation of the prostitution of others or other forms of sexual exploitation, forced labour or services, slavery or practices similar to slavery, servitude or the removal of organs." The consent of a victim of trafficking is irrelevant under the Protocol. When the victim is a child (a person under the age of 18), the "recruitment, transportation, transfer,

---

[34] 8 U.S.C. § 1154.

[35] *Available at* http://www2.ohchr.org/english/law/protocoltraffic.htm.

[36] Pub. L. No. 106-386, 114 Stat. 1464.

harbouring or receipt of a child for the purpose of exploitation shall be considered 'trafficking in persons' even if this does not involve" any of the prohibited means.

The Protocol provides that to the extent permitted by domestic law, the privacy and identity of victims of trafficking in persons should be protected, including by making legal proceedings relating to such trafficking confidential. The Protocol recommends that the participating countries "consider implementing measures to provide for the physical, psychological and social recovery of victims of trafficking in persons," including "[c]ounselling and information, in particular as regards their legal rights, in a language that the victims of trafficking in persons can understand."

Pursuant to the Protocol, the U.S. Department of Justice has issued regulations for a "T visa," which will enable certain trafficking victims to live and work legally in the United States for three years while their cases are investigated and prosecuted. The Department of Health and Human Services can provide certification letters to permit victims of trafficking to become eligible to apply for federal and certain state benefits to the same extent as refugees.

Commercial sex trafficking of children is considered to be a severe form of trafficking in persons under TVPA.[37]

§ 17.6.2 UN Convention on the Rights of the Child (CRC)

The United Nations Convention on the Rights of the Child (CRC)[38] was adopted by the UN General Assembly on November 20, 1989 and came into force on September 2, 1990. Beginning in January 1990 the CRC was open to ratification and accession. Within the first two years 100 state parties had ratified it. Among the nations of the world, *only* Somalia, which lacks a functioning government, and the United States have failed to ratify the CRC. The United States did sign the CRC on February 16, 1995, but despite several attempts, Congress has not yet ratified it.[39] Professor Benjamin Shmueli points out: "According to the Vienna Convention on the Law of Treaties, a signature alone does not make the United States a true state party. However, a signature obliges a state party to refrain from acts that would defeat the object and purpose of the treaty, until the state party declares an express intention not to become a party. The United States has not expressed such an intention so far."[40] Therefore, it is possible to make limited legal argument in reference to the CRC despite its lack of force within the United States.

---

[37] 22 U.S.C. § 7102(8)(A).

[38] *Available at* http://www2.ohchr.org/english/law/crc.htm.

[39] The United States did sign and ratify two optional protocols to the CRC dealing with the involvement of children in armed conflict and prohibition of the sale of children, child prostitution, and child pornography. *See* Optional Protocols to the Convention on the Rights of the Child, G.A. Res. 54/263, Annex II, U.N. GAOR, 54th Sess., U.N. Doc. A/RES/54/263 (June 26, 2000).

[40] Benjamin Shmueli, *The Influence of the United Nations Convention on the Rights of the Child on Corporal Punishment – A Comparative Study*, 10 OR. REV. INT'L L. 189, 236–37 (2008) (footnote omitted).

Among the rights secured for children by the CRC are the following, which are particularly relevant to child welfare proceedings:

Article 6

1. States Parties recognize that every child has the inherent right to life.

2. States Parties shall ensure to the maximum extent possible the survival and development of the child.

Article 7

1. The child shall be registered immediately after birth and shall have the right from birth to a name, the right to acquire a nationality and, as far as possible, the right to know and be cared for by his or her parents.

    . . .

Article 8

1. States Parties undertake to respect the right of the child to preserve his or her identity, including nationality, name and family relations as recognized by law without unlawful interference.

    . . .

Article 9

1. States Parties shall ensure that a child shall not be separated from his or her parents against their will, except when competent authorities subject to judicial review determine, in accordance with applicable law and procedures, that such separation is necessary for the best interests of the child. Such determination may be necessary in a particular case such as one involving abuse or neglect of the child by the parents, or one where the parents are living separately and a decision must be made as to the child's place of residence.

2. In any proceedings pursuant to paragraph 1 of the present article, all interested parties shall be given an opportunity to participate in the proceedings and make their views known.

3. States Parties shall respect the right of the child who is separated from one or both parents to maintain personal relations and direct contact with both parents on a regular basis, except if it is contrary to the child's best interests.

4. Where such separation results from any action initiated by a State Party, such as the detention, imprisonment, exile, deportation or death (including death arising from any cause while the person is in the custody of the State) of one or both parents or of the child, that State Party shall, upon request, provide the parents, the child or, if appropriate, another member of the family with the essential information concerning the whereabouts of the absent member(s) of the family

unless the provision of the information would be detrimental to the well-being of the child. States Parties shall further ensure that the submission of such a request shall of itself entail no adverse consequences for the person(s) concerned.

Article 10

1. In accordance with the obligation of States Parties under article 9, paragraph 1, applications by a child or his or her parents to enter or leave a State Party for the purpose of family reunification shall be dealt with by States Parties in a positive, humane and expeditious manner. States Parties shall further ensure that the submission of such a request shall entail no adverse consequences for the applicants and for the members of their family.

2. A child whose parents reside in different States shall have the right to maintain on a regular basis, save in exceptional circumstances, personal relations and direct contacts with both parents. Towards that end and in accordance with the obligation of States Parties under article 9, paragraph 1, States Parties shall respect the right of the child and his or her parents to leave any country, including their own, and to enter their own country. The right to leave any country shall be subject only to such restrictions as are prescribed by law and which are necessary to protect the national security, public order (order public), public health or morals or the rights and freedoms of others and are consistent with the other rights recognized in the present Convention.
   . . .

Article 12

1. States Parties shall assure to the child who is capable of forming his or her own views the right to express those views freely in all matters affecting the child, the views of the child being given due weight in accordance with the age and maturity of the child.

2. For this purpose, the child shall in particular be provided the opportunity to be heard in any judicial and administrative proceedings affecting the child, either directly, or through a representative or an appropriate body, in a manner consistent with the procedural rules of national law.
   . . .

Article 14

1. States Parties shall respect the right of the child to freedom of thought, conscience and religion.

2. States Parties shall respect the rights and duties of the parents and, when applicable, legal guardians, to provide direction to the child in the exercise of his or her right in a manner consistent with the evolving capacities of the child.

3. Freedom to manifest one's religion or beliefs may be subject only to such limitations as are prescribed by law and are necessary to protect public safety, order, health or morals, or the fundamental rights and freedoms of others.

. . .

Article 16

1. No child shall be subjected to arbitrary or unlawful interference with his or her privacy, family, or correspondence, nor to unlawful attacks on his or her honour and reputation.

2. The child has the right to the protection of the law against such interference or attacks.

. . .

Article 18

1. States Parties shall use their best efforts to ensure recognition of the principle that both parents have common responsibilities for the upbringing and development of the child. Parents or, as the case may be, legal guardians, have the primary responsibility for the upbringing and development of the child. The best interests of the child will be their basic concern.

2. For the purpose of guaranteeing and promoting the rights set forth in the present Convention, States Parties shall render appropriate assistance to parents and legal guardians in the performance of their child-rearing responsibilities and shall ensure the development of institutions, facilities and services for the care of children.

3. States Parties shall take all appropriate measures to ensure that children of working parents have the right to benefit from child-care services and facilities for which they are eligible.

Article 19

1. States Parties shall take all appropriate legislative, administrative, social and educational measures to protect the child from all forms of physical or mental violence, injury or abuse, neglect or negligent treatment, maltreatment or exploitation, including sexual abuse, while in the care of parent(s), legal guardian(s) or any other person who has the care of the child.

. . .

Article 20

1. A child temporarily or permanently deprived of his or her family environment, or in whose own best interests cannot be allowed to remain in that environment, shall be entitled to special protection and assistance provided by the State.

2. States Parties shall in accordance with their national laws ensure alternative care for such a child.

3. Such care could include, inter alia, foster placement, kafalah of Islamic law, adoption or if necessary placement in suitable institutions for the care of children. When considering solutions, due regard shall be paid to the desirability of continuity in a child's upbringing and to the child's ethnic, religious, cultural and linguistic background.

Article 21

States Parties that recognize and/or permit the system of adoption shall ensure that the best interests of the child shall be the paramount consideration and they shall:

(a) Ensure that the adoption of a child is authorized only by competent authorities who determine, in accordance with applicable law and procedures and on the basis of all pertinent and reliable information, that the adoption is permissible in view of the child's status concerning parents, relatives and legal guardians and that, if required, the persons concerned have given their informed consent to the adoption on the basis of such counselling as may be necessary;

(b) Recognize that inter-country adoption may be considered as an alternative means of child's care, if the child cannot be placed in a foster or an adoptive family or cannot in any suitable manner be cared for in the child's country of origin;

(c) Ensure that the child concerned by inter-country adoption enjoys safeguards and standards equivalent to those existing in the case of national adoption;

(d) Take all appropriate measures to ensure that, in inter-country adoption, the placement does not result in improper financial gain for those involved in it;

(e) Promote, where appropriate, the objectives of the present article by concluding bilateral or multilateral arrangements or agreements, and endeavour, within this framework, to ensure that the placement of the child in another country is carried out by competent authorities or organs.

. . .

Article 24

1. States Parties recognize the right of the child to the enjoyment of the highest attainable standard of health and to facilities for the treatment of illness and rehabilitation of health. States Parties shall strive to ensure that no child is deprived of his or her right of access to such health care services.

. . .

Article 25

States Parties recognize the right of a child who has been placed by the competent authorities for the purposes of care, protection or treatment of his or her physical or mental health, to a periodic review of the treatment provided to the child and all other circumstances relevant to his or her placement.

. . .

Article 27

1. States Parties recognize the right of every child to a standard of living adequate for the child's physical, mental, spiritual, moral and social development.

2. The parent(s) or others responsible for the child have the primary responsibility to secure, within their abilities and financial capacities, the conditions of living necessary for the child's development.

3. States Parties, in accordance with national conditions and within their means, shall take appropriate measures to assist parents and others responsible for the child to implement this right and shall in case of need provide material assistance and support programmes, particularly with regard to nutrition, clothing and housing.

4. States Parties shall take all appropriate measures to secure the recovery of maintenance for the child from the parents or other persons having financial responsibility for the child, both within the State Party and from abroad. In particular, where the person having financial responsibility for the child lives in a State different from that of the child, States Parties shall promote the accession to international agreements or the conclusion of such agreements, as well as the making of other appropriate arrangements.

Article 28

1. States Parties recognize the right of the child to education, and with a view to achieving this right progressively and on the basis of equal opportunity, they shall, in particular:

    (a) Make primary education compulsory and available free to all;

    (b) Encourage the development of different forms of secondary education, including general and vocational education, make them available and accessible to every child, and take appropriate measures such as the introduction of free education and offering financial assistance in case of need;

    (c) Make higher education accessible to all on the basis of capacity by every appropriate means;

    (d) Make educational and vocational information and guidance available and accessible to all children;

    (e) Take measures to encourage regular attendance at schools and the reduction of drop-out rates.

2. States Parties shall take all appropriate measures to ensure that school discipline is administered in a manner consistent with the child's human dignity and in conformity with the present Convention.

3. States Parties shall promote and encourage international cooperation in matters relating to education, in particular with a view to contributing to the elimination of ignorance and illiteracy throughout the world and facilitating access to scientific and technical knowledge and modern teaching methods. In this regard, particular account shall be taken of the needs of developing countries.
    . . .

Article 34

States Parties undertake to protect the child from all forms of sexual exploitation and sexual abuse. For these purposes, States Parties shall in particular take all appropriate national, bilateral and multilateral measures to prevent:

(a) The inducement or coercion of a child to engage in any unlawful sexual activity;

(b) The exploitative use of children in prostitution or other unlawful sexual practices;

(c) The exploitative use of children in pornographic performances and materials.
. . .

Article 39

States Parties shall take all appropriate measures to promote physical and psychological recovery and social reintegration of a child victim of: any form of neglect, exploitation, or abuse; torture or any other form of cruel, inhuman or degrading treatment or punishment; or armed conflicts. Such recovery and reintegration shall take place in an environment which fosters the health, self-respect and dignity of the child.
. . .

§ 17.7 Conclusion

The twenty-first century has seen an increase in the mobility of families. Many child welfare cases involve interstate or international issues. Whether there has been a divorce or paternity action in another state, a visiting child reveals abuse or neglect, or a child's parent lives in a foreign state or country, child welfare attorneys and courts must be aware of the various laws that constrain the exercise of local jurisdiction to protect children or to make placements across state lines.

Chapter 18: Confidentiality[*]

by Ann M. Haralambie[1]

§ 18.1 Introduction

Confidentiality in child welfare practice involves both state and federal laws. Not only does the law determine what matters are deemed confidential, but also who is entitled to assert or waive confidentiality and what formalities are required to obtain confidential records. Ordinarily, state law provides people with an evidentiary privilege that protects their communications with medical and mental health professionals. For the privilege to arise, it is generally required that the communication be made with the intention that it remain confidential, that the confidentiality be essential to the relationship, that the relationship be one that society wishes to foster, and that the injury of disclosure be greater than the benefit to be gained for the correct disposition of the litigation.[2] Wigmore took the position that privileges, being in derogation of common law, are disfavored and are to be strictly construed or eliminated altogether.[3] However, many courts are loath to lightly set aside privileges, and in some states some privileges are constitutionally protected privacy interests.[4] Exercise or waiver of privileges involves balancing the holder's privacy rights, the public policy benefits of extending privilege to encourage full disclosure in confidential settings, and the court's need to have complete information. Where a child's safety is concerned, the public policy scale may tip towards disclosure.

In general, adults control release of their own confidential records, and the parents or legal guardians generally control release of children's records. But when families are involved in child welfare proceedings, parents may lose the right to control access to their children's records, and it is not always clear who then steps into the parent's position: the agency, the child's attorney, or the court itself? Further, when the records were produced through the court process itself, such as in court-ordered evaluations, examinations, and therapy, there is a question about whether confidentiality ever attached to the professional relationships and records. The records of child protective services and of the dependency court proceedings themselves may be covered by

---

[*] This chapter is based in part on portions of several chapters in the first edition of this book.

[1] Ann M. Haralambie, J.D., is a certified family law specialist practicing in Tucson, Arizona. She is also an author and speaker in the fields of family and children's law.

[2] *See, e.g.*, JOHN H. WIGMORE, EVIDENCE IN TRIALS AT COMMON LAW 2285 (1961).

[3] *See, e.g.*, EDWARD J. IMWINKELRIED, THE NEW WIGMORE: EVIDENTIARY PRIVILEGES § 3.2.2 (2002).

[4] *See, e.g.*, People v. Hammon, 15 Cal. 4th 1117, 938 P.2d 986 (1997) (defendant in child sexual abuse prosecution denied access to his victim foster daughter's therapy records; therapist-patient privilege is an aspect of the constitutional right of privacy).

confidentiality laws. Finally, child welfare court proceedings may be deemed confidential, and not only the public in general, but non-party friends and relatives of the parents and children may be barred from attending the proceedings.

While the federal law has generally tightened confidentiality of the records it governs, states have been experimenting with loosening the restrictions on access to child welfare court proceedings.[5]

This chapter will deal briefly with the major ways in which confidentiality, other than confidentiality in the attorney-client relationship, is involved in the practice of child welfare law.

§ 18.2 When Confidentiality Generally Does Not Apply

§ 18.2.1 Court-Ordered Evaluations and Examinations

Court-ordered examinations and evaluations generally do not create confidential professional relationships that shield the patient from disclosure of information to the court.[6] This is because the reason for the professional examination or evaluation is explicitly to provide information to the court and parties for use in the legal proceeding. Nevertheless, the health care professional, as part of the standard informed consent procedure, should specifically inform the patient that nothing said or discovered during the examination or evaluation is confidential and that the results will be disclosed to the court, child welfare agency, and/or the other parties to the legal proceeding. The therapist-patient privilege might apply to communications made during court-ordered therapy.[7] The fact that a parent did or did not attend court-ordered therapy would not be deemed privileged. It would be helpful for the court ordering therapy to specify whether or not the sessions will be covered by privilege.

§ 18.2.2 Child Abuse and Neglect Reporting

All states have mandatory reporting statutes, but there are some differences among the various states concerning who must report and the circumstances under which reports must be made.[8] Typically, professionals who deal with children are required to report suspicion of abuse. If they fail to do so, they may suffer criminal or

---

[5] For a discussion of public access to child welfare proceedings, see § 18.5, Confidentiality of Juvenile Court Proceedings.

[6] *See* FED. R. EVID. 706 and the state rules patterned after it. *See also In re* Jones, 99 Ohio St. 3d 203, 790 N.E.2d 321 (2003) (statements made by mother to licensed psychologist or licensed social worker in the course of forensic examinations ordered for child dependency proceeding were not privileged).

[7] *See, e.g., In re* Jones, 99 Ohio St. 3d 203, 790 N.E.2d 321 (2003) (privilege applies for statements mother made to licensed independent social worker during therapy in child dependency proceeding, even though therapist was working primarily with the children because the participation was treatment-focused, with goal of getting mother to change her own behavior and develop healthy and constructive relationship with her children).

[8] *See generally* SETH C. KALICHMAN, MANDATED REPORTING OF SUSPECTED CHILD ABUSE: ETHICS, LAW & POLICY (1993).

civil penalties. Under some statutes, professionals are required to report suspicion of abuse if the suspicion originates from the professional's observation or examination of the child (as opposed to merely hearing about the abuse from a person other than the child). Doctors, nurses, teachers, psychologists, and daycare workers who have a reasonable *suspicion* of abuse generally must make a report, even if they would not be in a position to testify that they held a professional opinion that abuse had occurred. In other words, it is the duty of child protective services or law enforcement to investigate suspected abuse. It is not the reporter's obligation to conduct an investigation.

Professional privileges for confidential communications are generally abrogated by the mandatory reporting laws.[9] However, in some states a few privileges remain and excuse an otherwise mandated reporter from making a report if the source of the suspicion is a privileged communication. In Nevada and Ohio, for example, attorneys and clergy are mandated reporters. Both states, however, have exceptions for privileged communications between attorney and client, and between clergy and penitent. If the abuse is disclosed during a privileged conversation, these specific mandated reporters are not required to report it.

§ 18.3 Confidentiality of Records

Child welfare attorneys often deal with records of parents and children that are confidential under the law and therefore entitled to an evidentiary privilege.[10] If there is a non-privileged option through which the relevant information may be obtained, privileges are generally upheld, even in child welfare cases. Therefore, for example, courts may order parents to undergo evaluations or examinations, in which case there is no expectation of confidentiality, and no evidentiary privilege attaches to the communications. The results of the evaluation may obviate the need for obtaining the parent's private therapy records.

The most direct way to obtain such records is with the informed, written consent of the person about whom the records pertain or, if the person is a minor, the consent of the parent or legal guardian. However, for medical and psychotherapy records, the consent now required under federal law is something more than the typical authorization for release of information routinely used by attorneys, and specific information must be included. For example, where subpoenas are administratively issued, instead of being issued by a judge, a health care provider might not release the records or might send them to the court under seal for *in camera* inspection. The court can refuse

---

[9] *See generally* JOHN E. B. MYERS, EVIDENCE IN CHILD ABUSE AND NEGLECT CASES §§ 1.12–1.19 (2d ed. 1992); ANN M. HARALAMBIE, 2 HANDLING CHILD CUSTODY, ABUSE AND ADOPTION CASES 3D § 12:23 (West 2009).

[10] For a good discussion of accessing children's records in child welfare cases, see Kathleen McNaught, *Mythbusting: Breaking Down Confidentiality and Decision-Making Barriers to Meet the Education Needs of Children in Foster Care* (2005), *available at* http://www.abanet.org/child/education/publications/mythbusting2.pdf.

to disclose the records or can disclose only a redacted copy containing only what is necessary, maintaining as much confidentiality as possible.

Release of substance abuse treatment records are covered by a separate federal law that requires a specific release or court order with specific findings.[11] Therefore, even subpoenas and court orders may not be sufficient to obtain covered records unless they specifically comply with federal law.

In addition to the federal confidentiality laws discussed in this chapter, attorneys should be aware of their own state laws regarding confidentiality. The U.S. Department of Justice Office of Juvenile Justice and Delinquency Prevention (OJJDP) maintains a Web site collecting current state laws on juvenile justice and child welfare record privacy, particularly with respect to interagency information sharing.[12]

§ 18.3.1 Child Abuse and Neglect Records

Pursuant to CAPTA,[13] states must keep child abuse and neglect reports confidential except as explicitly provided by federal law.[14] Where certain disclosure is permitted, CAPTA prohibits re-disclosure of that confidential information without consent. Once the information is released to these authorized recipients, they become subject to the same confidentiality rules as the releasing agency. More than half the states permit public disclosure in the case of child fatalities or near fatalities,[15] which is explicitly permitted by CAPTA.[16] A few states permit disclosure if the abuser has been arrested or criminally charged.[17] Some states allow limited information to be provided to reporting sources summarizing the outcome of the investigation

---

[11] *See* § 18.3.3, Substance Abuse Treatment Records.

[12] See their Web page titled "State Statutes on Juvenile Interagency Information & Record Sharing" at http://dept.fvtc.edu/childprotectiontraining/states.htm.

[13] 42 U.S.C. § 5106a(b)(2)(A)(viii).

[14] Exceptions exist, *inter alia*, for disclosure to individuals who are the subject of the report, government entities that have a need for such information in order to carry out their responsibilities under law to protect children from abuse and neglect, child abuse citizen review panels, child fatality review panels, a grand jury or court, upon a finding that information in the record is necessary for the determination of an issue before the court or grand jury, and other entities or classes of individuals statutorily authorized by the State to receive such information pursuant to a legitimate State purpose. 42 U.S.C. § 5106a(b)(2)(A)(viii).

[15] Alabama, Arizona, Arkansas, Colorado, Connecticut, Florida, Georgia, Illinois, Indiana, Iowa, Kansas, Kentucky, Louisiana, Maine, Michigan, Mississippi, Missouri, Nebraska, Nevada, New Jersey, New Mexico, New York, Oregon, Rhode Island, South Dakota, West Virginia, and Wisconsin. *See* Child Welfare Information Gateway, *Disclosure of Confidential Child Abuse and Neglect Records* (2008), *available at* http://www.childwelfare.gov/systemwide/laws_policies/statutes/confide.cfm.

[16] 42 U.S.C. § 5106a(b)(2)(A)(x).

[17] Minnesota, North Carolina, Oklahoma, and Wisconsin. *See* Child Welfare Information Gateway, *Disclosure of Confidential Child Abuse and Neglect Records* (2008), *available at* http://www.childwelfare.gov/systemwide/laws_policies/statutes/confide.cfm.

conducted pursuant to the report.[18] The records, usually with the reporting source redacted, are generally available to the parties in the child welfare case and their attorneys. Some states also permit certain information to be shared with the child's foster parents.[19]

Courts may preclude parties from otherwise disclosing records they have received through the child welfare proceeding. Further, confidential child welfare records disclosed pursuant to Title IV-B of the Social Security Act or CAPTA may not be redisclosed by the recipients unless the redisclosure also complies with Title IV-B of the Social Security Act or CAPTA.[20] In other words, the recipient is governed by the same legal rules as the agency that initially released the information, and there are penalties for unauthorized redisclosure. It is prudent for attorneys to obtain an order allowing disclosure to independent consultants or experts as part of trial preparation. It can be argued that there is implied authorization for such further disclosure, but any secondary disclosure should be made with written restrictions on further disclosure by the third party.

§ 18.3.2 Health Records and HIPAA[21]

Congress enacted the Health Insurance Portability and Accountability Act of 1996[22] (HIPAA), in relevant part, to establish national standards for electronic health care transactions that ensure the security and privacy of patient information and to provide for patient access to their own health records. In addition to medical and dental records, psychotherapy notes are covered under HIPAA.[23] Because a violation of HIPAA can involve both civil and criminal penalties to a health care provider who

---

[18] Arkansas, California, Connecticut, Georgia, Iowa, Louisiana, Maine, Massachusetts, Minnesota, Mississippi, Nebraska, Nevada, New Hampshire, New Jersey, North Dakota, Ohio, Pennsylvania, Rhode Island, Vermont, Wisconsin, and Wyoming. *See* Child Welfare Information Gateway, *Disclosure of Confidential Child Abuse and Neglect Records* (2008), *available at* http://www.childwelfare.gov/systemwide/laws_policies/statutes/confide.cfm.

[19] For example, Arizona, Arkansas, Illinois, Kansas, Louisiana, Maine, Montana, New Hampshire, New Jersey, New Mexico, Oklahoma, Pennsylvania, South Carolina, South Dakota, Texas, and Wisconsin. *See* Child Welfare Information Gateway, *Disclosure of Confidential Child Abuse and Neglect Records* (2008), *available at* http://www.childwelfare.gov/systemwide/laws_policies/statutes/confide.cfm.

[20] *See, e.g.,* 45 C.F.R. § 205.50.

[21] This section was co-authored by Andrea Khoury, J.D. She is an Assistant Staff Director at the American Bar Association Center on Children and the Law. She has represented children in abuse and neglect proceedings for over twelve years.

[22] Pub. L. No. 104-191, 110 Stat. 1936 (codified as amended in scattered sections of 26, 29, 42 U.S.C.).

[23] "Psychotherapy notes means notes recorded (in any medium) by a health care provider who is a mental health professional documenting or analyzing the contents of conversation during a private counseling session or a group, joint, or family counseling session and that are separated from the rest of the individual's medical record. Psychotherapy notes excludes medication prescription and monitoring, counseling session start and stop times, the modalities and frequencies of treatment furnished, results of clinical tests, and any summary of the following items: Diagnosis, functional status, the treatment plan, symptoms, prognosis, and progress to date." 45 C.F.R. § 164.501.

releases records, most health care providers err on the side on nondisclosure to third parties when there is any question about authorization.

The Standards for Privacy of Individually Identifiable Health Information ("Privacy Rule"), enacted by the U.S. Department of Health and Human Services, incorporated federal privacy protection for individually identifiable health information held or transmitted by a covered entity or its business associate in any form or media, whether electronic, paper, or oral.[24] A covered entity (including health care providers) may not use or disclose protected health information (PHI) without authorization from the individual who is the subject of the PHI or for other permissible uses allowed under the Privacy Rule. "All authorizations must be in plain language, and contain specific information regarding the information to be disclosed or used, the person(s) disclosing and receiving the information, expiration, right to revoke in writing, and other data."[25]

Relevant exceptions to this rule are:

- HIPAA rules do not apply where the provision of state law provides for the reporting of disease or injury, child abuse, or for the conduct of a public health investigation.[26]

- A covered entity may use or disclose PHI for treatment, payment, or health care operations.[27]

- PHI can be disclosed in response to court or administrative orders or by subpoena, discovery request, or other lawful process.[28]

- A covered entity can disclose PHI to a "public health authority that is authorized by law to receive reports of child abuse or neglect."[29]

The Privacy Rule does not prevent reports of suspected abuse to the proper authorities when state law provides for reporting. In most states, the child welfare agency is the public health authority that receives the abuse and neglect reports.[30]

Child welfare professionals should seek an individual's authorization when attempting to receive protected health information. Many health care providers have

---

[24] United States Department of Health and Human Services, OCR Privacy Brief, *Summary of the HIPAA Privacy Rule* (2003), *available at* http://www.hhs.gov/ocr/privacy/hipaa/understanding/summary/index.html.

[25] United States Department of Health and Human Services, OCR Privacy Brief, *Summary of the HIPAA Privacy Rule,* p. 9 (2003), *available at* http://www.hhs.gov/ocr/privacy/hipaa/understanding/summary/index.html.

[26] 45 C.F.R. § 160.203(c).

[27] 45 C.F.R. § 164.506(a).

[28] 45 C.F.R. § 164.512(e) and (f).

[29] 45 C.F.R. § 164.512 (b)(1)(ii).

[30] Committee on Child Abuse and Neglect, *Policy Statement: Child abuse, Confidentiality and the Health Insurance Portability and Accountability Act*, 125/1 PEDIATRICS 197 (2010), *available at* http://pediatrics.aappublications.org/cgi/content/abstract/125/1/197.

their own authorization forms that comply with HIPAA and will be readily recognized by the records clerk responding to a request for confidential records. The authorization must describe the type of information that must be disclosed, the name of the person or agency to whom disclosure should be made, the purpose of the disclosure, and the date on which the authorization will expire. If the need for access to records extends beyond the expiration date, a new authorization must be obtained.

If the authorization is not forthcoming, access to a child's or parent(s)' PHI may be obtained through a judge-issued subpoena or court order. An administratively issued subpoena that was not signed by a judge is insufficient under HIPAA. Before obtaining a subpoena or court order, the Privacy Rule requires that the party seeking the information has made reasonable efforts to ensure that the individual who is the subject of the PHI has been given notice of the request and the opportunity to object[31] or that the individual seeking the information has sought a qualified protective order prohibiting the parties from using or disclosing the PHI for any purpose other than the proceeding for which the information was requested and requiring the destruction of the PHI (or return to the covered entity) at the end of the proceeding.[32] The child welfare professional should then retain a copy of the subpoena and document the information provided.

When a covered entity discloses PHI in compliance with a court order or subpoena issued by a judicial officer, the covered entity must ensure that the information sought is relevant and is limited in scope to satisfy the purpose for the information.[33] Therefore, the subpoena or court order must specify the scope of records sought to ensure that all relevant records are produced.

§ 18.3.3 Substance Abuse Treatment Records

Federal law, 42 C.F.R. Part 2, provides strengthened confidentiality protections specifically for records concerning substance abuse diagnosis or treatment, over and above the HIPAA protections for health care records in general.[34] "Records of the identity, diagnosis, prognosis, or treatment of any patient which are maintained in connection with the performance of any drug abuse prevention function conducted, regulated, or directly or indirectly assisted by any department or agency of the United States Substance abuse treatment records from facilities which receive federal funding, directly or indirectly,"[35] are confidential and may not be disclosed without

---

[31] 45 C.F.R. § 164.512(e).

[32] 45 C.F.R. § 164.512(e).

[33] 45 C.F.R. § 164.512(f).

[34] Substance abuse treatment programs that are subject to HIPAA must also comply with the HIPAA Privacy Rule. *See generally* United States Department of Health and Human Services, *The Confidentiality of Alcohol and Drug Abuse Patient Records Regulation and the HIPAA Privacy Rule: Implications for Alcohol and Substance Abuse Programs* (June 2004), *available at* http://www.hipaa.samhsa.gov/download2/SAMHSAPart2-HIPAAComparison2004.pdf.

[35] 42 U.S.C. § 290dd-2(a).

the patient's specific written consent or a court order based upon a specific showing of good cause.[36] The court may order disclosure of the patient's confidential communications only if the disclosure "is necessary to protect against an existing threat to life or of serious bodily injury, including circumstances which constitute suspected child abuse and neglect and verbal threats against third parties."[37] Any order permitting disclosure of protected records must also include appropriate safeguards against unauthorized disclosure.[38]

The federal regulations specify the procedure to be followed if the patient has not consented to disclosure:

> (a) *Application.* An order authorizing the disclosure of patient records for purposes other than criminal investigation or prosecution may be applied for by any person having a legally recognized interest in the disclosure which is sought. The application may be filed separately or as part of a pending civil action in which it appears that the patient records are needed to provide evidence. An application must use a fictitious name, such as John Doe, to refer to any patient and may not contain or otherwise disclose any patient identifying information unless the patient is the applicant or has given a written consent (meeting the requirements of these regulations) to disclosure or the court has ordered the record of the proceeding sealed from public scrutiny.

> (b) *Notice.* The patient and the person holding the records from whom disclosure is sought must be given:

> (1) Adequate notice in a manner which will not disclose patient identifying information to other persons; and

> (2) An opportunity to file a written response to the application, or to appear in person, for the limited purpose of providing evidence on the statutory and regulatory criteria for the issuance of the court order.

> (c) *Review of evidence: Conduct of hearing.* Any oral argument, review of evidence, or hearing on the application must be held in the judge's chambers or in some manner which ensures that patient identifying information is not disclosed to anyone other than a party to the proceeding, the patient, or the person holding the record, unless the patient requests an open hearing in a manner which meets the written consent requirements of these regulations. The proceeding

---

[36] 42 U.S.C. § 290dd–2(b) (there are also exceptions for medical emergencies and for disclosure of non-identifying information for scientific research, audits, or evaluations). *See also* 42 U.S.C. § 290dd-2(b)(2)(C); 42 U.S.C. § 290dd; 42 C.F.R. §§ 2.1, 2.2.

[37] 42 C.F.R. § 2.63(a)(1).

[38] 42 U.S.C. § 290dd-2(b)(2)(C).

may include an examination by the judge of the patient records referred to in the application.

(d) *Criteria for entry of order:* An order under this section may be entered only if the court determines that good cause exists. To make this determination the court must find that:

(1) Other ways of obtaining the information are not available or would not be effective; and

(2) The public interest and need for the disclosure outweigh the potential injury to the patient, the physician-patient relationship and the treatment services.

(e) *Content of order.* An order authorizing a disclosure must:

(1) Limit disclosure to those parts of the patient's record which are essential to fulfill the objective of the order;

(2) Limit disclosure to those persons whose need for information is the basis for the order; and

(3) Include such other measures as are necessary to limit disclosure for the protection of the patient, the physician-patient relationship and the treatment services; for example, sealing from public scrutiny the record of any proceeding for which disclosure of a patient's record has been ordered.[39]

State law cannot authorize disclosure of the protected records other than as provided by the federal regulations. Therefore, for example, a general statutory authorization or court order providing that a child's attorney or guardian ad litem will have access to all records would not by itself permit disclosure of protected records, even to the child patient's own attorney.

Substance abuse records are not subject to a subpoena unless the subpoena is accompanied by an order meeting the criteria listed above. Further, a provider is not required to, but may, disclose the confidential records based solely on an order that meets the criteria, unless the order is accompanied by a subpoena or other compulsory process.[40]

Disclosure or use of the confidential records in violation of the federal law or violation of any part of the relevant regulations subjects the violator to criminal penalties and fines. Therefore, an attorney seeking access to substance abuse records must be very careful to comply in all respects with 42 C.F.R. § 2.64. Because the records of most child welfare proceedings are sealed, a fictitious name will not ordinarily be necessary. However, some states are opening their child welfare

---

[39] 42 C.F.R. § 2.64.

[40] 42 C.F.R. § 2.61.

proceedings to the public,[41] and attorneys should be aware that under such circumstances they will be subject to criminal sanction if they do not use a fictitious name in their applications for substance abuse diagnostic or treatment records.

§ 18.3.4 School Records—FERPA

Confidentiality of school records is governed by the Family Education Rights and Privacy Act[42] (FERPA), as amended by the Improving America's School Act (IASA).[43] Generally, FERPA provides that parents have a right to access to their children's school records and that third parties do not have access to such records without proper authorization. When the child becomes an "eligible student,"[44] the parent's rights are transferred to the student,[45] and subject to some exceptions, the parent becomes a third party with respect to the need for authorization to access the student's records. Where certain disclosure is permitted without consent,[46] such as pursuant to a court order, FERPA prohibits re-disclosure of that confidential information unless consent is obtained. There is no prohibition to redisclosure for persons who have obtained school records with consent. There is also an exception to the general prohibition of redisclosure when the prior consent of the parent or "eligible student" is not required under 34 C.F.R. § 99.31, and the party complies with the reporting requirements found at 34 C.F.R. § 99.32(b).

FERPA defines a parent as "a parent of a student and includes a natural parent, a guardian, or an individual acting as a parent in the absence of a parent or guardian."[47] Even if the child is in the legal custody of the child welfare agency, that fact alone does not suspend the child's parent from also having access to school records unless

---

[41] For a discussion of public access to child welfare proceedings, see § 18.5, Confidentiality of Juvenile Court Proceedings.

[42] 20 U.S.C. §§ 1232g, 1232h.

[43] Pub. L. No. 103-382, 108 Stat. 3518 (1984).

[44] "Eligible student means a student who has reached 18 years of age or is attending an institution of postsecondary education." 34 C.F.R. § 99.3.

[45] 34 C.F.R. § 99.5. Therefore, a child who has reached the age of 18 or is in college has a right to access all of his or her school records and must consent to a third party's access.

[46] "The most relevant exceptions to child welfare professionals that permit disclosure without prior consent are to: [1] other school officials, including teachers, with legitimate educational interest in the child; [2] appropriate persons in connection with an emergency, when the information is needed to protect the health and safety of the student or other persons (Note: used for health and safety emergencies where immediate release of the information is necessary to control a serious situation); [3] officials of other schools when a student is transferring schools; [4] state and local authorities within the department of juvenile justice, if your state statute permits disclosure (Note: currently only Florida and Illinois have such statutes); and [5] appropriate persons when the release of information is needed to comply with a judicial order or subpoena." Kathleen McNaught, *Mythbusting: Breaking Down Confidentiality and Decision-Making Barriers to Meet the Education Needs of Children in Foster Care* (2005) [citations omitted], *available at* http://www.abanet.org/child/education/publications/mythbusting2.pdf.

[47] 34 C.F.R. § 99.3.

parental rights have been terminated or the parent's right to access has been restricted by court order.

§ 18.3.5 School Records—IDEA

Records concerning services received under the Individuals with Disabilities Education Act (IDEA),[48] are "education records" under FERPA and are therefore subject to the confidentiality provisions of FERPA. In addition, IDEA provides its own confidentiality requirements. In the process of determining whether or not a student is eligible for services under IDEA, the school may compile many records concerning the child and family that go beyond the normal school records. An agency or institution that collects, maintains, or uses personally identifiable information, or from which information is obtained, under Part B of IDEA is also a "participating agency"[49] subject to the Part B Confidentiality of Information requirements.[50] The school "must protect the confidentiality of personally identifiable information at collection, storage, disclosure, and destruction stages."[51] The Secretary of Education is required "to ensure the protection of the confidentiality of any personally identifiable data, information, and records collected or maintained by the Secretary and by State educational agencies and local educational agencies."[52]

The child's parents have a right to inspect and review the IDEA records and to consent to the release of the records to third parties. However, IDEA's definition of a parent is more specific and narrow than the definition of a parent in FERPA and includes:

> (A) a natural, adoptive, or foster parent of a child (unless a foster parent is prohibited by State law from serving as a parent);
>
> (B) a guardian (but not the State if the child is a ward of the State);
>
> (C) an individual acting in the place of a natural or adoptive parent (including a grandparent, stepparent, or other relative) with whom the child lives, or an individual who is legally responsible for the child's welfare; or
>
> (D) . . . an individual assigned ... to be a surrogate parent.[53]

Notably, IDEA specifically excludes the child welfare agency ("the State") from the definition of "guardian" for purposes of the Act, even if the agency is the child's legal guardian.

---

[48] 20 U.S.C. §§ 1400 *et seq.*, 34 C.F.R. Part 300. *See generally* Chapter 22, Education Goals for Children in Foster Care and the Role of Attorneys.

[49] *See* 34 C.F.R. § 300.611(c).

[50] Confidentiality of information is covered in 34 C.F.R. §§ 300.610–300.627.

[51] 34 C.F.R. § 300.623(a).

[52] 20 U.S.C. § 1417(c).

[53] 20 U.S.C. § 1401(23).

§ 18.4 Who May Assert or Waive Confidential Privileges

The Federal Rules of Evidence rejected a proposed rule that would have detailed various privileges and waiver of those privileges, instead deferring to common law and state law.[54] States that have adopted rules patterned after the Federal Rules of Evidence have generally added rules after Rule 501 relating to what matters are privileged and, sometimes, who may assert or waive them.

Generally, privileges may be asserted or waived by the holder of the privilege or that person's legal representative. Competent adults may assert or waive the professional privilege related to their own confidential communications and records. Children are generally also entitled to the evidentiary benefits of professional privileges.[55] Children who have been victimized by their parents may be especially harmed by the casual breach of their confidential relationships.[56]

Who has the authority to exercise or waive such privileges on behalf of children? In a few states it is provided for by statute, case law, or court order. The professional may always assert the privilege on behalf of the patient or client (and may have a duty to do so) but may not waive the privilege. In some cases, both the children and their parents or guardians have an ability to assert or waive the child's privileges. Generally, parents who have custodial rights can assert or waive these privileges; however, where the parents are in a legally adverse posture with the child, it is generally held that the parent should not be permitted to assert or waive the objection on behalf of the child over the child's objection or to protect the parent from evidence of the child's injuries.[57] Where the child has an attorney or guardian ad litem, that

---

[54] FED. R. EVID. 501 (and Advisory Committee Notes).

[55] *See, e.g.*, CAL. WELF. & INST. CODE § 317(f) (the child is the holder of the privilege, or the child's attorney is the holder of the privilege if the court finds the child not to be of sufficient age and maturity; if a mature child invokes the privilege, counsel may not waive it, but if counsel invokes the privilege, the mature child may waive it).

[56] A Florida appellate court has expressed this persuasively: "Many children involved with service agencies have suffered repeated violations of their sense of personal privacy. They have been abused by parents or relatives, or transferred from one foster care placement to another, or treated like commodities on an assembly line by harried or overworked agency staff. Respect for confidentiality rights is particularly crucial for such children. It allows them to exert some measure of control over their world, and to develop a degree of trust in those around them. . . . We recognize that a guardian ad litem has an interest in inquiring into the child's progress in therapy. Nevertheless, we conclude that [the child] has a right to assert the therapist/patient privilege." S.C. v. Guardian ad Litem, 845 So. 2d 953, 960 (Fla. App. 4 Dist. 2003).

[57] *See, e.g.*, *In re* Berg, 152 N.H. 658, 886 A.2d 980 (2005) (denying parent an automatic right to access to child's therapy records over child's objection in a custody proceeding, holding that the court must engage in fact-finding to determine whether waiver or assertion of the privilege is in the best interests of the child); McCormack v. Bd. of Educ. of Baltimore County, 158 Md. App. 292, 857 A.2d 159 (2004) (the test for determining whether the appointment of a guardian is necessary is whether there is a conflict of interest between parent and child so substantial that it imperils a significant interest of the child); *In re* Daniel C.H., 220 Cal. App. 3d 814, 269 Cal. Rptr. 624 (1990) (in a dependency proceeding, except in very special circumstances, if disclosure would have a detrimental effect on the child, a

person may be deemed the proper person to exercise the privilege on the child's behalf, but the child may have an independent right to notice and a hearing if he or she objects to a proposed waiver.[58] Courts may even appoint a guardian ad litem for the purpose of deciding whether to assert or waive the child's privilege.[59]

Where the child is a ward of the court—that is, where the court already has formal authority over the child—the court itself may have the power to assert or waive privileges,[60] or the agency having legal guardianship may have that power. In some jurisdictions, a judge other than the judge hearing the case will consider and rule on whether the privilege should be waived. Because state laws on these issues are generally not well developed, perhaps no one clearly possesses the legal authority to enter a waiver on behalf of a child.

Where local law permits children to waive confidentiality, or where the law is not clear, the attorney must determine whether the child has the capacity to make an informed waiver. Functional capacity exists on a continuum, even for adults. Many factors contribute to whether a child has sufficient capacity to make a waiver with respect to a particular issue at a particular time, and there is no bright line test for determining capacity.[61]

Children's capacity to waive rights has been considered most often in the context of juvenile delinquency cases. The United States Supreme Court has held that juveniles may have the capacity to waive their constitutional rights. In that context, mental health professionals and some courts have found that children's actual capacity to waive rights has been overestimated. In assessing whether a child has capacity to waive constitutional rights, a crucial issue is the child's ability to appreciate the consequences of the waiver. It is at the developmental stage of formal operations, which begins around age 12, when the child develops the ability to appreciate consequences of decisions. However, the protections offered by assertion of constitutional rights in a delinquency setting raise different concerns than the protections provided by ethical rules about conflict of interest or assertion of testimonial privileges.

---

parent may not waive the child's therapist-patient privilege); *In re* Adoption of Diane, 400 Mass. 196, 508 N.E.2d 837, 840 (1987) (in an adoption proceeding, where the parent and child may well have conflicting interests, the mother could not assert the child's therapist-patient privilege, especially where neither the child's attorney nor the guardian ad litem chose to exercise the privilege); *In re* M___ P___ S___, 342 S.W.2d 277 (Mo. App. 1961) (in neglect proceeding, mother could not invoke the child's privilege to bar the attending physician from testifying).

[58] *See, e.g.*, S.C. v. Guardian ad Litem, 845 So. 2d 953 (Fla. App. 4 Dist. 2003) (a 14-year-old dependent child may assert a psychotherapist/patient privilege to deny guardian ad litem access to therapeutic records; to the extent the court may have authority to invade the minor's privilege, its exercise must, at a minimum, include notice to the minor and an opportunity to be heard).

[59] *See, e.g.*, MD CODE, COURTS AND JUDICIAL PROCEEDINGS, § 9-109(c) (if a patient is incompetent to assert or waive the therapist-patient privilege, a guardian must be appointed and must act for the patient).

[60] *See, e.g., In re* D.K., 245 N.W.2d 644 (S.D. 1976) (it is within the court's power to waive the privilege on behalf of the neglected or dependent child to permit the physician to testify when the mother's treatment of the child was the critical question).

[61] *See* § 29.4, Determining Decision-Making Capacity.

Further, the goals of juvenile justice and the child welfare system are different, and statutory rights of confidentiality may not be the equivalent of constitutional rights.

Children's capacity to give informed consent has also been considered in the context of medical or mental health treatment. The United States Supreme Court and lower courts have adopted the doctrine of the "mature minor," who is permitted to make certain medical decisions without parental involvement. In obtaining informed consent on a child-friendly level, the medical or mental health professional will explain the consequences to the child. Similarly, the child's attorney must explain the likely or possible short- and long-term consequences of the child's direction. However, before the child has reached the stage of formal operations (and children in child welfare proceedings are often developmentally delayed or impaired), the child is not likely to have the capacity to appreciate the impact of the consequences on his or her life, even when the consequences have been explained.

Attorneys, by training, rarely have any specialized skills in judging a person's legal capacity. When undertaking such a task, it is easy to confuse capacity and wisdom. The fact that the child—or even an adult client—makes choices that the attorney disagrees with or that are foolish does not necessarily indicate that the child lacks capacity to make the choice. Further, the attorney may have a great deal of influence over how the child chooses to address waiver issues, with many children merely following the attorney's advice. It is tempting to assume that because the child is following the attorney's advice, the child must possess adequate capacity to make the decision. Therefore, the determination of capacity should be made thoughtfully, based on consideration of many factors, perhaps with the input of other adults who know the child well or have specialized training in the field, such as teachers or mental health professionals. Comment 6 to revised Rule 1.14 of the Model Rules of Professional Responsibility[62] provides:

> In determining the extent of the client's diminished capacity, the lawyer should consider and balance such factors as: the client's ability to articulate reasoning leading to a decision, variability of state of mind and ability to appreciate consequences of a decision; the substantive fairness of a decision; and the consistency of a decision with the known long-term commitments and values of the client. In appropriate circumstances, the lawyer may seek guidance from an appropriate diagnostician.

Most mental health professionals do not have adequate training to determine whether the child has adequate capacity to waive conflicts and privileges. That determination is very specialized. Child development experts may be aware of some means to assess the child's capacity, but as of the writing of this edition, there are no tests or batteries of tests that will provide a definitive answer. Whether or not a particular child can

---

[62] AMERICAN BAR ASSOCIATION, MODEL RULES OF PROFESSIONAL RESPONSIBILITY (2002).

give informed consent to waive a particular right will remain a problem for future resolution.

Even in situations where a child does not have the legal right to consent to disclosure of his or her own records, the child's attorney or guardian ad litem should consider obtaining the child's written consent in addition to the consent of the legal guardian or a court order. For a child old enough to appreciate the concept of confidentiality, it is a matter of respect to allow the child to consent. Of course, if the child withholds consent, the attorney must explain that other parties may be able to obtain the records without the child's consent. In appropriate circumstances, the attorney may want to interpose an objection to disclosure on the child's behalf.

§ 18.5 Confidentiality of Juvenile Court Proceedings[63]

Confidentiality of juvenile court proceedings and records has long been an element of the juvenile dependency court process. The longstanding assumption has been that maintaining the confidentiality of juvenile court proceedings, as well as maintaining confidentiality of juvenile court records, protects the children involved. More recently, critics have suggested that the secrecy created by closed courts is not healthy and is not the most conducive to good outcomes. Many states are debating the potential benefits of opening juvenile court proceedings and records. In the Child Abuse Prevention and Treatment Act (CAPTA) amendments of 2003, Congress provided states with the flexibility to allow public access to court proceedings that determine child abuse and neglect, so long as policies ensure the safety and well-being of the child, parents, and families.[64]

Historically, the Supreme Court has enforced the public's First Amendment right to access, requiring open court proceedings unless a court orders otherwise. The Court has applied a two-prong analysis to determine whether criminal proceedings should be open, considering the history of access to a proceeding and the function of the proceeding.[65] The rationale behind the Court's decision to open proceedings included the importance of increased public understanding and confidence in the judicial process.[66] In *Globe Newspaper Co. v. Superior Court*,[67] the Supreme Court rejected the Massachusetts Supreme Court's decision to close a sex offense trial during the testimony of minor victims. The court ruled that closing a criminal proceeding, even for a limited amount of time, violated the First Amendment.

---

[63] This section is updated from Chapter 13 of the first edition of this book, which was co-authored with Amanda George Donnelly.

[64] Child Abuse Prevention and Treatment Act (CAPTA), as amended by The Keeping Children and Families Safe Act of 2003, 42 U.S.C. § 5106a(b)(2)(D).

[65] *See* Richmond Newspaper, Inc. v. Virginia, 448 U.S. 555 (1980) (plurality opinion) (recognizing right of access to criminal trials through the First and Fourteenth Amendments).

[66] *See* Heidi S. Schellhas, *Children in the Law Issue: Contributors Open Child Protection Proceedings in Minnesota*, 26 WM. MITCHELL L. REV. 631, 642 (2000).

[67] 457 U.S. 596 (1982).

Family law matters have traditionally been viewed as private proceedings. Confidentiality restrictions in child welfare proceedings exist to protect children and families from public exposure of the intimate details of their lives.[68] Even states with open courtrooms generally permit closure of the court during sensitive portions of proceedings, for instance, when a child is testifying. Many states, however, are questioning the value of closed child welfare proceedings and considering the potential benefits of open proceedings.[69]

§ 18.5.1 Pros and Cons of Open Court Proceedings

In the mid-1960s, in the juvenile delinquency context, the United States Supreme Court put constraints on the informality of juvenile courts and proceedings done in the name of not stigmatizing children.[70] As the public has clamored for delinquents to be treated more harshly for their crimes, there has been a parallel call to open delinquency hearings to the public, removing the perceived ability of the juvenile to "hide" in juvenile court. Proponents of open dependency courts approach the issue from another side. They question whether the confidentiality of juvenile court has, in fact, protected its most vulnerable subjects.

Advocates for opening child welfare proceedings argue that the secrecy actually protects the abusive parents, child welfare agencies, attorneys, and judges more than the children. They argue that an open system will increase public awareness and accountability.[71] Others argue that open proceedings will motivate the public to improve the child welfare system.[72] Additionally, some view open proceedings as an opportunity for the court to receive more accurate information in child protection proceedings by allowing families, friends, and neighbors to participate as witnesses.[73]

The Minnesota Supreme Court Foster Care Task Force conducted a three-year pilot project mandating open proceedings and records for neglect and termination of parental rights proceedings.[74] Minnesota's pilot project permitted access to all

---

[68] *See* MARK I. SOLER, A. C. SHOTTON & J. R. BELL, GLASS WALLS: CONFIDENTIALITY PROVISIONS AND INTERAGENCY COLLABORATIONS (Youth Law Center 1993).

[69] *See* Heidi S. Schellhas, *Children in the Law Issue: Contributors Open Child Protection Proceedings in Minnesota*, 26 WM. MITCHELL L. REV. 631, 644 (2000).

[70] *See, e.g.*, *In re* Gault, 387 U.S. 1, 28 (1967) ("the condition of being a boy does not justify a kangaroo court"); Kent v. United States, 383 U.S. 541, 544 (1966) ("there is no place in our system of law for reaching a result of such tremendous consequences without ceremony—without hearing, without effective assistance of counsel, without a statement of reasons").

[71] EVERY CHILD MATTERS & THE LEGACY FAMILY INSTITUTE, BALANCING ACCOUNTABILITY AND CONFIDENTIALITY IN CHILD WELFARE: SOURCEBOOK, at II-36 (2003).

[72] Barbara White Stack, *Few Problems, Benefits in Open Proceedings*, PITTSBURGH POST-GAZETTE, Sept. 30, 2001, *available at* http://www.post-gazette.com/regionstate/20010930minn0930p8.asp.

[73] Heidi S. Schellhas, *Contributors Open Child Protection Proceedings in Minnesota*, 26 WM. MITCHELL L. REV. 631, 666 (2000).

[74] *See* FRED. L. CHEESMAN, MINNESOTA SUPREME COURT STATE COURT ADMINISTRATOR'S OFFICE, KEY FINDINGS FROM THE EVALUATION OF OPEN HEARINGS AND COURT RECORDS IN JUVENILE PROTECTION MATTERS: FINAL REPORT (2001).

documents, except those restricted by rules. Social Services and GAL files were not open, and judges could issue protective orders to keep any file closed. The National Center for State Courts evaluated Minnesota's project and concluded that "no devastating downsides or remarkable benefits" resulted from open proceedings.[75] In 2002, the Minnesota Supreme Court ordered dependency court proceedings presumptively open.[76]

State statues or court rules dictate access to proceedings and records in most jurisdictions. As of 2004, 16 states had open or presumptively open child welfare proceedings, and 10 states had presumptively closed, but judicial discretion to open proceedings; 19 states had closed proceedings for all cases, and 8 states had closed proceedings with some exceptions.[77] Each state with presumptively open proceedings has a provision to close the courtroom when it is determined to be in the best interest of the child involved.[78] A court could also be open but place restrictions on what observers could disclose outside of the courtroom. Judge Leonard Edwards argues that this provision allows the individual juvenile judge to balance the benefits with the specific needs of the family, especially the children.[79] A number of states have statutory regulations providing for presumptively closed proceedings with judicial discretion to open them.[80] Many jurisdictions, however, have continued with all closed proceedings.[81]

Opponents of open proceedings argue that open dependency proceedings could psychologically harm the children involved. A finding of the psychological analysis, developmental victimology, indicates that in sexual abuse cases a child's psychological distress is increased by self-blame for the abuse. Public exposure and the public's reaction to abuse appear to increase the child's self-blame, which impacts the duration and severity of the child's psychological trauma.[82]

---

[75] Barbara White Stack, *Few Problems, Benefits in Open Proceedings*, PITTSBURGH POST-GAZETTE, Sept. 30, 2001, *available at* http://www.post-gazette.com/regionstate/20010930minn0930p8.asp.

[76] State of Minnesota Supreme Court File No. C2-95-1476, "Order Mandating Public Access to Hearings and Records in Juvenile Protection Matters" (Dec. 26, 2001).

[77] *See* Kay Farley, National Center for State Courts, *Issue Brief: Public Access to Child Abuse and Neglect Proceedings* (May 2004), *available at* http://www.ncsconline.org/D_Gov/IssueBriefs/Brf-Opn-Crts-May-04.pdf.

[78] Lynne Tucker, *Open or Closed: A Survey of the Opinions and the Realities of Opening Juvenile Court Dependency Proceedings* (Barton Child Law and Policy Clinic at Emory University, Nov. 2000), *available at* http://www.childwelfare.net/activities/interns/2000summer/OpenCourts/.

[79] *See* Leonard P. Edwards, *Confidentiality and the Juvenile and Family Courts*, 55 JUV. & FAM. CT. J. 1 (2004).

[80] KAY FARLEY, PUBLIC ACCESS TO CHILD ABUSE AND NEGLECT PROCEEDINGS 3–4 (National Center for State Courts Issue Brief No. 5, 2003).

[81] *See* DIONNE MAXWELL ET AL., TO OPEN OR NOT TO OPEN: THE ISSUE OF PUBLIC ACCESS IN CHILD PROTECTION HEARINGS (NCJFCJ Technical Assistance Brief, 2004).

[82] *See* William Patton, *Revictimizing Child Abuse Victims: An Empirical Rebuttal to the Open Juvenile Dependency Court Reform Movement*, 38 SUFFOLK UNIV. L. REV. 303 (2005).

Additionally, opponents of open proceedings are concerned about the potential negative impact of open proceedings on the child welfare system. Advocates of closed proceedings note the risk for a decrease in admitting to allegations because the admissions would be made public. They are also concerned that open proceedings may cause more contested hearings and requests for closed hearings, resulting in increased costs and delayed placement of children.[83] The critics also point out that there are other mechanisms for overseeing the system, such as citizen review boards, which still maintain the family's confidentiality.

Critics of open proceedings doubt the value of the media's access to dependency proceedings. Many child advocates fear that the media will exploit children involved in dependency proceedings.[84] They argue that the media feeds on sensationalism and will likely expose identifying information of children involved. The media rarely report on dependency proceedings, and when they do they are under no ethical duty to withhold identifying information.[85]

NACC has adopted the position that courts should be presumptively closed, with the exception that judges should be allowed to open them on a case-by-case basis. The NACC position on Open Courts in Child Welfare Proceedings can be accessed on the NACC Web site.[86]

---

[83] William Patton, *Pandora's Box: Opening Child Protection Cases to the Press and Public*, 27 W. St. U. L. Rev. 181, 186 (1999/2000).

[84] Informal survey conducted on the NACC Listserv March 2003.

[85] *See* William Patton, *Revictimizing Child Abuse Victims: An Empirical Rebuttal to the Open Juvenile Dependency Court Reform Movement*, 38 Suffolk Univ. L. Rev. 303 (2005).

[86] *See* National Association of Counsel for Children, *Confidentiality of Juvenile Court Proceedings and Records* (NACC Policy Papers, adopted April 25, 1998), *available at* http://www.naccchildlaw.org/?page=Policy_Papers.

Chapter 19: Collateral Proceedings

by Ann M. Haralambie[1]

§ 19.1 Introduction

Although CAPTA requires that a child be represented in child protection cases,[2] many such children and youth may also be subject to other legal proceedings affecting their welfare or may have other legal remedies available to them that could address their safety and well-being. It is critical that the child's attorney become informed about, involved in, and perhaps even initiate such collateral proceedings as a way to meet the safety, permanency, and well-being needs of the client. Children's attorneys play a critical role in empowering children and ensuring that children's views are heard in legal proceedings that affect their lives. The following is a discussion of collateral proceedings commonly encountered by and available to children's attorneys.[3]

§ 19.2 Coordinating Legal Proceedings

Ideally, all legal proceedings affecting the same family will be heard by the same judge.[4] Although this "one-family one-judge" principle is reflected in policy recommendations[5] and in some state laws,[6] it is not universal. Some states have

---

[1]   Ann M. Haralambie, J.D., is a certified family law specialist practicing in Tucson, Arizona. She is also an author and speaker in the fields of family and children's law.

[2]   42 U.S.C. § 5106a(b)(2)(A)(xiii).

[3]   *See also* Chapter 20, Immigration Issues—Representing Children Who Are Not United States Citizens; Chapter 21, Advocacy for Foster Youth in Mental Health Commitment Proceedings; and Chapter 22, Education Goals for Children in Foster Care and the Role of Attorneys.

[4]   Of course, if the "one judge" is biased or uninformed, such a situation would be far from ideal.

[5]   *See* PERMANENCY PLANNING FOR CHILDREN DEPARTMENT, NATIONAL COUNCIL FOR JUVENILE AND FAMILY COURT JUDGES, RESOURCE GUIDELINES: IMPROVING COURT PRACTICE IN CHILD ABUSE & NEGLECT CASES (1995). There are 25 courts currently participating in the NCJFCJ national Child Victims Act Model Courts Project, including juvenile and family courts from Alexandria, VA; Buffalo, NY; Charlotte, NC; Chicago, IL; Cincinnati, OH; Des Moines, IA; El Paso, TX; Honolulu, HI; Indianapolis, IN; Los Angeles, CA; Louisville, KY; Miami, FL; Nashville, TN; New Orleans, LA; New York City, NY; Newark, NJ; Omaha, NE; Portland, OR; Reno, NV; Salt Lake City, UT; San Jose, CA; Toledo, OH; Tucson, AZ; Washington, DC; and the Tribal Court in Zuni, NM. *Id.*

[6]   *E.g.*, California, Illinois, Kentucky, and New Hampshire. *See* CAROL R. FLANGO , VICTOR E. FLANGO & H. TED RUBIN, HOW ARE COURTS COORDINATING FAMILY CASES? (National Center for State Courts, Sept. 1999), *available at* http://www.ncsconline.org/wc/courtopics/ResourceGuide.asp?topic=CasMan.

established "unified family courts," organized under a variety of models,[7] which seek to address the fragmentation of legal proceedings with which many parties involved in the child welfare system must deal. When proceedings are pending in both juvenile and family court, juvenile court proceedings are given priority in dealing with custody and visitation issues. Therefore, if a divorce or post-divorce proceeding occurs while the case is in juvenile court, the family court generally loses jurisdiction to address the custody and visitation issues. In some states, there are agreements or protocols for dealing with simultaneous proceedings. Sometimes the cases are consolidated for hearing in one court or the other. In some states, juvenile courts may enter "exit orders" that allow dismissal or termination of the child welfare proceeding in favor of final resolution in the family court, with the exit orders acting as a bridge to protect the child until the family court enters its final orders. It is important to understand the local law concerning simultaneous proceedings.

In 1999, the National Council of Juvenile and Family Court Judges issued its report, *Effective Intervention in Domestic Violence & Child Maltreatment Cases: Guidelines for Policy and Practice.* Among the Council's recommendations were that "[j]uvenile courts must collaborate with other courts" and that "[w]hen courts and agencies exchange information concerning family members, the safety and privacy concerns of all parties must be balanced carefully with the need for access to . . . information."[8] Judges in child welfare cases may be particularly open to requests for coordination with other courts addressing domestic violence in the family involved in the child welfare proceeding.

In some child welfare cases, aside from parallel criminal cases addressing the abuse or neglect of the child, there may be separate domestic violence proceedings filed against the abuser. These may be criminal prosecutions or civil proceedings for protection orders. The child may or may not be a victim or a witness in these proceedings. In states where different courts have jurisdiction to issue civil protection orders, some courts may not be able to include orders curtailing contact between the

---

[7] *See, e.g.*, Barbara A. Babb, *Reevaluating Where We Stand: A Comprehensive Survey of America's Family Justice Systems,* 46/2 FAM. CT. REV. 230 (2008); University of Baltimore School of Law, Center for Families, Children & the Courts, *Final Report of the Summit on Unified Family Courts: Serving Children and Families Efficiently, Effectively and Responsibly* (2008); James W. Bozzomo & Gregory Scolieri, *A Survey of Unified Family Courts: An Assessment of Different Jurisdictional Models*, 42/1 FAM. CT. REV. 12 (2004); John M. Greacen & Julia Hosford Barnes, *Unified Family Courts: Recent Developments in Twelve States*, 42/2 JUDGES' JOURNAL 10 (2003); American Institutes for Research, *Unified Family Court Evaluation: Literature Review* (2002), *available at* http://www.courtinfo.ca.gov/programs/cfcc/pdffiles/ufclitreview.pdf.

[8] NATIONAL COUNCIL OF JUVENILE AND FAMILY COURT JUDGES, EFFECTIVE INTERVENTION IN DOMESTIC VIOLENCE & CHILD MALTREATMENT CASES: GUIDELINES FOR POLICY AND PRACTICE 91–92 (1999), *available at* http://www.thegreenbook.info/. The report also recommends that "[c]hild protection services should avoid strategies that blame a non-abusive parent for the violence committed by others." (Recommendation 22). And it recommends that dependency should be based on witnessed domestic violence only if the evidence demonstrates that the child suffered significant emotional harm and that the non-abusing parent is unable to protect the child from that emotional abuse even with the assistance of available services, (Recommendation 59).

defendant and his or her children. If those provisions are desired, but the action has been filed in a court without adequate jurisdiction, it may be possible to transfer the case to a court that can grant full relief. It may also be possible to consolidate the civil protection case with the child welfare case.

In criminal cases, release orders or conditions of probation may regulate or prohibit contact between the offender and the child. If part of the child's case plan involves therapeutic or other contact with the offender, the criminal court's orders may conflict with the orders or plans in the child welfare case. Parties in both cases need to be made aware of the relevant orders existing in the other case. Ideally, the criminal court will be aware of the existing orders and case plan before entering its own orders. If possible, sentencing orders should coordinate with the child welfare case plan. The probation officer, prosecutor, and defense attorney should be provided with relevant information from the child welfare proceeding. The criminal justice system may have access to different resources than the juvenile court that can be used in sentencing in furtherance of the case plan. Criminal courts are often willing to carve out exceptions for contact that is undertaken pursuant to the juvenile court's orders or required by attendance at court hearings at which the victim will also be present.

Similarly, civil protection orders may carve out exceptions to no-contact orders to permit contact allowed by the juvenile court. The child's attorney or caseworker may be able to provide an affidavit or other information to be included in the petition to support the need for issuance of a protective order. Many civil protection orders are obtained *ex parte*, and the issuing judge may even be unaware of the child welfare proceeding, unaware that an agency has legal custody of the child, or unaware that orders regarding custody and access may already exist. Some states[9] permit appointment of an attorney for the child in a civil protection order case, and if the judge is aware that the child is represented in the child welfare proceeding, that attorney may be permitted to represent the child in the civil protection order case as well.

Defendants have a right to object to the civil protection order, and if they do so, information concerning the child welfare proceeding may be presented at that hearing. An application to modify the order may also be brought based on the needs of the case plan. In some jurisdictions, the child, guardian ad litem, or child welfare agency may be permitted to intervene to address the need for more or less contact in furtherance of the child's needs or to suggest how the limitations on contact might be structured.

The attorneys and the court hearing the child welfare proceeding should be made aware of the existence of any civil domestic violence proceedings and should be notified when orders of protection are issued, modified, dismissed, or expire in order to be sure that appropriate orders are in place at all times.

Where there is a choice of forum, juvenile courts are often better equipped to deal with the substantive analysis of the abuse-related allegations. In addition, the child is

---

[9]   *E.g.*, Alaska, California, Indiana, Massachusetts, Missouri, Montana, New Hampshire, North Dakota, and Washington.

more likely to have independent representation in a child welfare proceeding than in the family court proceeding. Further, juvenile courts generally have greater access to resources to protect the child and rehabilitate the family than the family court. However, child welfare proceedings are generally more intrusive into family life than family court proceedings and may stigmatize families in a way that family court proceedings do not. Under the right circumstances, divorce-child custody action in family court, a "private law" approach (where government is not a party), may be a more effective and less intrusive method of resolving a child protection case where the child would be placed with a non-offending parent under standing court orders that protect the child from the offending parent. Both the parent's attorney and child's attorney should consider these choices of forum options. A careful analysis should be made in comparing which forum will best meet the client's needs.

§ 19.3 Delinquency and Status Offenses

Many children involved in the child welfare system are also involved in the delinquency system. Often such children are "dually adjudicated," meaning that they have been found to be both dependent and delinquent. Changes in foster placements and placement in a shelter or group home setting may make it more likely that a dependent child will engage in delinquent behavior or be reported to police for infractions committed in the living environment that parents would not have reported to the police. Services available through the child's dependency case plan may address the underlying causes of the child's delinquent behavior. The fact that the child has a caseworker and services provided in the child welfare proceeding may make a prosecutor more willing to allow the child to participate in diversion programs to avoid a delinquency adjudication.[10]

Some courts have specific protocols for dealing with dually adjudicated children. In some jurisdictions, the same judge hears both the dependency and delinquency cases. In a few courts, the hearings in both cases are held jointly, with a coordinated disposition. Where such coordinated systems are not used, the case plan and services provided for in the dependency court may conflict with the terms of probation, incarceration, or parole of the juvenile from the delinquency court. The child may have different attorneys in each proceeding, in which case the attorney in the child welfare case should coordinate with the delinquency attorney. Resources that would benefit the child may be more readily available in one proceeding than the other, often because of different funding streams and "slots" or "beds" allocated to juvenile justice cases.

If the child is adjudicated delinquent, information from the child welfare proceeding will be very important to the disposition. Therefore, it is important to ensure that the defense attorney and probation officer have that information available

---

[10] For examples of such diversion programs, see ARIZ. REV. STAT. § 8-321 (2009); COLO. REV. STAT. § 19-2-303 (2009); MINN. STAT. ANN. § 388.24 (2009); OR. REV. STAT. § 419C.225 (2009).

and that the court considers it. Evaluations and reports prepared in child welfare cases are often broader in time and scope and more comprehensive than those that are prepared specifically for delinquency dispositions. Caseworkers and other professionals involved in the child welfare proceeding may be called to testify in the dispositional hearing. Foster parents and other care providers may also testify, although in some cases they may be the victims in the delinquency proceeding. Even if the two cases are not directly coordinated, it is often helpful to have joint staffing to determine what resources each system can bring to address the child's needs.

It is also important for the dependency court, caseworker, and attorneys to be kept apprised of the delinquency proceedings. It may be possible for copies of hearing notices, pleadings, and orders to be sent to the participants in both cases if the cases are not otherwise consolidated or coordinated.

If the child is sent to a secure facility as a part of the delinquency case, it is important to make arrangements for appropriate services to be continued to address the dependency case plan and the needs identified through the child welfare proceeding.

§ 19.4 Criminal Proceedings

Sometimes there is a parallel criminal prosecution arising out of the same facts as underlie the child welfare case. The attorneys in the child welfare case may or may not be directly involved in the criminal case, but they still should be aware of what is happening in the criminal case and may want to have some level of involvement.

§ 19.4.1 Interface Between Civil Child Protection and Criminal Prosecution

More serious forms of child abuse, neglect, and abandonment also constitute crimes under state and, sometimes, federal law. Some prosecutors choose not to prosecute cases that are being handled in the child welfare system. Sometimes cases are pursued in both forums, either simultaneously or seriatim. Parents' criminal defense attorneys may be hesitant to have a parent participate in services or testify in the child welfare case because of admissions that might be used in the criminal trial. Therefore, parents' child welfare attorneys often prefer that the criminal proceeding take place first so that their clients can fully participate in the child welfare proceeding. However, the clock on the various statutory time limits do not stop running while the criminal process plays itself out. Therefore, a parent who does not move forward with the child welfare proceedings in a timely manner may end up at a termination hearing without having had the time to demonstrate compliance with a reunification plan.

In some cases, the prosecutor may be willing to agree not to use admissions concerning the charged crime that are made in therapy or as part of other reunification services because the prosecutor believes that involving the defendant in such services minimizes damage to the child. This is particularly true with regard to "apology sessions" in which the parent apologizes to the child and takes full responsibility for the maltreatment. The parent's attorney, often with the support of the child's attorney, may be able to negotiate an agreement with the prosecutor not to use those statements in the criminal trial. However, in the absence of an agreement, evidence developed in the child welfare proceeding is generally available to the prosecutor in the criminal proceeding. Because of the confidentiality provisions surrounding many child welfare investigations and proceedings, the prosecutor may need to obtain a court order before getting direct access to some of the child welfare information and testimony.

A criminal conviction for the abuse or neglect alleged in the dependency or termination petition, because it is made based on proof beyond a reasonable doubt, can be used to establish the abuse or neglect in the child welfare proceeding. The reverse is not true, however, because of the difference in the burden of proof. Further, abuse or neglect sufficient to sustain a finding of dependency or termination may not fulfill the statutory elements of the crime.

The federal Children's Justice Act (CJA)[11] provides grants to states to improve the investigation, prosecution, and judicial handling of cases of child abuse and neglect, particularly child sexual abuse and exploitation. Among the programs qualifying for funding are establishing or enhancing child advocacy centers and other multi-disciplinary programs to serve child victims and their families in order to minimize trauma. Funds may also be used to support the enactment of laws to improve systems response, including allowing the admission of indirect testimony of children into evidence, making the courtroom setting less intimidating to children, increasing the penalties for sexual offenses against children, requiring mandatory sentencing, shortening the trial process, and permitting victims to make statements prior to sentencing.

Every state has a victims' bill of rights.[12] Child victims may also be entitled to some or all of these rights, which may include the right:

- To be notified of all criminal proceedings.

- To be kept apprised of the status of the defendant (including the release of the defendant from jail and the conditions of release or notice of escape).

- To confidentiality of the victim's address.

- To be present at certain criminal proceedings.

- To be consulted before a case is dismissed or a plea agreement entered.

---

[11] Children's Justice Act, 100 Stat. 903, 42 U.S.C. § 5101; *see also* CHILDREN'S BUREAU, U.S. DEPARTMENT OF HEALTH & HUMAN SERVICES, CHILDREN'S JUSTICE ACT FACT SHEET (2004), *available at* http://www.acf.hhs.gov/programs/cb/laws_policies/policy/cjafact.htm.

[12] *See, e.g.,* ARIZ. REV. STAT. §§ 13-4401 *et seq.* (2009); GA. CODE ANN. §§ 17-17-1 *et seq.* (2009); TENN. CODE ANN. §§ 40-38-101 *et seq.* (2009); MISS. CODE. ANN. §§ 99-43-1 *et seq.* (2009); R.I. GEN. LAWS §§ 12-28-1 *et seq.* (2009).

- To refuse to be interviewed by defense counsel or to have an advocate present during any interview by defense counsel.
- To a separate waiting area.
- To make a statement at sentencing or various pre- and post-trial release proceedings.
- To obtain restitution after the defendant is convicted.

Children may be required to exercise these rights through a legal guardian or guardian ad litem. In some states, the prosecutor may exercise the child victim's rights on behalf of the child.

In addition to providing victims' rights by statute, at least 32 states[13] have adopted amendments to their constitutions concerning victims' rights. Most of these bills of rights apply only to victims of adult perpetrators and not to victims of juvenile offenders who are being prosecuted in juvenile courts.

Children who are victims often end up being interviewed or testifying in conjunction with the criminal case. It is not always clear who has standing to assist the child through the process by asserting any rights the child may have, including asserting the child's privilege and confidential interests in his or her records.[14] A parent, particularly a non-offending parent whose parental rights have not been terminated, may be able to assert the child's rights. The agency that has legal custody pursuant to the child welfare proceeding may have the right and duty to protect the child's interests in the criminal proceeding. The child's attorney or guardian ad litem may have standing to assert the child's rights. It might be necessary or prudent for the respective parties and their counsel to seek a judicial determination in the child welfare case concerning who may and may not act on behalf of the child in the criminal proceeding. Where more than one person or entity has that right, such as the agency and the child's attorney, some effort should be made to coordinate a unified approach if possible.

Many states provide various accommodations for child witnesses, such as permitting the child to be accompanied by a support person or to have special procedures for taking the child's testimony. Whichever adult is helping the child through the criminal process should inquire about the availability of any such procedures.[15]

---

[13] Alabama, Alaska, Arizona, California, Colorado, Connecticut, Florida, Idaho, Illinois, Indiana, Kansas, Louisiana, Maryland, Michigan, Mississippi, Missouri, Montana, Nebraska, Nevada, New Jersey, New Mexico, North Carolina, Ohio, Oklahoma, Rhode Island, South Carolina, Tennessee, Texas, Utah, Virginia, Washington, and Wisconsin; a similar amendment in Oregon has been repealed. *See* VICTIMS' RIGHTS CONSTITUTIONAL AMENDMENTS (2004), *available at* http://www.ojp.usdoj.gov/ovc/ncvrw/1999/amend.htm.

[14] *See* Chapter 18, Confidentiality.

[15] *See* Chapter 30, Children in Court.

§ 19.4.2 The Child's Attorney or Guardian Ad Litem in the Criminal Case

If the child is represented by an attorney or guardian ad litem in the child welfare proceeding, that person may be permitted to appear in the criminal case. The attorney may be required to affirmatively seek the appointment from the judge in the criminal case. In addition to helping with preparing the child to testify, the attorney may be permitted to address the issue of sentencing, especially where the defendant is the child's parent. Many child victims are ambivalent about the abuser and feel guilty that their testimony has helped to convict the parent. The child may feel guilty because the prosecution of the abuser has resulted in financial detriment to the family and the *de facto* break-up the family. In some cases, it may be appropriate to advocate for a work-release sentence that permits the defendant to earn money during the work day while spending nights and weekends in jail.

The guardian ad litem in the criminal case can assist in minimizing the number of duplicate interviews and evaluations of the child. The prosecutor may not be aware of all of the information already gathered in the child welfare process. Some jurisdictions have joint child abuse investigations, including requiring that all child interviews be conducted at child advocacy centers where both the prosecutor (or law enforcement) and child protective services worker funnel their questions to one forensic interviewer, who is often on the other side of a one-way mirror in a room with the child. However, even in those situations, the prosecutor may not be kept informed of new information developed in the child welfare case. The guardian ad litem can ensure that the prosecutor is aware of such information on an on-going basis. In particular, the guardian ad litem can inform the prosecutor of any special needs the child might have with respect to testifying or sentencing. The guardian ad litem can assist in scheduling the child's interviews or testimony at times convenient to the child and any support person who will be accompanying the child.

Child witnesses are often attacked as being incompetent to testify, confused, or testifying based on contaminated memories. The guardian ad litem can assist in supporting the child's credibility by ensuring that the child is well prepared to testify, perhaps with therapeutic support.[16]

§ 19.4.3 Protective Orders

All states have statutes providing for domestic violence protection orders.[17] Children who have been victims of child abuse or exposed to domestic violence are proper beneficiaries of those protective orders. The Violence Against Women Act

---

[16] *See* Chapter 30, Children in Court; and Chapter 5, Investigative Interviewing of the Child.

[17] For a discussion of domestic violence orders of protection, see § 19.6.1.

(VAWA)[18] provides for full faith and credit for domestic violence protective orders that are entered by state or tribal courts in compliance with the Act. Therefore, it is important that any protective order issued comply with the requirements of VAWA.

In addition to domestic violence protective orders, the child's attorney can seek discovery protective orders, if appropriate, to maintain the privacy of the child's school, medical, and counseling records, as well as records generated within the child welfare proceeding. These records might be sought by both the prosecution and defense, and the child has a privacy interest in the records regardless of who is seeking them. The attorney can ask either that the records remain entirely confidential or that they be submitted to the criminal court judge for *in camera* inspection and redaction. Further, the attorney can request an order prohibiting further dissemination of released records.

§ 19.5 Divorce, Child Custody, and Visitation Proceedings

§ 19.5.1 Staying Together or Divorcing

For some parents, the decision either to stay in an abusive home or to leave is problematic. When child protective services workers investigate a family, they are concerned not only about an active abuser, but also about a parent who fails to protect the children from the abuse. However, when a non-abusive parent who has never been involved with the child welfare system leaves the abuser, files for divorce, and alleges child abuse by the abusive parent, the fact that the parties are involved in custody litigation may cause the professionals involved to view the protective parent's allegations with skepticism. While custody litigation may in fact spawn some false allegations of abuse and exaggerated reports, it is also true that good parenting may compel separation and divorce from an abuser. So a non-abusing parent may land in a no-win situation, where he or she is criticized as a bad parent for staying in the marriage, but disbelieved after leaving. The ultimate penalty for not being believed about abuse by the other parent is the loss of custody to the abuser. This is particularly likely to happen with respect to allegations of child sexual abuse.[19]

The American Psychological Association's Presidential Task Force on Violence and the Family found that batterers are twice as likely to seek custody as non-batterers.[20] So it should come as no surprise that domestic violence, child abuse, and

---

[18] The Violence Against Women Act (VAWA), 42 U.S.C. § 3796gg, Title IV of the Violent Crime Control and Law Enforcement Act of 1994, Pub. L. No. 103-322. *See* The Office on Violence Against Women Online Resources, http://www.vaw.umn.edu/library/.

[19] *See, e.g.*, JOHN E. B. MYERS, A MOTHER'S NIGHTMARE—INCEST: A PRACTICAL GUIDE FOR PARENTS AND PROFESSIONALS (1997); ANN M. HARALAMBIE, CHILD SEXUAL ABUSE IN CIVIL CASES: HANDLING CUSTODY AND TORT ACTIONS (American Bar Association 1999).

[20] *See* REPORT OF THE AMERICAN PSYCHOLOGICAL ASSOCIATION PRESIDENTIAL TASK FORCE ON VIOLENCE AND THE FAMILY (1996).

neglect may be issues in divorce, paternity, and custody cases as well as in post-decree modification actions. Many legal and mental health professionals become very frustrated at what have come to be called "high conflict divorce cases." Johnston and Campbell found that in approximately 75% of intractable custody conflicts there is a history of domestic violence.[21] Bancroft and Silverman suggest that "many of the characteristics that [Johnston and Campbell] consider to be inherent to 'high-conflict divorce' may actually be the dynamics of domestic violence."[22] Therefore, they believe that the assumption that high-conflict divorces are the result of both parents' inappropriate behaviors may be incorrect, and that one parent's abuse may actually be the cause of the intractability in many cases.

The time of separation and divorce can be particularly dangerous for victims of domestic violence.[23] Bancroft and Silverman write:

> In fact, we observe that many batterers' motivation to intimidate their victims through the children *increases* when the couple separates, because of the loss of other ways to exert control. In addition, the batterer's partner is no longer present to monitor his behavior toward the children. If there is litigation involving custody or visitation, her reports of physical abuse of the children by him may be dismissed by the courts as a divorce tactic, which may leave him feeling free to behave with impunity.[24]

The failure to accurately determine whether abuse has occurred places children in greater danger during and after the separation than before the separation for several reasons. Children are obviously in danger when they are being abused within the secrecy of their family life. Abuse is reported with the goal of obtaining protection for the children and rehabilitation of the parents where appropriate. When a parent attempts to obtain the protection of the child welfare and judicial system, but the courts do not believe that abuse has occurred, the would-be protector has no place else to turn. Each subsequent attempt to get help may be viewed as vindictiveness, paranoia, hypervigilance, or attempts to "alienate" the child from the other parent. Parents may actually be ordered not to make any further CPS reports or to first have a report screened by some other professional, even if such orders put parents who are mandated reporters at risk of violating mandatory reporting laws. Self-help may be dealt with even more severely. A parent who flees with the child risks not only a

---

[21] *See* JANET R. JOHNSTON & LINDA E. G. CAMPBELL, IMPASSES OF DIVORCE: THE DYNAMICS AND RESOLUTION OF FAMILY CONFLICT (Free Press 1988).

[22] *See* LUNDY BANCROFT & JAY G. SILVERMAN, THE BATTERER AS PARENT: ADDRESSING THE IMPACT OF DOMESTIC VIOLENCE ON FAMILY DYNAMICS 131 (Sage Publications 2002).

[23] *See, e.g.,* Jennifer L. Hardesty, *Separation Assault in the Context of Postdivorce Parenting: An Integrative Review of the Literature*, 8/5 VIOLENCE AGAINST WOMEN 597 (2002); Martha Mahoney, *Legal Images of Battered Women: Redefining the Issue of Separation*, 90 MICH. L. REV. 1 (1999).

[24] *See* LUNDY BANCROFT & JAY G. SILVERMAN, THE BATTERER AS PARENT: ADDRESSING THE IMPACT OF DOMESTIC VIOLENCE ON FAMILY DYNAMICS 44 (Sage Publications 2002).

contempt citation, but also loss of custody and criminal prosecution for custodial interference. If that parent takes the child across state lines, the matter becomes a federal criminal offense. The resources of local law enforcement, the FBI, and the National Center for Missing and Exploited Children are available to assist the left-behind (abusive) parent in obtaining return of the child and punishment of the protective parent. A child whose protective parent is incarcerated for attempting to protect the child and who is placed in the full-time custody of the abuser is being taught a disturbing lesson: seeking help for the abuse makes the situation much worse, not better.

Family court judges may tend to be more skeptical about child abuse allegations than juvenile or criminal court judges, who daily see parties who have committed violence or other abusive acts.[25] They are used to hearing litigants exaggerate trivial events that were accepted during the marriage but that take on the characterization of unacceptable abuse during the divorce trial. In addition to exaggerations, some divorce litigants lie outright in order to gain an advantage or punish the other parent. It is within this context that many domestic relations judges view allegations of child abuse. This same perspective holds true for some custody evaluators as well. These biases are particularly evident in child sexual abuse cases.[26] Even child protective services investigators tend to be more skeptical of abuse allegations made in the context of divorce proceedings, even where the parent making the allegations asserts that he or she left the marriage as a response to the abuse.[27]

§ 19.5.2 Child Welfare and Family Court Interaction

Family law attorneys may advise divorce litigants to make CPS reports when they suspect the other parent is abusing the child. In fact, parents are mandated reporters in many states. However, CPS investigators often complain that divorce litigants are trying to use them in the divorce case as a weapon to gain an advantage over the other party. With child welfare systems under increasing budgetary crises, investigation priorities tend to favor putting resources into families where neither party is willing to

---

[25] *See generally* ANN M. HARALAMBIE, CHILD SEXUAL ABUSE IN CIVIL CASES: A GUIDE TO CUSTODY AND TORT ACTIONS ch. 2 (American Bar Association 1999).

[26] *See generally* THE BACKLASH: CHILD PROTECTION UNDER FIRE (John E. B. Myers ed., Sage Publications 1994); BILLIE WRIGHT DZIECH & CHARLES B. SCHUDSON, ON TRIAL: AMERICA'S COURTS AND THEIR TREATMENT OF SEXUALLY ABUSED CHILDREN (Beacon Press 1989); DAVID HECHLER, THE BATTLE AND THE BACKLASH: THE CHILD SEXUAL ABUSE WAR (Lexington Books 1988).

[27] For example, one small study in Boulder, Colorado, looked at eighteen cases of sexual abuse allegations arising in family court custody litigation. Seventeen of the reports were deemed by the Sexual Abuse Team to be unfounded (the one "founded" allegation was admitted by the perpetrator). The same CPS workers reviewed the cases again, with no additional information, using an improved validation protocol and reclassified an additional seven as substantiated (having even overlooked physical evidence in two of the cases). The CPS workers admitted that they viewed allegations in a custody dispute context with greater skepticism. *See* J. Melbourne McGraw & Holly A. Smith, *Child Sexual Abuse Allegations Amidst Divorce and Custody Proceedings: Refining the Validation Process*, 1/1 J. CHILD SEXUAL ABUSE 49 (1992).

protect the child. A parent who recognizes the danger and is seeking family court assistance in protecting the child is not high on the list of cases to investigate. Further, as mentioned above, many CPS workers are skeptical of reports made in the context of a divorce case, believing many such allegations to be either fabricated or wildly exaggerated. This is particularly true when no allegations had been received before the initiation of the divorce action or post-decree litigation. Parents who lack the financial resources to obtain private evaluations, especially in jurisdictions where the family court does not have its own social service investigators, may have little hope of an expert investigation into allegations of abuse unless CPS conducts the investigation. However, CPS investigations into allegations arising during litigation may not be as thorough or objective as investigations done while the family was still together.

In many cases, there is inadequate coordination between the child welfare and family court systems and a lack of understanding of the implications of the findings of each. For example, most CPS investigators are required to label the results of an investigation in a very restrictive way (either "founded" or "unfounded," "substantiated" or "unsubstantiated") rather than along a continuum of confidence that abuse did or did not occur. Many custody evaluators, attorneys, and judges in the family court system construe "unfounded" or "unsubstantiated" findings as indications by CPS that the accused parent did not abuse the child. This undercuts the credibility of the protective parent, even where the initial report was made by a third party and not by that parent. Future allegations of abuse are likely to be met with increased skepticism based on the assumptions that: (1) CPS determined that the allegations lacked merit; and (2) if the child were deemed to be in danger, the child welfare agency would have sought judicial relief. However, where there is a parent willing and able to take protective action, the child welfare system generally does not intervene, and the dependency statute generally requires that a petition be filed only where there is not a parent protecting the child, even where abuse has occurred. Therefore, even if a CPS investigator believed that one parent was abusing the child, if the other parent has initiated a divorce and sought orders to protect the child, the CPS investigation is likely to be closed without taking any further action. The assumption is made that the child will be adequately protected in the family law case. The various professionals and judges involved in the family court case, however, may not understand that the allegations were credited by the neutral investigators.

Similarly, when family courts have addressed abuse allegations and found inadequate evidence to prove them or even that they were maliciously made, CPS investigators may assume that the allegations were thoroughly investigated by the family court and will be even more skeptical of future allegations made. In fact, the professionals involved in the family court case may not be experienced in investigating and litigating child abuse claims. Many custody evaluators do not have special training in the abuse field, and most family law attorneys do not routinely practice in juvenile courts or otherwise have experience dealing with abuse cases. Further, multidisciplinary evaluations are rare in family court. Therefore, whether the family court finds that abuse did or did not occur, child welfare professionals should not assume that the finding was based on a thorough, appropriate investigation into the merits of the case.

Failure to appreciate the weaknesses and biases of both the child welfare and family court systems can result in failure to protect a child from abuse. Therefore, in either arena, it is important for there to be an individualized determination of the underlying allegations and not merely an assumption that the decision has already been made correctly.

§ 19.6 Domestic Violence[28]

Child abuse is a particular type of domestic violence. Children who are exposed to domestic violence in their homes, even if they are not the targets of that abuse, also suffer harm by being in that environment.[29] In fact, a New York agency had adopted a policy of prosecuting abused mothers and summarily removing their children who had observed the domestic violence. The New York Court of Appeals held that the definition of a "neglected child" under the child welfare statute does not include instances in which the sole allegation of neglect is that the parent or other person legally responsible for the child's care allows the child to witness domestic abuse against the caretaker and that emergency removal should generally not be permitted without a court order.[30]

Responses to the problem of children witnessing domestic violence raise interesting policy considerations. Domestic violence advocates, in particular, criticize judicial findings that further penalize battered spouses who have difficulty in rescuing themselves and their children from violent situations. Leaving an abusive situation without having an appropriate safety plan and support system in place might even make things worse for the children and place the entire family in greater danger. The National Association of Public Child Welfare Administrators has summarized the tension between child welfare and domestic violence professionals as follows:

> Child welfare has largely viewed the domestic violence field as discounting the safety needs of children by focusing solely on adult victims. On the other hand, some domestic violence advocates may perceive child welfare as revictimizing adult victims through punitive and blaming assessment and intervention practices that erroneously result in charging adult victims with "failure to protect." Some domestic violence advocates often note that protecting adult victims

---

[28] This section is based in part on ANN M. HARALAMBIE, HANDLING CHILD CUSTODY, ABUSE, AND ADOPTION CASES 3d §§ 4:14 and 12:18 (West 2009).

[29] *See, e.g.*, Gregory K. Moffatt & Savannah L. Smith, *Childhood Exposure to Conjugal Violence: Consequences for Behavioral and Neural Development*, 56 DEPAUL L. REV. 879 (2007); Carolyn Copps Hartley, *The Co-occurrence of Child Maltreatment and Domestic Violence: Examining Both Neglect and Child Physical Abuse*, 7/4 CHILD MALTREAT. 349 (2002).

[30] *See* Nicholson v. Scoppetta, 3 N.Y.3d 357, 787 N.Y.S.2d 196, 820 N.E.2d 840 (2004).

is inextricably linked with protecting children and that the protective factors used by adult victims are not accurately assessed and accounted for during child protective services (CPS) intervention. In turn, child welfare's response may stress that the ultimate responsibility of providing protection, safety, and stability for children rests with their primary caretakers who have an obligation to provide this assurance by ameliorating any personal issues that are contributing to or presenting risk to their children.[31]

In divorce cases, all states except South Dakota and Utah provide that domestic violence, whether or not witnessed by the children, is a factor that at least should be considered or even explicitly that it should be weighed against custody being awarded to the abuser. Some states have rebuttable presumptions against physical custody or joint legal custody being awarded to an abuser. Congress encouraged this legislative trend in 1990 by unanimously adopting Concurrent Resolution 172, which recommended that in determining custody, "credible evidence of physical abuse of one's spouse should create a statutory presumption that it is detrimental to the child to be placed in the custody of the abusive spouse."[32]

§ 19.6.1 Orders of Protection

Most states have passed domestic violence laws that provide for ex parte restraining orders or orders of protection when there has been domestic violence and there is a current danger of continued violence. States differ on whether children can be included within the protections of a civil protection order, especially where the child's parent, but not the child, was a victim of the domestic violence. Many states permit children[33] or parties acting on their behalf[34] to seek orders of protection, especially where the child was a victim of the domestic violence. In most states, courts hearing civil protection order cases have expressed or implied authority to enter orders affecting custody. However, while a court may restrict contact more than an existing juvenile court order, a civil protection order generally cannot change custody or increase contact beyond what is permitted by an existing order in a child welfare proceeding. If the civil order of protection attempts to do so, the child welfare order generally takes precedence. In practice, law enforcement officers are likely to look at

---

[31] NATIONAL ASSOCIATION OF PUBLIC CHILD WELFARE ADMINISTRATORS, GUIDELINES FOR PUBLIC CHILD WELFARE AGENCIES SERVING CHILDREN AND FAMILIES EXPERIENCING DOMESTIC VIOLENCE 12 (2000).

[32] HR Con. Res. 172, 101st Congress, 2d Sess. (1990).

[33] *E.g.*, California, Connecticut, District of Columbia, Minnesota, Nevada, New Hampshire, New Jersey, New Mexico, North Dakota, Oklahoma, Oregon, Rhode Island, South Dakota, Tennessee, Utah, and Washington.

[34] *E.g.*, Alabama, Alaska, Arizona, Arkansas, California, Colorado, Delaware, Georgia, Hawaii, Idaho, Illinois, Indiana, Iowa, Kansas, Kentucky, Louisiana, Maine, Maryland, Minnesota, Mississippi, Montana, North Carolina, Ohio, Oklahoma, Pennsylvania, South Carolina, Texas, Vermont, and Washington.

and enforce the most recent order, so it is important to obtain a new order reconciling any inconsistencies.

A number of states have also adopted statutory address confidentiality programs (ACPs), which protect the address of a domestic violence victim from the abuser. When the abuser has a legal right to access to the child, provisions must be made for contact, which may require visitation exchanges at a public place or location other than at the victim parent's residence.

Orders of protection or restraining orders may be issued based on specialized statutes or as part of divorce or paternity cases. The National Conference of Commissioners on Uniform State Laws has promulgated the Uniform Interstate Enforcement of Domestic Violence Protection Orders Act.[35]

§ 19.7 Guardianships

Aside from guardianships that may be granted within the child welfare proceeding, there may also be guardianship actions heard by probate and other courts. Ideally these actions, although traditionally sent to separate courts, would be brought before and heard by the same judge, perhaps through a state's unified family court or by procedures that allow matters to be heard by the same judge. Where a child protection case is pending, the guardianship case generally involves the same people with the same factual context. Under the right circumstances, a guardianship may be an appropriate resolution to a child welfare case. A parent may be unable to care for his or her child, but another family member or close friend may be able to assume guardianship either for the long-term or temporarily while the parents resolve their issues. Attorneys for the parent or the child may find guardianship an attractive option that is less invasive than child protection jurisdiction and provides more power and autonomy to the family.

If a collateral guardianship proceeding is pending at the same time as a child welfare proceeding, it is important to ensure that both courts are aware of the other proceeding. Typically, only the child welfare system has the ability to provide comprehensive services to the child and family. Further, only the child welfare court is likely to be able to provide independent representation for the parties. If the attorney for the agency, parent, or child in the child welfare proceeding becomes aware of the collateral guardianship proceeding, that attorney may be able to intervene in the guardianship on behalf of the client or at least help coordinate one proceeding with the other.[36]

---

[35] As of the January 2010, the Act has been adopted by 16 states, the District of Columbia, and the Virgin Islands.

[36] For a more thorough discussion of guardianship, see Chapter 25, Establishing Legal Permanence for the Child.

Chapter 20: Immigration Issues—Representing Children Who Are Not United States Citizens

by Katherine Brady[1] and David B. Thronson[2]

§ 20.1 Introduction

Representing noncitizen children and their families presents both opportunities and challenges. Practitioners who identify immigration issues and seek timely assistance from immigration experts can make a tremendously positive impact. Lack of lawful immigration status has real consequences for children and families. In some instances, involvement with family courts and child welfare systems provides unique, often fleeting, opportunities for children to achieve legal immigration status. Recognizing immigration opportunities and seeking timely assistance from immigration experts may change a child's life.

At the same time, reliance on incorrect assumptions about the import of a noncitizen's immigration status can overemphasize the role of immigration status in the lives of noncitizen children. Those representing noncitizen children must be wary of claims that their clients do not have certain legal rights[3] or that they can be denied certain public privileges or benefits due to immigration status.[4] It is vital for attorneys to cultivate awareness of the real implications of immigration status to effectively represent noncitizen children and families.

Family law and immigration law constantly and inevitably interact. Family relationships, especially the parent-child relationship, play a critical role in the framework that delineates who is permitted to enter and remain in the United States under immigration and nationality law. In turn, the operation of immigration law has a tremendous impact on family integrity because it intrudes into decisions about where children and families live. Yet family law and immigration law are motivated by

---

[1] Katherine Brady, J.D., a senior staff attorney at the Immigration Legal Resource Center in San Francisco, California, is the author of several manuals and articles about immigration law.

[2] David B. Thronson, Professor of Law, Michigan State University College of Law, researches and writes about the intersection of immigration and family law.

[3] See David B. Thronson, *Custody and Contradictions: Exploring Immigration Law as Federal Family Law in the Context of Child Custody*, 59 HASTINGS L.J. 453 (2008).

[4] *See, e.g.*, Plyler v. Doe, 457 U.S. 202 (1982) (establishing that all children living in the United States, regardless of immigration status, have the right to K-12 public education in the United States); Special Supplemental Nutrition Program for Women, Infants, and Children (WIC), 42 U.S.C. § 1786, 7 C.F.R. §§ 246.1 *et seq.* (allowing anyone to access WIC, regardless of immigration status, so long as the applicant meets income eligibility standards and risk factor priorities set by each state).

divergent and often conflicting policies that often prove difficult, and on occasion impossible, to reconcile. A complete review of ways in which immigration issues impact the lives of children is far beyond the scope of this chapter. Yet awareness of some the ways that immigration law interacts with family law, coupled with a willingness to seek assistance from immigration attorneys, can be instrumental.

§ 20.2 Special Immigrant Juvenile Status

Special Immigrant Juvenile Status (SIJS) provides a means for children to obtain legal permanent residence status (a "green card") in the United States. Such status provides authorization to remain permanently in the United States, gives eligibility for employment authorization and student financial assistance, and places the child on a path to citizenship. Special Immigrant Juvenile Status is not conferred automatically on state dependents. To ensure that windows of opportunity to obtain permanent residence through this provision are not missed, it is important to identify eligible state dependent children who lack lawful immigration status. Applying for this status is not without risk. If an application to U.S. Citizenship and Immigration Services (USCIS) is denied, it is possible, although not likely, that the child might be referred for deportation proceedings. Therefore, it is highly advisable to seek the assistance of an immigration attorney to help children who appear to be eligible.

State dependency in itself does nothing to alter federal immigration status. Prior to 1990, undocumented children in state care routinely found themselves in an immigration predicament. They remained in state care until their majority, and then found themselves turned out to face the world without legal immigration status and all its associated benefits. In 1990, Congress created Special Immigrant Juvenile Status to provide an avenue of immigration relief for undocumented children who are juvenile court dependents.[5]

The process of obtaining Special Immigrant Juvenile Status uses a unique hybrid system of state and federal collaboration, incorporating state court child welfare expertise into federal decision-making on immigration matters. Federal immigration law places critical fact finding functions about the child's best interests and the possibility of family reunification with state "juvenile courts," defined as "court[s] located in the United States having jurisdiction under State law to make judicial determinations about the custody and care of juveniles."[6]

---

[5]   *See* 8 U.S.C. § 1101(a)(27)(J).

[6]   8 C.F.R. § 204.11(a). "The reliance upon state juvenile courts anticipated in the SIJ statutory scheme signals Congress' recognition that the states retain primary responsibility and administrative competency to protect child welfare." Gregory Zhong Tian Chen, *Elian or Alien? The Contradictions of Protecting Undocumented Children Under the Special Immigrant Juvenile Statute*, 27 HASTINGS CONST. L.Q. 597, 609 (2000). The federal government "lacks the professional staff and administrative support to make assessments of individual children's mental and physical conditions and their welfare needs." *Id.* at 611.

As a prerequisite for a child present in the United States to file for Special Immigrant Juvenile Status, a juvenile court must make the following three factual determinations:

(1) The child has been "declared dependent on a juvenile court" **or** the child has been "legally committed to, or placed under the custody of, an agency or department of a State, or an individual or entity appointed by a State or juvenile court located in the United States."

(2) The child's "reunification with [one] or both of the [child's] parents is not viable due to abuse, neglect, abandonment, or a similar basis found under State law."

(3) It "would not be in the [child's] best interest to be returned to the [child's] or parent's previous country of nationality or last habitual residence."[7]

In making these findings, the juvenile court does not make any immigration decision. Rather, these preliminary factual determinations are simply prerequisites to the filing of an application for immigration relief from USCIS. With these findings, an application for admission to the status of legal permanent resident status can be filed with USCIS.

§ 20.2.1 Juvenile Court Dependency

When a juvenile or family court accepts jurisdiction to make a decision about the care and custody of a child, for immigration purposes the child is dependent on a juvenile court. Establishing dependency on a juvenile court does not require state intervention or a decision to place the child in any particular form of care. A juvenile is dependent on the juvenile court if he or she "[h]as been the subject of judicial proceedings or administrative proceedings authorized or recognized by the juvenile court."[8] In other words, the

> acceptance of jurisdiction over the custody of a child by a juvenile court, when the child's parents have effectively relinquished control of the child, makes the child dependent upon the juvenile court, whether the child is placed by the court in foster care or, as here, in a guardianship situation.[9]

While children placed in formal foster care certainly are dependent on a juvenile court, so are children for whom a court has appointed a guardian. This longstanding interpretation of "state dependency" for Special Immigrant Juvenile purposes was confirmed in a 2008 amendment to the statutory language to specify eligibility for

---

[7]   8 U.S.C. § 1101(a)(27)(J).

[8]   8 C.F.R. § 204.11(c)(6).

[9]   *In re* Menjivar, 29 Immig. Rptr. B2-37 (1994).

children placed under the custody of "an *individual* . . . appointed by a State or juvenile court."[10] A child for whom a guardianship is established may qualify for Special Immigrant Juvenile Status even if he or she was never removed from a parent or placed in foster care.

Juvenile courts make decisions about the care and custody of children in a variety of ways, including but not limited to foster care placements and guardianship. Qualifying guardianships may be established through any court empowered under state law to make decisions regarding the care and custody of children, including probate courts in many jurisdictions. Moreover, among the courts that make decisions about the care and custody of children are those that adjudicate delinquency petitions. A decision adjudicating a child delinquent and making determinations about the custody of the child can serve to establish the requisite dependency on the juvenile court. The key here is that although the particular form or name of the proceeding may vary, a court is taking jurisdiction to make a decision about the care and custody of a child. In theory, even more limited forms of guardianship, such a testamentary guardianships or voluntary guardianship established for school residency purposes, might suffice to establish dependency if a juvenile court is involved. Such limited guardianships, however, are not likely to support the next required finding that reunification with a parent is not viable.

§ 20.2.2 Viability of Reunification with Parent

Eligibility for Special Immigrant Juvenile Status requires a finding that "reunification with [one] or both of the immigrant's parents is not viable due to abuse, neglect, abandonment, or a similar basis found under State law."[11] Previously, the statute required a finding that the child was "eligible for long-term foster care," a confusing term that was defined by federal immigration regulation to mean "that family reunification is no longer a viable option."[12] This statutory language was recently amended, and likely will be the subject of litigation to determine its scope and meaning. In particular, the shift in language from "family reunification" to "reunification with [one] or both parents" has great potential significance, yet was accomplished without a trace of legislative history.[13]

First, a finding for Special Immigrant Juvenile purposes that reunification is not viable does not require formal termination of parental rights or a determination that reunification will never be possible. While short separations from parents likely

---

[10] *See* 8 U.S.C. § 1101(a)(27)(J), as amended by the Trafficking Victims Protection Reauthorization Act of 2008, § 235(d), Pub. L. No. 110-457, 122 Stat. 5044 (2008), § 235(d). *See also* Donald Neufeld & Pearl Chang, *Trafficking Victims Protection Reauthorization Act of 2008: Special Immigrant Juvenile Status Provisions* (USCIS Memorandum, Mar. 24, 2009) (acknowledging Special Immigrant Juvenile eligibility for a child "on whose behalf a juvenile court appointed a guardian").

[11] 8 U.S.C. § 1101(a)(27)(J)(i).

[12] 8 C.F.R. § 204.11(a).

[13] Similarly, there is "no contemporaneous legislative history . . . which explains why SIJ status was originally created in 1990." Yu v. Brown, 92 F. Supp. 2d 1236, 1246 (D.N.M. 2000).

would not qualify for a finding that reunification is not viable, the possibility or even the stated goal of a child's return to a parent need not deter a finding that reunification presently is not viable. Given the lack of temporal specificity in the current statutory language, it is feasible to advocate that the requirement is satisfied based on any significant separation.

Second, reunification must not be viable "due to abuse, neglect, abandonment, or a similar basis found under State law." The words "due to abuse, neglect, or abandonment" were added to the statute in 1997.[14] The House Conference Report on this amendment states that "[t]he language has been modified in order to limit the beneficiaries of this provision to those juveniles for whom it was created, namely abandoned, neglected, or abused children."[15] This language prohibits establishing Special Immigrant Juvenile eligibility based on collusion to create juvenile court dependency for children not otherwise in need, but does not require that formal charges of abuse, neglect, or abandonment be levied against the parents. For example, a child for whom the court appoints a guardian can qualify without a separate proceeding against the parents alleging abuse, neglect, or abandonment. The 2008 addition of the language "or similar basis found under State law" accommodates the range of statutory language used in various jurisdictions to determine when a juvenile court can intervene to make decisions about the care and custody of children.[16]

Third, by rejecting the use of "family reunification" in favor of "reunification with one or both parents," the new statutory language appears to permit eligibility for Special Immigrant Juvenile Status on the basis of the nonviability of reunification with one parent due to abuse, neglect or abandonment, even while the child remains in the care of the other. Certainly, this language clarifies that children placed in kinship care can meet this requirement. While some such situations may well fall within the plain language of the statute, they fall outside more traditional conceptions of state dependent children for whom Special Immigrant Juvenile Status originally was conceived. Moreover, even if a child may qualify as a Special Immigrant Juvenile while still with one parent, the statutory provision remains that "no natural parent or prior adoptive parent of any alien provided special immigrant status under this subparagraph shall thereafter, by virtue of such parentage, be accorded any right, privilege, or status under this chapter."[17] This means that a child who receives lawful permanent resident status as a Special Immigrant Juvenile can never petition for a parent to receive such status, even later in life when the child has become an adult U.S. citizen, reflecting the origins of Special Immigrant Juvenile Status as a means to address the situation of children separated from parents. Whether Special Immigrant Juvenile Status now will extend to

---

[14] *See* Departments of Commerce, Justice, and State, the Judiciary, and Related Agencies Appropriations Act of 1998, Pub. L. No. 105-119, 111 Stat. 2440, 2460.

[15] H.R. Conf. Rep. No. 105-405, at 130 (1997), reprinted in 1997 U.S.C.C.A.N. 2941, 2981.

[16] *See* Trafficking Victims Protection Reauthorization Act of 2008, § 235(d), Pub. L. No. 110-457, 122 Stat. 5044 (2008), § 235(d).

[17] 8 U.S.C. § 1101(a)(27)(J)(iii)(II).

children separated from one parent but not the other remains unclear and is almost certainly an issue that will be litigated.

§ 20.2.3 Best Interests of the Child

Eligibility for Special Immigrant Juvenile Status requires a finding that it is not in the child's best interest to be returned to his or her "previous country of nationality or country of last habitual residence."[18] This is the only provision in U.S. immigration law in which eligibility for immigration status takes the best interests of the child into consideration, in part explaining why responsibility for this determination is placed with the juvenile court and not immigration authorities. In short, this is not an immigration determination but rather the sort of best interests calculation that family courts routinely make. In many cases, the lack of known appropriate family to care for the child in the home country alone is sufficient to determine that it is in the best interests of the child to maintain the status quo. Also, in this context it is entirely appropriate for the court to consider potential future opportunities for the child in the United States in comparison to the home country.

§ 20.2.4 Age and Continuing Dependency

To qualify for Special Immigration Juvenile Status, an applicant must be a child, defined for immigration purposes as unmarried and under age 21.[19] Historically, this meant that applicants needed to complete the immigration adjudication process prior to age 21. The Trafficking Victims Protection Reauthorization Act of 2008, however, provided age-out protection to Special Immigrant Juvenile applicants.[20] "*Officers must now consider the petitioner's age at the time of filing to determine whether the petitioner has met the age requirement.* Officers must not deny or revoke SIJ status based on age if the alien was a child on the date the SIJ petition was properly filed if it was filed on or after December 23, 2008, or if it was pending on December 23, 2008."[21]

This new age-out protection, however, is in tension with a regulatory interpretation of the statute requiring that until the end of the immigration processing the child must "continue to be dependent upon the juvenile court and eligible for long-term foster care, such declaration, dependency or eligibility not having been vacated, terminated, or otherwise ended."[22] In the past, this provision has meant that for many applicants in jurisdictions where courts did not maintain jurisdiction over them until age 21, the de facto age limit was set by the age at which the court relinquished

---

[18] 8 U.S.C. § 1101(a)(27)(J)(ii).

[19] 8 U.S.C. § 1101(b)(1); 8 C.F.R. § 204.11(c).

[20] Trafficking Victims Protection Reauthorization Act of 2008, § 235(d), Pub. L. No. 110-457, 122 Stat. 5044 (2008), § 235(d)(6).

[21] Donald Neufeld & Pearl Chang, *Trafficking Victims Protection Reauthorization Act of 2008: Special Immigrant Juvenile Status Provisions* (USCIS Memorandum, Mar. 24, 2009) (emphasis in original).

[22] 8 C.F.R. § 204.11(c)(5).

jurisdiction. Moreover, courts have been urged to delay finalization of adoptions for children with pending Special Immigrant Juvenile petitions to ensure continuing court dependency until the immigration processing is complete.

While it seems clear that that statute now intends to protect a child from aging out of eligibility, it remains to be seen if the age provision will force reconsideration of the regulatory requirement of continuing jurisdiction. The potential conflict may be minimized by another new mandate that requires U.S. Citizenship and Immigration Services to process SIJ applications within 180 days of filing.[23] Still, until clarification or regulatory reform is achieved it remains best practice to proceed as expeditiously as possible in pursuing Special Immigrant Juvenile Status to complete processing while the child continues to be court dependent.

§ 20.2.5 Application to USCIS and Grounds of Inadmissibility

After children receive the requisite juvenile court findings, they still must apply to U.S. Citizenship and Immigration Services for recognition as a Special Immigrant Juvenile and adjustment of status to legal permanent resident. This application involves completing immigration forms, obtaining a special medical exam, capturing biometrics including fingerprints and photographs, and providing proof of age.[24] The application must include a juvenile court order setting forth the findings discussed above.[25] Parts of the application involve hefty filing fees, but fee waivers are available. U.S. Citizenship and Immigration Services will schedule a date for an adjustment interview at which the application is reviewed and adjudicated, though the application can be granted without an interview.

This process includes scrutiny to see if applicants are disqualified from obtaining legal immigration status by any of the long listing of grounds of inadmissibility. Some of these grounds of inadmissibility are automatically waived for Special Immigrant Juveniles, and others are potentially waiveable upon application. For example, Special Immigrant Juveniles are exempted from grounds of inadmissibility related to becoming a public charge, working without labor certification, being present in the United States without inspection, misrepresentations to immigration authorities, stowing away, possessing certain documents, and being unlawfully present in the United States.[26]

Other grounds of inadmissibility are not waived and raise particular concerns for children in delinquency proceedings. In particular, activity involving the sale or possession of drugs is problematic under immigration law. Findings regarding prostitution or sex offenses also can cause difficulties. Other issues that serve as red flags include testing positive for HIV, past deportations or denied immigration

---

[23]   Trafficking Victims Protection Reauthorization Act of 2008, § 235(d), Pub. L. No. 110-457, 122 Stat. 5044 (2008), § 235(d)(2).

[24]   For the proof of age requirement, see 8 C.F.R. § 204.11(d)(1).

[25]   8 C.F.R. § 204.11(d).

[26]   8 U.S.C. § 1255(h).

applications, falsely claiming U.S. citizenship, and mental conditions posing a threat to self or others. Any child who is considering applying for Special Immigrant Juvenile status and who has delinquency adjudications or other red flags should seek expert immigration advice.

§ 20.3 VAWA, U and T Visas, and Other Immigration Relief

A number of provisions in immigration law provide avenues to obtain lawful immigration status for children who have been subjected to abuse or are victims of other crimes. Unlike Special Immigrant Juvenile Status discussed above, these provisions do not necessarily turn on the involvement of family courts or child welfare systems. The provisions, however, are highly applicable to many of the experiences that result in the involvement of child welfare and court systems in the lives of children. This section will not attempt to set forth these provisions in detail, but will provide brief descriptions of each for purposes of flagging situations in which the provisions might apply and for which consultation with an immigration attorney is advised.

§ 20.3.1 Violence Against Women Act

Immigration provisions in the Violence Against Women Act (VAWA) allow certain noncitizens to file for immigration relief when they have been battered or subjected to extreme mental cruelty by a parent or spouse who is a U.S. citizen or lawful permanent resident.[27] This is referred to as "self-petitioning" and can be accomplished without the abuser's assistance or knowledge. This form of immigration relief is applicable only where the abusive family member is a U.S. citizen or lawful permanent resident. VAWA, in essence, allows the abused person to access immigration benefits that the parent or spouse should be working to achieve for the abused person. The application process requires, among other things, proof of the abuse and that the abused person is of good moral character. The successful VAWA applicant first receives notice of approval of her prima facie case, then approval of the VAWA petition which permits adjustment of status to lawful permanent residence. Immigration relief under VAWA also can qualify recipients for some forms of public assistance at various stages in the application process, and can provide waivers to bars to benefits that apply to many lawful permanent residents who achieve their status through other provisions of immigration law.[28]

As with Special Immigrant Juveniles above, grounds of inadmissibility apply to VAWA petitioners, and careful screening by an immigration attorney usually is warranted. Waivers of some grounds of inadmissibility, such as public charge and

---

[27] 8 U.S.C § 1154(a)(1)(A)(iii), (B)(iii).

[28] *See, e.g.*, Tanya Broder, National Immigration Law Center, *Immigrant Eligibility for Public Benefits* (2005), *available at* http://www.nilc.org/immspbs/special/imm_elig_for_pub_bens_aila_0305.pdf.

unlawful presence, are available but waivers in this context are not as generous as in the Special Immigrant Juvenile context.

Importantly, derivative status is available under VAWA, so parents of children who qualify and children of parents who qualify also may obtain lawful immigration status. This establishes VAWA as an important option to help families stabilize their immigration status and maintain family integrity.

§ 20.3.2 U Visas

Congress authorized the U visa in the Trafficking Victims of Trafficking and Violence Protection Act of 2000.[29] These visas are available to noncitizens who have suffered substantial physical or mental abuse as a result of qualifying criminal activity that occurred in the United States or violated U.S. law; possess information concerning that activity; and have been helpful, are being helpful, or are likely to be helpful with the investigation or prosecution of the criminal activity.[30] The U visa provides authorization to remain in the United States, with employment authorization, for up to four years.[31] After three years in U visa status, the holder may qualify to adjust his or her status to lawful permanent residence.[32]

The range of criminal activity covered by this provision is broad, including many crimes against children and their parents. The list includes activity in violation of federal, state, or local laws relating to:

> rape; torture; trafficking; incest; domestic violence; sexual assault; abusive sexual contact; prostitution; sexual exploitation; female genital mutilation; being held hostage; peonage; involuntary servitude; slave trade; kidnapping; abduction; unlawful criminal restraint; false imprisonment; blackmail; extortion; manslaughter; murder; felonious assault; witness tampering; obstruction of justice; perjury; or attempt, conspiracy, or solicitation to commit any of the above mentioned crimes.[33]

Importantly, while cooperation with law enforcement is required, a prosecution and conviction related to the activity is not. The child, or in the case of children under age 16 a parent or guardian, must cooperate in the "investigation or prosecution" of the activity with a prosecutor, judge, or any law enforcement official investigating the activity.[34] This reaches child protective services investigations, without regard to whether criminal charges are ever filed.

---

[29] Pub. L. No. 106-386, 114 Stat. 1463 (Oct. 28, 2000).

[30] 8 U.S.C. § 1101(a)(15)(U)(i).

[31] 8 U.S.C. § 1184(p)(6).

[32] 8 U.S.C. § 1255(m)(1).

[33] 8 U.S.C. § 1101(a)(15)(U)(iii).

[34] 8 U.S.C. § 1101(a)(15)(U)(i)(III).

Unlike VAWA, U visas are available without regard to the immigration status of the person engaged in the criminal conduct, and no particular relationship with this person is required. For example, a child subjected to abuse would qualify even if the abuser is without lawful immigration status and is not the child's parent.

The U visa derivative provisions are the most generous in immigration law and permit the extension of U visa status from the direct victim to spouses, parents of children under 21, and even unmarried siblings under the age of 18 of children victims under the age of 21.[35] The reach of the U visa makes it an important tool to consider when immigration status concerns extend to other family members in the home.

As with VAWA, waivers of grounds of inadmissibility are potentially available upon application.[36]

§ 20.3.3 T Visas

Along with the U visa, Congress authorized the T visa through the Trafficking Victims of Trafficking and Violence Protection Act of 2000.[37] This visa is available to a person who is in the United States as a "victim of a severe form of human trafficking" and meets other criteria related to cooperation with law enforcement.[38] A severe form of human trafficking is defined as "sex trafficking in which a commercial sex act is induced by force, fraud, or coercion, or in which the person induced to perform such act has not attained 18 years of age" or "the recruitment, harboring, transportation, provision, or obtaining of a person for labor or services, through the use of force, fraud, or coercion for the purpose of subjection to involuntary servitude, peonage, debt bondage, or slavery."[39]

In design and operation, the T visa is comparable to the U visa described above, with its narrower range of victimizing activity. Indeed, any person who qualifies for a T visa likely qualifies for a U visa. Having a T visa can qualify recipients for some forms of public assistance and can provide waivers to bars to benefits that apply to persons who achieve lawful permanent resident status through other avenues.[40] As with all these forms of immigration relief, it is highly advisable to obtain the advice of immigration counsel regarding potential qualifications, disqualifications, and strategic advantages of various routes.

---

[35]   8 U.S.C. § 1101(a)(15)(U)(ii)

[36]   8 U.S.C. § 1255(m)(1).

[37]   Pub. L. No. 106-386, 114 Stat. 1463 (Oct. 28, 2000).

[38]   8 U.S.C. § 1101(a)(15)(T).

[39]   22 U.S.C. § 7102(8).

[40]   *See, e.g.*, Tanya Broder, National Immigration Law Center, *Immigrant Eligibility for Public Benefits* (2005), *available at* http://www.nilc.org/immspbs/special/imm_elig_for_pub_bens_aila_0305.pdf.

§ 20.3.4 Other Forms of Immigration Relief

In addition to the forms of relief discussed above that deal with children specifically or depend on particular forms of victimization, it is important not to reject outright the possibility that children may be eligible for immigration relief under more mainstream provisions. For example, when children have family members with lawful immigration status, it is important to learn how this status was obtained and research whether some immigration benefits might extend to the child. Moreover, children are eligible to apply for other extraordinary forms of relief that often are perceived as applicable to adults, such as asylum. Though children often are effectively handicapped in pursuing some forms of relief, they generally are not ineligible based on their age.[41]

§ 20.4 Immigration Issues in Child Custody Disputes

As the number of immigrants and children of immigrants in the United States grows,[42] it is increasingly common to find "mixed-status" families in which all family members do not share a common immigration or citizenship status.[43] In 2008, 16.3 million children in the United States, or 23.2% of the total population of U.S. children, had at least one immigrant parent.[44] The majority of these children in immigrant families, 59%, have at least one parent who is a U.S. citizen.[45] But about 5.5 million children have at least one parent who is an unauthorized immigrant.[46] Many of these children are U.S. citizens, though approximately 1.5 million unauthorized children live in the United States.[47] Differences in immigration status

---

[41] David B. Thronson, *Kids Will Be Kids? Reconsidering Conceptions of Children's Rights Underlying Immigration Law*, 63 Ohio St. L.J. 979 (2002).

[42] One in five children in the United States lives in an immigrant family, i.e., a family in which one or more parent is an immigrant. Federal Interagency Forum on Child and Family Statistics, *America's Children: Key National Indicators of Well-Being 2002*, *available at* http://www.childstats.gov/pdf/ac2002/ac_02.pdf.

[43] In fact, 85% of families with children and headed by a noncitizen are mixed-status families. Michael Fix, Wendy Zimmermann & Jeffrey Passel, *The Integration of Immigrant Families in the United States*, p. 15 (The Urban Institute 2001), *available at* http://www.urban.org/uploadedpdf/immig_integration.pdf.

[44] Aaron Terrazas & Jeanne Batalova, *Frequently Requested Statistics on Immigrants and Immigration in the United States* (Migration Policy Institute, Oct. 2009), *available at* http://www.migrationinformation.org/USfocus/display.cfm?ID=747#7.

[45] Donald J. Hernandez, *Generational Patterns in the U.S.: American Community Survey and other Sources* (2009), *available at* http://www.brown.edu/Departments/Education/paradox/documents/Hernandez.pdf.

[46] Aaron Terrazas & Jeanne Batalova, *Frequently Requested Statistics on Immigrants and Immigration in the United States* (Migration Policy Institute, Oct. 2009), *available at* http://www.migrationinformation.org/USfocus/display.cfm?ID=747#7.

[47] *Id.* at 6–7. Children in immigrant families live with two parents 82% of the time, compared with 71% of the time for native families. Donald J. Hernandez, *Generational Patterns in the U.S.: American*

within families and between parents can create difficulties in the best of times, but they present special challenges when families face the prospect of separation.

In decisions regarding child custody, judges and advocates can be "all too eager to attach exaggerated legal significance to immigration status with little explanation and no analysis."[48] While parties and courts often reflexively assume there is legal significance or advantage in the distinction, the logic of this presumed relevance rarely is explained. In general, courts "have demonstrated a willingness to consider immigration status issues in child custody disputes but have yet to articulate a rationale for whether this engagement is proper and to develop a workable framework for competent analysis if it is."[49]

Working with immigrant children and families can present new challenges for child welfare advocates and systems. "In any determination of child custody issues, vigilance against discrimination on the basis of immigration status is crucial, but a strict prohibition on raising immigration status issues in child custody matters would be difficult to maintain because immigration status does have an impact on the experiences of many immigrants and their families."[50] Rather than sweeping issues related to immigration under the table, it is important that when such considerations are at play, they are "acknowledged, understood, and, when appropriate, affirmatively addressed in legal representation."[51]

A full exploration of the manner in which immigration issues arise in child custody matters is beyond the scope of this chapter, but a baseline principle is important to keep in mind as a starting point: immigration status alone says nothing about a parent's fitness or the best interests of a child. Best interest determinations are highly contextual and fact specific, requiring individualized inquiry from an unbiased starting point. The presence of immigration issues rarely makes a matter simpler, but complexity and logistical difficulties must never provide cover to ignore fundamental rights of children and parents.[52]

§ 20.5 Resources

In most cases involving the immigration rights of children it is important to consult with immigration law experts. Given the risk of deportation inherent in

---

Community Survey and other Sources (2009), *available at*
http://www.brown.edu/Departments/Education/paradox/documents/Hernandez.pdf.

[48] David B. Thronson, *Of Borders and Best Interests: Examining the Experiences of Undocumented Immigrants in U.S. Family Courts*, 11 TEX. HISP. J.L. & POL'Y 45, 49 (2005).

[49] David B. Thronson, *Custody and Contradictions: Exploring Immigration Law as Federal Family Law in the Context of Child Custody*, 59 HASTINGS L.J. 453, 456 (2008).

[50] David B. Thronson, *Creating Crisis: Immigration Raids and the Destabilization of Immigrant Families*, 43 WAKE FOREST L. REV. 391, 416 (2008).

[51] David B. Thronson, *Custody and Contradictions: Exploring Immigration Law as Federal Family Law in the Context of Child Custody*, 59 HASTINGS L.J. 453, 472 (2008).

[52] David B. Thronson, *Creating Crisis: Immigration Raids and the Destabilization of Immigrant Families*, 43 WAKE FOREST L. REV. 391 (2008).

submitting to the immigration authorities an application for relief that is not meritorious, it is generally not advisable to contact immigration authorities about a child until the child's immigration possibilities and rights have been thoroughly researched. Some important sources of information can be found at:

- Immigrant Legal Resource Center – www.ilrc.org
- ASISTA – http://asistahelp.org
- Center for Gender and Refugee Studies – http://cgrs.uchastings.edu
- Families for Freedom – www.familiesforfreedom.org
- Kids In Need of Defense – http://www.supportkind.org
- National Immigration Law Center – www.nilc.org
- National Immigrant Project – http://www.nationalimmigrationproject.org/
- United States Citizenship & Immigration Services – www.uscis.gov

It often is difficult to find attorneys with experience in the practice of both immigration and family law. Some of the organizations above may be helpful in locating a qualified attorney in your area. Most serious immigration attorneys are members of the American Association of Immigration Attorneys, which may be able to provide referrals. Finally, many law school clinical programs are developing expertise in the representation of immigrant children and are important resources to explore.

Chapter 21: Advocacy for Foster Youth in Mental Health Commitment Proceedings[*]

by Bernard P. Perlmutter[1]

§ 21.1 Introduction

"Karina," a former foster care client of the University of Miami School of Law's Children & Youth Law Clinic, submitted the following comments to the Florida Supreme Court in 2002 on proposed Florida Rule of Juvenile Procedure 8.350 governing the commitment of dependent children to psychiatric facilities:

> I was placed in several treatment facilities over the years I was in foster care. . . I wish I would have had a lawyer during all the years I was kept in locked facilities. I think it would have made a big difference. I don't think that I would have been abused like I was if I would have had a lawyer. I don't think I would have even been in locked facilities as long as I was if I would have had a lawyer. If I hadn't finally gotten a lawyer, DCF would have kept me in a locked facility until I turned 18, and I never would have learned to live outside of a facility. . . .

> I think it's very important for a foster child to have a hearing before DCF sends them to a facility so they can talk to the judge. After I got my attorney, she made sure that I got a hearing and that I went to court. I was able to speak to the judge, and my lawyer told the judge why I shouldn't be placed in a facility. The judge said that I didn't need to be put in another facility. . . Also, I think it's very important for every foster child in a facility to have a lawyer. If a child doesn't have a lawyer, then there's no one to stand up for what the child

---

[*] This article was originally written by Bernard P. Perlmutter, J.D. and Carolyn S. Salisbury, J.D. and appeared as Chapter 12 (G) of the first edition of Child Welfare Law and Practice. The author is grateful to Carolyn Salisbury for her significant contribution to this chapter.

[1] Bernard P. Perlmutter, J.D., is Director and Associate Clinical Professor at the Children & Youth Law Clinic, University of Miami School of Law. Professor Perlmutter prepared the revised version of this chapter.

wants. This makes a child lose hope, which is how I felt for a long time.[2]

This chapter provides an overview of the legal framework governing the commitment of children like Karina to psychiatric residential treatment programs or facilities, the research on the effectiveness of residential treatment for emotionally disturbed children, the therapeutic jurisprudence considerations pertinent to the representation of children committed to these facilities, the ethical responsibilities of lawyers who represent these children, and the roles performed by attorneys both before and after a child's commitment to a psychiatric facility.

§ 21.2 Background

There has been growing skepticism about the effectiveness, necessity, and cost benefit value of the psychiatric commitment of emotionally disturbed or behaviorally disordered children and adolescents in state care like our client Karina.[3] In recent years, advocates have voiced and documented their concerns about the overuse and misuse of mental hospitals and residential treatment centers to institutionalize "troublesome youth" diagnosed with relatively mild adolescent disorders such as "conduct disorder," "oppositional defiant disorder," and "adolescent adjustment reaction."[4] While some children who have serious psychiatric disorders may need such care, many other state-dependent children are institutionalized in psychiatric facilities for a wide variety of antisocial teenage behaviors including running away,

---

[2] *See* Karina's Comments, Appendix to University of Miami School of Law Children & Youth Law Clinic Comments, in *In re Fla. R. Juv. P. 8.350* (*filed* Feb. 15, 2002). *See In re* Fla. Juv. P. 8.350, 804 So. 2d 1206, 1209 (Fla. 2001), 842 So. 2d 763 (Fla. 2003).

[3] *See* U.S. Department of Health and Human Services, *Mental Health: A Report of the Surgeon General* (1999), *available at* http://www.surgeongeneral.gov/library/mentalhealth/chapter3/sec7.html#treatment ("Concerns about residential care primarily relate to criteria for admission; inconsistency of community-based treatment . . .; the costliness of such services; the risks of treatment, including failure to learn behavior needed in the community; the possibility of trauma associated with the separation from the family; difficulty reentering the family or even abandonment by the family; victimization by RTC staff; and learning of antisocial or bizarre behavior from intensive exposure to other disturbed children.") (citations omitted).

[4] *See, e.g.,* Lois A. Weithorn, Note, *Mental Hospitalization of Troublesome Youth: An Analysis of Skyrocketing Admission Rates,* 40 STAN. L. REV. 773, 788–92 (1988) (noting that more than half of children in psychiatric facilities were "troublemakers" suffering from relatively mild psychological disorders, and children undergoing normal adolescent developmental phases, rather than children diagnosed with severe mental illness or psychotic disorders). *See also* Bernard P. Perlmutter & Carolyn S. Salisbury, *"Please Let Me Be Heard:" The Right of a Florida Foster Child to Due Process Prior to Being Committed to a Long-Term, Locked Psychiatric Institution,* 25 NOVA L. REV. 725, 731 (2001) (describing growing concerns over "misuse of private mental hospitals to institutionalize 'troublesome youth' diagnosed with relatively mild adolescent disorders").

aggression, opposition to parental values and rules, or "sexualized behaviors" such as teenage pregnancy or homosexuality.[5]

Nationally, studies have shown that many children and youth committed to psychiatric institutions are inappropriately placed.[6] Also, studies of the psychiatric commitment of adolescents have shown that fewer than one-third of those children admitted for inpatient mental health treatment were diagnosed as having severe or acute mental disorders of the type typically associated with such admissions (such as psychotic, serious depressive, or organic disorders).[7] Disturbingly, "the rising rates of psychiatric admission of children and adolescents reflect an increasing use of hospitalization to manage a population for whom such intervention is typically inappropriate: 'troublesome' youth who do not suffer from severe mental disorders."[8]

Erroneous placement in a residential treatment facility can have an extremely harmful and traumatic impact on a child:

A recent review of psychological research concluded that certain degrees of freedom of movement, association, and communication are critical to the psychological well-being of children and adolescents. Mental hospitalization may entail substantial periods of isolation, particularly in the case of recalcitrant children and adolescents, and may be characterized by involuntary administration of heavy doses of psychotropic medication (that is, medication used to alter psychological functioning), invasions of privacy, and social pressure to conform behavior to certain norms. . . . Certain aspects of mental hospitalization can be extremely frightening for

---

[5]   *See, e.g.*, Maribel Morey, Note *The Civil Commitment of State Dependent Minors: Resonating Discourses That Leave Her Heterosexuality and His Homosexuality Vulnerable to Scrutiny*, 81 N.Y.U. L. REV. 2129 (2006); Sarah E. Valentine, *Traditional Advocacy for Nontraditional Youth: Rethinking Best Interest for the Queer Child*, 2008 MICH. ST. L. REV. 1053, 1091–96 (2008).

[6]   *See, e.g.*, Bazelon Center for Mental Health Law, *Fact Sheet: Children in Residential Treatment Centers* (2006), *available at* http://cafety.org/research/121-research/142-fact-sheet-children-in-rtcs-from-the-bazelon-center-for-mental-health-law-and-policy ("RTCs are among the most restrictive mental health services and, as such, should be reserved for children whose dangerous behavior cannot be controlled except in a secure setting. Too often, however, child-serving bureaucracies hastily place children in RTCs because they have not made more appropriate community-based services available.") (citations omitted). *See also* Lois A. Weithorn, Note, *Mental Hospitalization of Troublesome Youth: An Analysis of Skyrocketing Admission Rates*, 40 STAN. L. REV. 773, 784 n. 72 (1988) (quoting J. KNITZER, UNCLAIMED CHILDREN: THE FAILURE OF PUBLIC RESPONSIBILITY TO CHILDREN AND ADOLESCENTS IN NEED OF MENTAL HEALTH SERVICES 46 (1982)). Inappropriateness was judged on the basis of "factors such as whether the 'children could have been served as outpatients' or in day treatment, and whether the severity of the children's diagnoses warranted inpatient treatment." *Id.*

[7]   Lois A. Weithorn, Note, *Mental Hospitalization of Troublesome Youth: An Analysis of Skyrocketing Admission Rates*, 40 STAN. L. REV. 773, 788 (1988); *see also* Maribel Morey, Note *The Civil Commitment of State Dependent Minors: Resonating Discourses That Leave Her Heterosexuality and His Homosexuality Vulnerable to Scrutiny*, 81 N.Y.U. L. REV. 2129, 2141–45 (2006) (listing examples of qualified evaluators focusing on minors' sexual behaviors as basis for recommending inpatient psychiatric commitment, without diagnosing clear evidence of emotional disturbance or psychiatric disorder).

[8]   Lois A. Weithorn, Note, *Mental Hospitalization of Troublesome Youth: An Analysis of Skyrocketing Admission Rates*, 40 STAN. L. REV. 773, 773–74 (1988).

some children. Children who are not seriously emotionally disturbed may be greatly upset by exposure to children who are.[9]

Many of the "troublesome" youth who are committed to psychiatric institutions are children who have been abused, abandoned, or neglected and placed in state foster care: "[A] very large proportion of children in mental hospitals and other residential treatment facilities are wards of the state . . . Once children are placed in state custody, a new set of problems emerge. Social service placements often are far from children's families and therefore, promote an institutional climate. Children find themselves amid a slow bureaucracy in which they are stuck in restrictive settings for long periods of time without effective recourse."[10]

Children who are committed to psychiatric institutions remain there indefinitely. In fact, once hospitalized, juvenile psychiatric patients remain in the institution approximately twice as long as do adults.[11] Additionally, foster children who are in state custody remain institutionalized for longer periods of time.[12]

§ 21.3 The Legal Framework

§ 21.3.1 *Parham v. J.R.*

In 1979, the United States Supreme Court decided *Parham v. J.R.*, a widely criticized decision in which the Court ruled that the Fourteenth Amendment to the United States Constitution does not require a court hearing prior to parents or the state

---

[9] *Id.* at 797 (citations omitted). For more recent study of the harmful impact of residential treatment on children, see Bazelon Center for Mental Health Law, *Fact Sheet: Children in Residential Treatment Centers* (2006), *available at* http://cafety.org/research/121-research/142-fact-sheet-children-in-rtcs-from-the-bazelon-center-for-mental-health-law-and-policy ("Children placed in RTCs have been sexually and physically abused, restrained for hours, over-medicated and subject to militaristic punishments; some have died.") (citations omitted); U.S. Government Accountability Office, GAO-08-146T, *Residential Treatment Programs: Concerns Regarding Abuse and Death in Certain Programs for Troubled Youth* (2007) (documenting thousands of allegations of abuse, some of which involved death, at residential treatment programs between 1990 and 2007).

[10] GARY B. MELTON, PHILLIP M. LYONS JR. & WILLIS J. SPAULDING, NO PLACE TO GO: THE CIVIL COMMITMENT OF MINORS 15–16 (1998) (citations omitted). "[A]t least 40% of children and youth in state hospitals could have been treated in less restrictive settings, *by the states' own admission*. This is true of residential treatment facilities as well." *Id.* at 37 (citing J. KNITZER, UNCLAIMED CHILDREN: THE FAILURE OF PUBLIC RESPONSIBILITY TO CHILDREN AND ADOLESCENTS IN NEED OF MENTAL HEALTH SERVICES 46 (1982)). *See also* Lois A. Weithorn, *Envisioning Second-Order Change in America's Responses to Troubled and Troublesome Youth*, 33 HOFSTRA L. REV.1305, 1497–1501 (2005) (observing how the inability of parents to afford mental health services for their severely behaviorally disordered children causes them to relinquish custody, and noting that these state-dependent children end up being admitted into mental hospitals for lengthy stays with little chance for reunification with their families); BAZELON CENTER FOR MENTAL HEALTH LAW, RELINQUISHING CUSTODY: THE TRAGIC RESULT OF FAILURE TO MEET CHILDREN'S MENTAL HEALTH NEEDS (2000) (same).

[11] Lois A. Weithorn, Note, *Mental Hospitalization of Troublesome Youth: An Analysis of Skyrocketing Admission Rates*, 40 STAN. L. REV. 773, 789 (1988).

[12] GARY B. MELTON, PHILLIP M. LYONS JR. & WILLIS J. SPAULDING, NO PLACE TO GO: THE CIVIL COMMITMENT OF MINORS 16 (1998)

committing a child to a psychiatric hospital.[13] The *Parham* court set forth the minimum due process that is required under the federal constitution when a child is committed to a psychiatric facility.

In *Parham*, the Court established that "[i]t is not disputed that a child, in common with adults, has a substantial liberty interest in not being confined unnecessarily for medical treatment and that the state's involvement in the commitment decision constitutes state action under the Fourteenth Amendment."[14] Accordingly, the Court "assume[d] that a child has a protectable interest not only in being free of unnecessary bodily restraints but also in not being labeled erroneously by some persons because of an improper decision by the state hospital superintendent."[15]

Under the Georgia statute challenged in *Parham*, a parent or guardian could admit a child for "observation and diagnosis."[16] The statute governing voluntary admissions further provided that if the superintendent of the hospital found "evidence of mental illness" and that the child was "suitable for treatment" in the hospital, the child could be admitted "for such period and under such conditions as may be authorized by law."[17] Although one of the plaintiffs in *Parham* had been voluntarily admitted to the mental hospital by his parents, the lead named plaintiff, J.R., was "declared a neglected child" and removed from his parents' care by the county. As a ward of the State of Georgia, J.R. had been admitted to the mental institution by the Georgia Department of Family and Children Services.[18]

The Court first discussed whether the procedure used by the State of Georgia violated due process when the child's parent admitted the child to the state mental hospital.[19] The Court determined that precedents permit parents to retain a substantial—if not the dominant—role in the decision, absent a finding of neglect or abuse, and that the traditional presumption that the parents act in the best interests of their child should apply. The Court also stated, however, that the child's rights and the nature of the commitment decision are such that parents cannot always have absolute and unreviewable discretion to decide whether to have a child institutionalized. The Court concluded that parents retain plenary authority to seek such care for their children, subject to a physician's independent examination and medical judgment.[20] In addition, the Court recognized that the State has "a significant interest in confining the use of its costly mental health facilities to cases of genuine need."[21]

---

[13] Parham v. J.R., 442 U.S. 584 (1979).

[14] *Id.* at 600.

[15] *Id.* at 601.

[16] *Id.* at 591.

[17] *Id.* at 590–91.

[18] *See id.*

[19] *Id.* at 589–617.

[20] *Id.* at 604.

[21] *Id.* at 604–05.

Answering the question, "What process protects adequately the child's constitutional rights?" the Court concluded that the risk of error inherent in the parental decision to have a child institutionalized for mental health care is sufficiently great that some kind of inquiry should be made by a "neutral factfinder" to determine whether the "statutory requirements for admission are satisfied."[22] That inquiry must carefully probe the child's background using all available sources, including, but not limited to, parents, schools, and other social agencies. The review must also include an interview with the child. It is necessary that the decision-maker have the authority to refuse to admit any child who does not satisfy the medical standards for admission. Finally, it is necessary that the child's continuing need for commitment be reviewed periodically by a similarly independent procedure.[23]

The Court next considered what process is due when the child is a ward of the state.[24] The Court indicated that when a child is in the custody of the state due to the parent's abuse or neglect, the state has a statutory duty to consider the best interests of the child with regard to commitment.[25] Although the majority recognized that "what process is due varies somewhat when the state, rather than a natural parent, makes the request for commitment," the Court concluded that "the differences in the two situations do not justify requiring different procedures at the time of the child's initial admission to the hospital."[26] However, the Court determined that "[i]t is possible that the procedures required in reviewing a ward's need for continuing care should be different from those used to review the need of a child with natural parents."[27]

Thus, the United States Supreme Court in *Parham* set forth three minimum due process requirements that must be provided when a child is committed: (1) an inquiry by a neutral factfinder, which is not required to be in the form of a judicial inquiry; (2) the inquiry must probe the child's background using all available resources; and (3) there must be periodic review by a neutral factfinder.[28] These minimum standards apply whether the child has been admitted by the state as the guardian of its ward or by a natural parent.[29]

---

[22] *Id.* at 606.

[23] *Id.* at 606–07 (emphasis added) (citations omitted).

[24] *See id.* at 617–21.

[25] *See id.* at 618–19.

[26] *Id.* at 617–18. Justice Brennan, joined by Justices Marshall and Stevens, strongly dissented on the issue of what procedures are constitutionally required when the child is a ward of the state. *See id.* at 636–39 (Brennan, J., concurring in part and dissenting in part). Justice Brennan wrote that "there is no justification for denying children committed by their social workers the prior hearings that the Constitution typically requires." *Id.* at 637. In addition, he observed that the social worker-child relationship is not deserving of the deference accorded the parent-child relationship, and that when a child is already in state custody, pre-hospitalization hearings will not prevent children from receiving needed care. *See id.* at 637–38.

[27] *Id.* at 619. The Court directed the district court to consider this issue on remand. *Id.*

[28] *Id.* at 606.

[29] *See id.* at 618–19. Although some would argue that U.S. Supreme Court cases regarding the scope of procedural due process protections in delinquency proceedings should accord minors facing civil

The *Parham* decision has been widely criticized for not mandating that children be provided with judicial due process safeguards prior to their commitment to psychiatric facilities,[30] as well as for relying on faulty assumptions about adolescent decision-making.[31] When the Court decided *Parham* in 1979, the Court relied on an *amicus curiae* brief submitted by the American Psychiatric Association that argued against providing judicial hearings prior to the minor's commitment. However, both the American Psychiatric Association and the American Psychological Association now strongly support judicial due process for adolescent minors facing psychiatric institutionalization, particularly when the minor is a ward of the state. Both associations have drafted model state commitment statutes or approved guidelines for

---

commitment greater due process (see, e.g., *In re Gault*, 387 U.S. 1 (1967) and *Kent v. United States*, 383 U.S. 541 (1966)), these decisions are not helpful because they were issued before the Court's ruling in *Parham*.

[30] As one commentator has noted, "[n]o modern U.S. Supreme Court civil case dealing with the rights of the mentally handicapped has been criticized as consistently or as thoroughly as [has] been *Parham*." MICHAEL L. PERLIN, MENTAL DISABILITY LAW: CIVIL AND CRIMINAL 428 (Lexis Law Publishing 1998–2003); *see also* Ira C. Lupu, *Mediating Institutions: Beyond the Public/Private Distinction: The Separation of Powers and the Protection of Children*, 61 U. CHI. L. REV. 1317 (1994) (discussing *Parham* and the mechanism for distributing decision-making authority over children); Bernard P. Perlmutter & Carolyn S. Salisbury, *"Please Let Me Be Heard:" The Right of a Florida Foster Child to Due Process Prior to Being Committed to a Long-Term, Locked Psychiatric Institution*, 25 NOVA L. REV. 725, 731–37 (2001) (summarizing research on residential treatment of "troublesome" youth in the wake of *Parham*); Lois A. Weithorn, Note, *Mental Hospitalization of Troublesome Youth: An Analysis of Skyrocketing Admission Rates*, 40 STAN. L. REV. 773, 826 (1988) (criticizing *Parham* as tolerating the inappropriate use of inpatient facilities, the result of "a combination of factors, including laissez-faire judicial policies, insurance coverage favoring inpatient treatment, the rise of corporate medicine, a mental health establishment willing to assume control over troublesome youth, and the symbolic appeal of a medical perspective on deviance").

[31] In *Parham*, Justice Burger stated that "[m]ost children, even in adolescence, simply are not able to make sound judgments concerning many decisions, including their need for medical care or treatment." *Parham*, 442 U.S. at 603. However, this dicta by the Supreme Court is one of a number of outmoded "assumptions" that the Court relied upon in its ruling. Indeed, the social science research now indicates that, at least in their reasoning about treatment decisions, adolescents are indistinguishable from adults. In a leading research study, clinical psychologists "presented hypothetical dilemmas about medical and psychological treatment decisions to nine, fourteen, eighteen, and twenty-one-year olds. The responses of the fourteen-year-olds could not be differentiated from those of the adult groups, according to any of the major standards of competency: evidence of choice; reasonable outcome or choice; reasonable decision making process; understanding the facts." *See* Gary B. Melton, *Toward "Personhood" for Adolescents: Autonomy and Privacy as Values in Public Policy*, 38/1 AM. PSYCHOL. 99 (1983). This empirical evidence indicates that "[t]here seems to be ample basis for reversal of current presumptions in favor of a view of adolescents as autonomous persons possessed of independent interests regarding liberty and privacy. Accordingly, psychologists should actively involve minors in decision making about treatment and research, and policy-makers should begin their analyses of issues involving adolescents with respect for their autonomy and privacy." *Id. See also* Jan C. Costello, *The Trouble is They're Growing, Therapeutic Jurisprudence and Adolescents' Participation in Mental Health Care Decisions*, 29 OHIO N.U. L. REV. 607, 638 (2003) (noting that "providing a 'growing' or 'grown' teen with greater participation in mental health care decisions may be highly therapeutic").

minors facing commitment to psychiatric facilities that provide the youth with substantial judicial due process prior to commitment.[32]

§ 21.3.2 State Laws

The *Parham* Court noted that states are free to provide additional due process safeguards for minors in mental health commitment proceedings.[33] State law varies widely in this area, and therefore children's attorneys need to familiarize themselves with the applicable case law and legislation in their states. Several state supreme courts have granted minors greater due process protections in mental health commitment proceedings.[34] In addition to state case law, legislation regulating minors' psychiatric commitment also varies by state:

---

[32] In 1981, two years after *Parham*, the American Psychiatric Association approved a set of guidelines for the psychiatric hospitalization of minors. The guidelines, prepared by the Association's Task Force on the Commitment of Minors, guarantee children over the age of 16 the right to contest an involuntary admission to a psychiatric facility, the right to an involuntary commitment hearing, and the right to counsel at the involuntary commitment hearing. At the involuntary commitment hearing, the child through the child's appointed counsel has the right to cross examine witnesses favoring commitment and the right to present testimony and evidence in opposition to commitment and/or in favor of less structured alternatives. In addition to these protections, the party seeking to commit the child against the child's will has the burden of showing the court by clear and convincing evidence that: (a) the child has a mental disorder; (b) the child is in need of treatment or care available at the institution to which involuntary commitment is sought; and (c) no less structured means are likely to be as effective in providing such treatment or care. If the court, after hearing the evidence presented, commits the child to a psychiatric program, the duration of the initial commitment cannot exceed 45 days, with the next commitment for 90 days, and subsequent commitments of 6 months. *See* American Psychiatric Association, *Guidelines for the Psychiatric Hospitalization of Minors*, § 4(C), 139/7 AM. J. PSYCHIATRY 971 (1982).

More recently, the American Psychological Association's Division of Child, Youth, and Family Services endorsed guidelines that provide significant judicial due process to youth facing psychiatric commitment. *See* GARY B. MELTON, PHILLIP M. LYONS JR. & WILLIS J. SPAULDING, NO PLACE TO GO: THE CIVIL COMMITMENT OF MINORS 17 (1998) (citing A MODEL ACT FOR THE MENTAL HEALTH TREATMENT OF MINORS, AMERICAN PSYCHOLOGICAL ASSOCIATION § 108). Both the guidelines by the American Psychological Association and the American Psychiatric Association apply even where the parent is seeking the youth's commitment.

[33] Parham v. J.R., 442 U.S. 584, 607 (1979).

[34] *See, e.g., In re* Roger S., 569 P.2d 1286 (Cal. 1977) (holding that no interest of the State sufficiently outweighs the liberty interest of a mature minor over age 14 to independently exercise his right to due process in a commitment to a mental hospital); *In re* P.F., Jr. v. Walsh, 648 P.2d 1067 (Colo. 1982) (holding that a minor has a substantial and protectable liberty interest in being free from the physical restraints attendant to commitment in a psychiatric hospital); Amendment to Rules of Juvenile Procedure, Fla. R. Juv. P. 8.350, 804 So. 2d 1206 (Fla. 2001), 842 So. 2d 763 (Fla. 2003) (adopting rule of court that provides a dependent child with an attorney and a pre-commitment hearing if the state seeks to involuntarily commit the child to a psychiatric facility); M.W. v. Davis, 756 So. 2d 90, 107–08 (Fla. 2000) (holding that "[a]n order approving the placement of a fifteen-year-old dependent child in a locked residential facility against the wishes of that child deprives the child of liberty" and directing the promulgation of a court rule that provides a dependent child "a meaningful opportunity to be heard" in psychiatric commitment proceedings); *In re* Commitment of N.N., 679 A.2d 1174 (N.J. 1996) (holding that even though the state has an interest in ensuring the mental health of its children, that interest is not sufficiently compelling to justify infringement upon a child's due process and liberty rights and ruling that a minor who is in need of intensive institutional psychiatric therapy

State legislation governing the admission of minors to psychiatric facilities can be classified into four general categories. One category includes states which merely abide by the informal admission process authorized in *Parham*. Other states go beyond the minimal requirements mandated in *Parham* by imposing additional pre-admission procedures. For example, some states require that consent be obtained from older children, while a few others implement a pre-admission review hearing. A third category is composed of several states which require some form of post-admission review procedure. A fourth classification includes those states which simply prohibit the voluntary psychiatric hospitalization by parents or other third parties.[35]

Since laws governing minors' psychiatric commitment vary widely among states, it is important for children's attorneys to familiarize themselves with the relevant law in their respective jurisdictions.

§ 21.3.3 Provisions Governing Psychiatric Commitment of Foster Children

Some states also have specific case law, legislation, or court rules regulating the psychiatric commitment of children in foster care,[36] and children's attorneys need to familiarize themselves with these provisions. Additionally, even in the absence of specific state law in this area, children's attorneys can use federal and state foster care law to protect the interests of their foster child clients who face commitment to psychiatric facilities.

---

may not be committed without a finding based on clear and convincing evidence that the minor without such care is a danger to others or self); State of Wash. *ex rel.* T.B. v. C.P.C. Fairfax Hosp., 918 P.2d 497 (Wash. 1996) (granting a 15-year-old mentally ill minor's petition for writ of habeas corpus on the ground that the involuntary incarceration of the minor in a mental hospital against her will violated Washington state law and the minor's constitutional right to liberty).

[35] Dennis E. Cichon, *Developing a Mental Health Code for Minors*, 13 T.M. COOLEY L. REV. 529, 561–62 (1996). For a survey of state legislation in effect at the time of the article's publication, *see id.* at 561–69; *see also* Jan C. Costello, *"The Trouble is They're Growing, The Trouble is They're Grown:" Therapeutic Jurisprudence and Adolescents' Participation in Mental Health Care Decisions*, 29 OHIO N.U. L. REV. 607 (2003) (surveying legislation in California, Illinois, and Ohio); Gary B. Sutnick, Comment, *"Reasonable Efforts" Revisited: Reforming Federal Financing of Children's Mental Health Services*, 68 N.Y.U. L. REV. 136, 149–54 (1993) (surveying select state legislation); Alexander V. Tsesis, *Protecting Children Against Unnecessary Institutionalization*, 39 S. TEX. L. REV. 995, 1019–21 (1998) (surveying select state legislation); Maribel Morey, Note *The Civil Commitment of State Dependent Minors: Resonating Discourses That Leave Her Heterosexuality and His Homosexuality Vulnerable to Scrutiny*, 81 N.Y.U. L. REV. 2129, 2134–38 (2006) (analyzing the civil commitment process of state-dependent minors, with a focus on Florida).

[36] *See, e.g.*, ARIZ. REV. STAT. § 36-518 (2009); CAL. WELF. & INST. CODE § 6552 (2009); CONN. GEN. STAT. ANN. § 17a-79 (2009); FLA. R. JUV. P. 8.350 (2009); OKLA. STAT. tit. 43A, § 5-503 (2009); TEX. HEALTH & SAFETY CODE § 572.001 (2009)*; see also In re* E., 538 P.2d 231 (Cal. 1975); Amendment to Rules of Juvenile Procedure, Fla. R. Juv. P. 8.350, 804 So. 2d 1206 (Fla. 2001), 842 So. 2d 763 (Fla. 2003); M.W. v. Davis, 756 So. 2d 90 (Fla. 2000); *In re* Commitment of N.N., 679 A.2d 1174 (N.J. 1996). For a more comprehensive, but now dated, list of statutory provisions on juvenile civil commitment, see DUE PROCESS PROTECTIONS FOR JUVENILES IN CIVIL COMMITMENT PROCEEDINGS app. A (Richard E. Redding et al. eds.,1991).

Under federal law, if a court has decided that a child cannot return home, then the court must also decide whether the state's proposed placement is the least restrictive, most family-like setting for the child and whether it is in as close proximity as possible to the parents' home.[37] Using foster care judicial review provisions, the child's attorney can argue that placement in a psychiatric facility is not the least restrictive, most family-like setting for the child. Usually, such placements are also not in close proximity to the home of the child's family.[38]

Additionally, federal law mandates that states must have a court-approved case plan for each foster child, which specifies tasks for each party, as well as the type of placement for the child.[39] Placements can range from a foster home, to kinship care, to institutional placement in a residential treatment center or psychiatric facility. Once case plans are adopted by the court, amendments require court approval.[40] Thus, if the state seeks to change a child's placement to commit the child to a psychiatric facility, the child's attorney can argue that this change in the type of placement for the child can only be accomplished through court approval amending the child's case plan, after notice and the opportunity to be heard.[41]

Children's attorneys should carefully examine their states' laws governing foster care judicial review proceedings and foster care case plans to develop arguments for providing foster children with judicial safeguards prior to the state committing the children to psychiatric facilities. Additionally, for children who have already been committed, children's attorneys should examine their states' laws regarding petitions for writs of habeas corpus to challenge the legality of their clients' commitments to these facilities.

§ 21.4 Therapeutic Jurisprudence Considerations

Prior to undertaking representation of a child in mental health commitment proceedings, it is important for children's attorneys to familiarize themselves with the therapeutic jurisprudence literature demonstrating the therapeutic and psychological benefits of ensuring that the child is provided with meaningful due process. Therapeutic jurisprudence is an interdisciplinary field of legal scholarship that seeks to "reshape legal rules and practices in ways that minimize their antitherapeutic effects and maximize their potential to enhance the emotional well-being of the

---

[37] *See* 42 U.S.C. § 675(5)(A).

[38] *See* Bazelon Center for Mental Health Law, *Fact Sheet: Children in Residential Treatment Centers* (2006), *available at* http://cafety.org/research/121-research/142-fact-sheet-children-in-rtcs-from-the-bazelon-center-for-mental-health-law-and-policy ("Children are usually far from home in RTCs, often out-of-state.") (citation omitted).

[39] *See* 42 U.S.C. § 675(1)(A) (requiring that the case plan include "[a] description of the type of home or institution in which a child is to be placed, including a discussion of the safety and appropriateness of the placement").

[40] *See* 42 U.S.C. § 675(5)(C).

[41] *Id.*

individual and society."[42] Therapeutic jurisprudence recognizes that people are more satisfied with and comply more with the outcome of legal proceedings when they perceive those proceedings to be fair and have an opportunity to participate in them.[43] Research on civil commitment hearings conducted by social psychologists and therapeutic jurisprudence scholars strongly favors procedures that "increase patients' perceptions of fairness, participation, and dignity."[44] Therapeutic jurisprudence research has shown that providing a minor with judicial due process in the context of mental health commitment enhances therapeutic and psychological benefits for the minor.

Research studies in the psychology of procedural justice have found that allowing children the opportunity to participate in adversarial court proceedings increases their perception of the fairness of the process.[45] Research indicates that "having some control over the process (a form of control inherent in a truly adversarial system) is likely to enhance a child's sense of perceived justice . . . and perhaps decrease resistance to treatment if it ultimately is ordered."[46] Significant clinical evidence exists showing a greater likelihood of the treatment succeeding when adolescents participate in the decision to begin treatment.[47]

An early research study found considerable benefits resulted from allowing adolescents to have judicial hearings prior to their commitment if they objected to

---

[42] Bruce J. Winick & Ginger Lerner-Wren, *Do Juveniles Facing Civil Commitment Have a Right to Counsel?: A Therapeutic Jurisprudence Brief*, 71 U. CIN. L. REV. 115 (2002); *see also* Jan C. Costello, *Why Have Hearings for Kids if You're not Going to Listen?: A Therapeutic Jurisprudence Approach to Mental Disability Proceedings for Minors*, 71 U. CIN. L. REV. 19 (2002); Bernard P. Perlmutter & Carolyn S. Salisbury, *"Please Let Me Be Heard:" The Right of a Florida Foster Child to Due Process Prior to Being Committed to a Long-Term, Locked Psychiatric Institution*, 25 NOVA L. REV. 725, 765–66 (2001) (proposing application of principles of therapeutic jurisprudence to civil commitment hearings for foster children); Carolyn S. Salisbury, *From Violence and Victimization to Voice and Validation: Incorporating Therapeutic Jurisprudence in a Children's Law Clinic*, 17 ST. THOMAS L. REV. 623, 671–90 (2005) (same).

[43] See Bruce J. Winick & Ginger Lerner-Wren, *Do Juveniles Facing Civil Commitment Have a Right to Counsel?: A Therapeutic Jurisprudence Brief*, 71 U. CIN. L. REV. 115, 115 (2002).

[44] Bruce J. Winick, *Therapeutic Jurisprudence and the Civil Commitment Hearing*, 10 J. CONTEMP. LEGAL ISSUES 37, 60 (1999).

[45] *See generally* Victoria Weisz, Twila Wingrove & April Faith-Slaker, *Children and Procedural Justice*, 44 CT. REV. 36 (2008) (citing studies applying procedural justice theories to demonstrate that children value fairness in court procedures); Tamar R. Birckhead, *Toward a Theory of Procedural Justice for Juveniles*, 57 BUFF. L. REV. 1447 (2009) (examining empirical studies in the area of procedural justice theory, exploring how children and adolescents develop ties to the law and legal actors, and demonstrating a causal relationship between juveniles' perceptions of fairness and their likelihood of reoffending).

[46] GARY B. MELTON, PHILLIP M. LYONS JR. & WILLIS J. SPAULDING, NO PLACE TO GO: THE CIVIL COMMITMENT OF MINORS 139–41 (1998).

[47] *See* Rochelle T. Bastien & Howard S. Adelman, *Noncompulsory Versus Legally Mandated Placement, Perceived Choice, and Response to Treatment Among Adolescents*, 52/2 J. CONSULT. CLIN. PSYCHOL. 171, 177 (1984).

hospitalization.[48] The researchers reported that hospital staff believed giving adolescents a hearing if they objected to hospitalization was "helpful to children" for the following reasons:

- The procedure gave the child the opportunity to tell how the child felt and to express his or her objection.

- The procedure made the child (and the family) confront the issue of whether or not the child really needed or wanted to be hospitalized.

- The procedure made the child feel that he or she had been treated fairly; if the child objected, the child would have an impartial hearing.

- The procedure afforded the child some measure of control over his or her own destiny.

- The procedure was a step in the patient's involvement in planning for his own care.

- The judge could only release the child if the child did not need to be hospitalized.[49]

The therapeutic jurisprudence literature also recognizes the vital role of the child's attorney as a zealous advocate for the child's wishes in psychiatric commitment proceedings:

> The attorney is the primary vehicle for effectuating the juvenile's participatory interests. Both the American Psychological Association and the American Psychiatric Association have recognized the therapeutic importance of having a juvenile represented by an attorney in their Model Act and Guidelines. Without representation [by an attorney] who is professionally bound to articulate the juvenile's wishes and preferences, juveniles will not experience the

---

[48] Alan Meisel & Loren H. Roth, *The Child's Right to Object to Hospitalization: Some Empirical Data*, 4 J. PSYCHIATRY & L. 377 (1976). This early study's finding were echoed in a more recent report on the impact of providing legal counsel and hearings for Florida foster children facing commitment by the court to Statewide Inpatient Psychiatric Programs (SIPPs), pursuant to Rule 8.350, Fla. R. Juv. P. *See* Lawyers for Children America, Inc., *Rule 8.350's First Year: The Impact of Legal Representation for SIPP Kids* (2004) (unpublished manuscript on file with the author). *See also* GARY B. MELTON, PHILLIP M. LYONS JR. & WILLIS J. SPAULDING, NO PLACE TO GO: THE CIVIL COMMITMENT OF MINORS 141 (1998) (summarizing systematic data collected in the 1980s regarding impact of children's participation in special education hearings at the therapeutic school at UCLA).

[49] Alan Meisel & Loren H. Roth, *The Child's Right to Object to Hospitalization: Some Empirical Data*, 4 J. PSYCHIATRY & L. 377, 384–85 (1976); *see also In re* Gault, 387 U.S. 1, 27 (1967) (observing that studies have shown that "the appearance as well as the actuality of fairness, impartiality and orderliness—in short, the essentials of due process—may be a more impressive and more therapeutic attitude so far as the juvenile is concerned").

sense of voice and participation in the proceedings that are essential to their having a positive response to the outcome of the hearing.[50]

Additionally, for both therapeutic and due process reasons, the child's attorney should seek to ensure that the court safeguards the child's right to assert the psychotherapist-patient privilege.[51] Asserting the privilege gives the child a voice and validation in the legal process and assures the integrity of the psychotherapist-patient relationship. Denying the child the right to assert the privilege can have profound anti-therapeutic consequences. The psychotherapist-patient privilege serves an important public interest by facilitating the provision of appropriate treatment for individuals suffering from mental or emotional problems. Foster children in particular, many of whom suffer for severe emotional disorders, must be given the assurance that they can trust their therapists with private disclosures, should be encouraged to seek mental health treatment, and must be able to establish clear boundaries of privacy within the framework of the psychotherapist relationship in order for treatment to succeed. Respect for confidentiality rights is particularly crucial for such children. It allows them to exert some measure of control over their world, and the ability to develop a degree of trust in those around them.[52]

§ 21.5 Ethical Role and Responsibilities of the Child's Attorney

Attorneys who represent children in mental health commitment proceedings have special obligations and challenges:

> For lawyers/advocates to provide effective legal representation they must be familiar with the client's legal rights under state and federal statutes and constitutions. They must have a clear understanding of their professional role and their unique duty to identify and pursue the client's *legal interests* and avoid functioning as a guardian ad litem or therapist. They must be comfortable with the language and concepts of mental health culture and be able to use them in communicating with mental health professionals and the court consistent with the client's *legal* interests. By skillful and zealous representation they

---

[50] Bruce J. Winick & Ginger Lerner-Wren, *Do Juveniles Facing Civil Commitment Have a Right to Counsel?: A Therapeutic Jurisprudence Brief,* 71 U. Cin. L. Rev. 115, 124–25 (2002) (internal citations omitted); *see also* Thomas E. Hopcroft, *Civil Commitment of Minors to Mental Institutions in the Commonwealth of Massachusetts,* 21/2 N. Engl. J. Crim. Civ. Confin. 543 (1995) (explaining that "representation by counsel at a commitment hearing should be as essential an element of due process for children as it is for adults").

[51] *See generally* Chapter 18, Confidentiality.

[52] *See generally S.C. v. GAL.,* 845 So. 2d 953 (Fla. Dist. Ct. App. 2003); David R. Katner, *Confidentiality and Juvenile Mental Health Records in Dependency Proceedings,* 12 Wm. & Mary Bill Rts. J. 511 (2004).

must seek to empower the child client and to help fashion for him or her a future filled with possibilities.[53]

A lawyer who serves as the child's attorney has a very different role from a guardian ad litem or an attorney who represents a guardian ad litem. Thus, prior to undertaking representation of a child client, it is of utmost importance for the child's attorney to understand his or her unique role in the context of representing a child facing commitment to a mental health facility.[54]

Rule 1.14 of the American Bar Association *Model Rules of Professional Conduct* mandates that attorneys who represent children and other clients with disabilities must, as far as reasonably possible, "maintain a normal client-lawyer relationship with the client." The Comment to the rule further states that "children as young as 5 or 6 years of age, and certainly those of 10 or 12, are regarded as having opinions that are entitled to weight in legal proceedings concerning their custody."

Additionally, in 1996, the American Bar Association promulgated *Standards of Practice for Lawyers Who Represent Children in Abuse and Neglect Cases* to clarify attorneys' ethical obligations in dependency proceedings.[55] Standard A-1 states: "The term 'child's attorney' means a lawyer who provides legal services for a child and who owes the same duties of undivided loyalty, confidentiality, and competent representation to the child as is due an adult client."[56] The Commentary to Standard A-1 adds that, "[t]o ensure that the child's independent voice is heard, the child's attorney must advocate the child's articulated position. Consequently, the child's attorney owes traditional duties to the child as client consistent with ER 1.14(a) of the

---

[53] Jan C. Costello, *Representing Children in Mental Disability Proceedings*, 1 J. Ctr. Child. & Cts. 101, 120 (1999); *see also* Joshua Cook, *Good Lawyering and Bad Role Models: The Role of Respondent's Counsel in a Civil Commitment Hearing*, 14 Geo. J. Legal Ethics 179, 182 (2000) (attempting to find a balance between the best interests approach and the adversarial approach to lawyering in civil commitment hearings); Janet B. Abisch, *Mediational Lawyering in the Civil Commitment Context: A Therapeutic Jurisprudence Solution to the Counsel Role Dilemma*, 1/1 Psychol. Pub. Pol'y & L. 120, 120 (1995) (advocating a model that incorporates the therapeutic aspects of adversarial and best interests representation); Henry Chen, *The Mediation Approach: Representing Clients with Mental Illness in Civil Commitment Proceedings*, 19 Geo. J. Legal Ethics 599, 610–12 (2006) (advocating a mediation approach to respondent representation in civil commitment hearings); Donald H. Stone, *Giving a Voice to the Silent Mentally Ill Client: An Empirical Study of the Role of Counsel in the Civil Commitment Hearing*, 70 UMKC L. Rev. 603, 605–09 (2002) (examining the results of an attorney survey showing that respondents' counsel are generally non-adversarial); Christyne E. Ferris, *The Search for Due Process in Civil Commitment Hearings: How Procedural Realities Have Altered Substantive Standards*, 61 Vand. L. Rev. 959 (2008) (arguing that the representation style used by an attorney in a civil commitment hearing can subvert the substantive standards mandated by due process); Michael L. Perlin, *A Critical Evaluation of the Role of Counsel In Mental Disability Cases*, 16/1 Law & Hum. Behav. 39, 56 (1992).

[54] *See generally* Chapter 29, Representing Children and Youth.

[55] The Standards are available at http://www.abanet.org/child/repstandwhole.pdf.

[56] ABA Standards of Practice for Lawyers Who Represent Children in Abuse and Neglect Cases (1996).

Model Rules of Professional Conduct."[57] Standard B-4 further mandates: "The child's attorney should elicit the child's preferences in a developmentally appropriate manner, advise the child, and provide guidance. The child's attorney should represent the child's expressed preferences and follow the child's direction throughout the course of litigation."

The lawyer who serves as the child's attorney in mental health commitment proceedings owes several important responsibilities to the child client. Prior to an initial commitment hearing, at the initial hearing, and at subsequent review hearings and appeals (if the child is committed), the child's attorney performs three critical responsibilities at each stage of the proceedings: (1) client counseling, (2) mediation and negotiation, and (3) zealous advocacy. The *ABA Standards of Practice for Lawyers Who Represent Children in Abuse and Neglect Cases* provide a lodestar to understand how the attorney's responsibilities should be fulfilled in representing the child facing commitment to these facilities.[58]

§ 21.5.1 Lawyer as Counselor

First, the child's lawyer must provide client-centered counseling to the child.[59] The Commentary to ABA Standard B-4 addresses this responsibility as follows:

> The lawyer has a duty to explain to the child in a developmentally appropriate way such information as will assist the child in having maximum input in determination of the particular position at issue. The lawyer should inform the child of the relevant facts and applicable laws and the ramifications of taking various positions, which may include the impact of such decisions on other family members or on future legal positions. The lawyer may express an opinion concerning the likelihood of the court or other parties accepting particular positions. The lawyer may inform the child of an expert's recommendations germane to the issue. . . .

---

[57] *Id.*

[58] *Id.*

[59] For discussions of the concept of client-centered counseling, which is based on deference to client autonomy and is designed to foster client decision-making, see DAVID A. BINDER ET AL., LAWYERS AS COUNSELORS: A CLIENT-CENTERED APPROACH 8–13 (2d ed. 2004) (describing the hallmarks of client-centered counseling and integrating client-centered counseling into the interviewing and counseling process); ROBERT M. BASTRESS & JOSEPH D. HARBAUGH, INTERVIEWING, COUNSELING, & NEGOTIATING SKILLS FOR EFFECTIVE REPRESENTATION 334–38 (1990); Robert D. Dinerstein, *Client-Centered Counseling: Reappraisal and Refinement*, 32 ARIZ. L. REV. 501 (1990). For a discussion of the therapeutic (client-centered, or Rogerian, therapy) derivations of this legal counseling model, which are based on the premise that individuals can achieve full potential or self-actualization when facilitated by a helping, empathic, and nonjudgmental person, see Bruce J. Winick, *Client Denial and Resistance in the Advance Directive Context: Reflections on How Attorneys Can Identify and Deal With a Psycholegal Soft Spot*, 4 PSYCHOL. PUB. POL'Y & L. 901, 916–17 (1998).

On the one hand, the lawyer has a duty to ensure that the child client is given the information necessary to make an informed decision, including advice and guidance. On the other hand, a lawyer has a duty not to overbear the will of the child. While the lawyer may attempt to persuade the child to accept a particular position, the lawyer may not advocate a position contrary to the child's expressed position except as provided by these Abuse and Neglect Standards or the Code of Professional Responsibility.

In proceedings involving a child's commitment to a psychiatric facility, the lawyer's client-counseling role is essential. To properly fulfill the client-counseling role, it is important for the attorney to become familiar with the child's background and special needs and to show special sensitivity to the child client. In a developmentally appropriate manner, "[t]he lawyer should first provide the client with the information necessary for an informed decision. After providing this information, the lawyer/advocate's task is to assist the client in reaching a decision. This means helping the client identify goals and weigh the pros and cons of the proposed course of action, answering the client's questions, and expressing a professional opinion on the practical effect of the client's decision. The lawyer's role is to facilitate the client's decision, not make it for the client."[60]

The child's lawyer needs to provide the child with an honest legal assessment of his or her case, a legal opinion as to whether the merits of the case are strong, and legal advice as to the chances of prevailing. If the merits of the child's case are not strong, then the lawyer may counsel the child that it may be in his or her best interests to waive the commitment hearing and voluntarily consent to placement. If the child wants to contest commitment, then the child's lawyer needs to proceed to engage in negotiation, mediation, and zealous advocacy on the child's behalf.

§ 21.5.2 Lawyer as Negotiator and Mediator

In addition to client counseling, the attorney serves an important role through the use of skills in negotiation and mediation with the state and other parties to explore and consider less restrictive alternatives to residential commitment. Indeed, "only the dependent child's own attorney can give meaning to the child's right to be heard by allowing the child to actively participate in such procedures as negotiating alternatives

---

[60] Jan C. Costello, *Representing Children in Mental Disability Proceedings*, 1 J. CTR. CHILD. & CTS. 101, 108 (1999). *See generally* Annette R. Appell, *Representing Children Representing What?: Critical Reflections On Lawyering For Children*, 39 COLUM. HUMAN RTS. L. REV. 573 (2008) (exploring how children's attorneys are beginning to critically assess their dominance and their approaches to the legal representation of children, developing methods to ensure that the child's viewpoint is expressed, and suggesting that lawyers pursue different methods for achieving justice for children that are more holistic and reflective of the norms of child clients, their families, and their communities); Annette R. Appell, *Children's Voice and Justice: Lawyering For Children in the Twenty-First Century*, 6 NEV. L. J. 692 (2006) (identifying differing approaches to best represent children).

with the GAL and the Department."[61] The Commentary to ABA Standards C-6 states that "[p]articularly in contentious cases, the child's attorney may effectively assist negotiations of the parties and their lawyers by focusing on the needs of the child."[62]

While ethically bound to advocate for the child's expressed wishes, children's lawyers should be prepared to interact with guardians ad litem, social workers, therapists, and other professionals who follow a best interests standard. "Because the best interests standard is prevalent in the child client's interactions with legal, medical, mental health, and social work institutions, the attorney cannot carry out effective representation without developing a sophisticated, principled understanding of the best interests of each client."[63]

In some cases, it may be possible to avoid the child's commitment if the child's attorney is able to mediate and negotiate community-based treatment alternatives that would be in the child's best interests. For example, in some cases, the child's attorney could help a treatment team to prepare a treatment plan that may involve placement in a therapeutic foster home (a foster home with fewer children and specially-trained foster parents), outpatient therapy, and enrollment in a special education school program. The child's attorney can play a vital role in negotiating treatment alternatives to commitment, as well as counseling the child to cooperate with these treatment alternatives.

Additionally, if commitment of the child seems inevitable or imminent, the child may be more likely to voluntarily agree to the commitment and waive a hearing, after consulting with counsel, if the lawyer mediates and negotiates concerns that are important to the child and asserts the child's legal rights. For many dependent children, it will be important to them to be placed in a residential treatment center or hospital that is as close as possible to their community. Additionally, it will also be important to many dependent children to have regularly scheduled visitations and phone contact with their parents or siblings, or both. The child's attorney can play a critical role in such issues as negotiating the frequency and duration of familial contact, ascertaining who will provide transportation for visits, and establishing whether the contact will be supervised or unsupervised.

§ 21.5.3 Lawyer as Zealous Advocate

Finally, the attorney for the child serves a vital advocacy role. The Commentary to ABA Standard B-1 emphasizes that: "The child's attorney should not be merely a fact-finder, but rather, should zealously advocate a position on behalf of the child. . . In furtherance of that advocacy, the child's attorney must be adequately prepared prior

---

[61] *In Re* Fla. R. Juv. P. 8.350, 804 So. 2d 1206, 1209 (Fla. 2001), 842 So. 2d 763 (Fla. 2003).

[62] ABA STANDARDS OF PRACTICE FOR LAWYERS WHO REPRESENT CHILDREN IN ABUSE AND NEGLECT CASES (1996).

[63] Jean Koh Peters, *The Roles and Content of Best Interests in Client-Directed Lawyering for Children in Child Protective Proceedings*, 64 FORDHAM L. REV. 1505, 1565 (1996).

to hearings. The lawyer's presence at and active participation in all hearings is absolutely critical."[64]

If the child objects to commitment, then the child's attorney has an important duty to represent the child at the hearings and present and rebut evidence to zealously contest the child's commitment. If the child agrees to commitment, then the attorney still has an important responsibility to ensure that the agreed order includes terms protecting the child's legal rights, including the general location of placement, the terms of family visitation, and other terms that the child's attorney achieved through negotiations with the parties.

If the child ultimately is committed to a facility, the role of the child's lawyer to provide zealous advocacy at review hearings is as important as at the initial commitment hearing, as many dependent children are forced to endure prolonged stays in residential treatment. ABA Standard D-13 provides that: "The child's attorney should seek to ensure continued representation of the child at all further hearings, including at administrative or judicial actions that result in changes to the child's placement or services, so long as the court maintains its jurisdiction."[65] Thus, not only does the child's attorney have vital roles of client counseling, mediation, negotiation, and zealous advocacy at the initial commitment hearing, but the child's attorney also fulfills these roles at the subsequent review hearings if the child is committed to a mental health facility.

In addition, ABA Standard F-1 provides that: "The child's attorney should consider and discuss with the child, as developmentally appropriate, the possibility of an appeal."[66] Thus, in addition to providing zealous advocacy at the initial commitment hearing and at subsequent review hearings, the child's attorney should, consistent with the child's wishes and the case merits, take all steps to preserve the trial court record to appeal adverse decisions, particularly when they implicate violations of the child's fundamental due process rights in these proceedings.[67]

---

[64] ABA STANDARDS OF PRACTICE FOR LAWYERS WHO REPRESENT CHILDREN IN ABUSE AND NEGLECT CASES (1996). *See also* Bruce J. Winick, *Therapeutic Jurisprudence and the Civil Commitment Hearing*, 10 J. CONTEMP. LEGAL ISSUES 37, 42–43 (1999) ("Lawyers in commitment hearings who take the paternalistic or best interest approach serve their clients inadequately in a number of respects. They often defer to the expert witness, performing little or no cross-examination. They frequently fail even to meet with the client prior to the hearing, or to perform any investigation of the facts that are alleged to justify the client's need for hospitalization. Many fail to controvert the allegation that the patient is mentally ill. They fail to explore alternatives to hospitalization or to obtain benefits for their clients that might avoid its necessity. Some attorneys play largely a clerical role, treating their function as just being 'to look through the paperwork to make sure it is in order, and thus give the false impression that the client has had the benefit of legal representation.' These lawyers 'roll over' in the hearing, deferring to the expert and even stipulating to the hospital's allegations and waiving the client's right to testify." (Citations omitted)).

[65] ABA STANDARDS OF PRACTICE FOR LAWYERS WHO REPRESENT CHILDREN IN ABUSE AND NEGLECT CASES (1996).

[66] *Id.*

[67] *See, e.g.*, G.T. v. Dep't of Children & Family Servs., 935 So. 2d 1245 (Fla. App. 1 Dist. 2006) (holding that DCFS failed to present competent evidence that dependent child was emotionally

§ 21.6 Protection of Children's Rights within Residential Treatment Centers and Hospitals

If the child is committed to a treatment facility, the child's attorney also has an important responsibility to help safeguard the child's rights while the child is in the facility. This requires the child's attorney to develop an understanding of children's psychiatric facilities and the laws governing those facilities.

Children's residential treatment centers and hospitals generally use behavioral modification techniques and employ a "level" and/or "point" system. Under the level/point system, the children gain or lose privileges and receive rewards or punishments, depending on how many points they accumulate in a day and what level they are on in the program. This system varies depending on the facility. Some facilities use the system to determine discretionary privileges like the child's bedtime, whether the child can have snacks, or whether the child can watch television or listen to a radio. However, some facilities attempt to use the level/point system not just to deny discretionary privileges, but also to deny basic legal rights, and this is an area that the child's attorney needs to be prepared to address.

For example, some facilities may attempt to prohibit the child from having any communication, including communication with the child's family, state caseworker, guardian ad litem, or attorney, and even including the ability to contact the state Abuse Registry, unless the child is on a suitably high behavioral level of the program or has acquired "enough" points to be able to exercise certain privileges. Such communication bans and other restrictions on freedom of association and communication "threaten due process generally and permit abusive conditions to go unchecked."[68] Children should not be denied communication with their families or their advocates as punishment because they do not have enough points or are not on a high enough tier or level. A particular communication (for example, with a family member) should only be denied if the court or treatment team determines the communication to be harmful to the child. Additionally, contact with a particular family member would be denied if the court has ordered no contact as part of the dependency proceeding.[69]

Some facilities also use the point/level system to determine whether the child is shackled with wrist and ankle restraints when transported to court or other hearings. Other facilities use the point/level system to determine whether children are allowed

---

disturbed or seriously emotionally disturbed for involuntary commitment to residential mental health treatment facility, where it offered no expert opinion testimony from a psychiatrist or psychologist, but only offered hearsay report by a psychologist); Dep't of Children & Family Servs. v. J.W., 890 So. 2d 337 (Fla. App. 2 Dist. 2004) (holding that the proper standard of proof in proceedings for involuntary commitment of a dependent child to a residential mental health treatment facility is clear and convincing evidence).

[68] GARY B. MELTON, PHILLIP M. LYONS JR. & WILLIS J. SPAULDING, NO PLACE TO GO: THE CIVIL COMMITMENT OF MINORS 62–63 (1998).

[69] *Id.*

to wear their own clothing or whether they must wear hospital gowns and whether or not they are allowed to keep personal items. Like other mental health patients, children should have the right to be transported without restraints and the right to wear their own clothing and to maintain their own personal items, unless there have been individual clinical determinations made about patient safety that bear directly on restraints, clothing and personal items.[70] Children cannot be forced to wear hospital gowns, to be transported in restraints, or to be denied their personal effects as punishment because they do not have enough points or are not on a high enough level. These can only occur if it they are for the safety of the child.

Further, concerns may arise regarding the administration of psychotropic medications to children in residential treatment centers. While some psychotropic drugs can be beneficial for a child, serious concerns have been expressed nationally regarding overmedication of foster children with psychotropic drugs, resulting in severe side effects for the children.[71] Therefore, it is important for the child's attorney to represent the child's interests when the facility seeks to administer psychotropic drugs to the child. Additionally, throughout the child's commitment to a facility, the child's attorney must be vigilant to ensure that the child is not being overmedicated or inappropriately medicated with psychotropic drugs.

Concerns may arise regarding the use of restraint and seclusion in the facility. It is important for the child's attorney to review the child's clinical record, which must be maintained by every mental health facility. Among other documents, the child's clinical record contains notes regarding the facility's use of restraints, seclusion, and psychotropic drugs. American Psychiatric Association guidelines and federal regulations governing the use of restraints and seclusion in psychiatric facilities are important tools for the child's attorney in monitoring the child's treatment in these settings. Indeed, it is generally accepted by medical and mental health professionals that shackling and physical restraints should only be used on children as a last resort and for limited durations.[72]

---

[70] *Id.* at 60–62. *See also* BRUCE J. WINICK, THE RIGHT TO REFUSE MENTAL HEALTH TREATMENT 51–59 (1997) (describing challenges to potential abuses and relative intrusiveness of behavioral therapy techniques in inpatient mental health programs).

[71] *See, e.g.*, Maggie Brandow, Note, *A Spoonful of Sugar Won't Help This Medicine Go Down: Psychotropic Drugs for Abused and Neglected Children*, 72 S. CAL. L. REV. 1151 (1999); Jan C. Costello, *Making Kids Take Their Medicine: The Privacy and Due Process Rights of De Facto Competent Minors*, 31 LOY. L.A. L. REV. 907, 912–18 (1998); Kate O'Leary, *An Advocate's Guide to the Use of Psychotropic Medications in Children and Adolescents*, 25 ABA CHILD L. PRAC. 81 (Aug. 2006); Stephen A. Talmadge, *Who Should Determine What is Best for Children in State Custody Who Object to Psychotropic Medication?*, 15/2 ANN. HEALTH LAW 183 (2006).

[72] *See, e.g.*, American Psychiatric Association, *The Use of Restraint and Seclusion in Correctional Mental Health Care*, p. 4 (2006), *available at* http://archive.psych.org/edu/other_res/lib_archives/archives/200605.pdf.

Additionally, U.S. Department of Health and Human Services general regulations for the use of restraints on patients in mental health facilities set forth explicit guidelines for determining when the use of physical restraints on patients in these facilities is appropriate. These guidelines emphasize the limited situations when physical restraints might be appropriate, the types of personnel who should

In addition to maintaining regular contact with the child, every attorney who represents a child in a residential treatment center or hospital needs to regularly review the child's clinical record to ensure that the child is receiving appropriate treatment and that the child's rights are being protected.

§ 21.7 Advocacy for Other Legal Entitlements and Services for the Child

Finally, the child's attorney has a vital role in advocating for the child's legal entitlements and needed services. In order to fully represent the child, the child's attorney should ensure that the child is receiving all services to which the child is entitled under the law. ABA Standard C-4 states that: "Consistent with the child's wishes, the child's attorney should seek appropriate services (by court order if necessary) to access entitlements, to protect the child's interests and to implement a service plan."[73] Additionally, specifically regarding a child with special needs, ABA Standard C-5 states that: "Consistent with the child's wishes, the child's attorney should assure that a child with special needs receives appropriate services to address physical, mental, or developmental disabilities."[74] These services should include Independent Living services and skills training pursuant to the federal Foster Care Independence Act of 1999, which created the John H. Chafee Foster Care Independence Program,[75] and special education and related services under the federal Individuals with Disabilities in Education Act (IDEA) and Section 504 of the Rehabilitation Act of 1973.[76]

Many foster youth with mental health needs or other disabilities are not provided with mandated independent living services or skills training to meet their special needs. Attorneys for foster youth with disabilities should zealously advocate for youth to be provided with the full range of independent living services to which they are

---

apply restraints, the duration for which restraints should be used, and appropriate follow-up care. *See* 42 C.F.R. § 482.13(e).

Thus, federal regulations prohibit the restraint of mental facility patients, whether adults or children, except in those situations in which there is no other available choice; federal regulations also require that restraints be removed at the earliest possible time. Significantly, the regulations prohibit the use of standing orders for restraint, 42 C.F.R. § 482.13(e)(6), and limit the duration of restraint to two hours for children and adolescents ages nine through seventeen, or one hour for patients under age nine. 42 C.F.R. § 482.13(e)(8)(i).

[73] ABA Standards of Practice for Lawyers Who Represent Children in Abuse and Neglect Cases (1996).

[74] *Id.*

[75] Pub. L. No. 106-169, 113 Stat. 1822 (1999) (codified at 42 U.S.C. § 677) (John H. Chafee Foster Care Independence Program, referred to here as Chafee Program or Act). *See generally* Chapter 23, Foster Youth: Transitioning from Foster Care into Self-Sufficient Adulthood.

[76] *See* Individuals With Disabilities Education Act ("IDEA"), 20 U.S.C. §§ 1400 *et seq.*, and Section 504 of the Rehabilitation Act (Section 504), 29 U.S.C. § 794. *See generally* Chapter 22, Education Goals for Children in Foster Care and the Role of Attorneys.

legally entitled under the Chafee Act.[77] Youth with disabilities may need additional and specialized programming to help them achieve independence, and state child welfare agencies must provide developmentally appropriate independent living services.[78]

Additionally, many foster youth with disabilities are in special education programs, and attorneys who represent these youth should ensure that appropriate educational services are coordinated with the youth's school. Pursuant to the Individuals with Disabilities Education Act (IDEA), every youth in a special education program must have an Individualized Education Plan (IEP).[79] For adolescent youth, the IEP must contain educational transition services to help the youth make the transition to adulthood.[80] Attorneys for these youth should advocate to ensure that the state child welfare agency coordinates its independent living plan for the youth with the school's IEP for the youth. Additionally, the child's lawyer can sometimes use the IDEA to advocate for the child's placement in a less restrictive residential or educational setting.[81] Further, attorneys for foster children committed to facilities should ensure that the client is provided with all independent living services that children outside of facilities receive. Title II of the Americans with Disabilities Act (ADA) of 1990[82] provides that "no qualified individual with a disability shall, by reason of such disability, be excluded from participation in or be denied the benefits of the services, programs, or activities of a public entity, or be subjected to discrimination by any such entity."[83] A public entity is defined under the ADA to include "any State or local government" and "any department, agency, special purpose district, or other instrumentality of a State or States or local government."[84] States are subject to the ADA and, in providing services to foster children, are required under the law to make "reasonable accommodations" for children with disabilities.[85]

---

[77] *See* 42 U.S.C. § 677.

[78] *See* JUVENILE LAW CENTER, DEPENDENT YOUTH AGING OUT OF FOSTER CARE IN PENNSYLVANIA: A JUDICIAL GUIDE 29 (3d ed. 2003), *available at* http://www.jlc.org/publications/8/dependent-youth-aging-out-of-f/. *See also* Bernard P. Perlmutter, *Avoiding Pot Holes on Florida's Road to Independence: Advocacy for Independent Living Services for Foster Youth* 22–25 (2006), *available at* http://www.law.miami.edu/cylc/cylc_clinic_03.php?op=4.

[79] *See* 20 U.S.C. § 1414.

[80] 20 U.S.C. § 1414(d)(1)(i)(VIII).

[81] Federal education law requires schools to ensure that "[t]o the maximum extent appropriate, children with disabilities, including children in public or private institutions or other care facilities, are educated with children who are not disabled." 20 U.S.C. § 1412(a)(5); *see also* 34 C.F.R. § 300.320(a)(4)(iii); 34 C.F.R. § 104.33(a). *See generally* Chapter 22, Education Goals for Children in Foster Care and the Role of Attorneys.

[82] 42 U. S. C. §§ 12201–12213.

[83] 42 U.S.C. § 12132.

[84] 42 U.S.C. § 12131.

[85] *Id.*; *see also* 42 U.S.C. § 12112.

The ADA defines a "qualified individual with a disability" as "an individual with a disability who, with or without reasonable modifications to rules, policies, or practices, the removal of architectural, communication, or transportation barriers, or the provision of auxiliary aids and services, meets the essential eligibility requirements for the receipt of services or the participation in programs or activities provide by a public entity."[86] The Foster Care Independence Act also "makes clear that Independent Living services . . . must be provided for youth 'at various stages of independence,' including those youth with disabilities."[87]

It is especially important for lawyers who represent children in these facilities to pay attention to adolescent youth with special needs, as they are at increased risk "for several of the least desirable outcomes such as poverty, early or unintended pregnancy and becoming a victim of sexual assault" in comparison to their non-special-needs peers.[88] State independent living programs must develop and provide services "in ways that address the multiple needs and learning styles of participants,"[89] and lawyers representing foster children in psychiatric facilities have special obligations to ensure that their clients in particular are provided independent living services and training so that they have the resources to live on their own after their discharge from these facilities and from foster care.

§ 21.8 Conclusion

By giving voice to the child's wishes, protecting the child's legal rights, and advocating the child's articulated position in all mental health commitment proceedings, the child's attorney fills a vital role. As Professor Jan Costello, an expert on the representation of children in mental health proceedings has concluded:

> Ultimately, the most therapeutic thing a lawyer can do is to empower the child client. That means treating the client with respect and building trust, trying to understand and communicate effectively with him or her, and resisting the temptation to coerce the client's compliance. It means encouraging others involved with the child, including parents, mental health professionals, and court personnel, to behave the same way. It means maximizing the client's understanding of and participation in legal or treatment proceedings by informing, listening, counseling, assisting in decision-making, and expressing

---

[86] 42 U.S.C. § 12131(2).

[87] *See* JUVENILE LAW CENTER, DEPENDENT YOUTH AGING OUT OF FOSTER CARE IN PENNSYLVANIA: A JUDICIAL GUIDE 29–30 (3d ed. 2003); *see also* Olmstead v. L.C., 527 U.S. 581 (1999) (mentally disabled institutionalized patients entitled to services that will enable them to develop skills to survive in community-based settings).

[88] SUSAN H. BADEAU ET AL., FREQUENTLY ASKED QUESTIONS II: ABOUT THE FOSTER CARE INDEPENDENCE ACT OF 1999 AND THE JOHN H. CHAFEE FOSTER CARE INDEPENDENCE PROGRAM 24 (2000), *available at* www.nationalfostercare.org/pdfs/ChafeeFAQII1.pdf.

[89] *Id.* at 25.

the client's unique individual perspective to the decision-maker. It means working to identify not just the legal issues involved in the immediate proceeding but also those that may be pursued in the future by or on behalf of the client. Finally, it means affirming to the client and to the outside world the inherent value of the child. In a system of law, the idea of rights, and the recognition that an individual has a right to something, is all but synonymous with a recognition that the person is worthy of respect. . . The assistance of a lawyer advocate affirms both the importance of the right and of the person.[90]

---

[90] Jan C. Costello, *Representing Children in Mental Disability Proceedings*, 1 J. Ctr. Child. & Cts. 101, 116 (1999).

Chapter 22: Education Goals for Children in Foster Care and the Role of Attorneys

by Janet Stotland,[1] Kathleen McNaught,[2] and Kristin Kelly[3]

§ 22.1 The Importance of Education Advocacy

Children in foster care, perhaps more than other children, need a solid education to help ensure a successful future. For the almost 800,000 children and youth involved in the foster care system each year, educational success can be a positive counterweight to their experiences of abuse, neglect, separation, and impermanence in their family and living situations. Unfortunately, the educational outcomes of most children in foster care are dismal.[4] Schools and child welfare agencies cannot be expected to address the needs of children in our system without input and advocacy from their attorneys.

Studies show that youth in foster care with unmet education needs are at higher risk for homelessness, poverty, public assistance, and juvenile or adult court involvement.[5] In contrast, one study shows that when school programs focus on education needs of children in care, the results are improved educational performance, decreased maladaptive behavior, and lower drop-out rates, all of which aid successful transitions to employment or higher education.[6]

Importantly, addressing education needs can also help achieve *permanency* for children in foster care.[7] Youth who are on track educationally, attending school

---

[1] Janet Stotland, J.D., is the co-director of the Education Law Center (PA).

[2] Kathleen McNaught, J.D., is an assistant director at the American Bar Association Center on Children and the Law and directs the Legal Center for Foster Care and Education, a national technical assistance resource and information clearinghouse on legal and policy matters affecting the education of children and youth in foster care.

[3] Kristin Kelly, J.D., is a staff attorney with the American Bar Association Center on Children and the Law and works on the Legal Center for Foster Care and Education.

[4] *See, e.g.*, National Working Group on Foster Care and Education, *Fact Sheet: Educational Outcomes for Children and Youth in Foster and Out-of-Home Care* (Dec. 2008), *available at* http://www.abanet.org/child/education/National_EdFactSheet_2008.pdf.

[5] *See* M. E. Courtney & A. Dworsky, *Midwest Evaluation of the Adult Functioning of Former Foster Youth: Outcomes at Age 19* (Chapin Hall Center for Children, Discussion Paper, May 2005).

[6] Robert H. Ayasse, *Addressing the Needs of Foster Children: The Foster Youth Services Program*, 17/4 SOC. WORK IN EDUC. 207 (1995).

[7] For a discussion of achieving permanence, see Chapter 25, Establishing Legal Permanence for the Child.

regularly, and not having behavior problems at school can be easier to return home or permanently place than youth who are having multiple school problems.

§ 22.2 Blueprint for Advocacy: Eight Goals

Advocating for a child's educational needs is critical to ensuring educational success for children in foster care. But what does that mean and where can you get started? The eight goals discussed in the following sections form the framework developed by the Legal Center for Foster Care and Education, *Blueprint for Change: Education Success for Children in Foster Care*.[8] When each of these goals is met, a child will receive the educational supports and services necessary to achieve positive education outcomes. Therefore, attorneys should ensure that they are addressing each of these goals in their representation of children, agencies, and parents.[9]

GOAL 1. *Youth have the opportunity to remain in their same school when in their best interest.* Youth in out-of-home care live, on average, in two to three different places each year.[10] When youth move, they often are forced to change schools. Studies indicate that frequent school changes negatively affect students' educational growth and graduation rates.[11] Youth in care are entitled to educational stability,[12] and efforts must be made to keep them in their same school whenever possible. School may be the one place where a youth has had (and can continue to have) consistency and continuity. As such, the first step towards achieving school success for children in foster care is maintaining school stability.

GOAL 2. *Youth have the seamless transitions between schools and school districts when school moves occur.* Although school stability is critical, sometimes school moves cannot be avoided or may be in the best interests of the child. These school moves should happen with minimal disruption to the youth's education. When state or local requirements delay enrollment, critical classroom time is lost. Youth need immediate enrollment in the new school and full access to all academic programs and other activities. All records and information about the student's prior schooling must

---

[8] The Legal Center for Foster Care and Education developed the *Blueprint for Change: Education Success for Children in Foster Care* to serve as a framework for advocates seeking to promote positive education outcomes for children in foster care. There are eight Goals for youth, with corresponding Benchmarks that indicate progress. The Goals and Benchmarks are intended to serve as a checklist for advocates in direct representation: What do children in care need to achieve positive education outcomes, and what can attorneys do to support their success? Following each Goal, there are National, State, and Local Examples of policies, programs, or laws that promote the Goals and Benchmarks. The Blueprint is available for download at www.abanet.org/child/education/blueprint/.

[9] For more information about laws that support these education goals, see § 22.6.2.

[10] U.S. Department of Health and Human Services, Administration for Children & Families, *The AFCARS Report: Final Estimates for FY 1998 through FY 2002* (2002).

[11] *See* Linda Jacobson, "Moving Targets," *Education Week*, p. 3 (April 4, 2001).

[12] For additional information on school stability and continuity, see § 22.3.

follow the youth to the new school, with appropriate credit given for work completed at the previous school.[13]

GOAL 3. *Young children enter school ready to learn.* All too often when thinking about how to meet the educational needs of children, we focus on school-age children. But it is crucial that we also consider the educational needs of younger children. According to the American Academy of Pediatrics, children in foster care have higher rates of physical, developmental, and mental health problems, and may enter into foster care with unmet medical and mental health needs.[14] These critical health needs must be addressed during the early years to ensure that young children are developing appropriately and will be ready to benefit from school. Critical to addressing the pre-learning needs of young children is linking them to the full range of screening and early intervention services available.

GOAL 4. *Youth have the opportunity and support to fully participate in all aspects of the school experience.* Unfortunately, youth in care are often prevented from accessing school services available to all other youth. Not only must youth in foster care receive *equal* treatment, they also frequently need *additional* supports. Family and educational instability combined with histories of abuse and neglect mean that youth in care experience higher rates of grade retention and lower academic achievement than their peers.[15] Effectively responding to these needs may require the creation of specific policies and additional supports designed to improve academic achievement and broaden their access to all aspects of the school experience.

GOAL 5. *Youth have supports to prevent school dropout, truancy, and disciplinary actions.* Studies indicate that youth in foster care have dropout, truancy, and disciplinary rates far higher than the general student population.[16] When youth are frustrated by frequent moves and rough transitions, they are more likely to act out, skip school, or drop out altogether. And, of course, children who have experienced abuse or neglect and have been removed from their parents often experience learning difficulties and other problems that interfere with school success. These youth need appropriate support, programs, and interventions to keep them engaged and in school.

---

[13] Linda Jacobson, "Moving Targets," *Education Week*, p. 3 (April 4, 2001).

[14] L. Leslie, M. Hurlburt, J. Landsverk, J. Rolls, P. Wood & K. Kelleher, *Comprehensive Assessments for Children Entering Foster Care: A National Perspective*, 112/1 PEDIATRICS 134 (2003).

[15] *See* M. Burley & M. Halpern, *Educational Attainment of Foster Youth: Achievement and Graduation Outcomes for Children in State Care* (Washington State Institute for Public Policy, Nov. 2001); Mark E. Courtney, Sherri Terao & Noel Bost, *Midwest Evaluation of the Adult Functioning of Former Foster Youth: Conditions of Youth Preparing to Leave State Care in Illinois* (Chapin Hall Center for Children 2004).

[16] *See* M. E. Courtney & A. Dworsky, *Midwest Evaluation of the Adult Functioning of Former Foster Youth: Outcomes at Age 19* (Chapin Hall Center for Children, Discussion Paper, May 2005); W. W. Blome, *What Happens to Foster Kids: Educational Experiences of a Random Sample of Foster Care Youth and a Matched Group of Non-Foster Care Youth*, 14/1 CHILD & ADOLESC. SOC. WORK J. 41 (1997).

In addition, youth in care need trained advocates who will ensure the best possible placement and increase the odds that the youth will complete their education.

GOAL 6. *Youth are involved and engaged in all aspects of their education and educational planning and are empowered to be advocates for their education needs and pursuits.* Encouraging youth to be engaged in education decision-making and planning helps them take an active role in their educational future and guide the professionals and adults advocating on their behalf. Participation in court proceedings, school meetings, the special education process, and transition planning for postsecondary education or jobs allows youth to become advocates on their own behalf. Appropriately trained professionals must facilitate this participation.

GOAL 7. *Youth have an adult who is invested in their education during and after their time in out-of-home care.* Youth need supportive adults to help them achieve their education goals and pursuits. It is critical that all students, and in particular students with disabilities, have an identified and available adult who has the authority to make education decisions on their behalf. Generally, this individual should be the child's parent, but in some cases another individual should be appointed.[17] Parents' and children's attorneys should ensure that an education decision-maker is always identified and, when necessary, advocate that one be appointed. It is also critical that youth have adults available to serve as mentors and to advocate for their rights and needs as they navigate the educational system. Trauma-sensitive training and a full understanding of federal disability law is necessary for any adult who advocates for a child in care or serves as a surrogate parent or authorized decision-maker.

GOAL 8. *Youth have supports to enter into and complete postsecondary education.* Like other students, youth in care want postsecondary education; however, studies indicate that they realize this dream less frequently than the general population.[18] To achieve their full potential, older youth in care and those exiting care need support and opportunities to participate in a wide range of postsecondary programs. Research shows that education outcomes improve when youth can stay in care beyond age 18.[19] In addition, these youth need career and college counseling,

---

[17] For more information about general and special education decision-making, please visit the series on this topic developed by the Legal Center for Foster Care and Education at http://www.abanet.org/child/education/publications/specialeducation.html.

[18] *See, e.g.,* M. E. Courtney, A. Dworsky, G. R. Cusick, J. Havlicek, A. Perez & T. Keller, *Midwest Evaluation of the Adult Functioning of Former Foster Youth: Outcomes at Age 21* (Chapin Hall Center for Children, Executive Summary, Dec. 2007); Mark E. Courtney, Sherri Terao & Noel Bost, *Midwest Evaluation of the Adult Functioning of Former Foster Youth: Conditions of Youth Preparing to Leave State Care in Illinois* (Chapin Hall Center for Children 2004); W. W. Blome, *What Happens to Foster Kids: Educational Experiences of a Random Sample of Foster Care Youth and a Matched Group of Non-Foster Care Youth,* 14/1 CHILD & ADOLESC. SOC. WORK J. 41 (1997).

[19] *See* C. M. Peters, A. Dworsky, M. E. Courtney & H. Pollack, *Extending Foster Care to Age 21: Weighing the Costs to Government Against the Benefits to Youth* (Chapin Hall Center for Children, Issue Brief, June 2009), *available at* http://www.chapinhall.org/sites/default/files/publications/Issue_Brief%2006_23_09.pdf.

assistance with applications and financial aid, and support while participating in their educational program of choice.

§ 22.3 School Stability and Continuity

§ 22.3.1 Importance of School Stability and Continuity

As mentioned above, one of the major educational challenges encountered by youth in foster care is a lack of school stability and continuity. When youth in foster care move, they face challenges unique to their situation. Many spend a significant amount of time out of school because of poor coordination between child welfare and school personnel, resulting in a failure to promptly enroll students in their new schools. Moreover, they often must repeat courses and even grades because of difficulties transferring all of their records and course credits from prior schools. Additionally, changing schools—challenging for any student —can be emotionally overwhelming for children in the foster care system who are simultaneously dealing with separation from their parents and siblings, neighborhoods, and everything that is familiar to them. As a result of these challenges, foster youth often fall behind their peers in school, lose hope, and ultimately drop out of school.

§ 22.3.2 Laws that Help Advocates Support School Stability and Continuity for Clients

Fostering Connections to Success and Increasing Adoptions Act

On October 7, 2008, the Fostering Connections to Success and Increasing Adoptions Act of 2008[20] (Fostering Connections Act) was signed into law. Among its provisions to address the needs of children and youth in foster care, it seeks to promote education stability for children in foster care.

Under the law, child welfare agencies must include "a plan for ensuring the educational stability of the child while in foster care" as part of every child's case plan.[21] As part of this plan, the agency must include assurances that: (1) the placement of the child in foster care takes into account the appropriateness of the current educational setting and the proximity to the school in which the child is enrolled at the time of placement; and (2) the state child welfare agency has coordinated with appropriate local educational agencies to *ensure* that the child remains in the school in which the child is enrolled at the time of placement.[22] Importantly, Fostering Connections also expands the definition of "foster care maintenance payments" to include reasonable transportation to a child's school, thus supporting the ability for child welfare agencies to ensure that children remain in their school.[23]

---

[20] Pub. L. No. 110-351 (codified at 42 U.S.C. §§ 621 *et seq.* and 42 U.S.C. §§ 671 *et seq.*).

[21] 42 U.S.C. § 675(1)(G).

[22] 42 U.S.C. § 675(1)(G).

[23] 42 U.S.C. § 675(4)(A).

Additionally, the law requires that if remaining in that school is *not* in the best interest of the child, the case plan must include assurances by the child welfare agency and the local educational agencies that they will: (1) provide immediate and appropriate enrollment in a new school; and (2) provide all of the educational records of the child to the school.[24]

Finally, Fostering Connections supports the well-being of children in foster care by requiring states to provide assurances in their Title IV-E state plans that every school-age child in foster care, and every school-age child receiving an adoption assistance or subsidized guardianship payment, is a full-time elementary or secondary school student or has completed secondary school.[25]

McKinney-Vento Homeless Assistance Education Act

The McKinney-Vento Homeless Assistance Education Act (McKinney-Vento Act)[26] is a federal law designed to increase the school enrollment, attendance, and success of children and youth who lack a fixed, regular and adequate nighttime residence. It provides modest grants to states to provide supplemental services to eligible youth. The McKinney-Vento Act applies to children and youth living in a wide variety of unstable or inadequate situations, including those children in emergency or transitional shelters, or those "awaiting foster care placement."[27] Although the Act does not define this term, many state and local child welfare agencies and education agencies have developed definitions of who is considered to be "awaiting foster care placement" in their state or locality.[28]

The McKinney-Vento Act's protections are invaluable in helping children in out-of-home care to succeed in school. Eligible children are entitled to many rights and services, including: (1) the right to remain in their school of origin,[29] even if their temporary living situation is located in another school district or attendance area, as long as remaining in that school is in their best interest;[30] (2) the right to receive transportation to and from the school of origin;[31] (3) the right to enroll in a new school and begin participating fully in all school activities immediately, even if they cannot produce normally required documents, such as birth certificates, proof of guardian-

---

[24] 42 U.S.C. § 675(1)(G)(ii)(II).

[25] 42 U.S.C. § 671(a)(30).

[26] Pub. L. No. 107-110; 42 U.S.C. §§ 11431 *et seq.*

[27] 42 U.S.C. § 11434a(2)(B)(i).

[28] For more information, see Patricia Julianelle, *The McKinney-Vento Act and Children and Youth Awaiting Foster Care Placement: Strategies for Improving Educational Outcomes Through School Stability* (National Association for the Education of Homeless Children and Youth 2008); Legal Center for Foster Care and Education, *States at a Glance: Awaiting Foster Care Placement Under the Mckinney-Vento Act, available at* http://www.abanet.org/child/education/publications/AFCPchart.pdf.

[29] "School of origin" is defined as the school the student attended when permanently housed, or the school in which the student was last enrolled. 42 U.S.C. § 11432(g)(3)(G).

[30] 42 U.S.C. § 11432(g)(3).

[31] 42 U.S.C. § 11432(g)(1)(J)(iii).

ship, school records, immunization records, or proof of residency;[32] and (4) supplemental services such as tutoring and mentorship.[33]

If an advocate suspects his or her client is eligible for services under the McKinney-Vento Act, the advocate should contact the McKinney-Vento homeless education liaison from the school district immediately. Every school district is required to designate a liaison who is responsible for determining eligibility under the Act and ensuring that services are provided. If the school or district office is unable to provide the liaison's contact information, the McKinney-Vento State Coordinator should have that information.[34] Many child welfare agencies also employ education specialists who can provide information about the McKinney-Vento Act and facilitate communication with the liaison.

Family Educational Rights and Privacy Act (FERPA)

Often, confidentiality concerns contribute to delays in enrollment and hinder advocates' access to the education records of their clients. Access to education records is critical to ensuring appropriate placements and services, and advocates must understand how to obtain records appropriately. Passed in 1974, FERPA is a federal law that protects the privacy interests of parents and students regarding students' education records.[35] Generally, FERPA protects the rights of parents to control who may access education records by preventing access to third parties without the written consent of the parent, but many exceptions exist.[36] The exceptions most relevant to child welfare cases permit disclosure without prior consent to: (1) other school officials, including teachers, with legitimate educational interest in the child;[37] (2) appropriate persons in connection with an emergency, when the information is needed to protect the health and safety of the student or other persons;[38] (3) officials of other schools when a student is transferring schools;[39] (4) state and local authorities within the department of juvenile justice, if your state has a statute permitting this disclosure;[40] and (5) appropriate persons when the release of information is needed to comply with a judicial order or subpoena.[41] If records are disclosed under one of these

---

[32] 42 U.S.C. § 11432(g)(3)(C).

[33] 42 U.S.C. §§ 11431 *et seq.*

[34] A list of State Coordinators is available on the University of North Carolina at Greensboro SERVE Center at http://www.serve.org/nche/downloads/sccontact.pdf.

[35] 20 U.S.C. § 1232g; 34 C.F.R. § 99. FERPA has been amended several times since its enactment in 1974, most recently by the No Child Left Behind Act of 2000.

[36] 20 U.S.C. § 1232g(b).

[37] 20 U.S.C. § 1232g(b)(1)(A).

[38] 20 U.S.C. § 1232g(b)(1)(I).

[39] 20 U.S.C. § 1232g(b)(1)(B).

[40] 20 U.S.C. § 1232g(b)(1)(E).

[41] 20 U.S.C. § 1232g(b)(1)(J).

exceptions, the recipient cannot redisclose the information unless the redisclosure fits under one of the FERPA exceptions.[42]

Applying FERPA, there are three ways that child welfare professionals or advocates can access education records. First, and most importantly, through parental consent. Advocates should always first attempt to obtain permission from a parent and have the parent sign a written consent. Where parents are unwilling or unavailable to sign a consent form, a representative from the child welfare agency may often obtain the records by qualifying as the child's "parent" for purposes of FERPA. This option will depend on the school's interpretation of the parent definition. FERPA regulations define a parent as "a natural parent, a guardian, or an individual acting as a parent in the absence of a parent or guardian."[43] Finally, child welfare professionals or advocates can obtain access to a child's school record through the court order exception. Because children in foster care are already under court jurisdiction, this is often the easiest way to gain access.

§ 22.3.3 Ways to Ensure School Stability and Continuity for Clients

- Ensure that the child welfare agency is maintaining and updating the child's case plan with the child's education records.

- Obtain records from the school to ensure the child is receiving appropriate educational supports and services.

- Consult with your client's teachers, guidance counselors, and resource providers before each hearing and secure their testimony if needed.

- Know who the education decision-maker is for your client and, if there is no such individual, ask to have one appointed.[44]

- Ensure that education stability is considered at all court hearings.

- Advocate to keep living placements stable whenever possible; when a youth must move, advocate for a living placement in the same school district.

- Help youth remain in their original school even when they move to a placement in a different school district; this includes advocating for youth to get transportation to their original school.

Title IV-E now clearly permits states to use foster care maintenance dollars to support reasonable school transportation.[45] Under the McKinney-Vento Act, when a child is eligible to remain in his or her school of origin, the school district must

---

[42] 34 C.F.R. § 99.33.

[43] 34 C.F.R. § 99.3.

[44] For more information on special education decision-makers, see the Legal Center for Foster Care and Education's publications page titled "Special Education Decisionmaking" at www.abanet.org/child/education/publications/specialeducation.html.

[45] *See* 42 U.S.C. § 675(4)(B).

provide transportation. Some state laws also provide a right to transportation.[46] If your state or locality should be providing transportation, advocate to make sure it happens. Even if there is no legal right to transportation, be proactive. Work with the agency and school district to consider other avenues: Could the foster parents or others be reimbursed for providing transportation? Is the school willing to add a new stop to the bus route, or use special education or magnet school transportation? Can the agency pay for taxis to transport your client?

- Clarify who can enroll the child and raise this issue at all hearings requiring a school change; insist on immediate enrollment of the child.

- Insist that your client's records be transferred immediately and advocate for proper credit transfers.

- Contact the McKinney-Vento liaison in the school, if applicable, or the foster care liaison, if one exists.

- Ensure your client's special education needs are being met, especially when there are school transfers.

§ 22.4 Special Education Advocacy

§ 22.4.1 Why Special Education Advocacy is Critical for Children in Foster Care

Numerous studies indicate that between 23% and 47% of children and youth in out-of-home care in the U.S. receive special education services at some point in their schooling.[47] Many others may need these services, but have not been identified. Still others have been identified inappropriately. As an advocate for children in the child welfare system, understanding how the federal Individuals with Disabilities Education Act (IDEA)[48]—the major law that governs the special education process—works can help you ensure that your clients with disabilities receive the special help they need.

Advocates must also familiarize themselves with their state special education laws. IDEA leaves some key questions to the states. For example, states can prohibit foster parents from serving as a child's special education decision-maker, or can set a

---

[46] *See* Legal Center for Foster Care and Education, *States at a Glance: Awaiting Foster Care Placement Under the Mckinney-Vento Act, available at* http://www.abanet.org/child/education/publications/ AFCPchart.pdf.

[47] *See* National Working Group on Foster Care and Education, *Fact Sheet: Educational Outcomes for Children and Youth in Foster and Out-of-Home Care* (Dec. 2008), *available at* http://www.abanet.org/child/education/National_EdFactSheet_2008.pdf

[48] 20 U.S.C. §§ 1400 *et seq.*; 34 C.F.R. Part 300. Other laws that provide protections for children with disabilities in the public education context are § 504 of the Rehabilitation act of 1973 and its implementing regulations, 29 U.S.C. § 794, 34 C.F.R. §§ 104.1 *et seq.*, and the Americans with Disabilities Act, 42 U.S.C. §§ 12101 *et seq.*, 28 C.F.R. Part 35. For more information about basic legal rights under IDEA and other federal laws related to education, see Kathleen McNaught, *Education Law Primer for Child Welfare Professionals*, 22 ABA Child L. Prac. 1, 1 (Parts 1 & 2) (2003).

timeline for school districts to complete special education evaluations that differs from the 60 calendar day deadline that otherwise applies. In addition, many states provide *more* protections than are required by IDEA. For example, in Pennsylvania "transition planning" begins during the school year in which a child turns 14, while the federal minimum is age 16.[49] Finally, IDEA has somewhat different rules for infants and toddlers who have disabilities.[50] For more information about IDEA's rules for younger children, check with your state's protection and advocacy system.[51]

§ 22.4.2 IDEA Overview

While some children in foster care have visible disabilities (e.g., orthopedic impairments or blindness), others have disabilities that are less obvious (e.g., specific learning and behavioral disabilities). Some children with disabilities have average or even above average intellectual capacity, while others have mildly or even severely impaired cognition.[52] To the extent possible, children with disabilities should learn what all students are learning, but for some the core of their education is functional academics and self-help skills. In short, youngsters with disabilities cannot be educated on a "one size fits all" model—they have a wide range of disabilities, talents, limitations, and needs. Their education and special education programs need to reflect this diversity.

Thus IDEA mandates that each child be comprehensively evaluated to determine if he or she has a disability that requires specialized instruction (that is, special education) in order for the child to learn effectively, and if so what services are needed. Following the evaluation, an Individualized Education Program (IEP) Team meets to develop a written plan called an IEP. The IEP includes the current academic and functional levels, the type and amount of services the child needs, the child's annual education goals and how progress towards those goals is to be measured, the extent to which the child will be educated with students without disabilities, and more.[53] The IDEA Parent must be invited to the IEP meeting, must be helped to participate, and must be a full partner in determining what should be included in the IEP.[54]

---

[49] 22 PA. Code § 14.131(a)(5).

[50] Part C of IDEA governs infants and toddlers with developmental delays and is at 20 U.S.C. §§ 1431 *et seq.* The Part C implementing regulations are at 34 C.F.R. Part 303.

[51] To find your state's protection and advocacy system, contact the National Disability Rights Network at http://www.ndrn.org/contactus.htm.

[52] For a list of the disabilities that qualify a child for special education, see 34 C.F.R. § 300.8(c).

[53] For details on what an IEP should contain and how it should be developed and periodically revised, see 34 C.F.R. §§ 300.320–300.324.

[54] For information on who qualifies as an IDEA Parent, see 34 C.F.R. §§ 300.30. *See also* § 22.4.3, Special Education Decision-Makers. Being a "parent" does not mean making the final decisions. After the deliberations have been concluded, it is the local education agency (usually the school district) that actually determines the IEP's content and offers it to the IDEA Parent for approval or disapproval. If the IDEA Parent disapproves the IEP (or for that matter disapproves any thing else about the process such as the results of the evaluation) the IDEA Parent can ask for mediation or

§ 22.4.3 Special Education Decision-Makers

Making sure that each child in the child welfare system has an "IDEA Parent" to make special education decisions on the child's behalf is absolutely pivotal if the child is to benefit from IDEA and any special education protections under state law. A "surrogate parent" is one type of IDEA Parent who must be appointed by a local education agency when no biological or adoptive parent can be located (when the parent is dead, missing, or parental rights have been terminated) or the child is a ward of the state under state law. In some situations a surrogate parent can be appointed by a juvenile court.[55] In any case, the advocate must make sure that the child he or she is representing has an IDEA Parent. In no case can the IDEA Parent be a person who is employed by an agency that is involved in the education or care of the child.[56]

Only an "IDEA Parent" can consent to the initial evaluation or for services to begin for the first time for a child. Only the IDEA Parent has a right to represent the child at the IEP team meetings and agree with the school district's proposal (or disagree and ask for mediation or a special education hearing). Often, the IDEA Parent is the child's birth or adoptive parent or other person with whom the child is living and who is caring for the child. For many children in the child welfare system, deciding who the IDEA Parent is can be complicated. It could be the birth or adoptive parent, but it could also be the foster parent if the birth parent is lost, is not "attempting to act as the parent," parental rights have been terminated, or a surrogate parent has been appointed by the school district (whenever feasible within 30 days).

IDEA mandates that every child who is eligible or thought to be eligible, including children in the child welfare system, must have an IDEA Parent.[57] However, the application of these principles can be very complicated, and it requires weaving IDEA's rules with various state law requirements.[58]

§ 22.4.4 Getting the Child Evaluated

When considering whether to have the child evaluated, gather information about the medical history of the family and the child. Watch for signs that the child is having school difficulties, such as: poor grades, difficulties with academic achievements, delays in developmental milestones, lack of interest in school, refusal to attend school, or behavior problems at school and at home.

---

request that an administrative hearing be convened to resolve the dispute. For more details on the IDEA's dispute resolution options, see § 22.4.5.

[55] 34 C.F.R. § 300.519(a), (c).

[56] 34 C.F.R. § 300.519(d)(2)(i).

[57] *See, e.g.,* 34 C.F.R. §§ 300.30, 300.45, and 300.519.

[58] For more information about special education decision-making, please see the series of articles and fact sheets on these topics developed by the Legal Center for Foster Care and Education and available at www.abanet.org/child/education/publications/specialeducation.html.

> *Caution:* In determining whether a child might have a learning disability and need a special education evaluation, consider whether more focused regular education services would get the child back on track. Many school districts offer a variety of remedial programs such as "response to intervention" (RTI), what IDEA calls "early inter-vening services," various Title I programs, and more. Every child who is struggling academically needs extra help, but not necessarily special education. Consult with the family and the health and behavioral health professionals who already know the child—what do they think is wrong and what do they think is needed?

An agency may have information from an evaluation it has already performed or records that could be helpful to the evaluation process. The advocate may also consider raising some specific questions to the evaluation team regarding a child's education needs. Also consider whether the agency, at its expense, should arrange for the child to be evaluated, or at least whether it can arrange for you to discuss the child with an expert. Such an evaluation or consultation can help you determine whether a special education referral is warranted. It can also help you understand the school district's evaluation report or whether the services the district is offering will meet the child's needs. The clinician may even serve as your expert if you end up in a special education hearing. Whenever possible, choose a clinician who is familiar with educational disabilities and the school system.

However, delaying your request for an evaluation conducted by the school district can be a risky strategy. The school and the IEP team must "consider" the independent evaluation, but they do not have to agree with its conclusions or recommendations. The school can (and usually does) insist on conducting its own evaluation of the child, and that will take time.

If you think that the child needs a special education evaluation, the parent or other person permitted by IDEA to act for the child should make a written request to the school district for an "initial evaluation." But remember, the timeline for the school to complete the evaluation does not start until the IDEA Parent has given written consent for the evaluation to begin—and the written request alone is not "consent." IDEA states that the school system has 60 calendar days to complete an evaluation from the date that the IDEA Parent signs the consent for the initial evaluation to begin.[59] But IDEA also permits states to adopt a different timeline, either longer or shorter.[60]

Two new IDEA rules are especially helpful to advocates for children in foster care. First, if a child changes school districts before the evaluation has been completed, the new school district must complete the evaluation within the timeline *unless* the district is "making sufficient progress to ensure a prompt completion of the

---

[59] 34 C.F.R. § 300.301(c)(1)(i).

[60] Pennsylvania, for example, has adopted a rule that gives school districts 60 calendar days to complete the evaluation and give the evaluation report to the family, but the 60 calendar days does not include the summer.

evaluation" and the IDEA Parent and the school district agree to a "specific time when the evaluation will be completed."[61] Second, for a child who is a "ward of the state,"[62] the judge can appoint any person[63] to consent to the initial evaluation of a child if the birth or adoptive parent's right to make education decisions has been "subrogated" by a judge.[64] This can expedite the process of determining whether the child is eligible. But remember that it still takes an IDEA Parent to consent to services beginning.

The evaluation must use a variety of assessment tools to gather functional, developmental, and academic information about the child (including information from the parent) to determine whether the child has a disability and needs special education and what should be in the Individualized Education Program (IEP) to enable the child to be involved in and progress in the general education curriculum.[65] The IDEA regulations include detailed rules to make sure that the evaluation is comprehensive, accurate, and non-discriminatory. For example, assessments must be provided and administered in the child's native language or mode of communication unless it is clearly not feasible to do so.[66] There are also new (and very complicated) rules that school districts must follow to identify a child as having a "specific learning disability."[67]

The IDEA Parent gets a free copy of the evaluation report and documentation of the team's eligibility determination.[68] If the IDEA Parent believes that the school district's evaluation is not appropriate, he or she may request in writing that an independent educational evaluation (IEE) be conducted at the school's expense. The school may either agree to this evaluation or take the case to a due process hearing to establish whether the school's original evaluation is sufficient.[69] The IDEA Parent can also ask for an administrative due process hearing to challenge the method or conclusions of the evaluators.

---

[61] 34 C.F.R. § 300.301(e).

[62] A "ward of the state" is a foster child, a ward of the state under state law, or a child in the custody of a child welfare agency who does not have a foster parent who is permitted by state law to serve as an IDEA Parent. 34 C.F.R. § 300.45.

[63] This is the sole exception to the general rule that persons appointed to serve as the IDEA Parent for a child (such as a surrogate parent) cannot be an employee of any agency that is involved in the education or care of the child. *See* 34 C.F.R. § 300.519(d)(2)(i).

[64] 34 C.F.R. § 300.300(a)(2)(iii).

[65] 34 C.F.R. § 300.304(b)(1).

[66] 34 C.F.R. § 300.304(c)(1)(ii).

[67] *See* 34 C.F.R. §§ 300.307–300.311. It is also important to remember that IDEA has specific definitions of qualifying disabilities. *See* 34 C.F.R. § 300.8(c). As the advocate, you must make sure that you are familiar with these definitions and that you share them with any clinicians who are evaluating the child.

[68] 34 C.F.R. § 300.306(a).

[69] 34 C.F.R. § 300.502.

Children must be re-evaluated at least every three years, although this can be waived by the IDEA Parent.[70] A re-evaluation should be conducted whenever conditions warrant re-evaluation or the child's parent or teacher requests one.[71] The IDEA Parent should not hesitate to request a reevaluation of a child if the parent feels it is warranted, but the parent can obtain a re-evaluation upon request no more frequently than annually.[72]

The school system cannot decide that a child is no longer eligible for special education services without first evaluating the child.[73] This protects the child from being terminated from special education erroneously and requires that termination be based on a thorough evaluation of the child. If you believe that a child who is receiving special education services may not need those services, request a reevaluation of the child. If the reevaluation finds the child no longer has a disability that requires special learning support, and the IDEA Parent concurs in this decision, the child will be discharged from special education.

§ 22.4.5 Getting the Child Special Education and Related Services in the Least Restrictive Environment

If the evaluation team concludes that the child is eligible for special education, the next step is for the school to convene an IEP Team meeting to decide what services, in what educational setting, the child should receive. The IEP must be developed within 30 days of a determination that the child is eligible for services,[74] and the child must start to receive services as soon as possible after the IEP has been completed.[75]

The IEP is the contract between the school district and the family that explains what "special education" and "related services"[76] the child will receive, when the services will start and end, how much of each service the child will receive (called duration and frequency), the educational annual goals that the IEP team expects the child to achieve, and how success will be measured. The IEP will also explain how IDEA's directive that the child be educated, to the maximum extent possible, together with peers who do not have disabilities will be achieved.[77]

---

[70] 34 C.F.R. § 300.303(b)(2).

[71] 34 C.F.R. § 300.303(a).

[72] 20 U.S.C. § 1414(a)(2)(B)(i); 34 C.F.R. § 300.303(b)(1).

[73] 34 C.F.R. § 300.305(e).

[74] 34 C.F.R. § 300.343(b)(2).

[75] 34 C.F.R. § 300.342(b)(1)(ii).

[76] "Related services" are the developmental, corrective, or other supportive services needed for a child to benefit from a special education program. The nonexclusive list in the IDEA is broad and includes, among many other things, therapies such as physical, occupational, and speech therapy, school health services, and medical services for determining a child's disability and the special education and related services the child needs. 34 C.F.R. § 300.34.

[77] *See* 34 C.F.R. §§ 300.320–300.324.

The IEP team must include the IDEA Parent, a regular education teacher, a special education teacher, a school system representative (who is qualified to provide or supervise instruction for children with disabilities and knows about the general curriculum and the availability of resources), and someone who can interpret the instructional implications of evaluation results (e.g., school psychologist, speech and language therapist).[78] One person can play more than one role. Remember, only the IDEA Parent has the right to participate in the evaluation and IEP process, and to agree or disagree with the school district's proposals or initiate mediation or the administrative hearing process.[79]

When planning for what will happen after the child graduates (called transition planning), which must occur for the IEP that will be in place when the child is 16 and every year thereafter, the child must be invited.[80] If the child does not attend, the school must take steps to ensure that the child's preferences and interests are considered.[81] With the IDEA Parent's consent, the school district must invite a representative of any agency that may be responsible for providing or paying for transition services.[82] This will likely mean that child welfare agency personnel will be included in these IEP meetings for older youth in care. All child welfare advocates need to ensure that the transition planning happening as part of a child's IEP is coordinated with the child's transition planning in the child welfare system.[83]

The IDEA Parent or the school district can invite a representative of the child welfare system (or any other person) to participate in the IEP meeting as a person "who has knowledge or special expertise regarding the child."[84] Even if you lack legal decision-making authority, the child's attorney or parent's attorney can still play a role advocating for the child's educational needs. But remember, the school district is still bound by FERPA and, unless the IDEA Parent or a court consents to your participation in the meeting, the school district cannot share with you the child's school records or information derived from the school records.[85] Make sure you establish your right to access all education records and information shared at the meeting through either parental consent or a court order permitting you access.

The IEP team must consider the child's strengths, the parents' concerns, the results of the most recent evaluations, and the academic, developmental, and functional needs of the child.[86] The team must also consider whether any of the

---

[78]   34 C.F.R. § 300.321.

[79]   *See* § 22.4.3, Special Education Decision-Makers.

[80]   34 C.F.R. § 300.29, Appendix A, Response to Question 11, 64 Fed. Reg. 12474 (March 12, 1999).

[81]   34 C.F.R. § 300.344(b)(2).

[82]   34 C.F.R. § 300.321(b).

[83]   For further discussion, see § 22.2. For a more complete discussion of advocating for children aging out of foster care, see Chapter 23.

[84]   34 C.F.R. § 300.321(a)(6).

[85]   *See generally* Chapter 18, Confidentiality.

[86]   34 C.F.R. § 300.324(a)(1).

following factors pertain, and if so address these needs in the IEP: (1) whether the child has behaviors that impede the child's learning or the learning of others, and if so what positive behavioral supports or interventions would help; (2) whether the child has limited English proficiency and has language needs; (3) whether the child has communication needs because the child is deaf or hard of hearing; (4) whether the child has needs because the child is blind or visually impaired; and (5) whether the child needs assistive technology.[87]

Key IEP elements include: (1) the child's present levels of educational and functional performance; (2) measurable annual goals (including short-term objectives for children who are taking alternative assessments aligned to alternate achievement standards); (3) a description of how the child's progress toward meeting the annual goals will be measured and when reports on progress will be provided to the IDEA Parent; (4) a statement of the special education and related services and supplementary aids and services (based on peer reviewed research); (5) program modifications and staff supports to be provided to help the child advance toward his or her annual goals and be involved in and make progress in the curriculum and extracurricular and non-academic activities provided to all students; and (6) a statement of accommodations the child needs to participate in state or district assessments of academic and functional performance (and any alternate assessment if appropriate).[88]

The IEP must also state the extent to which the child will participate in regular classrooms and activities with children who do not have disabilities.[89] This is what is known as the "least restrictive environment" requirement, or the child's right to be educated together with children who do not have disabilities in regular classrooms, with the "supplementary aids and services" they need to succeed in that setting—if possible, in the same school the child would attend if the child did not have a disabilities. School districts must offer a continuum of placement options, from a regular education classroom with support to a separate or even residential school. Removal of a student from a regular classroom should only be to the extent necessary for that student to succeed in his or her academic and functional goals (for example, for tutoring in math). Advocates should work with the IDEA Parent to enforce the school district's duty to provide supplementary aids and supports to help children with disabilities achieve their goals in regular school settings, and the advocate should make sure that these supports are included in detail in the child's IEP.[90]

Unfortunately, many children in the child welfare system change their living situations—and their schools—often. IDEA mandates that, when a child with an IEP transfers from another school district in the same state or another state and enrolls within the same school year in a new school, the new school district must provide the child with, at minimum, services comparable to the services described in the IEP from

---

[87] 34 C.F.R. § 300.324(a)(2).

[88] 34 C.F.R. § 300.320(a).

[89] 34 C.F.R. § 300.347(a)(4).

[90] 34 C.F.R. § 300.320(a)(5), 300.114–300.117.

the previous agency until the old IEP is adopted or a new IEP is developed and agreed to by the IDEA Parent.[91] To facilitate the child's transition, the new school district must take reasonable steps to obtain promptly the child's records, including the special education records, from the previous school.[92]

§ 22.4.6 How the IDEA Parent Should Prepare for an IEP Meeting

As noted above, it is the IDEA Parent who has the right to be invited to and participate in the child's IEP Team meeting and to agree to or reject the proposed IEP. However, other advocates for the child may have information that can help the IDEA Parent and the school district make the best decisions for the child. If the IDEA Parent permits these advocates to be included, the advocates can work with the IDEA Parent. Either way, the IDEA Parent should:

- Think about what the child should accomplish in the coming year. Consider listing the child's strengths, needs, and interests and your major concerns about the child's education.[93]

- Collect and bring any documentation describing the child's disability, behaviors, and school progress (e.g., evaluations, examples of the child's schoolwork).

- Review materials you have collected and any materials the school has sent you. Make sure that you have and have read the child's school records, in particular any evaluation reports, report cards, and other information on how well the child is doing. Review the evaluations and determine whether you agree with the conclusions and whether the described behavior in the evaluation matches what you know of the child.

- If the child has been receiving special education services, review the last few IEPs. What were the goals? Do they seem right from what you know or have learned about the child? What were the measures of success? Did the child achieve them?

- An attorney (even if the attorney is the surrogate parent) must notify the school that he or she will be attending the meeting. The school will then have the right to have a school attorney present at the meeting.

---

[91] 34 C.F.R. § 300.323(e), (f).

[92] 34 C.F.R. § 300.323(g).

[93] For more information on planning for an IEP meeting, see Families and Advocates Partnership for Education, Pacer Center Inc., *Planning Your Child's Individualized Education Program (IEP): Some Suggestions to Consider* (2001), *available at* http://www.fape.org/pubs/FAPE-25.pdf.

§ 22.4.7 Tasks the IDEA Parent or Advocate Performs at the Meeting

- Share your knowledge about the child and carefully listen to what others say about the child to be able to respond appropriately. If you do not understand something, ask for clarification.

- In many states, parents and their advocates are permitted to tape record IEP meetings. This is particularly important (and perhaps required) if there is a reason why the IDEA Parent could not otherwise participate effectively (for example, the parent has a disability or is not fluent in English—although in the latter case the parent also has the right to the help of an interpreter or other help).[94]

- If you are the IDEA Parent you will probably be asked to sign the IEP at the end of the meeting consenting to everything it contains. Be sure you understand fully what you are being asked to approve. If it is the child's first IEP, services cannot start without your written consent. If the IEP is for a child who is already receiving special education services, and you need more time to think things over before giving your consent, make sure that you understand how much time you have to make a decision before the school district can begin to implement its proposal without your written consent.

- Make sure the IDEA Parent is given a copy of the notes and all documents from the meeting. If anyone at the meeting has promised to provide additional information to the IDEA Parent, encourage him or her to follow up with that team member, preferably in writing.

- In a few cases the advocate might believe that the IDEA Parent is not acting in the child's best interest or is doing a poor job of advocating for the child. In that case, the advocate can ask the juvenile court to appoint an "education guardian" for the child, and then the school district must deal directly with the person appointed by the court.[95]

§ 22.4.8 How the IDEA Parent or Advocate Monitors the Student's Progress and the Implementation of the IEP

The child's advocate has many responsibilities—the most important being to ensure that the child is safe and, whenever possible, living in a supportive family setting. The child's education may seem a marginal concern in this context. Nevertheless, the child's future depends on getting a quality education, and if the child has a disability the stakes are even higher. If the advocate has accepted the role of the IDEA Parent, these items are clearly the advocate's responsibility. Even if the advocate is not the IDEA Parent, the following represents the gold standard to which

---

[94] 34 C.F.R. § 300.322(e).

[95] *See* 34 C.F.R. § 300.30(b).

advocates should aspire when they represent a child. If the advocate is not the IDEA Parent, the consent of the IDEA Parent may be required.

- After an IEP is in place, monitor how the services are working for the child. Review the child's assignments and tests when possible.

- Find out what the child thinks about the new services, whether the services are helpful, and what, if anything, needs to be changed.

- Communicate regularly with the child's teachers through phone calls, e-mails, or progress reports.

- An IDEA Parent can request an IEP meeting any time if there is reason to believe the IEP is not being implemented appropriately or if something needs to be added or changed. At a minimum, IDEA requires an annual review of the IEP to review achievement of past goals and establish goals and services for the coming year.

§ 22.5 Dispute Resolution and Enforcement

§ 22.5.1 Notice

If the IDEA Parent does not agree with a school district's proposal to make a change, or if the school district refuses to make a change that the parent requests, the school district must give the parent written notice that contains: (1) an explanation of the action or refusal to act and the reasons; (2) a statement that the parent has certain procedural rights and how to get the notice that describes the procedural rights; (3) information about where the parent can get help; and (4) other information as enumerated in IDEA.[96] The notice must be in language understandable to the parent, which can include, if feasible, providing the notice in the native language or other mode of communication that works best for the parent.[97]

Almost any issue can be the subject of IDEA dispute resolution (e.g., whether the child has a disability and which disability, what special education or related services the child needs, what school setting is the "least restrictive" educational setting for the child, and what supplementary aids and services the child needs in that setting). IDEA Parents (and school districts) can request mediation or a special education hearing to resolve disputes over any of these proposals or refusals. IDEA also requires states to maintain complaint systems through which IDEA Parents (or other persons or agencies that are concerned with a child) can complain to the state that a public agency is violating a child's or family's rights under federal or state special education law and get the problem corrected. The following sections provide a brief overview of the rules that govern these three options.

---

[96] 34 C.F.R. § 300.503(b).

[97] 34 C.F.R. § 300.503(c). In some situations, such as the request or referral of a child for an initial evaluation, the school district must automatically provide the procedural safeguard notice, which sets out in detail all of the IDEA's procedural protection. 34 C.F.R. § 300.504.

§ 22.5.2 Mediation

Mediation is a cheap, quick, and often effective way to resolve disputes. Every state must operate a system by which families and school districts can mediate disputes.[98] Mediation is voluntary,[99] which means that a school district can refuse to participate. Mediation cannot be used to deny or delay a parent's right to a hearing.[100] A qualified and impartial mediator must conduct the mediation,[101] and the mediation session must be held in a timely manner at a location that is convenient to the parties.[102] The state bears the cost of mediation.[103] All information shared in mediation is confidential and cannot be used in a later due process hearing or lawsuit.[104] If agreement can be reached during mediation, the terms of the agreement must be documented in writing, signed by the parties, and can be enforced in court.[105] Please note that unless a state has taken steps to fill the gap,[106] a request for mediation alone does not trigger the child's right to "pendency"—that is, once the child is identified and in the special education system, the school district can implement its proposed change even though mediation has not been concluded. However, that cannot happen if the family has filed a complaint requesting an impartial hearing, in which case "the child involved in the complaint must remain in his or her current educational placement."[107]

§ 22.5.3 Due Process Hearing

A due process hearing is a trial-like administrative proceeding where evidence and witnesses are presented and cross-examined. An impartial hearing officer presides over the hearing and issues a written ruling in the case. A successful result at a due process hearing may involve obtaining appropriate services or placement for a child, and also can involve receiving compensatory services (services to make up for the school's error or failures) and money to recoup costs and attorney fees.[108]

---

[98] 34 C.F.R. § 300.506(a).

[99] 34 C.F.R. § 300.506(b)(1)(i).

[100] 34 C.F.R. § 300.506(b)(1)(ii).

[101] 34 C.F.R. § 300.506(b)(1)(iii), (c).

[102] 34 C.F.R. § 300.506(b)(5).

[103] 34 C.F.R. § 300.506(b)(4).

[104] 34 C.F.R. § 300.506(b)(8).

[105] 34 C.F.R. § 300.506(b)(6), (7).

[106] For example, Pennsylvania regulations explicitly provide that a request for mediation triggers the family's right to pendency. Therefore, in Pennsylvania, a family who wants to mediate is not required also to request a special education hearing to make sure that the school district cannot implement an objectionable change until after the mediation has been concluded. 22 PA. Code §14.162(s).

[107] 34 C.F.R. § 300.518(a).

[108] Whether prevailing party fees can be obtained through the administrative hearing process depends on state law. Regardless, they can be obtained from a judge. 34 C.F.R. § 300.517.

To request a hearing, the IDEA Parent must file a "complaint," which can be challenged by the other side if it deems the complaint insufficient. The complaint must allege a violation that occurred not more than two years before the date the parent or the public agency "knew or should have known about the alleged action that forms the basis of the due process complaint" unless the state sets an alternate deadline. There are several exceptions to this deadline.[109] Unless the parties agree otherwise, either a mediation or a "resolution session" must be held to try to resolve the complaint before the hearing will be scheduled.

Due process hearings can be complicated. If you do not have experience pursuing these kinds of hearings, proceed with caution. IDEA Parents may appear unrepresented, but that is often unwise as these hearings can involve long and intense conflicts. School systems are frequently represented by attorneys with expertise in this area of law. An attorney without experience handling due process cases should ask an experienced education attorney for assistance, to co-counsel, or even handle the case. For children in foster care, you could ask the juvenile court overseeing the child welfare case to appoint an education attorney to represent the IDEA parent in these matters.

§ 22.5.4 Complaint to State Department of Education

Any individual or organization (this is not limited to the IDEA Parent) can file a complaint with the state department of education alleging a violation of federal or state special education law that occurred within the last year.[110] In addition to requesting that the state investigate and correct the legal violation, the complainant can ask for monetary reimbursement or compensatory education. In most cases the state must investigate and issue a written decision within 60 calendar days.[111]

The advantage of this type of complaint over a due process proceeding is that it is much faster and less costly. But this system works well only for clear legal violations that do not involve disputed facts (e.g., Were the appropriate team members present at the child's IEP meeting? Was the evaluation conducted within the timeline? Is the child getting all of the services listed in the IEP?). States vary in the quality of their investigations and decision-making, and this method is usually not effective in resolving quality issues (e.g., Is this speech language therapy adequately meeting the child's needs?).

---

[109] The exceptions are that the complaint was not filed due to specific misrepresentations by the local education agency that it had resolved the problem forming the basis of the complaint, or, that the local education agency withheld information from the parent that the IDEA required be provided to the parent. 34 C.F.R. § 300.511(e). For the detailed rules and timelines that pertain to hearing requests, hearings, and administrative or judicial appeals, see 34 C.F.R. §§ 300.507, 300.515–300.516.

[110] *See* 34 C.F.R. §§ 300.151–300.154. The complaint must allege a violation that occurred within one year before the date the complaint is received. 34 C.F.R. § 300.153(c),

[111] *See* 34 C.F.R. §§ 300.151–300.154.

§ 22.5.5 Filing an "Action" in State or Federal Court

If the IDEA Parent is not satisfied with the results of the Due Process hearing, in some states there is an administrative appeal process. In any case, when the administrative hearing and any administrative appeal process has been concluded, the "aggrieved party" can file an action in federal or state court challenging the decision.[112] The timeline for taking an appeal is 90 days from the date of a the final administrative decision.

§ 22.5.6 Conclusion

Beyond the scope of this section are other important IDEA rules, including those that govern school discipline for children with disabilities.[113] Advocacy is needed to prevent and minimize the effects of discipline for children in foster care, which ultimately affects their chances of achieving permanency and their futures.[114] Specifically, advocates should help prevent disciplinary measures from being necessary, protect the child's rights during disciplinary meetings and hearings, and help minimize the effects of disciplinary actions. If you are representing a child facing multiple suspensions, an expulsion, or an involuntary transfer to an "interim alternative educational setting" make sure that you check those rules carefully.[115]

Advocates can help link children in foster care to special education services and ensure those services are meeting the children's needs. Understanding IDEA and what services are available to children in the foster care system is critical to navigating the special education process. With child welfare systems struggling to provide all children in care with the services they need, failing to access services under IDEA is wasting an important source of education assistance for these children.

§ 22.6 Youth Engagement and Transition Planning and Postsecondary Planning

§ 22.6.1 Importance for Children in Foster Care

All too often, youth in foster care are not engaged or involved in their case planning and court hearings. Youth involvement in education planning and obtaining postsecondary education is critically important to their education planning and pursuits beyond high school. Youth must receive support to identify and develop further education aspirations, including services to help them prepare for, enter, and

---

[112] *See* 34 C.F.R. §§ 300.514–300.516.

[113] For information about school discipline, including the specific protections for children in special education, see Education Law Center, http://www.elc-pa.org/pubs/pubs_disabilities.html.

[114] For information about the importance of advocacy for children in foster care around school discipline generally, see KATHLEEN MCNAUGHT, LEARNING CURVES: EDUCATION ADVOCACY FOR CHILDREN IN FOSTER CARE (2004).

[115] *See* 34 C.F.R. §§ 300.530–300.536.

complete postsecondary education if that is their goal. Successful advocacy for older youth includes being aware of available services and supports, promoting higher education or vocational education aspirations, and supporting youth in attaining their postsecondary education or vocational goals.[116]

§ 22.6.2 Laws and Programs that Help Ensure Youth Can Enter and Complete Postsecondary Education

Child and Family Services Improvement Act of 2006

Recognizing the critical importance of youth being involved and engaged in their case planning and court hearings, the Child and Family Services Improvement Act of 2006[117] amended Title IV-B of the Social Security Act to require procedural safeguards to assure the court or administrative body conducting a permanency hearing involving older and transitioning youth consults with the youth about the proposed permanency or transition plan. These consultations must be conducted in an age-appropriate manner.

Because of this requirement, advocates must ensure that the child's perspective is shared with the court, and that the child attends court if he or she chooses. Critical to youth participation is ensuring that youth are well-prepared for court, that they are offered the opportunity to share their perspective, and that they are debriefed afterwards to make sure they understand the actions and orders of the court. While court involvement is critical for all children, it is especially critical for older and transitioning youth to ensure that their transition needs, including those related to education, are met.[118]

Foster Care Independence Act of 1999; Education Training Vouchers

The Social Security Act requires the child welfare agency to include as part of the case plan for children age 16 and older a "written description of the programs and services which will help such a child prepare for the transition from foster care to independent living."[119] This plan, often referred to as the "independent living plan" (ILP), should be created closely with the youth and should include information related to the youth's education.

Recognizing the need for improved planning and services for older youth in foster care, the Foster Care Independence Act of 1999 (FCIA)[120] increased the supports available to children, who are likely to leave the child welfare system at age 18, to continue their education, find employment, and obtain life skills to be successful

---

[116] For further discussion of assisting youth who are aging out of foster care, see Chapter 23.

[117] Pub. L. No. 109-288, 120 Stat. 1233.

[118] For further discussion, see Chapter 23, Foster Youth: Transitioning from Foster Care into Self-Sufficient Adulthood.

[119] 42 U.S.C. § 675(1)(D).

[120] Foster Care Independence Act of 1999, Pub. L. No. 106-169.

adults. It doubled the amount of federal funds (Chafee funds) provided to the states for services to older teens, and gives states increased flexibility in using the funds. States can use Chafee funds to aid education goals in the following ways: tuition, tutoring, education planning, financial aid, and other education expenses related to receiving a high school diploma, GED, or post-secondary education. For students in postsecondary education, education services may include assistance with tuition, room and board expenses, or personal support services needed to complete post-secondary education. In some states, Chafee program funds have been used to pay for the development of agreements with state colleges and universities for free housing and for counseling and other support for former youth in foster care. For those youth in care involved in the state's Chafee program, advocates should ensure that services are documented in the child's ILP.

Finally, Education and Training Vouchers (ETV)[121] provide funding of up to $5,000 per year for postsecondary education to youth who have aged out of foster care or entered guardianships or adoption after age 16. To apply for a voucher, youth should contact their regional or state Independent Living/Chafee program coordinator through the National Resource Center for Youth Development.[122] In addition to ETVs, many states have state tuition vouchers or waivers for children who were or are in foster care.[123] Advocates should be aware of available scholarship programs and tuition supports for older clients.

Fostering Connections Act

One way the Fostering Connections Act[124] makes significant strides toward improving outcomes for older youth in care is by requiring a "transition plan." The plan must be personalized and directed by the child and must include specific options for education.[125]

Additionally, Fostering Connections also permits states, at their option, to receive Title IV-E reimbursement for the cost of placement and services for youth until the age of 19, 20, or 21.[126] In order to remain in care, youth must be attending school, working, or involved in a program designed to remove barriers to working or education.[127] Prior to Fostering Connections, states could only receive Title IV-E reimbursement until a youth turned 18, or 19 for youth still in high school. The option to receive federal reimbursement past age 18 provides an important incentive to states

---

[121] Promoting Safe and Stable Families Amendments of 2001, Pub. L. No. 107-133.

[122] *See* http://www.nrcys.ou.edu/yd/.

[123] For a list of all state tuition vouchers, see the Web site of the National Resource Center for Youth Development at http://www.nrcys.ou.edu/yd/state_pages/search.php?search_option=tuition_waiver.

[124] Pub. L. No. 110-351 (codified as amended at 42 U.S.C. §§ 621 et seq. and 42 U.S.C. §§ 671 *et seq.*).

[125] 42 U.S.C. § 675(5)(H).

[126] 42 U.S.C. § 675(8)(B).

[127] 42 U.S.C. § 675(8)(B).

to extend care for youth over the age of 18, which for states that already provide this support, has translated to improved educational outcomes.[128]

For a full discussion of the Fostering Connections Act, see Chapter 23, Foster Youth: Transitioning from Foster Care into Self-Sufficient Adulthood.

Individuals with Disabilities Education Act (IDEA)

For children in foster care receiving special education services, an additional transition plan is required. Under the Individuals with Disabilities Education Act (IDEA), schools must develop Individualized Education Programs (IEPs) for all students receiving special education services. Beginning not later than the first IEP to be in effect when the child is 16, and updated annually thereafter, the IEP must include both of the following:

- Measurable postsecondary goals based on age-appropriate transition assessments related to training, education, employment, and, where appropriate, independent living skills

- Transition services (including courses of study) to help the child reach those goals

Recognizing the poor education outcomes of children transitioning out of the special education system, the 2004 IDEA Regulations added more protections for youth by defining and clarifying the required "transition services." The plan must be part of "a results-oriented process, that is focused on improving the academic and functional achievement of the child with a disability to facilitate the child's movement from school to post-school activities, including postsecondary education, vocational education, integrated employment (including supported employment), continuing and adult education, adult services, independent living, or community participation."[129] Further, the plan should be based on the child's needs, accounting for the child's strengths, preferences, and interests to achieve a post-school goal.[130] Finally, the plan should include required instruction, related services, community experiences, the development of employment and other post-school adult living objectives, help with daily living skills, and provision of a functional vocational evaluation.[131]

IDEA now requires that for transition planning youth must be invited to attend IEP meetings. If they are not able to come, the education agency must take other steps to ensure the child's preferences and interests are considered. Similar to the plans required by the child welfare agency, the education plan also requires that youth are actively engaged and empowered in their transition planning.

---

[128] C. M. Peters, A. Dworsky, M. E. Courtney & H. Pollack, *Extending Foster Care to Age 21: Weighing the Costs to Government Against the Benefits to Youth* (Chapin Hall Center for Children, Issue Brief, June 2009), *available at* http://www.chapinhall.org/sites/default/files/publications/Issue_Brief%2006_23_09.pdf.

[129] 34 C.F.R. § 300.43(a)(1).

[130] 34 C.F.R. § 300.43(a)(2).

[131] 34 C.F.R. § 300.43(a)(2).

In addition to the youth and the required members of the IEP team from the school, IDEA also provides that, at the discretion of the education agency or parent, other individuals with knowledge or special expertise about the child, including related services personnel, should be included in IEP meetings. For children in foster care, it is critical that people already involved in a youth's ILP and transition planning—including caseworkers, attorneys or GALs, CASAs, relatives of the child, and others—be consulted about a child's IEP. While many individuals help develop a child's IEP, only the child's IDEA Parent can approve the IEP. Therefore, the education decision-maker should be clearly identified and actively engaged throughout the process.[132]

Higher Education Opportunity Act

In August 2008, the Higher Education Opportunity Act[133] was enacted. This legislation reauthorized the Higher Education Act[134] and includes numerous amendments designed to increase foster students' access to postsecondary education. The law now makes youth in foster care (including youth who have left foster care after reaching age 13), automatically eligible for all TRIO programs. The TRIO programs are federal programs that support at-risk junior high and high school students to graduate from high school, enter college, and complete their degrees. These programs include Talent Search, Upward Bound, Student Support Services, Educational Opportunity Centers, Staff Development Activities, and Gaining Early Awareness and Readiness for Undergraduate Programs (GEAR-UP).

Finally, and importantly, the law also makes clear that Student Support Services funds can be used for "securing temporary housing during breaks in the academic year" for students who are (1) homeless or formerly homeless under McKinney or (2) in foster care or aging out of the foster care system.[135] Education advocates should use these provisions as a way to ensure youth access to these critical services for youth in foster care.

College Cost Reduction and Access Act of 2008

The complexities of the financial aid process often create a barrier for youth in foster care to apply to and enroll in higher education. The College Cost Reduction and Access Act of 2008[136] makes clear that for the purposes of federal financial aid, an "independent student" includes a youth who is "an orphan, in foster care, or a ward of the court, at any time when the individual is 13 years of age or older."[137] This

---

[132] For more on this topic, see the Legal Center for Foster Care and Education's special education decision-making series, *available at* http://www.abanet.org/child/education/publications/specialeducation.html.

[133] Pub. L. No. 110-315 (codified as amended at 20 U.S.C. §§ 1001 *et seq.*).

[134] Pub. L. No. 99-498 (codified as amended at 20 U.S.C. §§ 1070 *et seq.* and 42 U.S.C. §§ 2751 *et seq.*).

[135] 20 U.S.C. § 1070a-14(c)(5).

[136] Pub. L. No. 110-84, 121 Stat. 784.

[137] 20 U.S.C. § 1087vv(d)(1)(B).

provision significantly increases the number of former and current youth in care who may fall into this category. If a youth is considered "independent," only the youth's income, not that of a parent or guardian, is considered in determining eligibility for financial aid.[138]

§ 22.6.3 Ensuring that Youth Participate in Education Planning and Court Hearings and Receive Support to Enter and Complete Postsecondary Education

- Ensure that youth have a positive educational and learning environment and that school and child welfare agencies are supporting youth to succeed and flourish and providing the tools and supports to do so.

- Ensure clients have exposure and access to education and career opportunities, role models, mentors, and strong education advocates.

- Ensure youth are attending court.

- Ensure youth are actively engaged and empowered in their future planning, especially as related to their education goals and pursuits.

- Ensure youth have clear information and concrete help with obtaining and completing admission and financial aid documents; explain to clients that they qualify as independent students for FAFSA. Know how Chafee funds can be used, and advocate using these funds to help your clients.

- Advocate for youth to access ETVs and other financial supports for higher education pursuits. Be alert for news about the funding for new education and training voucher programs.

- Use the transition plan requirements to ensure older youth receive the supports they need. Each of the required transition plans creates an important tool for advocates. These plans provide an opportunity for advocates to enforce the rights of youth by:

  o Participating in the development of all plans and ensuring they are detailed and based on the client's needs

  o Ensuring that all plans actively engage and empower youth

  o Encouraging both the child welfare agency and education agency to engage the other in developing the plans, especially relating to education outcomes and transition services

  o Taking part in systemic advocacy to create a structure and policies that require the child welfare agency and schools to collaborate

---

[138] For more information about financial aid for "independent students," see *Providing Effective Financial Aid Assistance to Students from Foster Care and Unaccompanied Homeless Youth: A Key to Higher Education Access and Success* (2009), *available at* http://casey.org/Resources/Publications/pdf/ProvidingEffectiveFinancialAid.pdf.

- o Ensuring that the federal requirement that findings be made regarding the services needed to transition to independence is followed and findings are sufficiently detailed to gauge agency compliance

- o Advocating that presentation and approval of the child welfare ILP be required at all court hearings for youth 16 and older, and the transition plan at least 90 days before a child's discharge

- o Advocating for youth throughout the IEP process, and holding the education agency accountable for developing and implementing the transition plan, supporting the use of the dispute process when necessary

- Ensure that youth have access to academic, social, and emotional supports during and through completion of their postsecondary education.

- Advocate for the court and agency to extend jurisdiction so that youth can receive support and protection while pursuing postsecondary education or employment.

§ 22.7 Resources for Advocates

Organizations

- *Legal Center for Foster Care and Education* – www.abanet.org/child/education

The Legal Center for Foster Care and Education was launched on January 1, 2007, and is a collaboration between Casey Family Programs (www.casey.org) and the American Bar Association Center on Children and the Law (www.abanet.org/child/), with support from the National Resource Center on Legal and Judicial Issues, in conjunction with the Education Law Center-PA (www.elc-pa.org) and the Juvenile Law Center (www.jlc.org). The Legal Center's mission is to bring attention and important legal resources to bear on the educational needs of children and youth in the nation's foster care system. It is a national technical assistance resource and information clearinghouse on legal and policy matters affecting the education of children in the foster care system. The Legal Center provides expertise to states and constituents, facilitates networking to advance promising practices and reforms, and provides technical assistance and training to respond to the ever-growing demands for legal support and guidance.

The Legal Center focuses on supporting direct education advocacy efforts for children in foster care, as well as promoting federal, state, and local laws and policies that address the education needs of this population. The Legal Center builds on the ever-increasing momentum behind meeting the education needs of children in foster care—an issue that can help establish safety, perma-nency, and well-being for children involved with the child welfare system.

The Legal Center has a dedicated Web site, www.abanet.org/child/education, which contains up-to-date information on important legal and policy resources.

Publications

- Kathleen M. McNaught, *Learning Curves: Education Advocacy for Children in Foster Care* (ABA Center on Children and the Law and National Child Welfare Resource Center on Legal and Judicial Issues, 2004), *available at* http://www.abanet.org/abastore/index.cfm

- Kathleen M. McNaught, *Mythbusting: Breaking Down Confidentiality and Decision-Making Barriers to Meet the Education Needs of Children in Foster Care* (ABA Center on Children and the Law), *available at* http://www.abanet.org/child/education/other-pub.shtml

- Sophia I. Gatowski, Tracy Medina & Megan Warren, *Technical Assistance Brief: Asking the Right Questions II: Judicial Checklists to Meet the Educational Needs of Children and Youth in Foster Care* (National Council for Juvenile and Family Court Judges, Dec. 2008), *available at* http://www.casey.org/Resources/Publications/AskingQuestions.htm

- *National CASA E-Module: Education Advocacy* (National Court Appointed Special Advocate Program – CASA)

- *In School, the Right School, Finish School: A Guide to Improving Educational Opportunities for Court-Involved Youth* (National Children's Law Network, 2007), *available at* www.justice4all.org/files/NCLN%20Manual%2006-1-07.pdf

- *Addressing the Educational Needs of Children in Foster Care: A Guide for Judges, Advocates and Child Welfare Professionals* (New York State Permanent Judicial Commission on Justice for Children) www.nycourts.gov/ip/justiceforchildren/PDF/EducationalNeeds.pdf

- Casey Family Programs, *Endless Dreams* (a video and curriculum to educate teachers about foster care), *available at* http://www.casey.org/Resources/Initiatives/EndlessDreams/

- Casey Family Programs, *A Road Map for Learning: Improving Educational Outcomes in Foster Care* (2004) http://www.casey.org/Resources/Publications/RoadMapForLearning.htm

Chapter 23: Foster Youth: Transitioning from Foster Care into Self-Sufficient Adulthood

by Melanie Delgado[1] and Robert Fellmeth[2]

§ 23.1 Introduction

Effective representation of older foster youth who are preparing to age out of the foster care system requires an understanding of the challenges these youth will face after they leave the system.

Though statistics vary from state to state, former foster youth experience higher rates of homelessness, incarceration, mental illness, poverty, and unemployment than do their peers who have no history of foster care. For example, a national survey found that 25% of foster youth become homeless within 2.5 to 4 years after leaving care.[3] As another stark example, 25% to 35% of foster youth are incarcerated at some point after they leave care.[4] Foster youth experience clinically significant mental health diagnoses and chronic health problems (resulting from early abuse and neglect) at much higher rates than their non-foster care peers.[5] Finally, former foster youth

---

[1] Melanie Delgado is an attorney at the Children's Advocacy Institute (CAI) and director of CAI's Foster Youth Transition Project.

[2] Robert Fellmeth is the Price Professor of Public Interest Law, University of San Diego School of Law and Director of the Children's Advocacy Institute.

[3] Ronna Cook, *A National Evaluation of Title IV-E Foster Care Independent Living Programs for Youth* (Westat, Inc. 1991).

[4] Joanne O'Sullivan & Patricia Lussier-Duynstee, *Adolescent Homelessness, Nursing, and Public Health Policy*, 7/1 POL'Y POLIT. NURS. PRAC. 73 (2006). *See also* Casey Family Programs, *Improving Outcomes for Older Youth in Foster Care* (2008), p. 4, *available at* http://www.casey.org/Resources/Publications/pdf/WhitePaper_ImprovingOutcomesOlderYouth_FR.pdf.

[5] In one study, within the previous 12 months, more than half of the alumni (54.4%) had clinical levels of at least one mental health problem and one in five (19.9%) had three or more mental health problems. In this study "alumni" refers to foster care alumni (former foster youth) who were interviewed between 2000 and 2002. Casey Family Programs, *Improving Family Foster Care: Findings from the Northwest Foster Care Alumni Study* (2005), *available at* http://www.casey.org/Resources/Publications/pdf/ImprovingFamilyFosterCare_FR.pdf. Approximately 8% of general population youth in the same age group experience mental illness. California Department of Mental Health, *Estimates of Need for Mental Health Services by Age, Sex, and Race/Ethnicity for California Serious Mental Illness for 2000*, *available at* http://www.dmh.cahwnet.gov/Statistics_and_Data_Analysis/CNE2/Calif_CD/q5asr_htm/California/q5asr2k_wsmi01_ca000_p0.xls).

experience post-traumatic stress disorder at rates higher than war veterans.[6]

There is an enormous disparity in parental financial support between former foster youth and their non-foster care peers. One study found the median amount provided by private parents to their children after age 18 approximated $46,000, which is 5 to 6 times the amount available to emancipating foster youth from their public parent.[7] Not only do former foster youth receive substantially less monetary support than do their peers, they receive far less support in the area of time-help as well. Private parents dedicate an average of nine weeks of full-time (40 hours per week) help to their children after each child reaches the age of 18.[8] There are no statistics available that reflect how much personal, full-time help each foster youth receives after age 18, but even in the programs available to them, it is doubtful that the staff can dedicate that level of personal attention to each youth in the program.

§ 23.2 Federal Law

For a little over two decades, Congress has slowly been making modest changes in the law relating to foster youth ages 16 to 21. In 1986, Congress amended the Social Security Act (SSA) to include the Independent Living Initiative (ILI),[9] which provides funding to assist foster youth transitioning out of foster care to independent living. Until 1999, the ILI limited the funding to foster youth ages 16 to 18, and focused on teaching some of the basic skills necessary for self-sufficiency (such as cooking, opening a bank account, and paying taxes). The ILI prohibited funding for housing or for transitional housing programs for former foster youth. States had the option to continue services after the foster youth aged out, but had to pay for these services with state-only funding.

§ 23.2.1 Chafee Foster Care Independence Act 1999

By 1999, it became clear that simply teaching foster youth independent living skills was not sufficiently preparing them to live on their own at age 18. Congress responded to the mounting evidence that the ILI was inadequate by passing the John H. Chafee Foster Care Independence Act (Chafee FCIA).[10]

---

[6] Casey Family Programs, The Foster Care Alumni Studies, *Assessing the Effects of Foster Care: Mental Health Outcomes from the Casey National Alumni Study, available at* http://www.casey.org/Resources/Publications/pdf/CaseyNationalAlumniStudy_MentalHealth.pdf.

[7] Robert F. Schoeni & Karen E. Ross, *Material Assistance Received From Families During the Transition to Adulthood, in* ON THE FRONTIER OF ADULTHOOD: THEORY, RESEARCH, AND PUBLIC POLICY 396–416 (Richard A. Settersten, Jr., Frank F. Furstenberg Jr. & Ruben G. Rumbaut eds., 2005), *available at* www.transad.pop.upenn.edu/projects/frontier.htm. The average amount parents pay to assist their children post-18 is $38,340 in 2001 dollars; the figure is $46,444 in 2009 dollars.

[8] *Id.*

[9] 42 U.S.C. § 677 (2009).

[10] 42 U.S.C. § 677 (2009).

The purpose of the Chafee FCIA is to identify children who are likely to remain in foster care until 18 years of age and to help these children make the transition to self-sufficiency by providing services beyond the mechanics of the ILI. This extra assistance may now extend to age 21 and may include Independent Living Services (ILS) such as:

- Help to obtain a high school diploma
- Vocational training
- Job placement services
- Substance abuse prevention
- Preventive health activities (including smoking avoidance, nutrition education, and pregnancy prevention)
- Preparation to enter postsecondary training and education institutions
- Personal and emotional support (through mentors and the promotion of interactions with dedicated adults)

The law also authorizes financial, housing, counseling, employment, education, and other appropriate support and services to former foster care recipients between 18 and 21 years of age.[11] Chafee FCIA significantly changed independent living services available to foster youth by also imposing a mandate, upon which federal funding is contingent, that states use a portion of Chafee FCIA funding to serve current and former foster youth up to age 21.[12] States may use up to 30% of Chafee FCIA funding to provide housing assistance to youth who have left foster care and are between the ages 18 and 21.[13]

Finally, Chafee FCIA provides states with the option to extend Medicaid eligibility to former foster youth to age 21.[14] As with other Chafee programs, state laws differ on the age at which Medicaid eligibility ends. A dependency attorney should be familiar with his or her state law with regard to extended Medicaid eligibility and the process through which his or her clients must apply to maintain Medicaid after they reach age 18 or leave the foster care system.

§ 23.2.2 Chafee Educational and Training Vouchers (ETV)

Completing a college degree or some form of vocational education can help to ensure that a youth will be able to transition into a productive, independent adulthood. Unfortunately, many states still terminate foster care before age 21, leaving former foster youth to attempt to live independently, attend college or vocational training, and work without the familial safety net their peers enjoy. Only 50% of foster youth

---

[11] 42 U.S.C. § 677(a) (2009). These services may be available to foster children who are 16 or older when they exit the system to kin guardianship or adoption as well. 2 U.S.C. § 677(a)(7) (2009).

[12] 42 U.S.C. § 677(b)(3)(A) (2009).

[13] 42 U.S.C. § 677(b)(3)(B) (2009).

[14] 42 U.S.C. § 1396a(a)(10)(A)(ii)(XVII) (2009).

ever graduate from high school, compared to 76% of their peers who have no history in the foster care system. Only 20% of foster youth ever start college, whereas 60% of their peers do. Only 3% of foster youth ever complete a four-year degree, as compared to 27% of their peers.[15]

In 2002, Congress amended the Chafee FCIA to add Chafee Educational and Training Vouchers (ETV).[16] Congress provided $60 million for this program that makes available up to $5,000 per year for former foster youth to help pay for qualifying college or vocational education expenses. As with previous Chafee FCIA funding, states must provide a 20% match for these federal funds. A state's allotment of Chafee ETV funding is based on its foster care ratio.[17]

The Chafee ETV program is available to youth who are otherwise eligible for services under the state Chafee program or were adopted from foster care after their 16th birthday.[18] Youth who are participating in the ETV program on the day they turn 21 are eligible to continue participation until age 23 if they are enrolled in a post-secondary education program and making satisfactory progress toward completing that program.[19] Importantly, the amount of a Chafee voucher may be disregarded for the purposes of determining the recipient's eligibility for, or the amount of, any federal or federally-funded assistance.[20]

A dependency attorney should be aware of his or her state's Chafee FCIA-funded Independent Living Services and Educational and Training Voucher programs, make efforts to ensure that his or her eligible clients get the maximum benefit from these programs, and be watchful for state compliance issues.[21]

---

[15] Thomas R. Wolanin, *Higher Education Opportunities for Foster Youth: A Primer for Policymakers* (Dec. 2005), p. v, *available at* http://www.ihep.org/assets/files/publications/m-r/OpportunitiesFoster Youth.pdf.

[16] 42 U.S.C. § 677(i) (2009). Vouchers may be available to pay for the cost of attendance at an institution of higher education as defined at 20 U.S.C. § 1002 (2009). Vouchers shall not exceed the lesser of $5,000 per year or the total cost of attendance as defined at 20 U.S.C. § 1087 (2009).

[17] "State foster care ratio" means the ratio of the number of children in foster care under a program of the State in the most recent fiscal year for which information is available to the total number of children in foster care in all states for the most recent fiscal year. 42 U.S.C. § 677(c)(3)–(4) (2009).

[18] Youth who entered kinship care after their 16th birthday also may be eligible. 42 U.S.C. § 677(i)(2) (2009). Eligible youth may receive this assistance prior to their 18th birthday, as well as after they have aged out of the foster care system. 42 U.S.C. § 677(i)(2) (2009).

[19] 42 U.S.C. § 677(i)(3) (2009).

[20] 42 U.S.C. § 677(i)(5) (2009). The total amount of assistance under federal and federally supported programs must not exceed the total cost of attendance as defined at 20 U.S.C. § 1087; the state must take steps to prevent duplication of benefits. 42 U.S.C. § 677(i)(5) (2009).

[21] The University of Oklahoma maintains a Web site called the National Resource Center for Youth Development (http://www.nrcys.ou.edu/yd/state_pages.html) with information about Chafee and other services available to foster youth in each of the 50 states. The Web site is a good place to find a state contact who may be able to provide information on available Medicaid and Chafee funded services for foster youth in the state. Information can also be found on the Web site of the Department of Health and Human Services, Administration for Children and Families, Children's Bureau at http://www.acf.hhs.gov/programs/cb/. For information specific to state ETV requirements and contacts, see the Web site of the ETV Program at https://www.statevoucher.org/.

§ 23.2.3 Federal Chafee Act Coverage

Each year, about 20,000 youth age out of foster care in the United States, placing the total number of former foster youth from age 18 to 21 at approximately 60,000.[22] As of 2010, Chafee funding for Independent Living Services, discussed above, provides $140 million for eligible youth between ages 16 and 21.[23] At most, $102 million of this funding is provided to youth post-emancipation (between the ages of 18 and 21).[24]

As noted above, foster youth who attend college are eligible for the Chafee ETV grants of up to $5,000 annually, while the average annual tuition for a public college in the United States in 2008–09 was $18,326, and the average amount for out-of-state students was $29,193.[25]

If a foster youth receives $6,120 in general assistance federal Chafee funding (with its 20% state match) and receives the maximum $5,000 ETV grant for education each year over four years of college, the public subsidy would total $26,120, or just over half the median amount private parents provide in monies to their children after age 18 (in addition to room and other assistance) to achieve self-sufficiency as adults. However, $20,000 of that total is in the form of the ETV grants that are received by less than 15% of emancipating foster youth. The more typical $6,120 total available to the vast majority of foster youth after turning 18 represents about 13% of the median amount paid by private parents for early adulthood assistance.

Chafee Independent Living funding and ETV provide assistance to youth who age out of the system, but the significant shortfall *vis-a-vis* both need and levels extant from private parents underlines the importance of the new federal Fostering Connections to Success Act, its state-by-state implementation expected in 2010 to 2012, and state-only funded programs, all discussed below.

---

[22] *See* Mark Courtney, *Youth Aging out of Foster Care* (Network on Transitions to Adulthood Policy Brief, April 2005, Issue 19), *available at* http://www.transad.pop.upenn.edu/downloads/courtney--foster%20care.pdf (citing *On Your Own without a Net: The Transition to Adulthood for Vulnerable Populations* (D. Wayne Osgood, E. Michael Foster, Constance Flanagan & Gretchen Ruth eds., University of Chicago Press)).

[23] *See* the Web page of the U.S. Department of Health and Human Services, Administration for Children and Families, titled "The John H. Chafee Foster Care Independence Program: Program Description" at http://www.acf.hhs.gov/programs/cb/programs_fund/state_tribal/jh_chafee.htm.

[24] Such youth receive on average $1,700 per annum from Chafee, with a state match of 20% bringing the amount up to $2,040. Accordingly, at current levels, the total average amount received over three years per emancipated youth is $6,120.

[25] *See* National Resource Center for Youth Development's Web page titled "John H. Chafee Foster Care Independence Program" at http://www.nrcyd.ou.edu/federal-programs/chafee. A maximum recipient of Chafee grants will receive less than 30% of in-state tuition alone, and less than 20% of tuition when combined with expected living costs.

§ 23.2.4 The Near Future: The Fostering Connections to Success and Increasing Adoptions Act of 2008

The Fostering Connections to Success and Increasing Adoptions Act (the Act) was signed into law in October 2008.[26] The Act covers a number of different areas related to foster care, including kinship guardianships, tribal foster care, adoption incentives, educational stability, and health care oversight.

The provision most relevant to foster youth who are preparing to age out of the system allows states to continue foster care beyond age 18. Specifically, as of October 1, 2010, the law gives states the option to expand the definition of the term "child" to include youth in foster care up to age 21 who are engaged in one of several specified activities.[27] The significance of this change in the law is that it provides federal matching funds to states that choose to extend foster care eligibility up to age 19, 20, or 21, as they select. This new funding is uncapped entitlement funding.

Because it is appropriate for older youth to have a more independent and flexible placement type than their younger counterparts, the Act contains a conforming amendment providing that in the case of a child who has attained 18 years of age, foster care maintenance payments may be made on behalf of a child living in a supervised setting in which the individual is living independently, in accordance with regulations adopted by the DHHS Secretary.[28] Such a supervised setting satisfies the "in foster care" requirement of § 42 U.S.C. § 675(8)(B), as that statute provides as of October 1, 2010.

States must submit a IV-E plan to receive federal Title IV-E funding for child welfare services. The Act gives states the option to amend their IV-E plans to extend services to youth up to ages 19, 20, or 21.[29]

---

[26] Pub. L. No. 110-351 (2008).

[27] At the option of the state, the term "child" includes an individual who is in foster care under the responsibility of the state; who has reached 18 years of age; who has not reached 19, 20 or 21 years of age (as the state may elect); and who is
- completing a secondary education program or a program leading to an equivalent credential;
- enrolled in an institution which provides postsecondary or vocational education;
- participating in a program or activity designed to promote, or remove barriers to, employment;
- employed for at least 80 hours per month; or
- incapable of doing any of the above activities due to a medical condition, which incapability is supported by regularly updated information in the case plan of the child.

42 U.S.C. § 675(8)(B) (2009), effective October 1, 2010.

[28] Amendments to 42 U.S.C. § 672(c)(2), effective October 1, 2010, provide that in the case of a child who has attained 18 years of age, the term "child-care institution" shall include a supervised setting in which the individual is living independently, in accordance with such conditions as the DHHS Secretary shall establish in regulations, but the term shall not include detention facilities, forestry camps, training schools, or any other facility operated primarily for the detention of children who are determined to be delinquent.

[29] This extension is also available for an individual with respect to whom an adoption assistance agreement or a kinship guardianship assistance agreement is in effect if the individual had attained 16 years of age before the agreement became effective. 42 U.S.C. § 675(8)(B)(i)(II)–(III) (2009), effective October 1, 2010. This change is significant because many states currently have state-only

Some states may need to enact new legislation or amend their existing laws to comply with the new federal legislation in order to amend their IV-E plans to receive funding to expand foster care. For example, a state that currently provides assistance to youth only to age 18 would need to amend its law to extend coverage to age 19, 20, or 21 (at its option) before it can receive additional funding. A state that provides assistance post-18 but prohibits assistance to children eligible under federal law would need to amend its law to comply with the federal law in order to receive funding for the eligible post-18-year-old population.

When drafting any legislation that may be necessary to implement the Act, states should note that under the Act, a qualifying supervised setting for post-18-year-old youth includes one in which the youth is living independently. State laws should mirror the federal law and provide as much flexibility as possible in the supervised independent living placement for youth over age 18.

§ 23.3 Current Law and Programs: State General Assistance

§ 23.3.1 State Transitional Housing

Many states have developed housing programs for youth who age out of foster care. Because only 30% of a state's Chafee FCIA allotment may be used to provide housing assistance to youth ages 18 to 21, states have developed programs that utilize federal, state, and private funding sources in addition to Chafee to provide transitional housing for former foster youth.

One example of state-only funding for post-18 transitional housing comes from California. California's Transition Housing Placement Plus (THP-Plus) Program, funded solely with state general fund monies, provides transitional housing services to youth between the ages of 18 and 24 who have aged out of California's foster care system.[30] It is available for 24 months cumulatively.[31] THP-Plus is a county-run program, so the programs vary slightly from county to county. Some counties use THP-Plus funding in conjunction with federal Chafee Independent Living Services to provide comprehensive assistance to former foster youth who participate in the program.[32]

States also use federal funding sources, such as the U.S. Department of Housing and Urban Development (HUD), to provide housing for foster youth transitioning

---

funded kin guardianship programs. Making federal funds available for kin guardianship programs will free up some state money currently used for these programs; states could use this savings to offset the expense of extending foster care to age 21, possibly making such an extension of care cost-neutral, or at least substantially off-setting such costs.

[30] CAL. WELF. & INST. CODE § 11403.2(a)(2) (2009).

[31] CAL. WELF. & INST. CODE § 11403.2(a)(2) (2009).

[32] For more information on THP-Plus, including contact information for county coordinators in California, see http://www.thpplus.org/.

from foster care. For example, two Minnesota nonprofits used private funding together with money from HUD, the Minnesota Housing Finance Agency, the City of Minneapolis, and an investment from Fannie Mae to create the Lindquist Apartments, which serve youth aging out of foster care who face homelessness or chemical dependency.[33]

§ 23.3.2 State Education Assistance

Several states have programs that provide education assistance, separate from and in addition to Chafee ETV, discussed above. Many states provide fee waivers or exemptions for foster youth who attend state colleges and universities. Florida, for example, provides a state-funded fee exemption, valid for four years after the date of high school graduation, to youth who were in the custody of the Department of Children and Family Services at age 18.[34] California's state-funded Board of Governors Fee Waiver waives enrollment fees at California Community Colleges; youth who were in foster care or were a dependent or ward of the court may be eligible for this program.[35]

In addition to educational assistance from Chafee ETV and state fee waivers and exemptions, foster youth may qualify for state- and federally-funded grants based on income. For example, foster youth may qualify for Federal Pell grants.[36] Foster youth are generally considered to be independent; thus, when applying for aid, only the youth's income is considered. Finally, it is important to remember that many states have state counterparts to federal programs. California, for example, has the Cal-Grant Program for which foster youth may qualify based on their income.

§ 23.4 Laws and Policies Impeding Foster Youth Transition to Self-Sufficiency

In addition to the lack of a familial or financial safety net and the difficulties that they face as they attempt to live independently absent these important supports, foster youth often encounter additional obstacles to self sufficiency. Some of these obstacles

---

[33] For information about the Lindquist Apartments, see Roxana Torrico & Soumya Bhat, *Connected by 25: Financing Housing Supports for Youth Transitioning Out of Foster Care* (May 2009), p. 20, *available at* http://www.financeproject.org/publications/FinancingHousingSupport.pdf.

[34] FLA. STAT. § 1009.25(2)(c) (2009). This exemption also applies to youth who were in the custody of a relative under FLA. STAT. § 39.5085, who are adopted from the Department after May 5, 1997, or who, after spending at least six months in Department custody after reaching 16 years of age, were placed in a guardianship by the court. FLA. STAT. § 1009.25(2)(d) (2009).

[35] CAL. ED. CODE § 76300 (2009). For more information about California's fee waiver program, see the "About the Program" section of the program's Website: http://www.icanaffordcollege.org/index.cfm?navId=5. For an application for California's fee waiver, see http://www.icanaffordcollege.org/documents/BOGFW_application.pdf.

[36] Students apply for a Federal Pell Grant by completing the Free Application for Federal Student Aid (FAFSA), *available at* http://www.fafsa.ed.gov/. Information on Federal Pell Grants is available at http://ifap.ed.gov/sfahandbooks/0304Vol3PellGrant.html.

are put in place by federal and state laws and policies and restrict a foster youth's ability to acquire resources he or she needs to transition to a self-sufficient adulthood.

§ 23.4.1 Federal Restrictions on Foster Youth Resources

For example, pursuant to 42 U.S.C. § 672, foster children who receive Title IV-E foster care maintenance payments and do not receive Supplemental Security Income (SSI) benefits may accumulate only up to $10,000 in resources.

Further, 42 U.S.C. § 1382 states that foster youth who receive SSI benefits are generally limited to $2,000 in countable resources. This limit has not been increased since 1989. Although there are some options for accumulating resources in excess of the $2,000 limit (e.g., establishing an Individual Development Account or a Plan for Achieving Self-Support), funds saved pursuant to those devices are limited to specific purposes and have their own restrictions and conditions.

§ 23.4.2 State Interception of Foster Youth Social Security Benefits

Throughout the United States, approximately 30,000 children in foster care are entitled to receive Social Security benefits, such as SSI for disabled children or survivor benefits for children of workers who have died. Those benefits are intended for the "use and benefit of the beneficiary" and are within the regulatory definition of "current maintenance" (i.e., food, clothing, shelter, medical care, and personal comfort items).[37]

In many cases, the named "representative payee" for foster children who are Social Security beneficiaries is the state child welfare agency (despite being named last on the regulatory list setting forth the order of selection that should guide the Social Security Administration in selecting a payee). As representative payee, the agency is charged with using these proceeds for the benefit of the children as required by federal law. Private representative payees may interpret this obligation to mean that the funds should be used to provide additional special services or treatment (e.g., in the case of a disabled child receiving SSI) or should be set aside in a dedicated account for use by the children when they attain the age of 18 (e.g., in the case of a child receiving survivor benefits after a parent has passed away). However, nearly all state agencies designated as the representative payee for foster children use the child's Social Security benefits as a funding stream for child welfare spending—in other words, these states use a foster child's own Social Security benefits to pay for the cost of basic foster care.[38]

---

[37] *See* Adrienne Fernandes, Scott Szymendera & Emilie Stoltzfus, *Child Welfare: Social Security and Supplemental Security Income (SSI) Benefits for Children in Foster Care* (Congressional Research Bureau, Feb. 1, 2007), p. 1, *available at* https://www.policyarchive.org/handle/10207/3120.

[38] *Id.*

The U.S. Supreme Court addressed the state practice of intercepting and taking Social Security benefits in *Washington State Dep't of Soc.& Health Servs. v. Keffeler*[39] and concluded that a state agency's use of a foster child's Social Security benefits to reimburse itself, as a representative payee, for some of its initial expenditures in providing foster care for those children does not violate the anti-attachment provision of the Social Security Act (SSA).

§ 23.5 Specialized Federal and State Medical Programs for Foster Youth Aging Out: Medicaid

Medicaid is an entitlement program that provides health care for low-income individuals. Each state must submit a state plan that complies with the guidelines set forth in the federal statute.[40] This requirement results in differing eligibility and services from state to state.[41] However, to receive federal funding states are required to cover certain populations, including children and youth under age 19 in families that live below the poverty line.[42]

States are required to cover specified services as well. The Social Security Act requires state coverage of services such as Early and Periodic Screening, Diagnostic, and Treatment (EPSDT) to individuals under age 21,[43] hospitalization, pregnancy-related services, and nurse practitioner and physician services.[44] For foster youth who are preparing to age out of care and live independently, this medical coverage is indispensable. These youth have a disproportionately high rate of mental illness[45] and a higher rate of chronic physical health problems. These are a result of the abuse and neglect to which many were exposed at a very young age.[46]

---

[39] 537 U.S. 371 (2003).

[40] 42 U.S.C. § 1396a (2009).

[41] Contact information for state Medicaid offices can be found on the Web site of the Centers for Medicare and Medicaid Services at http://www.cms.hhs.gov/apps/contacts/.

[42] 42 U.S.C. § 1396a(e)(13)(G) (2009).

[43] 42 U.S.C. § 1396d (2009). EPSDT includes periodic screening, vision, dental, and hearing services. In addition, 42 U.S.C. § 1396d(r)(5) requires that any medically necessary health care service listed at 42 U.S.C. § 1396a be provided to an EPSDT recipient even if the service is not available under the state's Medicaid plan to the rest of the Medicaid population. These services include physical and mental illness and conditions discovered by the screening service.

[44] *Id.*

[45] Casey Family Programs, *Improving Outcomes for Older Youth in Foster Care* (2008) , p. 4, *available at* http://www.casey.org/Resources/Publications/pdf/WhitePaper_ImprovingOutcomesOlderYouth_FR.pdf.

[46] *See* Abigail English, Amy J. Stinnett & Elisha Dunn-Georgiou, *Healthcare for Adolescents and Young Adults Leaving Foster Care: Policy Options for Improving Access* (Center for Adolescent Health and the Law, Issue Brief, Feb. 2006), *available at* http://www.cahl.org/PDFs/FCIssueBrief.pdf; *see also* Mark D. Simms, Howard Dubowitz & Moira A. Szilagyi, *Health Care Needs of Children in the Foster Care System*, 106/4 PEDIATRICS 909 (2000), *available at* http://pediatrics.aappublications.org/cgi/content/full/106/4/S1/909 (requires subscription).

States are required to provide Medicaid to vulnerable groups including recipients of SSI and recipients of adoption assistance and foster care under Title IV-E.[47] The Chafee FCIA provides states with the option to expand Medicaid to foster youth who age out of care until age 21, regardless of income eligibility.[48] Many states have implemented this option,[49] though some states either have not extended Medicaid to age 21 or terminate Medicaid when the youth leaves foster care.

The requirements to maintain eligibility vary from state to state. An attorney should ensure that his or her clients are aware of the requirements to maintain eligibility in their state because there are several barriers youth may experience to continued health care coverage. First, some states require foster youth to reapply for Medicaid when they exit the system, even given their eligibility as former foster youth. This paperwork creates a barrier, particularly if the child welfare agency responsible for the youth is not required to ensure that the youth has applied.

Second, most states require Medicaid recipients to prove continuing eligibility by providing proof of residence or income on a regular basis.[50] This can present an obstacle for a young person who is on his or her own and must navigate the system alone, often in addition to juggling work, school, transportation, interpersonal relationships, and housing issues.

Third, although meeting the proof of residence requirement may appear to be easy, many foster youth become homeless, are transient, or have difficulty renting an apartment or establishing utility service in their name. Thus, counsel should be aware of governing state law regarding proof of residency requirements and facilitate that offer of proof by providing emancipating youth with appropriate paperwork. Similarly, the movement of foster youth between counties or states upon emancipation is common and may present Medicaid enrollment barriers. Where counsel knows that such movement will occur in advance, it may be prudent to arrange enrollment transfer under the procedures of the applicable jurisdiction.

The checklist section on Medicaid at the end of this chapter provides items for attorneys to consider as their clients prepare to age out of foster care.

---

[47] *See* 42 U.S.C. §§ 1396a and 1396d for information on mandatory populations. Information is also available at the Centers for Medicare and Medicaid Services Web page titled "Medicaid Eligibility: Overview" at http://www.cms.hhs.gov/MedicaidEligibility/.

[48] 42 U.S.C. § 1396a(a)(10)(A)(ii)(XVII) (2009).

[49] States that have implemented this program include Arizona, California, Connecticut, Iowa, Kansas, Texas, New Jersey, and several others. States may have differing eligibility and application requirements.

[50] This may vary by state, so an attorney should be aware of his or her state policies and procedures; see the Centers for Medicare and Medicaid Services Web page titled "Contacts Database" at http://www.cms.hhs.gov/apps/contacts/.

§ 23.6 Specialized Federal and State Disability Programs

§ 23.6.1 Supplemental Security Income (SSI)—Disability Benefits

Supplemental Security Income (SSI) is a means-tested federally administered entitlement program. SSI provides cash to meet the basic food, clothing, and shelter needs of aged, blind, and disabled people who have limited income. In addition to providing a monthly income to physically and mentally disabled people, it entitles them to Medicaid and other specialized services.[51]

A youth must be disabled to receive SSI benefits. The disability standards are different for adults and children. An individual under age 18 is considered disabled under the Social Security Act if he or she has a medically determinable physical or mental impairment, which results in marked and severe functional limitations, and which can be expected to result in death or which has lasted or can be expected to last for a continuous period of not less than twelve months.[52] An adult is disabled under the Social Security Act if he or she is unable to engage in any substantial gainful activity by reason of any medically determinable physical or mental impairment which can be expected to result in death or which has lasted or can be expected to last for a continuous period of not less than twelve months.[53]

Because SSI benefits for disabled youth who age out of foster care could mean the difference between a successful transition and an adulthood plagued with illness and homelessness, it is critical to that foster youth be screened for SSI eligibility before they age out of the system. Unfortunately, not every state does so. Mandated screening of foster youth for eligibility would ensure that foster youth have needed SSI assistance—to which they are entitled—that would help them avoid homelessness and the other negative outcomes they regularly face upon aging out of foster care.

Some states statutorily mandate that foster youth be screened before court jurisdiction is terminated. California, for example, requires that the state: (1) screen all youth who are in foster care and are between the ages of 16.5 and 17.5 years of age for a physical or mental disability; and (2) submit an SSI application on behalf of those youth who are determined likely eligible for benefits.[54] An attorney must know his or her state's laws with regard to screening foster youth for SSI eligibility, and should make every effort to ensure that clients who are approaching emancipation have been screened for SSI eligibility and have submitted an SSI application if they are found to be eligible.

---

[51] 42 U.S.C. § 1381a (2009).

[52] 42 U.S.C. § 1382c(a)(3)(C)(i) (2009).

[53] 42 U.S.C. § 1382c(a)(3)(A), (B) (2009).

[54] CAL. WELF. & INST. CODE § 13757 (2009).

Importantly, a policy instruction issued by the Social Security Administration in January 2010 allows it to accept an SSI application from a disabled youth in foster care up to 90 days before federal foster care payments are expected to end. To ensure continuity of services, attorneys for youth preparing to age out of foster care must be aware of this important and useful exception.[55]

§ 23.6.2 Special Needs and Self-Sufficiency Trusts

In some instances, assets accumulated by a foster youth from sources such as employment or an inheritance may exceed the asset limit set forth in the Social Security Act and disqualify a disabled youth who is otherwise eligible for SSI and would benefit from the resources SSI provides.[56] In this circumstance, a Special Needs Trust should be considered for the youth. A Special Needs Trust may be created by a parent, grandparent, legal guardian, or the court for the benefit of an individual under age 65 who is disabled.[57] In addition, a Special Needs Trust must include a provision repaying state Medicaid agencies for any benefits, payable at the death of the beneficiary.[58]

While a Special Needs Trust is structured such that a beneficiary would not be disqualified from receiving SSI, cash distributed from a Special Needs Trust directly to the beneficiary may be considered unearned income.[59] "Unearned income" is all income that is not earned and includes items such as periodic payments (pensions and annuities, for example), alimony, dividends, gifts, and in-kind support.[60] "In-kind support" is not cash but food, shelter, or anything the recipient receives that he or she can convert into these items.[61] Receipt of in-kind support and maintenance or other unearned income may also reduce SSI benefits despite the Special Needs Trust. Therefore, these trusts must be very carefully drafted to comply with the law in order to ensure that the youth maintains SSI eligibility.

Additionally, the increasingly available option of self-sufficiency trusts is not limited to special needs youth. This option may apply to foster youth post-18 years of age who need assistance for self-sufficiency with some continued adult and court support. These funds are administered under a court-approved trust agreement, subject to administration and guidance from a court-appointed trustee/mentor and are subject to periodic review and revision as needed.

The self-sufficiency trust mechanism does not require the mental illness or disability prerequisites that may apply to a special needs trust or to a conservatorship.

---

[55] *See* Social Security Online Program Operations Manuel System (POMS), Policy Instruction No. SI 00601.011, *available at* https://secure.ssa.gov/apps10/poms.nsf/lnx/0500601011!opendocument.

[56] *See* 42 U.S.C. § 1382b (2009).

[57] *See* 42 U.S.C. § 1396p(d)(4)(A) (2009).

[58] *See* 42 U.S.C. § 1396p(d)(4)(C)(iv) (2009).

[59] 20 C.F.R. §§ 416.1120, 416.1121 (2009).

[60] 20 C.F.R. §§ 416.1120, 416.1121 (2009).

[61] 20 C.F.R. §§ 416.1102, 416.1130 (2009).

It may be formulated in advance of emancipation, and the court-appointed trustee may assist the youth in achieving self-sufficiency and expending available funds for that purpose under court supervision—even if the youth is no longer directly under the court's supervision. Such a mechanism also allows a plan to be customized to the needs of individual clients and to be changed with court permission, as circumstances require.

These self-sufficiency trusts are explicitly authorized in California and some trusts have been established.[62] Other states have generic authority within juvenile court or probate court to fashion such arrangements. The financing for these trusts may come from charitable contributions, foundation funding, mental health benefits, or other special state appropriations. The broad language of the federal Fostering Connections Act (discussed above in § 23.2.4) allows a federal match for substantial assistance to foster youth up to age 21, making Social Security Act Title IV-E funds potentially available for such court-supervised trusts, depending on the implementing federal regulations and conforming state amendments.[63]

§ 23.7 Special Education Considerations

It is impossible to overemphasize the importance of education for youth preparing to age out of foster care and live independently.[64] It is crucial for a young person's attorney to be attentive to his or her client's education needs, particularly if the client has special education needs. As a youth prepares to age out of the foster care system, his or her dependency attorney should be aware of several important issues.

First, if the youth has an Individualized Education Program (IEP), it must include a transition plan to move the student from school to post-school life, including living skills, postsecondary education, and employment. Regulations under the federal Individuals with Disabilities Education Act (IDEA) require the IEP to include transition services.[65] Often, these transition plans are boilerplate provisions that are not individualized. Dependency attorneys should ensure that each client's transition

---

[62] *See* CAL. PROB. CODE § 1517(b). For a model court order and trust agreement, see http://caichildlaw.org/Misc/Model_TLC_Petition_and_Order.pdf (petition and order) and http://caichildlaw.org/Misc/Model_TLC_Trust_Agreement.pdf (trust agreement).

[63] The provisions of the Fostering Connections to Success Act, which are effective in October 2010, allow federal money for supervised arrangements in general to the extent they facilitate employment or the completion of secondary or postsecondary education. Counsel drafting trusts or other documents for the support of foster youth post-18 (whether in traditional foster care or care in the form of a trust or other state supervision as is consistent with the Act) should advisedly tailor such documents mindful of these provisions to optimize potential qualification for federal IV-E contribution.

[64] For a more complete discussion of educational advocacy for children, see Chapter 22.

[65] 34 C.F.R. § 300.320(b) (2009). The IEP must include: (1) appropriate measurable postsecondary goals based on age-appropriate transition assessments related to training, education, employment, and, where appropriate, independent living skills; and (2) the transition services (including courses of study) needed to assist the child in reaching those goals. 34 C.F.R. § 300.320(b) (2009).

plan is properly individualized, accurately represents the client's goals, and reflects a reasonable and sufficiently detailed plan to achieve those goals.

Second, the IEP will help the youth access services such as instruction, community experiences, development of employment and other post-school adult living objectives, acquisition of daily living skills if appropriate, and a functional vocational evaluation if appropriate.[66] These services are available until the youth is 22, provided the youth does not have a regular high school diploma. Once the youth receives his or her diploma, the services cease.[67]

Third, although some postsecondary institutions and vocational schools may offer services for these youth, there are no federally funded special education programs for postsecondary education. Nevertheless, the school district must identify appropriate programs and offer these to the student as part of the IEP.

Finally, an attorney must be aware of his or her state's laws and regulations regarding youth ages 18 to 21.[68] Some state laws may differ on the availability of services.

§ 23.8 Examples of State Assistance Regimes

State laws differ, so attorneys representing older foster youth should be especially familiar with their state's laws regarding jurisdiction, eligibility, and requirements for services for foster youth who are transitioning from foster care to independent living.

The table at § 23.10 contains the current status of the laws in each state as of September 2009; it is possible that these laws will change in 2010 or 2011 due to further implementation of the Fostering Connections to Success Act of 2008.

§ 23.8.1 State Example: California

Termination of Jurisdiction

Currently, California law allows the juvenile court to maintain jurisdiction over a foster youth until age 21.[69] However, like most states that allow jurisdiction until age 21, California usually terminates jurisdiction well before age 21, typically while the youth is 18. One exception to this practice occurs when a youth is attending high school or the equivalent level of vocational or technical training on a full-time basis, or is in the process of pursuing a high school equivalency certificate before his or her 18th birthday, in which case the youth may continue to receive aid following his or her 18th birthday (but only if the youth is reasonably expected to complete the

---

[66] 34 C.F.R. § 300.43(a)(2).

[67] 34 C.F.R. § 300.102(a)(3) (2009). The term "regular high school diploma" does not include an alternative degree that is not fully aligned with the state's academic standards, such as a certificate or a general educational development credential (GED). 34 C.F.R. § 300.102(a)(3)(iv) (2009).

[68] *See* 34 C.F.R. § 300.102(a)(1) (2009).

[69] CAL. WELF. & INST. CODE § 303 (2009).

educational or training program or to receive a high school equivalency certificate, before his or her 19th birthday).[70]

At a hearing to terminate jurisdiction over a child who has reached the age of majority, California law mandates that counties ensure that the youth is present in court or document efforts to locate the child when the youth is not available.[71] Further, the law requires the counties to submit a report verifying that the information, documents, and services have been provided to the youth.[72]

Counties must provide the child with written information concerning the child's dependency case, including:

- Any known information regarding the child's Indian heritage or tribal connections, if applicable

- The child's family history and placement history

- Any photographs of the child or his or her family in the possession of the county welfare department, other than forensic photographs

- The whereabouts of any siblings under the jurisdiction of the juvenile court (unless the court determines that sibling contact would jeopardize the safety or welfare of the sibling)

- Directions on how to access documents the child is entitled to inspect

- The date on which the jurisdiction of the juvenile court would be terminated[73]

Counties must provide the following documents to the youth:

- Social Security card

- Certified birth certificate

- Health and education summary

- Driver's license or identification card

- A letter prepared by the county welfare department that includes the child's name and date of birth

- The dates during which the child was within the jurisdiction of the juvenile court

- A statement that the child was a foster youth in compliance with state and federal financial aid documentation requirements

- The death certificate of the parent or parents, if applicable

- Proof of the child's citizenship or legal residence, if applicable[74]

---

[70] CAL. WELF. & INST. CODE § 11403 (2009).

[71] CAL. WELF. & INST. CODE § 391(a)(1) (2009).

[72] CAL. WELF. & INST. CODE § 391(a)(2) (2009).

[73] CAL. WELF. & INST. CODE § 391(a)(2)(A) (2009).

The county must provide the youth with assistance in completing an application for Medi-Cal, California's version of Medicaid, or assistance in obtaining other health insurance; referral to transitional housing, if available, or assistance in securing other housing; and assistance in obtaining employment or other financial support.[75]

The county must provide the youth with assistance in applying for admission to college, a vocational training program, or other educational institution, and must assist the youth in obtaining financial aid, where appropriate.[76]

Finally, the county must provide assistance to the youth in maintaining relationships with individuals who are important to a child who has been in out-of-home placement in a group home for six months or longer from the date the child entered foster care, based on the child's best interests.[77]

A juvenile court in California may continue jurisdiction if it finds that the county welfare department has not met the above requirements and that termination of jurisdiction would be harmful to the best interests of the child. If the court determines that continued jurisdiction is warranted, the continuation is only required for the period of time necessary for the county welfare department to meet the requirements. The court may terminate jurisdiction if the county welfare department has offered the required services and the youth either refused the services or, after reasonable efforts by the county welfare department, the youth cannot be located.

Health Care

California has opted to make Medi-Cal, the state's Medicaid program, available to foster youth until age 21. To remain eligible for Medi-Cal, the youth must complete an annual redetermination to verify he or she is still a resident and still wants Medi-Cal.

In 2004, California voters passed the Mental Health Services Act (MHSA),[78] which provides funding for prevention and early intervention services. The Act does not mandate that the counties create programs specifically for transition age foster youth. However, it does carve out the broader transition age youth population, defined as youth between the ages of 16 to 25, for services. Given the high rates at which foster youth and former foster youth experience significant mental illness, these programs have the potential to provide much needed services. Unfortunately, no county has used this funding to create comprehensive services specifically to serve transition age foster youth. Nevertheless, there are several MHSA-funded programs from which foster youth may benefit. Attorneys should be cognizant of laws like the MHSA that, while not designed specifically for transition age foster youth, may nonetheless provide beneficial resources for them.

---

[74] CAL. WELF. & INST. CODE § 391(a)(2)(B) (2009).

[75] CAL. WELF. & INST. CODE § 391(a)(2)(C) (2009).

[76] CAL. WELF. & INST. CODE § 391(a)(2)(D) (2009).

[77] CAL. WELF. & INST. CODE § 391(a)(2)(E) (2009).

[78] CAL. WELF. & INST. CODE §§ 5891 *et seq.*

Housing

As discussed above, California's Transitional Housing Placement Plus (THP-Plus) program provides transitional housing and services to former foster youth.[79] The program is available for 24 months, cumulatively, and former foster youth are eligible until age 24. California's THP-Plus program currently has capacity for 1,400 youth,[80] while each year approximately 4,300 youth age out of foster care in California.[81]

Education

California's Foster Youth Success Initiative[82] works to improve the ability of foster youth attending higher education to access postsecondary education and benefit from support services that are available but are often unknown to them. Each community college in California has a foster youth liaison on campus to assist foster youth attending that college.

In addition to eligibility for Chafee Educational and Training Vouchers, discussed above, California has several privately funded programs and public/private partnerships that address the need for foster youth to receive a college education. These programs offer a range of services such as a campus liaison, tutoring, and keeping campus housing open to foster youth during school breaks. The programs vary from campus to campus.[83]

§ 23.8.2 State Example: Illinois

Termination of Jurisdiction

Under Illinois law, dependency court jurisdiction terminates at age 19 unless a court determines that the best interest of the minor and the public require the continuation of wardship, in which case jurisdiction may continue until age 21.[84] Foster youth in Illinois routinely remain in care past age 18.[85]

Legislation to allow older youth to re-enter foster care after opting out will take effect on January 1, 2010.[86]

---

[79] CAL. WELF. & INST. CODE §§ 11403.1 *et seq.*

[80] THP-Plus online newsletter (Spring 2009), a*vailable at* http://www.thpplus.org/pdfs/THP-Plus%20Newsletter%20Spring%202009.pdf.

[81] *THP-Plus Annual Report 2006-2007*, p.4, *available at* http://www.thpplus.org/THP-PlusAnnual Report.pdf

[82] *See* CAL. EDUC. CODE §§ 89340 *et seq.*

[83] For more information on California's college programs for foster youth, see the Web site of California College Pathways at http://www.cacollegepathways.org/index.html.

[84] 705 ILL. COMP. STAT. 405/3-32.

[85] Amy Dworsky & Judy Havlicek, *Review of State Policies and Programs to Support Young People Transitioning Out of Foster Care* (Chapin Hall at the University of Chicago 2009), *available at* http://www.chapinhall.org/sites/default/files/Review_State_Policies_02_09.pdf.

[86] Illinois H.B. 4054 (2009) amended the following Illinois statutes effective Jan. 1, 2010: 20 ILL. COMP. STAT. 505/5, 705 ILL. COMP. STAT. 405/2-23, 705 ILL. COMP. STAT. 405/2-27, 705 ILL. COMP. STAT. 405/2-31, 705 ILL. COMP. STAT. 405/2-33.

Benchmark Hearings

Some Illinois jurisdictions, notably Cook County, where Chicago is located, have implemented "benchmark hearings," which monitor the progress of older foster youth toward achieving independence.

Benchmark hearings are held at least twice, when the youth is 14 and 17½, with additional benchmark hearings held as appropriate. The intent of the hearings is to engage the youth in articulating educational, employment, and other goals and to ensure that the Transition Living Plan is in place to achieve important outcomes prior to discharge. The benchmark hearings aim to ensure that older foster youth are prepared to live a healthy, productive adult life. As such, the hearings engage not only the youth, but also individuals important in his or her life, such as the caseworker, the youth's attorney, the Court Appointed Special Advocate, teachers, mentors, service providers, and adults with whom the youth has built or might build long-lasting relationships. A comprehensive benchmark hearing can take up to two hours.[87]

Education

In addition to Chaffee ETVs, Illinois provides the Youth in College Program, which provides a stipend to foster youth in college until they reach age 23, provided they maintain the required grade point average.

§ 23.8.3 State Example: New York

Termination of Jurisdiction

New York law allows foster care jurisdiction to extend to age 21 with the consent of the foster youth.[88] The state has a unique hybrid approach to emancipation, requiring a six-month trial discharge. During this period, the court maintains jurisdiction over the youth's case. The state must make all aftercare services available to the youth, and the youth's social worker must supervise and be available for appointments at the youth's request. The youth, however, is not considered to be a foster youth and may elect which services, if any, he or she will receive.[89]

The court has jurisdiction to re-designate the youth a foster youth and place the youth in a state authorized foster care placement if either (a) a triggering event, such as homelessness, occurs or (b) the youth requests to return to foster care.

---

[87] For more information about benchmark hearings, see *Benchmark Hearings – Milestones Toward Independence,* Child Protection Best Practices Bulletin, Innovative Strategies to Achieve Safety, Permanence, and Well-Being, *available at* http://ipl.unm.edu/childlaw/docs/0701/Benchmark Hearings.pdf.

[88] Jurisdiction ends at age 18, but with the child's consent may continue to age 21. *See* N.Y.C.L.S. Family Ct. Act § 1055.

[89] *See* N.Y. Comp. Codes R. & Regs. Tit. 18 § 430.12 (2009).

§ 23.9 Checklist for Attorneys

☐ Is the youth receiving ILP Services?
    ☐ Does your state/county allow ILP services prior to age 16?
    ☐ Does the youth have a plan for living independently?
    ☐ Does the youth know who his or her ILP coordinator is?
    ☐ Does the youth have the appropriate contact information for this person?
    ☐ Has the youth's social worker assisted the youth with applications that can be submitted prior to age 18?

☐ Does the youth have all the documentation he or she will need to apply for school, financial aid, housing, and other services he or she will need upon aging out of the system?
    ☐ Driver's license or state identification card
    ☐ Birth certificate
    ☐ Social Security card
    ☐ Educational history/records
    ☐ Health history
    ☐ An official letter or documentation confirming the youth's status as a foster youth for the purposes of applying for financial aid and other services
    ☐ Parent's death certificate (if applicable)
    ☐ Citizenship papers and documents (if applicable)

☐ Has the youth been screened for SSI eligibility?
    ☐ Has all of the applicable paperwork been submitted in a timely fashion?
    ☐ If it appears that there may be a gap in time between when the youth ages out of the system and when he or she will begin to receive SSI payments, consider advocating for jurisdiction to continue until such time as the youth begins to receive SSI payments.
    ☐ Is the youth aware of his or her responsibilities as far as SSI is concerned?
        ☐ Maintaining eligibility
        ☐ Reporting marriage
        ☐ Reporting change in circumstances
    ☐ Does the youth have a listing of names and contact information for all doctors, therapists, and hospital visits? (SSI generally contacts these facilities directly to get records so a youth will need to know who/where he or she has been treated, when, and the providers' address and phone number contacts.)

☐ Are there any special state-only programs that provide services for foster youth who have aged out of foster care?
    ☐ Has the youth applied for these services?

☐ Does the youth have Native American ancestry? If so, does he or she have the proper documentation so proving?

☐ Are there any immigration issues that need to be addressed?
    ☐ Has the youth applied for Special Immigrant Juvenile Status (if applicable)?

☐ Does the youth have a mentor or other continuous caring adult in his or her life?

☐ Is funding for a trust-type arrangement available?

Education

☐ Will the youth graduate from high school or have a GED before the court terminates jurisdiction?

    ☐ If not, is there a way to extend jurisdiction until the youth graduates or receives equivalent credentials?

    ☐ If so:
        ☐ Does the youth know what he or she wants to do after high school?
        ☐ College: Has the youth taken the proper entrance exams? (SAT, ACT. . .)
        ☐ Has the youth applied to college or a vocational school?
        ☐ Has the youth completed a Free Application for Federal Student Aid (FAFSA)?[90]

        ☐ Is the youth eligible for a Chafee ETV grant?
            ☐ Has the youth applied for a Chafee ETV grant? Check the state's Department of Education for information and an application

        ☐ Has the youth applied for other state/federal assistance?
            ☐ Pell Grants?
            ☐ State grants?
            ☐ Tuition or fee waivers for which the youth is eligible?
            ☐ Special state programs? (like California's Guardian Scholars)
            ☐ Provide the youth with a list of private scholarships from organizations such as the Orphan Foundation of America[91] and their contact information

☐ Does the youth have an appropriate IEP?
    ☐ Does the IEP include a transition plan that is individualized, with well-articulated goals and a reasonable, appropriate plan to achieve those goals (not boilerplate)?

---

[90] *See* http://www.fafsa.ed.gov/.

[91] *See* http://orphan.org/index.php.

Housing

- ☐ Does the youth have a safe and stable place to live when he or she emancipates from foster care?
  - ☐ Are there Chafee funded programs available? (Each state can use up to 30% of its Chafee funding for housing.) Be familiar with state law and check with state or county child welfare for local programs.
  - ☐ Are there special state programs available? Be familiar with state law and check with state or county child welfare.
  - ☐ Are there any HUD programs for which the youth may qualify?
  - ☐ Are there programs available at the college the youth will be attending? Some state colleges keep the dorms open for foster youth during breaks to provide year-round housing—is this a possibility?

Healthcare

- ☐ Does the youth have health insurance in place for after he or she emancipates?
  - ☐ Does the state have a Medicaid program that extends eligibility for foster youth to age 21?
  - ☐ If so, what kind of paperwork and documentation does the state require?
  - ☐ Does the youth have copies of any documentation he or she will need to maintain health insurance?
  - ☐ Does the youth understand his or her responsibilities with regard to maintaining health insurance?
  - ☐ If the state has not extended Medicaid, are there other health care insurance options?

- ☐ Does the youth qualify for Social Security disability benefits? Has he or she applied?
  - ☐ Will the youth begin to receive assistance immediately upon aging out, or will there be a period of time between the youth's aging out and commencement of benefits?
  - ☐ If there is a period of time between the youth's aging out of foster care and the commencement of disability benefits, can any action be taken to ensure the youth receives proper care and does not become homeless in the interim?

- ☐ Is a Special Needs Trust necessary and appropriate?

Employment

- ☐ Does the youth have the documentation required to apply for a job?
- ☐ Has the youth had any training with regard to the application and interview process?
- ☐ Does the youth have any work experience or job training?
- ☐ Does the youth have a resume, or know how to draft one?

§ 23.10 Table of State Foster Care Aging Out Statutes

The following table contains the current status of the laws in each state as of September 2009.

State	Age at Which Jurisdiction Ends
Alabama	The Court may continue jurisdiction to age 21. Ala. Code § 12-15-117 (2009).
Alaska	Currently, court jurisdiction may be continued to age 20 at the request of the child. Alaska has a bill pending (SB 105) that would extend support to age 21. Alaska Stat. § 47.10.100 (2009).
Arizona	Jurisdiction currently ends at 18. Ariz. Rev. Stat. § 8-202 (2009).
Arkansas	Jurisdiction terminates at 18, but can be expanded to 21 if the youth so requests. Ark. Code Ann. § 9-27-306 (2009).
California	Court may retain jurisdiction until age 21. Cal. Welf. & Inst. Code § 303 (2009).
Colorado	Jurisdiction ends at age 21. Colo. Rev. Stat. § 19-3-205 (2009).
Connecticut	Jurisdiction ends at age 18, or may end at 21 if the youth is in full-time attendance in a secondary school, a technical school, a college or a state-accredited job training program. Conn. Gen. Stat. § 17a-93 (2009).
Delaware	Jurisdiction may continue until age 18. (DEL. CODE ANN. Tit. 10 §§ 901, 921)
Florida	Jurisdiction ends at age 18. Fla. Stat. § 409.1451 (2009).
Georgia	Jurisdiction ends at age 18. Ga. Code Ann. § 15-11-2 (2009).
Hawaii	Jurisdiction ends at age 19, or until full term for any order entered expires. Haw. Rev. Stat. § 587-12 (2009).
Idaho	Jurisdiction ends at age 18. Idaho Code Ann. § 16-1604 (2009).
Illinois	Jurisdiction may continue until age 21. 20 Ill. Comp. Stat. § 505/5 (2009).
Indiana	Jurisdiction may continue until age 21. Ind. Code Ann. § 31-30-2-1 (2009).
Iowa	Jurisdiction ends at age 18. Iowa Code § 232.2 (2009).
Kansas	Jurisdiction ends at age 21 but youth can petition to be released at 18. Kan. Stat. Ann. §§ 38-2202, 38-2203 (2008).

State	Age at Which Jurisdiction Ends
Kentucky	Jurisdiction may continue until age 21. Ky. Rev. Stat. Ann. § 620.140 (2009).
Louisiana	Jurisdiction ends at age 18. La. C.C. Art. 303; La. C.C. Art. 29 (2009).
Maine	Jurisdiction ends at 18 but youth may sign a V-9 contract to continue until 21. 22-A M.R.S. § 215 (2009).
Maryland	Jurisdiction may continue until age 21. Md. Code, Courts and Judicial Proceedings § 3-804 (2009).
Massachusetts	Jurisdiction may continue until age 22 under some circumstances. Mass. Gen. Laws Ch. 119, § 23 (2009).
Michigan	Jurisdiction may continue in some circumstances where a youth has reached age 19, yet is still in a school or training program. Mich. Comp. Laws § 712A.2a (2009).
Minnesota	Jurisdiction ends at age 19. Minn. Stat. § 260C.193 (2009).
Mississippi	Jurisdiction may continue until age 20. Miss. Code. Ann. § 43-21-151 (2009).
Missouri	Jurisdiction may continue until age 21. Mo. Rev. Stat. § 211.041 (2009).
Montana	Jurisdiction ends at age 18. Mont. Code Anno. §§ 41-3-102, 41-3-103 (2009).
Nebraska	Jurisdiction ends at age 19. Neb. Rev. Stat. § 43-245 (2009).
Nevada	Jurisdiction ends at age 18. Nev. Rev. Stat. Ann. §§ 432B.040 , 432B.410 (2009).
New Hampshire	Jurisdiction can continue if the youth has not graduated from high school or completed his/her GED and is under the age of 21. N.H. Rev. Stat. Ann. § 169-C:4 (2009).
New Jersey	Jurisdiction ends at age 21. N.J. Rev. Stat. § 9:17B-3 (2009).
New Mexico	Jurisdiction ends at age 18. N.M. Stat. Ann. §§ 32A-1-8, 32A-4-24(F) (2009).
New York	Jurisdiction ends at age 18, but with the child's consent may continue to age 21. NY CLS Family Ct Act § 1055
North Carolina	Jurisdiction ends at age 18. N.C. Gen. Stat. §§ 7B-200, 7B-201 (2009).
North Dakota	Jurisdiction ends at age 20. N.D. Cent. Code § 27-20-36(2009).

State	Age at Which Jurisdiction Ends
Ohio	Jurisdiction generally ends at age 18; jurisdiction ends at age 21 if the child is mentally retarded, developmentally disabled, or physically impaired, or the child is adopted and a final decree of adoption is issued. The court may retain jurisdiction over the child for a specified period of time to enable the child to graduate from high school or vocational school. Ohio Rev. Code Ann. § 2151.353 (2009).
Oklahoma	Jurisdiction ends at age 18. Okla. Stat. tit. 10, § 7002-1.1 (2009).
Oregon	Jurisdiction ends at age 21. Or. Rev. Stat. § 419B.328 (2009).
Pennsylvania	Jurisdiction ends at age 21. 42 Pa. Cons. Stat. § 6302 (2009).
Rhode Island	Jurisdiction ends at age 18. R.I. Gen. Laws § 14-1-6 (2009).
South Carolina	Jurisdiction may continue until the child becomes 18 years of age, unless emancipated earlier. S.C. Code Ann. § 63-7-2520 (2009).
South Dakota	Jurisdiction generally ends at age 18 but may continue until age 21. S.D. Codified Laws § 26-7A-1 (2009).
Tennessee	Jurisdiction ends at age 18. Tenn. Code Ann. § 37-1-102 (2009).
Texas	Jurisdiction ends at age 18. Tex. Fam. Code § 264.101 (2009).
Utah	Jurisdiction ends at age 18. Utah Code Ann. § 78A-6-103 (2009).
Vermont	Jurisdiction generally ends at age 18. Vt. Stat. Ann. tit. 33, § 5103 (2009).
Virginia	Jurisdiction ends at age 18. Va. Code Ann. § 63.2-100 (2009).
Washington	Jurisdiction ends at age 18. Wash. Rev. Code § 13.34.030 (2009).
West Virginia	Jurisdiction generally ends at age 18. W. Va. Code § 49-2-2 (2009).
Wisconsin	Jurisdiction ends at age 18. Wis. Stat. §§ 48.13, 48.02 (2009).
Wyoming	Jurisdiction ends at age 18. Wyo. Stat. § 14-3-402 (2009).

Chapter 24: Non-Adversarial Case Resolution

by Donald N. Duquette[1]

§ 24.1 Introduction

A lawyer practicing in child welfare is increasingly likely to either want to refer a case to a Non-Adversarial Case Resolution (NACR) program or to be ordered into NACR by the court.[2] This chapter is intended to orient a lawyer to the most common forms of NACR in the United States today, prepare him or her to participate competently in that structure, and to encourage more widespread use of these promising alternatives.

Professionals who work with children and parents have become increasingly dissatisfied with the customary reliance on the traditional adversarial system in resolving family-related disputes, including cases involving children's protection, placement, and permanent care. The power struggle in contested cases and hearings relating to child welfare may foster hostility among the parties and dissipate money, energy, and attention that could otherwise be used to solve problems cooperatively. One leading expert said: "Few child welfare experts deny that the predominant approach to decision-making is inefficient, ineffective, and even toxic for children and families."[3] Parties may become polarized, open communication may be discouraged, and there may be little investment in information sharing and joint problem solving. Children may suffer when adversarial tensions escalate and ameliorative services are delayed.

On the other hand, the adversarial system is essential and well-suited to resolving conflicts when differences regarding the true facts of a child abuse or neglect case, or the differing views of the proper response to a family's problems related to child protection, are irreconcilable. The traditional protections of due process of law must

---

[1] Donald N. Duquette, J.D., is Clinical Professor of Law and Director of the Child Advocacy Law Clinic of the University of Michigan Law School.

[2] Howard Davidson, Director of the American Bar Association Center for Children and the Law, deserves credit for coining the term "Non-adversarial Case Resolution (NACR)" as it applies to the child welfare law context. The use of this term reflects the hope of many that perhaps someday in the future non-adversarial case resolution will become widespread enough so as not to be considered the *alternative* dispute resolution, but rather the more commonplace means of conflict resolution. *See* CHILDREN'S BUREAU, U.S. DEPARTMENT OF HEALTH & HUMAN SERVICES, ADOPTION 2002: THE PRESIDENT'S INITIATIVE ON ADOPTION AND FOSTER CARE, GUIDELINES FOR PUBLIC POLICY AND STATE LEGISLATION GOVERNING PERMANENCE FOR CHILDREN (1999), *available at* http://web.archive.org/web/20030224035115/www.acf.dhhs.gov/programs/cb/publications/adopt02/.

[3] Bernie Mayer, *Reflections on the State of Consensus-Based Decision Making in Child Welfare*, 47/1 FAM. CT. REV. 10, 11 (2009).

remain fully available to parents and children where the most fundamental rights of family relationships are at stake.

Most child abuse and neglect cases are resolved through informal settlement negotiations. Unfortunately, these settlements are often quickly made in courthouse hallways where the interests of all parties may not be carefully or fully considered. Hastily made agreements or stipulations made immediately prior to a hearing can do a disservice to both children and their families.

Courts traditionally encourage resolution of contested matters through pretrial hearings and party negotiations that narrow the issues in contention. These court-based approaches to avoid lengthy and contested case proceedings, including pretrial case settlement and case status conferences, are commonly used and often authorized by statute or court rule. But more formalized Alternative Dispute Resolution (or Non-Adversarial Case Resolution (NACR), the preferred term here) has become an accepted alternative to the traditional adversarial processes of the courts. It has also been widely adopted to resolve conflicts within government agencies and elsewhere. Surveys of court improvement projects indicate that one of the most popular reforms identified by the states is the use of alternative forms of dispute resolution.[4] Non-adversarial case resolution programs now exist in most states, and the popularity of these programs seems to be growing.[5]

In a related development, state efforts to improve family assessment and increase cooperative decision-making in child protection cases is one of the most dynamic and fast changing areas in the child welfare field. There is a great deal of policy development and experimentation that deals with the child welfare process from the first CPS contact with a family through investigation, risk analysis, assessment of family strengths and weaknesses, and development of safety plans. In some states, lawyers practicing child welfare law may encounter "Alternative Response" or "Differential Response," in which the traditional investigative approach is replaced with a problem-solving focus on assessing the strengths and needs of the family and child while ensuring the child's safety, usually without requiring a "substantiated" or "unsubstantiated" ("founded" or "unfounded") determination regarding maltreatment.[6]

---

[4] *See* National Child Welfare Resource Center on Legal and Judicial Issues summary of CIP progress reports which can be limited by subject (ADR, for example) at http://www.abanet.org/child/rclji; *see also* the National Evaluation of the CIP, Synthesis of 2005 CIP Reform and Activities, Final Report, July 2007), *available at* http://www.pal-tech.com/cip/index.cfm; NATIONAL COUNCIL OF JUVENILE & FAMILY COURT JUDGES, SUMMARIES OF TWENTY-FIVE STATE COURT IMPROVEMENT ASSESSMENT REPORTS (1998).

[5] For a list of state court Alternative Dispute Resolution Web sites, see RSI's Court ADR Resource Center at www.courtadr.org. *See also* American Humane Association, *A Compilation of State and Provincial Laws, Policies, Rules and Regulations on Family Group Decision Making and Other Family Engagement Approaches in Child Welfare Decision Making* (March 2009). For information on the practice of Family Group Decision Making, see the American Humane Association's Web page titled "Family Group Decision Making" at www.americanhumane.org/fgdm.

[6] Child Welfare Information Gateway, *Alternative Response as a Family-Centered Approach*, *available at* http://www.childwelfare.gov/famcentered/overview/approaches/alternative.cfm. Visit the National

In addition, agencies generally are trying to take a more subtle approach to risk assessment so the focus is to "remove the danger, not the child".[7] These are promising innovations that could significantly improve the state response to child welfare.

These innovations will also affect our legal practice and dispute resolution processes. Even though these new agency approaches have the effect of diverting cases from the court process, and they generally occur at a stage where lawyers are not appointed for children or parents, lawyers must be aware of these new approaches and the civil liberties concerns they raise. Although collaborative, less judgmental approaches to the family are promising and could be very beneficial, there remains a risk that parents (and their children) will be coerced to accept limits on their legal rights. While promising, these alternatives must respect the dignity and rights of the parents. Where participation is not truly voluntary, lawyers should insist on the full protection of the law and legal procedures.

This chapter will concentrate on two of the most common and more formalized dispute resolution processes that are more likely to occur after the lawyer for child, parent or agency is actively involved: mediation and family group conferencing.

§ 24.2 Mediation

§ 24.2.1 Definition

Mediation in the child welfare context is well established in many jurisdictions.[8] It is commonly defined as "an intervention into a dispute or negotiation by an acceptable, impartial and neutral third party who has no authoritative decision-making power but who assists the disputing parties in voluntarily reaching their own mutually acceptable settlement of disputed issues in a non-adversarial setting."[9] Mediation is widely used today in domestic relations custody disputes between parents, and it is increasingly found in many juvenile delinquency, juvenile status offender, and child welfare proceedings.[10] Mediation in the child welfare context has existed in Los Angeles and Orange Counties in California and in Connecticut since the mid-1980s. Child welfare mediation programs now exist in some form in a majority of

---

Quality Improvement Center on Differential Response in Child Protective Services at http://www.differentialresponseqic.org/.

[7] *See* Chapter 14, Child Safety: What Judges and Lawyers Need to Know; Chapter 13, The Practice of Child Welfare Casework: A Primer.

[8] Leonard Edwards, *Child Protection Mediation: A 25 Year Perspective,* 47/1 Fam. Ct. Rev. 69 (2009). The Family Court Review devotes the entire January 2009 issue to Mediation and Conferencing in Child Protection Disputes.

[9] Children's Bureau, U.S. Department of Health & Human Services, Adoption 2002: The President's Initiative on Adoption and Foster Care, Guidelines for Public Policy and State Legislation Governing Permanence for Children at V-2 (1999).

[10] *Id.* at V-2 to V-3.

jurisdictions.[11] Several states, including Arizona, California, Colorado, Delaware, and Florida, have state legislation authorizing the use of mediation in cases related to child welfare. Although court-affiliated dependency mediation programs began in the 1980s and there now exists 15 years of dependency mediation research, a recent survey found that most of the programs operating today are fairly new.[12]

§ 24.2.2 Philosophy and Principles

The adversarial process in child abuse and neglect cases can sometimes break down communications and create hostility, divisiveness, and rigid position-taking between participants, most notably between the parents and the child protective agency or the child's attorney. Mediation, on the other hand, brings all significant case participants together in a non-adversarial and problem-solving setting.[13] Mediation in child welfare cases typically has several central characteristics:

- Always focuses on preserving the safety and best interests of the children (and the safety of all family members), while simultaneously attempting to validate the concerns, points of view, feelings, and resources of all participants, especially family members.

- Involves discussions facilitated by one or more neutral, highly skilled and trained third-party mediators, involving all relevant case participants and attorneys at some point during the mediation.

- May occur at any stage in the history of the case. Typically the earlier it occurs once the most significant case information is available, the better.

- Can be used to resolve a broad range of disposition and post-disposition issues, as well as certain jurisdictional issues.

- Serves to orient and educate family members, clarify issues, facilitate exchange of the most current case information, and creatively intervene to resolve roadblocks to case resolution.

- Should be confidential with exceptions limited to new reports of suspected child abuse and neglect and threats to harm self or others.

- Usually results in agreements that become part of the court record and, if approved by the court, are entered as fully enforceable court orders.

- Seeks to leave family members with an experience of having been significant, respected, and understood participants in the court process,

---

[11] See the ABA Center on Children and the Law, National Child Welfare Resource Center on Legal and Judicial Issues at http://www.abanet.org/child/rclji/.

[12] Nancy Thoennes, *What We Know Now: Findings From Dependency Mediation Research*, 47/1 FAM. CT. REV. 21, 23 (2009).

[13] Leonard P. Edwards & Steven Baron, *Alternatives to Contested Litigation in Child Abuse and Neglect Cases*, 33 FAM. & CONCILIATION CTS. REV. 275 (1995).

with an investment in accepting and complying with the terms of the resolution or decisions of the court.

- Serves to reduce the degree of animosity held by family members toward "the system" and focuses the family's energy instead on child protection and parenting-related issues.[14]

§ 24.2.3 The Mediation Process

A child welfare lawyer representing a child, parent, or child welfare agency is very likely to have a case in mediation or to participate in mediation, either as a mediator or as a legal representative of one of the parties. The first stage in the process is to determine whether a particular case is suitable for mediation. Although mediation is successful in a large *number* of cases and in many *types* of cases, not every case is suitable. The case may be referred for voluntary mediation or court-ordered into mediation. Once the case is selected for mediation, the parties are identified, and the session is scheduled. The mediation steps are fairly simple, but the process itself can be complex. The nomenclature and outline may vary by local practice or depending on the unique variables of the case or the personalities of the individuals involved. A typical mediation will be structured as follows:[15]

Opening Statement

Mediations are held in a neutral place at a time convenient to the parties. Commonly, there are two mediators who open the session with a welcome and an explanation of the process. The mediators generally explain that they, the mediators, have no power to mandate a settlement but rather they are neutral facilitators who are charged with helping the parties come to an agreement if possible. The mediators try to establish an informal and relaxed atmosphere and get agreement on the basic "ground rules" of the mediation process such as that there should be no interruptions, shouting, threatening, abusive language and that all behavior must be honest and respectful. Mediators will get agreement on time schedules and ask each participant to agree to listen as carefully as they can to what the others are trying to say.

Uninterrupted Time

Sometimes this is called the "opening statement." Each person takes a turn speaking while everyone else listens. The statement is generally open-ended in response to a question like, "Tell us why you are here today." Typically the party, not the lawyer, speaks about anything that is relevant to the situation. Very commonly a mediator repeats back what the party has said in a neutral summary that reiterates the

---

[14] NATIONAL COUNCIL OF JUVENILE & FAMILY COURT JUDGES, RESOURCE GUIDELINES: IMPROVING COURT PRACTICE IN CHILD ABUSE AND NEGLECT CASES 133–38 (1995).

[15] *See* JENNIFER E. BEER & EILEEN STIEF, THE MEDIATOR'S HANDBOOK (3d ed.), developed by the Friends Conflict Resolution Programs. Copyright 1997 by New Society Publishing Company.

essential points—and communicates that the party has been respectfully and accurately heard.

The Exchange

Then the arguing and discussion begin. People commonly accuse each other and attempt to straighten out the other person on the facts. They explain why they are upset and make demands. The hostility and emotions come to the surface and are expressed. The mediators keep the discussion in bounds, making sure that each person is heard and each is protected. The mediators do not try to determine the truth or who is at fault. Rather, they listen for what matters to people and for possible areas of agreement. Sometimes the Exchange brings about a "turning point" of reconciliation.

Separate Meetings

Separate meetings, or caucuses, can occur at any time during the mediation and they have many uses, including checking out a person's concerns, confronting unhelpful behavior, or helping people think through their options. Typically the caucuses are confidential so that the mediator cannot share information obtained there without permission of the party. In some cases a shuttle diplomacy, with the mediators conveying information or options and offers, may help facilitate settlement.

Setting the Agenda

Once information is drawn out and, hopefully, heard by all sides, discussion turns to identifying the needs and interests of the parties, identifying and framing the issues, and setting and organizing the agenda for the remainder of the session.

Building the Agreement

The parties then work through each issue on the agenda, generating options, expanding options, and then weighing, adjusting, and testing the alternatives to craft a workable, mutually satisfactory solution.

Writing the Agreement and Closing

If the parties are able to settle their differences, the mediators write a formal agreement containing those decisions. Everyone present signs and takes a copy home. The mediators review what has been accomplished, remind people of next steps, congratulate them on their accomplishment, and wish them well.[16] In some jurisdictions the mediation agreement is submitted to the court and may be approved by the court or entered as a stipulated court order.

---

[16] *Id.* at 4–5.

§ 24.3 Family Group Conferencing

Family Group Conference (FGC) is a form of NACR that focuses on engaging the extended family in planning for a child and does not necessarily involve the mediating of disputes. It is a promising NACR model that has been recently imported to the U.S. from New Zealand. A Family Group Conference, whether it takes the form of Family Group Decision Making or a Family Unity Meeting, is characterized as a family-focused, strengths-oriented, and community-based process where parents, extended family members, and others come together to collectively make key decisions for children involved in the child welfare system.[17] Family Group Conference is often administered by the child welfare agency. FGC could also be a form of court-approved NACR.[18] The Annie E. Casey Foundation has included "Team Decision-Making," a form of Family Group Conferencing, as one of four elements of the Family to Family Initiative, now in its fourteenth year.[19] Family to Family and Team Decision Making (TDM) is now available in 17 states.

§ 24.3.1 Philosophy and Principles

The following principles and values characterize Family Group Conferences:

- Children are best raised in families.

- The primary responsibility for the care of children rests with their families, who should be respected, supported, and protected.

- Family groups can make safe decisions for their own children. Families have strengths and can change.

- Family groups are experts on themselves. Families have wisdom and solutions that are workable for them.

---

[17] LISA MERKEL-HOLGUIN, PUTTING FAMILIES BACK INTO THE CHILD PROTECTION PARTNERSHIP: FAMILY GROUP DECISION-MAKING (American Humane Association, Summer 1996); American Humane Association, *A Compilation of State and Provincial Laws, Policies, Rules and Regulations on Family Group Decision Making and Other Family Engagement Approaches in Child Welfare Decision Making*, (Mar. 2009). For more information, see the American Humane Association's Web page titled "Family Group Decision Making" at www.americanhumane.org/fgdm.

[18] *See* Jolene M. Lowry, *Family Group Conferences as a Form of Court-Approved Alternative Dispute Resolution in Child Abuse and Neglect Cases*, 31 U. MICH. J.L. REFORM 57 (1997).

[19] For a description of Family to Family, see the Annie E. Casey Foundation's Web page titled "Family to Family" at http://www.aecf.org/Home/MajorInitiatives/Family%20to%20Family.aspx. Family to Family is summarized as: "A family-centered, neighborhood-based system of foster care promoting permanence for all children." The Annie E. Casey Foundation's initiative is an example of the unity and coordination required among individual families, neighborhoods, public and private child welfare agencies, the courts, and the law. Child welfare is not the sole province of any single component of the community.

- The essence of family empowerment is the belief in self-determination: Those we help have a right and need to be free in making their own decisions and choices.[20]

§ 24.3.2 Structure of Family Group Conferencing

The Family Group Conference process comprises four main parts. The first is the referral, in which a coordinator or gatekeeper decides whether to hold a conference. The second is the preparation and planning. The third is the conference itself, which is generally divided into four stages of welcome, information sharing, family meeting, and decision. The fourth is writing, distribution, and implementation of the plan.[21]

There are two primary differences between the Family Group Decision Making (FGDM) and Family Unity models (FUM). FGDM discourages the practice of excluding any family members from the meeting, while the FUM permits parents to veto the participation of any family member, a practice that provides parents with more control over the process and with whom information will be shared. The second major difference is that the FUM model allows professionals and support persons to be present during the family discussion, while a key tenet of FGDM is that families, once briefed by the professionals, must have a private family meeting without the presence of any nonfamily persons.

For a compilation of state law and national resources, see the National Resource Center for Permanency and Family Connections.[22]

§ 24.4 Voluntary Relinquishment Counseling

Voluntary relinquishment counseling is a under-utilized child welfare NACR that should receive special attention. It may be employed as part of mediation or Family Group Conferencing, or it may occur separate from these mechanisms. Many professionals believe that it would be helpful for parents and children alike if parental counseling concerning the voluntary relinquishment of parental rights were readily available. Voluntary relinquishment can be more humane than contested termination proceedings by avoiding some trauma to parent and child. It can also avoid delay. In

---

[20] Kelly Browe Olson, *Family Group Conferencing and Child Protection Mediation: Essential Tools for Prioritizing Family Engagement in Child Welfare Cases,* 47 FAM. CT. REV. 53 (Jan. 2009); *see also* Elizabeth Cole, *Key Policy Decisions in Implementing Family Group Conferences: Observations Drawn from the New Zealand Model, in* MARK HARDIN, FAMILY GROUP CONFERENCES IN CHILD ABUSE AND NEGLECT CASES: LEARNING FROM THE EXPERIENCE IN NEW ZEALAND (ABA Center on Children and the Law 1996).

[21] Jolene M. Lowry, *Family Group Conferences as a Form of Court Approved Alternative Dispute Resolution in Child Abuse and Neglect Cases,* 31 U. MICH. J.L. REFORM 57, 66–76 (1997); LISA MERKEL-HOLGUIN, PUTTING FAMILIES BACK INTO THE CHILD PROTECTION PARTNERSHIP: FAMILY GROUP DECISION-MAKING 5–7 (American Humane Association, Summer 1996).

[22] http://www.hunter.cuny.edu/socwork/nrcfcpp/info_services/family-group-conferencing.html,

many cases, voluntary relinquishment of parental rights is preferable to contested termination because it reduces the financial, emotional, and time costs.

The use of NACR in the voluntary relinquishment process may also *add civil liberty protections* to the birth parents when compared with more common methods of working with birth parents on parental rights termination issues. By participating in NACR, parents may be more likely to feel that those within the "system" are consciously protecting their rights, rather than simply coercing them to "give up" their rights to their child. Also, where voluntary relinquishments are not made within the court, making them within a NACR process could provide protections to parents that are similar to those that should be provided to parents within more formal termination of parental rights proceedings. Parents should be aware of the possibility of voluntary relinquishment at all stages of the court process.

Voluntary relinquishment will be more attractive if options for permanency, such as cooperative adoption or adoption with contact, are available under state law.[23] Some parents will be more willing to relinquish parental rights if they can ensure that their child will be adopted by someone of whom they approve or if they know that siblings will be able to keep track of one another. Subject to the court finding that it is in the best interests of a child, some states permit parents involved in child protection proceedings to voluntarily relinquish their child for adoption by specified persons to the same extent that so-called direct-consent adoptions are permitted for other birth parents. Relinquishment under state law is generally of two types. In one type, often called surrender, the agency determines who the adoptive parents will be, subject to court approval. The other type involves direct or specific consent, in which the parents are allowed to relinquish the child to a designated individual, also with court approval.[24]

An amicable relationship between the birth parent and the new parent is also more likely under voluntary relinquishment. Further, if more contested terminations of parental rights could be converted into voluntary relinquishments, states would save considerable time and expense. Some voluntary relinquishment programs have involved elements of mediation, including the possibility of formal agreements concerning future contact between the birth parent and child. In such processes, parents' legal rights should be carefully protected. Parents should be legally represented, even though their lawyers might not participate in each stage of the relinquishment counseling or mediation.

§ 24.5 Uses of NACR in Child Welfare Cases

NACR techniques can be used in various ways and at various times in a child welfare case. Both mediation and Family Group Conferences can be used:

---

[23] Options for legal permanency are discussed in Chapter 25, Establishing Legal Permanence for the Child.

[24] *See* JOAN H. HOLLINGER ET AL., ADOPTION LAW AND PRACTICE (1988).

- To resolve conflicts between *child welfare agencies and parents* concerning proposed case plans and final case resolutions, to help divert cases from the court system, and to work out disputes over a child's supervision, placement, visitation, family reunification, and permanent plans for the child (e.g., mediated relinquishment of parental rights or guardianship, as well as facilitation of cooperative adoption agreements where appropriate and permitted by law).

- To increase intrafamilial involvement among *parents, relatives, and other extended (kinship) family members* in fashioning case resolutions and improving cooperation and coordination with government child protection and child welfare authorities.[25] Proponents of NACR in child welfare cases have seen it used successfully to help facilitate safety plans allowing children to stay with their birth parents, establish kinship placements, and expedite adoptions and guardianships for severely abused or neglected children.

Mediation can be used:

- To resolve conflicts among substitute care providers, foster care caseworkers and case reviewers, and children's court-appointed advocates about the needs of children during periods of substitute care.

- To resolve matters more promptly as part of the court process among the various attorneys and other advocates, caseworkers, therapists, other involved professionals, and the parents and other family members in child protection judicial proceedings. Mandatory case mediation facilitated by a trained independent mediator can help focus attention on collaborative problem solving on behalf of the child.[26]

Confidentiality is an essential component of NACR. The confidentiality provisions are intended to promote the free and unreserved discussion and sharing of information. Statements made in the NACR process should be treated under evidence rules as if they were statements made in the course of settlement discussions. Even when there is only partial agreement on the issues, the substance of the NACR discussion should not be used in the court process. When mediation is unsuccessful, neither the mediators nor other participants in the process should testify against any party in court nor should any product of the mediation be used in court, including whether in the mediator's opinion one party cooperated or failed to cooperate.[27]

---

[25] CHILDREN'S BUREAU, U.S. DEPARTMENT OF HEALTH & HUMAN SERVICES, ADOPTION 2002: THE PRESIDENT'S INITIATIVE ON ADOPTION AND FOSTER CARE, GUIDELINES FOR PUBLIC POLICY AND STATE LEGISLATION GOVERNING PERMANENCE FOR CHILDREN at Ch. V (1999).

[26] *Id.*

[27] NATIONAL COUNCIL OF JUVENILE & FAMILY COURT JUDGES, RESOURCE GUIDELINES: IMPROVING COURT PRACTICE IN CHILD ABUSE AND NEGLECT CASES 137 (1995); Gregory Firestone, *Empowering Parents in Child Protection Mediation: Challenges and Opportunities*, 47 FAM. CT. REV. 98 (2009).

As a corollary to confidentiality and also to ensure free and open discussion, sharing of information with all the participants is important. Information about the child and family can be shared, as appropriate, with members of the extended family during the NACR process, but the people who receive such information have a duty to treat it in confidence, and should be informed of that duty. Relevant information about the child, parents, and other family members is likely to be known only to certain individuals directly involved in child welfare agency or court actions related to the child. Ideally, the persons affected would voluntarily release such information for purposes of NACR, but the voluntary cooperation may not be forthcoming, especially when the court mandates NACR. If information about the child, parents, and other family members is withheld, the type of shared decision-making that is critical to successful NACR may be impossible.

On occasion, and where appropriate, children will be involved in the process, especially if they are older and reasonably mature. Exposure of children to NACR can help them recognize that their immediate families and relatives are truly interested in their welfare and that their own concerns are being heard and taken seriously.

The NACR process should not be delayed by strategic litigation concerns. The permanency timelines of Federal and State law must be met and delays in the formal process avoided. For example, in cases involving the abuse or neglect of a child, in which criminal charges are pending against a parent/party, mediation should not be delayed because the related criminal matter has not yet been resolved.[28]

Typically, any interested person is authorized to request NACR in a child welfare case. To avoid trivial issues taking up valuable time within NACR, court or agency gatekeepers or facilitators of these processes generally explain the ground rules to participants and indicate how matters inappropriate for resolution within NACR can be separately addressed. Because a Family Group Conference is more logistically complex and time consuming than mediation, the gatekeepers may be more cautious in convening the FGC. Some important questions must be addressed in any NACR program implementation. For example, do the parents have the right to consent to, or opt out of, the convening of a Mediation or Family Group Conference process? Who should be considered "family members" or other "interested persons" and therefore invited to participate? Should the coordinator or facilitator of the process have authority to exclude certain family members, such as those believed to be intimidating the child or other family members? Should there be mandatory timetables for convening and completing the NACR process?

To ensure that all parties consider it an objective process, some authorities recommend that mediators be independent of the child welfare agency or the judge,

---

[28] CHILDREN'S BUREAU, U.S. DEPARTMENT OF HEALTH & HUMAN SERVICES, ADOPTION 2002: THE PRESIDENT'S INITIATIVE ON ADOPTION AND FOSTER CARE, GUIDELINES FOR PUBLIC POLICY AND STATE LEGISLATION GOVERNING PERMANENCE FOR CHILDREN (1999).

even though the child welfare and court system must coordinate in the execution of these processes to ensure NACR is effectively implemented.[29]

Some also recommend that certification standards for NACR staff be established. NACR personnel should be trained in dispute resolution generally and on issues relevant to the child welfare NACR process. The training should include information on the following:

- Child abuse and neglect.
- Child development.
- Domestic violence and its impact on children.
- Substance abuse.
- Family functioning and family systems.
- Power imbalance concerns in mediating child welfare cases.
- Working with diverse communities.
- Access to community resources.

Because these are highly transferable skills, many in the community may want to be trained as mediators. All trainees should be monitored by more experienced NACR experts. Trainees should observe others in action.[30]

§ 24.6 Effectiveness of NACR

Evaluations of mediation programs have demonstrated that a variety of models proved effective, mediation can produce settlements at all *stages* of cases, and that all *types* of cases can be settled in mediation. Some argue that certain cases, such as domestic violence or child sexual abuse, are not appropriate for mediation, but Thoennes found no evidence to support blanket screening out of certain types of cases.[31] There is also widespread support for mediating both adjudicatory and dispositional case issues, although time constraints pose problems in doing both. Parents report that mediation gave them a place to be "heard" and to better understand what was required of them.[32]

---

[29] *Id.* at V-11.

[30] CHILDREN'S BUREAU, U.S. DEPARTMENT OF HEALTH & HUMAN SERVICES, ADOPTION 2002: THE PRESIDENT'S INITIATIVE ON ADOPTION AND FOSTER CARE, GUIDELINES FOR PUBLIC POLICY AND STATE LEGISLATION GOVERNING PERMANENCE FOR CHILDREN (1999).

[31] Nancy Thoennes, *What We Know Now: Findings From Dependency Mediation Research*, 47/1 FAM. CT. REV. 21, 23 (2009); Nancy Thoennes, *An Evaluation of Child Protection Mediation in Five California Courts*, 35/2 FAM. & CONCILIATION CTS. REV. 184 (1997).

[32] NANCY THOENNES & J. PEARSON, MEDIATION IN FIVE CALIFORNIA DEPENDENCY COURTS: A CROSS-SITE COMPARISON (Report to the California State Legislature, Denver, Colorado Center for Policy Research, 1995); Nancy Thoennes, *An Evaluation of Child Protection Mediation in Five California Courts*, 35/2 FAM. & CONCILIATION CTS. REV. 184 (1997).

Thoennes also reports that agreements produced in mediation were similar to outcomes promulgated by judges. The former were more likely, however, to include detailed visitation plans for children in out-of-home placement, to address communication problems between family members or between the family and the child welfare agency, and to result in parents specifically acknowledging the need for services. Mediated contested cases were also less likely than non-mediated contested cases to result in later contested hearings. Mediated settlements enjoy greater compliance by parents at least in the short run.[33]

Both mediation and Family Group Conferences are alternatives to traditional adversarial litigation case approaches and help divert children and families from the child welfare and court systems while engaging parents in a nonthreatening situation. NACR may enable parents who have been inappropriately denying or minimizing the impact of the children's abuse or neglect to safely acknowledge responsibility for the mistreatment and to willingly accept help. Within the NACR process, parents can be given choices of methods to solve the problems they and their children face. The informal and participatory setting of NACR can facilitate this problem-solving approach. Everyone benefits if disputes can be resolved earlier in the process when a child has been identified as abused or neglected.

The advantages to using NACR in child welfare cases include:

- Sharing of responsibility for child protection beyond the child welfare agency and the courts to include the child's immediate family, the child's extended family, and the child's community.

- Empowering parents in the decision-making process related to their children.

- Helping ensure that, in addition to parents, others with a strong interest in abused and neglected children are heard within the process of intervention.

- Facilitating parental compliance with agency case plans.

- Avoiding conflicts and delay, especially those harmful to children, which are associated with the adversarial process.

- Reducing crowded judicial case dockets.

- Circumventing the need for expensive, lengthy contested trials and case review hearings.

Additionally, family members often feel more comfortable raising the cultural, ethnic, or religious needs of the child in the more informal NACR process.

Several unique factors should be considered whenever NACR is considered for a matter involving child welfare. First, those involved with the process must remember that the safety of children must never be compromised or endangered through the use

---

[33] *Id.*

of any non-adversarial case approaches. Second, parents who participate in the NACR process must be competently represented in order to compensate for the potential power imbalance that can exist when government is intervening in a family's life. Third, NACR, if done properly within child welfare proceedings, may provide a beneficial process—but it will not be inexpensive. Programs must have adequate funding for properly trained mediators or family-group facilitators who can resolve cases in a timely manner.

§ 24.7 Compromising Child Safety or Well-Being

The principal goal of NACR in the child welfare context is to ensure the safety and protection of children through resolution of disputes without having to rely on the traditional adversarial court process. At the same time, the process should ensure that the parents' legal rights are properly protected. There should be no compromise on protection of parental rights.

NACR should also focus on child well-being and permanency, family empowerment, and community involvement in the process. NACR should not delay the resolution of cases nor create additional trauma for the child and family. NACR should empower parents and promote shared responsibility with the extended family and community to serve the best interests of the child effectively and more promptly.[34]

The greatest fear among critics of NACR in these cases is that child safety will be compromised or sacrificed during the process. Proponents and critics of such processes agree that child safety must never be sacrificed in the interests of reaching agreement or as part of any "plea bargains." Concerns about children being endangered through the use of NACR can be alleviated in several ways:

- NACR must assure that the child's "voice" is clearly heard within the process, either through the child's legal representative or through the child and the representative.

- NACR must permit the child's representative, the convenor/facilitator/ mediator, or others to veto any agreements reached through the process that compromise the child's safety or welfare.

- NACR should provide for an independent review of any mediated agreements, stipulations, or settlements by judges and child welfare agency supervisors.

- NACR should structure more frequent involvement by protective family members during the mediation processes and within mediated agreements.

---

[34] CHILDREN'S BUREAU, U.S. DEPARTMENT OF HEALTH & HUMAN SERVICES, ADOPTION 2002: THE PRESIDENT'S INITIATIVE ON ADOPTION AND FOSTER CARE, GUIDELINES FOR PUBLIC POLICY AND STATE LEGISLATION GOVERNING PERMANENCE FOR CHILDREN at V-8 (1999).

- NACR should be initiated promptly, and ideally a decision should be reached within 30 days of its initiation; in emergency situations, it should be completed even sooner.

- The NACR process should clarify how any agreement will be enforced and what will happen if the agreement fails.

- In addition to being ever conscious about the child safety issues in mediating case resolutions, those involved within the NACR process must constantly think about how the process, and its outcomes, will promote permanency for the child.

§ 24.8 Conclusion

Non-adversarial case resolution approaches are increasingly used throughout the child protection process—both before and after court intervention becomes necessary. NACR, while not inexpensive, is generally more expeditious and efficient than traditional litigation and can often resolve disputes without the hostile overtones characteristic of the court's adversarial process. When children are endangered, their extended families may provide invaluable resources to help fashion safe and permanent case resolutions.

NACR in the child welfare context can be structured to involve the parents and the child's extended family in responsible planning and decision-making for the child. Use of various forms of NACR can provide clients with the opportunity to vent, disagree and be heard, and to understand the points of view of others. Typically, the earlier in the process that NACR is implemented, the greater its chance for success.

Different forms of NACR can be useful at any stage of state intervention to facilitate the well being of children—from the initial identification of abuse and neglect through the final permanent placement of a child. Child welfare lawyers must understand the process and make judgments about whether and how NACR will serve the interests of their clients.

Chapter 25: Establishing
Legal Permanence for the Child

by Donald N. Duquette[1]

§ 25.1 Introduction

This chapter is intended to identify options for legal permanency that state law and the federal Adoption and Safe Families Act of 1997[2] (ASFA) commonly recognize to better serve children in foster care. Ideally, the child will ultimately return safely to his or her home of origin. But when a return home is not possible, the child welfare legal process should result in a safe and legally secure alternative permanent placement for the child. The emphasis on legally secure permanent placement is meant to provide the child with psychological stability and a sense of belonging and to limit the likelihood of future disruption of the parent-child relationship. All state laws authorize adoption of children, but traditional adoption does not meet the needs of all children in public foster care. Attorneys representing children, parents, or the government agency may seek other legal options for permanent and legally secure placement. Some authorities recommend that these options be broad enough to serve the needs of all children in care who are not able to return to their home of origin; options could include adoption, adoption with contact, permanent guardianship, subsidized guardianship, stand-by guardianship, and "another planned permanent living arrangement" (APPLA) such as permanent long-term foster care.[3]

For children who cannot be reared by one or both of their birth parents, adoption, by relatives or non-relatives, is the preferred option for a permanent legal placement. By providing children with a new family, adoption is most likely to ensure protection, stability, nurturing, and familial relationships that will last throughout their lives. Alternatives to adoption discussed here, such as permanent guardianship and subsidized guardianship, are generally appropriate only when adoption has been thoroughly explored and found unsuitable to meet the needs of a particular child.

---

[1] Donald N. Duquette, J.D., is Clinical Professor of Law and Director of the Child Advocacy Law Clinic of the University of Michigan Law School.

[2] Pub. L. No. 105-89, 111 Stat 2115.

[3] CHILDREN'S BUREAU, U.S. DEPARTMENT OF HEALTH & HUMAN SERVICES, ADOPTION 2002: THE PRESIDENT'S INITIATIVE ON ADOPTION AND FOSTER CARE, GUIDELINES FOR PUBLIC POLICY AND STATE LEGISLATION GOVERNING PERMANENCE FOR CHILDREN (1999), *available at:* http://web.archive.org/web/20030224035115/www.acf.dhhs.gov/programs/cb/publications/adopt02/.

§ 25.2 Priority for Permanence

A certain priority among these options for permanency is generally accepted and reflects a preference for permanent placement of foster children with their family of origin or relatives that is expressed in federal and most state laws. Termination of parental rights is not always appropriate and can lead to the unhappy outcome of making the child a legal orphan raised by the state. The generally accepted priority of permanency options is: (1) safe reunification with the biological parents or a suitable member of the family of origin;[4] (2) adoption; and (3) permanent guardianship. Long-term foster care is generally disfavored but may be appropriate for some children, particularly older children who have a connection with their biological families and strongly object to being adopted.[5]

This hierarchy of preference is not inflexible and requires individualized judgments based on the circumstances of each individual child. For example, if a child is psychologically attached to a relative and has been living for an extended time with that relative, but the relative cannot or will not adopt, a permanent guardianship with that relative may be preferable to moving the child to a recruited adoptive family. On the other hand, a relative with no established relationship with the child who offers to become a child's caretaker late in the court process may not be as appropriate for adoption as foster parents who have cared for the child for some time and who wish to adopt.

§ 25.3 Adoption

Adoption, the legal and permanent transfer of all parental rights and responsibilities to the adoptive parents, remains the placement of choice when a child cannot be returned to his or her birth family because it gives the child a new, permanent, legal family with the same legal standing and protection as a family created through birth. An adopted individual is entitled to inherit from and through the adoptive parents and is treated as the child of the adoptive parents for purposes of social security, insurance, retirement, pension, and all other public and private benefit programs. Conversely, adoptive parents acquire rights to inherit from and through the adopted child. Adoption thus provides, for the most part, the same autonomy, security, and durability of family relationships that children experience in their families of birth. Children, adoptive parents, birth parents, and the general public also

---

[4] See § 10.6, Fostering Connections to Success and Increasing Adoptions Act, for a discussion of the Fostering Connections to Success and Increasing Adoptions Act which, among other things, provides additional tools to maintain a child's ties with extended family.

[5] CHILDREN'S BUREAU, U.S. DEPARTMENT OF HEALTH & HUMAN SERVICES, ADOPTION 2002: THE PRESIDENT'S INITIATIVE ON ADOPTION AND FOSTER CARE, GUIDELINES FOR PUBLIC POLICY AND STATE LEGISLATION GOVERNING PERMANENCE FOR CHILDREN at II-2 (1999). For a discussion of services available to youth who do not exit the foster care system into permanent placement, see Chapter 23, Foster Youth: Transitioning from Foster Care into Self-Sufficient Adulthood.

understand and are familiar with this type of legal relationship. Children may be adopted by relatives, step-parents, foster parents, or persons previously unrelated or unknown to them.[6] Commonly, state laws permit a parent to release parental rights directly to a specific adoptive parent or parents or to surrender parental rights to a public or private agency who would then determine who the adoptive parents would be, subject to court approval.[7] However, parents whose rights have been terminated or whose children are legal wards of the court may lose the right to designate a specific adoptive placement.

§ 25.3.1 Adoption Subsidies

Adoption subsidies play an important role in achieving permanency for children. In the past, costs of care and services were major obstacles to individuals who would otherwise adopt.[8] The agency's reasonable efforts to finalize a permanency plan should include informing caregivers about adoption subsidies and securing them when appropriate. For many children, adoption assistance can make adoption possible.[9] Denial of the subsidy or an insufficient subsidy can be a barrier to permanency. In many states, adoption assistance can include regular monthly cash payments, Medicaid, social services to the family, and nonrecurring adoption expenses. The federal government and the state share the costs of adoption assistance for those children who meet federal eligibility requirements. For children who do not meet federal eligibility requirements, some states will pay the entire cost of the subsidy. For children who qualify, federal adoption assistance is an entitlement. Eligibility criteria are as follows[10]:

(1)   The child was eligible, before adoption, for assistance under one of two programs:

(a)   Foster care or adoption assistance under Title IV-E. The child (or the child's birth family) must have been eligible to receive federal AFDC. Even though AFDC was discontinued in 1996, a child's eligibility for Title IV-E is based on the states' AFDC eligibility standards as of July 16, 1996.[11]

---

[6]   For a useful guide for state legislatures regarding adoption from foster care, see STEVE CHRISTIAN & LISA EKMAN, A PLACE TO CALL HOME: ADOPTION AND GUARDIANSHIP FOR CHILDREN IN FOSTER CARE (National Conference of State Legislatures 2000).

[7]   *See* JOAN H. HOLLINGER ET AL., ADOPTION LAW AND PRACTICE (2001).

[8]   Child Welfare Information Gateway, *Adoption Assistance for Children Adopted From Foster Care: A Factsheet for Families* (2004), *available at* http://www.childwelfare.gov/pubs/f_subsid.cfm.

[9]   For a more detailed explanation of adoption assistance agreements, see Elizabeth Oppenheim et al., *Adoption Assistance for Children with Special Needs, in* ADOPTION LAW AND PRACTICE (Joan Hollinger ed., 2001). In New York, for example, subsidies are provided in over 80% of the adoptions that occur through the child welfare agency. *Id.*

[10] Child Welfare Information Gateway, *Adoption Assistance for Children Adopted From Foster Care: A Factsheet for Families* (2004), *available at* http://www.childwelfare.gov/pubs/f_subsid.cfm.

[11] 42 U.S.C. § 673(a)(2)(A), (B).

    (b)   Supplemental Security Income (SSI), a program for low-income people with disabilities.[12]

(2)   The child has special needs as defined by the state's definition of special needs.[13] Special needs may include certain medical, emotional, and mental health conditions and membership in a minority, sibling, or age group.[14]

(3)   The child could not be placed for adoption without a subsidy. In other words, a "reasonable, but unsuccessful, effort has been made to place the child with appropriate adoptive parents [without providing any assistance]."[15] This requirement can be waived if the child already has a significant relationship or significant emotional ties with the caregiver.[16]

(4)   There has been a judicial determination that the child cannot or should not be returned home. Obviously, if the child's parents' rights have been terminated, this requirement is satisfied.

Adoption assistance information by state is available at the Child Welfare Information Gateway.[17] The federal child welfare policy manual is also available online.[18] States may not impose additional eligibility criteria for federal assistance beyond what is required by federal law. Nearly all children adopted out of foster care in recent years received an adoption subsidy.[19]

§ 25.3.2 Post-Adoption Contact

Post-adoption contact between the child and the birth parents, siblings, or other people who are psychologically important to the child may serve the long-term interests of a child and is often arranged. Commonly, the adoptive parents, whether kin or non-kin, recognize that certain people are important to the child and that it is important for the child to maintain contact with them. Purely voluntary, "open adoptions" occur in all states, where the adoptive parents freely and voluntarily permit or even encourage contact with the child's natural networks. No force of law or court

---

[12] 42 U.S.C. §§ 673(a)(2)(A)(ii), 673(a)(2)(B)(iii).

[13] 42 U.S.C. § 673(a)(2)(C).

[14] *See* 42 U.S.C. § 673(c)(2)(A). Agencies and courts have traditionally referred to these children as "hard to place." The more common current term is "special needs."

[15] 42 U.S.C. § 673(c)(2)(A), 673(c)(2)(B).

[16] 42 U.S.C. § 673(c)(2)(B).

[17] http://www.childwelfare.gov/adoption/adopt_assistance/index.cfm.

[18] See the Web site of the U.S. Department of Health & Human Services, Administration for Children & Families, http://www.acf.hhs.gov/j2ee/programs/cb/laws_policies/laws/cwpm.

[19] HHS Office of the Assistant Secretary for Planning and Evaluation, *Understanding Adoption Subsidies: An Analysis of AFCARS Data* (Jan. 2005), *available at* http://aspe.hhs.gov/hsp/05/adoption-subsidies/.

order requires that such contact occur, and the adoptive parents may end such voluntary arrangements at will.[20]

State Laws

Approximately 23 states currently have "open" or "cooperative" adoption laws that provide some mechanism for approval and enforcement of post-adoption agreements.[21] Annette Appel reports:

> Though variable in specifics, these statutes are nearly identical in several respects: first, by definition, none permit a court to grant an adoption with contact unless the adoptive parents agree; second, each statute indicates who must approve of the agreement in order for it to be enforceable later; third, all but one (West Virginia) require the agreement to be in writing, either as a written contract, relinquishment, or court order; fourth, all of the statutes explicitly, or through court interpretation, provide for enforcement of the agreements unless there are grounds not to enforce or there are grounds to modify; finally, no statutes permit vacation of the adoption or withdrawal of relinquishment as a sanction for breach or modification of the agreement or order.

While most states make contact between the child and his or her natural networks available to all adoptees,[22] some state laws limit such post-adoption contact to children who have been in foster care.[23] California limits post-adoption contact to children adopted by relatives[24] while Indiana limits it to children age two and over.[25] Other states simply acknowledge that post-adoption contact can occur (e.g., Ohio)[26] or prohibit the court from forbidding such contact (e.g., Missouri).[27] At least one state

---

[20] "In general, state law does not prohibit postadoption contact or communication." Child Welfare Information Gateway, *Postadoption Contact Agreements Between Birth and Adoptive Families: Summary of State Laws, available at* http://www.childwelfare.gov/systemwide/laws_policies/statutes/cooperativeall.pdf.

[21] *Id.* States that permit enforceable contracts include Alaska, Arizona, California, Connecticut, Florida, Indiana, Louisiana, Maryland, Massachusetts, Minnesota, Montana, Nebraska, Nevada, New Hampshire, New Mexico, New York, Oklahoma, Oregon, Rhode Island, Texas, Vermont, Washington, and West Virginia. *See also* Annette R. Appell, *Survey of State Utilization of Adoption with Contact*, 6/4 ADOPTION QUARTERLY 75 (2003), *available at* http://www.haworthpress.com/store/product.asp?sku=J145.

[22] *E.g.*, MINN. STAT. ANN. § 259.58 ; MONT. CODE ANN. § 42-5-301; N.M. STAT. ANN. § 32A-5-35; (OR. REV. STAT. § 109.305; S.D. CODIFIED LAWS § 25-6-17; WASH. REV. CODE § 26.33.295; W. VA. CODE § 48-22-704.

[23] *See, e.g.*, NEB. REV. STAT. §§ 43-162 to 43-164; N.Y. SOC. SERV. LAW § 383-c.

[24] CAL. R. OF COURT 5.400(b) (2003) (formerly CAL. FAM. CODE § 8714.7 (renumbered 2003)).

[25] IND. CODE ANN § 31-19-16-2 (1997).

[26] OHIO REV. CODE ANN. § 3107.62.

[27] MO. REV. STAT. § 453.080(4).

(Florida) permits the court that is terminating parental rights to order post-termination contact to be reviewed upon the adoption of the child.[28] This may be a useful mechanism when: (1) the child has a need for post-termination or post-adoption contact; and (2) the adoptive parents have not been identified at the time of termination of parental rights; and (3) the birth parents will not be present at the adoption.

Benefits

Many foster children have psychological connections to their birth families, siblings, and other significant persons, such as foster parents, so that it would be in the child's interest to maintain some sort of contact even after adoption. The child may need to know and understand his or her ethnic background and heritage. There may be a need to share medical information and health histories. Preservation of an emotional tie may be beneficial to the child. Continued contact may relieve an older child's guilt or concerns about the birth parent. Contact may help the child come to terms with his or her past. A connection with a biological parent may be a positive, yet limited, influence, and may prevent the child from running away or disrupting a new place-ment when the child desires continuing ties. Continued contact may avoid the trauma of contested and prolonged termination of parental rights proceedings. Children generally benefit from contact with siblings. These needs may be recognized and agreed to by the new parents and approved by the court. The contact could be as simple as exchanging photos each year without any physical contact, but the arrange-ments could leave a door open for future relationships *when helpful to the child.*

Birth parents, when given a chance, can be tremendous resources in planning for their children, and their participation can have positive outcomes for adoption. For many years, certain adoption agencies have placed children in adoptions where birth parents and adoptive parents voluntarily maintain contact and exchange information. This happens with infant adoption, direct consent adoption, and in adoptions within the extended family. These "cooperative adoption" arrangements are often negotiated in the context of an adoption of older children, especially children with special needs, who have been in foster care before being placed for adoption. In appropriate situations, even where child protection proceedings have been initiated, state law and the parties to a child protection proceeding could encourage birth parents' involve-ment in planning for relinquishment of parental rights and adoption of the child.

Pitfalls

On the other hand, there may be pitfalls to maintaining ties between birth parents and their children after children are placed into new permanent homes. For example, the birth parents might only reluctantly accept the new placement and may later try to disrupt or undermine it. The birth parents might be dangerous to the child or the adoptive family or might constitute an abduction risk. The child may be fearful of or

---

[28] FLA. STAT. ANN. § 39.811(7)(b), 63.0427.

resistant to continuing contacts. The determination of whether an individual child needs a permanent placement with ongoing birth parent-child contacts or contacts with siblings or members of the extended family is a subtle and sophisticated task. Each case is unique and demands thoughtful and expert consideration.

Some experts recommend against any legally enforceable post-adoption rights of contact between a child and members of his or her family of origin, particularly with those against whom there was an adjudication or stipulation of child abuse or neglect. Others argue that contact should not be allowed if the child is fearful of the parent or fearful that he or she will be removed from the adoptive home and returned to the parent. Contact may also be contraindicated when the child has had many placements and does not have strong ties to the parent, or where there is evidence that post-adoption contact will undermine the integrity and security of the adoptive relationship.

Some argue that contact between the adoptive and biological families, if contact occurs at all, should remain entirely voluntary with no enforceability by the court. An enforceable right of contact, even when based on initial agreement among the parties, may erode the exclusive rights and prerogatives of the adopting parents. In this view, the government should not continue to be involved in the lives of families once an adoption is approved because adoptive families are entitled to as much autonomy as any other legally-recognized family.

Determining Whether Post-Adoption Contact Is Appropriate

To determine whether post-adoption contact is warranted, the primary concern is whether it will meet the child's needs, interests, and desires, not the needs and interests of the adults involved without necessarily benefiting the child. "Adoption with contact" will likely promote settlement of some termination of parental rights cases. The court, however, should not allow adoption with contact merely because it is a convenient settlement option for parents facing a strong termination of parental rights case. Nor should it be allowed merely because it is more expeditious and convenient for an agency that is unwilling to put time and energy into a difficult termination of parental rights case. "Adoption with contact" must serve the best interests of the child.

Elements of a Successful Post-Adoption Contact Agreement

Adoption with contact will be most successful when all of the parties to the contact agree on each of the following points:

- That the contact should occur.
- What type of contact should occur.
- How or where the contact will occur.
- How frequently the contact will occur.

Post-adoption contact agreements should be flexible enough to accommodate the changing needs and abilities of all the parties, particularly the child. The parties could agree simply that the adoptive parents will keep the birth parents informed about the child through voice, written, photographic, or videographic communication and that the birth parents will keep the adoptive parents updated about medical history. Or the parties could agree to face-to-face visitation. Or they could agree to any combination of the two simultaneously or chronologically. The important issue is that the parties are comfortable with the agreement.

The *Guidelines for Public Policy and State Legislation Governing Permanence for Children* [29] recommend that clarity within the statutes is important to give guidance to the court and parties and to diminish the likelihood of future litigation. States must strike a balance between enabling parties to change orders and making such actions so accessible that the parties will be in court unnecessarily. The *Guidelines* propose that only a party to the agreement may move to enforce it. Typically, the parties to the agreement will be the child, adoptive parent(s), and biological parent(s); in some cases, however, the parties to the agreement could include siblings, grandparents or other relatives, foster parents, or any other significant person in the child's life.

Enforcing the Agreement

Most courts have taken the position that post-adoption visitation agreements are valid and enforceable so long as the court deems the nature and frequency of contact to be in the child's best interests.[30] American Law Reports has a thorough annotation on "Postadoption visitation by natural parent."[31] For agreements to be enforceable, they must be approved by the court that has jurisdiction over the adoption. Five states require the written consent of the child who is age 12 or older.[32] Nine states require the parties to participate in mediation before petitions for enforcement or modifications are brought before the court.[33] Some courts have found post-adoption contact agreements to be invalid and unenforceable, generally concluding that such an agreement would conflict with the adoption of the child.[34]

---

[29] CHILDREN'S BUREAU, U.S. DEPARTMENT OF HEALTH & HUMAN SERVICES, ADOPTION 2002: THE PRESIDENT'S INITIATIVE ON ADOPTION AND FOSTER CARE, GUIDELINES FOR PUBLIC POLICY AND STATE LEGISLATION GOVERNING PERMANENCE FOR CHILDREN (1999).

[30] Child Welfare Information Gateway, *Postadoption Contact Agreements Between Birth and Adoptive Families: Summary of State Laws, available at* http://www.childwelfare.gov/systemwide/laws_policies/statutes/cooperativeall.pdf; Danny R. Veilleux, Annotation, *Postadoption Visitation by Natural Parent*, 78 A.L.R. 4th 218 (1990).

[31] Danny R. Veilleux, Annotation, *Postadoption Visitation by Natural Parent*, 78 A.L.R. 4th 218 (1990).

[32] Child Welfare Information Gateway, *Postadoption Contact Agreements Between Birth and Adoptive Families: Summary of State Laws, available at* http://www.childwelfare.gov/systemwide/laws_policies/statutes/cooperativeall.pdf. The five states are California, Connecticut, Indiana, Massachusetts, and Rhode Island.

[33] *Id.* The nine states are Arizona, California, Connecticut, Louisiana, Minnesota, New Hampshire, Oklahoma, Oregon, and Texas.

[34] Danny R. Veilleux, Annotation, *Postadoption Visitation by Natural Parent*, 78 A.L.R. 4th 218, § 5 (1990).

Many of the existing post-adoption contact statutes provide that the contact can be modified or terminated only (1) when the parties agree or circumstances have changed, and (2) it is in the child's best interests. This standard strikes an appropriate balance because it does not permit frivolous actions and protects the best interests of the child.[35]

§ 25.4 Permanent Guardianship

A legally secure permanent guardianship, particularly with a subsidy, could provide an appropriate permanent plan for those children whose return home or adoption is not appropriate or possible. Children in permanent guardianship would not require ongoing court or agency supervision. Parental rights might not be terminated, but the custodial rights of the parents would be transferred to the guardians. Unfortunately, although a number of distinct legal categories of custody and guardianship are available under state law, many are easily revoked and provide inadequate legal protections for the guardian or custodian as well as inadequate permanence for the child.[36] The forms of guardianship available in most states are too legally vulnerable to provide the permanency that is required.

The Adoption and Safe Families Act of 1997 (ASFA) allows the court, during a permanency hearing, to consider both adoption and legal guardianship as permanent placements.[37] Permanent guardianships under state law are not necessarily consistent with the Federal definition of legal guardianship in ASFA:

> The term "legal guardianship" means a judicially created relationship between child and caretaker which is intended to be permanent and self-sustaining as evidenced by the transfer to the caretaker of the following parental rights with respect to the child: protection, education, care and control of the person, custody of the person, and decision making. The term "legal guardian" means the caretaker in such a relationship.[38]

The Adoption 2002 *Guidelines for Public Policy and State Legislation Governing Permanence for Children* recommend that because the goal of permanent guardianship is to create a permanent *family* for the child, guardians for this purpose should be adult individuals or couples, rather than public or private agencies. Once a

---

[35] CHILDREN'S BUREAU, U.S. DEPARTMENT OF HEALTH & HUMAN SERVICES, ADOPTION 2002: THE PRESIDENT'S INITIATIVE ON ADOPTION AND FOSTER CARE, GUIDELINES FOR PUBLIC POLICY AND STATE LEGISLATION GOVERNING PERMANENCE FOR CHILDREN at II-8 (1999).

[36] *See* STEVE CHRISTIAN & LISA EKMAN, A PLACE TO CALL HOME: ADOPTION AND GUARDIANSHIP FOR CHILDREN IN FOSTER CARE (National Conference of State Legislatures 2000); Mark Hardin, *Legal Placement Options to Achieve Permanence for Children in Foster Care, in* FOSTER CHILDREN IN THE COURTS 128, 150–70 (Mark Hardin ed., 1983).

[37] Adoption and Safe Families Act of 1997, Pub. L. No. 105-89, § 302 amending 42 U.S.C. § 675(5)(C).

[38] ASFA, Pub. L. No. 105-89, § 101(b); 42 U.S.C. § 675(7).

permanent guardianship is established, there need not be any ongoing court review or agency supervision of the guardianship. The only exception is that the court could retain jurisdiction, just as it would in child custody determinations following divorce, to consider any subsequent motions to modify or terminate the guardianship or enforce orders of child support.[39]

In some jurisdictions, the judge handling the child protection proceeding has the authority to order a guardianship. An efficient legal process should address all of the needs of the child consistent with the principle of one child, one judge. In states where guardianship requires a separate proceeding in another court, there are formidable procedural barriers, and guardianship is sometimes avoided when it is most appropriate for the child and family. California, Michigan, and Rhode Island, among other states, authorize the courts that hear child protection cases to order guardianship.

The permanent guardian has full rights and responsibilities concerning the child, including the obligation to support the child. Birth parents could retain an obligation to contribute to the support of a child to the extent of their financial abilities if ordered to do so by the court. Courts could enter standing orders for support as part of the guardianship order, as appropriate in the circumstances. The court may reserve certain rights concerning the birth family in the decree of permanent guardianship, including rights of visitation with the birth parents, siblings, and extended family. The decree of permanent guardianship divests the birth parents or prior adoptive parents of legal custody and guardianship but does not terminate their parental rights. Thus, the decree of permanent guardianship differs from an adoption in that it does not affect a child's inheritance rights or rights to other government benefits (e.g., social security in certain cases) from and through the birth parents.[40] In fact, one legally significant difference between adoption with contact and permanent guardianship can be the survival of financial rights and benefits from the parents.

Permanent guardianship achieves a legally protected permanency without terminating parental rights. Some legal theorists distinguish between three levels of parental rights:

- Custody (to have physical possession and responsibility for daily care).
- Guardianship (the right to make the important decisions for the child).
- Residual rights (connection to the biological extended family, rights of inheritance, and the possibility of regaining custody or guardianship, should one lose them temporarily).

Termination of parental rights generally terminates all legal relation between the child and the extended biological family, whose legal connection is derived from the

---

[39] *See* CHILDREN'S BUREAU, U.S. DEPARTMENT OF HEALTH & HUMAN SERVICES, ADOPTION 2002: THE PRESIDENT'S INITIATIVE ON ADOPTION AND FOSTER CARE, GUIDELINES FOR PUBLIC POLICY AND STATE LEGISLATION GOVERNING PERMANENCE FOR CHILDREN, CH. II (1999).

[40] *See* Mark Hardin, *Legal Placement Options to Achieve Permanence for Children in Foster Care, in* FOSTER CHILDREN IN THE COURTS 128, 171–73 (Mark Hardin ed., 1983).

parents' rights, so that the child is no longer related and becomes a legal stranger to them. (Similarly, in adoption the child acquires a new set of parents and a new extended family.) In a permanent guardianship the child remains legally related for inheritance purposes and may receive government and other benefits from the biological mother and father and the extended biological family. Should the permanent guardianship be terminated, for example, by the death or disability of the guardian, the parents and extended family members retain their legal relationship with the child. They could have a right to be notified and an opportunity to show the court that the guardianship should be terminated completely, restoring the rights of the parent or parents, or that the court should appoint another relative or designated person as successor guardian for the child.

Obviously this legal status is not for every child. Adoption probably remains the preferred permanent placement for children who cannot be reunited with their biological parents. But permanent guardianship may serve some children very well. The judgment as to when this status is in the best interests of the child is legally and psychologically complex and should be made on a case-specific basis.

Because a "permanent guardianship" is legally secure and very difficult to set aside, fairness, particularly to the parents, warrants application of strict standards. Permanent guardianship is not a status to be entered into lightly. The court should make a record in support of the guardianship including, where applicable, the fact that prior to the permanent guardianship the child was in state custody as the result of parental abuse or neglect and the parents were not able to resume care. Developing a sound legal record in support of the permanent guardianship protects the status from challenges except on the grounds cited below.

Permanent guardianship may be based on the consent of the parties if a factual basis for the guardianship is preserved on the record. All parties need not consent to a permanent guardianship, however, and the court may order permanent guardianship following a contested hearing. In Washington, for instance, a form of guardianship may be ordered after proofs equivalent to those required for termination of parental rights.[41]

The court must also find that the proposed guardian is suitable. In cases where the child has been living with the guardian, the quality of care will help establish this suitability, along with a careful home study and criminal and other background checks. In cases where the child has not been living with the guardian, the agency and court might rely entirely on the home study and background check, or the court might delay a permanent decision until the child has been in the home for a trial period.

When an adult individual or couple has permanent legal guardianship of a child, the legal position of the guardian should be as secure as that of a typical birth parent or adoptive parent. That is, it should not be possible to remove the child from the guardian unless it is shown that continuing placement in the home is detrimental to the child. If there is a report of child abuse or neglect, the child protection agency will

---

[41] WASH. REV. CODE § 13.34.230.

have to provide the same evidence and proof that would be required against a biological parent.[42]

§ 25.5 Subsidized Guardianship

The Fostering Connections to Success and Increasing Adoptions Act of 2008[43] (Fostering Connections Act), which amends numerous provisions of Titles IV-B and IV-E, became law on October 7, 2008. Among its provisions is an expansion of subsidized guardianships—a policy change advocated by a number of groups, including the Children's Defense Fund.[44] For details on a particular state's implementation of Fostering Connections Act, a state-by-state summary is available online.[45] The federal requirements for funding guardianships can be found at the Children's Bureau Web site.[46]

The Fostering Connections Act permits each state to establish a subsidized kinship guardianship program under which "grandparents and other relatives" who have cared for a child in the role of foster parents and who are willing to make a permanent commitment to raising the child may become legal guardians of the child. This program would work much the same way as the adoption subsidy program. In summary, the adult relative would be given guardianship over the foster child that is intended to be permanent. The relative-guardian would receive financial assistance to provide care for that child, and the child would be eligible for Medicaid. Among other requirements, to be eligible for a subsidized guardianship, the relative must have cared for the child as a foster care provider for six consecutive months and the child should have a strong attachment to the prospective guardian. Siblings of children may also be eligible if placed in the same guardianship arrangement even if they are not otherwise eligible. Children 14 and older must be consulted about the guardianship, and some youths may be eligible beyond age 18. Additionally, the state can be reimbursed by the federal government for up to $2000 for nonrecurring expenses related to putting the guardianship in place (e.g., filing fees). Before placing a child in a kinship guardianship, the case worker must document: (1) the steps that were taken to determine that returning the child to the parent is not an appropriate permanency plan; (2) why placement with a relative in a permanent guardianship will serve the

---

[42] For recommendations for a state statute providing for permanent guardianship, see CHILDREN'S BUREAU, U.S. DEPARTMENT OF HEALTH & HUMAN SERVICES, ADOPTION 2002: THE PRESIDENT'S INITIATIVE ON ADOPTION AND FOSTER CARE, GUIDELINES FOR PUBLIC POLICY AND STATE LEGISLATION GOVERNING PERMANENCE FOR CHILDREN at II-9 (1999).

[43] Pub. L. No. 110-351, 122 Stat. 3949 (Oct. 7, 2008) (codified in scattered sections of 42 U.S.C.).

[44] *See* Children's Defense Fund, *States' Subsidized Guardianship Laws at a Glance* (Oct. 2004); THE PEW COMMISSION ON CHILDREN IN FOSTER CARE, FOSTERING THE FUTURE: SAFETY, PERMANENCE AND WELL-BEING FOR CHILDREN IN FOSTER CARE 20 (2005). For a fuller discussion of Fostering Connections Act, see § 10.6, Fostering Connections to Success and Increasing Adoptions Act.

[45] See the Web site of the National Association of Public Child Welfare Administrators at http://www.napcwa.org/Legislative/LG.asp.

[46] http://www.acf.hhs.gov/j2ee/programs/cb/laws_policies/laws/cwpm/policy.jsp?idFlag+2.

child's best interests; (3) that adoption by the relative has been discussed; (4) why adoption is not being pursued; and (5) the efforts that were made to discuss the matter with the child's parents.[47]

Research in Illinois, replicated in Wisconsin and Tennessee, indicates that federally subsidized guardianship "is a permanent and cost effective alternative to retaining children in long-term foster care."[48] Fewer children remained in long-term foster care, and thus the states saved the costs of on-going administrative oversight. Concerns have been raised that subsidized guardianship might undermine adoption as a permanency option. The National Council for Adoption recognizes that adoption may not be an appropriate exit from foster care alternative for all children. There are some instances, they say, "when even the most passionate adoption advocate can agree that guardianship is the best permanency option" including:

- When a child is being cared for by a relative who wishes and is able to make a legally binding commitment, but does not want to disrupt existing family relationships by terminating the parents' parental rights;

- When an adolescent 14 years of age or older who clearly understands his or her options chooses guardianship because he or she doesn't wish to be adopted, but wants to forge a permanent, legal connection with his or her caregiver;

- When it is in the best interests of a child below the age of 14 to maintain his or her relationship with a sibling under a guardian's care; and

- When a parent's physical, emotional, or cognitive disability prevent him or her from caring effectively for the child, but where termination of parental rights is undesired and unwarranted.[49]

§ 25.6 Standby Guardianship

Standby guardianship is a legal mechanism that transfers decision-making for children in those circumstances where a custodial parent suffering from a chronic or terminal illness is able to designate a person to care for the child during the time the parent is unable to care for the child or upon the parent's death.

With respect to Standby Guardianship, ASFA contains the following language:

SEC. 403 SENSE OF CONGRESS REGARDING STANDBY
GUARDIANS It is the sense of Congress that the States should have
in effect laws and procedures that permit any parent who is

---

[47] *See* §10.6, Fostering Connections to Success and Increasing Adoptions Act.

[48] Mark F. Testa, *Subsidized Guardianship: Testing the Effectiveness of an Idea Whose Time Has Finally Come*, Child and Family Research Center, The University of Illinois and Urbana-Champaign (May 2008).

[49] Marc Zappala & Thomas Atwood, *Guarding Adoption While Subsidizing Guardianship*, ADOPTION ADVOCATE (National Council for Adoption), February 2008.

chronically ill or near death, without surrendering parental rights, to designate a standby guardian for the parent's minor children, whose authority would take effect upon:

1) the death of the parent,

2) the mental incapacity of the parent, or

3) the physical debilitation and consent of the parent.

A parent can arrange for Standby Guardianship without immediately ending his or her parental rights. If the parent dies, the Standby Guardian can become guardian and also should have the option of applying for adoption. Standby Guardianship may be an appropriate option where parents are terminally ill (e.g., with cancer or HIV/AIDS) or when they suffer from a disease or disorder that will become incapacitating. Standby Guardianship allows terminally ill parents to choose who will become their child's guardian. It allows the parent to develop a practical plan for transition of responsibilities. It allows the identified guardian to take over the parental functions when the birth parent dies or becomes incapacitated. At least 25 states have enacted Standby Guardianship laws.[50] The National Conference of Commissioners on Uniform State Laws proposes a standby guardianship in its Uniform Guardianship and Protective Proceedings Act (1997), Section 202(b). Thus, there has now been significant experience with Standby Guardianship as a legal option for permanence.

California allows for "joint guardianship" for terminally ill parents, which is similar but not identical to Standby Guardianship.[51] Joint guardianship allows the parent and guardian to have decision-making authority for the child at the same time, while the parent is still alive and not yet incapacitated. It also allows the surviving joint guardian to automatically take over upon the parent's death or incapacity without confirmation by the court. Eliminating the requirement of court confirmation following the triggering event may create a smoother shift of authority than many

---

[50] *See* ANN M. HARALAMBIE, 2 HANDLING CHILD CUSTODY, ABUSE AND ADOPTION CASES § 11:6 (West 2009). *See, e.g.,* ARK. CODE § 28-65-221 (2008); CAL. PROB. CODE § 2105(f) (2008); CONN. GEN. STAT. ANN. §§ 45a-624 *et seq.* (2008); 13 DEL. CODE §§ 2361 *et seq.* (2008); D.C. STAT. §§ 16-4801 *et seq.* (2008); FLA. STAT. ANN. § 744.304 (2008); GA. STAT. §§ 29-2-10 *et seq.* (2007); 755 ILL. COMP. STAT. ANN. §§ 5/1-2.23, 5/11-13.1 (2008); IOWA CODE ANN. §633.560 (2008); KAN. STAT. ANN. § 59-3074 (2007); KY. REV. STAT. ANN. § 387.750 (2007); MD. CODE ANN., EST. & TRUST. §§ 13-901 *et seq.* (2008); MASS. GEN. LAWS ANN. ch 201 § 2B (2008); MICH. COMP. LAWS ANN. § 330.1640 (2008); NEB. REV. STAT. § 30-2608(c) (2007); N.C. GEN. STAT. ANN. §§ 35A-1370 *et seq.* (2008); N.J. STAT. ANN. §§ 3B:12-67 *et seq.* (2008); N.Y. SURR. CT. PROC. ACT § 1726 (2008); N.C. STAT. §§ 35A-1370 *et seq.* (2008); OHIO REV. CODE ANN. §§1337.09(D), 2111.121(D) (2008); 23 PA. CONS. STAT. ANN. §§ 5601 *et seq.* (2008); VA CODE §§ 16.1-349 *et seq.* (2008); WASH. REV. CODE ANN. §§11.88.125 *et seq.* (2008); W. VA. CODE § 44A-5-1 *et seq.* (2008); WIS. STAT. ANN. § 54.52 (2007); WYO. STAT. §3-2-108 (2008). *See also* Child Welfare Information Gateway, Standby Guardianship: Summary of State Laws (July 2008), *available at* http://www.childwelfare.gov/system wide/laws_policies/statutes/guardianshipall.pdf; YOLANDE SAMERSON, CHOICES FOR TERMINALLY ILL PARENTS: A GUIDE FOR STATE LAWMAKERS (ABA Center on Children and the Law 1997).

[51] CALIF. PROB. CODE § 2105.

Standby Guardianship procedures. New York's Standby Guardianship statute, however, permits immediate commencement of the guardian's authority without court confirmation if the parent provides written consent that is filed with the court within 90 days.[52]

§ 25.7 Another Planned Permanent Living Arrangement

"Another planned permanent living arrangement" (or APPLA) is recognized as a permanency option under the Adoption and Safe Families Act[53] (ASFA), but it is the least favored of the permanency options.[54] APPLA, defined as "any permanent living arrangement not enumerated in the statute," is intended to be *planned* and *permanent*.[55] The ABA Center on Children and the Law notes that the preferred permanency plans involve a specific adult or couple (not an organization), who will be in charge of the youngster and likely live with him or her. They give these examples of APPLAs:

- A 14-year-old child, Angela, is in a residential treatment facility. She spends some weekends and holidays with a family friend, Mrs. S., who she has known for years. Mrs. S. is unwilling to adopt Angela because she is concerned that the adoption subsidy would not adequately address Angela's significant mental health needs. Mrs. S. is open to the idea of adopting Angela after she turns 18, and possibly being the representative payee for Angela's SSI benefits. In addition to addressing her mental health needs, Angela's permanency plan would include a structure of regular visitation with Mrs. S., and would include Mrs. S. in Angela's treatment and therapy, as appropriate.

- A 16-year-old boy, Robert, lives in a supervised apartment and is receiving independent living services. He stays with his aunt and uncle every other weekend. They are unwilling to allow him to live there full time because they have three children under age 9. Robert has also had problems with drugs in the past, and they are concerned that he will be a negative influence on their young children. They do help him with school issues, and are in the process of helping him fill out applications for college. Robert's permanency plan would not only include the independent living services he needs, but would also address issues between him

---

[52] N.Y. Surr. Ct. Proc. Act § 1726(3)(e)(iii).

[53] 42 U.S.C. § 675(5)(C).

[54] *See* Cecilia Friemonte & Jennifer L. Renne, Making It Permanent: Reasonable Efforts to Finalize Permanency Plans for Foster Children 79–84 (ABA Center on Children and the Law 2002), *available at* http://www.abanet.org/child/rclji/pub.html.

[55] *Id.*

and his aunt and uncle so that those relationships are strengthened and nurtured.

- Termination of parental rights is not being pursued for an 8-year-old Native American child because the agency doesn't think they can meet the burden of proving beyond a reasonable doubt that continued custody of the child by the parent is likely to result in serious emotional or physical damage to the child. Consistent with tribal custom, the tribe has placed the child with a (nonrelative) tribe member who has agreed to be responsible for the child, and with whom the child will reside on a permanent basis.

- A sibling group, ages 6, 9, and 14 have been in foster care with Mr. and Mrs. J. for three years. They visit regularly with their biological mother, and the agency is not pursuing termination of parental rights. The children are bonded with Mr. and Mrs. J. who have committed to caring for the children on a permanent basis. This APPLA could be approved as "permanent foster care with Mr. and Mrs. J."[56]

Long-term foster care is the least desirable option among the permanent placement options when a foster child cannot safely return home. ASFA and its regulations explicitly discourage long-term foster care as an APPLA. The preamble to the ASFA regulations explains, "Far too many children are given the permanency goal of long-term foster care, which is not a permanent living situation for a child."[57] Foster care is generally not stable and may be disrupted, leading to frequent moves for the child and instability.

Emancipation, the legal process by which minors are granted legal adulthood, is also discouraged as an alternative permanent placement. "Emancipation and independent living are not permanency goals, they are services."[58] Emancipation lacks the permanency features spelled out in ASFA.

Nonetheless, some youth will not be adopted, and a long-term placement with a specific foster family may be in their long-range best interests. Each decision must be individualized and focus on the context and needs of a particular child. ASFA permits a long-term foster placement as an APPLA option if the agency demonstrates a "compelling reason" to the court. "If the agency concludes, after considering reunification, adoption, legal guardianship, or relative placement, that the most appropriate permanency plan is an APPLA, the agency must document to the court the compelling reasons for the alternate plan."[59]

---

[56] *Id.*

[57] Title IV-E Foster Care Eligibility Reviews and Child and Family Services State Plan Reviews, 65 Fed. Reg. 4020-1, 4036 (January 25, 2000).

[58] Brenda G. McGowan, *Facilitating Permanency for Youth, in* CHILD WELFARE FOR THE TWENTY-FIRST CENTURY: A HANDBOOK OF PRACTICES, POLICIES, AND PROGRAMS (Gerald Mallon & Peg McCartt Hess eds., Columbia University Press 2005).

[59] 45 C.F.R. § 1356.21(h)(3).

The regulations give three examples of a compelling reason for establishing an APPLA as a permanency plan:

(1) an older teen who specifically requests that emancipation be established as his/her permanency plan;

(2) the case of a parent and child who have a significant bond but the parent is unable to care for the child because of an emotional or physical disability and the child's foster parents have committed to raising him/her to the age of majority and to facilitate visitation with the disabled parent; or

(3) the Tribe has identified another planned permanent living arrangement for the child.[60]

Children in planned long-term living arrangements should continue to receive assistance from the state agency and supervision of the court, including continuing access to an attorney for the child. All should exercise great caution to support the foster family and child to prevent disruption of the placement.

Decisions resulting in permanent or long-term living arrangements should be based on a thorough assessment of the child's needs *and* the family's capacity to meet those needs *currently and into the child's future*. Simply meeting state licensing standards is not sufficient. A home study or an evaluation of the family, a written agreement between the agency and the family, the child's consent, and a statement of the family's intent to parent the child into adulthood should also be required. These materials should be discussed, developed, and agreed to by all parties, including the child, the foster parents, and the agency. Some states use a "permanent foster family agreement" (PFFA) to structure these arrangements.[61] Such agreements should be based on a thorough assessment of the family's capacity to meet the ongoing, lifelong developmental needs of the child.

§ 25.8 Re-establishing Parental Rights Post-Termination

The permanency planning philosophy of America sometimes results in termination of parental rights where the child is not adopted, the adoption is disrupted, or the child does not settle into some alternative permanent placement. The tight timelines of permanency planning and aggressive termination of parental rights have been criticized for not allowing enough individualized decision-making and for creating a certain number of "legal orphans." Guggenheim observes:

> Modern reforms aimed at helping families in need have resulted in creating the highest number of unnatural orphans in the history of the

---

[60] 45 C.F.R. § 1356.21(h)(3)(i), (ii), & (iii).

[61] *See, e.g.*, MICH. COMP. LAWS § 712A.13a(h).

United States. . . . Now is the time to re-examine a child protection system that relies on foster care as the most prominent child protection mechanism and that also creates more legal orphans than it appears to have the capacity to place in permanent, adoptive homes.[62]

Sometimes, after parental rights are severed and after a youth has been in foster care for some time, the situation changes—the child is older, there may have been unsuccessful or disrupted placements, and the parent's ability to provide for the child has improved. Youth occasionally vote with their feet and run from foster care to be with their extended family, including the parents whose parental rights were previously terminated. It sometimes happens that a reunification with the parent, even after all this history, is indeed in the interests of the child. With the passage of time and change of circumstances a legal, as well as a physical, reunification may be appropriate for the child.

Some state laws permit restoration of parental rights in those circumstances.[63] In other states parents may apply to adopt the child or to become the legal guardians of the child. Although restoration of parental rights is certainly not a common occurrence, it may serve the interests of a child, and we should be open to that possibility.

---

[62] Martin Guggenheim, *The Effects of Recent Trends to Accelerate the Termination of Parental Rights of Children in Foster Care: An Empirical Analysis in Two States*, 29 FAM. L. Q. 121, 140 (1995).

[63] *See, e.g.*, CAL. WELF. & INST. CODE § 366.26(i)(2); MICH. COMP. LAWS § 712A.20.

Chapter 26: Child Welfare Appellate Law and Practice*

by Donna Furth[1]

§ 26.1 Methods of Seeking Appellate Review

There are two basic methods of getting your case before a higher court: appeals and writs.

§ 26.1.1 Appeals and Appellate Jurisdiction

An appeal removes the entire cause from the court of original jurisdiction (the "superior" or "circuit" court) to a higher court and subjects both the facts and the law to review by the superior tribunal. The essential parties are: (1) the *appellant*, the party who lost in the trial court and is seeking relief in the higher court; and (2) the *appellee* or *respondent*, the party who prevailed in the lower court, who is expected to defend the judgment.

Thirty-eight states provide an *appeal of right* from the court of original jurisdiction to an intermediate appellate court and a *discretionary appeal* from the intermediate court to the state's highest court. The intermediate court functions as a *court of error*, to determine if the lower court erred and if its rulings must be reversed or modified; the highest court functions as a *court of review*, to adjudicate important questions of law and resolve conflicts between decisions of the intermediate courts. "It is the essential criterion of appellate jurisdiction, that it revises and corrects the proceedings in a cause already instituted, and does not create that cause."[2]

Twelve states (Mississippi, West Virginia, Nebraska, Maine, New Hampshire, Rhode Island, Nevada, Montana, South Dakota, Delaware, Vermont, and Wyoming) do not have an intermediate court. All of them except West Virginia and New Hampshire provide an appeal of right from the court of original jurisdiction to the state's highest court.[3]

---

* Reprinted from *Handling Child Custody, Abuse and Adoption Cases, Third Edition*, with permission of Thomson Reuters. For more information about this publication, please visit www.west.thomson.com. *Author's Note*: This chapter is abridged and adapted from Chapter 23, written by Donna Furth, in ANN M HARALAMBIE, 2 HANDLING CHILD CUSTODY, ABUSE AND ADOPTION CASES 3D (Thomson West 2009). More complete and detailed information about appeals and writs can be found in that chapter.

[1] Donna Furth practices law in San Francisco. She has authored the chapters on appeals and writs in several books.

[2] Marbury v. Madison, 1 Cranch 137, 175 (1803).

[3] ROBERT L. STERN, APPELLATE PRACTICE IN THE UNITED STATES § 1.3 at 7, n. 14; § 1.5 at 13-15 (2d ed.1989).

§ 26.1.2 Writs and Original Jurisdiction

Appellate courts also have *original jurisdiction* in certain instances, including original jurisdiction to issue prerogative writs. A writ is an original proceeding asking an appellate court to command an inferior tribunal to do something or to refrain from doing something. The parties in a writ proceeding are: (1) the *petitioner*, someone who is beneficially interested, but not necessarily a party to the lower court proceeding; (2) the *respondent*, the court and the judge of the court whose action is being challenged, generally a nominal party whose judgment is defended by the party who prevailed in the lower court; and (3) the *real party in interest*. To qualify for writ relief, the petitioner must show that: (1) he or she lacks a speedy and adequate remedy in the ordinary course of law (i.e., on appeal); and (2) failure to grant relief will place petitioner at risk of irreparable harm (i.e., harm that cannot be remedied by an appeal). Only in exceptional circumstances will courts depart from these requirements.

Note: Some courts characterize the jurisdiction to issue writs as the *"supervisory" or "superintending" jurisdiction* of appellate courts and the power to issue writs as the means by which appellate courts confine inferior tribunals within the jurisdiction accorded them. Some courts deem supervisory jurisdiction as ancillary to the court's appellate jurisdiction, whereas others deem it as an independent basis of jurisdiction, distinct from both appellate and original jurisdiction. The significant fact for our purposes is that *original or supervisory jurisdiction is equitable in nature and is "bounded only by the exigencies which call for its exercise."*[4] "[T]he *power* of the courts to grant extraordinary writs is very broad," even though it is exercised very narrowly.[5]

§ 26.1.3 Traditional Writs

The traditional writs are those that existed at common law: primarily writs of *mandamus, prohibition, certiorari*, and *habeas corpus*.

Mandamus and Prohibition

A writ of mandamus (or mandate) lies to compel the lower court to perform a duty that the law requires. "Where the act complained of involves judicial discretion . . . mandamus is appropriate 'only in those exceptional cases' where judicial power is usurped or the court clearly abuses its discretion."[6]

A writ of prohibition issues to restrain a threatened judicial act without or in excess of jurisdiction. "However, the concept of 'jurisdiction' within the context of prohibition is broad. It refers to fundamental 'subject matter' and 'personal'

---

[4]   Hutchins v. City of Des Moines, 176 Iowa 189, 157 N.W. 881, 889 (1916), italics added.

[5]   ROBERT L. STERN, EUGENE GRESSMAN & STEPHEN M. SHAPIRO, SUPREME COURT PRACTICE § 11.1 at 582 (8th ed. 2002).

[6]   Chrysler Corp. v. Makovec, 157 Vt. 84, 88–89, 596 A.2d 1284 (1991) (quoting Ley v. Dall, 150 Vt. 383, 386, 553 A.2d 562, 564 (1988)).

jurisdiction, *as well as the power to act in a particular manner*. Thus, the writ lies to restrain the exercise of any *unauthorized power* even though the respondent court has jurisdiction over the subject matter and the parties."[7] Mandamus is a prayer for an affirmative order; prohibition is a prayer for a negative order. Given that most issues can be framed either affirmatively or negatively, the distinction between mandate and prohibition is now blurred.

Certiorari

The writ of certiorari commands the lower court to certify its record to the reviewing court so that the superior tribunal can determine if the lower court acted in excess of, or without, jurisdiction. "Like prohibition, certiorari is available only to redress jurisdictional errors; but again, within the writ context, that term encompasses any action that exceeds the court's power to act in a particular manner."[8] The required showing is that: (1) petitioner has *no* appeal or other adequate remedy, and (2) the act challenged is a judicial act that has been completed (as opposed to threatened).[9] The appellate court reviews the principles of law on which the decision rests de novo.

Note: The common law writ of certiorari is distinguishable from the *discretionary writ of certiorari* issued by the United States Supreme Court and other supreme courts, which is a statutory writ, derived from, but not to be confused with, the common law writ.[10]

Habeas Corpus

"Habeas corpus is . . . a writ antecedent to statute, . . . throwing its root deep into the genesis of our common law. The writ appeared in English law several centuries ago, became an integral part of our common-law heritage by the time the Colonies achieved independence, and received explicit recognition in the Constitution, which forbids suspension of the Privilege of the Writ of Habeas Corpus . . . unless when in Cases of Rebellion or Invasion the public Safety may require it."[11] Its traditional role was to test the validity of imprisonment or other restraint of liberty. The seminal case of *In re Gault* [12] was initiated as a petition for writ of habeas corpus filed by the parents of 15-year-old Gerald Gault to challenge their son's six-year commitment to a state industrial school for making a "dirty" phone call.

---

[7] JON B. EISENBERG, ELLIS J. HORVITZ & JUSTICE HOWARD B. WIENER, CALIFORNIA PRACTICE GUIDE: CIVIL APPEALS AND WRITS § 15:57 at 15-36 (2009).

[8] *Id.* at § 15:72 at 15-41.

[9] *See, e.g., In re* General Adjudication of All Rights to Use Water in the Big Horn River System, 803 P.2d 61, 67 (Wyo. 1990).

[10] ROBERT L. STERN, EUGENE GRESSMAN & STEPHEN M. SHAPIRO, SUPREME COURT PRACTICE § 2.1 at 68 (8th ed. 2002).

[11] Rasul v. Bush, 542 U.S. 466, 473–74 (2004) (internal cites and quotation marks omitted).

[12] 387 U.S. 1 (1967).

The habeas writ was originally limited to cases of restraint made under color of law; however, it was in time extended to controversies regarding the custody of children, "which were governed, not so much by considerations of strictly legal rights, as by those of expediency and equity and, above all, the interests of the child."[13] "Where the custody of children is involved . . . the scope of the writ of habeas corpus is enlarged and invokes the broad equitable powers of the court."[14]

§ 26.1.4 Statutory Writs

All jurisdictions have statutes authorizing the review of particular orders by writ. These "statutory writs" are not an independent kind of writ. The term simply refers to particular situations in which review by a common law writ is authorized by statute.

The significant difference between traditional and statutory writs is that traditional writs are subject to equitable deadlines; an unreasonable delay in seeking relief by means of a traditional writ may bar relief on the ground of *laches*. "Laches is an equitable doctrine that may be invoked when delay by one party works to the disadvantage of the other, causing a change of circumstances that would make the grant of relief to the delaying party inequitable."[15] In contrast, the filing deadline for a statutory writ is often short and jurisdictional, i.e., failure to seek relief within the statutory period bars relief.

§ 26.1.5 Remedies in States that "Abolished" Writs

Some states have "abolished" traditional writs, at least in name, and have instituted special remedies for reviewing orders that would have been reviewable by writ at common law. A model for these provisions is a New York statute known as "Article 78": "Relief previously obtained by writs of certiorari . . . mandamus or prohibition shall be obtained in a proceeding under this article. Wherever in any statute reference is made to a writ or order of certiorari, mandamus or prohibition, such reference shall, so far as applicable, be deemed to refer to the proceeding authorized by this article."[16] Article 78 simplified and clarified the traditional writ procedures, but did not alter the substantive law on which the writs were based.

States with provisions similar to Article 78 are Arizona ("special action"),[17] Washington ("discretionary review")[18] and Tennessee ("application for extraordinary appeal").[19] Colorado too has abolished "special forms of pleadings and writs,"[20] but

---

[13] People *ex rel.* Riesner v. New York Nursery & Child's Hosp., 230 N.Y. 119, 124 (1920).

[14] Vanden Heuvel v. Vanden Heuvel, 254 Iowa 1391, 1399, 121 N.W.2d 216 (1963); *see In re* Kerry D., 144 N.H. 146, 148, 737 A.2d 662 (1999).

[15] State of Nevada v. Eighth Judicial Dist. Court of State of Nevada, 116 Nev. 127, 135, 994 P.2d 692 (2000).

[16] N.Y. CIV. PRAC. L. & R. § 7801 (McKinney's 1963).

[17] *See* 17B ARIZ. R. P. SPECIAL ACTIONS R. 1(a) (West 2002).

[18] *See* WASH. R. APP. P. 2.1.

[19] *See* TENN. R. APP. P. 9, 10.

the Colorado constitution vests the state supreme court with exclusive "power to issue writs of habeas corpus, mandamus, quo warranto, certiorari, injunction, and . . . other original and remedial writs . . . with authority to hear and determine the same."[21]

Such provisions "eliminate the historical, often technical, restrictions on the use of particular writs, and either leave the court with unfettered discretion to do what seems right, as in Arizona, or to substitute general standards which concentrate on the practical reasons why allowing review before termination of a case is reasonable in the circumstances."[22]

§ 26.2 Deciding Whether to Appeal

§ 26.2.1 Appealability: The "One Final Judgment" Rule

The first step in deciding to appeal is determining if the order in question is appealable. A core principle of appellate procedure, the "one final judgment rule," bars courts, in exercising appellate jurisdiction, from reviewing interlocutory rulings until final resolution of the case. In general, where no issue is left for future consideration except the fact of compliance or noncompliance, the order is *final*; however, where anything further in the nature of judicial action is required by the court to determine the rights of the parties, the order is *interlocutory*. There are many exceptions to the "one final judgment" rule, i.e., instances in which technically interlocutory orders are appealable by statute or in which courts deem interlocutory orders "final" for purposes of appeal.

Exception: Collateral Final Orders

"Final decisions" include collateral orders that do not terminate the litigation but are sufficiently important that they should be treated as final.[23] Such claims are "too important to be denied review and too independent of the cause itself to require that appellate consideration be deferred until the whole case is adjudicated."[24] The requirements for a collateral order appeal are that the order "'(1) conclusively determine the disputed question, (2) resolve an important issue completely separate from the merits of the action, and (3) be effectively unreviewable on appeal from a final judgment.'"[25]

---

[20] COLO. R. CIV. P. 106.

[21] COLO. CONST. art. 6, § 3.

[22] ROBERT L. STERN, APPELLATE PRACTICE IN THE UNITED STATES § 4.7 at 98 (2d ed. 1989).

[23] Will v. Hallock, 546 U.S. 345, 348 (2006).

[24] Cohen v. Beneficial Indus. Loan Corp., 337 U.S. 541, 546 (1949).

[25] Will v. Hallock, 546 U.S. 345, 347 (2006) (quoting Puerto Rico Aqueduct & Sewer Auth. v. Metcalf & Eddy, Inc., 506 U.S. 139, 144 (1993), quoting Coopers & Lybrand v. Livesay, 437 U.S. 463, 468 (1978)).

Exception: Orders in Dependency Cases

In dependency cases, the original dispositional order is often deemed the "final judgment" for purposes of appeal—which means the detention order and jurisdictional findings are reviewable on appeal from the *dispositional order.* [26] In fact, the dispositional order is usually one of several appealable orders in the dependency process.

For example, in Arizona, "final" orders in a dependency case include not only dispositional orders,[27] but also orders declaring children dependent, orders reaffirming findings that children are dependent, orders entered after review hearings, orders dismissing dependency proceedings, orders terminating or limiting parents' visitation rights,[28] and orders granting a motion to terminate parental rights.[29]

In Arkansas, where out-of-home placement has been ordered, appealable orders in a dependency are those from: "(A) adjudication and disposition hearings, (B) review and permanency planning hearings if the court directs entry of a final judgment as to one or more of the issues or parties and upon express determination that there is no just reason for delay of an appeal. . . ; and (C) termination of parental rights."[30]

In California, the dispositional order is directly appealable as a "judgment" and every post-dispositional order is appealable as an "order after judgment."[31]

In Maryland, an appeal may be taken from any interlocutory order "[d]epriving a parent, grandparent, or natural guardian of the care and custody of his child, or changing the terms of such an order."[32] "It is immaterial that the order appealed from emanated from the permanency planning hearing or from the periodic review hearing. If the change could deprive a parent of the fundamental right to care and custody of his or her child, whether immediately or in the future, the order is an appealable interlocutory order."[33]

In short, each state has different standards for determining which orders in a dependency are "final" and appealable and which are reviewable solely by writ. It is

---

[26] *See, e.g., In re* Daniel K., 61 Cal. App. 4th 661, 666, 71 Cal. Rptr. 2d 764 (1998); In Interest of Long, 313 N.W.2d 473, 477 (Iowa 1981); Sanchez v. Walker County Dep't of Family & Children Servs., 235 Ga. 817, 818, 221 S.E.2d 589 (1976); *In re* Murray, 52 Ohio St. 3d 155, 159–61, 556 N.E.2d 1169 (1990); *In re* M.D., 839 A.2d 1116, 1118 (Pa. Super. 2003); *In re* Dependency of Chubb, 112 Wash. 2d 719, 721–22, 773 P.2d 851 (1989).

[27] Lindsey M. v. Arizona Dep't of Econ. Sec., 212 Ariz. 43, 45, 127 P.3d 59 (Ariz. Ct. App., Div. 2, 2006).

[28] *Id.; see* Matter of Appeal In Maricopa County Juvenile Action No. JD-5312, 178 Ariz. 372, 374, 873 P.2d 710 (Ariz. App., Div. 1, 1994); Matter of Maricopa County Juvenile Action No. JD-500116, 160 Ariz. 538, 542–43, 774 P.2d 842 (Ariz. App., Div. 1, 1989).

[29] Monica C. v. Arizona Dep't of Econ. Sec., 211 Ariz. 89, 118 P.3d 37 (Ariz. App., Div. 1, 2005).

[30] ARK. R. APP. PROC. 2(c)(3).

[31] CAL. WELF. & INST. CODE § 395; *In re* Daniel K., 61 Cal. App. 4th 661, 668, 71 Cal. Rptr. 2d 764 (1998).

[32] MD. CODE, COURTS & JUDICIAL PROCEEDINGS § 12-303(3)(x); *see, e.g., In re* Joseph N., 407 Md. 278, 291, 965 A.2d 59 (2009); *In re* Samone H., 385 Md. 282, 315–16, 869 A.2d 370 (2005).

[33] *In re* Karl H., 394 Md. 402, 430, 906 A.2d 898 (2006).

critical that counsel research the pertinent statutes in his or her jurisdiction before deciding to appeal or *not* to appeal a particular order in a dependency case. Failure to appeal an appealable order within the required time limits constitutes a waiver of the claim.

Exception: Interlocutory Orders Appealable by Statute

All jurisdictions have statutes that permit interlocutory orders to be appealed under specified conditions. For example, in Massachusetts "temporary appellate relief from interlocutory orders" may be sought in "single justice" appeals, which are often heard in fewer than 30 days.[34]

New York allows appeals as of right from any interlocutory order which "involves some parts of the merits" or "affects a substantial right."[35] Commentaries to the statute conclude that "almost anything can be appealed to New York's intermediate appellate court," the Appellate Division.[36]

The Federal Interlocutory Appeals Act permits an interlocutory appeal if the district judge certifies that an interlocutory order "involves a controlling question of law as to which there is substantial ground for difference of opinion and that an immediate appeal from the order may materially advance the ultimate termination of the litigation."[37]

Several states—including Alaska, Illinois, Indiana, Michigan, New Jersey, Tennessee, Washington, and Wisconsin—have provisions modeled on the federal standards, but that deviate from them in that the guiding standard is phrased differently, application is made to the reviewing court, and/or application may be made to the reviewing court even if the trial court has refused to certify.[38]

§ 26.2.2 Time Limits

The appellant typically has 30 days from the date judgment is rendered to file a notice of appeal. The "date judgment is rendered" may be the oral pronouncement of the ruling, the filing of the judgment by the clerk of the court, or the service of the judgment on the parties to the matter. The time for filing may be extended by certain post-trial motions. For the permissible period in your jurisdiction and its proper calculation, check the rules of appellate procedure in your state. Every state maintains a Web site setting forth the most current version of its rules of appellate procedure.

---

[34] MASS. GEN. LAWS ANN. tit. 2, ch. 231, § 118 (West 2004); *see* John H. Henn, *Civil Interlocutory Appellate Review Under G.L.M. c. 231, § 118 and G.L.M. c. 211, § 3*, 81 MASS. L. REV. 24, 25 (1996).

[35] 8 N.Y. CIV. PRAC. L. & R. § 5701(a) (McKinney's 2004).

[36] ROBERT L. STERN, APPELLATE PRACTICE IN THE UNITED STATES § 4.2 at 79–80 (2d ed. 1989).

[37] 28 U.S.C. § 1292(b).

[38] ROBERT L. STERN, APPELLATE PRACTICE IN THE UNITED STATES § 4.5(b) at 84–88 (2d ed. 1989); *see, e.g.*, ALASKA R. APP. P. 402; ILL. SUP. CT. R. 308; IND. R. APP. PROC. 14(B); MICH. APP. R. 7.205; N.J. R. APP. P. 2:2-2; TENN. R. APP. P. 9(a); WASH R. APP. PROC. 2.3; and WISC. R. APP. P. 809.50.

§ 26.2.3 Standing to Appeal

"The issue of standing implicates [the reviewing] court's subject matter jurisdiction."[39] Thus, to have standing to appeal, the appellant must be an *aggrieved party*: (a) a party of record to the lower court proceeding (b) whose interests are directly, substantially, and injuriously affected by the judgment. In other words, an appellant is not permitted to raise an error affecting only another party who did not appeal. Where the interests of two parties are interrelated, both may have standing to raise issues that impact the related interests. Thus, children have been held to have standing to raise their parents' rights in termination of parental rights proceedings, and parents have been held to have standing in such proceedings to raise the child's constitutional rights and right to competent counsel.[40]

An aggrieved *nonparty*—someone who was not a party to the lower court proceeding, but is aggrieved by the judgment—may seek party status by filing a motion to intervene in the trial court and, if the motion is granted, file a notice of appeal as an aggrieved party. An aggrieved nonparty has, in any event, the right to seek writ review.

§ 26.2.4 Preservation of the Error: The Waiver Rule

"Appellate determination of reversible error is based on the presence of three interrelated circumstances: [1] specific rulings, acts or omissions by the trial tribunal constituting trial error; [2] which follow an objection by counsel or the grant or denial of an oral or written motion or submission; [3] accompanied by a proper and appropriate course of action recommended by the appellant that was rejected by the tribunal. *When all three elements are present, the issue has been properly preserved for review.*"[41]

If these elements are not present, the error is deemed "waived" or "forfeited." The rationale is that it is unfair to the trial judge and adverse parties for an appellate court to reverse for an error that could have been corrected had it been brought to the attention of the trial court in a timely manner.[42]

---

[39] *In re* Melody L., 290 Conn. 131, 155–56, 962 A.2d 81 (2009).

[40] *See, e.g., In re* Patricia E., 174 Cal. App. 3d 1, 7, 219 Cal. Rptr. 783 (1985), *disapproved on other grounds, In re* Celine R., 31 Cal. 4th 45, 1 Cal. Rptr. 3d 432 (2003); *In re* Melody L., 290 Conn. 131, 157, 962 A.2d 81 (2009); *In re* Christina M., 280 Conn. 474, 486–87, 908 A.2d 1073 (2006); Wright v. Alexandria Div. of Soc. Servs., 16 Va. App. 821, 825, 433 S.E.2d 500 (1993), *cert. denied*, 513 U.S. 1050 (1994).

[41] RUGGERO J. ALDISERT, WINNING ON APPEAL: BETTER BRIEFS AND ORAL ARGUMENT § 5.1 at 55 (2d ed. 2003), italics added.

[42] Doers v. Golden Gate Bridge, Highway & Transp. Dist., 23 Cal. 3d 180, 184–85 n. 1, 151 Cal. Rptr. 837 (1979); *see* Arnold v. Lebel, 941 A.2d 813, 818 (R.I. 2007); *In re* Adoption of E.N.R., 42 S.W.3d 26, 31–32 (Tenn. 2001).

Exception: When Issues May Be Raised the First Time on Appeal

The waiver rule is the general rule. It will be enforced "*unless due process forbids it.*"[43] Hence, courts depart from the waiver rule when the question to be presented is of a jurisdictional nature, when there has been "plain error," when the interest of justice so requires, and whether other unusual circumstances are involved.[44]

§ 26.2.5 Standards of Appellate Review

In a common law jurisdiction, the reviewing court does not reweigh the evidence presented in the trial court.[45] Instead, it reviews the record through *standards of review*, determined by the nature of the issue raised. The relevant standard of review is a significant factor in determining the likelihood of a reversal.

Findings of Fact

In the federal courts[46] and in most states, the standard for reviewing findings of facts is the *clearly erroneous standard*. "A finding is 'clearly erroneous' when although there is evidence to support it, *the reviewing court on the entire evidence is left with the definite and firm conviction that a mistake has been committed. . .* If the district court's account of the evidence is plausible in light of the record viewed in its entirety, the court of appeals may not reverse it even though convinced that had it been sitting as the trier of fact, it would have weighed the evidence differently. *Where there are two permissible views of the evidence, the factfinder's choice between them cannot be clearly erroneous.*"[47] The trial court's findings regarding the credibility of witnesses are entitled to similar deference. In addition, the appellate court is required to resolve all evidentiary conflicts in favor of the judgment of the lower court.

In a few jurisdictions, the standard for reviewing findings of fact is the *substantial evidence standard*. Here again, the reviewing court will not reweigh the evidence, re-evaluate the credibility of witnesses, or otherwise substitute its conclusions for those of the trial court. Rather, the reviewing court will draw all reasonable inferences in support of the trial court's findings (applying the presumption of correctness) and affirm the order if it is supported by substantial evidence, even if other evidence

---

[43] *In re* Janee J., 74 Cal. App. 4th 198, 208, 87 Cal. Rptr. 2d 634 (1999), italics added; *see* Wood v. Georgia, 450 U.S. 261, 264–65 (1980); State v. Golding, 213 Conn. 233, 239–40, 567 A.2d 823 (1989); Parrell-Sisters MHC, LLC v. Spokane County, 147 Wash. App. 356, 363–64, 195 P.3d 573 (2008).

[44] ROBERT L. STERN, APPELLATE PRACTICE IN THE UNITED STATES § 3.1 at 65 (2d ed. 1989).

[45] "In civil cases in Louisiana, the sole civil law jurisdiction in the United States, the state's court of appeal (the court of second instance) may review facts." RUGGERO J. ALDISERT, WINNING ON APPEAL: BETTER BRIEFS AND ORAL ARGUMENT § 5.6 at 65–66 (2d ed. 2003).

[46] *See* FED R. CIV. P. 52(a)(6).

[47] Anderson v. City of Bessemer City, N.C., 470 U.S. 564, 573–74 (1986), italics added and citations omitted; *see In re* Melody L., 290 Conn. 131, 148, 962 A.2d 81 (2009); *In re* A.C.G., 894 A.2d 436 (D.C. 2006); Trost-Steffen v. Steffen, 772 N.E.2d 500, 505 (Ind. App. 2002); *In re* Adoption of Roni, 56 Mass. App. Ct. 52, 58, 775 N.E.2d 419 (2002); *In re* A.D.T., 174 Vt. 369, 817 A.2d 20 (2002).

supports a contrary conclusion.[48] "[T]he power of an appellate court begins and ends with the determination as to whether there is any substantial evidence, contradicted or uncontradicted, which will support the finding of fact."[49]

Discretionary Decisions

The abuse of discretion standard is applicable in 30 states for custody and placement decisions.[50] It is also applicable to evidentiary rulings.[51] Under this standard, the appellate court will not substitute its judgment and discretion for that of the trial court except where the record reflects a "clear" or "manifest" abuse of discretion. "When a court has made a custody determination in a dependency proceeding, a reviewing court will not disturb that decision unless the trial court has exceeded the limits of legal discretion by making an arbitrary, capricious, or patently absurd determination. . . . The appropriate test for abuse of discretion is whether the trial court exceeded the bounds of reason. When two or more inferences can reasonably be deduced from the facts, the reviewing court has no authority to substitute its decision for that of the trial court."[52]

Note: Courts in a few states—including Arkansas, Iowa, Michigan, Nebraska, Oregon, Pennsylvania and Tennessee—apply a somewhat broader standard of review in custody and placement decisions. "Appellate courts in these states give a de novo review to custody cases and do not feel bound by the trial court's decision, although the appellate courts will give weight to the trial judge's decision if the trial judge gives a careful explanation for his decision."[53] The *de novo* standard is also applicable in Iowa to both the facts and the law in child-in-need of assistance (CINA) proceedings. The reviewing court gives weight to the trial court's findings, but is not bound by them.[54]

Issues of Law

Pure issues of law, including questions of statutory interpretation, are reviewed independently (*de novo*) by the appellate court. No deference is given to the trial

---

[48] *See, e.g., In re* Pima County Juvenile Action No. J-31853, 18 Ariz. App. 219, 220, 501 P.2d 395 (Div. 2 1972); Bowers v. Bernards, 150 Cal. App. 3d 870, 873–74, 197 Cal. Rptr. 925 (1984); *In re* S.M.H., 160 S.W.3d 355 (Mo. 2005).

[49] Green Trees Enters., Inc. v. Palm Springs Alpine Estates, Inc., 66 Cal. 2d 782, 784, 59 Cal. Rptr. 141 (1967).

[50] *See* LINDA D. ELROD, CHILD CUSTODY PRACTICE AND PROCEDURE § 14:27 at 14-34 to14-41 (2004–2009).

[51] *See, e.g., In re* Melody L., 290 Conn. 131, 148, 962 A.2d 81 (2009).

[52] *In re* Stephanie M., 7 Cal. 4th 295, 318–19, 27 Cal. Rptr. 2d 595, 608 (1994), citations omitted; *see* LINDA D. ELROD, CHILD CUSTODY PRACTICE AND PROCEDURE § 14:27 (2004–2009).

[53] Jeff Atkinson, *Criteria for Deciding Child Custody in the Trial and Appellate Courts*, 18 FAM. L. Q. 1, 41, n. 180 (1984).

[54] *See, e.g., In re* A.M.H., 516 N.W.2d 867, 870 (Iowa 1994); *In re* T.A.L., 505 N.W.2d 480, 482 (Iowa 1993).

court's determination. The reviewing court "makes an original appraisal of all the evidence to decide whether or not it believes the outcome should have been different."[55] Chances for reversal are most favorable under this standard. Hence, try to phrase your issue as a question of law (e.g., that the trial court *failed to exercise its discretion* or *exercised its discretion based on an improper factor*) rather than simply that it *abused its discretion.*

Mixed Questions of Law and Fact

Mixed questions are those in which the facts are established, the law is undisputed, and the issue is whether the law as applied to the established facts is violated.[56] Some courts hold that a mixed question is reviewed as a question of law, while other courts hold that, if the findings of fact are supported by competent, substantial evidence, the reviewing court will review the application of law to those facts *de novo.*[57] California employs a three-step process.[58] "Mixed questions" in dependency cases include whether "active efforts" were used to prevent the breakup of an Indian family, whether counsel rendered ineffective assistance, and if a "final ruling on dependency" is legally correct and factually supported.[59]

§ 26.2.6 Standards of Prejudice

Harmless Error

The appellate court will not reverse a judgment merely because an error occurred, even an error of constitutional dimension. The error must have materially affected the outcome or the substantial rights of the parties, or resulted in a miscarriage of justice, i.e., it must have been *prejudicial* error. Otherwise, it will be deemed *harmless.* Thus if the trial judge committed an error but there is substantial evidence to support the judgment, the error will be deemed harmless, and the appellate court will permit the decision to stand.[60]

Harmless Beyond a Reasonable Doubt

Errors that violate the federal constitution are evaluated under the standard articulated in *Chapman v. California*:[61] reversal is required unless the error is shown

---

[55] *In re* George T., 33 Cal. 4th 620, 631–32, 93 P.3d 1007 (2004).

[56] Annotation, *Mixed Questions of Law and Fact*, 5 AM. JUR. 2D *Appellate Review* § 631 (updated May 2009) (citing People v. Kennedy, 36 Cal. 4th 595 (2005), *cert. denied*, 547 U.S. 1076, 126 S.Ct. 1781 (2006)).

[57] *Id.* (citing Hendrix v. State, 908 So. 2d 412, 419–20 (Fla. 2005)).

[58] *See, e.g.*, Ghirardo v. Antonioli, 8 Cal. 4th 791, 799–800, 35 Cal. Rptr. 2d 418 (1994).

[59] *See, e.g.*, E.A. v. State Div. of Family & Youth Servs., 46 P.3d 986, 989 (Alas. 2002); *In re* K.B., 173 Cal. App. 4th 1275, 1286, 93 Cal. Rptr. 3d 751 (2009); *In re* S.M., 997 So. 2d 513, 515 (Fla. App., 2 Dist. 2008); State v. Green, 350 Mont. 141, 145, 205 P.3d 798 (2009).

[60] *See, e.g.*, Goldman v. Logue, 461 So. 2d 469, 472–73 (La. Ct. App. 1984); People v. Watson, 46 Cal. 2d 818, 836, 299 P.2d 243 (1956).

[61] 386 U.S. 18 (1967), *reh'g denied*, 386 U.S. 987.

to have been harmless beyond a reasonable doubt.[62] This standard is applied in criminal cases, but also has been applied in dependency cases raising federal due process issues.[63]

Reversible Per Se

The United States Supreme Court has distinguished constitutional errors that are *trial errors*—that occur during the presentation of the case, the effect of which can "be quantitatively assessed in the context of other evidence presented in order to determine whether [they were] harmless beyond a reasonable doubt"—from "*structural defect[s]* affecting the framework within which the trial proceeds" that "defy analysis by harmless-error standards" and can never be harmless.[64] Structural defects require automatic reversal because they involve basic protections without which a criminal trial "cannot reliably serve its function to determine guilt or innocence."[65] A structural error requires reversal "without regard to the strength of the evidence or other circumstances."[66] Most structural errors arise in criminal cases,[67] although a few courts have invoked the doctrine in dependency and adoption cases, in most instances for egregious violations of a parent's due process rights.[68]

§ 26.3 While the Appeal is Pending: Stays and Supersedeas

§ 26.3.1 General Rules Regarding Stays

Filing an appeal vests jurisdiction in the appellate court over the order appealed from. It thereby divests the trial court of jurisdiction over that order and suspends its

---

[62] *Id.* at 22; *see also* United States v. Hasting, 461 U.S. 499, 509 (1983).

[63] *See, e.g., In re* Stacey T., 52 Cal. App. 4th 1415, 1416, 26 Cal. Rptr. 3d 394 (1997); *In re* Dolly D., 41 Cal. App. 4th 440, 446, 48 Cal. Rptr. 2d 691 (1995); *In re* Amy M., 232 Cal. App. 3d 849, 848, 283 Cal. Rptr. 788 (1991).

[64] Arizona v. Fulminante, 499 U.S. 279, 307–10 (1991).

[65] *Id. at* 310; *see also* Neder v. United States, 527 U.S. 1, 9 (1999).

[66] *In re* Enrique G., 140 Cal. App. 4th 676, 685, 44 Cal.Rptr.3d 724, 731 (2006).

[67] *See* Arizona v. Fulminante, 499 U.S. 279, 309–10 (1991); United States v. Gonzalez-Lopez, 548 U.S. 140, 126 S.Ct. 2557, 2565 (2006).

[68] *See, e.g., In re* Adoption of B.J.M., 42 Kan. App. 2d 77, 209 P.3d 200 (2009) (biological father's due process rights were violated when he was prohibited from personally attending hearing on stepfather's adoption petition; error was structural error, entitling father to automatic reversal of order granting the adoption); *In re* Marriage of Carlsson, 163 Cal. App. 4th 281, 311–12, 77 Cal. Rptr. 3d 305 (2008) (trial judge's act of abandoning divorce trial in the middle of husband's case-in-chief deprived him of due process rights and was structural error requiring reversal); *In re* Jasmine G., 127 Cal. App. 4th 1109, 1114–16, 26 Cal. Rptr. 3d 394 (2005) (termination of parental rights without notice of the hearing at which termination could occur was structural error requiring reversal); *In re* J.M.B., 296 Ga. App. 786, 676 S.E.2d 9, 12 (2009) (waiver of right to counsel at termination of parental rights hearing that was not knowing, intelligent, and voluntary calls into question the very structural integrity of the fact-finding process).

power to modify or vacate the order. Filing an appeal may also stay enforcement of the order.

At common law, filing an appeal automatically stayed the order appealed from. That is still the rule in some jurisdictions, even in custody cases.[69] Thus, some courts hold that the trial court loses jurisdiction to modify a custody order once an appeal has been filed; however, the *appellate court* has jurisdiction to entertain such a motion. Some hold that the trial court retains *continuing* jurisdiction to modify a prior custody order because the child is always deemed within its inherent (equitable) jurisdiction, whereas others hold that both trial and appellate courts have jurisdiction to modify a prior custody order.

If filing an appeal does *not* effect an automatic stay of a custody order, of course—as occurs in some states and in the federal courts—the appellant must seek a *discretionary* stay.[70] In California: "The perfecting of an appeal shall *not* stay proceedings as to those provisions of a judgment or order which award, change, or otherwise affect the custody, including the right of visitation, of a minor child in any civil action, in an action filed under the Juvenile Court Law, or in a special proceeding.... *However, the trial court may in its discretion stay execution of these provisions pending review on appeal....*"[71] The California statute has been construed to embrace the issuance of discretionary stays in dissolution, dependency, guardianship, visitation, and adoption cases.[72]

§ 26.3.2 When a Discretionary Stay Merits Consideration

A stay of a trial court's order pending appellate review "is one of the most extraordinary remedies that an appellate court may issue. The stay is imposed without a full hearing on the merits of the case, and it has the effect of suspending the operation of the order under review."[73] Indeed, it may be a critical step in the litigation, in that failure to seek a stay may result in the very harm the appealing party is seeking to avoid.

Thus, the ABA Standards provide that if a child client wishes to appeal the order and the appeal has merit, "the lawyer should take all steps necessary to perfect the

---

[69] *See, e.g.,* Skinner v. Skinner, 172 Ga. App. 609, 610, 323 S.E.2d 905 (1984).

[70] *See* John Y. Gotanda, *The Emerging Standards for Issuing Appellate Stays*, 45 BAYLOR L. REV. 809, 811 (1993).

[71] CAL. CIV. PROC. CODE § 917.7 (West 2002), italics added. The statute also provides for automatic stays of short periods for orders allowing or eliminating restrictions against removal of the child from the state, excepting orders brought pursuant to (a) the UCCJEA (CAL. FAM. CODE §§ 3400 *et seq.* (West 2000)), (b) the PKPA of 1980 (28 U.S.C. § 1738A), or (c) the Hague Convention (42 U.S.C. §§ 11601 *et seq.*).

[72] *See* 9 WITKIN, CALIFORNIA PROCEDURE 5th, Appeal § 225 (Thomson/West 2008).

[73] John Y. Gotanda, *The Emerging Standards for Issuing Appellate Stays*, 45 BAYLOR L. REV. 809, 809 (1993).

appeal and *seek appropriate temporary orders or extraordinary writs necessary to protect the interests of the child during the pendency of the appeal.*"[74]

§ 26.3.3 Requesting a Stay

The initial stay request should be filed in the trial court. Whether the court will grant a discretionary stay in a child custody case depends on the potential for harm to the children in the current situation and the probable merits of the appeal. Counsel should also seek a *temporary* stay pending the trial court's ruling on the stay request. The factors considered in ruling on a stay request include: (1) the likelihood of hardship or harm to the child if the stay is denied; (2) whether the appeal has probable merit and is taken in good faith; (3) the harm, if any, to the nonmoving party if a stay is granted; and (4) other equitable considerations.[75]

If the trial court denies a stay, the petitioner may seek a stay (or writ of supersedeas) in the appellate court. This application is necessarily a more formal process in that it must not only inform the appellate court of the pertinent facts, but also must make the requisite showing for a stay to issue. The burden of persuasion is also greater, the motion having already received full consideration by the trial judge.

An appellate court has the inherent jurisdiction to issue a stay pending the determination of the merits of an appeal. It is deemed an incident of its *appellate* jurisdiction. Some states refer to the application for such a stay as a *petition for a writ of supersedeas*. The effect of a stay is to preserve the status quo; hence, the reviewing court cannot stay a judgment that has already been executed.

§ 26.4 Procedural Steps in an Appeal[76]

§ 26.4.1 Notice of Appeal

The initial step in perfecting an appeal of right to an intermediate appellate court (or, in states without an intermediate appellate court, to the state's highest court) is to file a notice of appeal within the time limits set forth in the pertinent statute or rule of court. This notice is filed with the clerk of the trial court and, in many states, must be sent to the court to which the appeal is taken. The notice must identify the appealing party or parties, the court to which the appeal is taken, the order or judgment being appealed (or the specific portion thereof from which the appeal is taken), and the relief sought.

---

[74] AMERICAN BAR ASSOCIATION STANDARDS OF PRACTICE FOR LAWYERS WHO REPRESENT CHILDREN IN ABUSE AND NEGLECT CASES (1996); Standard F-1, italics added.

[75] LINDA D. ELROD, CHILD CUSTODY PRACTICE AND PROCEDURE § 14.14 at 14-25 (2004–2009) (citing Alpers v. Alpers, 806 P.2d 1057 (N.M. App. 1990)).

[76] For more detailed information, the reader is directed to the author's more complete discussion in ANN M. HARALAMBIE, 2 HANDLING CHILD CUSTODY, ABUSE AND ADOPTION CASES 3D §§ 23:34–23:43 (Thomson West 2009).

The time within which a notice of appeal must be filed varies. The average time limit is 30 days from the "date judgment is rendered," which may be the oral pronouncement of the ruling, the filing of the judgment by the clerk of the court, or the service of the judgment on the parties to the matter.[77] The time for filing may be extended by certain post-trial motions.

§ 26.4.2 Designation of Appellate Record

The appealing party is required to designate the record to be prepared by the clerk of the court. The required components of the appellate record (and the alternative means by which it may be provided) will be set forth in the rules of court. Generally speaking, you must file a copy of the judgment from which you appealed and the entire trial court record.

Appellee may also seek augmentation of the record and/or transmission of exhibits.

§ 26.4.3 Briefs

The appellant's opening brief is the foundational document in any appeal, the roadmap for the parties and the court in determining the merits of the matter. The opening brief identifies the issues, the authority on which appellant seeks relief, and his or her legal reasoning. Its importance cannot be overemphasized.

States do not follow a uniform briefing system; hence, counsel should follow the state rules on requirements for the opening brief. However, some components should always be included, namely: (a) a table of contents drafted as an outline of the legal argument, in declarative sentences, so that the judge or law clerk can quickly refer to a particular section of your brief; (b) a jurisdictional statement identifying the law, and facts, that "render this original action, or this appeal, properly brought before that court;"[78] (c) a statement succinctly phrasing the issues to be decided, often as questions; (d) a legal memorandum including in *each* section an explanation of the lower court ruling, your objection to it, the standard of review for that issue, an exposition of the pertinent law, and an application of the law to the facts of your case;[79] and (e) a conclusion reiterating the precise relief sought.

The brief of the appellee (or respondent) follows the same format as appellant's opening brief, but addresses every point raised by appellant to demonstrate that it lacks legal merit or is unpersuasive. Appellee presents the facts, the legal issues, and the discussion from "a perspective of *affirmance*, casting the case in a manner that

---

[77] Linda D. Elrod, Child Custody Practice and Procedure § 14.7 at 14-15 (2004–2009).

[78] Antonin Scalia & Bryan A. Garner, Making Your Case: The Art of Persuading Judges § 1 at 4 (2008).

[79] *See* Carmela Simoncini & Cheryl Geyerman, *A Quick Guide to Structuring a Logical Argument in a Dependency Case*, Appellate Defenders Issues (June 2001), *available at* http://www.adi-sandiego.com/newsletters/2001_june.pdf.

shows reversal is *not* warranted."[80] Appellee is entitled to the benefit of the prejudicial error rule; hence he or she will generally urge that any error was harmless. More judgments are probably affirmed on the basis of harmless error than on any other ground.

Some jurisdictions permit appellant to file a reply to appellee's brief. New issues may not be raised in a reply; hence, reply briefs are effectively organized by paraphrasing appellant's premise and appellee's answer as to each issue, then explaining why appellee's answer is incorrect, misplaced, or irrelevant. Ideally, the reply brief is a "self-contained document, comprehensible without any reference to earlier writings. Why? Because many judges and law clerks have developed the habit of reading briefs in reverse order: reply first, then the responding brief, then the appellant's initial brief. . . . Assume that the judge has only your reply brief in hand. Do not send the judge to your adversary's brief to understand what the case is about."[81]

§ 26.4.4 Oral Argument

Appeals are generally won or lost on the briefs. Nonetheless, oral argument is the only opportunity for a dialogue between the parties and the justices who will decide the case. Parties are not required to exercise the right to oral argument; however, an appellant who waives oral argument might send the message that the appeal is unimportant or hopeless.

The chance of obtaining oral argument varies. Some courts clearly favor argument, while others clearly disfavor it.[82] The trend in both state and federal appellate courts is to dispense with oral argument.[83] Thus, if you are granted argument, know your case inside and out, and prepare with precise goals in mind: (1) identifying and addressing the court's concerns; (2) answering the court's questions; (3) focusing on the decisive points; and (4) presenting a broader picture, including policy issues.

§ 26.4.5 Petition for Rehearing

If the decision of the Court of Appeal is adverse to your client, you may wish to petition for rehearing. Petitions for rehearing are usually denied, some with a slight modification of the opinion. Nonetheless, there are three things that get a reviewing court's attention in a petition for rehearing: that the court (a) misstated a fact, (b) mis-cited a case, or (c) erred in its legal analysis. Also, if you intend to petition for

---

[80] Jon B. Eisenberg, Ellis J. Horvitz & Justice Howard B. Wiener, California Practice Guide: Civil Appeals and Writs § 9:68 at 9-22–9.22.1 (2009).

[81] Antonin Scalia & Bryan A. Garner, Making Your Case: The Art of Persuading Judges § 34 at 73-74 (2008).

[82] Ruggero J. Aldisert, Winning on Appeal: Better Briefs and Oral Argument § 1.4 at 16 (2d ed. 2003).

[83] Robert L. Stern, Appellate Practice in the United States § 13.1 at 368, n. 17 (2d ed. 1989).

discretionary review in the state's highest court, a petition for rehearing is recommended to demonstrate that you have exhausted all other available remedies.

§ 26.4.6 Petition for Certiorari or Discretionary Review

Review of the decision of the intermediate appellate court is generally sought by filing a petition for discretionary review in the state's highest court within the period set in the rules of court. The period most frequently chosen is 30 days from the judgment of the intermediate court.[84]

Brevity and conciseness are the watchwords for cert petitions. The factors considered by most courts in determining whether to grant discretionary review are the general importance of the question presented, the existence of a conflict between the decision sought to be reviewed and a decision of either the Supreme Court or of another division of the intermediate court, and the need for the exercise of the Supreme Court's supervisory authority.[85]

A petition seeking discretionary review should limit the number of questions presented and focus on their importance as matters of law. "To have a significant chance of success, you must show that the error you complain of consisted in the adoption of an erroneous rule of law, not merely the erroneous application of a rule correctly expressed."[86] If review is granted in the state's highest court, additional briefs are submitted to address the merits of the questions to be decided.

§ 26.4.7 Role of Amicus Curiae

An effective way to demonstrate that a case presents an issue worthy of the scrutiny of the state's highest court is for letters amici curiae to be filed in support of granting certiorari and, if review is granted, amicus briefs in support of one's position on the merits.[87] One recent study, which focused on a random sample of certiorari petitions in the U.S. Supreme Court, found that "when the United States does not participate at the certiorari stage . . . , the participation of *amicus* increased the acceptance rate from 8.5 percent to 26.7 percent."[88]

If you are writing an amicus brief, heed the admonition in Supreme Court Rule 37: "An *amicus curiae* brief that brings to the attention of the Court relevant matter not already brought to its attention by the parties may be of considerable help to the

---

[84] *Id.* at § 6.7(b) at 154–55.

[85] Gerald B. Cope, Jr., *Discretionary Review of the Decisions of Intermediate Appellate Courts: A Comparison of Florida's System With Those of the Other States and the Federal System*, 45 FLA. L. REV. 21, 46–62 (1993).

[86] ANTONIN SCALIA & BRYAN A. GARNER, MAKING YOUR CASE: THE ART OF PERSUADING JUDGES § 34 at 77 (2008).

[87] *See* Kent L. Richland, *Taming the Odds: Increasing the Chances of Getting Relief from the Supreme Court*, 5 CALIFORNIA LITIGATION 8 (Winter 1992).

[88] ROBERT L. STERN, EUGENE GRESSMAN & STEPHEN M. SHAPIRO, SUPREME COURT PRACTICE § 6.4 at 465 (8th ed. 2002)

Court. An *amicus curiae* brief that does not serve this purpose burdens the Court, and its filing is not favored."[89]

§ 26.5 Procedural Steps in Traditional Writ Proceeding[90]

§ 26.5.1 Writ Petition and Record

The petition to a reviewing court for issuance of any writ within its original jurisdiction is an original pleading filed in the appellate court. It is generally required to conform as far as possible to the rules applicable to briefs on appeal; however, there are some significant differences, namely: (1) the statement of facts is usually drafted as enumerated allegations of ultimate fact—including allegations identifying the parties, setting forth the facts of the case, the action taken by the lower court, and allegations showing the basis for writ relief (inadequate remedy at law and irreparable harm if writ denied); (2) statements in the petition are followed by citations to the writ record, *viz.*, the exhibits assembled by petitioner and attached to the petition or filed under separate cover; and (3) the petition must include a personal verification by either counsel or the petitioner and a prayer identifying the relief sought, *viz.*, an alternative or peremptory writ, or both, and must indicate whether the petitioner seeks a temporary stay.

§ 26.5.2 Alternatives Available to the Reviewing Court

Appellate courts are generally afforded maximum flexibility in responding to writ petitions on their individual basis; however, when an appellate court receives such a petition, it has three basic alternatives—each of which sets in motion its own procedural sequence.

- *If the petition appears facially without merit*, the court may deny it summarily, before or after receiving preliminary or formal opposition. The usual reason for a summary denial is failure to provide the court with a record sufficient to review the claims made.

- *If the petition makes a prima facie case for relief*, the court may request the filing of briefs or a formal answer, set the case for oral argument, and dispose of the matter in whatever manner seems appropriate.[91] In traditional writ terminology, it may issue an *alternative writ*, which commands the respondent to comply with the prayer of the petition or to show cause why it should not be ordered to do so. This order is an implicit command to the real party in interest to file an answer to the

---

[89] SUP. CT. R. 37(1).

[90] For more detailed information, the reader is directed to the author's more complete discussion in ANN M. HARALAMBIE, 2 HANDLING CHILD CUSTODY, ABUSE AND ADOPTION CASES 3D §§ 23:44–23:47 (Thomson West 2009).

[91] *See* ROBERT L. STERN, APPELLATE PRACTICE IN THE UNITED STATES § 4.7 at 98 (2d ed. 1989).

petition, called a *return*.[92] If the court determines after briefing and perhaps argument that the petitioner is entitled to relief, it will discharge the alternative writ and issue a *peremptory writ* requiring the performance of the act sought to be enforced.

- *If petitioner is entitled to relief based on the petition alone*, the court may grant a peremptory writ in the first instance, generally after having given notice to opposing parties of its intent to do so. This relief is granted "only when petitioner's entitlement to relief is so obvious that no purpose could reasonably be served by plenary consideration of the issue—for example, when such entitlement is conceded or when there has been clear error under well-settled principles of law and undisputed facts—or when there is an unusual urgency requiring acceleration of the normal process."[93]

§ 26.5.3 Responses Available to Real Party In Interest

When a real party in interest is served with a traditional writ petition, he or she may:

- *File no response at all* if the petition seems facially without merit.

- *File an unsolicited preliminary opposition*, particularly if the petition seems persuasive or contains factual inaccuracies.

- *File a formal opposition or "return"* after the reviewing court has issued an alternative writ. An alternative writ commands the respondent to perform the act sought in the writ petition or to show cause why it should not be compelled to do so. If the respondent chooses to comply with the order, the petition will be dismissed as moot. Otherwise, respondent or real party must show cause, by filing a responsive pleading, why the relief sought in the petition should not be granted. Hence, if respondent chooses not to comply, the respondent and/or real party must file a formal opposition or "return."

The "return" consists of enumerated responses to the allegations of the petition, each in the form of a verified answer, demurrer, or both, The due date for the return is usually specified in the order issuing the alternative writ; if not, file the return within a reasonable period of time after issuance of alternative writ or notice that the court is considering issuing a peremptory writ in the first instance.

---

[92] *See, e.g.*, FED. R. APP. P. 21(b)(1).

[93] Ng v. Superior Court, 4 Cal. 4th 29, 35, 13 Cal. Rptr. 2d 856 (1992).

§ 26.5.4 Oral Argument and Discretionary Review

If the intermediate court summarily denies the writ petition, the petitioner has no right to oral argument, and the order is usually final immediately. The petitioner will have a set period of time within which to seek discretionary review in the highest court.

If the intermediate court issues an alternative writ and receives opposition, petitioner may seek leave to file a reply, and the parties will generally have the right to argument and a written decision on the merits of the case. From the decision on the merits, the petitioner will generally have the same right to seek discretionary review as he or she did from a decision on the merits in an appeal.

§ 26.6 Informing the Court of Post-Judgment Events

§ 26.6.1 When Post-Judgment Evidence Becomes an Issue

As a general rule, an appellate court reviews the correctness of a judgment at the time of its rendition, upon a record of matters that were before the trial court and factual determinations made by the lower court. However, there are exceptions. If the appeal is mooted by subsequent events, for example, it is subject to dismissal. Counsel is required to inform the appellate court of any such event.[94] "Since the absence of a controversy is jurisdictional, the point is not one that counsel may waive or disregard by stipulation."[95] But note that appellate courts have the discretion to review technically moot questions presenting important questions of public interest that tend to evade review.[96]

Post-judgment events may also undermine the basis of the judgment or demonstrate that any error was harmless. A reviewing court "'cannot simply unwind a juvenile case and presume that circumstances cannot have changed in the interim. They always do.'"[97] In appropriate circumstances, such facts too must be brought to the attention of the appellate court.

§ 26.6.2 Bringing Post-Judgment Evidence to the Court's Attention

Post-judgment evidence may be brought to the attention of the appellate court by several means, each of which is discussed below.

---

[94] *See, e.g.*, Fusari v. Steinberg, 419 U.S. 379, 391 (1975) (Burger, C.J., concurring).

[95] ROBERT L. STERN, EUGENE GRESSMAN & STEPHEN M. SHAPIRO, SUPREME COURT PRACTICE § 18.4 at 828 (8th ed. 2002).

[96] *See, e.g., In re* William M., 3 Cal. 3d 16, 23, 89 Cal. Rptr. 33 (1970); Shannon by Shannon v. Hansen, 469 N.W.2d 412, 414 (Iowa 1991); Arnold v. Lebel, 941 A.2d 813, 818–19 (R.I. 2007); State v. G.A.H., 133 Wash. App. 567, 572–73, 137 P.3d 66 (2006).

[97] *In re* Isayah C., 118 Cal. App. 4th 684, 701, 13 Cal. Rptr. 3d 198 (2004) (quoting *In re* S. D., 99 Cal. App. 4th 1068, 1083, 121 Cal. Rptr. 2d 518 (2002)).

Motion to Take Judicial Notice

"The taking of judicial notice of a fact outside of the record is part of the inherent power and function of every court, whether a trial or appellate tribunal."[98] A judicially noticeable fact is one "not subject to reasonable dispute in that it is either (1) generally known within the territorial jurisdiction of the trial court or (2) capable of accurate and ready determination by resort to sources whose accuracy cannot reasonably be questioned."[99]

Note: Judicial notice is taken of *adjudicative facts*, those relevant to that particular case.[100] *A court is not restricted in taking judicial notice of legislative facts*, "those which have relevance to legal reasoning and the lawmaking process, whether in the formulation of a legal principle or ruling by a judge or court or in the enactment of a legislative body."[101] Thus, in *Muller v. Oregon*,[102] the U.S. Supreme Court relied on scientific writings demonstrating that long working hours were detrimental to women's health to uphold an Oregon law fixing maximum working hours for women.[103]

Motion to Take Additional Evidence

Some states permit appellate courts to take additional evidence of facts that may not be subject to judicial notice. For example, in Tennessee, a reviewing court has the discretion on its own motion or the motion of a party "to consider facts concerning the action that occurred after judgment."[104] Consideration generally will extend only to those facts, capable of ready demonstration, affecting the positions of the parties or the subject matter of the action such as mootness, bankruptcy, divorce, death, other judgments or proceedings, relief from the judgment requested or granted in the trial court and other similar matters.[105] In Washington, the appellate court may direct that additional evidence on the merits of the case be taken if six conditions are met.[106] In New Jersey, a provision of the state constitution has been construed to confer "a broader power in non-jury cases to admit incontrovertible evidence in aid of the final disposition of the controversy between the parties."[107] Similarly, in Louisiana, the general rule is "relaxed where facts occurring subsequent to the appeal are not denied. . . . [I]t would serve no useful purpose to remand a case for the purpose of

---

[98] ROBERT L. STERN, APPELLATE PRACTICE IN THE UNITED STATES § 10.12(a) at 276 (2d ed. 1989).

[99] FED. R. EVID. 201(b).

[100] FED. R. EVID. 201(a).

[101] ROBERT L. STERN, APPELLATE PRACTICE IN THE UNITED STATES § 10.12(a) at 277 (2d ed. 1989).

[102] 208 U.S. 412 (1908).

[103] *Id.* at 420–21; *see also* Planned Parenthood of Central Missouri v. Danforth, 428 U.S. 52, 71 (1976).

[104] TENN. R. APP. P. 14(b).

[105] TENN. R. APP. P. 14(a).

[106] WASH. R. APP. P. 9.11(a).

[107] Ballurio v. Castellini, 28 N.J. Super. 368, 373, 100 A.2d 678 (1953).

offering evidence in the court below of facts which are not denied."[108] California too permits appellate courts to take additional evidence in non-jury cases.[109] Although the California Supreme Court has disapproved using unsworn statements of counsel as "evidence" to reverse an order terminating parental rights,[110] it has approved considering post-judgment facts to "expedite the proceedings and promot[e] the finality of the juvenile courts orders."[111] Thus, California courts routinely consider post-judgment evidence in dependency cases for purposes other than reversing an order terminating parental rights.[112]

Motion to Dismiss Appeal: Fugitive Disentitlement Rule

Appellate courts have the discretion to dismiss an appeal of one who is a fugitive from justice during the pendency of the appeal, or who has refused to comply with the court's orders. "Courts employ the fugitive dismissal rule because of 'the difficulty of enforcement against one not willing to subject himself to the court's authority, the inequity of allowing that 'fugitive' to use the resources of the courts only if the outcome is an aid to him, the need to avoid prejudice to the nonfugitive party, and the discouragement of flights from justice.'"[113]

§ 26.7 Conclusion

Those who practice child welfare law are acutely aware of the inadequacy of the published case law. As a result, the same issues are perennially relitigated, often with different results, necessarily leaving some clients' rights along the way. The challenge is for those of us in the practice to bring unresolved legal questions to the attention of appellate courts and to support others in doing so by participating in important cases as amici curiae.

---

[108] Wilson v. Wilson, 205 La. 196, 203–04, 17 So.2d 249, 251 (1944).

[109] CAL. CIV. PROC. CODE § 909.

[110] *In re* Zeth S., 31 Cal. 4th 396, 73 P.3d 541 (2003).

[111] *In re* Josiah Z., 36 Cal. 4th 664, 676, 115 P.3d 1133, 1138 (2005).

[112] *See, e.g., In re* A.B., 164 Cal. App. 4th 832, 840–43, 79 Cal. Rptr. 3d 580 (2008); *In re* B.D., 159 Cal. App. 4th 1218, 1240–41, 72 Cal. Rptr. 3d 153 (2008); *In re* Sabrina H. 149 Cal. App. 4th 1403, 1417, 57 Cal. Rptr. 3d 863 (2007); *In re* Salvador M., 133 Cal. App. 4th 1415, 1421–22, 35 Cal. Rptr. 3d 577 (2005); *In re* Marina S.,132 Cal. App. 4th 158, 166, 33 Cal. Rptr. 3d 220 (2005); *In re* Karen G.,121 Cal. App. 4th 1384, 1390, 18 Cal. Rptr. 3d 301 (2004).

[113] Colombe v. Carlson, 757 N.W.2d 537, 540 (N.D. 2008) (quoting Moscona v. Shenhar, 50 Va. App. 238, 649 S.E.2d 191, 197 (2007)).

IV. THE ROLE AND DUTIES OF LEGAL COUNSEL

Chapter 27: Agency Attorneys and Caseworkers: Working Well Together[*]

by Mimi Laver[1]

§ 27.1 Introduction

How often have you heard:

Agency Attorney:

"Those social workers are so 'touchy/feely' they can't give the judge concrete facts?" or "The workers are always 'in the field,' where is that!?"

Child Welfare Agency Caseworker:

"Our agency attorneys are so arrogant and emotionally distant . . . ?" and "The attorneys care more about winning the case than about the kids?"

Attorney and Caseworker:

"They never return my call?" or "They just don't understand what I do . . . ?"

---

[*] This chapter was adapted from MIMI LAVER, FOUNDATIONS FOR SUCCESS: STRENGTHENING YOUR AGENCY ATTORNEY OFFICE (American Bar Association 1999):

Copyright 1999 by American Bar Association.
Mimi Laver
Director Legal Education
ABA Center on Children and the Law
740 15th St. NW
Washington, DC 20005
http://newabanet.org/child/
202-662-1720
Reprinted by permission.

Nonsubstantive changes were made to the text and formatting to reflect the style of this publication. Section numbers have also been added to reflect the style of this publication.

[1] Mimi Laver, J.D., is the Director of Legal Education at the ABA Center on Children and the Law, Washington, D.C. She previously was a Deputy City Solicitor representing the Department of Human Services and the Department of Health in Philadelphia, Pennsylvania.

As an agency attorney representing the Department of Human Services in Philadelphia, I often heard these kinds of comments. At times I felt like a cruise director: trying to keep caseworkers and attorneys happy by coordinating their activities and helping them work together better. Sometimes, "cheerleading" about working as a team would improve life, but usually just for a little while. What we needed was some real effort and communication to improve our relationships.

If you also hear these gripes in the halls of your office, read on for a "beyond cheerleading" discussion of ways to ease the tensions in attorney-caseworker relationships and to form positive working teams. There's more to it than saying, "Let's all be friends . . ."

§ 27.2 Roles of Attorneys and Social Workers

§ 27.2.1 Defining the Client

As an agency attorney, it is important that you identify who your client is. Many conflicts between attorneys and social workers stem from a misunderstanding of who the attorney represents. The models of agency representation vary by jurisdiction and should be defined by your state's law. Attorneys may be employed by local prosecutor's offices, state attorney general offices, local civil litigation offices, or the agency itself. Additionally, some agencies hire special prosecutors or contract attorneys.[2] If you are uncertain what your state legislation dictates, your state attorney general or comparable office should be able to advise.

Within each model, the view of who the client is differs. Some attorneys represent the agency as an entity, relying on the caseworker's opinions, but keeping the interests of the agency in mind at all times, and some, as in the prosecutor model, represent the "people." Each has its strengths and weaknesses.

If you represent the agency as an entity, as I did in my previous practice, there are two considerations. Sometimes the caseworkers feel the attorneys disregard their wishes, and do not represent them aggressively in court. What happens is the agency attorneys try to be mindful of agency policy, while listening to the individual caseworker's viewpoint. Sometimes the interests of the agency differ from those of individual caseworkers. Because the attorney represents the agency, not individual caseworkers, the attorney must defer to the agency.

The other concern is that if caseworkers make serious errors that conflict with agency policy and a contempt proceeding is held, the caseworkers' union attorney has to represent the caseworker, while the agency attorney represents the agency. In my experience, the benefits of this model outweighed the problems. We were able to

---

[2] Donald N. Duquette, *Lawyers' Roles in Child Protection*, *in* THE BATTERED CHILD (Mary Edna Helfer et al. eds., 5th ed. 1997); Henry J. Plum, *Legal Representation of Agencies Presentation Outline*, June 15-17, 1998.

consistently represent agency policy while advocating for the caseworkers' positions in court.

Several concerns about the prosecutor model make this method of representation particularly problematic. Often, the attorneys in these offices are new and choose to work in the prosecutor's office to practice criminal law. They rotate out of dependency cases quickly, and therefore never get proper training. As a result, the caseworkers often feel the representation is inadequate. Additionally, with this method the attorneys generally get the final word on whether a petition should be filed. This leaves the caseworker feeling as if his or her professional opinion is not considered. They may also fear that with attorneys making decisions about the caseworkers' clients, best social work practice will be ignored. The National Association of Social Workers (NASW) *Standards for Social Work Practice* in child protection set out· "The initiation of court action is an agency team decision requiring legal counsel and legal representation."[3] In the prosecutor model of representation, the collaborative decision-making process can get lost and can cause tension between you and the caseworker.

No matter which model your jurisdiction uses, it is important for you to identify the relationship with your client.[4] Further, it is important for your client to understand the scope of your representation.

§ 27.2.2 Remember Your Obligations

No matter who your client is, there are certain ethical obligations you have in your practice. You may need to communicate these rules to the caseworker from time to time. Your primary responsibility is as follows: "A lawyer shall provide competent representation to a client. Competent representation requires the legal knowledge, skill, thoroughness and preparation reasonably necessary for the representation."[5] Further, "[i]n representing a client, a lawyer shall exercise independent professional judgment and render candid advice. In rendering advice, a lawyer may refer not only to law but to other considerations such as moral, economic, social and political factors, which may be relevant to the client's situation."[6] As an agency attorney, you will often be asked to act as an advisor. You must provide the best counsel possible and then allow your client to reach a decision.

Often, attorneys worry that if the caseworkers are making major decisions about a case, the attorneys will be forced to do something unethical. If you and the caseworker or supervisor disagree about a decision, you have an obligation to try to work out a solution that is comfortable for you and the client. You are bound by the

---

[3]   NASW STANDARDS FOR SOCIAL WORK PRACTICE IN CHILD PROTECTION, Standard 21 (NASW 1997).

[4]   *See* MODEL RULES OF PROF'L CONDUCT R. 1.13 and cmt. (2009) ("A lawyer employed or retained by an organization [including a governmental organization] represents the organization acting through its duly authorized constituents.").

[5]   MODEL RULES OF PROF'L CONDUCT R. 1.1.

[6]   MODEL RULES OF PROF'L CONDUCT R. 2.1.

Model Rules of Professional Conduct, however, and may not act in an unethical manner. Generally, if you and your client discuss the matter, you will be able to reach a mutually acceptable outcome.

§ 27.2.3 Define Responsibilities

Decide which tasks you should handle and which should be handled by the caseworker. Decide what jobs should be shared. Deciding who has what responsibilities and sticking with it often causes tension in the attorney-caseworker relationship. Deciding together can make your team operate more smoothly.

Use the list of responsibilities in Section 27.8 when deciding who should handle various duties. Your needs may be different, and you may have additional tasks that should be considered when you and the caseworkers divide the workload.

You and the caseworkers should make your own list of jobs and openly discuss who should have primary responsibility for each. Consider creating protocols for some of the ongoing responsibilities you share. With the written protocol for termination petitions, for example, you, your staff, and the caseworker will have guidance about what jobs you must each complete and timeframes for completion.

§ 27.2.4 Decide Who Calls the Shots

Once you have defined your responsibilities, you and the caseworkers need to decide who makes the decisions. Some will be fairly obvious. For example, if an issue clearly involves a legal strategy, you get to make the final decision.[7] Similarly, if the question concerns social work or family specific treatment, the caseworker, on behalf of the agency, calls the shots. Most questions though, are not so clearly defined. Your strong communication and teamwork will be needed to discuss the issue with the caseworker and try to resolve the issue in a manner that satisfies both of your goals.

Additionally, you will need to keep in mind the answer to the "who is my client?" question. Generally, your client will be the agency and not the caseworker. You and the agency administration should have a system in place to resolve conflicts between you and individual caseworkers. Sometimes just having a calm conversation with the caseworker and both of your supervisors can help. Sometimes the issue has systemic impact, and the head of the agency needs to make the decision. If a dispute resolution system is implemented before a major conflict, none of the players will be offended if the system is used.[8] There are times when you will need to talk with the caseworker's supervisor for clarification. This should not be viewed as "tattling" on the caseworker, but as part of the process to improve and expand the team.

---

[7] *See* MODEL RULES OF PROF'L CONDUCT R. 1.2 and cmt.

[8] Donald N. Duquette, *Lawyers' Roles in Child Protection, in* THE BATTERED CHILD, 471–72 (Mary Edna Helfer et al. eds., 5th ed. 1997). *See also* Gene D. Skarin, *The Role of the Child Protective Agency's Attorney in Family Court*, 171 PLI/CRIM 431, 440–41 (1995).

§ 27.2.5 Think About Roles During Non-Adversarial Case Resolution

Many jurisdictions have or are working on implementing some form of non-adversarial case resolution such as mediation or family group decision-making into their systems. While these practices have proven effective in empowering families, helping them feel more engaged in the case, and improving permanency outcomes, changing the way a system operates is difficult. Many child welfare professionals, agency attorneys and caseworkers included, are hesitant to move away from a traditional adversarial system. In the video "Pathways to Permanency: Dependency Mediation" "an *agency attorney* admits she was skeptical when mediation was first introduced in her jurisdiction: 'It was something that was very new. I think as lawyers there's always a sense and fear that you're going to lose some control—that is something you work very hard to have in a trial process to make the case go the way you want it to.'"[9] During the video, and in jurisdictions around the country, professionals have found the positives for families, and the court system overall, become more important than the initial concerns.

For the agency attorney, caseworker, and agency director, the implementation of a new practice provides an excellent time to work together to identify each person's role and the overarching values the agency has about families and how to best work with them. As a group you can decide what your responsibilities will be during the non-adversarial case resolution. You and the other stakeholders should think through some of these questions while setting up your system:

- Will you and the other attorneys be in the room?
- Will you play a role in leading the session?
- Will you and the caseworker have time to confer during the session?
- If you and the caseworker are not satisfied with the outcome, what will happen?

Even if you and the agency are nervous about moving away from a traditional adversarial system, as you think about the outcomes you want for your children and their families, you may realize this new way of doing business will serve everyone's needs most effectively. Work with the agency, court, other attorneys and families to craft a system that works well for all of you.

§ 27.3 Need for Collaboration

As an agency attorney, you need good relationships with child welfare agency caseworkers to best serve children in the system. When you and the workers are busy complaining, your ability to work as a team and handle cases effectively and

---

[9] Claire Sandt, *You Want Me to . . . Mediate!?*, 20 CHILD L. PRAC. 42 (2001).

efficiently suffers. As a result, your cases may not be prepared thoroughly for court, your frustration about your job may increase, and the children on your caseload may remain in foster care longer than they should.

There are several characteristics of a strong working relationship: communication, mutual respect, trust, and teamwork.

§ 27.3.1 Communication

Open communication is a basic element of any good relationship. It is no different when working with caseworkers. Communicating effectively requires returning phone calls promptly, asking questions, addressing differences of opinion, and making time to talk about cases. Caseworkers should expect this of you and you of them.

Work with the caseworkers to devise a workable communication system. Do you all have e-mail, and are you using it? Is this a way to communicate that would save time and be reliable? Do you have an inter-office mail system? Are there mutually agreed upon times that you could be available to answer questions? Explore what, if any, complaints you each have about availability and level of communication, and then, together, find ways to improve. When you are all communicating, there is less likelihood that you will arrive in court not knowing what the caseworker's position is or what needs to be done for the child.

§ 27.3.2 Mutual Respect

Attorneys and caseworkers are both professionals with specific areas of expertise. You both have particular tasks to perform on all cases and are essential to a positive outcome in the case. Often, attorneys and caseworkers express that members of the other profession do not value their opinions and do not treat them courteously. When there is a lack of respect, incorrect assumptions about the other group emerge and add to negative feelings. It is essential that you each learn about the other's backgrounds and job responsibilities. With greater understanding of each other, an increased respect will grow.

§ 27.3.3 Trust

In addition to respect, you and the caseworkers need to trust each other. If you are a new attorney, it can be difficult to gain the trust of the caseworkers. The caseworkers may believe you do not know the answers to questions or are too new to advocate aggressively on their behalf. If you consistently provide good advice and perform well in court, the caseworkers will develop trust.

If you are an experienced attorney and have gained the caseworker's trust, keeping it requires that you are consistent and honest. When a trusting relationship exists, the caseworkers are more likely to call you with questions rather than acting first and then asking. Similarly, when you trust the caseworkers, you will have greater confidence in the cases you present in court.

§ 27.3.4 Teamwork

Out of the communication, respect, and trust comes a sense of teamwork.[10] When you and the caseworker know what the other person has been doing on a case, know what the other person thinks about the case, and value the other person's viewpoint, the case will be its strongest, and the child will benefit. Even if you and the caseworker do not agree about parts of the case, as a team you will be able to reach a mutually satisfactory decision. If you are functioning as a team, your representation will be its best, and the caseworker's efforts for the family will be most effective.

§ 27.4 Strengthening the Relationship

To improve the attorney-caseworker relationship, you need to talk and have more contact with each other. You and the caseworkers are probably overloaded in managing your day-to-day work, and the idea of trainings or group discussions may not be a pleasant one. However, taking time now will help improve the team for the long-term.

§ 27.4.1 Informal Sessions

Find Shared Beliefs

Meet with caseworkers and agency administrators to eliminate existing barriers and identify common goals. You will probably all realize that you share the ideal of improving the lives of children, parents, and families in your community, and working through your differences may become easier with this understanding.

The NASW Standards for Social Work Practice in Child Protection delineate specific values that are central to improving the child welfare system and the lives of children and families. These include:

- Recognizing the dignity of the child.
- Commitment to the child's family.
- Promoting permanent and consistent care for children.
- Recognizing people's capacity to change.[11]

Child welfare attorneys generally share these ideals and the caseworkers need to know that.

Facilitate in Comfort

Ask a neutral person with experience controlling discussions to facilitate a series of sessions that allow participants to express concerns and work towards concrete

---

[10] See Janet Weinstein, *And Never the Twain Shall Meet: The Best Interests of Children and the Adversary System*, 52 U. MIAMI L. REV. 79, 159 (Oct. 1997).

[11] NASW STANDARDS FOR SOCIAL WORK PRACTICE IN CHILD PROTECTION, Standard 2 and cmt.

remedies. If you do not have a person in your department with this kind of experience, consider contacting your local university's marketing department for referrals. Meet in a comfortable room. You and the caseworkers can alternate as hosts if your offices are not in the same place.

Be Concrete

These discussions may start as gripe-and-complaint sessions, but sometimes it is necessary for people to express their frustrations before being able to form positive resolutions. If complaining is permitted, the facilitator should set ground rules. For instance, names should not be used to bad mouth one another.

As an example of the need to be concrete, I remember an experience when I was an attorney in Philadelphia. The caseworkers and attorneys in my office attempted to have some sessions focused on improving our relationships. The attorneys often found them frustrating because there was too much talking with too few concrete results. While we cared how the caseworkers felt about us and the court process, we were more interested in trying to "fix" the problems right away. Needless to say, we were unable to do so without also talking about our view of the system and really listening to what the caseworkers were sharing. Similarly, the process could not work without the caseworkers joining us in trying to think of practical ways to improve our relationships.

Understand Each Others' Languages

There needs to be an understanding that, in general, attorneys and social workers think about things differently. They do not always use the same language. Attorneys are taught and are generally good at "multi-tasking," while caseworkers concentrate on single tasks, such as working on specific goals with a family. Attorneys often look at things on a macro or system level, while caseworkers focus on the child or family level. Attorneys have good intuitive adversarial skills, while caseworkers have intuitive social skills. These social skills are necessary for good social work, but may not be useful when it comes to testifying in a courtroom where the adversarial skills come in handy. Additionally, attorneys are not trained in social work practice while in law school, and caseworkers learn very little about the law during their educations. The law is pervasive in the child welfare system, which may be frustrating for caseworkers who focus on helping a family.[12] To improve the relationships, attorneys and caseworkers must acknowledge these differences and try to learn each others' languages.

---

[12] Telephone interview with Melissa Mitchell, J.D., General Counsel, Franklin County Children Services, Columbus, Ohio based on her discussions with the in-house attorneys at Franklin County Children Services, July 14, 1998.

Share Basic Information

Often attorneys and caseworkers complain that the other group does not understand what they do or their roles. During discussion sessions you could talk about how you came to your positions and what your jobs entail. A caseworker could describe a home visit and the feelings that accompany removing a child from the home. You could discuss how you prepare for a contested hearing and the difficulties involved when you get attached to one of the children. Let the workers know that "lawyers have feelings too!"

Reach Outcomes

You are busy and so are the caseworkers, but try not to let the discussions end until you have realized some positive outcomes. Other areas in which protocols could help are:

- When attorneys should attend meetings between the caseworker and a family.
- The expected responsibilities of the attorneys and workers in preparing a solid case for court.
- Procedures about disclosure of records to other attorneys on the case.
- When it is alright, and when it is not, for caseworkers to communicate with children's and parents' attorneys.
- Implementing an information system to inform everyone about changes in staff, law, and policy.
- How workers and attorneys will communicate: e-mail, written memos, telephone conferencing.
- What the dispute resolution system is and when it will be used.

If not all attorneys and caseworkers attend the sessions, develop a way to share the protocols and the other new approaches with the rest of the staff.

§ 27.4.2 Interdisciplinary Training

In addition to informal sessions, it is helpful for you and the caseworkers to attend substantive trainings in areas that relate to both of your practices. By participating in training together, you will all have the same knowledge base. You will also benefit from spending time together outside the courtroom. While interdisciplinary training cannot resolve all of the issues between you and the caseworkers and it will not provide you with all of the strictly legal knowledge that you need, it is an excellent way for all to develop their skills and knowledge.

Topics to consider for training include:

- Invite a local judge to discuss court practice, the type of testimony he or she prefers, what should be included in a petition, and his or her view of how the court process relates to the child welfare system as a whole.

- Invite a local doctor or other medical expert to talk about the medical evidence that points to abuse, factitious disorder (also known as Munchausen Syndrome by Proxy), failure to thrive, and other medical issues that relate to child welfare. The discussion can also focus on the ethical decisions involved when a parent withholds medical treatment for religious reasons.

- Have a psychiatrist or psychologist discuss mental health diagnoses and the implications for parents and foster children who suffer from the disorders.

- Learn about the substance abuse programs available in your community and how they can be accessed for the children and their parents.[13]

- Learn about other family preservation and reunification services, including special housing programs and how they are used to try to keep families together.

- Explore different ways to use relatives in achieving permanency, and familiarize yourself with local, state and federal law and policy on kinship care.

- Conduct a trial skills program which could include instruction for the caseworker about being a good witness, and practice for the attorneys on direct and cross examination, as well as other evidentiary issues.

§ 27.4.3 Multidisciplinary Teams

In Washington, the agency attorneys and caseworkers have improved their relationships and their effectiveness in cases through two types of multidisciplinary meetings. First, for children, especially young children under three years of age, who have been in foster care for three months, the agency has a prognostic staffing meeting. An attorney attends, and the team reviews the case to determine whether a concurrent plan should be implemented. The caseworkers appreciate having the attorney attend and have found these meetings help reduce the time the child remains in foster care. Because the attorney knows the state legislation, he or she can advise as to whether the case is ready for a termination of parental rights petition or another permanent plan. Additionally, the attorneys and caseworkers are getting to know each other better, which improves their teamwork in all cases.

The courts in Washington, as in many other jurisdictions, also have committees, which are made up of judges, agency attorneys, caseworkers or supervisors, and children's and parents' attorneys, to resolve procedural problems in the court.

---

[13] David J. Herring, *Interdisciplinary Training and Assessing Community Services Resources, in* AGENCY ATTORNEY TRAINING MANUAL: ACHIEVING TIMELY PERMANENCY FOR CHILDREN BY IMPLEMENTING THE PRIVATE MODEL OF LEGAL REPRESENTATION FOR THE STATE AGENCY IN CHILD ABUSE AND NEGLECT MATTERS (1992); *see also* Mimi Laver, *A Guide to Retaining Agency Attorneys,* 17 CHILD L. PRAC. 5, 73–75 (1998).

Through these committees, the court has reduced delays in cases, the participants have gained respect for each other, the judges have taken a positive leadership role, and all players work together to resolve the problems that affect the entire system.[14]

§ 27.5 Conclusion

No matter what kind of relationship you have with the caseworkers in your agency, there is probably room for improvement. While it is not easy and may be frustrating, through increased communication and a focus on mutual respect, you can work as a more effective team to benefit the children and families in your community.

---

[14] Telephone interview with Linda Katz, MSW, adjunct faculty at the University of Washington School of Social Work, Seattle, Washington, July 14, 1998.

§ 27.6 Sample Protocol for Termination Petitions

Sample Protocol for Termination Petitions

Step 1. A recommendation is made by the permanency planning committee, legal unit, or supervisor that a termination petition be filed.

Step 2. Within **30 days** of Step 1, the caseworker will send a completed information packet with referral form to the legal unit.

Step 3. For a permanent neglect, mental illness or mental retardation case, within **30 days** of Step 2, the attorney will either draft a petition or request more information from the caseworker. The attorney will forward the draft petition or request for information to the caseworker.

For an abandonment case, within **15 days** of Step 2, the attorney will either draft a petition or request more information from the caseworker. The attorney will forward the draft petition or request for information to the caseworker.

Step 4. If additional information is requested, the caseworker shall return the petition or provide the information to the attorneys within **7 days**. Once the petition is returned, the attorney shall file the petition within **7 days**.

Step 5. After receiving the additional information, for a permanent neglect, mental illness or mental retardation case, the attorneys shall file the petition within **30 days**.

After receiving the additional information, for an abandonment case, the attorney shall file the petition within **15 days**.

Step 6. The attorney and caseworker shall meet at least **2 weeks** prior to the trial date to prepare for trial.

Source: Albany County Permanency Planning Project, Attorney Caseworker Protocol for Termination Petitions. Developed by Anne Marie Lancour, J.D., Legal Training Director, ABA Center on Children and the Law. Washington, DC.

§ 27.7 Sample Protocol for Dispute Resolution Between Agency Attorney and Caseworker

---

**Sample Protocol for Dispute Resolution
Between Agency Attorney and Caseworker**

Step 1.   You and the caseworker thoroughly and calmly discuss the case or problem.

Step 2.   If you cannot resolve the problem, each of you go and discuss it with your supervisors. Pick a time to communicate again within two days.

Step 3.   Meet with your supervisors and determine whether you are taking the position of your agency. Try to work out other ways to view the issue. Find out when your supervisor is free to meet with the caseworker and supervisor if needed. This should be within one week, or sooner if the case is pending in court.

Step 4.   Keep the appointment to talk again and see if there has been a resolution.

Step 5.   If there was no resolution, pick a mutually convenient time for a meeting between you and the caseworker and your supervisors.

Step 6.   Have the meeting. Try to talk through the entire issue to reach an understanding.

Step 7.   If there is still no resolution, you will each need to go up your chain of command. If this is a policy issue, the head of your unit will need to discuss it with the head of the agency and find a reasonable position.

---

§ 27.8 Responsibilities of Attorney and Social Worker

RESPONSIBILITY	WHO SHOULD DO IT[15]
Investigate the report.	Caseworker.
Discuss the facts with police, medical professionals, and teachers.	Caseworker, who may have discussions with attorney.
Prepare the petition.	Legal assistant, with information from caseworker and supervision of attorney.
Notify the parties of the hearing.	Law office, by subpoena. Caseworker, if required.
Identify witnesses.	Caseworker gives information to attorney and attorney identifies witnesses after reviewing the file.
Prepare the witnesses.	Attorney, who may have help from legal assistant.
Prepare the child witness.	Attorney, who may have caseworker present to support the child emotionally. Remember to collaborate with the child's attorney or CASA.
Prepare any exhibits for the hearing.	Legal assistant and attorney. Caseworker should provide an organized case file.
Other court preparation.	Attorney, with conversations with caseworker.
Present the case in court.	Attorney.
Enter into agreements with the parents.	Caseworker and/or attorney can work with the parents and the other parties should be included before reaching a final agreement.
Ongoing documentation.	Caseworker.
Attend meetings with the family.	Caseworker and sometimes attorney.
Ongoing casework.	Caseworker.

---

[15] Source: Robin Russel, *Role Perceptions of Attorneys and Caseworkers in Child Abuse Cases in Juvenile Court*, CHILD WELFARE Vol. 67, No. 3, May-June 1988, 205–16. *See also* DAVID J. HERRING, AGENCY ATTORNEY TRAINING MANUAL: ACHIEVING TIMELY PERMANENCY FOR CHILDREN BY IMPLEMENTING THE PRIVATE MODEL OF LEGAL REPRESENTATION FOR THE STATE AGENCY IN CHILD ABUSE AND NEGLECT MATTERS (1992); Gene D. Skarin, *The Role of the Child Protective Agency's Attorney in Family Court*, 171 PLI/CRIM 431, 459–60 (1995).

Chapter 28: Representing Parents in Child Welfare Cases*

by Vivek S. Sankaran[1]

§ 28.1 Introduction

A parent's constitutional right to raise his or her child is one of the most venerated liberty interests safeguarded by the Constitution and the courts.[2] The law presumes parents to be fit, and it establishes that they do not need to be model parents to retain custody of their children.[3] If the state seeks to interfere with the parent-child relationship, the Constitution mandates that the state: (1) prove parental unfitness, a standard defined by state laws; and (2) follow certain procedures protecting the due process rights of parents. The constitutional framework for child welfare cases is premised on the belief that the interests of children are best served when children are in their parents' custody. For that reason, the state's evidence of parental unfitness must satisfy a high burden before the state may interfere with or permanently sever the parent-child relationship.

Attorneys who represent parents in child protective proceedings play a crucial role in safeguarding these liberty interests. This role manifests itself in many ways. Similar to criminal defense attorneys, parents' attorneys protect their clients from unjust accusations, ensure that their clients receive due process protections, and help to ensure that the entire judicial process affords their clients a fair opportunity to take advantage of its protections. In situations where temporary removal occurs, advocacy

---

* *Author's Note:* I based a large part of this chapter on a guidebook for parents' attorneys I co-wrote with Professor Frank Vandervort for the Michigan State Court Administrative Office. In addition to Professor Vandervort, I would like to thank David Meyers, Rich Cozzola, and Professor Chris Gottlieb for reviewing drafts of this chapter and providing invaluable feedback.

[1] Vivek S. Sankaran, J.D., C.W.L.S., is a clinical assistant professor of law in the Child Advocacy Law Clinic. Professor Sankaran's research and policy interests center on improving outcomes for children in child abuse and neglect cases by empowering parents and strengthening due process protections in the child welfare system. He currently sits on the Board of Trustees of the Detroit Metropolitan Bar Foundation and is Director of The Detroit Center for Family Advocacy.

[2] Troxel v. Granville, 530 U.S. 57, 65 (2000) ("[T]he interest of parents in the care, custody, and control of their children . . . is perhaps the oldest of the fundamental liberty interests recognized by this Court."); Michael H. v. Gerald D., 491 U.S. 110, 123–24 (1989) ("[T]he Constitution protects the sanctity of the family precisely because the institution of the family is deeply rooted in this Nation's history and tradition."); Prince v. Massachusetts, 321 U.S. 158 (1944); Pierce v. Society of Sisters, 268 U.S. 510 (1925); Meyer v. Nebraska, 262 U.S. 390 (1923).

[3] Santosky v. Kramer, 455 U.S. 745, 753 (1982) ("The fundamental liberty interest of natural parents in the care, custody, and management of their child does not evaporate simply because they have not been model parents or have lost temporary custody of their child to the State.").

by parents' counsel can expedite the safe reunification of the family by ensuring the prompt delivery of appropriate services to the family and by counseling parents about the ramifications of the choices they must make. If the parent is unable to care for the child, a parent's lawyer can serve the client by arranging for another temporary or permanent legal placement, such as a guardianship or an adoption, which will advance the parent's interests. In these and other situations, strong advocacy on behalf of parents furthers the best interests of children and improves outcomes for both children and their families.[4]

The challenges confronting parents' attorneys are daunting. Parents involved in child welfare cases often confront a host of seemingly insurmountable issues that transcend child welfare, including poverty, substance abuse, mental illness, and domestic violence. Those problems can make it difficult for an attorney to earn the client's trust and develop a successful litigation strategy. The attorney must master complex federal and state child welfare laws and become familiar with related laws in areas such as adoption, guardianship, and special education. The attorney must also engage in cooperative problem solving with a number of stakeholders, which can include the child protection authorities, the child's attorney or guardian ad litem (GAL), tribal representatives, CASA, and the court. But the attorney must always hold the client's interests paramount, which may necessitate formal and assertive courtroom advocacy. Too often, parents' attorneys must do all of this while receiving low compensation, handling high caseloads, and enduring criticism that their advocacy for their clients somehow harms their clients' children.[5] These and other challenges make representing parents among the most difficult and important areas in which to practice law.

§ 28.2 The Role of Parent's Counsel

In many ways, the role of the parent's attorney is no different than that of any attorney representing a client. Rules of professional conduct adopted in each state establish the basic parameters of the attorney-client relationship.[6] An attorney must zealously advocate on behalf of his or her client and maintain an undivided loyalty to the client's interests, regardless of the attorney's personal beliefs.[7] The attorney must

---

[4] *See, e.g.*, Bobbe J. Bridge & Joanne I. Moore, *Implementing Equal Justice for Parents in Washington: A Dual Approach*, 53/4 JUV. & FAM. CT. J. 31 (2002) (finding that strengthening parents' counsel increased family reunifications by 50% and stating that "the enhancement of parents' representation has the potential to save . . . millions in state funding on an annualized basis").

[5] *See, e.g.*, AMERICAN BAR ASSOCIATION CENTER ON CHILDREN AND THE LAW, LEGAL REPRESENTATION FOR PARENTS IN CHILD WELFARE PROCEEDINGS: A PERFORMANCE-BASED ANALYSIS OF MICHIGAN PRACTICE (2009) (describing problems in Michigan's system of parent representation).

[6] Attorneys representing parents should also consult the AMERICAN BAR ASSOCIATION, STANDARDS OF PRACTICE FOR ATTORNEYS REPRESENTING PARENTS IN ABUSE AND NEGLECT CASES (2006), *available at* http://www.abanet.org/child/clp/ParentStds.pdf.

[7] *See* MODEL RULES OF PROF'L CONDUCT R. 1.7 cmt. (1983) ("Loyalty and independent judgment are essential elements in the lawyer's relationship to a client.").

act with "reasonable diligence and promptness in representing a client"[8] and must not knowingly reveal a confidence or secret of a client except in narrowly defined circumstances.[9] Most rules of professional conduct require joint decision-making by the attorney and the client. While the client has the ultimate authority to determine the goals of the representation, the attorney typically decides how best to accomplish those goals after consulting with the client.[10] Because a clear distinction frequently cannot be drawn between the client's objectives and the tactical means to accomplish them, in many cases the client-lawyer relationship involves a joint undertaking.[11]

These and other requirements define the relationship between a parent's attorney and the parent. The requirements remain the same regardless of whether the attorney is appointed by the court or retained, and regardless of how much the attorney is paid. The interests and wishes of the client always remain paramount. Any attorney engaging in this work must read and understand the applicable rules of professional conduct adopted in his or her jurisdiction.

While having the same ethical obligations as all other lawyers, parents' attorneys confront unique challenges when representing their clients.[12] These challenges are discussed in the next several sections.

§ 28.2.1 Establishing Trust

Establishing mutual trust is crucial in forming any good attorney-client relationship. Trust allows clients to honestly discuss the facts of their cases, and it enables attorneys to render candid advice. Yet parents' attorneys often find it difficult to develop a trusting relationship with their clients. Forming such a relationship takes time and can rarely be achieved in the initial meeting.

Most of the parents come from traditionally disadvantaged populations.[13] Additionally, parents accused of child maltreatment may be frightened and may

---

[8] Model Rules of Prof'l Conduct R. 1.3 (1983).

[9] Model Rules of Prof'l Conduct R. 1.6 (1983).

[10] Model Rules of Prof'l Conduct R. 1.2 (1983).

[11] *See* Model Rules of Prof'l Conduct R. 1.2 cmt. (1983).

[12] *See generally* Jennifer L. Renne, Legal Ethics in Child Welfare Cases (2004).

[13] Statistics reveal that most families affected by the child welfare system are poor. According to the Third National Incidence Study of Child Abuse and Neglect (NIS-3), poor children were over 20 times more likely to be maltreated and over 40 times more likely to be neglected. Andrea J. Sedlak & Diane D. Broadhurst, United States Department of Health and Human Services, *Third National Incidence Study of Child Abuse and Neglect*, p. 4–5 (1996). Additionally, African-American children are disproportionately affected by the foster care system even though no evidence exists that African-American parents are any more likely to abuse or neglect their children. Despite only comprising 12% of the population, African-American children constituted 29% of children who had open cases and 40% of children in foster care. Children's Bureau, United States Department of Health and Human Services, *The AFCARS Report: Interim FY 2000 Estimates as of August 2002*, p. 2 (2002). A recent report in Michigan confirmed these findings. The Center for the Study of Social Policy, *Race Equity Review: Findings from a Qualitative Analysis of Racial Disproportionality and Disparity for African American Children and Families in Michigan's Child Welfare System* (2009).

appear hostile and confrontational. In responding to the petition and, in many cases, the actual removal of their children by Children's Protective Services, parents may distrust the child welfare system's authority figures, including their own attorneys.

Parents typically meet their attorneys for the first time in the courthouse immediately before or just following their initial removal hearing. In all likelihood, the attorney who claims to represent them was appointed (and will be paid) by the same court that authorized the children's removal. In the parent's mind, the attorney may appear as just another member of the establishment responsible for the child's removal from the home. The parent's attorney must recognize the barriers created by this, and other factors may make it difficult to earn the client's trust.

To remove those barriers, the attorney must, immediately upon appointment, clearly explain to the client that the attorney's job is to represent the parent's interests, and that the attorney's loyalty lies completely with the client, not with the court or the agency. Words alone will not engender trust, however. The attorney must be mindful of how the client perceives the attorney's actions. Taking some visible action on behalf of the client very early in the representation—for example, making positive statements about the client to the caseworker or the court—may help to establish a trusting relationship. In court, the attorney must never make any disparaging comments about the client; in addition to being unethical, doing so would undermine the client's still tentative confidence in counsel. Even counsel's casual conversations outside the courtroom with caseworkers, opposing counsel, or court staff may be interpreted by clients as signs that the attorney is working against their interests, even if those conversations are unrelated to their case. Acknowledging that these relationships exist and can be beneficial to the parent can often help mitigate these fears. In the early stages of the relationship, even the appearance of divided loyalties may irreparably impair the client's trust.

At the outset of the relationship, the attorney must listen patiently to the client's full story and avoid prejudging the parent based on the agency's allegations. Instead, the attorney should empathize with the client and, if appropriate, validate the client's emotional reaction to the situation. This will help to establish rapport with the client, which is a primary goal of the initial interview. Counsel should then use broad, open-ended questions to elicit information from the parent, reserving more specific questions about the case until after the client has had a full opportunity to tell his or her story.

Counsel must seek information about the client's family and should consider constructing a chart or genogram[14] to obtain a clear understanding of the extended family. Even though a client may not be willing to disclose relatives or extended family, early engagement of this support network can be the most effective tool a parent's attorney can employ to support the client through this process and ensure a continued connection to the child should reunification fail.

---

[14] A genogram is a graphic representation of the family tree with space for additional information related to a family. A program called GenoPro permits a lawyer to diagram the family tree, keep track of different individuals in the family and update it as relationships change. Genealogy Software: GenoPro, http://www.genopro.com.

The attorney should close the first interview by demonstrating an understanding of the client's goals and priorities, reviewing the next steps to be taken by both the client and counsel, and ensuring that the client knows how to reach the attorney. Throughout this process, counsel must reassure the client that, subject only to a few very limited disclosure exceptions, all conversations with the attorney are confidential.[15]

Meeting with the client on multiple occasions, especially at locations away from the courthouse, can be crucial to the trust-building process. In addition to meeting in the attorney's office, attorneys should meet with clients in places that are comfortable to the client such as the client's home, or public buildings with private rooms, such as a library. Letting the client choose the meeting location will help empower the client and reduce tension early in the relationship.

Once earned, the client's trust must be maintained. The attorney must stay in close contact with the client, which requires making and returning phone calls, scheduling regular meetings outside of court, and sending the client letters and copies of court orders. During each conversation, the attorney must carefully listen to the client's concerns before recommending the course of action that will best serve the client's interests. Providing information will also help to build and maintain trust. Sharing documents such as petitions, agency reports, motions, and court orders not only provides the client information he or she should have, but takes away some of the mystery of the court process and demonstrates that the attorney is working for the client. Explaining as fully as possible what the client should expect at each stage of the proceeding may make the situation less intimidating and avoid surprises. Letting the client know the attorney's strategy at various points also encourages the client to see the work as a collaborative effort and to see that his or her position is being represented vigorously.

By taking these steps, the attorney will show that the client's wishes and needs are paramount, and that open and honest communication will enhance the quality of the attorney's representation.

§ 28.2.2 Defining the Client's Goals

Soon after the case begins, parents' attorneys must help their clients define and clarify their goals. The typical overarching goal—reunifying the family—may be obvious, but the attorney must also identify the client's numerous short- and long-term goals on issues such as placement, visitation, and services. Even if the client denies the allegations in the petition, will the client agree to participate in services such as a parenting class? If the children cannot be returned home immediately, where should they live while the case proceeds? What type of visitation should occur? Is anyone else available to supervise those initial visits? What frequency of sibling visits does the client prefer?

---

[15] MODEL RULES OF PROF'L CONDUCT R. 1.6 (1983). For example, under Rule 1.6 of the Model Rules, an attorney may disclose information to "prevent reasonably certain death or substantial bodily harm."

The parent's attorney must help the client establish realistic goals for the representation. To that end, the attorney should provide objective feedback about the client's stated goals and guide the client toward goals that can be achieved. For example, where the evidence clearly shows that the parent seriously abused the child, the parent should not expect immediate reunification. Most parents want their attorney to analyze the likelihood of achieving their short- and long-term goals. Therefore, parents' attorneys must provide objective, carefully considered advice.

The attorney must also ascertain the extent to which the client wants the case to focus on the past or the future. This decision will significantly affect how the attorney handles the case. If the case is about the past—that is, about the veracity of the agency's allegations against the parent—then the pre-jurisdictional stage of the child protective case may resemble a criminal proceeding. The parent's attorney will act like defense counsel, trying to exonerate the client with the hope of obtaining a dismissal or at least a finding that the court does not have jurisdiction. In that situation, an attorney may take a more adversarial approach to the case, focusing on the traditional aspects of civil litigation such as formal discovery, depositions, and the trial.

On the other hand, many clients will decide that they do not want to focus on the past, preferring instead that the case be about the future. If so, then the parent's improvement becomes the goal and the attorney will try at every opportunity to demonstrate to the court and the agency that the parent has made progress and now can care for the child. Rather than pursuing the more adversarial techniques discussed above, this litigation strategy may acknowledge the court's jurisdiction and move on immediately to cooperative problem-solving and the parent's participation in services.

In other words, exonerating a parent may entail a different legal strategy than addressing the deficits identified by the court and the agency. For both, the goal is to reunify the family, but the attorney's strategy and tactics will differ markedly. In the abstract, one cannot determine which approach will be best for a client. A parent will likely elect to incorporate elements of both. But the one indispensable step is for the attorney to meet with the client to establish the parent's individualized goals and priorities.

Regardless of the client's specific litigation strategy, the parent's attorney should try to foster a healthy relationship between the client and the caseworker. That will benefit even those parents who disagree with the agency's actions and decide to challenge the factual and legal bases for the court taking jurisdiction over the child. A strong, working relationship with the caseworker will make it easier to resolve disputes regarding placement, visitation, and services to the family, which the courts often cannot resolve quickly unless the parties have already agreed on how to resolve them. The attorney must explain that it is often in the parent's interests to cooperate with the caseworker despite their disagreements on some specific issues. The attorney should express understanding of the challenges of working with the caseworker, but help the parent consider whether to risk the consequences of having a confrontational dynamic with a person who may greatly influence the direction of the case. The attorney should offer to intervene if the parent is having trouble working with the caseworker and encourage the parent to voice concerns to the attorney first if it is difficult to do so constructively with the caseworker.

§ 28.2.3 Defining the Scope of Representation

Defining the scope of the legal representation presents another challenge for parents' attorneys. Typically, parent's attorneys become involved in the case after receiving an appointment from the court. The appointment order will likely authorize legal advocacy both inside and outside the courtroom provided that the advocacy relates directly to the child welfare case. Yet, attorneys who do this work recognize that resolving collateral legal disputes and related issues can significantly affect the child welfare case. For example, a parent may need an attorney to file for custody or establish paternity, to provide criminal defense consultation, to expunge the parent's name from the central registry of child abuse and neglect, or to advocate for both the child and the parent in special education hearings. Without legal assistance on these collateral issues, the parent may not be able to take the necessary steps to move the child welfare case forward. Unfortunately, in many jurisdictions, court-appointed parents' attorneys do not get paid for assisting clients in these separate but related matters. Consequently, court-appointed parents' attorneys often confront the question, "How much more should I do for my client?"

Beyond representing the parent in the child welfare proceeding, which the appointment order typically mandates, each attorney must determine the scope of the representation and explain to the client exactly which other activities the attorney can and will undertake. This determination should be reflected in writing. Sometimes just a little work by counsel can make a huge difference in the child welfare case. Some examples include helping the client fill out standard court forms or merely advising a client on how to proceed in a related matter. If the attorney cannot directly assist the parent in the collateral matter, then the attorney should attempt to locate another lawyer, perhaps at a legal aid organization, to help the client. At a minimum, the attorney must try to provide the client with sufficient direction to enable the client to address the collateral legal issue without an attorney's assistance. Parents' attorneys must think broadly about their client's goals and act creatively to achieve those goals, even if that entails advising the client to pursue other legal avenues such as custody, adoption, or guardianship. These small counseling steps, taken when the attorney cannot do more, may help resolve the child welfare case.

§ 28.2.4 Institutional Pressures

Parents' attorneys often face enormous institutional pressures to undermine their own clients' interests. For example, low compensation and high case loads discourage active advocacy. Due to a court's docket backlog, parents' attorneys may face pressures to convince their clients to enter a plea giving the court jurisdiction rather than take a case to trial. This pressure may be compounded by a perceived need to please the judge, who may control the attorney's appointments in future cases. Even worse, parents' attorneys who press their clients' arguments aggressively may be chastised by other parties or outside observers who believe that the parent's goals conflict with they deem is the child's best interests.

Regardless of these pressures, parents' attorneys must remember that their paramount obligation, under the rules of professional conduct, is to zealously advocate on behalf of their client.[16] This responsibility remains despite external constraints such as low fees or pressure from third parties. If an attorney feels unable to fulfill his or her ethical responsibilities to the client, the attorney must immediately request permission to withdraw from the case.[17] Under no circumstances do the rules of professional conduct permit an attorney to deviate from the basic requirements set forth in those rules.[18]

§ 28.2.5 Representing Nonresident Fathers

For the most part, this chapter is geared towards attorneys representing custodial parents who stand accused of abusing or neglecting their children. But attorneys who practice child welfare law sometimes will represent "the other parent." This parent may be one who has done nothing wrong—or perhaps done nothing worse than failing to report the abusive parent to the authorities or not participating in the child's life. Because many of these parents are nonresident fathers, this section will focus on the unique challenges attorneys face when representing these individuals. Keep in mind, however, that much of the information presented elsewhere in the chapter will apply to these situations, too.

The Supreme Court has stated that nonresident fathers have rights protected by the Constitution when they maintain a sufficient involvement in their children's lives. "When an unwed father demonstrates a full commitment to the responsibilities of parenthood by coming forward to participate in the rearing of his child, his interest in personal contact with his child acquires substantial protection under the Due Process Clause."[19] For example, in *Caban v. Mohammed*,[20] the Court struck down a New York law that denied a father the right to object to an adoption to which the biological mother had already consented. The Court held that because the father was as involved in the children's upbringing as their mother, both parties had to be treated equally.[21] But, in *Lehr v. Robertson*, the Supreme Court upheld a New York law that did not require a father to be notified of his child's impending adoption because the father did not take meaningful steps to establish a parental relationship with his child.[22] In *Lehr*

---

[16] MODEL RULES OF PROF'L CONDUCT, Preamble, #2.

[17] MODEL RULES OF PROF'L CONDUCT R. 1.16

[18] MODEL RULES OF PROF'L CONDUCT R. 14–21.

[19] Lehr v. Robertson, 463 U.S. 248, 261 (1983) (internal citations and quotations omitted).

[20] 441 U.S. 380 (1979).

[21] *Id.* at 389.

[22] Lehr v. Robertson, 463 U.S. 248, 248 (1983).

and other similar cases, the Supreme Court has prevented fathers who failed to make efforts to establish a relationship with their children from using the Constitution to disrupt the child's permanent placement.[23]

Although the Supreme Court has never listed the specific actions a nonresident father must take to establish his constitutionally protected interest in his child, the Court's rulings clarify that the rights of fathers who have established relationships with their children are constitutionally protected from state interference absent proof of unfitness. Courts often consider a number of factors to determine whether a father has established a relationship with the child, including whether he: paid child support or provided other assistance to the mother, visited or lived with the child, sent the child cards or gifts, attended school meetings or took the child to doctor appointments, or listed his name on the birth certificate.[24]

In addition to providing guidance as to when relationships between fathers and their children are constitutionally protected, the Supreme Court has said that states must give all fathers the opportunity to establish parental relationships by allowing them to claim their interest in the child soon after the child's birth.[25] States have created several ways for fathers to assert parentage. In some states, fathers have to file an affidavit of paternity jointly with the child's mother[26] or institute a paternity suit.[27] Other states use putative father registries to let fathers assert their interests.[28] State practices vary on this issue, and attorneys representing nonresident fathers must know the options available to fathers in their state. Many courts have found that a father's failure to comply with state procedures constitutes a permanent waiver of the father's rights to his child.[29]

As the discussion above suggests, the extent of fathers' parental rights are often less clear under the law than mothers' rights, and the attorney must advise clients accordingly and help fathers take steps to solidify and protect their rights. The manner in which state laws protect the rights of nonresident fathers in child welfare cases varies considerably. Many states provide nonresident fathers the right to notice of proceedings and the opportunity to participate in hearings, the right to visitation with

---

23   *See, e.g.,* Lehr v. Robertson, 463 U.S. 248, 248 (1983); Quilloin v. Walcott, 434 U.S. 246, 255 (1977).

24   *See, e.g., In re* A.A.T., 287 Kan. 590, 609, 196 P.3d 1180, 1194 (2008) (noting that "to determine if a natural father of a newborn child has taken diligent, affirmative action, courts measure the putative father's efforts to make a financial commitment to the upbringing of the child, to legally substantiate his relationship with the child, and to provide emotional, financial, and other support to the mother during the pregnancy."). In the decision, the Kansas Supreme Court details case law from other jurisdictions on this issue.

25   Lehr v. Robertson, 463 U.S. 248, 262–63 (1983).

26   *See, e.g.,* MICH. COMP. LAWS § 722.1003.

27   *See, e.g.,* MICH. COMP. LAWS § 722.714.

28   *See, e.g.,* OHIO REV. CODE ANN. § 3107.062; FLA. STAT. § 63.054.

29   *See, e.g.,* Marco C. v. Sean C., 218 Ariz. 216, 181 P.3d 1137 (App. 2008) (refusing to permit fathers to assert parental rights where they did not comply with statutory requirements); Heidbreder v. Carton, 645 N.W.2d 355 (Minn. 2002) (same); Hylland v. Doe, 126 Or. App. 86, 867 P.2d 551 (1994) (same); Sanchez v. L.D.S. Soc. Servs., 680 P.2d 753 (Utah 1984) (same).

children, and the right to court-appointed counsel if indigent. States practices diverge, however, on a number of issues including whether putative fathers have standing to appear in the case, whether the child must be placed with the nonresident father absent proof of unfitness, and whether the court can order a fit nonresident father to comply with services it deems are in the child's best interests.[30] The first step an attorney must take is to acquire a comprehensive understanding of state laws and practices that address the rights of nonresident fathers. The attorney must determine if his or her client has standing to participate in the child welfare proceeding under state law and, if not, what steps must be taken to gain standing.

When representing the nonresident father in these situations, counsel should consider both constitutional and practice-based arguments. If the state seeks to deprive the nonresident father of custody and place the child in foster care, counsel should argue that the Constitution requires a finding of unfitness against the father before the custody deprivation can occur, assuming that he maintained a sufficiently close relationship with the child before the case.[31] Any attempt to strip an involved parent of his parental rights without such a finding of unfitness contravenes the Due Process Clause.[32] Attorneys raising this argument should file a written motion and stand ready to appeal immediately if the trial court denies the parent the right to an evidentiary hearing or refuses to return custody to the nonresident father.

In addition to framing arguments around the father's constitutional rights, attorneys must also put forward practical arguments to move their client's case forward. They must ensure that the court and the agency identify and locate their client early in the case and provide him with notice of all child welfare proceedings.[33] They must make sure that the agency moves expeditiously to complete home studies when required before a determination on custody or visitation.[34] The attorneys must also work with the agency to protect the father's right to be involved in case planning and creating the family's service plan, which will outline the services the father must complete. They may also consider filing a separate custody complaint or a motion to modify custody in a family law case, which may then be consolidated with the child

---

[30] *See* Vivek S. Sankaran, *Parens Patriae Run Amuck: The Child Welfare System's Disregard for the Constitutional Rights of Nonoffending Parents*, 82 TEMP. L. REV. 55 (Spring 2009).

[31] *See* Stanley v. Illinois, 405 U.S. 645, 649 (1972) ("[A]s a matter of due process of law, Stanley was entitled to a hearing on his fitness as a parent before his children were taken from him.").

[32] *See generally* Wisconsin v. Yoder, 406 U.S. 205 (1872); Moore v. Cleveland, 431 U.S. 494 (1977); Troxel v. Granville, 530 U.S. 57 (2000).

[33] *See In re* Rood, 483 Mich. 73, 763 N.W.2d 587 (2009) (reversing termination of parental rights decision where trial court failed to involve nonresident father in child welfare case).

[34] Practitioners may confront situations in which their parent client lives in a different state than the one in which the juvenile case is based. In such cases, child welfare agencies and courts often seek to apply the requirements of the Interstate Compact on the Placement of Children (ICPC). For arguments that the ICPC does not apply to placements with non-offending birth parents, see Vivek S. Sankaran, *Out of State and Out of Luck: The Treatment of Non-Custodial Parents Under the Interstate Compact on the Placement of Children*, 25 YALE L. & POL'Y REV. 63 (2006). For additional resources on advocating within the ICPC, see ICPC Advocacy, *available at* http://www.law.umich.edu/centersandprograms/ccl/specialprojects/Pages/ICPCAdvocacy.aspx.

welfare case. Finally, if the nonresident father cannot receive custody immediately, the attorney should request liberal visitation between the client and his child. Counsel should frame all these arguments in terms of the interests of children—that it serves the best interests of children to maintain relationships with their fathers and the extended paternal side of the family. These are some of the basic considerations that attorneys must think about when representing nonresident fathers.[35]

Although child welfare practice and terminology varies considerably pursuant to state laws, the essential stages of the case are similar across jurisdictions. The next sections aim to discuss strategic considerations for parents' attorneys at each stage.

§ 28.3 The Preliminary Hearing

In most jurisdictions, at the preliminary or emergency removal hearing, the court decides whether to authorize the agency's petition and whether to approve the child's temporary removal from the family home, if the agency has requested removal. This hearing bears some similarity to the arraignment and preliminary examination stages of a criminal case, but can be the most critical determinant of the case's ultimate outcome. If the court finds probable cause to believe the allegations of abuse or neglect in the petition, then the court will authorize the petition, which may result in a subsequent full-scale proceeding to determine whether the court has jurisdiction over the child.

In most jurisdictions, parents' attorneys will meet their clients for the first time just before the preliminary hearing. This is hardly ideal. If possible, the parents' attorney should meet the clients and prepare for the first hearing in advance. Typically, however, this meeting will takes place in the hallway outside the courtroom. The attorney will have very little time before the hearing to discuss the case with the new client, but many decisions of great consequence are made during the hearing. Studies reveal that a natural bias toward preserving the custodial status quo makes courts reluctant to quickly return children to their parents once the court has ordered the child's removal.[36] After a removal, the barriers to reunification increase and courts may be unwilling to reunify the family until every element of a service plan has been met. In many cases, due to a perceived emergency need for protection, the child will have been removed from the parent's home even before the preliminary hearing. If so, the preliminary hearing represents the first opportunity to remedy an erroneous removal decision. Regardless of a particular case's initiating events, what

---

[35] For a more comprehensive analysis on representing nonresident fathers, *see* Andrew L. Cohen, *Representing Nonresident Fathers in Dependency Cases*, *in* ANDREW L. COHEN ET AL., ADVOCATING FOR NONRESIDENT FATHERS IN CHILD WELFARE COURT CASES (2009). Additionally, the federal government has created a National Quality Improvement Center on Nonresident Fathers and the Child Welfare System. More information about the Center is available at http://www.abanet.org/child/fathers/.

[36] *See* Peggy Cooper Davis & Gautam Barua, *Custodial Choices for Children at Risk: Bias, Sequentiality, and the Law*, 2 U CHI L. SCH. ROUNDTABLE 139, 139–55 (1995) (observing a "sequentiality effect" in child protective decisions where decision-makers tend to favor the status quo once a child is removed from his or her home).

happens during the preliminary hearing may dictate where the child lives for many months. Therefore, strong, zealous advocacy by parents' attorneys is essential from the outset.

§ 28.3.1 Eliciting Information

Knowledge about the case empowers an attorney to represent a client effectively. Therefore, a parent's attorney must either meet a new client in advance or make the most out of the brief initial interview before the preliminary hearing. Counsel should acquire basic factual information about the case and advise the client on the decisions that the client must make immediately. The attorney should also obtain the client's personal information (e.g., date of birth, address, phone number, or membership or eligibility for membership in an Indian tribe or Alaskan Native Village[37]), the client's version of how the family became involved with protective services, any previous family involvement with the courts or the agency, whether the family currently receives services, whether the child has special needs, and the nature of outside resources available to the family, including alternative placement options if the court orders removal. To elicit this information, the attorney should use open-ended questions calling for narrative answers. More focused, clarifying questions should follow. At the end of the interview, the attorney should retell the story in the attorney's own words to verify an understanding of the client's version of the facts.

Also during the limited time available before the preliminary hearing, the attorney must obtain information from other people who are present for the hearing. These may include the Children's Protective Services worker, family members, and attorneys representing other parties. At a minimum, the attorney must obtain and review a copy of the petition, which usually will have been prepared and filed by an agency worker. A thorough reading of the petition will help the parent's attorney avoid surprises during the hearing. It also will allow the attorney to negotiate with the other parties to see if any agreements can be reached before the preliminary hearing.

§ 28.3.2 Client Counseling

In addition to gathering information, the parent's attorney should use the initial client interview to explain the two main decisions that the court will make at the preliminary hearing. First, the court will decide whether to authorize the petition, which is a finding that the petitioner has shown cause to believe that the facts in the petition may be true such that the case may come within the court's statutorily defined jurisdiction. Second, if the court does authorize the petition, the jurist then will decide where the child will live while the case proceeds to the adjudication phase. The parent-client must decide whether to contest the authorization of the petition. Unless the parent waives all objections, the court must determine whether the agency has

---

[37] If the client is a member or is eligible to be a member of an Indian tribe or an Alaskan Native Village, counsel should carefully review the provisions of the Indian Child Welfare Act to determine whether special procedures must be applied in the case. *See* 25 U.S.C. § 1901 (2006).

shown probable cause to believe that one or more of the allegations in the petition are true and are among the grounds for jurisdiction listed in the statute. To help the parent-client decide whether to contest the petition's authorization, the attorney must explain that the preliminary hearing is not a full-fledged trial. Even if the parent-client waives all objections to authorization, he or she will still have the right to contest the petition's allegations later, during a trial before a referee, judge, or jury, depending on state law. Authorizing the petition only allows the case to go forward; it does not confirm the allegations against the parent.

Challenging the authorization, however, may have negative consequences for the parent-client. The evidentiary showing required of the petitioner at the preliminary hearing is a very low standard of proof. Further, at a preliminary hearing, the petitioner can typically use hearsay evidence to satisfy that burden of proof. Typically, the rules of evidence do not apply at an emergency removal hearing and the testimony of the Children's Protective Services worker may suffice to meet the probable cause standard. Only rarely will a parent be able to convince the court that a petition should not be authorized.

Furthermore, if a parent does contest the authorization decision, that parent may later have difficulty convincing the court or the agency to side with the parent on issues involving placement and visitation. Much of the testimony and argument at a contested preliminary hearing will be devoted to the factual allegations in the petition. That will keep the court focused on the alleged abusive or neglectful acts by the parent, which the agency will recount using hearsay evidence that may not be admissible at a later trial. If the court hears that evidence during a preliminary hearing, the court may think less favorably of the parent at all subsequent stages.

Given the possible adverse consequences and the low likelihood of success, contesting probable cause may not be worth the risk. If, however, the allegations in the petition, even if true, seemingly fail to set forth a prima facie case of abuse or neglect, it may make sense for the parent to contest the petition's authorization for that reason. The argument then will hinge on the petition's legal sufficiency, not its factual accuracy. Framing the challenge in legal terms avoids prematurely exposing the court to all the factual details. To determine whether the alleged facts, if proven, are sufficient for the court to assert jurisdiction, the parent's attorney must know the legal standards for the court taking jurisdiction over a child.[38]

The child's placement pending trial is the second main decision that the court makes during the preliminary hearing. The parent-client must understand the distinction between a court's decision to authorize the petition and the separate decision about where to place the child. Even if the court finds probable cause and authorizes the petition, it may also decide that the child should remain in the parent's home. Ideally when it comes to the placement decision, the court will be looking to

---

[38] If the case involves a party from a different state, counsel should determine where jurisdiction is appropriate under the Uniform Child Custody and Jurisdiction Enforcement Act (UCCJEA). For more information about the UCCJEA, see Chapter 17, Interstate and International Issues.

assess the risk to the child and the parent's ability to control that risk. The court should be open to strategies that would "remove the danger and not the child."[39]

Therefore, before the hearing, the attorney must ascertain whether the parent wants the child back in the home and, if so, whether the parent is willing to accept conditions on the placement. For example, in order to keep the child at home, will the parent agree to random drug testing or accept agency services such as in-home reunification assistance or parenting classes? If the parent-client is not the alleged abuser, will he or she help enforce a court order requiring the alleged abuser to leave the home? Is the parent willing to take the children to services such as counseling and medical appointments? The attorney must convey to the parent-client that flexibility when it comes to conditions like those listed above will increase the likelihood that the court will let the child return home. The attorney must convey to the parent-client that accepting agency services does not indicate that the parent admits the allegations in the petition. Regardless of whether the client accepts services, he or she will have a right to a full evidentiary hearing if the case proceeds as far as an adjudication trial. All courts are required at this hearing to make the federal finding that "reasonable efforts were made to prevent or eliminate the need for removal."[40] This can be a useful tool for parent's attorneys to use when attempting to secure placement at this phase.

The attorney and parent-client should also discuss the parent's options if the court does not immediately return the child to the parent's custody. They should explore other placement possibilities that the parent considers more acceptable than foster care. For example, federal law requires that the court and agency consider placing the child with relatives,[41] which may allow the parent to see the child more frequently and in a more relaxed setting. The attorney and parent-client should identify relatives, friends, and others who could care for the child temporarily. When considering this type of placement, the court will look at factors such as the proposed caregiver's prior criminal or child protective history, the family's resources, the proposed caregiver's previous involvement in the child's life, and the proposed caregiver's willingness and ability to comply with any restrictions placed on the child's contact with the parent. The attorney and parent-client should discuss those factors before the preliminary hearing to assess the feasibility of these alternative placement options.

In addition to possible placements, the attorney should discuss visitation issues with the parent-client. What type of visitation would the client like? Where should the visits take place? How frequently should they occur? If visitation time must be supervised, does the client know someone who is willing to supervise the visits and can pass the agency's background checks and follow the agency's rules? When evaluating all of these possibilities, the attorney should view the client as a valuable collaborator who can help develop creative solutions to the various issues.

---

[39] *See* Chapter 14, Child Safety: What Judges and Lawyers Need to Know.

[40] *See* 42 U.S.C. § 671(a) (15)(B)(i).

[41] 42 U.S.C. § 671(a)(19) (2006).

Initial visitation will not occur often enough, and at first it will likely occur only at the offices of the agency that is supervising the child's court-ordered placement. If visitation must be supervised, the attorney should at least try to arrange more frequent parenting time in a more family-friendly setting. Several jurisdictions have standing court orders that dictate the minimum amount of visitation a parent should receive in any case, but given that the frequency of visitation is a direct tie to successful reunification, attorneys must always advocate for as much visitation as possible.

§ 28.3.3 Negotiating

Before the preliminary hearing, in addition to information gathering and client counseling, the parent's attorney should begin negotiating with the other parties and their attorneys.[42] The Children's Protective Services worker and the child's attorney will, in all likelihood, attend the preliminary hearing. In some jurisdictions, attorneys representing the caseworker, child, and the child's other parent may also appear. After ascertaining the client's goals, the parent's attorney should work with the other attorneys and the caseworker to resolve differences, identify agreements, and try to reach a consensus on how the case should proceed. Stipulations on issues such as authorization, placement, visitation, and services will give the client a greater sense of control over the process. If agreements cannot be reached, having conversations with opposing parties will at least reveal essential information about each party's position and reasoning. This knowledge will help the parent's attorney decide what strategy to use at the preliminary hearing.

To summarize the last several sections, the attorney's three primary tasks before the preliminary hearing are: information gathering, client counseling, and negotiating. Although the time for these activities may be limited, even brief conversations can help the attorney achieve the client's objectives. The next section focuses on advocacy during the preliminary hearing.

§ 28.3.4 Courtroom Advocacy

The goals articulated by the client during the first attorney-client meeting will guide the attorney's advocacy at the preliminary hearing. Under no circumstances should the attorney attempt to advocate on behalf of the client without first having discussed the case with the client and ascertained the client's position on the major issues. If there has not yet been sufficient time to consult with the client, the attorney should request that the case be "passed" until later that day (to preserve the possibility of the child's immediate return home) or until a later date (but only if a longer adjournment will allow time for proper preparation).

The preliminary hearing is the attorney's first chance to introduce the parent and the parent's story to the court. The court, the child's attorney, and the agency

---

[42] In some jurisdictions, attorneys may be able to participate in mediation programs or family group conferencing before the preliminary hearing.

caseworker will watch the parent's courtroom actions closely to determine whether the parent seems inclined to respond positively to the judicial intervention and whether the parent will prioritize the children's interests. The attorney must caution the parent that the parent's behavior and attitude will be scrutinized closely during the hearing. Behaviors such as hostility toward the caseworker or the judge may delay reunification. The parent's instinctively hostile or distraught reactions may be understandable or even justifiable, but they will rarely further the parent's goal of having the children returned. Thoroughly explaining beforehand what will occur during the preliminary hearing will help to prepare and potentially calm the client. The parent's attorney then should model appropriate courtroom etiquette for the client by maintaining a professional demeanor while asserting the client's rights. Additionally, the attorney can provide the client with appropriate opportunities to participate in the court hearing. For example, having a client write down objections to statements made by other parties may minimize the possibility of vocal outbursts when disagreements arise.

Generally speaking, the major issues addressed at the preliminary hearing are: (1) whether to authorize the petition; (2) the child's placement; (3) visitation; and (4) services for the family. Despite long-standing recommendations to the contrary,[43] due to busy dockets, the preliminary hearing may last for only a few minutes, but the decisions made will lay the foundation for the rest of the case. Parents' attorneys must ensure that they have opportunities to address each of those major issues and that the court considers each issue fully and separately.

The attorney may need to slow the pace of the hearing to ensure that everyone hears the client's full story. Judges try to use their bench time efficiently, and that may cause them to conflate the discussion of whether to authorize the petition with what should be the completely separate discussion of where to place the child if they do authorize the petition. Many judges assume that if they authorize the petition, they almost certainly will place the child in foster care. As explained above, that assumption is incorrect. After authorizing the petition, the court, in most jurisdictions, must then make a separate determination about where the child will be placed pending trial, which can include returning the child to one or both parents. If the parent wants the child to remain at home or to live with a relative, the parent's attorney must ensure that the court considers the placement issue fully, separately, and in its proper sequence. Evidence such as report cards, medical records, and statements from teachers, therapists, religious leaders, friends, neighbors, and family members may help the court make those decisions.

Additionally, to assuage the court's concerns about the child returning to a parent's home, the parent's attorney may want to suggest reasonable terms and conditions for a home placement. For example, courts may permit a child to remain in

---

[43] *See* National Center for Juvenile and Family Court Judges, *Resource Guidelines: Improving Practice in Child Abuse and Neglect Cases*, p. 42 (1995) (recommending that preliminary hearings last at least 60 minutes to cover basic issues).

the home if the parents are willing to accept services such as intensive in-home reunification programs, parenting classes, and counseling. Each jurisdiction has different service programs that may assist a family in danger of being separated. Parents' attorneys should become familiar with the local community's various programs for in-home and preventive services. They should consider all the programs available in the county—not just those typically used by the agency. Knowledge of these programs will enable the attorney to expand the court's placement options at the preliminary hearing.

Parent's attorneys should always keep in mind that the law requires the agency to make "reasonable efforts" to prevent the removal of the child from the home except in the most extreme circumstances.[44] This obligation requires accessing community resources that might avoid the need to place the child in foster care. The agency's failure to make "reasonable efforts" before seeking court authorization for a child's removal constitutes a valid argument against removal. In the right cases, parents' attorneys should advance that argument at the preliminary hearing.

The attorney also should explore placement alternatives to the typical foster care placement. For example, the court may order a home placement if a trusted family member offers to move into the parent's home or to allow the client and the client's children to move into that relative's home. If the parent-client was not the wrongdoer, the attorney may request that the court order the actual abuser to leave the home.

The attorney must explain to the client that accepting community services or agreeing to special living arrangements does not represent an admission of wrong-doing or waive the right to a trial. At the same time, the attorney must emphasize the importance of complying with the court's orders because, in many situations, the only way to keep the child at home will be to identify the court's concerns and address those concerns by making some concessions.

If the court does order an out-of-home placement, then counsel should advocate for frequent and family-friendly visitation. As with placement issues, the attorney's role regarding visitation is to expand the court's options. In many child welfare cases, the standard protocol is to allow parents an hour of supervised visitation per week, with the visits occurring at the agency's office. This standard practice, in all likeli-hood, may not suit a particular family's needs. Having the agency supervise visitation may not be necessary. Attorneys should push for unsupervised visits when they can argue that such visits do not pose a danger to the child. For example, many child protective proceedings arise out of poverty-based neglect; in those cases, the issues that led to the child's removal may be related to the condition of the home. In such situations, day visits, with restrictions on where the parent may take the child, may suffice to protect the child.

Even if visitation must be supervised, the attorney should advocate for options that are more family-friendly and less restrictive than the common arrangement under which the parent and child see each other only at the agency office. For example,

---

[44] 42 U.S.C. § 671(a)(15)(B).

relatives, friends, clergy, community members, or foster parents may be willing to supervise the visits. Visits can also take place at nonagency sites such as a library, church, school, or even the client's home.

The court must also determine the frequency of visitation. Studies have shown that frequent visitation significantly increases the likelihood that reunification will occur.[45] Parents afforded the opportunity to see their children regularly have an added incentive to comply with the service plan. They receive reassurance that their children are doing well in foster care. Regular visitation also preserves the parent-child bond, which, especially for younger children, has important developmental consequences.[46]

Services for the family are the fourth main issue (after authorization, placement, and visitation) that may be discussed at the preliminary hearing. If the parent will accept services immediately, the attorney should request that the court order the agency to begin providing those services by a specified date. Because the first permanency planning hearing must be held within 12 months of a child's removal,[47] parents should try to begin their participation in services immediately. That will maximize the services provided within the first 12 months, and thus maximize the parents' opportunity to regain custody of the child. Some clients may hesitate to accept services prior to the jurisdiction trial because they fear that information revealed during services such as a parenting class or a counseling session could be used against them at trial. If this concern exists, counsel should consider requesting a protective order that limits the disclosure of that sensitive information until the dispositional stage of the case—if the case proceeds that far. Such an order will encourage the client to begin participating in services immediately.

In practice, the court may make all of the decisions described above in a matter of minutes, but their import for the future course of the child protective case and the child's life cannot be overstated. Although parents' attorneys often request a summary dismissal at the preliminary hearing, courts seldom dismiss cases outright at that point. More often, the case next enters the pretrial phase. The next section discusses the strategic issues that arise during that phase.

---

[45] *See* DAVID FANSHEL & EUGENE B. SHINN, CHILDREN IN FOSTER CARE: A LONGITUDINAL INVESTIGATION (1978) (finding that more frequent visitation increased the emotional well-being and developmental progress of foster children and resulted in a higher likelihood that children were reunified with their parents). Research has also shown that frequent visitation prior to reunification increases the likelihood that the reunification will succeed. *See* Elaine Farmer, *Family Reunification with High Risk Children: Lessons From Research*, 18/4-5 CHILD & YOUTH SERVS. REV. 287 (1996).

[46] John Bowlby, a developmental psychologist and a leader in the field of attachment, described the effect of separating a young child from his or her parent. He wrote, "Whenever a young child who has had an opportunity to develop an attachment to a mother-figure is separated from her unwillingly, he shows distress; and should he also be placed in a strange environment and cared for by a succession of strange people, such distress is likely to be intense." John Bowlby, 2 ATTACHMENT AND LOSS: SEPARATION : ANXIETY AND ANGER 26 (1973). From the child's perspective, placement in foster care is typically an unwilling separation from a person to whom a child is attached. Visitation is one way to ameliorate the child's distress.

[47] 42 U.S.C. § 675(5)(C) (2006).

§ 28.4 Pre-Adjudication Proceedings

§ 28.4.1 Pre-Adjudication Counseling

During the pre-adjudication phase, the attorney should focus first on the parent-client's immediate needs—on issues such as placement, visitation, and services. After that, the focus will shift to resolving the allegations in the petition and preparing for a trial on jurisdiction if the parties cannot resolve the case without a trial.

If the court authorizes the child's removal at the preliminary hearing, then the period immediately following that hearing is crucial. The parent may feel alienated, disempowered, and frustrated. The loss of control often makes parents want to disengage from the process completely. The parent's attorney can counter these understandable but self-defeating tendencies by ensuring that the agency keeps the parent involved in the child's life. As a first step, the attorney must explain the importance of the parent attending each scheduled visit with the child. If the parent has to miss a visit, the parent must notify the caseworker as soon as possible so the child will not be transported to the visitation site and then be disappointed when the parent fails to appear. If scheduling difficulties arise frequently, then the attorney and the parent should discuss those issues with the agency supervising the case. For its part, the agency should ensure that transportation difficulties do not impede a parent's efforts to visit the child and offer transportation assistance when necessary.

The attorney can help to preserve the parent's involvement in other ways. Even after a child is removed from a parent's home, the parent still retains important parental decision-making rights. For example, parental consent is typically necessary for some types of medical care.[48] Similarly, parents retain the right to make major educational decisions for a child.[49] They may attend educational planning meetings. In addition, they retain the right to decide whether the child will receive special education services.[50] The parent's attorney should encourage the parent to attend school meetings, doctor appointments, and therapy sessions, unless the court order prohibits such involvement. At a minimum, the attorney should make sure that the parent continues to receive updated information about the child from the service providers. Keeping the parent involved in the child's life will show the court that the parent remains concerned about the child's well-being and wants the child to return home even though the child has been temporarily placed elsewhere.

---

[48] *See, e.g.,* MICH. COMP. LAWS § 722.124a(1) (requiring parental consent for nonroutine or elective medical treatment of the foster child).

[49] *See* 34 C.F.R. § 300.519 (stating that a surrogate parent is needed only when a foster child is made a "ward of the State").

[50] *Id.*

§ 28.4.2 Maximizing the Parent's Opportunity to Receive Agency Services

Making sure that the agency complies with all court orders, statutes, and departmental policies will help keep the parent invested in the process. Therefore, the parent's attorney should actively monitor and enforce the court's orders related to placement, visitation, and services. The attorney should encourage the client to call immediately if any problems arise. If the agency fails to implement court orders in a timely manner despite requests from the parent and attorney, then the attorney should file a motion requesting that the court hold the agency in contempt of court. Depending on the date of the next scheduled court hearing, the attorney may ask the court to hear the contempt motion even earlier, at a specially scheduled hearing.

In all cases, federal law requires that the agency do certain things within specified intervals after the child's removal or the preliminary hearing. Within 60 days of removal, the agency must prepare an initial service plan specifying the services that the agency will recommend that the parent complete before the child can be returned home.[51] The service plan must specify measurable objectives the parent is expected to achieve.[52] Additionally, the agency must encourage the parent to actively participate in developing the service plan, which includes the ability to suggest and challenge requirements.[53] If the parents do not participate, the plan that the agency submits must document the reasons for a parent's nonparticipation.[54] Any delay in providing services to parents jeopardizes reunification. Therefore, if the agency does not prepare the plan within the time allowed, or if the parent is not sufficiently involved in the planning process, the parent's attorney should follow up with the appropriate persons. If necessary, the attorney should request that the court review a placement order or the initial services plan and modify those orders and plan if modification is in the client's interests.

§ 28.4.3 Exploring Settlement Possibilities

Attempting an informal resolution of the petition's allegations constitutes the attorney's second major task during the pretrial phase. The attorney should first consider whether some resolution short of the court assuming jurisdiction is possible and appropriate. The alternatives include dismissing the case with a voluntary agreement that the parent will participate in services, holding the petition in abeyance while the parent complies with services, or asking the parent whether he or she will consider ceding custodial rights to another caregiver, either temporarily or permanently. If so, then the attorney should consider arrangements like a guardianship, a direct placement adoption, or a voluntary relinquishment of parental rights. But those

---

[51] 45 C.F.R. § 1356.21(g) (2008).

[52] 45 C.F.R. § 1356.21(g) (2008).

[53] 45 C.F.R. § 1356.21(g)(1) (2008).

[54] 65 Fed. Reg. 4057 (Jan. 25, 2000).

options can have major collateral consequences that the parent must consider. For example, in some states, if the parent agrees to voluntarily relinquish parental rights to one child, that act can be grounds for the court later terminating that parent's rights to a future child.[55] Also, ceding custodial rights to another caregiver may make it very difficult for the parent to regain custody of the child in the future. Regardless, all options must be explored and the attorney must review the consequences of the decision with the client. Then, if a settlement possibility exists, the attorney must negotiate with the other parties to ascertain whether a mutually agreeable resolution can be reached without a jurisdiction trial.

The attorney and parent-client should also discuss the possibility of entering a limited plea or stipulation that allows the court to take jurisdiction over the child. The attorney should first assess the strength of the agency's case and estimate the parent's chances of prevailing at trial on the jurisdictional issue. A plea that allows the court to take jurisdiction may be appropriate when the facts alleged in the petition are undisputed and clearly establish a statutory basis for jurisdiction. In addition the parent may prefer that the child remain out of the home temporarily while services are provided. Entering a plea that allows the court to take jurisdiction may create positive strategic momentum for the parent by causing the other parties and the court to view the parent as cooperative.

Additionally, the plea will avoid a jurisdiction trial, which often carries negative consequences for the parent. During a trial, the agency may present detailed evidence of abuse or neglect by the parent. That will inevitably focus everyone's attention on the parent's past mistakes. A trial may also exacerbate hostilities between the parent and the caseworker, service providers, and any family members who testify about the parent's past conduct. Entering a plea that allows the court to take jurisdiction may avoid some of these consequences because the plea will allow the case to move directly to the dispositional phase, where the goal will likely be to reunify the family.

Despite the possible advantages of entering a jurisdictional plea, attorneys must also advise their parent-clients about some possible negative consequences. By entering a plea, the parent waives, among other things, the right to a jurisdiction trial. Many parents will view this trial as their first real opportunity to tell their story, and they will want to exercise that right regardless of the possible negative consequences. Also, if the parent waives the right to a jurisdiction trial by entering a plea, the court's power over the family increases significantly. All future decisions regarding place-ment, visitation, or closure of the case will then rest with the court. The court may also use the parent's jurisdictional plea as evidence in a later proceeding to terminate parental rights.

Ultimately, after being advised by his or her attorney, it will be the parent-client who must decide whether to settle the jurisdiction issue or proceed to trial. Under no circumstances should anyone, including the attorney, try to force the parent to enter a plea.

---

[55] *See, e.g.*, MICH. COMP. LAWS § 712A.19b(3)(m) (2008).

If the parent-client will at least consider entering a jurisdictional plea, the attorney should negotiate the plea's details with the prosecutor and the other parties. In most jurisdictions, the parent can either admit to all or some of the allegations in the petition or plead "no contest" to the allegations in either the original petition or a petition that the agency has amended after negotiations with the parent's attorney. The attorney should review these options with the client and then propose to the agency's lawyer the plea language that the client finds acceptable. Before reviewing the options with the client, counsel must determine the consequences of the plea, including both those noted above and others determined by local practices. For example, despite the usual expectation that "no contest" means neither admitting nor denying the allegations in the petitions but being willing to accept the court's jurisdiction, in some jurisdictions, a no contest plea is treated as a finding by the court that the petition's allegations are true. In those jurisdictions, the agency and the court then may be able to use those not-contested "facts" against the parent at a later termination of parental rights hearing. Other judges will expect a parent who has pled no contest on the jurisdictional issue to (later) make explicit admissions during the dispositional phase. These judges view the belated admissions as evidence that the parent now fully appreciates the wrongfulness of the previous conduct, which indicates to these judges that the parent has made real progress in treatment. Understanding these differing local practices will allow the attorney to better evaluate the possible plea deals discussed during negotiations.

§ 28.4.4 Preparing for a Jurisdiction Trial or Fact-Finding Hearing

If the parent wishes to proceed to a jurisdiction trial, much of the pretrial phase will be consumed by trial preparation similar to that in any case. The attorney should thoroughly investigate the matter by interviewing potential witnesses and reviewing relevant documents. There may be alternate explanations for the alleged abuse or neglect and the context in which something occurred may be determinative of the need for state intervention. Potential witnesses may include medical or psychological experts, teachers, neighbors, police officers, and family members. To obtain information from non-parties, attorneys can use their subpoena power if necessary. Attorneys should also obtain a copy of the complete child protective files which—if not already allowed by state statute or court rule—they should be able to obtain with a subpoena and a release signed by the parent-client. If the agency will not open its files, the parent's attorney should first seek to resolve that issue with the attorney representing the agency. If negotiating fails, counsel should then request a court order compelling disclosure.

Attorneys should also use formal discovery procedures to uncover the details of other sides' case—if that right is available under state law—so that no information unknown to the parent's attorney will be presented at trial. Discovery procedures may include interrogatories, requests for production of documents, depositions, and requests for admissions. As part of this inquiry, the attorney should also interview the guardian ad litem, the children's attorney, and all of the witnesses testifying on behalf of the state. Some states have mandatory disclosure procedures in lieu of or in addition to the availability of discovery.

§ 28.4.5 The Pretrial Hearing

The pretrial hearing presents another opportunity for the parent's attorney to resolve issues concerning placement, visitation, and services. Generally these issues may be addressed at any hearing in a child welfare case. Updated information regarding the parent—including compliance with services, changes in employment, changes in living situation, or successful visitation—may cause the court to revisit orders entered at the preliminary hearing. At every hearing, it is critical that the attorney make the court aware, through testimony, exhibits, and argument, that the parent is making continued progress, something that is crucial to creating and maintaining positive momentum.

The pretrial hearing also allows the jurist and the attorneys to anticipate and resolve issues that may arise during the jurisdiction trial. The parent's attorney should inform the court whether the parent-client is willing to enter into a plea admitting jurisdiction or if the client wants a trial. At the pretrial hearing, attorneys may file trial-related motions or enter stipulations regarding particular pieces of evidence. For example, if the agency has failed to respond to a discovery request, the pretrial hearing affords a good opportunity to raise that issue with the jurist and, if necessary, request that discovery be compelled by the court. If the petition contains factual allegations that have no relevance to the jurisdiction determination, the attorney should request that the agency amend the petition by striking the irrelevant allegations. The pretrial hearing may also resolve motions in limine on issues such as the admissibility of specific pieces of evidence or the manner in which children's testimony or out-of-court statements will be presented at trial.

At the pretrial hearing, the parent's attorney should give the court an estimate of how many witnesses will testify at trial and what exhibits will be introduced. A thorough pretrial investigation and discovery effort will have prepared the attorney to provide that information. The attorney should also request that the court's pretrial order include deadlines for exchanging witness and exhibit lists and for filing any remaining motions. At the end of the pretrial hearing, the court will set a trial date if it has not already done so.

Through zealous advocacy at the pretrial stage, the parent's attorney can achieve or advance the parent-client's goals by facilitating a mutually agreeable plea bargain or assembling a strong case for trial. If the allegations cannot be resolved completely during the pretrial phase, then a trial regarding jurisdiction will be necessary. The next section addresses the issues that may arise at a jurisdiction trial.

§ 28.5 The Jurisdiction Trial

§ 28.5.1 Use Traditional Trial Practice Techniques

The role of the parent's attorney during the jurisdiction trial resembles that of a defense attorney in a criminal case. The agency bears the burden of proving the petition's allegations by a standard of proof defined by state law, and the parent's attorney usually will offer an alternate case theory to dispute the agency's allegations. As appropriate, counsel should call witnesses, cross-examine the agency's witnesses, and introduce exhibits that support the parent-client's position. If the client is going to testify, it is crucial that the attorney prepare the client to present the testimony as sympathetically as possible. At a minimum, the attorney must meet with the client to practice the direct exam and likely cross exam questions and advise the client on the disadvantages of appearing hostile or inconsistent. If there is a possibility of a parallel criminal trial, the decision to testify should be coordinated with the criminal defense attorney. Ultimately, the referee, judge, or jury will determine whether the agency has proven that grounds exist for the court to take jurisdiction of the child. If the court does assume jurisdiction, the case will proceed to its dispositional phase, which is discussed below in § 28.6.

A comprehensive guide to trial practice is beyond the scope of this chapter. To prepare for trial, parents' attorneys may wish to review a trial practice manual to familiarize themselves with such basics as delivering opening statements and closing arguments, asking direct and cross-examination questions, and introducing documents into evidence. [56] Parent's counsel should also inquire about a county's local practices. He or she should try to ascertain the judge's preferences on procedural matters such as marking exhibits, submitting witness and exhibit lists, and entering stipulations.

In all jurisdiction trials, the parent's attorney has two overarching tasks in addition to other responsibilities: (1) develop and present a coherent theory of the case; and (2) preserve trial errors for later appellate review.

§ 28.5.2 Theory of the Case

To tell the client's "story" effectively at trial, the parent's attorney must develop a coherent theory of the case that adapts the client's story to the case's legal issues. A successful theory speaks directly to the case's legal issues and is logical, simple, and easy to believe. In Chapter 32, Steven Lubet and John Myers suggest three questions for attorneys to ask when developing and expressing their case theory: What happened? Why did it happen? Why does that mean the client should win?

An ideal case theory can be expressed in a single paragraph. For example, if the agency alleges that a mother left her ten-year-old child unsupervised for several hours while she was at work, the mother's case theory could be: "Being poor does not make

---

[56] *See generally* STEVEN LUBET, MODERN TRIAL ADVOCACY: ANALYSIS AND PRACTICE (4th ed. 2009); THOMAS A. MAUET, TRIAL TECHNIQUES (7th ed. 2007). *See also* Chapter 32, Trial Advocacy.

one a neglectful parent. Ms. Smith is a hardworking, single parent who was forced by emergency circumstances to leave her child alone. Court supervision, however, is not needed to protect this child."

The attorney can formulate a solid case theory only after conducting a thorough investigation that has uncovered both the good and bad facts of the case. The theory must then address both the positive and negative aspects of the case. Attorneys preparing for trial will often draft several case theories before settling on the one that best explains their client's actions.

A coherent theory of the case will guide the attorney's tactical decisions at trial. Should a specific witness be called? What types of cross-examination questions should the attorney ask? Should a document be introduced into evidence? Should the attorney object to a particular line of questioning? The parent's attorney can make better trial decisions by always considering which actions best support the prepared theory of the case.

§ 28.5.3 Preserving Issues for Appeal

The need to preserve issues for appeal also will determine some of the attorney's actions at trial. If the parent loses the jurisdiction trial, the court will then enter a dispositional order, which most jurisdictions consider an appealable final order. A parent who wishes to appeal the trial court's assumption of jurisdiction must act quickly. Inexperienced parents' attorneys often make the mistake of waiting until the client's parental rights have been terminated (a much later phase of some child welfare cases) before challenging the court's initial decision to take jurisdiction, and often these appeals are deemed moot.[57] Attorneys must know at what points in their states appeals are available as a matter of right or within the court's discretion, and must know the applicable deadlines for filing notices of appeal.[58]

For the parent to have any significant chance of prevailing on appeal, the parent's trial attorney must have preserved the appellate issues during the trial. An attorney can preserve issues for appeal by clearly presenting them to the trial court and requesting rulings during the trial. The attorney usually should raise the issue with a timely objection or a motion *in limine*. That gives the trial court the first opportunity to decide the issue, something that appellate courts almost always insist upon before they will rule on an issue. This general rule applies to both procedural and evidentiary rulings. Appellate courts routinely decline to consider unpreserved issues unless they conclude that the error was both plain and substantially affected the party's rights. In practice, that is a nearly insurmountable appellate standard. Trial attorneys must take care to preserve all potential appellate issues with timely objections or motions.

As a practical matter, the steps required to preserve an issue for appeal are straightforward. The precise steps will vary by state law. But generally speaking, if

---

[57] *See, e.g., In re* Hatcher, 443 Mich. 426, 505 N.W.2d 834 (1993).

[58] *See* Chapter 26, Child Welfare Appellate Law and Practice.

the parent's attorney disagrees with an evidentiary ruling, the attorney need only present a timely objection or motion to strike that states the specific ground for the objection. If the objection involves admitting or excluding a particular piece of evidence that the court has not yet heard or seen, the attorney must also ensure that the court knows the substance of the evidence. Once the court makes a definitive ruling on the record either admitting or excluding evidence, the attorney does not need to object repeatedly or make a formal offer of proof in order to preserve the question for appeal.

Similarly, for a procedural ruling such as one involving service of process, or how to present testimony by a child witness, the attorney need only state the objection, ensure that the court understands the basis for the objection, and request a ruling on the issue.

To create the clearest possible record for the appellate court, the best practice often will be to file a written motion in limine before the issue actually arises, or a written motion for reconsideration if the court has already ruled. Filing written motions will eliminate any uncertainty as to whether the issue has been properly preserved for appeal. The same considerations about preserving issues for appeal apply at termination of parental rights hearings, which are discussed in Section 28.10.

Through zealous advocacy at the jurisdiction trial, the parent's counsel will further the interests of both the parent and the child by ensuring that the court intervenes only in appropriate cases. Winning a dismissal at the conclusion of the jurisdiction trial will end the attorney's involvement in the case. If, however, the court decides to assume jurisdiction over the child, then the case will proceed to the dispositional phase, where different tactical considerations arise. These are discussed below.

§ 28.6 Dispositional Hearing

If the court finds—based on either the parent's plea or the agency's trial evidence—that a child comes within the court's jurisdiction, the case then moves to the dispositional phase.[59] At the initial dispositional hearing, the court typically decides who should have custody of the child, who is entitled to services, and what steps must be taken to resolve the issues that led to the adjudication of abuse or neglect. The hearing is crucial because at its conclusion, the plan ordered by the court will guide the future of the case. Quite often, the subsequent termination of a parent's rights is based on his or her failure to comply with the dispositional plan. Thus, attorneys representing parents must be very diligent in ensuring that the plan is narrowly tailored to address the specific issues that led to the child's adjudication.

---

[59] Some courts may consolidate the evidence in one trial and make adjudicatory and dispositional findings and orders at the end of the trial while others may have separate phases sequentially within the same trial or set a separate dispositional hearing.

One of the first steps the attorneys should take in preparing for a dispositional hearing is to ascertain the agency's goals. Most states require the agency to submit a detailed, written dispositional report or service plan for the court to consider. Federal law requires a case service plan to be developed within 60 days of the child's removal.[60] The parent's attorney must obtain all agency reports well in advance of each hearing, read them carefully, and then review them with the client. The agency's reports and treatment plans should detail both the services provided or planned for the parent and the behavioral changes that the agency expects to result from the parent's participation in those services. If the attorney cannot obtain a copy of the report before the hearing, he or she should consider requesting a short adjournment of the proceeding. The attorney should also obtain copies of other reports filed by other individuals including the guardian ad litem or children's attorney, the court-appointed special advocate, and mental health professionals. The attorney should also meet with and provide relevant information to the child's legal representative and should consider permitting that individual to meet directly with the parent.

To assess the appropriateness of the agency's recommendations, the attorney should conduct an independent investigation of the client's circumstances. At a minimum, this should include regularly discussing the case with the client and asking the client to sign releases so the attorney can obtain additional information directly from service providers. The parent's attorney also should obtain the service providers' written documentation of the client's progress. Throughout the dispositional and review phases of the proceedings, the parent's attorney should communicate regularly with anyone who may have information that will help the attorney advocate for the client. That list includes, at a minimum, the caseworker, the child's guardian ad litem or children's attorney, the state's attorney, and other participants such as the child's court-appointed special advocate.

During this investigation it may become apparent that the client has needs that are not being met. For example, the attorney may learn that the client is developmentally delayed or has a previously undisclosed substance abuse problem or mental health diagnosis. In such circumstances, the parent's attorney must meet with the client and explain that additional evaluations and services may identify deficits that have impaired the client's ability to parent. But the attorney also must explain that coming forward with such information may further delay reunification or make it less likely. Parents' attorneys should counsel their clients carefully about the risks and advantages that accompany each course of action.

The parent's attorney should obtain official documentation showing that the client has complied with or completed services. In addition, the attorney should advise clients to document their own efforts. For example, the attorney may suggest that the parent keep a journal of dates, times and details of: (1) interactions with the caseworker or other professionals; (2) attempted or made phone calls to service providers; (3) attendance at services; and (4) visits with their children. Any

---

[60]   45 C.F.R. § 1356.21(g).

documentation that the parent has benefited from services will be especially helpful. Examples of that include certificates from parenting classes, residence leases (to show that the parent has obtained proper housing), and sign-in sheets for substance abuse treatment programs. Counsel should present copies of these documents to the court at the initial dispositional hearing and at subsequent review hearings. Counsel should also share this information with the guardian ad litem or children's attorney and all other parties before the hearing because the information may affect the recommendation those parties make to the court.

As during the other phases of a child welfare case, client counseling is crucial before and after the dispositional hearing. The parent's attorney should encourage the client to cooperate with the agency's efforts to provide services directed at reunification, and should explain the consequences of failing to cooperate. The parent's attorney should also advise the client that, although reunification will not occur unless the parent complies with the agency's recommendations, compliance alone will not ensure reunification. The parent must also demonstrate that he or she has benefited from the services. If the agency worker does not agree that the parent has benefitted from services and made progress, the parent's attorney should explore with the client ways to convince the court that the client has benefited. For example, if possible, the attorney should retain a social worker to observe a visit and testify or write a report, or encourage one of the service providers to observe a visit for that purpose.

The attorney should also counsel the parent about alternative dispositional options that could resolve the case. For example, if the child has been placed temporarily with a relative, the attorney might discuss trying to resolve the case through a custody or guardianship agreement or through an adoption, if the client wishes to do so. In some cases, a change of custody to the child's other parent may resolve a child welfare case. Finally, if the attorney concludes that the parent does not wish to take any steps to regain custody of the child, the attorney should consider counseling the parent about releasing his or her parental rights so that the child will be eligible for adoption. Of course, the attorney must discuss with the parent the potential pros and cons of any dispositional alternatives.

At the actual dispositional hearing, the parent's attorney should zealously advocate for a plan that meets the client's objectives. Where the client believes that the agency report includes inaccurate information, the attorney should explain the disagreement to the court and request an explicit finding as to which version is true. If the court finds that a statement made in a written report is inaccurate, the parent's attorney should request that the report be amended. A failure to take those steps will allow the inaccurate information to become part of the court's continuing record that the court may rely on at later stages in the proceeding. Parents' attorneys should also consider submitting into evidence their own written reports that summarize their clients' views regarding participation in services, the benefits derived from that participation, the child's best interests, and other relevant matters. For example, a report filed by a parent's attorney could include information regarding the parent's efforts to comply with and benefit from the following components of the court-ordered service plan: visitation with the child, participation in counseling, substance abuse treatment, parenting programs, and other services. The parent's report also could direct the court's attention to any difficulties the parent has encountered in accessing agency services or contacting the caseworker. Finally, the report may also include the attorney's requests that the court order additional or different services (or eliminate the requirement of compliance with a service). The submission of an independent report can do much to counterbalance inaccurate or incomplete information in the agency's report. It also serves to balance the entire written record of the case, which could be vitally important if the court reviews its file in a subsequent termination proceeding.

Parents' attorneys should also advocate for the services that best suit the client's individual needs. To do this effectively, an attorney should learn everything possible about the local community's service providers. Regardless of the client's apparent capacity to parent, if reunification is the articulated goal, the agency has a statutory duty to make reasonable efforts to provide services that address the parent's deficits. This means that the services must address the primary barriers to reunification in the particular case. That may require more than the agency's favored boilerplate services, which often will not address a particular client's identified parenting deficits. The attorney should be prepared to use cross examination of the caseworker or to submit evidence from experts or service providers to support an argument for services individualized to the client's needs.

The agency must offer services of sufficient quality, duration, and intensity to allow a parent who complies with the service plan a fair chance to demonstrate that he or she has made the needed changes. When services do not address the parent's needs, are not of sufficient quality, do not last long enough, or are not sufficiently intense, parents' attorneys should argue that the agency has failed to make reasonable efforts to reunify the family.

Some clients' parenting deficits result from conditions covered by the Americans with Disabilities Act (ADA).[61] If so, the agency must provide services that go beyond the general "reasonable efforts" requirement.[62] The ADA additionally requires the agency to make "reasonable accommodations" to address that parent's specific disability.[63] For example, a developmentally delayed parent should attend parenting classes that are hands-on rather than classes that use a lecture format. To give developmentally delayed parents a fair opportunity to learn and integrate the necessary parenting information, they usually need to attend more class sessions over a longer period of time. The parent's attorney should track the agency's compliance with the ADA throughout the dispositional and review hearing process.

---

[61] *See* 42 U.S.C. § 12101 (2006).

[62] *See, e.g., In re* Terry, 240 Mich. App. 14, 610 N.W.2d 563 (2000).

[63] *See In re* Terry, 240 Mich. App. 14, 610 N.W.2d 563, 570 (2000).

Parents who have two or more co-existing problems (e.g., substance abuse and a mental illness) may be required to engage in multiple services. That will require substantial time commitments, which can be especially difficult for parents who work. Those competing demands may cause conflicts or transportation difficulties. Therefore, counsel may have to ask the agency (or the court, if the agency refuses) to prioritize the services schedule in a way that gives the parent a fair chance to comply.

Visitation aims to maintain and strengthen the parent-child attachment, which is crucial to a child's development and successful reunification. The visitation schedule must be tailored to the individual needs of the child. Particularly for infants and young children, weekly, supervised one-hour visits at the agency's office will not suffice to maintain the parent-child relationship.[64] The parent's attorney should advocate for maximum visitation in order to develop, preserve, or enhance the natural bonding between parent and child.

The parent's attorney must consider two additional issues concerning services. First, the attorney must advocate for the availability of services to parents at times outside traditional office hours, which is particularly important because many parents do not have jobs that allow for much time off or for flexibility. This means that agencies sometimes must accommodate the parent's or child's need for services in the evenings and on weekends. Second, the service location may present problems because many parents do not have ready access to reliable transportation. The attorney should know the community's public transportation options and advocate for services in convenient locations or for special transportation services that will allow the parent to travel to and from the service providers.

After the court has concluded a dispositional review hearing, the parent's attorney should obtain and carefully review the dispositional order. If the order does not accurately reflect the hearing's outcome, the attorney should immediately ask the court to amend the order. The attorney should provide the client a copy of the order and review it with the client to ensure that the client understands what the order requires and the possible consequences of failing to comply with it.

§ 28.7 Advocacy Between Hearings

After the dispositional hearing, the next court hearing—the review hearing—will occur approximately three to six months later. During the intervals between court hearings, agency personnel often make critically important decisions. In many states, administrative meetings occur on a regular basis at which many issues are discussed including modifications to the case service plan such as additional services for the family, selection of treatment/service professionals, and changes to the visitation schedule. Ideally, attorneys for parents should attend these meetings and view them as

---

[64] *See* National Council of Juvenile and Family Court Judges, *Child Development: A Judge's Reference Guide*, p. 22–24 (1993) (discussing attachment and bonding and noting that a primary ingredient of healthy development is time with the parent).

opportunities to solve problems before heading to court. At the very least, parent's attorneys should closely monitor these developments through in-person and phone contacts with the client, the caseworker, and service delivery personnel. Because these decisions will often be ratified by the court an attorney can dramatically improve case outcomes by advocating for the client between court hearings. If formal conferences are not routinely held, the parent's attorney should request opportunities to address issues as they arise. Ideally, the attorney should seek to convene a meeting before *every* court hearing to attempt to resolve issues.

In some states, before making a placement or any change in the child's placement between hearings, the agency convenes Team Decision-making Meetings (TDM) that include the parent, caseworkers, the guardian ad litem or children's attorney, and other family members.[65] Critical decisions about placement, visitation, and services are made at TDM meetings, and, because there will be an inherent power imbalance if a parent attends alone, the parent's attorney should try to attend TDMs and ensure that the parent has additional support persons in attendance. Even when the parent's attorney cannot attend the TDM, the attorney should encourage the parent to attend and to work cooperatively with the team members to ensure that the parent's voice is heard. These administrative meetings provide additional opportunities for parents to stay involved in their children's lives and for attorneys to address their client's concerns.

§ 28.8 Review Hearings

Review hearings are post-disposition proceedings at which the judge assesses the progress of the case and determines whether any changes need to be made to the service plan. Typically, the primary issues addressed at a review hearing are placement, services, and visitation. The court will determine whether the agency has met its obligations to provide services and facilitate visitation under the statute and the court order and will ascertain whether the parent has made progress towards remedying the factors that led to the adjudication. At each hearing, the court should also be assessing whether the grounds for dependency continue to exist.

Preparing for a review hearing is similar to getting ready for the initial dispositional hearing. The attorney should obtain a copy of the agency's report and all documents prepared by other parties and interested actors in the case. The attorney should review the documents with his or her client and should also independently speak to all of the service providers working with the client to determine who may be able to provide the court with information helpful to the parent. Potential service providers may include the parenting class instructor, the mental health therapist or the visitation supervisor. Once these individuals are identified, the attorney should obtain

---

[65] Team decision-making meetings are a key component of the Family to Family initiative pioneered by the Annie E. Casey Foundation. For more information about the Family to Family program, visit the page titled "Family to Family Resources" on the Web site of the Annie E. Casey Foundation at http://www.aecf.org/MajorInitiatives/Family%20to%20Family/Resources.aspx.

written reports from them and should consider subpoenaing them for the hearing so that they can provide testimony to the court. As is the case before the initial dispositional hearing, the attorneys should also consider filing a written report documenting the client's progress towards fulfilling the case service plan.

At the review hearing, the attorney should request modifications to the service plan and court orders—including changes in placement and visitation—that the client requests. Counsel should advocate for return of the child to the parent's custody where the risk to the child is eliminated, the child is no longer vulnerable to risk or the parent have sufficient protective capacities to manage or control the threats of danger to the child.[66] Parent's counsel should use every opportunity to demonstrate to the court that progress is being made and should ensure that the court focuses on the parent's strengths and successes, not just on the shortcomings that the other parties may dwell on. Counsel should also ensure that the agency's actions are consistent with state and federal mandates and that the state made reasonable efforts towards reunification. Additionally, if the grounds for dependency no longer exist, counsel should request the immediate closure of the case.

After the hearing, the attorney should carefully review the order with the parent to ensure that the court did not err in its findings and that the parent understands exactly what is expected by the court and the agency.

§ 28.9 Permanency Planning Hearing

Federal law requires the court to hold a permanency planning hearing (PPH) within 12 months after the child's removal from the home or within 30 days of a determination that no reunification efforts are necessary. The requirement to hold a PPH was intended to make courts expedite a permanent placement for the child, which may include reunification, adoption, or a legal guardianship, among other options. At the PPH, the court may direct the agency to file a petition to terminate the parent's legal rights to the child. The specific decisions that are made at the PPH and the legal standards may vary from state to state.

Parents' attorneys should begin thinking about the permanency plan at the inception of the child welfare case, when they counsel their clients about complying with the case service plan. A parent's failure to comply with the court-ordered service plan is typically considered evidence that the child will be at risk if returned to the parent's custody. Conversely, where a parent has substantially complied with the ordered services, the parent's attorney should be prepared to make an argument that any risk of harm has been reduced or eliminated and that the child should be returned home.

To prepare for a PPH, the parent's attorney should consider how best to demonstrate that returning the child home would not subject the child to harm—even if the parent has not completed all treatment services. Counsel should informally

---

[66] *See* Chapter 14, Child Safety: What Judges and Lawyers Need to Know.

lobby the caseworker to recommend a return home or, at least allow more time for the parent to complete the court-ordered services.

Before a PPH, the attorney should interview all the service providers to assess the client's compliance with and benefit from services. If the providers offer helpful information, the parent's attorney should subpoena them to testify at the hearing.

The service providers often can clarify a parent's issues in ways that caseworkers cannot or will not do. If sympathetic providers cannot testify in person at a PPH, the attorney should solicit letters or affidavits from them to help the court understand the parent's progress in the treatment program. Hearsay is typically admissible at the hearing.

Just as evidence provided by those working directly with the parent can impact the court's permanency planning determination, the views of the guardian ad litem or children's attorney, who works directly with the child, also will carry considerable influence. Before a PPH (and ideally before every hearing), the parent's attorney should consult with the child's attorney regarding the permanency recommendation. The parent's attorney should try to persuade the child's legal representative to support the child's return home or, at least, continued efforts to reunify the family. This conversation also should include a realistic assessment of other permanency options and their likely effects on the child. Questions to ask the GAL may include the following: What is the long term permanency goal? Is adoption likely? If so, has the GAL already identified a viable adoptive placement? Does the child have special needs that would make adoption difficult to arrange? If the plan is for the child to transition to adulthood from foster care, how would termination of parental rights further the child's best interests?

In addition to advocating for the client when meeting with the GAL, the parent's attorney should consider permitting the GAL to meet with the parent so the GAL can independently assess the parent's progress. Counsel may want to be present if such a meeting occurs.

Also before the permanency planning hearing, the parent's attorney should counsel the client about all possible options. In cases in which reunification appears unlikely, the attorney should consider discussing with the client the possibility of consenting to a legal guardianship, custody order, or adoption decree, or of relinquishing his or her parental rights. Where reunification appears in doubt, pursuing one of these options may enable the client to avoid the involuntary termination of his or her rights. If the client decides to relinquish his or her parental rights, counseling may be appropriate and the attorney can help construct a therapeutic process so that the parent and the child can say goodbye in the least detrimental way possible.

At the hearing itself, the attorney should zealously advocate to achieve the client's objectives. Attorneys should use state statutory language to request that a child be returned home if return does not pose a substantial risk of harm to the child.[67] If the

---

[67] *See, e.g.*, MICH. COMP. LAWS § 712A.19a(5) (child must be returned home unless return home would cause a "substantial risk of harm to the child's life, physical health, or mental well-being").

agency is seeking permission to file a petition to terminate parental rights, the attorney should argue that a petition is premature. Although federal law requires that a petition be filed if a child has been in foster care for 15 of the most recent 22 months, certain exceptions apply, including the placement of the child with a relative or the state's failure to provide appropriate services to the family.[68] The attorney should be prepared to argue that one of these exceptions applies or that compelling reasons demonstrate why filing the petition would be contrary to the child's best interests.[69] For example, termination of parental rights may not be appropriate in the case of an older child who does not wish to be adopted or for a child living with a relative who does not wish to adopt him or her. The attorney should also consider having the parent testify if he or she could persuasively testify as to steps taken to address the issues that led to the foster care placement.

§ 28.10 Termination of Parental Rights

§ 28.10.1 Investigation and Analysis

After the permanency planning hearing, the court, often acting on the agency's recommendation, may order the agency to file a petition to terminate the parent's rights. Generally speaking, a termination order permanently severs the legal relationship between the child and the parent. After the issuance of the order, the parent has no legal right to visit, plan for, or contact the child. Due to the severity of the sanction sought by the state, termination cases require the parent's attorney to confront a new series of difficult legal and strategic challenges. Counsel must carefully identify the issues presented in the individual case and address each issue in turn.

When the agency files a termination petition, the parent's attorney should meet with the client to review each factual allegation and the corresponding legal basis for termination cited in the petition, which the state must prove by at least clear and convincing evidence.[70] After hearing the client's response to each factual and legal allegation, the attorney should then work with the client to develop a list of potential witnesses. For example, the client's mental health evaluator, substance abuse counselor, or therapist might provide important testimony that will challenge the termination petition's factual or legal allegations.

After developing the list of potential witnesses, the attorney should contact and interview each one. To interview some witnesses (e.g., therapists), the attorney will first need to have the client sign a release that authorizes the witness to reveal confidential information to the attorney. Counsel will need permission from the guardian ad litem or children's attorney to interview the client's children. After interviewing the potential witnesses, the parent's attorney will need to decide which

---

[68] 42 U.S.C. § 675(5)(E).

[69] 42 U.S.C. § 675(5)(E)(ii).

[70] In *Santosky v. Kramer*, 455 U.S. 745 (1982), the United State Supreme Court held that a clear and convincing standard of proof was constitutionally required in termination of parental rights cases.

witnesses' testimony will bolster the parent's theory of the case. The attorney should subpoena those witnesses and develop direct-examination questions that will elicit the information that the court needs to understand the parent's theory of the case. The parent's attorney should also obtain the witness and exhibit lists prepared by the agency and the guardian ad litem or children's attorney. The attorney should interview those potential adverse witnesses and obtain copies of all documents that the other parties will seek to introduce into evidence. This advance preparation will allow the parents' attorney to develop a theory as to each adverse witness and a strategy for cross-examining that witness. The parent's attorney should also gather documentary evidence that supports the parent's case. As part of that effort, the attorney should request (and subpoena if necessary) the caseworker's file. The attorney must review the file's contents and make copies of important documents. When reviewing the history of the case, the attorney should identify the original basis for the court's jurisdiction over the child and the services ordered by the court, and assess the agency's efforts to work with the client and provide the required services. If the agency resists providing this information, the parent's attorney should file a discovery motion seeking access to the information as permitted under state law.

§ 28.10.2 Pretrial Motions

While conducting a thorough investigation of the case, the parent's attorney should evaluate whether any pretrial motions are required. If the state intends to call witnesses whose sole basis of knowledge comes from hearsay evidence, the attorney should file a motion *in limine* to exclude the testimony. The attorney may also determine that expert evaluations are necessary to assess the relationships between the child, the foster parent, and the birth parents or to determine the parent's capacity to take care of the child. In some states, the court or the agency may be required to pay for such evaluations where the parent is indigent. Whether an attorney wants to take the risk inherent in requesting an evaluation of the parent may depend on the strength of the case. Where the facts are strong, the evaluation may be unnecessary and may only threaten to undermine the case. However, where the case is weak, the attorney may determine that a good evaluation may be crucial (and worth the risk) to prevent the termination of the client's parental rights.

§ 28.10.3 Theory of the Case

As with the jurisdiction trial, the parent's attorney must develop a coherent theory of the parent's case.[71] The theory should present a short and logical summary of the case's facts and the parent's legal position. An ideal theory distills both the client's story and the applicable law. For example, the following might be the parent's theory of the case for a termination case: "The existing attachment between this mother and her daughter is such that a severing of the existing bond would be severely

---

[71] *See* Chapter 32, Trial Advocacy.

detrimental to the child." Other theories may involve the feasibility of other, less drastic, permanency options such as guardianship, custody, or placement in a "planned permanent living arrangement" as defined by federal law.[72] Developing a coherent and comprehensive theory will help the attorney organize the facts and will provide a framework for determining which witnesses to call, what evidence to present, and what questions to ask. To make sure that the judge understands the theory and sees how the evidence supports it, the attorney should outline the theory during both the opening statement and the closing argument.

§ 28.11 Appellate Advocacy

When a court issues an adverse ruling at any point in the child welfare cases, attorneys will be confronted with a decision as to whether to appeal the order. After determining whether the order is one that is appealable under state law,[73] the attorney should counsel the client on the likely outcome of the appeal. The attorney should carefully review the record, including all transcripts and the court records, and should make an initial determination of what potential issues can be raised on appeal. The attorney should consider constitutional claims, statutory arguments, and abuses of discretion by the trial court. To be a successful appellate attorney, counsel must be well-versed in the substantive and procedural constitutional rights afforded to parents by the Fourteenth Amendment, federal and state child welfare laws, and the intricacies of appellate practice.[74]

If the parent's attorney determines that legitimate claims exist for an appeal, then the attorney should counsel the client on the pros and cons of appealing. The attorney should advise the client about the length of time an appeal is likely to take in the jurisdiction and how the delay may affect the family's situation. At times, appealing a determination of jurisdiction will slow efforts toward reunification; during an appeal of a termination of parental rights, the parent may not be allowed to see the child.

Ultimately, after counseling the client about the pros and cons of going forward with the appeal, it is the parent's decision whether or not the claim should be pursued. If a parent wishes to go forward, the attorney should take all steps permitted under state law to expedite the completion of the process.

§ 28.12 Conclusion

Parents have a constitutionally protected right to the care, custody, and control of their children. The state may interfere with these rights only by following proper procedures, and only after showing that the parent is unfit to parent his or her child.

---

[72] 42 U.S.C. § 675(5)(C).

[73] Typically, state laws permit the appeal of the initial dispositional order and the final termination of parental rights decision. Other appeals may be discretionary.

[74] *See* Chapter 26, Child Welfare Appellate Law and Practice.

Parents' attorneys must use the law to protect these critically important rights, working with the parent to establish the goals of the representation, which usually are to minimize the state's interference with parental rights. The parent's attorney must be a zealous advocate for the parent and must counsel the client based on a comprehensive knowledge of the law and a detailed understanding of the particular case. The parent's attorney must carefully investigate the case at every stage and advise the client regarding all the options at each stage, but ultimately let the client determine the goals to be achieved. By taking these steps, the parent's attorney will fully explore all aspects of the case, protect the parent's interests, ensure that the need for court involvement continues to exist, and increase the likelihood that the court makes a decision that serves the best interests of the child.

Chapter 29 Representing Children and Youth*

by Donald N. Duquette[1] and Ann Haralambie[2]

§ 29.1 Introduction

The role of the child's attorney is unique in American jurisprudence and not yet clearly defined by law or tradition. There is a growing consensus, however, that children in dependency cases should have lawyers who are as active and as involved in their cases as are lawyers for any other party in any other litigation. Yet there continues to be confusion and debate over the role and duties of the lawyer, particularly as to what voice the child should have in determining the direction and goals of the litigation. Policy makers have differed as to whether the child's lawyer should represent the best interests of the child as determined by the lawyer or the expressed wishes of the child. The two competing views, the "best interests" model or the "client directed" model, are not yet resolved in American law.

Nevertheless, there is a strong agreement as to the duties of the child's lawyer— no matter how the decision-making authority for the litigation is defined. This chapter is based on the law as it is today or reasonably could be interpreted to be. We attempt to identify what governing legal authority currently exists on the role and duties of the child's advocate and leave the policy debate to another time and place.[3]

---

* This chapter is based on an earlier work by Donald N. Duquette and Marvin Ventrell that appeared in the first edition of Child Welfare Law and Practice.

[1] Donald N. Duquette, J.D., is Clinical Professor of Law and Director of the Child Advocacy Law Clinic of the University of Michigan Law School.

[2] Ann Haralambie, J.D., is a certified family law specialist practicing in Tucson, Arizona. She is also an author and speaker in the fields of family and children's law.

[3] *See, e.g.,* American Bar Association, *Report and Working Draft of a Model Act Governing the Representation of Children in Abuse, Neglect, and Dependency Proceedings,* 42 FAM. L.Q. 145 (Spring 2008); Barbara Ann Atwood, *The Uniform Representation of Children in Abuse, Neglect, and Custody Proceedings Act: Bridging the Divide Between Pragmatism and Idealism,* 42 FAM. L.Q. 63 (Spring 2008); Linda D. Elrod, *Client-Directed Lawyers for Children: It Is the "Right" Thing to Do,* 27 PACE L. REV. 869 (2007); *Proceedings of the UNLV Conference on Representing Children in Families: Children's Advocacy and Justice Ten Years After Fordham: Recommendations of the Conference,* 6 NEV. L.J. 592 (2006); Barbara Ann Atwood, *Representing Children: The Ongoing Search for Clear and Workable Standards,* 19 J. AM. ACAD. MATRIM. LAW. 183 (2005); JEAN KOH PETERS, REPRESENTING CHILDREN IN CHILD PROTECTIVE PROCEEDINGS 2007: ETHICAL AND PRACTICAL DIMENSIONS (3d ed. 2007); Donald Duquette, *Legal Representation for Children in Protection Proceedings: Two Distinct Lawyer Roles Are Required,* 34 FAM. L.Q. 441 (2000); *Proceedings of the Conference on Ethical Issues in the Legal Representation of Children: Recommendations of the Conference,* 64 FORDHAM L. REV. 1301 (1996); Annette R. Appell, *Decontextualizing the Child Client: The Efficacy of the Attorney-Client Model for Very Young Children,* 64 FORDHAM L. REV.

In Section 29.2 below, we begin this chapter by discussing the federal, state, and local law that defines the duties of the child advocate, along with recent court decisions on a child's right to counsel. Because binding rules of ethics in your jurisdiction are likely to provide helpful guidance to the lawyer, we discuss ethical rules in Section 29.3. In Sections 29.4, 29.5, and 29.6 we discuss we discuss giving voice and weight to the child's stated wishes; even if your jurisdiction is a "best interests" jurisdiction and has not adopted a client-directed approach to child representation, the child's wishes and views are always relevant to the court, no matter how young, immature, or erratic the child may appear. In Section 29.7 we articulate the widely accepted duties of the child's lawyer as found in the ABA Standards and in many state and local standards, which anticipate a child's lawyer who is competent, independent, and zealous. Some of the special challenges facing a child's lawyer are discussed in Sections 29.8 and 29.9. Finally in Section 29.10 we discuss the current developments in the organization and delivery of legal services to children.

§ 29.2 Federal and State Law Governing the Child's Advocate

§ 29.2.1 Federal Statutory Law

Children have been represented in the child welfare cases for a relatively short time. Prior to the 1970s, children were infrequently represented by counsel, but today children are nearly always represented under some model of representation.[4] Unlike delinquency law, which mandates independent legal counsel under *In re Gault*,[5] there is no such federal or constitutional mandate in dependency court.[6] Guidance comes primarily from the Federal Child Abuse Prevention and Treatment Act (CAPTA). As a condition for receiving Federal child abuse related funds, CAPTA requires that each

---

1955 (1996); Katherine Hunt Federle, *The Ethics of Empowerment: Rethinking the Role of Lawyers in Interviewing and Counseling the Child Client*, 64 FORDHAM L. REV. 1655 (1996); Martin Guggenheim, *A Paradigm for Determining the Role of Counsel for Children*, 64 FORDHAM L. REV. 1399 (1996); Ann M. Haralambie, *The Role of the Child's Attorney in Protecting the Child Throughout the Litigation Process*, 71 N.D. L. REV. 939, 944 (1995); Marvin R. Ventrell, *Rights & Duties: An Overview of the Attorney-Child Client Relationship*, 26 LOY. U. CHI. L.J. 259 (1995); ANN M. HARALAMBIE, THE CHILD'S ATTORNEY (1993).

[4] First Star & Children's Advocacy Institute, *A Child's Right to Counsel: A National Report Card on Legal Representation for Abused and Neglected Children, Second Edition* (2009); U.S. Department of Health and Human Services, Children's Bureau, *Representation of Children in Child Abuse and Neglect Proceedings: Summary of State Laws* (Child Welfare Information Gateway 2009), *available at* http://www.childwelfare.gov/systemwide/laws_policies/statutes/representall.pdf.

[5] 387 U.S. 1 (1967).

[6] A few states have improved on the problem by determining that a child has a constitutional right to legal representation in child welfare proceedings. *See* Kenny A. *ex rel.* Winn v. Perdue, 356 F. Supp. 2d 1353 (N.D. Ga. 2005); *In re* Jamie TT, 191 A.D.2d 132, 599 N.Y.S.2d 892 (1993). *See generally* Erik Pitchal, *Children's Constitutional Right to Counsel in Dependency Cases*, 15 TEMP. POL. & CIV. RTS. L. REV. 663 (2006); Jacob E. Smiles, *A Child's Due Process Right to Legal Counsel in Abuse and Neglect Dependency Proceedings*, 37 FAM. L.Q. 485 (2003).

state appoint a guardian ad litem for a child in every case involving an abused or neglected child that results in a judicial proceeding.[7] CAPTA permits the courts to appoint a guardian ad litem, who is an attorney or a lay advocate or both. It also requires the guardian ad litem to obtain, first-hand, a clear understanding of the situation and needs of the child and make recommendations to the court concerning the best interests of the child. The 2003 amendments to CAPTA require that the states receiving federal funds certify that each court-appointed lawyer or GAL "has received training appropriate to the role."[8] Federal law has recently expanded the availability of Federal funds for attorney training.[9] Yet only about half the states require attorneys to have training prior to appointment or to have continuing legal education in the field.[10]

If the child is an "Indian Child" under the Indian Child Welfare Act (ICWA),[11] the child has a discretionary right to appointed counsel, and where there is no state provision authorizing payment, the federal government will pay reasonable attorney's fees and expenses.[12] ICWA is silent on which model of representation applies; therefore, whatever model the state uses applies to ICWA cases as well.

§ 29.2.2 State Law and Local Standards

Most states provide for appointment of attorneys, with various titles and roles, for children in dependency[13] and termination[14] cases. A guardian ad litem can, in some situations, serve a dual role as both the guardian ad litem and the juvenile's attorney.[15] But when a guardian ad litem recommends a disposition that conflicts with the juvenile's wishes, the juvenile court may appoint independent counsel to represent the child if the child is of sufficient age and maturity to make an informed decision about a potential termination of the child's relationship with his or her parents.[16] CAPTA is a reasonable starting place but does not constitute a comprehensive model. The result of implementing CAPTA in the states has been the creation of numerous—and oftentimes inconsistent and unclear—models of representation. It can be argued that no two models of child representation among the various U.S. jurisdictions are alike. Further, within jurisdictions, there is often considerable disagreement as to which

---

[7]   42 U.S.C. § 5106a(b)(2)(A)(xiii).

[8]   *Id.*

[9]   Fostering Connections to Success and Increasing Adoptions Act, Pub. L. No. 110-351.

[10] *See* First Star & Children's Advocacy Institute, *A Child's Right to Counsel: A National Report Card on Legal Representation for Abused and Neglected Children, Second Edition* (2009).

[11] 25 U.S.C. §§ 1901 *et seq.*

[12] 25 U.S.C. § 1912(b).

[13] *See* First Star & Children's Advocacy Institute, *A Child's Right to Counsel: A National Report Card on Legal Representation for Abused and Neglected Children, Second Edition* (2009).

[14] *See* ANN M. HARALAMBIE, 3 HANDLING CHILD CUSTODY, ABUSE, AND ADOPTION CASES 3D at 667 (2009).

[15] *See, e.g.,* IOWA CODE § 232.89(2).

[16] *See, e.g.,* IOWA CODE § 232.89.

model is used and what the role of the representative is within the model. In the absence of clear statutory guidance or court rules, the expectations on the attorney may be up to the individual judge or even left totally to the attorney's own judgment. This confusion has undoubtedly contributed to the poor quality of representation children frequently receive in our system.[17]

The conscientious attorney who wishes to rest his or her representation on solid legal authority is hard pressed to find it in many states. To determine what precisely are the role and duties of the child's lawyer in dependency cases, the careful lawyer must draw on a range of legal authority and guidance. First look to state law for controlling authority. The role of the child's lawyer may be set forth in state statutes, case law, court rules, state's ethics codes, or appointment orders and contracts. In Colorado, for example, state statute mandates the appointment of a guardian ad litem and further requires that the GAL be an attorney.[18] The representation model is further defined by a body of case law, a supreme court directive, and the state ethics code.[19] Taken together, these authorities provide the legal framework for the child's representation. New York has a comprehensive set of standards for what New York calls "law guardians."[20] However, other states have no law that sets out the duties of the child's representative in one statute or rule. The child's attorney may need to look broadly and carefully for that authority. Moreover, some state laws offer very little guidance to the child's lawyer even after a careful search. Fortunately there is a developing body of national authority to help guide the practitioner. By drawing on the authority of national ethics and practice standards, the dependency court child's attorney can fill in the gaps that may be left by his or her state law.

---

[17] *Id.*; *America's Children at Risk: A National Agenda for Legal Action*, 1993 REPORT OF THE ABA PRESIDENTIAL WORKING GROUP ON THE UNMET LEGAL NEEDS OF CHILDREN AND THEIR FAMILIES.

[18] COLO. REV. STAT. §§ 19-1-111(1), 19-1-103(59), 19-3-203(3).

[19] *See In re* J.E.B., 854 P.2d 1372 (Colo. App. 1973); Supreme Court of Colorado Directive 04-06, "Court Appointments Through the Office of the Child's Representative" (2004); Colorado Rules of Professional Conduct.

[20] *See* COMMITTEE ON CHILDREN AND THE LAW, NEW YORK STATE BAR ASSOCIATION, LAW GUARDIAN REPRESENTATION STANDARDS (2005).

Authority for Dependency Court Legal Representation

- State Statute.
- Administrative Regulations.
- State Ethics Code.
- Case Law.
- State and Local Court Rule.
- Appointment Order.
- Appointment Contract with State Oversight Authority.
- State Standards of Practice or Guidelines.
- The Child Abuse Prevention and Treatment Act.
- NACC Recommendations for Representation of Children in Abuse and Neglect Cases.
- ABA Standards (and ABA NACC Revised Version) of Practice for Lawyers Who Represent Children in Abuse and Neglect Cases.
- Department of Health and Human Services Guidelines for Public Policy and State Legislation Governing Permanence for Children.
- Treatises and Literature.

---

§ 29.3 Ethical Rules

§ 29.3.1 Presumption that Ethical Responsibility to a Child Client is the Same as to an Adult

Another authoritative foundation for the general rules of lawyer duties to a child client is the ABA Model Code of Professional Responsibility or Model Rules. Each state has adopted a version of one of the ABA Model Code of Professional Responsibility or Model Rules of Professional Conduct. The Model Code and Model Rules define the lawyer's basic responsibility of independent, competent, zealous advocacy.[21] These basic duties, including knowledge, skill, thoroughness, and preparation apply equally to lawyers representing children. No jurisdiction has created a blanket exception to the duty to abide by them for children's lawyers. Lawyers appointed to represent children, therefore, owe the same duties to the child client as he or she would to an adult client unless the state provides a specific exception, such as in the case of client confidentiality under some state's guardian ad litem provisions.

---

[21] *See* MODEL RULES OF PROF'L CONDUCT Preamble, R. 1.1; MODEL CODE OF PROF'L RESPONSIBILITY EC 7-1, EC 7-12, DR 6-101.

Likewise, if one accepts that the duty to provide competent representation requires a lawyer to know his or her client, it would be a breach of the duty and a violation of the lawyer's ethics to fail to meet with the child client.

§ 29.3.2 Conflict of Interest

In addition to the typical situations involving conflict of interest, the representation of children may involve some particular circumstances worth considering separately. The first of these regards the representation of sibling groups.

Representation of Siblings

Representation of siblings does not, *per se,* create a conflict of interest. Possible conflicts may arise when the siblings want different outcomes in the case, such as wanting to live with different parents. If the reasons for the differences in preference do not undermine the other sibling's preference, there would not appear to be a conflict. A more difficult situation arises when the siblings' differences go to issues that would affect each other. This may occur, for example, where the children take contrary positions with respect to whether or not there has been abuse or neglect. Similarly, siblings may all have witnessed domestic violence in the home, with some siblings wanting to testify about what they saw and the others denying that it happened in order to preserve the family or because of primary loyalty to the parents. In these cases, the attorney must carefully assess whether there is a conflict of interest that would preclude representing the siblings.

If the children are in counseling, a therapist may be able to help the attorney determine whether there is a conflict of interest. Sometimes the issues that are in conflict are areas being dealt with in therapy, and those conflicts may be resolved during the course of therapy. If the attorney is already appointed when the conflict arises, and there is no immediate need for the attorney to take a position on behalf of one or more of the children, the attorney may be able to wait until the therapy has reached a point where the conflict is resolved. However, an attorney who is not functioning as a guardian ad litem will probably be unable to continue multiple representation of the siblings who retain such incompatible positions.

DR 5-105(A) of the American Bar Association's Model Code of Professional Responsibility prohibits employment if the attorney's "exercise of his professional judgment on behalf of a client will be or is likely to be adversely affected by the acceptance of the proffered employment, or if it would be likely to involve him in representing differing interests, except to the extent permitted by DR 5-105(C)." DR 5-105(C) permits an attorney to continue multiple representation "if it is obvious that he can adequately represent the interest of each and if each consents to the representation after full disclosure of the possible effect of such representation on the exercise of his independent professional judgment on behalf of each."

Rule 1.7 of the American Bar Association's Model Rules of Professional Conduct sets forth the general rule on conflicts of interest:

(a)   A lawyer shall not represent a client if the representation of that client will be directly adverse to another client, unless:

> (1) the lawyer reasonably believes the representation will not adversely affect the relationship with the other client; and
>
> (2) each client consents after consultation.

(b)   A lawyer shall not represent a client if the representation of that client may be materially limited by the lawyer's responsibilities to another client or to a third person, or by the lawyer's own interests, unless:

> (1) the lawyer reasonably believes the representation will not be adversely affected; and
>
> (2) the client consents after consultation. When representation of multiple clients in a single matter is undertaken, the consultation shall include explanation of the implications of the common representation and the advantages and risks involved.

When the Model Rules were modified in 2002, Rule 1.7 was rewritten to read:

(a)   Except as provided in paragraph (b), a lawyer shall not represent a client if the representation involves a concurrent conflict of interest. A concurrent conflict of interest exists if:

> (1) the representation of one client will be directly adverse to another client; or
>
> (2) there is a significant risk that the representation of one or more clients will be materially limited by the lawyer's responsibilities to another client, a former client or a third person or by a personal interest of the lawyer.

(b)   Notwithstanding the existence of a concurrent conflict of interest under paragraph (a), a lawyer may represent a client if:

> (1) the lawyer reasonably believes that the lawyer will be able to provide competent and diligent representation to each affected client;
>
> (2) the representation is not prohibited by law;
>
> (3) the representation does not involve the assertion of a claim by one client against another client represented by the lawyer in the same litigation or other proceeding before a tribunal; and
>
> (4) each affected client gives informed consent, confirmed in writing.

Under any set of American Bar Association ethics rules, the attorney is prohibited from providing more than direct advocacy against another client. Comment 1 to

Model Rule 1.7 states that "[l]oyalty to a client is also impaired when a lawyer cannot consider, recommend or carry out an appropriate course of action for the client because of the lawyer's other responsibilities or interests. The conflict in effect forecloses alternatives that would otherwise be available to the client." Comment 1 to the revised Rule 1.7 provides that "[l]oyalty and independent judgment are essential elements in the lawyer's relationship to a client." Comment 6 to the revised Rule 1.7 provides that "a directly adverse conflict may arise when a lawyer is required to cross-examine a client who appears as a witness in a lawsuit involving another client, as when the testimony will be damaging to the client who is represented in the lawsuit."

Confidentiality

Confidentiality concerns, as well as compromised advocacy, also come into play with representation of multiple parties. Comment 31 to revised Rule 1.7 provides that "continued common representation will almost certainly be inadequate if one client asks the lawyer not to disclose to the other client information relevant to the common representation. This is so because the lawyer has an equal duty of loyalty to each client, and each client has the right to be informed of anything bearing on the representation that might affect that client's interests and the right to expect that the lawyer will use that information to that client's benefit."

Waiver

The attorney must be candid with the clients about the effect their differences may have on the attorney's ability to continue to represent them. In general, clients may waive conflicts of interest so long as they have full disclosure about the conflict and provide informed consent. Comment 18 to the revised Rule 1.7 provides that informed consent "requires that each affected client be aware of the relevant circumstances and of the material and reasonably foreseeable ways that the conflict could have adverse effects on the interests of that client. . . . The information required depends on the nature of the conflict and the nature of the risks involved. When representation of multiple clients in a single matter is undertaken, the information must include the implications of the common representation, including possible effects on loyalty, confidentiality and the attorney-client privilege and the advantages and risks involved." Comment 19 provides that "when the lawyer represents different clients in related matters and one of the clients refuses to consent to the disclosure necessary to permit the other client to make an informed decision, the lawyer cannot properly ask the latter to consent."

Older children may be able to appreciate the ethical dilemma of the attorney and may be competent to sign statements waiving the conflict. It is doubtful, however, that young children are competent to appreciate the conflict of interest sufficiently to waive it. If the children are in counseling, it is recommended that the therapist be consulted about the competence of the children to waive the conflict before the attorney relies on any such waiver. Children's legal competence to knowingly waive a potential or actual conflict of interest is problematic and presents unique questions of law and process.

Payment of Attorney Fees by a Third Party

Another situation in which conflict of interest may arise is in cases where a third party pays the child's attorney fees. In some cases the court, state, or county may pay for the services of the child's attorney. Under such circumstances, it is understood that the attorney is an independent agent representing the child. Even when the court appoints an attorney for the child and orders that some other party, such as the child's parents, pay the fees, the third party payors generally understand that they have not retained the attorney and cannot direct the representation, especially if a fee award is not made until the end of the case. However, conflicts may arise when a third party privately retains an attorney to act on behalf of the child. It is not clear who has standing to retain an attorney for the child privately. Some courts have prohibited parents from retaining counsel to represent their children in custody or abuse cases because of the conflict between the parents' interests and the children's interests.

ER 1.8(f) of the Model Rules of Professional Conduct and DR 5-107(A)(1) of the Model Code of Professional Responsibility prohibit third-party payment unless the client consents after consultation, there is no interference with the attorney's independence of judgment or with the attorney-client relationship, and the confidentiality of client information is protected. The Comment to revised Rule 1.8 provides:

> [11] Lawyers are frequently asked to represent a client under circumstances in which a third person will compensate the lawyer, in whole or in part. The third person might be a relative or friend, an indemnitor (such as a liability insurance company) or a co-client (such as a corporation sued along with one or more of its employees). Because third-party payers frequently have interests that differ from those of the client, including interests in minimizing the amount spent on the representation and in learning how the representation is progressing, lawyers are prohibited from accepting or continuing such representations unless the lawyer determines that there will be no interference with the lawyer's independent professional judgment and there is informed consent from the client. See also Rule 5.4(c) (prohibiting interference with a lawyer's professional judgment by one who recommends, employs or pays the lawyer to render legal services for another).

> [12] Sometimes, it will be sufficient for the lawyer to obtain the client's informed consent regarding the fact of the payment and the identity of the third-party payer. If, however, the fee arrangement creates a conflict of interest for the lawyer, then the lawyer must comply with Rule. 1.7. The lawyer must also conform to the

requirements of Rule 1.6 concerning confidentiality. Under Rule 1.7(a), a conflict of interest exists if there is significant risk that the lawyer's representation of the client will be materially limited by the lawyer's own interest in the fee arrangement or by the lawyer's responsibilities to the third-party payer (for example, when the third-party payer is a co-client). Under Rule 1.7(b), the lawyer may accept or continue the representation with the informed consent of each affected client, unless the conflict is nonconsentable under that paragraph. Under Rule 1.7(b), the informed consent must be confirmed in writing.

It is particularly helpful to obtain a significant trust account deposit in advance in cases of third party representation. In that way, the third party cannot use the leverage of withholding payment to influence the attorney's representation. It is also important to have the third party sign a retainer agreement that explicitly states that the third party is not the client, cannot direct the representation, and will not receive confidential information concerning the case. A more difficult issue is the child's ability to provide an informed consent.[22]

§ 29.3.3 Attorney-Client Privilege

DR 4-101 of the Model Code of Professional Responsibility and ER 1.6(a) of the Model Rules of Professional Responsibility, including the 2002 revisions, provide for the confidentiality of attorney-client communications. While DR 4-101 protects only communications that occur directly between the attorney and client, ER 1.6(a) extends the confidentiality to all client information "relating to the representation." All states provide an evidentiary privilege for attorney-client communications. The attorney's role may determine whether a child's communications with the attorney are privileged. Where the attorney is appointed as legal counsel, communication should remain privileged. However, if the attorney is appointed as the child's guardian ad litem, this privilege may not apply.

Where allegations of abuse are raised during confidential communications between children and attorneys, the judge's right to be fully informed may conflict with the attorney-client relationship. When and how information about abuse should be presented creates a problem for lawyers. State law may cover this issue. DR 5-102 of the Model Code of Professional Responsibility and ER 3.7 of the Model Rules of Professional Conduct discourage an attorney from acting as both a witness and an advocate. Mandatory child abuse reporting statutes may abrogate all privileges except the attorney-client privilege, and in some states the attorney-client privilege may also be abrogated. An attorney acting as a guardian ad litem may not be covered by the privilege, depending on local law. Some state statutes specifically require a duty of

---

[22] See the discussion of waiver in § 29.3.4, Waiver of Rights.

confidence for the lawyer (e.g., Michigan), while other states specifically eliminate the duty (e.g., Alaska requires the attorney to report suspected child abuse and neglect).

The original Model Rule 1.6(b)(1) permitted revealing client confidences "to prevent the client from committing a criminal act that the lawyer believes is likely to result in imminent death or substantial bodily harm." This provision did not seem to directly permit the child's attorney to reveal confidences to prevent the child client from becoming the victim of such a crime at the hands of another. It would seem anomalous to permit disclosure of confidential information designed to protect a third party from harm at the client's hand but not to permit an attorney to reveal confidential information designed to protect the client from death or substantial bodily harm. The new Rule 1.6(b)(1) permits disclosure of client confidences "to prevent reasonably certain death or substantial bodily harm," without making reference to a crime or to harm to a third party. Comment 6 to the new Rule 1.6, amending Comment 9 to Model Rule 1.6, states that the new provision "recognizes the overriding value of life and physical integrity and permits disclosure reasonably necessary to prevent reasonably certain death or substantial bodily harm. Such harm is reasonably certain to occur if it will be suffered imminently or if there is a present and substantial threat that a person will suffer such harm at a later date if the lawyer fails to take action necessary to eliminate the threat." Unlike the original Comment to the Model Rules, which discusses only the client who intends harm to a third person, the new Comment is broad enough to encompass harm to the client as well as harm to a third person.

§ 29.3.4 Waiver of Rights

Many of the ethical rules cited above require a knowing and informed waiver, sometimes in writing, of potential or actual conflicts of interest.

Since state laws on who can waive conflicts of interest on behalf of a child are generally not well-developed, perhaps no one possesses the legal authority to enter a waiver on behalf of a child. The court may be in the odd position of having to appoint separate counsel for siblings for want of legal authority to enter a waiver.

Where local law permits children to waive conflicts and privileges, or where the law is not clear, the attorney must determine whether the child has the capacity to make an informed waiver. Functional capacity exists on a continuum, even for adults. Many factors contribute to whether a child has sufficient capacity to make a waiver with respect to a particular issue at a particular time, and there is no bright line test for determining capacity.

Children's capacity to waive rights has been considered most often in the context of juvenile delinquency cases. The United States Supreme Court has held that juveniles may have the capacity to waive their constitutional rights.[23] In that context,

---

[23] *See, e.g.,* Fare v. Michael C., 442 U.S. 707 (1979) (finding that the totality-of-the-circumstances approach is adequate to determine whether there has been a waiver even where interrogation of juveniles is involved); *In re* Gault, 387 U.S. 1, 55 (1967) ("We appreciate that special problems may arise with respect to waiver of the privilege by or on behalf of children, and that there may well be

mental health professionals[24] and some courts have found that children's actual capacity to waive rights has been overestimated. In assessing whether a child has capacity to waive constitutional rights, a crucial issue is the child's ability to appreciate the consequences of the waiver. It is at the developmental stage of formal operations, which begins around age 12, when the child develops the ability to appreciate consequences of decisions.[25] However, the protections offered by assertion of constitutional rights in a delinquency setting raise different concerns than the protections provided by ethical rules about conflict of interest of assertion of testimonial privileges. Further, the goals of juvenile justice and the child welfare system are different. Most mental health professionals do not have adequate training to determine whether the child has adequate capacity to waive conflicts and privileges. That determination is very specialized. Therefore, it is difficult for attorneys without mental health training to make this decision independently. Whether a particular child can give informed consent to waive a particular right will remain a problem for future resolution. For a discussion of informed consent and waiver in the context of confidentiality decisions, see § 18.4.

§ 29.4 Determining Decision-Making Capacity

Attorneys should be vigilant and thoughtful about maximizing the child client's participation in determining the positions to be taken in the case. Even an attorney acting in the role of a best interest attorney or guardian ad litem should allow the child to participate in the decision-making process to the extent that the child is able to do so. As is true with the issue of waiver, functional capacity to direct representation or contribute to positions taken exists on a continuum, even for adults. The attorney should consider whether the child client has sufficient capacity to make a decision or to give significant input with respect to a particular issue at a particular time, and there is no bright line test for determining capacity.[26]

When it comes to accommodating a child's wishes and preferences, perhaps the best an attorney can do is to really listen to the child, understand what is important from the child's perspective and how decisions will impact on the child's experience of his or her life, and act with humility when considering taking a position that significantly differs from the child's expressed wishes.[27] Professor Jean Koh Peters

---

some differences in technique—but not in principle—depending upon the age of the child and the presence and competence of parents").

[24] *See, e.g.*, THOMAS GRISSO, JUVENILES' WAIVER OF RIGHTS: LEGAL AND PSYCHOLOGICAL COMPETENCE (1981); YOUTH ON TRIAL: A DEVELOPMENTAL PERSPECTIVE ON JUVENILE JUSTICE (Thomas Grisso & Robert G. Schwartz eds., 2000).

[25] *See, e.g.*, JEAN PAIGET & BARBEL INHELDER, THE PSYCHOLOGY OF THE CHILD (1969).

[26] *See* §18.4, Who May Assert or Waive Confidential Privileges.

[27] *See generally* Ann M. Haralambie, *Humility and Child Autonomy in Child Welfare and Custody Representation of Children*, 28 HAMLINE J. PUB. L. & POL'Y 177 (2006); Susan L. Brooks, *Representing Children in Families*, 6 NEV. L.J. 724 (2006) (stating five basic principles of best practices in representing children: (1) respect the dignity of all individuals and families; (2) approach

states it most succinctly: the child's attorney must understand "how this client speaks, how this client sees the world, what this client values, and what shows this client respect."[28]

§ 29.5 Determining the Goals of the Case: Client with "Diminished Capacity"

The American Bar Association's old Model Code of Professional Responsibility[29] did not provide any direct guidance for the attorney representing a child. The newer Model Rules of Professional Conduct[30] address the issue of dealing with a client under a disability. Rule 1.14(a) of the Model Rules provides: "When a client's ability to make adequately considered decisions is impaired, whether because of minority, mental disability or for some other reason, the lawyer shall, as far as reasonably possible, maintain a normal client-lawyer relationship with the client. The commentary to Rule 1.14 says: "Furthermore, to an increasing extent the law recognizes intermediate degrees of competence. For example, children as young as five or six years of age, and certainly those of ten or twelve, are regarded as having opinions that are entitled to weight in legal proceedings governing their custody." The default position, therefore, is for the child's lawyer to maintain as normal an attorney-client relationship as possible.

Rule 1.14(b) says: "A lawyer may seek the appointment of a guardian or take other protective action with respect to a client, only when the lawyer reasonably believes that the client cannot act in the client's own interest."

In August 2002, the American Bar Association adopted revised ethical rules with the "Ethics 2000" project.[31] The new Rule 1.14(a) of the Model Rules, now referring to a client with *diminished capacity*, provides: "When a client's capacity to make adequately considered decisions in connection with a representation is diminished, whether because of minority, mental impairment or for some other reason, the lawyer

---

every child as a member of a family system; (3) respect individual, family, and cultural differences; (4) adopt a nonjudgmental posture that focuses on identifying strengths and empowering families; and (5) appreciate that families are not replaceable); Ann M. Haralambie, *Recognizing the Expertise of Children and Families*, 6 NEV. L.J. 1277 (2006) (arguing: "Children have their own world view. They alone know what is of greatest subjective importance to them. They know what relationships matter to them. They know what activities they want to remain involved with. They can often provide valuable information on family interactions and other family resources. If we really listen to them, we may be surprised at the insights they have about what does and does not work in their families. We need to go beyond finding out what they want and explore their reasons for what they want, which may lead the attorney-client partnership in an entirely different direction. Further, we need to consider how alternative proposed placements will feel from the child's perspective. The 'cure' may be worse for the child than the family dysfunction from which we seek to extricate the child.").

[28] JEAN KOH PETERS, REPRESENTING CHILDREN IN CHILD PROTECTIVE PROCEEDINGS: ETHICAL AND PRACTICAL DIMENSIONS 258 (1997).

[29] MODEL CODE OF PROF'L RESPONSIBILITY (American Bar Association 1969).

[30] MODEL RULES OF PROF'L CONDUCT (American Bar Association 1983).

[31] MODEL RULES OF PROF'L CONDUCT (2002).

shall, as far as reasonably possible, maintain a normal client-lawyer relationship with the client."

Rule 1.14(b) provides: "When the lawyer reasonably believes that the client has diminished capacity, is at risk of substantial physical, financial or other harm unless action is taken and cannot adequately act in the client's own interest, the lawyer may take reasonably necessary protective action, including consulting with individuals or entities that have the ability to take action to protect the client and, in appropriate cases, seeking the appointment of a guardian ad litem, conservator or guardian." The new Rule 1.14(b) gives the child's attorney broader guidance on what "other protective action" might be appropriate, including allowing consultation with other persons or entities. Further, the new Rule 1.14(b) provides more guidance regarding the previous trigger for acting ("only when the lawyer reasonably believes that the client cannot act in the client's own interest") to include situations in which the client "is at risk of substantial physical, financial or other harm unless action is taken and cannot adequately act in the client's own interest." This change reflects the Ethics 2000 loosening of the confidentiality rules under some circumstances.

The Comment to the new Rule 1.14 provides much greater guidance to the child's attorney wishing to take protective action on behalf of the child client:

[5] If a lawyer reasonably believes that a client is at risk of substantial physical, financial or other harm unless action is taken, and that a normal client-lawyer relationship cannot be maintained as provided in paragraph (a) because the client lacks sufficient capacity to communicate or to make adequately considered decisions in connection with the representation, then paragraph (b) permits the lawyer to take protective measures deemed necessary. Such measures could include: consulting with family members, using a reconsideration period to permit clarification or improvement of circumstances, using voluntary surrogate decision-making tools such as durable powers of attorney or consulting with support groups, professional services, adult-protective agencies or other individuals or entities that have the ability to protect the client. In taking any protective action, the lawyer should be guided by such factors as the wishes and values of the client to the extent known, the client's best interests and the goals of intruding into the client's decision-making autonomy to the least extent feasible, maximizing client capacities and respecting the client's family and social connections.

[6] In determining the extent of the client's diminished capacity, the lawyer should consider and balance such factors as: the client's ability to articulate reasoning leading to a decision, variability of state of mind and ability to appreciate consequences of a decision; the substantive fairness of a decision; and the consistency of a decision with the known long-term commitments and values of the client. In

appropriate circumstances, the lawyer may seek guidance from an appropriate diagnostician.

[7] If a legal representative has not been appointed, the lawyer should consider whether appointment of a guardian ad litem, conservator or guardian is necessary to protect the client's interests. Thus, if a client with diminished capacity has substantial property that should be sold for the client's benefit, effective completion of the transaction may require appointment of a legal representative. In addition, rules of procedure in litigation sometimes provide that minors or persons with diminished capacity must be represented by a guardian or next friend if they do not have a general guardian. In many circumstances, however, appointment of a legal representative may be more expensive or traumatic for the client than circumstances in fact require. Evaluation of such circumstances is a matter entrusted to the professional judgment of the lawyer. In considering alternatives, however, the lawyer should be aware of any law that requires the lawyer to advocate the least restrictive action on behalf of the client.

The new Comment 4 to Rule 1.14, modifying Comment 3 to Model Rule 1.14, provides that in "matters involving a minor, whether the lawyer should look to the parents as natural guardians may depend on the type of proceeding or matter in which the lawyer is representing the minor." In the child welfare context, it is likely that the child's attorney would not be looking to the parents for direction on the central questions of custody, although the parents could be helpful on collateral questions such as placement, education and health care.

§ 29.6 The Child's Wishes Are Always Relevant

The national authorities that have addressed the child preferences reflect a consensus on this issue, too.[32] Regardless of whether or not a child is competent to direct the attorney, and even if the role of the attorney is defined as other than purely client-directed, the wishes and preferences of the child are always relevant and should be communicated to the court unless limited by privilege. No matter what weight is given to the child's preferences in determining the goals of advocacy, the attorney should elicit the child's preferences in a developmentally appropriate manner, advise

---

[32] These include the ABA STANDARDS OF PRACTICE FOR LAWYERS WHO REPRESENT CHILDREN IN ABUSE AND NEGLECT CASES, AND THE NACC REVISED VERSION; ADOPTION 2002, THE PRESIDENT'S INITIATIVE ON ADOPTION AND FOSTER CARE, GUIDELINES FOR PUBLIC POLICY AND STATE LEGISLATION GOVERNING PERMANENCE FOR CHILDREN (1999); *Proceedings of the Conference on Ethical Issues in the Legal Representation of Children: Recommendations of the Conference*, 64 FORDHAM L. REV. 1301 (1996); and *Proceedings of the UNLV Conference on Representing Children in Families: Children's Advocacy and Justice Ten Years After Fordham: Recommendations of the Conference*, 6 NEV. L.J. 592 (2006).

the child, and provide guidance. The child's attorney should communicate the child's wishes and preferences to the court. The lawyer also has a duty to explain to the child in a developmentally appropriate way information that will help the child have maximum input in the determination of the particular position at issue. According to the child's ability to understand, the lawyer should inform the child of the relevant facts, the applicable laws, and the ramifications of taking various positions, which may include the impact of such decisions on other family members or on future legal proceedings.

State law may provide authoritative guidance on how the stated wishes and preferences of the child are to be presented to the court, if at all. Maine provides an example:

> The guardian ad litem shall make the wishes of the child known to the court if the child has expressed his wishes, regardless of the recommendation of the guardian ad litem.[33]

Florida requires the guardian ad litem to file a written report that must include "a statement of the wishes of the child."[34]

In any event, the child's wishes are to be elicited and taken seriously. The lawyer is expected to play a counseling role, advising the child client of the risks and benefits of various options and, particularly, the likely consequences of the client's expressed choices. This discussion and counseling will, in many cases, produce agreement between client and lawyer about what they perceive to be in the client's best interests.

Assuming that the child's stated preferences are determined and elicited by the lawyer and communicated to the court, how much weight should the lawyer for the child attach to those stated preferences in determining the goals of the litigation? The vast majority of legal scholars and authorities who have addressed this issue recommend that a lawyer should take direction from his or her child client if the child is determined to have developed the cognitive capacity to engage in reasoned decision making. The national trend is in the direction of a more traditional lawyer role, giving more deference to the child's wishes and preferences, and turning to a more objective process for determining the child's position when that is required. Determining the decision-making capacity of any particular child and the weight to be given to that child's preferences remains a difficult and elusive question, however. The ABA Model Rules of Professional Responsibility, discussed above, especially the 2002 amendments, will provide some guidance. In the case of the very young child or the older child, the question of competence to instruct counsel may not be so difficult. If the client is an infant and cannot speak, the client cannot instruct counsel. If a client is a normally developed 15- or 16-year-old, however, he or she is quite likely to have clear and reasonable views as to the proper decisions to be made affecting his or her life that should be aggressively argued to the court. But determining capacity for the

---

[33] ME. REV. STAT. tit. 22, §4005(1)(E).

[34] FLA. STAT. § 39.807(2)(b)(1).

middle-years child, from 8 to 12 for instance, and the weight to be given to that child's preferences is perhaps the most difficult question in child advocacy today, and it does not yet have a clear answer.

The weight given to a child's stated wishes and preferences generally depend on the child's capacity, on his or her mental competence and maturity. But how should that capacity be assessed? Especially for the middle-years child, capacity is not an either-or proposition. Children mature at different rates and may be capable for some judgments and not for others. Professor Jean Koh Peters creates the image of a sliding scale or "dimmer switch" in which the child's capability is not an "on or off" phenomenon where a child is either capable of directing the lawyer or not.[35] "Competency, in this context, is a dimmer switch: the client can shed light on some aspects of the representation, even though she cannot participate in all of it."[36] A child's capacity, then, is a broader spectrum where children may be able to contribute various amounts to guide the representation if the lawyer properly incorporates the child's unique individuality.

State law and practice may incorporate the "dimmer switch" concept in authoritative directions to the lawyer. If the lawyer is appointed to represent the "best interests of the child," for instance, the statute may recognize the child's growing capacity. In Michigan, for example, the duties of the lawyer/GAL include:

> (h) To make a determination regarding the child's best interests and advocate for those best interests according to the lawyer-guardian ad litem's understanding of those best interests, regardless of whether the lawyer-guardian ad litem's determination reflects the child's wishes. *The child's wishes are relevant to the lawyer-guardian ad litem's determination of the child's best interests, and the lawyer-guardian ad litem shall weigh the child's wishes according to the child's competence and maturity.* Consistent with the law governing attorney-client privilege, the lawyer-guardian ad litem shall inform the court as to the child's wishes and preferences. (emphasis added)

Under Michigan law, the lawyer, when formulating a best interest goal, is to give increasing weight to the preferences of the child according to the child's age and maturity. At some point the best interests and wishes of the child merge, and the lawyer/GAL ends up representing the stated wishes of the child. If, however, a conflict remains between the child and the lawyer/GAL regarding the child's best interests, the lawyer/GAL should bring the matter to the court, which may appoint an attorney for the child who serves in addition to the lawyer/GAL.[37]

---

[35] JEAN KOH PETERS, REPRESENTING CHILDREN IN CHILD PROTECTIVE PROCEEDINGS: ETHICAL AND PRACTICAL DIMENSIONS 53–54 (1997).

[36] *Id.*

[37] MICH. COMP. LAWS § 712A.17d(1)(h). Where there is a disagreement between the lawyer-guardian ad litem and the child as to the child's best interests, the lawyer is to bring the question before the court,

§ 29.7 The Child's Lawyer: Duty of Competent, Independent, and Zealous Advocacy

No matter how the goals of the advocacy are determined, whether as directed by the child-client or as determined by a "best interest of the child" judgment of the lawyer, there is widespread agreement that the lawyer for the child should be an active and aggressive advocate. Few continue to argue that a lawyer representing a child client is absolved from the fundamental duties of thorough communication with the client or case investigation and preparation. While recognizing the difficulty of determining the goals of litigation in the face of a client of limited capacity, there is agreement that certain duties are fundamental.

Beyond the "child's attorney" role designation of the ABA Standards, the focus of the Standards is on the basic obligations and required actions of the lawyer for the child that most policy makers support, regardless of their view of the dilemma. These obligations also appear in NACC Recommendations for Representation of Children in Abuse and Neglect Cases and the NACC revised version of the standards.[38] They are also affirmed by the federal government in *Guidelines for Public Policy and State Legislation Governing Permanence for Children*.[39] The duties of the child's attorney, from the ABA Standards are very full and ambitious. See Appendix A for a full statement of the duties and obligations of the children's lawyer.

Whether the lawyer takes his or her direction from the child or makes a best interest judgment as to what the goals of the litigation should be, the list of activities in the ABA Standards is what is expected of the lawyer in implementing the goals, once they are determined.

§ 29.8 Special Challenges for the Child's Lawyer

The lawyer has many duties to a child client, one of which is the duty to identify the child's permanency-related needs. The lawyer also has a duty to protect the child's important affiliations, property, records, and social history. Additionally, lawyers should advocate for therapeutically appropriate closure in cases where the child does not return home. These needs and interests may change based on the child's changing developmental needs.

---

and the court may appoint an *attorney* for the child who has the same duty of zealous representation as for an adult and serves in addition to the lawyer-guardian ad litem. MICH. COMP. LAWS § 712A.17d(2).

[38] *See* Appendix A.

[39] ADOPTION 2002: THE PRESIDENT'S INITIATIVE ON ADOPTION AND FOSTER CARE, GUIDELINES FOR PUBLIC POLICY AND STATE LEGISLATION GOVERNING PERMANENCE FOR CHILDREN (1999).

§ 29.8.1 Identifying Permanency Needs and Protecting Important Affiliations

The permanency needs of infants and very young children require that decisions be made comparatively quickly because of the way they experience time. Six months for a six-month-old child is his or her entire lifetime. A young child's need to form a secure attachment may be impaired by a delayed or ill-timed change of placement. At certain developmental stages, a change of placement—whether removal from a family, change to a different placement, or return home—is particularly problematic. When dealing with preschool-aged children, it is particularly important for the attorney to seek appropriate expert input on any decision to change the child's placement. Further, very young children who are separated from their parents but will likely return home need to have very frequent contact with their parents. Child welfare resources may not exist for daily visits, but attorneys should seek other potential supervisors to supplement agency-supervised visits where that is possible and appropriate. Where there are relatives or other people who have been close to the child and may be considered as placements, visitation may be appropriate for those persons, as well as the parents, to ensure the child's ongoing familiarity with them.

Older children are better able to tolerate longer separations and to understand adults' explanations of delays in the child welfare process. However, even older children generally need things to move more quickly than the system moves, and one task of the attorney is to ensure that things move along as quickly as possible. Older children also often have a wider range of people to whom they feel connected and a wider range of activities that are important to them. To the extent possible, these connections should be nurtured and continued unless they would specifically be detrimental to the child. As children become older, their peers and extracurricular activities take on increased importance. Their sense of affiliation with their families may also increase, and many states require children of a certain age, typically 12, to consent to their adoption. An older child who does not want to be adopted, even if he or she will probably not be returned home, deserves to have that need for affiliation with his or her family of origin considered.

§ 29.8.2 Maintaining the Child's Property, Records, and Social History

Children in care often have nobody to maintain their social history, including their developmental milestones, photographs, important school papers and projects, and other documentary evidence of their progress through childhood. This early history can be preserved to some extent by preparing and maintaining "life books." Some child welfare agencies have programs for this, and some communities have volunteers who will compile records for the child's life book. These records should be accessible to the child and must be supplemented throughout the time the child is in care. Further, the information should be maintained in such a way that it is not lost as the child moves into different placements.

Older children need to have access to some discretionary money or allowance. They need to be able to participate in extracurricular activities, field trips, and functions such as school proms. Teenagers need to be given training in life skills that will prepare them for independence and financial autonomy, particularly if they will not be returned home or adopted.[40]

§ 29.8.3 Sibling Association

The child welfare system often attempts to place siblings together, but siblings are separated in many instances. They may not only be placed separately, but they may even be adopted by different families. For children who have been removed from home, their siblings may be the only continuity of family relationships they have. Siblings may represent the only people in their living circumstances who are not strangers, the only people with whom they share a history and memories, the only people who really understand what they have lived through and what they now miss. Of course, there are circumstances where sibling contact is not in the best interests of one or more of the siblings, and such contact might even be detrimental.

Maintaining sibling relations during any periods of separation may be very difficult, but unless there is a demonstrable reason for limiting contact, it is a valuable goal. Courts have been slow to recognize any constitutional right to sibling association.[41] Some states have statutes permitting sibling visitation. Where fit parents object to the visitation, there may be a constitutional challenge to a court's ordering visitation without affording some special weight to the parent's objection.[42] However, in child welfare cases, the courts are not generally dealing with "fit" parents. Therefore, the court may have greater latitude in ordering sibling visitation regardless of parental objection, especially when all of the involved children are in care. It is certainly appropriate to make ongoing sibling contact part of the family's case plan.

Because adoption creates a new legal family, it may be more difficult to provide any formal right to post-adoption sibling visitation. If such rights are to be secured, it is prudent to explore the possibility of an open adoption agreement providing explicitly for post-adoption contact with siblings. Even if no formal agreement is reached, it may be possible for the adoptive parents to allow ongoing contact on an informal basis. Children who at least know the new names and contact information for their siblings who were adopted by other families are in a better position to re-establish a relationship upon reaching majority.

---

[40] For a discussion of Chafee Funds and transitional living services, *see* Chapter10, Federal Child Welfare Legislation, and Chapter 23, Foster Youth: Transitioning from Foster Care into Self-Sufficient Adulthood.

[41] *See generally* William Wesley Patton, *The Status of Siblings' Rights: A View into the New Millennium*, 51 DePaul L. Rev. 1 (2001).

[42] *See* Troxel v. Granville, 530 U.S. 57, 70 (2000) (addressing grandparent visitation).

§ 29.8.4 LGBTQ Children

Lesbian, Gay, Bisexual, Transgendered or Questioning (LGBTQ) youth are disadvantaged in foster care for a variety of reasons. For most child clients, sexual orientation and gender identity are not a significant issue—the child is either too young to have formed a sexual identity or is heterosexual. But the ABA Opening Doors Project research estimates that 4 to 10% of youth in care identify as LGBTQ and that this status can have a profound effect on the youth's experience in foster care. The project reports that 70% of LGBTQ youth in group homes report violence based on their sexuality, and 100% of LGBTQ youth in group homes report verbal harassment. In addition, 78% of youth were removed or ran away from placement because of hostility to their LGBTQ status, and 30% of LGBTQ youth report physical violence by their family after coming out. Verbal harassment at school was reported by 80% of LGBTQ students, 70% felt unsafe, and 28% dropped out.[43]

The youth's sexual orientation does not define him or her as a person or frame the needs the child may have in the foster care system. Other areas of the child's life may take priority. But as these few statistics demonstrate, the youth's sexual orientation could seriously compromise the experience in foster care. The youth's lawyer should not assume that the child is heterosexual.

One of the most important things the lawyer for the child can do is to communicate acceptance, sensitivity, and respect about sexual orientation and gender identity. The lawyer must be aware of his or her own attitudes. Some law offices communicate this acceptance by prominent display of posters and symbols. Some have pamphlets available to youth on a variety of topics, including LGBTQ issues, and give them to the client saying some of these may be relevant to you, some may not be.

The lawyer should not be shy about finding out the client's orientation because it could be a significant factor in their child welfare system experience. A strong relationship between the youth and lawyer is essential if the youth is to trust the lawyer to help. "If a youth feels she is being judged based on her sexual orientation, or her advocate has negative beliefs about homosexuality, she is likely to withhold information that may jeopardize her safety and permanency."[44]

The Opening Doors survey indicates that judges recognize that LGBTQ youth may be harder to place than heterosexual youth because of the lack of tolerance and acceptance of their status.[45] Mimi Laver writes:

> Finding permanent homes for teens is a challenge. Agency workers and other professionals often give up on helping LGBTQ youth achieve permanency. Like other teens, these youth can and should go

---

[43] Mimi Laver & Andrea Khoury, OPENING DOORS FOR LGBTQ YOUTH IN FOSTER CARE: A GUIDE FOR LAWYERS AND JUDGES 1 (ABA Center on Children and the Law 2008).

[44] *Id.* at 11.

[45] *Id.* at 73.

home with appropriate supports. If not they should be placed in adoptive homes or with guardians. They should also have at least one positive adult connection that will continue after they leave foster care. As the judge or lawyer, you can make this happen.[46]

§ 29.9 Advocating for Appropriate Closure After Termination

When termination is ordered, the child may still have unfinished business. Even if there has not been visitation, the child may need to face the parent or otherwise deal with the finality of the termination. The child may need individualized therapeutic help to determine how to find closure and deal with any remaining issues of grief or anger. The attorney should consider getting current information on the parents' whereabouts in case the child wants to re-establish contact upon reaching adulthood. Similarly, the attorney should obtain any available information on how to contact relatives or other people who have been important while the child was in care. Even after adoption, children may have a desire to visit parents, siblings, other relatives, or other children with whom they have been in care. To the extent appropriate, the attorney may make arrangements to maintain these affiliations and associations.

Some states authorize legally enforceable "open adoptions" in which relatives and individuals with significant emotional ties to a child may have ongoing contact with the child even after an adoption.[47] In other states, informal agreements for this kind of contact are common, even where the agreements may not be legally enforceable.

§ 29.10 Delivery of Legal Services for Children

As child welfare law has matured as a profession, the issues of how legal services for children are organized and delivered have also come to the forefront. Not many years ago it was rare for a jurisdiction to have a specialty office devoted to child representation. By far the most common means of delivering legal services to children was the ad hoc appointment of counsel by the local court from a list of lawyers willing to take such assignments. The few staff attorney offices had astronomically high caseloads. Training and supervision and general quality control were quite limited, and there was little or no systematic attention paid to either attorney compensation or caseloads. Today, despite the presence of excellent individual child lawyers and certain superb offices, the organization and delivery of child representation still draws considerable criticism across the nation.

However, there is growing appreciation for the importance of an organizational structure to support the individual child advocate. The 1996 ABA Standards detail the

---

[46] *Id.* at 47.

[47] *See* Chapter 25, Establishing Legal Permanence for the Child.

role and duties of the advocate, but they also emphasize the importance of a supportive administrative structure in achieving good representation for children:

> . . . [N]o matter how carefully a bar association, legislature, or court defines the duties of lawyers representing children, practice will only improve if judicial administrators and trial judges play a stronger role in the selection, training, oversight, and prompt payment of court-appointed lawyers in child abuse/neglect . . . cases.[48]

The NACC has nurtured the development of specialty law offices devoted to the delivery of legal services to children and youth:

> The delivery of high quality child welfare legal services requires a practice infrastructure which provides the attorney with the necessary time, compensation, and resources. The NACC believes, therefore, that one of the best mechanisms for delivery of high quality legal services to children is an institutional structure that allows multiple attorneys to focus their attention on the representation of children in general and the representation of children in child welfare law proceedings in particular – in other words, a dedicated child welfare law office.[49]

Across the county there is an increasing number of such specialty offices or statewide contract systems of child attorneys.[50] Attorneys representing children, courts, and the larger community realize the benefit of institutional support for training, supervision, quality control, case consultation, mentoring, and peer support.

The organization and delivery of legal services for children will get a boost from the National Quality Improvement Center on the Representation of Children in the Child Welfare System (QIC), a five-year project funded by the U.S. Children's Bureau in 2009. The QIC will assess the state of child representation in the nation, identify promising models of child representation, and conduct empirical research on the effectiveness of various approaches. "The overriding goals are to gather, develop, and communicate knowledge on child representation that presents the strengths and weaknesses of varying methods of representing children, promotes consensus on the role of the child's legal representative, and provides an empirically based analysis of

---

[48] AMERICAN BAR ASSOCIATION, STANDARDS OF PRACTICE FOR LAWYERS WHO REPRESENT CHILDREN IN ABUSE AND NEGLECT CASES, Part II, Enhancing the Judicial Role in Child Representation, Preface.

[49] NACC, CHILD WELFARE LAW OFFICE GUIDEBOOK (2006).

[50] Some specialty offices include: KidsVoice of Pittsburgh (www.kidsvoice.org); Children's Law Center of Los Angeles (www.clcla.org); and Children's Law Center in Washington, D.C. (www.childrenslawcenter.org). Examples of statewide offices representing children include: Connecticut Commission on Child Protection (http://www.ct.gov/CCPA/site/default.asp); and Colorado's Office of the Child's Representative (http://www.coloradochildrep.org/).

how legal representation for the child might best be delivered."[51] Visit the website for progress reports on efforts and lessons learned.[52]

§ 29.11 Conclusion

A child welfare legal system that serves and protects children must include independent legal counsel for all parties, including children. The practice of law for children has evolved over a relatively short period of time from a cottage age industry to a sophisticated legal specialty. That specialty includes new guidelines and standards of practice that guide the practitioner toward providing children with the full benefit of legal counsel. Despite some disagreement over the nuances of practice, there is widespread consensus on the primary duties of the child's lawyer. A national model of practice that serves the special needs of child clients has emerged.

---

[51] National Quality Improvement Center on the Representation of Children in the Child Welfare System at http://www.law.umich.edu/centersandprograms/ccl/Pages/NationalQualityImprovementCenteron theRepresentationofChildrenintheChildWelfareSystem.aspx.

[52] The Child Advocacy Law Clinic at the University of Michigan Law School is named the National Quality Improvement Center for Representation of Children in the Child Welfare System. Visit the Web site at http://www.law.umich.edu/centersandprograms/ccl/calc/Pages/default.aspx. Don Duquette is the Project Director.

V. COURTROOM ADVOCACY

Chapter 30: Children in Court

by John E. B. Myers[1]

§ 30.1 Introduction

This chapter discusses children as witnesses and hearsay declarants. The following topics are addressed: suggestibility, testimonial competence, impact on children of testifying, techniques to help children testify, hearsay, and whether children should be in court during hearings.

§ 30.2 Suggestibility

This section summarizes findings of suggestibility research that are relevant to the investigation and litigation of child abuse.

§ 30.2.1 Age and Suggestibility

There is no simple relationship between age and suggestibility.[2] Psychologists Karen Saywtiz, Thomas Lyon, and Gail Goodman observe, "[I]ndividual differences in suggestibility proneness exist at every age . . . ."[3] Suggestibility on a particular occasion depends on a host of situational, developmental, and personality factors, including the type of event, how well it is remembered, the type of information sought by the interviewer (e.g., central details versus peripheral details), the way the interview is conducted and the language used, whether or not the questioner intimidates the subject, and a host of other influences before and during the interview.

As a group, young children, particularly children under age six, are more suggestible than older children and adults.[4] Saywitz, Lyon, and Goodman conclude,

---

[1]   John E. B. Myers, J.D., is Professor of Law at University of the Pacific, McGeorge School of Law.

[2]   *See* MEMORY AND SUGGESTIBILITY IN THE FORENSIC INTERVIEW (Mitchell L. Eisen et al. eds., 2002); Gail S. Goodman & Beth M. Schwartz-Kenny, *Why Knowing a Child's Age is Not Enough: Influences of Cognitive, Social, and Emotional Factors on Children's Testimony, in* CHILDREN AS WITNESSES 15, 22 (Helen Dent & Rhona Flin eds., 1992).

[3]   Karen J. Saywitz, Thomas D. Lyon & Gail S. Goodman, *Interviewing Children, in* THE APSAC HANDBOOK ON CHILD MALTREATMENT (John E. B. Myers ed., 3d ed. 2010).

[4]   *See* Maggie Bruck, Stephen J. Ceci, Emmett Francoeur & Ronald Barr, *I Hardly Cried When I Got My Shot!: Influencing Children's Reports About a Visit to Their Pediatrician*, 66/1 CHILD DEV. 193 (1995); Stephen J. Ceci & Mary Lyn Crotteau Huffman, *How Suggestible Are Preschool Children? Cognitive and Social Factors*, 36/7 J. AM. ACAD. CHILD ADOLESC. PSYCHIATRY 948 (1997); Jodi A.

"overall young children are particularly likely to fall sway to suggestive pressures." Psychologists Lindsay Malloy and Jodi Quas add, "The most reliable factor that affects children's memory, ability to describe events that they have experienced or witnessed, and suggestibility, is age. The statement, 'with age, children's memory accuracy improves and suggestibility decreases,' holds for virtually all events and eyewitness contexts."[5] By the time children near adolescence, most approach adult levels of suggestibility.[6] This is not to say, of course, that older children are not suggestible. The point is that with older children and adolescents, concerns about suggestibility are less acute.

Despite the fact that young children as a group are at increased risk of being misled by suggestive questions, preschoolers are not invariably suggestible.[7] Children can resist suggestive questions.[8] Stephen Ceci and his colleagues wrote, "When the adults who have access to preschool children do not attempt to usurp their memories through repeated suggestions over long intervals, even very young children do very well."[9] Gary Melton and his colleagues added, "Age does have some relation to suggestibility, but probably less than often has been assumed."[10] Jodi Quas and her

---

Quas, Gail S. Goodman, Simona Ghetti & Allison D. Redlich, *Questioning the Child Witness: What Can We Conclude From the Research Thus Far?*, 1/3 Trauma, Violence & Abuse 223, 225 (2000) ("Across studies of children's memory and suggestibility, the most consistent and robust predictor of differences in children's performance is age. Older children generally remember more than younger children do, and older children are less susceptible to false suggestion. However, young children still can and do remember their experiences."); Karen J. Saywitz, *Developmental Underpinnings of Children's Testimony*, in Children's Testimony: A Handbook of Psychological Research and Forensic Practice 3, 11 (Helen L. Westcott et al. eds., 2002) ("Younger children (especially 3-5-year-olds) are much more suggestible than older children and older children are much less suggestible than younger ones."); *see also In re* G.B., 838 A.2d 529, 530 n.1 (2004) ("children in the three to four-year-old age group are most vulnerable to suggestions by the questioner").

[5] Lindsay C. Malloy & Jodi A. Quas, *Children's Suggestibility: Areas of Consensus and Controversy*, in The Evaluation of Child Sexual Abuse Allegations: A Comprehensive Guide to Assessment and Testimony 268 (Kathryn Kuehnle & Mary Connell eds., 2009).

[6] *See* Karen J. Saywitz & Lynn Snyder, *Improving Children's Testimony with Preparation*, in Gail S. Goodman & Bette L. Bottoms, Child Victims, Child Witnesses: Understanding and Improving Testimony (1993).

[7] *See* Gail S. Goodman, Jennifer M. Batterman-Faunce, Jennifer M. Schaaf & Robert Kenney, *Nearly Four Years After an Event: Children's Eyewitness Memory and Adults' Perceptions of Children's Accuracy*, 26/8 Child Abuse & Neglect 849 (2002).

[8] *See* Elisa Krackow & Steven Jay Lynn, *Is There Touch in the Game of Twister? The Effects of Innocuous Touch and Suggestive Questions on Children's Eyewitness Memory*, 27/6 Law & Hum. Behav. 589, 592 (2003) ("Studies of abused and nonabused children's responses to both stressful and nonstressful events have indicated that for the most part preschool children do not falsely assent to questions that imply they were touched."); Jodi A. Quas, Jianjian Qin, Jennifer M. Schaaf & Gail S. Goodman, *Individual Differences in Children's and Adults' Suggestibility and False Event Memory*, 9/4 Learning & Individual Differences 359 (1997).

[9] Stephen J. Ceci & Mary Lyn Crotteau Huffman, *How Suggestible Are Preschool Children? Cognitive and Social Factors*, 36/7 J. Am. Acad. Child Adolesc. Psychiatry 948, 957 (1997) (original emphasis omitted).

[10] Gary B. Melton, G. S. Goodman, S. C. Kalichman, M. Levine, K. J. Saywitz & G. P. Koocher, *Empirical Research on Child Maltreatment and the Law*, 24 J. Clin. Child Psychol. 47, 59 (1995).

colleagues wrote, "Although young children can be misled to report inaccurate information about their experiences, they are more resistant to false suggestions about negative and abuse-related activities than false suggestions about other never-experienced activities."[11]

§ 30.2.2 Questioning by Authority Figures; The Social Demands of Interviews

Children are sometimes more suggestible when questioned by an authority figure.[12] Moreover, young children, particularly preschoolers, appear less able than older children to withstand the social demands of the interview.[13] Thus, because they find it difficult to "stand their ground" in the face of suggestive questions, young children are at greater risk of going along with the adult's suggestions.[14]

§ 30.2.3 Central Details vs. Peripheral Details

Children, like adults, are more likely to be suggestible about peripheral details of events than about central, salient, memorable details.[15] Child abuse is typically salient, and a child who is questioned about abuse may be less suggestible than a child questioned about an innocuous event.[16] Gail Goodman and Karen Saywitz wrote,

---

[11] Jodi A. Quas, Jianjian Qin, Jennifer M. Schaaf & Gail S. Goodman, *Individual Differences in Children's and Adults' Suggestibility and False Event Memory*, 9/4 LEARNING & INDIVIDUAL DIFFERENCES 359, 362 (1997).

[12] *See* Michael E. Lamb, Kathleen J. Sternberg & Phillip W. Esplin, *Factors Influencing the Reliability and Validity of Statements Made by Young Victims of Sexual Maltreatment*, 15/2 J. APPLIED DEV. PSYCHOL. 255, 265 (1994) ("Misleading or suggestive questioning can manipulate both young and old witnesses. Such questions are most likely to be influential when the memory is not rich or recent, when the questions themselves are so complicated that the witness is confused, and when the interviewer appears to have such authority or status that the witness feels compelled to accept his or her implied construction of events.").

[13] *See* William S. Cassel, Claudia E. M. Roebers & David F. Bjorklund, *Developmental Patterns of Eyewitness Responses to Repeated and Increasingly Suggestive Questions*, 61/2 J. EXPERIMENTAL PSYCHOL. 116 (1996).

[14] *See* Gary B. Melton, G. S. Goodman, S. C. Kalichman, M. Levine, K. J. Saywitz & G. P. Koocher, *Empirical Research on Child Maltreatment and the Law*, 24 J. CLIN. CHILD PSYCHOL. 47 (1995); Karen J. Saywitz, Thomas D. Lyon & Gail S. Goodman, *Interviewing Children*, *in* THE APSAC HANDBOOK ON CHILD MALTREATMENT (John E. B. Myers ed., 3d ed. 2010).

[15] *See* Michael E. Lamb, Kathleen J. Sternberg & Phillip W. Esplin, *Factors Influencing the Reliability and Validity of Statements Made by Young Victims of Sexual Maltreatment*, 15/2 J. APPLIED DEV. PSYCHOL. 255, 264 (1994) ("there is agreement that suggestions are less likely to be effective when they pertain to central or salient details"); Gary B. Melton, G. S. Goodman, S. C. Kalichman, M. Levine, K. J. Saywitz & G. P. Koocher, *Empirical Research on Child Maltreatment and the Law*, 24 J. CLIN. CHILD PSYCHOL. 47, 59 (1995) ("Generally, children are more resistant to suggestion about salient actions than peripheral details, including abuse-related events like physical assault or removal of clothes.").

[16] Gary B. Melton, G. S. Goodman, S. C. Kalichman, M. Levine, K. J. Saywitz & G. P. Koocher, *Empirical Research on Child Maltreatment and the Law*, 24 J. CLIN. CHILD PSYCHOL. 47, 59 (1995)

"Children, similar to adults, are more likely to give incorrect reports and to be more suggestible about peripheral information than about more salient, memorable information. Abusive genital contact is likely to be a fairly salient event for a child, and therefore children are likely to be less suggestible about such actions."[17]

§ 30.2.4 Ambiguous Body Touch

The touching involved in sexual abuse is sometimes ambiguous. For example, touching a young child's genitals may be entirely proper care taking or a felony, depending on the intention of the adult. Young children may be particularly suggestible regarding acts that are ambiguous, especially when they are questioned by a biased interviewer.[18] A child who is unsure how to interpret an event—"good touch" or "bad touch"—may go along with an adult's interpretation.[19]

Although children may go along with suggestive questions about the *meaning* of ambiguous events, children are likely to be less suggestible regarding the facts they observed.[20] Thus, although a child might be led astray about the interpretation of an ambiguous event, the child is likely to be accurate about what happened.

§ 30.2.5 Participant vs. Bystander

Participating in an event, as opposed to watching from the sidelines, sometimes lowers suggestibility, probably because the participant has a stronger memory for the event.[21] Ann Tobey and Gail Goodman observed, "Participation can both strengthen children's recollections of an event and their ability to resist suggestion."[22]

("Generally, children are more resistant to suggestion about salient actions than peripheral details, including abuse-related events like physical assault or removal of clothes.").

[17] Gail S. Goodman & Karen J. Saywitz, *Memories of Abuse; Interviewing Children When Sexual Victimization is Suspected*, 3/4 CHILD & ADOLESC. PSYCHIATR. CLIN. N. AM. 645, 648 (1994).

[18] *See* William C. Thompson, K. Alison Clarke-Stewart & Stephen J. Lepore, *What Did the Janitor Do? Suggestive Interviewing and the Accuracy of Children's Accounts*, 21 LAW & HUM. BEHAV. 405 (1997).

[19] *See* Karen J. Saywitz, *Developmental Underpinnings of Children's Testimony*, in CHILDREN'S TESTIMONY: A HANDBOOK OF PSYCHOLOGICAL RESEARCH AND FORENSIC PRACTICE 3, 9–10 (Helen L. Westcott et al. eds., 2002) ("One reason for heightened suggestibility is that young children are particularly deferential to adults' beliefs. Adults may convey their view of events to children through the question they ask, the comments they make, and through their demeanor. At an early age children recognize adults' superior knowledge base.").

[20] *See* Gail S. Goodman & Alison Clarke-Stewart, *Suggestibility in Children's Testimony: Implications for Sexual Abuse Investigations, in* THE SUGGESTIBILITY OF CHILDREN'S RECOLLECTIONS: IMPLICATIONS FOR EYEWITNESS TESTIMONY 92–105 (John Doris ed., 1991).

[21] *See* Gail S. Goodman et al., *Children's Concerns and Memory: Issues of Ecological Validity in the Study of Children's Eyewitness Testimony, in* KNOWING AND REMEMBERING IN YOUNG CHILDREN 249–84 (Robyn Fivush & Judith A. Hudson eds., 1990).

[22] Ann E. Tobey & Gail S. Goodman, *Children's Eyewitness Memory: Effects of Participation and Forensic Context*, 16/6 CHILD ABUSE & NEGLECT 779, 792 (1992).

§ 30.2.6 Negative Stereotypes and Accusatory Atmosphere

Interviewers should avoid creating an atmosphere that is accusatory regarding a particular person.[23] Nor should interviewers describe individuals in terms of negative stereotypes. Negative stereotypes and an accusatory atmosphere cause some interviewees—children and adults—to be suggestible regarding the object of the unflattering commentary.[24]

Ann Tobey and Gail Goodman examined the effect on non-abused four-year-old children of questioning by a police officer.[25] The children in the study played with a research assistant who was described to the children as a "baby sitter." Eleven days later, the children were interviewed about the experience. Some of the children were interviewed in a neutral fashion by a research assistant, while other children were interviewed by a police officer who said, "I am very concerned that something bad might have happened the last time that you were here. I think that the babysitter you saw here last time might have done some bad things, and I am trying to find out what happened the last time you were here when you played with the babysitter." Questioning by the police officer had a deleterious impact on some children's accuracy, although "only two children in the police condition seemed to be decisively misled by the police officer's suggestion that the babysitter may have done some bad things."[26]

Michelle Leichtman and Stephen Ceci designed an experiment to highlight the dangers of negative stereotypes during interviews of young children.[27] In this study, one group of preschool children was told on several occasions about a man named Sam Stone, who, according to the story, was very clumsy. Thus, the children were inculcated with a stereotype of a clumsy Sam Stone. Other children in the study did not receive this stereotyping information. Some time later, Sam Stone visited the children's preschool classroom. He stayed about two minutes, but did nothing clumsy or unusual. Following Sam Stone's uneventful visit to the classroom, the children in both groups were interviewed once a week for four successive weeks—some with leading questions—about Sam Stone's visit. The leading questions contained an implication that Sam ripped a book and soiled a teddy bear. Finally, at a fifth interview, the researchers examined the impact of leading questions on the children who had been told that Sam Stone was clumsy. Children who received the stereotyping message about Sam were more likely than other children to provide inaccurate information in response to leading questions. Leichtman and Ceci's study

---

[23] For examples of how not to interview children, see *State v. Michaels*, 642 A.2d 1372, 1385, 1391 (1994) (presenting appendix to court's opinion containing portions of several interviews).

[24] *See* Michelle D. Leichtman & Stephen J. Ceci, *The Effects of Stereotypes and Suggestions on Preschoolers' Reports*, 31/4 DEV. PSYCHOL. 568 (1995).

[25] Ann E. Tobey & Gail S. Goodman, *Children's Eyewitness Memory: Effects of Participation and Forensic Context*, 16/6 CHILD ABUSE & NEGLECT 779 (1992).

[26] *Id.* at 790.

[27] *See* Michelle D. Leichtman & Stephen J. Ceci, *The Effects of Stereotypes and Suggestions on Preschoolers' Reports*, 31/4 DEV. PSYCHOL. 568 (1995).

underscores the importance of avoiding interview practices that stereotype possible perpetrators.

It is generally inappropriate for an interviewer to tell a child what others said about the suspect or the facts under investigation.[28] John Shaw and his colleagues used the term "co-witness information" to describe the situation in which interviewers tell interviewees what others said. Describing their research on "co-witness information," Shaw wrote, "As expected, co-witness information had an immediate impact on the accuracy of the participant-witness' memory reports. In all three experiments, when participants received incorrect information about co-witnesses' responses to a question just before they provided their own response to that same question, the participants were more likely to give the same incorrect responses as the co-witness (or co-witnesses) than they were if they received no co-witness information."[29]

§ 30.2.7 Lowering Suggestibility

Interviewers can lower children's suggestibility.[30] Children can be instructed to pay close attention and to report only what "really happened." Children can be informed that some questions may be difficult to understand, and that the child should not guess or make up answers. Helen Dent advises telling children that the interviewer does not know what happened, and that the child is free to say "I don't know."[31]

Karen Saywitz and her colleagues suggest that children be given instructions such as these: "There may be some questions that you do not know the answers to. That's okay. Nobody can remember everything. If you don't know the answer to a question, then tell me 'I don't know,' but do not make anything up. It is very important to tell me only what you really remember. Only what really happened." "If you do not want to answer some of the questions, you don't have to. That's okay. Tell me 'I don't want to answer that question.'" "If you don't know what something I ask you means, tell me 'I don't understand' or 'I don't know what you mean.' Tell me to say it in new words." "I may ask you some questions more than one time. Sometimes I forget that I already asked you that question. You don't have to change your answer, just tell me what you remember the best you can."[32] Statements like these are helpful during

---

[28] *See* John S. Shaw III, Sena Garvin & James M. Wood, *Co-Witness Information Can Have Immediate Effects on Eyewitness Memory Reports*, 21/5 Law & Hum. Behav. 503 (1997).

[29] *Id.* at 516.

[30] *See* Karen J. Saywitz, Thomas D. Lyon & Gail S. Goodman, *Interviewing Children*, in The APSAC Handbook on Child Maltreatment (John E. B. Myers ed., 3d ed. 2010); Kathy Pezdek & Jeolle Greene, *Testing Eyewitness Memory: Developing a Measure that is More Resistant to Suggestibility*, 17/3 Law & Hum. Behav. 361 (1993); Amye Warren, Katherine Hulse-Trotter & Ernest C. Tubbs, *Inducing Resistance to Suggestibility in Children*, 15/3 Law & Hum. Behav. 273 (1991).

[31] Helen R. Dent, *Experimental Studies of Interviewing Child Witnesses*, in The Suggestibility of Children's Recollections: Implications for Eyewitness Testimony 138–46 (John Doris ed., 1991).

[32] Karen J. Saywitz, R. Edward Geiselman & Gail K. Bornstein, *Effects of Cognitive Interviewing and Practice on Children's Recall Performance*, 77/5 J. Applied Psychol. 744 (1992). *See also* Karen J.

interviews. At trial, however, an attorney should not tell a child, "If you don't want to answer, you don't have to."[33]

§ 30.3 Testimonial Competence

To testify, a child must possess the capacity to observe, sufficient intelligence, adequate memory, ability to communicate, awareness of the difference between truth and falsehood, and an appreciation of the obligation to tell the truth in court.[34] A child of any age who possesses these characteristics may testify. There is no minimum age below which children are automatically disqualified as witnesses.

Rule 601 of the Federal Rules of Evidence provides, "Every person is competent to be a witness except as otherwise provided in these rules."[35] A majority of states have adopted the Federal Rules, including Rule 601. In states that have not adopted the Federal Rules, evidence codes generally provide that competence is presumed. Thus, California Evidence Code § 700 provides that "every person, irrespective of age, is qualified to be a witness."[36] New York Criminal Procedure Law § 60.20 states that "[a]ny person may be a witness in a criminal proceeding."[37] A small number of states retain the older view that children below a specified age (e.g., 10 or 12) are presumed incompetent until the contrary is established. In Federal Court, Section 3509(c) of Title 18 provides: "A child is presumed to be competent."[38] Despite Rule 601's pronouncement that "every person is competent to be a witness," trial judges have authority to hold competency examinations when legitimate questions arise about testimonial competence.

§ 30.3.1 Capacity to Observe

To testify, a child must have the physical and mental capacity to observe. Courts sometimes refer to this as the ability to receive correct impressions by the senses.[39] Children's observational capacity develops rapidly during the first year of life, and the capacity to observe almost never poses a barrier to testimony.

Saywitz, Thomas D. Lyon & Gail S. Goodman, *Interviewing Children, in* THE APSAC HANDBOOK ON CHILD MALTREATMENT (John E. B. Myers ed., 3d ed. 2010).

[33] *See In re* Pers. Restraint Petition of Grasso, 84 P.3d 859 (Wash. 2004).

[34] *See* Walters v. McCormick, 108 F.3d 1165 (9th Cir. 1997); State v. Pham, 75 Wash. App. 626, 879 P.2d 321 (1994) ("The age of the child is not determinative of his or her capacity as a witness.").

[35] FED. R. EVID. 601.

[36] CAL. EVID. CODE § 700.

[37] N.Y. CRIM. PROC. LAW § 60.20.

[38] 18 U.S.C. § 3509(c)(2).

[39] *See* State v. Earl, 252 Neb. 127, 560 N.W.2d 491 (1997); State v. Segerberg, 131 Conn. 546, 41 A.2d 101, 102 (1945) ("The principle…is that the child shall be sufficiently mature to receive correct impressions by her senses…"); State v. Guy, 227 Neb. 610, 419 N.W.2d 152, 155 (1988) (trial court must determine whether child is sufficiently mature to receive correct impressions by senses).

§ 30.3.2 Memory

Children have good memory capacity. Psychologist Michael Lamb and his colleagues observe, "Although young children tend to provide briefer narrative accounts of their experiences than do older children and adults, these accounts are generally quite accurate . . . . From the time they are two or three years of age, it is clear that young children can remember and verbally recount a great deal of information about many of their experiences when questioned after both short delays of, for example, one month or less and sometimes also after much longer delays."[40] The basic capacity to recall events should almost never pose a barrier to testimonial competence. Whether a child's memory for particular events is accurate is a matter of credibility, not testimonial competence.[41]

§ 30.3.3 Capacity to Communicate

To be competent as a witness, a child must be able to communicate so as to be understood. In nearly all cases, children possess the capacity to communicate.

§ 30.3.4 Intelligence

To testify, a witness must possess a threshold level of intelligence. Normal intelligence is not required for testimonial competence, and children with below-average intelligence may testify if they possess the ability to observe, recollect, and relate in a manner that assists the trier of fact.[42]

§ 30.3.5 Understanding the Difference Between Truth and Falsehood

To testify, a child must understand the difference between truth and falsehood.[43] The child need not comprehend the finer points of truth and falsity, nor must the child understand the concept of perjury.[44] The child may articulate the necessary understanding in childlike terms. The fact that a child makes mistakes or is to some degree inconsistent does not render the child incompetent.[45] When judges and attorneys use

---

[40] MICHAEL E. LAMB, IRIT HERSHKOWITZ, YAEL ORBACH & PHILLIP W. ESPLIN, TELL ME WHAT HAPPENED: STRUCTURED INVESTIGATIVE INTERVIEWS OF CHILD VICTIMS AND WITNESSES 24 (2008).

[41] *See* Robyn Fivush & Jennifer R. Shukat, *Content, Consistency, and Coherence of Early Autobiographical Recall, in* MEMORY AND TESTIMONY IN THE CHILD WITNESS 5–23 (Maria S. Zaragoza et al. eds., 1995). *See also* United States v. Frederick, 78 F.3d 1370 (9th Cir. 1996).

[42] *See* United States v. Benn, 476 F.2d 1127 (D.C. Cir. 1972).

[43] Bett N. Gordon, Kenneth G. Jens, Richard Hollings & Thomas P. Watson, *Remembering Activities Performed Versus Those Imagined: Implications for Testimony of Children with Mental Retardation,* 23/3 J. CLIN. CHILD PSYCHOL. 239, 248 (1994).

[44] *See* Ricketts v. State, 488 A.2d 856, 857 (Del. 1985) (six-year-old who did not understand concept of perjury, but knew difference between truth and falsehood, was found competent to testify).

[45] *See* People v. Norfleet, 142 Mich. App. 745, 371 N.W.2d 438 (1985); State v. Ybarra, 24 N.M. 413, 174 P.212, 214 (1918); State v. Pettis, 488 A.2d 704, 706 (R.I. 1985).

developmentally appropriate methods to question children, most youngsters demonstrate the necessary understanding.

Although children understand the difference between truth and lies, judges and attorneys are sometimes not very good at eliciting children's understanding. Psychologists Thomas Lyon and Karen Saywitz have done important research on children's understanding of the difference between truth and lies, and on developmentally appropriate methods to showcase children's understanding.[46] Lyon and Saywitz note that three techniques are commonly employed to question children about truth and falsehood. First, the adult may ask the child to define the truth and a lie. For example, the adult might ask, "What is the truth?" Although a young child probably understands the difference, the child may not be able to define truth and lies.[47] Thus, it is generally advisable to avoid asking young children questions like, "What is the truth?" or "What is a lie?" Many young children find it difficult to generate examples of truthful statements and lies. Second, judges and attorneys sometimes ask young children to explain the difference between the truth and a lie. Explaining the difference between things presupposes understanding of the word "difference." Moreover, even if a child understands the word "difference," explaining the difference between truth and lies is linguistically and cognitively challenging. Although many children perform well on this task, others who know the difference between truth and falsehood stumble over providing a self-generated explanation. The third approach to questioning young children about truth and lies is more closely attuned to children's developmental capabilities. Rather than ask the child to define truth and lie, or to explain the difference, the adult provides simple examples of lies and truthful statements, and asks the child to identify them. Children as young as three perform well on this task. Thus, the adult might say, "Sally, if someone[48] told you this pen is blue, would that be the truth or a lie?" or "Billy, take a look at the shirt I'm wearing. If someone said this shirt is green, would that be the truth or a lie?"

Lyon and Saywitz developed a simple and developmentally appropriate procedure to use with young children to determine their understanding of the difference between truth and falsehood. The entire procedure can be obtained by going to Dr. Lyon's publication website.[49]

---

[46] *See* Thomas D. Lyon & Karen J. Saywitz, *Young Maltreated Children's Competence to Take the Oath*, 3 APPLIED DEV. SCIENCE 16 (1999). The research can be obtained on line by going to Dr. Lyon's Web page at the University of Southern California Law School, http://lawweb.usc.edu/who/faculty/directory/contactInfo.cfm?detailID=232.

[47] *See* Thomas D. Lyon, Nathalie Carrick & Jodi A. Quas, *Young Children's Competency to Take the Oath: Effects of Task, Maltreatment, and Age*, 34 LAW & HUM. BEHAV. 141 (2010) ("Prior research has demonstrated that children's ability to recognize 'truth' and 'lies' far exceeds their ability to define the terms."), *available at* http://works.bepress.com/thomaslyon/62/.

[48] Anne Graffam Walker points out in her workshops that children will be less likely to identify something as a lie if asked "if *I* told you" rather than if asked "if *someone* told you."

[49] Thomas D. Lyon & Karen J. Saywitz, *Qualifying Children to Take the Oath: Materials for Interviewing Professionals*, available on Dr. Lyon's Web page at the University of Southern California Law School, bepress page: http://works.bepress.com/thomaslyon/9/.

Show the child one of the drawings and proceed as follows:

Here's a picture. Look at this animal—what kind of animal is this?

Ok, that's a [child's label].

[Pointing to child on the left] Listen to what this boy says about the [child's label]. This boy says it's a [child's label]. Did he tell the truth?

[Pointing to the child on the right]. Listen to what this boy says about the [child' label]. This boy says it's a dog. Did he tell the truth?

[Repeat the procedure with three or four pictures to make sure the child is not guessing].

§ 30.3.6 Duty to Testify Truthfully

To testify, a child must understand the duty to tell the truth in court.[50] Children as young as three and four comprehend the duty to tell the truth. For young children, telling the truth means reporting what they saw. If the judge is concerned about a child's understanding of the obligation to testify truthfully, the judge may instruct the child.[51]

In addition to understanding the obligation to tell the truth, a child must realize that untruthful testimony can result in punishment.[52] By age three or four, children understand they can be punished for lying. It is not necessary that the child understand or believe in divine punishment for false swearing. Nor must the child comprehend the concept of perjury. The anticipated punishment may come from any source, including God, the judge, or a parent, and the child may describe the punishment in childlike terms.[53]

---

[50] *See* Richardson v. State, 33 Ark. App. 128, 803 S.W.2d 557 (1991); Hester v. State, 187 Ga. App. 873, 371 S.E.2d 684, 685(1988); Hodges v. State, 524 N.E.2d 774, 780 (Ind. 1988).

[51] *See* Hester v. State, 187 Ga. App. 873, 371 S.E.2d 684, 685 (1988).

[52] 2 John H. Wigmore, Evidence in Trials at Common Law § 506, at 513 (James H. Chadbourn rev. ed., Little Brown & Co. 1979).

[53] *See* State v. Dunn, 731 S.W.2d 297, 301 (Mo. Ct. App. 1987); State v. Higginbottom, 312 N.C. 760, 324 S.E.2d 834, 839 (1985).

Lyon and Saywitz's procedure for evaluating children's testimonial competence is useful in evaluating a child's understanding of the importance of telling the truth. An example of their procedure follows:

Here's a judge. She wants to know what happened to these boys. Well, one of these boys is gonna get in trouble for what he says, and you'll tell me which boy is gonna get in trouble.

[Point to boy on the left]. This boy tells the truth.

[Point to boy on the right]. This boy tells a lie.

Which boy is gonna get in trouble?

§ 30.3.7 Burden of Proof Regarding Testimonial Competence

In jurisdictions where "every person is competent to be a witness,"[54] the party challenging a child's competence has the burden of establishing incompetence.[55] The opponent of a child's testimony must make timely objection.[56] Failure to object

---

[54] FED. R. EVID. 601.

[55] *See* Mitchell v. State, 473 So. 2d. 591, 596 (Ala. Crim. App. 1985); Richardson v. State, 33 Ark. App. 128, 803 S.W.2d 557, 559 (1991). *See also* 18 U.S.C. § 3509(c)(3) (in federal court, party opposing child's competency must file written motion and offer proof of incompetency).

[56] FED. R. EVID. 103(a)(1); *see also* 81 AM. JUR. 2D *Witnesses* § 134, at 175–76 (1976).

constitutes a waiver unless permitting the child to testify was plain error.[57] In the small number of jurisdictions where children below a specified age are presumed incompetent, the proponent of a child below the specified age has the burden of rebutting the presumption.[58]

§ 30.3.8 Oath or Affirmation

To testify, a witness must take a religious oath or a secular affirmation. The oath or affirmation is "calculated to awaken the witness' conscience and impress the witness' mind with the duty" to tell the truth.[59] A judge may question a child to ascertain the child's understanding of the oath.[60] A child need not define the word "oath." Most children are unable to define "oath" until adolescence. A childlike understanding of the oath and the consequences of untruthful testimony are permissible.[61] No particular form of words is required for an oath.[62] The judge or clerk may simplify the language of the oath, and may take the time to ensure complete understanding.[63] A child may be asked to "promise to tell the truth." Several states have statutes allowing children to testify without an oath.[64] Thomas Lyon and Joyce Dorado write, "A child-friendly version of the oath increases testimonially competent maltreated children's true disclosures without increasing false disclosures."[65]

An affirmation is a secular undertaking to testify truthfully. As with an oath, an affirmation may take any form calculated to awaken the child's conscience and impress the child with the duty to tell the truth.[66]

---

[57] FED. R. EVID 103(d); *see also* People v. Burton, 55 Cal. 2d 328, 359 P.2d 433, 11 Cal. Rptr. 65 (1961); State v Gordon, 316 N.C. 497, 342 S.E.2d 509, 511–12 (1986).

[58] *See, e.g.*, PA. STAT. ANN. tit. 42 § 5911; *see* COLO. REV. STAT. § 13-90-106(b) and MO. ANN. STAT. § 491.060(2) (children under the age of ten who appear incapable of receiving just impressions and relating them truly are incompetent except in child abuse cases, in which all child victims are competent).

[59] FED. R. EVID. 603.

[60] 6 JOHN H. WIGMORE, EVIDENCE IN TRIALS AT COMMON LAW § 1821, at 406 (James H. Chadbourn rev. ed., Little Brown & Co. 1979).

[61] *See* Huggins v. State, 184 Ga. App. 540, 362 S.E.2d 120 (1987); *In re* Ralph D., 557 N.Y.S.2d 1003, 1005 (App. Div. 1990).

[62] *See* CAL. EVID. CODE § 710; COLO. REV. STAT. § 13-90-117.5 (1990).

[63] *See* State v. Dwyer, 149 Wis. 2d 850, 440 N.W.2d 344, 347 (1989); *In re* R.R., 79 N.J. 97, 398 A.2d 76, 83 (1979).

[64] FLA. STAT. ANN. § 90.605(2); N.Y. CRIM. PROC. LAW § 60.20.

[65] Thomas D. Lyon & Joyce S. Dorado, *Truth Induction in Young Maltreated Children: The Effects of Oath-Taking and Reassurance on True and False Disclosures*, 32/7 CHILD ABUSE & NEGLECT 738, 745 (2008).

[66] FED. R. EVID. 603.

§ 30.4 The Effects of Testifying on Children: Psychological Research

Psychologists began studying the effects of testifying on children in the 1980s.[67] Based on the empirical work to date, "no agreement has been reached as to whether the effect of testimony on children is positive or negative."[68] Desmond Runyan and his colleagues found that for some children, testifying in juvenile court is a positive experience.[69] Runyan concluded that juvenile court "testimony may improve the child's sense of control and treat the sense of powerlessness induced by the abuse." Gail Goodman and her colleagues followed 218 children during the two years it took their sexual abuse cases to progress through Denver, Colorado's criminal justice system.[70] Of the children who testified, "On average, the short-term effects on the children's behavioral adjustments, as reported by their caretakers, were more harmful than helpful. In contrast, by the time the cases were resolved, the behavioral adjustment of most, but not all, children who testified was similar to that of children who did not take the stand. The general course for these children, as for the control children, was gradual improvement." Debra Whitcomb and her colleagues reviewed research up to 1994 and wrote, "Virtually all of the children improved emotionally, regardless of their experiences in court. At worst, testifying may impede the improvement process for some children; at best, it may enhance their recovery."[71]

§ 30.5 While Children Are on the Witness Stand

Certain factors help children cope with testifying. These are discussed below.

§ 30.5.1 Emotional Support

Children who have emotional support are more likely to cope well with testifying than children lacking such support. Children benefit from the supportive presence of a non-offending parent, loved one, or victim advocate. Children who are emotionally supported while testifying are often better able to cope with the stress of facing the accused. On direct examination, emotionally supported children may be better able to answer questions than children lacking support. During cross-examination,

---

[67] The most thorough discussion of the issue is found in SUSAN R. HALL & BRUCE D. SALES, COURTROOM MODIFICATIONS FOR CHILD WITNESSES: LAW AND SCIENCE IN FORENSIC EVALUATIONS (2008).

[68] *See* Committee on Psychosocial Aspects of Child & Family Health, American Academy of Pediatrics, *The Child in Court: A Subject Review*, 104/5 PEDIATRICS 1145, 1146 (1999).

[69] Desmond K. Runyan, Mark D. Everson, Gail A. Edelsohn, Wanda M. Hunter & Martha L. Coulter, *Impact of Legal Intervention on Sexually Abused Children*, 113/4 J. PEDIATR. 647, 652 (1988).

[70] Gail S. Goodman, Elizabeth P. Taub, David P.H. Jones, Patricia England, Linda K. Port, Leslie Rudy & Lydia Prado, *Testifying in Criminal Court*, 57/5 MONOGR. SOC. RES. CHILD DEV. 1 (1992).

[71] U.S. DEPARTMENT OF JUSTICE, DEBRA WHITCOMB ET AL., THE EMOTIONAL EFFECTS OF TESTIFYING ON SEXUALLY ABUSED CHILDREN 5 (Research in Brief NCJ 146414, 1994).

emotionally supported children tend to provide more consistent testimony. In sum, emotional support helps children testify.

§ 30.5.2 Preparing Children to Testify

Preparing children to testify lowers their stress, increases their capacity to answer questions, and helps them understand the nature and seriousness of the proceeding.

§ 30.5.3 Scheduling a Young Child's Testimony

Young children perform best when they are rested. Up to age five, many children nap in the afternoon. A young child's testimony should be scheduled to accommodate naptime. Testifying in the morning is a good solution for many young children. With school-age children, it is usually best to schedule testimony during school hours. Few children are dismayed at the prospect of missing a little school. More importantly, a child who testifies following a full school day is tired and has spent the day worrying about going to court. It is better to take the child's testimony early in the day.

§ 30.5.4 Leading on Direct

Traditional practice restricts leading questions on direct examination. Rule 611(c) of the Federal Rules of Evidence provides, "Leading questions should not be used on the direct examination of a witness except as may be necessary to develop the witness' testimony."[72] Courts allow leading on direct regarding preliminary and undisputed matters (e.g., name, address, relationship to the events or parties). Leading is often permitted to introduce new topics or to rekindle memory. The judge may allow leading questions on embarrassing topics. Judges routinely permit leading questions during the direct examination of children who experience difficulty testifying due to fear, timidity, embarrassment, confusion, or reluctance. The better practice is to begin with nonleading questions and to move to leading questions if the child is unable to proceed.

§ 30.5.5 Testimonial Aids

Many children can show what they cannot tell, and children may use dolls or other props to help them testify. Anatomical dolls are helpful to illustrate penetration. It is not necessary that a child be completely unable to testify before using a testimonial aid. The question is whether the aid will assist the child to describe events.

§ 30.5.6 Allowing a Child Witness to Have a Comfort Item

Many children derive comfort from a favorite toy, stuffed animal, or blanket, and children should be permitted to bring their particular favorite with them to the witness stand.

---

[72] FED. R. EVID. 611(c).

§ 30.5.7 Recesses During Child's Testimony

Judges have discretion to recess the proceedings during a child's testimony, and they should do so when a child shows signs of fatigue, loss of concentration, or unmanageable stress. It is not sufficient to tell a child, "If you want a break, just ask." Children will not take the initiative to request a recess. Moreover, young children have difficulty monitoring their own needs. A five-year-old is more likely to stop answering questions or cry than to ask for a rest. The responsibility should be on the court and counsel to monitor the child's needs.

Recesses during direct examination pose few problems. Interruptions during cross-examination are another matter; although, it is during cross-examination that children often are most uncomfortable and in need of rest. The court has authority to recess the proceedings at reasonable intervals during cross-examination.[73] To avoid the complaint that recesses interfere with cross-examination, the court may inform counsel ahead of time that recesses will occur at regular intervals, for example, every 20 minutes.

§ 30.6 Hearsay[74]

Hearsay is important in child abuse litigation for three reasons:

- The child's out-of-court statements are often powerful evidence of abuse.

- In many cases, the importance of the child's out-of-court statements is magnified by a paucity of physical evidence and eyewitnesses.

- Although most children have the capacity to testify, some children are ineffective witnesses, and some cannot take the stand at all.

§ 30.6.1 Hearsay Defined

Rule 801(c) of the Federal Rules of Evidence defines hearsay as "a statement, other than one made by the declarant while testifying at the trial or hearing, offered in evidence to prove the truth of the matter asserted."[75] For hearsay purposes, a "statement" is an oral or written assertion or nonverbal conduct that is intended as an assertion.[76] A child makes an assertion when the child speaks, writes, acts, or fails to act with the intent to express some fact or opinion. Nonverbal conduct intended as an assertion is hearsay when offered to prove the matter asserted.[77] Suppose, for

---

[73] *See* State v. Hillman, 613 So. 2d 1053, 1058–59 (La. Ct. App. 1993).

[74] For up-to-date cases and developments regarding hearsay, see the annually supplemented JOHN E. B. MYERS, MYERS ON EVIDENCE IN CHILD, DOMESTIC AND ELDER ABUSE (Aspen Publishers, 4th ed. 2005 & 2010 Supp.).

[75] FED. R. EVID. 801(c).

[76] FED. R. EVID. 801(c).

[77] *See* State v. Hall, 946 P.2d 712 (Utah Ct. App. 1997); MUELLER & KIRKPATRICK, FEDERAL EVIDENCE § 369 (2d ed. 1995); *see also* State v. Egger, 8 Neb. App. 740, 601 N.W.2d 785 (1999).

example, that a physician who is examining a child for possible sexual abuse asks, "Did anyone touch you in your private parts?" The child nods her head up and down. This nonverbal conduct is the equivalent of words and is hearsay when offered to prove that the child was touched.

An out-of-court statement is hearsay only if it is offered to prove the truth of the matter asserted. If a statement is offered for some other purpose, it is not hearsay. Suppose a four-year-old makes the following out-of-court statement, "Daddy's private was hard, and white pee came out that tasted really yucky." If this disturbing statement is offered for the truth of the matter asserted, it is hearsay. If the child's statement meets the requirements of an exception to the hearsay rule, then the statement is admissible for the truth. Even if the statement does not fall within an exception, it may be admissible if it is relevant for some purpose other than proving the truth of the matter asserted. The child's statement demonstrates sexual knowledge one would not expect in a four-year-old, and developmentally unusual sexual knowledge can constitute circumstantial evidence of sexual abuse. Offered to prove sexual knowledge, the statement is not hearsay because it is not offered for the truth. A second non-hearsay use of a child's out-of-court statement is to establish the timing and circumstances in which a child reported abuse. Third, a child's out-of-court statement may reveal knowledge of a place, person, or thing that the child could not know unless the child had prior contact with the place, person, or thing. Finally, children's out-of-court statements are sometimes offered to establish why the police or social services began an investigation. The problem with the latter use of out-of-court statements is that, in most circumstances, the reason for the investigation is irrelevant.

§ 30.6.2 Exceptions to the Hearsay Rule

Although there are many exceptions to the hearsay rule, only a handful play a day-to-day role in child abuse and neglect litigation. Relevant exceptions are briefly described below.

Prior Inconsistent Statements

A witness's testimony may be impeached with evidence that the witness told a different story prior to testifying.[78] When a prior inconsistent statement is used solely to impeach, it is not offered for the truth of the matter asserted, and is not hearsay.[79] A prior inconsistent statement that is offered both to impeach and for the truth is hearsay.[80]

---

[78] State v. Gomez, 131 N.M. 118, 33 P.3d 669 (Ct. App. 2001); *see* United States v. Hale, 422 U.S. 171, 176 (1975) ("a basic rule of evidence provides that prior inconsistent statements may be used to impeach the credibility of a witness"); Commonwealth v. Brown, 538 Pa. 410, 648 A.2d 1177, 1185 (1994).

[79] State v. Patterson, 742 So. 2d 50 (La. Ct. App. 1999) (discussion of foundation for impeachment with prior inconsistent statement); *State v. Wood*, 126 Idaho 241, 880 P.2d 771, 778 (Ct. App. 1994).

[80] *See* People v. Sambo, 197 Ill. App. 3d 574, 554 N.E.2d 1080, 1086 (1990); State v. Mancine, 124 N.J. 232, 590 A.2d 1107 (1991).

Under the Federal Rules of Evidence, prior inconsistent statements are generally admissible to impeach. However, only a limited class of prior inconsistent statements are admissible for the truth as well as to impeach. Under Federal Rule 801(d)(1)(A), only prior inconsistent statements that were "given under oath subject to the penalty of perjury at a trial, hearing, or other proceeding, or in a deposition"[81] are admissible for the truth of the matter asserted. In some states, all or nearly all prior inconsistent statements are admissible for the truth of the matter asserted as well as to impeach.[82]

Prior Consistent Statements

Prior consistent statements that are admitted solely to rehabilitate a witness's credibility are not offered for the truth, and are not hearsay.[83] When a prior consistent statement is offered for the truth as well as to rehabilitate, it is hearsay. States have hearsay exceptions for prior consistent statements. Rule 801(d)(1)(B) of the Federal Rules of Evidence governs admissibility of prior consistent statements offered for the truth in federal court, and provides: "A statement is not hearsay if . . . [t]he declarant testifies at the trial or hearing and is subject to cross-examination concerning the statement, and the statement is . . . consistent with the declarant's testimony and is offered to rebut an express or implied charge against the declarant of recent fabrication or improper influence or motive."[84]

To gain admission as a prior consistent statement, an out-of-court statement must be consistent with trial testimony. The prior statement does not have to be identical to trial testimony. Some children disclose abuse gradually, revealing additional details over time.[85] A child's trial testimony may contain more, less, or slightly different information than out-of-court disclosures. If the gist of the child's out-of-court statements is consistent with the child's trial testimony, the out-of-court statements are consistent.

Rehabilitation with prior consistent statements must await impeachment. The following modes of impeachment can open the door for rehabilitation with prior consistent statements.

Charge of Fabrication

An express or implied assertion that a witness's testimony is fabricated paves the way for rehabilitation with prior consistent statements. When the witness is a child,

---

[81] FED. R. EVID. 801(d)(1)(A).

[82] *See, e.g.*, CAL. EVID. CODE § 1235 (West); 725 ILL. COMP. STAT. 5/115-10.1; N.J. R. EVID. 803(a)(1). *See also* State v. Borrelli, 227 Conn. 153, 629 A.2d 1105 (1993).

[83] MCCORMICK ON EVIDENCE § 49, at 118 (Edward W. Leary ed., 1984).

[84] FED. R. EVID. 801(d)(1)(B).

[85] *See generally* JOHN E. B. MYERS, MYERS ON EVIDENCE IN CHILD, DOMESTIC AND ELDER ABUSE § 6.04 (Aspen Publishers, 4th ed. 2005); Thomas D. Lyon, *Scientific Support for Expert Testimony on Child Sexual Abuse Accommodation, in* CRITICAL ISSUES IN CHILD SEXUAL ABUSE: HISTORICAL, LEGAL, AND PSYCHOLOGICAL PERSPECTIVES 107 (Jon R. Conte ed., 2002).

the cross-examiner may suggest that the child was coached during questioning by parents, police, social workers, or an attorney.

When the cross-examiner asserts fabrication, the majority rule is that prior consistent statements are admissible only if they were uttered before the motive or pressure to fabricate arose.[86] The logic of the "prior to motive" rule is that consistent statements uttered before there was a motive to fabricate have rehabilitative value, while statements uttered after the motive to fabricate arose lack rehabilitative value. Sometimes it is difficult to tell when an alleged improper influence or motive to fabricate arose. When the impeaching attorney concentrates heavily on fabrication, the need for rehabilitation increases, and courts are more likely to admit prior consistent statements despite uncertainty regarding when the influence or motive arose.

Impeachment by Contradiction

Impeachment by contradiction sometimes triggers rehabilitation with prior consistent statements, especially when the cross-examiner implies fabrication.

Impeachment by Evidence of Untruthful Character

Most authorities hold that impeachment that attacks a witness's character for truthfulness (e.g., impeachment by conviction (Rule 609))[87] or specific acts of untruthfulness (Rule 608(b))[88] does not trigger rehabilitation with prior consistent statements.[89]

Impeachment with Prior Inconsistent Statements

Impeachment by a prior inconsistent statement sometimes amounts to a charge of fabrication, triggering rehabilitation with prior consistent statements.

Impeachment Charging Lapse of Memory

The cross-examiner sometimes hopes to undermine a child's testimony by implying that the child's memory is faulty. The impeaching attorney emphasizes inconsistencies between the child's trial testimony and earlier statements on the theory that the earlier statements were accurate and the child's memory faded in the

---

[86] *See* Tome v. United States, 513 U.S. 150, 156, 115 S.Ct. 696, 700 (1995) ("The prevailing common-law rule for more than a century before adoption of the Federal Rules of Evidence was that a prior consistent statement introduced to rebut a charge of recent fabrication or improper influence or motive was admissible if the statement had been made before the alleged fabrication, influence, or motive came into being, but it was inadmissible if made afterwards."); Noel v. Commonwealth, 76 S.W.3d 923, 928 (Ky. 2002); Commonwealth v. Cruz, 53 Mass. App. Ct. 393, 759 N.E.2d 723 (2001).

[87] FED. R. EVID. 609.

[88] FED. R. EVID. 608(b).

[89] *See* McCORMICK ON EVIDENCE § 49, at 118 (Edward W. Leary ed., 1984); MUELLER & KIRKPATRICK, FEDERAL EVIDENCE § 406, at 186–87 (2d ed. 1995).

interim. Faced with such impeachment, courts often admit prior consistent statements uttered close in time to the event, when the child's memory was fresh.[90]

Present Sense Impressions

Rule 803(1) of the Federal Rules of Evidence creates a hearsay exception for "[a] statement describing or explaining an event or condition made while the declarant was perceiving the event or condition, or immediately thereafter."[91] The present sense impression exception has three requirements:

- The declarant must perceive an event or condition. The event need not be startling or shocking, and the declarant need not be a participant in the event.

- The statement must describe or explain the perceived event.[92]

- The statement must be made while the declarant was perceiving the event or condition, or immediately afterwards.[93]

The time element is strict. A statement made during the event qualifies.[94] Difficulty arises when the statement is uttered shortly after the event. A few moments delay between the event and the statement should not disqualify a statement as a present sense impression. When delay extends into minutes, however, the statement is not a present sense impression.[95]

Excited Utterances

The excited utterance exception is codified at Rule 803(2) of the Federal Rules of Evidence,[96] and provides that the hearsay rule does not exclude statements relating to a startling event made while the declarant was under the stress of excitement caused by the event. The rationale for the excited utterance exception is that statements made under the stress of a startling event are unlikely to be the product of conscious reflection or fabrication.

---

[90] State v. Bakken, 604 N.W.2d 106 (Minn. Ct. App. 2000); Applebaum v. American Export Isbrandsten Lines, 472 F.2d 56, 61–62 (2d Cir. 1972); United States v. Keller, 145 F. Supp. 692, 697 (D.N.J. 1956); State v. Bruggeman, 161 Ariz. 508, 779 P.2d 823, 825 (Ct. App. 1989).

[91] FED. R. EVID. 803(1).

[92] *See* United States v. Portsmouth Paving Corp., 694 F.2d 312, 323 (4th Cir. 1982) ("We perceive events with our ears as much as with our eyes…").

[93] MUELLER & KIRKPATRICK, FEDERAL EVIDENCE § 434, at 387 (2d ed. 1995).

[94] Territory of Guam v. Ignacio, 10 F.3d 608 (9th Cir. 1993) (three-year-old's statement during bath that her vaginal area hurt was admissible as present sense impression); State v. Perry, 95 N.M. 179, 619 P.2d 855 (Ct. App. 1980) (rape of adult took place in motel room; declarant in neighboring room heard victim scream and called motel office to complain about noise; declarant's statement to manager was admitted as present sense impression).

[95] *See* Hilyer v. Howat Concrete Co., 578 F.2d 422, 426 n.7 (D.C. Cir. 1978) (delay of 15 to 45 minutes too long); Tucker v. State, 264 Ark. 890, 575 S.W.2d 684, 685 (1979) (delay of three days too long).

[96] FED. R. EVID. 803(2).

The excited utterance exception has three requirements:

- There must be a startling or exciting event.
- The out-of-court statement must relate to the event.
- The statement must be made while the child is under the stress of excitement induced by the event.[97]

To determine whether the child was under the stress of excitement when the statement was made, courts consider the following factors: spontaneity of the statement, nature of the event, type of questions used to elicit the statement, how much time elapsed between the startling event and the child's statement, the child's emotional and physical condition when the statement was made (e.g., child crying, physically injured, or in pain), the words spoken that may indicate excitement, pressured or hurried speech that may indicate excitement, and the child's age.[98]

Fresh Complaint of Rape or Sexual Abuse

In rape and sexual assault prosecutions, it has long been the law that when the victim testifies, her fresh complaint of rape or sexual assault is admissible to support her credibility.[99] With the exception of Tennessee,[100] the fresh complaint doctrine applies when the victim is a child. The fresh complaint doctrine is not found in the Federal Rules of Evidence or in most state evidence codes, although several states have statutes codifying the doctrine.

The fresh complaint doctrine is based on the idea that evidence of the victim's complaint is needed to forestall jurors from improperly discounting the victim's trial testimony. Some jurors believe that a victim of rape or sexual assault will naturally report the crime shortly after it occurs. Unless such jurors are informed that the victim spoke out promptly, these jurors may infer that no report was made and, since no report was made, no crime occurred.

Although a fresh complaint is an out-of-court statement, it is not hearsay. The report is not admitted for the truth, but to corroborate the victim's testimony. A few decisions and statutes define fresh complaint evidence as hearsay within an exception.[101]

---

[97] FED. R. EVID. 803(2); *see also* MUELLER & KIRKPATRICK, FEDERAL EVIDENCE § 435, at 390 (2d ed. 1995).

[98] Barnett v. State, 757 So. 2d 323 (Miss. Ct. App. 2000); *see also* United States v. Renville, 779 F.2d 430, 440 (8th Cir. 1985); People v. Hackney, 183 Mich. App. 516, 455 N.W.2d 358, 362 (1990).

[99] *See* Russel M. Coombs, *Reforming New Jersey Evidence Law on Fresh Complaint of Rape*, 25 RUT. L.J 699 (1994); Michael H. Graham, *The Cry of Rape: The Prompt Complaint Doctrine and the Federal Rules of Evidence*, 19 WILLAMETTE L. REV. 489–512 (1983). *See also* State v, Dabkowski, 199 Conn. 193, 506 A.2d 118 (1986).

[100] Ruff v. State, 978 S.W.2d 95 (Tenn. 1998); State v. Speck, 944 S.W.2d 598 (Tenn. 1997).

[101] State v. Joel H., 755 A.2d 520 (Me. 2000); *see* Commonwealth v. Bailey, 370 Mass. 388, 348 N.E.2d 746 (1976); State v. Sanders, 691 S.W.2d 566, 568 (Tenn. Crim. App. 1984) (statements by five-year-old victim "were admissible under the fresh complaint exception to the hearsay rule"); OR. EVID. CODE 803(18a); LOUISIANA CODE EVID. 801(D)(1)(d).

Fresh complaint evidence is admissible during the state's case-in-chief. As a general rule, the victim must testify before a fresh complaint is admissible. Impeachment is not a condition precedent to admission of the victim's fresh complaint. Under the traditional view, evidence of fresh complaint is limited to the statement of complaint. Details are not admissible. The court may permit more than one fresh complaint witness. As the name suggests, the fresh complaint doctrine requires a complaint to be made promptly.[102] A complaint satisfies this requirement if it is made within a reasonable time. Delay in reporting may be explained.[103]

Diagnosis or Treatment Exception

Certain hearsay statements that are made for purposes of obtaining a diagnosis or treatment are admissible under Federal Rule of Evidence 803(4) and similar state rules. The rationale for the diagnosis or treatment exception is that statements to secure diagnosis or treatment are reliable because the declarant has an incentive to be truthful with the doctor or nurse.

Do young children understand the importance of telling the truth to the doctor or nurse? Psychologists have studied children's understanding of illness, medical care, and the role of medical professionals. As one would expect, children's understanding follows a developmental progression.[104] In general, the understanding of older children about illness and its causes is more complex than that of younger children. Yet, even some very young children have the capacity to meet the medical hearsay exception. Assessment of children's understanding should proceed case-by-case.

Not everything that is said to a doctor or nurse is admissible under the medical diagnosis or treatment exception. The exception reaches only statements that are "pertinent" to diagnosis or treatment. Any information that assists a professional in reaching diagnostic or treatment decisions is pertinent. The exception includes statements describing past as well as present symptoms. Thus, the patient's medical history is admissible under the exception. The exception also embraces the patient's description of the cause of illness or injury. In child abuse litigation, most courts hold that a child's statement identifying the perpetrator can be pertinent to diagnosis or

---

[102] *See* People v. Baggett, 185 Ill. App. 3d 1007, 541 N.E. 2d 1266, 1273 (1989); Commonwealth v. Lamontagne, 42 Mass. App. 213, 675 N.E.2d 1169 (1997); Commonwealth v. Swain, 36 Mass. App. Ct. 433, 632 N.E.2d 848 (1994).

[103] Brown v. Commonwealth, 37 Va. App. 169, 554 S.E.2d 711 (2001) (two-year delay in reporting was not unreasonable given the circumstances of this case); Folse v. Folse, 738 So. 2d 1040 (La. 1999); State v. Marshall, 246 Conn. 799, 717 A.2d 1224 (1998).

[104] *See* Janice L. Genevro, Carol J. Andreassen & Marc H. Bornstein, *Young Children's Understanding of Routine Medical Care and Strategies for Coping with Stressful Medical Experiences, in* CHILD DEVELOPMENT AND BEHAVIORAL PEDIATRICS 59–83 (Marc H. Bornstein & Janice L. Genevro eds., 1996); *see also* Pamela M. Kato, Thomas D. Lyon & Christina Rasco, *Reasoning About Moral Aspects of Illness and Treatment by Preschoolers Who Are Healthy or Who Have Chronic Illness,* 19/2 J. DEV. BEHAV. PEDIATR. 68 (1998).

treatment, and admissible under the exception.[105] Most courts admit selected statements to mental health professionals.[106]

Residual and Child Hearsay Exceptions

The Rule 807 of the Federal Rules of Evidence contains an exception[107] for reliable hearsay that does not fall within one of the traditional exceptions. This is the so-called residual or catch-all exception. Of states that have adopted the Federal Rules, a majority have a version of the residual exception. In addition to a residual exception, most states have a special catch-all exception for children's hearsay in child abuse cases.

When hearsay is offered under a residual or child hearsay exception, the primary issue usually is whether the hearsay is sufficiently reliable. In criminal cases, the starting place for analysis of reliability is the U.S. Supreme Court's decision in *Idaho v. Wright*.[108] In that case, the Supreme Court ruled that under the Confrontation Clause of the Sixth Amendment, reliability is assessed in light of "the totality of the circumstances." Yet, the Court divided this totality into two categories: (1) circumstances "that surround the making of the statement and that render the declarant particularly worthy of belief;" and (2) circumstances that corroborate the statement but do not surround it. The Court ruled that the Confrontation Clause allows judges assessing reliability to consider circumstances that surround the statement, but forbids consideration of corroborating evidence such as medical or physical evidence of abuse, the defendant's opportunity to commit the offense, or the testimony of another witness identifying the defendant as the perpetrator.

In civil litigation, including dependency cases in juvenile court, the Sixth Amendment Confrontation Clause does not apply. One can argue that *Idaho v. Wright's*[109] distinction between immediately surrounding factors and corroborating factors is inapplicable in civil cases and that the court may consider all factors shedding light on reliability, including corroborating factors.

A judge evaluating the reliability of hearsay offered under a residual or child hearsay exception considers the following factors:

- Whether the child was testimonially competent when the statement was uttered. The fact that a child possessed or lacked the competence to testify *at the time* an out-of-court statement was uttered may impact reliability.

---

[105] *See, e.g.*, State v. Telford, 948 A.2d 350, 354 (Conn. App. 2008); Morgan v. State, 995 So. 2d 812 (Miss. App. 2008); *Ex parte* C.L.Y., 928 So. 2d 1069, 1073 (Ala. 2005); Anthony v. State, 23 So. 3d 611 (Miss. App. 2009).

[106] *See, e.g.*, United States v. Kappell, 418 F.3d 550, 556 (6th Cir. 2005); Anthony v. State, 23 So. 3d 611 (Miss. App. 2009); State v. Moses, 129 Wash. App. 718, 119 P.3d 906 (2005).

[107] FED. R. EVID. 807.

[108] 497 U.S. 805 (1990).

[109] 497 U.S. 805 (1990).

- Whether the child is testimonially competent at the time of trial. The fact that a child lacks testimonial competence at trial may or may not impact the reliability of the child's out-of-court statements. One must ask *why* the child is incompetent to testify at trial. If the child lacks the ability to distinguish truth from lies, this incapacity may or may not have existed when the out-of-court statement was made. On the other hand, if the only reason the child cannot testify is fear of the defendant, then the child's lack of testimonial competence has no bearing on the reliability of out-of-court statements.

- The more spontaneous a statement, the less likely it was a product of fabrication.

- The reliability of an out-of-court statement may be influenced by the type of questions used to elicit the statement. When questions are leading, the possibility exists that the questioner influenced the statement.

- Reliability may be enhanced when a child's out-of-court statements are consistent.

- Young children lack the experience required to fabricate detailed accounts of sex acts. A four-year-old cannot describe fellatio, including ejaculation, unless the child has experienced fellatio or witnessed it. Naturally, care must be taken to rule out innocent explanations for a child's developmentally unusual sexual knowledge.

- Evidence that a child had or lacked a motive to fabricate impacts reliability. The motivation of adults is also relevant.[110]

In addition to the foregoing factors, the following factors may corroborate a child's statement:

- A child's statement may be corroborated by medical, laboratory, scientific, or physical evidence.[111]

- When a child's behavior changes in a way that corroborates the child's hearsay description of abuse, it may be appropriate to place increased confidence in the hearsay.[112]

- In some cases, a young child's developmentally unusual sexual knowledge surrounds the child's out-of-court statement and may be

---

[110] *See* Daniel B. Lord, Note, *Determining Reliability Factors in Child Hearsay Statements: Wright and Its Progeny Confront the Psychological Research*, 79 Iowa L. Rev. 1149 (1994); Gilles Renaud, *A Thematic Review of "Principled Hearsay" in Child Sex Abuse Cases*, 37 Crim. L. Q. 277 (1995); *see also* United States v. Harrison, 296 F.3d 994 (10th Cir. 2002); State v. Peterson, 557 N.W.2d 389 (S.D. 1996).

[111] Morgan v. Foretich, 846 F.2d 941 (4th Cir. 1988).

[112] *See* State v. Robinson, 153 Ariz. 191, 735 P.2d 801 (1987); State v. Ritchey, 107 Ariz. 552, 490 P.2d 558 (1971); People v. Bowers, 801 P.2d 511 (Colo. 1990).

considered in assessing reliability.[113] In other cases, the child's developmentally unusual sexual knowledge corroborates the child's statement.[114]

The fact that the defendant had the opportunity to commit the act described in a child's statement may increase the reliability of the statement.[115]

§ 30.6.3 Hearsay and the Confrontation Clause

The hearsay rule and the Confrontation Clause of the Sixth Amendment share the goal of excluding unreliable evidence. In criminal trials, when a declarant testifies at trial and is subject to cross-examination, the Confrontation Clause is satisfied and raises no barrier to hearsay. When the declarant does not testify at trial, admission of hearsay against the defendant in a criminal trial is governed by *Crawford v. Washington*.[116] Under *Crawford*, if the hearsay is "testimonial," it is inadmissible unless the defendant had a prior opportunity to cross-examine the declarant. If the hearsay is not testimonial, admissibility is governed the principles laid down in *Ohio v. Roberts*.[117]

In *Crawford*, the Supreme Court did not provide a definitive definition of "testimonial." But the Court did provide the following examples of testimonial hearsay:

- A formal declaration made for the purpose of proving a fact.

- Prior testimony (including grand jury testimony) that the defendant had no opportunity to cross-examine.

- An affidavit.

- A statement by a person in police custody in response to formal police interrogation.

- Hearsay statements that the declarant would reasonably expect to be used in later court proceedings.

The Court's principal concern in *Crawford* was limiting the admissibility of hearsay generated by government officials with an eye toward prosecution.

In *Crawford*, the Court provided the following example of nontestimonial statements: off-hand, casual remarks to friends or family members. Thus, a child's hearsay statements to parents, babysitters, teachers, or friends are nontestimonial.

---

[113] *See* People v. Bowers, 801 P.2d 511 (Colo. 1990).

[114] *See In re* Stephen "GG," 279 A.D.2d 651, 719 N.Y.S. 2d 167 (2001); *In re* Nicole V., 71 N.Y.2d 112, 518 N.E.2d 914 (1987).

[115] *See* State v. Bellotti, 383 N.W.2d 308 (Minn. Ct. App. 1986); State v. Booth, 124 Ore. App. 282, 862 P.2d 518 (1993).

[116] 541 U.S. 36 (2004).

[117] 448 U.S. 56 (1980), *overruled by* Crawford v. Washington, 541 U.S. 36 (2004).

Crawford v. Washington is a Sixth Amendment decision, and does not apply in civil litigation. Thus, *Crawford*'s limitations on the admissibility of hearsay should not apply in juvenile court protective proceedings.

§ 30.7 Should Children Attend Court Hearings?

An issue that divides judges and attorneys in juvenile court protective proceedings is whether the child should attend court hearings. Obviously, if the child is scheduled to testify, the child must attend. But what about the numerous hearings where the child's testimony is not required? Reasonable minds differ on whether children should attend such hearings.

Those who believe children should attend all or most hearings point out that the case is about the child—the child's future is at stake—and the child should be present when decisions are made. Having the child present is a mark of respect for the child. Children often have useful information to contribute, regardless of whether they are scheduled to testify. When a child is present in the courtroom, the hearing comes alive. The hearing is no longer about a stack of papers—it is about a living, breathing child whose presence in the courtroom focuses the attention of the professionals. Having the child in court ensures that the hearing is treated with the seriousness and respect it deserves.

Those who believe children generally do not need to attend hearings point out that many hearings are perfunctory, lasting only a few minutes and accomplishing important but routine matters. Children have little or nothing to add to such proceedings. Yet, requiring the child's attendance disrupts the child's routine, including school attendance, as well as the routines of foster parents, social workers, and others. At some hearings, sensitive information is discussed that the child should not hear. For example, does a child benefit when unflattering information is disclosed about the child's parents. Is it wise for a child to be present when a psychotherapist discusses the child's mental health problems?

As with many controversial issues, there may be a middle ground when it comes to children's attendance at court hearings. When a child is old enough to understand and contribute to proceedings, the child's presence is generally warranted for the reasons discussed above. If the child's attorney, the judge, or another professional believes the child's attendance at a particular hearing is contraindicated, the adult can raise the issue before the hearing, or the child can be excused during portions of the hearing. As for young children, attendance at hearings may have little utility in the run of cases. NACC has adopted a policy on children's presence in the courtroom.[118]

---

[118] *NACC Policy Statement: Confidentiality of Juvenile Court Proceedings and Records* (adopted by NACC Board of Directors on April 25, 1998), *available at* http://www.naccchildlaw.org/?page= Policy_Papers.

Chapter 31: Special Evidentiary Issues

by John E. B. Myers[1]

§ 31.1 Selected Evidence Issues

This chapter discusses expert testimony and syndrome evidence.[2]

§ 31.2 Expert Testimony

Expert testimony from mental health and medical experts plays an important role in child maltreatment litigation.

§ 31.2.1 Qualifications to Testify as Expert Witness

To qualify as an expert, a witness must possess sufficient "knowledge, skill, experience, training, or education."[3] Unless a medical or mental health professional is clearly unqualified, deficiencies in qualifications go to the weight accorded the expert's testimony rather than admissibility.[4] A professional need not be the foremost authority on child maltreatment, nor must the witness understand every aspect of the subject. In *State v. Best*,[5] the defendant challenged the qualifications of two physicians. One was an orthopedic surgeon and the other a radiologist. The orthopedic surgeon testified that the victim's fractured arm was probably the result of child abuse. The radiologist testified that the twisting force required to produce the fracture could not have resulted from getting an arm caught in crib bars. Defendant claimed that the surgeon was not qualified in the area of child abuse and that the radiologist was not qualified on the force needed to produce a fracture. The South Dakota Supreme Court rejected both challenges, noting that experts do not have to be expert in every aspect of a subject.

In *Deese v. State*,[6] the victim died of Shaken Baby Syndrome. The prosecution's expert was a pediatrician specializing in pediatric emergency medicine. Although not

---

[1] John E. B. Myers, J.D., is Professor of Law at University of the Pacific, McGeorge School of Law.

[2] For a comprehensive treatise on evidentiary issues in child abuse and neglect cases, see JOHN E. B. MYERS, MYERS ON EVIDENCE IN CHILD, DOMESTIC AND ELDER ABUSE (Aspen Publishers, 4th ed. 2005). For a discussion of evidentiary issues involving children's hearsay statements, see Chapter 30.

[3] FED. R. EVID. 702.

[4] *See* FED. R. EVID. 702, Commentary ("Courts have not required a party to show that the witness is an outstanding expert, or to show that the witness is well-known or respected in the field; these are generally questions of weight.").

[5] 232 N.W.2d 447 (1975).

[6] 786 A.2d 751 (2001).

a pathologist, the doctor was qualified to offer an opinion on the cause of the child's death. The Maryland Court of Appeals wrote, "Assuming, *arguendo*, that the most relevant field of expertise was forensic pathology, as distinct from pediatrics and pediatric emergency medicine, previous decisions have affirmed a trial court's admission of expert testimony when the expert, although not a specialist in the field having the most sharply focused relevancy to the issue at hand, nevertheless could assist the jury in light of the witness's 'formal education, professional training, personal observations, and actual experience.'"[7]

Many pediatricians, radiologists, pathologists, emergency room physicians, psychiatrists, psychologists, and social workers possess the training and experience required to testify as experts.

§ 31.2.2 Bases for Expert Opinion

Expert witnesses may base their testimony on a broad range of facts and data.[8] An expert may state an opinion without specifying the factual basis for the opinion.[9] As a practical matter, however, experts nearly always provide the factual data on which testimony is based. This information may precede or follow the expert's opinion.

In many child abuse and neglect cases, the expert has firsthand knowledge of the child because the expert examined or treated the child. Firsthand knowledge is not always required, however, and in the right circumstances, an expert may render an opinion without personally examining the child. For example, an expert may base an opinion on review of records. In *State v. Moyer*,[10] defendant argued that expert testimony should be excluded because the doctor had not personally examined the child. The doctor reviewed records and photographs of the child. The court rejected defendant's argument, writing, "We find no requirement and do not consider it imperative that the doctor actually examine the child. [The doctor] was an expert, he understood the [battered child] syndrome and he knew what factors to look for. He had sufficient evidence before him from which he could formulate his expert opinion."[11]

Experts may base opinions on information that is not admissible in evidence, provided such information is "of a type reasonably relied upon by experts in the particular field in forming opinions or inferences upon the subject."[12] For example, a doctor evaluating the possibility of physical abuse may consider the caretaker's prior violence toward the child.[13] Although the caretaker's violent history may be character

---

[7] *Id.* at 756 (citations omitted).

[8] *See* FED. R. EVID. 703.

[9] *See* FED. R. EVID. 705.

[10] 727 P.2d 31 (Ariz. Ct. App. 1986).

[11] *Id.* at 34.

[12] FED. R. EVID. 703.

[13] *See* People v. Gordon, 738 P.2d 404, 406 (Colo. App. 1987) (noting expert considered defendant's "prior violent behavior toward the child").

evidence, the doctor's reliance on character is clinically appropriate. Expert testimony may be based in part on hearsay. Written hearsay includes medical and psychological records, consultation reports, and documents prepared by police and social services agencies. Verbal hearsay plays an important role in diagnosis. The patient's history—which often lies at the heart of diagnosis—is hearsay. With children, the history is often provided by a parent or caretaker. A doctor or therapist acts properly when the professional bases court testimony partly on a medical history.

Although an expert's opinion may be based on inadmissible evidence, Rule 703 of the Federal Rule of Evidence provides, "Facts or data that are otherwise inadmissible shall not be disclosed to the jury by the proponent of the opinion or inference unless the court determines that their probative value in assisting the jury to evaluate the expert's opinion substantially outweighs their prejudicial effect."

§ 31.3 Syndrome Evidence

Expert testimony describing syndrome evidence is often admitted in child maltreatment litigation, including testimony on Battered Child Syndrome, Shaken Baby Syndrome, Munchausen Syndrome by Proxy, Child Sexual Abuse Accommodation Syndrome, and Posttraumatic Stress Disorder. These and additional syndromes are addressed below, following a discussion of the use and abuse of syndrome evidence.

Dorland's Medical Dictionary defines syndrome as "a set of symptoms which occur together."[14] The word "syndrome" is not the only term that is used to describe concurring symptoms. The word "profile" is occasionally found in the literature to describe a set of symptoms, characteristics, or behaviors. The American Psychiatric Association's *Diagnostic and Statistical Manual of Mental Disorders*[15] (DSM) uses the word "disorder" rather than "syndrome." The DSM acknowledges, however, that "Each of the mental disorders is conceptualized as a clinically significant behavioral or psychological syndrome or pattern."[16]

Many diseases and some syndromes share the feature of diagnostic value. That is, the disease or syndrome points with some degree of certainty to a particular cause or etiology. The clinician reasons backward as follows: "In my patient I observe symptoms A, B, and C. These symptoms comprise Disease X or Syndrome Y. From the presence of Disease X or Syndrome Y, I reason backward to the cause or etiology of the symptoms." The ability to reason backward from symptoms to etiology is diagnostic value.

With diseases, the relationship between symptoms and etiology is often clear. Thus, many diseases have high diagnostic value. The same is true for some

---

[14] DORLAND'S ILLUSTRATED MEDICAL DICTIONARY 1632 (28th ed. 1994).

[15] AMERICAN PSYCHIATRIC ASSOCIATION, DIAGNOSTIC AND STATISTICAL MANUAL OF MENTAL DISORDERS, TEXT REVISION (4th ed. 2000).

[16] *Id.*

syndromes, that is, the relationship between the symptoms comprising the syndrome and the etiology is clear. With many syndromes, however, the relationship between symptoms and etiology is unclear or unknown. When it is not possible to reason backward from symptoms to etiology, the syndrome lacks diagnostic value.

Nearly all of the psychological syndromes that find their way into child maltreatment litigation lack diagnostic value. In other words, nearly all psychological syndromes are nondiagnostic. One cannot reason backward from the syndrome to its etiology.

Focusing for the moment on syndromes that do have diagnostic value, it is important to understand that diagnostic value varies from syndrome to syndrome. Syndromes with diagnostic value are on a continuum of diagnostic certainty. Some diagnostic syndromes point with greater certainty to their etiology than others. Two syndromes that are used in litigation illustrate the continuum of diagnostic certainty: Battered Child Syndrome and Rape Trauma Syndrome. A child with Battered Child Syndrome is very likely to have suffered nonaccidental injury. Battered Child Syndrome points convincingly to abuse. The doctor can reason backward from symptoms to cause. Battered Child Syndrome has high diagnostic value.

Compare the high diagnostic value of Battered Child Syndrome with the decidedly low diagnostic value of Rape Trauma Syndrome. Rape Trauma Syndrome consists of symptoms and behaviors that are caused by a broad range of events including, but not limited to, rape. Rape Trauma Syndrome may have no diagnostic value at all. Even if the Syndrome has some diagnostic value, it is low, which accounts for the fact that nearly all courts hold that Rape Trauma Syndrome is not admissible to prove lack of consent.

Lawyers and judges sometimes fail to appreciate that some syndromes have diagnostic value and others do not. As stated above, many syndromes do not point with *any* degree of certainty to a particular cause. The term "nondiagnostic syndrome" is useful to describe syndromes that have no diagnostic value. To repeat, nearly all of the psychological syndromes used in court are nondiagnostic.

A further example will nail down the distinction between diagnostic and nondiagnostic syndromes. Compare two syndromes—one nondiagnostic, the other diagnostic. The nondiagnostic syndrome is Child Sexual Abuse Accommodation Syndrome (CSAAS), which appeared in the literature in 1983.[17] Psychiatrist Roland Summit coined the term CSAAS to describe how children react (accommodate) to ongoing sexual abuse. Children "learn to accept the situation and to survive. There is no way out, no place to run. The healthy, normal, emotionally resilient child will learn to accommodate to the reality of continuing sexual abuse."[18] Summit described five aspects of CSAAS: (1) secrecy, (2) helplessness, (3) entrapment and accommodation, (4) delayed, conflicted, and unconvincing disclosure, and (5) retraction or recantation.

---

[17] Roland C. Summit, *The Child Sexual Abuse Accommodation Syndrome*, 7/2 CHILD ABUSE & NEGLECT 177 (1983).

[18] *Id.* at 184.

CSAAS is nondiagnostic because one cannot reason backward from CSAAS to sexual abuse. The fact that a child demonstrates one or more aspects of CSAAS does not provide substantive evidence of sexual abuse. For example, the fact that a child delayed reporting and then recanted is hardly evidence of abuse. Summit observed, "The accommodation syndrome is neither an illness nor a diagnosis, and it can't be used to measure whether or not a child has been sexually abused."[19] CSAAS was not designed to prove that abuse occurred. Rather, CSAAS was intended to explain how children who are abused may react to their maltreatment.

Contrast CSAAS, which lacks diagnostic value, to Battered Child Syndrome, which has high diagnostic value. Battered Child Syndrome points decisively to physical abuse. With Battered Child Syndrome, we reason backward from the presence of certain injuries to the cause of the injuries.

To sum up, the common feature of nondiagnostic syndromes is that they do not point with any certainty to a cause. The cause must be ascertained through other means. The purpose of nondiagnostic syndromes is *not* to establish cause, but to describe reactions to *known* causes. When evidence of a syndrome is offered, the first step is to determine whether the syndrome is diagnostic or nondiagnostic. Determining whether a syndrome is diagnostic is essentially a question of logical relevance, that is, does the presence of certain symptoms have any tendency to make the existence of a particular etiology more probable? If the answer is yes, the syndrome is diagnostic. If it is not possible to draw a logical inference from symptoms to etiology, the syndrome is nondiagnostic. If the syndrome is nondiagnostic, it should not be used to establish the etiology of a person's symptoms.

When a new syndrome or a syndrome of dubious scientific merit is offered, a *Frye* or *Daubert* hearing is an ideal venue to test the validity and reliability of the syndrome. A *Frye* or *Daubert* hearing allows inquiry into whether the syndrome is diagnostic or nondiagnostic. If nondiagnostic, care can be taken to ensure that the syndrome is not used as substantive evidence. If the syndrome is diagnostic, the hearing affords an opportunity to locate the syndrome along the continuum of diagnostic certainty.

§ 31.3.1 Battered Child Syndrome

Expert testimony on Battered Child Syndrome is frequently offered to prove nonaccidental injury. The term Battered Child Syndrome was coined in 1962 by pediatrician Henry Kempe and his colleagues.[20] Kempe described the syndrome:

> The battered-child syndrome may occur at any age, but, in general the affected children are younger than 3 years. In some instances the clinical manifestations are limited to those resulting from a single

---

[19] Mary B. Meinig, *Profile of Roland Summit*, 1 VIOLENCE UPDATE 6, 6 (1991).

[20] C. Henry Kempe, Frederic N. Silverman, Brandt F. Steele, William Droegemueller & Henry K. Silver, *The Battered-Child Syndrome*, 181/1 JAMA 17 (1962).

episode of trauma, but more often the child's general health is below par, and he shows evidence of neglect including poor skin hygiene, multiple soft tissue injuries, and malnutrition. One often obtains a history of previous episodes suggestive of parental neglect or trauma. A marked discrepancy between clinical findings and historical data as supplied by the parents is a major diagnostic feature of the battered-child syndrome. . . . Subdural hematoma, with or without fracture of the skull . . . is an extremely frequent finding even in the absence of fractures of the long bones. . . . The characteristic distribution of these multiple fractures and the observation that the lesions are in different stages of healing are of additional value in making the diagnosis.[21]

Not all battered children have injuries in different stages of healing. Kempe noted, for example, that abusive injury sometimes results from "a single episode of trauma." Moreover, many child abuse fatalities lack a pattern of repeated injury.

Battered Child Syndrome is an accepted medical diagnosis. Pediatrician David Chadwick and his colleagues wrote, "Diagnosis of classical 'battered children' who are presented for care with multiple injuries in differing stages of healing is relatively simple for experienced physicians."[22] Expert testimony on Battered Child Syndrome is routinely approved.[23] As the U.S. Supreme Court observed in *Estelle v. McGuire*,[24] the "syndrome exists when a child has sustained repeated and/or serious injuries by nonaccidental means. . . . [E]vidence demonstrating battered child syndrome helps to prove that the child died at the hands of another and not by falling off a couch, for example; it also tends to establish that the 'other,' whoever it may be, inflicted the injuries intentionally."[25] The Minnesota Supreme Court wrote, "Child abuse was recognized as a medical diagnosis at least as early as 1962 with the publication of Dr. C. Henry Kempe's report, 'The Battered Child Syndrome.'"[26]

A finding of nonaccidental injury can be premised partially or entirely on expert testimony on Battered Child Syndrome. The Battered Child Syndrome is not novel scientific evidence, and is not subject to *Frye* or *Daubert*.

§ 31.3.2 Battering Parent Syndrome

There is no personality profile of a "typical" child abuser. Thus, there is no Battering Parent Syndrome or Battering Parent Profile that can determine whether

---

[21] *Id.* at 17–18, *cited in* United States v. Boise, 916 F.2d 497, 503 n.14 (9th Cir. 1990).

[22] David L. Chadwick, Steven Chin, Connie Salerno, John Landsverk & Louann Kitchen, *Deaths from Falls in Children: How Far Is Fatal?*, 31/10 J. TRAUMA 1353, 1354 (1991).

[23] *See* United States v. Boise, 916 F.2d 497, 503 (9th Cir. 1990); Milton Roberts, Annotation, *Admissibility of Expert Medical Testimony on Battered Child Syndrome*, 98 A.L.R.3d 306 (1980).

[24] 502 U.S. 62 (1991).

[25] *Id.* at 66, 68.

[26] Becker v. Mayo Foundation, 737 N.W.2d 200, 207–08 (Minn. 2007).

someone abused a child. In the few instances where prosecutors offered expert testimony on a purported Battering Parent Syndrome or Battering Parent Profile, courts rejected the evidence.[27]

§ 31.3.3 Munchausen Syndrome by Proxy

Munchausen Syndrome in *adults* is "a condition characterized by habitual presentation for hospital treatment of an apparent acute illness, the patient giving a plausible and dramatic history, all of which is false."[28] English pediatrician Sir Roy Meadow coined the term Munchausen Syndrome by Proxy in 1977 to describe adults who use a child as the vehicle for fabricated illness or injury.[29] Pediatrician Donna Rosenberg defined Munchausen Syndrome by Proxy as "illness in a child [that] is persistently and secretly simulated (lied about or faked) and/or produced by a parent or someone who is *in loco parentis*, and the child repeatedly presented for medical assessment and care."[30] The Iowa Supreme Court described the Syndrome as "a form of child abuse in which a parent repeatedly presents their child for unnecessary medical treatments by simulating or producing symptoms in the child."[31] Some say the constellation of behaviors generally referred to as Munchausen by Proxy actually consists of two perspectives—the pediatric diagnosis of child abuse and a psychiatric diagnosis of the perpetrator.[32] The DSM-IV-TR identifies the phenomenon from the perspective of the child victim as "Pediatric Condition Falsification" (PCF) and as "Factitious Disorder by Proxy" (FDP) from the perspective of the perpetrator.[33]

The prevalence of Munchausen Syndrome by Proxy is unknown, although it appears to be uncommon. Mothers are the most frequent perpetrators of the

---

[27] *See* United States v. Harrow, 65 M.J. 190 (C.A.A.F. 2007); State v. Maule, 667 P.2d 96 (Wash. Ct. App. 1983) (finding it reversible error to permit testimony in statutory rape case that majority of child abuse cases involved male parent figure, with biological parents in the majority); State v. Steward, 660 P.2d 278, 280 (Wash. Ct. App. 1983) (finding it reversible error to admit "expert" testimony in a second degree murder prosecution of a babysitting boyfriend that "serious injuries to children were often inflicted by either live-in or babysitting boyfriends."); *see also* Gregory G. Sarno, Annotation, *Admissibility at Criminal Prosecution of Expert Testimony on Battering Parent Syndrome*, 43 A.L.R.4th 1203 (1986).

[28] Dorland's Illustrated Medical Dictionary 1635 (28th ed. 1994).

[29] *See* Roy Meadow, *Munchausen Syndrome by Proxy: The Hinterland of Child Abuse*, 2 Lancet 343 (1977); Roy Meadow, *False Allegations of Abuse and Munchausen Syndrome by Proxy*, 68/4 Arch. Dis. Child. 444 (1993) (describing 14 children in 7 families where allegations of child abuse were fabricated by parent as part of syndrome).

[30] Donna Andrea Rosenberg, *Munchausen Syndrome by Proxy*, in Child Abuse: Medical Diagnosis & Management 513 (Robert M. Reece & Cindy W. Christian eds., 3d ed. 2009).

[31] Geringer v. Iowa Dep't of Human Servs., 521 N.W.2d 730, 730–31 (Iowa 1994).

[32] American Psychiatric Association, Diagnostic and Statistical Manual of Mental Disorders, Text Revision (4th ed. 2000); Catherine C. Ayoub & Randell Alexander, *Definitional Issues in Munchausen*, 11 APSAC Advisor 11 (1998).

[33] American Psychiatric Association, Diagnostic and Statistical Manual of Mental Disorders, Text Revision (4th ed. 2000).

Syndrome. Boys and girls are victimized in roughly equal numbers. Most victims are babies or toddlers.

There is no psychological test that detects Munchausen Syndrome by Proxy. Nor is there a personality profile that describes the "typical" perpetrator of this bizarre form of child abuse. Psychiatrist Herbert Schreier wrote, "The primary motivation seems to be an intense need for attention from, and manipulation of, powerful professionals, most frequently, but not exclusively a physician."[34]

Munchausen Syndrome by Proxy manifests itself in many ways, including smothering, poisoning, injecting contaminants into the child (e.g., drugs, saliva, salt, urine, feces), inducing fever, inducing vomiting, fabricating symptoms, and in other ways.

For survivors of Munchausen Syndrome by Proxy, there may be long-lasting psychological and physical sequelae. The efficacy of psychotherapy for perpetrators of Munchausen Syndrome by Proxy is an open question. Therapy may work for parents who admit they have a problem.

When Munchausen Syndrome by Proxy occurs, the child is at risk of serious injury or death, and removing the child from the custody of the suspected offender is typically the only way to ensure safety. Moreover, separating the child from the suspect, and documenting that the child's symptoms abate following separation, is often the best way to confirm the diagnosis of Munchausen Syndrome by Proxy. For children in the hospital, covert video surveillance can be life saving, and is often the only way to catch the abuser in the act.

Expert testimony is necessary to prove Munchausen Syndrome by Proxy, and courts allow such testimony.[35] In *People v. Phillips*,[36] for example, the California Court of Appeal approved expert psychiatric testimony on the syndrome to establish the defendant's motive to poison her baby by putting large amounts of salt in the baby's food.

Munchausen Syndrome by Proxy is an accepted diagnosis. In *State v. Hocevar*,[37] where a mother was accused of poisoning her young child, and two of her other children died of smothering, the court noted that:

> The expert testimony regarding MSBP is neither novel nor scientific. The term "Munchausen Syndrome by Proxy" has appeared in medical literature since at least 1977. . . .While this Court has not previously addressed the admissibility of MSBP evidence, other courts have considered such evidence since 1981. . . . A Westlaw search reveals that the term "Munchausen Syndrome by Proxy" has appeared in over

---

[34] Herbert Schreier, *Munchausen by Proxy Defined*, 110/5 PEDIATRICS 985, 985 (2002).

[35] *See* People v. Phillips, 175 Cal. Rptr. 703 (Cal. Ct. App. 1981); *In re* Colin R., 493 A.2d 1083 (Md. Ct. App. 1985); State v. Hocevar, 7 P.3d 329 (Mont. 2000) (suggesting Munchausen Syndrome by Proxy is beyond the ken of jurors).

[36] 175 Cal. Rptr. 703 (1981).

[37] 7 P.3d 329, 342 (Mont. 2000).

forty state and federal cases since then. Thus testimony regarding MSBP is not novel to the field of pediatrics or law.[38]

Courts hold that expert testimony on the Syndrome is either not subject to analysis under *Frye* or *Daubert*, or that is passes muster.[39] In *Reid v. State*,[40] defendant was charged with murdering her infant child. The prosecution offered expert testimony on Munchausen Syndrome by Proxy. The Texas Court of Appeals provided a thorough analysis of the scientific reliability of expert testimony on the Syndrome, concluding, "the trial court did not err in determining the scientific reliability of MSBP testimony."[41]

§ 31.3.4 Shaken Baby Syndrome

The average infant spends two to three hours a day crying. Frustrated caretakers sometimes grasp young children by the shoulders or under the arms and shake them. Violent shaking can cause direct injury to brain tissue. Babies are particularly susceptible to such injury because they have weak neck muscles and because the infant brain is not as solid as the brain in older children and adults.

Neurological damage caused by shaking is called Shaken Baby Syndrome, Whiplash Shaken Infant Syndrome, or Shake-Impact Syndrome. Pediatrician Robert Reece writes, The term Shaken Baby Syndrome is often used to describe head injuries when shaking is the likely explanation. Another widely used term is Shaken Impact Syndrome which denotes a child shaken and slammed against a hard surface. The terms Shaken Baby Syndrome and Shaken Impact Syndrome are slowly being replaced with the following terms: abusive head trauma, inflicted traumatic brain injury, inflicted childhood neurotrauma, non-accidental head injury, and inflicted head injury.[42] The American Academy of Pediatrics recommends discontinuation of the term "Shaken Baby Syndrome" and use instead of the term abusive head trauma.[43]

Many experts believe that shaking alone—without impact on a hard surface—can cause Shaken Baby Syndrome, with resultant severe injury or death. Other experts believe that in most cases of Shaken Baby Syndrome, the damage results from a combination of violent shaking plus impact, as when the out-of-control adult shakes the baby and slams it down on a surface. Whatever the precise mechanism of injury, it

---

[38] *Id.* (citations omitted).

[39] *See id.*

[40] 964 S.W.2d 723 (Tex. App. 1998).

[41] *Id.* at 729.

[42] Robert M. Reece, *Medical Evaluation of Physical Abuse*, in THE APSAC HANDBOOK ON CHILD MALTREATMENT (John E. B. Myers ed., 3d ed. 2010).

[43] Cindy W. Christian, Robert Block & American Academy of Pediatrics Committee on Child Abuse and Neglect, *Abusive Head Trauma in Infants and Children (Organizational Principles)*, 123/5 PEDIATRICS 1409 (2009).

is clear that this form of child abuse causes enormous damage, often resulting in death.

Although not all physicians agree with Shaken Baby Syndrome, the Syndrome is an accepted medical diagnosis. The Syndrome is not novel, and is not subject to *Frye* or *Daubert*.[44] Courts routinely approve expert testimony on Shaken Baby Syndrome.[45]

Shaking can cause bleeding in the eye, especially retinal hemorrhages. Quite a few babies are born with retinal hemorrhages, although birth-related retinal hemorrhages disappear within a few weeks. Although retinal hemorrhages are not diagnostic of abusive head injury, retinal hemorrhages are seen much more frequently with inflicted head injury than with accidental head injury.

There is some disagreement over whether cardiopulmonary resuscitation can cause retinal hemorrhages. Byard and Cohle wrote in 2004, "More recent studies have supported the concept that retinal hemorrhages occur rarely, if ever, from cardio-pulmonary resuscitation."[46]

§ 31.3.5 Posttraumatic Stress Disorder

Posttraumatic Stress Disorder (PTSD) is a psychiatric diagnosis describing the reaction some people experience to extreme trauma, including rape and sexual assault. The American Psychiatric Association observed that PTSD "may be especially severe or long lasting when the stressor is of human design (e.g., torture, rape)."[47] PTSD is a well-established diagnosis. The diagnostic Criteria for PTSD are set forth in the fourth edition of the American Psychiatric Association's *Diagnostic and Statistical Manual of Mental Disorders* (DSM-IV-TR):

> A. The person has been exposed to a traumatic event in which both of the following were present: (1) the person experienced, witnessed, or was confronted with an event or events that involved actual or threatened death or serious injury, or a threat to the physical integrity of self or others; (2) the person's response involved intense fear, helplessness, or horror. Note: In children, this may be expressed instead by disorganized or agitated behavior.

---

[44] *See* People v. Martinez, 74 P.3d 316, 323 (Colo. 2003) ("we assume, as it is not in dispute, that the scientific principles of shaken-impact syndrome and subdural hematomas resulting from extreme accidents are reasonably reliable."); State v. McClary, 541 A.2d 96, 102 (1988) (stating shaken baby syndrome is generally accepted by medical science).

[45] *See* United States v. Vallo, 238 F.3d 1242 (10th Cir. 2001); Steggall v. State, 8 S.W.3d 538 (Ark. 2000); People v. Malfavon, 125 Cal. Rptr. 2d 618 (Ct. App. 2002) (involving fatal shaking of a seven-month-old infant); People v. Dunaway, 88 P.3d 619 (Colo. 2004).

[46] Roger W. Byard & Stephen D. Cohle, *Homicide and Suicide, in* SUDDEN DEATH IN INFANCY, CHILDHOOD, AND ADOLESCENCE 77, 142 (Roger W. Byard ed., 2d ed. 2004).

[47] AMERICAN PSYCHIATRIC ASSOCIATION, DIAGNOSTIC AND STATISTICAL MANUAL OF MENTAL DISORDERS, TEXT REVISION 464 (4th ed. 2000).

B. The traumatic event is persistently reexperienced in one (or more) of the following ways: (1) recurrent and intrusive distressing recollections of the event, including images, thoughts, or perceptions. Note: In young children, repetitive play may occur in which themes or aspects of the trauma are expressed. (2) recurrent distressing dreams of the event. Note: In children, there may be frightening dreams without recognizable content. (3) acting or feeling as if the traumatic event were recurring (includes a sense of reliving the experience, illusions, hallucinations, and dissociative flashback episodes, including those that occur on awakening or when intoxicated.) Note: In young children, trauma-specific reenactment may occur. (4) intense psychological distress at exposure to internal or external cues that symbolize or resemble an aspect of the traumatic event. (5) physiological reactivity on exposure to internal or external cues that symbolize or resemble an aspect of the traumatic event.

C. Persistent avoidance of stimuli associated with the trauma and numbing of general responsiveness (not present before the trauma), as indicated by three (or more) of the following: (1) efforts to avoid thoughts, feelings, or conversations associated with the trauma; (2) efforts to avoid activities, places, or people that arouse recollections of the trauma; (3) inability to recall an important aspect of the trauma; (4) markedly diminished interest or participation in significant activities; (5) feeling of detachment or estrangement from others; (6) restricted range of affect (e.g., unable to have loving feelings) (7) sense of a foreshortened future (e.g., does not expect to have a career, marriage, children, or a normal life span).

D. Persistent symptoms of increased arousal (not present before the trauma), as indicated by two (or more) of the following: (1) difficulty falling or staying asleep; (2) irritability or outbursts of anger; (3) difficulty concentrating; (4) hypervigilance; (5) exaggerated startle response.

E. Duration of the disturbance (symptoms in Criteria B, C, and D) is more than 1 month.

F. The disturbance causes clinically significant distress or impairment in social, occupational, or other important areas of functioning.

Children can experience PTSD. The DSM provides, "For children, sexually traumatic events may include developmentally inappropriate sexual experiences without threatened or actual violence or injury."[48] As the DSM criteria explain, the symptoms displayed by young children differ in some respects from those observed in adolescents and adults. The DSM states, "In younger children, distressing dreams of the event may, within several weeks, change into generalized nightmares of monsters, of rescuing others, or of threats to self or others. Young children usually do not have the sense that they are reliving the past; rather, the reliving of the trauma may occur through repetitive play . . . . Children may also exhibit various physical symptoms, such as stomachaches and headaches."[49]

§ 31.3.6 Posttraumatic Stress Disorder in Litigation

There are thousands of civil PTSD cases. Individuals with PTSD resort to the courts in search of money damages, workers' compensation, and government benefits. The present focus is limited to the use of PTSD in proving rape, sexual assault, and child abuse. In the context of such litigation, the question is whether a diagnosis of PTSD has probative value. In other words, is PTSD a diagnostic syndrome? Upon reading the diagnostic criteria for PTSD, one quickly sees a roadblock to using PTSD as diagnostic of trauma. The criteria for PTSD presuppose a traumatic event. That is, to reach a diagnosis of PTSD, the clinician must accept the fact that the patient has experienced a traumatic event. Yet, if the diagnosis depends on acknowledging a traumatic event, how can the diagnosis prove the event? The circularity of such reasoning is obvious. Given the definitional requirements of PTSD, a diagnosis of PTSD has little probative value as substantive evidence of trauma.

If the diagnostic label PTSD has little probative value in proving trauma, what about the symptoms that make up PTSD? Do the symptoms themselves have a tendency to prove trauma? To be diagnosed with PTSD, an individual must experience intense fear, helplessness, or horror. The traumatic event must be persistently reexperienced (e.g., recurrent dreams, distress when thinking about the trauma), and the person must avoid stimuli associated with the trauma. Additionally, there must be symptoms of increased arousal (e.g., difficulty sleeping, hyper-vigilance). PTSD symptoms can indicate that something traumatic occurred.

Symptoms of PTSD can take on probative value when independent evidence establishes the date of onset for the symptoms, and when the symptoms represent a marked departure from the individual's long-established behavior. Consider, for example, a sixth grade student who claims she was raped in a park near her school on March 1, 2010. Evidence establishes that prior to March 1 the girl was high functioning, self-confident, happy, outgoing, and not inordinately fearful. After March 1, however, she routinely expressed intense fear of men, feelings of helplessness, nightmares in which she is assaulted, intense distress whenever she approaches the park where she says she was attacked, difficulty concentrating on schoolwork, and a

---

[48] *Id.*

[49] *Id.* at 466.

steep downturn in academic performance. All these are symptoms of PTSD, and when their sudden onset is considered in conjunction with the girl's prior behavior, the symptoms have considerable probative force. Although the symptoms are not specific for rape, the symptoms have a tendency to prove trauma at the relevant time.

In sum, because of the circularity issue discussed above, a diagnosis of PTSD has little probative value in itself. The symptoms of PTSD, standing alone, say little about the timing and cause of the symptoms. When PTSD symptoms are considered with other evidence, however, the symptoms can assume probative force.

Several courts recognize that a diagnosis of PTSD does not prove trauma. In *Hutton v. State*,[50] the Maryland Court of Appeals wrote:

> [D]etermining from the symptoms that PTSD is the proper diagnosis ordinarily does not answer the question of what traumatic event caused it; the symptoms, in other words, are not reliable identifiers of the specific cause of the disorder. . . . The literature concludes that a PTSD diagnosis is essentially a therapeutic aid, rather than a tool for the detection of sexual abuse . . . . Because causes other than sexual abuse may trigger PTSD—the traumatic event being unable to be verified objectively, its occurrence must necessarily be assumed—a diagnosis of PTSD does not reliably prove the nature of the stressor.[51]

Similarly, the Louisiana Supreme Court wrote in *State v. Chauvin*:[52]

> [T]he psychiatric procedures used in developing the diagnosis of PTSD are designed for therapeutic purposes and are not reliable as fact-finding tools to determine whether sexual abuse has in fact occurred. . . . [T]he potential for prejudice looms large because the jury may accord too much weight to expert opinions stating medical conclusions which were drawn from diagnostic methods having limited merit as fact-finding devices. . . . [W]e find expert testimony of PTSD is inadmissible for the purpose of substantively proving that sexual abuse occurred.[53]

The court added, "Although PTSD is widely accepted among professionals as an anxiety disorder attributable to some type of trauma, it has not been proven to be a reliable indicator that sexual abuse is the trauma underlying the disorder or that sexual abuse has even occurred."[54] The Louisiana court ruled that expert testimony on PTSD

---

[50] 663 A.2d 1289 (Md. 1995).

[51] *Id.* at 1294–95 (citations omitted).

[52] 846 So. 2d 697 (La. 2003).

[53] *Id.* at 707–08 (citations omitted).

[54] *Id.* at 707.

offered as substantive evidence of abuse did not "pass the *Daubert* threshold test of reliability."[55]

Illinois, by statute, makes evidence of PTSD admissible.[56]

§ 31.3.7 Acute Distress Disorder

In addition to PTSD, the *Diagnostic and Statistical Manual of Mental Disorders* contains the closely related diagnosis of Acute Distress Disorder. "The essential feature of Acute Stress Disorder is the development of characteristic anxiety, dissociative, and other symptoms that occurs within 1 month after exposure to an extreme traumatic stressor."[57] The DSM provides, "Acute Stress Disorder is distinguished from Posttraumatic Stress Disorder because the symptom pattern in Acute Stress Disorder must occur within 4 weeks of the traumatic event and resolve within that 4-week period. If the symptoms persist for more than 1 month and meet criteria for Posttraumatic Stress Disorder, the diagnosis is changed from Acute Stress Disorder to Posttraumatic Stress Disorder."[58]

§ 31.3.8 Child Sexual Abuse Accommodation Syndrome

As discussed above, Child Sexual Abuse Accommodation Syndrome (CSAAS) was described in 1983 by psychiatrist Roland Summit.[59] Summit described five characteristics observed in many sexually abused children, particularly incest victims:

- Secrecy.
- Helplessness.
- Entrapment and accommodation.
- Delayed, conflicted, and unconvincing disclosure.
- Retraction.

Summit's purpose in describing CSAAS was to provide a "common language" for professionals working to protect sexually abused children. Summit did not intend CSAAS as a device to detect or diagnose sexual abuse.

CSAAS is a nondiagnostic syndrome. The Indiana Supreme Court observed in *Steward v. State*[60] that CSAAS "was not intended as a diagnostic device and does not

---

[55] *Id.* at 708.

[56] 725 ILL. COMP. STAT. 5/115-7.2 provides: "In a prosecution for an illegal sexual act perpetrated upon a victim . . . testimony by an expert, qualified by the court relating to any recognized and accepted form of post-traumatic stress syndrome shall be admissible as evidence."

[57] AMERICAN PSYCHIATRIC ASSOCIATION, DIAGNOSTIC AND STATISTICAL MANUAL OF MENTAL DISORDERS, TEXT REVISION 469 (4th ed. 2000).

[58] *Id.* at 467.

[59] Roland C. Summit, *The Child Sexual Abuse Accommodation Syndrome*, 7/2 CHILD ABUSE & NEGLECT 177 (1983).

[60] 652 N.E.2d 490 (Ind. 1995).

detect sexual abuse."[61] The syndrome assumes that abuse occurred and helps explain the child's reaction to it. The Mississippi Supreme Court noted in *Hall v. State*[62] that the accommodation syndrome "was not meant to be used as a diagnostic device to show that abuse had, in fact, occurred. . . . Thus, any attempt to show that a child had been abused because he exhibits some signals of CSAAS is an improper usage of Dr. Summit's theory."[63]

CSAAS has a role to play in child sexual abuse litigation, but not as substantive evidence of abuse. Expert testimony on CSAAS is admissible to rehabilitate a child's credibility following impeachment focused on delayed reporting, inconsistency, or recantation. Such rehabilitation is appropriate to explain that delayed reporting, recantation, and inconsistency are relatively common among sexually abused children.[64]

§ 31.3.9 Parental Alienation Syndrome

In contested child custody litigation, one parent sometimes alienates the children from the other parent. Psychiatrist Richard Gardner coined the term Parental Alienation Syndrome (PAS) to describe this phenomenon.[65] Gardner defined PAS as follows: "In this disorder we see not only programming ('brainwashing') of the child by one parent to denigrate the other parent, but self-created contributions by the child in support of the preferred parent's campaign of denigration against the non-preferred parent."[66]

Gardner pointed out that if the child was abused, the child *should* feel alienated from the abuser. Gardner wrote, "When bona fide abuse does exist, then the child's responding hostility is warranted and the concept of the parental alienation syndrome is *not* applicable."[67] One finds occasional reference to PAS is reported decisions, primarily custody cases.[68]

---

[61] *Id.* at 493.

[62] 611 So. 2d 915 (Miss. 1992).

[63] *Id.* at 919 (citations omitted).

[64] On the proper use of accommodation syndrome and information on the disclosure process see Thomas D. Lyon & Elizabeth C. Ahern, *Disclosure of Child Sexual Abuse: Implications for Interviewing*, in THE APSAC HANDBOOK ON CHILD MALTREATMENT (John E. B. Myers ed., 3d ed. 2010); Thomas D. Lyon, *Abuse Disclosure: What Adults Can Tell*, in CHILDREN AS VICTIMS, WITNESSES, AND OFFENDERS: PSYCHOLOGICAL SCIENCE AND THE LAW (Bette L. Bottoms et al. eds., 2009); Thomas D. Lyon, *False Denials: Overcoming Methodological Biases in Abuse Disclosure Research*, in CHILD SEXUAL ABUSE: DISCLOSURE, DELAY, AND DENIAL 41 (Margaret-Ellen Pipe et al. eds., 2007).

[65] RICHARD A. GARDNER, THE PARENTAL ALIENATION SYNDROME: A GUIDE FOR MENTAL HEALTH AND LEGAL PROFESSIONALS (1992).

[66] *Id.* at xv.

[67] *Id.* at xviii.

[68] *See* Pearson v. Pearson, 5 P.3d 239 (Alas. 2000); *In re* Paternity of V.A.M.C., 768 N.E.2d 990 (Ind. Ct. App. 2002); Ellis v. Ellis, 840 So. 2d 806 (Miss. Ct. App. 2003) (involving child custody and visitation dispute).

PAS is nondiagnostic.[69] Kathleen Faller wrote, "Because the parental alienation syndrome is a nondiagnostic syndrome, it is only useful for mental health professionals in explaining the symptom presentation if they know from other information that an abuse allegation is a deliberately made, false accusation. The syndrome cannot be used to decide whether the child has been sexually abused. As a consequence, it is of little probative value to courts making decisions about the presence or absence of sexual abuse."[70] Because PAS is nondiagnostic, it sheds no light on whether allegations of abuse are true or false. Any use of PAS for diagnostic purposes is a misuse of the syndrome that does not pass muster under *Frye* or *Daubert*.[71]

PAS has been criticized.[72] The American Psychological Association wrote, "There are no data to support the phenomenon called parental alienation syndrome."[73] Carol Bruch wrote, "PAS as developed and purveyed by Richard Gardner has neither a logical nor a scientific basis. It is rejected by responsible social scientists and lacks solid grounding in psychological theory or research."[74] Kathleen Faller stated, "A fundamental flaw in the syndrome, as described by Gardner is that it fails to take into account alternative explanations for the child's and mother's behavior, including the veracity of the allegations or that the mother has made an honest mistake."[75]

---

[69] *See* Kathleen Coulborn Faller, *The Parental Alienation Syndrome: What Is It and What Data Support It?*, 3 CHILD MALTREAT. 100, 111 (1998).

[70] *Id.*

[71] *See* C.J.L. v. M.W.B., 879 So. 2d 1169, 1178 (Ala. Civ. App. 2003) ("Although we might, if faced squarely with the question whether evidence concerning an actual diagnosis of PAS was admissible under *Frye*'s 'general acceptance' test, be inclined to agree with the mother and find that PAS had not been generally accepted in the scientific community, we do not need to make that decision in this case."); People v. Sullivan, 2003 WL 1785921 (Cal. Ct. App. Apr. 3, 2003) (not officially published) (finding no need for expert testimony that in contested custody cases parents sometimes alienate children; this is within the ken of the jury); People v. Fortin, 289 A.D.2d 590, 590 (N.Y. App. Div. 2001) ("The County Court was correct in determining that the defendant failed in his burden of demonstrating that 'Parental Alienation Syndrome' was generally accepted in the relevant scientific communities. In making that determination, the County Court properly considered that the defendant's sole witness at the *Frye* hearing [Dr. Richard Gardner] had a significant financial interest in having his theory accepted." (internal citations omitted)); Zafran v. Zafran, 740 N.Y.S.2d 596 (N.Y. Sup. Ct. 2002) (granting *Frye* hearing on PAS).

[72] *See* Carol S. Bruch, *Parental Alienation Syndrome and Parental Alienation: Getting It Wrong in Child Custody Cases*, 35 FAM. L. Q. 527 (2001).

[73] AMERICAN PSYCHOLOGICAL ASSOCIATION, VIOLENCE AND THE FAMILY 40 (1996).

[74] Carol S. Bruch, *Parental Alienation Syndrome and Parental Alienation: Getting It Wrong in Child Custody Cases*, 35 FAM. L. Q. 527, 550 (2001).

[75] Kathleen Coulborn Faller, *The Parental Alienation Syndrome: What Is It and What Data Support It?*, 3/2 CHILD MALTREAT. 100, 112 (1998).

Chapter 32: Trial Advocacy[*]

by Steven Lubet[1] and John E. B. Myers[2]

§ 32.1 Case Analysis

§ 32.1.1 The Idea of a Persuasive Story

Trials as Stories

Trials allow the parties to persuade the judge by recounting their versions of the historical facts. Each party has the opportunity to tell a story, albeit through the stilted devices of direct and cross examination and introduction of evidence. The framework for the stories—or their grammar—is set by the rules of procedure and evidence. The conclusion of the stories—the end to which they are directed—is controlled by the elements of the applicable substantive law. The content of the stories is governed by the truth, or at least by so much of the truth as is available to the advocate. The party who tells the most persuasive story generally wins.

But what is persuasive storytelling in the context of a trial? A persuasive story can establish an affirmative case if it has these characteristics: (1) it is told about people who have reasons for the way they act; (2) it accounts for or explains the known or undeniable facts; (3) it is told by credible witnesses; (4) it is supported by details; (5) it accords with common sense and contains no implausible elements; and (6) it is organized in a way that makes each succeeding fact increasingly more likely. On the other hand, the opponent tells a "counter story" that negates the above.

An advocate's task when preparing for trial is to conceive of and structure a true story—comprising admissible evidence and containing all of the elements of a claim or defense—that is most likely to be believed by the trier of fact. This is a creative process because the facts will seldom lead to a single, undisputed interpretation. To carry through this process the lawyer must first "imagine" a series of alternative

---

[*] This material appears in Modern Trial Advocacy: Analysis and Practice, 4th Edition (© 2009 NITA). Reproduced with permission from the **National Institute for Trial Advocacy**. The NACC is grateful to NITA for permitting the use of these materials as a gift to the child advocacy community. The NACC highly recommends the full publication of *Modern Trial Advocacy* and additional NITA trial skills training materials, available at **www.nita.org** or by calling NITA's publishing partner **LexisNexis** at **800-533-1637**. *Editor's Note:* Nonsubstantive changes have been made to the text and formatting to reflect the style of this publication. Section numbers have also been added to reflect the style of this publication. Material has been condensed and where possible, examples have been replaced by Professor John E. B. Myers with child welfare examples.

[1] Steven Lubet, J.D., is Williams Memorial Professor of Law and Director of the Bartlit Center for Trial Strategy at Northwestern University School of Law in Chicago, Illinois.

[2] John E. B. Myers, J.D., is a Professor of Law at University of the Pacific McGeorge School of Law in Sacramento, California.

scenarios, assessing each for its clarity, simplicity, and believability, as well as for its legal consequences.

A Hypothetical Case—In re A.C.

The following hypothetical juvenile court dependency case of *In re A.C.* will be referred to throughout this chapter.

Five-month-old A.C. was reported to Child Protective Services (CPS) by a public health nurse following a visit to A.C.'s home. The nurse reported that the two bedroom apartment was dirty, with spoiled food in the sink and the refrigerator, dog feces in several rooms, and roaches throughout. What most concerned the nurse, however, was that A.C. had a number of bruises on her head. A.C.'s eighteen-year-old mother, Eve, explained that the bruises occurred when A.C. rolled off the couch onto the hardwood floor. In addition to the head bruises, the nurse noticed what appeared to be a healing cigarette burn on sole of A.C.'s foot. Eve is unmarried and the mother of two children, A.C. and three-year-old D.C. Neither father is involved with their child. Eve's live-in boyfriend, Dell, baby sits the children while Eve works in a restaurant from 5:00 a.m. to noon. Dell works at a hotel from 3:00 p.m. to midnight.

CPS investigates. There is no evidence that three-year-old D.C. is abused. The worker asked about the bruises on A.C.'s head, and Eve repeated the explanation that the baby rolled off the couch. When asked about the burn on A.C.'s foot, Eve had no explanation, but denied inflicting a burn. The worker asked Eve to take A.C. to a doctor for an examination but Eve refused, stating, "We don't have medical insurance, and we can't afford to see a doctor."

The CPS worker found marijuana and cocaine in the apartment. Eve and Dell deny using illegal drugs and state that the marijuana and cocaine belongs to a friend. Eve and Dell acknowledge that they drink quite a bit and like to "party." On four previous occasions while drunk, Dell struck Eve during arguments. Dell has two prior misdemeanor convictions for DUI.

There is no doubt that Eve loves her children and that they love her. Eve is overwhelmed with the responsibilities of parenthood, work, and her often strained relationship with Dell. Eve is probably depressed. Three-year-old D.C. is attached to Dell and calls him "daddy." Dell appears to be concerned about the children and to provide adequate care for them.

CPS workers in this jurisdiction use a Structured Decision Making Model (SDM) to assess safety and risk.[3] The CPS worker conducted an initial safety assessment and concluded that both children should be removed from the home and placed in foster care. The decision was based on Eve's refusal to take A.C. to the doctor, the worker's

---

[3] Structured decision-making (SDM) refers to a series of assessment tools designed as a framework to guide consistent decisions across agencies such as Child Protective Services or juvenile courts. A single assessment tool can take forms such as a decision tree or a score sheet on which various criteria are rated. Angeline Spain & National Evaluation and TA Center for the Education of Children and Youth Who Are Neglected, Delinquent, or At-Risk, *Structured Decision Making: An Overview*, *available at* www.neglected-delinquent.org.

belief that the bruises and burn might be inflicted rather than accidental, drugs in the apartment, the children's exposure to domestic violence, and the condition of the apartment. The following day, a juvenile court judge approved emergency removal of the children.

Immediately following removal, a doctor examined A.C. and found a number of old bruises on A.C.'s bottom as well as the bruises on her head. In the doctor's opinion, the bruises on the bottom were a result of spanking. The doctor could not determine what caused the bruises on A.C.'s head, but concluded they were "suspicious for abuse." Eve admits that she "spanks" the children to discipline them, but denies causing bruises. Dell says he never spanked the children. The doctor concluded the burn on A.C.'s foot is consistent with an inflicted cigarette burn.

CPS filed a petition in juvenile court alleging: (1) Eve and/or Dell physically abused A.C. by striking and burning her; (2) if one of the adults did not actually strike or burn A.C., then that adult neglected A.C. by failing to protect the child; (3) Eve and Dell neglected both children by exposing them to illegal drugs in the home; (4) Dell is neglecting both children by inflicting domestic violence on Eve, and Eve is failing to protect the children by permitting them to be exposed to the domestic violence; (5) the home is unsuitable due to its condition.

Efforts to settle the case have failed and the matter is set for a contested adjudicatory hearing. At the hearing the attorney for CPS plans to offer testimony from the CPS worker, the doctor who examined A.C., and the landlord, who will describe loud parties, drinking in the apartment, and domestic violence. Eve and Dell deny any maltreatment and want the children returned to their custody. Counsel for Eve must prepare to undermine the evidence presented by CPS. Eve's counsel must determine whether it will be necessary to retain an expert to counter the physician's testimony. Perhaps a thorough cross examination will suffice and an expert will not be required.

A "best interests" attorney was appointed for the children.

§ 32.1.2 Preparing a Persuasive Trial Story: Your Theory, Theme, and Frame

Assume that you have decided on the story that you want to tell. It is persuasive. It is about people who have reasons for the way they act. It accounts for all of the known facts. It is told by credible witnesses. It is supported by details. It accords with common sense. It can be organized in a way that makes each succeeding fact more likely. How do you put your story in the form of a trial?

Your case must have a theory, a theme, and a frame.

Theory

Your theory is the adaptation of your story to the legal issues in the case. A theory of the case should be expressed in a single paragraph that combines an account of the facts and the law in such a way as to lead to the conclusion that your client should win. A successful theory contains these elements:

- *It is logical.* A winning theory has internal logical force. It is based on a foundation of undisputed or otherwise provable facts, all of which lead in a single direction. The facts on which your theory is based should reinforce each other. Indeed, they should lead to each other, each fact or premise implying the next, in an orderly and inevitable fashion. The attorney for CPS will tie together the various instances of maltreatment— physical abuse, neglect, illegal drugs, domestic violence—to form an overall picture of harm. Counsel for Eve may have difficulty disputing all of the evidence, and so may build a case theory that rests on denying the more serious accusations and downplaying any risk to the children. The children's attorney will conduct an investigation and may align with one side or the other, or propose an alternative theory.

- *It speaks to the legal elements of your case.* All of your trial persuasion must be in aid of a "legal" conclusion. Your theory *therefore* must be directed to prove every legal element that is necessary both to justify a decision on your behalf and to preserve it on appeal.

- *It is simple.* A good theory *makes* maximum use of undisputed facts. It relies as little as possible on evidence that may be hotly controverted, implausible, inadmissible, or otherwise difficult to prove.

- *It is easy to believe.* Even "true" theories may be difficult to believe because they contradict everyday experience. You must strive to eliminate implausible elements from your theory. An airtight theory is able to encompass the entirety of the other side's case and still result in your victory by sheer logical force. To develop and express your theory, ask these three questions: What happened? Why did it happen? Why does that mean that my client should win? If your answer is longer than one paragraph, your theory may be logical and true, but it is probably too complicated.

Theme

A theme is a rhetorical device. It gives persuasive force to your arguments. The most compelling themes appeal to shared values or common motivations. The theme can be succinctly expressed and repeated during the trial. If you are representing the state at the termination stage of a child welfare case, for example, your theory will account for all of the facts surrounding the parent's failure to adequately protect the child, as well as the relevant law. Your theme will reinforce your theory by under-scoring your argument (e.g., why termination is the right thing to do). Whatever your theme, you want to introduce it during your opening statement, reinforce it during direct and cross examinations, and drive it home during your final argument.

Frame

It is often said that compelling facts speak for themselves, but that is not really accurate. Because no case occurs in a vacuum, every fact—and every argument—is subject to interpretation. A story frame provides the setting in which facts are received—the environment in which they are accepted, rejected, emphasized, or discounted.

§ 32.1.3 Planning Your Final Argument

Good trial preparation begins at the end. It makes great sense to plan your final argument first, because that aspect of the trial is the most similar to storytelling: it is the single element of the trial where it is permissible for you to suggest conclusions, articulate inferences, and otherwise present your theory to the trier of fact as an uninterrupted whole. In other words, during final argument you are most allowed to say exactly what you want to say, limited only by the requirement that all arguments be supported by evidence contained in the trial record.

Thus, by planning your final argument at the beginning of your preparation, you will then be able to plan the balance of your case so as to ensure that the record contains every fact that you will need for summation.

Ask yourself these two questions: What do I want to say at the end of the case? What evidence must I introduce or elicit in order to be able to say it? The answers will give you the broad outline of your entire case.

§ 32.1.4 Planning Your Case-in-Chief

Your goal during your case-in-chief is to persuade the trier of fact as to the correctness of your theory, constantly appealing to a compelling frame while invoking your theme.

Consider Potential Witnesses and Exhibits

Your first step is to list the legal elements of every claim you hope to establish. Next, list the evidence that you have available to support each element. Most likely the bulk of your evidence will be in the form of witness testimony, but some of it will consist of documents, tangible objects, and other real evidence. For each exhibit, note the witness through whom you will seek its introduction. In *In re A.C.*, the CPS worker has personal knowledge of the apartment and will describe the conditions in which the family lived. If the worker took photographs, the worker can lay the foundation necessary for their admission by testifying that each photo is a fair and accurate representation of the apartment at a particular date and time.

Evaluate Each Witness

With every potential witness, ask: What does this witness contribute to my theory? What facts can I introduce through this witness? Are other witnesses available for the same facts? Is this witness an effective vehicle for my theme? What can I say about this witness that will be persuasive?

Once you have assembled the positive information about each witness, you must consider all possible problems and weaknesses:

- *Factual Weaknesses.* Are there likely to be inconsistencies or gaps in the witness's testimony? Does the witness have damaging information that is likely to be elicited on cross examination? If the answer to either question is affirmative, how can you minimize these problems? Can you resolve the inconsistencies by reevaluating your theory? Can another witness fill the gaps? Can you defuse the potentially damaging facts by bringing them out on direct examination?

- *Evidentiary Problems.* Each witness's testimony must be evaluated for possible evidentiary problems. Do not assume that an item of evidence or testimony is automatically admissible. Instead, you must be able to state a positive theory of admissibility for everything that you intend to offer during your case in chief. To prepare for objections ask yourself, "How would I try to keep this information out of evidence?" Then plan your response.

- *Credibility Problems.* How is the witness likely to be impeached? Is the witness subject to challenge for bias or interest? Will perception be in issue? Does the witness have a substance abuse problem? Is there potential for impeachment by prior inconsistent statements? Can you structure your direct examination so as to avoid or minimize these problems?

Decide Which Witnesses to Call and in Which Order

Having evaluated the contributions, strengths, and weaknesses of your potential witnesses, you are in a position to decide which ones you will call to the stand. Your central concern will be to make sure that all of your necessary evidence is admitted. You must call any witness who is the sole source of a crucial piece of information. Except in rare or compelling circumstances, you will also want to call any witness whose credibility or appearance is central to the internal logic of your case.

Nonessential witnesses must be evaluated according to their strengths and weaknesses. You will want to consider eliminating witnesses whose testimony will be cumulative. You must also be willing to dispense with calling witnesses whose credibility is suspect.

If you represent the parent accused of maltreatment, you must assess how your client will perform on the witness stand. Some parents make poor witnesses while others perform well, especially with preparation.

Will the child(ren) testify? Jurisdictions vary in the extent to which children testify in civil child protection matters.

Once you have arrived at your list of witnesses, arrange them in the order that will be most helpful to your case. Although there are no hard and fast rules for determining witness order, the following principles should help you decide:

- *Retention.* You want your evidence not only to be heard, but also to be retained. Studies suggest that judges and juries tend to best remember evidence they hear at the beginning and the end of the trial. With this principle in mind, you may decide to call your most important witness first and your next most important witness last. Start fast and end strong.

- *Progression.* The "first and last" principle must occasionally give way to the need for logical progression. Some witnesses provide the foundation for the testimony of others. Thus, it may be necessary to call "predicate" witnesses early in the trial as a matter of both logical development and legal admissibility. You may also wish to arrange your witnesses so that accounts of key events are given in chronological order.

- *Impact.* You may order your witnesses to maximize their dramatic impact. A necessary witness who is impeachable may be buried in the middle of your case.

§ 32.1.5 Planning Your Cross Examinations

It is inherently more difficult to plan a cross examination than it is to prepare for direct. It is impossible to safeguard yourself against all surprises, but the following steps will help keep surprises to a minimum.

First, compile a list of every potential adverse witness. Imagine why the witness is likely to be called. Ask yourself, "How can this witness most hurt my case?" Always prepare for the worst possible alternative.

Second, consider whether there is a basis for keeping the witness off the stand. Is the witness competent to testify? Is it possible to invoke a privilege? Then consider whether any part of the expected testimony might be excludable. For every statement that the witness might make, imagine all reasonable evidentiary objections. Do the same thing concerning all exhibits that might be offered through the witness. For each objection, plan your argument and prepare for the likely counterargument. You will not want to make every possible objection, but you will want to be prepared.

Third, consider the factual weaknesses of each opposing witness. Are there inconsistencies that can be exploited or enhanced? Is the witness's character subject to attack? Can the witness be impeached from prior statements? How can the witness be used to amplify your own theme?

Finally, catalog the favorable information that you hope to obtain from opposing witnesses.

§ 32.1.6 Reevaluate Everything

Now that you have planned your case-in-chief and cross examinations, it is imperative that you go back and reevaluate every aspect of your case. Do your direct examinations fully support and establish your theory? Do they leave any logical gaps? Are you satisfied that all of your necessary evidence will be admissible? Will it be credible? Do the potential cross examinations raise issues with which you cannot cope? Will you be able to articulate your theme during most or all of the direct and cross examinations? If you are unable to answer these questions satisfactorily, you may need to readjust your theory or theme.

Assuming that you are satisfied with your theory, you should now have an excellent idea of what the evidence at trial will be. With this in mind, go back again and rework your final argument. Make sure that it is completely consistent with the expected evidence and that it makes maximum use of the uncontroverted facts. Consider eliminating any parts of the argument that rest too heavily on evidence that you anticipate will be severely contested. Be sure that you structure your argument so that you can begin and end with your theme, and invoke it throughout. Finally, outline your opening statement, again beginning and ending with your theme, and raising each of the points to which you will return on final argument.

§ 32.2 Evidentiary Foundations

§ 32.2.1 The Requirement of Foundation

Before evidence can be considered at trial there must be a basis for believing it to be relevant and admissible. This basis is called the foundation. Depending on the nature of the evidence, the foundation may be complex or simple. The law of evidence determines which facts form the predicate for the admission of testimony and exhibits.

Regarding testimony, the foundation is so obvious that it is almost overlooked as a formal aspect of the trial. For example, the basic foundation for eyewitness testimony is that the witness observed relevant events and is able to recall them. The foundation is typically established as a means of introducing the witness. For example:

> Q: Were you on duty on December the 20th?
>
> A: Yes.
>
> Q: Did you have occasion on that date to respond to a report of possible child abuse?
>
> A: Yes.
>
> Q: What was the first thing you did after receiving the report?
>
> A: I drove to the home located at 123 Maple Street here in the City.

Q. Then what did you do?

A. I entered the premises and spoke to the people living there.

It has now been shown that the witness has personal knowledge of relevant facts. On the basis of this foundation, and in the absence of some objection that is not apparent from the example, the witness should be allowed to describe the investigation. Of course, not all foundations are so straightforward. Many foundations require the proof of predicate facts as a condition precedent to admissibility of evidence.

§ 32.2.2 Components of Foundation

There are three aspects to evidentiary foundations. To be admitted, evidence must be (1) relevant, (2) authentic, and (3) admissible under the rules of evidence.[4]

Relevance

Relevance defines the relationship between proffered evidence and some fact that is at issue in the case. Evidence will not be admitted simply because it is interesting. Rather, it must be shown to be probative in the sense that it makes some disputed fact either more or less likely.[5] The relevance of most evidence is generally made apparent from the context of the case, but occasionally it must be demonstrated by the establishment of foundational facts.

Authenticity

The concept of authenticity refers to the requirement of proof that the evidence actually is what the proponent claims it to be.[6] In other words, evidence is not to be admitted until there has been a threshold showing that it is "the real thing." The judge decides whether an item of evidence has been sufficiently authenticated, and the criteria vary according to the nature of the evidence involved.[7]

We generally think of authentication as it applies to tangible evidence such as documents, physical objects, or photographs. Thus, is this the belt that was used for punishment? Does the photograph fairly and accurately depict the child's injuries? Is this the child's medical record? Before an exhibit can be received, a foundation must be established that adequately supports the proponent's claim of authenticity.

Specific Admissibility

While evidence will generally be received if it is relevant and authentic, the law of evidence contains a host of specific provisions that govern the admissibility of various sorts of proof.[8] In many cases evidence can be admitted only following the

---

[4]   FED. R. EVID. 401, 901, 105.

[5]   FED. R. EVID. 401, 402.

[6]   FED. R. EVID. 901(a).

[7]   FED. R. EVID. 902.

[8]   FED. R. EVID. 105.

establishment of foundational facts. Exceptions to the hearsay rule, for example, require such a preliminary showing.[9] It is impossible to generalize about such prerequisites except to say that the advocate must be aware of the rule of evidence under which each item of evidence is proffered.

§ 32.3 Direct Examination

§ 32.3.1 The Role of Direct Examination

Cases are won as a consequence of direct examination. Direct examination is your opportunity to present the substance of your case. It is the time to offer the evidence to establish the facts that you need to prevail. Having planned your persuasive story, you must now prove the facts on which it rests by eliciting the testimony of witnesses.

Direct examination, then, is the heart of your case. It is the fulcrum of the trial— the aspect on which all else turns. Every other aspect of the trial is derivative of direct examination. Opening statements and final arguments are simply the lawyer's opportunity to comment on what the witnesses have to say; cross examination exists solely to allow the direct examination to be challenged.

§ 32.3.2 Introduce Undisputed Facts

In most trials there are many facts that are not in dispute. Nonetheless, such facts cannot be considered by the judge, and will not be part of the record on appeal, until they have been placed in evidence through a witness's testimony or the introduction of a document. Failing to include undisputed facts in direct examination could lead to an unfavorable decision or reversal on appeal.

§ 32.3.3 Enhance the Likelihood of Disputed Facts

Direct examination is your opportunity to put forward your client's version of the disputed facts. You must not only introduce evidence on disputed points, you must do so persuasively. The art of direct examination consists in large part of establishing the certainty of facts that the other side claims are uncertain or untrue.

§ 32.3.4 Reflect on the Credibility of Witnesses

The credibility of a witness is always in issue. Thus, every direct examination, whatever its ultimate purpose, must attend to the credibility of the witness. For this reason, most direct examinations begin with some background information about the witness. What does she do for a living? Where did she go to school? How long has

---

[9] FED. R. EVID. 803. *See, e.g.*, FED. R. EVID. 803 (1), Present sense impression. A statement describing or explaining an event or condition made while the declarant was perceiving the event or condition, or immediately thereafter.

she lived in the community? Even if the witness's credibility will not be challenged, this sort of information helps to humanize the witness.

In juvenile court, the same professionals (e.g., CPS workers) often testify repeatedly before the same judge, and it is unnecessary to take time to familiarize the judge with the witness. It is possible in such cases to get quickly "down to business." If the case might be appealed, however, and if an expert witness supports your position, you will want to introduce the witness's resume or obtain a stipulation as to specific qualifications.

§ 32.3.5 Competence of Witnesses

Under the rules of evidence, every person is presumed competent to testify.[10] Issues of testimonial competence usually arise only with child witnesses.

§ 32.3.6 Non-leading Questions

The principal rule of direct examination is that the attorney may not "lead" the witness.[11] A leading question is one that suggests its own answer. Because the party calling a witness to the stand is presumed to have conducted an interview and to know what the testimony will be, leading questions are disallowed to insure that the testimony is in the witness's own words.

Whether a question is leading is frequently an issue of tone or delivery, as much as form. The distinction, moreover, is often finely drawn. For example, there is no doubt that this question is leading: "Of course, you inspected every room in the home, didn't you?" Not only does the question contain its own answer, its format virtually requires that it be answered in the affirmative. On the other hand, this question is not leading: "Did you inspect every room in the home?" Although the question is specific and calls for a "yes or no" answer, it does not control the witness's response. Finally, this question falls in the middle: "Didn't you inspect every room in the home?" If the examiner's tone of voice and inflection indicate that this is meant as a true query, the question probably will not be considered leading. If the question is stated more as an assertion, however, it will violate the leading question rule.

There are exceptions to the rule against leading on direct. A lawyer is generally permitted to lead a witness on preliminary matters, on issues that are not in dispute, in order to direct the witness's attention to a specific topic, expedite the testimony on nonessential points, and refresh a witness's recollection.[12] In addition, it is usually permissible to lead witnesses who are young, old, infirm, confused, or frightened.[13]

---

[10] FED. R. EVID. 601.

[11] FED. R. EVID. 611(c).

[12] FED. R. EVID. 612.

[13] *See* JOHN E. B. MYERS, MYERS ON EVIDENCE IN CHILD, DOMESTIC AND ELDER ABUSE § 3.02[F] at 148 (Aspen Publishers, 4th ed. 2005).

Although many judges allow leading questions during direct examination of expert witnesses, this may make the testimony hard to follow and hard to digest. Finally, it is within the trial judge's discretion to permit leading questions to make the examination effective for the ascertainment of the truth, avoid needless consumption of time, protect the witness from harassment or undue embarrassment, or as is otherwise necessary to develop the testimony.[14]

In the absence of abuse, most lawyers do not object to the occasional use of leading questions on direct. It is most common to object to leading questions that are directed to the central issues of the case or that are used to substitute the statements of counsel for that of the witness.

§ 32.3.7 Narratives

Witnesses on direct examination may not testify in "narrative" form.[15] The term narrative has no precise definition, but it is usually taken to mean an answer that goes beyond responding to a specific question. Questions that invite a lengthy or run-on reply are said to "call for a narrative answer."An example of a non-narrative question is, "What did you do next?" The narrative version would be, "Tell us everything that you did that day."

As with leading questions, the trial judge has discretion to permit narrative testimony.[16] Narratives are often allowed when the witness is an expert.

§ 32.3.8 The Lay Witness Opinion Rule

Witnesses are expected to testify as to their sensory observations.[17] What did the witness see, hear, smell, touch, taste, or do? Witnesses other than experts generally are not allowed to offer opinions or to characterize events or testimony.[18] A lay witness, however, is allowed to give opinions that are "rationally based upon the perception of the witness."[19] Thus, witnesses are usually permitted to draw conclusions on issues such as cleanliness, odor, noise volume, distance, time, weight, temperature, and weather conditions. Similarly, lay witnesses may characterize the behavior of others as angry, drunken, affectionate, busy, frightened, or even insane.[20]

§ 32.3.9 Refreshing Recollection

Although witnesses are expected to testify in their own words, they are not expected to have perfect recall. The courtroom can be an unfamiliar and intimidating

---

[14] FED. R. EVID. 611(a).

[15] FED. R. EVID. 611(a).

[16] FED. R. EVID. 611(a).

[17] FED. R. EVID. 701.

[18] FED. R. EVID. 701.

[19] FED. R. EVID. 701(a).

[20] FED. R. EVID. 701.

place, and witnesses can suffer memory lapses due to stress, fatigue, discomfort, or simple forgetfulness. Under these circumstances it is permissible for the direct examiner to refresh the witness's recollection.[21] It is common to rekindle a witness's memory through the use of a document such as the witness's prior report. It may also be permissible to use a photograph, an object, or a leading question.

To refresh recollection with a document, you must first establish that the witness's memory is exhausted concerning a specific issue or event. You must then determine that her memory might be refreshed by reference to a writing. Next, show the writing to the witness, allow her time to examine it, and inquire as to whether her memory has returned. If the answer is yes, remove the document and request the witness to continue her testimony. Note that in this situation the testimony ultimately comes from the witness's own restored memory. The document is not offered in evidence. Thus, a document used for the limited purpose of refreshing recollection does not have to satisfy the best evidence rule, does not have to be authenticated, and is not hearsay.

§ 32.3.10 Planning Direct Examinations

There are three fundamental aspects to every direct examination: content, organization, and technique.

Your principal tool in presenting a persuasive direct examination is knowledge of the witness. If the underlying content of the examination is not accurate and believable, the lawyer's technique is unlikely to make any noticeable difference. Your primary concern, then, must be content—the facts you intend to prove.

The content of a direct examination can be enhanced through the use of organization, language, focus, pacing, and rapport. Effective organization requires sequencing an examination in a manner that provides for logical development, while emphasizing important points and minimizing damaging ones. Questions should be asked in language that directs the progress of the examination without putting words in the witness's mouth. A direct examination uses focus to underscore and expand on crucial issues. Pacing varies the tone, speed, and intensity of the testimony to insure that it does not become boring. Finally, the positive rapport of the direct examiner with the witness is essential to establish the witness's overall trustworthiness and believability.

§ 32.3.11 Content

Content—what the witness says—is the driving force of every direct examination. The examination must have a central purpose. It must either establish some aspect of your theory, or it must contribute to the persuasiveness of your theme. Preferably, it will do both.

---

[21] *See* FED. R. EVID. 612.

Begin by asking yourself: Why am I calling this witness? Which elements of my claims or defenses will the witness address? How can the witness be used to controvert an element of the other side's case? What exhibits can be introduced through the witness? How can the witness bolster or detract from the credibility of others who will testify? How can the witness add strength to the presentation of the case?

Since a witness might be called for any or all of the above reasons, you must determine all of the possible useful information. List every conceivable thing that the witness might say to explain or help your case.

In direct examination, length is your enemy. Work to eliminate all nonessential facts that are questionable, subject to impeachment, cumulative, distasteful, implausible, distracting, or just plain boring.

Go through a process of inclusion. List the witness's facts that are necessary to the establishment of your theory. What is the single most important thing that the witness has to say? What are the witness's collateral facts that will make the central information more plausible? What is the next most important part of the potential testimony? What secondary facts make that testimony more believable? Continue this process for every element of your case. You must also be sure to include those "thematic" facts that give persuasive force to your arguments.

In addition to central facts and supporting details, your "content checklist" should include consideration of the following sorts of information:

- *Reasons.* Recall that stories are more persuasive when they include reasons for the way people act. A direct examination usually should include the reasons for the witness's own actions. Some witnesses can also provide reasons for the actions of another.

- *Explanations.* When a *witness's* testimony is not self-explanatory, or where it raises obvious questions, simply ask the witness to explain.

- *Credibility.* The credibility of a witness is always in issue. Some part of every direct examination should be devoted to *establishing* the credibility of the witness. You can enhance credibility in numerous ways. Show that the witness is neutral and disinterested. Demonstrate that the witness had an adequate opportunity to observe. Allow the witness to deny any expected charges of bias or misconduct. Elicit the witness's personal background of probity and honesty.

What to Exclude

Having identified the facts that most support your theory and most strengthen your theme, you may now begin the process of elimination. It should go without saying that you must omit those facts that are "untrue." While you are not required to assure yourself beyond reasonable doubt of the probity of each witness, neither may you knowingly elicit testimony that you believe to be false.[22] By the time you are preparing your direct examinations, you certainly will have abandoned any legal or factual theory that rests on evidence of this sort.

More realistically, unless you have an extraordinarily compelling reason to include them, you will need to consider discarding facts that fall into the following categories: clutter, unprovables, implausibles, impeachables, and door openers. Each of these is discussed below.

CLUTTER. This may be the single greatest vice in direct examination. Details are essential to the corroboration of important evidence, and they are worse than useless virtually everywhere else. Aimless detail will detract from your true corroboration.

How do you determine whether a certain fact is clutter? Ask what it contributes to the persuasiveness of your story. Does it supply a reason for the way someone acted? Does it make an important fact more or less likely? Does it affect the credibility or authority of a witness? Does it enhance the moral value of your story? If all of the answers are negative, you are looking at clutter.

UNPROVABLES. These are facts that can successfully be disputed. While not "false," they may be subjected to such vigorous and effective dispute as to make them unusable. Is the witness the only person who claims to have observed a certain event, while many other credible witnesses swear to the precise contrary? Is the witness less than certain? Is the testimony contradicted by credible documentary evidence? It is usually better to pass up a line of inquiry than to pursue it and ultimately have it rejected. This is not, however, a hard and fast rule. Many true facts will be disputed by the other side, and your case will virtually always turn upon your ability to persuade the trier of fact that your version is correct. Sometimes your case will depend entirely on the testimony of a single witness who, though certain and truthful, will come under massive attack. Still, you must be willing to evaluate all of the potential testimony against the standards of provability and need. If you can't prove it, don't use it. Especially if you don't need it.

IMPLAUSIBLES. Some facts need not be disputed to collapse under their own weight. They might be true, they might be useful, they might be free from possible contradiction, but they just won't fly.

IMPEACHABLES. These are statements open to contradiction by the witness's own prior statements. By the time of trial many witnesses will have given oral and/or written statements in the form of interviews, reports, and depositions. Many also will have signed or authored documents, correspondence, and other writings. With some limitations, the witnesses' previous words may be used to cast doubt on their credibility; this is called impeachment by a prior inconsistent statement. The demonstration that a witness has previously made statements that contradict her trial testimony is often one of the most dramatic, and damning, aspects of cross

---

[22] MODEL RULES OF PROF'L CONDUCT R. 3.3(a)(3) (2002) (candor toward the tribunal).

examination. Unless you can provide an extremely good explanation of why the witness has changed, or seems to have changed, his or her story, it is usually best to omit "impeachables" from direct testimony.

DOOR OPENERS. Some direct testimony is said to "open the door" for inquiries on cross examination that otherwise would not be allowed. The theory here is that fairness requires that the cross examiner be allowed to explore any topic that was deliberately introduced on direct.

§ 32.3.12 Organization and Structure

Organization is the tool through which you translate the witness's memory of events into a coherent and persuasive story. The keys to this process are primacy and recency, duration, and repetition. Primacy and recency refer to the widely accepted phenomenon that people tend best to remember those things that they hear first and last. Following this principle, the important parts of a direct examination should be brought out at its beginning and again at its end. Less important information should be sandwiched in the middle. Duration refers to the amount of time you spend on various aspects of the direct examination. As a general rule you should dwell on the more important points. Important points should be repeated to increase the likelihood that they will be retained.

§ 32.3.13 Direct Examination of the CPS Worker and Doctor in *In re A.C.*

The attorney for CPS realizes that success depends on the testimony of the CPS worker and the doctor. The landlord is the least important witness but may, if credible, add detail by describing the loud parties, drinking, and domestic violence. On the other hand, if the landlord has "baggage" that could be spotlighted on cross examination (e.g., convictions, a drinking or drug problem of his own), the attorney for CPS may decide against calling him. If the landlord is called, it would be wise to sandwich him between the CPS worker and the doctor, thus taking advantage of primacy and recency.

A CPS worker testifying in juvenile court dependency litigation is an unusual—in some respects unique—witness. The worker is a lay witness insofar as the worker has personal knowledge of relevant facts (e.g., bruises, messy house). At the same time, the worker may be qualified as an expert witness. The worker is knowledgeable about risk and safety assessment, standards of maltreatment, and related matters. In the relatively informal environs of dependency cases, where the legal and non-legal professionals are well acquainted with each other, and where there is no jury, it is common for CPS workers to combine lay and expert testimony.

The CPS worker's testimony will establish CPS's theory and theme of the case— these young children are maltreated and in danger. The CPS worker will paint a broad picture of the family, describing all aspects of the investigation. The worker can describe Dell's relationship with the children, which is evidence that he has assumed a parental role and thus a duty to care for the children. The CPS worker can repeat Eve's damaging admissions for the record. The worker can lay the foundation for the CPS report. In addition, if allowable under local evidence rules, the worker may be able to lay the foundation for the hospital record (under the business and/or public records exceptions to the hearsay rule.[23] Many courts expect the parties to agree prior to trial on foundation issues such as authentication and the best evidence rule.

In preparing for direct examination of the CPS worker, counsel must think through the possible cross examination strategies for the defense. Are there holes in the investigation? Did the CPS investigator cross all the t's and dot all the i's? If there are gaps in the report or the investigation, how can direct examination preempt cross examination? Perhaps the CPS worker had a good reason for omitting certain information from the report. If so, bring this fact out on direct.

The doctor will testify as an expert to describe the bruises and cigarette burn. Photographs that help the doctor to describe the child's injuries are admissible, and the doctor can lay the necessary foundation by testifying that the photographs are a fair and accurate representation of the injuries. So long as the doctor saw the injuries, the doctor does not have to be the photographer.[24]

§ 32.4 Cross Examination

§ 32.4.1 The Role of Cross Examination

Cross examination must be approached with great care. A common saying among trial attorneys is that you cannot win your case on cross examination, but you sure can lose it. A poor direct examination may be aimless and boring, but the witness is generally helpful. Your worst fear on direct examination is usually that you have left something out. A poor cross examination, on the other hand, can be disastrous. Witnesses on cross examination range from cooperative to hostile. On cross you run the risk of adding weight or sympathy to the other side's case. The witness may argue with you. The witness may fill in gaps that were left in the direct testimony. Whatever damage you do on cross may be immediately cured on redirect examination.

None of these problems can be avoided entirely, but they can be minimized. You need not cross every witness. Pick your battles and set realistic goals. Many trial lawyers suggest that cross examination be limited to three or four points. Although there may be reasons to depart from this guideline, the short cross examination has much to commend it.

---

[23] Fed. R. Evid. 803(6) and (8).

[24] *See* John E. B. Myers, Myers on Evidence in Child, Domestic and Elder Abuse § 4.26 at 310 (Aspen Publishers, 4th ed. 2005).

§ 32.4.2 Leading Questions Permitted

The most obvious distinction between direct and cross examination is the permissible use of leading questions on cross.[25]

§ 32.4.3 Cross Examination Limited by the Scope of Direct; Plus Impeachment

The general rule is that cross examination is limited to the scope of the direct examination.[26] That is, the scope of cross is restricted to subjects that were raised during direct examination. The definition of "scope" varies from jurisdiction to jurisdiction, and even from courtroom to courtroom. A narrow application of the "scope of direct" rule can limit the cross examiner to the precise events and occurrences that the witness discussed on direct. A broader approach allows questioning on related events. There is a trend toward a generous approach to the "scope" issue, especially in bench trials.

The rule that cross examination is limited by the scope of direct examination does not govern impeachment.[27] Thus the cross-examiner may be free to impeach a witness regardless of the scope of subjects discussed on direct examination.

§ 32.4.4 Content of Cross Examination

The first question concerning any cross examination is whether it should be brief or extensive. Most witnesses are cross examined at least to some extent. Perhaps there are opportunities to use cross examination to establish positive points to help your client.

In preparation for cross examination, consider the potential direct examination. What do you expect the witness to say on direct, and how, if at all, will you need to challenge or add to the direct? At trial you must make a further determination. Did the actual direct examination proceed as you expected? Was it more or less damaging than you anticipated? Reevaluate your cross examination strategy in light of the direct testimony that was produced.

§ 32.4.5 Purposes of Cross Examination

Cross examination should be undertaken only to serve some greater purpose within your theory of the case. A useful cross examination should promise to fulfill at least one of the following objectives:

- *Repair or Minimize Damage.* Did the direct examination hurt your case? If so, can the harm be rectified or minimized? Can the witness be made to retract or back away from certain testimony? Can additional facts be

---

[25] FED. R. EVID. 611(c).

[26] FED. R. EVID. 611(b).

[27] FED. R. EVID. 611(b).

elicited that will minimize the witness's impact? In *In re A.C.*, for example, might the doctor acknowledge that the burn on A.C.'s foot could be something other than an inflicted cigarette burn?

- *Enhance Your Case.* Can cross examination be used to further one of your claims or defenses? Are there positive facts that can be brought out that will support or contribute to your version of events? Could the CPS worker in *In re A.C.* be convinced to describe the good aspects of the relationship between Eve, Dell, and the kids? The worker's direct examination is likely to focus on the negatives about this family. Yet, there are positives too, especially the attachment between the children and the adults. The worker will almost certainly concede that removing the children will disrupt their lives.

- *Detract From the Opponent's Case.* Can the cross examination be used to establish facts that are detrimental to your opponent's case? Can it be used to create inconsistencies among the other side's witnesses?

- *Impeach the Witness.* Can the witness be impeached? Impeachment techniques are summarized in § 32.5.

The length of your cross examination will generally depend on how many of the above goals you expect to fulfill. It is not necessary, and it may not be possible, to achieve them all. You often stand to lose more by over-reaching than you can gain by seeking to cover all of the bases in cross examination. Be selective.

§ 32.4.6 Organization of Cross Examination

As with direct examination, the organization of a cross examination can be based on the principles of primacy and recency, repetition, and duration. Unlike direct examination, however, on cross examination you will often have to deal with a recalcitrant witness. You may therefore have to temper your plan in recognition of this reality, occasionally sacrificing maximum clarity and persuasion to avoid "telegraphing" your strategy to the uncooperative witness. Thus, we must include the principles of indirection and misdirection when planning cross examinations.

Three further concepts are basic to the organization, presentation, and technique of cross examination.

First, cross examination is your opportunity to tell part of your client's story in the middle of the other side's case. Your object is to focus attention away from the witness's direct testimony and onto matters that you believe are helpful. On cross examination, YOU want to tell the story, not the witness. To do so, you must control the witness.

Second, cross examination is generally not the time to gather new information. Seldom will you ask a witness on cross examination a question simply to find out the answer. Rather, cross examination is used to establish or enhance the facts that favor your client.

Finally, an effective cross examination often succeeds through the use of implication and innuendo. It is not necessary, and it is often harmful, to ask a witness the "ultimate question." Final argument is your opportunity to point out the relationship between facts, make characterizations, and draw conclusions based on the accumulation of details.

Lay the groundwork for your eventual argument, then stop. This technique is premised on the assumption that many witnesses will be reluctant to concede facts that will later prove to be damaging or embarrassing. Thus, it may be necessary to avoid informing the witness of the ultimate import of the particular inquiry. This can be accomplished through indirect questioning, which seeks first to establish small and uncontrovertible factual components of a theory and only later addresses the theory itself.

For example, a witness may be loath to admit having read a document before signing it; perhaps the written statement contains damaging admissions that the witness would prefer to disclaim. Direct questioning would be unlikely to produce the desired result. The witness, if asked, may deny having read the item in question. Indirect questioning, however, may be able to establish the point:

Q: You are a social worker?

A: Correct.

Q: Many documents cross your desk?

A: True.

Q: It is your job to read and respond to them?

A: Many of them, yes.

Q: Your agency relies on you to be accurate?

A: Of course.

Q: You often must send written replies?

A: Yes.

Q: Important decisions are based on the replies you send?

A: Often.

Q: You have an obligation to be careful?

A: Yes.

Q: So you must be careful about what you write?

A: Yes.

Q: Of course, that includes your signature?

A: Yes.

The questions have obtained through indirection that which the witness would not have conceded directly. The final question should be superfluous.

Misdirection is a relative of indirection; used when the witness is thought to be deceptive or untruthful. Here the cross examiner not only conceals the object of the examination, but attempts to take advantage of the witness's inclination to be uncooperative. Knowing that the witness will tend to fight the examination, the lawyer creates and then exploits a "misdirected" image.

§ 32.4.7 Progressive Approach to Cross Examination

Topical organization is essential in cross examination. Your goal on cross examination is not to retell the witness's story, but rather to establish a small number of additional or discrediting points. A topical format will be the most effective in allowing you to move from area to area. Moreover, topical organization also allows you to take maximum advantage of apposition, indirection, and misdirection. You can use it to cluster facts in the same manner that you would on direct examination or to separate facts to avoid showing your hand to the witness.

Because almost all cross examinations are topical, there can be no standard or prescribed form of organization. The following format is designed to maximize witness cooperation and is useful in many cases.

Begin with a Friendly Approach

Begin by asking questions that the witness regards as nonthreatening. As soon as a witness feels attacked, the witness's guard comes up and the witness hesitates to cooperate. Ask questions that add to your case rather than tear down the opposition's case.

Get the Details First

Details are, if anything, more important on cross examination than they are on direct. On direct examination a witness will always be able to tell the gist of the story; details are used in a secondary manner to add strength and veracity to the basic testimony. On cross examination, however, the witness will frequently disagree with the gist of the story that you want to tell, and use of details becomes the primary method of making your points. You may elicit details to lay the groundwork for future argument, to draw out internal inconsistencies in the witness's testimony, to point out inconsistencies between witnesses, to lead the witness into implausible assertions, or to create implications that the witness will be unable to deny later.

In each segment of your cross examination, it is usually preferable to get the details first. No matter what your goal, the witness is far more likely to agree with a series of small, incremental facts before the thrust of the examination has been made apparent. After you have challenged, confronted, or closely questioned a witness, it is extremely difficult to go back and fill in the details necessary to make the challenge stick.

Uncontrovertible Information

If you need to proceed beyond the "friendly" component of cross, you can begin with questions that damage the opposition's case or detract from the witness's testimony but that cannot be denied.

Challenge the Witness's Information

The next step is to challenge some or many aspects of the witness's testimony. A witness is unlikely to cooperate with you after you begin challenging his or her testimony.

Impeach the Witness

When necessary, impeach the witness's credibility with the techniques described in § 32.5.

§ 32.4.8 Control the Witness

The essential technique of cross examination is witness control. As noted above, your object on cross examination is to tell your client's story. You do not want to give the witness another opportunity to tell your opponent's story. How do you control the witness? With leading questions—often questions that require a "yes" or "no" answer. If the witness tries to expand beyond a simple yes or no, you might interrupt politely and say, "The question calls for a yes or no response. Please answer yes or no." If the witness persists in attempting to explain, you may ask the judge to "admonish the witness to answer the question." Judges conducting bench trials have differing approaches to this issue. Some judges require the witness to limit the answer, while other judges allow witnesses to explain.

To maintain witness control, avoid asking the witness "how" and "why" questions. Such questions nearly always relinquish control to the witness.

§ 32.5 Impeachment Techniques

As discussed above, the goal of cross examination is not invariably to undermine the witness's credibility. With some witnesses the cross examiner is able to elicit favorable information in a non-confrontational, even friendly manner. Yet, with many witnesses the cross examiner must shake the trier of fact's confidence in a witness's testimony. Impeachment techniques fall into two categories. First, some impeachment techniques assert that the witness is not telling the truth (e.g., impeachment by conviction of a crime). Second, other impeachment techniques do not attack the witness's truthfulness, but assert that even though the witness is trying to tell the truth, the witness is wrong (e.g., the witness has forgotten details of what happened). This section describes seven common modes of impeachment.

§ 32.5.1 Prior Inconsistent Statement

A witness may be impeached with a prior out of court statement that is inconsistent with his or her trial testimony.[28] The out of court statement may be oral or in writing. By tradition, the impeaching attorney lays the following foundation before confronting a witness with a prior inconsistent statement: (1) ask the witness if he or she made a statement at a particular time; (2) at a particular place; (3) who was present; and (4) the subject matter of the statement. Jurisdictions and judges differ in the extent to which they require the traditional foundation. Once the foundation questions are asked, the witness is questioned about the prior inconsistent statement. For example, assume that the CPS worker's direct testimony was that "I inspected every room in the home." The cross examiner might ask, "Isn't it true that your report states that you never entered the second bedroom?"

A prior statement offered for the limited purpose of impeachment is not hearsay because it is not offered for the truth of the matter asserted (TOMA). When a prior inconsistent statement *is* offered for the truth of the matter asserted *as well as* to impeach, then the statement *may be* hearsay and it cannot be admitted for TOMA unless it falls under at least one of the many exceptions to the hearsay rule. In some states (e.g., California), all prior inconsistent statements are admissible both to impeach *and* for TOMA, without regard to any other hearsay exception.

If the witness admits making the prior inconsistent statement, then the impeachment is complete. Suppose, however, that the witness denies making the prior inconsistent statement. If the prior statement is in writing, the judge should allow the cross examiner to hand the document to the witness and question him or her about it.

If the prior inconsistent statement denied by the witness was oral, the question becomes: May the cross-examiner call as a witness the person to whom the prior inconsistent statement was made and ask the person to repeat the statement? This scenario—where extrinsic evidence is offered to prove a prior inconsistent statement that has been denied on cross examination—raises the so-called collateral fact rule.[29] If the prior inconsistent statement is collateral, the second witness may not testify about it. On the other hand, if the prior inconsistent statement is relevant to some issue in the case *other* than impeachment, then it is not collateral and the witness may testify. Some states have abolished the formal collateral fact rule. In these states the judge determines on a case-by-case basis whether it is worth taking the time required to admit the extrinsic evidence of a prior inconsistent statement.

§ 32.5.2 Contradiction

There are two types of impeachment by contradiction. The first type is where the witness says one thing during direct examination and the cross examiner gets the witness to contradict himself or herself—self-contradiction. Recall that in *In re A.C.*,

---

[28] FED. R. EVID. 613.

[29] FED. R. EVID. 405(a), 608(b).

Eve and Dell deny using illegal drugs and state that the marijuana and cocaine found in their apartment belonged to a friend. On direct examination by her attorney, Eve explains that the marijuana and cocaine belonged to the friend, and that she and Dell did not use illegal drugs. On cross-examination of Eve, the attorney for CPS proceeds as follows:

> Q: You knew the marijuana was in your apartment, right?
>
> A: Yes, but it wasn't ours.
>
> Q: The marijuana had been there for at least a week, isn't that so?
>
> A: Maybe a week. I'm not sure.
>
> Q: You have smoked marijuana, haven't you?
>
> A: Once or twice, but that was before I had kids.
>
> Q: Did you ask your friend to remove the drugs?
>
> A: No.
>
> Q: You had the opportunity to smoke some of the marijuana if you wanted to, isn't that right?

Eve is obviously not inclined to admit she smoked marijuana in the apartment with her children. If she fesses up under the pressure of cross examination, her credibility is damaged in two ways: first, she used illegal drugs; second, she contradicted herself.

The second way to impeach a witness by contradiction is to offer the testimony of another witness who contradicts the first witness. For example, Eve and Dell's friend might testify that the drugs are not his, or another witness may have seen Eve use illegal drugs at home.

§ 32.5.3 Specific Acts of Untruthfulness

A witness who has lied in the past may be lying now, on the witness stand. Federal Rule of Evidence 608(b) and similar rules in most states allow a cross examiner to ask a witness about specific untruthful acts—lies—that the witness committed in the past. Under Rule 608(b), if the witness denies the lie, the cross examiner must accept the witness's answer and cannot offer another witness to testify that the person really did tell the lie.

§ 32.5.4 Conviction Used to Impeach

The theory behind impeachment by conviction is that a person who has been convicted of a crime is more likely to lie on the witness stand than a person who has not suffered a conviction. Obviously, some crimes tell us more about whether a person will testify falsely that other crimes. Perjury, for example, says a great deal about lying under oath. Assault and battery, on the other hand, are crimes of violence that say little about truthfulness.

Federal Rule of Evidence 609 governs impeachment by conviction. It is a complex rule. Basically, a witness may always be impeached with a conviction for a crime that involved lying or false statement (e.g., fraud, embezzlement). Regarding other crimes, such as battery or drug sales, the judge must weigh the probative value of the conviction against the danger of unfair prejudice.

All states have a rule on impeachment by conviction. Quite a few states have adopted Federal Rule of Evidence 609 verbatim. Other states use a variety of approaches.

If the witness who suffered a conviction is the parent accused of maltreatment, the conviction could be used for two purposes. First, as described above, it can be used to impeach credibility. Second, because character is in issue in dependency cases,[30] the fact that the parent/witness has been convicted of one or more crimes may be relevant to whether he or she poses a risk to the child.

§ 32.5.5 Bias

A witness who is biased for or against a party may be impeached.[31] The experienced cross examiner does not ask the witness if they are biased. Instead, the examiner brings out the reasons why the witness is biased, and lets the trier of fact draw its own conclusion. Consider, for example, the following cross examination of a doctor:

> Q: Now doctor, you are employed by Children's Hospital, isn't that correct?
>
> A: Right.
>
> Q: At the hospital, are you a member of the multidisciplinary team that investigates allegations of child abuse?

---

[30] *See* JOHN E. B. MYERS, MYERS ON EVIDENCE IN CHILD, DOMESTIC AND ELDER ABUSE § 8.02[B] at 667 (Aspen Publishers, 4th ed. 2005):

> One can argue that parental character should always be "in issue" in protective litigation. In criminal litigation, the focus is exclusively on the past: Did defendant do it? The prosecutor may not prove defendant's guilt with evidence that he is a bad man. By contrast, in dependency proceedings, the principle concern is the future, not the past. The state seeks to prove what happened in the past in order to protect the child in the future. Thus, the overriding issue in protective litigation is the child's future safety, and evidence of parental character is often relevant in this regard. The future-oriented purpose of protective litigation, coupled with the relevance of character to future conduct, the fact that protective proceedings are tried to the court and not a jury, and that fact that the purpose of the litigation is not to punish the parent but to protect the child, support the argument that parental character should be 'in issue' in protective litigation in juvenile court.

[31] FED. R. EVID. 408.

A: The team performs medical examinations and interviews. We do not investigate. The police investigate. But yes, I am a member of the hospital's multidisciplinary child abuse team.

Q: Your team regularly performs investigative examinations and interviews at the request of the prosecuting attorney's office, isn't that correct?

strictly theoretical

Q: When you complete your investigation for the prosecutor, you prepare a report for the prosecutor, don't you?

A: A report and recommendation is prepared and placed in the child's medical record. On request, the team provides a copy of the report to the prosecutor and, I might add, to the defense.

Q: After your team prepares its report and provides a copy to the prosecutor, you often come to court to testify as an expert witness for the government in child abuse cases, isn't that right, doctor?

A: Yes.

Q: Do you usually testify for the government rather than the defense?

A: Correct.

Q: In fact, would I be correct in saying that you always testify for the government and never for the defense?

A: I would be willing to testify for the defense, but so far I have always testified for the government.

Q: Thank you, doctor. I have no further questions.

The cross examiner seeks to portray the doctor as biased in favor of the government, but the cross examiner does not ask, "Well then, doctor, isn't it a fact that because of your close working relationship with the government, you are biased in favor of the government?" The cross examiner knows the answer is "No," so the cross examiner simply plants seeds of doubt about the doctor's objectivity.

§ 32.5.6 Opportunity to Observe

The cross examiner may bring out facts that indicate a witness did not correctly perceive an event. For example, if a witness described a car speeding down a street, the cross examiner might bring out that the night was dark and that the witness saw the car only briefly. If the witness admits these facts, the attorney can argue that the witness's testimony should be discounted because the witness "didn't get a good look at the car."

§ 32.5.7 Memory

No one has perfect memory for an event that happened weeks, months, or years ago. The cross examiner may bring out facts—particularly peripheral facts—that the witness cannot recall in an effort to shake confidence in the witness's memory.

§ 32.6 Expert Testimony

Rule 702 of the Federal Rules of Evidence and similar state rules provide that expert testimony is admissible where the expert's "scientific, technical, or other specialized knowledge will assist the trier of fact to understand the evidence or to determine a fact in issue."

§ 32.6.1 Expert Testimony on Ultimate Issues

Federal Rule of Evidence 704(a) provides that expert testimony "is not objectionable because it embraces an ultimate issue to be decided by the trier of fact." There are two kinds of ultimate issues: (1) ultimate facts, and (2) the ultimate legal issue. Experts are allowed to opine on ultimate issues of fact but not ultimate legal issues. For example, in a child sexual abuse case, one issue may be whether the child was penetrated. An expert could testify, "In my opinion the child's genitals were penetrated." Penetration is an issue of ultimate fact. The expert should not testify, "In my opinion the child was raped." This is the ultimate legal issue.

In child maltreatment litigation, the line separating ultimate facts from ultimate legal issues can be difficult to maintain. For example, should a CPS worker be permitted to testify that a child is at risk of maltreatment at home and should be removed? The answer should be yes. The testimony goes to ultimate issues, but the issue is particularly within the competence of CPS professionals. Moreover, the testimony, although embracing an ultimate issue, is primarily factual. On the other hand, the CPS worker should not testify, "The court has jurisdiction over the child." This is the ultimate legal issue for the court to decide.

In *In re A.C.*, should the doctor be permitted to testify that the burn on A.C.'s foot is a nonaccidental cigarette burn? Yes. Should the doctor be allowed to testify that the injury was the result of child abuse? Is such an opinion one of ultimate fact or ultimate law? In reality it is both. There are many appellate cases approving such testimony from physicians.[32]

---

[32] *See* State v, Smallwood, 264 Kan. 69, 955 P.2d 1209, 1221 (1998); Fairchild v. State, 992 P.2d 350 (Okla. Crim. App. 1999); State v. Smith, 359 S. C. 481, 597 S.E.2d 888 (Ct. App. 2004). These cases are discussed in JOHN E. B. MYERS, MYERS ON EVIDENCE IN CHILD, DOMESTIC AND ELDER ABUSE § 4.09 (Aspen Publishers, 4th ed. 2005).

§ 32.6.2 Qualification

To testify as an expert, a witness must be qualified by reason of knowledge, skill, experience, training, or education.[33] This is a threshold question for the judge.[34] The establishment of basic qualifications, however, should not be counsel's entire objective. It is equally if not more important to go on to qualify the witness as persuasively as possible.

Persuasive Qualification

The technical qualification of an expert merely allows the witness to testify in the form of an opinion. Counsel's ultimate goal is to ensure that the opinion is accepted by the trier of fact. Persuasive qualification is particularly important in cases involving competing experts, since their relative qualifications may be one basis on which the judge will decide which expert to believe.

It is a mistake to think that more qualifications are necessarily more persuasive. An endless repetition of degrees, publications, awards, and appointments may easily overload the judge's ability, not to mention desire, to pay careful attention. It is often better to introduce the witness's detailed resume or curriculum vitae and to use the qualification portion of the actual examination to focus on several salient points.

It is usually more persuasive to concentrate on a witness's specific expertise, as opposed to his or her more generic or remote qualifications. Every pediatrician, for example, is a medical doctor, so there is comparatively little advantage to be gained by spending time expounding your expert's academic degree. But not every pediatrician has forensic training in child abuse. Similarly, there is usually scant reason to go into matters such as the subject of the witness's doctoral thesis, unless it bears directly on some issue in the case.

On the other hand, an expert's credibility can be greatly enhanced by singling out qualifications that relate specifically to the particular case. Thus, it would be important to point out that the witness has published several articles directly relevant to the issues in the case. It would be less useful to take the witness through a long list of extraneous articles, even if they appeared in prestigious journals. Other case-specific qualifications may include direct experience, consulting work, or teaching that is concentrated on an issue in the case.

Experience is often more impressive than academic background. So, for example, a medical expert who has actually practiced in the applicable specialty may be more impressive than one who has strictly theoretical knowledge. When presenting a witness with practical experience, then, counsel should typically dwell on the witness's experience, pointing out details such as the number of procedures the witness has performed, the hospitals where he or she is on staff, and the number of other physicians who have consulted him or her.

---

[33] FED. R. EVID. 702.

[34] FED. R. EVID. 703.

Finally, it is frequently effective to emphasize areas of qualification where you know the opposing expert to be lacking. If your expert has a superior academic background, use the direct examination to point out why academic training is important. If your expert holds a certification that the opposing expert lacks, have your expert explain how difficult it is to become certified.

§ 32.6.3 Opinion and Theory

Federal Rule of Evidence 705 provides that an expert "may testify in terms of opinion or inference and give reasons therefor without first testifying to the underlying facts or data, unless the court requires otherwise." The expert may state his or her opinion without first detailing the basis for the opinion. After the opinion is delivered, the expert proceeds to describe the information and analysis that supports the opinion. Alternatively the expert may "build up" to the opinion by first describing the basis for the opinion.

§ 32.6.4 Cross Examination of Expert Witnesses

Experts may be impeached with the techniques described in § 32.5 (e.g., prior inconsistent statement, bias). One of the most effective cross-examination techniques with expert witnesses is to elicit the facts, inferences, and conclusions that support the expert's opinion, and then dispute or undermine one or more of those facts, inferences, or conclusions. Consider a case where a physician testifies that a child probably experienced vaginal penetration. The cross examiner begins by committing the doctor to the facts and assumptions underlying the opinion:

> Q: So doctor, your opinion is based exclusively on the history and the physical examination. Is that correct?
>
> A: Yes, that's correct.
>
> Q: And there is nothing else you relied on to form your opinion. Is that correct?
>
> A: That's correct.

The cross-examiner has now committed the physician to a specific set of facts and assumptions. When the cross-examiner disputes those facts or assumptions, the doctor's opinion cannot be justified on some other basis.

Once the cross-examiner pins down the basis of the doctor's opinion, counsel may attack the opinion by disputing one or more of the facts, inferences, or conclusions that support it. The cross examiner might ask whether the doctor's opinion would change if certain facts were different (a hypothetical question). The cross examiner might press the doctor to acknowledge alternative explanations for the doctor's conclusion. The examiner might ask whether other experts could arrive at different conclusions based on the same facts.

Rather than attack the doctor directly, counsel may limit the cross examination to the establishment of certain baseline facts or inferences. Once the witness has left the stand, counsel can offer other experts to contradict the doctor's testimony.

The cross examiner may also seek to undermine an expert's testimony by confronting the witness with books or articles (learned treatises) that contradict the expert's direct testimony.[35] The rules on cross-examination with learned treatises vary from state to state. When an expert is confronted with a sentence or a paragraph selected by an attorney from an article or chapter, the witness has the right to put the selected passage in context by reading surrounding material. The expert might say to the cross-examiner, "Counsel, I cannot comment on the sentence you have selected unless I first read the entire article. If you will permit me to read the article, I'll be happy to comment on the sentence that interests you."

§ 32.6.5 Cross Examination of the CPS Worker and the Doctor in *In re A.C.*

The CPS Worker

Parents' counsel must have a case theory. Given the facts in In re A.C., a two-stage theory seems plausible. Stage one—there was no maltreatment and the court should dismiss the petition. Stage two—if the court finds maltreatment, out-of-home placement is unnecessary.

At stage one, the theory may be that CPS overreacted to a situation that did not pose a serious threat to the well-being of A.C. or D.C. Eve loves her children and they love her. Dell has a good relationship with the children. He is not perfect, but he is not dangerous. Is it possible to prove that the bruises are not serious? Could it be that the burn on A.C.'s foot was accidental? Did CPS make any efforts—let alone reasonable efforts—to keep this family together?

The theme of cross-examination may be to undermine the thoroughness of the CPS investigation and thus its conclusions. If the CPS worker filled out the risk assessment form required by a Structured Decision Making (SDM) Model, did the worker make mistakes? Is the worker's removal decision supported by the SDM form? What steps did the worker fail to take that could have provided a basis for keeping the children at home?

At stage two, parent's counsel should argue that out-of-home placement is not needed, and that it would be harmful to the children. Hopefully, the attorney has counseled effectively with Eve and Dell, and will be able to inform the court that they are taking all necessary steps to keep the children safe.

The Doctor

The doctor concluded that the bruises on A.C.'s bottom were caused by spanking. Eve admits she spanked the child. When Eve testifies, she should state that she now

---

[35] *See* FED. R. EVID. 803(18).

understands that spanking is ineffective with very young children, and that she will not spank in the future. As for the doctor, Eve's attorney will attempt to have the doctor acknowledge that the bruises were not serious. The doctor could not determine the cause of the bruises on A.C.'s head. Might the doctor admit that the bruises could have been caused by a fall off a couch onto a hardwood floor as described by Eve? The burn on A.C.'s foot is very worrisome. If it really is an inflicted cigarette burn, it is a red flag for abuse. Eve and Dell deny they did it. What is counsel to do? The doctor testified on direct that the burn is *"consistent* with an inflicted cigarette burn," but that is not a definitive statement of causation. Are there possible benign explanations for the burn? Could it have been an accident? Before trial the attorney will have consulted an expert to discover possible non-abusive explanations. If there is something in the medical literature that supports a benign explanation, the attorney may decide to confront the doctor with the relevant books or articles.

§ 32.7 Conclusion

Although proceedings in juvenile court are generally informal, adversarial litigation is sometimes necessary, and the attorneys who work in juvenile court need to be competent trial counsel. We hope this brief chapter will help attorneys hone their advocacy skills.

Chapter 33: Case Assessment and Planning: Dimensions of Child Advocacy

by Colene Flynn Robinson[1]

§ 33.1 Introduction

The complexities, fluctuating factual basis, and potentially subjective nature of child welfare cases require attorneys to engage in thoughtful, dynamic case analysis for every case. Case analysis includes developing a theory of the case and then developing positions consistent with the theory of the case. An attorney should be prepared to answer the question "what is your theory of the case" for each case, at each stage, for each child. This chapter describes how to analyze a case, develop an appropriate theory of the case, develop positions consistent with that theory, and the steps an attorney must take in litigation to present the theory of the case.

§ 33.2 Investigating the Facts

Case analysis involves several steps, but is always based on a thorough fact investigation. Children's advocates must independently gather facts for their cases. This includes talking to witnesses, observing the scene, reading reports, and talking to collateral sources such as teachers, doctors, service providers, neighbors, family members, and respondents when possible. Obtaining adequate discovery is a key part of investigating the facts. For example, relevant items of discovery might include school records, treatment provider records, drug toxicologies, mental health records, Department of Social Services (Department) records, criminal background information, health records, and requesting evaluations when necessary. Think creatively about discovery. For example, if a key element in a case is determining whether the respondent mother is still having contact with her incarcerated boyfriend, the prison's visitation and phone logs might be very helpful. Subpoenas are enormously helpful in getting records or talking to individuals to verify or expand on information.

As a note of caution, it is imprudent to rely solely on the information the Department provides: too often it is inaccurate or incomplete, and attorneys have an independent ethical obligation to conduct an investigation.[2]

---

[1] Colene Flynn Robinson, J.D., is an Associate Clinical Professor at the University of Colorado Law School and the director of the Juvenile Law Clinic. From 2001 to 2004 she was Senior Staff Attorney at the National Association of Counsel for Children.

While undergoing discovery, the lawyer simultaneously turns to developing a theory of the case, which is one of the most important actions that trial lawyers take. From the theory flows the rest of the coherent, persuasive, story of the child's position.[3]

§ 33.3 Developing a Theory of the Case: Case Example with Focus Questions

Assume that the child lawyer's[4] client, Dorothy, is five years old. She has allegedly been sexually abused by her mother's live-in boyfriend, who also physically abuses Dorothy's mom, Sarah. The Department has filed a neglect petition against Sarah for failing to protect Dorothy from the abuse by her boyfriend. The case has been filed in a jurisdiction where the child's lawyer is charged with representing what is in the child's best interests, and not the child's stated wishes.

Developing a theory of the case, and positions which support it, requires asking a series of basic focus questions. These questions are:

1. What is the child advocate's role in the jurisdiction?
2. What is the child's position?
3. What is the permanency goal?
4. At what stage is the case?
5. What is the cause of action (the grounds for abuse or neglect)?
6. What is the individual child like?
7. What will serve the child's well-being and maintain her safety?
8. What other facts are relevant to the theory of the case or the position?
9. What does the child's lawyer think of his or her tentative position?
10. Has the attorney's subjective bias influenced her decisions?

By answering the above focus questions while developing a theory of the case, the lawyer accounts for and addresses the most important factors. A well-reasoned and well-presented theory of the case increases the likelihood of the court adopting recommendations that support it. Each of the focus questions is discussed in detail below.

---

[2]   MODEL RULES OF PROF'L CONDUCT, PMBL. 2 (2002); MODEL RULES OF PROF'L CONDUCT, R. 1.1 (2002); STANDARDS OF PRACTICE FOR LAWYERS WHO REPRESENT CHILDREN IN ABUSE AND NEGLECT CASES, R. C-2, (ABA 1996), *available at* http://www.abanet.org/child/repstandwhole.pdf.

[3]   For further discussion of the theory of the case, see Chapter 32, Trial Advocacy.

[4]   The "child's lawyer" will be used in this chapter to generically refer to an attorney representing a child in a child welfare action.

§ 33.3.1 Role of the Child's Advocate

Case analysis, at first glance, is not as straightforward for children's lawyers as it is for other lawyers in the system. Before beginning a case analysis, the child's lawyer must understand his or her role, ethical obligations, and the child's age and maturity—and how all these factors will impact the theory of the case. In some jurisdictions, the attorney is charged with representing what is in the child's best interests, typically as a guardian ad litem (GAL). In other jurisdictions, the attorney must advocate for the child's wishes. Other jurisdictions use a combination of these approaches, and in some jurisdictions, the role of the child's advocate is unclear.[5] The theory of the case must be consistent with whichever role is applicable in the jurisdiction.

GALs representing what is in the child's best interests should, when possible, take the child's position as their starting point. From there, GALs analyze the child's wishes to determine if pursuing the child's wishes would serve the child's well-being. If the child's wishes and best interests are aligned, then the GAL can develop a theory of the case that is consistent. If they are not aligned, the GAL must craft a theory of the case that advocates for what is in the child's best interests, even if the result is contrary to what the child wants. The GAL still should inform the court of the child's position, however.

For attorneys representing a child's wishes, the theory of the case is consistent with the child's position as that position is developed after a period of legal counseling, just as with an adult client.[6]

Other parties' roles in the case also dictate their theory of the case. In the example case of domestic violence and the sexual abuse of Dorothy, the mother's attorney's theory of the case may be: "This is a case about a loving mother, who desperately wanted to leave an abusive relationship but lacked the emotional and financial support to do so, and feared she or her child would be more severely hurt if she tried to leave. Now that she has the assistance of the Department, she is able to leave the relationship safely." Yet the Department attorney's theory might be: "This is a case about a mother who chose, and will continue to choose, her abusive boyfriend over her child's safety." The GAL's theory might be: "This is a case about a mother who loves her daughter but due to emotional and physical abuse by her boyfriend, has been unable

---

[5]   *See NACC Recommendations and Standards of Practice for the Legal Representation of Children in Abuse and Neglect Cases, available at* http://www.naccchildlaw.org/resource/resmgr/resource_center/ nacc_standards_and_recommend.pdf. For a thorough discussion of the different roles of children's attorneys, see Ann Haralambie, The Child's Attorney: A Guide to Representing Children in Custody, Adoption, and Protection Cases (American Bar Association 1993).

[6]   The case analysis below, using the sample fact pattern, is written assuming the child's lawyer is acting as a GAL. When the result might be different, based on the attorney's role, the difference is highlighted.

to protect her daughter and needs to prove over time that she can protect her child before reunification can happen."[7]

§ 33.3.2 Determine the Child's Position

Part of the child advocate's investigation includes speaking with the client, if the client is old enough, to determine his or her position.[8] Each child has a position, and each child must be interviewed separately. Do not assume that an older child speaks for his or her younger siblings. For children too young to express a thoughtful opinion, the lawyer tries to determine what they would want, if they could come to a thoughtful opinion, given the circumstances, their relationship and bond with other family members, and other developmental factors. This is not the same as what the lawyer believes is in the child's best interests, even though the lawyer may be charged with representing the child's best interests. At this stage in the analysis, the lawyer tries to determine what the child would want if the child could form and articulate an opinion. The child's position is the starting point for determining what the advocate's position will be.[9]

In our example case, Dorothy wants to have overnight visits with her mother, even though Sarah's boyfriend still lives with Sarah. The GAL counsels Dorothy about the risks involved and alternatives, but Dorothy continues to state that her desire is to have overnight visits with her mom. Remember that Dorothy is five.

Once the lawyer has determined the child's position, it must be analyzed given the lawyer's role in the jurisdiction. If charged with representing what is in the child's best interests, then test the child's position through that lens. The child's position influences what the theory of the case is and what positions will be taken. Remember, even GALs should always present the child's position to the court, even if the child's position on best interests is different than the GAL's position. After factoring the lawyer's role and the child's position, the analysis then moves to the permanency goal.

---

[7]   In the example above, the child's lawyer's position would probably change if he or she was representing the child's wishes, and not best interests, and the client did not think her mother had failed to keep her safe and wanted to return home immediately. In that case, the child's lawyer and mother's lawyer would probably share the same theory of the case.

[8]   If the client is not old enough to speak with, the attorney still has an obligation to see the client and observe his or her interactions with family members and caregivers. *See* NACC, *NACC Recommendations for Representation of Children in Abuse and Neglect Cases* (2001), Part III (B)(2).

[9]   Your role as an attorney does not merely require you to ask the child what his or her position is. No matter what role you play, your obligations as an attorney require you to counsel your client on the choices he or she is making and the ramifications of those choices, and provide advice and guidance regarding that choice. *See* NACC, *NACC Recommendations for Representation of Children in Abuse and Neglect Cases* (2001). *See* Chapter 6, Interviewing and Counseling Legal Clients Who Are Children.

§ 33.3.3 Permanency Goal

Depending on the stage of the case, the theory of the case may well be a statement of the permanency goal and the reasons for it. Even from the very beginning of a case, the lawyer needs to have an idea of what the permanency goal is and must take positions in the case that are consistent with that goal, or advocate for changing it. As the case develops and the facts change, so may the permanency goal, and consequently the theory of the case.

In the case of Dorothy, the parties have agreed that the permanency goal is reunification.

§ 33.3.4 Stage of the Litigation

The next question is at what stage is the case? Is it at the preliminary hearing stage, the fact-finding stage, a review stage, or the termination of parental rights trial stage? Each stage will impact the lawyer's position differently.

If our example case is at the preliminary hearing stage, enough may not be known about the mother, or her ability to keep her boyfriend out of the house for one night, to know whether overnight visits are realistic. If our example case is at the termination stage, overnight visits might be harder for Dorothy if she is about to lose all contact with her mother.

§ 33.3.5 Grounds for Abuse or Neglect

The allegations in the petition impact the position as well. Decisions about appropriate permanency goals and treatment plans depend entirely on the specific allegations in the petition and later on the court's findings. A position that drug testing must be a part of a treatment plan for someone in a case with no drug allegations or findings is obviously unsupportable.

§ 33.3.6 Individual Child's Characteristics

The individual child and his or her strengths, weaknesses, and individual characteristics also impact the theory of the case. How old is the client? Is the client developmentally on track? What disabilities or medical needs, if any, does the client have? Has the client had previous experiences that impact the lawyer's position? What strengths and skills does the client have? The lawyer's position must be individually tailored to each child, considering many factors about that child's mental health, developmental abilities, and strengths and weaknesses.[10]

---

[10] For a further discussion of a child's developmental abilities as they impact decision-making, see Chapter 6. For more on understanding children in context, see JEAN KOH PETERS, REPRESENTING CHILDREN IN CHILD PROTECTIVE PROCEEDINGS 2007: ETHICAL AND PRACTICAL DIMENSIONS (3d ed. 2007).

In our example case, Dorothy is five and is developmentally on target. She does not have any special educational, developmental, or medical needs. She is articulate and able to express her opinions and feelings to professionals involved in the case.

§ 33.3.7 Child's Safety and Well-Being

The child's safety and well-being must also factor into the development of a theory of the case. The lawyer's role in the jurisdiction may complicate this analysis—a direct advocacy attorney at times may have a theory of the case that appears, and may be, at odds with what some would consider to be best for the child's well-being. In determining what provides the greatest well-being and safety for the client, the attorney must understand and consider the child's context, including the people, animals, and activities that are important to the child. While searching for a working idea of what is optimal for the child, the lawyer must be attentive to his or her own subjective interpretation, potentially rife with class bias, for example. Once a working idea is formed, the lawyer then attempts to fashion a theory that addresses those factors yet is consistent with the attorney's role.

In our example case, the goal will be to protect Dorothy from further harm by Sarah's boyfriend.

§ 33.3.8 Investigation of Other Relevant Facts

Other facts will influence the lawyer's position, such as additional information gathered through investigation, therapy reports, or the client's wishes. In our example case, Dorothy's lawyer has learned several things during the fact investigation that impact the question of overnight visits. In speaking with Dorothy's therapist, Dorothy's lawyer learned that it would be therapeutic for Dorothy to: (1) have experiences with her mother where her mother is able to be protective of her, (2) sleep safely in her own bed at home, and (3) spend more time with her mother. Overnight visits would potentially offer all of these benefits.

§ 33.3.9 Analysis of Child's Lawyer's Tentative Position

Now the child's lawyer identifies a tentative position—that overnight visits are appropriate, in Dorothy's case—and analyzes it against all the facts. The attorney should look at each fact and see if it supports the position or detracts from it. Looking first to the facts that do not support the lawyer's position, it is obvious that the fact that the abuser is still in the home is dangerous for the client, and the attorney's position will have to account for this. Dorothy is also very young – only five – and does not have the skills necessary to protect herself, emotionally or physically.

One fact which supports the GAL's position is Dorothy's relationship with her therapist, who advocates for her and can provide help. Another is that Dorothy's mother wants overnight visits and is motivated to do what is necessary to obtain them.

How does the child's lawyer address the bad facts? The boyfriend cannot be in the home, or Dorothy won't be safe. Dorothy's mother must agree to keeping him out of the home, and the GAL and the court must be confident she will comply. One way to do that may be to have Mother join Dorothy in therapy for several sessions, and the three of them explore the possibility of overnight visits and the importance of keeping Dorothy safe and strategies for doing so. Perhaps the therapist and the mother can draft a safety contract that the Mother signs. The therapist can also work with Dorothy regarding ways to keep herself safe.[11]

The developing facts may also change a child's lawyer's theory of the case. As the mother proves herself capable of protecting Dorothy, the lawyer's theory might become "This is a case about a loving mother who lacked the skills and resources to protect her child from an abusive boyfriend. But after receiving services and support, she has proven she can protect her child."

The lawyer's position has grown through analysis of all the facts. Like the theory of the case, the lawyer's position should be about one sentence long, incorporate good and bad facts, and follow common sense. In the example, the GAL's position for visitation is 'Dorothy should have overnight visits with her mother provided that boyfriend is not present at any time, mother signs a safety contract and cooperates with Dorothy's therapist, and it continues to be therapeutically recommended.'

§ 33.3.10 Subjective Bias

Also, at every stage, the child's lawyer must check his or her position for any subjective bias that he or she might be imposing unwittingly. While it is impossible to eliminate our personal subjective biases, it is important to try to limit the impact of our personal history and assumptions about culture, race, economic status, gender, sexual orientation, age, or religion on our decision-making.[12]

§ 33.4 Litigation Strategy

Once the lawyer has developed a well-considered position, he or she must plan how and when to present it to the court. Consider all the litigation options available: written motion, oral application during a regularly scheduled hearing, requesting a special hearing, a show cause order, or other practice options in the jurisdiction.

Then consider what evidence is needed to support the position. In the case of Dorothy, the following evidentiary considerations come to mind: Will a signed safety contract be enough for the court? Should the therapist be available to answer the court's questions? Or should the lawyer plan to call the therapist as a witness? Should the boyfriend be called as a witness to discuss his treatment, his understanding of his culpability, and his willingness to comply with the plans so that Dorothy can have an overnight visit with her mother?

The lawyer should carefully consider the timing and manner of the presentation of his or her position to create the greatest chance of getting appropriate orders. These

---

[11] *See* Chapter 14, Child Safety: What Judges and Lawyers Need to Know.

[12] *See* Chapter 8, Cultural Context in Abuse and Neglect Practice: Tips for Attorneys.

tactical decisions will obviously depend greatly on the local practice and the particular fact finder.

§ 33.5 Conclusion

The child's lawyer's theory of the case guides decision-making and should point to a position on most questions that may come up in the life of the case. The theory, however, is dynamic and adaptable, changing in course as new facts develop. A thorough analysis provides the foundation for litigation preparation and assists in examining witnesses, entering evidence, and making opening and closing arguments. A clear, well-examined theory of the case greatly improves advocacy effectiveness.

Addendum: Child Welfare Case Checklist

Developing a generic checklist for the work that needs to be done in each child welfare case is difficult. So much depends on the role of the attorney, local practice, the type of case, and all of the individual factors that dictate the appropriate course of action in a particular case. It is possible, however, to walk through the steps that should be considered in every case and applied when appropriate. The checklist below does just that: ask these questions and follow these steps for a thorough assessment of the case and the litigation options.

Before getting to the checklist, however, it is important to note that the attorney should always focus on permanency, safety, and well-being for each client. When following the checklist, the attorney should place the questions and answers in the context of what permanency means for the client, what safety is required for the client, and whether the client's well-being is being served.

QUESTIONS

From the beginning of a case to the end, consider these preliminary questions:

- [ ] When was the case filed?
- [ ] Who called in the report?
- [ ] What are the results of the CPS investigation?
- [ ] Does the family have any prior child welfare history?
- [ ] Has the child's father been identified?
- [ ] Are his whereabouts known?
- [ ] What is his role in the child's life, including legal status?
- [ ] If the child was removed from the home, why?
- [ ] Where is the child placed?
- [ ] When was the child placed there?
- [ ] What is the visitation plan for the parents?
- [ ] Are there siblings? Where are they?
- [ ] If the siblings have been separated, why?
- [ ] What is the plan for reunifying them?
- [ ] What is the visitation plan for the siblings?
- [ ] Will the child be staying in the current placement? Get contact information.
- [ ] Are there any other family members? Get contact information.
- [ ] Are other family members available as a placement option?
- [ ] Where does the child go to school?
- [ ] What are the child's needs (e.g., education, health care)?

☐ What services is the family currently receiving? Get contact information for service providers.

☐ Are there any other people in the child's life who play a significant role (e.g., babysitter, neighbor, family friend)?

☐ What is the child's position?

☐ What is the social worker recommending, why, and what evidence or support is there?

☐ What is the parent's position, why, and what evidence or support is there?

☐ Does the child have Native American ancestry?

☐ If a criminal background check has been done on anyone involved in the case, what are the results?

ACTIONS

As Soon as Possible

☐ Meet with clients and caregivers.

☐ Visit the family home if possible and appropriate.

☐ Interview the respondents if possible and appropriate.

☐ Speak with collateral sources, such as teachers, neighbors, and family members.

☐ Obtain releases from the respondents, if possible and appropriate, for drug or other treatment providers.

☐ Obtain discovery, including but not limited to Department records, police reports, medical and school records, and witness statements.

At the Initial Hearing

☐ Advocate your position.

☐ Always apprise the court of the child's wishes, even if different from your position.

☐ Present evidence when necessary.

☐ Request any necessary orders for discovery.

☐ Request any necessary orders for services for parents.

☐ Request any necessary orders for services for children.

☐ Request any necessary orders for visitation with parents, siblings, other family, and important individuals.

☐ When necessary for compliance or enforcement, get written orders even when everyone agrees to a service. Present such requests as, for example, "Upon consent of all parties, the child will receive a speech and language evaluation by one month from today."

☐ Request any orders necessary to ensure continuity of school and medical care.

☐ Request orders that children remain in the current placement home absent a court order or emergency.

☐ Request an order that attorney be notified prior to a client's change in placement.

☐ Clarify the court's orders and reduce them to writing.

After the Initial Hearing

☐ Get a copy of the court's order.

☐ Make sure the social worker and any other collateral sources who need the information have a copy of court's order. Get consent or a court order for disclosure to collateral sources.

☐ Monitor compliance with the court order.

☐ Visit the client and explain the order and determine your position for adjudication.

Preparing for the Adjudication

☐ Investigate the facts.

☐ Investigate potential placement options, particularly kinship placements.

☐ Obtain discovery.

☐ Develop your theory of the case.

☐ Develop your litigation strategy.

☐ Interview the respondents if possible and appropriate.

☐ Interview witnesses.

☐ Conduct depositions or send interrogatories when appropriate.

☐ Subpoena witnesses.

☐ Order independent evaluations when necessary.

☐ Participate in pretrial conferences.

    ○ Present your position.

    ○ Settle when possible: if not on entire case, then on certain issues.

    ○ Agree on stipulations when possible, and reduce them to writing when necessary.

☐ Prepare the exhibits.

☐ Prepare the direct and cross examinations of witnesses.

☐ Prepare the witnesses.

☐ Prepare the closing argument.

☐ Develop a permanency position.

At Adjudication

☐ Advocate your position, and always present the child's position, even when it is not your own.

☐ Examine the witnesses.

☐ Present evidence when necessary.

At Disposition

☐ Advocate your position, and always present the child's position, even when it is not your own.

☐ Examine the witnesses.

☐ Present evidence when necessary.

☐ Report to the court on compliance issues, and seek appropriate orders.

☐ Report to the court and seek appropriate orders on essential needs of child: placement issues, food, clothing, shelter or health needs, educational status, sibling relationships, visitation issues.

After Adjudication and Disposition

☐ Obtain copies of court orders and distribute them to the necessary people.

☐ Monitor compliance with the court orders by the respondents and the Department.

☐ Reassess your permanency position.

☐ Visit and counsel the client and explain the court's findings and orders. Determine the client's position for the review and permanency hearings.

☐ Speak to the foster parents, therapists, and other service providers. Update them on the court orders and gather information.

Preparing for Review Hearings/Permanency Hearings

☐ Investigate the facts. This includes observing visits when appropriate, speaking to the child's caregivers and other collateral sources, and interviewing witnesses.

☐ Meet with and counsel the client.

☐ Determine your position.

☐ Determine whether the child is in a potentially permanent placement; if not, advocate with the Department for a transfer.

☐ Subpoena witnesses.

☐ Obtain court reports from the Department and other discovery.

☐ Investigate any new placement options.

☐ Obtain the other parties' stipulations when appropriate.

☐ Make a home visit if possible and appropriate.

☐ Interview the parents if possible and appropriate.

At Review/Permanency Hearings

☐ Advocate your position; the child's lawyer should always state the child's position, even when it is not your own.

☐ Present evidence when necessary.

☐ Seek necessary orders consistent with your position, for example, an order to file a TPR or order that a trial discharge plan be developed.

☐ Report to the court on compliance issues; seek appropriate orders.

☐ Report to the court and seek appropriate orders on essential needs of the child: placement issues, food, clothing, shelter or health needs, educational status, sibling relationships, visitation issues.

☐ Seek orders for services for the parents and child when necessary.

After Review/Permanency Hearings

☐ Obtain copies of court orders and distribute to the necessary people.

☐ Monitor compliance with the court orders by the respondents and the Department.

☐ Reassess your permanency position if need be.

☐ Visit and counsel the client and explain the court's findings and orders. Determine the client's position for a termination hearing if appropriate.

☐ Speak to the foster parents, therapists, other service providers. Update them on the court orders and gather information.

Before Termination of Parental Rights Trial

☐ Meet with and counsel the client.

☐ Obtain a certified copy of the adjudication findings if necessary.

☐ Obtain an adjudication transcript/record if necessary.

☐ Order a certified copy of criminal or other collateral proceedings if necessary.

☐ Obtain and analyze discovery.

☐ Obtain independent evaluations if necessary.

☐ Develop a litigation strategy.

☐ Interview the respondents if possible and appropriate.

☐ Interview witnesses.

☐ Conduct depositions or send interrogatories when appropriate.

☐ Subpoena witnesses.

☐ Participate in pretrial conferences.

    ○ Present your position.

- o Settle when possible: if you cannot settle the entire case, then settle on certain issues such as visitation, suspended judgment, and placement with relatives.
- o Agree on stipulations when possible, and reduce them to writing when necessary.
- ☐ Prepare the exhibits.
- ☐ Prepare stipulations when possible.
- ☐ Prepare the direct and cross examinations.
- ☐ Prepare the closing argument.

At Termination of Parental Rights Trial

- ☐ Advocate your position: always state the child's wishes, even if not your position.
- ☐ Participate in the trial: conduct examinations of witnesses and present evidence.
- ☐ Seek appropriate orders, including orders for sibling or parental visitation, placement, expediting the adoption, or other orders if appropriate and necessary.

After TPR Trial

- ☐ Obtain court orders and distribute them to the necessary people.
- ☐ Monitor compliance with court orders by the Department, or by the respondents if the TPR was not granted.
- ☐ Visit and counsel the client and explain the court's findings and orders.
- ☐ Speak to the foster parents, therapists, and other service providers. Update them on the court orders and gather information.
- ☐ If the children are in an adoptive home, work with the adoption attorney to see that the adoption is filed.
- ☐ If the children are not in an adoptive home, work with the agency to identify an adoptive home and ensure a smooth transition to the new home. Then work with the adoption attorney.
- ☐ Prepare a court report if required.

Before Post-Termination Review

- ☐ Investigate the facts. This will involve speaking to the child's caregivers and other collateral sources and interviewing witnesses.
- ☐ Meet with and counsel the client.
- ☐ Determine your position.
- ☐ Determine whether the children are in the most appropriate placement; if not, advocate with the Department for a transfer or file a motion.

☐ File motions for compliance with court orders when necessary.

☐ Subpoena witnesses if necessary.

☐ Obtain court reports from the Department and other discovery.

☐ Investigate any new placement options.

Appendix A

NACC Recommendations for Representation of Children in Abuse and Neglect Cases

NATIONAL ASSOCIATION OF COUNSEL FOR CHILDREN

Funded by a Grant from The Anschutz Foundation

National Association of Counsel for Children (NACC)
13123 E. 16th Avenue, B390
Aurora, CO 80045
303/864-5320
1/888-828-NACC
Fax 303/864-5351
E-mail advocate@NACCchildlaw.org
Web NACCchildlaw.org

NACC Recommendations for Representation of Children in Abuse and Neglect Cases was produced as part of the NACC's objective to establish the practice of law for children as a legitamate profession and legal specialty. As part of that objective, the NACC periodically produces standards of practice or guidelines for the representation of children.

The document was drafted by the NACC Program Committee and the prinipal authors listed below.

The document was adopted by a unanimous vote of the NACC Board of Directors on April 28, 2001.

Principal Authors
> David Katner
> Philip (Jay) McCarthy, Jr.
> Miriam Rollin
> Marvin Ventrell

NACC Drafting Committee Members
> Angela Adams
> Donald Bross
> Donald Duquette
> Ann Haralambie
> Katherine Holliday
> Ellen Jones
> Laoise King
> Patricia Macias
> Philip (Jay) McCarthy, Jr.
> John Myers
> Jacqueline Parker
> Henry Plum
> Miriam Rollin
> John Stuemky
> Marvin Ventrell
> Christopher Wu

Funding for this project was provided by The Anschutz Foundation, Denver, Colorado.

For additional copies or reprint permission, contact the NACC 1-888-828-NACC or advocate@NACCchildlaw.org

CONTENTS

EXECUTIVE SUMMARY

The lack of standards of practice or guidelines for attorneys representing children in child protection proceedings has frequently been cited as a major cause of substandard and ineffective legal representation of children. Unlike more traditional areas of practice where the model of representation and the lawyer code of conduct are essentially uniform from state to state, the practice of law for children has no commonly accepted uniform model or code, and many states provide inadequate guidance for attorneys doing this work. This is the case in part because the practice of law for children is a unique and relatively recent development, and because the evolution has occurred on a state by state basis. Additionally, there has been significant disagreement as to whether representation for children should take a traditional client directed ("expressed wishes"), or an advocate directed ("best interests") form, making it difficult to adopt a model.

Important progress was made toward the creation of a uniform model of representation with the creation of the *ABA Standards of Practice for Lawyers Who Represent Children in Abuse and Neglect Cases* in 1996. Still, jurisdictions struggle to adopt clear and comprehensive guidelines for children's attorneys, frequently because of the long-standing debate over the form of representation.

The *NACC Recommendations for Representation of Children in Abuse and Neglect Cases* is a document designed to assist jurisdictions in the selection and implementation of a model of child representation. Rather than urging jurisdictions to choose a particular model, this document sets out a checklist of children's needs that should be met by whatever representation scheme is chosen. It is the NACC's hope that this approach will allow jurisdictions to focus on what matters, serving the child client, and avoid becoming mired in the debate over best interests and expressed wishes.

The NACC believes that children's legal service needs can be met by both client directed ("expressed wishes") and advocate directed ("best interest") models of representation. In an effort to help jurisdictions understand various models, this document includes a section describing the various models of representation.

Whatever form of representation jurisdictions choose, the NACC believes that every child subject to a child protection proceeding must be provided an independent, competent, and zealous attorney, trained in the law of child protection and the art of trial advocacy, with adequate time and resources to handle the case.

NACC RECOMMENDATIONS FOR REPRESENTATION OF CHILDREN IN ABUSE AND NEGLECT CASES

I.   Introduction

This document is designed to assist children's attorneys, courts, and policy makers working to improve the legal representation of children. The focus is on the representation of children in abuse and neglect proceedings. The document also has application in private custody and adoption matters.

Rather than prescribing one specific model of representation, this document provides a policy framework for the legal representation of children, followed by a checklist of children's needs that representation should meet, whatever form of representation states choose. The document describes various models of representation in an effort to help the reader appreciate the strengths and weaknesses of each.

The NACC is aware of the debate in the child advocacy community over the two primary models of representing children - the attorney guardian *ad litem* (advocate directed "best interests" model) and the traditional attorney (client directed "expressed wishes" model). While this debate can be useful, the NACC suggests that rather than spending time and resources debating the merits of the various models, states should focus on ensuring that the model of representation used meets the children's needs checklist.

II.   Children's Legal Representation Policy

A.   Overview

The NACC believes that each child must be valued as a unique human being, regardless of race, ethnicity, religion, age, social class, physical or mental disability, gender, or sexual orientation. Each child is vested with certain fundamental rights, including a right to physical and emotional health and safety. In order to achieve the physical and emotional well being of children, we must promote legal rights and remedies for children. This includes empowering children by ensuring that courts hear and consider their views in proceedings that affect their lives.

Children's attorneys play a critical role in empowering children and ensuring that children's views are heard in legal proceedings. Outcomes in our adversarial process are directly tied to the quality of legal representation. Additionally, the presence of children's attorneys is critical to ensuring the timeliness of proceedings.

The NACC believes that attorneys representing children should have a combination of knowledge, training, experience, and ability which allows them to effectively discharge their duties to their clients. The NACC supports federal, state, and local programs to enhance the competence of these attorneys.

B.   Child Welfare Cases

The NACC believes that in order for justice to be done in child abuse and neglect related court proceedings, all parties, including children, must be represented by independent *legal* counsel[1]. The children who are the subjects of these proceedings are usually the most profoundly affected by the decisions made, and these children are usually the least able to voice their views effectively on their own. In many jurisdictions, however, courts do not appoint independent attorneys for all children in abuse and neglect related proceedings. NACC believes that federal, state, and local law must mandate that independent attorneys be appointed to represent the interests of children in all such proceedings.

C.   Private Custody and Adoption Cases

The NACC believes that while legal representation is not required for every child who is the subject of a child custody determination, the judge *should* appoint an attorney to represent the child in certain cases: when there are certain substantive allegations that make child representation necessary – i.e., when there is an allegation of child neglect or abuse (physical, sexual, or emotional) by a parent or household member, when there is a culture of violence between the parents, when there is an allegation of substance abuse by a parent, when there are allegations of non-paternity, or when there is an allegation of or fear about child snatching – as well as when there are certain procedural situations which make child representation necessary – e.g., when a child will be a witness or when the case develops an extremely adversarial nature. In addition, the judge *should consider* appointing an attorney to represent the child in certain other cases: when there is an allegation of mental illness on the part of a parent, when a custodial parent is relocating geographically, when child representation can reduce undue harm to the child from the litigation itself, when the child has exceptional physical or mental health needs, when the child expresses a strong desire to make his or her opinions known to the judge, when there is a *pro se* parent, when there is a third-party custody action against a parent (e.g., by a grandparent), or when the failure to appoint a representative for the child would otherwise impede the judge's capacity to decide the case properly. (Attorneys can be instrumental in ensuring that judges have the necessary data upon which to make an informed decision.)

---

[1]   The U.S. Department of Health and Human Services supports this principle. *Adoption 2002: The President's Initiative on Adoption and Foster Care. Guidelines for Public Policy and State Legislation Governing Permanence for Children*, U.S. Dept. of HHS ACF ACYF Children's Bureau, 1999.

III. Needs Checklist for Children Involved in Abuse and Neglect Cases

The NACC encourages jurisdictions to adopt a system of legal representation of children which satisfies the following checklist. The representation scheme should ensure that each of the following children's rights or needs are satisfied through a combination of systemic safeguards, advocacy duties, and basic advocacy issues.

A. Systemic Safeguards

☐ 1. Children need competent, independent, and zealous attorneys. The system of representation must require the appointment of competent, independent, zealous attorneys for every child at every stage of the proceedings. The same attorney should represent the child for as long as the child is subject to the court's jurisdiction.

Comment A: Competence is the foundation of all legal representation. The fundamental requirements of competency as defined in each jurisdiction, combined with the ability to function without constraint or obligation to any party other than the child client is of paramount importance. (See, ABA Model Rules of Professional Conduct (Model Rules): Preamble; 1.14(a); ABA Model Code of Professional Responsibility (Model Code): EC 7-1; EC 7-12; ABA Standards of Practice for Lawyers who Represent Children in Abuse and Neglect Cases (ABA Standards): Preface; A-1.)

Comment B: Competent representation includes knowledge, skill, thoroughness, and preparation. This includes knowledge of placements and services available for the child, and services available to the child's family. (See, Model Rule: 1.1; Model Code DR 6-101(A)(1)(2); ABA Standards B-1; C.) Jurisdictions should provide special initial and periodic training to all attorneys in child welfare proceedings covering substantive law (federal, state, statutory, regulatory, and case law), procedure, trial advocacy, child welfare and child development.

Comment C: Continuity of representation is important to the child. The same lawyer should represent the child for as long as the child is under the jurisdiction of the court. Temporary substitution of counsel, although often unavoidable, should be discouraged. Any substitute counsel must be familiar with the child and the child's case.

☐ 2. Children need attorneys with adequate time and resources. The system of representation must include reasonable caseload limits and at the same time provide adequate compensation for attorneys representing children.

Comment A: The NACC recommends that a full time attorney represent no more than 100 individual clients at a time, assuming a caseload that includes clients at various stages of cases, and recognizing that some clients may be part of the same sibling group. This is the same cap recommended by the U.S. Dept. of HHS Children's Bureau and the American Bar Association[2]. One hundred cases averages to 20 hours per case in a 2000-hour year.

---

[2]   ABA Standards of Practice for Lawyers Who Represent Children in Abuse and Neglect Cases, §§L-1, L-2; The U.S. Department of Health and Human Services supports this principle. *Adoption 2002: The President's Initiative on Adoption and Foster Care. Guidelines for Public Policy and State*

Comment B: For the sake of the child client and the interests of the system, attorneys must be provided appropriate and reasonable compensation. The NACC adopts the following position of the Dept. of HHS on this point: "Primary causes of inadequate legal representation of the parties in child welfare cases are low compensation and excessive caseloads. Reasonable compensation of attorneys for this important work is essential. Rather than a flat per case fee, compensate lawyers for time spent. This will help to increase their level of involvement in the case and should help improve the image of attorneys who are engaged in this type of work. When attorneys are paid a set fee for complicated and demanding cases, they cope either by providing less service than the child-client requires or by providing representation on a pro bono or minimum wage basis. Neither of these responses is appropriate. Rates should also reflect the level of seniority and level of experience of the attorneys. In some offices, lawyers handling child welfare cases receive lower pay than other attorneys. This is inappropriate. Compensation of attorneys handling children's cases should be on a par with other lawyers in the office handling legal matters of similar demand and complexity. The need for improved compensation is not for the purpose of benefiting the attorney, but rather to ensure that the child receives the intense and expert legal services required."[3]

☐ 3.   Children need attorneys who understand their role and duties. The system of representation of children must be well defined by statute, bar standards, administrative guidelines, supreme court directive or other documents such that every attorney appointed for a child can understand his/her precise role and duties, and such that an attorney can be held accountable for performance of those duties.

Comment: It is helpful here to distinguish between role and duties. Role refers to whether, for example, the attorney is client directed (traditional attorney model or child's attorney models) while duties refer to those actions to be taken by the attorney (investigation, calling witnesses, etc.). Although duties are in part dependent on role, most commentators agree that certain fundamental duties should apply regardless of role. See ABA and ABA / NACC Revised Standards § C Actions to be Taken.

☐ 4.   Children need an opportunity to present their positions to the court through counsel. The system of representation must provide the child with an opportunity for his/her needs and wishes to be expressed to the court.

Comment: Children have an independent perspective and may have information and positions to present to the court on a wide range of issues including but extending beyond the issue of placement. Other parties and the court may otherwise be unaware of the child's perspective or of how certain decisions subjectively affect the child.

Legislation Governing Permanence for Children, U.S. Dept. of HHS ACF ACYF Children's Bureau, 1999, page VII-5.

[3]   *Adoption 2002: The President's Initiative on Adoption and Foster Care. Guidelines for Public Policy and State Legislation Governing Permanence for Children*, U.S. Dept. of HHS ACF ACYF Children's Bureau, 1999, page VII-4.

☐ 5. Children need confidential communication with their attorneys. The attorney has a duty to explain the extent of confidentiality in developmentally appropriate language.

Comment A: Every child should have the right to communicate confidentially with the representative. (See, Model Rules: 1.6, 3.7; Model Code: DR 4-101; 5-102; ABA Standards: A-1; Comment B-2(2).)

Comment B: But see Alaska Ethics Op. 854. Some jurisdictions include attorneys as mandatory reporters, and pure confidentiality may be precluded with a GAL - advocate directed representation system.

☐ 6. Children need to be involved as litigants in the entire litigation process, including any post disposition, termination of parental rights, and adoption proceedings. The system of representation must recognize the child as a party to the litigation and must include the child in all phases of the litigation, including the opportunity to participate in arguments and jury selection where applicable, offer exhibits, call witnesses, examine and cross examine witnesses and engage in motions and discovery processes. The child must also be given notice of all proceedings and copies of all pleadings.

Comment: The child should be physically present early in the proceedings, so as to allow all parties and their representatives the opportunity to become acquainted with the child as an individual. Although the child's presence may not be required at every court hearing, it should not be waived by the representative, unless the child has already been introduced to the court and his/her presence is not required by law, custom, or practice in that jurisdiction. Every child should be notified through counsel of every court hearing, every agency meeting, and every case conference or negotiation among the various professionals involved in the case and the child's attorney should be notified concerning any change in the child's welfare, placement, education, or status. Every child should be considered a party to the litigation, and should therefore, be entitled to any and all benefits under the law granted to any other party. Every child should have access to sufficient information to allow his/her representative to provide competent representation including the child's representative having access to social services, psychiatric, psychological, drug and alcohol, medical, law enforcement, school and other records relevant to the case, and opportunity for interviewing child welfare caseworkers, foster parents and other caretakers, school personnel, health professionals, law enforcement, and other persons with relevant information. This access may require the representative to file motions for discovery, subpoenas, subpoenas duces tecum, depositions and interrogatories, according to the discovery mechanisms available in the jurisdiction. Every child should have the opportunity to present his/her witnesses in the court proceedings. This requires the representative to investigate facts, identify and communicate with witnesses, and issue subpoenas to ensure that witnesses appear in court.

☐ 7. Children need judicial review of adverse decisions. The system of representation must provide an opportunity to appeal an adverse ruling.

Comment: Children need to have access to the court after the adjudication occurs. This may require the representative to forego informal resolution of issues at the review stage of the litigation. See State ex rel. Jeanette H., 529 S.E. 2d 865 (2000).

☐ 8. Children need to be able to hold their attorneys accountable. The system of representation must provide recourse for ineffective assistance of counsel.

Comment: Every child should be able to hold the representative accountable for providing less than competent representation.

☐ 9. Children need an attorney with a fair opportunity to be effective in the court system. The system of representation must include a court system that devotes adequate time and resources to cases.

Comment: Courts cannot be "rubber stamp" agencies for social service agencies and must be equipped to handle caseloads responsibly. See, *Resource Guidelines, Improving Court Practice in Child Abuse and Neglect Cases*, National Council of Juvenile and Family Court Judges, © 1995 NCJFCJ, Reno, NV

B. Advocacy Duties

☐ 1. Children need attorneys who fully understand their cases. The attorney must perform a full and independent case investigation.

Comment: The child's attorney has a duty of full investigation of the case. (See, Model Rule: 4.2; Model Code: DR 7-104 (A) (1); ABA Standards: C-2(4); C-6.)

☐ 2. Children need meaningful communication with their attorneys. The attorney must observe the child, and dependent upon the child's age and capabilities, interview the child. The attorney must engage in regular and meaningful communication with the child. Children need to participate in making decisions that affect their cases. The attorney has a duty to involve the child client in the process, whether under a client directed model or advocate directed model. The attorney has a duty to explain his/her role to the child in developmentally appropriate language.

Comment A: Under a client directed model, the scope of representation by the child's attorney includes the duty to abide by the client's decision concerning the objectives of the representation. (See, Model Rule: 1.2(a); Model Code: DR 7-101(A)(1); EC 7-7; EC 7-8; ABA Standards: B-4.)

Comment B: This is a universal need, and it applies whether or not the child is pre-verbal. Visual encounters with children who are represented, even with pre-verbal children, are crucial to the representation. Otherwise, the representative is limited by relying upon the mental impressions of third parties. The child's attorney has a duty of effective, thorough, and developmentally appropriate communication with the client, including the duty to meet with the client. (See, Model Rules: 1.4 (a), (b); Model Code: EC 7-8; 9-2; ABA Standards: C-1; A-3; B-1(5); D-2; E-2; F-4.)

Comment C: Children need education about the law and all options available under the legal system. This need is restricted to developmentally appropriate clients, capable of communication.

Comment D: The child client must be informed about the responsibilities and obligations of the representative, as well as the ability and requirements of the representative to accomplish these things.

☐ 3.   Children need loyal attorneys. The child's attorney is prohibited from representation that would constitute a conflict of interest.

Comment: Attorneys must be aware of the potential for conflict while representing a sibling group. Additionally, the child's attorney must be sensitive to the age and maturity of the client where waiver is an issue. (See, Model Rules: 1.7; Model Code: DR 5-101 (A); 5-105(A), (C); 5-107 (B); ABA Standards: B-2(2).)

☐ 4.   Children need the full benefit of legal counsel. The attorney must provide competent, independent and zealous representation for each client. The attorney must have adequate time and resources to devote to the child's case, and to understanding his/her role and duties, insuring confidentiality, and full active participation in all stages of the child's case.

C.   Advocacy Issues

☐ 1.   Children need permanence. The attorney must advocate for timely resolution and permanent resolution (absent compelling reasons to the contrary) of the case.

Comment: The child's attorney has a duty of diligent and prompt representation, and a duty to expedite litigation, especially where placement of a young child is at issue. (See, Model Rule: 1.3; 3.2; Model Code: DR 6-101(A)(3); EC 6-4; ABA Standards: B-1(4); C-6.)

☐ 2.   Children need their immediate and basic needs met. The attorney must advocate for food, shelter, clothing, and safety, including a safe temporary placement where necessary and for educational, medical, mental health, and dental needs.

Comment: The child's most immediate physical needs must be addressed and should be the highest priority for the child's representative. After the immediate needs of sustaining life have been addressed, the child's education, mental health, medical, and dental needs must be addressed. Children's attorneys should act as a kind of "watchdog" for the children's needs, insuring that services are provided.

☐ 3.   Children need family relationships. The attorney must advocate for continuation of appropriate familial relationships and family preservation services where appropriate.

Comment: Without jeopardizing the child's physical or emotional safety, arrangements to maintain familial relationships (including siblings) which are not deemed to be harmful to the child should be established as soon as practicable. Family services may include visitation and services for family members: parenting education, medical and mental health care, drug and alcohol treatment, housing, etc. Such family services may also be appropriate to continue other meaningful relationships and ongoing activities where feasible.

☐ 4. Children need to be protected from unnecessary harm that can result from legal proceedings. The attorney must advocate for the utilization of court processes that minimize harm to the child, and make certain that the child is properly prepared and emotionally supported where the child is a witness.

IV. Representation Models

The following representation models are presented to assist states in evaluating and formulating models of representation. States should consider the requirements of the federal Child Abuse Prevention and Treatment Act (CAPTA) regarding the appointment of representation for the child. The U.S. Department of Health and Human Services, Children's Bureau has indicated that although CAPTA requires a GAL best interests representative, that role may be filled by either an attorney GAL or more traditional client directed attorney.[4]

A. Advocate Directed Representation

1. The Attorney Guardian *ad Litem* Hybrid[5] Model.
This model provides an attorney to represent the child and instructs the attorney to represent the child's "best interests." The attorney GAL advocates for a result which he/she believes (not necessarily what the child believes) is in the child's "best interests." Rather than taking direction from the client, as is the case in traditional attorney representation of adults, the attorney GAL is charged with forming the client's position by using his/her own judgment. Under this model, the attorney GAL's judgment as to the child's "best interests" takes precedence over the client's wishes.

Pros: This model is favored by many as the traditional model of representing children, particularly young children who cannot meaningfully participate in their litigation. It is also thought to protect older children from the harm of their own bad choices.

---

[4] *Adoption 2002: The President's Initiative on Adoption and Foster Care. Guidelines for Public Policy and State Legislation Governing Permanence for Children*, U.S. Dept. of HHS ACF ACYF Children's Bureau, 1999, p. VII-21.

[5] Ann M. Haralambie identifies and discusses the "hybrid' role in *The Child's Attorney, A Guide to Representing Children in Custody, Adoption and Protection Cases*, ABA 1993 at p. 37.

Cons: Critics charge that this is an "old fashioned," paternalistic model of representation that treats children as chattel rather than empowering them in the system. Critics charge that advocate directed representation is wrong by definition because: 1) attorneys are not ethically allowed to disregard their clients directives; 2) attorneys are not qualified to make "best interests" determinations; and 3) the legal system requires that attorneys be zealous advocates for a client's position, not agents of the court. Critics also charge that the system results in "relaxed advocacy" where attorneys appointed as GAL feel, and are treated, as relieved of their traditional lawyering responsibilities. Critics argue that this model has contributed to sub standard representation of children across the country.

Jurisdictions Using a Form of This Model: Approximately 60% of the U/S jurisdictions use a form of this model.[6]

Source: The Colorado version is comprised of the following sources: Colorado Revised Statutes §§ 19-1-103, 19-1-111, 19-3-203; The Colorado Rules of Professional Conduct at CRS, Volume 12 - pages 711-831; Supreme Court of Colorado Chief Justice Directive 97-02; Colorado GAL Standards of Practice.

2. **The Lay Guardian *ad Litem* Model**
    This advocate directed model provides for a non-attorney to "represent" the child's "best interests." This person, usually a non-professional volunteer, advocates for what he/she believes (not necessarily what the child believes) is in the child's "best interests." The lay GAL "stands" in the proceeding for the presumptively incompetent child. The focus is the protection of the child by an adult who attempts to know and then articulate the child's best interests.

    The NACC discourages the use of this as an exclusive model. Children, even more than adults, require trained legal representation and this model, by definition, is not legal representation. While the NACC recognizes the value of non-legal advocacy for children, whether in the form of lay GAL or CASA, we stress that it cannot be a substitute for trained professional attorneys for children. On this point, the NACC and National CASA have agreed. Non-legal advocates play an important role

---

[6] *Child Abuse and Neglect Cases: Representation as a Critical Component of Effective Practice.*
NCJFCJ Permanency Planning for Children Project, Technical Assistance Bulletin, 1999, page 45.

in the process, and jurisdictions should consider implementing such programs *in addition* to appointing attorneys.

Due to the substantial shortcomings of this model, states which use this model of representation frequently appoint an attorney to represent the child or the lay GAL.

Pros: The model has value when used in conjunction with legal counsel.

Cons: Assuming this is the only "representation" provided, the child has no legal counsel. Lay GALs are unable to provide "legal" counsel and cannot, for example, present evidence, examine witnesses, appeal adverse decisions, or advise the client of the ramifications of legal matters. Lay GALs attempting to serve in the role of legal counsel are engaging in the unauthorized practice of law. Additionally, lay representatives are less accountable than professionals for their actions because their conduct is not governed by ethical and legal standards.

Jurisdictions Using a Form of this Model Include: Florida, Hawaii, Maine

Sources: Florida uses a lay volunteer Guardian *ad litem* model. Florida's Guardian *Ad Litem* Program includes an attorney who advises volunteers on the protection of children's rights and represents the program in contested court proceedings. Fla. Stat. § 39.820 (2000).

In Hawaii, children in dependency cases are generally represented by volunteer lay guardians *ad litem* and CASAs called Volunteer Guardians *Ad Litem* (VGAL). Children *may also* be represented by an Attorney Guardian *Ad Litem*. H.R.S § 587-40.

Maine law calls for a GAL who is usually an attorney but is not required to be by statute. The GAL is considered a party and has the right to call and cross examine witnesses and has access to discovery. Should the GAL be an attorney, he/she essentially functions in the hybrid role of Attorney GAL defined in IV. A. 1. above. It is not clear how such duties can be performed competently or without violating the law against unauthorized practice of law if the appointment is of a lay person. Maine Supreme Judicial Court Rules for Guardians *Ad Litem*; 22 M.R.S. § 4005; 4 M.R.S. §1501.

3.   **The "Two Distinct Lawyer Roles" Model.**

A single lawyer model, either advocate directed (best interests) or client directed, may not meet the needs of all children, given their developing and varied capacities from infants to mature and articulate teens. This model would require appointment of a best interest lawyer-guardian *ad litem* or a traditional attorney under certain circumstances as set out in law.

In 1998, Michigan passed a version of this model that creates two separate and distinct roles for the lawyer representing children: attorney and lawyer-guardian *ad litem*. Michigan requires the appointment of a lawyer-GAL in every case and the lawyer-GAL is to represent the best interests of the child. The statute permits the court to appoint an attorney where the mature child and lawyer-GAL are in conflict about identification of the child's interests. The model prescribes aggressive duties for the lawyer-GAL and provides for attorney-client privilege. It requires the lawyer-GAL to tell the court the wishes and preferences of the child even if the lawyer-GAL advocates for a different view and requires the lawyer-GAL to weigh the child's wishes in making the best interests determination according to the age and maturity of the client. When a lawyer is appointed as "attorney," however, the attorney owes the same duties of undivided loyalty, confidentiality and zealous representation of the child's express wishes as the attorney would to an adult client. Some proponents of the Two Distinct Lawyer Role model urge that the law *require* appointment of an attorney instead of a lawyer-GAL at a certain age (unless the child is mentally handicapped), rather than leave attorney appointment to the discretion of the court.

Pros: Proponents argue that the pure forms of either advocate directed ("best interests") or client directed ("expressed wishes") models are deficient when applied to all children, so that a model which provides clear lawyer duties depending on the age and maturity of the child better serves the child client. This model is also well defined by statute and lessens the tendency toward "relaxed advocacy." This model also reduces the risk inherent in the ABA and NACC models that a lawyer appointed as "attorney" would find an exception to (or water down) the duty of aggressive and client-directed advocacy.

Cons: Critics argue that, at its foundation, this is just an attorney directed model with most of the shortcomings of model A. 1. above. The appointment of an attorney GAL is the rule, not the exception, and an attorney is appointed only in rare circumstances. Also, under rare circumstances the child could be represented by both an attorney and a lawyer-guardian *ad litem* which adds to the cost. The test for appointing one or the other lawyer roles remains unsettled.

Jurisdictions Using the Model: Michigan

Source: MCL 712A.13a(1)(b) (for definition of "attorney") and MCL 712A.17d (for duties of lawyer-guardian *ad litem*)

B.   **Client Directed Representation.**

1.   **Traditional Attorney.**
A traditional attorney functions as a client directed advocate. He/she advocates for the expressed wishes of the client and is bound by the client's directives concerning the objectives of representation. The model does not prohibit the attorney from acting in his/her capacity as counselor for the client, and state ethics codes include the counseling function. Attorneys are not required, without first counseling their client as to more appropriate options, to blindly follow directives that are clearly harmful to the client. Further, the model does not require attorneys to advocate positions not supported by facts and the law.

Pros: The model is thought to give voice and autonomy to the client and to empower the child within the system. It allows attorneys to function in a familiar setting. Proponents believe it produces good outcomes for children because it encourages independent, zealous advocacy, and the attorney is not confused by the role or duties.

Cons: Critics charge that the model does not work for young children who cannot meaningfully direct their litigation or for older children who may misdirect their litigation.

Jurisdictions Using a Form of This Model Include: Oregon uses a traditional attorney, but not in all cases. Additionally, a CASA appointment is required in Oregon. Likewise, in many cases a traditional attorney is used in Massachusetts, but in conjunction with a Guardian *ad Litem.*

Sources: Oregon Revised Statutes §§ 419A.170; 419A.012; 419B.195; Ethics provision 3.3. Mass. Gen. Laws ch. 119, § 29; Mass. Ethics Opinion 93-6. ABA Model Rules of Professional Conduct (Model Rules): Preamble; 1.14(a); ABA Model Code of Professional Responsibility (Model Code): EC 7-1; EC 7-12.

2. **Child's Attorney (ABA Standards Model)**

The following selected provisions from the *ABA Standards of Practice for Lawyers Who Represent Children in Abuse and Neglect Cases* define the model. "The term 'child's attorney' means a lawyer who provides legal services for a child and who owes the same duties of undivided loyalty, confidentiality, and competent representation to the child as is due an adult client. The child's attorney should elicit the child's preferences in a developmentally appropriate manner, advise the child, and provide guidance. The child's attorney should represent the child's expressed preferences and follow the child's direction throughout the course of litigation. To the extent that a child cannot express a preference, the child's attorney shall make a good faith effort to determine the child's wishes and advocate accordingly or request appointment of a guardian *ad litem*. To the extent that a child does not or will not express a preference about particular issues, the child's attorney should determine and advocate the child's legal interests. If the child's attorney determines that the child's expressed preference would be seriously injurious to the child (as opposed to merely being contrary to the lawyer's opinion of what would be in the child's interests), the lawyer may request appointment of a separate guardian *ad litem* and continue to represent the child's expressed preference, unless the child's position is prohibited by law or without any factual foundation."

Pros: Proponents see the model as the most significant advance in child representation in many years. They see the model as an evolution from the GAL model of the 1970s. The model is a detailed roadmap for representation taking role and duty confusion out of the picture. The model also discourages relaxed advocacy.

Cons: Critics argue the model still does not work well for young children and that the directive to resort to representation of the child's "legal interests" in some cases is not a meaningful directive. Critics complain that focusing on the child's so-called "legal interests" is unsatisfactory because the legal interests of the child may be unclear or contradictory. For example, a child has a legal interest in being protected from abusive or neglectful parents. The ABA Standards are also criticized for including broad exceptions to the client-directed ideal and thus giving the lawyer unfettered and unreviewed discretion identifying the goals of the child - the same sort of unbridled discretion that critics complain about in the best interests substituted judgment model.

Jurisdictions Using a Form of This Model Include: At the time of the preparation of this document, no jurisdiction had adopted the ABA Standards as the exclusive system of representation. A number of jurisdictions have adopted many of the "duties" requirements of the standards (e.g., case investigation, motion practice) as opposed to the "role" requirements. As to "role" of counsel, Oregon uses a traditional attorney similar to this model.

Source: *ABA Standards of Practice for Lawyers Who Represent Children in Abuse & Neglect Cases,* © 1996 American Bar Association, Chicago, IL

3.   **Child's Attorney (ABA / NACC Model)**
The *ABA Standards* were adopted by the ABA in 1996. The following year, the NACC adopted the standards with reservation as to Standard B-4. Standard B-4 is the critical client direction language of the standards and some members of the NACC board believed the *ABA Standards* gave too much autonomy to the child client and was unrealistic where young children were concerned. The *ABA Standards (NACC Revised Version)*, is the NACC's attempt to achieve a better balance of client autonomy and protection within standard B-4. This child's attorney model places the attorney in the role of traditional attorney and addresses the needs of the young child through the application of an objective best interests evaluation in limited situations. The model requires that the attorney assume the traditional role of zealous advocate and not GAL to avoid any propensity toward relaxed advocacy. At the same time, it recognizes that some children are not capable of directing their litigation. The model allows for a degree of advocate direction so long as it is the exception to the rule, and based on objective criteria.

The distinction between the *ABA Standards* and the *NACC Revised ABA Standards* is that where the ABA remained consistent with the client directed attorney throughout, the NACC carved out a significant exception where the client cannot meaningfully participate in the formulation of his or her position. In such cases, the NACC's version calls for a GAL type judgment using objective criteria. Additionally, the NACC's version *requires* the attorney to request the appointment of a separate GAL, after unsuccessful attempts at counseling the child, when the child's wishes are considered to be seriously injurious to the child.

Pros: Proponents believe this is the best blending of the traditional attorney and attorney / GAL, providing the best of both options.

Cons: One critic has suggested that, by blending the attorney and GAL roles, this model dilutes both. The NACC model is also criticized for giving the lawyer unfettered and unreviewed discretion identifying the goals of the child - the same sort of unbridled discretion that critics complain about in the best interests advocate directed model.

Jurisdictions Using a Form of This Model Include: At the time of the preparation of this document, no jurisdiction had adopted the ABA NACC Revised Standards as the exclusive system of representation. A number of jurisdictions have adopted many of the "duties" requirements of the model (e.g., case investigation, motion practice) as opposed to the "role" requirements. As to "role" of counsel, Oregon uses a traditional attorney similar to this model.

Source: *ABA Standards of Practice for Lawyers Who Represent Children in Abuse & Neglect Cases*, (NACC Revised Version) NACC Children's Law Manual Series, 1999 Edition, p. 177.

V. Resources

ABA Standards of Practice for Lawyers Who Represent Children in Abuse & Neglect Cases, © 1996 American Bar Association, Chicago, IL. Available on line at http://www.abanet.org/child

ABA Standards of Practice for Lawyers Who Represent Children in Abuse & Neglect Cases, (NACC Revised Version) NACC Children's Law Manual Series, 1999 Edition, p. 177. Available on line at http://naccchildlaw.org

Adoption 2002: The President's Initiative on Adoption and Foster Care, Guidelines for Public Policy and State Legislation Governing Permanence for Children. US Dept. of HHS, Administration on Children, Youth and Families, June 1999. Available on line at http://www.acf.dhhs.gov/

Advocating for the Child in Protection Proceedings: A Handbook for Lawyers and Court Appointed Special Advocates, by Donald Duquette, © Jossey-Bass, Inc., San Francisco, CA

Child Abuse and Neglect Cases: Representation as a Critical Component of Effective Practice. Technical Assistance Bulletin, NCJFCJ / OJJDP, © 1998.

Coming to Praise, Not to Bury, The New ABA Standards of Practice for Lawyers Who Represent Children in Abuse and Neglect Cases, by David Katner, NACC Children's Law Manual, 1997 Edition, page 247.

The Courts and Child Maltreatment, by Howard A. Davidson, page 482 in *The Battered Child*, Fifth Edition, edited by Helfer, Kempe and Krugman, © 1997 University of Chicago Press, Chicago, IL

The Child's Attorney, by Ann M. Haralambie, © 1993 American Bar Association, ABA Section of Family Law, Chicago, IL (Call 303/864-5320)

Ethical Issues in the Legal Representation of Children, Fordham Law Review, Vol. LXIV No. 4 March 1996.

Facts About Children and the Law, American Bar Association Division for Media Relations and Public Affairs

Handling Child Custody, Abuse and Adoption Cases, by Ann M. Haralambie, Second Edition © 1993 Shepard's McGraw-Hill, Colorado Springs, CO, now published by Clark, Boardman, Callaghan, Deerfield, IL

Independent Representation for the Abused and Neglected Child: The Guardian Ad Litem, by B. Fraser, 13 *California Western Law Review* 16 (1976)

A Judges Guide to Improving Legal Representation of Children, edited by Kathi Grasso, ABA Center on Children and the Law, © ABA May 1998.

Lawyers' Roles in Child Protection, by Donald N. Duquette, page 460 in *The Battered Child*, Fifth Edition, edited by Helfer, Kempe, and Krugman, © 1997 University of Chicago Press, Chicago, IL

Legal Representation for Children in Protection Proceedings: Two Distinct Lawyer Roles are Required, by Donald N. Duquette, *FAMILY LAW QUARTERLY*, (Fall 2000)

Legal Representation of Children in Dependency Court: Toward A Better Model - The ABA (NACC Revised) Standards of Practice, by Marvin Ventrell, NACC Children's Law Manual Series, 1999 Edition.

Representing Children in Child Protective Proceedings: Ethical and Practical Dimensions, by Jean Koh Peters, © 1997, LEXIS Law Publishing, Charlottesville, VA

Representing the Child Client, by Dale, Soler, Shotton, Bell, Jameson, Shauffer, Warboys, © 2000, Mathew Bender and Company, Inc., New York, NY

Resource Guidelines, Improving Court Practice in Child Abuse and Neglect Cases, National Council of Juvenile and Family Court Judges, © 1995 NCJFCJ, Reno, NV

Rights and Duties: An Overview of the Attorney-Child Client Relationship, by Marvin Ventrell, Loyola University of Chicago Law Journal, Vol. 26 No. 2 Winter 1995

Appendix B: Resources

Books

Adoption Law and Practice, by Joan H. Hollinger, Mathew Bender & Co., Inc., New York, NY, 1995.

The Backlash, *Child Protection Under Fire*, edited by John E. B. Myers, Sage Publications, Thousand Oaks, CA, 1994.

The Battered Child (5th ed.), edited by Helfer, Kempe & Krugman, University of Chicago Press, Chicago, IL, 1997.

The Best Interests of the Child, The Least Detrimental Alternative, *The Landmark Trilogy of Beyond the Best Interests of the Child, Before the Best Interests of the Child, and In the Best Interests of the Child*, by Goldstein, Solnit, Goldstein & Freud, The Free Press, New York, NY, 1996.

Cases and Materials in Juvenile Law, by J. Eric Smithburn, Anderson Publishing Co., Cincinnati, OH, 2002.

The Child Abuse-Delinquency Connection, by David N. Sandberg, Lexington Books, Lexington, MA, 1989.

Child Abuse and the Legal System, by Inger J. Sagatun & Leonard P. Edwards, Nelson-Hall, Inc., Chicago, IL, 1995.

Child Abuse and Neglect: Cases and Materials, by Robert D. Goldstein, West Group, American Casebook Series, St. Paul, MN, 1999.

Child Maltreatment: A Clinical Guide and Reference, by James Monteleone & Armand E. Brodeur, G.W. Medical Publishing, Inc., St. Louis, MO, 1994.

Child Rights and Remedies: How the U.S. Legal System Affects Children, by Robert C. Fellmeth, Clarity Press, Atlanta, GA, 2002.

Child Safety: A Guide for Judges and Attorneys, by Therese Roe Lund & Jennifer Renne, ABA Publishing, Washington, DC, 2009. Available at: http://www.nrccps.org/resources/ guide_judges_attorneys.php.

Child Sexual Abuse in Civil Cases: A Guide to Custody and Tort Actions, by Ann M. Haralambie, American Bar Association, ABA Section of Family Law, Chicago, IL, 1999.

The Child's Attorney, by Ann M. Haralambie, American Bar Association, ABA Section of Family Law, Chicago, IL, 1993.

Children & the Law: Rights and Obligations, by Thomas A. Jacobs, Clark Boardman Callaghan, Deerfield, IL, 1995.

Classic Papers in Child Abuse, edited by Anne Cohn Donnelly & Kim Oates, Sage Publications, Thousand Oaks, CA, 2000.

Desk Reference to the Diagnostic Criteria From DSM-IV-TR (Fourth Edition, Text Revision), by American Psychiatric Association, Washington, DC, 2000.

Diagnostic and Statistical Manual of Mental Disorders, Fourth Edition – DSM-IV, by American Psychiatric Association, Washington, DC, 2000.

Diagnostic Imaging of Child Abuse (2d ed.), by Paul K. Kleinman, Mosby, St. Louis, MO, 1998.

A Digest of Cases of the United States Supreme Court as to Juveniles and Family Law, edited by the National Council of Juvenile and Family Court Judges, 2001.

Expert Witnesses in Child Abuse Cases, edited by Stephen J. Ceci & Helene Hembrooke, American Psychological Association, Washington, D.C. 1998.

Facts About Children and the Law, by American Bar Association, Division for Media Relations and Public Affairs, Chicago, IL.

Families by Law: An Adoption Reader, edited by Naomi R. Cahn & Joan Heifetz Hollinger, New York University Press, New York, NY, 2004.

Glass Walls: Confidentiality Provisions and InterAgency Collaborations, by Mark I. Soler, Alice C. Shotton & James R. Bell, Youth Law Center, San Francisco, CA, 1993.

Handbook on Questioning Children: A Linguistic Perspective (2d ed.), by Anne Groffam Walker, Ph.D., American Bar Association, Chicago, IL, 1999.

Handling Child Custody, Abuse and Adoption Cases (3d ed.), by Ann M. Haralambie, Thomson-West, Eagan, MN, 2009.

A History of Child Protection in America, by John E. B. Myers, 2004.

Juvenile Sexual Offending: Causes, Consequences, and Correction, by Gail D. Ryan & Sandy L. Lane, Lexington Books, Lexington, MA, 1991.

Legal Ethics in Child Welfare Cases, by Jennifer Renne. ABA Center on Children and the Law, Washington, DC, 2004.

Legal Issues in Child Abuse and Neglect (2d ed.), by John E. B. Myers, Sage Publications, Thousand Oaks, CA, 1998.

Legal Rights of Children (2d. ed.), by Donald T. Kramer, Shepard's McGraw-Hill, Colorado Springs, CO, now published by Clark, Boardman, Callaghan, Deerfield, IL, 1994.

Modern Trial Advocacy, Analysis and Practice (4th ed.), by Steven Lubet, National Institute for Trial Advocacy, Louisville, CO, 2009.

Myers on Evidence in Child Abuse and Neglect Cases (3d ed.), by John E. B. Myers, Aspen Publishers, New York, NY, 2005.

Recognizing Child Abuse, by Douglas J. Besharov, The Free Press, New York, NY, 1990.

Representing the Child Client, by Dale, Soler, Shotton, Bell, Jameson, Shauffer & Warboys, Lexis Publishing, New York, NY, 2000.

Representing Children in Child Protective Proceedings: Ethical and Practical Dimensions (3d ed.), by Jean K. Peters, Mathew Bender & Company, Inc., A Member of LexisNexis Group, New York, NY, 2007.

The Spectrum of Child Abuse: Assessment, Treatment, and Prevention, by R. Kim Oates, M.D., Brunner/Mazel, Inc. New York, NY, 1996.

Trial Manual for Defense Attorneys in Juvenile Court, by Heartz, Gugenheim & Amsterdam, ALI-ABA, Philadelphia, PA, 1991.

What Are My Rights?, by Thomas A. Jacobs, Free Spirit Publishing, Minneapolis, MN, 1997.

What's Wrong with Children's Rights?, by Martin Guggenheim, Harvard University Press Boston, MA, 2007.

Technical Assistance

ABA Standards of Practice for Attorneys Representing Parents in Abuse and Neglect Cases, American Bar Association, Chicago, IL. Available at: http://www.abanet.org/child/clp/ParentStds.pdf

ABA Standards of Practice for Lawyers Who Represent Children in Abuse & Neglect Cases, by American Bar Association, Chicago, IL, 1996. Available at: http://www.abanet.org/child/repstandwhole.pdf

ABA Standards of Practice for Lawyers Representing Child Welfare Agencies, by American Bar Association, Chicago, IL, 2004. Available at: http://www.abanet.org/child/agency-standards.pdf

ABA (NACC Revised) Standards of Practice for Lawyers Who Represent Children in Abuse & Neglect Cases, 1999. Available at: http://www.naccchildlaw.org/default.asp?page=PracticeStandards

Adoption 2002: Guidelines For Public Policy and State Legislation Governing Permanence For Children, by Donald N. Duquette & Mark Hardin, Department of Health and Human Services, 1999.

Advocacy For Children by Foster Parents, by Shari Shink & Seth Grob, A Project of the Rocky Mountain Children's Law Center, Denver, CO, 1997.

America's Children at Risk, A Report of the Presidential Working Group on the Unmet Legal Needs of Children and Their Families, American Bar Association, Chicago, IL, 1993.

America's Children Still at Risk, A Report of the Steering Committee on the Unmet Legal Needs of Children, American Bar Association, Chicago, IL, 2001.

Child Abuse and Neglect: State Statutes Series, by U.S. Department of Health and Human Services, Washington, D.C., 1997.

Child Maltreatment: Reports from the States to the National Center on Child Abuse and Neglect, published annually by U.S. Department of Health and Human Services, NCCAN, Washington, DC.

Child Development, A Judges Reference Guide, by Cassady, Durst, Greydnus, Russ, Schonberg, Sikorski, & Stein, National Counsel of Juvenile and Family Court Judges, Reno, NV, 1993.

Children in the States 2000, by the Children's Defense Fund, Washington, D.C. 2000.

The Children's Law Manual Series, by the National Association of Counsel for Children, produced annually from 1989 to present, NACC, Denver, CO.

Building a Better Court, Measuring and Improving Court Performance and Judicial Workload in Child Abuse and Neglect Cases, by The National Council of Juvenile and Family Court Judges, American Bar Association, Washington, D.C.

Defending Child Abuse and Neglect Cases: Representing Parents in Civil Proceedings, by Douglas J. Besharov, The District of Columbia Bar, Washington, DC, 1987.

Foundations for Success: Strengthening Your Agency Attorney Office, by Mimi Laver, American Bar Association, 1999.

The National Directory of Children, Youth, and Families Services 2004-2005 (20th ed.), by The National Directory of Children, Youth, and Families Services, Englewood, CO, 2004.

Preparing Children for Court: A Practitioner's Guide, by Lynn M. Copen, Sage Publications, Inc., Thousand Oaks, CA, 2000.

The Prosecuting Attorney in Dependency Proceeding in Juvenile Court, *Defining and Assessing Critical Role in Child Abuse and Neglect Cases*, Meghan Scahill, Esq., National Center for Juvenile Justice, Pittsburgh, PA, 2000.

Recommendations of the UNLV Conference on Representing Children in Families: Child Advocacy and Justice Ten Years After Fordham, 6 Nev. L. J. 592 (2006).

Resource Guidelines, Improving Court Practice in Child Abuse and Neglect Cases, National Council of Juvenile and Family Court Judges, National Counsel of Juvenile and Family Court Judges, Reno, NV, 1995.

A Sourcebook on Child Sexual Abuse, by David Finkelhor, Sage Publications, Inc., Newbury Park, CA, 1986.

The State of America's Children Yearbook, published annually by the Children's Defense Fund, CDF, Washington, DC.

Journals

Child Abuse & Neglect, The International Journal, Official Monthly Publication of the International Society for Prevention of Child Abuse and Neglect, Denver, CO

Child Law Practice, Monthly Publication of the ABA Center on Children and the Law, Washington, DC

Child Maltreatment, Quarterly Publication of American Professional Society on the Abuse of Children, Chicago, IL

Children's Legal Rights Journal, Quarterly Publication of the American Bar Association on Children & the Law and Loyola University Chicago School of Law in cooperation with the National Association of Counsel for Children, Buffalo, NY.

Conference on Representing Children in Families: Children's Advocacy and Justice Ten Years After Fordham: UNLV Children's Conference, 6 Nev. L. J. 571-1408 (2006).

Conference on the Ethical Issues in Representation of Children, 64 Fordham L. Rev. 1281-2131 (1996).

Family Law Quarterly, Quarterly Publication of the ABA Section of Family Law, Chicago, IL

The Guardian, Quarterly Newsletter of the National Association of Counsel for Children, Denver, CO

Juvenile and Family Court Journal, Quarterly Publication of the National Council of Juvenile and Family Court Judges, Reno, NV

Juvenile and Family Law Digest, Monthly Publication of the National Council of Juvenile and Family Court Judges, Reno, NV

The Quarterly Update, Reviews of Current Child Abuse Medical Research, Quarterly Publication, Norwich, VT.

Organizations

American Academy of Adoption Attorneys
> P.O. Box 33053, Washington, DC 20033
> Ph: (202) 832-2222 / info@adoptionattorneys.org
> http://adoptionattorneys.org/

American Academy of Pediatrics
> 141 Northwest Point Blvd., Elk Grove Village, IL, 60007
> Ph: (847) 434-4000
> http://www.aap.org/

American Bar Association Center on Children and the Law
> 740 15th Street, NW. Washington, DC 20005
> Ph: (202) 662-1720 / ctrchildlaw@abanet.org
> http://www.apanet.org/child

American Bar Association Section of Litigation Children's Rights Litigation Committee
> Current Chair Catherine Krebs, Washington, DC
> Ph: (202) 547-3060 / krebsc@staff.abanet.org
> http://www.abanet.org/litigation/committees/childrights/

ABA Steering Committee on the Unmet Legal Needs of Children
> 740 15th Street, NW, Washington, D.C. 20005-1022
> Ph: (202) 662-1675 / murphym@staff.abanet.org
> http://www.abanet.org/unmet/home.html

American Humane, Children's Services
> 63 Inverness Drive East, Englewood, CO 80112
> Ph: (800) 227-4645 / info@americanhumane.org
> http://www.americanhumane.org/protecting-children/

American Professional Society on the Abuse of Children
> 350 Poplar Avenue, Elmhurst, IL 60126
> Ph: (630) 941-1235 / apsac@apsac.org
> http://www.apsac.org

American Psychological Association
> 750 First Street NE, Washington, DC 20002-4242
> Ph: (800) 374-2721
> http://www.apa.org/

Association of Family and Conciliation Courts
> 6525 Grand Teton Plaza, Madison, WI 53719
> Ph: (608) 664-3750 / afcc@afccnet.org
> http://www.afccnet.org/

Child Welfare League of America
  2345 Crystal Drive, Suite 250, Arlington, VA 22202
  Ph: (703) 413-2400
  http://www.cwla.org/

Children's Defense Fund
  25 E Street NW, Washington, D.C. 20001
  Ph: (800) 233-1200 / cdfinfo@childrensdefense.org
  http://www.childrensdefense.org/

First Star
  1666 K Street Northwest, Suite 300, Washington, D.C. 20006
  Ph: (202) 293-3703 / contact@firststar.org
  http://www.firststar.org/

Immigrant Legal Resource Center
  1663 Mission Street, Suite 602, San Francisco, CA 94103
  Ph: (415) 255-9499
  http://www.ilrc.org

International Society for Prevention of Child Abuse and Neglect
  13123 E. 16th Ave., B390, Aurora, CO 80045-7106, USA
  Ph: (303) 864-5220 / ispcan@ispcan.org
  http://www.ispcan.org/

Judicial Council of California Center for Families, Children and the Courts
  455 Golden Gate Ave., 6th Floor, San Francisco, CA 94102-3660
  Ph: (415) 865-7739 / CFCC@jud.ca.gov
  http://www.courtinfo.ca.gov/programs/cfcc/

Juvenile Law Center
  The Philadelphia Building, 4th floor, 1315 Walnut Street, Philadelphia, PA 19107
  Ph: (800) 875-8887
  http://www.jlc.org/

Kempe Children's Center
  The Gary Pavilion at The Children's Hospital, 13123 E 16th Ave B390, Aurora, CO 80045
  Ph: (303) 864-5300 / questions@kempe.org
  http://www.kempecenter.org/

National Association of Counsel for Children
  The Gary Pavilion at The Children's Hospital, 13123 E 16th Ave B390, Aurora, CO 80045
  Ph: (888) 828-6222 / advocate@naccchildlaw.org
  http://www.naccchildlaw.org/

National Center for Juvenile Justice
  3700 South Water Street, Suite 200, Pittsburgh, PA, 15203
  Ph: (412) 227-6950 / ncjj@ncjj.org
  http://ncjj.servehttp.com/NCJJWebsite/main.htm

National Center for Prosecution of Child Abuse
44 Canal Center Plaza, Suite 110, Alexandria, VA 22314
Ph: (703) 549-9222 / ncpca@ndaa.org
http://www.ndaa.org/ncpca_home.html

National Center for State Courts
300 Newport Avenue, Williamsburg VA 23185
Ph: (800) 616-6164
http://www.ncsconline.org/

National Council of Juvenile and Family Court Judges
P.O. Box 8970 Reno, NV 89507
Ph: (775) 784-6012 / staff@ncjfcj.org
http://www.ncjfcj.org/

National CASA
100 West Harrison, North Tower, Suite 500, Seattle, WA 98119
(800) 628-3233
http://www.casaforchildren.org/

National Institute of Trial Advocacy
361 Centennial Parkway, Suite 220, Louisville, CO 80027
Ph: (800) 225-6482 / customerservice@nita.org
http://www.nita.org/

U.S. Department of Health and Human Services, Children's Bureau
Administration for Children & Families/National Clearinghouse on Child Abuse and
Neglect Information
Children's Bureau/ACYF, 1250 Maryland Avenue, SW, Eighth Floor,
Washington, DC 20024
Ph: (800) 394-3366 / info@childwelfare.gov
http://www.childwelfare.gov/

Zero to Three
2000 M St. NW, Suite 200, Washington, DC 20036
Ph: (202) 638-1144
http://www.zerotothree.org/

Index